Lecture Notes in Computer Science 11205

Commenced Publication in 1973
Founding and Former Series Editors:
Gerhard Goos, Juris Hartmanis, and Jan van Leeuwen

Editorial Board

David Hutchison
  Lancaster University, Lancaster, UK
Takeo Kanade
  Carnegie Mellon University, Pittsburgh, PA, USA
Josef Kittler
  University of Surrey, Guildford, UK
Jon M. Kleinberg
  Cornell University, Ithaca, NY, USA
Friedemann Mattern
  ETH Zurich, Zurich, Switzerland
John C. Mitchell
  Stanford University, Stanford, CA, USA
Moni Naor
  Weizmann Institute of Science, Rehovot, Israel
C. Pandu Rangan
  Indian Institute of Technology Madras, Chennai, India
Bernhard Steffen
  TU Dortmund University, Dortmund, Germany
Demetri Terzopoulos
  University of California, Los Angeles, CA, USA
Doug Tygar
  University of California, Berkeley, CA, USA
Gerhard Weikum
  Max Planck Institute for Informatics, Saarbrücken, Germany

More information about this series at http://www.springer.com/series/7412

Vittorio Ferrari · Martial Hebert
Cristian Sminchisescu · Yair Weiss (Eds.)

Computer Vision – ECCV 2018

15th European Conference
Munich, Germany, September 8–14, 2018
Proceedings, Part I

 Springer

Editors
Vittorio Ferrari
Google Research
Zurich
Switzerland

Martial Hebert
Carnegie Mellon University
Pittsburgh, PA
USA

Cristian Sminchisescu
Google Research
Zurich
Switzerland

Yair Weiss
Hebrew University of Jerusalem
Jerusalem
Israel

ISSN 0302-9743   ISSN 1611-3349   (electronic)
Lecture Notes in Computer Science
ISBN 978-3-030-01245-8   ISBN 978-3-030-01246-5   (eBook)
https://doi.org/10.1007/978-3-030-01246-5

Library of Congress Control Number: 2018955489

LNCS Sublibrary: SL6 – Image Processing, Computer Vision, Pattern Recognition, and Graphics

© Springer Nature Switzerland AG 2018
This work is subject to copyright. All rights are reserved by the Publisher, whether the whole or part of the material is concerned, specifically the rights of translation, reprinting, reuse of illustrations, recitation, broadcasting, reproduction on microfilms or in any other physical way, and transmission or information storage and retrieval, electronic adaptation, computer software, or by similar or dissimilar methodology now known or hereafter developed.
The use of general descriptive names, registered names, trademarks, service marks, etc. in this publication does not imply, even in the absence of a specific statement, that such names are exempt from the relevant protective laws and regulations and therefore free for general use.
The publisher, the authors and the editors are safe to assume that the advice and information in this book are believed to be true and accurate at the date of publication. Neither the publisher nor the authors or the editors give a warranty, express or implied, with respect to the material contained herein or for any errors or omissions that may have been made. The publisher remains neutral with regard to jurisdictional claims in published maps and institutional affiliations.

This Springer imprint is published by the registered company Springer Nature Switzerland AG
The registered company address is: Gewerbestrasse 11, 6330 Cham, Switzerland

Foreword

It was our great pleasure to host the European Conference on Computer Vision 2018 in Munich, Germany. This constituted by far the largest ECCV event ever. With close to 2,900 registered participants and another 600 on the waiting list one month before the conference, participation more than doubled since the last ECCV in Amsterdam. We believe that this is due to a dramatic growth of the computer vision community combined with the popularity of Munich as a major European hub of culture, science, and industry. The conference took place in the heart of Munich in the concert hall Gasteig with workshops and tutorials held at the downtown campus of the Technical University of Munich.

One of the major innovations for ECCV 2018 was the free perpetual availability of all conference and workshop papers, which is often referred to as open access. We note that this is not precisely the same use of the term as in the Budapest declaration. Since 2013, CVPR and ICCV have had their papers hosted by the Computer Vision Foundation (CVF), in parallel with the IEEE Xplore version. This has proved highly beneficial to the computer vision community.

We are delighted to announce that for ECCV 2018 a very similar arrangement was put in place with the cooperation of Springer. In particular, the author's final version will be freely available in perpetuity on a CVF page, while SpringerLink will continue to host a version with further improvements, such as activating reference links and including video. We believe that this will give readers the best of both worlds; researchers who are focused on the technical content will have a freely available version in an easily accessible place, while subscribers to SpringerLink will continue to have the additional benefits that this provides. We thank Alfred Hofmann from Springer for helping to negotiate this agreement, which we expect will continue for future versions of ECCV.

September 2018

Horst Bischof
Daniel Cremers
Bernt Schiele
Ramin Zabih

Preface

Welcome to the proceedings of the 2018 European Conference on Computer Vision (ECCV 2018) held in Munich, Germany. We are delighted to present this volume reflecting a strong and exciting program, the result of an extensive review process. In total, we received 2,439 valid paper submissions. Of these, 776 were accepted (31.8%): 717 as posters (29.4%) and 59 as oral presentations (2.4%). All oral presentations were presented as posters as well. The program selection process was complicated this year by the large increase in the number of submitted papers, +65% over ECCV 2016, and the use of CMT3 for the first time for a computer vision conference. The program selection process was supported by four program co-chairs (PCs), 126 area chairs (ACs), and 1,199 reviewers with reviews assigned.

We were primarily responsible for the design and execution of the review process. Beyond administrative rejections, we were involved in acceptance decisions only in the very few cases where the ACs were not able to agree on a decision. As PCs, and as is customary in the field, we were not allowed to co-author a submission. General co-chairs and other co-organizers who played no role in the review process were permitted to submit papers, and were treated as any other author is.

Acceptance decisions were made by two independent ACs. The ACs also made a joint recommendation for promoting papers to oral status. We decided on the final selection of oral presentations based on the ACs' recommendations. There were 126 ACs, selected according to their technical expertise, experience, and geographical diversity (63 from European, nine from Asian/Australian, and 54 from North American institutions). Indeed, 126 ACs is a substantial increase in the number of ACs due to the natural increase in the number of papers and to our desire to maintain the number of papers assigned to each AC to a manageable number so as to ensure quality. The ACs were aided by the 1,199 reviewers to whom papers were assigned for reviewing. The Program Committee was selected from committees of previous ECCV, ICCV, and CVPR conferences and was extended on the basis of suggestions from the ACs. Having a large pool of Program Committee members for reviewing allowed us to match expertise while reducing reviewer loads. No more than eight papers were assigned to a reviewer, maintaining the reviewers' load at the same level as ECCV 2016 despite the increase in the number of submitted papers.

Conflicts of interest between ACs, Program Committee members, and papers were identified based on the home institutions, and on previous collaborations of all researchers involved. To find institutional conflicts, all authors, Program Committee members, and ACs were asked to list the Internet domains of their current institutions. We assigned on average approximately 18 papers to each AC. The papers were assigned using the affinity scores from the Toronto Paper Matching System (TPMS) and additional data from the OpenReview system, managed by a UMass group. OpenReview used additional information from ACs' and authors' records to identify collaborations and to generate matches. OpenReview was invaluable in refining conflict definitions and in generating quality matches. The only glitch is that, once the matches were generated, a small percentage of papers were unassigned because of discrepancies between the OpenReview conflicts and the conflicts entered in CMT3. We manually assigned these papers. This glitch is revealing of the challenge of using multiple systems at once (CMT3 and OpenReview in this case), which needs to be addressed in future.

After assignment of papers to ACs, the ACs suggested seven reviewers per paper from the Program Committee pool. The selection and rank ordering were facilitated by the TPMS affinity scores visible to the ACs for each paper/reviewer pair. The final assignment of papers to reviewers was generated again through OpenReview in order to account for refined conflict definitions. This required new features in the OpenReview matching system to accommodate the ECCV workflow, in particular to incorporate selection ranking, and maximum reviewer load. Very few papers received fewer than three reviewers after matching and were handled through manual assignment. Reviewers were then asked to comment on the merit of each paper and to make an initial recommendation ranging from definitely reject to definitely accept, including a borderline rating. The reviewers were also asked to suggest explicit questions they wanted to see answered in the authors' rebuttal. The initial review period was five weeks. Because of the delay in getting all the reviews in, we had to delay the final release of the reviews by four days. However, because of the slack included at the tail end of the schedule, we were able to maintain the decision target date with sufficient time for all the phases. We reassigned over 100 reviews from 40 reviewers during the review period. Unfortunately, the main reason for these reassignments was reviewers declining to review, after having accepted to do so. Other reasons included technical relevance and occasional unidentified conflicts. We express our thanks to the emergency reviewers who generously accepted to perform these reviews under short notice. In addition, a substantial number of manual corrections had to do with reviewers using a different email address than the one that was used at the time of the reviewer invitation. This is revealing of a broader issue with identifying users by email addresses that change frequently enough to cause significant problems during the timespan of the conference process.

The authors were then given the opportunity to rebut the reviews, to identify factual errors, and to address the specific questions raised by the reviewers over a seven-day rebuttal period. The exact format of the rebuttal was the object of considerable debate among the organizers, as well as with prior organizers. At issue is to balance giving the author the opportunity to respond completely and precisely to the reviewers, e.g., by including graphs of experiments, while avoiding requests for completely new material or experimental results not included in the original paper. In the end, we decided on the two-page PDF document in conference format. Following this rebuttal period, reviewers and ACs discussed papers at length, after which reviewers finalized their evaluation and gave a final recommendation to the ACs. A significant percentage of the reviewers did enter their final recommendation if it did not differ from their initial recommendation. Given the tight schedule, we did not wait until all were entered.

After this discussion period, each paper was assigned to a second AC. The AC/paper matching was again run through OpenReview. Again, the OpenReview team worked quickly to implement the features specific to this process, in this case accounting for the existing AC assignment, as well as minimizing the fragmentation across ACs, so that each AC had on average only 5.5 buddy ACs to communicate with. The largest number was 11. Given the complexity of the conflicts, this was a very efficient set of assignments from OpenReview. Each paper was then evaluated by its assigned pair of ACs. For each paper, we required each of the two ACs assigned to certify both the final recommendation and the metareview (aka consolidation report). In all cases, after extensive discussions, the two ACs arrived at a common acceptance decision. We maintained these decisions, with the caveat that we did evaluate, sometimes going back to the ACs, a few papers for which the final acceptance decision substantially deviated from the consensus from the reviewers, amending three decisions in the process.

We want to thank everyone involved in making ECCV 2018 possible. The success of ECCV 2018 depended on the quality of papers submitted by the authors, and on the very hard work of the ACs and the Program Committee members. We are particularly grateful to the OpenReview team (Melisa Bok, Ari Kobren, Andrew McCallum, Michael Spector) for their support, in particular their willingness to implement new features, often on a tight schedule, to Laurent Charlin for the use of the Toronto Paper Matching System, to the CMT3 team, in particular in dealing with all the issues that arise when using a new system, to Friedrich Fraundorfer and Quirin Lohr for maintaining the online version of the program, and to the CMU staff (Keyla Cook, Lynnetta Miller, Ashley Song, Nora Kazour) for assisting with data entry/editing in CMT3. Finally, the preparation of these proceedings would not have been possible without the diligent effort of the publication chairs, Albert Ali Salah and Hamdi Dibeklioğlu, and of Anna Kramer and Alfred Hofmann from Springer.

September 2018

Vittorio Ferrari
Martial Hebert
Cristian Sminchisescu
Yair Weiss

Organization

General Chairs

Horst Bischof — Graz University of Technology, Austria
Daniel Cremers — Technical University of Munich, Germany
Bernt Schiele — Saarland University, Max Planck Institute for Informatics, Germany
Ramin Zabih — CornellNYCTech, USA

Program Committee Co-chairs

Vittorio Ferrari — University of Edinburgh, UK
Martial Hebert — Carnegie Mellon University, USA
Cristian Sminchisescu — Lund University, Sweden
Yair Weiss — Hebrew University, Israel

Local Arrangements Chairs

Björn Menze — Technical University of Munich, Germany
Matthias Niessner — Technical University of Munich, Germany

Workshop Chairs

Stefan Roth — TU Darmstadt, Germany
Laura Leal-Taixé — Technical University of Munich, Germany

Tutorial Chairs

Michael Bronstein — Università della Svizzera Italiana, Switzerland
Laura Leal-Taixé — Technical University of Munich, Germany

Website Chair

Friedrich Fraundorfer — Graz University of Technology, Austria

Demo Chairs

Federico Tombari — Technical University of Munich, Germany
Joerg Stueckler — Technical University of Munich, Germany

Publicity Chair

Giovanni Maria   University of Catania, Italy
  Farinella

Industrial Liaison Chairs

Florent Perronnin   Naver Labs, France
Yunchao Gong   Snap, USA
Helmut Grabner   Logitech, Switzerland

Finance Chair

Gerard Medioni   Amazon, University of Southern California, USA

Publication Chairs

Albert Ali Salah   Boğaziçi University, Turkey
Hamdi Dibeklioğlu   Bilkent University, Turkey

Area Chairs

Kalle Åström   Lund University, Sweden
Zeynep Akata   University of Amsterdam, The Netherlands
Joao Barreto   University of Coimbra, Portugal
Ronen Basri   Weizmann Institute of Science, Israel
Dhruv Batra   Georgia Tech and Facebook AI Research, USA
Serge Belongie   Cornell University, USA
Rodrigo Benenson   Google, Switzerland
Hakan Bilen   University of Edinburgh, UK
Matthew Blaschko   KU Leuven, Belgium
Edmond Boyer   Inria, France
Gabriel Brostow   University College London, UK
Thomas Brox   University of Freiburg, Germany
Marcus Brubaker   York University, Canada
Barbara Caputo   Politecnico di Torino and the Italian Institute
                          of Technology, Italy
Tim Cootes   University of Manchester, UK
Trevor Darrell   University of California, Berkeley, USA
Larry Davis   University of Maryland at College Park, USA
Andrew Davison   Imperial College London, UK
Fernando de la Torre   Carnegie Mellon University, USA
Irfan Essa   GeorgiaTech, USA
Ali Farhadi   University of Washington, USA
Paolo Favaro   University of Bern, Switzerland
Michael Felsberg   Linköping University, Sweden

Sanja Fidler	University of Toronto, Canada
Andrew Fitzgibbon	Microsoft, Cambridge, UK
David Forsyth	University of Illinois at Urbana-Champaign, USA
Charless Fowlkes	University of California, Irvine, USA
Bill Freeman	MIT, USA
Mario Fritz	MPII, Germany
Jürgen Gall	University of Bonn, Germany
Dariu Gavrila	TU Delft, The Netherlands
Andreas Geiger	MPI-IS and University of Tübingen, Germany
Theo Gevers	University of Amsterdam, The Netherlands
Ross Girshick	Facebook AI Research, USA
Kristen Grauman	Facebook AI Research and UT Austin, USA
Abhinav Gupta	Carnegie Mellon University, USA
Kaiming He	Facebook AI Research, USA
Martial Hebert	Carnegie Mellon University, USA
Anders Heyden	Lund University, Sweden
Timothy Hospedales	University of Edinburgh, UK
Michal Irani	Weizmann Institute of Science, Israel
Phillip Isola	University of California, Berkeley, USA
Hervé Jégou	Facebook AI Research, France
David Jacobs	University of Maryland, College Park, USA
Allan Jepson	University of Toronto, Canada
Jiaya Jia	Chinese University of Hong Kong, SAR China
Fredrik Kahl	Chalmers University, USA
Hedvig Kjellström	KTH Royal Institute of Technology, Sweden
Iasonas Kokkinos	University College London and Facebook, UK
Vladlen Koltun	Intel Labs, USA
Philipp Krähenbühl	UT Austin, USA
M. Pawan Kumar	University of Oxford, UK
Kyros Kutulakos	University of Toronto, Canada
In Kweon	KAIST, South Korea
Ivan Laptev	Inria, France
Svetlana Lazebnik	University of Illinois at Urbana-Champaign, USA
Laura Leal-Taixé	Technical University of Munich, Germany
Erik Learned-Miller	University of Massachusetts, Amherst, USA
Kyoung Mu Lee	Seoul National University, South Korea
Bastian Leibe	RWTH Aachen University, Germany
Aleš Leonardis	University of Birmingham, UK
Vincent Lepetit	University of Bordeaux, France and Graz University of Technology, Austria
Fuxin Li	Oregon State University, USA
Dahua Lin	Chinese University of Hong Kong, SAR China
Jim Little	University of British Columbia, Canada
Ce Liu	Google, USA
Chen Change Loy	Nanyang Technological University, Singapore
Jiri Matas	Czech Technical University in Prague, Czechia

Yasuyuki Matsushita	Osaka University, Japan
Dimitris Metaxas	Rutgers University, USA
Greg Mori	Simon Fraser University, Canada
Vittorio Murino	Istituto Italiano di Tecnologia, Italy
Richard Newcombe	Oculus Research, USA
Minh Hoai Nguyen	Stony Brook University, USA
Sebastian Nowozin	Microsoft Research Cambridge, UK
Aude Oliva	MIT, USA
Bjorn Ommer	Heidelberg University, Germany
Tomas Pajdla	Czech Technical University in Prague, Czechia
Maja Pantic	Imperial College London and Samsung AI Research Centre Cambridge, UK
Caroline Pantofaru	Google, USA
Devi Parikh	Georgia Tech and Facebook AI Research, USA
Sylvain Paris	Adobe Research, USA
Vladimir Pavlovic	Rutgers University, USA
Marcello Pelillo	University of Venice, Italy
Patrick Pérez	Valeo, France
Robert Pless	George Washington University, USA
Thomas Pock	Graz University of Technology, Austria
Jean Ponce	Inria, France
Gerard Pons-Moll	MPII, Saarland Informatics Campus, Germany
Long Quan	Hong Kong University of Science and Technology, SAR China
Stefan Roth	TU Darmstadt, Germany
Carsten Rother	University of Heidelberg, Germany
Bryan Russell	Adobe Research, USA
Kate Saenko	Boston University, USA
Mathieu Salzmann	EPFL, Switzerland
Dimitris Samaras	Stony Brook University, USA
Yoichi Sato	University of Tokyo, Japan
Silvio Savarese	Stanford University, USA
Konrad Schindler	ETH Zurich, Switzerland
Cordelia Schmid	Inria, France and Google, France
Nicu Sebe	University of Trento, Italy
Fei Sha	University of Southern California, USA
Greg Shakhnarovich	TTI Chicago, USA
Jianbo Shi	University of Pennsylvania, USA
Abhinav Shrivastava	UMD and Google, USA
Yan Shuicheng	National University of Singapore, Singapore
Leonid Sigal	University of British Columbia, Canada
Josef Sivic	Czech Technical University in Prague, Czechia
Arnold Smeulders	University of Amsterdam, The Netherlands
Deqing Sun	NVIDIA, USA
Antonio Torralba	MIT, USA
Zhuowen Tu	University of California, San Diego, USA

Tinne Tuytelaars	KU Leuven, Belgium
Jasper Uijlings	Google, Switzerland
Joost van de Weijer	Computer Vision Center, Spain
Nuno Vasconcelos	University of California, San Diego, USA
Andrea Vedaldi	University of Oxford, UK
Olga Veksler	University of Western Ontario, Canada
Jakob Verbeek	Inria, France
Rene Vidal	Johns Hopkins University, USA
Daphna Weinshall	Hebrew University, Israel
Chris Williams	University of Edinburgh, UK
Lior Wolf	Tel Aviv University, Israel
Ming-Hsuan Yang	University of California at Merced, USA
Todd Zickler	Harvard University, USA
Andrew Zisserman	University of Oxford, UK

Technical Program Committee

Hassan Abu Alhaija	Peter Anderson	Arunava Banerjee
Radhakrishna Achanta	Juan Andrade-Cetto	Atsuhiko Banno
Hanno Ackermann	Mykhaylo Andriluka	Aayush Bansal
Ehsan Adeli	Anelia Angelova	Yingze Bao
Lourdes Agapito	Michel Antunes	Md Jawadul Bappy
Aishwarya Agrawal	Pablo Arbelaez	Pierre Baqué
Antonio Agudo	Vasileios Argyriou	Dániel Baráth
Eirikur Agustsson	Chetan Arora	Adrian Barbu
Karim Ahmed	Federica Arrigoni	Kobus Barnard
Byeongjoo Ahn	Vassilis Athitsos	Nick Barnes
Unaiza Ahsan	Mathieu Aubry	Francisco Barranco
Emre Akbaş	Shai Avidan	Adrien Bartoli
Eren Aksoy	Yannis Avrithis	E. Bayro-Corrochano
Yağız Aksoy	Samaneh Azadi	Paul Beardlsey
Alexandre Alahi	Hossein Azizpour	Vasileios Belagiannis
Jean-Baptiste Alayrac	Artem Babenko	Sean Bell
Samuel Albanie	Timur Bagautdinov	Ismail Ben
Cenek Albl	Andrew Bagdanov	Boulbaba Ben Amor
Saad Ali	Hessam Bagherinezhad	Gil Ben-Artzi
Rahaf Aljundi	Yuval Bahat	Ohad Ben-Shahar
Jose M. Alvarez	Min Bai	Abhijit Bendale
Humam Alwassel	Qinxun Bai	Rodrigo Benenson
Toshiyuki Amano	Song Bai	Fabian Benitez-Quiroz
Mitsuru Ambai	Xiang Bai	Fethallah Benmansour
Mohamed Amer	Peter Bajcsy	Ryad Benosman
Senjian An	Amr Bakry	Filippo Bergamasco
Cosmin Ancuti	Kavita Bala	David Bermudez

Jesus Bermudez-Cameo
Leonard Berrada
Gedas Bertasius
Ross Beveridge
Lucas Beyer
Bir Bhanu
S. Bhattacharya
Binod Bhattarai
Arnav Bhavsar
Simone Bianco
Adel Bibi
Pia Bideau
Josef Bigun
Arijit Biswas
Soma Biswas
Marten Bjoerkman
Volker Blanz
Vishnu Boddeti
Piotr Bojanowski
Terrance Boult
Yuri Boykov
Hakan Boyraz
Eric Brachmann
Samarth Brahmbhatt
Mathieu Bredif
Francois Bremond
Michael Brown
Luc Brun
Shyamal Buch
Pradeep Buddharaju
Aurelie Bugeau
Rudy Bunel
Xavier Burgos Artizzu
Darius Burschka
Andrei Bursuc
Zoya Bylinskii
Fabian Caba
Daniel Cabrini Hauagge
Cesar Cadena Lerma
Holger Caesar
Jianfei Cai
Junjie Cai
Zhaowei Cai
Simone Calderara
Neill Campbell
Octavia Camps

Xun Cao
Yanshuai Cao
Joao Carreira
Dan Casas
Daniel Castro
Jan Cech
M. Emre Celebi
Duygu Ceylan
Menglei Chai
Ayan Chakrabarti
Rudrasis Chakraborty
Shayok Chakraborty
Tat-Jen Cham
Antonin Chambolle
Antoni Chan
Sharat Chandran
Hyun Sung Chang
Ju Yong Chang
Xiaojun Chang
Soravit Changpinyo
Wei-Lun Chao
Yu-Wei Chao
Visesh Chari
Rizwan Chaudhry
Siddhartha Chaudhuri
Rama Chellappa
Chao Chen
Chen Chen
Cheng Chen
Chu-Song Chen
Guang Chen
Hsin-I Chen
Hwann-Tzong Chen
Kai Chen
Kan Chen
Kevin Chen
Liang-Chieh Chen
Lin Chen
Qifeng Chen
Ting Chen
Wei Chen
Xi Chen
Xilin Chen
Xinlei Chen
Yingcong Chen
Yixin Chen

Erkang Cheng
Jingchun Cheng
Ming-Ming Cheng
Wen-Huang Cheng
Yuan Cheng
Anoop Cherian
Liang-Tien Chia
Naoki Chiba
Shao-Yi Chien
Han-Pang Chiu
Wei-Chen Chiu
Nam Ik Cho
Sunghyun Cho
TaeEun Choe
Jongmoo Choi
Christopher Choy
Wen-Sheng Chu
Yung-Yu Chuang
Ondrej Chum
Joon Son Chung
Gökberk Cinbis
James Clark
Andrea Cohen
Forrester Cole
Toby Collins
John Collomosse
Camille Couprie
David Crandall
Marco Cristani
Canton Cristian
James Crowley
Yin Cui
Zhaopeng Cui
Bo Dai
Jifeng Dai
Qieyun Dai
Shengyang Dai
Yuchao Dai
Carlo Dal Mutto
Dima Damen
Zachary Daniels
Kostas Daniilidis
Donald Dansereau
Mohamed Daoudi
Abhishek Das
Samyak Datta

Achal Dave
Shalini De Mello
Teofilo deCampos
Joseph DeGol
Koichiro Deguchi
Alessio Del Bue
Stefanie Demirci
Jia Deng
Zhiwei Deng
Joachim Denzler
Konstantinos Derpanis
Aditya Deshpande
Alban Desmaison
Frédéric Devernay
Abhinav Dhall
Michel Dhome
Hamdi Dibeklioğlu
Mert Dikmen
Cosimo Distante
Ajay Divakaran
Mandar Dixit
Carl Doersch
Piotr Dollar
Bo Dong
Chao Dong
Huang Dong
Jian Dong
Jiangxin Dong
Weisheng Dong
Simon Donné
Gianfranco Doretto
Alexey Dosovitskiy
Matthijs Douze
Bruce Draper
Bertram Drost
Liang Du
Shichuan Du
Gregory Dudek
Zoran Duric
Pınar Duygulu
Hazım Ekenel
Tarek El-Gaaly
Ehsan Elhamifar
Mohamed Elhoseiny
Sabu Emmanuel
Ian Endres

Aykut Erdem
Erkut Erdem
Hugo Jair Escalante
Sergio Escalera
Victor Escorcia
Francisco Estrada
Davide Eynard
Bin Fan
Jialue Fan
Quanfu Fan
Chen Fang
Tian Fang
Yi Fang
Hany Farid
Giovanni Farinella
Ryan Farrell
Alireza Fathi
Christoph Feichtenhofer
Wenxin Feng
Martin Fergie
Cornelia Fermuller
Basura Fernando
Michael Firman
Bob Fisher
John Fisher
Mathew Fisher
Boris Flach
Matt Flagg
Francois Fleuret
David Fofi
Ruth Fong
Gian Luca Foresti
Per-Erik Forssén
David Fouhey
Katerina Fragkiadaki
Victor Fragoso
Jan-Michael Frahm
Jean-Sebastien Franco
Ohad Fried
Simone Frintrop
Huazhu Fu
Yun Fu
Olac Fuentes
Christopher Funk
Thomas Funkhouser
Brian Funt

Ryo Furukawa
Yasutaka Furukawa
Andrea Fusiello
Fatma Güney
Raghudeep Gadde
Silvano Galliani
Orazio Gallo
Chuang Gan
Bin-Bin Gao
Jin Gao
Junbin Gao
Ruohan Gao
Shenghua Gao
Animesh Garg
Ravi Garg
Erik Gartner
Simone Gasparin
Jochen Gast
Leon A. Gatys
Stratis Gavves
Liuhao Ge
Timnit Gebru
James Gee
Peter Gehler
Xin Geng
Guido Gerig
David Geronimo
Bernard Ghanem
Michael Gharbi
Golnaz Ghiasi
Spyros Gidaris
Andrew Gilbert
Rohit Girdhar
Ioannis Gkioulekas
Georgia Gkioxari
Guy Godin
Roland Goecke
Michael Goesele
Nuno Goncalves
Boqing Gong
Minglun Gong
Yunchao Gong
Abel Gonzalez-Garcia
Daniel Gordon
Paulo Gotardo
Stephen Gould

Venu Govindu
Helmut Grabner
Petr Gronat
Steve Gu
Josechu Guerrero
Anupam Guha
Jean-Yves Guillemaut
Alp Güler
Erhan Gündoğdu
Guodong Guo
Xinqing Guo
Ankush Gupta
Mohit Gupta
Saurabh Gupta
Tanmay Gupta
Abner Guzman Rivera
Timo Hackel
Sunil Hadap
Christian Haene
Ralf Haeusler
Levente Hajder
David Hall
Peter Hall
Stefan Haller
Ghassan Hamarneh
Fred Hamprecht
Onur Hamsici
Bohyung Han
Junwei Han
Xufeng Han
Yahong Han
Ankur Handa
Albert Haque
Tatsuya Harada
Mehrtash Harandi
Bharath Hariharan
Mahmudul Hasan
Tal Hassner
Kenji Hata
Soren Hauberg
Michal Havlena
Zeeshan Hayder
Junfeng He
Lei He
Varsha Hedau
Felix Heide

Wolfgang Heidrich
Janne Heikkila
Jared Heinly
Mattias Heinrich
Lisa Anne Hendricks
Dan Hendrycks
Stephane Herbin
Alexander Hermans
Luis Herranz
Aaron Hertzmann
Adrian Hilton
Michael Hirsch
Steven Hoi
Seunghoon Hong
Wei Hong
Anthony Hoogs
Radu Horaud
Yedid Hoshen
Omid Hosseini Jafari
Kuang-Jui Hsu
Winston Hsu
Yinlin Hu
Zhe Hu
Gang Hua
Chen Huang
De-An Huang
Dong Huang
Gary Huang
Heng Huang
Jia-Bin Huang
Qixing Huang
Rui Huang
Sheng Huang
Weilin Huang
Xiaolei Huang
Xinyu Huang
Zhiwu Huang
Tak-Wai Hui
Wei-Chih Hung
Junhwa Hur
Mohamed Hussein
Wonjun Hwang
Anders Hyden
Satoshi Ikehata
Nazlı Ikizler-Cinbis
Viorela Ila

Evren Imre
Eldar Insafutdinov
Go Irie
Hossam Isack
Ahmet Işcen
Daisuke Iwai
Hamid Izadinia
Nathan Jacobs
Suyog Jain
Varun Jampani
C. V. Jawahar
Dinesh Jayaraman
Sadeep Jayasumana
Laszlo Jeni
Hueihan Jhuang
Dinghuang Ji
Hui Ji
Qiang Ji
Fan Jia
Kui Jia
Xu Jia
Huaizu Jiang
Jiayan Jiang
Nianjuan Jiang
Tingting Jiang
Xiaoyi Jiang
Yu-Gang Jiang
Long Jin
Suo Jinli
Justin Johnson
Nebojsa Jojic
Michael Jones
Hanbyul Joo
Jungseock Joo
Ajjen Joshi
Amin Jourabloo
Frederic Jurie
Achuta Kadambi
Samuel Kadoury
Ioannis Kakadiaris
Zdenek Kalal
Yannis Kalantidis
Sinan Kalkan
Vicky Kalogeiton
Sunkavalli Kalyan
J.-K. Kamarainen

Martin Kampel
Kenichi Kanatani
Angjoo Kanazawa
Melih Kandemir
Sing Bing Kang
Zhuoliang Kang
Mohan Kankanhalli
Juho Kannala
Abhishek Kar
Amlan Kar
Svebor Karaman
Leonid Karlinsky
Zoltan Kato
Parneet Kaur
Hiroshi Kawasaki
Misha Kazhdan
Margret Keuper
Sameh Khamis
Naeemullah Khan
Salman Khan
Hadi Kiapour
Joe Kileel
Chanho Kim
Gunhee Kim
Hansung Kim
Junmo Kim
Junsik Kim
Kihwan Kim
Minyoung Kim
Tae Hyun Kim
Tae-Kyun Kim
Akisato Kimura
Zsolt Kira
Alexander Kirillov
Kris Kitani
Maria Klodt
Patrick Knöbelreiter
Jan Knopp
Reinhard Koch
Alexander Kolesnikov
Chen Kong
Naejin Kong
Shu Kong
Piotr Koniusz
Simon Korman
Andreas Koschan

Dimitrios Kosmopoulos
Satwik Kottur
Balazs Kovacs
Adarsh Kowdle
Mike Krainin
Gregory Kramida
Ranjay Krishna
Ravi Krishnan
Matej Kristan
Pavel Krsek
Volker Krueger
Alexander Krull
Hilde Kuehne
Andreas Kuhn
Arjan Kuijper
Zuzana Kukelova
Kuldeep Kulkarni
Shiro Kumano
Avinash Kumar
Vijay Kumar
Abhijit Kundu
Sebastian Kurtek
Junseok Kwon
Jan Kybic
Alexander Ladikos
Shang-Hong Lai
Wei-Sheng Lai
Jean-Francois Lalonde
John Lambert
Zhenzhong Lan
Charis Lanaras
Oswald Lanz
Dong Lao
Longin Jan Latecki
Justin Lazarow
Huu Le
Chen-Yu Lee
Gim Hee Lee
Honglak Lee
Hsin-Ying Lee
Joon-Young Lee
Seungyong Lee
Stefan Lee
Yong Jae Lee
Zhen Lei
Ido Leichter

Victor Lempitsky
Spyridon Leonardos
Marius Leordeanu
Matt Leotta
Thomas Leung
Stefan Leutenegger
Gil Levi
Aviad Levis
Jose Lezama
Ang Li
Dingzeyu Li
Dong Li
Haoxiang Li
Hongdong Li
Hongsheng Li
Hongyang Li
Jianguo Li
Kai Li
Ruiyu Li
Wei Li
Wen Li
Xi Li
Xiaoxiao Li
Xin Li
Xirong Li
Xuelong Li
Xueting Li
Yeqing Li
Yijun Li
Yin Li
Yingwei Li
Yining Li
Yongjie Li
Yu-Feng Li
Zechao Li
Zhengqi Li
Zhenyang Li
Zhizhong Li
Xiaodan Liang
Renjie Liao
Zicheng Liao
Bee Lim
Jongwoo Lim
Joseph Lim
Ser-Nam Lim
Chen-Hsuan Lin

Shih-Yao Lin
Tsung-Yi Lin
Weiyao Lin
Yen-Yu Lin
Haibin Ling
Or Litany
Roee Litman
Anan Liu
Changsong Liu
Chen Liu
Ding Liu
Dong Liu
Feng Liu
Guangcan Liu
Luoqi Liu
Miaomiao Liu
Nian Liu
Risheng Liu
Shu Liu
Shuaicheng Liu
Sifei Liu
Tyng-Luh Liu
Wanquan Liu
Weiwei Liu
Xialei Liu
Xiaoming Liu
Yebin Liu
Yiming Liu
Ziwei Liu
Zongyi Liu
Liliana Lo Presti
Edgar Lobaton
Chengjiang Long
Mingsheng Long
Roberto Lopez-Sastre
Amy Loufti
Brian Lovell
Canyi Lu
Cewu Lu
Feng Lu
Huchuan Lu
Jiajun Lu
Jiasen Lu
Jiwen Lu
Yang Lu
Yujuan Lu

Simon Lucey
Jian-Hao Luo
Jiebo Luo
Pablo Márquez-Neila
Matthias Müller
Chao Ma
Chih-Yao Ma
Lin Ma
Shugao Ma
Wei-Chiu Ma
Zhanyu Ma
Oisin Mac Aodha
Will Maddern
Ludovic Magerand
Marcus Magnor
Vijay Mahadevan
Mohammad Mahoor
Michael Maire
Subhransu Maji
Ameesh Makadia
Atsuto Maki
Yasushi Makihara
Mateusz Malinowski
Tomasz Malisiewicz
Arun Mallya
Roberto Manduchi
Junhua Mao
Dmitrii Marin
Joe Marino
Kenneth Marino
Elisabeta Marinoiu
Ricardo Martin
Aleix Martinez
Julieta Martinez
Aaron Maschinot
Jonathan Masci
Bogdan Matei
Diana Mateus
Stefan Mathe
Kevin Matzen
Bruce Maxwell
Steve Maybank
Walterio Mayol-Cuevas
Mason McGill
Stephen Mckenna
Roey Mechrez

Christopher Mei
Heydi Mendez-Vazquez
Deyu Meng
Thomas Mensink
Bjoern Menze
Domingo Mery
Qiguang Miao
Tomer Michaeli
Antoine Miech
Ondrej Miksik
Anton Milan
Gregor Miller
Cai Minjie
Majid Mirmehdi
Ishan Misra
Niloy Mitra
Anurag Mittal
Nirbhay Modhe
Davide Modolo
Pritish Mohapatra
Pascal Monasse
Mathew Monfort
Taesup Moon
Sandino Morales
Vlad Morariu
Philippos Mordohai
Francesc Moreno
Henrique Morimitsu
Yael Moses
Ben-Ezra Moshe
Roozbeh Mottaghi
Yadong Mu
Lopamudra Mukherjee
Mario Munich
Ana Murillo
Damien Muselet
Armin Mustafa
Siva Karthik Mustikovela
Moin Nabi
Sobhan Naderi
Hajime Nagahara
Varun Nagaraja
Tushar Nagarajan
Arsha Nagrani
Nikhil Naik
Atsushi Nakazawa

P. J. Narayanan
Charlie Nash
Lakshmanan Nataraj
Fabian Nater
Lukáš Neumann
Natalia Neverova
Alejandro Newell
Phuc Nguyen
Xiaohan Nie
David Nilsson
Ko Nishino
Zhenxing Niu
Shohei Nobuhara
Klas Nordberg
Mohammed Norouzi
David Novotny
Ifeoma Nwogu
Matthew O'Toole
Guillaume Obozinski
Jean-Marc Odobez
Eyal Ofek
Ferda Ofli
Tae-Hyun Oh
Iason Oikonomidis
Takeshi Oishi
Takahiro Okabe
Takayuki Okatani
Vlad Olaru
Michael Opitz
Jose Oramas
Vicente Ordonez
Ivan Oseledets
Aljosa Osep
Magnus Oskarsson
Martin R. Oswald
Wanli Ouyang
Andrew Owens
Mustafa Özuysal
Jinshan Pan
Xingang Pan
Rameswar Panda
Sharath Pankanti
Julien Pansiot
Nicolas Papadakis
George Papandreou
N. Papanikolopoulos

Hyun Soo Park
In Kyu Park
Jaesik Park
Omkar Parkhi
Alvaro Parra Bustos
C. Alejandro Parraga
Vishal Patel
Deepak Pathak
Ioannis Patras
Viorica Patraucean
Genevieve Patterson
Kim Pedersen
Robert Peharz
Selen Pehlivan
Xi Peng
Bojan Pepik
Talita Perciano
Federico Pernici
Adrian Peter
Stavros Petridis
Vladimir Petrovic
Henning Petzka
Tomas Pfister
Trung Pham
Justus Piater
Massimo Piccardi
Sudeep Pillai
Pedro Pinheiro
Lerrel Pinto
Bernardo Pires
Aleksis Pirinen
Fiora Pirri
Leonid Pischulin
Tobias Ploetz
Bryan Plummer
Yair Poleg
Jean Ponce
Gerard Pons-Moll
Jordi Pont-Tuset
Alin Popa
Fatih Porikli
Horst Possegger
Viraj Prabhu
Andrea Prati
Maria Priisalu
Véronique Prinet

Victor Prisacariu
Jan Prokaj
Nicolas Pugeault
Luis Puig
Ali Punjani
Senthil Purushwalkam
Guido Pusiol
Guo-Jun Qi
Xiaojuan Qi
Hongwei Qin
Shi Qiu
Faisal Qureshi
Matthias Rüther
Petia Radeva
Umer Rafi
Rahul Raguram
Swaminathan Rahul
Varun Ramakrishna
Kandan Ramakrishnan
Ravi Ramamoorthi
Vignesh Ramanathan
Vasili Ramanishka
R. Ramasamy Selvaraju
Rene Ranftl
Carolina Raposo
Nikhil Rasiwasia
Nalini Ratha
Sai Ravela
Avinash Ravichandran
Ramin Raziperchikolaei
Sylvestre-Alvise Rebuffi
Adria Recasens
Joe Redmon
Timo Rehfeld
Michal Reinstein
Konstantinos Rematas
Haibing Ren
Shaoqing Ren
Wenqi Ren
Zhile Ren
Hamid Rezatofighi
Nicholas Rhinehart
Helge Rhodin
Elisa Ricci
Eitan Richardson
Stephan Richter

Gernot Riegler
Hayko Riemenschneider
Tammy Riklin Raviv
Ergys Ristani
Tobias Ritschel
Mariano Rivera
Samuel Rivera
Antonio Robles-Kelly
Ignacio Rocco
Jason Rock
Emanuele Rodola
Mikel Rodriguez
Gregory Rogez
Marcus Rohrbach
Gemma Roig
Javier Romero
Olaf Ronneberger
Amir Rosenfeld
Bodo Rosenhahn
Guy Rosman
Arun Ross
Samuel Rota Bulò
Peter Roth
Constantin Rothkopf
Sebastien Roy
Amit Roy-Chowdhury
Ognjen Rudovic
Adria Ruiz
Javier Ruiz-del-Solar
Christian Rupprecht
Olga Russakovsky
Chris Russell
Alexandre Sablayrolles
Fereshteh Sadeghi
Ryusuke Sagawa
Hideo Saito
Elham Sakhaee
Albert Ali Salah
Conrad Sanderson
Koppal Sanjeev
Aswin Sankaranarayanan
Elham Saraee
Jason Saragih
Sudeep Sarkar
Imari Sato
Shin'ichi Satoh

Torsten Sattler
Bogdan Savchynskyy
Johannes Schönberger
Hanno Scharr
Walter Scheirer
Bernt Schiele
Frank Schmidt
Tanner Schmidt
Dirk Schnieders
Samuel Schulter
William Schwartz
Alexander Schwing
Ozan Sener
Soumyadip Sengupta
Laura Sevilla-Lara
Mubarak Shah
Shishir Shah
Fahad Shahbaz Khan
Amir Shahroudy
Jing Shao
Xiaowei Shao
Roman Shapovalov
Nataliya Shapovalova
Ali Sharif Razavian
Gaurav Sharma
Mohit Sharma
Pramod Sharma
Viktoriia Sharmanska
Eli Shechtman
Mark Sheinin
Evan Shelhamer
Chunhua Shen
Li Shen
Wei Shen
Xiaohui Shen
Xiaoyong Shen
Ziyi Shen
Lu Sheng
Baoguang Shi
Boxin Shi
Kevin Shih
Hyunjung Shim
Ilan Shimshoni
Young Min Shin
Koichi Shinoda
Matthew Shreve

Tianmin Shu
Zhixin Shu
Kaleem Siddiqi
Gunnar Sigurdsson
Nathan Silberman
Tomas Simon
Abhishek Singh
Gautam Singh
Maneesh Singh
Praveer Singh
Richa Singh
Saurabh Singh
Sudipta Sinha
Vladimir Smutny
Noah Snavely
Cees Snoek
Kihyuk Sohn
Eric Sommerlade
Sanghyun Son
Bi Song
Shiyu Song
Shuran Song
Xuan Song
Yale Song
Yang Song
Yibing Song
Lorenzo Sorgi
Humberto Sossa
Pratul Srinivasan
Michael Stark
Bjorn Stenger
Rainer Stiefelhagen
Joerg Stueckler
Jan Stuehmer
Hang Su
Hao Su
Shuochen Su
R. Subramanian
Yusuke Sugano
Akihiro Sugimoto
Baochen Sun
Chen Sun
Jian Sun
Jin Sun
Lin Sun
Min Sun

Qing Sun
Zhaohui Sun
David Suter
Eran Swears
Raza Syed Hussain
T. Syeda-Mahmood
Christian Szegedy
Duy-Nguyen Ta
Tolga Taşdizen
Hemant Tagare
Yuichi Taguchi
Ying Tai
Yu-Wing Tai
Jun Takamatsu
Hugues Talbot
Toru Tamak
Robert Tamburo
Chaowei Tan
Meng Tang
Peng Tang
Siyu Tang
Wei Tang
Junli Tao
Ran Tao
Xin Tao
Makarand Tapaswi
Jean-Philippe Tarel
Maxim Tatarchenko
Bugra Tekin
Demetri Terzopoulos
Christian Theobalt
Diego Thomas
Rajat Thomas
Qi Tian
Xinmei Tian
YingLi Tian
Yonghong Tian
Yonglong Tian
Joseph Tighe
Radu Timofte
Massimo Tistarelli
Sinisa Todorovic
Pavel Tokmakov
Giorgos Tolias
Federico Tombari
Tatiana Tommasi

Chetan Tonde
Xin Tong
Akihiko Torii
Andrea Torsello
Florian Trammer
Du Tran
Quoc-Huy Tran
Rudolph Triebel
Alejandro Troccoli
Leonardo Trujillo
Tomasz Trzcinski
Sam Tsai
Yi-Hsuan Tsai
Hung-Yu Tseng
Vagia Tsiminaki
Aggeliki Tsoli
Wei-Chih Tu
Shubham Tulsiani
Fred Tung
Tony Tung
Matt Turek
Oncel Tuzel
Georgios Tzimiropoulos
Ilkay Ulusoy
Osman Ulusoy
Dmitry Ulyanov
Paul Upchurch
Ben Usman
Evgeniya Ustinova
Himanshu Vajaria
Alexander Vakhitov
Jack Valmadre
Ernest Valveny
Jan van Gemert
Grant Van Horn
Jagannadan Varadarajan
Gul Varol
Sebastiano Vascon
Francisco Vasconcelos
Mayank Vatsa
Javier Vazquez-Corral
Ramakrishna Vedantam
Ashok Veeraraghavan
Andreas Veit
Raviteja Vemulapalli
Jonathan Ventura

Matthias Vestner
Minh Vo
Christoph Vogel
Michele Volpi
Carl Vondrick
Sven Wachsmuth
Toshikazu Wada
Michael Waechter
Catherine Wah
Jacob Walker
Jun Wan
Boyu Wang
Chen Wang
Chunyu Wang
De Wang
Fang Wang
Hongxing Wang
Hua Wang
Jiang Wang
Jingdong Wang
Jinglu Wang
Jue Wang
Le Wang
Lei Wang
Lezi Wang
Liang Wang
Lichao Wang
Lijun Wang
Limin Wang
Liwei Wang
Naiyan Wang
Oliver Wang
Qi Wang
Ruiping Wang
Shenlong Wang
Shu Wang
Song Wang
Tao Wang
Xiaofang Wang
Xiaolong Wang
Xinchao Wang
Xinggang Wang
Xintao Wang
Yang Wang
Yu-Chiang Frank Wang
Yu-Xiong Wang

Zhaowen Wang
Zhe Wang
Anne Wannenwetsch
Simon Warfield
Scott Wehrwein
Donglai Wei
Ping Wei
Shih-En Wei
Xiu-Shen Wei
Yichen Wei
Xie Weidi
Philippe Weinzaepfel
Longyin Wen
Eric Wengrowski
Tomas Werner
Michael Wilber
Rick Wildes
Olivia Wiles
Kyle Wilson
David Wipf
Kwan-Yee Wong
Daniel Worrall
John Wright
Baoyuan Wu
Chao-Yuan Wu
Jiajun Wu
Jianxin Wu
Tianfu Wu
Xiaodong Wu
Xiaohe Wu
Xinxiao Wu
Yang Wu
Yi Wu
Ying Wu
Yuxin Wu
Zheng Wu
Stefanie Wuhrer
Yin Xia
Tao Xiang
Yu Xiang
Lei Xiao
Tong Xiao
Yang Xiao
Cihang Xie
Dan Xie
Jianwen Xie

Jin Xie
Lingxi Xie
Pengtao Xie
Saining Xie
Wenxuan Xie
Yuchen Xie
Bo Xin
Junliang Xing
Peng Xingchao
Bo Xiong
Fei Xiong
Xuehan Xiong
Yuanjun Xiong
Chenliang Xu
Danfei Xu
Huijuan Xu
Jia Xu
Weipeng Xu
Xiangyu Xu
Yan Xu
Yuanlu Xu
Jia Xue
Tianfan Xue
Erdem Yörük
Abhay Yadav
Deshraj Yadav
Payman Yadollahpour
Yasushi Yagi
Toshihiko Yamasaki
Fei Yan
Hang Yan
Junchi Yan
Junjie Yan
Sijie Yan
Keiji Yanai
Bin Yang
Chih-Yuan Yang
Dong Yang
Herb Yang
Jianchao Yang
Jianwei Yang
Jiaolong Yang
Jie Yang
Jimei Yang
Jufeng Yang
Linjie Yang

Michael Ying Yang
Ming Yang
Ruiduo Yang
Ruigang Yang
Shuo Yang
Wei Yang
Xiaodong Yang
Yanchao Yang
Yi Yang
Angela Yao
Bangpeng Yao
Cong Yao
Jian Yao
Ting Yao
Julian Yarkony
Mark Yatskar
Jinwei Ye
Mao Ye
Mei-Chen Yeh
Raymond Yeh
Serena Yeung
Kwang Moo Yi
Shuai Yi
Alper Yılmaz
Lijun Yin
Xi Yin
Zhaozheng Yin
Xianghua Ying
Ryo Yonetani
Donghyun Yoo
Ju Hong Yoon
Kuk-Jin Yoon
Chong You
Shaodi You
Aron Yu
Fisher Yu
Gang Yu
Jingyi Yu
Ke Yu
Licheng Yu
Pei Yu
Qian Yu
Rong Yu
Shoou-I Yu
Stella Yu
Xiang Yu

Yang Yu
Zhiding Yu
Ganzhao Yuan
Jing Yuan
Junsong Yuan
Lu Yuan
Stefanos Zafeiriou
Sergey Zagoruyko
Amir Zamir
K. Zampogiannis
Andrei Zanfir
Mihai Zanfir
Pablo Zegers
Eyasu Zemene
Andy Zeng
Xingyu Zeng
Yun Zeng
De-Chuan Zhan
Cheng Zhang
Dong Zhang
Guofeng Zhang
Han Zhang
Hang Zhang
Hanwang Zhang
Jian Zhang
Jianguo Zhang
Jianming Zhang
Jiawei Zhang
Junping Zhang
Lei Zhang
Linguang Zhang
Ning Zhang
Qing Zhang

Quanshi Zhang
Richard Zhang
Runze Zhang
Shanshan Zhang
Shiliang Zhang
Shu Zhang
Ting Zhang
Xiangyu Zhang
Xiaofan Zhang
Xu Zhang
Yimin Zhang
Yinda Zhang
Yongqiang Zhang
Yuting Zhang
Zhanpeng Zhang
Ziyu Zhang
Bin Zhao
Chen Zhao
Hang Zhao
Hengshuang Zhao
Qijun Zhao
Rui Zhao
Yue Zhao
Enliang Zheng
Liang Zheng
Stephan Zheng
Wei-Shi Zheng
Wenming Zheng
Yin Zheng
Yinqiang Zheng
Yuanjie Zheng
Guangyu Zhong
Bolei Zhou

Guang-Tong Zhou
Huiyu Zhou
Jiahuan Zhou
S. Kevin Zhou
Tinghui Zhou
Wengang Zhou
Xiaowei Zhou
Xingyi Zhou
Yin Zhou
Zihan Zhou
Fan Zhu
Guangming Zhu
Ji Zhu
Jiejie Zhu
Jun-Yan Zhu
Shizhan Zhu
Siyu Zhu
Xiangxin Zhu
Xiatian Zhu
Yan Zhu
Yingying Zhu
Yixin Zhu
Yuke Zhu
Zhenyao Zhu
Liansheng Zhuang
Zeeshan Zia
Karel Zimmermann
Daniel Zoran
Danping Zou
Qi Zou
Silvia Zuffi
Wangmeng Zuo
Xinxin Zuo

Contents – Part I

Learning for Vision

Convolutional Networks with Adaptive Inference Graphs

Andreas Veit[(✉)] and Serge Belongie

Department of Computer Science and Cornell Tech, Cornell University,
New York, NY, USA
{av443,sjb344}@cornell.edu
https://tech.cornell.edu/

Abstract. Do convolutional networks really need a fixed feed-forward structure? What if, after identifying the high-level concept of an image, a network could move directly to a layer that can distinguish fine-grained differences? Currently, a network would first need to execute sometimes hundreds of intermediate layers that specialize in unrelated aspects. Ideally, the more a network already knows about an image, the better it should be at deciding which layer to compute next. In this work, we propose convolutional networks with adaptive inference graphs (ConvNet-AIG) that adaptively define their network topology conditioned on the input image. Following a high-level structure similar to residual networks (ResNets), ConvNet-AIG decides for each input image on the fly which layers are needed. In experiments on ImageNet we show that ConvNet-AIG learns distinct inference graphs for different categories. Both ConvNet-AIG with 50 and 101 layers outperform their ResNet counterpart, while using 20% and 33% less computations respectively. By grouping parameters into layers for related classes and only executing relevant layers, ConvNet-AIG improves both efficiency and overall classification quality. Lastly, we also study the effect of adaptive inference graphs on the susceptibility towards adversarial examples. We observe that ConvNet-AIG shows a higher robustness than ResNets, complementing other known defense mechanisms.

1 Introduction

Often, convolutional networks (ConvNets) are already confident about the high-level concept of an image after only a few layers. This raises the question of what happens in the remainder of the network that often comprises hundreds of layers for many state-of-the-art models. To shed light on this, it is important to note that due to their success, ConvNets are used to classify increasingly large sets of visually diverse categories. Thus, most parameters model high-level features that, in contrast to low-level and many mid-level concepts, cannot be broadly shared across categories. As a result, the networks become larger and slower as the number of categories rises. Moreover, for any given input image the number of computed features focusing on unrelated concepts increases.

© Springer Nature Switzerland AG 2018
V. Ferrari et al. (Eds.): ECCV 2018, LNCS 11205, pp. 3–18, 2018.
https://doi.org/10.1007/978-3-030-01246-5_1

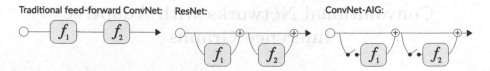

Fig. 1. ConvNet-AIG (right) follows a high level structure similar to ResNets (center) by introducing identity skip-connections that bypass each layer. The key difference is that for each layer, a gate determines whether to execute or skip the layer. This enables individual inference graphs conditioned on the input.

What if, after identifying that an image contains a bird, a ConvNet could move directly to a layer that can distinguish different bird species, without executing intermediate layers that specialize in unrelated aspects? Intuitively, the more the network already knows about an image, the better it could be at deciding which layer to compute next. This shares resemblance with decision trees that employ information theoretic approaches to select the most informative features to evaluate. Such a network could decouple inference time from the number of learned concepts. A recent study [31] provides a key insight towards the realization of this scenario. The authors study residual networks (ResNets) [11] and show that almost any individual layer can be removed from a trained ResNet without interfering with other layers. This leads us to the following research question: *Do we really need fixed structures for convolutional networks, or could we assemble network graphs on the fly, conditioned on the input?*

In this work, we propose ConvNet-AIG, a convolutional network that adaptively defines its inference graph conditioned on the input image. Specifically, ConvNet-AIG learns a set of convolutional layers and decides for each input image which layers are needed. By learning both general layers useful to all images and expert layers specializing on subsets of categories, it allows to only compute features relevant to the input image. It is worthy to note that ConvNet-AIG does not require special supervision about label hierarchies and relationships.

Figure 1 gives an overview of our approach. ConvNet-AIG follows a structure similar to a ResNet. The key difference is that for each residual layer, a gate determines whether the layer is needed for the current input image. The main technical challenge is that the gates need to make discrete decisions, which are difficult to integrate into convolutional networks that we would like to train using gradient descent. To incorporate the discrete decisions, we build upon recent work [4,18,24] that introduces differentiable approximations for discrete stochastic nodes in neural networks. In particular, we model the gates as discrete random variables over two states: to execute the respective layer or to skip it. Further, we model the gates conditional on the output of the previous layer. This allows to construct inference graphs adaptively based on the input and to train both the convolutional weights and the discrete gates jointly end-to-end.

In experiments on ImageNet [5], we demonstrate that ConvNet-AIG effectively learns to generate inference graphs such that for each input only relevant features are computed. In terms of accuracy both ConvNet-AIG 50 and ConvNet-AIG 101 outperform their ResNet counterpart, while at the same time using 20% and 33% less computations. We further show that, without specific supervision, ConvNet-AIG discovers parts of the class hierarchy and learns specialized layers focusing on subsets of categories such as animals and man-made objects. It even learns distinct inference graphs for some mid-level categories such as birds, dogs and reptiles. By grouping parameters for related classes and only executing relevant layers, ConvNet-AIG both improves efficiency and overall classification quality. Lastly, we also study the effect of adaptive inference graphs on susceptibility towards adversarial examples. We show that ConvNet-AIG is consistently more robust than ResNets, independent of adversary strength and that the additional robustness persists even when applying additional defense mechanisms.

2 Related Work

Our study is related to work in multiple fields. Several works have focused on **neural network composition** for visual question answering (VQA) [1, 2, 19] and zero-shot learning [25]. While these approaches include convolutional networks, they focus on constructing a fixed computational graph up front to solve tasks such as VQA. In contrast, the focus of our work is to construct a convolutional network conditioned on the input image on the fly during execution.

Our approach can be seen as an example of **adaptive computation** for neural networks. Cascaded classifiers [32] have a long tradition for computer vision by quickly rejecting "easy" negatives. Recently, similar approaches have been proposed for neural networks [22, 33]. In an alternative direction, [3, 26] propose to adjust the amount of computation in fully-connected neural networks. To adapt computation time in convolutional networks, [14, 30] propose architectures that add classification branches to intermediate layers. This allows stopping a computation early once a satisfying level of confidence is reached. Most closely related to our approach is the work on spatially adaptive computation time for residual networks [6]. In that paper, a ResNet adaptively determines after which layer to stop computation. Our work differs from this approach in that we do not perform early stopping, but instead determine which subset of layers to execute. This is key as it allows the grouping of parameters that are relevant for similar categories and thus enables distinct inference graphs for different categories.

Our work is further related to network **regularization with stochastic noise**. By randomly dropping neurons during training, Dropout [27] offers an effective way to prevent neural networks from over-fitting. Closely related is the work on stochastic depth [16], where entire layers of a ResNet are randomly removed during each training iteration. Our work resembles this approach in that it also includes stochastic nodes that decide whether to execute layers. However, in contrast to our work, layer removal in stochastic depth is independent from the input and aims to *increase* redundancy among layers. In our work, we construct the inference graph conditioned on the input image to *reduce* redundancy and allow the network to learn layers specialized on subsets of the data.

Lastly, our work can also be seen as an example of an **attention mechanism** in that we select specific layers of importance for each input image to assemble the inference graph. This is related to approaches such as highway networks [28] and squeeze-and-excitation networks [13] where the output of a residual layer is rescaled according to the layer's importance. This allows these approaches to emphasize some layers and pay less attention to others. In contrast to our work, these are soft attention mechanisms and still require the execution of every single layer. Our work is a hard attention mechanism and thus enables decoupling computation time from the number of categories.

3   Adaptive Inference Graphs

Traditional feed-forward ConvNets can be considered as a set of N layers which are sequentially applied to an input image. Formally, let $\mathcal{F}_l(\cdot)$, $l \in \{1, ..., N\}$ denote the function computed by the lth layer. With $\mathbf{x}_0$ as input image and $\mathbf{x}_l$ as output of the lth layer, such a network can be recursively defined as

$$\mathbf{x}_l = \mathcal{F}_l(\mathbf{x}_{l-1}) \tag{1}$$

ResNets [11] change this definition by introducing identity skip-connections that bypass each layer, i.e., the input to each layer is also added to its output. This has been shown to greatly ease optimization during training. As gradients can propagate directly through the skip-connection, early layers still receive sufficient learning signal even in very deep networks. A ResNet can be defined as

$$\mathbf{x}_l = \mathbf{x}_{l-1} + \mathcal{F}_l(\mathbf{x}_{l-1}) \tag{2}$$

In a follow-up study [31] on the effects of the skip-connection, it has been shown that, although all layers are trained jointly, they exhibit a high degree of independence. Further, almost any individual layer can be removed from a trained ResNet without harming performance and interfering with other layers.

3.1   Gated Inference

Inspired by the observations in [31], we design ConvNet-AIG, a network that can define its topology on the fly. The architecture follows the basic structure of a ResNet with the key difference that instead of executing all layers, the network determines for each input image which subset of layers to execute. In particular, with layers focusing on different subgroups of categories, it can select only those layers necessary for the specific input. A ConvNet-AIG can be defined as

$$\mathbf{x}_l = \mathbf{x}_{l-1} + z(\mathbf{x}_{l-1}) \cdot \mathcal{F}_l(\mathbf{x}_{l-1})$$
$$\text{where } z(\mathbf{x}_{l-1}) \in \{0, 1\} \tag{3}$$

where $z(\mathbf{x}_{l-1})$ is a gate that, conditioned on the input to the layer, decides whether to execute the next layer. The gate chooses between two discrete states: 0 for 'off' and 1 for 'on', which can be seen as a *hard attention mechanism*.

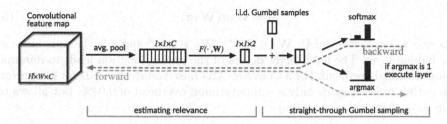

Fig. 2. Overview of gating unit. Each gate comprises two parts. The first part estimates the relevance of the layer to be executed. The second part decides whether to execute the layer given the estimated relevance. In particular, the Gumbel-Max trick and its softmax relaxation are used to allow for the propagation of gradients through the discrete decision.

For the gate to be effective, it needs to address a few key challenges. First, to estimate the relevance of its layer, the gate needs to understand its input features. To prevent mode collapse into trivial solutions that are independent of the input features, such as always or never executing a layer, we found it to be of key importance for the gate to be stochastic. We achieve this by adding noise to the estimated relevance. Second, the gate needs to make a discrete decision, while still providing gradients for the relevance estimation. We achieve this with the Gumbel-Max trick and its softmax relaxation. Third, the gate needs to operate with low computational cost. Figure 2 provides and overview of the two key components of the proposed gate. The first one efficiently estimates the relevance of the respective layer for the current image. The second component makes a discrete decision by sampling using Gumbel-Softmax [18,24].

3.2 Estimating Layer Relevance

The goal of the gate's first component is to estimate its layer's relevance given the input features. The input to the gate is the output of the previous layer $x_{l-1} \in \mathbb{R}^{W \times H \times C}$. Since operating on the full feature map is computationally expensive, we build upon recent studies [13,17,23] which show that much of the information in convolutional features is captured by the statistics of the different channels and their interdependencies. In particular, we only consider channel-wise means gathered by global average pooling. This compresses the input features into a $1 \times 1 \times C$ channel descriptor.

$$z_c = \frac{1}{H \times W} \sum_{i=1}^{H} \sum_{j=1}^{W} x_{i,j,c} \qquad (4)$$

To capture the dependencies between channels, we add a simple non-linear function of two fully-connected layers connected with a ReLU [7] activation function. The output of this operation is the relevance score for the layer. Specifically, it is a vector β containing unnormalized scores for the two actions of (a) computing and (b) skipping the following layer, respectively.

$$\beta = \mathbf{W}_2 \sigma(\mathbf{W}_1 \mathbf{z}) \tag{5}$$

where σ refers to the ReLU, $\mathbf{W}_1 \in \mathbb{R}^{d \times C}$, $\mathbf{W}_2 \in \mathbb{R}^{2 \times d}$ and d is the dimension of the hidden layer. The lightweight design of the gating function leads to minimal computational overhead. For a ConvNet-AIG based on ResNet 101 for ImageNet, the gating function adds only a computational overhead of 0.04%, but allows to skip 33% of its layers on average.

3.3 Greedy Gumbel Sampling

The goal of the second component is to make a discrete decision based on the relevance scores. For this, we build upon recent work that propose approaches for propagating gradients through stochastic neurons [4,20]. In particular, we utilize the Gumbel-Max trick [9] and its recent continuous relaxation [18,24].

A naïve attempt would be to choose the maximum of the two relevance scores to decide whether to execute or skip the layer. However, this approach leads to rapid mode collapse as it does not account for the gate's uncertainty and it is further not differentiable. Ideally, we would like to choose among the two options proportional to their relevance scores. A standard way to introduce such stochasticity is to add noise to the scores.

We choose the Gumbel distribution for the noise, because of its key property that is known as the Gumbel-Max trick [9]. A random variable G follows a Gumbel distribution if $G = \mu - \log(-\log(U))$, where μ is a real-valued location parameter and U a sample from the uniform distribution $U \sim \text{Unif}[0, 1]$. Then, the Gumbel-Max trick states that if we samples from K Gumbel distributions with location parameters $\{\mu_{k'}\}_{k'=1}^{K}$, the outcome of the kth Gumbel is the largest exactly with the softmax probability of its location parameter

$$P(\text{k is largest} | \{\mu_{k'}\}_{k'=1}^{K}) = \frac{e^{\mu_k}}{\sum_{k'=1}^{K} e^{\mu_{k'}}} \tag{6}$$

With this we can parameterize discrete distributions in terms of Gumbel random variables. In particular, let X be a discrete random variable with probabilities $P(X = k) \propto \alpha_k$ and let $\{G_k\}_{k \in \{1,\dots,K\}}$ be a sequence of i.i.d. Gumbel random variables with location $\mu = 0$. Then, we can sample from the discrete variable X by sampling from the Gumbel random variables

$$X = \underset{k \in \{1,\dots,K\}}{\arg\max} \left(\log \alpha_k + G_k \right) \tag{7}$$

A drawback of this approach is that the argmax operation is not continuous. To address this, a continuous relaxation of the Gumbel-Max trick has been proposed [18,24], replacing the argmax with a softmax. Note that a discrete random variable can be expressed as a one-hot vector, where the realization of the variable is the index of the non-zero entry. With this notation, a sample from the Gumbel-Softmax relaxation can be expressed by the vector $\hat{X}$ as follows:

$$\hat{X}_k = \text{softmax} \left((\log \alpha_k + G_k) / \tau \right) \tag{8}$$

where $\hat{X}_k$ is the kth element in $\hat{X}$ and τ is the temperature of the softmax. With $\tau \to 0$, the softmax function approaches the argmax function and Eq. 8 becomes equivalent to the discrete sampler. For $\tau \to \infty$ it becomes a uniform distribution. Since softmax is differentiable and G_k is independent noise, we can propagate gradients to the probabilities α_k. To generate samples, we set the log probabilities to the estimated relevance scores, $\log \alpha = \beta$.

One option to employ the Gumbel-softmax estimator is to use the continuous version from Eq. 8 during training and obtain discrete samples with Eq. 7 during testing. An alternative is the *straight-through* version [18] of the Gumbel-softmax estimator. There, during training, for the forward pass we get discrete samples from Eq. 7, but during the backwards pass we compute the gradient of the softmax relaxation in Eq. 8. Note that the estimator is biased due to the mismatch between forward and backward pass. However, we observe that empirically the straight-through estimator performs better and leads to inference graphs that are more category-specific. We illustrate the two different paths during the forward and backward pass in Fig. 2.

3.4   Training Loss

For the network to learn when to use which layer, we constrain how often each layer is allowed to be used. Specifically, we use soft constraints by introducing an additional loss term that encourages each layer to be executed at a certain target rate t. This guides the optimization to solutions in which parameters that are relevant only to subsets of related categories are grouped together in separate layers, which minimizes the amount of unnecessary features to be computed. We approximate the execution rates for each layer over each mini-batch and penalize deviations from the target rate. Let $\bar{z}_l$ denote the fraction of images within a mini-batch that layer l is executed. Then, the target rate loss is defined as

$$\mathcal{L}_{target} = \sum_{l=1}^{N} (\bar{z}_l - t)^2 \qquad (9)$$

The target rate provides an easy instrument to adjust computation time. ConvNet-AIG is robust to a wide range of target rates. We study the effect of the target rate on classification accuracy and inference time in the experimental section. With the standard multi-class logistic loss, $\mathcal{L}_{MC}$, the overall training loss is

$$\mathcal{L}_{AIG} = \mathcal{L}_{MC} + \mathcal{L}_{target} \qquad (10)$$

We optimize this joint loss with mini-batch stochastic gradient descent.

4   Experiments

We perform a series experiments to evaluate the performance of ConvNet-AIG and whether it learns specialized layers and category-specific inference graphs. Lastly, we study its robustness by analyzing the effect of adaptive inference graphs on the susceptibility towards adversarial attacks.

Table 1. Test error on CIFAR 10 in %. ConvNet-AIG 110 clearly outperforms ResNet 110 while only using a subset of 82% of the layers. When executing all layers (ConvNet-AIG 110*), it also outperforms stochastic depth.

Model	Error	#Params (10^6)	FLOPs (10^9)
ResNet 110 [11]	6.61	1.7	0.5
Pre-ResNet 110 [12]	6.37	1.7	0.5
Stochastic Depth ResNet 110 [16]	5.25	1.7	0.5
ConvNet-AIG 110	5.76	1.78	0.41
ConvNet-AIG 110*	**5.14**	1.78	0.5

4.1 Results on CIFAR

We first perform a set of experiments on CIFAR-10 [21] to validate the proposed gating mechanism and its effectiveness to distribute computation among layers.

Model Configurations and Training Details. We build ConvNet-AIG based on the original ResNet 110 [11]. Besides the added gates, ConvNet-AIG follows the same architecture as ResNet 110. For the gates, we choose a hidden state of size $d = 16$. The additional gate per residual block, adds a fixed overhead of 0.01% more floating point operations and 4.8% more parameters compared to the standard ResNet-110. We follow a similar training scheme as [11] with momentum 0.9 and weight decay 5×10^{-4}. All models are trained for 350 epochs with a mini-batch size of 256. We use a step-wise learning rate starting at 0.1 and decaying by 10^{-1} after 150 and 250 epochs. We adopt a standard data-augmentation scheme, where images are padded with 4 pixels on each side, randomly cropped to 32×32 and with probability 0.5 horizontally flipped.

Results. Table 1 shows test error on CIFAR 10 for ResNet [11], pre-activation ResNet [12], stochastic depth [16] and their ConvNet-AIG counterpart. The table also shows the number of model parameters and floating point operations (multiply-adds). We compare two variants: For standard ConvNet-AIG, we only execute layers with open gates. As a second variant, which we indicate by " * ", we execute all layers and analogous to Dropout [27] and stochastic depth [16] the output of each layer is scaled by its expected execution rate.

From the results, we observe that ConvNet-AIG clearly outperforms its ResNet counterparts, even when using only a subset of the layers. In particular, ConvNet-AIG 110 with a target-rate of 0.7 uses only 82% of the layers in expectation. Since ResNet 110 might be over-parameterized for CIFAR-10, the regularization induced by dropping layers could be a key factor to performance. We observe that ConvNet-AIG 110* outperforms stochastic depth, implying benefits of adaptive inference graphs beyond regularization. In fact, ConvNet-AIG learns to identify layers of key importance such as downsampling layers and learns to always execute them, although they incur computation cost. We do not observe any downward outliers, i.e. layers that are dropped every time.

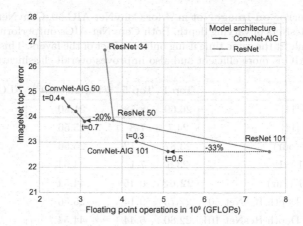

Fig. 3. Top-1 accuracy vs. computational cost on ImageNet. ConvNet-AIG 50 outperforms ResNet 50, while skipping 20% of its layers in expectation. Similarly, ConvNet-AIG 101 outperforms ResNet 101 while requiring 33% less computations. It is often more effective to decrease the target rate than to reduce the number of layers.

4.2   Results on ImageNet

In experiments on ImageNet [5], we study whether ConvNet-AIG learns to group parameters such that for each image only relevant features are computed. ImageNet is well suited for this study, as it contains a large set of categories with a wide variety including man-made objects, food, and many different animals.

Model Configurations and Training Details. We build ConvNet-AIGs based on ResNet 50 and ResNet 101 [11]. Again, we follow the same architectures as the original ResNets, with the sole exception of the added gates. The size of the hidden state is again $d = 16$, adding a fixed overhead of 3.9% more parameters and 0.04% more floating point operations. For ConvNet-AIG 50, all 16 residual layers have gates. For ConvNet-AIG 101, we fix the early layers up to the second downsampling operation to be always executed. The main reason is that early layers to not yet distinguish between object categories.

We follow the standard ResNet training procedure, with mini-batch size of 256, momentum of 0.9 and weight decay of 10^{-4}. All models are trained for 100 epochs with step-wise learning rate starting at 0.1 and decaying by 10^{-1} every 30 epochs. We use the data-augmentation procedure as in [11] and at test time first rescale images to 256×256 followed by a 224×224 center crop. The gates are initialized to open at a rate of 85% at the beginning of training.

Quantitative Comparison. Figure 3 shows top-1 error on ImageNet and computational cost in terms of GFLOPs for ConvNet-AIG with 50 and 101 layers and the respective ResNets of varying depth. We further show the impact of different target rates on performance and efficiency. We use target rates from 0.4

Table 2. Test error on ImageNet in % for ConvNet-AIG 50, ConvNet-AIG 101 and the respective ResNets of varying depth. Both ConvNet-AIGs outperform their ResNet counterpart, while at the same time using only a subset of the layers. This demonstrates that ConvNet-AIG is more efficient and also improves overall classification quality.

Model	Top 1	Top 5	#Params (10^6)	FLOPs (10^9)
ResNet 34 [11]	26.69	8.58	21.80	3.6
ResNet 50 [11]	24.7	7.8	25.56	3.8
ResNet 50 (our)	23.87	7.12	25.56	3.8
ResNet 101 [11]	23.6	7.1	44.54	7.6
ResNet 101 (our)	**22.63**	6.45	44.54	7.6
Stochastic Depth ResNet 50	27.75	9.14	25.56	3.8
Stochastic Depth ResNet 101	22.80	6.44	44.54	7.6
ConvNet-AIG 50 [t = 0.4]	24.75	7.61	26.56	2.56
ConvNet-AIG 50 [t = 0.5]	24.42	7.42	26.56	2.71
ConvNet-AIG 50 [t = 0.6]	24.22	7.21	26.56	2.88
ConvNet-AIG 50 [t = 0.7]	**23.82**	**7.08**	26.56	3.06
ConvNet-AIG 101 [t = 0.3]	23.02	6.58	46.23	4.33
ConvNet-AIG 101 [t = 0.5]	**22.63**	**6.26**	46.23	5.11

to 0.7 for ConvNet-AIG 50 and 0.3 to 0.5 for ConvNet-AIG 101. Details about the models' complexities and further baselines are presented in Table 2.

From the results we make the following key observations. Both ConvNet-AIG 50 and ConvNet-AIG 101 outperform their ResNet counterpart, while also using only a subset of the layers. In particular, ConvNet-AIG 50 with a target rate of 0.7 saves about 20% of computation. Similarly, ConvNet-AIG 101 outperforms its respective ResNet while using 33% less computations.

Figure 3 also visualizes the effect of the target rate. As expected, decreasing the target rate reduces computation time. Interestingly, penalizing computation first improves accuracy, before lowering the target rate further decreases accuracy. This demonstrates that ConvNet-AIG both improves efficiency and overall classification quality. Further, it appears often more effective to decrease the target rate compared to reducing layers in standard ResNets.

Due to surface resemblance, we also compare to stochastic depth [16]. We observe that for smaller ResNet models stochastic depth does not provide competitive results. Only very large models see benefits from stochastic depth regularization. The paper on stochastic depth [16] reports that even for the very large ResNet 152 performance remains below a basic ResNet. This highlights the opposite goals of ConvNet-AIG and stochastic depth. Stochastic depth aims to create redundant features by enforcing each subset of layers to model the whole dataset [31]. ConvNet-AIG aims to separate parameters that are relevant to different subsets of the dataset into different layers.

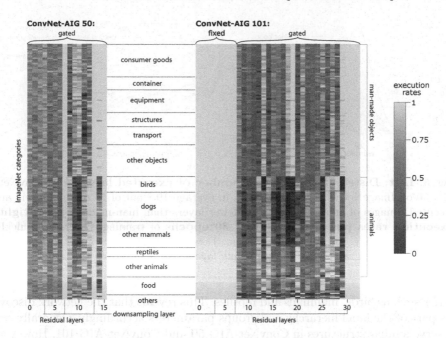

Fig. 4. Learned inference graphs on ImageNet. The histograms show for ConvNet-AIG 50 (left) and ConvNet-AIG 101 (right) how often each residual layer (x-axis) is executed for each of the 1000 classes in ImageNet (y-axis). We observe a clear difference between layers used for man-made objects and for animals and even for some mid-level categories such as birds, mammals and reptiles. Without specific supervision, the network discovers parts of the class hierarchy. Further, downsampling layers and the last layers appear of key importance and are executed for all images. Lastly, the left histogram shows that early layers are mostly agnostic to the different classes. Thus, we set early layers in ConvNet-AIG 101 to be always executed. The remaining layers are sufficient to provide different inference graphs for the various categories.

These results indicates that *convolutional networks do not need a fixed feed-forward structure* and that ConvNet-AIG is an effective means to enable adaptive inference graphs that are conditioned on the input image.

Analysis of Learned Inference Graphs. To analyze the learned inference graphs, we study the rates at which different layers are executed for images of different categories. Figure 4 shows the execution rates of each layer for ConvNet-AIG 50 on the left and ConvNet-AIG 101 on the right. The x-axis indicates the residual layers and the y-axis breaks down the execution rates by the 1000 classes in ImageNet. Further, the figure shows high-level and mid-level categories that contain large numbers of classes. The color in each cell indicates the percentage of validation images from a given category that the respective layer is executed.

From the figure, we see a clear difference between man-made objects and animals. Moreover, we even observe distinctions between mid-level animal cate-

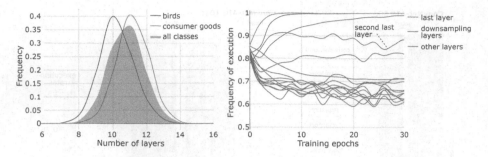

Fig. 5. Left: Distribution over the number of executed layers. For ConvNet-AIG 50 on ImageNet with target rate 0.4, in average 10.8 out of 16 residual layers are executed. Images of animals tend to use fewer layers than man-made objects. **Right: Execution rates per layer over first 30 epochs** of training. Layers are quickly separated into key and less critical layers. Downsampling layers and the last layer increase execution rate, while the remaining layers slowly approach the target rate.

gories such as birds, mammals and reptiles. This reveals that the network discovers part of the label hierarchy and groups parameters accordingly. Generally, we observe similar structures in ConvNet-AIG 50 and ConvNet-AIG 101. However, the grouping of the mid-level categories is more distinct in ConvNet-AIG 101 due to the larger number of layers that can capture high-level features. This result demonstrates that ConvNet-AIG successfully learns layers that focus on specific subsets of categories. It is worthy to note that the training objective does not include an incentive to learn category specific layers. The specialization appears to emerge naturally when the computational budget gets constrained.

Further, we observe that downsampling layers and the last layers deviate significantly from the target rate and are executed for all images. This demonstrates their key role in the network (as similarly observed in [31]) and shows how ConvNet-AIG learns to effectively trade-off computational cost for accuracy.

Lastly, the figure shows that for ConvNet-AIG 50, inter-class variation is mostly present in the later layers of the network after the second downsampling layer. One reason for this could be that features from early layers are useful for all categories. Further, early layers might not yet capture sufficient semantic information to discriminate between categories. Thus, we keep the early layers of ConvNet-AIG 101 fixed to be always executed. The remaining layers still provide sufficient flexibility for different inference paths for the various categories.

Figure 5 shows on the right a typical trajectory of the execution rates during training for ConvNet-AIG 50. The layers are initialized to execute a rate of 85% at the start of training. The figure shows the first 30 training epochs and highlights how the layers are quickly separated into key layers and less critical layers. Important layers such as downsampling and the last layers increase their execution rate, while the remaining layers slowly approach the target rate.

Fig. 6. Validation images from ImageNet that use the fewest layers (top) and the most layers (bottom) within the categories of birds, dogs and musical instruments. The examples illustrate how instance difficulty translates into layer usage.

Variable Inference Time. Due to the adaptive inference graphs, computation time varies across images. Figure 5 shows on the left the distribution over how many of the 16 residual layers in ConvNet-AIG 50 are executed over all ImageNet validation images. On average 10.81 layers are executed with a standard deviation of 1.11. The figure also highlights the mid-level categories of birds and consumer goods. In expectation, images of birds use one layer less than images of consumer goods. From Fig. 4 we further know the two groups also use different sets of layers. Figure 6 shows the validation images that use the fewest and the most layers within the categories of birds, dogs and musical instruments. The examples highlight that easy instances with iconic views require only a few layers. Difficult instances that are small or occluded need more computation.

4.3   Robustness to Adversarial Attacks

In a third set of experiments we aim to understand the effect of adaptive inference graphs on the susceptibility towards adversarial attacks. On one hand, if adversarial perturbations change the inference graph such that key layers of the network are skipped, performance might degrade. On the other hand, the stochasticity of the graph might improve robustness.

We perform a Fast Gradient Sign Attack [8] on ResNet 50 and ConvNet-AIG 50, both trained on ImageNet. The results are presented in Fig. 7. In the graph on the left, the x-axis shows the strength of the adversary measured in the amount each pixel can to be changed. The y-axis shows top-1 accuracy on ImageNet. We observe that ConvNet-AIG is consistently more robust, independent of adversary strength. To investigate whether this additional robustness complements other defenses [10], we perform JPEG compression on the adversarial examples. We follow [10] and use a JPEG quality setting of 75%. While both networks greatly benefit from the defense, ConvNet-AIG remains more robust, indicating that the additional robustness can complement other defenses.

To understand the effect of the attack on the gates, we look at the execution rates before and after the attack. On the right side, Fig. 7 shows the average execution rates per layer over all bird categories for ConvNet-AIG 50 before and after a FGSM attack with epsilon 0.047. Although the accuracy of the network

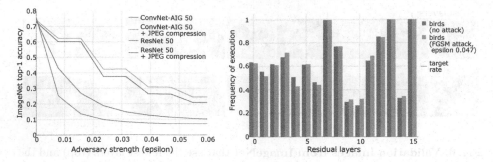

Fig. 7. Adversarial attack using Fast Gradient Sign Method. Left: ConvNet-AIG is consistently more robust than the plain ResNet, independent of adversary strength. The additional robustness persists even when applying additional defense mechanisms. **Right:** Average execution rates per layer for images of birds before and after the attack. The execution rates remain mostly unaffected by the attack.

drops from 74.62% to 11%, execution rates remain similar. One reason for the gates' resilience might be the stochasticity induced by the Gumbel noise which might outweigh the noise introduced by the attack. Further, the global average pooling operation might cancel out some of the adversarial perturbations.

5 Conclusion

In this work, we have shown that convolutional networks do not need fixed feed-forward structures. With ConvNet-AIG, we introduced a ConvNet that adaptively assembles its inference graph on the fly based on the input image. Experiments on ImageNet show that ConvNet-AIG groups parameters for related classes into specialized layers and learns to only execute those layers relevant to the input. This allows decoupling inference time from the number of learned concepts and improves both efficiency as well as overall classification quality.

This work opens up numerous paths for future work. With respect to network architecture, it would be intriguing to extend this work beyond ResNets to other structures such as densely-connected [15] or inception-based [29] networks. From a practitioner's point of view, it might be exciting to extend this work into a framework where the set of executed layers is adaptive, but their number is fixed so as to achieve constant inference times. Further, we have seen that the gates are largely unaffected by basic adversarial attacks. For an adversary, it could be interesting to investigate attacks that specifically target the gating functions.

Acknowledgements. We would like to thank Ilya Kostrikov, Daniel D. Lee, Kimberly Wilber, Antonio Marcedone and Yiqing Hua for insightful discussions and feedback. This work was supported in part by the Oath Laboratory for Connected Experiences, a Google Focused Research Award, AWS Cloud Credits for Research and a Facebook equipment donation.

References

1. Andreas, J., Rohrbach, M., Darrell, T., Klein, D.: Learning to compose neural networks for question answering. In: Proceedings of NAACL-HLT (2016)
2. Andreas, J., Rohrbach, M., Darrell, T., Klein, D.: Neural module networks. In: Conference on Computer Vision and Pattern Recognition (CVPR) (2016)
3. Bengio, E., Bacon, P.L., Pineau, J., Precup, D.: Conditional computation in neural networks for faster models. arXiv preprint arXiv:1511.06297 (2015)
4. Bengio, Y., Léonard, N., Courville, A.: Estimating or propagating gradients through stochastic neurons for conditional computation. arXiv preprint arXiv:1308.3432 (2013)
5. Deng, J., Dong, W., Socher, R., Li, L.J., Li, K., Fei-Fei, L.: ImageNet: a large-scale hierarchical image database. In: Conference on Computer Vision and Pattern Recognition (CVPR) (2009)
6. Figurnov, M., et al.: Spatially adaptive computation time for residual networks. In: Conference on Computer Vision and Pattern Recognition (CVPR) (2017)
7. Glorot, X., Bordes, A., Bengio, Y.: Deep sparse rectifier neural networks. In: International Conference on Artificial Intelligence and Statistics (AISTATS) (2011)
8. Goodfellow, I.J., Shlens, J., Szegedy, C.: Explaining and harnessing adversarial examples. arXiv preprint arXiv:1412.6572 (2014)
9. Gumbel, E.J.: Statistical theory of extreme values and some practical applications: a series of lectures. No. 33, US Govt. Print. Office (1954)
10. Guo, C., Rana, M., Cisse, M., van der Maaten, L.: Countering adversarial images using input transformations. arXiv preprint arXiv:1711.00117 (2017)
11. He, K., Zhang, X., Ren, S., Sun, J.: Deep residual learning for image recognition. In: Conference on Computer Vision and Pattern Recognition (CVPR) (2016)
12. He, K., Zhang, X., Ren, S., Sun, J.: Identity mappings in deep residual networks. In: Leibe, B., Matas, J., Sebe, N., Welling, M. (eds.) ECCV 2016. LNCS, vol. 9908, pp. 630–645. Springer, Cham (2016). https://doi.org/10.1007/978-3-319-46493-0_38
13. Hu, J., Shen, L., Sun, G.: Squeeze-and-excitation networks. arXiv preprint arXiv:1709.01507 (2017)
14. Huang, G., Chen, D., Li, T., Wu, F., van der Maaten, L., Weinberger, K.Q.: Multi-scale dense convolutional networks for efficient prediction. arXiv preprint arXiv:1703.09844 (2017)
15. Huang, G., Liu, Z., Weinberger, K.Q., van der Maaten, L.: Densely connected convolutional networks. In: Conference on Computer Vision and Pattern Recognition (CVPR) (2017)
16. Huang, G., Sun, Y., Liu, Z., Sedra, D., Weinberger, K.Q.: Deep networks with stochastic depth. In: Leibe, B., Matas, J., Sebe, N., Welling, M. (eds.) ECCV 2016. LNCS, vol. 9908, pp. 646–661. Springer, Cham (2016). https://doi.org/10.1007/978-3-319-46493-0_39
17. Huang, X., Belongie, S.: Arbitrary style transfer in real-time with adaptive instance normalization. In: International Conference on Computer Vision (ICCV) (2017)
18. Jang, E., Gu, S., Poole, B.: Categorical reparameterization with gumbel-softmax. arXiv preprint arXiv:1611.01144 (2016)
19. Johnson, J., et al.: Inferring and executing programs for visual reasoning. In: International Conference on Computer Vision (ICCV) (2017)
20. Kingma, D.P., Welling, M.: Auto-encoding variational bayes. arXiv preprint arXiv:1312.6114 (2013)

21. Krizhevsky, A., Hinton, G.: Learning multiple layers of features from tiny images (2009)
22. Li, H., Lin, Z., Shen, X., Brandt, J., Hua, G.: A convolutional neural network cascade for face detection. In: Conference on Computer Vision and Pattern Recognition (CVPR) (2015)
23. Li, Y., Wang, N., Liu, J., Hou, X.: Demystifying neural style transfer. arXiv preprint arXiv:1701.01036 (2017)
24. Maddison, C.J., Mnih, A., Teh, Y.W.: The concrete distribution: A continuous relaxation of discrete random variables. arXiv preprint arXiv:1611.00712 (2016)
25. Misra, I., Gupta, A., Hebert, M.: From red wine to red tomato: Composition with context. In: Conference on Computer Vision and Pattern Recognition (CVPR) (2017)
26. Shazeer, N., et al.: Outrageously large neural networks: The sparsely-gated mixture-of-experts layer. arXiv preprint arXiv:1701.06538 (2017)
27. Srivastava, N., Hinton, G.E., Krizhevsky, A., Sutskever, I., Salakhutdinov, R.: Dropout: a simple way to prevent neural networks from overfitting. J. Mach. Learn. Res. (JMLR) 15(1), 1929–1958 (2014)
28. Srivastava, R.K., Greff, K., Schmidhuber, J.: Highway networks. arXiv preprint arXiv:1505.00387 (2015)
29. Szegedy, C., et al.: Going deeper with convolutions. In: Conference on Computer Vision and Pattern Recognition (CVPR)
30. Teerapittayanon, S., McDanel, B., Kung, H.: BranchyNet: fast inference via early exiting from deep neural networks. In: Conference onPattern Recognition (ICPR) (2016)
31. Veit, A., Wilber, M.J., Belongie, S.: Residual networks behave like ensembles of relatively shallow networks. In: Advances in Neural Information Processing Systems (NIPS) (2016)
32. Viola, P., Jones, M.J.: Robust real-time face detection. Int. J. Comput. Vis. (IJCV) 57(2), 137–154 (2004)
33. Yang, F., Choi, W., Lin, Y.: Exploit all the layers: fast and accurate CNN object detector with scale dependent pooling and cascaded rejection classifiers. In: Conference on Computer Vision and Pattern Recognition (CVPR) (2016)

Progressive Neural Architecture Search

Chenxi Liu[1]($\boxtimes$), Barret Zoph[2], Maxim Neumann[2], Jonathon Shlens[2],
Wei Hua[2], Li-Jia Li[2], Li Fei-Fei[2,3], Alan Yuille[1], Jonathan Huang[2],
and Kevin Murphy[2]

[1] Johns Hopkins University, Baltimore, USA
cxliu@jhu.edu
[2] Google AI, Mountain View, USA
[3] Stanford University, Stanford, USA

Abstract. We propose a new method for learning the structure of convolutional neural networks (CNNs) that is more efficient than recent state-of-the-art methods based on reinforcement learning and evolutionary algorithms. Our approach uses a sequential model-based optimization (SMBO) strategy, in which we search for structures in order of increasing complexity, while simultaneously learning a surrogate model to guide the search through structure space. Direct comparison under the same search space shows that our method is up to 5 times more efficient than the RL method of Zoph et al. (2018) in terms of number of models evaluated, and 8 times faster in terms of total compute. The structures we discover in this way achieve state of the art classification accuracies on CIFAR-10 and ImageNet.

1 Introduction

There has been a lot of recent interest in automatically learning good neural net architectures. Some of this work is summarized in Sect. 2, but at a high level, current techniques usually fall into one of two categories: evolutionary algorithms (see e.g. [24,28,35]) or reinforcement learning (see e.g., [2,5,39–41]). When using evolutionary algorithms (EA), each neural network structure is encoded as a string, and random mutations and recombinations of the strings are performed during the search process; each string (model) is then trained and evaluated on a validation set, and the top performing models generate "children". When using reinforcement learning (RL), the agent performs a sequence of actions, which specifies the structure of the model; this model is then trained and its validation performance is returned as the reward, which is used to update the RNN

C. Liu—Work done while an intern at Google.

Electronic supplementary material The online version of this chapter (https://doi.org/10.1007/978-3-030-01246-5_2) contains supplementary material, which is available to authorized users.

controller. Although both EA and RL methods have been able to learn network structures that outperform manually designed architectures, they require significant computational resources. For example, the RL method in [41] trains and evaluates 20,000 neural networks across 500 P100 GPUs over 4 days.

In this paper, we describe a method that is able to learn a CNN which matches previous state of the art in terms of accuracy, while requiring 5 times fewer model evaluations during the architecture search. Our starting point is the structured search space proposed by [41], in which the search algorithm is tasked with searching for a good convolutional "cell", as opposed to a full CNN. A cell contains B "blocks", where a block is a combination operator (such as addition) applied to two inputs (tensors), each of which can be transformed (e.g., using convolution) before being combined. This cell structure is then stacked a certain number of times, depending on the size of the training set, and the desired running time of the final CNN (see Sect. 3 for details). This modular design also allows easy architecture transfer from one dataset to another, as we will show in experimental results.

We propose to use heuristic search to search the space of cell structures, starting with simple (shallow) models and progressing to complex ones, pruning out unpromising structures as we go. At iteration b of the algorithm, we have a set of K candidate cells (each of size b blocks), which we train and evaluate on a dataset of interest. Since this process is expensive, we also learn a model or surrogate function which can predict the performance of a structure without needing to training it. We expand the K candidates of size b into $K' \gg K$ children, each of size $b + 1$. We apply our surrogate function to rank all of the K' children, pick the top K, and then train and evaluate them. We continue in this way until $b = B$, which is the maximum number of blocks we want to use in our cell. See Sect. 4 for details.

Our progressive (simple to complex) approach has several advantages over other techniques that directly search in the space of fully-specified structures. First, the simple structures train faster, so we get some initial results to train the surrogate quickly. Second, we only ask the surrogate to predict the quality of structures that are slightly different (larger) from the ones it has seen (c.f., trust-region methods). Third, we factorize the search space into a product of smaller search spaces, allowing us to potentially search models with many more blocks. In Sect. 5 we show that our approach is 5 times more efficient than the RL method of [41] in terms of number of models evaluated, and 8 times faster in terms of total compute. We also show that the structures we discover achieve state of the art classification accuracies on CIFAR-10 and ImageNet.[1]

---

[1] The code and checkpoint for the PNAS model trained on ImageNet can be downloaded from the TensorFlow models repository at http://github.com/tensorflow/models/. Also see https://github.com/chenxi116/PNASNet.TF and https://github.com/chenxi116/PNASNet.pytorch for author's reimplementation.

2 Related Work

Our paper is based on the "neural architecture search" (NAS) method proposed in [40,41]. In the original paper [40], they use the REINFORCE algorithm [34] to estimate the parameters of a recurrent neural network (RNN), which represents a policy to generate a sequence of symbols (actions) specifying the structure of the CNN; the reward function is the classification accuracy on the validation set of a CNN generated from this sequence. [41] extended this by using a more structured search space, in which the CNN was defined in terms of a series of stacked "cells". (They also replaced REINFORCE with proximal policy optimization (PPO) [29].) This method was able to learn CNNs which outperformed almost all previous methods in terms of accuracy vs speed on image classification (using CIFAR-10 [19] and ImageNet [8]) and object detection (using COCO [20]).

There are several other papers that use RL to learn network structures. [39] use the same model search space as NAS, but replace policy gradient with Q-learning. [2] also use Q-learning, but without exploiting cell structure. [5] use policy gradient to train an RNN, but the actions are now to widen an existing layer, or to deepen the network by adding an extra layer. This requires specifying an initial model and then gradually learning how to transform it. The same approach, of applying "network morphisms" to modify a network, was used in [12], but in the context of hill climbing search, rather than RL. [26] use parameter sharing among child models to substantially accelerate the search process.

An alternative to RL is to use evolutionary algorithms (EA; "neuro-evolution" [32]). Early work (e.g., [33]) used EA to learn both the structure and the parameters of the network, but more recent methods, such as [21,24,27,28,35], just use EA to search the structures, and use SGD to estimate the parameters.

RL and EA are local search methods that search through the space of fully-specified graph structures. An alternative approach, which we adopt, is to use heuristic search, in which we search through the space of structures in a progressive way, from simple to complex. There are several pieces of prior work that explore this approach. [25] use Monte Carlo Tree Search (MCTS), but at each node in the search tree, it uses random selection to choose which branch to expand, which is very inefficient. Sequential Model Based Optimization (SMBO) [17] improves on MCTS by learning a predictive model, which can be used to decide which nodes to expand. This technique has been applied to neural net structure search in [25], but they used a flat CNN search space, rather than our hierarchical cell-based space. Consequently, their resulting CNNs do not perform very well. Other related works include [23], who focus on MLP rather than CNNs; [33], who used an incremental approach in the context of evolutionary algorithms; [40] who used a schedule of increasing number of layers; and [13] who search through the space of latent factor models specified by a grammar. Finally, [7,16] grow CNNs sequentially using boosting.

Several other papers learn a surrogate function to predict the performance of a candidate structure, either "zero shot" (without training it) (see e.g., [4]), or after training it for a small number of epochs and extrapolating the learning curve (see e.g., [3,10]). However, most of these methods have been applied to fixed sized structures, and would not work with our progressive search approach.

3   Architecture Search Space

In this section we describe the neural network architecture search space used in our work. We build on the hierarchical approach proposed in [41], in which we first learn a cell structure, and then stack this cell a desired number of times, in order to create the final CNN.

3.1   Cell Topologies

A cell is a fully convolutional network that maps an $H \times W \times F$ tensor to another $H' \times W' \times F'$ tensor. If we use stride 1 convolution, then $H' = H$ and $W' = W$; if we use stride 2, then $H' = H/2$ and $W' = W/2$. We employ a common heuristic to double the number of filters (feature maps) whenever the spatial activation is halved, so $F' = F$ for stride 1, and $F' = 2F$ for stride 2.

The cell can be represented by a DAG consisting of B blocks. Each block is a mapping from 2 input tensors to 1 output tensor. We can specify a block b in a cell c as a 5-tuple, (I_1, I_2, O_1, O_2, C), where $I_1, I_2 \in \mathcal{I}_b$ specifies the inputs to the block, $O_1, O_2 \in \mathcal{O}$ specifies the operation to apply to input I_i, and $C \in \mathcal{C}$ specifies how to combine O_1 and O_2 to generate the feature map (tensor) corresponding to the output of this block, which we denote by H_b^c.

The set of possible inputs, $\mathcal{I}_b$, is the set of all previous blocks in this cell, $\{H_1^c, \ldots, H_{b-1}^c\}$, plus the output of the previous cell, H_B^{c-1}, plus the output of the previous-previous cell, H_B^{c-2}.

The operator space $\mathcal{O}$ is the following set of 8 functions, each of which operates on a single tensor[2]:

- 3x3 depthwise-separable convolution
- 5x5 depthwise-separable convolution
- 7x7 depthwise-separable convolution
- 1x7 followed by 7x1 convolution
- identity
- 3x3 average pooling
- 3x3 max pooling
- 3x3 dilated convolution

This is less than the 13 operators used in [41], since we removed the ones that their RL method discovered were never used.

For the space of possible combination operators $\mathcal{C}$, [41] considerd both elementwise addition and concatenation. However, they discovered that the RL method never chose to use concatenation, so to reduce our search space, we always use addition as the combination operator. Thus in our work, a block can be specified by a 4-tuple.

We now quantify the size of the search space to highlight the magnitude of the search problem. Let the space of possible structures for the b'th block be $\mathcal{B}_b$; this has size $|\mathcal{B}_b| = |\mathcal{I}_b|^2 \times |\mathcal{O}|^2 \times |\mathcal{C}|$, where $|\mathcal{I}_b| = (2 + b - 1)$, $|\mathcal{O}| = 8$ and

---

[2] The depthwise-separable convolutions are in fact two repetitions of ReLU-SepConv-BatchNorm; 1x1 convolutions are also inserted when tensor sizes mismatch.

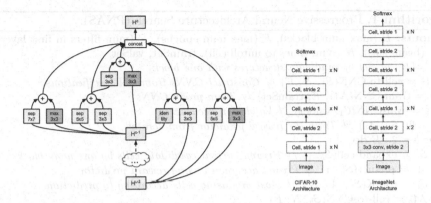

Fig. 1. *Left*: The best cell structure found by our Progressive Neural Architecture Search, consisting of 5 blocks. *Right*: We employ a similar strategy as [41] when constructing CNNs from cells on CIFAR-10 and ImageNet. Note that we learn a single cell type instead of distinguishing between Normal and Reduction cell.

$|\mathcal{C}| = 1$. For $b = 1$, we have $\mathcal{I}_1 = \{H_B^{c-1}, H_B^{c-2}\}$, which are the final outputs of the previous two cells, so there are $|\mathcal{B}_1| = 256$ possible block structures.

If we allow cells of up to $B = 5$ blocks, the total number of cell structures is given by $|\mathcal{B}_{1:5}| = 2^2 \times 8^2 \times 3^2 \times 8^2 \times 4^2 \times 8^2 \times 5^2 \times 8^2 \times 6^2 \times 8^2 = 5.6 \times 10^{14}$. However, there are certain symmetries in this space that allow us to prune it to a more reasonable size. For example, there are only 136 unique cells composed of 1 block. The total number of unique cells is $\sim 10^{12}$. This is much smaller than the search space used in [41], which has size 10^{28}, but it is still an extremely large space to search, and requires efficient optimization methods.

3.2   From Cell to CNN

To evaluate a cell, we have to convert it into a CNN. To do this, we stack a predefined number of copies of the basic cell (with the same structure, but untied weights), using either stride 1 or stride 2, as shown in Fig. 1 (right). The number of stride-1 cells between stride-2 cells is then adjusted accordingly with up to N number of repeats. At the top of the network, we use global average pooling, followed by a softmax classification layer. We then train the stacked model on the relevant dataset.

In the case of CIFAR-10, we use 32×32 images. In the case of ImageNet, we consider two settings, one with high resolution images of size 331×331, and one with smaller images of size 224×224. The latter results in less accurate models, but they are faster. For ImageNet, we also add an initial 3×3 convolutional filter layer with stride 2 at the start of the network, to further reduce the cost.

The overall CNN construction process is identical to [41], except we only use one cell type (we do not distinguish between Normal and Reduction cells, but instead emulate a Reduction cell by using a Normal cell with stride 2), and the cell search space is slightly smaller (since we use fewer operators and combiners).

Algorithm 1. Progressive Neural Architecture Search (PNAS).

Inputs: B (max num blocks), E (max num epochs), F (num filters in first layer), K (beam size), N (num times to unroll cell), trainSet, valSet.
$S_1 = B_1$ // *Set of candidate structures with one block*
$M_1 = $ cell-to-CNN(S_1, N, F) // *Construct CNNs from cell specifications*
$C_1 = $ train-CNN(M_1, E, trainSet) // *Train proxy CNNs*
$A_1 = $ eval-CNN(C_1, valSet) // *Validation accuracies*
$\pi = $ fit(S_1, A_1) // *Train the reward predictor from scratch*
for $b = 2 : B$ **do**
    $S_b' = $ expand-cell(S_{b-1}) // *Expand current candidate cells by one more block*
    $\hat{A}_b' = $ predict(S_b', π) // *Predict accuracies using reward predictor*
    $S_b = $ top-K(S_b', $\hat{A}_b'$, K) // *Most promising cells according to prediction*
    $M_b = $ cell-to-CNN(S_b, N, F)
    $C_b = $ train-CNN(M_b, E, trainSet)
    $A_b = $ eval-CNN(C_b, valSet)
    $\pi = $ update-predictor(S_b, A_b, π) // *Finetune reward predictor with new data*
end for
Return top-K(S_B, A_B, 1)

---

4   Method

4.1   Progressive Neural Architecture Search

Many previous approaches directly search in the space of full cells, or worse, full CNNs. For example, NAS uses a 50-step RNN[3] as a controller to generate cell specifications. In [35] a fixed-length binary string encoding of CNN architecture is defined and used in model evolution/mutation. While this is a more direct approach, we argue that it is difficult to directly navigate in an exponentially large search space, especially at the beginning where there is no knowledge of what makes a good model.

As an alternative, we propose to search the space in a progressive order, simplest models first. In particular, we start by constructing all possible cell structures from B_1 (i.e., composed of 1 block), and add them to a queue. We train and evaluate all the models in the queue (in parallel), and then expand each one by adding all of the possible block structures from B_2; this gives us a set of $|B_1| \times |B_2| = 256 \times 576 = 147,456$ candidate cells of depth 2. Since we cannot afford to train and evaluate all of these child networks, we refer to a learned predictor function (described in Sect. 4.2); it is trained based on the measured performance of the cells we have visited so far. (Our predictor takes negligible time to train and apply.) We then use the predictor to evaluate all the candidate cells, and pick the K most promising ones. We add these to the queue, and repeat the process, until we find cells with a sufficient number B of blocks. See Algorithm 1 for the pseudocode, and Fig. 2 for an illustration.

---

[3] 5 symbols per block, times 5 blocks, times 2 for Normal and Reduction cells.

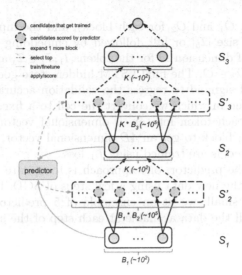

Fig. 2. Illustration of the PNAS search procedure when the maximum number of blocks is $B = 3$. Here $\mathcal{S}_b$ represents the set of candidate cells with b blocks. We start by considering all cells with 1 block, $\mathcal{S}_1 = \mathcal{B}_1$; we train and evaluate all of these cells, and update the predictor. At iteration 2, we expand each of the cells in $\mathcal{S}_1$ to get all cells with 2 blocks, $\mathcal{S}'_2 = \mathcal{B}_{1:2}$; we predict their scores, pick the top K to get $\mathcal{S}_2$, train and evaluate them, and update the predictor. At iteration 3, we expand each of the cells in $\mathcal{S}_2$, to get a subset of cells with 3 blocks, $\mathcal{S}'_3 \subseteq \mathcal{B}_{1:3}$; we predict their scores, pick the top K to get $\mathcal{S}_3$, train and evaluate them, and return the winner. $B_b = |\mathcal{B}_b|$ is the number of possible blocks at level b and K is the beam size (number of models we train and evaluate per level of the search tree).

4.2 Performance Prediction with Surrogate Model

As explained above, we need a mechanism to predict the final performance of a cell before we actually train it. There are at least three desired properties of such a predictor:

- *Handle variable-sized inputs*: We need the predictor to work for variable-length input strings. In particular, it should be able to predict the performance of any cell with $b + 1$ blocks, even if it has only been trained on cells with up to b blocks.
- *Correlated with true performance*: we do not necessarily need to achieve low mean squared error, but we do want the predictor to rank models in roughly the same order as their true performance values.
- *Sample efficiency*: We want to train and evaluate as few cells as possible, which means the training data for the predictor will be scarce.

The requirement that the predictor be able to handle variable-sized strings immediately suggests the use of an RNN, and indeed this is one of the methods we try. In particular, we use an LSTM that reads a sequence of length $4b$

(representing I_1, I_2, O_1 and O_2 for each block), and the input at each step is a one-hot vector of size $|\mathcal{I}_b|$ or $|\mathcal{O}|$, followed by embedding lookup. We use a shared embedding of dimension D for the tokens $I_1, I_2 \in \mathcal{I}$, and another shared embedding for $O_1, O_2 \in \mathcal{O}$. The final LSTM hidden state goes through a fully-connected layer and sigmoid to regress the validation accuracy. We also try a simpler MLP baseline in which we convert the cell to a fixed length vector as follows: we embed each token into an D-dimensional vector, concatenate the embeddings for each block to get an $4D$-dimensional vector, and then average over blocks. Both models are trained using L_1 loss.

When training the predictor, one approach is to update the parameters of the predictor using the new data using a few steps of SGD. However, since the sample size is very small, we fit an ensemble of 5 predictors, each fit (from scratch) to 4/5 of all the data available at each step of the search process. We observed empirically that this reduced the variance of the predictions.

In the future, we plan to investigate other kinds of predictors, such as Gaussian processes with string kernels (see e.g., [1]), which may be more sample efficient to train and produce predictions with uncertainty estimates.

5   Experiments and Results

5.1   Experimental Details

Our experimental setting follows [41]. In particular, we conduct most of our experiments on CIFAR-10 [19]. CIFAR-10 has 50,000 training images and 10,000 test images. We use 5000 images from the training set as a validation set. All images are whitened, and 32×32 patches are cropped from images upsampled to 40×40. Random horizontal flip is also used. After finding a good model on CIFAR-10, we evaluate its quality on ImageNet classification in Sect. 5.5.

For the MLP accuracy predictor, the embedding size is 100, and we use 2 fully connected layers, each with 100 hidden units. For the RNN accuracy predictor, we use an LSTM, and the hidden state size and embedding size are both 100. The embeddings use uniform initialization in range $[-0.1, 0.1]$. The bias term in the final fully connected layer is initialized to 1.8 (0.86 after sigmoid) to account for the mean observed accuracy of all $b = 1$ models. We use the Adam optimizer [18] with learning rate 0.01 for the $b = 1$ level and 0.002 for all following levels.

Algorithm 2. Evaluating performance of a predictor on a random dataset.

for $b = 1 : B - 1$ do
    for $t = 1 : T$ do
        $\mathcal{S}_{b,t,1:K}$ = random sample of K models from $\mathcal{U}_{b,1:R}$
        $\pi_{b,t}$ = fit($\mathcal{S}_{b,t,1:K}$, $A(\mathcal{S}_{b,t,1:K})$) // *Train or finetune predictor*
        $\hat{A}_{b,t,1:K}$ = predict($\pi_{b,t}$, $\mathcal{S}_{b,t,1:K}$) // *Predict on same b*
        $\hat{A}_{b+1,t,1:R}$ = predict($\pi_{b,t}$, $\mathcal{U}_{b+1,1:R}$) // *Predict on next b*
    end for
end for

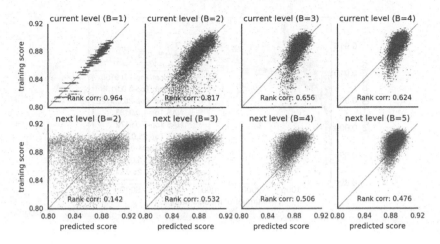

Fig. 3. Accuracy of MLP-ensemble predictor. Top row: true vs predicted accuracies on models from the training set over different trials. Bottom row: true vs predicted accuracies on models from the set of all unseen larger models. Denoted is the mean rank correlation from individual trials.

Table 1. Spearman rank correlations of different predictors on the training set, $\hat{\rho}_b$, and when extrapolating to unseen larger models, $\tilde{\rho}_{b+1}$. See text for details.

Method	$b = 1$		$b = 2$		$b = 3$		$b = 4$	
	$\hat{\rho}_1$	$\tilde{\rho}_2$	$\hat{\rho}_2$	$\tilde{\rho}_3$	$\hat{\rho}_3$	$\tilde{\rho}_4$	$\hat{\rho}_4$	$\tilde{\rho}_5$
MLP	0.938	0.113	0.857	0.450	0.714	0.469	0.641	0.444
RNN	0.970	**0.198**	**0.996**	0.424	0.693	0.401	**0.787**	0.413
MLP-ensemble	**0.975**	0.164	0.786	**0.532**	0.634	**0.504**	0.645	**0.468**
RNN-ensemble	0.972	0.164	0.906	0.418	**0.801**	0.465	0.579	0.424

Our training procedure for the CNNs follows the one used in [41]. During the search we evaluate $K = 256$ networks at each stage (136 for stage 1, since there are only 136 unique cells with 1 block), we use a maximum cell depth of $B = 5$ blocks, we use $F = 24$ filters in the first convolutional cell, we unroll the cells for $N = 2$ times, and each child network is trained for 20 epochs using initial learning rate of 0.01 with cosine decay [22].

5.2   Performance of the Surrogate Predictors

In this section, we compare the performance of different surrogate predictors. Note that at step b of PNAS, we train the predictor on the observed performance of cells with up to b blocks, but we apply it to cells with $b+1$ blocks. We therefore consider predictive accuracy both for cells with sizes that have been seen before (but which have not been trained on), and for cells which are one block larger than the training data.

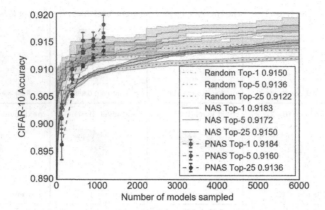

Fig. 4. Comparing the relative efficiency of NAS, PNAS and random search under the same search space. We plot mean accuracy (across 5 trials) on CIFAR-10 validation set of the top M models, for $M \in \{1, 5, 25\}$, found by each method vs number of models which are trained and evaluated. Each model is trained for 20 epochs. Error bars and the colored regions denote standard deviation of the mean.

More precisely, let $\mathcal{U}_{b,1:R}$ be a set of randomly chosen cells with b blocks, where $R = 10,000$. (For $b = 1$, there are only 136 unique cells.) We convert each of these to CNNs, and train them for $E = 20$ epochs. (Thus in total we train $\sim (B - 1) \times R = 40,000$ models for 20 epochs each.) We now use this random dataset to evaluate the performance of the predictors using the pseudocode in Algorithm 2, where $A(\mathcal{H})$ returns the true validation set accuracies of the models in some set $\mathcal{H}$. In particular, for each size $b = 1 : B$, and for each trial $t = 1 : T$ (we use $T = 20$), we do the following: randomly select $K = 256$ models (each of size b) from $\mathcal{U}_{b,1:R}$ to generate a training set $\mathcal{S}_{b,t,1:K}$; fit the predictor on the training set; evaluate the predictor on the training set; and finally evaluate the predictor on the set of all unseen random models of size $b + 1$.

The top row of Fig. 3 shows a scatterplot of the true accuracies of the models in the training sets, $A(\mathcal{S}_{b,1:T,1:K})$, vs the predicted accuracies, $\hat{A}_{b,1:T,1:K}$ (so there are $T \times K = 20 \times 256 = 5120$ points in each plot, at least for $b > 1$). The bottom row plots the true accuracies on the set of larger models, $A(\mathcal{U}_{b+1,1:R})$, vs the predicted accuracies $\tilde{A}_{b+1,1:R}$ (so there are $R = 10K$ points in each plot). We see that the predictor performs well on models from the training set, but not so well when predicting larger models. However, performance does increase as the predictor is trained on more (and larger) cells.

Figure 3 shows the results using an ensemble of MLPs. The scatter plots for the other predictors look similar. We can summarize each scatterplot using the Spearman rank correlation coefficient. Let $\hat{\rho}_b = \text{rank-correlation}(\hat{A}_{b,1:T,1:K}, A(\mathcal{S}_{b,1:T,1:K}))$ and $\tilde{\rho}_{b+1} = \text{rank-correlation}(\tilde{A}_{b+1,1:R}, A(\mathcal{U}_{b+1,1:R}))$. Table 1 summarizes these statistics across different levels. We see that for predicting the training set, the RNN does better than the MLP, but for predicting the performance on unseen larger models (which is the setting we care about in practice),

Table 2. Relative efficiency of PNAS (using MLP-ensemble predictor) and NAS under the same search space. B is the size of the cell, "Top" is the number of top models we pick, "Accuracy" is their average validation accuracy, "# PNAS" is the number of models evaluated by PNAS, "# NAS" is the number of models evaluated by NAS to achieve the desired accuracy. Speedup measured by number of examples is greater than speedup in terms of number of models, because NAS has an additional reranking stage, that trains the top 250 models for 300 epochs each before picking the best one.

B	Top	Accuracy	# PNAS	# NAS	Speedup (# models)	Speedup (# examples)
5	1	0.9183	1160	5808	5.0	8.2
5	5	0.9161	1160	4100	3.5	6.8
5	25	0.9136	1160	3654	3.2	6.4

the MLP seems to do slightly better. This will be corroborated by our end-to-end test in Sect. 5.3, and is likely due to overfitting. We also see that for the extrapolation task, ensembling seems to help.

5.3   Search Efficiency

In this section, we compare the efficiency of PNAS to two other methods: random search and the NAS method. To perform the comparison, we run PNAS for $B = 5$, and at each iteration b, we record the set S_b of $K = 256$ models of size b that it picks, and evaluate them on the CIFAR-10 validation set (after training for 20 epochs each). We then compute the validation accuracy of the top M models for $M \in \{1, 5, 25\}$. To capture the variance in performance of a given model due to randomness of the parameter initialization and optimization procedure, we repeat this process 5 times. We plot the mean and standard error of this statistic in Fig. 4. We see that the mean performance of the top $M \in \{1, 5, 25\}$ models steadily increases, as we search for larger models. Furthermore, performance is better when using an MLP-ensemble (shown in Fig. 4) instead of an RNN-ensemble (see supplementary material), which is consistent with Table 1.

For our random search baseline, we uniformly sample 6000 cells of size $B = 5$ blocks from the random set of models $U_{5,1:R}$ described in Sect. 5.2. Fig. 4 shows that PNAS significantly outperforms this baseline.

Finally, we compare to NAS. Each trial sequentially searches 6000 cells of size $B = 5$ blocks. At each iteration t, we define H_t to be the set of all cells visited so far by the RL agent. We compute the validation accuracy of the top M models in H_t, and plot the mean and standard error of this statistic in Fig. 4. We see that the mean performance steadily increases, but at a slower rate than PNAS.

To quantify the speedup factor compared to NAS, we compute the number of models that are trained and evaluated until the mean performance of PNAS and NAS are equal (note that PNAS produces models of size B after evaluating $|\mathcal{B}_1| + (B - 1) \times K$ models, which is 1160 for $B = 5$). The results are shown in

Table 3. Performance of different CNNs on CIFAR test set. All model comparisons employ a comparable number of parameters and exclude cutout data augmentation [9]. "Error" is the top-1 misclassification rate on the CIFAR-10 test set. (Error rates have the form $\mu \pm \sigma$, where μ is the average over multiple trials and σ is the standard deviation. In PNAS we use 15 trials.) "Params" is the number of model parameters. "Cost" is the total number of examples processed through SGD ($M_1E_1 + M_2E_2$) before the architecture search terminates. The number of filters F for NASNet-{B, C} cannot be determined (hence N/A), and the actual E_1, E_2 may be larger than the values in this table (hence the range in cost), according to the original authors.

Model	B	N	F	Error	Params	M_1	E_1	M_2	E_2	Cost
NASNet-A [41]	5	6	32	3.41	3.3M	20000	0.9M	250	13.5M	21.4-29.3B
NASNet-B [41]	5	4	N/A	3.73	2.6M	20000	0.9M	250	13.5M	21.4-29.3B
NASNet-C [41]	5	4	N/A	3.59	3.1M	20000	0.9M	250	13.5M	21.4-29.3B
Hier-EA [21]	5	2	64	3.75±0.12	15.7M	7000	5.12M	0	0	35.8B[a]
AmoebaNet-B [27]	5	6	36	3.37±0.04	2.8M	27000	2.25M	100	27M	63.5B[b]
AmoebaNet-A [27]	5	6	36	3.34±0.06	3.2M	20000	1.13M	100	27M	25.2B[c]
PNASNet-5	5	3	48	3.41±0.09	3.2M	1160	0.9M	0	0	1.0B

[a]In Hierarchical EA, the search phase trains 7K models (each for 4 times to reduce variance) for 5000 steps of batch size 256. Thus, the total computational cost is 7K × 5000 × 256 × 4 = 35.8B.
[b]The total computational cost for AmoebaNet consists of an architecture search and a reranking phase. The architecture search phase trains over 27K models each for 50 epochs. Each epoch consists of 45K examples. The reranking phase searches over 100 models each trained for 600 epochs. Thus, the architecture search is 27K × 50 × 45K = 60.8B examples. The reranking phase consists of 100 × 600 × 45K = 2.7B examples. The total computational cost is 60.8B + 2.7B = 63.5B.
[c]The search phase trains 20K models each for 25 epochs. The rest of the computation is the same as AmoebaNet-B.

Table 2. We see that PNAS is up to 5 times faster in terms of the number of models it trains and evaluates.

Comparing the number of models explored during architecture search is one measure of efficiency. However, some methods, such as NAS, employ a secondary reranking stage to determine the best model; PNAS does not perform a reranking stage but uses the top model from the search directly. A more fair comparison is therefore to count the total number of examples processed through SGD throughout the search. Let M_1 be the number of models trained during search, and let E_1 be the number of examples used to train each model.[4] The total number of examples is therefore M_1E_1. However, for methods with the additional reranking stage, the top M_2 models from the search procedure are trained using E_2 examples each, before returning the best. This results in a total cost of $M_1E_1 + M_2E_2$. For NAS and PNAS, $E_1 = 900K$ for NAS and PNAS since they use 20 epochs on a training set of size 45K. The number of models searched to

---

[4] The number of examples is equal to the number of SGD steps times the batch size. Alternatively, it can be measured in terms of number of epoch (passes through the data), but since different papers use different sized training sets, we avoid this measure. In either case, we assume the number of examples is the same for every model, since none of the methods we evaluate use early stopping.

achieve equal top-1 accuracy is $M_1 = 1160$ for PNAS and $M_1 = 5808$ for NAS. For the second stage, NAS trains the top $M_2 = 250$ models for $E_2 = 300$ epochs before picking the best.[5] Thus we see that PNAS is about 8 times faster than NAS when taking into account the total cost.

5.4   Results on CIFAR-10 Image Classification

We now discuss the performance of our final model, and compare it to the results of other methods in the literature. Let PNASNet-5 denote the best CNN we discovered on CIFAR using PNAS, also visualized in Fig. 1 (left). After we have selected the cell structure, we try various N and F values such that the number of model parameters is around 3M, train them each for 300 epochs using initial learning rate of 0.025 with cosine decay, and pick the best combination based on the validation set. Using this best combination of N and F, we train it for 600 epochs on the union of training set and validation set. During training we also used auxiliary classifier located at 2/3 of the maximum depth weighted by 0.4, and drop each path with probability 0.4 for regularization.

The results are shown in Table 3. We see that PNAS can find a model with the same accuracy as NAS, but using 21 times less compute. PNAS also outperforms the Hierarchical EA method of [21], while using 36 times less compute. Though the the EA method called "AmoebaNets" [27] currently give the highest accuracies (at the time of writing), it also requires the most compute, taking 63 times more resources than PNAS. However, these comparisons must be taken with a grain of salt, since the methods are searching through different spaces. By contrast, in Sect. 5.3, we fix the search space for NAS and PNAS, to make the speedup comparison fair.

5.5   Results on ImageNet Image Classification

We further demonstrate the usefulness of our learned cell by applying it to ImageNet classification. Our experiments reveal that CIFAR accuracy and ImageNet accuracy are strongly correlated ($\rho = 0.727$; see supplementary material).

To compare the performance of PNASNet-5 to the results in other papers, we conduct experiments under two settings:

- *Mobile*: Here we restrain the representation power of the CNN. Input image size is 224×224, and the number of multiply-add operations is under 600M.
- *Large*: Here we compare PNASNet-5 against the state-of-the-art models on ImageNet. Input image size is 331×331.

In both experiments we use RMSProp optimizer, label smoothing of 0.1, auxiliary classifier located at 2/3 of the maximum depth weighted by 0.4, weight decay of 4e-5, and dropout of 0.5 in the final softmax layer. In the *Mobile* setting, we use distributed synchronous SGD with 50 P100 workers. On each worker,

---

[5] This additional stage is quite important for NAS, as the NASNet-A cell was originally ranked 70th among the top 250.

Table 4. ImageNet classification results in the *Mobile* setting.

Model	Params	Mult-Adds	Top-1	Top-5
MobileNet-224 [14]	4.2M	569M	70.6	89.5
ShuffleNet (2x) [37]	5M	524M	70.9	89.8
NASNet-A ($N = 4, F = 44$) [41]	5.3M	564M	74.0	91.6
AmoebaNet-B ($N = 3, F = 62$) [27]	5.3M	555M	74.0	91.5
AmoebaNet-A ($N = 4, F = 50$) [27]	5.1M	555M	74.5	92.0
AmoebaNet-C ($N = 4, F = 50$) [27]	6.4M	570M	75.7	92.4
PNASNet-5 ($N = 3, F = 54$)	5.1M	588M	74.2	91.9

Table 5. ImageNet classification results in the *Large* setting.

Model	Image Size	Params	Mult-Adds	Top-1	Top-5
ResNeXt-101 (64x4d) [36]	320 × 320	83.6M	31.5B	80.9	95.6
PolyNet [38]	331 × 331	92M	34.7B	81.3	95.8
Dual-Path-Net-131 [6]	320 × 320	79.5M	32.0B	81.5	95.8
Squeeze-Excite-Net [15]	320 × 320	145.8M	42.3B	82.7	96.2
NASNet-A ($N = 6, F = 168$) [41]	331 × 331	88.9M	23.8B	82.7	96.2
AmoebaNet-B ($N = 6, F = 190$) [27]	331 × 331	84.0M	22.3B	82.3	96.1
AmoebaNet-A ($N = 6, F = 190$) [27]	331 × 331	86.7M	23.1B	82.8	96.1
AmoebaNet-C ($N = 6, F = 228$) [27]	331 × 331	155.3M	41.1B	83.1	96.3
PNASNet-5 ($N = 4, F = 216$)	331 × 331	86.1M	25.0B	82.9	96.2

batch size is 32, initial learning rate is 0.04, and is decayed every 2.2 epochs with rate 0.97. In the *Large* setting, we use 100 P100 workers. On each worker, batch size is 16, initial learning rate is 0.015, and is decayed every 2.4 epochs with rate 0.97. During training, we drop each path with probability 0.4.

The results of the *Mobile* setting are summarized in Table 4. PNASNet-5 achieves slightly better performance than NASNet-A (74.2% top-1 accuracy for PNAS vs 74.0% for NASNet-A). Both methods significantly surpass the previous state-of-the-art, which includes the manually designed MobileNet [14] (70.6%) and ShuffleNet [37] (70.9%). AmoebaNet-C performs the best, but note that this is a different model than their best-performing CIFAR-10 model. Table 5 shows that under the *Large* setting, PNASNet-5 achieves higher performance (82.9% top-1; 96.2% top-5) than previous state-of-the-art approaches, including SENet [15], NASNet-A, and AmoebaNets under the same model capacity.

6   Discussion and Future Work

The main contribution of this work is to show how we can accelerate the search for good CNN structures by using progressive search through the space of increasingly complex graphs, combined with a learned prediction function to efficiently identify the most promising models to explore. The resulting models achieve the same level of performance as previous work but with a fraction of the computational cost.

There are many possible directions for future work, including: the use of better surrogate predictors, such as Gaussian processes with string kernels; the use of model-based early stopping, such as [3], so we can stop the training of "unpromising" models before reaching E_1 epochs; the use of "warm starting", to initialize the training of a larger $b+1$-sized model from its smaller parent; the use of Bayesian optimization, in which we use an acquisition function, such as expected improvement or upper confidence bound, to rank the candidate models, rather than greedily picking the top K (see e.g., [30,31]); adaptively varying the number of models K evaluated at each step (e.g., reducing it over time); the automatic exploration of speed-accuracy tradeoffs (cf., [11]), etc.

Acknowledgements. We thank Quoc Le for inspiration, discussion and support; George Dahl for many fruitful discussions; Gabriel Bender, Vijay Vasudevan for the development of much of the critical infrastructure and the larger Google Brain team for the support and discussions. CL also thanks Lingxi Xie for support.

References

1. Baisero, A., Pokorny, F.T., Ek, C.H.: On a family of decomposable kernels on sequences. CoRR abs/1501.06284 (2015)
2. Baker, B., Gupta, O., Naik, N., Raskar, R.: Designing neural network architectures using reinforcement learning. In: ICLR (2017)
3. Baker, B., Gupta, O., Raskar, R., Naik, N.: Accelerating neural architecture search using performance prediction. CoRR abs/1705.10823 (2017)
4. Brock, A., Lim, T., Ritchie, J.M., Weston, N.: SMASH: one-shot model architecture search through hypernetworks. In: ICLR (2018)
5. Cai, H., Chen, T., Zhang, W., Yu, Y., Wang, J.: Efficient architecture search by network transformation. In: AAAI (2018)
6. Chen, Y., Li, J., Xiao, H., Jin, X., Yan, S., Feng, J.: Dual path networks. In: NIPS (2017)
7. Cortes, C., Gonzalvo, X., Kuznetsov, V., Mohri, M., Yang, S.: AdaNet: adaptive structural learning of artificial neural networks. In: ICML (2017)
8. Deng, J., Dong, W., Socher, R., Li, L., Li, K., Fei-Fei, L.: Imagenet: a large-scale hierarchical image database. In: CVPR (2009)
9. Devries, T., Taylor, G.W.: Improved regularization of convolutional neural networks with cutout. CoRR abs/1708.04552 (2017)
10. Domhan, T., Springenberg, J.T., Hutter, F.: Speeding up automatic hyperparameter optimization of deep neural networks by extrapolation of learning curves. IJCAI (2015)
11. Dong, J.D., Cheng, A.C., Juan, D.C., Wei, W., Sun, M.: PPP-Net: platform-aware progressive search for pareto-optimal neural architectures. In: ICLR Workshop (2018)
12. Elsken, T., Metzen, J.H., Hutter, F.: Simple and efficient architecture search for convolutional neural networks. CoRR abs/1711.04528 (2017)

13. Grosse, R.B., Salakhutdinov, R., Freeman, W.T., Tenenbaum, J.B.: Exploiting compositionality to explore a large space of model structures. In: UAI (2012)
14. Howard, A.G., et al.: MobileNets: efficient convolutional neural networks for mobile vision applications. CoRR abs/1704.04861 (2017)
15. Hu, J., Shen, L., Sun, G.: Squeeze-and-excitation networks. CoRR abs/1709.01507 (2017)
16. Huang, F., Ash, J.T., Langford, J., Schapire, R.E.: Learning deep resnet blocks sequentially using boosting theory. CoRR abs/1706.04964 (2017)
17. Hutter, F., Hoos, H.H., Leyton-Brown, K.: Sequential model-based optimization for general algorithm configuration. In: Coello, C.A.C. (ed.) LION 2011. LNCS, vol. 6683, pp. 507–523. Springer, Heidelberg (2011). https://doi.org/10.1007/978-3-642-25566-3_40
18. Kingma, D.P., Ba, J.: Adam: a method for stochastic optimization. In: ICLR (2015)
19. Krizhevsky, A., Hinton, G.: Learning multiple layers of features from tiny images. Technical report, University of Toronto (2009)
20. Lin, T.-Y., et al.: Microsoft COCO: common objects in context. In: Fleet, D., Pajdla, T., Schiele, B., Tuytelaars, T. (eds.) ECCV 2014. LNCS, vol. 8693, pp. 740–755. Springer, Cham (2014). https://doi.org/10.1007/978-3-319-10602-1_48
21. Liu, H., Simonyan, K., Vinyals, O., Fernando, C., Kavukcuoglu, K.: Hierarchical representations for efficient architecture search. In: ICLR (2018)
22. Loshchilov, I., Hutter, F.: SGDR: stochastic gradient descent with restarts. In: ICLR (2017)
23. Mendoza, H., Klein, A., Feurer, M., Springenberg, J.T., Hutter, F.: Towards Automatically-Tuned neural networks. In: ICML Workshop on AutoML, pp. 58–65, December 2016
24. Miikkulainen, R., et al.: Evolving deep neural networks. CoRR abs/1703.00548 (2017)
25. Negrinho, R., Gordon, G.J.: DeepArchitect: automatically designing and training deep architectures. CoRR abs/1704.08792 (2017)
26. Pham, H., Guan, M.Y., Zoph, B., Le, Q.V., Dean, J.: Efficient neural architecture search via parameter sharing. CoRR abs/1802.03268 (2018)
27. Real, E., Aggarwal, A., Huang, Y., Le, Q.V.: Regularized evolution for image classifier architecture search. CoRR abs/1802.01548 (2018)
28. Real, E., et al.: Large-scale evolution of image classifiers. In: ICML (2017)
29. Schulman, J., Wolski, F., Dhariwal, P., Radford, A., Klimov, O.: Proximal policy optimization algorithms. CoRR abs/1707.06347 (2017)
30. Shahriari, B., Swersky, K., Wang, Z., Adams, R.P., de Freitas, N.: Taking the human out of the loop: a review of bayesian optimization. Proc. IEEE **104**(1), 148–175 (2016)
31. Snoek, J., Larochelle, H., Adams, R.P.: Practical bayesian optimization of machine learning algorithms. In: NIPS (2012)
32. Stanley, K.O.: Neuroevolution: a different kind of deep learning, July 2017
33. Stanley, K.O., Miikkulainen, R.: Evolving neural networks through augmenting topologies. Evol. Comput. **10**(2), 99–127 (2002)
34. Williams, R.: Simple statistical gradient-following algorithms for connectionist reinforcement learning. Mach. Learn. **8**, 229–256 (1992)
35. Xie, L., Yuille, A.L.: Genetic CNN. In: ICCV (2017)
36. Xie, S., Girshick, R.B., Dollár, P., Tu, Z., He, K.: Aggregated residual transformations for deep neural networks. In: CVPR (2017)
37. Zhang, X., Zhou, X., Lin, M., Sun, J.: ShuffleNet: an extremely efficient convolutional neural network for mobile devices. CoRR abs/1707.01083 (2017)

38. Zhang, X., Li, Z., Loy, C.C., Lin, D.: PolyNet: a pursuit of structural diversity in very deep networks. In: CVPR (2017)
39. Zhong, Z., Yan, J., Liu, C.L.: Practical network blocks design with Q-learning. In: AAAI (2018)
40. Zoph, B., Le, Q.V.: Neural architecture search with reinforcement learning. In: ICLR (2017)
41. Zoph, B., Vasudevan, V., Shlens, J., Le, Q.V.: Learning transferable architectures for scalable image recognition. In: CVPR (2018)

Diverse Image-to-Image Translation
via Disentangled Representations

Hsin-Ying Lee[1]([⊠]), Hung-Yu Tseng[1], Jia-Bin Huang[2], Maneesh Singh[3],
and Ming-Hsuan Yang[1,4]

[1] University of California, Merced, USA
hlee246@ucmerced.edu
[2] Virginia Tech, Blacksburg, USA
[3] Verisk Analytics, Jersey City, USA
[4] Google Cloud, Merced, USA

Abstract. Image-to-image translation aims to learn the mapping between two visual domains. There are two main challenges for many applications: (1) the lack of aligned training pairs and (2) multiple possible outputs from a single input image. In this work, we present an approach based on disentangled representation for producing diverse outputs without paired training images. To achieve diversity, we propose to embed images onto two spaces: a domain-invariant content space capturing shared information across domains and a domain-specific attribute space. Using the disentangled features as inputs greatly reduces mode collapse. To handle unpaired training data, we introduce a novel cross-cycle consistency loss. Qualitative results show that our model can generate diverse and realistic images on a wide range of tasks. We validate the effectiveness of our approach through extensive evaluation.

1 Introduction

Image-to-Image (I2I) translation aims to learn the mapping between different visual domains. Many vision and graphics problems can be formulated as I2I translation problems, such as colorization [21,43] (grayscale → color), super-resolution [20,23,24] (low-resolution → high-resolution), and photorealistic image synthesis [6,39] (label → image). Furthermore, I2I translation has recently shown promising results in facilitating domain adaptation [3,15,30,33].

Learning the mapping between two visual domains is challenging for two main reasons. First, aligned training image pairs are either difficult to collect (e.g., day scene ↔ night scene) or do not exist (e.g., artwork ↔ real photo). Second, many such mappings are inherently multimodal — a single input may correspond to multiple possible outputs. To handle multimodal translation, one possible approach is to inject a random noise vector to the generator for modeling the data distribution in the target domain. However, mode collapse may still occur easily since the generator often ignores the additional noise vectors.

H.-Y. Lee and H.-Y. Tseng—Equal contribution.

© Springer Nature Switzerland AG 2018
V. Ferrari et al. (Eds.): ECCV 2018, LNCS 11205, pp. 36–52, 2018.
https://doi.org/10.1007/978-3-030-01246-5_3

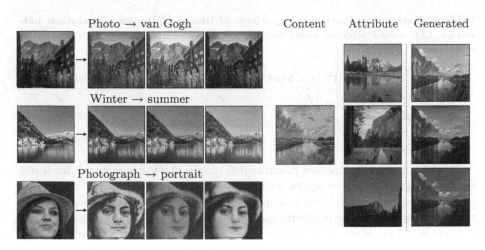

Fig. 1. Unpaired diverse image-to-image translation. (*Left*) Our model performs diverse translation between two collections of images without aligned training pairs. (*Right*) Example-guided translation.

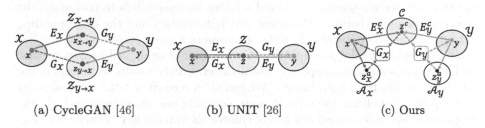

(a) CycleGAN [46]   (b) UNIT [26]   (c) Ours

Fig. 2. Comparisons of unsupervised I2I translation methods. Denote x and y as images in domain $\mathcal{X}$ and $\mathcal{Y}$: (a) CycleGAN [45] and DiscoGAN [18] map x and y onto *separated* latent spaces. (b) UNIT [25] assumes x and y can be mapped onto a *shared* latent space. (c) Our approach disentangles the latent spaces of x and y into a shared content space $\mathcal{C}$ and an attribute space $\mathcal{A}$ of each domain.

Several recent efforts have been made to address these issues. Pix2pix [17] applies conditional generative adversarial network to I2I translation problems. Nevertheless, the training process requires paired data. A number of recent work [9,25,35,41,45] relaxes the dependency on paired training data for learning I2I translation. These methods, however, produce a single output conditioned on the given input image. As shown in [17,46], simply incorporating noise vectors as additional inputs to the generator does not lead the increased variations of the generated outputs due to the mode collapsing issue. The generators in these methods are inclined to overlook the added noise vectors. Very recently, BicycleGAN [46] tackles the problem of generating diverse outputs in I2I problems by encouraging the one-to-one relationship between the output and the latent vector. Nevertheless, the training process of BicycleGAN requires paired images.

Table 1. Feature-by-feature comparison of image-to-image translation networks. Our model achieves multimodal translation without using aligned training image pairs.

Method	Pix2Pix [17]	CycleGAN [45]	UNIT [25]	BicycleGAN [46]	Ours
Unpaired	-	✓	✓	-	✓
Multimodal	-	-	-	✓	✓

In this paper, we propose a disentangled representation framework for learning to generate *diverse* outputs with *unpaired* training data. Specifically, we propose to embed images onto two spaces: (1) a domain-invariant content space and (2) a domain-specific attribute space as shown in Fig. 2. Our generator learns to perform I2I translation conditioned on content features and a latent attribute vector. The domain-specific attribute space aims to model the variations within a domain given the same content, while the domain-invariant content space captures information across domains. We achieve this representation disentanglement by applying a content adversarial loss to encourage the content features *not* to carry domain-specific cues, and a latent regression loss to encourage the invertible mapping between the latent attribute vectors and the corresponding outputs. To handle unpaired datasets, we propose a *cross-cycle consistency loss* using the disentangled representations. Given a pair of unaligned images, we first perform a cross-domain mapping to obtain intermediate results by swapping the attribute vectors from both images. We can then reconstruct the original input image pair by applying the cross-domain mapping one more time and use the proposed cross-cycle consistency loss to enforce the consistency between the original and the reconstructed images. At test time, we can use either (1) randomly sampled vectors from the attribute space to generate diverse outputs or (2) the transferred attribute vectors extracted from existing images for example-guided translation. Figure 1 shows examples of the two testing modes.

We evaluate the proposed model through extensive qualitative and quantitative evaluation. In a wide variety of I2I tasks, we show diverse translation results with randomly sampled attribute vectors and example-guided translation with transferred attribute vectors from existing images. We evaluate the realism of our results with a user study and the diversity using perceptual distance metrics [44]. Furthermore, we demonstrate the potential application of unsupervised domain adaptation. On the tasks of adapting domains from MNIST [22] to MNIST-M [12] and Synthetic Cropped LineMod to Cropped LineMod [14,40], we show competitive performance against state-of-the-art domain adaptation methods.

We make the following contributions:

(1) We introduce a disentangled representation framework for image-to-image translation. We apply a content discriminator to facilitate the factorization of domain-invariant content space and domain-specific attribute space, and a cross-cycle consistency loss that allows us to train the model with unpaired data.

(2) Extensive qualitative and quantitative experiments show that our model compares favorably against existing I2I models. Images generated by our model are both diverse and realistic.

(3) We demonstrate the application of our model on unsupervised domain adaptation. We achieve competitive results on both the MNIST-M and the Cropped LineMod datasets.

Our code, data and more results are available at https://github.com/HsinYingLee/DRIT/.

2   Related Work

Generative Adversarial Networks. Recent years have witnessed rapid progress on generative adversarial networks (GANs) [2,13,31] for image generation. The core idea of GANs lies in the adversarial loss that enforces the distribution of generated images to match that of the target domain. The generators in GANs can map from noise vectors to realistic images. Several recent efforts explore *conditional* GAN in various contexts including conditioned on text [32], low-resolution images [23], video frames [38], and image [17]. Our work focuses on using GAN conditioned on an input image. In contrast to several existing conditional GAN frameworks that require paired training data, our model produces diverse outputs without paired data. This suggests that our method has wider applicability to problems where paired training datasets are scarce or not available.

Image-to-Image Translation. I2I translation aims to learn the mapping from a source image domain to a target image domain. Pix2pix [17] applies a conditional GAN to model the mapping function. Although high-quality results have been shown, the model training requires paired training data. To train with unpaired data, CycleGAN [45], DiscoGAN [18], and UNIT [25] leverage cycle consistency to regularize the training. However, these methods perform generation conditioned solely on an input image and thus produce one single output. Simply injecting a noise vector to a generator is usually not an effective solution to achieve multimodal generation due to the lack of regularization between the noise vectors and the target domain. On the other hand, BicycleGAN [46] enforces the bijection mapping between the latent and target space to tackle the mode collapse problem. Nevertheless, the method is only applicable to problems with paired training data. Table 1 shows a feature-by-feature comparison among various I2I models. Unlike existing work, our method enables I2I translation with diverse outputs in the absence of paired training data.

Very recently, several concurrent works [1,5,16,27] (all independently developed) also adopt a disentangled representation similar to our work for learning diverse I2I translation from unpaired training data. We encourage the readers to review these works for a complete picture.

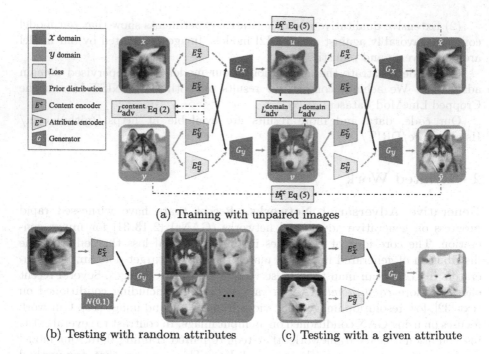

(a) Training with unpaired images

(b) Testing with random attributes   (c) Testing with a given attribute

Fig. 3. Method overview. (a) With the proposed content adversarial loss $L_{adv}^{content}$ (Sect. 3.1) and the cross-cycle consistency loss L_1^{cc} (Sect. 3.2), we are able to learn the multimodal mapping between the domain $\mathcal{X}$ and $\mathcal{Y}$ with unpaired data. Thanks to the proposed disentangled representation, we can generate output images conditioned on either (b) random attributes or (c) a given attribute at test time.

Disentangled Representations. The task of learning disentangled representation aims at modeling the factors of data variations. Previous work makes use of labeled data to factorize representations into class-related and class-independent components [8,19,28,29]. Recently, the unsupervised setting has been explored [7,10]. InfoGAN [7] achieves disentanglement by maximizing the mutual information between latent variables and data variation. Similar to DrNet [10] that separates time-independent and time-varying components with an adversarial loss, we apply a content adversarial loss to disentangle an image into domain-invariant and domain-specific representations to facilitate learning diverse cross-domain mappings.

Domain Adaptation. Domain adaptation techniques focus on addressing the domain-shift problem between a source and a target domain. Domain Adversarial Neural Network (DANN) [11,12] and its variants [4,36,37] tackle domain adaptation through learning domain-invariant features. Sun et al. [34] aims to map features in the source domain to those in the target domain. I2I translation has been recently applied to produce simulated images in the target domain by translating images from the source domain [11,15]. Different from the afore-mentioned I2I based domain adaptation algorithms, our method does not utilize source domain annotations for I2I translation.

3 Disentangled Representation for I2I Translation

Our goal is to learn a multimodal mapping between two visual domains $\mathcal{X} \subset \mathbb{R}^{H \times W \times 3}$ and $\mathcal{Y} \subset \mathbb{R}^{H \times W \times 3}$ without paired training data. As illustrated in Fig. 3, our framework consists of content encoders $\{E_{\mathcal{X}}^c, E_{\mathcal{Y}}^c\}$, attribute encoders $\{E_{\mathcal{X}}^a, E_{\mathcal{Y}}^a\}$, generators $\{G_{\mathcal{X}}, G_{\mathcal{Y}}\}$, and domain discriminators $\{D_{\mathcal{X}}, D_{\mathcal{Y}}\}$ for both domains, and a content discriminators D_{adv}^c. Take domain $\mathcal{X}$ as an example, the content encoder $E_{\mathcal{X}}^c$ maps images onto a shared, domain-invariant content space $(E_{\mathcal{X}}^c : \mathcal{X} \rightarrow \mathcal{C})$ and the attribute encoder $E_{\mathcal{X}}^a$ maps images onto a domain-specific attribute space $(E_{\mathcal{X}}^a : \mathcal{X} \rightarrow \mathcal{A}_{\mathcal{X}})$. The generator $G_{\mathcal{X}}$ generates images conditioned on both content and attribute vectors $(G_{\mathcal{X}} : \{\mathcal{C}, \mathcal{A}_{\mathcal{X}}\} \rightarrow \mathcal{X})$. The discriminator $D_{\mathcal{X}}$ aims to discriminate between real images and translated images in the domain $\mathcal{X}$. Content discriminator D^c is trained to distinguish the extracted content representations between two domains. To enable multimodal generation at test time, we regularize the attribute vectors so that they can be drawn from a prior Gaussian distribution $N(0,1)$.

In this section, we first discuss the strategies used to disentangle the content and attribute representations in Sect. 3.1 and then introduce the proposed cross-cycle consistency loss that enables the training on unpaired data in Sect. 3.2. Finally, we detail the loss functions in Sect. 3.3.

3.1 Disentangle Content and Attribute Representations

Our approach embeds input images onto a shared content space $\mathcal{C}$, and domain-specific attribute spaces, $\mathcal{A}_{\mathcal{X}}$ and $\mathcal{A}_{\mathcal{Y}}$. Intuitively, the content encoders should encode the common information that is *shared* between domains onto $\mathcal{C}$, while the attribute encoders should map the remaining domain-specific information onto $\mathcal{A}_{\mathcal{X}}$ and $\mathcal{A}_{\mathcal{Y}}$.

$$\begin{aligned}
\{z_x^c, z_x^a\} &= \{E_{\mathcal{X}}^c(x), E_{\mathcal{X}}^a(x)\} & z_x^c \in \mathcal{C}, z_x^a \in \mathcal{A}_{\mathcal{X}} \\
\{z_y^c, z_y^a\} &= \{E_{\mathcal{Y}}^c(y), E_{\mathcal{Y}}^a(y)\} & z_y^c \in \mathcal{C}, z_y^a \in \mathcal{A}_{\mathcal{Y}}
\end{aligned} \quad (1)$$

To achieve representation disentanglement, we apply two strategies: weight-sharing and a content discriminator. First, similar to [25], based on the assumption that two domains share a common latent space, we share the weight between the last layer of $E_{\mathcal{X}}^c$ and $E_{\mathcal{Y}}^c$ and the first layer of $G_{\mathcal{X}}$ and $G_{\mathcal{Y}}$. Through weight sharing, we force the content representation to be mapped onto the same space. However, sharing the same high-level mapping functions cannot guarantee the same content representations encode the same information for both domains. Therefore, we propose a content discriminator D^c which aims to distinguish the domain membership of the encoded content features z_x^c and z_y^c. On the other hand, content encoders learn to produce encoded content representations whose domain membership cannot be distinguished by the content discriminator D^c. We express this content adversarial loss as:

$$L_{\text{adv}}^{\text{content}}(E_{\mathcal{X}}^c, E_{\mathcal{Y}}^c, D^c) = \mathbb{E}_x[\frac{1}{2}\log D^c(E_{\mathcal{X}}^c(x)) + \frac{1}{2}\log(1 - D^c(E_{\mathcal{X}}^c(x)))]$$
$$+ \mathbb{E}_y[\frac{1}{2}\log D^c(E_{\mathcal{Y}}^c(y)) + \frac{1}{2}\log(1 - D^c(E_{\mathcal{Y}}^c(y)))] \qquad (2)$$

3.2 Cross-Cycle Consistency Loss

With the disentangled representation where the content space is shared among domains and the attribute space encodes intra-domain variations, we can perform I2I translation by combining a content representation from an arbitrary image and an attribute representation from an image of the target domain. We leverage this property and propose a *cross-cycle consistency*. In contrast to cycle consistency constraint in [45] (i.e., $\mathcal{X} \rightarrow \mathcal{Y} \rightarrow \mathcal{X}$) which assumes one-to-one mapping between the two domains, the proposed cross-cycle constraint exploit the disentangled content and attribute representations for cyclic reconstruction.

Our cross-cycle constraint consists of two stages of I2I translation.

Forward Translation. Given a non-corresponding pair of images x and y, we encode them into $\{z_x^c, z_x^a\}$ and $\{z_y^c, z_y^a\}$. We then perform the first translation by swapping the attribute representation (i.e., z_x^a and z_y^a) to generate $\{u, v\}$, where $u \in \mathcal{X}, v \in \mathcal{Y}$.

$$u = G_{\mathcal{X}}(z_y^c, z_x^a) \quad v = G_{\mathcal{Y}}(z_x^c, z_y^a) \qquad (3)$$

Backward Translation. After encoding u and v into $\{z_u^c, z_u^a\}$ and $\{z_v^c, z_v^a\}$, we perform the second translation by once again swapping the attribute representation (i.e., z_u^a and z_v^a).

$$\hat{x} = G_{\mathcal{X}}(z_v^c, z_u^a) \quad \hat{y} = G_{\mathcal{Y}}(z_u^c, z_v^a) \qquad (4)$$

Here, after two I2I translation stages, the translation should reconstruct the original images x and y (as illustrated in Fig. 3). To enforce this constraint, we formulate the *cross-cycle consistency loss* as:

$$L_1^{cc}(G_{\mathcal{X}}, G_{\mathcal{Y}}, E_{\mathcal{X}}^c, E_{\mathcal{Y}}^c, E_{\mathcal{X}}^a, E_{\mathcal{Y}}^a) = \mathbb{E}_{x,y}[\|G_{\mathcal{X}}(E_{\mathcal{Y}}^c(v), E_{\mathcal{X}}^a(u)) - x\|_1$$
$$+ \|G_{\mathcal{Y}}(E_{\mathcal{X}}^c(u), E_{\mathcal{Y}}^a(v)) - y\|_1], \qquad (5)$$

where $u = G_{\mathcal{X}}(E_{\mathcal{Y}}^c(y)), E_{\mathcal{X}}^a(x))$ and $v = G_{\mathcal{Y}}(E_{\mathcal{X}}^c(x)), E_{\mathcal{Y}}^a(y))$.

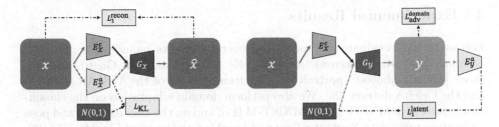

Fig. 4. Loss functions. In addition to the cross-cycle reconstruction loss L_1^{cc} and the content adversarial loss $L_{adv}^{content}$ described in Fig. 3, we apply several additional loss functions in our training process. The self-reconstruction loss L_1^{recon} facilitates training with self-reconstruction; the KL loss L_{KL} aims to align the attribute representation with a prior Gaussian distribution; the adversarial loss L_{adv}^{domain} encourages G to generate realistic images in each domain; and the latent regression loss L_1^{latent} enforces the reconstruction on the latent attribute vector. More details can be found in Sect. 3.3.

3.3 Other Loss Functions

Other than the proposed content adversarial loss and cross-cycle consistency loss, we also use several other loss functions to facilitate network training. We illustrate these additional losses in Fig. 4. Starting from the top-right, in the counter-clockwise order:

Domain Adversarial Loss. We impose adversarial loss L_{adv}^{domain} where $D_{\mathcal{X}}$ and $D_{\mathcal{Y}}$ attempt to discriminate between real images and generated images in each domain, while $G_{\mathcal{X}}$ and $G_{\mathcal{Y}}$ attempt to generate realistic images.

Self-Reconstruction Loss. In addition to the cross-cycle reconstruction, we apply a self-reconstruction loss L_1^{rec} to facilitate the training. With encoded content/attribute features $\{z_x^c, z_x^a\}$ and $\{z_y^c, z_y^a\}$, the decoders $G_{\mathcal{X}}$ and $G_{\mathcal{Y}}$ should decode them back to original input x and y. That is, $\hat{x} = G_{\mathcal{X}}(E_{\mathcal{X}}^c(x), E_{\mathcal{X}}^a(x))$ and $\hat{y} = G_{\mathcal{Y}}(E_{\mathcal{Y}}^c(y), E_{\mathcal{Y}}^a(y))$.

KL Loss. In order to perform stochastic sampling at test time, we encourage the attribute representation to be as close to a prior Gaussian distribution. We thus apply the loss $L_{KL} = \mathbb{E}[D_{KL}((z_a)\|N(0,1))]$, where $D_{KL}(p\|q) = -\int p(z) \log \frac{p(z)}{q(z)} dz$.

Latent Regression Loss. To encourage invertible mapping between the image and the latent space, we apply a latent regression loss L_1^{latent} similar to [46]. We draw a latent vector z from the prior Gaussian distribution as the attribute representation and attempt to reconstruct it with $\hat{z} = E_{\mathcal{X}}^a(G_{\mathcal{X}}(E_{\mathcal{X}}^c(x), z))$ and $\hat{z} = E_{\mathcal{Y}}^a(G_{\mathcal{Y}}(E_{\mathcal{Y}}^c(y), z))$.

The full objective function of our network is:

$$\min_{G,E^c,E^a} \max_{D,D^c} \lambda_{adv}^{content} L_{adv}^c + \lambda_1^{cc} L_1^{cc} + \lambda_{adv}^{domain} L_{adv}^{domain} + \lambda_1^{recon} L_1^{recon}$$
$$+ \lambda_1^{latent} L_1^{latent} + \lambda_{KL} L_{KL} \tag{6}$$

where the hyper-parameters λs control the importance of each term.

4   Experimental Results

Datasets. We evaluate our model on several datasets include Yosemite [45] (summer and winter scenes), artworks [45] (Monet and van Gogh), edge-to-shoes [42] and photo-to-portrait cropped from subsets of the WikiArt dataset[1] and the CelebA dataset [26]. We also perform domain adaptation on the classification task with MNIST [22] to MNIST-M [12], and on the classification and pose estimation tasks with Synthetic Cropped LineMod to Cropped LineMod [14,40].

Compared Methods. We perform the evaluation on the following algorithms:

- **DRIT:** We refer to our proposed model, Disentangled Representation for Image-to-Image Translation, as DRIT.
- **DRIT w/o D^c:** Our proposed model without the content discriminator.
- **CycleGAN** [45], **UNIT** [25], **BicycleGAN** [46]
- **Cycle/Bicycle:** As there is no previous work addressing the problem of multimodal generation from unpaired training data, we construct a baseline using

Input   Generated images

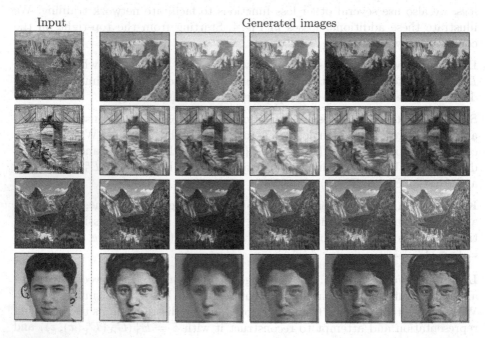

Fig. 5. Sample results. We show example results produced by our model. The left column shows the input images in the source domain. The other five columns show the output images generated by sampling random vectors in the attribute space. The mappings from top to bottom are: Monet → photo, van Gogh → Monet, winter → summer, and photograph → portrait.

---

[1] https://www.wikiart.org/.

a combination of CylceGAN and BicycleGAN. Here, we first train CycleGAN on unpaired data to generate corresponding images as *pseudo* image pairs. We then use this pseudo paired data to train BicycleGAN.

4.1 Qualitative Evaluation

Diversity. We first demonstrate the diversity of the generated images on several different tasks in Fig. 5. In Fig. 6, we compare the proposed model with other methods. Both our model without D^c and Cycle/Bicycle can generate diverse results. However, the results contain clearly visible artifacts. Without the content discriminator, our model fails to capture domain-related details (e.g., the color of tree and sky). Therefore, the variations take place in global color difference. Cycle/Bicycle is trained on pseudo paired data generated by CycleGAN. The quality of the pseudo paired data is not uniformly ideal. As a result, the generated images are of ill-quality.

To have a better understanding of the learned domain-specific attribute space, we perform linear interpolation between two given attributes and generate the corresponding images as shown in Fig. 7. The interpolation results verify the

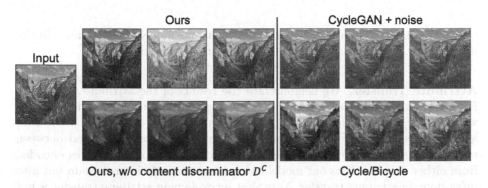

Fig. 6. Diversity comparison. On the winter → summer translation task, our model produces more diverse and realistic samples over baselines.

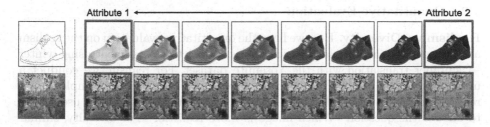

Fig. 7. Linear interpolation between attribute vectors. Translation results with linear-interpolated attribute vectors between attributes (highlighted in red). (Color figure online)

Content   Attribute   Output   Content   Attribute   Output

(a) Inter-domain attribute transfer   (b) Intra-domain attribute transfer

Fig. 8. Attribute transfer. At test time, in addition to random sampling from the attribute space, we can also perform translation with the query images with the desired attributes. Since the content space is shared across the two domains, we not only can achieve (a) inter-domain, but also (b) intra-domain attribute transfer. Note that we do not explicitly involve intra-domain attribute transfer during training.

continuity in the attribute space and show that our model can generalize in the distribution, rather than memorize trivial visual information.

Attribute Transfer. We demonstrate the results of the attribute transfer in Fig. 8. Thanks to the representation disentanglement of content and attribute, we are able to perform attribute transfer from images of desired attributes, as illustrated in Fig. 3(c). Moreover, since the content space is shared between two domains, we can generate images conditioned on content features encoded from either domain. Thus our model can achieve not only inter-domain but also intra-domain attribute transfer. Note that intra-domain attribute transfer is not explicitly involved in the training process.

4.2   Quantitative Evaluation

Realism vs. Diversity. Here we have the quantitative evaluation on the realism and diversity of the generated images. We conduct the experiment using winter → summer translation with the Yosemite dataset. For realism, we conduct a user study using pairwise comparison. Given a pair of images sampled from real images and translated images generated from various methods, users need to answer the question "Which image is more realistic?" For diversity, similar to [46], we use the LPIPS metric [44] to measure the similarity among images. We compute the distance between 1000 pairs of randomly sampled images translated from 100 real images.

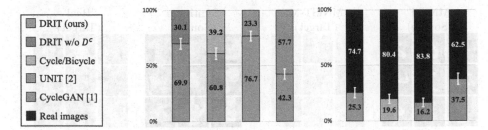

Fig. 9. Realism preference results. We conduct a user study to ask subjects to select results that are *more realistic* through pairwise comparisons. The number indicates the percentage of preference on that comparison pair. We use the winter → summer translation on the Yosemite dataset for this experiment.

Table 2. Diversity. We use the LPIPS metric [44] to measure the diversity of generated images on the Yosemite dataset.

Method	Diversity
Real images	.448 ± .012
DRIT	**.424** ± .010
DRIT w/o D^c	.410 ± .016
UNIT [25]	.406 ± .022
CycleGAN [45]	.413 ± .008
Cycle/Bicycle	.399 ± .009

Table 3. Reconstruct error. We use the edge-to-shoes dataset to measure the quality of our attribute encoding. The reconstruction error is $\|y - G_{\mathcal{Y}}(E_{\mathcal{X}}^c(x), E_{\mathcal{Y}}^a(y))\|_1$. *BicycleGAN uses *paired* data for training.

Method	Reconstruct error
BicycleGAN [46]*	**0.0945**
DRIT	0.1347
DRIT, w/o D^c	0.2076

Figure 9 and Table 2 show the results of realism and diversity, respectively. UNIT obtains low realism score, suggesting that their assumption might not be generally applicable. CycleGAN achieves the highest scores in realism, yet the diversity is limited. The diversity and the visual quality of Cycle/Bicycle are constrained by the data CycleGAN can generate. Our results also demonstrate the need for the content discriminator.

Reconstruction Ability. In addition to diversity evaluation, we conduct an experiment on the edge-to-shoes dataset to measure the quality of the disentangled encoding. Our model was trained using unpaired data. At test time, given a paired data $\{x, y\}$, we can evaluate the quality of content-attribute disentanglement by measuring the reconstruction errors of y with $\hat{y} = G_{\mathcal{Y}}(E_{\mathcal{X}}^c(x), E_{\mathcal{Y}}^a(y))$.

We compare our model with BicycleGAN, which requires paired data during training. Table 3 shows our model performs comparably with BicycleGAN despite training without paired data. Moreover, the result suggests that the content discriminator contributes greatly to the quality of disentangled representation.

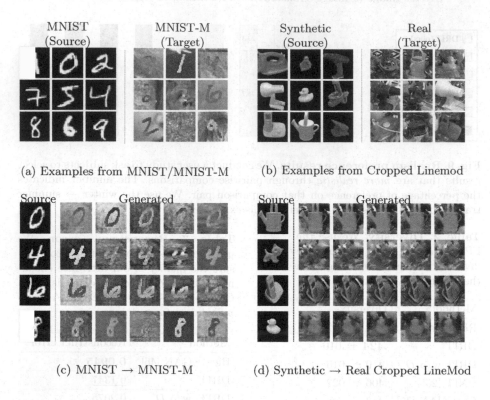

(a) Examples from MNIST/MNIST-M   (b) Examples from Cropped Linemod

(c) MNIST → MNIST-M   (d) Synthetic → Real Cropped LineMod

Fig. 10. Domain adaptation experiments. We conduct the experiment on (a) MNIST to MNIST-M, and (b) Synthetic to Realistic Cropped LineMod. (c) (d) Our method can generate diverse images that benefit the domain adaptation.

4.3   Domain Adaptation

We demonstrate that the proposed image-to-image translation scheme can benefit unsupervised domain adaptation. Following PixelDA [3], we conduct experiments on the classification and pose estimation tasks using MNIST [22] to MNIST-M [12], and Synthetic Cropped LineMod to Cropped LineMod [14,40]. Several example images in these datasets are shown in Fig. 10(a) and (b). To evaluate our method, we first translate the labeled source images to the target domain. We then treat the generated labeled images as training data and train the classifiers of each task in the target domain. For a fair comparison, we use the classifiers with the same architecture as PixelDA. We compare the proposed method with CycleGAN, which generates the most realistic images in the target domain according to our previous experiment, and three state-of-the-art domain adaptation algorithms: PixelDA, DANN [12] and DSN [4].

We present the quantitative comparisons in Table 4 and visual results from our method in Fig. 10(c) and (d). Since our model can generate diverse output, we generate one time, three times, and five times (denoted as ×1, ×3, ×5) of target images using the same amount of source images. Our results validate that the

Table 4. Domain adaptation results. We report the classification accuracy and the pose estimation error on MNIST to MNIST-M and Synthetic Cropped LineMod to Cropped LineMod. The entries "Source-only" and "Target-only" represent that the training uses either image only from the source and target domain. Numbers in parenthesis are reported by PixelDA, which are slightly different from what we obtain.

(a) MNIST-M		(b) Cropped LineMod		
Model	Classification Accuracy (%)	Model	Classification Accuracy (%)	Mean Angle Error (°)
Source-only	56.6	Source-only	42.9 (47.33)	73.7 (89.2)
CycleGAN [46]	74.5	CycleGAN [46]	68.18	47.45
Ours, ×1	86.93	Ours, ×1	95.91	42.06
Ours, ×3	90.21	Ours, ×3	97.04	37.35
Ours, ×5	**91.54**	Ours, ×5	**98.12**	**34.4**
DANN [13]	77.4	DANN [13]	99.9	56.58
DSN [4]	83.2	DSN [4]	100	53.27
PixelDA [3]	**95.9**	PixelDA [3]	99.98	**23.5**
Target-only	96.5	Target-only	100	12.3 (6.47)

proposed method can simulate diverse images in the target domain and improve the performance in target tasks. While our method does not outperform PixelDA, we note that unlike PixelDA, we do not leverage label information during training. Compared to CycleGAN, our method performs favorably even with the same amount of generated images (i.e., ×1). We observe that CycleGAN suffers from the mode collapse problem and generates images with similar appearances, which degrade the performance of the adapted classifiers.

5   Conclusions

In this paper, we present a novel disentangled representation framework for diverse image-to-image translation with unpaired data. We propose to disentangle the latent space to a content space that encodes common information between domains, and a domain-specific attribute space that can model the diverse variations given the same content. We apply a content discriminator to facilitate the representation disentanglement. We propose a cross-cycle consistency loss for cyclic reconstruction to train in the absence of paired data. Qualitative and quantitative results show that the proposed model produces realistic and diverse images. We also apply the proposed method to domain adaptation and achieve competitive performance compared to the state-of-the-art methods.

Acknowledgements. This work is supported in part by the NSF CAREER Grant #1149783, the NSF Grant #1755785, and gifts from Verisk, Adobe and Nvidia.

References

1. Almahairi, A., Rajeswar, S., Sordoni, A., Bachman, P., Courville, A.: Augmented cyclegan: learning many-to-many mappings from unpaired data. arXiv preprint arXiv:1802.10151 (2018)
2. Arjovsky, M., Chintala, S., Bottou, L.: Wasserstein GAN. In: ICML (2017)
3. Bousmalis, K., Silberman, N., Dohan, D., Erhan, D., Krishnan, D.: Unsupervised pixel-level domain adaptation with generative adversarial networks. In: CVPR (2017)
4. Bousmalis, K., Trigeorgis, G., Silberman, N., Krishnan, D., Erhan, D.: Domain separation networks. In: NIPS (2016)
5. Cao, J., et al.: DiDA: disentangled synthesis for domain adaptation. arXiv preprint arXiv:1805.08019 (2018)
6. Chen, Q., Koltun, V.: Photographic image synthesis with cascaded refinement networks. In: ICCV (2017)
7. Chen, X., Duan, Y., Houthooft, R., Schulman, J., Sutskever, I., Abbeel, P.: Info-GAN: interpretable representation learning by information maximizing generative adversarial nets. In: NIPS (2016)
8. Cheung, B., Livezey, J.A., Bansal, A.K., Olshausen, B.A.: Discovering hidden factors of variation in deep networks. In: ICLR Workshop (2015)
9. Choi, Y., Choi, M., Kim, M., Ha, J.W., Kim, S., Choo, J.: StarGAN: unified generative adversarial networks for multi-domain image-to-image translation. In: CVPR, vol. 1711 (2018)
10. Denton, E.L., Birodkar, V.: Unsupervised learning of disentangled representations from video. In: NIPS (2017)
11. Ganin, Y., Lempitsky, V.: Unsupervised domain adaptation by backpropagation. In: ICML (2015)
12. Ganin, Y., et al.: Domain-adversarial training of neural networks. JMLR **17**, 1–35 (2016)
13. Goodfellow, I., et al.: Generative adversarial nets. In: NIPS (2014)
14. Hinterstoisser, S., et al.: Model based training, detection and pose estimation of texture-less 3D objects in heavily cluttered scenes. In: Lee, K.M., Matsushita, Y., Rehg, J.M., Hu, Z. (eds.) ACCV 2012. LNCS, vol. 7724, pp. 548–562. Springer, Heidelberg (2013). https://doi.org/10.1007/978-3-642-37331-2_42
15. Hoffman, J., et al.: CyCADA: cycle-consistent adversarial domain adaptation. In: ICML (2018)
16. Huang, X., Liu, M.Y., Belongie, S., Kautz, J.: Multimodal unsupervised image-to-image translation. In: ECCV (2018)
17. Isola, P., Zhu, J.Y., Zhou, T., Efros, A.A.: Image-to-image translation with conditional adversarial networks. In: CVPR (2017)
18. Kim, T., Cha, M., Kim, H., Lee, J., Kim, J.: Learning to discover cross-domain relations with generative adversarial networks. In: ICML (2017)
19. Kingma, D.P., Rezende, D., Mohamed, S.J., Welling, M.: Semi-supervised learning with deep generative models. In: NIPS (2014)
20. Lai, W.S., Huang, J.B., Ahuja, N., Yang, M.H.: Deep laplacian pyramid networks for fast and accurate superresolution. In: CVPR (2017)

21. Larsson, G., Maire, M., Shakhnarovich, G.: Learning representations for automatic colorization. In: Leibe, B., Matas, J., Sebe, N., Welling, M. (eds.) ECCV 2016. LNCS, vol. 9908, pp. 577–593. Springer, Cham (2016). https://doi.org/10.1007/978-3-319-46493-0_35
22. LeCun, Y., Bottou, L., Bengio, Y., Haffner, P.: Gradient-based learning applied to document recognition. Proc. IEEE 86(11), 2278–2324 (1998)
23. Ledig, C., et al.: Photo-realistic single image super-resolution using a generative adversarial network. In: CVPR (2017)
24. Li, Y., Huang, J.-B., Ahuja, N., Yang, M.-H.: Deep joint image filtering. In: Leibe, B., Matas, J., Sebe, N., Welling, M. (eds.) ECCV 2016. LNCS, vol. 9908, pp. 154–169. Springer, Cham (2016). https://doi.org/10.1007/978-3-319-46493-0_10
25. Liu, M.Y., Breuel, T., Kautz, J.: Unsupervised image-to-image translation networks. In: NIPS (2017)
26. Liu, Z., Luo, P., Wang, X., Tang, X.: Deep learning face attributes in the wild. In: ICCV (2015)
27. Ma, L., Jia, X., Georgoulis, S., Tuytelaars, T., Van Gool, L.: Exemplar guided unsupervised image-to-image translation. arXiv preprint arXiv:1805.11145 (2018)
28. Makhzani, A., Shlens, J., Jaitly, N., Goodfellow, I., Frey, B.: Adversarial autoencoders. In: ICLR Workshop (2016)
29. Mathieu, M., Zhao, J., Sprechmann, P., Ramesh, A., LeCun, Y.: Disentangling factors of variation in deep representation using adversarial training. In: NIPS (2016)
30. Murez, Z., Kolouri, S., Kriegman, D., Ramamoorthi, R., Kim, K.: Image to image translation for domain adaptation. In: CVPR (2018)
31. Radford, A., Metz, L., Chintala, S.: Unsupervised representation learning with deep convolutional generative adversarial networks. In: ICLR (2016)
32. Reed, S., Akata, Z., Yan, X., Logeswaran, L., Schiele, B., Lee, H.: Generative adversarial text to image synthesis. In: ICML (2016)
33. Shrivastava, A., Pfister, T., Tuzel, O., Susskind, J., Wang, W., Webb, R.: Learning from simulated and unsupervised images through adversarial training. In: CVPR (2017)
34. Sun, B., Feng, J., Saenko, K.: Return of frustratingly easy domain adaptation. In: AAAI (2016)
35. Taigman, Y., Polyak, A., Wolf, L.: Unsupervised cross-domain image generation. In: ICLR (2017)
36. Tsai, Y.H., Hung, W.C., Schulter, S., Sohn, K., Yang, M.H., Chandraker, M.: Learning to adapt structured output space for semantic segmentation. In: CVPR (2018)
37. Tzeng, E., Hoffman, J., Zhang, N., Saenko, K., Darrell, T.: Deep domain confusion: maximizing for domain invariance. arXiv preprint arXiv:1412.3474 (2014)
38. Vondrick, C., Pirsiavash, H., Torralba, A.: Generating videos with scene dynamics. In: NIPS (2016)
39. Wang, T.C., Liu, M.Y., Zhu, J.Y., Tao, A., Kautz, J., Catanzaro, B.: High-resolution image synthesis and semantic manipulation with conditional GANs. In: CVPR (2018)
40. Wohlhart, P., Lepetit, V.: Learning descriptors for object recognition and 3D pose estimation. In: CVPR (2015)
41. Yi, Z., Zhang, H.R., Tan, P., Gong, M.: DualGAN: unsupervised dual learning for image-to-image translation. In: ICCV (2017)

42. Yu, A., Grauman, K.: Fine-grained visual comparisons with local learning. In: CVPR (2014)
43. Zhang, R., Isola, P., Efros, A.A.: Colorful image colorization. In: Leibe, B., Matas, J., Sebe, N., Welling, M. (eds.) ECCV 2016. LNCS, vol. 9907, pp. 649–666. Springer, Cham (2016). https://doi.org/10.1007/978-3-319-46487-9_40
44. Zhang, R., Isola, P., Efros, A.A., Shechtman, E., Wang, O.: The unreasonable effectiveness of deep networks as a perceptual metric. In: CVPR (2018)
45. Zhu, J.Y., Park, T., Isola, P., Efros, A.A.: Unpaired image-to-image translation using cycle-consistent adversarial networks. In: ICCV (2017)
46. Zhu, J.Y., et al.: Toward multimodal image-to-image translation. In: NIPS (2017)

Lifting Layers: Analysis and Applications

Peter Ochs[1], Tim Meinhardt[2], Laura Leal-Taixe[2], and Michael Moeller[3]([✉])

[1] Saarland University, Saarbrücken, Germany
ochs@math.uni-sb.de
[2] Technical University of Munich, Munich, Germany
{tim.meinhardt,leal.taixe}@tum.de
[3] University of Siegen, Siegen, Germany
michael.moeller@uni-siegen.de

Abstract. The great advances of learning-based approaches in image processing and computer vision are largely based on deeply nested networks that compose linear transfer functions with suitable non-linearities. Interestingly, the most frequently used non-linearities in imaging applications (variants of the rectified linear unit) are uncommon in low dimensional approximation problems. In this paper we propose a novel non-linear transfer function, called *lifting*, which is motivated from a related technique in convex optimization. A *lifting layer* increases the dimensionality of the input, naturally yields a linear spline when combined with a fully connected layer, and therefore closes the gap between low and high dimensional approximation problems. Moreover, applying the lifting operation to the loss layer of the network allows us to handle non-convex and flat (zero-gradient) cost functions. We analyze the proposed lifting theoretically, exemplify interesting properties in synthetic experiments and demonstrate its effectiveness in deep learning approaches to image classification and denoising.

Keywords: Machine learning · Deep learning · Interpolation
Approximation theory · Convex relaxation · Lifting

1 Introduction

Deep Learning has seen a tremendous success within the last 10 years improving the state-of-the-art in almost all computer vision and image processing tasks significantly. While one of the main explanations for this success is the replacement of handcrafted methods and features with data-driven approaches, the architectures of successful networks remain handcrafted and difficult to interpret.

The use of some common building blocks, such as convolutions, in imaging tasks is intuitive as they establish translational invariance. The composition of

---

Electronic supplementary material The online version of this chapter (https://doi.org/10.1007/978-3-030-01246-5_4) contains supplementary material, which is available to authorized users.

© Springer Nature Switzerland AG 2018
V. Ferrari et al. (Eds.): ECCV 2018, LNCS 11205, pp. 53–68, 2018.
https://doi.org/10.1007/978-3-030-01246-5_4

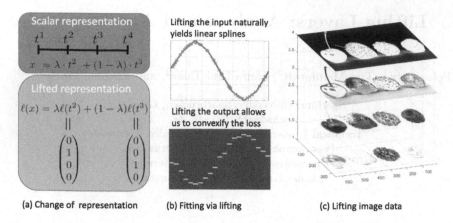

(a) Change of representation   **(b)** Fitting via lifting   **(c)** Lifting image data

Fig. 1. The proposed lifting identifies predefined labels $t^i \in \mathbb{R}$ with the unit vectors e_i in $\mathbb{R}^L$, $L \geq 2$. As illustrated in (a), a number x that is represented as a convex combination of t^i and t^{i+1} has a natural representation in a higher dimensional *lifted* space, see (3). When a lifting layer is combined with a fully connected layer it corresponds to a linear spline, and when both the input as well as the desired output are *lifted* it allows non-convex cost functions to be represented as a convex minimization problem (b). Finally, as illustrated in (c), coordinate-wise lifting yields an interesting representation of images, which allows textures of different intensities to be filtered differently.

linear transfer functions with non-linearities is a natural way to achieve a simple but expressive representation, but the choice of non-linearity is less intuitive: Starting from biologically motivated step functions or their smooth approximations by sigmoids, researchers have turned to rectified linear units (ReLUs),

$$\sigma(x) = \max(x, 0) \tag{1}$$

to avoid the optimization-based problem of a vanishing gradient. The derivative of a ReLU is $\sigma'(x) = 1$ for all $x > 0$. Nonetheless, the derivative remains zero for $x < 0$, which does not seem to make it a natural choice for an activation function, and often leads to "dead" ReLUs. This problem has been partially addressed with ReLU variants, such as leaky ReLUs [1], parameterized ReLUs [2], or maxout units [3]. These remain amongst the most popular choice of non-linearities as they allow for fast network training in practice.

In this paper we propose a novel type of non-linear layer, which we call *lifting layer* ℓ. In contrast to ReLUs (1), it does not discard large parts of the input data, but rather *lifts* it to different channels that allow the input x to be processed independently on different intervals. As we discuss in more detail in Sect. 3.4, the simplest form of the proposed lifting non-linearity is the mapping

$$\sigma(x) = \begin{pmatrix} \max(x, 0) \\ \min(x, 0) \end{pmatrix}, \tag{2}$$

which essentially consists of two complementary ReLUs and therefore neither discards half of the incoming inputs nor has intervals of zero gradients.

More generally, the proposed non-linearity depends on *labels* $t^1 < \ldots < t^L \in \mathbb{R}$ (typically linearly spaced) and is defined as a function $\ell \colon [t^1, t^L] \to \mathbb{R}^L$ that maps a scalar input $x \in \mathbb{R}$ to a vector $\ell(x) \in \mathbb{R}^L$ via

$$\ell(x) = \Big(0, \ldots, 0, \underbrace{\frac{t^{l+1} - x}{t^{l+1} - t^l}}_{l\text{-th coordinate}}, \frac{x - t^l}{t^{l+1} - t^l}, 0, \ldots, 0\Big)^T \quad \text{for } x \in [t^l, t^{l+1}]. \quad (3)$$

The motivation of the proposed lifting non-linearity is illustrated in Fig. 1. In particular, we highlight the following *contributions*:

1. The concept of representing a low dimensional variable in a higher dimensional space is a well-known optimization technique called *functional lifting*, see [4]. Non-convex problems are reformulated as the minimization of a convex energy in the higher dimensional 'lifted' space. While the **introduction of lifting layers** does not directly correspond to the optimization technique, some of the advantageous properties carry over as we detail in Sect. 3.
2. ReLUs are commonly used in deep learning for imaging applications, however their low dimensional relatives of interpolation or regression problems are typically tackled differently, e.g. by fitting (piecewise) polynomials. We show that a lifting layer followed by a fully connected layer **yields a linear spline**, which **closes the gap between low and high dimensional interpolation problems**. In particular, the aforementioned architecture can **approximate any continuous function** $f \colon \mathbb{R} \to \mathbb{R}$ to arbitrary precision and can still be trained **by solving a *convex* optimization problem** whenever the loss function is convex, a favorable property that is, for example, not shared even by the simplest ReLU-based architecture.
3. By additionally lifting the desired output of the network, one can **represent non-convex cost functions in a convex fashion**. Besides handling the non-convexity, such an approach allows for the minimization of cost functions with large areas of zero gradients such as truncated linear costs.
4. We demonstrate that the proposed lifting **improves the test accuracy in comparison to similar ReLU-based architectures in several experiments** on image classification and produces state-of-the-art image denoising results, making it an attractive universal tool in the design of neural networks.

2   Related Work

Lifting in Convex Optimization. One motivation for the proposed non-linearity comes from a technique called *functional lifting* which allows particular types of non-convex optimization problems to be reformulated as convex problems in a higher dimensional space, see [4] for details. The recent advances in functional lifting [5] have shown that (3) is a particularly well-suited discretization of the continuous model from [4]. Although, the techniques differ significantly, we hope for the general idea of an easier optimization in higher dimensions to carry over. Indeed, for simple instances of neural network architecture, we prove several favorable properties for our lifting layer that are related to properties of functional lifting. Details are provided in Sects. 3 and 4.

Non-linearities in Neural Networks. While many non-linear transfer functions have been studied in the literature (see [6, Sect. 6.3] for an overview), the ReLU in (1) remains the most popular choice. Unfortunately, it has the drawback that its gradient is zero for all $x < 0$, thus preventing gradient based optimization techniques to advance if the activation is zero (dead ReLU problem). Several variants of the ReLU avoid this problem by either utilizing smoother activations such as softplus [7] or exponential linear units [8], or by considering

$$\sigma(x; \alpha) = \max(x, 0) + \alpha \min(x, 0), \tag{4}$$

e.g. the absolute value rectification $\alpha = -1$ [9], leaky ReLUs with a small $\alpha > 0$ [1], randomized leaky ReLUs with randomly choosen α [10], parametric ReLUs in which α is a learnable parameter [2]. Self-normalizing neural networks [11] use scaled exponential LUs (SELUs) which have further normalizing properties and therefore replace the use of batch normalization techniques [12]. While the activation (4) seems closely related to the simplest case (2) of our lifting, the latter allows to process $\max(x, 0)$ and $\min(x, 0)$ separately, avoiding the problem of predefining α in (4) and leading to more freedom in the resulting function.

Another related non-linear transfer function are maxout units [3], which (in the 1-D case we are currently considering) are defined as

$$\sigma(x) = \max_j(\theta_j x + b_j). \tag{5}$$

They can represent any piecewise linear *convex* function. However, as we show in Proposition 1, a combination of the proposed lifting layer with a fully connected layer drops the restriction to *convex* activation functions, and allows us to learn *any* piecewise linear function.

Universal Approximation Theorem. As an extension of the universal approximation theorem in [13], it has been shown in [14] that the set of feedforward networks with one hidden layer, i.e., all functions $\mathcal{N}$ of the form

$$\mathcal{N}(x) = \sum_{j=1}^{N} \theta_j^1 \sigma(\langle \theta_j^2, x \rangle + b_j) \tag{6}$$

for some integer N, and weights $\theta_j^1 \in \mathbb{R}$, $\theta_j^2 \in \mathbb{R}^n$, $b_j \in \mathbb{R}$ are dense in the set of continuous functions $f \colon [0, 1]^n \to \mathbb{R}$ if and only if σ is not a polynomial. While this result demonstrates the expressive power of all common activation functions, the approximation of some given function f with a network $\mathcal{N}$ of the form (6) requires optimization for the parameters θ^1 and (θ^2, b) which inevitably leads to a non-convex problem. We prove the same expressive power of a lifting based architecture (see Corollary 1), while, remarkably, our corresponding learning problem is a convex optimization problem. Moreover, beyond the qualitative density result for (6), we may quantify the approximation quality depending on a simple measure for the "complexity" of the continuous function to be approximated (see Corollary 1 and the supplementary material).

3   Lifting Layers

In this section, we introduce the proposed lifting layers (Sect. 3.1) and study their favorable properties in a simple 1-D setting (Sect. 3.2). The restriction to 1-D functions is mainly for illustrative purposes and simplicity. All results can be transferred to higher dimensions via a vector valued lifting (Sect. 3.3). The analysis provided in this section does not directly apply to deep networks, however it provides an intuition for this setting. Section 3.4 discusses some practical aspects and reveals a connection to ReLUs. All proofs are provided in the supplementary material.

3.1   Definition

The following definition formalizes the lifting layer from the introduction.

Definition 1 (Lifting).   *We define the lifting of a variable $x \in [\underline{t}, \overline{t}]$, $\underline{t}, \overline{t} \in \mathbb{R}$, with respect to the Euclidean basis $\mathcal{E} := \{e^1, \dots, e^L\}$ of $\mathbb{R}^L$ and a knot sequence $\underline{t} = t^1 < t^2 < \dots < t^L = \overline{t}$, for some $L \in \mathbb{N}$, as a mapping $\ell \colon [\underline{t}, \overline{t}] \to \mathbb{R}^L$ given by*

$$\ell(x) = (1 - \lambda_l(x))e^l + \lambda_l(x)e^{l+1} \quad \text{with } l \text{ such that } x \in [t^l, t^{l+1}], \tag{7}$$

where $\lambda_l(x) := \frac{x - t^l}{t^{l+1} - t^l} \in \mathbb{R}$. The (left-)inverse mapping $\ell^\dagger \colon \mathbb{R}^L \to \mathbb{R}$ of ℓ, which satisfies $\ell^\dagger(\ell(x)) = x$, is defined by

$$\ell^\dagger(z) = \sum_{l=1}^{L} z_l t^l. \tag{8}$$

Note that while liftings could be defined with respect to an arbitrary basis $\mathcal{E}$ of $\mathbb{R}^L$ (with a slight modification of the inverse mapping), we decided to limit ourselves to the Euclidean basis for the sake of simplicity. Furthermore, we limit ourselves to inputs x that lie in the predefined interval $[\underline{t}, \overline{t}]$. Although, the idea extends to the entire real line by linear extrapolation, i.e., by allowing $\lambda_1(x) > 1$, $\lambda_2(x) < 0$, respectively, $\lambda_L(x) > 1$, $\lambda_{L-1}(x) < 0$, it requires more technical details. For the sake of a clean presentation, we omit these details.

3.2   Analysis in 1D

Although, here we are concerned with 1-D functions, these properties and examples provide some intuition for the implementation of the lifting layer into a deep architecture. Moreover, analogue results can be stated for the lifting of higher dimensional spaces.

Proposition 1 (Prediction of a Linear Spline).   *The composition of a fully connected layer $z \mapsto \langle \theta, z \rangle$ with $\theta \in \mathbb{R}^L$, and a lifting layer, i.e.,*

$$\mathcal{N}_\theta(x) := \langle \theta, \ell(x) \rangle, \tag{9}$$

yields a linear spline (continuous piecewise linear function). Conversely, any linear spline can be expressed in the form of (9).

Although the architecture in (9) does not fall into the class of functions covered by the universal approximation theorem, well-known results of linear spline interpolation still guarantee the same results.

Corollary 1 (Prediction of Continuous Functions). *Any continuous function $f \colon [\underline{t}, \overline{t}] \to \mathbb{R}$ can be represented arbitrarily accurate with a network architecture $\mathcal{N}_\theta(x) := \langle \theta, \ell(x) \rangle$ for sufficiently large L, and $\theta \in \mathbb{R}^L$.*

Furthermore, as linear splines can of course fit any (spatially distinct) data points exactly, our simple network architecture has the same property for a particular choice of labels t^i. On the other hand, this result suggests that using a small number of labels acts as regularization of the type of linear interpolation.

Corollary 2 (Overfitting). *Let (x_i, y_i) be training data, $i = 1, \ldots, N$ with $x_i \neq x_j$ for $i \neq j$. If $L = N$ and $t^i = x_i$, there exists θ such that $\mathcal{N}_\theta(x) := \langle \theta, \ell(x) \rangle$ is exact at all data points $x = x_i$, i.e. $\mathcal{N}_\theta(x_i) = y_i$ for all $i = 1, \ldots, N$.*

Note that Proposition 1 highlights two crucial differences of the proposed nonlinearity to the maxout function in (5): (i) maxout functions can only represent convex piecewise linear functions, while liftings can represent arbitrary piecewise linear functions; (ii) The maxout function is non-linear w.r.t. its parameters (θ_j, b_j), while the simple architecture in (9) (with lifting) is linear w.r.t. its parameters (θ, b). The advantage of a lifting layer compared to a ReLU, which is less expressive and also non-linear w.r.t. its parameters, is even more significant.

Remarkably, the optimal approximation of a continuous function by a linear spline (for any choice of t^i), yields a convex minimization problem.

Proposition 2 (Convexity of a simple Regression Problem). *Let training data $(x_i, y_i) \in [\underline{t}, \overline{t}] \times \mathbb{R}$, $i = 1, \ldots, N$, be given. Then, the solution of the problem*

$$\min_\theta \sum_{i=1}^N \mathcal{L}(\langle \theta, \ell(x_i) \rangle ; y_i) \tag{10}$$

yields the best linear spline fit of the training data with respect to the loss function $\mathcal{L}$. In particular, if $\mathcal{L}$ is convex, then (10) is a convex optimization problem.

As the following example shows, this is not true for ReLUs and maxout functions.

Example 1. The convex loss $\mathcal{L}(z; 1) = (z-1)^2$ composed with a ReLU applied to a linear transfer function, i.e., $\theta \mapsto \max(\theta x_i, 0)$ with $\theta \in \mathbb{R}$, leads to a non-convex objective function, e.g. for $x_i = 1$, $\theta \mapsto (\max(\theta, 0) - 1)^2$ is non-convex.

Therefore, in the light of Proposition 2, the proposed lifting closes the gap between low dimensional approximation and regression problems (where linear splines are extremely common), and high dimensional approximation/learning problems, where ReLUs have been used instead of linear spline type of functions. In this one-dimensional setting, the proposed approach in fact represents a kernel method with a particular feature map ℓ from (1) that gives rise to linear splines. It is interesting to see that approximations by linear splines recently arose as an optimal architecture choice for second-order total variation minimization in [15].

3.3 Vector-Valued Lifting Layers

A vector-valued construction of the lifting similar to [16] allows us to naturally extend all our previous results for functions $f: [\underline{t}, \overline{t}] \to \mathbb{R}$ to functions $f: \Omega \subset \mathbb{R}^d \to \mathbb{R}$. Definition 1 is generalized to d dimensions by triangulating the compact domain Ω, and identifying each vertex of the resulting mesh with a unit vector in a space $\mathbb{R}^N$, where N is the total number of vertices. The lifted vector contains the barycentric coordinates of a point $x \in \mathbb{R}^d$ with respect its surrounding vertices. The resulting lifting remains a continuous piecewise linear function when combined with a fully connected layer (cf. Proposition 1), and yields a convex problem when looking for the best piecewise linear fit on a given triangular mesh (cf. Proposition 2).

Unfortunately, discretizing a domain $\Omega \subset \mathbb{R}^d$ with L labels per dimension leads to $N = L^d$ vertices, which makes a vector-valued lifting prohibitively expensive for large d. Therefore, in high dimensional applications, we turn to narrower and deeper network architectures, in which the scalar-valued lifting is applied to each component separately. The latter sacrifices the convexity of the overall problem for the sake of a high expressiveness with comparably few parameters. Intuitively, the increasing expressiveness is explained by an exponentially growing number of kinks for the composition of layers that represent linear splines. A similar reasoning can be found in [17].

3.4 Scaled Lifting

We are free to scale the lifted representation defined in (7), when the inversion formula in (8) compensates for this scaling. For practical purposes, we found it to be advantageous to also introduce a **scaled lifting** by replacing (7) in Definition 1 by

$$\ell_s(x) = (1 - \lambda_l(x))t^l e^l + \lambda_l(x)t^{l+1}e^{l+1} \quad \text{with } l \text{ such that } x \in [t^l, t^{l+1}], \quad (11)$$

where $\lambda_l(x) := \frac{x - t^l}{t^{l+1} - t^l} \in \mathbb{R}$. The inversion formula reduces to the sum over all components of the vector in this case. We believe that such a scaled lifting is often advantageous: (i) The magnitude/meaning of the components of the lifted vector is preserved and does not have to be learned; (ii) For an uneven number of equally distributed labels in $[-\overline{t}, \overline{t}]$, one of the labels t^l will be zero, which allows us to omit it and represent a scaled lifting into $\mathbb{R}^L$ with $L - 1$ many entries. For $L = 3$ for example, we find that $t^1 = -\overline{t}$, $t^2 = 0$, and $t^3 = \overline{t}$ such that

$$\ell_s(x) = \begin{cases} \left(1 - \dfrac{x + \overline{t}}{0 + \overline{t}}\right)(-\overline{t})e^1 = xe^1 & \text{if } x \leq 0, \\[3mm] \dfrac{x - 0}{\overline{t} - 0}\, \overline{t}\, e^3 = xe^3 & \text{if } x > 0. \end{cases} \quad (12)$$

As the second component remains zero, we can introduce an equivalent more memory efficient variant of the scaled lifting which we already stated in (2).

4 Lifting the Output

So far, we considered liftings as a non-linear layer in a neural network. However, motivated by lifting-based optimization techniques, which seek a tight convex approximation to problems involving non-convex loss functions, this section presents a convexification of non-convex loss functions by lifting in the context of neural networks. This goal is achieved by approximating the loss by a linear spline and predicting the output of the network in a lifted representation. The advantages of this approach are demonstrated at the end of this section in Example 2 for a robust regression problem with a vast number of outliers.

Consider a loss function $\mathcal{L}_y \colon \mathbb{R} \to \mathbb{R}$ defined for a given output y (the total loss for samples (x_i, y_i), $i = 1, \ldots, N$, may be given by $\sum_{i=1}^{N} \mathcal{L}_{y_i}(x_i)$). We achieve the tight convex approximation by a lifting function $\ell_y \colon [\underline{t}_y, \overline{t}_y] \to \mathbb{R}^{L_y}$ for the range of the loss function $\mathrm{im}(\mathcal{L}_y) \subset \mathbb{R}$ with respect to the standard basis $\mathcal{E}_y = \{e_y^1, \ldots, e_y^{L_y}\}$ and a knots $\underline{t}_y = t_y^1 < \ldots < t_y^{L_y} < \overline{t}_y$ following Definition 1.

The goal of the convex approximation is to predict the lifted representation of the loss, i.e. a vector $z \in \mathbb{R}^{L_y}$. However, in order to assign the correct loss to the lifted variable, it needs to lie in $\mathrm{im}(\ell_y)$. In this case, the following lemma proves a one-to-one representation of the loss between $[\underline{t}_y, \overline{t}_y]$ and $\mathrm{im}(\ell_y)$.

Lemma 1 (Characterization of the range of ℓ). *The range of the lifting $\ell \colon [\underline{t}, \overline{t}] \to \mathbb{R}^L$ is given by*

$$\mathrm{im}(\ell) = \left\{ z \in [0,1]^L \; : \; \exists! l \colon z_l + z_{l+1} = 1 \text{ and } \forall k \notin \{l, l+1\} \colon z_k = 0 \right\} \tag{13}$$

and the mapping ℓ is a bijection between $[\underline{t}, \overline{t}]$ and $\mathrm{im}(\ell)$ with inverse $\ell^\dagger$.

Since the range of ℓ_y is not convex, we relax it to a convex set, actually to the smallest convex set that contains $\mathrm{im}(\ell_y)$, the convex hull of $\mathrm{im}(\ell_y)$.

Lemma 2 (Convex Hull of the range of ℓ). *The convex hull $\mathrm{conv}(\mathrm{im}(\ell))$ of $\mathrm{im}(\ell)$ is the unit simplex in $\mathbb{R}^L$.*

Putting the results together, using Proposition 1, we obtain a tight convex approximation of the (possibly non-convex) loss $\mathcal{L}_y(x)$ by $\langle l_y, z \rangle$ with $z \in \mathrm{im}(\ell_y)$, for some $l_y \in \mathbb{R}^{L_y}$. Instead of evaluating the network $\mathcal{N}_\theta(x)$ by $\mathcal{L}_y(\mathcal{N}_\theta(x))$, we consider a network $\widetilde{\mathcal{N}}_\theta(x)$ that predicts a point in $\mathrm{conv}(\mathrm{im}(\ell_y)) \subset \mathbb{R}^{L_y}$ and evaluate the loss $\langle l_y, \widetilde{\mathcal{N}}_\theta(x) \rangle$. As it is hard to incorporate range-constraints into the network's prediction, we compose the network with a lifting layer ℓ_x, i.e. we consider $\langle l_y, \tilde{\theta} \ell_x(\widetilde{\mathcal{N}}_\theta(x)) \rangle$ with $\tilde{\theta} \in \mathbb{R}^{L_y \times L_x}$, for which simpler constraints may be derived. The following proposition states the convexity of the relaxed problem.

Proposition 3 (Convex Approximation of a simple non-convex regression problem). *Let $(x_i, y_i) \in [\underline{t}, \overline{t}] \times [\underline{t}_y, \overline{t}_y]$ be training data, $i = 1, \ldots, N$. Moreover, let ℓ_y be a lifting of the common image $[\underline{t}_y, \overline{t}_y]$ of the loss $\mathcal{L}_{y_i}$, $i = 1, \ldots, N$,*

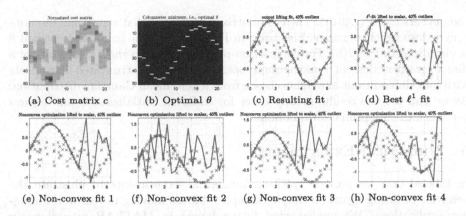

(a) Cost matrix c   (b) Optimal θ   (c) Resulting fit   (d) Best ℓ^1 fit

(e) Non-convex fit 1   (f) Non-convex fit 2   (g) Non-convex fit 3   (h) Non-convex fit 4

Fig. 2. Visualization of Example 2 for a regression problem with 40% outliers. Our lifting of a (non-convex) truncated linear loss to a convex optimization problem robustly fits the function nearly optimally (see (c)), whereas the most robust convex formulation (without lifting) is severely perturbed by the outliers (see (d)). Trying to optimize the non-convex cost function directly yields different results based on the initialization of the weights and is prone to getting stuck in suboptimal local minima, see (e)–(h).

and ℓ_x is the lifting of $[\underline{t}, \overline{t}]$. Let $l_{y_i} \in \mathbb{R}^{L_y}$ be such that $t_y \mapsto \langle l_{y_i}, \ell_y(t_y) \rangle$ is a piecewise linear spline approximation of $t_y \mapsto \mathcal{L}_{y_i}(t_y)$, for $t_y \in [\underline{t}_y, \overline{t}_y]$. Then

$$\min_{\theta} \sum_{i=1}^{N} \langle l_{y_i}, \theta \ell_x(x_i) \rangle \quad s.t. \ \theta_{p,q} \geq 0, \ \sum_{p=1}^{L_y} \theta_{p,q} = 1, \ \begin{cases} \forall p = 1, \ldots, L_y, \\ \forall q = 1, \ldots, L_x. \end{cases} \tag{14}$$

is a convex approximation of the (non-convex) loss function, and the constraints guarantee that $\theta \ell_x(x_i) \in \mathrm{conv}(\mathrm{im}(\ell_y))$.

The objective in (14) is linear (w.r.t. θ) and can be written as

$$\sum_{i=1}^{N} \langle l_{y_i}, \theta \ell_x(x_i) \rangle = \sum_{i=1}^{N} \sum_{p=1}^{L_y} \sum_{q=1}^{L_x} \theta_{p,q} \ell_x(x_i)_q (l_{y_i})_p =: \sum_{p=1}^{L_y} \sum_{q=1}^{L_x} c_{p,q} \theta_{p,q} \tag{15}$$

where $c := \sum_{i=1}^{N} l_{y_i} \ell_x(x_i)^{\top}$.

Moreover, the closed-form solution of (14) is given for all $q = 1, \ldots, L_x$ by $\theta_{p,q} = 1$, if the index p minimizes $c_{p,q}$, and $\theta_{p,q} = 0$ otherwise.

Example 2 (Robust fitting). For illustrative purposes of the advantages of this section, we consider a regression problem with 40% outliers as visualized in Fig. 2(c) and (d). Statistics motivates us to use a robust non-convex loss function. Our lifting allows us to use a robust (non-convex) truncated linear loss in a convex optimization problem (Proposition 3), which can easily ignore the outliers and achieve a nearly optimal fit (see Fig. 2(c)), whereas the most robust convex loss (without lifting), the ℓ_1-loss, yields a solution that is severely perturbed by the outliers (see Fig. 2(d)). The cost matrix c from (15) that represents the non-convex loss (of this example) is shown in Fig. 2(a) and the computed optimal θ is visualized in Fig. 2(b). For comparison purposes we also show the results of a direct (gradient descent + momentum) optimization of the truncated linear costs with four different initial weights chosen from a zero mean Gaussian distribution. As we can see the results greatly differ for different initializations and always got stuck in suboptimal local minima.

5   Numerical Experiments

In this section we provide synthetic numerical experiments to illustrate the behavior of lifting layers on simple examples, before moving to real-world imaging applications. We implemented lifting layers in MATLAB as well as in PyTorch with https://github.com/michimoeller/liftingLayers containing all code for reproducing the experiments in this paper. A description of the presented network architectures is provided in the supplementary material.

5.1   Synthetic Examples

The following results were obtained using a stochastic gradient descent (SGD) algorithm with a momentum of 0.9, using minibatches of size 128, and a learning rate of 0.1. Furthermore, we use weight decay with a parameter of 10^{-4}. A squared ℓ^2-loss (without lifting the output) was used.

1-D Fitting. To illustrate our results of Proposition 2, we first consider the example of fitting values $y_i = \sin(x_i)$ from input data x_i sampled uniformly in $[0, 2\pi]$. We compare the lifting-based architecture $\mathcal{N}_\theta(x) = \langle \theta, \ell_9(x) \rangle$ (Lift-Net) including an unscaled lifting ℓ_9 to $\mathbb{R}^9$ with the standard design architecture $\mathrm{fc}_1(\sigma(\mathrm{fc}_9(x)))$ (Std-Net), where $\sigma(x) = \max(x, 0)$ applies coordinate-wise and fc_n denotes a fully connected layer with n output neurons. Figure 3 shows the resulting functions after 25, 75, 200, and 2000 epochs of training.

2-D Fitting. While the above results were expected based on the favorable theoretical properties, we now consider a more difficult test case of fitting

$$f(x_1, x_2) = \cos(x_2 \sin(x_1)) \tag{16}$$

on $[0, 2\pi]^2$. Note that although a 2-D input still allows for a vector-valued lifting, our goal is to illustrate that even a coordinate-wise lifting has favorable properties (beyond being able to approximate any separable function with a single layer which is a simple extension of Corollary 1). Hence, we compare two networks

$$f_{\text{Lift-Net}}(x_1, x_2) = \mathrm{fc}_1(\sigma(\mathrm{fc}_{20}([\ell_{20}(x_1), \ell_{20}(x_2)]))), \tag{Lift-Net}$$

$$f_{\text{Std-Net}}(x_1, x_2) = \mathrm{fc}_1(\sigma(\mathrm{fc}_{20}(\mathrm{fc}_{40}([x_1, x_2])))), \tag{Std-Net}$$

where the notation $[u, v]$ in the above formula denotes the concatenation of the two vectors u and v, and the subscript of the lifting ℓ denotes the dimension L we

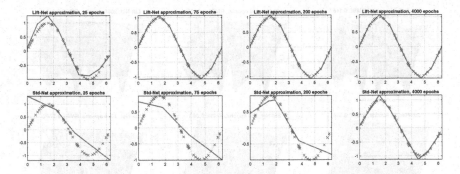

Fig. 3. Illustrating the results of approximating a sine function on $[0, 2\pi]$ with 50 training examples after different number of epochs. While the proposed architecture with lifting yields a convex problem for which SGD converges quickly (upper row), the standard architecture based on ReLUs yields a non-convex problem which leads to slower convergence and a suboptimal local minimum after 4000 epochs (lower row).

lift to. The corresponding training problems are non-convex. As we see in Fig. 4 the general behavior is similar to the 1-D case: Increasing the dimensionality via lifting the input data yields faster convergence and a more precise approximation than increasing the dimensionality with a parameterized filtering. For the sake of completeness, we have included a vector valued lifting with an illustration of the underlying 2-D triangulation in the bottom row of Fig. 4.

5.2   Image Classification

As a real-world imaging example we consider the problem of image classification. To illustrate the behavior of our lifting layer, we use the "Deep MNIST for expert model" (*ME-model*) by TensorFlow[1] as a simple convolutional neural network (CNN) architecture which applies a standard ReLU activation. To improve its accuracy, we use an additional batch-normalization (BN) layer and denote the corresponding model by *ME-model+BN*.

Our corresponding lifting model (*Proposed*) is created by replacing all ReLUs with a scaled lifting layer (as introduced in Sect. 3.4) with $L = 3$. In order to allow for a meaningful combination with the max pooling layers, we scaled with the absolute value $|t^i|$ of the labels. We found the comparably small lifting of $L = 3$ to yield the best results, and provided a more detailed study for varying L in the supplementary material. Since our model has almost twice as many free parameters as the two *ME* models, we include a forth model *Large ME-model+BN* larger than our lifting model with twice as many convolution filters and fully-connected neurons.

Figure 5 shows the results each of these models obtains on the CIFAR-10 and CIFAR-100 image classification problems. As we can see, the favorable behavior of the synthetic experiments carried over to the exemplary architectures in

---

[1] https://www.tensorflow.org/tutorials/layers.

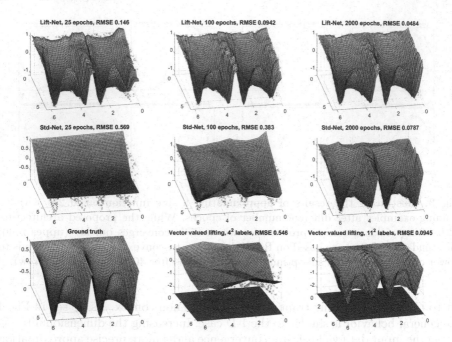

Fig. 4. Illustrating the results of approximating the function in (16) with the standard network in (Std-Net) (middle row) and the architecture in (Lift-Net) based on lifting the input data (upper row). The red markers illustrate the training data, the surface represents the overall network function, and the RMSE measures its difference to the true underlying function (16), which is shown in the bottom row on the left. Similar to the results of Fig. 3, our lifting based architecture converges more quickly and yields a better approximation of the true underlying function (lower left) after 2000 epochs. The middle and right approximations in the bottom row illustrate a vector valued lifting (see Sect. 3.3) into 4^2 (middle) and 11^2 (right) dimensions. The latter can be trained by solving a linear system. We illustrate the triangular mesh used for the lifting below the graph of the function to illustrate that the approximation is indeed piecewise linear (as stated in Proposition 1).

image classification: Our proposed lifting architecture has the smallest test error and loss in both experiments. Both common strategies, i.e. including batch normalization and increasing the size of the model, improved the results, but both ReLU-based architectures remain inferior to the lifting-based architecture.

5.3   Maxout Activation Units

To also compare the proposed lifting activation layer with the maxout activation, we conduct a simple MNIST image classification experiment with a fully connected one-hidden-layer architecture, applying either a ReLU, maxout or lifting as activations. For the maxout layer we apply a feature reduction by a factor of 2 which has the capabilities of representing a regular ReLU and a lifting layer

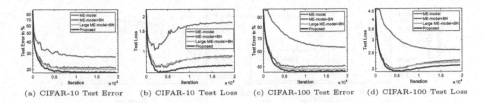

(a) CIFAR-10 Test Error   (b) CIFAR-10 Test Loss   (c) CIFAR-100 Test Error   (d) CIFAR-100 Test Loss

Fig. 5. Comparing different approaches for image classification on CIFAR-10 and CIFAR-100. The proposed architecture with lifting layers shows a superior performance in comparison to its ReLU-based relatives in both cases.

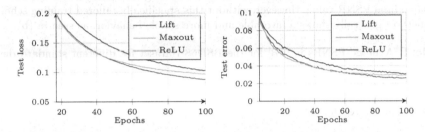

Fig. 6. MNIST image classification comparison of our lifting activation with the standard ReLU and its maxout generalization. The ReLU, maxout and lifting architectures (79510, 79010 and 76485 trainable parameters) achieved a best test error of 3.07%, 2.91% and 2.61%, respectively. The proposed approach behaves favorably in terms of the test loss from epoch 50 on, leading to a lower overall test error after 100 epochs.

as in (2). Due to the nature of the different activations - maxout applies a max pooling and lifting increases the number of input neurons in the subsequent layer - we adjusted the number of neurons in the hidden layer to make for an approximately equal and fair amount of trainable parameters.

The results in Fig. 6 are achieved after optimizing a cross-entropy loss for 100 training epochs by applying SGD with learning rate 0.01. Particularly, each architecture was trained with the identical experimental setup. While both the maxout and our lifting activation yield a similar convergence behavior better than the standard ReLU, our proposed method exceeds in terms of the final lowest test error.

5.4   Image Denoising

To also illustrate the effectiveness of lifting layers for networks mapping images to images, we consider the problem of Gaussian image denoising. We designed the *Lift-46* architecture with 16 blocks each of which consists of 46 convolution filters of size 3×3, batch normalization, and a lifting layer with $L = 3$ following the same experimental reasoning for deep architectures as in Sect. 5.2. As illustrated in Fig. 7(a), a final convolutional layer outputs an image we train to approximate the residual, i.e., noise-only, image. Due to its state-of-the-art performance in image denoising we adopted the same training pipeline as for the

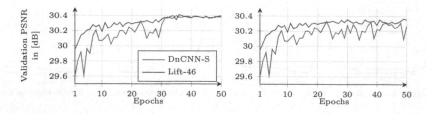

Fig. 7. To demonstrate the robustness of our lifting activation, we illustrate the validation PSNR for denoising Gaussian noise with $\sigma = 25$ for two different training schemes. In (a) both networks plateau - after a learning rate decay at 30 epochs - to the same final PSNR value. However, without this specifically tailored training scheme our method generally shows a favorable and more stable behavior, as seen in (b).

Table 1. Average PSNRs in [dB] for the BSD68 dataset for different standard deviations σ of the Gaussian noise on all of which our lifting layer based architecture is among the leading methods. Please note that (most likely due to variations in the random seeds) our reproduced DnCNN-S results are different - in the second decimal place - from the results reported in [18].

Reconstruction PSNR in [dB]

σ	Noisy	BM3D [19]	WNNM [20]	EPLL [21]	MLP [22]	CSF [23]	TNRD [24]	DnCNN-S [18]	Our
15	24.80	31.07	31.37	31.21	-	31.24	31.42	**31.72**	**31.72**
25	20.48	28.57	28.83	28.68	28.96	28.74	28.92	**29.21**	**29.21**
50	14.91	25.62	25.87	25.67	26.03	-	25.97	26.21	**26.23**

DnCNN-S architecture from [18] which resembles our Lift-46 network but implements a regular ReLU and 64 convolution filters. The two architectures contain an approximately equal amount of trainable parameters.

Table 1 compares our architecture with a variety of denoising methods most notably the DnCNN-S [18] and shows that we produce state-of-the-art performance for removing Gaussian noise of different standard deviations σ. In addition, the development of the test PSNR in Fig. 7(b) suggests a more stable and favorable behavior of our method compared to DnCNN-S.

6   Conclusions

We introduced lifting layers as a favorable alternative to ReLU-type activation functions in machine learning. Opposed to the classical ReLU, liftings have nonzero derivative almost everywhere, and can represent any continuous piecewise linear function. We demonstrated several advantageous properties of lifting, for example, we can handle non-convex and partly flat loss functions. Our numerical experiments in image classification and reconstruction showed that lifting layers are an attractive building block in various neural network architectures, and we improved the performance of corresponding ReLU-based architectures.

Acknowledgements. This research was partially funded by the Humboldt Foundation through the Sofja Kovalevskaja Award.

References

1. Maas, A., Hannun, A., Ng, A.: Rectifier nonlinearities improve neural network acoustic models. In: ICML (2013)
2. He, K., Zhang, X., Ren, S., Sun, J.: Delving deep into rectifiers: surpassing human-level performance on imagenet classification. In: ICCV (2015)
3. Goodfellow, I., Warde-Farley, D., Mirza, M., Courville, A., Bengio, Y.: Maxout networks. In: ICML (2013)
4. Pock, T., Cremers, D., Bischof, H., Chambolle, A.: Global solutions of variational models with convex regularization. SIAM J. Imaging Sci. 3(4), 1122–1145 (2010)
5. Möllenhoff, T., Laude, E., Moeller, M., Lellmann, J., Cremers, D.: Sublabel-accurate relaxation of nonconvex energies. In: CVPR (2016)
6. Goodfellow, I., Bengio, Y., Courville, A.: Deep Learning. The MIT Press (2016)
7. Dugas, C., Bengio, Y., Bélisle, F., Nadeau, C., Garcia, R.: Incorporating second-order functional knowledge for better option pricing. In: NIPS (2001)
8. Clevert, D.A., Unterthiner, T., Hochreiter, S.: Fast and accurate deep network learning by exponential linear units (ELUs). In: ICLR (2016)
9. Jarrett, K., Kavukcuoglu, K., Ranzato, M., LeCun, Y.: What is the best multi-stage architecture for object recognition? In: CVPR (2009)
10. Xu, B., Wang, N., Chen, T., Li, M.: Empirical evaluation of rectified activations in convolutional network (2015). ICML Deep Learning Workshop. https://arxiv.org/abs/1505.00853
11. Klambauer, G., Unterthiner, T., Mayr, A., Hochreiter, S.: Self-normalizing neural networks. In: NIPS (2017)
12. Ioffe, S., Szegedy, C.: Batch normalization: accelerating deep network training by reducing internal covariate shift. In: ICML (2015)
13. Cybenko, G.: Approximation by superpositions of a sigmoidal function. Math. Control Sig. Syst. 2(4), 303–314 (1989)
14. Leshno, M., Lin, V., Pinkus, A., Schocken, S.: Multilayer feedforward networks with a nonpolynomial activation function can approximate any function. Neural Netw. 6(6), 861–867 (1993)
15. Unser, M.: A representer theorem for deep neural networks (2018). Preprint at https://arxiv.org/abs/1802.09210
16. Laude, E., Möllenhoff, T., Moeller, M., Lellmann, J., Cremers, D.: Sublabel-accurate convex relaxation of vectorial multilabel energies. In: Leibe, B., Matas, J., Sebe, N., Welling, M. (eds.) ECCV 2016. LNCS, vol. 9905, pp. 614–627. Springer, Cham (2016). https://doi.org/10.1007/978-3-319-46448-0_37
17. Montúfar, G., Pascanu, R., Cho, K., Bengio, Y.: On the number of linear regions of deep neural networks. In: NIPS (2014)
18. Zhang, K., Zuo, W., Chen, Y., Meng, D., Zhang, L.: Beyond a gaussian denoiser: residual learning of deep CNN for image denoising. IEEE Trans. Image Process. 26(7), 3142–3155 (2017)
19. Dabov, K., Foi, A., Katkovnik, V., Egiazarian, K.: Image denoising by sparse 3-D transform-domain collaborative filtering. IEEE Trans. Image Process. 16(8), 2080–2095 (2007)
20. Gu, S., Zhang, L., Zuo, W., Feng, X.: Weighted nuclear norm minimization with application to image denoising. In: CVPR (2014)

21. Zoran, D., Weiss, Y.: From learning models of natural image patches to whole image restoration. In: ICCV (2011)
22. Burger, H., Schuler, C., Harmeling, S.: Image denoising: can plain neural networks compete with BM3D? In: CVPR (2012)
23. Schmidt, U., Roth, S.: Shrinkage fields for effective image restoration. In: CVPR (2014)
24. Chen, Y., Pock, T.: On learning optimized reaction diffusion processes for effective image restoration. In: ICCV (2015)

Learning with Biased Complementary Labels

Xiyu Yu[1](✉), Tongliang Liu[1], Mingming Gong[2,3], and Dacheng Tao[1]

[1] UBTECH Sydney AI Centre, SIT, FEIT,
The University of Sydney, Sydney, Australia
xiyu0300@uni.sydney.edu.ac, {tongliang.liu,dacheng.tao}@sydney.edu.au
[2] Department of Philosophy, Carnegie Mellon University, Pittsburgh, USA
[3] Department of Biomedical Informatics, University of Pittsburgh, Pittsburgh, USA
mig73@pitt.edu

Abstract. In this paper, we study the classification problem in which we have access to easily obtainable surrogate for true labels, namely complementary labels, which specify classes that observations do **not** belong to. Let Y and $\bar{Y}$ be the true and complementary labels, respectively. We first model the annotation of complementary labels via transition probabilities $P(\bar{Y} = i|Y = j), i \neq j \in \{1, \cdots, c\}$, where c is the number of classes. Previous methods implicitly assume that $P(\bar{Y} = i|Y = j), \forall i \neq j$, are identical, which is not true in practice because humans are biased toward their own experience. For example, as shown in Fig. 1, if an annotator is more familiar with monkeys than prairie dogs when providing complementary labels for meerkats, she is more likely to employ "monkey" as a complementary label. We therefore reason that the transition probabilities will be different. In this paper, we propose a framework that contributes three main innovations to learning with **biased** complementary labels: (1) It estimates transition probabilities with no bias. (2) It provides a general method to modify traditional loss functions and extends standard deep neural network classifiers to learn with biased complementary labels. (3) It theoretically ensures that the classifier learned with complementary labels converges to the optimal one learned with true labels. Comprehensive experiments on several benchmark datasets validate the superiority of our method to current state-of-the-art methods.

Keywords: Multi-class classification · Biased complementary labels Transition matrix · Modified loss function

1 Introduction

Large-scale training datasets translate supervised learning from theories and algorithms to practice, especially in deep supervised learning. One major assumption that guarantees this successful translation is that data are accurately

Electronic supplementary material The online version of this chapter (https://doi.org/10.1007/978-3-030-01246-5_5) contains supplementary material, which is available to authorized users.

© Springer Nature Switzerland AG 2018
V. Ferrari et al. (Eds.): ECCV 2018, LNCS 11205, pp. 69–85, 2018.
https://doi.org/10.1007/978-3-030-01246-5_5

labeled. However, collecting true labels for large-scale datasets is often expensive, time-consuming, and sometimes impossible. For this reason, some weak but cheap supervision information has been exploited to boost learning performance. Such supervision includes side information [33], privileged information [29], and weakly supervised information [15] based on semi-supervised data [6,9,37], positive and unlabeled data [23], or noisy labeled data [4,8,10,11,19,30]. In this paper, we study another weak supervision: the complementary label which specifies a class that an object does **not** belong to. Complementary labels are sometimes easily obtainable, especially when the class set is relatively large. Given an observation in multi-class classification, identifying a class label that is incorrect for the observation is often much easier than identifying the true label.

True Label   Meerkat   Prairie Dog   Monkey

Complementary
Label   Not "monkey"   Not "meerkat"   Not "prairie dog"

Fig. 1. A comparison between true labels (top) and complementary labels (bottom).

Complementary labels carry useful information and are widely used in our daily lives: for example, to identify a language we do not know, we may say "not English"; to categorize a new movie without any fighting, we may say "not action"; and to recognize an image of a previous American president, we may say "not Trump". Ishida et al. [13] then proposed learning from examples with only complementary labels by assuming that a complementary label is uniformly selected from the $c-1$ classes other than the true label class ($c > 2$). Specifically, they designed an unbiased estimator such that learning with complementary labels was asymptotically consistent with learning with true labels.

Sometimes, annotators provide complementary labels based on both the content of observations and their own experience, leading to the biases in complementary labels. Thus, complementary labels are mostly non-uniformly selected from the remaining

$c-1$ classes, some of which even have no chance of being selected for certain cases. Regarding the bias governed by the observation content, let us take labeling digits 0-9 as an example. Since digit 1 is much more dissimilar to digit 3 than digit 8, the complementary labels of "3" are more likely to be assigned with "1" rather than "8". Regarding the bias governed by annotators' experience, taking our example above, we can see that if one is more familiar with monkeys than other animals, she may be more likely to use "monkey" as a complementary label.

Motivated by the cause of biases, we here model the biased procedure of annotating complementary labels via probabilities $P(\bar{Y} = i|Y = j), i \neq j \in$

$\{1, \cdots, c\}$. Note that the assumption that a complementary label is uniformly selected from the remaining $c-1$ classes implies $P(\bar{Y} = i|Y = j) = 1/(c-1), i \neq j \in \{1, \cdots, c\}$. However, in real applications, the probabilities should not be $1/(c-1)$ and can differ vastly. How to estimate the probabilities is a key problem for learning with complementary labels.

We therefore address the problem of learning with biased complementary labels. For effective learning, we propose to estimate the probabilities $P(\bar{Y} = i|Y = j), i \neq j \in \{1, \cdots, c\}$ without biases. Specifically, we prove that given a clear observation $\mathbf{x}_j$ for the j-th class, i.e., the observation satisfying $P(Y = j|\mathbf{x}_j) = 1$, which can be easily identified by the annotator, it holds that $P(\bar{Y} = i|Y = j) = P(\bar{Y} = i|\mathbf{x}_j), i \in \{1, \cdots, j-1, j, \cdots, c\}$. This implies that probabilities $P(\bar{Y} = i|Y = j), i \neq j \in \{1, \cdots, c\}$ can be estimated without biases by learning $P(\bar{Y} = i|\mathbf{x}_j)$ from the examples with complementary labels. To obtain these clear observations, we assume that a small set of easily distinguishable instances (e.g., 10 instances per class) is usually not expensive to obtain.

Given the probabilities $P(\bar{Y}|Y)$, we modify traditional loss functions proposed for learning with true labels so that the modifications can be employed to efficiently learn with biased complementary labels. We also prove that by exploiting examples with complementary labels, the learned classifier converges to the optimal one learned with true labels with a guaranteed rate. Moreover, we also empirically show that the convergence of our method benefits more from the biased setting than from the uniform assumption, meaning that we can use a small training sample to achieve a high performance.

Comprehensive experiments are conducted on benchmark datasets including UCI, MNIST, CIFAR, and Tiny ImageNet, which verifies that our method significantly outperforms the state-of-the-art methods with accuracy gains of over 10%. We also compare the performance of classifiers learned with complementary labels to those learned with true labels. The results show that our method almost attains the performance of learning with true labels in some situations.

2   Related Work

Learning with Complementary Labels. To the best of our knowledge, Ishida et al. [13] is the first to study learning with complementary labels. They assumed that the transition probabilities are identical and then proposed modifying traditional one-versus-all (OVA) and pairwise-comparison (PC) losses for learning with complementary labels. The main differences between our method and [13] are: (1) Our work is motivated by the fact that annotating complementary labels are often affected by human biases. Thus, we study a different setting in which transition probabilities are different. (2) In [13], modifying OVA and PC losses is naturally suitable for the uniform setting and provides an unbiased estimator for the expected risk of classification with true labels. In this paper, our method can be generalized to many losses such as cross-entropy loss and directly provides an unbiased estimator for the risk minimizer. Due to these differences, [13] often achieves promising performance in the uniform setting while our method achieves good performance in both the uniform and non-uniform setting.

Learning with Noisy Labels. In the setting of label noise, transition probabilities are introduced to statistically model the generation of noisy labels. In classification and transfer learning, methods [18,21,32,35] employ transition probabilities to modify loss functions such that they can be robust to noisy labels. Similar strategies to modify deep neural networks by adding a transition layer have been proposed in [22,26]. However, this is the first time that this idea is applied to the new problem of learning with biased complementary labels. Different from label noise, here, all diagonal entries of the transition matrix are zeros and the transition matrix sometimes may be not required to be invertible in empirical.

3   Problem Setup

In multi-class classification, let $\mathcal{X} \in \mathbb{R}^d$ be the feature space and $\mathcal{Y} = [c]$ be the label space, where d is the feature space dimension; $[c] = \{1, \cdots, c\}$; and $c > 2$ is the number of classes. We assume that variables $(X, Y, \bar{Y})$ are defined on the space $\mathcal{X} \times \mathcal{Y} \times \mathcal{Y}$ with a joint probability measure $P(X, Y, \bar{Y})$ ($P_{XY\bar{Y}}$ for short).

In practice, true labels are sometimes expensive but complementary labels are cheap. This work thus studies the setting in which we have a large set of training examples with biased complementary labels and a very small set of correctly labeled examples. The latter is only used for estimating transition probabilities. Our aim is to learn the optimal classifier with respect to the examples with true labels by exploiting the examples with complementary labels.

For each example $(\mathbf{x}, y) \in \mathcal{X} \times \mathcal{Y}$, a complementary label $\bar{y}$ is selected from the complement set $\mathcal{Y} \setminus \{y\}$. We assign a probability for each $\bar{y} \in \mathcal{Y} \setminus \{y\}$ to indicate how likely it can be selected, i.e., $P(\bar{Y} = \bar{y}|X = \mathbf{x}, Y = y)$. In this paper, we assume that $\bar{Y}$ is independent of feature X conditioned on true label Y, i.e., $P(\bar{Y} = \bar{y}|X = \mathbf{x}, Y = y) = P(\bar{Y} = \bar{y}|Y = y)$. This assumption considers the bias which depends only on the classes, e.g., if the annotator is not familiar with the features in a specific class, she is likely to assign complementary labels that she is more familiar with. We summarize all the probabilities into a transition matrix $\mathbf{Q} \in \mathbb{R}^{c \times c}$, where $Q_{ij} = P(\bar{Y} = j|Y = i)$ and $Q_{ii} = 0, \forall i, j \in [c]$. Here, Q_{ij} denotes the entry value in the i-th row and j-th column of $\mathbf{Q}$. Note that transition matrix is also widely exploited in Markov chains [7] and has many applications in machine learning, such as learning with label noise [21,22,26].

If complementary labels are uniformly selected from the complement set, then $\forall i, j \in [c]$ and $i \neq j$, $Q_{ij} = \frac{1}{c-1}$. Previous work [13] has proven that the optimal classifier can be found under the uniform assumption. Sometimes, this is not true in practice due to human biases. Therefore, we focus on situations in which $Q_{ij}, \forall i \neq j$, are different. We mainly study the following problems: how to modify loss functions such that the classifier learned with these biased complementary labels can converge to the optimal one learned with true labels; the speed of the convergence; and how to estimate transition probabilities.

4 Methodology

In this section, we study how to learn with biased complementary labels. We first review how to learn optimal classifiers from examples with true labels. Then, we modify loss functions for complementary labels and propose a deep learning based model accordingly. Lastly, we theoretically prove that the classifier learned by our method is consistent with the optimal classifier learned with true labels.

4.1 Learning with True Labels

The aim of multi-class classification is to learn a classifier $f(\mathbf{x})$ that predicts a label y for a given observation $\mathbf{x}$. Typically, the classifier is of the following form:

$$f(X) = \arg\max_{i \in [c]} g_i(X), \tag{1}$$

where $\mathbf{g} : \mathcal{X} \to \mathbb{R}^c$ and $g_i(X)$ is the estimate of $P(Y = i|X)$.

Various loss functions $\ell(f(X), Y)$ have been proposed to measure the risk of predicting $f(X)$ for Y [1]. Formally, the expected risk is defined as.

$$R(f) = \mathbb{E}_{(X,Y) \sim P_{XY}}[\ell(f(X), Y)]. \tag{2}$$

The optimal classifier is the one that minimizes the expected risk; that is,

$$f^* = \arg\min_{f \in \mathcal{F}} R(f), \tag{3}$$

where $\mathcal{F}$ is the space of f.

However, the distribution P_{XY} is usually unknown. We then approximate $R(f)$ by using its empirical counterpart: $R_n(f) = \frac{1}{n}\sum_{i=1}^{n} \ell(f(\mathbf{x}_i), y_i)$, where $\{(\mathbf{x}_i, y_i)\}_{1 \leq i \leq n}$ are i.i.d. examples drawn according to P_{XY}.

Similarly, the optimal classifier is approximated by $f_n = \arg\min_{f \in \mathcal{F}} R_n(f)$.

4.2 Learning with Complementary Labels

True labels, especially for large-scale datasets, are often laborious and expensive to obtain. We thus study an easily obtainable surrogate; that is, complementary labels. However, if we still use traditional loss functions ℓ when learning with these complementary labels, similar to Eq.(1), we can only learn a mapping $\mathbf{q} : \mathcal{X} \to \mathbb{R}^c$ that tries to predict conditional probabilities $P(\bar{Y}|X)$ and the corresponding classifier that predicts a $\bar{y}$ for a given observation $\mathbf{x}$.

Therefore, we need to modify these loss functions such that the classifier learned with biased complementary labels can converge to the optimal one learned with true labels. Specifically, let $\bar{\ell}$ be the modified loss function. Then, the expected and empirical risks with respect to complementary labels are defined as $\bar{R}(f) = \mathbb{E}_{(X,\bar{Y}) \sim P_{X\bar{Y}}}[\bar{\ell}(f(X), \bar{Y})]$ and $\bar{R}_n(f) = \frac{1}{n}\sum_{i=1}^{n} \bar{\ell}(f(\mathbf{x}_i), \bar{y}_i)]$, respectively. Here, $\{(\mathbf{x}_i, \bar{y}_i)\}_{1 \leq i \leq n}$ are examples with complementary labels.

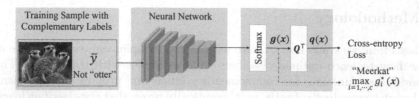

Fig. 2. An overview of our method. We modify the deep neural network by adding a layer that multiplies the output of the softmax function by $\mathbf{Q}^\top$.

Denote $\bar{f}^*$ and $\bar{f}_n$ as the optimal solution obtained by minimizing $\bar{R}(f)$ and $\bar{R}_n(f)$, respectively. They are $\bar{f}^* = \arg\min_{f \in \mathcal{F}} \bar{R}(f)$ and $\bar{f}_n = \arg\min_{f \in \mathcal{F}} \bar{R}_n(f)$.

We hope that the modified loss function $\bar{\ell}$ can ensure that $\bar{f}_n \xrightarrow{n} f^*$, which implies that by learning with complementary labels, the classifier we obtain can also approach to the optimal one defined in (3).

Recall that in transition matrix $\mathbf{Q}$, $Q_{ij} = P(\bar{Y} = j | Y = i)$ and $Q_{ii} = P(\bar{Y} = i | Y = i) = 0, \forall i \in [c]$. We observe that $P(Y|X)$ can be transferred to $P(\bar{Y}|X)$ by using the transition matrix $\mathbf{Q}$; that is, $\forall j \in [c]$,

$$
\begin{aligned}
P(\bar{Y} = j | X) &= \sum_{i \neq j} P(\bar{Y} = j, Y = i | X) \\
&= \sum_{i \neq j} P(\bar{Y} = j | Y = i, X) P(Y = i | X) \\
&= \sum_{i \neq j} P(\bar{Y} = j | Y = i) P(Y = i | X).
\end{aligned}
\tag{4}
$$

Intuitively, if $q_i(X)$ tries to predict the probability $P(\bar{Y} = i | X)$, $\forall i \in [c]$, then $\mathbf{Q}^{-\top} \mathbf{q}$ can predict the probability $P(Y|X)$. To enable end-to-end learning rather than transferring after training, we let

$$
\mathbf{q}(X) = \mathbf{Q}^\top \mathbf{g}(X),
\tag{5}
$$

where $\mathbf{g}(X)$ is now an intermediate output, and $f(X) = \arg\max_{i \in [c]} g_i(X)$.

Then, the modified loss function $\bar{\ell}$ is

$$
\bar{\ell}(f(X), \bar{Y}) = \ell(\mathbf{q}(X), \bar{Y}).
\tag{6}
$$

In this way, if we can learn an optimal $\mathbf{q}^*$ such that $q_i^*(X) = P(\bar{Y} = i | X), \forall i \in [c]$, meanwhile, we can also find the optimal $\mathbf{g}^*$ and the classifier f^*.

This loss modification method can be easily applied to deep learning. As shown in Fig. 2, we achieve this simply by adding a linear layer to the deep neural network. This layer outputs $\mathbf{q}(X)$ by multiplying the output of the softmax function (i.e., $\mathbf{g}(X)$) by the transposed transition matrix $\mathbf{Q}^\top$. With sufficient training examples with complementary labels, this deep neural network often simultaneously learns good classifiers for both $(X, \bar{Y})$ and (X, Y).

Note that, in our modification, the forward process does not need to compute $\mathbf{Q}^{-\top}$. Even though the subsequent analysis for identification requires the transition matrix to be invertible, sometimes, we may have no such requirement in practice. We also show an example in the Supplementary Material that even with singular transition matrices, high classification performance can also be achieved if no column of $\mathbf{Q}$ is all-zero.

5 Identification of the Optimal Classifier

In this section, we aim to prove that the proposed loss modification method ensures the identifiability of the optimal classifier under a reasonable assumption:

Assumption 1. By minimizing the expected risk $R(f)$, the optimal mapping $\mathbf{g}^*$ satisfies $g_i^*(X) = P(Y = i|X), \forall i \in [c]$.

Based on Assumption 1, we can prove that $\bar{f}^* = f^*$ by the following theorem:

Theorem 1. Suppose that $\mathbf{Q}$ is invertible and Assumption 1 is satisfied, then the minimizer $\bar{f}^*$ of $\bar{R}(f)$ is also the minimizer f^* of $R(f)$; that is, $\bar{f}^* = f^*$.

Please find the detailed proof in the Supplementary Material. Given sufficient training data with complementary labels, $\bar{f}_n$ can converge to $\bar{f}^*$, which can be proved in the next section. According to Theorem 1, this also implies that $\bar{f}_n$ also converges to the optimal classifier f^*.

Examples of Loss Functions. The proof of Theorem 1 relies on Assumption 1. However, for many loss functions, Assumption 1 can be provably satisfied. Here, we take the cross-entropy loss as an example to demonstrate this fact. The cross-entropy loss is widely used in deep supervised learning and is defined as

$$\ell(f(X), Y) = -\sum_{i=1}^{c} 1(Y = i) \log(g_i(X)), \tag{7}$$

where $1(\cdot)$ is an indicator function; that is, if the input statement is true, it outputs 1; otherwise, 0. For the cross-entropy loss, we have the following lemma:

Lemma 1. Suppose ℓ is the cross-entropy loss and $\mathbf{g}(X) \in \Delta^{c-1}$, where Δ^{c-1} refers to a standard simplex in $\mathbb{R}^c$; that is, $\forall \mathbf{x} \in \Delta^{c-1}$, $x_i \geq 0, \forall i \in [c]$ and $\sum_{i=1}^{c} x_i = 1$. By minimizing the expected risk $R(f)$, we have $g_i^*(X) = P(Y = i|X), \forall i \in [c]$.

Please see the detailed proof in the Supplementary Material. In fact, losses such as square-error loss $\ell(f(X), Y) = \sum_{j=1}^{c} (1(Y = j) - g_j(X))^2$, also satisfy Assumption 1. The readers can prove it themselves using similar strategy. Combined with Theorem 1, we can see, by applying the proposed method to loss functions such as cross-entropy loss, we can prove that the optimal classifier f^* can be found even when learning with biased complementary labels.

6 Convergence Analysis

In this section, we show an upper bound for the estimation error of our method. This upper bound illustrates a convergence rate for the classifier learned with complementary labels to the optimal one learned with true labels. Moreover, with the derived bound, we can clearly see that the estimation error could further benefit from the setting of biased complementary labels under mild conditions.

Since $\bar{f}^* = f^*$, we have $|\bar{f}_n - f^*| = |\bar{f}_n - \bar{f}^*|$. We will upper bound the error $|\bar{f}_n - \bar{f}^*|$ via upper bounding $\bar{R}(\bar{f}_n) - \bar{R}(\bar{f}^*)$; that is, when $\bar{R}(\bar{f}_n) - \bar{R}(\bar{f}^*) \to 0$, $|\bar{f}_n - \bar{f}^*| \to 0$. Specifically, it has been proven that

$$
\begin{aligned}
\bar{R}(\bar{f}_n) - \bar{R}(\bar{f}^*) &= \bar{R}(\bar{f}_n) - \bar{R}_n(\bar{f}_n) + \bar{R}_n(\bar{f}_n) - \bar{R}_n(\bar{f}^*) + \bar{R}_n(\bar{f}^*) - \bar{R}(\bar{f}^*) \\
&\leq \bar{R}(\bar{f}_n) - \bar{R}_n(\bar{f}_n) + \bar{R}_n(\bar{f}^*) - \bar{R}(\bar{f}^*) \\
&\leq 2 \sup_{f \in \mathcal{F}} |\bar{R}(f) - \bar{R}_n(f)|,
\end{aligned}
\tag{8}
$$

where the first inequality holds because $\bar{R}_n(\bar{f}_n) - \bar{R}_n(\bar{f}^*) \leq 0$ and the error in the last line is called the generalization error.

Let $(X_1, \bar{Y}_1), \cdots, (X_n, \bar{Y}_n)$ be independent variables. By employing the concentration inequality [3], the generalization error can be upper bounded by using the method of Rademacher complexity [2].

Theorem 2. ([2]) Let the loss function be upper bounded by M. Then, for any $\delta > 0$, with the probability $1 - \delta$, we have

$$
\sup_{f \in \mathcal{F}} |\bar{R}(f) - \bar{R}_n(f)| \leq 2\Re_n(\bar{\ell} \circ \mathcal{F}) + M\sqrt{\frac{\log 1/\delta}{2n}},
\tag{9}
$$

where $\Re_n(\bar{\ell} \circ \mathcal{F}) = \mathbb{E}\left[\sup_{f \in \mathcal{F}} \frac{1}{n} \sum_{i=1}^{n} \sigma_i \bar{\ell}(f(X_i), \bar{Y}_i)\right]$ is the Rademacher complexity; $\{\sigma_1, \cdots, \sigma_n\}$ are Rademacher variables uniformly distributed from $\{-1, 1\}$.

Before upper bounding $\Re_n(\bar{\ell} \circ \mathcal{F})$, we need to discuss the specific form of the employed loss function $\bar{\ell}$. By exploiting the well-defined binary loss functions, one-versus-all and pairwise-comparison loss functions [36] have been proposed for multi-class learning. In this section, we discuss the modified loss function $\bar{\ell}$ defined by Eqs. (6) and (7), which can be rewritten as,

$$
\begin{aligned}
\bar{\ell}(f(X), \bar{Y}) &= -\sum_{i=1}^{c} \mathbb{1}(\bar{Y} = i) \log\left((\mathbf{Q}^{\top} \mathbf{g})_i(X)\right) \\
&= -\sum_{i=1}^{c} \mathbb{1}(\bar{Y} = i) \log\left(\frac{\sum_{j=1}^{c} Q_{ji} \exp(h_j(X))}{\sum_{k=1}^{c} \exp(h_k(X))}\right),
\end{aligned}
\tag{10}
$$

where $(\mathbf{Q}^{\top} \mathbf{g})_i$ denotes the i-th entry of $\mathbf{Q}^{\top} \mathbf{g}$; $\mathbf{h} : \mathcal{X} \to \mathbb{R}^c$, $h_i(X) \in \mathcal{H}, \forall i \in [c]$; and $g_i(X) = \frac{\exp(h_i(X))}{\sum_{k=1}^{c} \exp(h_k(X))}$.

Usually, the convergence rates of generalization bounds of multi-class learning are at most $O(c^2/\sqrt{n})$ with respect to c and n [13,20]. To reduce the dependence on c of our derived convergence rate, we rewrite $\bar{R}(f)$ as follows:

$$\bar{R}(f) = \int_X \sum_{i=1}^c P(\bar{Y}=i)P(X|\bar{Y}=i)\bar{\ell}(f(X),\bar{Y}=i)dX$$

$$= \sum_{i=1}^c P(\bar{Y}=i) \int_X P(X|\bar{Y}=i)\bar{\ell}(f(X),\bar{Y}=i)dX \tag{11}$$

$$= \sum_{i=1}^c \bar{\pi}_i \bar{R}_i(f),$$

where $\bar{R}_i(f) = \mathbb{E}_{X \sim P(X|\bar{Y}=i)}\bar{\ell}(f(X),\bar{Y}=i)$ and $\bar{\pi}_i = P(\bar{Y}=i)$.

Similar to Theorem 2, we have the following theorem.

Theorem 3. *Suppose $\bar{\pi}_i = P(\bar{Y}=i)$ is given. Let the loss function be upper bounded by M. Then, for any $\delta > 0$, with the probability $1 - c\delta$, we have*

$$\bar{R}(\bar{f}_n) - \bar{R}(\bar{f}^*) \le 2 \sup_{f \in \mathcal{F}} |\bar{R}(f) - \bar{R}_n(f)|$$

$$\le 2 \sum_{i=1}^c \bar{\pi}_i \sup_{f \in \mathcal{F}} |\bar{R}_i(f) - \bar{R}_{i,n_i}(f)|$$

$$\le 2 \sum_{i=1}^c \bar{\pi}_i \left(2\Re_{n_i}(\bar{\ell} \circ \mathcal{F}) + M\sqrt{\frac{\log 1/\delta}{2n_i}} \right) \tag{12}$$

$$= \sum_{i=1}^c \left(4\bar{\pi}_i\Re_{n_i}(\bar{\ell} \circ \mathcal{F}) + 2\bar{\pi}_i M\sqrt{\frac{\log 1/\delta}{2n_i}} \right),$$

where $\Re_{n_i}(\bar{\ell} \circ \mathcal{F}) = \mathbb{E}\left[\sup_{f \in \mathcal{F}} \frac{1}{n_i} \sum_{j=1}^{n_i} \sigma_j \bar{\ell}(f(X_j),\bar{Y}_j=i)\right]$ and $\bar{R}_{i,n_i}(f)$ is the empirical counterpart of $\bar{R}_i(f)$, and $n_i, i \in [c]$, represents the numbers of X whose complementary labels are $\bar{Y}=i$.

Due to the fact that $\bar{\ell}$ is actually defined with respect to $\mathbf{h}$ rather than f, we would like to bound the error by the Rademacher complexity of $\mathcal{H}$. We observe that the relationship between $\Re_{n_i}(\bar{\ell} \circ \mathcal{F})$ and $\Re_{n_i}(\mathcal{H})$ is:

Lemma 2. *Let $\bar{\ell}(f(X),\bar{Y}=i) = -\log\left(\frac{\sum_{k=1}^c Q_{ki} \exp(h_k(X))}{\sum_{k=1}^c \exp(h_k(X))}\right)$ and suppose that $h_i(X) \in \mathcal{H}, \forall i \in [c]$, we have $\Re_{n_i}(\bar{\ell} \circ \mathcal{F}) \le c\Re_{n_i}(\mathcal{H})$.*

The detailed proof can be found in the Supplementary Material. Combine Theorem 3 and Lemma 2, we have the final result:

Corollary 1. *Suppose $\bar{\pi}_i = P(\bar{Y}=i)$ is given. Let the loss function be upper bounded by M. Then, for any $\delta > 0$, with the probability $1 - c\delta$, we have*

$$\bar{R}(\bar{f}_n) - \bar{R}(\bar{f}^*) \le \sum_{i=1}^c \left(4c\bar{\pi}_i\Re_{n_i}(\mathcal{H}) + 2\bar{\pi}_i M\sqrt{\frac{\log 1/\delta}{2n_i}} \right). \tag{13}$$

In current state-of-the-art methods [13], the convergence rate of $\mathfrak{R}_n(\bar{\ell}\circ\mathcal{F})$ is of order $O(c^2/\sqrt{n})$ with respect to c and n while our derived bound $\sum_i^c 4c\bar{\pi}_i\mathfrak{R}_{n_i}(\mathcal{H})$ is of order $max_{i\in[c]}O(c/\sqrt{n_i})$. Since our error bound depends on n_i, the bound would be loose if n_i (or $\bar{\pi}_i$) is small. However, if $\bar{\pi}_i$ is balanced and n_i is about n/c, our convergence rate is of order $O(c\sqrt{c}/\sqrt{n})$, which is smaller than the error bounds provided by previous methods if c is very large.

Remark. Theorem 3 and Corollary 1 aim to provide the proof of uniform convergence for general losses and show how the convergence rate can benefit from the biased setting under mild conditions. Thus, assuming the loss is upper-bounded is reasonable for many loss functions such as the square-error loss. If the readers would like to derive specific error bound for the cross-entropy loss, strategies in [31] can be employed. If we assume that the transition matrix Q is invertible, we can derive similar results as those in Lemma 1-3 [31] for the modified loss function, which can be finally deployed to derive generalization error bound similar to Corollary 1.

7   Estimating Q

In the aforementioned method, transition matrix $\mathbf{Q}$ is assumed to be known, which is not true. Here, we thus provide an efficient method to estimate $\mathbf{Q}$.

When learning with complementary labels, we completely lose the information of true labels. Without any auxiliary information, it is impossible to estimate the transition matrix which is associated with the class priors of true labels. On the other hand, although it is costly to annotate a very large-scale dataset, a small set of easily distinguishable observations are assumed to be available in practice. This assumption is also widely used in estimating transition probabilities in label noise problem [28] and class priors in semi-supervised learning [34]. Therefore, in order to estimate $\mathbf{Q}$, we manually assign true labels to 5 or 10 observations in each class. Since these selected observations are often easy to classify, we further assume that they satisfy the anchor set condition [18]:

Assumption 2 (Anchor Set Condition). For each class y, there exists an anchor set $\mathcal{S}_{\mathbf{x}|y} \subset \mathcal{X}$ such that $P(Y = y|X = \mathbf{x}) = 1$ and $P(Y = y'|X = \mathbf{x}) = 0$, $\forall y' \in \mathcal{Y} \setminus \{y\}, \mathbf{x} \in \mathcal{S}_{\mathbf{x}|y}$.

Here, $\mathcal{S}_{\mathbf{x}|y}$ is a subset of features in class y. Given several observations in $\mathcal{S}_{\mathbf{x}|y}, y \in [c]$, we are ready to estimate the transition matrix $\mathbf{Q}$. According to Eq. (4),

$$P(\bar{Y} = \bar{y}|X) = \sum_{y' \neq \bar{y}} P(\bar{Y} = \bar{y}|Y = y')P(Y = y'|X). \qquad (14)$$

Suppose $\mathbf{x} \in \mathcal{S}_{\mathbf{x}|y}$, then $P(Y = y|X = \mathbf{x}) = 1$ and $P(Y = y'|X = \mathbf{x}) = 0, \forall y' \in \mathcal{Y} \setminus \{y\}$. We have

$$P(\bar{Y} = \bar{y}|X = \mathbf{x}) = P(\bar{Y} = \bar{y}|Y = y). \qquad (15)$$

That is, the probabilities in $\mathbf{Q}$ can be obtained via $P(\bar{Y}|X)$ given the observations in the anchor set of each class. Thus, we need only to estimate this conditional probability, which has been proven to be achievable in Lemma 1. In this paper, with the training sample $\{(x_i, \bar{y}_i)\}_{1 \le i \le n}$, we estimate $P(\bar{Y}|X)$ by training a deep neural network with the softmax function and cross-entropy loss. After obtaining these conditional probabilities, each probability $P(\bar{Y} = \bar{y}|Y = y)$ in the transition matrix can be estimated by averaging the conditional probabilities $P(\bar{Y} = \bar{y}|X = \mathbf{x})$ on the anchor data $\mathbf{x}$ in class y.

8   Experiments

We evaluate our algorithm on several benchmark datasets including the UCI datasets, USPS, MNIST [16], CIFAR10, CIFAR100 [14], and Tiny ImageNet[1]. All our experiments are trained on neural networks. For USPS and UCI datasets, we employ a one-hidden-layer neural network (d-3-c) [13]. For MNIST, LeNet-5 [17] is deployed, and ResNet [12] is exploited for the other datasets. All models are implemented in PyTorch[2].

UCI and USPS. We first evaluate our method on USPS and six UCI datasets: WAVEFORM1, WAVEFORM2, SATIMAGE, PENDIGITS, DRIVE, and LETTER, downloaded from the UCI machine learning repository. We apply the same strategies of annotating complementary labels, standardization, validation, and optimization with those in [13]. The learning rate is chosen from $\{10^{-5}, \cdots, 10^{-1}\}$, weight decay from $\{10^{-7}, 10^{-4}, 10^{-1}\}$, batch size 100.

For fair comparison in these experiments, we assume the transition probabilities are identical and known as prior. Thus, no examples with true labels are required here. All results are shown in Table 1. Our loss modification (LM) method is compared to a partial label (PL) method [5], a multi-label (ML) method [24], and "PC/S" (the pairwise-comparison formulation with sigmoid loss), which achieved the best performance in [12]. We can see, "PC/S" achieves very good performances. The relatively higher performance of our method may be due to that our method provides an unbiased estimator for risk minimizer.

MNIST. MNIST is a handwritten digit dataset including 60,000 training images and 10,000 test images from 10 classes. To evaluate the effectiveness of our method, we consider the following three settings: (1) for each image in class y, the complementary label is uniformly selected from $\mathcal{Y} \setminus \{y\}$ ("**uniform**"); (2) the complementary label is non-uniformly selected, but each label in $\mathcal{Y} \setminus \{y\}$ has non-zero probability to be selected ("**without0**"); (3) the complementary label is non-uniformly selected from a small subset of $\mathcal{Y} \setminus \{y\}$ ("**with0**").

To generate complementary labels, we first give the probability of each complementary label to be selected. In the "uniform" setting, $P(\bar{Y} = j|Y = i) = \frac{1}{9}, \forall i \ne j$. In the "without0" setting, for each class y, we first randomly split

---

[1] The dataset is available at http://cs231n.stanford.edu/tiny-imagenet-200.zip.
[2] http://pytorch.org.

Table 1. Classification accuracy on USPS and UCI datasets: the means and standard deviations of classification accuracy over 20 trials in percentages are reported. "#train" is the number of training and validation examples in each class. "#test" is the number of test examples in each class.

Dataset	c	d	#train	#test	PC/S	PL	ML	LM (ours)
WAVEFORM1	$1 \sim 3$	21	1226	398	**85.8 (0.5)**	85.7 (0.9)	79.3 (4.8)	85.1 (0.6)
WAVEFORM2	$1 \sim 3$	40	1227	408	84.7 (1.3)	84.6 (0.8)	74.9 (5.2)	**85.5 (1.1)**
SATIMAGE	$1 \sim 7$	36	415	211	**68.7 (5.4)**	60.7 (3.7)	33.6 (6.2)	69.3 (3.6)
PENDIGITS	$1 \sim 5$	16	719	336	87.0 (2.9)	76.2 (3.3)	44.7 (9.6)	**92.7 (3.7)**
	$6 \sim 10$		719	335	78.4 (4.6)	71.1 (3.3)	38.4 (9.6)	**85.8 (1.3)**
	even #		719	336	**90.8 (2.4)**	76.8 (1.6)	43.8 (5.1)	90.0 (1.0)
	odd #		719	335	76.0 (5.4)	67.4 (2.6)	40.2 (8.0)	**86.5 (0.5)**
	$1 \sim 10$		719	335	38.0 (4.3)	33.2 (3.8)	16.1 (4.6)	**62.8 (5.6)**
DRIVE	$1 \sim 5$	48	3955	1326	89.1 (4.0)	77.7 (1.5)	31.1 (3.5)	**93.3 (4.6)**
	$6 \sim 10$		3923	1313	88.8 (1.8)	78.5 (2.6)	30.4 (7.2)	**92.8 (0.9)**
	even #		3925	1283	81.8 (3.4)	63.9 (1.8)	29.7 (6.3)	**84.3 (0.7)**
	odd #		3939	1278	85.4 (4.2)	74.9 (3.2)	27.6 (5.8)	**85.9 (2.1)**
	$1 \sim 10$		3925	1269	40.8 (4.3)	32.0 (4.1)	12.7 (3.1)	**75.1 (3.2)**
LETTER	$1 \sim 5$	16	565	171	**79.7 (5.4)**	75.1 (4.4)	28.3 (10.4)	84.3 (1.5)
	$6 \sim 10$		550	178	76.2 (6.2)	66.8 (2.5)	34.0 (6.9)	**84.4 (1.0)**
	$11 \sim 15$		556	177	78.3 (4.1)	67.4 (3.4)	28.6 (5.0)	**88.3 (1.9)**
	$16 \sim 20$		550	184	77.2 (3.2)	68.4 (2.1)	32.7 (6.4)	**85.2 (0.7)**
	$21 \sim 25$		585	167	80.4 (4.2)	75.1 (1.9)	32.0 (5.7)	**82.5 (1.0)**
	$1 \sim 25$		550	167	**5.1 (2.1)**	5.0 (1.0)	5.2 (1.1)	7.0 (3.6)
USPS	$1 \sim 5$	256	652	166	**79.1 (3.1)**	70.3 (3.2)	44.4 (8.9)	86.4 (4.5)
	$6 \sim 10$		542	147	69.5 (6.5)	66.1 (2.4)	37.3 (8.8)	**88.1 (2.7)**
	even #		556	147	67.4 (5.4)	66.2 (2.3)	35.7 (6.6)	**79.5 (5.4)**
	odd #		542	147	77.5 (4.5)	69.3 (3.1)	36.6 (7.5)	**86.3 (3.1)**
	$1 \sim 10$		542	127	30.7 (4.4)	26.0 (3.5)	13.3 (5.4)	**37.2 (5.4)**

Table 2. Classification accuracy on MNIST: the means and standard deviations of classification accuracy over five trials in percentages are reported. "TL" denotes the result of learning with true labels. "LM/T" and "LM/E" refer to our method with the true $\mathbf{Q}$ and the estimated one, respectively.

Method	Uniform	Without0	With0
TL	99.12	99.12	99.12
PC/S	86.59 ± 3.99	76.03 ± 3.34	29.12 ± 1.94
LM/T	97.18 ± 0.45	97.65 ± 0.15	98.63 ± 0.05
LM/E	96.33 ± 0.31	97.04 ± 0.31	98.61 ± 0.05

$\mathcal{Y} \setminus \{y\}$ to three subsets, each containing three elements. Then, for each complementary label in these three subsets, the probabilities are set to $\frac{0.6}{3}$, $\frac{0.3}{3}$, and $\frac{0.1}{3}$, respectively. In the "with0" setting, for each class y, we first randomly selected three labels in $\mathcal{Y} \setminus \{y\}$, and then randomly assign them with three probabilities whose summation is 1. After $\mathbf{Q}$ is given, we assign complementary label to

Table 3. Classification accuracy on CIFAR10: the means and standard deviations of classification accuracy over five trials in percentages are reported. "TL" denotes the result of learning with true labels. "LM/T" and "LM/E" refer to our method with the true $\mathbf{Q}$ and the estimated one, respectively.

Method	Uniform	Without0	With0
TL	90.78	90.78	90.78
PC/S	41.19 ± 0.04	42.97 ± 3.00	18.12 ± 1.45
LM/T	73.38 ± 1.06	78.80 ± 0.45	85.32 ± 1.11
LM/E	42.96 ± 0.76	70.56 ± 0.34	84.60 ± 0.14

each image based on these probabilities. Finally, we randomly set aside 10% of training data as validation set.

In all experiments, the learning rate is fixed to $1e-4$; batch size 128; weight decay $1e-4$; maximum iterations 60,000; and stochastic gradient descend (SGD) with momentum $\gamma = 0.9$ [27] is applied to optimize deep models. Note that, as shown in [13] and previous experiments, [13] and our method have surpassed baseline methods such as PL and ML. In the following experiments, we will not again make comparisons with these baselines.

The results are shown in Table 2. The means and standard deviations of classification accuracy over five trials are reported. Note that the digit data features are not too entangled, making it easier to learn a good classifier. However, we can still see the differences in the performance caused by the change of settings for annotating complementary labels. According to the results shown in Table 2, "PC/S" [13] works relatively well under the uniform assumption but the accuracy deteriorates in other settings. Our method performs well in all settings. It can also be seen that due to the accurate estimates of these probabilities, "LM/E" with the estimated transition matrix $\mathbf{Q}$ is competitive with "LM/T" which exploits the true one.

CIFAR10. We evaluate our method on the CIFAR10 dataset under the aforementioned three settings. CIFAR10 has totally 10 classes of tiny images, which includes 50,000 training images and 10,000 test images. We leave out 10% of the training data as validation set. In these experiments, ResNet-18 [12] is deployed. We start with an initial learning rate 0.01 and divide it by 10 after 40 and 80 epochs. The weight decay is set to $5e-4$, and other settings are the same as those for MNIST. Early stopping is applied to avoid overfitting.

We apply the same process as MNIST to generate complementary labels. The results in Table 3 verify the effectiveness of our method. "PC/S" achieves promising performance when complementary labels are uniformly selected, and our method outperforms "PC/S" in other settings. In the "uniform" setting, $P(\bar{Y}|X)$ is not well estimated. As a result, the transition matrix is also poorly estimated. "LM/E" thus performs relatively badly.

The results of our method under the "uniform" and "without0" settings (shown in Table 3) are usually worse than that of "with0". For a certain amount

Table 4. Classification accuracy on CIFAR100 and Tiny ImageNet under the setting "with0": the means and standard deviations of classification accuracy over five trials in percentages are reported. "TL" denotes the result of learning with true labels. "LM/T" and "LM/E" refer to our method with the true Q and the estimated one, respectively.

Method	CIFAR100	Tiny ImageNet
TL	69.55	63.26
PC/S	8.95 ± 1.47	N/A
LM/T	62.84 ± 0.30	52.71 ± 0.71
LM/E	60.27 ± 0.28	49.70 ± 0.78

of training images, the empirical results show that in the "uniform" and "without0" setting, the proposed method converges at a slower rate than in the "with0" setting. This phenomenon may be caused by the fact that the uncertainty involved with the transition procedure in the "with0" setting is less than that in "uniform" and "without0" settings, making it easier to learn in the former setting. This phenomenon also indicates that, for images in each class, annotators need not to assign all possible complementary labels, but can provide the labels following the criteria, i.e., each label in the label space should be assigned as complementary label for images in at least one class. In this way, we can reduce the number of training examples to achieve high performance.

CIFAR100. CIFAR100 also presents a collection of tiny images including 50,000 training images and 10,000 test images. But CIFAR100 has totally 100 classes, each with only 500 training images. Due to the label space being very large and the number of training data being limited, in both "uniform" and "without0" settings, few training data are assigned as j for images in each class i, $\forall i \neq j$. Both the proposed method and "PC/S" cannot converge. Here, we only conduct the experiments under the "with0" setting. To generate complementary labels, for each class y, we randomly selected 5 labels from $\mathcal{Y} \setminus \{y\}$, and assign them with non-zero probabilities. Others have no chance to be selected.

In these experiments, ResNet-34 is deployed. Other experimental settings are the same with those in CIFAR10. Results are shown in the second column of Table 4. "PC/S" can hardly obtains a good classifier, but our method achieves high accuracies that are comparable to learning with true labels.

Tiny ImageNet. Tiny ImageNet represents 200 classes with 500 images in each class from ImageNet dataset [25]. Images are cropped to 64×64. Detailed information is lost during the down-sampling process, making it more difficult to learn. ResNet-18 for ImageNet [12] is deployed. Instead of using the original first convolutional layer with a 7×7 kernel and the subsequent max pooling layer, we replace them with a convolutional layer with a 3×3 kernel, stride=1, and no padding. The initial learning rate is 0.1, divided by 10 after 20,000 and 40,000 iterations. The batch size is 256 and weight decay is $5e - 4$. Other settings are the same as CIFAR100. The experimental results are shown in the third column of Table 4. We also only test our method under the setting "with0". "PC/S" cannot converge here, but our method still achieves promising performance.

9   Conclusion

We address the problem of learning with biased complementary labels. Specifically, we consider the setting that the transition probabilities $P(\bar{Y} = j | Y = i)$, $\forall i \neq j$ vary and most of them are zeros. We devise an effective method to estimate the transition matrix given a small amount of data in the anchor set. Based on the transition matrix, we proposed to modify traditional loss functions such that learning with complementary labels can theoretically converge to the optimal classifier learned from examples with true labels. Comprehensive experiments on a wide range of datasets verify that the proposed method is superior to the current state-of-the-art methods.

Acknowledgement. This work was supported by Australian Research Council Projects FL-170100117, DP-180103424, and LP-150100671. This work was partially supported by SAP SE and research grant from Pfizer titled "Developing Statistical Method to Jointly Model Genotype and High Dimensional Imaging Endophenotype". We are also grateful for the computational resources provided by Pittsburgh Super Computing grant number TG-ASC170024.

References

1. Bartlett, P.L., Jordan, M.I., McAuliffe, J.D.: Convexity, classification, and risk bounds. J. Am. Stat. Assoc. **101**(473), 138–156 (2006)
2. Bartlett, P.L., Mendelson, S.: Rademacher and gaussian complexities: risk bounds and structural results. J. Mach. Learn. Res. **3**(Nov), 463–482 (2002)
3. Boucheron, S., Lugosi, G., Massart, P.: Concentration Inequalities: A Nonasymptotic Theory of Independence. Oxford University Press, Oxford (2013)
4. Cheng, J., Liu, T., Ramamohanarao, K., Tao, D.: Learning with bounded instance- and label-dependent label noise. arXiv preprint arXiv:1709.03768 (2017)
5. Cour, T., Sapp, B., Taskar, B.: Learning from partial labels. J. Mach. Learn. Res. **12**(May), 1501–1536 (2011)
6. Ehsan Abbasnejad, M., Dick, A., van den Hengel, A.: Infinite variational autoencoder for semi-supervised learning. In: CVPR, July 2017
7. Gagniuc, P.A.: Markov Chains: From Theory to Implementation and Experimentation. Wiley, Hoboken (2017)
8. Gong, C., Zhang, H., Yang, J., Tao, D.: Learning with inadequate and incorrect supervision. In: ICDM, pp. 889–894. IEEE (2017)
9. Haeusser, P., Mordvintsev, A., Cremers, D.: Learning by association: a versatile semi-supervised training method for neural networks. In: CVPR (2017)
10. Han, B., Tsang, I.W., Chen, L., Celina, P.Y., Fung, S.F.: Progressive stochastic learning for noisy labels. IEEE Trans. Neural Netw. Learn. Syst. **99**, 1–13 (2018)

11. Han, B., et al.: Co-teaching: robust training deep neural networks with extremely noisy labels. arXiv preprint arXiv:1804.06872 (2018)
12. He, K., Zhang, X., Ren, S., Sun, J.: Deep residual learning for image recognition. In: CVPR, pp. 770–778 (2016)
13. Ishida, T., Niu, G., Sugiyama, M.: Learning from complementary labels. In: NIPS (2017)
14. Krizhevsky, A., Hinton, G.: Learning multiple layers of features from tiny images (2009)
15. Law, M.T., Yu, Y., Urtasun, R., Zemel, R.S., Xing, E.P.: Efficient multiple instance metric learning using weakly supervised data. In: CVPR, July 2017
16. LeCun, Y., Corinna, C., Christopher, B.J.: The MNIST database of handwritten digits. http://yann.lecun.com/exdb/mnist/
17. LeCun, Y., Bottou, L., Bengio, Y., Haffner, P.: Gradient-based learning applied to document recognition. Proc. IEEE **86**(11), 2278–2324 (1998)
18. Liu, T., Tao, D.: Classification with noisy labels by importance reweighting. IEEE Trans. Pattern Anal. Mach. Intell. **38**(3), 447–461 (2016)
19. Misra, I., Lawrence Zitnick, C., Mitchell, M., Girshick, R.: Seeing through the Human reporting bias: visual classifiers from noisy Human-centric labels. In: CVPR, pp. 2930–2939 (2016)
20. Mohri, M., Rostamizadeh, A., Talwalkar, A.: Foundations of Machine Learning. MIT press, Cambridge (2012)
21. Natarajan, N., Dhillon, I.S., Ravikumar, P.K., Tewari, A.: Learning with noisy labels. In: NIPS, pp. 1196–1204 (2013)
22. Patrini, G., Rozza, A., Menon, A., Nock, R., Qu, L.: Making neural networks robust to label noise: a loss correction approach. In: CVPR (2017)
23. du Plessis, M.C., Niu, G., Sugiyama, M.: Analysis of learning from positive and unlabeled data. In: NIPS, pp. 703–711 (2014)
24. Read, J., Pfahringer, B., Holmes, G., Frank, E.: Classifier chains for multi-label classification. Mach. Learn. **85**(3), 333–359 (2011)
25. Russakovsky, O., et al.: ImageNet large scale visual recognition challenge. Int. J. Comput. Vis. **115**(3), 211–252 (2015). https://doi.org/10.1007/s11263-015-0816-y
26. Sukhbaatar, S., Bruna, J., Paluri, M., Bourdev, L., Fergus, R.: Training convolutional networks with noisy labels. arXiv preprint arXiv:1406.2080 (2014)
27. Sutskever, I., Martens, J., Dahl, G., Hinton, G.: On the importance of initialization and momentum in deep learning. In: ICML, pp. 1139–1147 (2013)
28. Vahdat, A.: Toward robustness against label noise in training deep discriminative neural networks. In: NIPS, pp. 5596–5605 (2017)
29. Vapnik, V., Vashist, A.: A new learning paradigm: learning using privileged information. Neural Netw. **22**(5), 544–557 (2009)
30. Veit, A., Alldrin, N., Chechik, G., Krasin, I., Gupta, A., Belongie, S.: Learning from noisy large-scale datasets with minimal supervision. In: CVPR, July 2017
31. Wan, L., Zeiler, M., Zhang, S., Le Cun, Y., Fergus, R.: Regularization of neural networks using dropconnect. In: ICML, pp. 1058–1066 (2013)
32. Wang, R., Liu, T., Tao, D.: Multiclass learning with partially corrupted labels. IEEE Trans. Neural Netw. Learn. Syst. **29**(6), 2568–2580 (2018)
33. Xing, E.P., Jordan, M.I., Russell, S.J., Ng, A.Y.: Distance metric learning with application to clustering with side-information. In: NIPS, pp. 521–528 (2003)
34. Yu, X., Liu, T., Gong, M., Batmanghelich, K., Tao, D.: An efficient and provable approach for mixture proportion estimation using linear independence assumption. In: CVPR, pp. 4480–4489 (2018)

35. Yu, X., Liu, T., Gong, M., Zhang, K., Tao, D.: Transfer learning with label noise. arXiv preprint arXiv:1707.09724 (2017)
36. Zhang, T.: Statistical analysis of some multi-category large margin classification methods. J. Mach. Learn. Res. **5**(Oct), 1225–1251 (2004)
37. Zhu, X.: Semi-supervised learning literature survey (2005)

Poster Session

Semi-convolutional Operators
for Instance Segmentation

David Novotny[1,2]($\boxtimes$) (iD), Samuel Albanie[1] (iD), Diane Larlus[2],
and Andrea Vedaldi[1] (iD)

[1] Visual Geometry Group, Department of Engineering Science,
University of Oxford, Oxford, UK
{david,albanie,vedaldi}@robots.ox.ac.uk
[2] Computer Vision Group, NAVER LABS Europe, Meylan, France
diane.larlus@naverlabs.com

Abstract. Object detection and instance segmentation are dominated
by region-based methods such as Mask RCNN. However, there is a growing interest in reducing these problems to pixel labeling tasks, as the
latter could be more efficient, could be integrated seamlessly in image-
to-image network architectures as used in many other tasks, and could
be more accurate for objects that are not well approximated by bounding
boxes. In this paper we show theoretically and empirically that constructing dense pixel embeddings that can separate object instances cannot be
easily achieved using convolutional operators. At the same time, we show
that simple modifications, which we call semi-convolutional, have a much
better chance of succeeding at this task. We use the latter to show a connection to Hough voting as well as to a variant of the bilateral kernel
that is spatially steered by a convolutional network. We demonstrate that
these operators can also be used to improve approaches such as Mask
RCNN, demonstrating better segmentation of complex biological shapes
and PASCAL VOC categories than achievable by Mask RCNN alone.

Keywords: Instance embedding · Object detection
Instance segmentation · Coloring · Semi-convolutional

1 Introduction

State-of-the-art methods for detecting objects in images, such as R-CNN [18,19,
46], YOLO [44], and SSD [38], can be seen as variants of the same paradigm:
a certain number of candidate image regions are proposed, either dynamically
or from a fixed pool, and then a convolutional neural network (CNN) is used

D. Novotny and S. Albani—Equal contribution.

Electronic supplementary material The online version of this chapter (https://
doi.org/10.1007/978-3-030-01246-5_6) contains supplementary material, which is
available to authorized users.

© Springer Nature Switzerland AG 2018
V. Ferrari et al. (Eds.): ECCV 2018, LNCS 11205, pp. 89–105, 2018.
https://doi.org/10.1007/978-3-030-01246-5_6

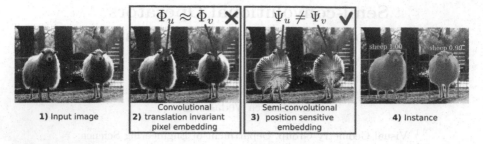

Fig. 1. Approaches for instance segmentation based on dense coloring via convolutional pixel embeddings cannot easily distinguishing identical copies of an object. In this paper, we propose a novel semi-convolutional embedding that is better suited for instance segmentation.

to decide which of these regions tightly enclose an instance of the object of interest. An important advantage of this strategy, which we call *propose & verify* (P&V), is that it works particularly well with standard CNNs. However, P&V also has several significant shortcomings, starting from the fact that rectangular proposals can only approximate the actual shape of objects; segmenting objects, in particular, requires a two-step approach where, as in Mask R-CNN [23], one first detects object instances using simple shapes such as rectangles, and only then refines the detections to pixel-accurate segmentations.

An alternative to P&V that can overcome such limitations is to label directly individual pixels with an identifier of the corresponding object occurrence. This approach, which we call *instance coloring* (IC), can efficiently represent any number of objects of arbitrary shape by predicting a single label map. Thus IC is in principle much more efficient than P&V. Another appeal of IC is that it can be formulated as an image-to-image regression problem, similar to other image understanding tasks such as denoising, depth and normal estimation, and semantic segmentation. Thus this strategy may allow to more easily build *unified architectures* such as [25, 27] that can solve instance segmentations together with other problems.

Despite the theoretical benefits of IC, however, P&V methods currently dominate in terms of overall accuracy. The goal of this paper is to explore some of the reasons for this gap and to suggest workarounds. Part of the problem may be in the nature of the dense labels. The most obvious way of coloring objects is to number them and "paint" them with their corresponding number. However, the latter is a global operation as it requires to be aware of all the objects in the image. CNNs, which are *local and translation invariant*, may therefore be ill-suited for direct enumeration. Several authors have thus explored alternative coloring schemes more suitable for convolutional networks. A popular approach is to assign an arbitrary color (often in the guise of a real vector) to each object occurrence, with the only requirement that different colors should be used for different objects [6, 15, 28]. The resulting color *affinities* can then be used to easily enumerate object a posteriori via a non-convolutional algorithm.

In this paper, we argue that even the latter technique is insufficient to make IC amenable to computation by CNNs. The reason is that, since CNNs are translation invariant, they must still assign the same color to identical copies of an object, making replicas indistinguishable by convolutional coloring. This argument, which is developed rigorously in Sect. 3.6, holds in the limit since in practice the receptive field size of most CNNs is nearly as large as the whole image; however, it suggests that the convolutional structure of the network is at least an unnatural fit for IC.

In order to overcome this issue, we suggest that an architecture used for IC should not be translation invariant; while this may appear to be a significant departure from convolutional networks, we also show that a small modification of standard CNNs can overcome the problem. We do so by defining *semi-convolutional* operators which mix information extracted from a standard convolutional network with information about the global location of a pixel (Sect. 3.1 and Fig. 1). We train the latter (Sect. 3.2) so that the response of the operator is about the same for all pixels that belong to the same object instance, making this embedding naturally suited for IC. We show that, if the mixing function is additive, then the resulting operator bears some resemblance to Hough voting and related detection approaches. After extending the embedding to incorporate standard convolutional responses that capture appearance cues (Sect. 3.3), we use it to induce pixel affinities and show how the latter can be interpreted as a steered version of a bilateral kernel (Sect. 3.4). Finally, we show how such affinities can also be integrated in methods such as Mask RCNN (Sect. 3.5).

We assess our method with several experiments. We start by investigating the limit properties of our approach on simple synthetic data. Then, we show that our semi-convolutional feature extractor can be successfully combined with state-of-the-art approaches to tackle parsing of biological images containing overlapping and articulated organisms (Sect. 4.2). Finally, we apply the latter to a standard instance segmentation benchmark PASCAL VOC (Sect. 4.3). We show in all such cases that the use of semi-convolutional features can improve the performance of state-of-the-art instance segmentation methods such as Mask RCNN.

2 Related Work

The past years have seen large improvements in object detection, thanks to powerful baselines such as Faster-RCNN [46], SSD [38] or other similar approaches [11,34,44], all from the *propose & verify* strategy.

Following the success of object detection and semantic segmentation, the challenging task of instance-level segmentation has received increasing attention. Several very different families of approaches have been proposed.

Proposal-Based Instance Segmentation. While earlier methods relied on bottom-up segmentations [9,18], the vast majority of recent instance-level approaches combine segment proposals together with powerful object classifiers. In general, they implement a multi-stage pipeline that first generates region proposals or class agnostic boxes, and then classifies them [7,10,20,29,32,42,43].

For instance DeepMask [42] and follow-up approaches [8,43] learn to propose segment candidates that are then classified. The MNC approach [10], based on Faster-RCNN [46], repeats this process twice [10] while [32] does it multiple times. [22] extends [10] to model the shape of objects. The fully convolutional instance segmentation method of [31] also combines segmentation proposal and object detection using a position sensitive score map.

Some methods start with semantic segmentation first, and then cut the regions obtained for each category into multiple instances [4,26,37], possibly involving higher-order CRFs [3].

Among the most successful methods to date, Mask-RCNN [23] extends Faster R-CNN [46] with a small fully convolutional network branch [40] producing segmentation masks for each region of interest predicted by the detection branch. Despite its outstanding results, Mask-RCNN does not come without shortcomings: it relies on a small and predefined set of region proposals and non-maximum suppression, making it less robust to strong occlusions, crowded scenes, or objects with fundamentally non-rectangular shapes (see detailed discussion in Sect. 3.6).

Instance-Sensitive Embeddings. Some works have explored the use of pixel-level embeddings in the context of clustering tasks, employing them as a soft, differentiable proxy for cluster assignments [12,15,21,28,41,53]. This is reminiscent of unsupervised image segmentation approaches [16,48]. It has been used for body joints [41], semantic segmentation [1,6,21] and optical flow [1], and, more relevant to our work, to instance segmentation [6,12,15,28].

The goal of this type of approaches is to bring points that belong to the same instance close to each other in an embedding space, so that the decision for two pixels to belong to the same instance can be directly measured by a simple distance function. Such an embedding requires a high degree of invariance to the interior appearance of objects.

Among the most recent methods, [15] combines the embedding with a greedy mechanism to select seed pixels, that are used as starting points to construct instance segments. [6] connects embeddings, low rank matrices and densely connected random fields. [28] embeds the pixels and then groups them into instances with a variant of mean-shift that is implemented as a recurrent neural network. All these approaches are based on convolutions, that are local and translation invariant by construction, and consequently are inherently ill-suited to distinguish several identical instances of the same object (see more details about the convolutional coloring dilemma in Sect. 3.6). A recent work [25] employs position sensitive convolutional embeddings that regress the location of the centroid of each pixel's instance. We mainly differ by allowing embeddings to regress an unconstrained representative point of each instance.

Among other approaches using a clustering component, [49] leverages a coverage loss and [50,51,55] make use of depth information. In particular, [51] trains a network to predict each pixel direction towards its instance center along with monocular depth and semantic labeling. Then template matching and proposal fusion techniques are applied.

Other Instance Segmentation Approaches. Several methods [24,33,42,43] move away from box proposals and use Faster-RCNN [46] to produce "centerness" scores on each pixel instead. They directly predict the mask of each object in a second stage. An issue with such approaches is that objects do not necessarily fit in the receptive fields.

Recurrent approaches sequentially generate a list of individual segments. For instance, [2] uses an LSTM for detection with a permutation invariant loss while [47] uses an LSTM to produce binary segmentation masks for each instance. [45] extends [47] by refining segmentations in each window using a box network. These approaches are slow and do not scale to large and crowded images.

Some approaches use watershed algorithms. [4] predicts pixel-level energy values and then partition the image with a watershed algorithm. [26] combines a watershed algorithm with an instance aware boundary map. Such methods create disconnected regions, especially in the presence of occlusion.

3 Method

3.1 Semi-convolutional Networks for Instance Coloring

Let $\mathbf{x} \in \mathcal{X} = \mathbb{R}^{H \times W \times 3}$ be an image and $u \in \Omega = \{1, \ldots, H\} \times \{1, \ldots, W\}$ a pixel. In instance segmentation, the goal is to map the image to a collection $\mathcal{S}_\mathbf{x} = \{S_1, \ldots, S_{K_\mathbf{x}}\} \subset 2^\Omega$ of image regions, each representing an occurrence of an object of interest. The symbol $S_0 = \Omega - \cup_k S_k$ will denote the complementary region, representing background. The regions as well as their number are a function of the image and the goal is to predict both.

In this paper, we are interested in methods that reduce instance segmentation to a pixel-labeling problem. Namely, we seek to learn a function $\Phi : \mathcal{X} \rightarrow \mathcal{L}^\Omega$ that associates to each pixel u a certain label $\Phi_u(\mathbf{x}) \in \mathcal{L}$ so that, as a whole, labels encode the segmentation $\mathcal{S}_\mathbf{x}$. Intuitively, this can be done by painting different regions with different "colors" (aka pixel labels) making objects easy to recover in post-processing. We call this process *instance coloring* (IC).

A popular IC approach is to use real vectors $\mathcal{L} = \mathbb{R}^d$ as colors, and then require that the colors of different regions are sufficiently well separated. Formally, there should be a margin $M > 0$ such that:

$$\forall u, v \in \Omega : \quad \begin{cases} \|\Phi_u(\mathbf{x}) - \Phi_v(\mathbf{x})\| \leq 1 - M, & \exists k : u, v \in S_k, \\ \|\Phi_u(\mathbf{x}) - \Phi_v(\mathbf{x})\| \geq 1 + M, & \text{otherwise.} \end{cases} \quad (1)$$

If this is the case, clustering colors trivially reconstructs the regions.

Unfortunately, it is difficult for a convolutional operator Φ to satisfy constraint (1) or analogous ones. While this is demonstrated formally in Sect. 3.6, for now an intuition suffices: if the image contains replicas of the same object, then a convolutional network, which is translation invariant, must assign the same color to each copy.

If convolutional operators are inappropriate, then, we must abandon them in favor of non-convolutional ones. While this sounds complex, we suggest that very simple modifications of convolutional operators, which we call *semi-convolutional*, may suffice. In particular, if $\Phi_u(\mathbf{x})$ is the output of a convolutional operator at pixel u, then we can construct a non-convolutional response by mixing it with information about the pixel location. Mathematically, we can define a semi-convolutional operator as:

$$\Psi_u(\mathbf{x}) = f(\Phi_u(\mathbf{x}), u) \tag{2}$$

where $f : \mathcal{L} \times \Omega \to \mathcal{L}'$ is a suitable mixing function. As our main example of such an operator, we consider a particularly simple type of mixing function, namely addition. With it, Eq. (2) specializes to:

$$\Psi_u(\mathbf{x}) = \Phi_u(\mathbf{x}) + u, \qquad \Phi_u(\mathbf{x}) \in \mathcal{L} = \mathbb{R}^2. \tag{3}$$

While this choice is restrictive, it has the benefit of having a very simple interpretation. Suppose in fact that the resulting embedding can perfectly separate instances, in the sense that $\Psi_u(\mathbf{x}) = \Psi_v(\mathbf{x}) \Leftrightarrow \exists k : (u, v) \in S_k$. Then for all the pixels of the region S_k we can write in particular:

$$\forall u \in S_k : \quad \Phi_u(\mathbf{x}) + u = c_k \tag{4}$$

where $c_k \in \mathbb{R}^2$ is an *instance-specific point*. In other words, we see that the effect of learning this semi-convolutional embedding for instance segmentation is to predict a *displacement field* $\Phi(\mathbf{x})$ that maps all pixels of an object instance to an instance-specific centroid c_k. An illustration of the displacement field can be found Fig. 2.

Relation to Hough Voting and Implicit Shape Models. Equations (3) and (4) are reminiscent of well known detection methods in computer vision: Hough voting [5,13] and implicit shape model (ISM) [30]. Recall that both of these methods map image patches to votes for the parameters θ of possible object occurrences. In simple cases, $\theta \in \mathbb{R}^2$ can be the centroid of an object, and casting votes may have a form similar to Eq. 4.

This establishes, a clear link between voting-based methods for object detection and coloring methods for instance segmentation. At the same time, there are significant differences. First, the goal here is to group pixels, not to reconstruct the parameters of an object instance (such as its centroid and scale). Equation (3) may have this interpretation, but the more general version Eq. (2) does not. Second, in methods such as Hough or ISM the centroid is defined a-priori as the actual center of the object; here the centroid c_k has no explicit meaning, but is automatically inferred as a useful but arbitrary reference point. Third, in traditional voting schemes voting integrates local information extracted from individual patches; here the receptive field size of $\Phi_u(\mathbf{x})$ may be enough to comprise the whole object, or more. The goal of Eqs. (2) and (3) is not to pool local information, but to solve a representational issue.

Fig. 2. Semi-convolutional embedding. The first two dimensions of the embedding $\Phi_u(\mathbf{x})$ are visualized as arrows starting from the corresponding pixel location u. Arrows from the same instance tend to point towards a *instance-specific* location c_k.

3.2   Learning Additive Semi-convolutional Features

Learning the semi-convolutional features of Eq. (2) can be formulated in many different ways. Here we adopt a simple direct formulation inspired by [12] and build a loss by considering, for each image $\mathbf{x}$ and instance $S \in \mathcal{S}$ in its segmentation, the distance between the embedding of each pixel $u \in S$ and the segment-wise mean of these embeddings:

$$\mathcal{L}(\Psi|\mathbf{x}, \mathcal{S}) = \sum_{S \in \mathcal{S}} \frac{1}{|S|} \sum_{u \in S} \left\| \Psi_u(\mathbf{x}) - \frac{1}{|S|} \sum_{u \in S} \Psi_u(\mathbf{x}) \right\|. \tag{5}$$

Note that while this quantity resembles the variance of the embedding values for each segment, it is not as the distance is not squared; this was found to be more robust.

Note also that this loss is simpler than the margin condition (1) and than the losses proposed in [12], which resemble (1) more closely. In particular, this loss only includes an "attractive" force which encourages embeddings for each segment to be all equal to a certain mean value, but does not explicitly encourage different segments to be assigned different embedding values. While this can be done too, empirically we found that minimizing Eq. (5) is sufficient to learn good additive semi-convolutional embeddings.

3.3   Coloring Instances Using Individuals' Traits

In practice, very rarely an image contains exact replicas of a certain object. Instead, it is more typical for different occurrences to have some distinctive individual traits. For example, different people are generally dressed in different ways, including wearing different colors. In instance segmentation, one can use such cues to tell right away an instance from another. Furthermore, these cues can be extracted by conventional convolutional operators.

In order to incorporate such cues in our additive semi-convolutional formulation, we still consider the expression $\Psi_u(x) = \hat{u} + \Phi_u(\mathbf{x})$. However, we relax $\Phi_u(\mathbf{x}) \in \mathbb{R}^d$ to have more than two dimensions $d > 2$. Furthermore, we define $\hat{u}$ as the pixel coordinates of u, u_x and u_y, extended by zero padding:

$$\hat{u} = \begin{bmatrix} u_x \ u_y \ 0 \dots 0 \end{bmatrix}^\top \in \mathbb{R}^d. \tag{6}$$

In this manner, the last $d - 2$ dimensions of the embedding work as conventional convolutional features and can extract instance-specific traits normally.

3.4 Steered Bilateral Kernels

The pixel embedding vectors $\Psi_u(\mathbf{x})$ must ultimately be decoded as a set of image regions. Again, there are several possible strategies, starting from simple K-means clustering, that can be used to do so. In this section, we consider transforming embeddings in an affinity matrix between two pixels, as the latter can be used in numerous algorithms.

In order to define the affinity between pixels $u, v \in \Omega$, consider first the Gaussian kernel

$$K(u, v) = \exp\left(-\frac{\|\Psi_u(\mathbf{x}) - \Psi_v(\mathbf{x})\|^2}{2}\right). \tag{7}$$

If the augmented embedding Eq. (6) is used in the definition of $\Psi_u(\mathbf{x}) = \hat{u} + \Phi_u(\mathbf{x})$, we can split $\Phi_u(\mathbf{x})$ into a geometric part $\Phi_u^g(\mathbf{x}) \in \mathbb{R}^2$ and an appearance part $\Phi_u^a(\mathbf{x}) \in \mathbb{R}^{d-2}$ and expand this kernel as follows:

$$K(u, v) = \exp\left(-\frac{\|(u + \Phi_u^g(\mathbf{x})) - (v + \Phi_v^g(\mathbf{x}))\|^2}{2}\right) \exp\left(-\frac{\|\Phi_u^a(\mathbf{x}) - \Phi_v^a(\mathbf{x})\|^2}{2}\right). \tag{8}$$

It is interesting to compare this definition to the one of the *bilateral kernel*:[1]

$$K_{\text{bil}}(u, v) = \exp\left(-\frac{\|u - v\|^2}{2}\right) \exp\left(-\frac{\|\Phi_u^a(\mathbf{x}) - \Phi_v^a(\mathbf{x})\|^2}{2}\right). \tag{9}$$

The bilateral kernel is very popular in many applications, including image filtering and mean shift clustering. The idea of the bilateral kernel is to consider pixels to be similar if they are close in both space and appearance. Here we have shown that kernel (8) and hence kernel (7) can be interpreted as a generalization of this kernel where spatial locations are steered (distorted) by the network to move pixels that belong to the same underlying object instance closer together.

In a practical implementation of these kernels, vectors should be rescaled before being compared, for example in order to balance spatial and appearance components. In our case, since embeddings are trained end-to-end, the network can learn to perform this balancing automatically, but for the fact that (4)

---

[1] In the bilateral kernel, a common choice is to set $\Phi_u^a(\mathbf{x}) = \mathbf{x}_u \in \mathbb{R}^3$ as the RGB triplet for the appearance features.

implicitly defines the scaling of the spatial component of the kernel. Hence, we modify Eq. (7) in two ways: by introducing a learnable scalar parameter σ and by considering a Laplacian rather than a Gaussian kernel:

$$K_\sigma(u, v) = \exp\left(-\frac{\|\Psi_u(\mathbf{x}) - \Psi_v(\mathbf{x})\|}{\sigma}\right). \tag{10}$$

This kernel is more robust to outliers (as it uses the Euclidean distance rather than its square) and is still positive definite [17]. In the next section we show an example of how this kernel can be used to perform instance coloring.

3.5   Semi-convolutional Mask-RCNN

The semi-convolutional framework we proposed in Sect. 3.1 is very generic and can be combined with many existing approaches. Here, we describe how it can be combined with the Mask-RCNN (MRCNN) framework [23], the current state-of-the-art in instance segmentation.

MRCNN is based on the RCNN *propose & verify* strategy and first produces a set of rectangular regions $\mathcal{R}$, where each rectangle $R \in \mathcal{R}$ tightly encloses an instance candidate. Then a fully convolutional network (FCN) produces foreground/background segmentation inside each region candidate. In practice, it labels every pixel u_i in R with a foreground score logit $s(u_i) \in \mathbb{R}$. However, this is not an optimal strategy for articulated objects or occluded scenes (as validated in Sect. 4.2), as it is difficult for a standard FCN to perform individual foreground/background predictions. Hence we leverage our pixel-level translation sensitive embeddings in order to improve the quality of the predictions $s(u_i)$.

Extending MRCNN. Our approach is based on two intuitions: first, some points are easier to be recognized as foreground than others, and, second, once one such *seed point* has been determined, its affinity with other pixels can be used to cut out the foreground region.

In practice, we first identify a seed pixel u_s in each region R using the MRCNN foreground confidence score map $\mathbf{s} = [s(u_1), \ldots, s(u_{|R|})]$. We select the *most confident* seed point as $u_s = \operatorname{argmax}_{1 \leq i \leq |R|} s(u_i)$, evaluate the steered bilateral kernel $K_\sigma(u_s, u)$ after extracting the embeddings Ψ_{u_s} for the seed and Ψ_{u_i} of each pixel u_i in the region, and then defining updated scores $\hat{s}(u_i)$ as $\hat{s}(u_i) = s(u_i) + \log K_\sigma(u_s, u_i)$. The combination of the scores and the kernel is performed in the log-space due to improved numerical stability. The final per-pixel foreground probabilities are obtained as in [23] with sigmoid($\hat{s}(u_i)$).

The entire architecture —the region selection mechanism, the foreground prediction, and the pixel-level embedding —is trained end-to-end. For differentiability, this requires the following modifications: we replace the maximum operator with a soft maximum over the scores $\mathbf{p}_s = \operatorname{softmax}(\mathbf{s})$ and we obtain the seed embedding Ψ_{u_s} as the expectation over the embeddings Ψ_u under the probability density $\mathbf{p}_s$. The network optimizer minimizes, together with the MRCNN losses, the image-level embedding loss $\mathcal{L}(\Psi|\mathbf{x}, \mathcal{S})$ and further attaches a secondary binary cross entropy loss that, similar to the MRCNN mask predictor, minimizes binary cross entropy between the kernel output $K_\sigma(u_s, u_i)$ and the ground truth instance masks.

The predictors of our semi-convolutional features Ψ_u were implemented as an output of a shallow subnetwork, shared between all the FPN layers. This subnet consists of a 256-channel 1×1 convolutional filter followed by ReLU and a final 3×3 convolutional filter producing $D = 8$ dimensional embedding Ψ_u. Due to an excessive sensitivity of the RPN component to perturbations of the underlying FPN representation, we downscale the gradients that are generated by the shallow subnetwork and received by the shared FPN tensors by a factor of 10.

3.6 The Convolutional Coloring Dilemma

In this section, we prove some properties of convolutional operators in relation to solving instance segmentation problems. In order to do this, we need to start by formalizing the problem.

We consider signals (images) of the type $\mathbf{x} : \Omega \to \mathbb{R}$, where the domain Ω is either $\mathbb{Z}^m$ or $\mathbb{R}^m$.[2] In segmentation, we are given a family $\mathbf{x} \in \mathcal{X}$ of such signals, each of which is associated to a certain partition $\mathcal{S}_\mathbf{x} = \{S_1, \ldots, S_{K_\mathbf{x}}\}$ of the domain Ω. The goal is to construct a *segmentation algorithm* $\mathcal{A} : \mathbf{x} \mapsto \mathcal{S}_\mathbf{x}$ that computes this function. We look in particular at algorithms that pre-process the signal by assigning a label $\Phi_u(\mathbf{x}) \in \mathcal{L}$ to each point $u \in \Omega$ of the domain. Furthermore, we assume that this labeling operator Φ is *local and translation invariant*[3] so as to be implementable with a convolutional neural network.

There are two families of algorithms that can be used to segment signals in this manner, discussed next.

Propose and Verify. The first family of algorithms submits all possible regions $S_r \subset \Omega$, indexed for convenience by a variable r, to a labeling function $\Phi_r(\mathbf{x}) \in \{0,1\}$ that *verifies* which ones belong to the segmentation $\mathcal{S}_\mathbf{x}$ (i.e. $\Phi_r(\mathbf{x}) = 1 \Leftrightarrow S_r \in \mathcal{S}_\mathbf{x}$). Since in practice it is not possible to test all possible subsets of Ω, such an algorithm must focus on a smaller set of proposal regions. A typical choice is to consider all translated squares (or rectangles) $S_u = [-H, H]^m + u$. Since the index variable $u \in \Omega$ is now a translation, the operator $\Phi_u(\mathbf{x})$ has the form discussed above, although it is not necessarily local or translation invariant.

Instance Coloring. The second family of approaches directly colors (labels) pixels with the index of the corresponding region, i.e. $\Phi_u(\mathbf{x}) = k \Leftrightarrow u \in S_k$. Differently from P&V, this can efficiently represent arbitrary shapes. However, the map Φ needs implicitly to decide which number to assign to each region, which is a global operation. Several authors have sought to make this more amenable to convolutional networks. A popular approach [12,15] is to color pixels arbitrarily (for example using vector embeddings) so that similar colors are assigned

---

[2] We assume that the domain extends to infinity to avoid having to deal explicitly with boundary conditions.

[3] We say that Φ is translation invariant if $\Phi_u(\mathbf{x}(\cdot - \tau)) = \Phi_{u-\tau}(\mathbf{x})$ for all translations $\tau \in \Omega$. We say that it is also local if there exists a constant $M > 0$ such that $x_u = x_{u'}$ for all $|u - u'| < M$ implies that $\Phi_u(\mathbf{x}) = \Phi'_u(\mathbf{x})$.

to pixels in the same region and different colors are used between regions, as already detailed in Eq. (1).

Convolutional Coloring Dilemma.
Here we show that, even with the variants discussed above, IC cannot be approached with convolutional operators even for cases where these would work with P&V.

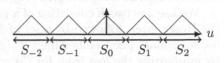

We do so by considering a simple 1D example. Let $\mathbf{x}$ be a signal of period 2 (i.e. $x_{u+2} = x_u$) where for $u \in [-1, 1]$ the signal is given by $x_u = \min(1-u, 1+u)$. Suppose that the segmentation associated to $\mathbf{x}$ is $\mathcal{S} = \{[-1, 1] + 2k, k \in \mathbb{Z}\}$. If we assume that a necessary condition for a coloring-based algorithm is that at least some of the regions are assigned different colors, we see that this cannot be achieved by a convolutional operator. In fact, due to the periodicity of $\mathbf{x}$, any translation invariant function will assign exactly the same color to pixels $2k, k \in \mathbb{Z}$. Thus *all* regions have at least one point with the same color.

On the other hand, this problem can be solved by P&V using the proposal set $\{[-1, 1] + u, u \in \Omega\}$ and the local and translation invariant verification function $\Phi_u(\mathbf{x}) = [x_u = 1]$, which detects the center of each region.

The latter is an extreme example of a convolutional coloring dilemma: namely, a local and translation invariant operator will naturally assign the same color to identical copies of an object even if when they are distinct occurrences (c.f. interesting concurrent work that explores related convolutional dilemmas [36]).

Solving the Dilemma. Solving the coloring dilemma can be achieved by using operators that are *not* translation invariant. In the counterexample above, this can be done by using the semi-convolutional function $\Phi_u(x) = u + (1 - x_u)\dot{x}_u$. It is easy to show that $\Phi_u(x) = 2k$ colors each pixel $u \in S_k = [-1, 1] + 2k$ with twice the index of the corresponding region by moving each point u to the center of the closest region. This works because such displacements can be computed by looking only locally, based on the shape of the signal.

4   Experiments

We first conduct experiments on synthetic data in order to clearly demonstrate inherent limitations of convolutional operators for the task of instance segmentation. In the ensuing parts we demonstrate benefits of the semi-convolutional operators on a challenging scenario with a high number of overlapping articulated instances and finally we compare to the competition on a standard instance segmentation benchmark.

4.1   Synthetic Experiments

In Sects. 3.6 and 3.1 we suggested that convolution operators are unsuitable for instance segmentation via coloring, but that semi-convolutional ones can do.

These experiments illustrate this point by learning a deep neural network to segment a synthetic image x_S where object instances correspond to identical dots arranged in a regular grid (Fig. 3 (a)).

We use a network consisting of a pretrained ResNet50 model truncated after the Res2c layer, followed by a set of 1×1 filters that, for each pixel u, produce 8-dimensional pixel embeddings $\Phi_u(x_S)$ or $\Psi_u(x_S)$. We optimize the network by minimizing the loss from Eq. (5) with stochastic gradient descent. Then, the embeddings corresponding to the foreground regions are extracted and clustered with the k-means algorithm into K clusters, where K is the true number of dots present in the synthetic image.

Figure 3 visualizes the results. Clustering the features consisting of the position invariant convolutional embedding $\Phi_u(x_S)$ results in nearly random clusters (Fig. 3 (c)). On the contrary, the semi-convolutional embedding $\Psi_u(x_S) = \Phi_u(x_S) + u$ allows to separate the different instances almost perfectly when compared to the ground truth segmentation masks (Fig. 3 (d)).

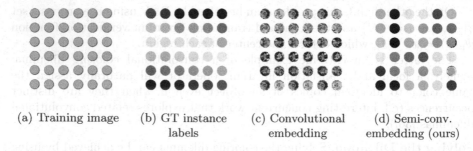

(a) Training image   (b) GT instance   (c) Convolutional   (d) Semi-conv.
labels   embedding   embedding (ours)

Fig. 3. Experiment on synthetic data. An instance segmentation pixel embedding is trained for a synthetic training image consisting of a regular dot pattern (a). After training a model on that image, the produced embeddings are clustered using k-means, encoding the corresponding cluster assignments with consistent pixel colors. A standard convolutional embedding (c) cannot successfully embed each dot into a unique location due to its translational invariance. Our proposed semi-convolutional operator (d) naturally embeds dots with identical appearance but distinct location into distinct regions in the feature space and hence allows for successful clustering of the instances. (Color figure online)

4.2   Parsing Biological Images

The second set of experiments considers the parsing of biological images. Organisms to be segmented present non-rigid pose variations, and frequently form clusters of overlapping instances, making the parsing of such images challenging. Yet, this scenario is of crucial importance for many biological studies.

Dataset and Evaluation. We evaluate our approach on the C. Elegans dataset (illustrated Fig. 4), a subset of the Broad Biomedical Benchmark collection [39]. The dataset consists of 100 bright-field microscopy images. Following standard practice [52,54], we operate on the binary segmentation of the microscopy

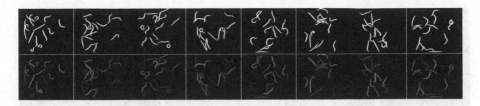

Fig. 4. Sample image crops (top) and corresponding ground-truth (bottom) from the *C. Elegans* dataset.

images. However, since there is no publicly defined evaluation protocol for this dataset, a fair numerical comparison with previously published experiments is infeasible. We therefore compare our method against a very strong baseline (MRCNN) and adopt the methodology introduced by [54] in which the dataset is divided into 50 training and 50 test images. We evaluate the segmentation using average precision (AP) computed using the standard COCO evaluation criteria [35]. We compare our method against the MRCNN FPN-101 model from [23] which attains results on par with state of the art on the challenging COCO instance segmentation task.

Results. The results are given in Table 1. We observe that the semi-convolutional embedding Ψ_u brings improvements in all considered instance segmentation metrics. The improvement is more significant at higher IoU thresholds which underlines the importance of utilizing position sensitive embedding in order to precisely delineate an instance within an MRCNN crop.

Table 1. Average precision (AP) for instance segmentation on *C. Elegans* reporting the standard COCO evaluation metrics [35]

AP	AP	$AP_{0.5}$	$AP_{0.75}$	AP_S	AP_M
Ours	**0.569**	**0.885**	**0.661**	**0.511**	**0.671**
MRCNN [24]	0.559	0.865	0.641	0.502	0.650

4.3   Instance Segmentation

The final experiment compares our method to competition on the instance segmentation task on a standard large scale dataset, PASCAL VOC 2012 [14].

As in the previous section, we base our method on the MRCNN FPN-101 model. Because we observed that the RPN component is extremely sensitive to changes in the base architecture, we employed a multistage training strategy. First, MRCNN FPN-101 model is trained until convergence and then our embeddings are attached and fine-tuned with the rest of the network . We follow [23] and learn using 24 SGD epochs, lowering the initial learning rate of 0.0025 tenfold after the first 12 epochs. Following other approaches, we train on the training set of VOC 2012 and test on the validation set.

Fig. 5. Instance segmentation on Pascal VOC 2012. Each pair of rows visualizes instance segmentations produced with method, together with the corresponding semi-convolutional embeddings

Table 2. Instance-level segmentation comparison using mean APr metric at 0.5 IoU on the PASCAL VOC 2012 validation set

SDS [20]	PFN [33]	DIN [3]	MNC [10]	FCIS [31]	R2-IOS [32]	DML [15]	R. Emb. [28]	BAIS [22]	MRCNN [24]	**Ours**
43.8	58.7	61.7	63.5	65.7	66.7	62.1	64.5	65.7	69.0	**69.9**

Results. The results are given in Table 2. Our method attains state of the art on PASCAL VOC 2012 which validates our approach. We further compare in detail against MRCNN in Table 3 using the standard COCO instance segmentation metrics from [35]. Our method outperforms MRCNN on the considered metrics, confirming the contribution of the proposed semi-convolutional embedding.

Table 3. Average precision (AP) for instance segmentation on PASCAL VOC 2012 reporting the standard COCO evaluation metrics [35]

AP	AP	$AP_{0.5}$	$AP_{0.75}$	AP_S	AP_M	AP_L
Ours	**0.412**	**0.699**	**0.424**	0.107	**0.317**	**0.538**
MRCNN [24]	0.401	0.690	0.412	**0.111**	0.313	0.525

5   Conclusions

In this paper, we have considered dense pixel embeddings for the task of instance-level segmentation. Departing from standard approaches that rely on translation invariant convolutional neural networks, we have proposed semi-convolutional operators which can be easily obtained with simple modifications of the convolutional ones. On top of their theoretical advantages, we have shown empirically that they are much more suited to distinguish several identical instances of the same object, and are complementary to the standard Mask-RCNN approach.

Acknowledgments. We gratefully acknowledge the support of Naver, EPSRC AIMS CDT, AWS ML Research Award, and ERC 677195-IDIU.

References

1. Harley, A.W., Derpanis, K.G., Kokkinos, I.: Segmentation-aware convolutional networks using local attention masks. In: Proceedings of the ICCV (2017)
2. Andriluka, M., Stewart, R., Ng, A.Y.: End-to-end people detection in crowded scenes. In: Proceeding of the CVPR (2016)
3. Arnab, A., Torr, P.H.S.: Pixelwise instance segmentation with a dynamically instantiated network. In: Proceedings of the CVPR (2017)
4. Bai, M., Urtasun, R.: Deep watershed transform for instance segmentation. In: Proceedings of the CVPR (2017)
5. Ballard, D.H.: Generalizing the hough transform to detect arbitrary shapes. In: Readings in Computer Vision: Issues, Problems, Principles, and Paradigms, pp. 714–725. Morgan Kaufmann Publishers Inc., San Francisco (1987)
6. Chandra, S., Usunier, N., Kokkinos, I.: Dense and low-rank gaussian CRFs using deep embeddings. In: Proceedings of the ICCV (2017)
7. Chen, Y.T., Liu, X., Yang, M.H.: Multi-instance object segmentation with occlusion handling. In: Proceedings of the CVPR (2015)
8. Dai, J., He, K., Li, Y., Ren, S., Sun, J.: Instance-sensitive fully convolutional networks. In: Leibe, B., Matas, J., Sebe, N., Welling, M. (eds.) ECCV 2016. LNCS, vol. 9910, pp. 534–549. Springer, Cham (2016). https://doi.org/10.1007/978-3-319-46466-4_32
9. Dai, J., He, K., Sun, J.: Convolutional feature masking for joint object and stuff segmentation. In: Proceedings of the CVPR (2015)
10. Dai, J., He, K., Sun, J.: Instance-aware semantic segmentation via multi-task network cascades. In: Proceedings of the CVPR (2016)
11. Dai, J., Li, Y., He, K., Sun, J.: R-FCN: Object detection via region-based fully convolutional networks. In: Proceedings of the NIPS (2016)
12. De Brabandere, B., Neven, D., Van Gool, L.: Semantic instance segmentation with a discriminative loss function. arXiv preprint arXiv:1708.02551 (2017)
13. Duda, R.O., Hart, P.E.: Use of the hough transformation to detect lines and curves in pictures. Commun. ACM **15**(1), 11–15 (1972)
14. Everingham, M., Van Gool, L., Williams, C.K.I., Winn, J., Zisserman, A.: The PASCAL Visual Object Classes Challenge 2012 (VOC2012) Results. http://www.pascal-network.org/challenges/VOC/voc2012/workshop/index.html
15. Fathi, A., et al.: Semantic instance segmentation via deep metric learning. CoRR abs/1703.10277 (2017)

16. Felzenszwalb, P.F., Huttenlocher, D.P.: Efficient graph-based image segmentation. IJCV **59**(2), 167–181 (2004)
17. Feragen, A., Lauze, F., Hauberg, S.: Geodesic exponential kernels: when curvature and linearity conflict. In: Proceedings of the CVPR (2015)
18. Girshick, R.: Fast r-CNN. In: Proceedings of the ICCV (2015)
19. Girshick, R., Donahue, J., Darrell, T., Malik, J.: Rich feature hierarchies for accurate object detection and semantic segmentation. In: Proceedings of the CVPR (2014)
20. Hariharan, B., Arbeláez, P., Girshick, R., Malik, J.: Simultaneous detection and segmentation. In: Fleet, D., Pajdla, T., Schiele, B., Tuytelaars, T. (eds.) ECCV 2014. LNCS, vol. 8695, pp. 297–312. Springer, Cham (2014). https://doi.org/10.1007/978-3-319-10584-0_20
21. Harley, A.W., Derpanis, K.G., Kokkinos, I.: Learning dense convolutional embeddings for semantic segmentation. In: Proceedings of the ICLR (2016)
22. Hayder, Z., He, X., Salzmann, M.: Boundary-aware instance segmentation. In: Proceedings of the CVPR (2017)
23. He, K., Gkioxari, G., Dollár, P., Girshick, R.: Mask r-CNN. In: Proceedings of the ICCV (2017)
24. Hu, H., Lan, S., Jiang, Y., Cao, Z., Sha, F.: Fastmask: segment multi-scale object candidates in one shot. In: Proceedings of the CVPR (2017)
25. Kendall, A., Gal, Y., Cipolla, R.: Multi-task learning using uncertainty to weigh losses for scene geometry and semantics. In: Proceedings of the CVPR (2017)
26. Kirillov, A., Levinkov, E., Andres, B., Savchynskyy, B., Rother, C.: Instancecut: from edges to instances with multicut. In: Proceedings of the CVPR, July 2017
27. Kokkinos, I.: Ubernet: training a universal convolutional neural network for low-, mid-, and high-level vision using diverse datasets and limited memory. In: Proceedings of the CVPR (2017)
28. Kong, S., Fowlkes, C.: Recurrent pixel embedding for instance grouping. In: Proceedings of the CVPR (2018)
29. Ladický, L., Sturgess, P., Alahari, K., Russell, C., Torr, P.H.S.: What, where and how many? Combining object detectors and CRFs. In: Daniilidis, K., Maragos, P., Paragios, N. (eds.) ECCV 2010. LNCS, vol. 6314, pp. 424–437. Springer, Heidelberg (2010). https://doi.org/10.1007/978-3-642-15561-1_31
30. Leibe, B., Schiele, B.: Interleaving object categorization and segmentation. In: Christensen, H.I., Nagel, H.-H. (eds.) Cognitive Vision Systems. LNCS, vol. 3948, pp. 145–161. Springer, Heidelberg (2006). https://doi.org/10.1007/11414353_10
31. Li, Y., Qi, H., Dai, J., Ji, X., Wei, Y.: Fully convolutional instance-aware semantic segmentation. In: Proceedings of the CVPR (2017)
32. Liang, X., Wei, Y., Shen, X., Jie, Z., Feng, J., Lin, L., Yan, S.: Reversible recursive instance-level object segmentation. In: Proceedings of the CVPR (2016)
33. Liang, X., Wei, Y., Shen, X., Yang, J., Lin, L., Yan, S.: Proposal-free network for instance-level object segmentation. PAMI (2017)
34. Lin, T., Dollar, P., Girshick, R., He, K., Hariharan, B., Belongie, S.: Feature pyramid networks for object detection. In: Proc. CVPR (2017)
35. Lin, T.-Y., et al.: Microsoft COCO: common objects in context. In: Fleet, D., Pajdla, T., Schiele, B., Tuytelaars, T. (eds.) ECCV 2014. LNCS, vol. 8693, pp. 740–755. Springer, Cham (2014). https://doi.org/10.1007/978-3-319-10602-1_48
36. Liu, R., et al.: An intriguing failing of convolutional neural networks and the coordconv solution. arXiv preprint arXiv:1807.03247 (2018)
37. Liu, S., Jia, J., Fidler, S., Urtasun, R.: Sgn: Sequential grouping networks for instance segmentation. In: Proceeding of the ICCV (2017)

38. Liu, W., Anguelov, D., Erhan, D., Szegedy, C., Reed, S., Fu, C.-Y., Berg, A.C.: SSD: single shot multibox detector. In: Leibe, B., Matas, J., Sebe, N., Welling, M. (eds.) ECCV 2016. LNCS, vol. 9905, pp. 21–37. Springer, Cham (2016). https:// doi.org/10.1007/978-3-319-46448-0_2

39. Ljosa, V., Sokolnicki, K.L., Carpenter, A.E.: Annotated high-throughput microscopy image sets for validation. Nat. Methods **9**(7), 637 (2012)

40. Long, J., Shelhamer, E., Darrell, T.: Fully convolutional networks for semantic segmentation. In: Proceedings of the CVPR (2015)

41. Newell, A., Huang, Z., Deng, J.: Associative embedding: end-to-end learning for joint detection and grouping. In: Proceedings of the NIPS (2017)

42. Pinheiro, P.O., Collobert, R., Dollár, P.: Learning to segment object candidates. In: Proceedings of the NIPS (2015)

43. Abaev, P., Gaidamaka, Y., Samouylov, K.E.: Queuing model for loss-based over-load control in a SIP server using a hysteretic technique. In: Andreev, S., Balandin, S., Koucheryavy, Y. (eds.) NEW2AN/ruSMART -2012. LNCS, vol. 7469, pp. 371–378. Springer, Heidelberg (2012). https://doi.org/10.1007/978-3-642-32686-8_34

44. Redmon, J., Farhadi, A.: YOLO9000: better, faster, stronger. In: Proceedings of the CVPR (2017)

45. Ren, M., Zemel, R.S.: End-to-end instance segmentation with recurrent attention. In: Proceedings of the CVPR (2017)

46. Ren, S., He, K., Girshick, R., Sun, J.: Faster R-CNN: Towards real-time object detection with region proposal networks. In: Proceedings of the NIPS (2015)

47. Romera-Paredes, B., Torr, P.H.S.: Recurrent instance segmentation. In: Leibe, B., Matas, J., Sebe, N., Welling, M. (eds.) ECCV 2016. LNCS, vol. 9910, pp. 312–329. Springer, Cham (2016). https://doi.org/10.1007/978-3-319-46466-4_19

48. Shi, J., Malik, J.: Normalized cuts and image segmentation. PAMI **22**(8), 888–905 (2000)

49. Silberman, N., Sontag, D., Fergus, R.: Instance segmentation of indoor scenes using a coverage loss. In: Fleet, D., Pajdla, T., Schiele, B., Tuytelaars, T. (eds.) ECCV 2014. LNCS, vol. 8689, pp. 616–631. Springer, Cham (2014). https://doi.org/10. 1007/978-3-319-10590-1_40

50. Tighe, J., Niethammer, M., Lazebnik, S.: Scene parsing with object instances and occlusion ordering. In: Proceedings of the CVPR (2014)

51. Uhrig, J., Cordts, M., Franke, U., Brox, T.: Pixel-Level encoding and depth layering for instance-level semantic labeling. In: Rosenhahn, B., Andres, B. (eds.) GCPR 2016. LNCS, vol. 9796, pp. 14–25. Springer, Cham (2016). https://doi.org/10.1007/ 978-3-319-45886-1_2

52. Wählby, C., et al.: Resolving clustered worms via probabilistic shape models. In: 2010 IEEE International Symposium on Biomedical Imaging: From Nano to Macro, pp. 552–555. IEEE (2010)

53. Wang, L., Lu, H., Ruan, X., Yang, M.H.: Deep networks for saliency detection via local estimation and global search. In: Proceedings of the CVPR, June 2015

54. Yurchenko, V., Lempitsky, V.: Parsing images of overlapping organisms with deep singling-out networks. In: Proceedings of the CVPR (2017)

55. Zhang, Z., Schwing, A.G., Fidler, S., Urtasun, R.: Monocular object instance segmentation and depth ordering with cnns. In: Proceedings of the ICCV (2015)

Skeleton-Based Action Recognition with Spatial Reasoning and Temporal Stack Learning

Chenyang Si[1,3] , Ya Jing[1,3] , Wei Wang[1,3(✉)] , Liang Wang[1,2,3] ,
and Tieniu Tan[1,2,3]

[1] Center for Research on Intelligent Perception and Computing (CRIPAC),
National Laboratory of Pattern Recognition (NLPR), Beijing, China
{chenyang.si,ya.jing}@cripac.ia.ac.cn,
{wangwei,wangliang,tnt}@nlpr.ia.ac.cn
[2] Center for Excellence in Brain Science and Intelligence Technology (CEBSIT),
Institute of Automation, Chinese Academy of Sciences (CASIA), Beijing, China
[3] University of Chinese Academy of Sciences (UCAS), Beijing, China

Abstract. Skeleton-based action recognition has made great progress recently, but many problems still remain unsolved. For example, the representations of skeleton sequences captured by most of the previous methods lack spatial structure information and detailed temporal dynamics features. In this paper, we propose a novel model with spatial reasoning and temporal stack learning (SR-TSL) for skeleton-based action recognition, which consists of a spatial reasoning network (SRN) and a temporal stack learning network (TSLN). The SRN can capture the high-level spatial structural information within each frame by a residual graph neural network, while the TSLN can model the detailed temporal dynamics of skeleton sequences by a composition of multiple skip-clip LSTMs. During training, we propose a clip-based incremental loss to optimize the model. We perform extensive experiments on the SYSU 3D Human-Object Interaction dataset and NTU RGB+D dataset and verify the effectiveness of each network of our model. The comparison results illustrate that our approach achieves much better results than the state-of-the-art methods.

Keywords: Skeleton-based action recognition · Spatial reasoning
Temporal stack learning · Clip-based incremental loss

1 Introduction

Human action recognition is an important and challenging problem in computer vision research. It plays an important role in many applications, such as intelligent video surveillance, sports analysis and video retrieval. Human action recognition can also help robots to have a better understanding of human behaviors, thus robots can interact with people much better [1, 21, 30].

© Springer Nature Switzerland AG 2018
V. Ferrari et al. (Eds.): ECCV 2018, LNCS 11205, pp. 106–121, 2018.
https://doi.org/10.1007/978-3-030-01246-5_7

Recently, there have existed many approaches to recognize human actions, the input data type of which can be grossly divided into two categories: RGB videos [25] and 3D skeleton sequences [4]. For RGB videos, spatial appearance and temporal optical flow generally are applied to model the motion dynamics. However, the spatial appearance only contains 2D information that is hard to capture all the motion information, and the optical flow generally needs high computing costs. Compared to RGB videos, Johansson et al. [11] have explained that 3D skeleton sequences can effectively represent the dynamics of human actions. Furthermore, the skeleton sequences can be obtained by the Microsoft Kinect [33] and the advanced human pose estimation algorithms [3]. Over the years, skeleton-based human action recognition has attracted more and more attention [2,4,26]. In this paper, we focus on recognizing human actions from 3D skeleton sequences.

For sequential data, recurrent neural networks (RNNs) perform a strong power in learning the temporal dependencies. There has been a lot of work successfully applying RNNs for skeleton-based action recognition. Hierarchical RNN [4] is proposed to learn motion representations from skeleton sequences. Shahroudy et al. [24] introduce a part-aware LSTM network to further improve the performance of the LSTM framework. To model the discriminative features, a spatial-temporal attention model [26] based on LSTM is proposed to focus on discriminative joints and pay different attentions to different frames. Despite the great improvement in performance, there exist two urgent problems to be solved. First, human behavior is accomplished in coordination with each part of the body. For example, walking requires legs to walk, and it also needs the swing of arms to coordinate the body balance. It is very difficult to capture the high-level spatial structural information within each frame if directly feeding the concatenation of all body joints into networks. Second, these methods utilize RNNs to directly model the overall temporal dynamics of skeleton sequences. The hidden representation of the final RNN is used to recognize the actions. For long-term sequences, the last hidden representation cannot completely contain the detailed temporal dynamics of sequences.

In this paper, we propose a novel model with spatial reasoning and temporal stack learning (SR-TSL) for this task, which can effectively solve the above challenges. Figure 1 shows the overall pipeline of our model that contains a spatial reasoning network (SRN) and a temporal stack learning network (TSLN). First, we propose a spatial reasoning network to capture the high-level spatial structural features within each frame. The body can be decomposed into different parts, e.g. two arms, two legs and one trunk. The concatenation of joints of each part is transformed into individual spatial feature with a linear layer. These individual spatial features of body parts are fed into a residual graph neural network (RGNN) to capture the high-level structural features between the different body parts, where each node corresponds to a body part. Second, we propose a temporal stack learning network to model the detailed temporal dynamics of the sequences, which consists of three skip-clip LSTMs. For a long-term sequence, it is divided into multiple clips. The short-term temporal information of each clip is

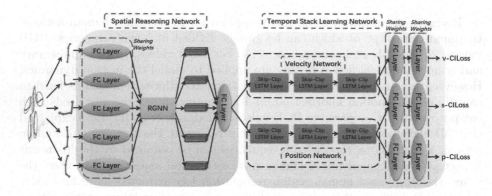

Fig. 1. The overall pipeline of our model which contains a spatial reasoning network and a temporal stack learning network. In the spatial reasoning network, a residual graph neural network (RGNN) is used to capture the high-level spatial structural information between the different body parts. The temporal stack learning network can model the detailed temporal dynamics for skeleton sequence. During training, the proposed model is efficiently optimized with the clip-based incremental losses (CIloss)

modeled with an LSTM layer shared among the clips in a skip-clip LSTM layer. When feeding a clip into shared LSTM, the initial hidden of shared LSTM is initialized with the sum of the final hidden state of all previous clips, which can inherit previous dynamics to maintain the dependency between clips. We propose a clip-based incremental loss to further improve the ability of stack learning. Therefore, our model can also effectively solve the problem of long-term sequence optimization. Experimental results show that the proposed SR-TSL speeds up the model convergence and improve the performance.

The main contributions of this paper are summarized as follows:

1. We propose a spatial reasoning network for each skeleton frame, which can effectively capture the high-level spatial structural information between the different body parts using a residual graph neural network.
2. We propose a temporal stack learning network to model the detailed temporal dynamics of skeleton sequences by a composition of multiple skip-clip LSTMs.
3. The proposed clip-based incremental loss further improves the ability of temporal stack learning, which can effectively speed up convergence and obviously improve the performance.
4. Our method obtains the state-of-the-art results on the SYSU 3D Human-Object Interaction dataset and NTU RGB+D dataset.

2   Related Work

In this section, we briefly review the existing literature that closely relates to the proposed method.

Skeleton Based Action Recognition. There have been amounts of work proposed for skeleton-based action recognition, which can be divided into two classes. The first class is to focus on designing handcrafted features to represent the information of skeleton motion. Wang et al. [29] exploit a new feature called local occupancy pattern, which can be treated as the depth appearance of joints, and propose an actionlet ensemble model to represent each action. Hussein et al. [10] use the covariance matrix for skeleton joint locations over time as a discriminative descriptor for a sequence. Vemulapalli et al. [27] utilize rotations and translations to represent the 3D geometric relationships of body parts in Lie group.

The second class is to use deep neural networks to recognize human actions. [12,13] exploit the Convolutional Neural Networks (CNNs) for skeleton-based action recognition. Recently, most of methods utilize the Recurrent Neural Networks (RNNs) for this task. Du et al. [4] first propose an end-to-end hierarchical RNN for skeleton-based action recognition. Zhu et al. [34] design a fully connected deep LSTM network with a regularization scheme to learn the co-occurrence features of skeleton joints. An end-to-end spatial and temporal attention model [26] learns to selectively focus on discriminative joints of the skeleton within each frame of the inputs and pays different levels of attention to the outputs of different frames. Zhang et al. [32] exploit a view adaptive model with LSTM architecture, which enables the network to adapt to the most suitable observation viewpoints from end to end. A two-stream RNN architecture is proposed to model both temporal dynamics and spatial configurations for skeleton-based action recognition in [28]. The most similar work to ours is [16] which proposes an ensemble temporal sliding LSTM (TS-LSTM) networks for skeleton-based action recognition. They utilize an ensemble of multi-term temporal sliding LSTM networks to capture short-term, medium-term, long-term temporal dependencies and even spatial skeleton pose dependency. In this paper, we design a spatial reasoning network and temporal stack learning network, which can capture the high-level spatial structural information and the detailed temporal dynamics of skeleton sequences, separately.

Graph Neural Networks. Recently, more and more works have used the graph neural networks (GNNs) to the graph-structured data, which can be categorized into two broad classes. The first class is to apply Convolutional Neural Networks (CNNs) to graph, which improves the traditional convolution network on graph. [5,6] utilize the CNNs in the spectral domain relying on the graph Laplacian. [15,20] apply the convolution directly on the graph nodes and their neighbors, which construct the graph filters on the spatial domain. Yan et al. [31] are the first to apply the graph convolutional neural networks for skeleton-based action recognition. The second class is to utilize the recurrent neural networks to every node of the graph. [23] proposes to recurrently update the hidden state of each node of the graph. Li et al. [17] propose a model based on Graph Neural Networks for situation recognition, which can efficiently capture joint dependencies between roles using neural networks defined on a graph. Qi et al. [22] use 3D graph neural networks for RGBD semantic segmentation. In this paper, a residual graph neural network is utilized to model the high-level spatial structural information between different body parts.

3   Overview

In this section, we briefly review the Graph Neural Networks (GNNs), the Recurrent Neural Networks (RNNs) and Long Short-Term Memory (LSTM), which are utilized in our framework.

3.1   Graph Neural Network

Graph Neural Network (GNN) is introduced in [23] as a generalization of recursive neural networks, which can deal with a more general class of graphs. The GNNs can be defined as an ordered pair $G = \{V, E\}$, where V is the set of nodes and E is the set of edges. At time step t, the hidden state of the i-th $(i \in \{1, ..., |V|\})$ node is s_i^t, and the output is o_i^t. The set of nodes Ω_v stands for the neighbors of node v.

For a GNN, the input vector of each node $v \in V$ is based on the information contained in the neighborhood of node v, and the hidden state of each node is updated recurrently. At time step t, the received messages of a node are calculated with the hidden states of its neighbors. Then the received messages and previous state s_i^{t-1} are utilized to update the hidden state s_i^t. Finally, the output o_i^t is computed with s_i^t. The GNN formulation at time step t is defined as follows:

$$m_i^t = f_m \left(\{ s_{\hat{i}}^{t-1} | \hat{i} \in \{1, ..., |\Omega_{v_i}|\} \right) \tag{1}$$

$$s_i^t = f_s \left(m_i^t, s_i^{t-1} \right) \tag{2}$$

$$o_i^t = f_o \left(s_i^t \right) \tag{3}$$

where m_i^t is the sum of all the messages that the neighbors Ω_{v_i} send to node v_i, f_m is the function to compute the incoming messages, f_s is the function that expresses the state of a node and f_o is the function to produce the output. Similar to RNNs, these functions are the learned neural networks and are shared among different time steps.

3.2   RNN and LSTM

Recurrent Neural Networks (RNNs) are the powerful models to capture the dependencies of sequences via cycles in the network of nodes, which are suitable for the sequence tasks. However, there exist two difficult problems of vanishing gradient and exploding gradient when the standard RNN is used for long-term sequences.

The advanced RNN architecture of Long Short-Term Memory (LSTM) is proposed by Hochreiter et al. [7]. LSTM neuron contains an input gate, a forget gate, an output gate and a cell, which can promote the ability to learn long-term dependencies.

4   Model Architecture

In this paper, we propose an effective model for skeleton-based action recognition, which contains a spatial reasoning network and a temporal stack learning network. The overall pipeline of our model is shown in Fig. 1. In this section, we will introduce these networks in detail.

4.1   Spatial Reasoning Network

Rich inherent structures of the human body that are involved in action recognition task, motivate us to design an effective architecture called spatial reasoning network to model the high-level spatial structural information within each frame. According to the general knowledge, the body can be decomposed into K parts, e.g. two arms, two legs and one trunk (shown in Fig. 2(a)), which express the knowledge of human body configuration.

For spatial structures, the spatial reasoning network encodes the coordinate vectors via two steps (see Fig. 1) to capture the high-level spatial features of skeleton structural relationships. First, the preliminary encoding process maps the coordinate vector of each part into the individual part feature e_k, $k \in \{1, ..., K\}$ with a linear layer that is shared among different body parts. Second, all part features e_k are fed into the proposed residual graph neural network (RGNN) to model the structural relationships between these body parts. Figure 2(b) shows a RGNN with three nodes.

For a RGNN, there are K nodes that correspond to the human body parts. At time step t, each node has a relation feature vector $r_k^t \in R^t$, where $R^t = \{r_1^t, ..., r_K^t\}$. And r_k^t denotes the spatial structural relationships of the part k with other parts. We initialize the r_k^t with the individual part feature e_k, such that $r_k^0 = e_k$. We use m_{ik}^t to denote the received message of node k from node

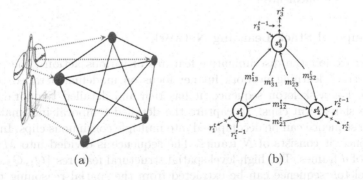

(a)   (b)

Fig. 2. The architecture of residual graph neural network (RGNN). (a) illustrates five human pose parts and a corresponding RGNN. (b) shows the principle of a RGNN with three nodes

i at time step t, where $i \in \{1, ..., K\}$. Furthermore, the received messages m_k^t of node k from all the neighbors Ω_{v_k} at time step t is defined as follows:

$$m_k^t = \sum_{i \in \Omega_{v_k}} m_{ik}^t$$

$$= \sum_{i \in \Omega_{v_k}} W_m s_i^{t-1} + b_m \qquad (4)$$

where s_i^{t-1} is the state of node i at time step $t - 1$, and a shared linear layer of weights W_m and biases b_m will be used to compute the messages for all nodes. After aggregating the messages, updating function of the node hidden state can be defined as follows:

$$s_k^t = f_{lstm}\left(r_k^{t-1}, m_k^t, s_k^{t-1}\right) \qquad (5)$$

where $f_{lstm}(\cdot)$ denotes the LSTM cell function. Then, we calculate the relation representation r_k^t at time step t via:

$$r_k^t = r_k^{t-1} + s_k^t \qquad (6)$$

The residual design of Eq. 6 aims to add the relationship features between each part based on the individual part features, so that the representations contain the fusion of both features.

After the RGNN is updated T times, we extract node-level output as the spatial structural relationships r_k^T of each part within each frame. Finally, the high-level spatial structural information q of human body for a frame can be computed as follows:

$$r^T = concat\left([r_1^T, r_2^T, ..., r_k^T]\right), \forall k \in K \qquad (7)$$

$$q = f_r\left(r^T\right) \qquad (8)$$

where $f_r(\cdot)$ is a linear layer.

4.2   Temporal Stack Learning Network

To further exploit the discriminative features of various actions, the proposed temporal stack learning network further focus on modeling detailed temporal dynamics. For a skeleton sequence, it has rich and detailed temporal dynamics in the short-term clips. To capture the detailed temporal information, the long-term sequence can be decomposed into multiple continuous clips. In a skeleton sequence, it consists of N frames. The sequence is divided into M clips at intervals of d frames. The high-level spatial structural features $\{Q_1, Q_2, ..., Q_M\}$ of the skeleton sequence can be extracted from the spatial reasoning network. $Q_m = \{q_{md+1}, q_{md+2}, ..., q_{(m+1)d}\}$ is the set of features of clip m, and q_n denotes the high-level spatial structural features of the skeleton frame $n, n \in \{1, ..., N\}$.

Our proposed temporal stack learning network is a two stream network: position network and velocity network (see Fig. 1). The two networks have the same architecture, which is composed of three skip-clip LSTM layers (shown in Fig. 3). The inputs of position network are the high-level spatial structural features $\{Q_1, Q_2, ..., Q_M\}$. The inputs of velocity network are the temporal differences $\{V_1, V_2, ..., V_M\}$ of the spatial features between two consecutive frames, where $V_m = \{v_{md+1}, v_{md+2}, ..., v_{(m+1)d}\}$. $v_n = q_n - q_{n-1}$ denotes the temporal difference of high-level spatial features for the skeleton frame n.

Skip-Clip LSTM Layer. In the skip-clip LSTM layer, there is an LSTM layer shared among the continuous clips (see Fig. 3). For the position network, the spatial features of continuous skeleton frames in the clip m will be fed into the shared LSTM to capture the short-term temporal dynamics in the first skip-clip LSTM layers:

$$h'_m = f_{LSTM}(Q_m)$$
$$= f_{LSTM}\left(\{q_{md+1}, q_{md+2}, ..., q_{(m+1)d}\}\right) \tag{9}$$

where h'_m is the last hidden state of shared LSTM for the clip m, $f_{LSTM}(\cdot)$ denotes the shared LSTM in the skip-clip LSTM layer.

Note that the inputs of LSTM cell between the first skip-clip LSTM layer and the other layers are different (see Fig. 3). In order to gain more dependency between two adjacent frames, the input x_t^l of LSTM cell for the l ($l \geq 2$) layer at time step t is defined as follows:

$$x_t^l = concat\left(h_{t-1}^{l-1}, h_t^{l-1}\right) \tag{10}$$

where h_t^{l-1} is the hidden state of the $l-1$ LSTM layer at time step t.

Then the representation of clip dynamics can be calculated as follows:

$$H_m = H_{m-1} + h'_m$$
$$= \sum_{i=1}^{m} h'_i \tag{11}$$

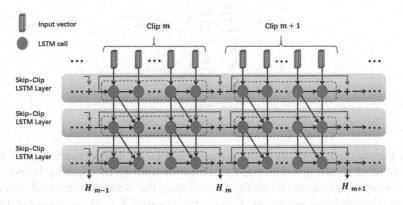

Fig. 3. The architecture of three skip-clip LSTM layers

where $\boldsymbol{H}_{m-1}$ and $\boldsymbol{H}_m$ denote the representations of clip $m-1$ and m, respectively. The representation $\boldsymbol{H}_m$ is to aggregate all the detailed temporal dynamics of the m-th clip and all previous clips to represent the long-term sequence. When feeding the clip m into the shared LSTM layer, we initialize the initial hidden state $\boldsymbol{h}_m^0$ of the shared LSTM with the $\boldsymbol{H}_{m-1}$, such that $\boldsymbol{h}_m^0 = \boldsymbol{H}_{m-1}$, which can inherit previous dynamics to learn the short-term dynamics of the m-th clip to maintain the dependency between clips.

The skip-clip LSTM layer can capture the temporal dynamics of the short-term clip based on the temporal information of previous clips. And the larger m is, the richer temporal dynamics $\boldsymbol{H}_m$ contains.

Learning the Classier. Finally, two linear layers are used to compute the scores for C classes:

$$\boldsymbol{O}_m = F_o(\boldsymbol{H}_m) \tag{12}$$

where $\boldsymbol{O}_m$ is the score of clip m and $\boldsymbol{O}_m = (o_{m1}, o_{m2}, ..., o_{mC})$, F_o denotes the two linear layers. And the output is fed to a softmax classifier to predict the probability being the ith class:

$$\hat{y}_{mi} = \frac{e^{o_{mi}}}{\sum_{j=1}^{C} e^{o_{mj}}}, i = 1, ..., C \tag{13}$$

where $\hat{y}_{mi}$ indicates the probability that the clip m is predicted as the ith class. And $\hat{\boldsymbol{y}}_m = (\hat{y}_{m1}, ..., \hat{y}_{mC})$ denotes the probability vector of clip m.

Our proposed temporal stack learning network is a two stream network, so the clip dynamic representations ($\boldsymbol{H}_m^p$, $\boldsymbol{H}_m^v$ and $\boldsymbol{H}_m^s$) of three modes will be captured. $\boldsymbol{H}_m^p$ and $\boldsymbol{H}_m^v$ denote the dynamic representations extracted from the position and velocity for the clip m, respectively. And $\boldsymbol{H}_m^s$ is the sum of $\boldsymbol{H}_m^p$ and $\boldsymbol{H}_m^v$. The probability vectors ($\hat{\boldsymbol{y}}_m^p$, $\hat{\boldsymbol{y}}_m^v$ and $\hat{\boldsymbol{y}}_m^s$) can be predicted from the network.

In order to optimize the model, we propose the clip based incremental losses for a skeleton sequence:

$$\mathcal{L}_p = -\sum_{m=1}^{M} \frac{m}{M} \sum_{i=1}^{C} y_i log \hat{y}_{mi}^p \tag{14}$$

$$\mathcal{L}_v = -\sum_{m=1}^{M} \frac{m}{M} \sum_{i=1}^{C} y_i log \hat{y}_{mi}^v \tag{15}$$

$$\mathcal{L}_s = -\sum_{m=1}^{M} \frac{m}{M} \sum_{i=1}^{C} y_i log \hat{y}_{mi}^s \tag{16}$$

where $\boldsymbol{y} = (y_1, ..., y_C)$ denotes the groundtruth label. The richer temporal information the clip contains, the greater the coefficient $\frac{m}{M}$ is. The clip-based incremental loss will promote the ability of modeling the detailed temporal dynamics for long-term skeleton sequences. Finally, the training loss of our model is defined as follows:

$$\mathcal{L} = \mathcal{L}_p + \mathcal{L}_v + \mathcal{L}_s \qquad (17)$$

Due to the mechanisms of skip-clip LSTM (see the Eq. 11), the representation H_M^s of clip M aggregates all the detailed temporal dynamics of the continuous clips from the position sequences and velocity sequences. In the testing process, we only use the probability vector $\hat{y}_M^s$ to predict the class of the skeleton sequence.

5   Experiments

To verify the effectiveness of our proposed model for skeleton-based action recognition, we perform extensive experiments on the NTU RGB+D dataset [24] and the SYSU 3D Human-Object Interaction dataset [8]. We also analyze the performance of our model with several variants.

5.1   Datasets and Experimental Settings

NTU RGB+D Dataset (NTU). This is the current largest action recognition dataset with joints annotations that are collected by Microsoft Kinect v2. It has 56880 video samples and contains 60 action classes in total. These actions are performed by 40 distinct subjects. It is recorded with three cameras simultaneously in different horizontal views. The joints annotations consist of 3D locations of 25 major body joints. [24] defines two standard evaluation protocols for this dataset: Cross-Subject and Cross-View. For Cross-Subject evaluation, the 40 subjects are split into training and testing groups. Each group consists of 20 subjects. For Cross-View evaluation, all the samples of camera 2 and 3 are used for training while the samples of camera 1 are used for testing.

SYSU 3D Human-Object Interaction Dataset (SYSU). This dataset contains 480 video samples in 12 action classes. These actions are performed by 40 subjects. There are 20 joints for each subject in the 3D skeleton sequences. There are two standard evaluation protocols [8] for this dataset. In the first setting (setting-1), for each activity class, half of the samples are used for training and the rest for testing. In the second setting (setting-2), half of subjects are used to train model and the rest for testing. For each setting, there is 30-fold cross validation.

Experimental Settings. In all our experiments, we set the hidden state dimension of RGNN to 256. For the NTU dataset, the human body is decomposed into $K = 8$ parts: two arms, two hands, two legs, one trunk and one head. For the SYSU dataset, there are $K = 5$ parts: two arms, two legs, and one trunk. We set the length $N = 100$ of skeleton sequences for the two datasets. The neuron size of LSTM cell in the skip-clip LSTM layer is 512. The learning rate, initiated with 0.0001, is reduced by multiplying it by 0.1 every 30 epochs. The batch sizes for the NTU dataset and the SYSU dataset are 64 and 10, respectively. The network is optimized using the ADAM optimizer [14]. Dropout with a probability of 0.5 is utilized to alleviate overfitting during training.

Table 1. The comparison results on NTU RGB+D dataset with Cross-Subject and Cross-View settings in accuracy (%)

Methods	Cross-Subject	Cross-View
HBRNN-L [4] (2015)	59.1	64.0
Part-aware LSTM [24] (2016)	62.9	70.3
Trust Gate ST-LSTM [18] (2016)	69.2	77.7
Two-stream RNN [28] (2017)	71.3	79.5
STA-LSTM [26] (2017)	73.4	81.2
Ensemble TS-LSTM [16] (2017)	74.6	81.3
Visualization CNN [19] (2017)	76.0	82.6
VA-LSTM [32] (2017)	79.4	87.6
ST-GCN [31] (2018)	81.5	88.3
SR-TSL (Ours)	**84.8**	**92.4**

5.2 Experimental Results

We compare the performance of our proposed model against several state-of-the-art approaches on the NTU dataset and SYSU dataset in Tables 1 and 2. These methods for skeleton-based action recognition can be divided into two categories: CNN-based methods [19,31] and LSTM-based methods [16,26,32].

As shown in Table 1, we can see that our proposed model achieves the best performances of 84.8% and 92.4% on the current largest NTU dataset. Our performances significantly outperform the state-of-the-art CNN-based method [31] by about 3.3% and 4.1% for cross-subject evaluation and cross-view evaluation, respectively. Our model belongs to the LSTM-based methods. Compared with VA-LSTM [32] that is the current best LSTM-based method for action recognition, our results are about 5.4% and 4.8% better than VA-LSTM on the NTU dataset. Ensemble TS-LSTM [16] is the most similar work to ours. The results of our model outperform by 10.2% and 11.1% compared with [16] in cross-subject evaluation and cross-view evaluation, respectively. As shown in Table 2, our proposed model achieves the best performances of 80.7% and 81.9% on SYSU dataset, which significantly outperforms the state-of-the-art approach [32] by about 3.8% and 4.4% for setting-1 and setting-2, respectively.

Table 2. The comparison results on SYSU dataset in accuracy (%)

Methods	Setting-1	Setting-2
LAFF [9] (2016)	-	54.2
Dynamic Skeletons [8] (2015)	75.5	76.9
VA-LSTM [32] (2017)	76.9	77.5
SR-TSL (Ours)	**80.7**	**81.9**

Table 3. The comparison results on NTU and SYSU dataset in accuracy (%). We compare the performances of several variants and our proposed model to verify the effectiveness of our model

Methods	NTU		SYSU	
	Cross-Subject	Cross-View	Setting-1	Setting-2
FC + LSTM	77.0	84.7	39.9	40.7
SRN + LSTM	78.7	87.3	42.1	44.4
FC + TSLN	83.8	91.6	77.3	77.4
SR-TSL(Position)	78.8	88.2	77.1	76.9
SR-TSL(Velocity)	82.2	90.6	71.7	71.8
SR-TSL (Ours)	**84.8**	**92.4**	**80.7**	**81.9**

5.3   Model Analysis

We analyze the proposed model by comparing it with several baselines. The comparison results demonstrate the effectiveness of our model. There are two key ingredients in the proposed model: spatial reasoning network (SRN) and temporal stack learning network (TSLN). To analyze the role of each component, we compare our model with several combinations of these components. Each variant is evaluated on NTU dataset.

FC+LSTM. For this model, the coordinate vectors of each body part are encoded with the linear layer and three LSTM layers are used to model the sequence dynamics. It is also a two stream network to learn the temporal dynamics from position and velocity.

SRN+LSTM. Compared with FC+LSTM, this model uses spatial reasoning network to capture the high-level spatial structural features of skeleton sequences within each frame.

FC+TSLN. Compared with FC+LSTM, the temporal stack learning network replaces three LSTM layers to learn the detailed sequence dynamics for skeleton sequences.

SR-TSL (Position). Compared with our proposed model, the temporal stack learning network of this model only contains the position network.

SR-TSL (Velocity). Compared with our proposed model, the temporal stack learning network of this model only contains the velocity network.

SR-TSL. It denotes our proposed model.

Table 3 shows the comparison results of the variants and our proposed model on NTU and SYSU dataset. We can observe that our model can obviously increase the performances on both datasets. And the increased performances showed in Table 3 illustrate that the spatial reasoning network and temporal stack learning network are effective for the skeleton based action recognition, especially the temporal stack learning network. Furthermore, the two stream architecture of temporal stack learning network is efficient to learn the temporal dynamics from the velocity sequence and position sequence. Figure 4 shows

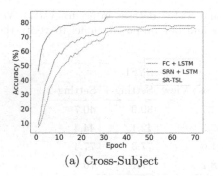 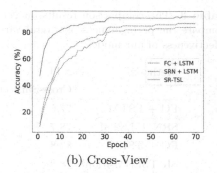

(a) Cross-Subject   (b) Cross-View

Fig. 4. The accuracy of the baselines and our model on the testing set of NTU RGB+D dataset during learning phase. (a) shows the comparison results for cross-subject evaluation, and (b) is for cross-view evaluation

the accuracy of the baselines and our model on the testing set of NTU RGB+D dataset during learning phase. We can see that our proposed model can speed up convergence and obviously improve the performance. We also show the process of temporal stack learning in Fig. 5. With the increase of m, the much richer temporal information is contained in the representation of a sequence. And the network can consider more temporal dynamics of the details to recognize human action, so as to improve the accuracy. The above results illustrate the proposed SR-TSL can effectively speed up convergence and obviously improve the performance.

We also discuss the effect of two important hyper-parameters: the time step T of the RGNN and the length d of clips. The comparison results are shown in Tables 4 and 5. For the time step T, we can find that the performance increases by a small amount when increasing T, and saturates soon. We think that the high-level spatial structural features between a small number of body parts can be learned quickly. For the length d of clips, with the increase of d, the perfor-

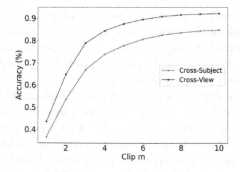

Fig. 5. The accuracy of the increasing clips on the testing set of NTU RGB+D dataset

Table 4. The comparison results on NTU dataset in accuracy (%). We compare several models that have different time steps for the RGNN to show the improvements achieved at every step

RGNN	Cross-Subject	Cross-View
$T = 1$	84.1	92.0
$T = 2$	84.4	92.2
$T = 3$	84.5	**92.4**
$T = 4$	84.7	92.3
$T = 5$	**84.8**	92.3
$T = 6$	84.7	92.2

Table 5. The comparison results on NTU dataset in accuracy (%). We compare the performances of several proposed models that have different the length d of clips

TSLN	Cross-Subject	Cross-View
$d = 2$	81.6	90.6
$d = 4$	84.1	91.4
$d = 6$	84.5	**92.4**
$d = 8$	84.5	92.3
$d = 10$	**84.8**	92.1
$d = 15$	84.7	92.2
$d = 20$	84.4	92.1

mance is significantly improved and then saturated. The reason of saturation is that learning short-term dynamic does not require too many frames. The above experimental results illustrate that our proposed model is effective for skeleton-based action recognition.

6   Conclusions

In this paper, we propose a novel model with spatial reasoning and temporal stack learning for long-term skeleton based action recognition, which achieves much better results than the state-of-the-art methods. The spatial reasoning network can capture the high-level spatial structural information within each frame, while the temporal stack learning network can model the detailed temporal dynamics of skeleton sequences. We also propose a clip-based incremental loss to further improve the ability of stack learning, which provides an effective way to solve long-term sequence optimization. With extensive experiments on the current largest NTU RGB+D dataset and SYSU dataset, we verify the effectiveness of our model for the skeleton based action recognition. In the future, we will further analyze the error samples to improve the model, and consider more contextual information, such as interactions, to aid action recognition.

Acknowledgements. This work is jointly supported by National Key Research and Development Program of China (2016YFB1001000), National Natural Science Foundation of China (61525306, 61633021, 61721004, 61420106015, 61572504), Scientific Foundation of State Grid Corporation of China.

References

1. Aggarwal, J.K., Ryoo, M.S.: Human activity analysis: a review. ACM Comput. Surv. **43**(3), 16 (2011)
2. Aggarwal, J.K., Xia, L.: Human activity recognition from 3d data: a review. Pattern Recognit. Lett. **48**, 70–80 (2014)
3. Cao, Z., Simon, T., Wei, S.E., Sheikh, Y.: Realtime multi-person 2d pose estimation using part affinity fields. In: CVPR (2017)
4. Du, Y., Wang, W., Wang, L.: Hierarchical recurrent neural network for skeleton based action recognition. In: CVPR (2015)
5. Duvenaud, D.K., et al.: Convolutional networks on graphs for learning molecular fingerprints. In: NIPS (2015)
6. Henaff, M., Bruna, J., LeCun, Y.: Deep convolutional networks on graph-structured data. arXiv preprint arXiv:1506.05163 (2015)
7. Hochreiter, S., Schmidhuber, J.: Long short-term memory. Neural Comput. **9**(8), 1735–1780 (1997)
8. Hu, J.F., Zheng, W.S., Lai, J., Zhang, J.: Jointly learning heterogeneous features for RGB-D activity recognition. In: CVPR (2015)
9. Hu, J.-F., Zheng, W.-S., Ma, L., Wang, G., Lai, J.: Real-time RGB-D activity prediction by soft regression. In: Leibe, B., Matas, J., Sebe, N., Welling, M. (eds.) ECCV 2016. LNCS, vol. 9905, pp. 280–296. Springer, Cham (2016). https://doi.org/10.1007/978-3-319-46448-0_17
10. Hussein, M.E., Torki, M., Gowayyed, M.A., El-Saban, M.: Human action recognition using a temporal hierarchy of covariance descriptors on 3d joint locations. In: IJCAI (2013)
11. Johansson, G.: Visual perception of biological motion and a model for its analysis. Percept. Psychophys. **14**(2), 201–211 (1973)
12. Ke, Q., Bennamoun, M., An, S., Sohel, F., Boussaid, F.: A new representation of skeleton sequences for 3d action recognition. In: CVPR (2017)
13. Kim, T.S., Reiter, A.: Interpretable 3d human action analysis with temporal convolutional networks. In: CVPR Workshops (2017)
14. Kingma, D.P., Ba, J.: Adam: a method for stochastic optimization. In: ICLR (2015)
15. Bruna, J., Zaremba, W., Szlam, A., LeCun, Y.: Spectral networks and locally connected networks on graphs. In: ICLR (2014)
16. Lee, I., Kim, D., Kang, S., Lee, S.: Ensemble deep learning for skeleton-based action recognition using temporal sliding LSTM networks. In: ICCV (2017)
17. Li, R., Tapaswi, M., Liao, R., Jia, J., Urtasun, R., Fidler, S.: Situation recognition with graph neural networks. In: ICCV (2017)
18. Liu, J., Shahroudy, A., Xu, D., Wang, G.: Spatio-temporal LSTM with trust gates for 3D human action recognition. In: Leibe, B., Matas, J., Sebe, N., Welling, M. (eds.) ECCV 2016. LNCS, vol. 9907, pp. 816–833. Springer, Cham (2016). https://doi.org/10.1007/978-3-319-46487-9_50
19. Liu, M., Liu, H., Chen, C.: Enhanced skeleton visualization for view invariant human action recognition. Pattern Recognit. **68**, 346–362 (2017)
20. Niepert, M., Ahmed, M., Kutzkov, K.: Learning convolutional neural networks for graphs. In: ICML (2016)
21. Poppe, R.: A survey on vision-based human action recognition. Image Vis. Comput. **28**(6), 976–990 (2010)
22. Qi, X., Liao, R., Jia, J., Fidler, S., Urtasun, R.: 3d graph neural networks for RGBD semantic segmentation. In: ICCV (2017)

23. Scarselli, F., Gori, M., Tsoi, A.C., Hagenbuchner, M., Monfardini, G.: The graph neural network model. IEEE Trans. Neural Netw. **20**(1), 61–80 (2009)
24. Shahroudy, A., Liu, J., Ng, T.T., Wang, G.: NTU RGB+D: a large scale dataset for 3d human activity analysis. In: CVPR (2016)
25. Simonyan, K., Zisserman, A.: Two-stream convolutional networks for action recognition in videos. In: NIPS (2014)
26. Song, S., Lan, C., Xing, J., Zeng, W., Liu, J.: An end-to-end spatio-temporal attention model for human action recognition from skeleton data. In: AAAI (2017)
27. Vemulapalli, R., Arrate, F., Chellappa, R.: Human action recognition by representing 3d skeletons as points in a lie group. In: CVPR (2014)
28. Wang, H., Wang, L.: Modeling temporal dynamics and spatial configurations of actions using two-stream recurrent neural networks. In: CVPR (2017)
29. Wang, J., Liu, Z., Wu, Y., Yuan, J.: Mining actionlet ensemble for action recognition with depth cameras. In: CVPR (2012)
30. Weinland, D., Ronfard, R., Boyer, E.: A survey of vision-based methods for action representation, segmentation and recognition. Comput. Vis. Image Underst. **115**(2), 224–241 (2011)
31. Yan, S., Xiong, Y., Lin, D., Tang, X.: Spatial temporal graph convolutional networks for skeleton-based action recognition. In: AAAI (2018)
32. Zhang, P., Lan, C., Xing, J., Zeng, W., Xue, J., Zheng, N.: View adaptive recurrent neural networks for high performance human action recognition from skeleton data. In: ICCV (2017)
33. Zhang, Z.: Microsoft kinect sensor and its effect. IEEE Multimedia **19**(2), 4–10 (2012)
34. Zhu, W., et al.: Co-occurrence feature learning for skeleton based action recognition using regularized deep LSTM networks. In: AAAI (2016)

Fictitious GAN: Training GANs with Historical Models

Hao Ge[(✉)], Yin Xia, Xu Chen, Randall Berry, and Ying Wu

Northwestern University, Evanston, IL, USA
{haoge2013,yinxia2012,chenx}@u.northwestern.edu,
{rberry,yingwu}@northwestern.edu

Abstract. Generative adversarial networks (GANs) are powerful tools for learning generative models. In practice, the training may suffer from lack of convergence. GANs are commonly viewed as a two-player zero-sum game between two neural networks. Here, we leverage this game theoretic view to study the convergence behavior of the training process. Inspired by the fictitious play learning process, a novel training method, referred to as Fictitious GAN, is introduced. Fictitious GAN trains the deep neural networks using a mixture of historical models. Specifically, the discriminator (resp. generator) is updated according to the best-response to the *mixture* outputs from a sequence of previously trained generators (resp. discriminators). It is shown that Fictitious GAN can effectively resolve some convergence issues that cannot be resolved by the standard training approach. It is proved that asymptotically the average of the generator outputs has the same distribution as the data samples.

1 Introduction

1.1 Generative Adversarial Networks

Generative adversarial networks (GANs) are a powerful framework for learning generative models. They have witnessed successful applications in a wide range of fields, including image synthesis [23,25], image super-resolution [14,15], and anomaly detection [28]. A GAN maintains two deep neural networks: the discriminator and the generator. The generator aims to produce samples that resemble the data distribution, while the discriminator aims to distinguish the generated samples and the data samples.

Mathematically, the standard GAN training aims to solve the following optimization problem:

$$\min_{G} \max_{D} V(G, D) = \mathsf{E}_{\boldsymbol{x} \sim p_d(\boldsymbol{x})}\{\log D(\boldsymbol{x})\} + \mathsf{E}_{\boldsymbol{z} \sim p_z(\boldsymbol{z})}\{\log(1 - D(G(\boldsymbol{z})))\}. \quad (1)$$

Y. Wu—First three authors have equal contributions.

Electronic supplementary material The online version of this chapter (https://doi.org/10.1007/978-3-030-01246-5_8) contains supplementary material, which is available to authorized users.

© Springer Nature Switzerland AG 2018
V. Ferrari et al. (Eds.): ECCV 2018, LNCS 11205, pp. 122–137, 2018.
https://doi.org/10.1007/978-3-030-01246-5_8

The global optimum point is reached when the generated distribution p_g, which is the distribution of $G(z)$ given $z \sim p_z(z)$, is equal to the data distribution. The optimal point is reached based on the assumption that the discriminator and generator are *jointly* optimized. Practical training of GANs, however, may not satisfy this assumption. In some training process, instead of ideal joint optimization, the discriminator and generator seek for best response by turns, namely the discriminator (resp. generator) is alternately updated with the generator (resp. discriminator) fixed.

Another conventional training methods are based on a gradient descent form of GAN optimization. In particular, they simultaneously take small gradient steps in both generator and discriminator parameters in each training iteration [9]. There have been some studies on the convergence behaviors of gradient-based training. The local convergence behavior has been studied in [11,18]. The gradient-based optimization is proved to converge assuming that the discriminator and the generator is convex over the network parameters [20]. The inherent connection between gradient-based training and primal-dual subgradient methods for solving convex optimizations is built in [4].

Despite the promising practical applications, a lot of works still witness the lack of convergence behaviors in training GANs. Two common failure modes are oscillation and mode collapse, where the generator only produces a small family of samples [3,9,16]. One important observation in [17] is that such non convergence behaviors stem from the fact that each generator update step is a partial collapse towards a delta function, which is the best response to the objective function. This motivates the study of this paper on the dynamics of best-response training and the proposal of a novel training method to address these convergence issues.

1.2   Contributions

In this paper, we view GANs as a two-player zero-sum game and the training process as a repeated game. For the optimal solution to Eq. (1), the corresponding generated distribution and discriminator (p_g^*, D^*) is shown to be the unique Nash equilibrium in the game. Inspired by the well-established fictitious play mechanism in game theory, we propose a novel training algorithm to resolve the convergence issue and find this Nash equilibrium.

The proposed training algorithm is referred to as Fictitious GAN, where the discriminator (resp. generator) is updated based on the mixed outputs from the sequence of historical trained generators (resp. discriminators). The previously trained models actually carry important information and can be utilized for the updates of the new model. We prove that Fictitious GAN achieves the optimal solution to Eq. (1). In particular, the discriminator outputs converge to the optimum discriminator function and the mixed output from the sequence of trained generators converges to the data distribution.

Moreover, Fictitious GAN can be regarded as a meta-algorithm that can be applied on top of existing GAN variants. Both synthetic data and real-world image datasets are used to demonstrate the improved performance due to the fictitious training mechanism.

2 Related Works

The idea of training using multiple GAN models have been considered in other works. In [1,12], the mixed outputs of multiple generators is used to approximate the data distribution. The multiple generators with a modified loss function have been used to alleviate the mode collapse problem [7]. In [17], the generator is updated based on a sequence of unrolled discriminators. In [19], dual discriminators are used to combine the Kullback-Leibler (KL) divergence and reverse KL divergences into a unified objective function. Using an ensemble of discriminators or GAN models has shown promising performance [6,27]. One distinguishing difference between the above-mentioned methods and our proposed method is that in our method only a *single* deep neural network is trained at each training iteration, while multiple generators (resp. discriminators) only provide inputs to a single discriminator (resp. generators) at each training stage. Moreover, the outputs from multiple networks is simply uniformly averaged and serves as input to the target training network, while other works need to train the optimal weights to average the network models. The proposed method thus has a much lower computational complexity.

The use of historical models have been proposed as a heuristic method to increase the diversity of generated samples [24], while the theoretical convergence guarantee is lacking. Game theoretic approaches have been utilized to achieve a resource-bounded Nash equilibrium in GANs [21]. Another closely related work to this paper is the recent work [10] that applies the Follow-the-Regularized-Leader (FTRL) algorithm to train GANs. In their work, the historical models are also utilized for online learning. There are at least two distinct features in our work. First, we borrow the idea of fictitious play from game theory to prove convergence to the Nash equilibrium for any GAN architectures assuming that networks have enough capacity, while [10] only proves convergence for semi-shallow architectures. Secondly, we prove that a *single* discriminator, instead of a mixture of multiple discriminators, asymptotically converges to the optimal discriminator. This provides important design guidelines for the training, where asymptotically a single discriminator needs to be maintained.[1]

3 Toy Examples

In this section, we use two toy examples to show that both the best-response approach and the gradient-based training approach may oscillate for simple minimax optimization problems.

---

[1] Due to space constraints, all the proofs in the paper are omitted and can be found in the Supplementary materials.

Take the GAN framework for instance, for the best-response training approach, the discriminator and the generator are updated to the optimum point at each iteration. Mathematically, the discriminator and the generator is alternately updated according to the following rules:

$$\max_{D} \mathsf{E}_{x \sim p_d(x)} \{\log D(x)\} + \mathsf{E}_{z \sim p_z(z)} \{\log(1 - D(G(z)))\} \qquad (2)$$

$$\min_{G} \mathsf{E}_{z \sim p_z(z)} \{\log(1 - D(G(z)))\} \qquad (3)$$

Example 1. Let the data follow the Bernoulli distribution $p_d \sim$ Bernoulli (a), where $0 < a < 1$. Suppose the initial generated distribution $p_g \sim$ Bernoulli (b), where $b \neq a$. We show that in the best-response training process, the generated distribution oscillates between $p_g \sim$ Bernoulli (1) and $p_g \sim$ Bernoulli (0).

We show the oscillation phenomenon in training using best-response training approach. To minimize (3), it is equivalent to find p_g such that $\mathsf{E}_{x \sim p_g(x)} \{\log(1 - D(x))\}$ is minimized. At each iteration, the output distribution of the updated generator would concentrate all the probability mass at $x = 0$ if $D(0) > D(1)$, or at $x = 1$ if $D(0) < D(1)$. Suppose $p_g(x) = 1\{x = 0\}$, where $1\{\cdot\}$ is the indicator function, then by solving (2), the discriminator at the next iteration is updated as

$$D(x) = \frac{p_d(x)}{p_d(x) + p_g(x)}, \qquad (4)$$

which yields $D(1) = 1$ and $D(0) < D(1)$. Therefore, the generated distribution at the next iteration becomes $p_g(x) = 1\{x = 1\}$. The oscillation between $p_g \sim$ Bernoulli (1) and $p_g \sim$ Bernoulli (0) continues by induction. A similar phenomenon can be observed for Wasserstein GAN.

The first toy example implies that the oscillation behavior is a fundamental problem to the iterative best-response training. In practical training of GANs, instead of finding the best response, the discriminator and generator are updated based on gradient descent towards the best-response of the objective function. However, the next example adapted from [8] demonstrates the failure of convergence in a simple minimax problem using a gradient-based method.

Example 2. Consider the following minimax problem:

$$\min_{-10 \leq y \leq 10} \max_{-10 \leq x \leq 10} xy. \qquad (5)$$

Consider the gradient based training approach with step size Δ. The update rule of x and y is:

$$\begin{bmatrix} x_{n+1} \\ y_{n+1} \end{bmatrix} = \begin{bmatrix} 1 & \Delta \\ -\Delta & 1 \end{bmatrix} \begin{bmatrix} x_n \\ y_n \end{bmatrix}. \qquad (6)$$

By using the knowledge of eigenvalues and eigenvectors, we can obtain

$$\begin{bmatrix} x_n \\ y_n \end{bmatrix} = \begin{bmatrix} -c_1^n c_2 \sin(n\theta + \beta) \\ c_1^n c_2 \cos(n\theta + \beta) \end{bmatrix}, \qquad (7)$$

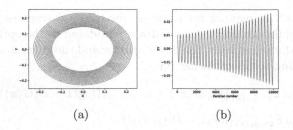

(a)   (b)

Fig. 1. Performance of gradient method with fixed step size for Example 2. (a) illustrates the choices of x and y as iteration processes, the red point $(0.1, 0.1)$ is the initial value. (b) illustrates the value of xy as a function of iteration numbers.

where $c_1 = \sqrt{1 + \Delta^2} > 1$ and c_2, θ, β are constants depending on the initial (x_0, y_0). As $n \to \infty$, since $c_1 > 1$, the process will not converge.

Figure 1 shows the performance of gradient based approach, the initial value $(x_0, y_0) = (0.1, 0.1)$ and step size is 0.01. It can be seen that both players' actions do not converge. This toy example shows that even the gradient based approach with arbitrarily small step size may not converge.

We will revisit the convergence behavior in the context of game theory. A well-established learning mechanism in game theory naturally leads to a training algorithm that resolves the non-convergence issues of these two toy examples.

4   Nash Equilibrium in Zero-Sum Games

In this section, we introduce the two-player zero-sum game and describe the learning mechanism of fictitious play, which provably achieves a Nash equilibrium of the game. We will show that the minimax optimization of GAN can be formulated as a two-player zero-sum game, where the optimal solution corresponds to the unique Nash equilibrium in the game. In the next section we will propose a training algorithm which simulates the fictitious play mechanism and provably achieves the optimal solution.

4.1   Zero-Sum Games

We start with some definitions in game theory. A game consists of a set of n players, who are rational and take actions to maximize their own utilities. Each player i chooses a pure strategy s_i from the strategy space $S_i = \{s_{i,0}, \cdots, s_{i,m-1}\}$. Here player i has m strategies in her strategy space. A utility function $u_i(s_i, s_{-i})$, which is defined over all players' strategies, indicates the outcome for player i, where the subscript $-i$ stands for all players excluding player i. There are two kinds of strategies, pure and mixed strategy. A pure strategy provides a specific action that a player will follow for any possible situation in a game, while a mixed strategy $\mu_i = (p_i(s_{i,0}), \cdots, p_i(s_{i,m-1}))$ for player i is a probability distribution over the m pure strategies in her strategy space with $\sum_j p_i(s_{i,j}) = 1$. The set of possible mixed strategies available to player i is denoted by ΔS_i. The expected utility of mixed strategy (μ_i, μ_{-i}) for player i is

$$\mathsf{E}\{u_i(\mu_i, \mu_{-i})\} = \sum_{s_i \in S_i} \sum_{s_{-i} \in S_{-i}} u_i(s_i, s_{-i}) p_i(s_i) p_{-i}(s_{-i}). \tag{8}$$

For ease of notation, we write $u_i(\mu_i, \mu_{-i})$ as $\mathsf{E}\{u_i(\mu_i, \mu_{-i})\}$ in the following. Note that a pure strategy can be expressed as a mixed strategy that places probability 1 on a single pure strategy and probability 0 on the others. A game is referred to as a finite game or a continuous game, if the strategy space is finite or nonempty and compact, respectively. In a continuous game, the mixed strategy indicates a probability density function (pdf) over the strategy space.

Definition 1. *For player i, a strategy μ_i^* is called a best response to others' strategy μ_{-i} if $u_i(\mu_i^*, \mu_{-i}) \geq u_i(\mu_i, \mu_{-i})$ for any $\mu_i \in \Delta S_i$.*

Definition 2. *A set of mixed strategies $\mu^* = (\mu_1^*, \mu_2^*, \cdots, \mu_n^*)$ is a Nash equilibrium if, for every player i, μ_i^* is a best response to the strategies μ_{-i}^* played by the other players in this game.*

Definition 3. *A zero-sum game is one in which each player's gain or loss is exactly balanced by the others' loss or gain and the sum of the players' payoff is always zero.*

Now we focus on a continuous two-player zero-sum game. In such a game, given the strategy pair (μ_1, μ_2), player 1 has a utility of $u(\mu_1, \mu_2)$, while player 2 has a utility of $-u(\mu_1, \mu_2)$. In the framework of GAN, the training objective (1) can be regarded as a two-player zero-sum game, where the generator and discriminator are two players with utility functions $-V(G, D)$ and $V(G, D)$, respectively. Both of them aim to maximize their utility and the sum of their utilities is zero.

Knowing the opponent is always seeking to maximize its utility, Player 1 and 2 choose strategies according to

$$\mu_1^* = \operatorname*{argmax}_{\mu_1 \in \Delta S_1} \min_{\mu_2 \in \Delta S_2} u(\mu_1, \mu_2) \tag{9}$$

$$\mu_2^* = \operatorname*{argmin}_{\mu_2 \in \Delta S_2} \max_{\mu_1 \in \Delta S_1} u(\mu_1, \mu_2). \tag{10}$$

Define $\underline{v} = \max_{\mu_1 \in \Delta S_1} \min_{\mu_2 \in \Delta S_2} u(\mu_1, \mu_2)$ and $\bar{v} = \min_{\mu_2 \in \Delta S_2} \max_{\mu_1 \in \Delta S_1} u(\mu_1, \mu_2)$ as the lower value and upper value of the game, respectively. Generally, $\underline{v} \leq \bar{v}$. Sion [26] showed that these two values coincide under some regularity conditions:

Theorem 1 (Sion's Minimax Theorem [26]). *Let X and Y be convex, compact spaces, and $f: X \times Y \to \mathbb{R}$. If for any $x \in X$, $f(x, \cdot)$ is upper semi-continuous and quasi-concave on Y and for any $y \in Y$, $f(\cdot, y)$ is lower semi-continuous and quasi-convex on X, then $\inf_{x \in X} \sup_{y \in Y} f(x, y) = \sup_{y \in Y} \inf_{x \in X} f(x, y)$.*

Hence, in a zero-sum game, if the utility function $u(\mu_1, \mu_2)$ satisfies the conditions in Theorem 1, then $\underline{v} = \bar{v}$. We refer to $v = \underline{v} = \bar{v}$ as the *value of the game*. We further show that a Nash equilibrium of the zero-sum game achieves the value of the game.

Corollary 1. *In a two-player zero-sum game with the utility function satisfying the conditions in Theorem 1, if a strategy (μ_1^*, μ_2^*) is a Nash equilibrium, then $u(\mu_1^*, \mu_2^*) = v$.*

Corollary 1 implies that if we have an algorithm that achieves a Nash equilibrium of a zero-sum game, we may utilize this algorithm to optimally train a GAN. We next describe a learning mechanism to achieve a Nash equilibrium.

4.2   Fictitious Play

Suppose the zero-sum game is played repeatedly between two rational players, then each player may try to infer her opponent's strategy. Let $s_i^n \in S_i$ denote the action taken by player i at time n. At time n, given the previous actions $\{s_2^0, s_2^1, \cdots, s_2^{n-1}\}$ chosen by player 2, one good hypothesis is that player 2 is using stationary mixed strategies and chooses strategy s_2^t, $0 \le t \le n - 1$, with probability $\frac{1}{n}$. Here we use the empirical frequency to approximate the probability in mixed strategies. Under this hypothesis, the best response for player 1 at time n is to choose the strategy μ_1^* satisfying:

$$\mu_1^* = \underset{\mu_1 \in \Delta S_1}{\text{argmax}}\, u(\mu_1, \mu_2^n), \tag{11}$$

where μ_2^n is the empirical distribution of player 2's historical actions. Similarly, player 2 can choose the best response assuming player 1 is choosing its strategy according to the empirical distribution of the historical actions.

Notice that the expected utility is a linear combination of utilities under different pure strategies, hence for any hypothesis μ_{-i}^n, player i can find a pure strategy s_i^n as a best response. Therefore, we further assume each player plays the best pure response at each round. In game theory this learning rule is called *fictitious play*, proposed by Brown [2].

Danskin [5] showed that for any continuous zero-sum games with any initial strategy profile, fictitious play will converge. This important result is summarized in the following theorem.

Theorem 2. *Let $u(s_1, s_2)$ be a continuous function defined on the direct product of two compact sets S_1 and S_2. The pure strategy sequences $\{s_1^n\}$ and $\{s_2^n\}$ are defined as follows: s_1^0 and s_2^0 are arbitrary, and*

$$s_1^n \in \underset{s_1 \in S_1}{\text{argmax}}\, \frac{1}{n} \sum_{k=0}^{n-1} u(s_1, s_2^k), \quad s_2^n \in \underset{s_2 \in S_2}{\text{argmin}}\, \frac{1}{n} \sum_{k=0}^{n-1} u(s_1^k, s_2), \tag{12}$$

then

$$\lim_{n \to \infty} \frac{1}{n} \sum_{k=0}^{n-1} u(s_1^n, s_2^k) = \lim_{n \to \infty} \frac{1}{n} \sum_{k=0}^{n-1} u(s_1^k, s_2^n) = v, \tag{13}$$

where v is the value of the game.

4.3   Effectiveness of Fictitious Play

In this section, we show that fictitious play enables the convergence of learning to the optimal solution for the two counter-examples in Sect. 3.

Example 1: Figure 2 shows the performance of the best-response approach, where the data follows a Bernoulli distribution $p_d \sim$ Bernoulli (0.25), the initialization is $D(x) = x$ for $x \in [0, 1]$ and the initial generated distribution $p_g \sim$ Bernoulli (0.1). It can be seen that the generated distribution based on best responses oscillates between $p_g(x = 0) = 1$ and $p_g(x = 1) = 1$.

Assuming best response at each iteration n, under fictitious play, the discriminator is updated according to $D_n = \arg\max_D \frac{1}{n} \sum_{w=0}^{n-1} V(p_{g,w}, D)$ and the generated distribution is updated according to $p_{g,n} = \arg\max_{p_g} \frac{1}{n} \sum_{w=0}^{n-1} V(p_g, D_w)$. Figure 2 shows the change of D_n and the empirical mean of the generated distributions $\bar{p}_{g,n} = \frac{1}{n} \sum_{w=0}^{n-1} p_{g,w}$ as training proceeds. Although the best-response generated distribution at each iteration oscillates as in Fig. 2a, the learning mechanism of fictitious play makes the empirical mean $\bar{p}_{g,n}$ converge to the data distribution.

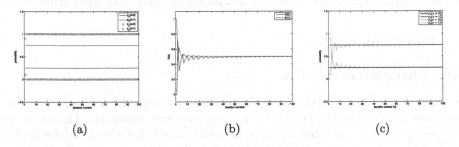

(a)   (b)   (c)

Fig. 2. Performance of best-response training for Example 1. (a) is Bernoulli distribution of p_g assuming best-response updates. (b) illustrates $D(x)$ in Fictitious GAN assuming best response at each training iteration. (c) illustrates the average of $p_g(x)$ in Fictitious GAN assuming best response at each training iteration.

Example 2: At each iteration n, player 1 chooses $x = \arg\max_x \frac{1}{n} \sum_{i=0}^{n-1} xy_i$, which is equal to $10 * \text{sign}(\sum_{i=0}^{n-1} y_i)$. Similarly, player 2 chooses y according to $y = -10 * \text{sign}(\sum_{i=0}^{n-1} x_i)$. Hence regardless of what the initial condition is, both players will only choose 10 or -10 at each iteration. Consequently, as iteration goes to infinity, the empirical mixed strategy only proposes density on 10 and -10. It is proved in the Supplementary material that the mixed strategy (σ_1^*, σ_2^*) that both players choose 10 and -10 with probability $\frac{1}{2}$ is a Nash equilibrium for this game. Figure 3 shows that under fictitious play, both players' empirical mixed strategy converges to the Nash equilibrium and the expected utility for each player converges to 0.

One important observation is fictitious play can provide the Nash equilibrium if the equilibrium is unique in the game. However, if there exist multiple Nash

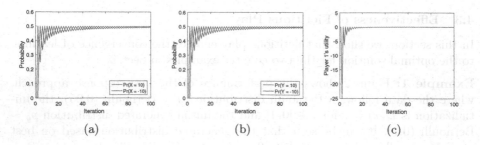

Fig. 3. (a) and (b) illustrate the empirical distribution of x and y at 10 and -10, respectively. (c) illustrates the expected utility for player 1 under fictitious play.

equilibriums, different initialization may yield different solutions. In the above example, it is easy to check $(0,0)$ is also a Nash equilibrium, which means both players always choose 0, but fictitious play can lead to this solution only when the initialization is $(0,0)$. The good thing we show in the next section is, due to the special structure of GAN (the utility function is linear over generated distribution), fictitious play can help us find the desired Nash equilibrium.

5   Fictitious GAN

5.1   Algorithm Description

As discussed in the last section, the competition between the generator and discriminator in GAN can be modeled as a two-player zero-sum game. The following theorem proved in the supplementary material shows that the optimal solution of (1) is actually a unique Nash equilibrium in the game.

Theorem 3. *Consider* (1) *as a two-player zero-sum game. The optimal solution of* (1) *with* $p_g^* = p_d$ *and* $D^*(x) = 1/2$ *is a unique Nash equilibrium in this game. The value of the game is* $-\log 4$.

By relating GAN with the two-player zero-sum game, we can design a training algorithm to simulate the fictitious play such that the training outcome converges to the Nash equilibrium

Fictitious GAN, as described in Algorithm 1, adapts the fictitious play learning mechanism to train GANs. We use two queues $\mathcal{D}$ and $\mathcal{G}$ to store the historically trained models of the discriminator and the generator, respectively. At each iteration, the discriminator (resp. generator) is updated according to the best response to $V(G, D)$ assuming that the generator (resp. discriminator) chooses a historical strategy uniformly at random. Mathematically, the discriminator and generator are updated according to (14) and (15), where the outputs due to the generator and the discriminator is mixed uniformly at random from the previously trained models. Note the back-propagation is still performed on a single neural network at each training step. Different from standard training approaches, we perform k_0 gradient descent updates when training the discriminator and the generator in order to achieve the best response. In practical learning, queues $\mathcal{D}$ and $\mathcal{G}$ are maintained with a fixed size. The oldest model is discarded if the queue is full when we update the discriminator or the generator.

Algorithm 1. Fictitious GAN training algorithm.

Initialization: Set $\mathcal{D}$ and $\mathcal{G}$ as the queues to store the historical models of the discriminators and the generators, respectively.

while the stopping criterion is not met **do**

    for $k = 1, \cdots, k_0$ **do**

        Sample data via minibatch $x_1, \cdots, x_m$.

        Sample noise via minibatch $z_1, \cdots, z_m$.

        Update the discriminator via gradient ascent:

$$\nabla_{\boldsymbol{\theta}_d} \frac{1}{m} \sum_{i=1}^{m} \left[\log(D(\boldsymbol{x}_i)) + \frac{1}{|\mathcal{G}|} \sum_{G_w \in \mathcal{G}} \log(1 - D(G_w(\boldsymbol{z}_i))) \right]. \qquad (14)$$

    end for

    for $k = 1, \cdots, k_0$ **do**

        Sample noise via minibatch $z_1, \cdots, z_m$.

        Update the generator via gradient descent:

$$\nabla_{\boldsymbol{\theta}_g} \left[\frac{1}{m|\mathcal{G}|} \sum_{i=1}^{m} \sum_{D_w \in \mathcal{D}} \log(1 - D_w(G(\boldsymbol{z}_i))) \right]. \qquad (15)$$

    end for

    Insert the updated discriminator and the updated generator into $\mathcal{D}$ and $\mathcal{G}$, respectively.

end while

The following theorem provides the theoretical convergence guarantee for Fictitious GAN. It shows that assuming best response at each update in Fictitious GAN, the distribution of the mixture outputs from the generators converge to the data distribution. The intuition of the proof is that fictitious play achieves a Nash equilibrium in two-player zero-sum games. Since the optimal solution of GAN is a unique equilibrium in the game, fictitious GAN achieves the optimal solution.

Theorem 4. *Suppose the discriminator and the generator are updated according to the best-response strategy at each iteration in Fictitious GAN, then*

$$\lim_{n \to \infty} \frac{1}{n} \sum_{w=0}^{n-1} p_{g,w}(\boldsymbol{x}) = p_d(\boldsymbol{x}), \qquad (16)$$

$$\lim_{n \to \infty} D_n(\boldsymbol{x}) = \frac{1}{2}, \qquad (17)$$

where $D_w(\boldsymbol{x})$ is the output from the w-th trained discriminator model and $p_{g,w}$ is the generated distribution due to the w-th trained generator.

5.2   Fictitious GAN as a Meta-Algorithm

One advantage of Fictitious GAN is that it can be applied on top of existing GANs. Consider the following minimax problem:

$$\min_{G} \max_{D} V(G, D) = \mathsf{E}_{\boldsymbol{x} \sim p_d(\boldsymbol{x})}\{f_0(D(\boldsymbol{x}))\} + \mathsf{E}_{\boldsymbol{z} \sim p_z(\boldsymbol{z})}\{f_1(D(G(\boldsymbol{z})))\}, \quad (18)$$

where $f_0(\cdot)$ and $f_1(\cdot)$ are some quasi-concave functions depending on the GAN variants. Table 1 shows the family of f-GAN [4, 20] and Wasserstein GAN.

We can model these GAN variants as two-player zero-sum games and the training algorithms for these variants of GAN follow by simply changing $f_0(\cdot)$ and $f_1(\cdot)$ in the updating rule accordingly in Algorithm 1. Following the proof in Theorem 4, we can show that the time average of generated distributions will converge to the data distribution and the discriminator will converge to D^* as shown in Table 1.

Table 1. Variants of GANs under the zero-sum game framework.

Divergence metric	$f_0(D)$	$f_1(D)$	D^*	value of the game
Kullback-Leibler	$\log(D)$	$1 - D$	1	0
Reverse KL	$-D$	$\log D$	1	-1
Pearson χ^2	D	$-\frac{1}{4}D^2 - D$	0	0
Squared Hellinger χ^2	$1 - D$	$1 - 1/D$	1	0
Jensen-Shannon	$\log(D)$	$\log(1 - D)$	$\frac{1}{2}$	$-\log 4$
WGAN	D	$-D$	0	0

6   Experiments

Our Fictitious GAN is a meta-algorithm that can be applied on top of existing GANs. To demonstrate the merit of using Fictitious GAN, we apply our meta-algorithm on DCGAN [22] and its extension conditional DCGAN. Conditional DCGAN allows DCGAN to use external label information to generate images of some particular classes. We evaluate the performance on a synthetic dataset and three widely adopted real-world image datasets. Our experiment results show that Fictitious GAN could improve visual quality of both DCGAN and conditional GAN models.

Image dataset. (1) **MNIST:** contains 60,000 labeled images of 28 × 28 grayscale digits. (2) **CIFAR-10:** consists of colored natural scene images sized at 32 × 32 pixels. There are 50,000 training images and 10,000 test images in 10 classes. (3) **CelebA:** is a large-scale face attributes dataset with more than 200K celebrity images, each with 40 attribute annotations.

Parameter Settings. We used Tensorflow for our implementation. Due to GPU memory limitation, we limit number of historical models to 5 in real-world image dataset experiments. More architecture details are included in supplementary material.

6.1 2D Mixture of Gaussian

Figure 4 shows the performance of Fictitious GAN for a mixture of 8 Gaussain data on a circle in 2 dimensional space. We use the network structure in [17] to evaluate the performance of our proposed method. The data is sampled from a mixture of 8 Gaussians uniformly located on a circle of radius 1.0. Each has standard deviation of 0.02. The input noise samples are a vector of 256 independent and identically distributed (i.i.d.) Gaussian variables with mean zero and unit standard deviation.

While the original GANs experience mode collapse [17,19], Fictitious GAN is able to generate samples over all 8 modes, even with a single discriminator asymptotically.

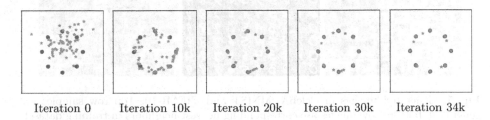

Iteration 0   Iteration 10k   Iteration 20k   Iteration 30k   Iteration 34k

Fig. 4. Performance of Fictitious GAN on 2D mixture of Gaussian data. The data samples are marked in blue and the generated samples are marked in orange. (Color figure online)

6.2 Qualitative Results for Image Generation

We show visual quality of samples generated by DCGAN and conditional DCGAN, trained by proposed Fictitious GAN. In Fig. 5 first row corresponds to generated samples. We apply train DCGAN on CelebA dataset, and train conditional DCGAN on MNIST and CIFAR-10. Each image in the first row corresponds to the image in the same grid position in second row of Fig. 5. The second row shows the nearest neighbor in training dataset computed by Euclidean distance. The samples are randomly drawn without cherry picking, they are representative of model output distribution.

In CelebA, we can generate face images with various genders, skin colors and hairstyles. In MNIST dataset, all generated digits have almost visually identical samples. Also, digit images have diverse visual shapes and fonts. CIFAR-10 dataset is more challenging, images of each object have large visual appearance variance. We observe some visual and label consistency in generated images and the nearest neigbhors, especially in the categories of airplane, horse and ship. Note that though we theoretical proved that Fictitious GAN could improve robustness of training in best response strategy, the visual quality still depends on the baseline GAN architecture and loss design, which in our case is conditional DCGAN.

Fig. 5. Generated images in CelebA, MNIST and CIFAR-10. Top row samples are generated, bottom row images are corresponding nearest neighbors in training dataset.

6.3   Quantitative Results

In this section, we quantitatively show that DCGAN models trained by our Fictitious GAN could gain improvement over traditional training methods. Also, we may have a better performance by applying Fictitious gan on other existing gan models. The results of comparison methods are directly copied as reported.

Metric. The visual quality of generated images is measured by the widely used Inception score metric [24]. It measures visual objectiveness of generated image and correlates well with human scoring of the realism of generated images. Following evaluation scheme of [24] setup, we generate 50,000 images from our model to compute the score.

As shown in Table 2, Our method outperforms recent state-of-the-art methods. Specifically, we improve baseline DCGAN from 6.16 to 6.63; and conditional DCGAN model from 7.16 to 7.27. It sheds light on the advantage of training with the proposed learning algorithm. Note that in order to highlight the performance improvement gained from fictitious GAN, the inception score of reproduced DCGAN model is 6.72, obtained without using tricks as [24]. Also, we did not use any regularization terms such as conditional loss and entropy loss to

Table 2. Inception Score on CIFAR-10.

Method	Score
Fictitious cDCGAN*	**7.27 ± 0.10**
DCGAN* [13] (best variant)	7.16 ± 0.10
MIX+WGAN* [1]	4.04 ± 0.07
Fictitious DCGAN	6.63 ± 0.06
DCGAN [13]	**6.16 ± 0.07**
GMAN [6]	6.00 ± 0.19
WGAN [1]	3.82 ± 0.06
Real data	11.24 ± 0.12

Note: * denotes models that use labels for training.

train DCGAN, as in [13]. We expect higher inception score when more training tricks are used in addition to Fictitious GAN.

6.4 Ablation Studies

One hyperparameter that affects the performance of Fictitious GAN is the number of historical generator (discriminator) models. We evaluate the performance of Fictitious GAN with different number of historical models, and report the inception scores on the 150-th epoch in CIFAR-10 dataset in Fig. 6. We keep the number of historical discriminators the same as the number of historical generators. We observe a trend of performance boost with an increasing number of historical models in 2 baseline GAN models. The mean of inception score slightly drops for Jenson-Shannon divergence metric when the copy number is 4, due to random initialization and random noise generation in training.

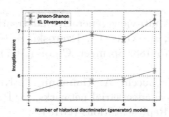

Fig. 6. We show that Fictitious-GAN can improve Inception score as a meta-algorithm with larger number of historical models, We select 2 divergence metrics from Table 1: Jenson-Shanon and KL divergence.

7   Conclusion

In this paper, we relate the minimax game of GAN to the two-player zero-sum game. This relation enables us to leverage the mechanism of fictitious play to design a novel training algorithm, referred to as fictitious GAN. In the training algorithm, the discriminator (resp. generator) is alternately updated as best response to the mixed output of the stale generator models (resp. discriminator). This novel training algorithm can resolve the oscillation behavior due to the pure best response strategy and the inconvergence issue of gradient based training in some cases. Real world image datasets show that applying fictitious GAN on top of the existing DCGAN models yields a performance gain of up to 8%.

References

1. Arora, S., Ge, R., Liang, Y., Ma, T., Zhang, Y.: Generalization and equilibrium in generative adversarial nets (GANs). In: International Conference on Machine Learning, pp. 224–232 (2017)
2. Brown, G.W.: Iterative solution of games by fictitious play. Act. Anal. Prod. Alloc. **13**(1), 374–376 (1951)
3. Che, T., Li, Y., Jacob, A.P., Bengio, Y., Li, W.: Mode regularized generative adversarial networks. In: Proceedings of International Conference on Learning Representations (2017)
4. Chen, X., Wang, J., Ge, H.: Training generative adversarial networks via primal-dual subgradient methods: a Lagrangian perspective on GAN. In: Proceedings of International Conference on Learning Representations (2018)
5. Danskin, J.M.: Fictitious play for continuous games. Nav. Res. Logist. (NRL) **1**(4), 313–320 (1954)
6. Durugkar, I., Gemp, I., Mahadevan, S.: Generative multi-adversarial networks. arXiv preprint arXiv:1611.01673 (2016)
7. Ghosh, A., Kulharia, V., Namboodiri, V., Torr, P.H., Dokania, P.K.: Multi-agent diverse generative adversarial networks. arXiv preprint arXiv:1704.02906 (2017)
8. Goodfellow, I.: Nips 2016 tutorial: generative adversarial networks. arXiv preprint arXiv:1701.00160 (2016)
9. Chen, M., Denoyer, L.: Multi-view generative adversarial networks. In: Ceci, M., Hollmén, J., Todorovski, L., Vens, C., Džeroski, S. (eds.) ECML PKDD 2017. LNCS, vol. 10535, pp. 175–188. Springer, Cham (2017). https://doi.org/10.1007/978-3-319-71246-8_11
10. Grnarova, P., Levy, K.Y., Lucchi, A., Hofmann, T., Krause, A.: An online learning approach to generative adversarial networks. In: Proceedings of International Conference on Learning Representations (2018)
11. Heusel, M., Ramsauer, H., Unterthiner, T., Nessler, B., Hochreiter, S.: GANs trained by a two time-scale update rule converge to a local nash equilibrium. In: Advances in Neural Information Processing Systems, pp. 6626–6637 (2017)
12. Hoang, Q., Nguyen, T.D., Le, T., Phung, D.: Multi-generator gernerative adversarial nets. arXiv preprint arXiv:1708.02556 (2017)
13. Huang, X., Li, Y., Poursaeed, O., Hopcroft, J., Belongie, S.: Stacked generative adversarial networks. In: IEEE Conference on Computer Vision and Pattern Recognition (CVPR), vol. 2, p. 4 (2017)

14. Johnson, J., Alahi, A., Fei-Fei, L.: Perceptual losses for real-time style transfer and super-resolution. In: Leibe, B., Matas, J., Sebe, N., Welling, M. (eds.) ECCV 2016. LNCS, vol. 9906, pp. 694–711. Springer, Cham (2016). https://doi.org/10.1007/978-3-319-46475-6_43

15. Ledig, C., et al.: Photo-realistic single image super-resolution using a generative adversarial network. In: IEEE Conference on Computer Vision and Pattern Recognition (CVPR), pp. 105–114 (2017)

16. Li, J., Madry, A., Peebles, J., Schmidt, L.: Towards understanding the dynamics of generative adversarial networks. arXiv preprint arXiv:1706.09884 (2017)

17. Metz, L., Poole, B., Pfau, D., Sohl-Dickstein, J.: Unrolled generative adversarial networks. In: Proceedings of International Conference on Learning Representations (2017)

18. Nagarajan, V., Kolter, J.Z.: Gradient descent GAN optimization is locally stable. In: Advances in Neural Information Processing Systems, pp. 5585–5595 (2017)

19. Nguyen, T., Le, T., Vu, H., Phung, D.: Dual discriminator generative adversarial nets. In: Advances in Neural Information Processing Systems, pp. 2667–2677 (2017)

20. Nowozin, S., Cseke, B., Tomioka, R.: f-GAN: training generative neural samplers using variational divergence minimization. In: Advances in Neural Information Processing Systems, pp. 271–279 (2016)

21. Oliehoek, F.A., Savani, R., Gallego, J., van der Pol, E., Gross, R.: Beyond local nash equilibria for adversarial networks. arXiv preprint arXiv:1806.07268 (2018)

22. Radford, A., Metz, L., Chintala, S.: Unsupervised representation learning with deep convolutional generative adversarial networks. In: Proceedings of International Conference on Learning Representations (2016)

23. Reed, S., Akata, Z., Yan, X., Logeswaran, L., Schiele, B., Lee, H.: Generative adversarial text to image synthesis. In: International Conference on Machine Learning, pp. 1060–1069 (2016)

24. Salimans, T., Goodfellow, I., Zaremba, W., Cheung, V., Radford, A., Chen, X.: Improved techniques for training GANs. In: Advances in Neural Information Processing Systems, pp. 2234–2242 (2016)

25. Shrivastava, A., Pfister, T., Tuzel, O., Susskind, J., Wang, W., Webb, R.: Learning from simulated and unsupervised images through adversarial training. In: The IEEE Conference on Computer Vision and Pattern Recognition (CVPR), vol. 3, p. 6 (2017)

26. Sion, M.: On general minimax theorems. Pac. J. Math. **8**(1), 171–176 (1958)

27. Tolstikhin, I.O., Gelly, S., Bousquet, O., Simon-Gabriel, C.J., Schölkopf, B.: ADA-GAN: boosting generative models. In: Advances in Neural Information Processing Systems, pp. 5424–5433 (2017)

28. Zhai, S., Cheng, Y., Lu, W., Zhang, Z.: Deep structured energy based models for anomaly detection. In: International Conference on Machine Learning, pp. 1100–1109 (2016)

Bi-box Regression for Pedestrian Detection and Occlusion Estimation

Chunluan Zhou[1,2(✉)] (iD) and Junsong Yuan[2] (iD)

[1] Nanyang Technological University, Singapore, Singapore
czhou002@e.ntu.edu.sg
[2] The State University of New York at Buffalo, Buffalo, USA
jsyuan@buffalo.edu

Abstract. Occlusions present a great challenge for pedestrian detection in practical applications. In this paper, we propose a novel approach to simultaneous pedestrian detection and occlusion estimation by regressing two bounding boxes to localize the full body as well as the visible part of a pedestrian respectively. For this purpose, we learn a deep convolutional neural network (CNN) consisting of two branches, one for full body estimation and the other for visible part estimation. The two branches are treated differently during training such that they are learned to produce complementary outputs which can be further fused to improve detection performance. The full body estimation branch is trained to regress full body regions for positive pedestrian proposals, while the visible part estimation branch is trained to regress visible part regions for both positive and negative pedestrian proposals. The visible part region of a negative pedestrian proposal is forced to shrink to its center. In addition, we introduce a new criterion for selecting positive training examples, which contributes largely to heavily occluded pedestrian detection. We validate the effectiveness of the proposed bi-box regression approach on the Caltech and CityPersons datasets. Experimental results show that our approach achieves promising performance for detecting both non-occluded and occluded pedestrians, especially heavily occluded ones.

Keywords: Pedestrian detection · Occlusion handling · Deep CNN

1 Introduction

Pedestrian detection has a wide range of applications including autonomous driving, robotics and video surveillance. Many efforts have been made to improve its performance in recent years [3–6, 8, 17, 33, 34, 37, 39–41]. Although reasonably good performance has been achieved on some benchmark datasets for detecting non-occluded or slightly occluded pedestrians, the performance for detecting heavily occluded pedestrians is still far from being satisfactory. Take the Caltech dataset [9] for example. One of the top-performing approaches, SDS-RCNN [4], achieves a miss rate of about 7.4% at 0.1 false positives per image (FPPI) for non-occludexd or slightly occluded pedestrian detection, but its miss rate

© Springer Nature Switzerland AG 2018
V. Ferrari et al. (Eds.): ECCV 2018, LNCS 11205, pp. 138–154, 2018.
https://doi.org/10.1007/978-3-030-01246-5_9

increases dramatically to about 58.5% at 0.1 FPPI for heavily occluded pedestrian detection (See Fig. 6). Occlusions occur frequently in real-world applications. For example, pedestrians on a street are often occluded by other objects like cars and they may also occlude each other when walking closely. Therefore, it is important for a pedestrian detection approach to robustly detect partially occluded pedestrians.

Fig. 1. Detection examples of our approach. The red and blue boxes on each detection represent the estimated full body and visible part respectively. For a pedestrian detection, its visible part is estimated normally as shown in columns 1 and 2. For a non-pedestrian detection, its visible part is estimated to be the center of its corresponding pedestrian proposal as shown in column 3. Since the red box of each detection is obtained by adding estimated offsets to its corresponding pedestrian proposal, the blue box of a non-pedestrian detection is often not exactly at the center of the red box. (Color figure online)

Recently, part detectors are commonly used to handle occlusions for pedestrian detection [21–23,25,31,43,44]. One drawback of these approaches is that parts are manually designed and therefore may not be optimal. In [21,22,25,31, 43], part detectors are learned separately and then integrated to handle occlusions. For these approaches, the computational cost for testing the part detectors grows linearly with the number of part detectors. A deep convolutional neural network (CNN) is designed to jointly learn and integrate part detectors [23]. However, this approach does not use part annotations for learning the part detectors, which may limit its performance. In [44], a multi-label learning approach is proposed to learn part detectors jointly so as to improve the performance for heavily occluded pedestrian detection and reduce the computational cost of applying the part detectors, but for non-occluded or slightly occluded pedestrian detection, it does not perform as well as state-of-the-art approaches. In addition, for a pedestrian, all these approaches only output one bounding box which specifies the full body region of the pedestrian but does not explicitly estimate which part of the pedestrian is visible or occluded. Occlusion estimation is not well explored in the pedestrian detection literature, but it is critical for applications like robotics which often requires occlusion reasoning to perform interactive tasks.

In this paper, we propose a novel approach to simultaneous pedestrian detection and occlusion estimation by regressing two bounding boxes for full body and visible part estimation respectively. Deep CNNs [4, 10, 34] have achieved promising performance for non-occluded or slightly occluded pedestrian detection, but their performance for heavily occluded pedestrian detection is far from being satisfactory. This motivates us to explore how to learn a deep CNN for accurately detecting both non-occluded and occluded pedestrians. We thus adapt the Fast R-CNN framework [4, 16, 34] to learn a deep CNN for simultaneous pedestrian classification, full body estimation and visible part estimation. Our deep CNN consists of two branches, one for full body estimation and the other for visible part estimation. Each branch performs classification and bounding box regression for pedestrian proposals. We treat the two branches differently during training such that they produce complementary outputs which can be further fused to boost detection performance. The full body estimation branch is trained to regress full body regions only for positive pedestrian proposals as in the original Fast R-CNN framework, while the visible part estimation branch is trained to regress visible part regions for both positive and negative pedestrian proposals. The visible part region of a negative pedestrian proposal is forced to shrink to its center. Figure 1 shows some detection examples of our approach. For training a deep CNN, positive pedestrian proposals are usually selected based on their overlaps with full body annotations [4, 5, 20, 34, 37, 39, 41], which would include poorly aligned pedestrian proposals for heavily occluded pedestrians (See Fig. 4(b)). To address this issue, we introduce a new criterion which exploits both full body and visible part annotations for selecting positive pedestrian proposals to improve detection performance on heavily occluded pedestrians.

The proposed bi-box regression approach has two advantages: (1) It can provide occlusion estimation by regressing the visible part of a pedestrian; (2) It exploits both full body and visible part regions of pedestrians to improve the performance of pedestrian detection. We demonstrate the effectiveness of our approach on the Caltech [9] and CityPersons [41] datasets. Experimental results show that our approach has comparable performance to the state-of-the-art for detecting non-occluded pedestrians and achieves the best performance for detecting occluded pedestrians, especially heavily occluded ones.

The contributions of this paper are three-fold: (1) A bi-box regression approach is proposed to achieve simultaneous pedestrian detection and occlusion estimation by learning a deep CNN consisting of two branches, one for full body estimation and the other for visible part estimation; (2) A training strategy is proposed to improve the complementarity between the two branches such that their outputs can be fused to improve pedestrian detection performance; (3) A new criterion is introduced to select better positive pedestrian proposals, contributing to a large performance gain for heavily occluded pedestrian detection.

2   Related Work

Recently, deep CNNs have been widely adopted for pedestrian detection [1, 4–6, 10, 17, 20, 23, 31, 32, 34, 37–39, 41] and achieved state-of-the-art performance [4, 10, 34]. In [38, 39], a set of decision trees are learned by boosting to form a pedestrian detector using features from deep CNNs. A complexity-aware cascaded pedestrian detector [6] is learned by taking into account the computational cost and discriminative power of different types of features (including CNN features) to achieve a trade-off between detection accuracy and speed. A cascade of deep CNNs are proposed in [1] to achieve real-time pedestrian detection by first using tiny deep CNNs to reject a large number of negative proposals and then using large deep CNNs to classify remaining proposals. In [23, 31], a set of part detectors are learned and integrated to handle occlusions. A deep CNN is learned to jointly optimize pedestrian detection and other semantic tasks to improve pedestrian detection performance [32]. In [4, 5, 20, 34, 37, 41], Fast R-CNN [16] or Faster R-CNN [27] is adapted for pedestrian detection. In this paper, we explore how to learn a deep CNN to improve performance for detecting partially occluded pedestrians.

Many efforts have been made to handle occlusions for pedestrian detection. A common framework for occlusion handling is learning and integrating a set of part detectors to handle a variety of occlusions [11, 12, 21–23, 25, 28, 31, 36, 43, 44]. The parts used in these approaches are usually manually designed, which may not be optimal. For approaches (e.g. [21, 31, 43]) which use a large number of part detectors, the computational cost of applying the learned part detector could be a bottleneck for real-time pedestrian detection. In [23], part detectors are learned and integrated with a deep CNN, which can greatly reduce the detection time. However, the part detectors in this approach are learned in a weakly supervised way, which may limit its performance. In [44], a multi-label learning approach is proposed to both improve the reliability of part detectors and reduce the computational cost of applying part detectors. Different part detector integration approaches are explored and compared in [43]. Different from these approaches, we learn a deep CNN without using parts to handle various occlusions. There are also some other approaches to occlusion handling. In [18], an implicit shape model is adopted to generate a set of pedestrian proposals which are further refined by exploiting local and global cues. The approach in [35] models a pedestrian as a rectangular template of blocks and performs occlusion reasoning by estimating the visibility statuses of these blocks. Several approaches [24, 26, 30] are specially designed to handle occlusion situations in which multiple pedestrians occlude each other. A deformable part model [13] and its variants [2, 15, 42] can also be used for handling occlusions.

3   Proposed Approach

Given an image, we want to detect pedestrians in it and at the same time estimate the visible part of each pedestrian. Specifically, our approach produces for each pedestrian two bounding boxes which specify its full body and visible part regions respectively. Considering promising performance achieved by deep CNNs for pedestrian detection [4,5,20,34,37,39,41], we adapt the Fast R-CNN framework [16] for our purpose. Figure 2 shows the overview of the proposed bi-box regression approach. A set of region proposals which possibly contain pedestrians are generated for an input image by a proposal generation approach (e.g. [4,39]). These pedestrian proposals are then fed to a deep CNN which performs classification, full body estimation and visible part estimation for each proposal.

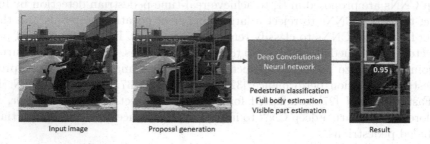

Fig. 2. Overview of our bi-box regression approach.

3.1   Network Structure

We adapt a commonly used deep CNN, VGG-16 [29], to achieve simultaneous pedestrian detection and occlusion estimation. Figure 3 shows the structure of our deep CNN. We keep convolution layers 1 through 4 in VGG-16 unchanged. It is reported in [5,39] that a feature map with higher resolution generally improves detection performance. As in [5,39], we remove the last max pooling layer and convolution layer 5 from VGG-16. A deconvolution layer (Deconv5), which is implemented by bilinear interpolation, is added on top of Conv4-3 to increase the resolution of the feature map from Conv4-3. Following Deconv5 is a ROI pooling layer on top of which are two branches, one for full body estimation and the other for visible part estimation. Each branch performs classification and bounding box regression as in Fast R-CNN [16].

3.2   Pedestrian Detection

For detection, an image and a set of pedestrian proposals are fed to the deep CNN for classification, full body estimation and visible part estimation. Let $P = (P^x, P^y, P^w, P^h)$ be a pedestrian proposal, where P^x and P^y specify the coordinates of the center of P in the image, and P^w and P^h are the width and height of P respectively. For the pedestrian proposal P, the full body estimation branch outputs two probabilities $p_1 = (p_1^0, p_1^1)$ (from the Softmax1 layer) and four offsets $f = (f^x, f^y, f^w, f^h)$ (from the FC11 layer). The visible part estimation branch also outputs two probabilities $p_2 = (p_2^0, p_2^1)$ (from the Softmax2 layer) and four offsets $v = (v^x, v^y, v^w, v^h)$ (from the FC13 layer). p_1^1 and $p_1^0 = 1 - p_1^1$ represent the probabilities of P containing and not containing a pedestrian, respectively. p_2^0 and p_2^1 are similarly defined. f^x and f^y specify the scale-invariant translations from the center of P to that of the estimated full body region, while f^w and f^h specify the log-space translations from the width and height of P to those of the estimated full body region respectively. v^x, v^y, v^w and v^h are similarly defined for visible part estimation. We define f and v following [16]. With f and v, we can compute the full body and visible part regions for the pedestrian proposal P (See [16] for more details).

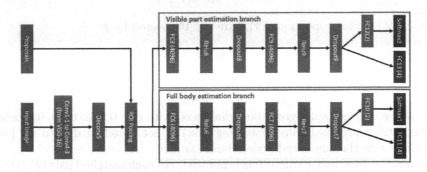

Fig. 3. Network architecture. The number in each fully connected (FC) layer is its output dimensionality. Softmax1 and Softmax2 perform the same task, pedestrian classification. FC11 is for full body estimation and FC13 is for visible part estimation.

We consider three ways to score a pedestrian proposal P. Let $s_1 = (s_1^0, s_1^1)$ and $s_2 = (s_2^0, s_2^1)$ be the raw scores from FC10 and FC12 respectively. The first way scores P with $p_1^1 = \frac{\exp(s_1^1)}{\exp(s_1^1)+\exp(s_1^0)}$ and the second way scores P with $p_2^1 = \frac{\exp(s_2^1)}{\exp(s_2^1)+\exp(s_2^0)}$. The third way fuses the raw scores from the two branches with a softmax operation $\hat{p}^1 = \frac{\exp(s_1^1+s_2^1)}{\exp(s_1^1+s_2^1)+\exp(s_1^0+s_2^0)}$. It can be proved that $\hat{p}^1 - p_1^1 > 0$ if $p_2^1 > 0.5$, i.e. $s_2^1 > s_2^0$. When two branches agree on a positive example, i.e. $p_1^1 > 0.5$ and $p_2^1 > 0.5$, the fused score $\hat{p}^1$ becomes stronger, i.e. $\hat{p}^1 > p_1^1$ and $\hat{p}^1 > p_2^1$. When one branch gives a low score ($p_1^1 < 0.5$) to the positive example, the other branch can increase its detection score if it gives a high score ($p_2^1 > 0.5$). This guides us to increase the complementarity between the two branches so to improve detections robustness as described in next section.

3.3 Network Training

To train our deep CNN, each pedestrian example is annotated with two bounding boxes which specify its full body and visible part regions respectively. Figure 4(a) shows an example of pedestrian annotation. Besides these annotated pedestrian examples, we also collect some pedestrian proposals for training. To achieve this, we match pedestrian proposals in a training image to annotated pedestrian examples in the same image. Let $Q = (\bar{F}, \bar{V})$ be an annotated pedestrian example in an image, where $\bar{F} = (\bar{F}^x, \bar{F}^y, \bar{F}^w, \bar{F}^h)$ and $\bar{V} = (\bar{V}^x, \bar{V}^y, \bar{V}^w, \bar{V}^h)$ are the full body and visible part regions respectively. A pedestrian proposal P is matched to Q if it aligns well with Q. Specifically, P and Q form a pair if they satisfy

$$\text{IOU}(P, \bar{F}) \geq \alpha \text{ and } \text{C}(P, \bar{V}) \geq \beta, \tag{1}$$

where $\text{IOU}(P, \bar{F})$ is the intersection over union of the two regions P and $\bar{F}$:

$$\text{IOU}(P, \bar{F}) = \frac{\text{Area}(P \cap \bar{F})}{\text{Area}(P \cup \bar{F})}, \tag{2}$$

and $\text{C}(P, \bar{V})$ is the proportion of the area of $\bar{V}$ covered by P:

$$\text{C}(P, \bar{V}) = \frac{\text{Area}(P \cap \bar{V})}{\text{Area}(\bar{V})}. \tag{3}$$

In Fig. 4(b), the pedestrian proposal (red bounding box) is matched to the annotated pedestrian example (green bounding box) with $\alpha = 0.5$ and $\beta = 0.5$, while the pedestrian proposal (blue bounding box) is not matched due to its poor alignment with the annotated pedestrian example.

Denote by I the image where P is generated. For each matched pair (P, Q), we construct a positive training example $X^+ = (I, P, c, \bar{f}, \bar{v})$, where $c = 1$ indicating P contains a pedestrian, and $\bar{f} = (\bar{f}^x, \bar{f}^y, \bar{f}^w, \bar{f}^h)$ and $\bar{v} = (\bar{v}^x, \bar{v}^y, \bar{v}^w, \bar{v}^h)$ are regression targets for full body and visible part estimation respectively.

As in [14,16], we define $\bar{f}$ as

$$\bar{f}^x = \frac{\bar{F}^x - P^x}{P^w}, \quad \bar{f}^y = \frac{\bar{F}^y - P^y}{P^h},$$
$$\bar{f}^w = \log(\frac{\bar{F}^w}{P^w}), \quad \bar{f}^h = \log(\frac{\bar{F}^h}{P^h}). \tag{4}$$

Similarly, $\bar{v}$ is defined as

$$\bar{v}^x = \frac{\bar{V}^x - P^x}{P^w}, \quad \bar{v}^y = \frac{\bar{V}^y - P^y}{P^h},$$
$$\bar{v}^w = \log(\frac{\bar{V}^w}{P^w}), \quad \bar{v}^h = \log(\frac{\bar{V}^h}{P^h}). \tag{5}$$

We consider P as a negative pedestrian proposal if $\text{IOU}(P, \bar{F}) < 0.5$ for all annotated pedestrian examples Q in the same image. There are two types of negative pedestrian proposals: background proposals which have no visible part region and poorly aligned proposals $(0 < \text{IOU}(P, \bar{F}) < 0.5)$. To better distinguish negative pedestrian proposals from positive ones, we choose to shrink the visible part regions of negative pedestrian proposals to their centers. Specifically, for each negative pedestrian proposal P, we construct a negative example $X^- = (I, P, c, \bar{f}, \bar{v})$, where $c = 0$ indicating P does not contain a pedestrian, $\bar{f} = (0, 0, 0, 0)$ and $\bar{v} = (0, 0, a, a)$ with $a < 0$. Since the height and width of the

(a)   (b)

Fig. 4. Pedestrian annotation and positive pedestrian proposal selection. (a) The green and yellow bounding boxes specify the full body and visible part of a pedestrian example respectively. (b) The red bounding box is a good pedestrian proposal and the blue bounding box is a bad pedestrian proposal. (Color figure online)

visible part region are both 0, i.e. $\bar{V}^{\mathrm{w}} = 0$ and $\bar{V}^{\mathrm{h}} = 0$, we have $\bar{v}^{\mathrm{w}} = -\infty$ and $\bar{v}^{\mathrm{h}} = -\infty$ according to the definition of $\bar{v}$ in Eq. (5). Ideally, a should be set to $-\infty$. In experiments, we find that if a is too small, it can cause numerical instability. Thus, we set $a = -3$ which is sufficient for the visible part region of a negative pedestrian proposal to shrink to a small region ($\sim \frac{1}{400}$ of the proposal region) at its center.

Let $\mathcal{D} = \{X_i = (I_i, P_i, c_i, \bar{f}_i, \bar{v}_i) | 1 \leq i \leq N\}$ be a set of training examples. Denote by W the model parameters of the deep CNN. Let p_{1i}, p_{2i}, f_i, and v_i be the outputs of the network for the training example X_i. We learn the model parameters W by minimizing the following multi-task training loss:

$$L(W, \mathcal{D}) = L_{\mathrm{C1}}(W, \mathcal{D}) + \lambda_{\mathrm{F}} L_{\mathrm{F}}(W, \mathcal{D}) + \lambda_{\mathrm{C2}} L_{\mathrm{C2}}(W, \mathcal{D}) + \lambda_{\mathrm{V}} L_{\mathrm{V}}(W, \mathcal{D}), \quad (6)$$

where L_{C1} and L_{F} are the classification loss and bounding box regression loss respectively for the full body estimation branch, and L_{C2} and L_{V} are the classification loss and bounding box regression loss respectively for the visible part estimation branch. L_{C1} is a multinomial logistic loss defined by

$$L_{\mathrm{C1}}(W, \mathcal{D}) = \frac{1}{N} \sum_{i=1}^{N} -\log(p_{1i}^*), \quad (7)$$

where $p_{1i}^* = p_{1i}^0$ if $c_i = 0$ and $p_{1i}^* = p_{1i}^1$ otherwise. Similarly, L_{C2} is defined by

$$L_{C2}(W, \mathcal{D}) = \frac{1}{N} \sum_{i=1}^{N} - \log(p_{2i}^*), \tag{8}$$

where $p_{2i}^* = p_{2i}^0$ if $c_i = 0$ and $p_{2i}^* = p_{2i}^1$ otherwise. For L_F and L_V, we use the smooth L1 loss proposed for bounding box regression in Fast R-CNN [16]. The bounding box regression loss L_F is defined by

$$L_F(W, \mathcal{D}) = \frac{1}{N} \sum_{i=1}^{N} c_i \sum_{* \in \{x,y,w,h\}} \text{Smooth}_{L1}(\bar{f}_i^* - f_i^*), \tag{9}$$

where for $s \in \mathbb{R}$

$$\text{Smooth}_{L1}(s) = \begin{cases} 0.5s^2 & \text{if } |s| < 1; \\ |s| - 0.5 & \text{otherwise.} \end{cases} \tag{10}$$

Similarly, L_V is defined by

$$L_V(W, \mathcal{D}) = \frac{1}{N} \sum_{i=1}^{N} \sum_{* \in \{x,y,w,h\}} \text{Smooth}_{L1}(\bar{v}_i^* - v_i^*). \tag{11}$$

The difference between L_F and L_V is that negative examples are not considered in L_F since $c_i = 0$ for these examples in Eq. (9), while both positive and negative examples are taken into account in L_V. During training, the visible part regions of negative examples are forced to shrink to their centers. In this way, the visible part estimation branch and the full body estimation branch are learned to produce complementary outputs which can be fused to improve detection performance. If the visible part estimation branch is trained to only regress visible parts for positive pedestrian proposals, the training of this branch would be dominated by pedestrian examples which are non-occluded or slightly occluded. For these pedestrian proposals, their ground-truth visible part and full body regions overlap largely. As a result, the estimated visible part region of a negative pedestrian proposal is often close to its estimated full body region and the difference between the two branches after training would not be as large as the case in which the visible part regions of negative examples are forced to shrink to their centers. As shown in our experiments, forcing the visible part regions of negative examples to shrink to their centers achieves a larger performance gain than not doing this when the two branches are fused.

We adopt stochastic gradient descent to minimize the multi-task training loss L in Eq. (6). We initialize layers Conv1-1 to Conv4-3 from a VGG-16 model pre-trained on ImageNet [7]. The other layers are randomly initialized by sampling weights from Gaussian distributions. In our experiments, we set $\lambda_F = \lambda_{C2} = \lambda_V = 1$. Each training mini-batch consists of 120 pedestrian proposals collected from one training image. The ratio of positive examples to negative examples in a training mini-batch is set to $\frac{1}{6}$.

3.4   Discussion

Our bi-box regression approach is closely related to Fast R-CNN [4,16,39]. The major difference between our approach and Fast R-CNN is that the deep CNN used in our approach has the additional visible part estimation branch. This branch brings two advantages. First, it can provide occlusion estimation for a pedestrian by regressing its visible part. Second, it can be properly trained to be complementary to the full body estimation branch such that their outputs can be further fused to improve detection performance. This is achieved by training the visible part estimation branch to regress visible part regions for positive pedestrian proposals normally but force the visible part regions of negative pedestrian proposals to shrink to their centers. To train the visible part estimation branch, we introduce visible part annotations. Also, we exploit both visible part and full body annotations to select better positive pedestrian proposals. Typically, Fast R-CNN selects a pedestrian proposal P as a positive training example if it has large overlap with the full body region of a annotated pedestrian example $Q = (\bar{F}, \bar{V})$, i.e. $IOU(P, \bar{F}) > \alpha$. This is a weak criterion for selecting positive pedestrian proposals for partially occluded pedestrian examples as illustrated in Fig. 4(b). For $\alpha = 0.5$, the blue bounding box which poorly aligns with the groud-truth pedestrian example is also selected as a positive training example. With visible part annotations, we can use the stronger criterion defined in Eq. (1). According to this criterion, the blue bounding box would be rejected since it does not cover a large portion of the visible part region.

4   Experiments

We evaluate our approach on two pedestrian detection benchmark datasets: Caltech [9] and CityPersons [41]. Both datasets provide full body and visible part annotations which are required for training our deep CNN.

4.1   Experiments on Caltech

The Caltech dataset [9] contains 11 sets of videos. The first six video sets S0–S5 are used for training and the remaining five video sets S6–S10 are used for testing. In this dataset, around 2,300 unique pedestrians are annotated and over 70% unique pedestrians are occluded in at least one frame. We evaluate our approach on three subsets: Reasonable, Partial and Heavy. The Reasonable subset is widely used for evaluating pedestrian detection approaches. In this subset, only pedestrian examples at least 50 pixels tall and not occluded more than 35% are used for evaluation. In the Partial and Heavy subsets, pedestrians used for evaluation are also at least 50 pixels tall but have different ranges of occlusions. The occlusion range for the Partial subset is 1–35%, while the occlusion range for the Heavy subset is 36–80%. The Heavy subset is most difficult among the three subsets. For each subset, the detection performance is summarized by a log-average miss rate which is calculated by averaging miss rates at 9 false positives per image (FPPI) points evenly spaced between 10^{-2} and 10^0 in log space.

Implementation Details. We sample training images at an interval of 3 frames from the training video sets S0-S5 as in [4,17,34,39,41,44]. Ground-truth pedestrian examples which are at least 50 pixels tall and are occluded less than 70% are selected for training as in [44]. For pedestrian proposal generation, we train a region proposal network [4] on the training set. ~1000 pedestrian proposals per image are collected for training and ~400 pedestrian proposals per image are collected for testing. We train the deep CNN in Fig. 3 with stochastic gradient decent which iterates 120,000 times. The learning rate is set to 0.0005 initially and decreases by a factor of 0.1 every 60,000 iterations. Since Fast R-CNN is the most relevant baseline for our approach, we also implement Fast R-CNN using the full body estimation branch of our deep CNN.

Influence of Positive Pedestrian Proposals. We first analyze the influence of positive pedestrian proposals on Fast R-CNN. We conduct a group of experiments in which Fast R-CNN uses the criterion defined in Eq. (1) with α set to 0.5 and β set to 0.1, 0.3, 0.5, 0.7 and 0.9 respectively. The results on the Reasonable, Partial and Heavy subsets are shown in Table 1. We can see that Fast R-CNN works reasonably well with $\beta = 0.5$. When α is fixed, β controls the quality and number of positive pedestrian proposals for training. When β is small, more poorly aligned pedestrian proposals are included. A large β excludes poorly aligned pedestrian proposals but reduces the number of positive training examples. From the results in Table 1, we can see that both the quality and number of positive pedestrian proposals are important for Fast R-CNN. $\beta = 0.5$ achieves a good trade-off between the two factors. In the remaining experiments, we use $\alpha = 0.5$ and $\beta = 0.5$ unless otherwise mentioned.

Ablation Study. Table 2 shows the results of different approaches on the Caltech dataset. FRCN is a standard implementation of Fast R-CNN using the full

Table 1. Results of Fast R-CNN with varying β. Numbers are log-average miss rates.

	$\beta = 0.1$	$\beta = 0.3$	$\beta = 0.5$	$\beta = 0.7$	$\beta = 0.9$
Reasonable	10.6	10.5	10.1	**9.9**	10.2
Partial	19.1	18.1	**17.2**	18.5	19.2
Heavy	48.9	48.4	**46.1**	48.1	50.6

Table 2. Results of different approaches on the Caltech dataset. Numbers refer to log-average miss rates.

	FRCN	FRCN+	VPE	FBE	PDOE-	PDOE	PDOE+RPN
Reasonable	10.3	10.1	9.8	10.0	9.7	9.4	**7.6**
Partial	19.1	17.2	17.5	17.7	16.4	14.6	**13.3**
Heavy	49.4	46.1	45.5	45.3	45.1	**43.9**	44.4

body estimation branch with $\alpha = 0.5$ and $\beta = 0$ for positive pedestrian proposal selection. FRCN+ uses the same network as FRCN but sets $\alpha = 0.5$ and $\beta = 0.5$. We can see that FRCN+ performs better than FRCN on all the three subsets since it uses a sufficient number of better positive pedestrian proposals for training. VPE, FBE and PDOE are three approaches which use the same deep CNN learned by the proposed approach, but score pedestrian proposals in different ways as described in Sect. 3.2. They score a pedestrian proposal by the visible part estimation branch (VPE), by the full body estimation branch (FBE) and by combining the outputs from both branches (PDOE) respectively. FRCN+, VPE and FBE have similar performances since they uses the same network structure. PDOE outperforms VPE and FBE on all the three subsets, which shows that the full body and visible part estimation branches complement each other to achieve better pedestrian classification. To demonstrate the effectiveness of forcing the estimated visible parts of negative pedestrian proposals to shrink to their centers, we implement a baseline PDOE- in which negative examples are ignored in the training loss L_V in Eq. (11). Although PDOE- also outperforms VPE and FBE, the performance gain achieved by PDOE- is not as significant as that achieved by PDOE. It is pointed out in [4] that the output from a region proposal network can be fused with the output from a detection network to further improve detection performance. As in [4], we further fuse the outputs from the two networks to score a pedestrian proposal P by $\bar{p}^1 = \frac{\exp(s_1^1 + s_2^1 + s_3^1)}{\exp(s_1^1 + s_2^1 + s_3^1) + \exp(s_1^0 + s_2^0 + s_3^0)}$, where $s_1 = (s_1^0, s_1^1)$ and $s_2 = (s_2^0, s_2^1)$ are raw scores from the pedestrian detection network and $s_3 = (s_3^0, s_3^1)$ are raw scores from the region proposal network. We call this approach PDOE+RPN. PDOE+RPN further improves the performance over PDOE on the Reasonable and Partial subsets.

Comparison with Occlusion Handling Approaches. To demonstrate the effectiveness of our approach for occlusion handling, we compare it with two most competitive occlusion handling approaches on the Caltech dataset, DeepParts [31] and JL-TopS [44]. Both approaches use part detectors to handle occlusions. Figure 5 shows the results of our approach and the two approaches on the Caltech dataset. Our approach, PDOE, outperforms the two approaches on all the three subsets. Particularly, PDOE outperforms JL-TopS by 0.6%, 2.0% and 5.3% on the Reasonable, Partial and Heavy subsets respectively. The performance improvement on the Heavy subset is significant, which demonstrates that our deep CNN has the potential to handle occlusions reasonably well. PDOE+RPN outperforms JL-TopS on the three subsets with performance improvements of 2.4%, 3.3% and 4.8% respectively. Besides performance improvement over DeepParts and JL-TopS, our approach is able to perform occlusion estimation by regressing visible part regions for pedestrians.

Comparison with State-of-the-Art Results. In Fig. 6, we compare our approach with some state-of-the-art approaches including DeepParts [31],

CompACT-Deep [6], SA-FastRCNN [19], MS-CNN [5], RPN+BF [39], F-DNN [10], F-DNN+SS [10], PCN [34], JL-TopS [44], SDS-RCNN [4]. Our approach PDOE+RPN performs slightly worse (0.2%) than SDS-RCNN on the Reasonable subset, but outperforms it by 1.6% and 14.1% on the Partial and Heavy subsets, respectively. The performance gain on the Heavy subset is significant. PCN and F-DNN+SS are two competitive approaches which work fairly well for detecting both non-occluded and occluded pedestrians. Our approach works better than the two approaches on all the three subsets. Note that as our approach, all F-DNN+SS, PCN and SDS-RCNN integrate two or more networks for pedestrian classification. For heavily occluded pedestrian detection, our approach outperforms JL-TopS by 4.8% on the Heavy subset.

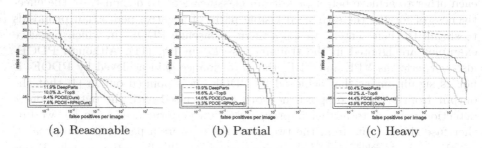

(a) Reasonable   (b) Partial   (c) Heavy

Fig. 5. Comparison of our approach with two competitive occlusion handling approaches on the Caltech dataset. Numbers in legends refer to log-average miss rates.

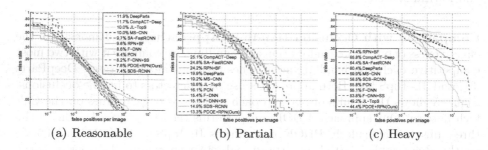

(a) Reasonable   (b) Partial   (c) Heavy

Fig. 6. Comparison of our approach and state-of-the-art approaches on the Caltech dataset. Numbers in legends refer to log-average miss rates.

4.2   Experiments on CityPersons

The CityPersons dataset [41] is a recently released pedestrian detection dataset which is diverse in terms of the numbers of countries, cities and seasons it covers. The dataset has a higher pedestrian density than Caltech. This dataset is split into three sets, Train, Val and Test which contain 2975, 500 and 1575 images respectively. Persons in this dataset are classified into six categories: ignored region, pedestrian, rider, group of people, sitting person and other. Results are reported for four setups: Reasonable, Small, Heavy and All. In the Reasonable setup, pedestrian examples which are at least 50 pixels tall and are not occluded more than 35% are used for evaluation. In the Small setup, the height and visibility ranges of pedestrian examples are [50, 75] and [0.65, 1] respectively. In the Heavy setup, the height and visibility ranges of pedestrian examples are [50, ∞] and [0.2, 0.65] respectively. In the All setup, the height and visibility ranges of pedestrian examples are [20, ∞] and [0.2, 1] respectively. As for the Caltech dataset, detection performance is summarized by the log-average miss rate.

Table 3. Results of different approaches on the CityPersons dataset. Numbers refer to log-average miss rates.

	FasterRCNN	FRCN	FRCN+	VPE	FBE	PDOE-	PDOE	PDOE+RPN
Reasonable	12.81	12.93	12.62	13.01	12.51	12.14	11.53	**11.24**
Small	-	50.12	49.81	50.02	49.65	49.16	47.84	**47.35**
Heavy	-	48.91	47.30	47.54	47.61	46.94	44.91	**44.15**
All	-	46.70	46.20	46.03	45.95	44.90	43.89	**43.41**

Implementation Details. We use the Train set for training and the Val set for testing. As in [41], we only use pedestrian examples to collect positive pedestrian proposals and ignore other person examples. Specifically, ground-truth pedestrian examples which are at least 50 pixels tall and are occluded less than 70% are used for training. We also train a region proposal network on the Train set to generate ~1000 pedestrian proposals per image for training and ~400 pedestrian proposals per image for testing. Stochastic gradient descent iterates 90,000 times and the learning rate is set to 0.001 initially and decreases by a factor of 0.1 every 45,000 iterations.

Results. Table 3 shows the results of different approaches on the CityPersons dataset. Our implementation of Fast R-CNN, FRCN, performs slightly worse than FasterRCNN [41] in the Reasonable setup. With better positive pedestrian proposals for training, FRCN+ outperforms FRCN in all the four setups. FRCN+, VPE and FBE have comparable log-average miss rates due to the same network structure they use. PDOE outperforms both VPE and FBE since the full body estimation branch and visible part estimation branch produce complementary scores which can be further fused to boost detection performance. Compared with PDOE, the performance of the downgraded version of our approach, PDOE-, decreases by 0.61%, 1.32%, 2.03% and 1.01% in the Reasonable, Small, Heavy and All setups respectively. PDOE outperforms the baseline FRCN by 1.4%, 2.28%, 4% and 2.81% in the four setups respectively. Fusing the detection network and region proposal network, PDOE+RPN achieves the best performance.

5 Conclusion

In this paper, we propose an approach to simultaneous pedestrian detection and occlusion estimation by regressing two bounding boxes to localize the full body and visible part of a pedestrian respectively. To achieve this, we learn a deep CNN consisting of two branches, one for full body estimation and the other for visible part estimation. The two branches are properly learned and further fused to improve detection performance. We also introduce a new criterion for positive pedestrian proposal selection, which contributes to a large performance gain for heavily occluded pedestrian detection. The effectiveness of the proposed bi-box regression approach is validated on the Caltech and CityPersons datasets.

Acknowledgement. This work is supported in part by Singapore Ministry of Education Academic Research Fund Tier 2 MOE2015-T2-2-114 and start-up grants of University at Buffalo.

References

1. Angelova, A., Krizhevsky, A., Vanhoucke, V., Ogale, A., Ferguson, D.: Real-time pedestrian detection with deep network cascades. In: British Machine and Vision Conference (BMVC) (2015)
2. Azizpour, H., Laptev, I.: Object detection using strongly-supervised deformable part models. In: Fitzgibbon, A., Lazebnik, S., Perona, P., Sato, Y., Schmid, C. (eds.) ECCV 2012. LNCS, vol. 7572, pp. 836–849. Springer, Heidelberg (2012). https://doi.org/10.1007/978-3-642-33718-5_60
3. Benenson, R., Mathias, M., Tuytelaars, T., Van Gool, L.: Seeking the strongest rigid detector. In: IEEE Conference on Computer Vision and Pattern Recognition (CVPR) (2013)
4. Brazil, G., Yin, X., Liu, X.: Illuminating pedestrians via simultaneous detection and segmentation. In: International Conference on Computer Vision (ICCV) (2017)
5. Cai, Z., Fan, Q., Feris, R.S., Vasconcelos, N.: A unified multi-scale deep convolutional neural network for fast object detection. In: Leibe, B., Matas, J., Sebe, N., Welling, M. (eds.) ECCV 2016. LNCS, vol. 9908, pp. 354–370. Springer, Cham (2016). https://doi.org/10.1007/978-3-319-46493-0_22
6. Cai, Z., Saberian, M., Vasconcelos, N.: Learning complexity-aware cascades for deep pedestrian detection. In: International Conference on Computer Vision (ICCV) (2015)
7. Deng, J., Dong, W., Socher, R., Li, L.J., Li, K., Fei-Fei, L.: Imagenet: a large-scale hierarchical image database. In: IEEE Conference on Computer Vision and Pattern Recognition (CVPR) (2009)
8. Dollar, P., Appel, R., Belongie, S., Perona, P.: Fast feature pyramids for object detection. IEEE Trans. Pattern Anal. Mach. Intell. (PAMI) **36**, 1532–1545 (2014)
9. Dollar, P., Wojek, C., Schiele, B., Perona, P.: Pedestrian detection: an evaluation of the state of the art. IEEE Trans. Pattern Anal. Mach. Intell. (PAMI) **34**, 743–761 (2012)
10. Du, X., El-Khamy, M., Lee, J., Davis, L.S.: Fused DNN: a deep neural network fusion approach to fast and robust pedestrian detection. CoRR (2016). http://arxiv.org/abs/1610.03466

11. Duan, G., Ai, H., Lao, S.: A structural filter approach to human detection. In: Daniilidis, K., Maragos, P., Paragios, N. (eds.) ECCV 2010. LNCS, vol. 6316, pp. 238–251. Springer, Heidelberg (2010). https://doi.org/10.1007/978-3-642-15567-3_18

12. Enzweiler, M., Eigenstetter, A., Schiele, B., Gavrila, D.: Multi-cue pedestrian classification with partial occlusion handling. In: IEEE Conference on Computer Vision and Pattern Recognition (CVPR) (2010)

13. Felzenszwalb, P., Girshick, R., McAllester, D., Ramanan, D.: Object detection with discriminatively trained part-based models. IEEE Trans. Pattern Anal. Mach. Intell. (PAMI) **32**, 1627–1645 (2010)

14. Girshick, R., Donahue, J., Darrel, T., Malik, J.: Rich feature hierarchies for accurate object detection and semantic segmentation. In: IEEE Conference on Computer Vision and Pattern Recognition (CVPR) (2014)

15. Girshick, R., Felzenszwalb, P., McAllester, D.: Object detection with grammar models. In: Advances in Neural Information Processing Systems (NIPS) (2011)

16. Girshick, R.: Fast R-CNN. In: International Conference on Computer Vision (ICCV) (2015)

17. Hosang, J., Omran, M., Benenson, R., Schiele, B.: Taking a deeper look at pedestrians. In: IEEE Conference on Computer Vision and Pattern Recognition (CVPR) (2015)

18. Leibe, B., Seemann, E., Schiele, B.: Pedestrian detection in crowded scenes. In: IEEE Conference on Computer Vision and Pattern Recogntion (CVPR) (2005)

19. Li, J., Liang, X., Shen, S., Xu, T., Yan, S.: Scale-aware fast R-CNN for pedestrian detection. CoRR (2015)

20. Mao, J., Xiao, T., Jiang, Y., Cao, Z.: What can help pedestrian detection? In: IEEE Conference on Computer Vision and Pattern Recognition (CVPR) (2017)

21. Mathias, M., Benenson, R., Timofte, R., Van Gool, L.: Handling occlusions with franken-classfiers. In: International Conference on Computer Vision (ICCV) (2013)

22. Ouyang, W., Wang, X.: A discriminative deep model for pedestrian detection with occlusion handling. In: IEEE Conference on Computer Vision and Pattern Recognition (CVPR) (2012)

23. Ouyang, W., Wang, X.: Joint deep learning for pedestrian detection. In: International Conference on Computer Vision (ICCV) (2013)

24. Ouyang, W., Wang, X.: Single-pedestrian detection aided by multi-pedestrian detection. In: IEEE Conference on Computer Vision and Pattern Recognition (CVPR) (2013)

25. Ouyang, W., Zeng, X., Wang, X.: Modeling mutual visibility relationship in pedestrian detection. In: IEEE Conference on Computer Vision and Pattern Recognition (CVPR) (2013)

26. Pepik, B., Stark, M., Gehler, P., Schiele, B.: Occlusion patterns for object class detection. In: IEEE Conference on Computer Vision and Pattern Recognition (CVPR) (2013)

27. Ren, S., He, K., Girshick, R., Sun, J.: Faster R-CNN: towards real-time object detection with region proposal networks. In: Advances in Neural Information Processing Systems (NIPS) (2015)

28. Shet, V., Neumann, J., Ramesh, V., Davis, L.: Bilattice-based logical reasoning for human detection. In: IEEE Conference on Computer Vision and Pattern Recognition (CVPR) (2007)

29. Simonyan, K., Zisserman, A.: Very deep convolutional networks for large-scale image recognition. CoRR (2014)

30. Tang, S., Andriluka, M., Schiele, B.: Detection and tracking of occluded people. In: British Machine Vision Conference (BMVC) (2012)
31. Tian, Y., Luo, P., Wang, X., Tang, X.: Deep learning strong parts for pedestrian detection. In: International Conference on Computer Vision (ICCV) (2015)
32. Tian, Y., Luo, P., Wang, X., Tang, X.: Pedestrian detection aided by deep learning semantic tasks. In: IEEE Conference on Computer Vision and Pattern Recognition (CVPR) (2015)
33. Tu, Z., Xie, W., Dauwels, J., Li, B., Yuan, J.: Semantic cues enhanced multi-modality multi-stream CNN for action recognition. IEEE Trans. Circuits Syst. Video Technol. (TCSVT) **PP**(99), 1 (2018)
34. Wang, S., Cheng, J., Liu, H., Tang, M.: PCN: part and context information for pedestrian detection with CNNs. In: British Machine Vision Conference (BMVC) (2017)
35. Wang, X., Han, T., Yan, S.: An HOG-LBP human detector with partial occlusion handling. In: International Conference on Computer Vision (ICCV) (2009)
36. Wu, B., Nevatia, R.: Detection of multiple, partially occluded humans in a single image by Bayesian combination of edgelet part detectors. In: International Conference on Computer Vision (ICCV) (2005)
37. Xu, D., Ouyang, W., Ricci, E., Wang, X., Sebe, N.: Learning cross-model deep representations for robust pedestrian detection. In: IEEE Conference on Computer Vision and Pattern Recognition (CVPR) (2017)
38. Yang, B., Yan, J., Lei, Z., Li, S.: Convolutional channel features. In: International Conference on Computer Vision (ICCV) (2015)
39. Zhang, L., Lin, L., Liang, X., He, K.: Is faster R-CNN doing well for pedestrian detection? In: Leibe, B., Matas, J., Sebe, N., Welling, M. (eds.) ECCV 2016. LNCS, vol. 9906, pp. 443–457. Springer, Cham (2016). https://doi.org/10.1007/978-3-319-46475-6_28
40. Zhang, S., Benenson, R., Omran, M., Hosang, J., Schiele, B.: How far are we from solving pedestrian detection? In: IEEE Conference on Computer Vision and Pattern Recognition (CVPR) (2016)
41. Zhang, S., Benenson, R., Schiele, B.: Citypersons: a diverse dataset for pedestrian detection. In: IEEE Conference on Computer Vision and Pattern Recognition (CVPR) (2017)
42. Zhou, C., Yuan, J.: Non-rectangular part discovery for object detection. In: British Machine Vision Conference (BMVC) (2014)
43. Zhou, C., Yuan, J.: Learning to integrate occlusion-specific detectors for heavily occluded pedestrian detection. In: Lai, S.-H., Lepetit, V., Nishino, K., Sato, Y. (eds.) ACCV 2016. LNCS, vol. 10112, pp. 305–320. Springer, Cham (2017). https://doi.org/10.1007/978-3-319-54184-6_19
44. Zhou, C., Yuan, J.: Multi-label learning of part detectors for heavily occluded pedestrian detection. In: International Conference on Computer Vision (ICCV) (2017)

C-WSL: Count-Guided Weakly Supervised Localization

Mingfei Gao[1](✉), Ang Li[2], Ruichi Yu[1], Vlad I. Morariu[3], and Larry S. Davis[1]

[1] University of Maryland, College Park, USA
{mgao,richyu,lsd}@umiacs.umd.edu
[2] DeepMind, Mountain View, CA, USA
anglili@google.com
[3] Adobe Research, College Park, USA
morariu@adobe.com

Abstract. We introduce count-guided weakly supervised localization (C-WSL), an approach that uses per-class object count as a new form of supervision to improve weakly supervised localization (WSL). C-WSL uses a simple count-based region selection algorithm to select high-quality regions, each of which covers a single object instance during training, and improves existing WSL methods by training with the selected regions. To demonstrate the effectiveness of C-WSL, we integrate it into two WSL architectures and conduct extensive experiments on VOC2007 and VOC2012. Experimental results show that C-WSL leads to large improvements in WSL and that the proposed approach significantly outperforms the state-of-the-art methods. The results of annotation experiments on VOC2007 suggest that a modest extra time is needed to obtain per-class object counts compared to labeling only object categories in an image. Furthermore, we reduce the annotation time by more than 2× and 38× compared to center-click and bounding-box annotations.

Keywords: Weakly supervised localization · Count supervision

1 Introduction

Convolutional neural networks (CNN) have achieved state-of-the-art performance on the object detection task [12,20,21,23,27–29,32,33,37–39]. However, these detectors are trained in a strongly supervised setting, requiring a large number of bounding box annotations and huge amounts of human labor.

To ease the burden of human annotation, weakly supervised localization (WSL) methods train a detector using weak supervision, e.g., image-level supervision, instead of tight object bounding boxes. The presence of an object category in an image can be obtained on the Internet nearly for free, so most existing WSL architectures require only object categories as supervision.

A. Li and V. I. Morariu—The work was done while the author was at the University of Maryland.

© Springer Nature Switzerland AG 2018
V. Ferrari et al. (Eds.): ECCV 2018, LNCS 11205, pp. 155–171, 2018.
https://doi.org/10.1007/978-3-030-01246-5_10

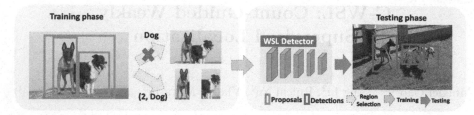

Fig. 1. Given a set of object proposals and the per-class object count label, we select high-quality positive regions (that tightly cover a single object) to train a WSL detector. Count information significantly reduces detected bounding boxes that are loose and contain two or more object instances, one of the most common errors produced by weakly supervised detectors (Color figure online)

Existing methods [1,3,5,14–16,19,24,30,34–36,40] have proposed different architectures to address the WSL problem. However, there is still a large performance gap between weakly and strongly supervised detectors [23,28,29] on standard object detection benchmarks [9,10,22]. Often, this is due to the limited information provided by object-category supervision. One major unsolved problem of WSL is that high confidence detections tend to include multiple objects instead of one. As shown in Fig. 1 (red cross branch), since training images containing multiple dogs are labeled just as "Dog", detectors tend to learn the composite appearance of multiple dogs as if they were one dog and group multiple dogs as a single instance at test time. To resolve this ambiguity, we use per-class object count information to supervise detector training.

Object count is a type of image-level supervision which is much weaker and cheaper than instance-level supervisions, such as center clicks [26] and bounding boxes. Unlike center click and bounding box annotations, which require several well-trained annotators to specify the center and tight box of each object, object count contains no location information and can be obtained without actually clicking on an object. Moreover, a widely studied phenomenon in psychology, called subitizing [4] suggests that humans are able to determine the number of objects without pointing to or fixating on each object sequentially if the total number of objects in the image is small (typically 1–4) [2]. Thus, people may be able to specify the object count with just a glance. To demonstrate the inexpensiveness of count annotation, we conduct annotation experiments on Pascal VOC2007. Experimental results show that only a small amount of extra time is needed to obtain per-class object counts compared to labeling just object categories in an image and the response time of the count annotation is much less than that of object center and bounding box.

Our proposed method, Count-guided WSL (C-WSL), is illustrated in Fig. 1. During the training process, C-WSL makes use of per-class object count supervision to identify the correct high-scoring object bounding boxes from a set of object proposals. Then, a weakly supervised detector is refined with these high-quality regions as pseudo ground-truth (GT) bounding boxes. This strategy is similar to existing WSL methods that refine detectors using automatically identified bounding boxes [14,19,35]. However, since these methods do not make use of object count supervision, they treat only the top-scoring region as the pseudo GT box, regardless of the number of object instances present in the image. This sometimes leads to multiple object instances being grouped into a single pseudo GT box, which hurts the detector's ability to localize individual objects. With the guidance of the object count label, C-WSL selects tight box regions that cover individual objects as shown in Fig. 1 (the "(2, Dog)" branch).

The main contribution of C-WSL is that it uses per-class object count, a cheap and effective form of image-level supervision, to address a common failure case in WSL where one detected bounding box contains multiple object instances. To implement C-WSL, we develop a simple Count-based Region Selection (CRS) algorithm and integrate it into two existing architectures—alternating detector refinement (ADR) and online detector refinement (ODR)—to significantly improve WSL. Experimental results on Pascal VOC2007 [9] and VOC2012 [10] show that C-WSL significantly improves WSL detection and outperforms state-of-the-art methods.

2 Related Works

MIL-based CNN Methods. Most existing WSL methods [1,3,5,14,15,19,24,35, 36] are based on multiple instance learning (MIL) [6]. In the MIL setting, a bag is defined as a collection of regions within an image. A bag is labeled as positive if at least one instance in the bag is positive and labeled as negative if all of its samples are negative. Bilen *et al.* [1] proposed a two-stream CNN architecture to classify and localize simultaneously and train the network in an end-to-end manner. Following [1], Kantorov *et al.* [15] added *additive* and *contrastive* models to improve localization on object boundaries instead of local parts. Singh *et al.* [34] proposed the 'Hide-and-Seek' framework which hides informative patches to encourage WSL to detect complete object instances. In [19], Li *et al.* conducted progressive domain adaption and significantly improved the localization ability of the baseline detector. Diba *et al.* [5] performed WSL in two/three cascaded stages to find the best candidate location based on a generated class activation map. Jie *et al.* proposed a self-taught learning approach in [14] which alternates between classifier training and online supportive sample harvesting. Similarly, in [35], Tang *et al.* designed an online classifier refinement pipeline to progressively locate the most discriminative region of an image. [14] and [35] are most related to our approach since we also conduct alternating and online detector refinement. However, instead of using the top-scoring detection as the positive label [35] or mining confident regions by solving a complex dense subgraph discovery problem [14], we use per-class object count, a cheap form of supervision, to guide region selection and progressively obtain better positive training regions.

WSL with Different Supervisions. [25] proposed a novel framework where an annotator verifies predicted results instead of manually drawing boxes.

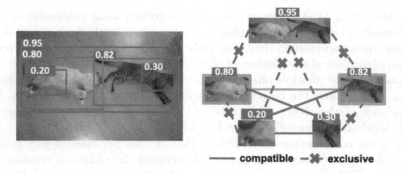

Fig. 2. A common failure case of WSL methods (left) and graph representation of our region selection formulation (right). Our goal is to select the two green boxes, each of which tightly covers one object, as the positive training samples for WSL detectors. We achieve this by analyzing the confidence scores and spatial constraints among regions (Color figure online)

Kolesnikov *et al.* [17] assigned object or distractor labels to co-occuring objects in images to improve WSL. Papadopoulos *et al.* [26] proposed click supervision and integrated it into existing MIL-based methods to improve localization performance. However, these methods either highly depend on the produced results and require frequent interactions with annotators or require annotators to search for and click on each instance in an image. In contrast, object count is an image-level annotation which contains no location information at all. It can be obtained with no clicks and few interactions, thus requires much less annotation time.

3   Proposed Approach

C-WSL selects regions covering a single object with the help of per-class object count supervision and then refines the WSL detector using these regions as the pesudo GT bounding boxes. We first introduce a simple Count-based Region Selection (CRS) algorithm that C-WSL relies on to select high-quality regions from object proposals on training images. Then, we integrate CRS into two detector refinement structures to improve weakly supervised detectors.

3.1   Count-Based Region Selection (CRS)

As shown in Fig. 2 (left), without object count information, previous methods often select the top-scoring box in training images as the positive training sample to refine the WSL detector [14,19,35]. Their detection performance is degraded because in many cases the top-scoring box contains multiple objects from the same category, *e.g.*, two cats. Our goal is to select distinct regions, each covering a single object as positive training samples with the help of object count constraints so that the detector will learn the appearance of a single cat.

We formulate the problem as a region selection problem. Given a set of boxes $\mathbf{B} = \{b_1, ..., b_N\}$ and the corresponding confidence scores $\mathbf{P} = \{p_1, ..., p_N\}$ (*e.g.*, the detection score of a region in each detector refinement iteration), a subset $\mathbf{G}$ is selected as the set of positive training regions where $|\mathbf{G}| = C$ and C indicates the per-class object count. We identify a good subset $\mathbf{G}$ using a greedy algorithm applied to a graphical representation of the set of boxes. Each box is represented as a node in the graph, and two nodes are connected if the spatial overlap of their corresponding boxes is below a threshold (See solid line in Fig. 2). The greedy algorithm provides an approximation to the following optimization problem:

$$\mathbf{G}^* = \arg \max_{\mathbf{G}} \sum_{b_k \in \mathbf{G}} p_k, \tag{1}$$

$$s.t. \ |\mathbf{G}| = C, \ a_o(b_i, b_j) < T \ \forall b_i, b_j \in \mathbf{G}, i \neq j.$$

To encourage selecting regions containing just one object, we use the asymmetric area of overlap, i.e., $a_o(b_i, b_j) = \frac{area(b_i \cap b_j)}{area(b_j)}$, which has been proposed in [7,8] to model spatial overlap between two boxes, where b_i is a box previously selected by the greedy algorithm and b_j indicates a box considered for selection. T is the overlap threshold. If the algorithm has previously added a large box to the solution, thresholding on a_o will discourage the selection of its subregions, regardless of their sizes.[1] So, to deliver a high total score, the algorithm prefers C small high-scoring boxes to one large box, even though the large box may have the highest score.

Algorithm 1. Count-based Region Selection (CRS)

Input : $\mathbf{B} = \{b_1, ..., b_N\}$, $\mathbf{P} = \{p_1, ..., p_N\}$, T, C;
            $\mathbf{B}$ is a list of candidate boxes;
            $\mathbf{P}$ is the corresponding scores;
            T is the overlap threshold;
            C indicates the object count;
Initialization: Sort (descend) $\mathbf{B}$ based on $\mathbf{P}$;
$\mathbf{G}^* \leftarrow \emptyset$; $s_{max} \leftarrow 0$;
Output: $\mathbf{G}^*$
for $i \in \{1, ..., N\}$ do
$\quad$ $\mathbf{G} \leftarrow b_i$; $s \leftarrow p_i$;
$\quad$ for $j \in \{i+1, ..., N\}$ do
$\quad\quad$ if $a_o(b_k, b_j) < T (\forall b_k \in \mathbf{G})$ then
$\quad\quad\quad$ $\mathbf{G} \leftarrow \mathbf{G} \cup \{b_j\}$; $s \leftarrow s + p_j$
$\quad\quad\quad$ if $|\mathbf{G}| == C \ or \ j == N$ then
$\quad\quad\quad\quad$ if $s > s_{max}$ then
$\quad\quad\quad\quad\quad$ $s_{max} \leftarrow s$; $\mathbf{G}^* \leftarrow \mathbf{G}$
$\quad\quad\quad\quad$ break;

---

[1] The commonly used symmetric intersection-over-union measure would select sufficiently small regions even if they were fully overlapped by an existing large box.

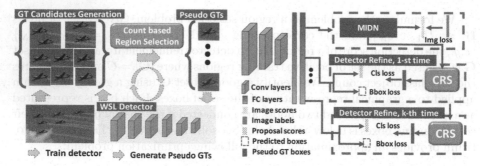

(a) Alternating detector refinement   (b) Online detector refinement w/ CRS

Fig. 3. (a): Count-based Region Selection (*CRS*) is applied to select high-quality positive training regions from the ground-truth (GT) candidate boxes generated by a WSL detector. The WSL detector is then refined using these regions. (b): The Multiple Instance Detection Network(*MIDN*) [1,35] and multiple detector networks share the same feature representation to refine the detector at all stages together. *Cls loss* indicates the classification loss and *Bbox loss* indicates bounding box regression loss

We conduct region selection after applying non-maximum suppression on a complete set of the detection boxes, so the number of nodes is limited to a reasonable number, and the computation cost is low in practice. The algorithm is summarized in Algorithm 1.

3.2   Detector Refinement Structures with CRS

Alternating Detector Refinement (ADR). We first integrate CRS into an alternating WSL refinement architecture, where a poor weakly supervised detector can be refined iteratively. The architecture is shown in Fig. 3, where a WSL detector alternates between generating high-quality regions as pseudo ground-truth (GT) boxes and refining itself using these GT boxes. Some WSL methods are based on a strategy like this [3,14]. The major difference is that we use CRS to select multiple high-quality regions as the GT boxes.

Initialization Phase. We first generate a set of box candidates from the training data using a pre-trained WSL detector. This set of box candidates is treated as the initialized pseudo GTs and will be refined iteratively afterwards.

Alternating Training Phase. We use Fast R-CNN [13] as our WSL network. Starting from the initialized pseudo GT boxes, Fast R-CNN alternates between improving itself via retraining with the pseudo GT boxes generated by CRS and generating a refined set of GT candidate boxes on the training images.

Online Detector Refinement (ODR). As argued in [35], the alternating strategy has two potential limitations: (1) it is time consuming to alternate between training on the fixed labels and generating labels by the trained model;

(2) separating refinements into different iterations might harm performance since it hinders the procedure from sharing image representations across iterations.

Based on [35], we propose an online detector refinement framework integrated with CRS. An illustration of the proposed method is shown in Fig. 3. A Multiple Instance Detection Network (MIDN) and several detector refinement stages share the same feature representation extracted from a backbone structure. The MIDN utilizes an object-category label to supervise its training as in [1,35]. Each detector refinement network outputs the classification score and predicted bounding box for each region proposal. The predicted boxes with scores at each stage will be used to select pseudo GTs for the next stage refinement. Compared to [35], we have two major differences: (1) we use CRS to generate high-quality regions as pseudo GTs rather than just choosing the top-scoring region; (2) we use both classification loss and bounding box regression loss for detector refinement, just as RCNNs do. Note that the inputs to CRS produced by MIDN are the proposals with scores before the summation over proposals.

4   Experiments

We compare with the existing WSL methods which are trained by object class labels to show the advantage of per-class count supervision. It may seem an 'unfair' comparison, since the per-class count provides more information compared to object class. However, we demonstrate via our annotation experiment that the cost of the additional information is very low, which makes it reasonable to determine how much improvement can be gained by adding this information.

4.1   Experimental Setup

Datasets and Evaluate Metrics. Comparisons with state-of-the-art methods are conducted on VOC2007 [9] and VOC2012 [10] which contain 20 object categories. For VOC2007, all the models are trained on the *trainval* set which contains 5,011 images and evaluated on *test* set which includes 4,952 images. For VOC2012, models are trained on 5,717 images of the *train* set and evaluated on 5,823 images in the *val* set. We use two widely used metrics for localization evaluation: Correct localization (CorLoc) [24] and Average Precision (AP) [11]. CorLoc evaluates localization accuracy by measuring if the maximum response point of a detection is inside the ground truth bounding box. AP evaluates models by comparing IoU between output and ground truth bounding boxes.

Implementation Details. We fix $T = 0.1$ for all models at all the iterations on both datasets. Note that our experiments show that the method is robust to T, *e.g.*, varying T from 0.1 to 1 with step 0.1, we achieved (Mean, Std) = (47.2%, 0.42%) mAP. Following [14,35], we set the total iteration number to 3 and use *VGG16* [31] as the backbone structure for both ADR and ODR. For fair comparison, the existing works also use *VGG16* except for [3] which utilizes *AlexNet*. In ADR, we strictly follow the steps of training Fast-RCNN at each iteration and use all the released default training parameters except that we use the generated pseudo GT boxes instead of the bounding box labels. In ODR, we follow the basic MIDN structure and training process from [35], and use the parameters released by the author. Note that we use the same classification and bounding box regression loss in ODR as in [13].

Variants of Our Approach. C-WSL:WSLPDA/OICR+ADR indicates ADR initialized with a pre-trained WSLPDA [19] (or OICR [35]) model where CRS is used to select confident GT boxes in each iteration. Then, a Fast-RCNN is alternatively refined as we mentioned in Sect. 3.2. *C-WSL:ODR* indicates the structure shown in Fig. 3(b). *C-WSL:ODR+FRCNN* denotes a Fast RCNN trained with the top-scoring region generated by *C-WSL:ODR* to improve results (inspired by [19, 35]). *C-WSL** indicates models trained by our annotated counts.

4.2   Annotation Time vs. Detection Accuracy

Object counting is very straightforward. The user interface includes an image and 15 buttons indicating the count numbers. We cap object count with 15 since it is very rare to have a count of the same class bigger than 15. Similar to the click experiments [21], an annotator was given a category and was asked to click the count corresponding to that category. Following [26], given an object category, we measure the response time of counting the object instances from the moment the image appears until the count is determined.

Annotation evaluations are conducted on the full *trainval* set with 20 categories of VOC2007 [9]. The average response time of counting a single object per class per image is 0.90 s. Average response time per image of annotating a single image class is from 1.5 s to 1.9 s [18] and that of annotating count given object class is 1.48s, so obtaining per-class object count from an image only needs $1.48/1.9 = 78\%$ to $1.48/1.5 = 99\%$ more time compared to annotating just the object class.

Annotation time of object counts per image increases as the number of objects increases. However, it might not always be helpful to count all the objects, especially for images with many objects, since these images are more likely to depict complex scenes, *e.g.*, significant occlusions and small object instances, and for such images the generated GT candidates might not include all the objects in the first place. Thus, we evaluate the detection accuracy of our model using at most K per-class objects annotation, where K is the upper bound of per-class object instances that are counted for each image. Obviously, K has positive

Table 1. Accuracy vs. cost among bounding box, clicks and count supervisions on VOC2007. We use [29] as a reference of fully supervised detector

Method	Faster-RCNN [29]	Two-clicks [26]	One-click [26]	C-WSL*: ODR+FRCNN
mAP(%)	69.9	49.1(AlexNet)/57.5(VGG16)	45.9(AlexNet)	48.2(VGG16)
Annotation cost	34.5s/img+anno. train+re-draw rejected boxes	3.74s/img+anno. train+re-click rejected clicks	1.87s/img+anno. train+re-click rejected clicks	0.90s/img

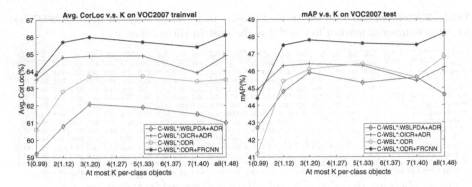

Fig. 4. Detection accuracy analysis when at most K per-class objects are counted in an image. Average annotation time (in seconds) per image under each K is shown in the parentheses. Detection accuracy becomes stable when $K = 3$

correlation with annotation time, since annotators may not be able to subitize for high values of K and will need to spend an amount of time proportional to K in order to produce an accurate count. Analysis of mAP and average $CorLoc$ vs. K is shown in Fig. 4. The results suggest that the detection accuracy reaches the highest point when at most 3 per-class objects are counted per image. Average annotation time per image for images with at most 3 per-class objects is 1.20 s which is 63%–80% overhead compared to object category annotations.

We compare our models trained by our annotated counts and those obtained from the VOC2007 annotations in Tables 2 and 3. The results demonstrate that models trained by the two sets of annotations have comparable performance, which suggests that our annotation is as useful as the VOC2007 annotations. Thus, in the following analysis, we just use (C-WSL) VOC2007 annotations.

Accuracy and cost comparisons among box, clicks and count supervisions are shown in Table 1. Although the accuracy of our approach does not outperform supervised and two-click methods, we have achieved a significant reduction in annotation cost. We are 38× and 4× faster regarding to response time for labeling a single image. In addition, box and clicks annotations require additional repeated annotator training to accurately locate objects and lengthy quality control processes. Our annotation does not require knowing the location of an object so it avoids the sensitivity to location noise. Consequently, we do not need annotator training and quality control in our experiments.

4.3 Comparison with State-of-the-art (SOTA) Approaches

Comparison in terms of mAP on the VOC2007 *test* set and $CorLoc$ on the VOC2007 *trainval* set are shown in Tables 2 and 3, respectively. Overall, the proposed C-$WSL:ODR+FRCNN$ outperforms all the existing SOTA methods using both $CorLoc$ and mAP measurements.

Tables 4 and 5 compare our variants with the two baseline detectors, *i.e.*, WSLPDA [19] and OICR [35]. The results suggest that even the simple ADR

Table 2. Comparison with the state-of-the-art in terms of mAP on the VOC2007 *test* set. Our number is marked in red if it is the best in the column

Methods	are	bik	brd	boa	btl	bus	car	cat	cha	cow	tbl	dog	hrs	mbk	prs	plt	shp	sfa	trn	tv	mAP
Cinbis et al. [3]	39.3	43.0	28.8	20.4	8.0	45.5	47.9	22.1	8.4	33.5	23.6	29.2	38.5	47.9	20.3	20.0	35.8	30.8	41.0	20.1	30.2
Wang et al. [36]	48.8	41.0	23.6	12.1	11.1	42.7	40.9	35.5	11.1	36.6	18.4	35.3	34.8	51.3	17.2	17.4	26.8	32.8	35.1	45.6	30.9
Jie et al. [14]	52.2	47.1	35.0	26.7	15.4	61.3	66.0	54.3	3.0	53.6	24.7	43.6	48.4	65.8	6.6	18.8	51.9	43.6	53.6	62.4	41.7
WSDDN [1]	39.4	50.1	31.5	16.3	12.6	64.5	42.8	42.6	10.1	35.7	24.9	38.2	34.4	55.6	9.4	14.7	30.2	40.7	54.7	46.9	34.8
WSDDN+Context [15]	57.1	52.0	31.5	7.6	11.5	55.0	53.1	34.1	1.7	33.1	49.2	42.0	47.3	56.6	15.3	12.8	24.8	48.9	44.4	47.8	36.3
WSDDN-Ens. [1]	46.4	58.3	35.5	25.9	14.0	66.7	53.0	39.2	8.9	41.8	26.6	38.6	44.7	59.0	10.8	17.3	40.7	49.6	56.9	50.8	39.3
WCCN-3stage [5]	49.5	60.6	38.6	29.2	16.2	70.8	56.9	42.5	10.9	44.1	29.9	42.2	47.9	64.1	13.8	23.5	45.9	54.1	60.8	54.5	42.8
WSLPDA [19]	54.5	47.4	41.3	20.8	17.7	51.9	63.5	46.1	21.8	57.1	22.1	34.4	50.5	61.8	16.2	29.9	40.7	15.9	55.3	40.2	39.5
OICR [35]	58.0	62.4	31.1	19.4	13.0	65.1	62.2	28.4	24.8	44.7	30.6	25.3	37.8	65.5	15.7	24.1	41.7	46.9	64.3	62.6	41.2
OICR-Ens.+FRCNN[a] [35]	64.5	64.4	44.1	25.9	16.9	67.8	68.4	33.2	9.0	57.5	46.4	21.7	57.8	64.3	10.0	23.7	50.6	60.9	64.7	58.0	45.5
C-WSL:ODR	62.7	63.7	40.0	25.5	17.7	70.1	68.3	38.9	25.4	54.5	41.6	29.9	37.9	64.2	11.3	27.4	49.3	54.7	61.4	67.4	45.6
C-WSL*:ODR	62.9	64.8	39.8	28.1	16.4	69.5	68.2	47.0	27.9	55.8	43.7	31.2	43.8	65.0	10.9	26.1	52.7	55.3	60.2	66.6	46.8
C-WSL:ODR+FRCNN	61.9	61.9	48.6	28.7	23.3	71.1	71.3	38.7	28.5	60.6	45.4	26.3	49.7	65.5	7.2	27.3	54.7	61.6	63.2	59.5	47.8
C-WSL*:ODR+FRCNN	62.9	68.3	52.9	25.8	16.5	71.1	69.5	48.2	26.0	58.6	44.5	28.2	49.6	66.4	10.2	26.4	55.3	59.9	61.6	62.2	48.2

[a] The numbers are reproduced by using the code released by the author.

Table 3. Comparison with the state-of-the-art in terms of CorLoc (%) on the VOC2007 *trainval* set. Our number is marked in red if it is the best in the column

Methods	are	bik	brd	boa	btl	bus	car	cat	cha	cow	tbl	dog	hrs	mbk	prs	plt	shp	sfa	trn	tv	Avg.
Cinbis et al. [3]	65.3	55.0	52.4	48.3	18.2	66.4	77.8	35.6	26.5	67.0	46.9	48.4	70.5	69.1	35.2	35.2	69.6	43.4	64.6	43.7	52.0
Wang et al. [36]	80.1	63.9	51.5	14.9	21.0	55.7	74.2	43.5	26.2	53.4	16.3	56.7	58.3	69.5	14.1	38.3	58.8	47.2	49.1	60.9	48.5
Jie et al. [14]	72.7	55.3	53.0	27.8	35.2	68.6	81.9	60.7	11.6	71.6	29.7	54.3	64.3	88.2	22.2	53.7	72.2	52.6	68.9	75.5	56.1
WSDDN [1]	65.1	58.8	58.5	33.1	39.8	68.3	60.2	59.6	34.8	64.5	30.5	43.0	56.8	82.4	25.5	41.6	61.5	55.9	65.9	63.7	53.5
WSDDN+Context [15]	83.3	68.6	54.7	23.4	18.3	73.6	74.1	54.1	8.6	65.1	47.1	59.5	67.0	83.5	35.3	39.9	67.0	49.7	63.5	65.2	55.1
WSDDN-Ens. [1]	68.9	68.7	65.2	42.5	40.6	72.6	75.2	53.7	29.7	68.1	33.5	45.6	65.9	86.1	27.5	44.9	76.0	62.4	66.3	66.8	58.0
WCCN-3stage [5]	83.9	72.8	64.5	44.1	40.1	65.7	82.5	58.9	33.7	72.5	25.6	53.7	67.4	77.4	26.8	49.1	68.1	27.9	64.5	55.7	56.7
SP-VGGNet [40]	85.3	64.2	67.0	42.0	16.4	71.0	64.7	88.7	20.7	63.8	58.0	84.1	84.7	80.0	60.0	29.4	56.3	68.1	77.4	30.5	60.6
WSLPDA [19]	78.2	67.1	61.8	38.1	36.1	61.8	78.8	55.2	28.5	68.8	18.5	49.2	64.1	73.5	21.4	47.4	64.6	22.3	60.9	52.3	52.4
OICR [35]	81.7	80.4	48.7	49.5	32.8	81.7	85.4	40.1	40.6	79.5	35.7	33.7	60.5	88.8	21.8	57.9	76.3	59.9	75.3	81.4	60.6
OICR-Ens.+FRCNN[2] [35]	85.8	78.8	62.8	48.9	38.9	83.2	85.4	50.0	21.9	77.4	45.6	41.9	79.3	91.6	12.6	60.8	86.6	70.2	80.2	79.9	64.2
C-WSL:ODR	86.3	80.4	58.3	50.0	36.6	85.8	86.2	47.1	42.7	81.5	42.2	42.6	50.7	90.0	14.3	61.9	85.6	64.2	77.2	82.4	63.3
C-WSL*:ODR	85.8	81.2	64.9	50.5	32.1	84.3	85.9	54.7	43.4	80.1	42.2	42.6	60.5	90.4	13.7	57.5	82.5	61.8	74.1	82.4	63.5
C-WSL:ODR+FRCNN	85.8	78.0	61.6	52.1	44.7	81.7	88.4	49.1	50.0	82.9	44.1	44.4	63.9	92.4	14.3	60.4	86.6	68.3	80.6	82.8	65.6
C-WSL*:ODR+FRCNN	87.5	81.6	65.5	52.1	37.4	83.8	87.9	57.6	50.3	80.8	44.9	44.4	65.6	92.8	14.9	61.2	83.5	68.5	77.6	83.5	66.1

[a] The numbers are reproduced by using the code released by the author.

Table 4. Comparison with baselines in terms of mAP on the VOC2007 *test* set. The table contains two comparison groups separated by double solid lines. Each group shows how much ADR and C-WSL improve each baseline. Underline is used if the C-WSL variant outperforms its baselines

Methods	are	bik	brd	boa	btl	bus	car	cat	cha	cow	tbl	dog	hrs	mbk	prs	plt	shp	sfa	trn	tv	mAP
WSLPDA [19]	54.5	47.4	41.3	20.8	17.7	51.9	63.5	46.1	21.8	57.1	22.1	34.4	50.5	61.8	16.2	29.9	40.7	15.9	55.3	40.2	39.5
WSLPDA+ADR	57.9	68.3	47.8	20.3	12.2	52.9	67.6	68.8	24.6	50.0	24.9	49.8	54.8	63.5	14.1	27.4	41.2	19.5	57.1	30.7	42.7
C-WSL:WSLPDA+ADR	60.5	70.1	52.5	24.7	24.4	63.6	71.8	58.1	26.0	66.4	26.5	34.7	55.0	65.8	8.8	31.9	51.6	20.4	60.0	41.8	45.7
OICR [35]	58.0	62.4	31.1	19.4	13.0	65.1	62.2	28.4	24.8	44.7	30.6	25.3	37.8	65.5	15.7	24.1	41.7	46.9	64.3	62.6	41.2
OICR+ADR	58.1	61.2	43.3	24.4	19.4	65.5	67.1	34.3	3.6	56.5	45.5	26.4	61.9	60.7	10.4	23.6	49.2	62.1	61.4	64.2	44.9
C-WSL:OICR+ADR	61.7	66.8	45.6	21.1	23.5	67.2	73.8	32.5	10.6	54.6	42.9	16.6	59.2	63.3	11.0	25.4	55.3	61.3	67.4	67.8	46.4

Table 5. Comparison with the baseline detectors in terms of CorLoc (%) on the VOC2007 *trainval* set. The table contains two comparison groups separated by double solid lines. Each group shows how much ADR and C-WSL improve each baseline. Underline is used if the C-WSL variant outperforms its baselines

Methods	are	bik	brd	boa	btl	bus	car	cat	cha	cow	tbl	dog	hrs	mbk	prs	plt	shp	sfa	trn	tv	Avg.
WSLPDA [19]	78.2	67.1	61.8	38.1	36.1	61.8	78.8	55.2	28.5	68.8	18.5	49.2	64.1	73.5	21.4	47.4	64.6	22.3	60.9	52.3	52.4
WSLPDA+ADR	84.6	76.9	69.7	41.0	21.8	68.5	83.2	77.6	34.4	76.7	19.8	73.7	75.2	84.7	26.3	53.8	70.1	22.3	73.8	50.9	59.2
C-WSL:WSLPDA+ADR	83.3	80.0	70.9	51.6	41.2	73.6	85.3	67.7	40.7	79.5	20.9	54.7	79.6	87.1	24.5	56.8	83.5	20.7	76.0	60.2	61.9
OICR [35]	81.7	80.4	48.7	49.5	32.8	81.7	85.4	40.1	40.6	79.5	35.7	33.7	60.5	88.8	21.8	57.9	76.3	59.9	75.3	81.4	60.6
OICR+ADR	85.8	76.9	65.8	49.5	38.5	83.2	84.8	49.7	14.0	79.5	46.8	41.2	80.3	89.2	15.0	60.1	84.5	66.4	78.3	80.6	63.5
C-WSL:OICR+ADR	85.4	78.0	65.5	49.5	43.5	84.3	87.5	48.0	23.6	80.8	43.3	38.8	79.9	92.8	15.8	60.1	87.6	66.4	81.0	80.3	64.6

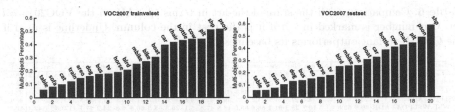

Fig. 5. Image number of multiple-objects over image number of non-zero objects. Note that "pson" means "person", "plt" means "plant" and "shp" denotes "sheep". C-WSL works better on most classes with high multiple-objects percentage. See Sect. 4.3

strategy can significantly improve the results. Moreover, if we use object count information, we can largely improve WSLPDA by 6.2% *mAP* (9.5% average *CorLoc*) and OICR by 5.2% *mAP* (4.0% average *CorLoc*). C-WSL improves the results of *WSLPDA+ADR* on 17 (15) out of 20 categories and the results of *OICR+ADR* on 10 (10) out of 20 categories in terms of *mAP* on the VOC2007 *test* set (in terms of *CorLoc* on the VOC2007 *trainval* set).

As stated in Sect. 1, the object count information is helpful to avoid a detector localizing on multiple objects. To demonstrate this point, we first calculate the percentage of images that have more than one per-class object (multi-objects percentage) in VOC2007. As shown in Fig. 5, "bottle", "car", "chair", "cow", "person", "plant" and "sheep" have a high percentage of images which include more than one object in the corresponding category. As shown in Tables 2 and 3, *C-WSL:ODR+FRCNN* outperforms SOTA methods for 5 out of these 7 categories. When looking into the effect of object count supervision on WSLPDA and OICR, we see significant improvement on these categories as shown in Tables 4 and 5. Consider the "sheep" category for example. *C-WSL:WSLPDA+ADR* improves *WSLPDA+ADR* by 13.4% *CorLoc* and 10.4% *AP*. *C-WSL:OICR+ADR* improves *OICR+ADR* by 3.1% *CorLoc* and 6.1% *AP*. Figure 6 shows some examples of training regions selected by *OICR+CRS* and *OICR*. OICR tends to select regions containing multiple instances, while object count helps to obtain regions including a single instance. Qualitative comparison between our *C-WSL:ODR+FRCNN* and *OICR-Ens.+FRCNN* on the VOC2007 *test* set is shown in Fig. 8, demonstrating that our approach achieves more precise localization when multiple per-class objects appear in an image. We will further analyze our approach on images with different numbers of objects in Sect. 4.4.

Tables 6 and 7 show the comparison of C-WSL with the SOTA on VOC2012. Note that results of WSLPDA and OICR models are reproduced by running the pretrained model and the code released by the authors. The results suggest that our method outperforms the SOTA method (*OICR-Ens.+FRCNN*) by 2.6% in *mAP* on the VOC2012 *val* set and by 2.8% in *CorLoc* on the VOC2012 *train* set. C-WSL improves the results of *WSLPDA+ADR* on 12 (10) out of 20 categories and the results of *OICR+ADR* on 10 (12) out of 20 categories in terms of *mAP* on the VOC2012 *val* set (in terms of *CorLoc* on the VOC2012 *train* set).

Table 6. Comparison with the state-of-the-art in terms of mAP on the VOC2012 *val* set. Our number is marked in red if it is the best in the column. Underline is used if the C-WSL variant outperforms its baselines

Methods	are	bik	brd	boa	btl	bus	car	cat	cha	cow	tbl	dog	hrs	mbk	prs	plt	shp	sfa	trn	tv	mAP
Jie et al. [14]	60.9	53.3	31.0	16.4	18.2	58.2	50.5	55.6	9.1	42.1	12.1	43.4	45.3	64.6	7.4	19.3	44.8	39.3	51.4	57.2	39.0
OICR-Ens.+FRCNN [35]	71.0	68.2	52.7	20.1	27.2	57.3	57.1	19.0	8.0	50.6	30.2	34.5	63.3	69.5	1.2	20.5	48.5	55.2	41.1	60.4	42.8
WSLPDA [19]	42.2	27.8	32.7	4.2	13.7	52.1	35.8	48.3	11.8	31.7	4.9	30.4	45.3	51.8	11.5	13.4	33.5	7.2	45.6	38.4	29.1
WSLPDA+ADR	70.0	65.6	46.3	14.4	22.8	57.5	54.2	67.5	16.1	45.0	4.4	40.0	51.7	71.8	5.8	27.7	38.3	11.7	55.2	34.1	40.0
C-WSL:WSLPDA+ADR	69.8	62.8	52.7	16.7	28.3	61.1	56.6	58.0	18.5	47.8	5.1	36.3	53.3	66.8	6.8	24.2	47.1	11.0	60.1	43.4	41.3
OICR [35]	71.0	59.1	42.3	27.4	20.2	58.7	46.4	18.6	18.1	45.7	21.7	20.5	53.1	68.5	1.8	15.7	42.7	40.0	41.0	61.5	38.7
OICR+ADR	67.0	63.1	50.8	12.8	23.8	55.3	55.1	16.1	5.2	47.2	23.4	28.2	55.9	69.2	1.9	21.5	46.5	49.9	35.9	63.8	39.6
C-WSL:OICR+ADR	71.3	68.3	50.9	17.1	24.8	60.9	56.4	13.9	14.5	54.6	22.2	25.7	57.7	70.4	1.6	20.0	55.8	46.0	35.7	62.9	41.5
C-WSL:ODR	74.0	67.3	45.6	29.2	26.8	62.5	54.8	21.5	22.6	50.6	24.7	25.6	57.4	71.0	2.4	22.8	44.5	44.2	45.2	66.9	43.0
C-WSL:ODR+FRCNN	75.3	71.6	52.6	32.5	29.9	62.9	56.9	16.9	24.5	59.0	28.9	27.6	65.4	72.6	1.4	23.0	49.4	52.3	42.4	62.2	45.4

Table 7. Comparison with the state-of-the-art in terms of *CorLoc* on the VOC2012 *train* set. Our number is marked in red if it is the best in the column. Underline is used if the C-WSL variant outperforms its baselines

Methods	are	bik	brd	boa	btl	bus	car	cat	cha	cow	tbl	dog	hrs	mbk	prs	plt	shp	sfa	trn	tv	Avg.
OICR-Ens.+FRCNN [35]	85.4	81.5	70.4	44.7	46.6	83.6	78.4	33.9	29.3	83.2	51.6	50.5	86.1	88.0	11.0	56.7	82.5	69.1	65.1	83.6	64.1
WSLPDA [19]	80.5	63.7	64.4	34.1	29.3	76.7	71.5	62.8	30.3	76.1	23.0	55.3	75.2	77.7	18.7	56.4	66.7	25.1	66.5	54.8	55.4
WSLPDA+ADR	87.2	79.7	72.4	38.6	40.9	82.6	75.2	79.8	35.1	81.3	18.9	62.1	82.4	83.9	21.6	60.9	75.4	29.5	74.5	55.5	61.9
C-WSL:WSLPDA+ADR	85.7	77.2	73.4	38.6	46.4	84.9	75.8	69.1	43.0	76.8	20.1	58.6	79.8	79.6	20.3	57.8	79.5	35.4	76.4	61.9	62.0
OICR [35]	86.6	80.4	65.2	57.6	42.1	85.4	72.5	28.0	45.7	79.4	46.2	34.0	78.2	87.2	7.5	55.0	83.6	58.5	62.2	84.3	62.0
OICR+ADR	84.5	79.0	72.4	39.0	47.1	83.6	79.9	31.9	25.0	84.5	48.7	48.3	87.8	88.7	13.3	55.0	82.5	67.4	65.1	83.9	63.4
C-WSL:OICR+ADR	86.6	80.8	73.9	43.2	44.4	87.7	76.2	32.2	34.0	87.1	49.1	46.2	88.2	91.2	12.1	57.1	78.4	65.5	65.1	85.3	64.2
C-WSL:ODR	90.9	81.1	64.9	57.6	84.9	78.1	29.8	49.7	83.9	50.9	42.6	78.6	87.6	10.4	58.1	85.4	61.0	64.7	86.6	64.9	
C-WSL:ODR+FRCNN	92.1	84.3	69.9	58.3	53.9	86.8	80.4	30.6	52.6	83.9	54.7	45.8	83.2	90.1	12.7	56.4	86.0	64.9	66.5	84.3	66.9

Fig. 6. Examples of the training regions selected by *OICR+CRS* (red) and *OICR* (yellow). The regions selected by *OICR* contain multiple object instances. Object count information helps to select regions, each covering a single instance (Color figure online)

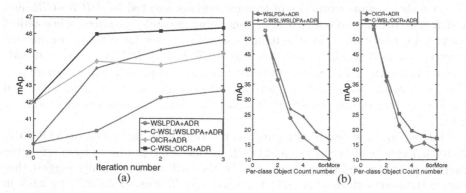

Fig. 7. (a): Model improvement as the number of *ADR* iterations increases on the VOC2007 *test* set. *C-WSL* approaches improve faster than others. (b): Evaluation on images with different per-class object counts on VOC2007. Our approach outperforms the WSL detectors in the presence of multiple instances in a test image

We also evaluated our methods and baselines (pre-trained on the VOC2007 trainval set) on the common 20 classes in MS COCO [22] 35k-val2014 set using COCO mAP@0.5 metric. Although not fine-tuned on COCO, our approaches still outperform the baseline methods. The results are that C-WSL:WSLPDA improves WSLPDA [19] from 17.9% to 19.6%. C-WSL:OICR+ADR improves OICR [35] from 18.7% to 20.1% and C-WSL:ODR+FRCNN improves OICR-Ens.+FRCNN [35] from 19.0% to 20.0%.

4.4 Ablation Analysis

Two major components contribute to the success of our approach. One is the iterative training process (alternating/online) and the other one is the per-class object count supervision. In Tables 4 and 5, we can see the improvement by adding ADR and object count into the system. For WSLPDA [19], iterative training (ADR) improves mAP by 3.2% and the count information (CRS) increases it by 3%. For OICR [35], ADR helps by increasing 3.7% mAP and CRS contributes 1.5%. In the following, we analyze each component in detail.

Number of iterations. ADR performances as a function of the number of iterations using the WSLDPA and OICR models is shown in Fig. 7(a). Generally, models improve as the number of iterations increases. When adding object count supervision into the framework, the results of both WSLDPA and OICR models improve faster, which demonstrates the advantage of count information in WSL.

Fig. 8. Qualitative comparison between our *CWSL:ODR+FRCNN* (red boxes) and *OICR+FRCNN* (yellow boxes) on the VOC2007 *test* set over the 20 classes. Our detector detects much tighter bounding boxes, yields much fewer boxes with multiple objects in them, and finds instances more accurately (Color figure online)

Fig. 9. Some examples of the common failure cases of our approach (*C-WSL: ODR+FRCNN*) on the "person" category of the VOC2007 *test* set

Number of object instances per image. Adding the object count constraint helps a detector focus on a single object rather than multiple objects. To demonstrate this, we partition images in the VOC2007 *test* set based on their per-class object count and re-evaluate our approaches on each subset.

The results are shown in Fig. 7(b). For both WSLPDA and OICR, the performance is much better under C-WSL. Generally, the gaps between curves of with and without C-WSL are bigger as the object count number increases.

4.5 Error Analysis

The results shown in Tables 2, 3, 6 and 7 suggest that most existing WSL detectors perform poorly on the "person" category: strongly supervised detectors achieve more than 76% AP on the VOC2007 *test* set (*e.g.*, 76.6% [23] and 76.3% [29]), while the best WSL detection result on "person" is 20.3% (see Table 2). This result is likely due to the large appearance variations of persons in the dataset. Without constraints provided by tight bounding boxes, rigid parts are easier to learn and mostly sufficient to differentiate the object from others. So, WSL detectors focus on local parts instead of the whole object as shown in Fig. 9.

Intuitively, this can be overcome if we can roughly estimate the size of object instances. We conducted a preliminary experiment as follows. Suppose that we know the size of the smallest instance of an object category in an image and assume all the object parts are smaller than the smallest object. This assumption is not generally true and we use it just as a proof-of-concept. We preprocess the region candidates by removing all boxes whose size is smaller than the smallest object and then conduct *C-WSL:WSLPDA+ADR* on VOC2007. The *AP* on "person" improves to 40.0% and the *mAP* over all the classes improves to 52.7%.

5 Conclusions

We proposed a Count-guided Weakly Supervised Localization (C-WSL) framework where a cheap and effective form of image-level supervision, *i.e.*, per-class object count, is used to select training regions each of which tightly covers a single object instance for detector refinement. As a part of C-WSL, we proposed a Count-based Region Selection (CRS) algorithm to perform high-quality region selection. We integrated CRS into two detector refinement architectures to improve WSL detectors. Experimental results demonstrate the effectiveness of C-WSL. To prove the inexpensiveness of the per-class object count annotation, we conduct annotation experiments on VOC2007. The results show that only a small amount of time is needed to obtain the count information in an image and that we reduce the annotation time of center click and bounding box by more than $2\times$ and $38\times$ respectively.

Acknowledgement. The research was supported by the Office of Naval Research under Grant N000141612713: Visual Common Sense Reasoning for Multi-agent Activity Prediction and Recognition. The authors would like to thank Eddie Kessler for proofreading the manuscript.

References

1. Bilen, H., Vedaldi, A.: Weakly supervised deep detection networks. In: The IEEE Conference on Computer Vision and Pattern Recognition (CVPR), June 2016
2. Chattopadhyay, P., Vedantam, R., Selvaraju, R.R., Batra, D., Parikh, D.: Counting everyday objects in everyday scenes. In: CVPR (2017)
3. Cinbis, R.G., Verbeek, J., Schmid, C.: Weakly supervised object localization with multi-fold multiple instance learning. IEEE Trans. Pattern Anal. Mach. Intell. **39**(1), 189–203 (2017)
4. Clements, D.H.: Subitizing: what is it? why teach it? Teach. Child. Math. **5**(7), 400 (1999)
5. Diba, A., Sharma, V., Pazandeh, A., Pirsiavash, H., Van Gool, L.: Weakly supervised cascaded convolutional networks. In: Proceedings of the 2017 IEEE Conference on Computer Vision and Pattern Recognition (CVPR), pp. 5131–5139 (2017)
6. Dietterich, T.G., Lathrop, R.H., Lozano-Pérez, T.: Solving the multiple instance problem with axis-parallel rectangles. Artif. Intell. **89**(1), 31–71 (1997)
7. Dollár, P., Tu, Z., Perona, P., Belongie, S.: Integral channel features. In: BMVC (2009)
8. Dollar, P., Wojek, C., Schiele, B., Perona, P.: Pedestrian detection: an evaluation of the state of the art. IEEE Trans. Pattern Anal. Mach. Intell. **34**(4), 743–761 (2012)
9. Everingham, M., Van Gool, L., Williams, C.K.I., Winn, J., Zisserman, A.: The PASCAL visual object classes challenge 2007 (VOC2007) results. http://www.pascal-network.org/challenges/VOC/voc2007/workshop/index.html
10. Everingham, M., Van Gool, L., Williams, C.K.I., Winn, J., Zisserman, A.: The PASCAL visual object classes challenge 2012 (VOC2012) results. http://www.pascal-network.org/challenges/VOC/voc2012/workshop/index.html
11. Everingham, M., Van Gool, L., Williams, C.K., Winn, J., Zisserman, A.: The pascal visual object classes (voc) challenge. Int. J. Comput. Vis. **88**(2), 303–338 (2010)
12. Gao, M., Yu, R., Li, A., Morariu, V.I., Davis, L.S.: Dynamic zoom-in network for fast object detection in large images. In: IEEE Conference on Computer Vision and Pattern Recognition (CVPR) (2018)
13. Girshick, R.: Fast R-CNN. In: Proceedings of the IEEE International Conference on Computer Vision, pp. 1440–1448 (2015)
14. Jie, Z., Wei, Y., Jin, X., Feng, J., Liu, W.: Deep self-taught learning for weakly supervised object localization. In: IEEE CVPR (2017)

15. Kantorov, V., Oquab, M., Cho, M., Laptev, I.: ContextLocNet: context-aware deep network models for weakly supervised localization. In: Leibe, B., Matas, J., Sebe, N., Welling, M. (eds.) ECCV 2016. LNCS, vol. 9909, pp. 350–365. Springer, Cham (2016). https://doi.org/10.1007/978-3-319-46454-1_22

16. Kim, D., Yoo, D., Kweon, I.S., et al.: Two-phase learning for weakly supervised object localization. In: Proceedings of the IEEE International Conference on Computer Vision (ICCV) (2017)

17. Kolesnikov, A., Lampert, C.H.: Improving weakly-supervised object localization by micro-annotation. In: BMVC (2016)

18. Krishna, R.A., et al.: Embracing error to enable rapid crowdsourcing. In: Proceedings of the 2016 CHI Conference on Human Factors in Computing Systems, pp. 3167–3179. ACM (2016)

19. Li, D., Huang, J.B., Li, Y., Wang, S., Yang, M.H.: Weakly supervised object localization with progressive domain adaptation. In: The IEEE Conference on Computer Vision and Pattern Recognition (CVPR), June 2016

20. Lin, T.Y., Dollár, P., Girshick, R., He, K., Hariharan, B., Belongie, S.: Feature pyramid networks for object detection. In: CVPR (2017)

21. Lin, T.Y., Goyal, P., Girshick, R., He, K., Dollár, P.: Focal loss for dense object detection. In: ICCV (2017)

22. Lin, T.-Y., et al.: Microsoft COCO: common objects in context. In: Fleet, D., Pajdla, T., Schiele, B., Tuytelaars, T. (eds.) ECCV 2014. LNCS, vol. 8693, pp. 740–755. Springer, Cham (2014). https://doi.org/10.1007/978-3-319-10602-1_48

23. Liu, W., et al.: SSD: single shot multibox detector. In: Leibe, B., Matas, J., Sebe, N., Welling, M. (eds.) ECCV 2016. LNCS, vol. 9905, pp. 21–37. Springer, Cham (2016). https://doi.org/10.1007/978-3-319-46448-0_2

24. Oquab, M., Bottou, L., Laptev, I., Sivic, J.: Is object localization for free?-weakly-supervised learning with convolutional neural networks. In: Proceedings of the IEEE Conference on Computer Vision and Pattern Recognition, pp. 685–694 (2015)

25. Papadopoulos, D.P., Uijlings, J.R., Keller, F., Ferrari, V.: We don't need no bounding-boxes: training object class detectors using only human verification. In: Proceedings of the IEEE Conference on Computer Vision and Pattern Recognition, pp. 854–863 (2016)

26. Papadopoulos, D.P., Uijlings, J.R., Keller, F., Ferrari, V.: Training object class detectors with click supervision. In: CVPR (2017)

27. Redmon, J., Divvala, S., Girshick, R., Farhadi, A.: You only look once: unified, real-time object detection. In: Proceedings of the IEEE Conference on Computer Vision and Pattern Recognition, pp. 779–788 (2016)

28. Redmon, J., Farhadi, A.: YOLO9000: better, faster, stronger. In: 2017 IEEE Conference on Computer Vision and Pattern Recognition, CVPR 2017, Honolulu, HI, USA, 21–26 July 2017, pp. 6517–6525 (2017)

29. Ren, S., He, K., Girshick, R., Sun, J.: Faster R-CNN: towards real-time object detection with region proposal networks. In: Advances in Neural Information Processing Systems, pp. 91–99 (2015)

30. Shi, M., Caesar, H., Ferrari, V.: Weakly supervised object localization using things and stuff transfer. In: Proceedings of the IEEE International Conference on Computer Vision (ICCV) (2017)

31. Simonyan, K., Zisserman, A.: Very deep convolutional networks for large-scale image recognition. CoRR abs/1409.1556 (2014)

32. Singh, B., Davis, L.S.: An analysis of scale invariance in object detection-snip. In: Proceedings of the IEEE Conference on Computer Vision and Pattern Recognition, pp. 3578–3587 (2018)

33. Singh, B., Li, H., Sharma, A., Davis, L.S.: R-FCN-3000 at 30fps: decoupling detection and classification. In: Proceedings of the IEEE Conference on Computer Vision and Pattern Recognition, pp. 1081–1090 (2018)
34. Singh, K.K., Lee, Y.J.: Hide-and-seek: forcing a network to be meticulous for weakly-supervised object and action localization. In: The IEEE International Conference on Computer Vision (ICCV) (2017)
35. Tang, P., Wang, X., Bai, X., Liu, W.: Multiple instance detection network with online instance classifier refinement. In: CVPR (2017)
36. Wang, C., Ren, W., Huang, K., Tan, T.: Weakly supervised object localization with latent category learning. In: Fleet, D., Pajdla, T., Schiele, B., Tuytelaars, T. (eds.) ECCV 2014. LNCS, vol. 8694, pp. 431–445. Springer, Cham (2014). https://doi.org/10.1007/978-3-319-10599-4_28
37. Yang, F., Choi, W., Lin, Y.: Exploit all the layers: fast and accurate CNN object detector with scale dependent pooling and cascaded rejection classifiers. In: Proceedings of the IEEE Conference on Computer Vision and Pattern Recognition, pp. 2129–2137 (2016)
38. Yu, R., Chen, X., Morariu, V.I., Davis, L.S.: The role of context selection in object detection. In: British Machine Vision Conference (BMVC) (2016)
39. Yu, R., Li, A., Morariu, V.I., Davis, L.S.: Visual relationship detection with internal and external linguistic knowledge distillation. In: IEEE International Conference on Computer Vision (ICCV) (2017)
40. Zhu, Y., Zhou, Y., Ye, Q., Qiu, Q., Jiao, J.: Soft proposal networks for weakly supervised object localization. In: Proceedings of the IEEE International Conference on Computer Vision (ICCV), pp. 1841–1850 (2017)

Attributes as Operators: Factorizing Unseen Attribute-Object Compositions

Tushar Nagarajan[1(✉)] and Kristen Grauman[2]

[1] The University of Texas at Austin, Austin, USA
tushar@cs.utexas.edu
[2] Facebook AI Research, Austin, USA
grauman@fb.com

Abstract. We present a new approach to modeling visual attributes. Prior work casts attributes in a similar role as objects, learning a latent representation where properties (e.g., *sliced*) are recognized by classifiers much in the way objects (e.g., *apple*) are. However, this common approach fails to separate the attributes observed during training from the objects with which they are composed, making it ineffectual when encountering new attribute-object compositions. Instead, we propose to model attributes as *operators*. Our approach learns a semantic embedding that explicitly factors out attributes from their accompanying objects, and also benefits from novel regularizers expressing attribute operators' effects (e.g., *blunt* should undo the effects of *sharp*). Not only does our approach align conceptually with the linguistic role of attributes as modifiers, but it also generalizes to recognize unseen compositions of objects and attributes. We validate our approach on two challenging datasets and demonstrate significant improvements over the state of the art. In addition, we show that not only can our model recognize unseen compositions robustly in an open-world setting, it can also generalize to compositions where objects themselves were unseen during training.

1 Introduction

Attributes are semantic descriptions that convey an object's properties—such as its materials, colors, patterns, styles, expressions, parts, or functions. Attributes have proven to be an effective representation for faces and people [26,29,32,36,44,45,49], catalog products [4,17,24,56], and generic objects and scenes [1,11,19,27,28,37]. Because they are expressed in natural language, attributes facilitate human-machine communication about visual content,

---

K. Grauman—On leave from University of Texas at Austin (grauman@cs.ute
xas.edu).

Electronic supplementary material The online version of this chapter (https://
doi.org/10.1007/978-3-030-01246-5_11) contains supplementary material, which is
available to authorized users.

© Springer Nature Switzerland AG 2018
V. Ferrari et al. (Eds.): ECCV 2018, LNCS 11205, pp. 172–190, 2018.
https://doi.org/10.1007/978-3-030-01246-5_11

e.g., for applications in image search [24,26], zero-shot learning [1], narration [25], or image generation [54].

Attributes and objects are fundamentally different entities: objects are physical things (nouns), whereas attributes are properties of those things (adjectives). Despite this fact, existing methods for attributes largely proceed in the same manner as state-of-the-art object recognition methods. Namely, image examples labeled according to the attributes present are used to train discriminative models, *e.g.*, with a convolutional neural network [29,32,45,47,49,56].

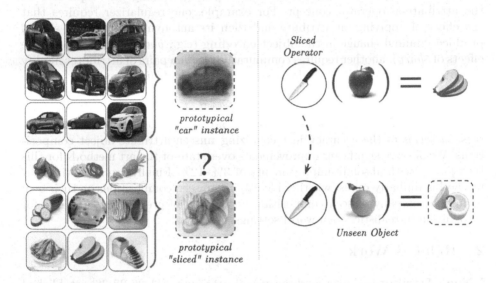

Fig. 1. Conceptual overview of our idea. Left: Unlike for objects, it is difficult to learn a predictable visual prototype for an attribute (*e.g.*, "sliced"as shown here). Furthermore, standard visual recognition pipelines are prone to overfit to those object-attribute pairings observed during training. Right: We propose to model attributes as operators, learning how they *transform objects* rather than what they themselves look like. Once learned, the effects of the attribute operators are generalizable to new, unseen object categories.

The latent vector encoding learned by such models is expected to capture an *object-agnostic* attribute representation. Yet, achieving this is problematic, both in terms of data efficiency and generalization. Specifically, it assumes during training that (1) the attribute has been observed in combination with all potential objects (unrealistic and not scalable), and/or (2) an attribute's influence is manifested similarly across all objects (rarely the case, *e.g.*, "old" influences church and shoe differently). We observe that with the attribute's meaning so intrinsically tied to the object it describes, an ideal attribute vector encoding may not exist. See Fig. 1, left.

In light of these issues, we propose to model attributes as *operators* — with the goal of learning a model *for attribute-object composition itself* capable of explicitly factoring out the attributes' effect from their accompanying object representations.

First, rather than encode an attribute as a point in some embedding space, we encode it as a (learned) transformation that, when applied to an object encoding, modifies it to appropriately transform its appearance (see Fig. 1, right). In particular, we formulate an embedding objective where compositions and images project into the same semantic space, allowing recognition of unseen attribute-object pairings in novel images.[1]

Second, we introduce novel regularizers during training that capitalize on the attribute-as-operator concept. For example, one regularizer requires that the effect of applying an attribute and then its antonym to an object should produce minimal change in the object encoding (e.g., *blunt* should "undo" the effects of *sharp*); another requires commutativity when pairs of attributes modify an object (e.g., a *sliced red* apple is equivalent to a *red sliced* apple).

We validate our approach on two challenging datasets: MIT-States [33] and UT-Zappos [55]. Together, they span hundreds of objects, attributes, and compositions. The results demonstrate the advantages of attributes as operators, in terms of the accuracy in recognizing unseen attribute-object compositions. We observe significant improvements over state-of-the-art methods for this task [5,33], with absolute improvements of 3%–12%. Finally, we show that our method is similarly robust whether identifying unseen compositions on their own or in the company of seen compositions—which is of great practical value for recognition in realistic, open world settings.

2   Related Work

Visual Attributes. Early work on visual attributes [11,26,28,36] established the task of inferring mid-level semantic descriptions from images. The research community has since explored many applications for attributes, including image search [24,26,44], zero-shot object categorization [1,21,28], sentence generation [25] and fashion image analysis [4,17,18]. Throughout, the standard approach to learn attributes is very similar to that used to learn object categories: discriminative classifiers with labeled examples. In particular, today's best accuracies are obtained by training a deep convolutional neural network to classify attributes [29,32,45,47,49]. Multi-task attribute training methods account for correlations between different attributes [19,23,32,44]. Our approach is a fundamental departure from all of the above: rather than consider attribute instances as points in some high-dimensional space that can be classified, we consider attributes as *operators* that transform visual data from one condition to another.

Composition in Language and Vision. In natural language processing, the composition of adjectives and nouns is modeled as single compositions [13,34] or transformations (*i.e.*, an adjective transformation applied to the noun vector)

---

[1] We stress that this differs from traditional zero-shot object recognition [1,21,28], where an *unseen object* is defined by its (previously learned and class-agnostic) attributes. In our case, we have *unseen compositions* of objects and attributes.

[3,46]. Bridging such linguistic concepts to visual data, some work explores the correlation between similarity scores for color-object pairs in the language and visual domains [35].

Composition in vision has been studied in the context of modeling compound objects [39] (clipboard = clip + board), verb-object interactions [42,57] (riding a horse = person + riding + horse), and adjective-noun combinations [5,9,33] (fluffy towel = towel modified by fluffy). All these approaches leverage the key insight that the characteristics of the composed entities could be very different from their constituents; however, they all subscribe to the traditional notion of representing constituents as vectors, and compositions as black-box modifications of these vectors. Instead, we model compositions as unique operators conditioned on the constituents (e.g., for attribute-object composition, a different modification for each attribute).

Limited prior work on attribute-object compositions considers *unseen compositions*, that is, where each constituent is seen during training, but new unseen compositions are seen at test time [5,33]. Both methods construct classifiers for composite concepts using pre-trained linear classifiers for the "seen" primitive concepts, either with tensor completion [5] or neural networks [33]. Recent work extends this notion to expressions connected by logical operators [9]. We tackle unseen compositions as well. However, rather than treat attributes and objects alike as classifier vectors and place the burden of learning on a single network, we propose a factored representation of the constituents, modeling attribute-object composition as an attribute-specific invertible *transformation* on object vectors. Our formulation also enables novel regularizers based on the attributes' linguistic meaning. Our model naturally extends to compositions where the objects themselves are unseen during training, unlike [5,33] which requires an SVM classifier to be trained for every new object. In addition, rather than exclusively predict unseen compositions as in [33], we also study the more realistic scenario where *all* compositions are candidates for recognition.

Visual Transformations. The notion of visual "states" has been explored from several angles. Given a collection of images [20] or time-lapse videos [27,59], methods can discover transformations that map between object states in order to create new images or visualize their relationships. Given video input, action recognition can be posed as learning the visual state transformation, *e.g.*, how a person manipulates an object [2,12] or how activity preconditions map to postconditions [51]. Given a camera transformation, other methods visualize the scene from the specified new viewpoint [22,58]. While we share the general concept of capturing a visual transformation, we are the first to propose modeling attributes as operators that alter an object's state, with the goal of recognizing unseen compositions.

Low-shot Learning with Sample Synthesis. Recent work explores ways to generate synthetic training examples for classes that rarely occur, either in terms of features [10,14,31,52,60] or entire images [8,56]. One part of our novel regularization approach also involves hypothetical attribute-transformed examples. However, whereas prior work explicitly generates samples offline to augment the dataset, our feature generation is an implicit process to regularize learning and works in concert with other novel constraints like inverse consistency or commutativity (see Sect. 3.3).

3   Approach

Our goal is to identify attribute-object compositions (*e.g.*, sliced banana, fluffy dog) in an image. Conventional classification approaches suffer from the long-tailed distribution of complex concepts [30,42] and a limited capacity to generalize to unseen concepts. Instead, we model the composition process itself. We factorize out the underlying primitive concepts (attributes and objects) seen during training, and use them as building blocks to identify unseen combinations during inference. Our approach is driven by the fundamental narrative: *if we've seen a sliced orange, a sliced banana, and a rotten banana, can we anticipate what a rotten orange looks like?*

We model the composition process around the functional role of attributes. Rather than treat objects and attributes equally as vectors, we model attributes as invertible operators, and composition as an attribute-conditioned transformation *applied* to object vectors. Our recognition task then turns into an embedding learning task, where we project images and compositions into a common semantic space to identify the composition present. We guide the learning with novel regularizers that are consistent with the linguistic behavior of attributes.

In the following, we start by formally describing the embedding learning problem in Sect. 3.1. We then describe the details of our embedding scheme for attributes and objects in Sect. 3.2. We present our optimization objective and auxiliary loss terms in Sect. 3.3. Finally, we describe our training methodology in Sect. 3.4.

3.1   Unseen Pair Recognition as Embedding Learning

We train a model that learns a mapping from a set of images $\mathcal{X}$ to a set of attribute-object pairs $\mathcal{P} = \mathcal{A} \times \mathcal{O}$. For example, "old-dog" is one attribute-object pairing. We divide the set of pairs into two disjoint sets: $\mathcal{P}_s$, which is a set of pairs that is seen during training and is used to learn a factored composition model, and $\mathcal{P}_u$, which is a set of pairs unseen during training, yet perfectly valid to encounter at test time. While $\mathcal{P}_s$ and $\mathcal{P}_u$ are completely disjoint, their constituent attributes and objects are observed in some (other) composition during training. Our images contain objects with a single attribute label associated with them, *i.e.*, each image has a unique pair label $p \in \mathcal{P}$.

During training, given an image $x \in \mathcal{X}$ and its corresponding pair label $p \in \mathcal{P}_s$, we learn two embedding functions $f(x)$ and $g(p)$ to project them into a *common semantic space*. For $f(x)$, we use a pretrained ResNet18 [15] followed by a linear layer. For $g(p)$, we introduce an attribute-operator model, described in detail in Sect. 3.2.

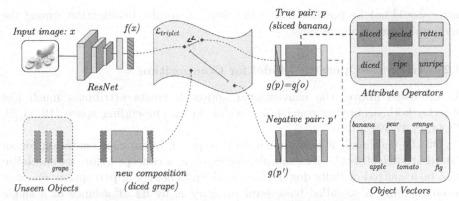

(a) **Proposed model**. We propose a factorized model for attribute-object composition where objects are vectors (*e.g.*, GloVe [38] vectors, bottom right), attributes are operators (top right matrices), and composition is an attribute-specific transformation of an object vector ($g(p)$). We embed images x and compositions p in a space where distances represent compatibility between them (center). Because of the way compositions are factorized, known attributes may be *assembled* with unseen objects, allowing our model to recognize new, unseen compositions in images (bottom left). Note that here *object vectors* are category-level embeddings, not images.

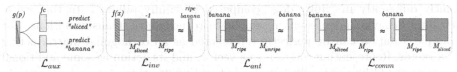

(b) **Proposed regularizers**. We propose several regularizers that conform with the linguistic meaning of attributes. $\mathcal{L}_{aux}$ ensures that the identity of the attribute/object is not lost during composition; $\mathcal{L}_{inv}$ *swaps out* attributes to implicitly synthesize new compositions for training; $\mathcal{L}_{ant}$ models antonyms ("unripe" should *undo* the effects of "ripe"); and $\mathcal{L}_{comm}$ models the commutative property of attributes (a *ripe sliced* banana is the same as a *sliced ripe* banana).

Fig. 2. Overview of proposed approach. Best viewed in color

We learn the embedding functions such that in this space, the Euclidean distance between the image embedding $f(x)$ and the correct pair embedding $g(p)$ is minimized, while the distance to all incorrect pairs is maximized. Distance in this space represents *compatibility*—*i.e.*, a low distance between an image and pair embedding implies the pair is present in the image. Critically, once $g(p)$ is learned, even an unseen pair can be projected in this semantic space, and its compatibility with an image can be assessed. See Fig. 2a.

During inference, we compute and store the pair embeddings of *all* potential pair candidates from $\mathcal{P}$ using our previously learned composition function $g(.)$. When presented with a new image, we embed it as usual using $f(.)$, and identify which of the pair embeddings is closest to it. Note how $\mathcal{P}$ includes both pairs seen in training as well as unseen attribute-object compositions; recognizing the latter would not be possible if we were doing a simple classification among the previously seen combinations.

3.2   Attribute-Operator Model for Composition

As discussed above, the conventional approach treats attributes much like objects, both occupying some point/region in an embedding space [19, 23, 29, 32, 44, 45, 47, 49].

On the one hand, it is meaningful to conjure a latent representation for an "attribute-free object"—for example, *dog* exists as a concept before we specialize it to be a spotted or fluffy dog. In fact, in the psychology of perception, one way to characterize a so-called basic-level category is by its affordance of a single mental prototype [40]. On the other hand, however, it is problematic to conjure an "object-free attribute". What does it mean to map "fluffy" as a concept in a semantic embedding space? What is the visual prototype of "fluffy"? See Fig. 1.

We contend that a more natural way of describing attributes is in how they *modify* the objects they refer to. Images of a "dog" and a "fluffy dog" help us estimate what the concept "fluffy" refers to. Moreover, these modifications are strongly conditioned on the object they describe ("fluffy" exhibits itself significantly differently in "fluffy dog" compared to "fluffy pillow"). In this sense, attribute behavior bears some resemblance to geometric transformations. For example, rotation can be perfectly represented as an orthogonal matrix acting on a vector. Representing rotation as a vector, and its action as some additional function, would be needlessly complicated and unintuitive.

With this in mind, we represent each object category $o \in \mathcal{O}$ as a D-dimensional vector, which denotes a prototypical object instance. Specifically, we use GloVe word embeddings [38] for the object vector space. Each attribute $a \in \mathcal{A}$ is a parametrized function $g_a : \mathcal{R}^D \to \mathcal{R}^D$ that modifies an object representation to exhibit that attribute, and brings it to the semantic space where images reside. For simplicity, we consider a linear transform for g_a, represented by a $D \times D$ matrix M_a:

$$g(p) = g_a(o) = M_a o, \tag{1}$$

though the proposed framework (excluding the inverse consistency regularizer) naturally supports more complex functions for g_a as well. See Fig. 2a, top right.

Interesting properties arise from our attribute-operator design. First, factorizing composition as a matrix-vector product facilitates transfer: an unseen pair can be represented by applying a learned attribute operator to an appropriate object vector (Fig. 2a, bottom left). Secondly, since images and compositions reside in the same space, it is possible to *remove* attributes from an image by applying the inverse of the transformation; multiple attributes can be applied consecutively to images; and the structure of the attribute space can be coded into how the transformations behave. Below we discuss how we leverage these properties to regularize the learning process (Sect. 3.3).

3.3 Learning Objective for Attributes as Operators

Our training set consists of n images and their pair labels, $\{(x_1, p_1), \ldots, (x_n, p_n)\}$. We design a loss function to efficiently learn to project images and composition pairs to a common embedding space. We begin with a standard triplet loss. The loss for an image x with pair label $p = (a, o)$ is given by:

$$\mathcal{L}_{triplet} = \max\left(0, d(f(x), M_a o) - d(f(x), M_{a'} o') + m\right), \forall\, a' \neq a \vee o' \neq o, \quad (2)$$

where d denotes Euclidean distance, and m is the margin value, which we keep fixed at 0.5 for all our experiments. In other words, the embedded image ought to be closer to its object transformed by the specified attribute a than other attribute-object pairings.

Thus far, the loss is similar in spirit to embedding based zero-shot learning methods [53], and more generally to triplet-loss based representation learning methods [7,16,43]. We emphasize that our focus is on learning a model for the composition operation; a triplet-loss based embedding is merely an appropriate framework that facilitates this. In the following, we extend this framework to effectively accommodate attributes as operators and inject our novel linguistic-based regularizers.

Object and Attribute Auxiliaries. In our model, both the attribute operator and object vector, and thereby their composition, are learnable parameters. It is possible that one element of the composition (either attributes or objects) will dominate during optimization, and try to capture all the information instead of learning a factorized model. This could lead to a composition representation, where one component does not adequately feature. To address this, we introduce an auxiliary loss term that forces the composed representation to be discriminative, *i.e.*, it must be able to predict both the attribute and object involved in the composition:

$$\mathcal{L}_{aux} = -\sum_{i \in \mathcal{A}} \delta_{ai} \, log(p_a^i) - \sum_{i \in \mathcal{O}} \delta_{oi} \, log(p_o^i), \quad (3)$$

where $\delta_{yi} = 1$ iff $y = i$, and p_a and p_o are the outputs of softmax linear classifiers trained to discriminate the attributes and objects, respectively. This auxiliary supervision ensures that the identity of the attribute and the object are not lost in the composed representation—in effect, strongly incentivizing a factorized representation.

Inverse Consistency. We exploit the invertible nature of our attributes to implicitly synthesize new training instances to regularize our model further. More specifically, we *swap out* an actual attribute a from the training example for a randomly selected one a', and construct another triplet loss term to account for the new composition:

$$\begin{aligned} f(x') &:= M_{a'} M_a^{-1} f(x) \\ \mathcal{L}_{inv} &= \max\left(0, d(f(x'), M_{a'} o) - d(f(x'), M_a o) + m\right), \end{aligned} \quad (4)$$

where the triplet loss notation is in the same form as Eq. 2.

Here $M_{a'}M_a^{-1}$ represents the removal of attribute a to arrive at the "prototype object" description of an image, and then the application of attribute a' to imbue the object with a new attribute. As a result, $f(x')$ represents a pseudo-instance with a new attribute-object pair, helping the model generalize better.

The pseudo-instances generated here are inherently noisy, and factoring them in directly (as a new instance) may obstruct training. To mitigate this, we select our negative example to target the more direct, and thus simpler consequence of this swapping. For example, when we swap out "sliced" for "ripe" from a *sliced banana* to make a *ripe banana*, we focus on the more obvious fact—that it is no longer "sliced"—by picking the original composition (*sliced banana*) as the negative, rather than sampling a completely new one.

Commutative Attribute Operators. Next we constrain the attributes to respect the commutative property. For example, applying the "sliced" operator after the "ripe" operator is the same as applying "ripe" after "sliced", or in other words a *ripe sliced* banana is the same as a *sliced ripe* banana. This commutative loss is expressed as:

$$\mathcal{L}_{comm} = \sum_{a,b \in \mathcal{A}} \| M_a(M_b o) - M_b(M_a o) \|_2 . \tag{5}$$

This loss forces the attribute transformations to respect the notion of *attribute composability* we observe in the context of language.

Antonym Consistency. The final linguistic structure of attributes we aim to exploit is antonyms. For example, we hypothesize that the "blunt" operator should *undo* the effects of the "sharp" operator. To that end, we consider a loss term that operates over pairs of antonym attributes (a, a'):

$$\mathcal{L}_{ant} = \sum_{a,a' \in \mathcal{A}} \| M_{a'}(M_a o) - o \|_2 . \tag{6}$$

For the MIT-States dataset (cf. Sect. 4), we manually identify 30 antonym pairs like ancient/modern, bent/straight, blunt/sharp. Figure 2b recaps all the regularizers.

3.4   Training and Inference

We minimize the combined loss function ($\mathcal{L}_{triplet} + \mathcal{L}_{aux} + \mathcal{L}_{inv} + \mathcal{L}_{comm} + \mathcal{L}_{ant}$) over all the training images, and train our network end to end. The learnable parameters are: the linear layer for $f(x)$, the matrices for every attribute M_a, $\forall a \in \mathcal{A}$, the object vectors $\forall o \in \mathcal{O}$ and the two fully-connected layers for the auxiliary classifiers.

During training, we embed each labeled image x in a semantic space using $f(x)$, and apply its attribute operator g_a to its object vector o to get a composed representation $g_a(o)$. The triplet loss pushes these two representations close together, while pushing incorrect pair embeddings apart. Our regularizers further make sure compositions are discriminative; attributes obey the commutative property; they undo the effects of their antonyms; and we implicitly synthesize instances with new compositions.

For inference, we compute and store the embeddings for all candidate pairs, $g_a(o)$, $\forall o \in \mathcal{O}$ and $\forall a \in \mathcal{A}$. When a new image q arrives, we sort the pre-computed embeddings by their distance to the image embedding $f(q)$, and identify the compositions with the lowest distances. The distance calculations can be performed quickly on our dataset with a few thousand pairs. Intelligent pruning strategies may be employed to reduce the search space for larger attribute/object vocabularies. We stress that the novel image can be assigned to an unseen composition absent in training images. We evaluate accuracy on the nearest composition $\hat{p}_q = (o_q, a_q)$ as our datasets support instances with single attributes.

4   Experiments

Our experiments explore the impact of modeling attributes as operators, particularly for recognizing unseen combinations of objects and attributes.

4.1   Experimental Setup

Datasets. We evaluate our method on two datasets:

- **MIT-States** [20]: This dataset has 245 object classes, 115 attribute classes and ~53K images. There is a wide range of objects (*e.g.*, *fish, persimmon, room*) and attributes (*e.g.*, *mossy, deflated, dirty*). On average, each object instance is modified by one of the 9 attributes it affords. We use the *compositional* split described in [33] for our experiments, resulting in disjoint sets of pairs—about 1.2 K pairs in $\mathcal{P}_s$ for training and 700 pairs in $\mathcal{P}_u$ for testing.

- **UT-Zappos50k** [56]: This dataset contains 50 K images of shoes with attribute labels. We consider the subset of ~33K images that contain annotations for material attributes of shoes (*e.g.*, *leather, sheepskin, rubber*); see Supp. The object labels are shoe types (*e.g.*, *high heel, sandal, sneaker*). We split the data randomly into disjoint sets, yielding 83 pairs in $\mathcal{P}_s$ for training and 33 pairs in $\mathcal{P}_u$ for testing, over 16 attribute classes and 12 object classes.

The datasets are complementary. While MIT-States covers a wide array of everyday objects and attributes, UT-Zappos focuses on a fine-grained domain of shoes. In addition, object annotations in MIT-States are very sparse (some classes have just 4 images), while the UT-Zappos subset has at least 200 images per object class.

Evaluation Metrics. We report top-1 accuracy on recognizing pair compositions. We report this accuracy in two forms: (1) Over only the unseen pairs, which we refer to as the **closed world setting**. During test time, we compute the distance between our image embedding and only the pair embeddings of the unseen pairs $\mathcal{P}_u$, and select the nearest one. The closed world setting artificially reduces the pool of allowable labels at test time to *only* the unseen pairs. This is the setting in which [33] report their results. (2) Over both seen and unseen pairs, which we call the **open world setting**. During test time, we consider all pair embeddings in $\mathcal{P}$ as candidates for recognition. This is more realistic and challenging, since no assumptions are made about the compositions present. We aim for high accuracy in both these settings. We report the *harmonic mean* of these accuracies given by $h\text{-}mean = 2 * (open * closed)/(open + closed)$, as a consolidated metric. Unlike the arithmetic mean, it penalizes large performance discrepancies between settings. The harmonic mean is recommended to handle a similar discrepancy between seen/unseen accuracies in "generalized" zero-shot learning [53], and is now widely adopted as an evaluation metric [6,48,50,52].

Implementation Details. For all experiments, we use an ImageNet [41] pre-trained ResNet-18 [15] for $f(x)$. For fair comparison, we do not finetune this network. We project our images and compositions to a $D = 300$-dim. embedding space. We initialize our object and attribute embeddings with GloVe [38] word vectors where applicable, and initialize attribute operators with the identity matrix as this leads to more stable training. All models are implemented in PyTorch. ADAM with learning rate $1e - 4$ and batch size 512 is used. The attribute operators are trained with learning rate $1e - 5$ as they encounter larger changes in gradient values. Our code is available at github.com/attributes-as-operators.

Baselines and Existing Methods. We compare to the following methods:

- **VisProd** uses independent classifiers on the image features to predict the attribute and object. It represents methods that do not explicitly model the composition operation. The probability of a pair is simply the product of the probability of each constituent: $P(a, o) = P(a)P(o)$. We report two versions, differing in the choice of the classifier used to generate the aforementioned probabilities: VisProd(SVM) uses a Linear SVM (as used in [33]), and VisProd(NN) uses a single layer softmax regression model.
- **AnalogousAttr** [5] trains a linear SVM classifier for each seen pair, then uses Bayesian Probabilistic Tensor Factorization (BPTF) to infer classifier weights for unseen compositions. We use the same existing code[2] as [5] to recreate this model.
- **RedWine** [33] trains a neural network to transform linear SVMs for the constituent concepts into classifier weights for an unseen combination. Since the authors' code was not available, we implement it ourselves following the paper closely. We train the SVMs with image features consistent with our models. We verify we could reproduce their results with VGG (network they employed), then upgrade its features to ResNet to be more competitive with our approach.

---

[2] https://www.cs.cmu.edu/~lxiong/bptf/bptf.html.

- **LabelEmbed** is like the REDWINE model, except it composes word vector representations rather than classifier weights. We use pretrained GloVe [38] word embeddings. This is the LabelEmbed baseline designated in [33].
- **LabelEmbed+** is an improved version of LABELEMBED where (1) We embed both the constituent inputs *and* the image features using feed-forward networks into a semantic embedding space of dimension D, and (2) We allow the input representations to be optimized during training. See Supp. for details.

To our knowledge [5,33] are the most relevant methods for comparison, as they too address recognition of unseen object-attribute pairs. For all methods, we use the same ResNet-18 image features used in our method; this ensures any performance differences can be attributed to the model rather than the CNN architecture. For all neural models, we ensure that the number of parameters and model capacity are similar to ours.

Table 1. Accuracy (%) on unseen pair detection. Our method outperforms all previous methods in the open world setting. It also is strongest in the consolidated harmonic mean (h-mean) metric that accounts for both the open and closed settings. Our method's gain is significantly wider when we eliminate the pressure caused by scarce object training data, by providing oracle object labels during inference to all methods ("+obj"). The harmonic mean is calculated over the open and closed settings only (it does not factor in +obj).

	MIT-States				UT-Zappos			
	closed	open	+obj	h-mean	closed	open	+obj	h-mean
CHANCE	0.1	0.05	0.9	0.1	3.0	0.9	6.3	1.3
VISPROD(SVM)	11.1	2.4	21.6	3.9	46.8	4.1	17.8	7.5
VISPROD(NN)	13.9	2.8	22.6	4.7	**49.9**	4.8	18.1	8.8
ANALOGOUSATTR [5]	1.4	0.2	22.4	0.4	18.3	3.5	16.9	5.9
REDWINE [33]	12.5	3.1	18.3	5.0	40.3	2.1	10.5	4.0
LABELEMBED	13.4	3.3	18.8	5.3	25.8	5.2	11.1	8.7
LABELEMBED+	**14.8**	5.7	27.2	8.2	37.4	9.4	19.4	15.0
OURS	12.0	**11.4**	**49.3**	**11.7**	33.2	**23.4**	**38.3**	**27.5**

4.2 Quantitative Results: Recognizing Object-Attribute Compositions

Detecting Unseen Compositions. Table 1 shows the results. Our method outperforms all previously reported results and baselines on both datasets by a large margin—around 6% on MIT-States and 14% on UT-Zappos in the open world setting—indicating that it learned a strong model for visual composition.

The absolute accuracies on the two datasets are fairly different. Compared to UT-Zappos, MIT-States is more difficult owing to a larger number of attributes, objects, and unseen pairs. Moreover, it has fewer training examples for primitive object concepts, leading to a lower accuracy overall.

Indeed, if an oracle provides the true object label on a test instance, the accuracies are much more consistent across both datasets ("+obj" in Table 1). This essentially trims the search space down to the attribute afforded by the object in question, and serves as an upper bound for each method's accuracy. On MIT-States, without object labels, the gap between the strongest baseline and our method is about 6%, which widens significantly to about 22% when object labels are provided (to all methods). On UT-Zappos, all methods improve with the object oracle, yet the gap is more consistent with and without (14% vs. 19%). This is consistent with the datasets' disparity in label distribution; the model on UT-Zappos learns a good object representation by itself.

ANALOGOUSATTR [5] varies significantly between the two datasets; it relies on having a partially complete set of compositions in the form of a tensor, and uses that information to "fill in the gaps". For UT-Zappos, this tensor is 43% complete, making completion a relatively simpler task compared to MIT-States, where the tensor is only 4% complete. We believe that over-fitting due to this extreme sparsity is the reason we observe low accuracies for ANALOGOUSATTR on this dataset.

In the closed world setting, our method does not perform as well as some of the other baselines. However, this setting is contrived and arguably a weaker indication of model performance. In the closed world, it is easy for a method to produce biased results due to the artificially pruned label space during infer-ence. For example, the attribute "young" occurs in only *one* unseen composition during test time—"young iguana". Since all images during test time that con-tain iguanas *are* of "young iguanas", an attribute-blind model is also perfectly capable of classifying these instances correctly, giving a false sense of accuracy. In practical applications, the separation into seen and unseen pairs arises from natural data scarcity. In that setting, the ability to identify unseen compositions *in the presence of known compositions*, *i.e.*, the open world, is a critical metric.

The lower performance in the closed world appears to be a side-effect of preventing overfitting to the subset of closed-world compositions. All models except ours have a large difference between the closed and open world accuracy. Our model operates robustly in both settings, maintaining similar accuracies in each. Our model outperforms the other models in the harmonic mean metric as well by about 3% and 12% on MIT-States and UT-Zappos, respectively.

Effect of Regularizers. Table 2 examines the effects of each proposed regular-izer on the performance of our model. We see that the auxiliary classification loss stabilizes the learning process significantly, and results in a large increase in accuracy on both datasets. For MIT-States, including the inverse consistency and the commutative operator regularizers provide small boosts and a reasonable increase when used together. For UT-Zappos, the effect of inverse consistency is less pronounced, possibly because the abundance of object training data makes it redundant. The commutative regularizer provides the biggest improvement of 4%. Antonym consistency is not very helpful on MIT-States, perhaps due to

Table 2. Ablation study of regularizers used. The auxiliary classifier loss is essential to our method. Adding other regularizers that are consistent with how attributes function also produces boosts in accuracy in most cases, highlighting the merit of thinking of *attributes as operators*.

	MIT-States			UT-Zappos		
	closed	open	h-mean	closed	open	h-mean
BASE	**14.2**	2.1	3.7	**46.2**	13.1	20.4
+INV	14.0	2.7	4.5	45.7	14.2	21.7
+AUX	10.3	9.5	9.9	33.2	26.5	29.5
+AUX+INV	10.4	9.8	10.1	33.1	26.2	29.2
+AUX+COMM	11.4	10.8	11.1	38.1	**29.7**	**33.4**
+AUX+ANT	8.9	8.8	8.8	-	-	-
+AUX+INV+COMM	12.0	**11.4**	**11.7**	33.2	23.4	27.5

the wide visual differences between some antonyms. For example, "ripe" and "unripe" for fruits produce vibrant color changes, and *undoing* one color change does not directly translate to *applying* the other *i.e.*, "ripe" may not be the *visual inverse* of "unripe".[3] These ablation experiments show the merits of pushing our model to be consistent with how attributes operate.

Overall, the results on two challenging and diverse datasets strongly support our idea to model attributes as operators. Our method consistently outperforms state-of-the-art methods. Furthermore, we see the promise of injecting novel linguistic/semantic operations into attribute learning.

4.3 Qualitative Results: Retrieving Images for Unseen Descriptions

Next, we show examples of our approach at work to recognize unseen compositions.

Image Retrieval for Unseen Compositions. With a learned composition model in place, our method can retrieve relevant images for textual queries for object-attribute pairs unseen during training. The query itself is in the form of an attribute a and an object o; we embed them, and all the image candidates x, in our semantic space, and select the ones that are nearest to our desired composition. We stress that these compositions are completely new and arise from our model's factored representation of composition.

Figure 3 shows examples. The query is shown in text, and the top 5 nearest images in embedding space are shown alongside. Our method accurately distinguishes between attribute "states" of the same object to retrieve relevant images for the query. The last row shows failure cases. We observe characteristic failures for compositions involving some under-represented object classes in

---

[3] Attributes for UT-Zappos are centered around materials of shoes (*leather*, *cotton*) and so lack antonyms, preventing us from experimenting with that regularizer.

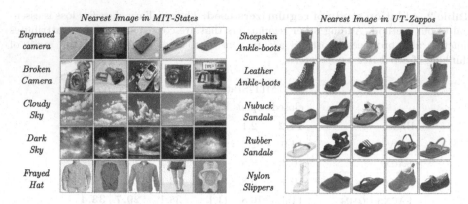

Fig. 3. Top retrieval results for unseen compositions. Unseen compositions are posed as textual queries on MIT-States (left) and UT-Zappos (right). These attribute-object pairs are completely unseen during training; the representation for them is generated using our factored composition model. We highlight correctly retrieved instances with a green border, and incorrect ones with red. Last row shows failure cases. (Color figure online)

training pairs. For example, compositions involving "hat" are poorly learned as it features in only two training compositions. We also observe common failures involving ambiguous labels (examples of *moldy bread* are also often *sliced* in the data).

Image Retrieval for Out-of-Domain Compositions. Figure 4 takes this task two steps further. First, we perform retrieval on an image database disjoint from training to demonstrate robustness to domain shift in the open world setting. Figure 4 (left) shows retrievals from the ImageNet validation set, a set of 50 K images disjoint from MIT-States. Even across this dataset, our model can retrieve images with unseen compositions. As to be expected, there is much more variation. For example, bottle-caps in ImageNet—an object class that is not present in MIT-States—are misconstrued as coins.

Second, we perform retrieval on the disjoint database *and* issue queries for compositions that are in neither the training nor test set. For example, the objects *barn* or *cycle* are never seen in MIT-States, under any attribute composition. We refer to these compositions as *out-of-domain*. Our method handles them by applying attribute operators to GloVe object vectors. Figure 4 (right) shows examples. This generalization is straightforward with our method, whereas it is prohibited by the existing methods REDWINE [33] and ANALOGOUSATTR [5]. They rely on having pre-trained SVMs for all constituent concepts. In order to allow an out-of-domain composition with a new object category, those methods would need to gather labeled images for that object, train an SVM, and repeat their full training pipelines.

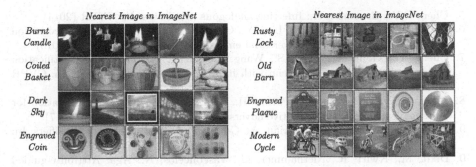

Fig. 4. Top retrieval results in the out-of-domain setting. Images are retrieved from an unseen domain, ImageNet. Left: Our method can successfully retrieve unseen compositions from images in the wild. Right: Retrievals on out-of-domain compositions. Compositions involving objects that are not even present in our dataset (like lock and barn) can be retrieved using our model's factorized representation.

5   Conclusion

We presented a model of attribute-object composition built around the idea of "attributes as operators". We modeled this composition as an attribute-conditioned transformation of an object vector, and incorporated it into an embedding learning model to identify unseen compositions. We introduced several linguistically inspired auxiliary loss terms to regularize training, all of which capitalize on the operator model for attributes. Experiments show considerable gains over existing models. Our method generalizes well to unseen compositions, in open world, closed world, and even out-of-domain settings. In future work we plan to explore extensions to accommodate relative attribute comparisons and to deal with compositions involving multiple attributes.

Acknowledgments. This research is supported in part by ONR PECASE N00014-15-1-2291 and an Amazon AWS Machine Learning Research Award. We gratefully acknowledge Facebook for a GPU donation.

References

1. Al-Halah, Z., Tapaswi, M., Stiefelhagen, R.: Recovering the missing link: predicting class-attribute associations for unsupervised zero-shot learning. In: CVPR (2016)
2. Alayrac, J.B., Sivic, J., Laptev, I., Lacoste-Julien, S.: Joint discovery of object states and manipulating actions. In: ICCV (2017)
3. Baroni, M., Zamparelli, R.: Nouns are vectors, adjectives are matrices: representing adjective-noun constructions in semantic space. In: EMNLP (2010)
4. Berg, T.L., Berg, A.C., Shih, J.: Automatic attribute discovery and characterization from noisy web data. In: Daniilidis, K., Maragos, P., Paragios, N. (eds.) ECCV 2010. LNCS, vol. 6311, pp. 663–676. Springer, Heidelberg (2010). https://doi.org/10.1007/978-3-642-15549-9_48

5. Chen, C.Y., Grauman, K.: Inferring analogous attributes. In: CVPR (2014)
6. Chen, L., Zhang, H., Xiao, J., Liu, W., Chang, S.F.: Zero-shot visual recognition using semantics-preserving adversarial embedding network. In: CVPR (2018)
7. Cheng, D., Gong, Y., Zhou, S., Wang, J., Zheng, N.: Person re-identification by multi-channel parts-based cnn with improved triplet loss function. In: CVPR (2016)
8. Choe, J., Park, S., Kim, K., Park, J.H., Kim, D., Shim, H.: Face generation for low-shot learning using generative adversarial networks. In: ICCVW (2017)
9. Cruz, R.S., Fernando, B., Cherian, A., Gould, S.: Neural algebra of classifiers. In: WACV (2018)
10. Dixit, M., Kwitt, R., Niethammer, M., Vasconcelos, N.: Aga: Attribute-guided augmentation. In: CVPR (2017)
11. Farhadi, A., Endres, I., Hoiem, D., Forsyth, D.: Describing objects by their attributes. In: CVPR (2009)
12. Fathi, A., Rehg, J.M.: Modeling actions through state changes. In: CVPR (2013)
13. Guevara, E.: A regression model of adjective-noun compositionality in distributional semantics. In: ACL Workshop on Geometrical Models of Natural Language Semantics (2010)
14. Hariharan, B., Girshick, R.: Low-shot visual recognition by shrinking and hallucinating features. In: ICCV (2017)
15. He, K., Zhang, X., Ren, S., Sun, J.: Deep residual learning for image recognition. In: CVPR (2016)
16. Hoffer, E., Ailon, N.: Deep metric learning using triplet network. In: Feragen, A., Pelillo, M., Loog, M. (eds.) SIMBAD 2015. LNCS, vol. 9370, pp. 84–92. Springer, Cham (2015). https://doi.org/10.1007/978-3-319-24261-3_7
17. Hsiao, W.L., Grauman, K.: Learning the latent look: Unsupervised discovery of a style-coherent embedding from fashion images. In: ICCV (2017)
18. Huang, J., Feris, R., Chen, Q., Yan, S.: Cross-domain image retrieval with a dual attribute-aware ranking network. In: ICCV (2015)
19. Huang, S., Elhoseiny, M., Elgammal, A., Yang, D.: Learning hypergraph-regularized attribute predictors. In: CVPR (2015)
20. Isola, P., Lim, J.J., Adelson, E.H.: Discovering states and transformations in image collections. In: CVPR (2015)
21. Jayaraman, D., Grauman, K.: Zero-shot recognition with unreliable attributes. In: NIPS (2014)
22. Jayaraman, D., Grauman, K.: Learning image representations tied to ego-motion. In: ICCV (2015)
23. Jayaraman, D., Sha, F., Grauman, K.: Decorrelating semantic visual attributes by resisting the urge to share. In: CVPR (2014)
24. Kovashka, A., Parikh, D., Grauman, K.: Whittlesearch: image search with relative attribute feedback. In: CVPR (2012)
25. Kulkarni, G., et al.: Babytalk: understanding and generating simple image descriptions. TPAMI **35**, 2891–2903 (2013)
26. Kumar, N., Belhumeur, P., Nayar, S.: FaceTracer: a search engine for large collections of images with faces. In: Forsyth, D., Torr, P., Zisserman, A. (eds.) ECCV 2008. LNCS, vol. 5305, pp. 340–353. Springer, Heidelberg (2008). https://doi.org/10.1007/978-3-540-88693-8_25
27. Laffont, P.Y., Ren, Z., Tao, X., Qian, C., Hays, J.: Transient attributes for high-level understanding and editing of outdoor scenes. In: SIGGRAPH (2014)
28. Lampert, C.H., Nickisch, H., Harmeling, S.: Learning to detect unseen object classes by between-class attribute transfer. In: CVPR (2009)

29. Liu, Z., Luo, P., Wang, X., Tang, X.: Deep learning face attributes in the wild. In: ICCV (2015)
30. Lu, C., Krishna, R., Bernstein, M., Fei-Fei, L.: Visual relationship detection with language priors. In: ECCV (2016)
31. Lu, J., Li, J., Yan, Z., Zhang, C.: Zero-shot learning by generating pseudo feature representations. arXiv preprint arXiv:1703.06389 (2017)
32. Lu, Y., Kumar, A., Zhai, S., Cheng, Y., Javidi, T., Feris, R.: Fully-adaptive feature sharing in multi-task networks with applications in person attribute classification. In: CVPR (2017)
33. Misra, I., Gupta, A., Hebert, M.: From red wine to red tomato: composition with context. In: CVPR (2017)
34. Mitchell, J., Lapata, M.: Vector-based models of semantic composition. In: HLT, ACL (2008)
35. Nguyen, D.T., Lazaridou, A., Bernardi, R.: Coloring objects: adjective-noun visual semantic compositionality. In: ACL Workshop on Vision and Language (2014)
36. Parikh, D., Grauman, K.: Relative attributes. In: ICCV (2011)
37. Patterson, G., Hays, J.: Sun attribute database: discovering, annotating, and recognizing scene attributes. In: CVPR (2012)
38. Pennington, J., Socher, R., Manning, C.: Glove: global vectors for word representation. In: EMNLP (2014)
39. Pezzelle, S., Shekhar, R., Bernardi, R.: Building a bagpipe with a bag and a pipe: exploring conceptual combination in vision. In: ACL Workshop on Vision and Language (2016)
40. Rosch, E., Mervis, C.B., Gray, W.D., Johnson, D.M., Boyes-Braem, P.: Basic objects in natural categories. Cogn. Psychol. 8(3), 382–439 (1976)
41. Russakovsky, O., et al.: Imagenet large scale visual recognition challenge. IJCV 115(3), 211–252 (2015)
42. Sadeghi, M.A., Farhadi, A.: Recognition using visual phrases. In: CVPR (2011)
43. Schroff, F., Kalenichenko, D., Philbin, J.: Facenet: a unified embedding for face recognition and clustering. In: CVPR (2015)
44. Siddiquie, B., Feris, R.S., Davis, L.S.: Image ranking and retrieval based on multi-attribute queries. In: CVPR (2011)
45. Singh, K.K., Lee, Y.J.: End-to-end localization and ranking for relative attributes. In: ECCV (2016)
46. Socher, R., et al.: Recursive deep models for semantic compositionality over a sentiment treebank. In: EMNLP (2013)
47. Su, C., Zhang, S., Xing, J., Gao, W., Tian, Q.: Deep attributes driven multi-camera person re-identification. In: Leibe, B., Matas, J., Sebe, N., Welling, M. (eds.) ECCV 2016. LNCS, vol. 9906, pp. 475–491. Springer, Cham (2016). https://doi.org/10.1007/978-3-319-46475-6_30
48. Verma, V.K., Arora, G., Mishra, A., Rai, P.: Generalized zero-shot learning via synthesized examples. In: CVPR (2018)
49. Wang, J., Cheng, Y., Schmidt Feris, R.: Walk and learn: facial attribute representation learning from egocentric video and contextual data. In: CVPR (2016)
50. Wang, Q., Chen, K.: Alternative semantic representations for zero-shot human action recognition. In: ECML (2017)
51. Wang, X., Farhadi, A., Gupta, A.: Action's transformations. In: CVPR (2016)
52. Xian, Y., Lorenz, T., Schiele, B., Akata, Z.: Feature generating networks for zero-shot learning. In: CVPR (2018)
53. Xian, Y., Schiele, B., Akata, Z.: Zero-shot learning-the good, the bad and the ugly. In: CVPR (2017)

54. Yan, X., Yang, J., Sohn, K., Lee, H.: Attribute2image: Conditional image generation from visual attributes. In: ECCV (2016)
55. Yu, A., Grauman, K.: Fine-grained visual comparisons with local learning. In: CVPR (2014)
56. Yu, A., Grauman, K.: Semantic jitter: dense supervision for visual comparisons via synthetic images. In: ICCV (2017)
57. Zhang, H., Kyaw, Z., Chang, S.F., Chua, T.S.: Visual translation embedding network for visual relation detection. In: CVPR (2017)
58. Zhou, T., Tulsiani, S., Sun, W., Malik, J., Efros, A.A.: View synthesis by appearance flow. In: ECCV (2016)
59. Zhou, Y., Berg, T.L.: Learning temporal transformations from time-lapse videos. In: Leibe, B., Matas, J., Sebe, N., Welling, M. (eds.) ECCV 2016. LNCS, vol. 9912, pp. 262–277. Springer, Cham (2016). https://doi.org/10.1007/978-3-319-46484-8_16
60. Zhu, Y., Elhoseiny, M., Liu, B., Elgammal, A.: Imagine it for me: generative adversarial approach for zero-shot learning from noisy texts. In: CVPR (2018)

Product Quantization Network for Fast Image Retrieval

Tan Yu[1]([⊠]), Junsong Yuan[2], Chen Fang[3], and Hailin Jin[3]

[1] Nanyang Technological University, Singapore, Singapore
tyu008@e.ntu.edu.sg
[2] State University of New York at Buffalo, Buffalo, USA
jsyuan@buffalo.edu
[3] Adobe Research, San Jose, USA
{cfang,hljin}@adobe.com

Abstract. Product quantization has been widely used in fast image retrieval due to its effectiveness of coding high-dimensional visual features. By extending the hard assignment to soft assignment, we make it feasible to incorporate the product quantization as a layer of a convolutional neural network and propose our product quantization network. Meanwhile, we come up with a novel asymmetric triplet loss, which effectively boosts the retrieval accuracy of the proposed product quantization network based on asymmetric similarity. Through the proposed product quantization network, we can obtain a discriminative and compact image representation in an end-to-end manner, which further enables a fast and accurate image retrieval. Comprehensive experiments conducted on public benchmark datasets demonstrate the state-of-the-art performance of the proposed product quantization network.

1 Introduction

Image retrieval has been a fundamental research topic in computer vision. Given a query image, it aims to find the relevant images from a database. Precision and efficiency are two key aspects for a retrieval system. These two key aspects also drives the image retrieval research to progress in two directions.

One direction is to design or learn a more effective image representation for a higher retrieval precision [2–5,11,18,28,30,31,40]. Good image representation maintains a large distance between irrelevant images in feature space and keeps a close distance between relevant images. Traditional image retrieval systems generated image representation by aggregating hand-craft local features like SIFT and the research focuses on designing a more effective aggregation method [18,30,31]. With the progress of deep learning, the convolutional neural network provides an effective image representation [2,3,28,38,41], which is trained by the semantic information and is robust to low-level image transformations.

On the other hand, to achieve a satisfactory efficiency in image retrieval, especially when dealing with a large-scale dataset, a compact image representation is necessary. Generically speaking, there are two types of schemes to gain

© Springer Nature Switzerland AG 2018
V. Ferrari et al. (Eds.): ECCV 2018, LNCS 11205, pp. 191–206, 2018.
https://doi.org/10.1007/978-3-030-01246-5_12

a compact image representation, hashing and quantization. Hashing maps the real-value vectors into binary codes, which enables a faster distance computation and lower memory cost. One of most widely used hashing method is locality sensitivity hashing (LSH) [7]. Nevertheless, LSH is data-independent, which ignores the data distribution and is sub-optimal to a specific dataset. To further improve the performance, some hashing methods [10, 32, 36] learn the projection from the data, which caters better to a specific dataset and achieves higher retrieval precision. Traditional hashing methods are based on off-the-shelf visual features. They optimize the feature extraction and Hamming embedding independently. More recently, inspired by the progress of deep learning, some deep hashing methods [22, 23, 25, 37] are proposed, which simultaneously conduct the feature learning and compression through a unified network.

Nevertheless, hashing methods are only able to produce a few distinct distances, limiting its capability of describing the distance between data points. In parallel to hashing methods, another widely used data compression method in image retrieval is product quantization. It represents each feature vector by a Cartesian product of several codewords. Thanks to the asymmetric distance calculation mechanism, it enables a more accurate distance calculation than hashing methods using the same code length. The product quantization (PQ) [17] and its optimized versions like OPQ [9], CKmeans [29], APQ [1] and CQ [12, 43] are originally designed for an unsupervised scenario where no labeling data are provided. SQ [35] extends product quantization to a supervised scenario. However, SQ is based on the hand-crafted features or CNN features from the pretrained model, therefore it might not be optimal with respect to the a specific dataset.

To simultaneously optimize the feature learning and quantization, Cao *et al.* [6] propose a deep quantization network (DQN) which can be trained in an end-to-end manner. It optimizes a weighted sum of similarity-preserve loss and product quantization loss. It iteratively updates codewords and other parameters of a neural network. Therefore, in each iteration, the codewords are directly updated by k-means whereas the label information is ignored. Recently, Klein *et al.* [20] propose a deep product quantization (DPQ). They learn a cascade of two fully-connected layers followed by a softmax layer to determine a soft codeword assignment. It is different from original product quantization, the codeword assignment is no longer determined by distance between the original feature and codewords. Nevertheless, the additional parameters introduced in the cascade of fully-connected layers make DPQ more prone to over-fitting.

In this paper, we also attempt to incorporate the product quantization in a neural network and train it in an end-to-end manner. We propose a soft product quantization layer which is differentiable and the original product quantization is a special case of the proposed soft product quantization when $\alpha \to +\infty$. Different from DPQ, we no longer need fully-connected layers to obtain the codebook assignment, instead, in our method, the codeword assignement is determined by the similarity between the original feature and the codewords. Therefore, we significantly reduce the number of parameters to be trained, making our PQN more immune to over-fitting compared with DPQ. Meanwhile, inspired by the success of the triplet loss in metric learning and the triumph of the asymmetric similarity measurement in feature compression, we propose a novel asymmetric triplet loss to directly optimize the asymmetric similarity measurement in an end-to-end manner. In summary, the contribution of our work is three-fold:

- We introduce a novel soft product quantization layer, which is a generalized version of the original product quantization. It is differentiable and thus brings an end-to-end training of the product quantization network.
- We propose a novel asymmetric triplet loss, which directly optimizes the asymmetric distance brought based on product quantization. It enables a more effective training of the convolutional neural network.
- Due to its simplicity, effectiveness and efficiency, we provide the image retrieval community a strong baseline. Some more sophisticated image retrieval methods can be further built upon the proposed framework.

2   Related Work

Hashing [7,10,13–15,22,23,25,32,36,37,39] aims to map a feature vector into a short code consisting of a sequence of bits, which enables a fast distance computation mechanism as well as a light memory cost. Traditional hashing methods like locality sensitivity hashing (LSH) [7], spetral hashing (SH) [36] and iterative quantization (ITQ) [10] first obtain real-value image features and then compress the features into binary codes. They conduct the representation learning and the feature compression separately and the mutual influence between them is ignored. Recently, motivated by the success of deep learning, some works [22,23,25,37] propose deep hashing methods by incorporating hashing as a layer into a deep neural network. The end-to-end training mechanism of deep hashing simultaneously optimizes the representation learning and feature compression, achieving better performance than the traditional hashing methods.

Since the hashing methods are only able to produce a few distinct distances, it has limited capability of describing the distance between data points. Parallelly, another scheme termed product quantization (PQ) [17] decomposes the space into a Cartesian product of subspaces and quantizes each subspace individually. Some following works [1,9,43] further optimize the product quantization through reducing the distortion errors and achieve higher retrieval precision. Note that production quantization and its optimized versions such as OPQ [9], AQ [1] and CQ [43] are originally designed for an unsupervised scenario where no label information is provided.

Wang et al. [35] propose supervised quantization (SQ) by exploiting the label information. Nevertheless, SQ conducts feature extraction and quantization individually, whereas the interaction between these two steps are ignored. To simultaneously learn image representation and product quantization, deep quantization network (DQN) [6] adds a fully connected bottleneck layer in the convolutional network. It optimizes a combined loss consisting of a similarity-preserving loss and a product quantization loss. Nevertheless, the codebook in

DPQ is trained through k-means clustering and thus the supervised information is ignored. Recently, deep product quantization (DPQ) [20] is proposed where the codebook as well as the parameters are learned in an end-to-end manner. Different from original product quantization which determines the codeword assignment according to the distance between the original feature and codewords, DPQ determines the codeword assignment through a fully-connected layer whose parameters are learned from data. Nevertheless, the additional parameters in the cascade of fully-connected layers will make the network more prone to overfitting.

Our work is also an attempt of incorporating the product quantization in a neural network. We propose a soft product quantization layer and build our product quantization network (PQN), which can be trained in an end-to-end manner. Different from DPQ, our PQN determines the codeword assignment according to the similarity between the feature for coding and codewords, which can be seen as a soft extension of original product quantization. Unlike DPQ, we do not need additional fully-connected layers to determine the codeword assignment and the parameters in our soft product quantization layer are only the codewords. Therefore, the number of parameters in our quantization layer is considerably less than that of DPQ, which mitigates the over-fitting. As shown in experiments, our PQN consistently outperforms DPQ by a large margin (Fig. 1).

3   Product Quantization Network

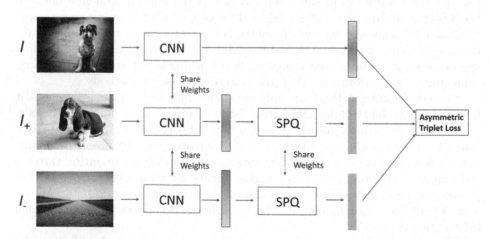

Fig. 1. The overview of the proposed product quantization network, where CNN represents the convolutional neural network and SPQ represents the proposed soft product quantization layer. The asymmetric triplet loss takes as input a triplet consisting of the CNN feature of an anchor image (I), the SPQ feature of a positive sample (I_+) and the SPQ feature of a negative sample (I_-).

3.1   From Hard Quantization to Soft Quantization

Let us denote by $\mathbf{x} \in \mathbb{R}^d$ the feature of an image I, we divide the feature $\mathbf{x}$ into M subvectors $[\mathbf{x}_1, \cdots, \mathbf{x}_m, \cdots, \mathbf{x}_M]$ in the feature space where $\mathbf{x}_m \in \mathbb{R}^{d/M}$ is a subvector. The product quantization further approximates $\mathbf{x}$ by

$$\mathbf{q} = [q_1(\mathbf{x}_1), \cdots, q_m(\mathbf{x}_m), \cdots, q_M(\mathbf{x}_M)], \tag{1}$$

where $q_m(\cdot)$ is the quantizer for $\mathbf{x}_m$ defined as

$$q_m(\mathbf{x}_m) = \sum_k \mathbb{1}(k = k^*)\mathbf{c}_{mk}, \tag{2}$$

where $k^* = \underset{k}{\arg\min} \|\mathbf{c}_{mk} - \mathbf{x}_m\|_2$, $\mathbb{1}(\cdot)$ is the indicator function and $\mathbf{c}_{mk}$ is the k-th codeword from the m-th codebook. The hard assignment makes it infeasible to derive its derivative and thus it can not be incorporated in a neural network. This embarrassment motivates us to replace the hard assignment $\mathbb{1}(k = k^*)$ by the soft assignment $e^{-\alpha\|\mathbf{x}_m - \mathbf{c}_{mk}\|_2^2} / \sum_{k'} e^{-\alpha\|\mathbf{x}_m - \mathbf{c}_{mk'}\|_2^2}$ and obtain

$$\mathbf{s} = [s_1(\mathbf{x}_1), \cdots, s_m(\mathbf{x}_m), \cdots, s_M(\mathbf{x}_M)], \tag{3}$$

where $s_m(\cdot)$ is the soft quantizer for m-th subvector defined as

$$s_m(\mathbf{x}_m) = \sum_k \frac{e^{-\alpha\|\mathbf{x}_m - \mathbf{c}_{mk}\|_2^2}\mathbf{c}_{mk}}{\sum_{k'} e^{-\alpha\|\mathbf{x}_m - \mathbf{c}_{mk'}\|_2^2}}. \tag{4}$$

It is not difficult to observe that

$$\mathbb{1}(k = k^*) = \lim_{\alpha \to +\infty} \frac{e^{-\alpha\|\mathbf{x}_m - \mathbf{c}_{mk}\|_2^2}}{\sum_{k'} e^{-\alpha\|\mathbf{x}_m - \mathbf{c}_{mk'}\|_2^2}} \tag{5}$$

Therefore, when $\alpha \to +\infty$, the soft quantizer $s_m(\mathbf{x}_m)$ will be equivalent to the hard quantizer $q_m(\mathbf{x}_m)$. Since the soft quantization operation is differentiable and thus it can be readily incorporated into a network as a layer.

3.2   Soft Product Quantization Layer

Before we conduct soft product quantization in the network, we first pre-process the original feature $\mathbf{x} = [\mathbf{x}_1, \cdots, \mathbf{x}_m, \cdots, \mathbf{x}_M]$ through intra-normalization and conduct ℓ_2-normalization on codewords $\{\mathbf{c}_{mk}\}_{m=1,k=1}^{M,K}$:

$$\mathbf{x}_m \leftarrow \mathbf{x}_m / \|\mathbf{x}_m\|_2 \tag{6}$$

$$\mathbf{c}_{mk} \leftarrow \mathbf{c}_{mk} / \|\mathbf{c}_{mk}\|_2 \tag{7}$$

The pre-processing step is motivated by two reasons: (1) intra-normalization and ℓ_2-normalization can balance the contribution of each sub-vector and each codeword; (2) it simplifies the gradient computation.

Forward Pass. After intra-normalization on original features and ℓ_2-normalization on the codewords, we can obtain $\|\mathbf{x}_m - \mathbf{c}_{mk}\|_2^2 = 2 - 2\langle \mathbf{x}_m, \mathbf{c}_{mk} \rangle$, where $\langle \cdot, \cdot \rangle$ denotes the inner product between two vectors. Based on the above property, we can rewrite Eq. (4) into:

$$s_m(\mathbf{x}_m) = \sum_k \frac{e^{2\alpha\langle \mathbf{x}_m, \mathbf{c}_{mk} \rangle} \mathbf{c}_{mk}}{\sum_{k'} e^{2\alpha\langle \mathbf{x}_m, \mathbf{c}_{mk'} \rangle}}. \tag{8}$$

Backward Pass. To elaborate the backward pass of the soft quantization layer, we introduce an immediate variable a_{mk} defined as

$$a_{mk} = \frac{e^{2\alpha\langle \mathbf{x}_m, \mathbf{c}_{mk} \rangle}}{\sum_{k'} e^{2\alpha\langle \mathbf{x}_m, \mathbf{c}_{mk'} \rangle}}. \tag{9}$$

Based on the above definition, Eq. (8) will be converted into

$$s_m(\mathbf{x}_m) = \sum_k a_{mk} \mathbf{c}_{mk}. \tag{10}$$

Through chain rule, we can obtain the derivative of loss with respect to $\mathbf{c}_{mk}$ by

$$\frac{\partial L}{\partial \mathbf{c}_{mk}} = a_{mk} \frac{\partial L}{\partial s_m(\mathbf{x}_m)} + \sum_{k'} \frac{\partial a_{mk'}}{\partial \mathbf{c}_{mk}} \left(\frac{\partial s_m(\mathbf{x}_m)}{\partial a_{mk'}} \right)^{\top} \frac{\partial L}{\partial s_m(\mathbf{x}_m)}, \tag{11}$$

where

$$\frac{\partial s_m(\mathbf{x}_m)}{\partial a_{mk'}} = \mathbf{c}_{mk'}, \tag{12}$$

and

$$\frac{\partial a_{mk'}}{\partial \mathbf{c}_{mk}} = \begin{cases} \dfrac{-e^{2\alpha\langle \mathbf{x}_m, \mathbf{c}_{mk'} \rangle} e^{2\alpha\langle \mathbf{x}_m, \mathbf{c}_{mk} \rangle} 2\alpha \mathbf{x}_m}{(\sum_{k''} e^{2\alpha\langle \mathbf{x}_m, \mathbf{c}_{mk''} \rangle})^2}, & k \neq k' \\ \dfrac{\sum_{k' \neq k} e^{2\alpha\langle \mathbf{x}_m, \mathbf{c}_{mk'} \rangle} e^{2\alpha\langle \mathbf{x}_m, \mathbf{c}_{mk} \rangle} 2\alpha \mathbf{x}_m}{(\sum_{k''} e^{2\alpha\langle \mathbf{x}_m, \mathbf{c}_{mk''} \rangle})^2}, & k = k' \end{cases} \tag{13}$$

By plugging Eqs. (12) and (13) into Eq. (11), we can obtain $\frac{\partial L}{\partial \mathbf{c}_{mk}}$.

3.3 Initialization

We initialize the parameters of convolutional layers by fine-tuning a standard convolutional neural network without quantization, e.g., Alexnet, on the specific dataset. Note that, we add an intra-normalization layer to fine-tune the network to make it compatible with our deep product quantization network. After the initialization of convolutional layers, we extract the features from the fine-tuned network and conduct k-means followed by ℓ_2-normalization to obtain the initialized codewords $\{\mathbf{c}_{mk}\}_{k=1,m=1}^{K,M}$ in the soft product quantization layer.

3.4   Asymmetric Triplet Loss

We propose a novel asymmetric triplet loss to optimize the parameters of the network. We define (I, I_+, I_-) as a training triplet, where I_- and I_+ represent a relevant image and an irrelevant image with respect to the anchor image I. We denote by $\mathbf{x}_I$ as the feature of I before soft product quantization and denote by $\mathbf{s}_{I_+}$ and $\mathbf{s}_{I_-}$ the features of I_+ and I_- after soft product quantization. We define asymmetric similarity between I and $I+$ as $\langle \mathbf{x}_I, \mathbf{s}_{I_+} \rangle$, where $\langle \cdot, \cdot \rangle$ denotes the inner-product operation. The proposed asymmetric triplet loss is defined as

$$l = \langle \mathbf{x}_I, \mathbf{s}_{I_-} \rangle - \langle \mathbf{x}_I, \mathbf{s}_{I_+} \rangle. \tag{14}$$

Intuitively, it aims to increase the asymmetric similarity between the pairs of relevant images and decrease that of pairs consisting of irrelevant images. It is a natural extension of original triplet loss on the condition of asymmetric distance. The difference is that, a training triplet used in original triplet loss consists of three features of the same type, whereas a training triplet used in the proposed asymmetric triplet loss consists of one feature without quantization and two features after quantization. In fact, our experiments show that a better performance is achieved by processing above loss through sigmoid function and a revised loss function is defined as Eq. (15). The better performance might be contributed by the fact that the sigmoid function can normalize the original loss so that the training will not be biased by some samples causing huge loss.

$$l = \frac{1}{1 + e^{\langle \mathbf{x}_I, \mathbf{s}_{I_+} \rangle - \langle \mathbf{x}_I, \mathbf{s}_{I_-} \rangle}}. \tag{15}$$

3.5   Encode and Retrieval

After training the proposed product quantization network, the reference images in the database will be encoded by hard product quantization. We define the layer before the soft product quantization layer as embedding layer. Given a reference image I of the database, we obtain its output from embedding layer $\mathbf{x} = [\mathbf{x}_1, \cdots, \mathbf{x}_m, \cdots, \mathbf{x}_M]$ and further obtain its product quantization code $\mathbf{b} = [b_1, \cdots, b_m, \cdots, b_M]$ where b_m is computed by

$$b_m = \underset{k}{\arg\max} \langle \mathbf{x}_m, \mathbf{c}_{mk} \rangle, \tag{16}$$

where $\{\mathbf{c}_{mk}\}_{m=1,k=1}^{M,K}$ are codewords learned from our product quantization network. In the retrieval phase, we obtain the query feature from the embedding layer $\mathbf{q} = [\mathbf{q}_1, \cdots, \mathbf{q}_m, \cdots, \mathbf{q}_M]$. The relevance between the query image and a reference image represented by its product quantization code $\mathbf{b} = [b_1, \cdots, b_m, \cdots, b_M]$ is computed by the asymmetric similarity $s(\mathbf{q}, \mathbf{b})$ defined as

$$s(\mathbf{q}, \mathbf{b}) = \sum_{m=1}^{M} \langle \mathbf{q}_m, \mathbf{c}_{mb_m} \rangle. \tag{17}$$

Since $\langle \mathbf{q}_m, \mathbf{c}_{mb_m} \rangle$ is computed only once for all the reference images in the database and thus obtaining $s(\mathbf{q}, \mathbf{b})$ only requires to sum up the pre-computed similarity scores in the look-up table, considerably speeding up the image retrieval process. Meanwhile, storing the product quantization code $\mathbf{b}$ only requires $M \log_2 K$ bits, which considerably reduces the memory cost.

3.6 Relation to Existing Methods

DQN [6] is the first attempt of incorporating product quantization in the neural network. It alternatively optimizes codewords and other parameters of the network. It is worth noting that when updating codewords, it only minimizes the quantizaition errors through k-means. Therefore, when learning codewords, the supervision information is ignored and the solution might be sub-optimal.

SUBIC [16] integrates the one-hot block encoding layer in the deep neural network. It represents each image by a product of one-hot blocks, following the spirit of product quantization. Nevertheless, the sparse property limits its representation capability, making it perform not as well as ours.

DPQ [20] is another attempt of incorporating the product quantization into the neural network. It determines the codeword assignment through a cascade of two fully-connected layers. In contrast, our method determines the codeword assignment according to the similarity between original feature and the codewords. Note that, the additional parameters from these two fully-connected layers in DPQ no only increase the computation complexity in training the neural network but also are more prone to over-fitting. Our experiments show that our proposed PQN considerably outperforms DPQ.

4   Experiments

We evaluate the performance of our PQN on two public benchmark datasets, CIFAR-10 and NUS-WIDE. CIFAR-10 [21] is a dataset containing $60,000$ color images in 10 classes, and each class has $6,000$ images in size 32×32. Different from CIFAR-10, NUS-WIDE [8] is a dataset for evaluating multi-class classification, in which one sample is assigned to one or multiple labels. We follow the settings in [6,22] and use the subset of $195,834$ images that are associated with the 21 most frequent concepts, where each concept consists of at least $5,000$ images. We resize all images into 256×256.

On the CIFAR-10 dataset, the performance reported by different baselines are based on different base convolutional neural networks, making it unfair to directly compare their reported retrieval accuracy. To make a fair comparison, we evaluate our method based on two types of convolutional neural networks. The first convolutional neural network we use is 3CNet which is also used by SUBIC [16] and DQN [20]. 3CNet is proposed in [25], which consists of $L = 3$

convolutional layers with 32, 32 and 64 filters of size 5×5 respectively, followed by a fully connected layer with $d = 500$ nodes. The second convolutional neural network we choose is AlexNet. It is worth noting that the baselines we compare may apply different models. For example, DQN [6] adopts AlexNet whereas other work [23,34] adopt VGG-F model. These two models are similar in the architecture. To be specific, both the CNN-F and AlexNet consist of five convolutional layers and two fully connected layers. As shown in [19], the CNN-F generally performs better than Alexnet in image retrieval, therefore, the better performance of ours based on AlexNet than existing state-of-art methods based on CNN-F is not owing to better base network. In other words, our method can achieve better performance even with an inferior base network. On the NUS-WIDE dataset, we also adopt AlexNet as our base model. On both datasets, we report the performance of the proposed method through mAP, which is a standard metric in evaluating the performance of retrieval algorithms.

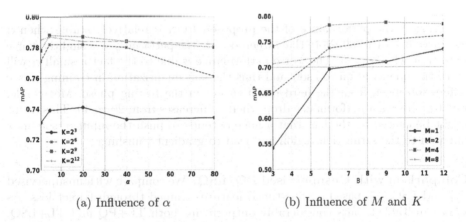

(a) Influence of α (b) Influence of M and K

Fig. 2. The influence of parameters on CIFAR-10 dataset using 3CNet.

4.1 CIFAR-10 Using 3CNet

Following the experimental setup in SUBIC [16] and DPQ [20], the training is conducted on 50K image training set. The test set is split into 9K database images and 1K query images (100 per class).

Influence of M and K. In this section, we evaluate the influence of the number of subvectors M and the number of codewords per sub-codebook K on the retrieval precision of the proposed PQN. We vary M among $\{1, 2, 4, 8\}$, and vary $B = log_2 K$ among $\{3, 6, 9, 12\}$. As shown in Fig. 2(a), the proposed method achieves the best performance when $M = 4$. By default, we set $M = 4$ on CIFAR-10 Dataset. Note that when $M = 1$ and $M = 2$, the performance of the proposed PQN increases as B increases. This is expected since the larger B can partition

Table 1. Comparisons with PQ and LSQ.

method	4bits	8bits	16bits	24bits	32bits
TL+Full			0.779		
TL+PQ	0.503	0.621	0.741	0.773	0.780
TL+LSQ	0.511	0.720	0.752	0.753	0.763
PQN(Ours)	**0.574**	**0.729**	**0.778**	**0.782**	**0.786**

the feature space into finer cells. Nevertheless, when $M = 4$, the performance drops when B increases from 9 to 12. Meanwhile, when $M = 8$, there is also a performance drop when K increases from 6 to 9. The worse performance might be caused by over-fitting when both M and K are large.

Influence of α. α controls the quantization softness of the soft product quantization layer. We evaluate the performance of our method when α varies. We test the influence of α when $M = 4$ and K varies among $\{2^3, 2^6, 2^9, 2^{12}\}$. As shown in Fig. 2(b), the performance of the proposed PQN is relatively stable when α increases from 1 to 80. Note that, when $\alpha = 1$, the performance is slightly worse than that when $\alpha = 5$. The worse performance is due to the fact a small α will make the quantization too soft and thus the soft quantization in training phase differs too much from the hard quantization in the testing phase. Meanwhile, we also observe a performance drop when α increases from 20 to 40. This drops might be caused by the fact that a huge α tends to push the input of soft-max function to the saturation region and lead to gradient vanishing.

Comparison with Unsupervised PQ/LSQ. We compare with unsupervised PQ and LSQ [27] based on fine-tuned features trained through triplet loss. As shown in Table 1, ours considerably outperforms both TL+PQ and TL+LSQ. Meanwhile, we also show the performance of original features trained through triplet loss without quantization (TL+Full) in Table 1. The performance of ours is even better than that of features without quantization, this is owing to the regularization imposed by quantization, which suppresses over-fitting.

Effectiveness of Asymmetric Triplet Loss. Meanwhile, in order to show the effectiveness of the proposed asymmetric triplet loss, we compare with two alternatives, cross-entropy loss (CEL) and triplet loss (TL). To make a fair comparison, we only change the loss function and keep the other parts of the network unchanged. As shown in Fig. 3, the proposed assymetric loss consistently outperforms the cross-entropy loss and triplet loss when L varies among $\{12, 24, 36, 48\}$. For instance, when $L = 36$, our ATL achieves a 0.787 mAP whereas TL only achieves a 0.778 mAP and CEL only achieves a 0.768 mAP.

Compare with State-of-the-art Methods. We compare our method with two state-of-the-art methods (SUBIC and DPQ), which adopt the same 3CNet as well as the same experimental settings. We change bit length L among $\{12, 24, 36, 48\}$. We set $M = 4$ and $K = 8, 64, 512, 4096$, respectively. Since SUBIC adopts cross-entropy loss, it is unfair to directly compare it with ours using asymmetric triplet loss. Therefore, we report the performance of our PQN based on the cross-entropy loss (CEL) as well as the proposed asymmetric triplet loss (ATL). As shown in Table 2, our method based on both CEL and ATL significantly outperform the existing state-of-the-art methods including SUBIC and DPQ. For instance, when $L = 24$, ours achieves a 0.771 mAP based on the cross-entropy loss and a 0.782 mAP using the proposed asymmetric triplet loss whereas SUBIC only achieves a 0.672 mAP and DPQ only achieves a 0.692 mAP.

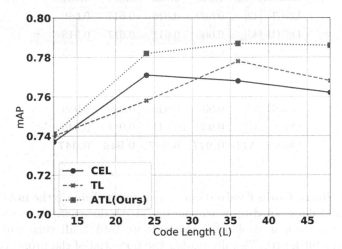

Fig. 3. Comparisons of our asymmetric triple loss (ATL) with cross-entropy loss (CEL) and triplet loss (TL).

4.2 CIFAR-10 Using AlexNet

Following the experimental settings in [23,34], we randomly sample 1000 images per class (10000 images in total) as the testing query images, and the remaining 50000 images are used as the training set as well as reference images in the database. We set $M = 4$ and vary K among $\{2^4, 2^6, 2^9, 2^{12}\}$, and thus the code length L varies among $\{16, 24, 36, 48\}$.

Table 2. mAP comparisons with state-of-the-art methods using 3CNet.

Method	12 bits	24 bits	36 bits	48 bits
SUBIC [16]	0.635	0.672	0.682	0.686
DPQ [20]	0.673	0.692	0.695	0.693
Ours+CEL	**0.737**	**0.771**	**0.768**	**0.762**
Ours+ATL	**0.741**	**0.782**	**0.787**	**0.786**

Comparions with State-of-the-art Methods. As shown in Table 3, ours consistently outperforms the existing state-of-the-art methods, especially when the bit length is small. For instance, when the bit length is 16, our method based on asymmetric triplet loss (Ours+ATL) achieves a 0.947 mAP whereas the second best method, DSDH, only achieves a 0.935 mAP.

Table 3. mAP comparisons with existing state-of-the-art methods using AlexNet base model on the CIFAR10 dataset.

Method	16 bits	24 bits	36 bits	48 bits
DRSCH [42]	0.615	0.622	0.629	0.631
DSCH [42]	0.609	0.613	0.617	0.686
DSRH [45]	0.608	0.611	0.617	0.618
VDSH [44]	0.845	0.848	0.844	0.845
DPSH [24]	0.903	0.885	0.915	0.911
DTSH [34]	0.915	0.923	0.925	0.926
DSDH [23]	0.935	0.940	0.939	0.939
Ours + CE	0.939	0.941	0.941	0.940
Ours + ATL	**0.947**	**0.947**	**0.946**	**0.947**

Extremely Short Code Evaluation. As shown in Table 3, the mAP achieved by our method does not drop when the bit length decreases from 48 to 16. In contrast, the performance of other methods in Table 3 all turn worse due to decrease of the bit length. To fully exploit the potential of the proposed product quantization network on the CIAFR-10 dataset, we evaluate it by setting the code length L extremely small. We vary M among 1, 2 and 4, and meanwhile vary the code length (bit number) L within $\{4, 6, 8, 10, 12\}$. As shown in Fig. 4, when code length is extremely small, e.g., $L = 4$, the performance of PQN when $M = 1$ significantly outperforms that when $M = 2, 4$. Meanwhile, when $M = 1$, there is not significant performance drop when L decreases from 12 to 4. Note that, when $M = 1$, the proposed PQN achieves a 0.945 mAP when using only 4 bits per code. It considerably outperforms the existing state-of-art method DSDH [23] which only achieves 0.935 mAP using 16 bits.

4.3   NUS-WIDE

Following the experiment setup in [23,34], we randomly sample 100 images per class (2100 images in total) as the test query set and the remaining images are used as database images. 500 database images per label are randomly sampled as training images. The mAP is calculated based on the top 5000 returned neighbors. Due to multi-label settings, the cross-entropy loss used in SUBIC [16] and the softmax loss in DPQ [20] are no longer feasible, which explains neither SUBIC [16] nor DPQ [20] conducts the experiments on NUS-WIDE dataset. Inspired by the success of label embedding proposed in [23], we also adopt a combined loss,

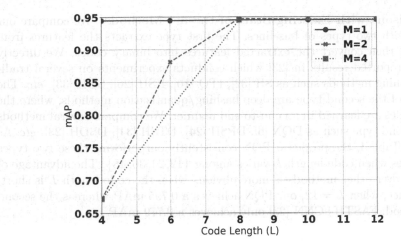

Fig. 4. Evaluation on the extremely short code.

Table 4. mAP comparisons with existing state-of-the-art methods using AlexNet base model on the NUS-WIDE dataset. The mAP is based on top 5000 nearest neighbors.

Method	12 bits	24 bits	36 bits	48 bits
SH + CNN [23]	0.621	0.616	0.615	0.612
ITQ + CNN [23]	0.719	0.739	0.747	0.756
LFH + CNN [23]	0.695	0.734	0.739	0.759
KSH + CNN [23]	0.768	0.786	0.790	0.799
SDH+ CNN [23]	0.780	0.804	0.815	0.824
FASTH+CNN [23]	0.779	0.807	0.816	0.825
CNNH [37]	0.611	0.618	0.625	0.608
NINH [22]	0.674	0.697	0.713	0.715
DHN [46]	0.708	0.735	0.748	0.758
DQN [6]	0.768	0.776	0.783	0.792
DPSH [24]	0.752	0.790	0.794	0.812
DTSH [34]	0.773	0.808	0.812	0.824
DSDH [23]	0.776	0.808	0.820	0.829
Ours	**0.795**	**0.819**	**0.823**	**0.830**

which is a weighed sum of our asymmetric triplet loss and a mean square loss defined as

$$l = \frac{1}{1 + e^{\langle \mathbf{x}_I, \mathbf{s}_{I_+} \rangle - \langle \mathbf{x}_I, \mathbf{s}_{I_-} \rangle}} + \beta \|\mathbf{W}\mathbf{s}_I - \mathbf{y}_I\|_2^2, \tag{18}$$

where $\mathbf{W}$ is the parameter in an additional FC layer after the soft product quantization layer and $\mathbf{y}_I$ is the label of the sample I. We set $\beta = 10$ by default.

Comparisons with Existing State-of-the-art Methods. We compare our method with two types of baselines. The first type extracts the features from CNN and then convert the extracted features into binary codes. We directly copy the reported results in [23] which conducts experiments on several traditional hashing methods such as SH [32], ITQ [10], KSH [26], SDH [33], *etc.* The baselines of the second type are deep hashing/quantization methods, where the binary codes are learned in an end-to-end manner. We compare several methods of the second type such as DQN [6], DPSH [24], DTSH [34], DSDH [23], *etc.* As shown in Table 4, the proposed PQN consistently outperforms these two types of baselines when code length L varies among $\{12, 24, 36, 48\}$. The advantage of our PQN over other methods is more obvious when the code length L is short. For instance, when $L = 12$, our PQN achieves a 0.795 mAP whereas the second best method, FASTH+CNN [23] only achieves a 0.779 mAP.

5   Conclusion

In this paper, by incorporating product quantization in the neural network, we propose product quantization nework (PQN) to learn a discriminative and compact image representation in an end-to-end manner. Meanwhile, we propose a novel asymmetric triplet loss, which directly optimizes the image retrieval based on asymmetric distance to train our network more effectively. Systematic experiments conducted on benchmark datasets demonstrate the state-of-the-art performance of the proposed PQN.

Acknowledgement. This work is supported in part by start-up grants of University at Buffalo, Computer Science and Engineering Department. This work is supported in part by Singapore Ministry of Education Academic Research Fund Tier 2 MOE2015-T2-2-114. This research was carried out at the ROSE Lab of Nanyang Technological University, Singapore. The ROSE Lab is supported by the National Research Foundation, Prime Ministers Office, Singapore. We gratefully acknowledge the support of NVAITC (NVIDIA AI Technology Centre) for their donation for our research.

References

1. Babenko, A., Lempitsky, V.: Additive quantization for extreme vector compression. In: CVPR, pp. 931–938 (2014)
2. Babenko, A., Lempitsky, V.: Aggregating local deep features for image retrieval. In: ICCV, pp. 1269–1277 (2015)
3. Babenko, A., Slesarev, A., Chigorin, A., Lempitsky, V.: Neural codes for image retrieval. In: Fleet, D., Pajdla, T., Schiele, B., Tuytelaars, T. (eds.) ECCV 2014. LNCS, vol. 8689, pp. 584–599. Springer, Cham (2014). https://doi.org/10.1007/978-3-319-10590-1_38
4. Bai, S., Bai, X., Tian, Q., Latecki, L.J.: Regularized diffusion process on bidirectional context for object retrieval. TPAMI (2018)
5. Bai, S., Zhou, Z., Wang, J., Bai, X., Latecki, L.J., Tian, Q.: Ensemble diffusion for retrieval

6. Cao, Y., Long, M., Wang, J., Zhu, H., Wen, Q.: Deep quantization network for efficient image retrieval. In: AAAI (2016)
7. Charikar, M.S.: Similarity estimation techniques from rounding algorithms. In: Proceedings of the Thiry-Fourth Annual ACM Symposium on Theory of Computing, pp. 380–388 (2002)
8. Chua, T.S., Tang, J., Hong, R., Li, H., Luo, Z., Zheng, Y.: NUS-wide: a real-world web image database from national university of Singapore. In: Proceedings of the ACM International Conference on Image and Video Retrieval, p. 48 (2009)
9. Ge, T., He, K., Ke, Q., Sun, J.: Optimized product quantization for approximate nearest neighbor search. In: CVPR, pp. 2946–2953. IEEE (2013)
10. Gong, Y., Lazebnik, S., Gordo, A., Perronnin, F.: Iterative quantization: a procrustean approach to learning binary codes for large-scale image retrieval. IEEE T-PAMI $35(12)$, 2916–2929 (2013)
11. Gordo, A., Almazán, J., Revaud, J., Larlus, D.: Deep image retrieval: learning global representations for image search. In: Leibe, B., Matas, J., Sebe, N., Welling, M. (eds.) ECCV 2016. LNCS, vol. 9910, pp. 241–257. Springer, Cham (2016). https://doi.org/10.1007/978-3-319-46466-4_15
12. Hong, W., Meng, J., Yuan, J.: Distributed composite quantization. In: AAAI (2018)
13. Hong, W., Meng, J., Yuan, J.: Tensorized projection for high-dimensional binary embedding. In: AAAI (2018)
14. Hong, W., Yuan, J.: Fried binary embedding: from high-dimensional visual features to high-dimensional binary codes. IEEE Trans. Image Process. $27(10)$ (2018)
15. Hong, W., Yuan, J., Bhattacharjee, S.D.: Fried binary embedding for high-dimensional visual features. CVPR 11, 18 (2017)
16. Jain, H., Zepeda, J., Perez, P., Gribonval, R.: Subic: a supervised, structured binary code for image search. In: ICCV, pp. 833–842 (2017)
17. Jegou, H., Douze, M., Schmid, C.: Product quantization for nearest neighbor search. IEEE T-PAMI $33(1)$, 117–128 (2011)
18. Jégou, H., Douze, M., Schmid, C., Pérez, P.: Aggregating local descriptors into a compact image representation. In: CVPR, pp. 3304–3311 (2010)
19. Jiang, Q.Y., Li, W.J.: Asymmetric deep supervised hashing. In: AAAI (2018)
20. Klein, B., Wolf, L.: In defense of product quantization. arXiv preprint arXiv:1711.08589 (2017)
21. Krizhevsky, A.: Learning multiple layers of features from tiny images (2009)
22. Lai, H., Pan, Y., Liu, Y., Yan, S.: Simultaneous feature learning and hash coding with deep neural networks. arXiv preprint arXiv:1504.03410 (2015)
23. Li, Q., Sun, Z., He, R., Tan, T.: Deep supervised discrete hashing. In: NIPS, pp. 2479–2488 (2017)
24. Li, W.J., Wang, S., Kang, W.C.: Feature learning based deep supervised hashing with pairwise labels. arXiv preprint arXiv:1511.03855 (2015)
25. Liu, H., Wang, R., Shan, S., Chen, X.: Deep supervised hashing for fast image retrieval. In: CVPR, pp. 2064–2072 (2016)
26. Liu, W., Wang, J., Ji, R., Jiang, Y.G., Chang, S.F.: Supervised hashing with kernels. In: CVPR, pp. 2074–2081 (2012)
27. Martinez, J., Clement, J., Hoos, H.H., Little, J.J.: Revisiting additive quantization. In: Leibe, B., Matas, J., Sebe, N., Welling, M. (eds.) ECCV 2016. LNCS, vol. 9906, pp. 137–153. Springer, Cham (2016). https://doi.org/10.1007/978-3-319-46475-6_9
28. Ng, J.Y.H., Yang, F., Davis, L.S.: Exploiting local features from deep networks for image retrieval. arXiv preprint arXiv:1504.05133 (2015)
29. Norouzi, M., Fleet, D.J.: Cartesian k-means. In: CVPR, pp. 3017–3024 (2013)

30. Perronnin, F., Liu, Y., Sánchez, J., Poirier, H.: Large-scale image retrieval with compressed fisher vectors. In: CVPR, pp. 3384–3391 (2010)
31. Philbin, J., Chum, O., Isard, M., Sivic, J., Zisserman, A.: Object retrieval with large vocabularies and fast spatial matching. In: CVPR, pp. 1–8 (2007)
32. Salakhutdinov, R., Hinton, G.: Semantic hashing. RBM **500**(3), 500 (2007)
33. Shen, F., Shen, C., Liu, W., Shen, H.T.: Supervised discrete hashing. IEEE T-PAMI **35**(12), 2916–2929 (2013)
34. Wang, X., Shi, Y., Kitani, K.M.: Deep supervised hashing with triplet labels. In: Lai, S.-H., Lepetit, V., Nishino, K., Sato, Y. (eds.) ACCV 2016. LNCS, vol. 10111, pp. 70–84. Springer, Cham (2017). https://doi.org/10.1007/978-3-319-54181-5_5
35. Wang, X., Zhang, T., Qi, G.J., Tang, J., Wang, J.: Supervised quantization for similarity search. In: CVPR, pp. 2018–2026 (2016)
36. Weiss, Y., Torralba, A., Fergus, R.: Spectral hashing. In: NIPS, pp. 1753–1760 (2009)
37. Xia, R., Pan, Y., Lai, H., Liu, C., Yan, S.: Supervised hashing for image retrieval via image representation learning. In: AAAI, pp. 2156–2162. AAAI Press (2014)
38. Yu, T., Meng, J., Yuan, J.: Is my object in this video? reconstruction-based object search in videos. In: Proceedings of the 26th International Joint Conference on Artificial Intelligence, pp. 4551–4557. AAAI Press (2017)
39. Yu, T., Wang, Z., Yuan, J.: Compressive quantization for fast object instance search in videos. In: ICCV, pp. 833–842 (2017)
40. Yu, T., Wu, Y., Bhattacharjee, S.D., Yuan, J.: Efficient object instance search using fuzzy objects matching. In: AAAI (2017)
41. Yu, T., Wu, Y., Yuan, J.: Hope: hierarchical object prototype encoding for efficient object instance search in videos. In: Proceedings of the IEEE Conference on Computer Vision and Pattern Recognition, pp. 2424–2433 (2017)
42. Zhang, R., Lin, L., Zhang, R., Zuo, W., Zhang, L.: Bit-scalable deep hashing with regularized similarity learning for image retrieval and person re-identification. IEEE TIP **24**(12), 4766–4779 (2015)
43. Zhang, T., Du, C., Wang, J.: Composite quantization for approximate nearest neighbor search. In: ICML, no. 2, pp. 838–846 (2014)
44. Zhang, Z., Chen, Y., Saligrama, V.: Efficient training of very deep neural networks for supervised hashing. In: CVPR, pp. 1487–1495 (2016)
45. Zhao, F., Huang, Y., Wang, L., Tan, T.: Deep semantic ranking based hashing for multi-label image retrieval. In: CVPR, pp. 1556–1564 (2015)
46. Zhu, H., Long, M., Wang, J., Cao, Y.: Deep hashing network for efficient similarity retrieval. In: AAAI (2016)

Cross-Modal Hamming Hashing

Yue Cao[1,2], Bin Liu[1,2], Mingsheng Long[1,2(✉)], and Jianmin Wang[1,2]

[1] School of Software, Tsinghua University, Beijing, China
caoyue10@gmail.com, liubinthss@gmail.com,
{mingsheng,jimwang}@tsinghua.edu.cn
[2] National Engineering Laboratory for Big Data Software, Beijing National Research Center for Information Science and Technology, Beijing, China

Abstract. Cross-modal hashing enables similarity retrieval across different content modalities, such as searching relevant images in response to text queries. It provide with the advantages of computation efficiency and retrieval quality for multimedia retrieval. Hamming space retrieval enables efficient constant-time search that returns data items within a given Hamming radius to each query, by hash lookups instead of linear scan. However, Hamming space retrieval is ineffective in existing cross-modal hashing methods, subject to their weak capability of concentrating the relevant items to be within a small Hamming ball, while worse still, the Hamming distances between hash codes from different modalities are inevitably large due to the large heterogeneity across different modalities. This work presents Cross-Modal Hamming Hashing (CMHH), a novel deep cross-modal hashing approach that generates compact and highly concentrated hash codes to enable efficient and effective Hamming space retrieval. The main idea is to penalize significantly on similar cross-modal pairs with Hamming distance larger than the Hamming radius threshold, by designing a pairwise focal loss based on the exponential distribution. Extensive experiments demonstrate that CMHH can generate highly concentrated hash codes and achieve state-of-the-art cross-modal retrieval performance for both hash lookups and linear scan scenarios on three benchmark datasets, NUS-WIDE, MIRFlickr-25K, and IAPR TC-12.

Keywords: Deep hashing · Cross-modal hashing
Hamming space retrieval

1 Introduction

With the explosion of big data, large-scale and high-dimensional data has been widespread in search engines and social networks. As relevant data items from different modalities may convey semantic correlations, it is significant to support cross-modal retrieval, which returns semantically-relevant results from one modality in response to a query of another modality. Recently, a popular and advantageous solution to cross-modal retrieval is learning to hash [1], an approach to approximate nearest neighbors (ANN) search across different modal-

© Springer Nature Switzerland AG 2018
V. Ferrari et al. (Eds.): ECCV 2018, LNCS 11205, pp. 207–223, 2018.
https://doi.org/10.1007/978-3-030-01246-5_13

ities with both computation efficiency and search quality. It transforms high-dimensional data into compact binary codes with similar binary codes for similar data, largely reducing the computational burdens of distance calculation and candidates pruning on large-scale high-dimensional data. Although the semantic gap across low-level descriptors and high-level semantics [2] has been reduced by deep learning, the intrinsic heterogeneity across modalities remains another challenge.

Previous cross-modal hashing methods capture the relations across different modalities in the process of hash function learning and transform cross-modal data into an isomorphic Hamming space, where the cross-modal distances can be directly computed [3–13]. Existing approaches can be roughly categorized into unsupervised methods and supervised methods. Unsupervised methods are general to different scenarios and can be trained without semantic labels or relevance information, but they are subject to the semantic gap [2] that high-level semantic labels of an object differ from low-level feature descriptors. Supervised methods can incorporate semantic labels or relevance information to mitigate the semantic gap [2], yielding more accurate and compact hash codes to improve the retrieval accuracy. However, without learning deep representations in the process of hash function learning, existing cross-modal hashing methods cannot effectively close the heterogeneity gap across different modalities.

To improve the retrieval accuracy, deep hashing methods [14–16] learn feature representation and hash coding more effectively using deep networks [17,18]. For cross-modal retrieval, deep cross-modal hashing methods [8,19–24] have shown that deep networks can capture nonlinear cross-modal correlations more effectively and yielded state-of-the-art cross-modal retrieval performance. Existing deep cross-modal hashing methods can be organized into unsupervised methods and supervised methods. The unsupervised deep cross-modal hashing methods adopt identical deep architecture for different modalities, e.g. MMDBM [20] uses Deep Boltzmann Machines, MSAE [8] uses Stacked Auto-Encoders, and MMNN [19] uses Multilayer Perceptrons. In contrast, the supervised deep cross-modal hashing methods [22–24] adopt hybrid deep architectures, which can be effectively trained with supervision to ensure best architecture for each modality, e.g. Convolutional Networks for images [17,18,25], Multilayer Perceptrons for texts [26–28] and Recurrent Networks for audio [29]. The supervised methods significantly outperform the unsupervised methods for cross-modal retrieval.

However, most existing methods focus on data compression instead of candidates pruning, i.e., they are designed to maximize retrieval performance by linear scan over the generated hash codes. As linear scan is still costly for large-scale database even using compact hash codes, we may deviate from our original goal towards hashing, i.e. maximizing search speedup under acceptable retrieval accuracy. With the prosperity of powerful hashing methods that perform well with linear scan, we should now return to our original ambition of hashing: enable efficient *constant-time* search using hash lookups, a.k.n. Hamming space retrieval [30]. More precisely, in Hamming space retrieval, we return data points within a given Hamming radius to each query in constant-time, by hash lookups instead of

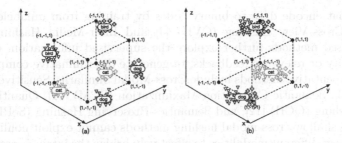

Fig. 1. Illustration of the bottleneck in cross-modal Hamming space retrieval. Different colors denote different categories (e.g. dog, cat, and bird) and different markers denote different modalities (e.g. triangles for images and crosses for texts). Due to the large intrinsic heterogeneity across different modalities, existing cross-modal hashing methods will generate hash codes of different modalities with very large Hamming distances, since their mis-specified losses cannot penalize different modalities of the same category to be similar enough in the Hamming distances, as shown in plot (a). We address this bottleneck by proposing a well-specified pairwise focal loss based on the exponential distribution, which penalizes significantly on similar cross-modal pairs with Hamming distances larger than the Hamming radius, as shown in plot (b). *Best viewed in color.* (Color figure online)

linear scan. Unfortunately, existing cross-modal hashing methods generally fall short in the capability of concentrating relevant cross-modal pairs to be within a small Hamming ball due to their mis-specified loss functions. This results in their ineffectiveness for cross-modal Hamming space retrieval. The bottleneck of existing cross-modal hashing methods is intuitively depicted in Fig. 1.

Towards a formal solution to the aforementioned heterogeneity bottleneck in Hamming space retrieval, this work presents Cross-Modal Hamming Hashing (CMHH), a novel deep cross-modal hashing approach that generates compact and highly concentrated hash codes to enable efficient and effective Hamming space retrieval. The main idea is to penalize significantly on similar cross-modal pairs with Hamming distances larger than the Hamming radius threshold, by designing a pairwise focal loss based on the exponential distribution. CMHH simultaneously learns similarity-preserving binary representations for images and texts, and formally controls the quantization error of binarizing continuous representations to binary hash codes. Extensive experiments demonstrate that CMHH can generate highly concentrated hash codes and achieve state-of-the-art cross-modal retrieval performance for both hash lookups and linear scan scenarios on three benchmark datasets, NUS-WIDE, MIRFlickr-25K, and IAPR TC-12.

2   Related Work

Cross-modal hashing has been an increasingly important and powerful solution to multimedia retrieval [31–36]. A latest survey can be found in [1].

Previous cross-modal hashing methods include unsupervised methods and supervised methods. Unsupervised cross-modal hashing methods learn hash functions that encode data to binary codes by training from unlabeled paired data, e.g. Cross-View Hashing (CVH) [4] and Inter-Media Hashing (IMH) [7]. Supervised methods further explore the supervised information, e.g. pairwise similarity or relevance feedbacks, to generate discriminative compact hash codes. Representative methods include Cross-Modal Similarity Sensitive Hashing (CMSSH) [3], Semantic Correlation Maximization (SCM) [11], Quantized Correlation Hashing (QCH) [12], and Semantics-Preserving Hashing (SePH) [37].

Previous shallow cross-modal hashing methods cannot exploit nonlinear correlations across different modalities to effectively bridge the intrinsic cross-modal heterogeneity. Deep multimodal embedding methods [38–41] have shown that deep networks can bridge different modalities more effectively. Recent deep hashing methods [14–16,42–44] have given state-of-the-art results on many image retrieval datasets, but they only support single-modal retrieval. There are several cross-modal deep hashing methods that use hybrid deep architectures for representation learning and hash coding, i.e. Deep Visual-Semantic Hashing (DVSH) [22], Deep Cross-Modal Hashing (DCMH) [23], and Correlation Hashing Network (CHN) [24]. DVSH is the first deep cross-modal hashing method that enables efficient image-sentence cross-modal retrieval, but it does not support the cross-modal retrieval between images and tags. DCMH and CHN are parallel works, which adopt pairwise loss functions to preserve cross-modal similarities and control quantization errors within hybrid deep architectures.

Previous deep cross-modal hashing methods fall short for Hamming space retrieval [30], i.e. hash lookups that discard irrelevant items out of the Hamming ball of a pre-specified small radius by early pruning instead of linear scan. Note that the number of hash buckets will grow exponentially with the Hamming radius and large Hamming ball will not be acceptable. The reasons for inefficient Hamming space retrieval are two folds. First, the existing methods adopt misspecified loss functions that penalize little when two similar points have large Hamming distance. Second, the huge heterogeneity across different modalities introduces large cross-modal Hamming distances. As a consequence, they cannot concentrate relevant points to be within the Hamming ball with small radius. This paper contrasts from existing methods by novel well-specified loss functions based on the exponential distribution, which shrinks the data points within small Hamming balls to enable effective hash lookups. To our best knowledge, this work is the first deep cross-modal hashing approach towards Hamming space retrieval.

3   Cross-Modal Hamming Hashing

In cross-modal retrieval, the database consists of objects from one modality and the query consists of objects from another modality. We capture the nonlinear correlation across different modalities by deep learning from a training set of N_x images $\{x_i\}_{i=1}^{N_x}$ and N_y texts $\{y_j\}_{j=1}^{N_y}$, where $x_i \in \mathbb{R}^{D_x}$ denotes the D_x-dimensional feature vector of the image modality, and $y_j \in \mathbb{R}^{D_y}$ denotes the D_y-dimensional feature vector of the text modality, respectively. Some pairs of images and texts are associated with similarity labels s_{ij}, where $s_{ij} = 1$ implies

x_i and y_j are similar and $s_{ij} = 0$ indicates x_i and y_j are dissimilar. Deep cross-modal hashing learns modality-specific hash functions $f_x(x) : \mathbb{R}^{D_x} \mapsto \{-1, 1\}^K$ and $f_y(y) : \mathbb{R}^{D_y} \mapsto \{-1, 1\}^K$ through deep networks, which encode each object x and y into compact K-bit hash codes $h^x = f_x(x)$ and $h^y = f_y(y)$ such that the similarity relations conveyed in the similarity pairs $\mathcal{S}$ is maximally preserved. In supervised cross-modal hashing, $\mathcal{S} = \{s_{ij}\}$ can be constructed from the semantic labels of data objects or relevance feedbacks in click-through behaviors.

Definition 1 (Hamming Space Retrieval). *For binary codes of K bits, the number of distinct hash buckets to examine is $N(K, r) = \sum_{k=0}^{r} \binom{K}{k}$, where r is the Hamming radius. $N(K, r)$ grows exponentially with r and when $r \leq 2$, it only requires $O(1)$ time for each query to find all r-neighbors. Hamming space retrieval refers to the constant-time retrieval scenario that directly returns points in the hash buckets within Hamming radius r to each query, by hash lookups.*

Definition 2 (Cross-Modal Hamming Space Retrieval). *Assuming there is an isomorphic Hamming space across different modalities, we return objects of one modality within Hamming radius r to a query of another modality, by hash lookups instead of linear scan in the modality-isomorphic Hamming space.*

This paper presents Cross-Modal Hamming Hashing (**CMHH**), a unified deep learning framework for cross-modal Hamming space retrieval, as shown in Fig. 2. The proposed deep architecture accepts pairwise inputs $\{(x_i, y_j, s_{ij})\}$ and processes them through an end-to-end pipeline of deep representation learning and binary hash coding: **(1)** an image network to extract discriminative visual representations, and a text network to extract good text representations; **(2)** two fully-connected hashing layers for transforming the deep representations of each modality into K-bit hash codes $h_i^x, h_j^y \in \{1, -1\}^K$, **(3)** a new exponential focal loss based on the exponential distribution for similarity-preserving learning, which uncovers the isomorphic Hamming space to bridge different modalities, and **(4)** a new exponential quantization loss for controlling the binarization error and improving the hashing quality in the modality-isomorphic Hamming space.

3.1 Hybrid Deep Architecture

The hybrid deep architecture of CMHH is shown in Fig. 2. **For image modality**, we extend AlexNet [17], a deep convolutional network with five convolutional layers *conv1–conv5* and three fully-connected layers *fc6–fc8*. We replace the classifier layer *fc8* with a hash layer *fch* of K hidden units, which transforms the *fc7* representation into K-dimensional continuous code $z_i^x \in \mathbb{R}^K$ for each image x_i. We obtain hash code h_i^x through sign thresholding $h_i^x = \text{sgn}(z_i^x)$. Since it is hard to optimize the sign function due to ill-posed gradient, we adopt the hyperbolic tangent (tanh) function to squash the continuous code z_i^x within $[-1, 1]$, reducing the gap between the continuous code z_i^x and the final binary hash code h_i^x. **For text modality**, we follow [23,24] and adopt a two-layer Multilayer Perceptron (MLP), with the same dimension and activation function

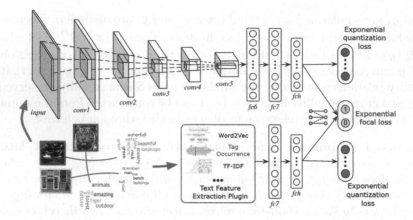

Fig. 2. The architecture of Cross-Modal Hamming Hashing (CMHH) consists of four modules: **(1)** a convolutional network for image representation and a multilayer perceptron for text representation; **(2)** two hashing layers (*fch*) for hash code generation, **(3)** an exponential focal loss for learning the isomorphic Hamming space, and **(4)** an exponential quantization loss for controlling the hashing quality. *Best viewed in color.*

as *fc7* and *fch* in the image network. We obtain the hash code h_j^y for each text y_j also through sign thresholding $h_j^y = \text{sgn}(z_j^y)$. To further guarantee the quality of hash codes for efficient Hamming space retrieval, we preserve the similarity between the training pairs $\{(x_i, y_j, s_{ij}) : s_{ij} \in \mathcal{S}\}$ and control the quantization error, both performed in an isomorphic Hamming space. Towards this goal, this paper proposes a pairwise exponential focal loss and a pointwise exponential quantization loss, both derived in the Maximum a Posteriori (MAP) framework.

3.2   Bayesian Learning Framework

In this paper, we propose a Bayesian learning framework to perform deep cross-modal hashing from similarity data by jointly preserving similarity relationship of image-text pairs and controlling the quantization error. Given training pairs with pairwise similarity labels as $\{(x_i, y_j, s_{ij}) : s_{ij} \in \mathcal{S}\}$, the logarithm Maximum a Posteriori (MAP) estimation of the hash codes $H^x = [h_1^x, \ldots, h_{N_x}^x]$ and $H^y = [h_1^y, \ldots, h_{N_y}^y]$ for N_x training images and N_y training texts is derived as

$$\log P(H^x, H^y | \mathcal{S}) \propto \log P(\mathcal{S} | H^x, H^y) P(H^x) P(H^y)$$
$$= \sum_{s_{ij} \in \mathcal{S}} w_{ij} \log P(s_{ij} | h_i^x, h_j^y) + \sum_{i=1}^{N_x} \log P(h_i^x) + \sum_{j=1}^{N_y} \log P(h_j^y)$$

$$(1)$$

where $P(\mathcal{S} | H^x, H^y) = \prod_{s_{ij} \in \mathcal{S}} \left[P(s_{ij} | h_i^x, h_j^y) \right]^{w_{ij}}$ is the weighted likelihood function [45], and w_{ij} is the weight for each training pair (x_i, y_j, s_{ij}). For each pair, $P(s_{ij}|\boldsymbol{h}_i^x, \boldsymbol{h}_j^y)$ is the conditional probability of similarity s_{ij} given a pair of hash codes $\boldsymbol{h}_i^x$ and $\boldsymbol{h}_j^y$, which can be defined based on the Bernoulli distribution,

$$P\left(s_{ij}|\boldsymbol{h}_i^x, \boldsymbol{h}_j^y\right) = \begin{cases} \sigma\left(\mathrm{d}\left(\boldsymbol{h}_i^x, \boldsymbol{h}_j^y\right)\right), & s_{ij} = 1 \\ 1 - \sigma\left(\mathrm{d}\left(\boldsymbol{h}_i^x, \boldsymbol{h}_j^y\right)\right), & s_{ij} = 0 \end{cases} \tag{2}$$
$$= \sigma(\mathrm{d}\left(\boldsymbol{h}_i^x, \boldsymbol{h}_j^y\right))^{s_{ij}} \left(1 - \sigma\left(\mathrm{d}\left(\boldsymbol{h}_i^x, \boldsymbol{h}_j^y\right)\right)\right)^{1-s_{ij}}$$

where $\mathrm{d}\left(\boldsymbol{h}_i^x, \boldsymbol{h}_j^y\right)$ denotes the Hamming distance between hash codes $\boldsymbol{h}_i^x$ and $\boldsymbol{h}_j^y$, and σ is a probability function to be elaborated in the next subsection. Similar to binary-class logistic regression for pointwise data, we require in Eq. (2) that the smaller $\mathrm{d}\left(\boldsymbol{h}_i^x, \boldsymbol{h}_j^y\right)$ is, the larger $P\left(1|\boldsymbol{h}_i^x, \boldsymbol{h}_j^y\right)$ will be, implying that the image-text pair $\boldsymbol{x}_i$ and $\boldsymbol{y}_j$ should be classified as similar; otherwise, the larger $P\left(0|\boldsymbol{h}_i^x, \boldsymbol{h}_j^y\right)$ will be, implying that the image-text pair should be classified as dissimilar. Thus, this is a natural extension of binary-class logistic regression to pairwise classification scenario with binary similarity labels $s_{ij} \in \{0, 1\}$.

Motivated by the focal loss [46], which yields state-of-the-art performance for object detection tasks, we focus our model more on hard and misclassified image-text pairs, by defining the weighting coefficient w_{ij} for each pair $(\boldsymbol{x}_i, \boldsymbol{y}_j, s_{ij})$ as

$$w_{ij} = \begin{cases} \left(1 - \sigma\left(\mathrm{d}\left(\boldsymbol{h}_i^x, \boldsymbol{h}_j^y\right)\right)\right)^\gamma, & s_{ij} = 1 \\ \left(\sigma\left(\mathrm{d}\left(\boldsymbol{h}_i^x, \boldsymbol{h}_j^y\right)\right)\right)^\gamma, & s_{ij} = 0 \end{cases} \tag{3}$$

where $\gamma \geq 0$ is a hyper-parameter to control the relative weight for misclassified pairs. In Fig. 3(a), we plot the focal loss with different $\gamma \in [0, 5]$. When $\gamma = 0$, the focal loss degenerates to the standard cross-entropy loss. As γ gets larger, the focal loss gets smaller on the highly confident pairs (easy pairs), resulting in relatively more focus on the less confident pairs (hard and mis-specified pairs).

3.3 Exponential Hash Learning

With the Bayesian learning framework, any probability function σ and distance function d can be used to instantiate a specific hashing model. Previous state-of-the-art deep cross-modal hashing methods, such as DCMH [23], usually adopt the sigmoid function $\sigma\left(x\right) = 1/(1 + e^{-\alpha x})$ as the probability function, where $\alpha > 0$ is a hyper-parameter controlling the saturation zone of the sigmoid function. To comply with the sigmoid function, we need to adopt inner product as a surrogate to quantify the Hamming distance, i.e. $\mathrm{d}\left(\boldsymbol{h}_i^x, \boldsymbol{h}_j^y\right) = \langle \boldsymbol{h}_i^x, \boldsymbol{h}_j^y \rangle$.

However, we discover a key *mis-specification* problem of the sigmoid function as illustrated in Fig. 3. We observe that the probability of the sigmoid function stays high when the Hamming distance between hash codes is much larger than 2 and only starts to decrease obviously when the Hamming distance becomes close to $K/2$. This implies that previous deep cross-modal hashing methods are ineffective to pull the Hamming distance between the hash codes of similar points to be smaller than 2, because the probabilities for different Hamming distances smaller than $K/2$ are not discriminative enough. This is a severe disadvantage

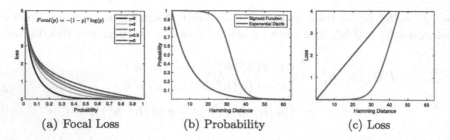

(a) Focal Loss   (b) Probability   (c) Loss

Fig. 3. [**Focal Loss**] The values of the focal loss (a) with respect to the conditional probability of similar data points ($s_{ij} = 1$). [**Exponential Distribution**] The values of Probability (b) and Loss (c) with respect to Hamming Distance between the hash codes of similar data points ($s_{ij} = 1$). The Probability (Loss) based on sigmoid function is large (small) even for Hamming distance much larger than 2, which is ill-specified for Hamming space retrieval. As a desired property, our loss based on the exponential distribution penalizes significantly on similar data pairs with larger Hamming distances.

of the existing cross-modal hashing methods, which makes hash lookup search inefficient. Note that for each query in the Hamming space retrieval, we can only return objects within the Hamming ball with a small radius (e.g. 2).

Towards the aforementioned mis-specification problem of sigmoid function, we propose a novel probability function based on the exponential distribution:

$$\sigma \left(\mathrm{d} \left(\boldsymbol{h}_i^x, \boldsymbol{h}_j^y \right) \right) = \exp \left(-\beta \cdot \mathrm{d} \left(\boldsymbol{h}_i^x, \boldsymbol{h}_j^y \right) \right), \qquad (4)$$

where β is the scaling parameter of the exponential distribution, and d is the Hamming distance. In Fig. 3(b), (c), the probability of the exponential distribution decreases very fast when the Hamming distance gets larger than 2, and the similar points will be pulled to be within small Hamming radius. The decaying speed of the probability will be even faster by using a larger β, which imposes more force to concentrate similar points to be within small Hamming balls. Thus the scaling parameter β is crucial to control the tradeoff between precision and recall. By simply varying β, we can support a variety of Hamming space retrieval scenarios with different Hamming radiuses for different pruning ratios.

As discrete optimization of Eq. (1) with binary constraints $\boldsymbol{h}_i^* \in \{-1, 1\}^K$ is challenging, continuous relaxation is applied to the binary constraints for ease of optimization, as adopted by most previous hashing methods [1,16,23]. To control the quantization error $\|\boldsymbol{h}_i^* - \mathrm{sgn}(\boldsymbol{h}_i^*)\|$ caused by continuous relaxation and to learn high-quality hash codes, we propose a novel prior distribution for each hash codes $\boldsymbol{h}_i^*$ based on a symmetric variant of the exponential distribution as

$$P \left(\boldsymbol{h}_i^* \right) = \exp \left(-\lambda \cdot \mathrm{d} \left(|\boldsymbol{h}_i^*|, \mathbf{1} \right) \right), * \in \{x, y\}, \qquad (5)$$

where λ is the scaling parameter of the symmetric exponential distribution, and $\mathbf{1} \in \mathbb{R}^K$ is the vector of ones. By using the continuous relaxation, we need to replace the Hamming distance with its best approximation on continuous codes.

Here we adopt Euclidean distance as the approximation of Hamming distance,

$$\mathrm{d}\left(\boldsymbol{h}_i^x, \boldsymbol{h}_j^y\right) = \left\|\boldsymbol{h}_i^x - \boldsymbol{h}_j^y\right\|_2^2. \tag{6}$$

By taking Eqs. (2)–(5) into the MAP estimation in (1), we obtain the optimization problem of the proposed Cross-Modal Hamming Hashing (CMHH):

$$\min_{\Theta} L + \lambda Q, \tag{7}$$

where λ is a hyper-parameter to trade-off the exponential focal loss L and the exponential quantization loss Q, and Θ denotes the set of network parameters to be optimized. Specifically, the proposed *exponential focal loss L* is derived as

$$L = \sum_{s_{ij} \in S} \left[s_{ij}\left(1 - \exp\left(-\beta \mathrm{d}\left(\boldsymbol{h}_i^x, \boldsymbol{h}_j^y\right)\right)\right)^\gamma \beta \mathrm{d}\left(\boldsymbol{h}_i^x, \boldsymbol{h}_j^y\right) \right.$$
$$\left. - (1 - s_{ij})\left(\exp\left(-\beta \mathrm{d}\left(\boldsymbol{h}_i^x, \boldsymbol{h}_j^y\right)\right)\right)^\gamma \log\left(1 - \exp\left(-\beta \mathrm{d}\left(\boldsymbol{h}_i^x, \boldsymbol{h}_j^y\right)\right)\right) \right], \tag{8}$$

and similarly, the proposed *exponential quantization loss* is derived as

$$Q = \sum_{i=1}^{N_x} \mathrm{d}\left(\left|\boldsymbol{h}_i^x\right|, \mathbf{1}\right) + \sum_{j=1}^{N_y} \mathrm{d}\left(\left|\boldsymbol{h}_j^y\right|, \mathbf{1}\right), \tag{9}$$

where $\mathrm{d}(\cdot, \cdot)$ is the Hamming distance between the hash codes or the Euclidean distance between the continuous codes. Since the quantization error will be controlled by the proposed exponential quantization loss, for ease of optimization, we can use continuous relaxation for hash codes $\boldsymbol{h}_i^*$ during training. Finally, we obtain K-bit binary codes by sign thresholding $\boldsymbol{h} \leftarrow \mathrm{sgn}(\boldsymbol{h})$, where $\mathrm{sgn}(\boldsymbol{h})$ is the sign function on vectors that for $i = 1, \ldots, K$, $\mathrm{sgn}(h_i) = 1$ if $h_i > 0$, otherwise $\mathrm{sgn}(h_i) = -1$. Note that, since we have minimized the quantization error during training, the final binarization step will incur negligible loss of retrieval accuracy.

4 Experiments

We conduct extensive experiments to evaluate the efficacy of the proposed CMHH with several state-of-the-art cross-modal hashing methods on three benchmark datasets: **NUS-WIDE** [47], **MIRFlickr-25K** [48] and **IAPR TC-12** [49].

4.1 Setup

NUS-WIDE [47] is a public image dataset containing 269,648 images. Each image is annotated by some of the 81 ground truth concepts (categories). We follow similar experimental protocols as [8,50], and use the subset of 195,834 image-text pairs that belong to some of the 21 most frequent concepts.

MIRFlickr-25K [48] consists of 25,000 images coupled with complete manual annotations, where each image is labeled with some of the 38 concepts.

IAPR TC-12 [49] consists of 20,000 images with 255 concepts. We follow [23] to use the entire dataset, with each text represented as a 2912-dimensional bag-of-words vector.

We follow dataset split as [24]. In NUS-WIDE, we randomly select 100 pairs per class as the query set, 500 pairs per class as the training set and 50 pairs per class as the validation set, with the rest as the database. In MIRFlickr-25K and IAPR TC-12, we randomly select 1000 pairs as the query set, 4000 pairs as the training set and 1000 pairs as the validation set, with the rest as the database.

Following standard protocol as in [11, 23, 24, 37], the similarity information for hash learning and for ground-truth evaluation is constructed from semantic labels: if the image i and the text j share at least one label, they are similar and $s_{ij} = 1$; otherwise, they are dissimilar and $s_{ij} = 0$. Note that, although we use semantic labels to construct the similarity information, the proposed approach CMHH can learn hash codes when only similarity information is available.

We compare CMHH with eight state-of-the-art cross-modal hashing methods: two unsupervised methods **IMH** [7] and **CVH** [4] and six supervised methods **CMSSH** [3], **SCM** [11], **SePH** [37], **DVSH** [22], **CHN** [24] and **DCMH** [23], where **DVSH**, **CHN** and **DCMH** are deep cross-modal hashing methods.

To verify the effectiveness of the proposed CMHH approach, we first evaluate the comparison methods in the **general setting** of cross-modal retrieval widely adopted by previous methods: using linear scan instead of hash lookups. We follow [23, 24, 37] and adopt two evaluation metrics: Mean Average Precision (**MAP**) with MAP@R = 500, and precision-recall curves (**P@R**).

Then we evaluate **Hamming space retrieval**, following evaluation methods in [30], consisting of two consecutive steps: (**1**) **Pruning**, to return data points within Hamming radius 2 for each query using hash lookups; (**2**) **Scanning**, to re-rank the returned data points in ascending order of their distances to each query using the continuous codes. To evaluate the effectiveness of Hamming space retrieval, we report two standard evaluation metrics to measure the quality of the data points within Hamming radius 2: Precision curves within Hamming Radius 2 (**P@H$\leq$2**), and Recall curves within Hamming Radius 2 (**R@H$\leq$2**).

For shallow hashing methods, we use AlexNet [17] to extract 4096-dimensional deep $fc7$ features for each image. For all deep hashing methods, we directly use raw image pixels as the input. We adopt AlexNet [17] as the base architecture, and implement CMHH in **TensorFlow**. We fine-tune the ImageNet-pretrained AlexNet and train the hash layer. For the text modality, all deep methods use tag occurrence vectors as the input and adopt a two-layer Multilayer Perceptron (MLP) trained from scratch. We use mini-batch SGD with 0.9 momentum and cross-validate the learning rate from 10^{-5} to 10^{-2} with a multiplicative step-size $10^{\frac{1}{2}}$. We fix the mini-batch size as 128 and the weight decay as 0.0005. We select the hyper-parameters λ, β and γ of the proposed CMHH by cross-validation. We also select the hyper-parameters of each comparison method by cross-validation.

Table 1. Mean Average Precision (MAP) of all methods for cross-modal retrieval.

Task	Method	NUS-WIDE			MIRFlickr-25K			IAPR TC-12		
		16 bits	32 bits	64 bits	16 bits	32 bits	64 bits	16 bits	32 bits	64 bits
$I \rightarrow T$	CMSSH [3]	0.445	0.457	0.535	0.493	0.511	0.565	0.345	0.337	0.348
	CVH [4]	0.433	0.421	0.418	0.662	0.680	0.675	0.379	0.369	0.362
	IMH [7]	0.517	0.599	0.580	0.651	0.669	0.673	0.463	0.490	0.510
	SCM [11]	0.663	0.695	0.729	0.668	0.683	0.679	0.588	0.611	0.628
	SePH [37]	0.575	0.582	0.576	0.721	0.744	0.747	0.507	0.513	0.515
	DVSH [22]	-	-	-	-	-	-	0.570	0.632	0.696
	CHN [24]	0.701	0.719	0.736	0.764	0.787	0.814	0.563	0.613	0.652
	DCMH [23]	0.697	0.715	0.728	0.748	0.771	0.798	0.578	0.606	0.631
	CMHH	**0.733**	**0.738**	**0.774**	**0.783**	**0.814**	**0.821**	**0.603**	**0.657**	**0.703**
$T \rightarrow I$	CMSSH [3]	0.401	0.478	0.411	0.425	0.433	0.458	0.363	0.377	0.365
	CVH [4]	0.418	0.403	0.406	0.568	0.592	0.579	0.379	0.367	0.364
	IMH [7]	0.601	0.653	0.687	0.597	0.611	0.616	0.516	0.526	0.534
	SCM [11]	0.642	0.688	0.711	0.583	0.598	0.605	0.588	0.605	0.620
	SePH [37]	0.581	0.587	0.603	0.618	0.624	0.633	0.471	0.480	0.481
	DVSH [22]	-	-	-	-	-	-	0.604	0.640	0.681
	CHN [24]	0.671	0.712	0.736	0.719	0.748	0.761	0.647	0.683	0.695
	DCMH [23]	0.678	0.723	0.750	0.731	0.763	0.784	0.659	0.674	0.691
	CMHH	**0.719**	**0.749**	**0.778**	**0.758**	**0.782**	**0.793**	**0.667**	**0.689**	**0.710**

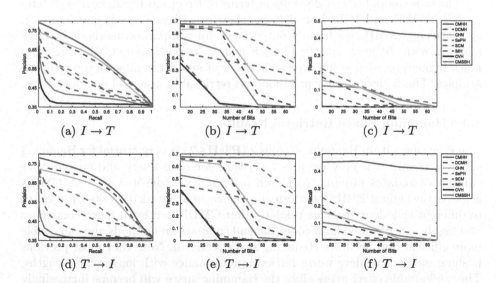

(a) $I \rightarrow T$ (b) $I \rightarrow T$ (c) $I \rightarrow T$

(d) $T \rightarrow I$ (e) $T \rightarrow I$ (f) $T \rightarrow I$

Fig. 4. Precision-recall (P@R) (a) (d), Precision within Hamming Radius 2 (P@H≤2) (b) (e) and Recall within Hamming Radius 2 (R@H≤2) (c) (f) on NUS-WIDE @ 32 bits.

4.2   General Setting Results

The **MAP** results of all the comparison methods are demonstrated in Table 1, which shows that the proposed CMHH substantially outperforms all the comparison methods by large margins. Specifically, compared to SCM, the best shallow cross-modal hashing method with deep features as input, CMHH achieves absolute increases of **5.3%/7.9%**, **12.5%/19.0%** and **4.6%/8.5%** in average MAP for two cross-modal retrieval tasks $I{\to}T/T{\to}I$ on NUS-WIDE, MIRFlickr-25K, and IAPR TC-12 respectively. CMHH outperforms DCMH, the state-of-the-art deep cross-modal hashing method, by large margins of **3.5%/4.3%**, **2.9%/2.6%** and **5.0%/1.4%** in average MAP on the three benchmark datasets, respectively. Note that, compared to DVSH, the state-of-the-art deep cross-modal hashing method with well-designed architecture for image-sentence retrieval, CMHH still outperforms DVSH of **2.2%/4.7%** in average MAP for two retrieval tasks on image-sentence dataset, IAPR TC-12. This validates that CMHH is able to learn high-quality hash codes for cross-modal retrieval based on linear scan.

The proposed CMHH improves substantially from the state-of-the-art DVSH, CHN and DCMH by two key perspectives: **(1)** CMHH enhances deep learning to hash by the novel exponential focal loss motivated from the Weighted Maximum Likelihood (WML), which puts more focus on hard and misclassified examples to yield better cross-modal search performance. **(2)** CMHH learns the isomorphic Hamming space and controls the quantization error, which better approximates the cross-modal Hamming distance and learns higher-quality hash codes.

The cross-modal retrieval results in terms of Precision-Recall curves (**P@R**) on NUS-WIDE and MIRFlickr-25K are shown in Figs. 4(a), (d) and 5(a), (d), respectively. CMHH significantly outperforms all comparison methods by large margins with different lengths of hash codes. In particular, CMHH achieves much higher precision at lower recall levels or at smaller number of top returned samples. This is desirable for precision-first retrieval in practical search systems.

4.3   Hamming Space Retrieval Results

The Precision within Hamming Radius 2 (**P@H≤2**) is very crucial for Hamming space retrieval, as it only requires $O(1)$ time for each query and enables very efficient candidates pruning. As shown in Figs. 4(b), (e), 5(b) and (e), CMHH achieves the highest P@H≤2 performance on the benchmark datasets with regard to different code lengths. This validates that CMHH can learn much compacter and highly concentrated hash codes than all comparison methods and can enable more efficient and accurate Hamming space retrieval. Note that most previous hashing methods achieve worse retrieval performance with longer code lengths. This undesirable effect arises since the Hamming space will become increasingly sparse with longer code lengths and fewer data points will fall in the Hamming ball of radius 2. It is worth noting that CMHH achieves a relatively mild decrease or even an increase in accuracy using longer code lengths, validating that CMHH can concentrate hash codes of similar points together to be within Hamming radius 2, which is beneficial to Hamming space retrieval.

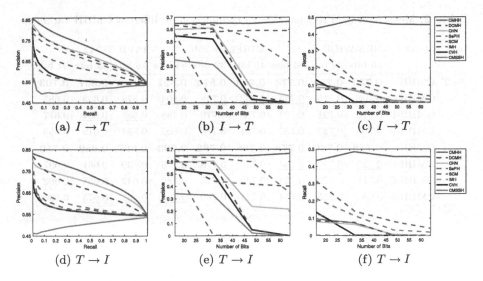

(a) $I \to T$ (b) $I \to T$ (c) $I \to T$

(d) $T \to I$ (e) $T \to I$ (f) $T \to I$

Fig. 5. Precision-recall (P@R) (a) (d), Precision within Hamming Radius 2 (P@H$\leq$2) (b) (e) and Recall within Hamming Radius 2 (R@H$\leq$2) (c) (f) on MIRFlickr @ 32 bits.

The Recall within Hamming Radius 2 (**R@H$\leq$2**) is more critical in Hamming space retrieval, since it is possible that all data points will be pruned out due to the highly sparse Hamming space. As shown in Fig. 4(c), (f), 5(c) and (f), CMHH achieves the highest R@H$\leq$2 results on both benchmark datasets with different code lengths. This validates that CMHH successfully concentrates more relevant points to be within the Hamming ball of radius 2.

It is important to note that, as the Hamming space becomes sparser using longer hash codes, most hashing baselines incur intolerable performance drop on R@H$\leq$2, i.e. **their R@H$\leq$2 approaches zero!** This special result reveals that existing cross-modal hashing methods cannot concentrate relevant points to be within Hamming ball with small radius, which is key to Hamming space retrieval. By introducing the novel exponential focal loss and exponential quantization loss, the proposed CMHH incurs very small performance drop on R@H$\leq$2 as the hash codes become longer, showing that CMHH can concentrate more relevant points to be within Hamming ball with small radius even using longer code lengths. The ability to adopt longer codes gives CMHH the flexibility to tradeoff accuracy and efficiency, while this is impossible for all previous cross-modal hashing methods.

4.4 Empirical Analysis

Ablation Study. We investigate three variants of CMHH: (1) **CMHH-E** is the variant by replacing the exponential focal loss with the popular cross-entropy loss [23]; (2) **CMHH-F** is the variant without using the focal reweight, namely $w_{ij} = 1$ in Eq. (3); (3) **CMHH-Q** is the variant without using the exponential

Table 2. Mean Average Precision (MAP) comparison of different CMHH variants.

Task	Method	NUS-WIDE			MIRFlickr-25K			IAPR TC-12		
		16 bits	32 bits	64 bits	16 bits	32 bits	64 bits	16 bits	32 bits	64 bits
$I \to T$	CMHH	**0.733**	**0.738**	**0.774**	**0.783**	**0.814**	**0.821**	**0.603**	**0.657**	**0.703**
	CMHH-Q	0.708	0.715	<u>0.765</u>	<u>0.762</u>	<u>0.788</u>	<u>0.804</u>	0.578	0.623	<u>0.685</u>
	CMHH-F	<u>0.710</u>	0.721	0.753	0.755	0.779	0.798	<u>0.589</u>	<u>0.631</u>	0.677
	CMHH-E	0.705	<u>0.722</u>	0.736	0.751	0.780	0.802	0.584	0.619	0.653
$T \to I$	CMHH	**0.719**	**0.749**	**0.778**	**0.758**	**0.782**	**0.793**	**0.667**	**0.689**	**0.710**
	CMHH-Q	<u>0.722</u>	<u>0.728</u>	<u>0.763</u>	0.733	<u>0.778</u>	0.786	0.639	0.661	<u>0.697</u>
	CMHH-F	0.718	0.720	0.758	<u>0.742</u>	0.771	0.780	0.642	0.658	0.682
	CMHH-E	0.684	0.725	0.754	0.737	0.769	<u>0.788</u>	<u>0.661</u>	<u>0.675</u>	0.695

quantization loss (9), namely $\lambda=0$; The MAP results of the three variants on the three datasets are reported in Table 2 (general setting by linear scan).

Exponential Focal Loss. (1) CMHH outperforms CMHH-E by margins of **2.7%/3.9%**, **2.4%/2.1%** and **3.6%/1.2%** in average MAP for cross-modal retrieval on NUS-WIDE, MIRFlickr-25K and IAPR TC-12, respectively. The exponential focal loss (8) leverages the exponential distribution to concentrate relevant points to be within small Hamming ball to enable effective cross-modal retrieval, while the sigmoid cross-entropy loss cannot achieve this desired effect. (2) CMHH outperforms CMHH-F by margins of **2.0%/2.8%**, **2.5%/2.1%** and **2.2%/2.8%** in average MAP for cross-modal tasks on the three datasets. The exponential focal loss enhances deep hashing by putting more focus on the hard and misclassified examples, and obtain better cross-modal search accuracy.

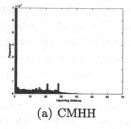
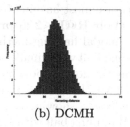

(a) CMHH   (b) DCMH

Fig. 6. Histogram of Hamming distances on similar pairs @ 64 bits of CMHH & DCMH.

Exponential Quantization Loss. CMHH outperforms CMHH-Q by **1.9% /2.2%**, **1.7%/ 2.0%** and **2.6%/2.3%** on the three datasets, respectively. These results validate that the exponential quantization loss (9) can boost the pruning efficiency and improve the performance of constant-time cross-modal retrieval.

Statistics Study. We compute the histogram of Hamming distances (0–64 for 64 bits codes) over all cross-modal pairs with $s_{ij} = 1$, as shown in Fig. 6. Due to the large heterogeneity across images and texts, the cross-modal Hamming distances computed based on the baseline DCMH hash codes are generally much larger than the Hamming ball radius (typically 2). This explains its nearly zero R@H≤2 in Figs. 4 and 5. In contrast, the majority of the cross-modal Hamming distances computed based on our CMHH hash codes are smaller than the Hamming ball radius, which enables successful cross-modal Hamming space retrieval.

5 Conclusion

This paper establishes constant-time cross-modal Hamming space retrieval by presenting a novel Cross-Modal Hamming Hashing (CMHH) approach that can generate compacter and highly concentrated hash codes. This is done by jointly optimizing a novel exponential focal loss and an exponential quantization loss in a Bayesian learning framework. Experiments show that CMHH yields state-of-the-art cross-modal retrieval results for Hamming space retrieval and linear scan scenarios on the three datasets, NUS-WIDE, MIRFlickr-25K, and IAPR TC-12.

Acknowledgements. This work is supported by National Key R&D Program of China (2016YFB1000701), and National Natural Science Foundation of China (61772299, 61672313, 71690231).

References

1. Wang, J., Zhang, T., Sebe, N., Shen, H.T., et al.: A survey on learning to hash. IEEE Trans. Pattern Anal. Mach. Intell. **40**, 769–790 (2017)
2. Smeulders, A.W., Worring, M., Santini, S., Gupta, A., Jain, R.: Content-based image retrieval at the end of the early years. TPAMI **22**, 1349–1380 (2000)
3. Bronstein, M., Bronstein, A., Michel, F., Paragios, N.: Data fusion through cross-modality metric learning using similarity-sensitive hashing. In: CVPR. IEEE (2010)
4. Kumar, S., Udupa, R.: Learning hash functions for cross-view similarity search. In: IJCAI (2011)
5. Zhen, Y., Yeung, D.: Co-regularized hashing for multimodal data. In: NIPS, pp. 1385–1393 (2012)
6. Zhen, Y., Yeung, D.Y.: A probabilistic model for multimodal hash function learning. In: SIGKDD. ACM (2012)
7. Song, J., Yang, Y., Yang, Y., Huang, Z., Shen, H.T.: Inter-media hashing for large-scale retrieval from heterogeneous data sources. In: SIGMOD. ACM (2013)
8. Wang, W., Ooi, B.C., Yang, X., Zhang, D., Zhuang, Y.: Effective multi-modal retrieval based on stacked auto-encoders. VLDB **7**, 649–660 (2014)
9. Yu, Z., Wu, F., Yang, Y., Tian, Q., Luo, J., Zhuang, Y.: Discriminative coupled dictionary hashing for fast cross-media retrieval. In: SIGIR. ACM (2014)
10. Liu, X., He, J., Deng, C., Lang, B.: Collaborative hashing. In: CVPR. IEEE (2014)
11. Zhang, D., Li, W.: Large-scale supervised multimodal hashing with semantic correlation maximization. In: AAAI (2014)

12. Wu, B., Yang, Q., Zheng, W., Wang, Y., Wang, J.: Quantized correlation hashing for fast cross-modal search. In: Proceedings of the Twenty-Fourth International Joint Conference on Artificial Intelligence, IJCAI 2015, Buenos Aires, Argentina, 25–31 July 2015 (2015)
13. Long, M., Cao, Y., Wang, J., Yu, P.S.: Composite correlation quantization for efficient multimodal retrieval. In: SIGIR (2016)
14. Xia, R., Pan, Y., Lai, H., Liu, C., Yan, S.: Supervised hashing for image retrieval via image representation learning. In: Proceedings of the AAAI Conference on Artificial Intellignece (AAAI). AAAI (2014)
15. Lai, H., Pan, Y., Liu, Y., Yan, S.: Simultaneous feature learning and hash coding with deep neural networks. In: CVPR (2015)
16. Zhu, H., Long, M., Wang, J., Cao, Y.: Deep hashing network for efficient similarity retrieval. In: Proceedings of the AAAI Conference on Artificial Intellignece (AAAI). AAAI (2016)
17. Krizhevsky, A., Sutskever, I., Hinton, G.E.: Imagenet classification with deep convolutional neural networks. In: Advances in Neural Information Processing Systems (NIPS) (2012)
18. Lin, M., Chen, Q., Yan, S.: Network in network. In: International Conference on Learning Representations (ICLR 2014) arXiv:1409.1556 (2014)
19. Masci, J., Bronstein, M.M., Bronstein, A.M., Schmidhuber, J.: Multimodal similarity-preserving hashing. IEEE Trans. Pattern Anal. Mach. Intell. **36**, 824–830 (2014)
20. Srivastava, N., Salakhutdinov, R.: Multimodal learning with deep boltzmann machines. JMLR **15**, 2949–2980 (2014)
21. Wan, J., Wang, D., Hoi, S.C.H., Wu, P., Zhu, J., Zhang, Y., Li, J.: Deep learning for content-based image retrieval: a comprehensive study. In: MM. ACM (2014)
22. Cao, Y., Long, M., Wang, J., Yang, Q., Yu, P.S.: Deep visual-semantic hashing for cross-modal retrieval. In: SIGKDD, pp. 1445–1454 (2016)
23. Jiang, Q., Li, W.: Deep cross-modal hashing. In: CVPR 2017, pp. 3270–3278 (2017)
24. Cao, Y., Long, M., Wang, J.: Correlation hashing network for efficient cross-modal retrieval. In: BMVC (2017)
25. Bengio, Y., Courville, A., Vincent, P.: Representation learning: A review and new perspectives. TPAMI **35**, 1798–1828 (2013)
26. Mikolov, T., Sutskever, I., Chen, K., Corrado, G.S., Dean, J.: Distributed representations of words and phrases and their compositionality. In: Advances in Neural Information Processing Systems (2013)
27. Le, Q.V., Mikolov, T.: Distributed representations of sentences and documents. In: Advances in Neural Information Processing Systems (2014)
28. Rumelhart, D.E., Hinton, G.E., Williams, R.J.: Parallel Distributed Processing: Explorations in the Microstructure of Cognition, vol. 1. MIT Press, Cambridge (1986)
29. Graves, A., Jaitly, N.: Towards end-to-end speech recognition with recurrent neural networks. In: ICML, pp. 1764–1772. ACM (2014)
30. Fleet, D.J., Punjani, A., Norouzi, M.: Fast search in hamming space with multi-index hashing. In: CVPR. IEEE (2012)
31. Wu, F., Yu, Z., Yang, Y., Tang, S., Zhang, Y., Zhuang, Y.: Sparse multi-modal hashing. IEEE Trans. Multimed. **16**(2), 427–439 (2014)
32. Ou, M., Cui, P., Wang, F., Wang, J., Zhu, W., Yang, S.: Comparing apples to oranges: a scalable solution with heterogeneous hashing. In: SIGKDD. ACM (2013)
33. Ding, G., Guo, Y., Zhou, J.: Collective matrix factorization hashing for multimodal data. In: CVPR (2014)

34. Wang, D., Gao, X., Wang, X., He, L.: Semantic topic multimodal hashing for cross-media retrieval. In: Proceedings of the Twenty-Fourth International Joint Conference on Artificial Intelligence, IJCAI 2015, Buenos Aires, Argentina, 25–31 July 2015 (2015)

35. Hu, Y., Jin, Z., Ren, H., Cai, D., He, X.: Iterative multi-view hashing for cross media indexing. In: MM. ACM (2014)

36. Wei, Y., Song, Y., Zhen, Y., Liu, B., Yang, Q.: Scalable heterogeneous translated hashing. In: SIGKDD. ACM (2014)

37. Lin, Z., Ding, G., Hu, M., Wang, J.: Semantics-preserving hashing for cross-view retrieval. In: CVPR (2015)

38. Donahue, J., Hendricks, L.A., Guadarrama, S., Rohrbach, M., Venugopalan, S., Saenko, K., Darrell, T.: Long-term recurrent convolutional networks for visual recognition and description. In: CVPR (2015)

39. Frome, A., Corrado, G.S., Shlens, J., Bengio, S., Dean, J., Mikolov, T., et al.: Devise: A deep visual-semantic embedding model. In: NIPS, pp. 2121–2129 (2013)

40. Kiros, R., Salakhutdinov, R., Zemel, R.S.: Unifying visual-semantic embeddings with multimodal neural language models. In: NIPS (2014)

41. Gao, H., Mao, J., Zhou, J., Huang, Z., Wang, L., Xu, W.: Are you talking to a machine? dataset and methods for multilingual image question answering. In: NIPS (2015)

42. Cao, Y., Long, M., Wang, J., Zhu, H., Wen, Q.: Deep quantization network for efficient image retrieval. In: Proceedings of the AAAI Conference on Artificial Intellignece (AAAI). AAAI (2016)

43. Cao, Z., Long, M., Wang, J., Yu, P.S.: Hashnet: Deep learning to hash by continuation. In: ICCV 2017 (2017)

44. Liu, B., Cao, Y., Long, M., Wang, J., Wang, J.: Deep triplet quantization. In: MM. ACM (2018)

45. Dmochowski, J.P., Sajda, P., Parra, L.C.: Maximum likelihood in cost-sensitive learning: model specification, approximations, and upper bounds. J. Mach. Learn. Res. (JMLR) **11**(Dec), 3313–3332 (2010)

46. Lin, T., Goyal, P., Girshick, R.B., He, K., Dollár, P.: Focal loss for dense object detection. In: ICCV 2017 (2017)

47. Chua, T.S., Tang, J., Hong, R., Li, H., Luo, Z., Zheng, Y.T.: NUS-WIDE: a real-world web image database from national university of Singapore. In: CIVR. ACM (2009)

48. Huiskes, M.J., Lew, M.S.: The MIR FLICKR retrieval evaluation. In: ICMR. ACM (2008)

49. Grubinger, M., Clough, P., Müller, H., Deselaers, T.: The IAPR TC-12 benchmark: a new evaluation resource for visual information systems. In: International Workshop OntoImage, pp. 13–23 (2006)

50. Zhu, X., Huang, Z., Shen, H.T., Zhao, X.: Linear cross-modal hashing for efficient multimedia search. In: MM. ACM (2013)

Deep Video Quality Assessor: From Spatio-Temporal Visual Sensitivity to a Convolutional Neural Aggregation Network

Woojae Kim[1], Jongyoo Kim[2], Sewoong Ahn[1], Jinwoo Kim[1],
and Sanghoon Lee[1(✉)]

[1] Department of Electrical and Electronic Engineering,
Yonsei University, Seoul, Republic of Korea
{wooyoa,anse3832,jw09191,slee}@yonsei.ac.kr
[2] Microsoft Research, Beijing, China
jongk@microsoft.com

Abstract. Incorporating spatio-temporal human visual perception into video quality assessment (VQA) remains a formidable issue. Previous statistical or computational models of spatio-temporal perception have limitations to be applied to the general VQA algorithms. In this paper, we propose a novel full-reference (FR) VQA framework named Deep Video Quality Assessor (DeepVQA) to quantify the spatio-temporal visual perception via a convolutional neural network (CNN) and a convolutional neural aggregation network (CNAN). Our framework enables to figure out the spatio-temporal sensitivity behavior through learning in accordance with the subjective score. In addition, to manipulate the temporal variation of distortions, we propose a novel temporal pooling method using an attention model. In the experiment, we show DeepVQA remarkably achieves the state-of-the-art prediction accuracy of more than 0.9 correlation, which is ~5% higher than those of conventional methods on the LIVE and CSIQ video databases.

Keywords: Video quality assessment · Visual sensitivity
Convolutional neural network · Attention mechanism · HVS
Temporal pooling

1 Introduction

With the explosive demand for video streaming services, it is vital to provide videos with high quality under unpredictable network conditions. Accordingly, video quality prediction plays an essential role in providing satisfactory streaming services to users. Since the ultimate receiver of video contents is a human, it is essential to develop a model or methodology to pervade human perception into the design of video quality assessment (VQA).

© Springer Nature Switzerland AG 2018
V. Ferrari et al. (Eds.): ECCV 2018, LNCS 11205, pp. 224–241, 2018.
https://doi.org/10.1007/978-3-030-01246-5_14

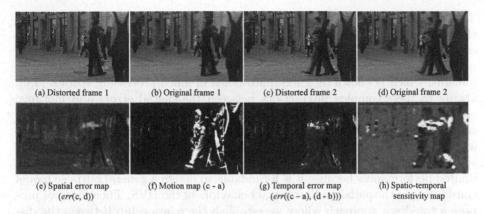

(a) Distorted frame 1   (b) Original frame 1   (c) Distorted frame 2   (d) Original frame 2

(e) Spatial error map   (f) Motion map (c - a)   (g) Temporal error map   (h) Spatio-temporal
   (*err*(c, d))   (*err*((c - a), (d - b)))   sensitivity map

Fig. 1. Example of predicted sensitivity map: (a) and (c) are a set of consecutive distorted frames; (b) and (d) are the original frames of (a) and (c); (e) is the spatial error map of (c), calculated by an error function $err(c, d)$; (f) is the motion map of distorted frame (c), calculated as subtraction of (c) and (a); (g) is the temporal error map between the distorted frames' motion map (f) and orginal motion map (d−b); (h) is the predicted spatio-temporal sensitivity map of the distorted frame (c).

In this paper, we seek to measure the video quality by modeling a mechanism of the human visual system (HVS) by using convolutional neural networks (CNNs). When the HVS perceives a video, the perceived quality is determined by the combination of the spatio-temporal characteristics and the spatial error signal. For example, a local distortion can be either emphasized or masked by visual sensitivity depending on the spatio-temporal characteristics [1–3]. For image quality assessment (IQA), deep learning-based visual sensitivity was successfully applied to extract perceptual behavior on spatial characteristics [3]. In contrast, a video is a set of consecutive frames that contain various motion properties. The temporal variation of contents strongly affects the visual perception of the HVS, thus the problem is much more difficult than IQA. Moreover, several temporal quality pooling strategies have been attempted on VQA, but none of them could achieve high correlation as demonstrated for IQA, which still remains as a challenging issue to build a methodology to characterize the temporal human perception. In this respect, we explore a data-driven deep scheme to improve video quality remarkably from the two major motivations: *Temporal motion effect* and *Temporal memory for quality judgment*.

Temporal Motion Effect. Our major motivation comes from the combined masking effects caused by spatial and temporal characteristics of a video. Figures 1(a)–(d) show a set of consecutive distorted frames and their originals and Figs. 1(e)–(g) show key examples of the spatial error map, a motion map, and a temporal error map of the distorted frame in (c). Each map will be explained in detail in Sect. 3.2. Being seen as a snapshot, several blocking artifacts induced by wireless network distortion are noticeable around pedestrians as shown in (a). However, they are hardly observable if they are shown in a playing video.

This is due to a temporal masking effect which explains the phenomenon that the changes in hue, luminance, and size are less visible to humans when there exist large motions [4]. On the other hand, when a severe error in the motion map occurs as demonstrated in Fig. 1(g), spatial errors become more visible to humans, which is known as a mosquito noise in video processing studies [5,6]. Owing to these complex interactions between the spatial errors and motions, conventional IQA methods usually result in inaccurate predictions of the perceptual quality of distorted videos. In the meantime, among VQA studies, many attempts have been made to address the above phenomena by modeling the spatio-temporal sensitivity of the HVS [7–10]. However, these studies yielded limited performances because it is formidable to design a general purpose model considering both spatial and temporal behaviors of the HVS. Therefore, we propose a top-down approach where we establish the relationship between the distortions and perceptual scores first, then it is followed by pixel-wise sensitivities considering both spatial and temporal factors. Figure 1(h) is an example of the predicted spatio-temporal sensitivity map by ours. The dark regions such as the pedestrians are predicted less sensitively by the strong motion in Fig. 1(f), while the bright regions have high weights by the temporal error component in Fig. 1(g).

Temporal Memory for Quality Judgment. In addition, as our second motivation, we explore the retrospective quality judgment patterns of humans given the quality scores of the frames in a video, which is demonstrated in Fig. 2. If there exist severely distorted frames in a video (Video B), humans generally determine that it has lower quality than a video having uniform quality distribution (Video A) even though both of them have the same average quality. Accordingly, a simple statistical temporal pooling does not work well in VQA [1,11,12]. Therefore, there has been a demand for an advanced temporal pooling strategy which reflects humans' retrospective decision behavior on video quality.

Our framework, which we call as Deep Video Quality Assessor (DeepVQA), fully utilizes the advantages of a convolutional neural network. To predict the spatio-temporal sensitivity map, a fully convolutional model is employed to extract useful information regarding visual perception which is embedded in a VQA database. Moreover, we additionally develop a novel pooling algorithm by borrowing an idea from an 'attention mechanism', where a neural network model focuses on only specific parts of an input [13–15]. To weight the predicted quality score of each frame adaptively, the proposed scheme uses a convolution operation, which we named a convolutional neural aggregation network (CNAN). Rather than taking a single frame quality score, our pooling method considers the distribution of predicted scores. Our contributions are summarized as follows:

1. The spatio-temporal sensitivity map is predicted through self-training without any prior knowledge of the HVS. In addition, a temporal pooling method is adaptively performed by utilizing the CNAN network.

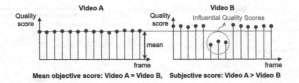

Fig. 2. Example of temporal quality variation and its effect on quality judgment.

2. Since the spatio-temporal sensitivity map and temporal pooling weight are derived as intermediate results, it is able to infer and visualize an important cue of human perception based on the correlation between the subjective and objective scores from the reverse engineering perspective, which is totally different from modeling based conventional methods.
3. Through achieving the state-of-the-art performance via end-to-end optimization, the human perception can be more clearly verified by the CNN/Attention based full reference (FR) VQA framework.

2 Related Works

2.1 Spatio-Temporal Visual Sensitivity

Numerous VQA models have been developed with respect to the human visual sensitivity. From these works, masking effects have been explained by a spatio-temporal contrast sensitivity function (CSF) [16–18]. According to the spatio-temporal CSF which resembles a band-pass filter, humans are not sensitive to signals with very low or high frequencies. Therefore, if strong contrast or motions exist, distortions are less noticeable in accordance with the masking effects [4,19, 20]. Based on these observations, various VQA methods have been developed. Saad *et al.* [7] used motion coherency and ego-motion as features that affect temporal masking. Mittal *et al.* [21] introduced a natural video statistics (NVS) theory, which is based on experimental results that pixel distributions can affect the visual sensitivity. However, there is a limitation in reflecting the complicated behavior of the HVS into the visual sensitivity models by these prior knowledge. Therefore, we design a learning-based model that learns human visual sensitivity autonomously from visual cues that affect the HVS.

Recently, there have been attempts to learn visual sensitivity by using deep-learning in I/VQA [3,22,23]. However, they did not consider motion properties when they extracted quality features. Therefore, a limitation still exists in predicting the effect of large motion variance.

2.2 Temporal Pooling

Temporal quality pooling methods have been studied in the VQA field. As mentioned, the simple strategy of taking the average has been employed in many

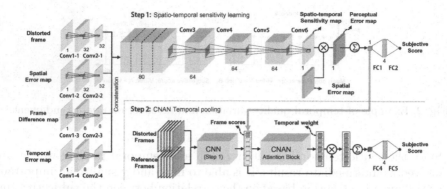

Fig. 3. Architecture of DeepVQA. The model takes a distorted frame, the spatial error map, the frame difference map and the temporal error map as input. Step 1: The CNN model is regressed onto a subjective score by the average pooling. Step 2: the overall frame scores are pooled using the CNAN and regressed onto the subjective score.

VQA algorithms [24–26]. Other studies have analyzed the score distribution and adaptively pooled the temporal scores from the HVS perspective [12]. However, since these naive pooling strategies utilize only limited temporal features, it is difficult to generalize to practical videos.

Recently, the attention mechanism has been developed in machine learning field [13,15]. Attention mechanisms in neural networks are based on the visual attention in the HVS. The attention-based method essentially allows the model to focus on specific regions and adjust focus over the temporal axis. Motivated by this, there was a study to solve temporal pooling through attention feature embedding [14]. However, since it adaptively embeds a weight vector to each independent score feature vector, it is difficult to effectively utilize the scheme for video temporal quality pooling due to the lack of consideration of the temporal score context. Instead, we use the convolution operation to detect specific patterns of score distribution, so it adaptively weights and combines the temporal scores as shown in Fig. 2.

3   DeepVQA Framework

3.1   Architecture

Visual sensitivity indicates which area of a given spatial error signal is perceived more sensitively to the HVS. The most intuitive way to learn visual sensitivity is to extract the weight map for a given spatial error map. As mentioned in Sect. 1, the visual sensitivity of a video content is determined by the spatial and temporal factors. Hence, by putting the sufficient information containing these factors as inputs, the model is able to learn visual sensitivity that reflects spatial and temporal masking effects. The proposed framework is depicted in Fig. 3. In our method, the spatio-temporal sensitivity map is first learned in step 1, then, a sensitivity weighted error map for each frame is temporally aggregated by the CNAN in step 2. As shown in Fig. 3, the CNAN takes a set of video frame scores in step 1 and computes a single pooled score as output.

A deep CNN with 3×3 filters is used for step 1 inspired by the recent CNN based work [3] for IQA. To generate the spatio-temporal sensitivity map without losing the location information, the model contains only convolutional layers. In the beginning, the distorted frames and spatial error maps are fed to spatial sensitivity representation. In addition, the model takes the frame difference and temporal error maps into account for a temporal factor. Each set of the input maps goes through independent convolutional layers, and feature maps are concatenated after the second convolutional layer. Zero-padding is applied before each convolution to preserve the feature map size. Two stridden convolutions are used for subsampling. Therefore the size of the final output is $1/4$ compared to that of the original frame, and the ground-truth spatial error maps are downscaled to $1/4$ correspondingly. At the end of the model in step 1, two fully connected layers are used to regress features onto the subjective scores.

In step 2, the proposed CNAN is trained using the pre-trained CNN model in step 1 and regressed onto the subjective video score as shown in Fig. 3. Once each feature is derived from the previous CNN independently, they are fed into the CNAN. By the CNAN, an aggregated score yields the final score. After then, two fully connected layers are used to regress the final score.

Frame Normalization. From the HVS perspective, each input in Fig. 3 is preprocessed to make the necessary properties stand out. Since the CSF shows a band-pass filter shape peaking at around 4 cycles per degree, and sensitivity drops rapidly at low-frequency [27]. Therefore, the distorted frames are simply normalized by subtracting the lowpass filtered frames from its grey scaled frames (range in $[0, 1]$). The normalized frames are denoted by $\hat{I}_r^t$ and $\hat{I}_d^t$ for given distorted I_d^t and reference I_r^t frames where t is frame index.

Patch-Based Video Learning. In the previous deep-learning based IQA works, a patch-based approach was successfully applied [3,23,28–30]. In our model, each video frame is split into patches, and then all the sensitivity patches in one frame are extracted. Next, these are used to reconstruct the sensitivity map as shown in Fig. 3. To avoid the overlapped regions of the predicted perceptual error map, the step of the sliding window is determined as $step_{patch} = size_{patch} - (N_{ign} \times 2 \times R)$, where N_{ign} is the number of ignored pixels, and R is the size ratio of the input and the perceptual error map. In the experiment, the ignored pixel N_{ign} was setted 4, and the patch size $size_{patch}$ was 112×112. To train the model, one video was split into multiple patches, which were then used as one training sample. In step 1, 12 frames per video were uniformly sampled, and 120 frames were used to train the model in step 2.

3.2 Spatio-Temporal Sensitivity Learning

The goal of spatio-temporal sensitivity learning is to derive an importance of each pixel for a given error map. To achieve this, we utilize the distorted frame and

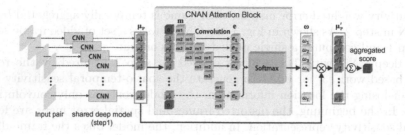

Fig. 4. Architecture of convolutional neural aggregation network.

spatial error map as the spatial factors. Also, the frame difference and temporal error maps are used as the temporal factor. We define a spatial error map e_s^t as a normalized log difference, as in [3],

$$e_s^t = \frac{\log(1/((\hat{I}_r^t - \hat{I}_d^t)^2 + \epsilon/255^2))}{\log(255^2/\epsilon)}, \tag{1}$$

where $\epsilon = 1$ for the experiment. To represent motion map, the frame difference is calculated along the consecutive frames. Since each video contains different frames per second (fps), the frame difference map considering fps variation is simply defined as $\boldsymbol{f}_d^t = |I_d^{t+\delta} - I_d^t|$ where $\delta = \lfloor fps/25 \rfloor$. In a similar way, the temporal error map, which is the difference between the motion information of the distorted and reference frames, is defined as $e_T^t = |\boldsymbol{f}_d^t - \boldsymbol{f}_r^t|$, where $\boldsymbol{f}_r^t$ is the frame difference of the reference frame. Then, the spatio-temporal sensitivity map $\mathbf{s}^t$ is obtained from the CNN model of step 1 as

$$\mathbf{s}^t = CNN_{s1}(\hat{I}_d^t, e_s^t, \boldsymbol{f}_d^t, e_T^t; \theta_{s1}), \tag{2}$$

where CNN_{s1} is the CNN model of step 1 with parameters θ_{s1}. To calculate a global score of each frame, the perceptual error map is defined by $\mathbf{p}^t = \mathbf{s}^t \odot e_s^t$, where $\odot$ is element-wise product.

Because we use zero-padding before each convolution, we ignore border pixels which tend to be zero. Each four rows and columns for each border are excluded in the experiment. Therefore, the spatial score $\mu_{\mathbf{p}}^t$ is derived by averaging the cropped perceptual error map $\mathbf{p}^t$ as

$$\mu_{\mathbf{p}}^t = \frac{1}{(H-8) \cdot (W-8)} \sum_{(i,j) \in \Omega} \mathbf{p}^t, \tag{3}$$

where H and W are the height and width of $\mathbf{p}^t$, (i,j) is a pixel index in cropped region Ω. Then, the score in step 1 is obtained by average pooling over spatial scores as $\mu_{s1} = \sum_t \mu_{\mathbf{p}}^t$. The pooled score is, then, fed into two fully connected layers to rescale the prediction. Then the final objective loss function is defined by a weighted summation of loss function and the regularization term as

$$\mathcal{L}_{step1}(\hat{\mathbf{I}}_d, \mathbf{e}_s, \boldsymbol{f}_d, \mathbf{e}_T; \theta_{s1}, \phi_1) = ||f_{\phi_1}(\mu_{s1}) - \mathbf{s}_{sub}||_2^2 + \lambda_1 TV + \lambda_2 L_2,$$

where $\hat{\mathbf{I}}_d, \mathbf{e}_s, \mathbf{f}_d, \mathbf{e}_T$ are sequences of each input, $f(\cdot)$ is a regression function with parameters ϕ_1 and s_{sub} is the ground-truth subjective score of the distorted video. In addition, a total variation (TV) and L_2 norm of the parameters are used to relieve high-frequency noise in the spatio-temporal sensitivity map and to avoid overfitting [3]. λ_1 and λ_2 are their weight parameters, respectively.

3.3 Convolutional Neural Aggregation Network

In step 1, the average of the perceptual error maps over spatial and temporal axes is regressed to a global video score. As mentioned, simply applying a mean pooling results in inaccurate predictions. To deal with this problem, we conduct temporal pooling for each frame's predicted score using the CNAN in step 2.

The memory attention mechanism has been successfully applied in various applications to pool spatial or temporal data [13–15]. Likewise, the CNAN is designed to predict human patterns of score judgment over all the frames' scores. The basic idea is to use a convolutional neural model to learn external memories through a differentiable addressing/attention scheme. Then the learned memories adaptively weight and combine scores across all frames.

Figure 4 shows the architecture of the CNAN for temporal pooling. The overall frame scores from step 1 are represented by a single vector $\boldsymbol{\mu_p}$. We then define a set of corresponding significance $\mathbf{e}$ in the attention block using the memory kernel $\mathbf{m}$. To generate the significance $\mathbf{e}$, one dimensional convolution is performed on the given $\boldsymbol{\mu_p}$ using the memory kernel $\mathbf{m}$. In other words, the significance is designed to learn a specific pattern of score variation during a certain filter length. This operation can be described as a simple convolution $\mathbf{e} = \mathbf{m} * \boldsymbol{\mu_p}$. To maintain the dimension of weights equal to $\boldsymbol{\mu_p}$, we padded zeros to the border of input $\boldsymbol{\mu_p}$. They are then passed to the softmax operator to generate positive temporal weights ω_t with $\sum_t \omega_t = 1$ as

$$\omega_t = \frac{\exp(e_t)}{\sum_j \exp(e_j)}. \tag{4}$$

Finally, the temporal weight ω_t derived from the attention block, is applied to the origin score vector to generate the final aggregated video score as $\mu_{s2} = \sum_t \omega_t \mu_{\mathbf{p}}^t$. Therefore, the objective function in step 2 is represented as

$$\mathcal{L}_{step2}(\hat{\mathbf{I}}_d, \mathbf{e}_s, \mathbf{f}_d, \mathbf{e}_T; \theta_{s1}, \phi_2) = ||f_{\phi_2}(\mu_{s2}) - \mathbf{s}_{sub}||_2^2 \tag{5}$$

where, $f_{\phi_2}(\cdot)$ represents a nonlinear regression function with parameters ϕ_2, and θ_{s1} refers to parameters in step 1.

4 Experimental Results

Since our goal is to learn spatio-temporal sensitivity and to aggregate frame scores via the CNAN, we chose the baseline model which takes only two spatial inputs (DeepQA [3]). Moreover, to study the effect of the temporal input, two

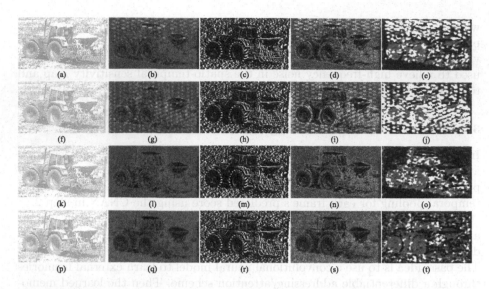

Fig. 5. Examples of the predicted sensitivity maps; (a), (f), (k), and (p) are distorted frames with Wireless, IP, H.264 compression, and MPEG-2 compression; (b), (g), (l), and (q) are the objective error maps; (c), (h), (m), and (r) are the frame difference maps; (d), (i), (n), and (s) are the temporal error maps; (e), (j), (o), and (t) are the predicted spatio-temporal sensitivity maps.

simpler models of DeepVQA without CNAN are defined. First, DeepVQA-*3ch* takes only two spatial inputs and the frame difference map. Second, DeepVQA-*4ch* takes all input maps. For both models, average pooling was conducted as described in step 1. We indicate the complete model as DeepVQA-*CNAN*.

4.1 Dataset

To evaluate the proposed algorithm, two different VQA databases were used: LIVE VQA [11], and CSIQ [31] databases. The LIVE VQA database contains 10 references and 150 distorted videos with four distortion types: wireless, IP, H.264 compression and MPEG-2 compression distortions. The CSIQ database includes 12 references and 216 distorted videos with six distortion types: motion JPEG (MJPEG), H.264, HEVC, wavelet compression using SNOW codec, packet-loss in a simulated wireless network and additive white Gaussian noise (AWGN). In the experiment, the ground-truth subjective scores were rescaled to the range [0, 1]. For differential mean opinion score (DMOS) values, their scale was reversed so that the larger values indicate perceptually better videos. Following the recommendation from the video quality experts group [32], we evaluated the performance of the proposed algorithm using two standard measures, i.e., Spearman's rank order correlation coefficient (SROCC) and Pearson's linear correlation coefficient (PLCC).

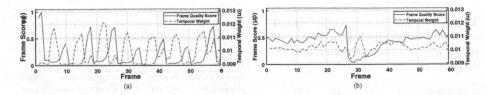

Fig. 6. Examples of frame quality scores μ_p and its temporal weight ω from the CNAN. (a) shows first 60 frames of "st02_25fps.yuv" in the LIVE video database; (b) shows first 60 frames of "mc13_50fps.yuv" in the LIVE video database.

4.2   Spatio-Temporal Sensitivity Prediction

To study the relevance of trained DeepVQA-*4ch* to the HVS, the predicted spatio-temporal sensitivity maps are shown in Fig. 5. Here, DeepVQA-*4ch* was trained with $\lambda_1 = 0.02$, $\lambda_2 = 0.005$. An example frames with four types of artifacts (wireless, IP, H.264 and MPEG-2) are represented in Figs. 5(a), (f), (k) and (p). Figures 5(b), (g), (l) and (q) are the spatial error maps, (c), (h), (m) and (r) are the frame difference maps, (d), (i), (n) and (s) are the temporal error maps, and (e), (j), (o) and (t) are the predicted sensitivity maps. In Fig. 5, darker regions indicate that pixel values are low. In case of wireless and IP distortions, temporal errors ((d) and (i)) are large in overall areas. Since humans are very sensitive to this motion variation cues, predicted sensitivity values ((e) and (j)) are high in all areas. Conversely, for H.264 and M-JPEG2 distortions, temporal errors ((n) and (s)) are relatively lower than those of wireless and IP distortions. In this case, the frame difference map which contains the motion information is a dominant factor in predicting the sensitivity map. In Fig. 5, a foreground object is being tracked in a video. Therefore, the motion maps ((m) and (r)) in the background region have higher values than those of the object. Finally, the value of background regions in the predicted sensitivity maps ((o) and (t)) is relatively low. These results are consistent with the previous studies on the temporal masking effect, which cannot be obtained only by considering spatial masking effect. Therefore, it can be concluded that the temporal information, as well as spatial error, is important to quantify the visual quality of videos.

4.3   CNAN Temporal Pooling

To evaluate the CNAN, we analyzed the relationship between the temporal pooling weight ω computed in the attention block and the normalized spatial score μ_p computed in step 1. Here, the size of kernel **m** was set to 21×1 experimentally. Figures 6(a) and (b) show two predicted temporal score distributions of μ_p (straight line) and its temporal weights ω (dotted line). In Fig. 6(a), the scores tend to rise or fall sharply at about every 5 frames. Conversely, the temporal weight has a higher value when the predicted score is low. This is because, as mentioned in Sect. 1, the human rating is highly affected by negative peak experiences than the overall average quality [7,12]. Therefore, it is obvious that the learned model mimics the temporal pooling mechanism of a human.

Table 1. Comparison of computational cost and median SROCC according to the number of sampled frames in LIVE database.

# of sampled frame	6	12	48	120
SROCC (120 epochs)	0.8787	0.8812	0.8772	0.8704
Computational time (1 epoch)	69 s	201 s	796 s	1452 s

Table 2. Cross dataset comparison on the LIVE video database (SROCC).

Models	Wireless	IP	H.264	MPEG-2	ALL
DeepVQA-*4ch*	0.8134	0.8023	0.8726	0.8439	0.8322
DeepVQA-*CNAN*	0.8211	0.8214	0.8748	0.8624	0.8437

Figure 6(b) shows that the scores are uniformly distributed except for the middle region. As explained before, the CNAN shows the filter response for a particular pattern by memory kernel **m**. Thus, the filter response of a monotonous input signal also tends to be monotonous. However, at near the 30th frame, the temporal pooling weight ω is large when the frame score abruptly changes. Therefore, the CNAN enables to reflect the behavior of scoring appropriately and leads to a performance improvement in Tables 3 and 4.

4.4   Number of Frames vs. Computation Cost

The number of video frames used for training the DeepVQA model has a great impact on a computational cost. As shown in Fig. 6, although the quality scores vary for each frame, the distribution shows certain patterns. Therefore, it is feasible to predict a quality score by using only a few sampled frames. To study the computational cost, we measure the performance according to the sampling rate.

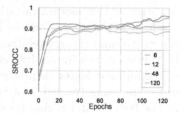

Fig. 7. Comparison of SROCC curves according to the number of sampled frames (6, 12, 48 and 120 frames).

For the simulation, a machine powered by a Titan X and equipped with the Theano. SROCC over 130 epochs with the 4 subset frames (6, 12, 48 and 120) is depicted in Fig. 7. When the number of sampled frames was 12, the SROCC was slightly higher than those of the other cases with a faster convergence speed. However, when the sampled frame was 120, the model suffered overfitting after 70 epochs, showing performance degradation. As shown in Table 1, DeepVQA obviously shows higher performance and lower execution time when using a video subset which contains a small number of frames.

4.5   Ablation Study

We verify the ablation of each input map and CNAN in our framework. To evaluate the ablation set, we tested each model (DeepQA (*2ch* [3]), DeepVQA-*3ch*, DeepVQA-*4ch* and DeepVQA-*CNAN*) on the LIVE and CSIQ databases.

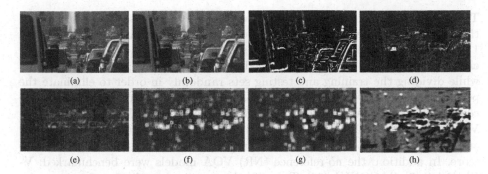

Fig. 8. Examples of the predicted sensitivity maps with different channel inputs: (a) is the distorted frame; (b) is the original frame; (c) is the frame difference map; (d) is the temporal error map; (e) is the spatial error map (f)–(h) are its predicted sensitivity maps from DeepQA (*2ch*) [3], DeepVQA-*3ch* and DeepVQA-*4ch*, respectively.

The experimental settings will be explained in Sect. 4.6 and the comparison results are tabulated in Tables 3 and 4. DeepQA [3] using only the distorted frame and spatial error map yielded lower performance than DeepVQA-*3ch* and *4ch*. Since DeepQA only infers the visual sensitivity of the spatial masking effect, it is strongly influenced by the spatial error signals. However, the performances of DeepVQA-*3ch* and *4ch* which were designed to infer the temporal motion effects were gradually improved. Moreover, the DeepVQA model combined with CNAN showed the highest performance since it considers the human patterns of quality judgment.

To study the effect of each channel input, we visualized the spatio-temporal sensitivity maps over different channel input. Figure 8 shows the predicted sensitivity map with different channel inputs. Figures 8(a), (b) and (e) are the distorted frame, its original and the spatial error map, respectively. In the case of Fig. 8(f), the local region of the sensitivity map looks similar to the spatial blocking artifact. However, when the frame difference map (Fig. 8(c)) is added in the model as Fig. 8 (g), the sensitivity is decreased for the regions with strong motions (darker region) as we expected. Finally, as Fig. 8(h), when all the four inputs including the temporal error map (Fig. 8(d)) are used, the sensitivity map is learned to consider all of the motion effects as described in Sect. 1. In addition, as the number of channels increases, the predicted sensitivity map tends to be smoother, which agrees with the HVS well [3].

4.6   Performance Comparison

To evaluate the performances, we compared DeepVQA with state-of-the-art I/VQA methods on the LIVE and CSIQ databases. We first randomly divided the reference videos into two subsets (80% for training and 20% for testing) and their corresponding distorted videos were divided in the same way so that there was no overlap between the two sets. DeepVQA was trained in a non-distortion-specific way so that all the distortion types were used simultaneously.

The training stage of step 1 (step 2) iterated 300 (20) epochs, then a model with the lowest validation error was chosen over the epochs. The accuracy of step 1 mostly saturated after 200 epochs as shown in Fig. 7. The correlation coefficients of the testing model are the median values of 20 repeated experiments while dividing the training and testing sets randomly in order to eliminate the performance bias. DeepVQA-*3ch*, DeepVQA-*4ch* and DeepVQA-*CNAN* were compared to FR I/VQA models: PSNR, SSIM [33], VIF [34], ST-MAD [35], ViS3 [36], MOVIE [25] and DeepQA [3]. For IQA metrics (PSNR, SSIM, VIF and DeepQA), we took an average pooling for each frame score to get a video score. In addition, the no-reference (NR) VQA models were benchmarked: V-BLIINDS [7], SACONVA [26]. To verify the temporal pooling performance, we further compare the existing temporal pooling method: VQPooling [12].

Tables 3 and 4 show the PLCC and SROCC comparisons for individual distortion types on the LIVE and CSIQ databases. The last column in each table reports overall SROCC and PLCC for all the distortion types, and the top three models for each criterion are shown in bold. Since our proposed model is a non-distortion specific model, the model should work well for overall performance when various distortion types coexist in the dataset. In our experiment, the highest SROCC and PLCC of overall distortion types were achieved by DeepVQA-*CNAN* in all the databases. In addition, DeepVQA-*CNAN* are generally competitive in most distortion types, even when each type of distortion is evaluated separately. Because the most of the distortion types in LIVE and CSIQ is distorted by video compression, which cause local blocking artifacts, there are many temporal errors in the databases. For this reason, the spatio-temporal sensitivity map is excessively activated in the large-scale block distortion type such as Fig. 5(j). Therefore, DeepVQA achieved relatively low performance in face of Wireless and IP distortions which include a large size of blocking artifacts. As shown in Table 4, since AWGN causes only spatial distortion, it shows a relatively low performance compared to the other types having blocking artifacts. Nevertheless, DeepVQA achieved a competitive and consistent accuracy across all the databases. Also, comparing the DeepVQA-*4ch* and DeepQA, we can infer that using the temporal inputs helps the model to extract useful features leading to an increase in an accuracy. Furthermore, VQPooling (DeepVQA-*VQPooling*) showed a slight improvement compared to DeepVQA-*4ch*, but CNAN showed approximately ∼2% improvement. Therefore, it can be concluded that temporal pooling via the CNAN improves performance the overall prediction.

4.7   Cross Dataset Test

To test the generalization capability of DeepVQA, the model was trained using the subset of the CSIQ video database, and tested on the LIVE video database. Since the CSIQ video database contains broader kinds of distortion types, we selected four distortion types (H.264, MJPEG, PLoss, and HEVC) which are similar in the LIVE database. The results are shown in Table 2, where both DeepVQA and DeepVQA-CNAN show nice performances. We can conclude that this models do not depend on the databases.

Table 3. Median PLCC and SROCC comparison on the LIVE VQA Database. *Italics* indicate full-reference (FR) methods.

Metrics	PLCC					SROCC				
	Wireless	IP	H.264	MPEG-2	ALL	Wireless	IP	H.264	MPEG-2	ALL
PSNR	0.7274	0.6395	0.7359	0.6545	0.7499	0.7381	0.6000	0.7143	0.6327	0.6958
SSIM [33]	0.7969	0.8269	0.7110	0.7849	0.7883	0.7381	0.7751	0.6905	0.7846	0.7211
VIF [34]	0.7473	0.6925	0.6983	0.7504	0.7601	0.7143	0.6000	0.5476	0.7319	0.6861
STMAD [35]	**0.8887**	**0.8956**	0.9209	0.8992	0.8774	0.8257	0.7721	0.9323	0.8733	0.8301
ViS3 [36]	0.8597	0.8576	0.7809	0.7650	0.8251	0.8257	0.7712	0.7657	0.7962	0.8156
MOVIE [25]	0.8392	0.7612	0.7902	0.7578	0.8112	0.8113	0.7154	0.7644	0.7821	0.7895
V-BLIINDS [7]	**0.9357**	**0.9291**	0.9032	0.8757	0.8433	0.8462	0.7829	0.8590	0.9371	0.8323
SACONVA [26]	0.8455	0.8280	0.9116	0.8778	0.8714	**0.8504**	0.8018	**0.9168**	0.8614	0.8569
DeepQA [3]	0.8070	0.8790	0.8820	0.8830	0.8692	0.8290	0.7120	0.8600	0.8940	0.8678
DeepVQA-3ch	0.8723	0.8661	**0.9254**	**0.9222**	0.8754	0.8376	**0.8615**	0.9014	**0.9543**	0.8723
DeepVQA-4ch	0.8867	0.8826	**0.9357**	**0.9416**	0.8813	0.8494	**0.8716**	**0.9193**	0.9664	**0.8913**
DeepVQA-VQPooling	–	–	–	–	0.8912	–	–	–	–	**0.8987**
DeepVQA-CNAN	**0.8979**	**0.8937**	0.9421	0.9443	0.8952	0.8674	0.8820	0.9200	0.9729	0.9152

Table 4. Median PLCC and SROCC comparison on the CSIQ VQA Database. *Italics* indicate full-reference (FR) methods.

Metrics	PLCC							SROCC						
	H.264	PLoss	MJPEG	Wavelet	AWGN	HEVC	ALL	H.264	PLoss	MJPEG	Wavelet	AWGN	HEVC	ALL
PSNR	0.9208	0.8246	0.6705	**0.9235**	0.9321	0.9237	0.7137	0.8810	0.7857	0.6190	0.8810	0.8333	0.8571	0.7040
SSIM [33]	0.9527	0.8471	0.8047	0.8907	**0.9748**	**0.9652**	0.7627	0.9286	0.8333	0.6905	0.8095	**0.9286**	0.9148	0.7616
VIF [34]	0.9505	**0.9212**	0.9114	**0.9241**	**0.9604**	**0.9624**	0.7282	0.9048	0.8571	0.8095	0.8571	0.8810	0.9012	0.7256
STMAD [35]	**0.9619**	0.8793	0.8957	0.8765	0.8931	0.9274	0.8254	0.9286	0.8333	0.8333	0.8095	0.8095	0.8810	0.8221
ViS3 [36]	0.9356	0.8299	0.8110	**0.9303**	0.9373	**0.9677**	0.8100	0.9286	0.8095	0.7857	0.9048	0.8571	0.9025	0.8028
MOVIE [25]	0.9035	0.8821	0.8792	0.8981	0.8562	0.9372	0.7886	0.8972	0.8861	**0.8874**	0.9012	0.8392	0.9331	0.8124
V-BLIINDS [7]	0.9413	0.7681	0.8536	0.9039	0.9318	0.9214	0.8494	0.9048	0.7481	0.8333	0.8571	**0.9048**	0.8810	0.8586
SACONVA [26]	0.9133	0.8115	0.8565	0.8529	0.9028	0.9068	0.8668	0.9048	0.7840	0.7857	0.8333	0.8810	0.8333	0.8637
DeepQA [3]	0.8753	0.8456	0.8460	0.9103	**0.9423**	0.9213	0.8723	0.8921	0.9013	**0.8623**	0.8010	**0.9021**	0.9566	0.8752
DeepVQA-3ch	0.9398	0.9009	**0.9159**	0.8621	0.8090	0.8756	0.8827	0.9622	0.9501	0.8103	0.9134	0.8145	**0.9718**	0.8854
DeepVQA-4ch	**0.9579**	**0.9241**	**0.9375**	0.8856	0.8271	0.8894	0.9013	0.9732	0.9662	0.8390	0.9344	0.8314	**0.9925**	**0.9043**
DeepVQA-4ch-VQPooling	-	-	-	-	-	-	**0.9057**	-	-	-	-	-	-	**0.9067**
DeepVQA-4ch-CNAN	**0.9633**	**0.9335**	**0.9401**	0.8853	0.8153	0.8897	**0.9135**	**0.9777**	**0.9672**	0.8510	0.9243	0.8106	**0.9950**	**0.9123**

5   Conclusion

In this paper, we proposed a novel FR-VQA framework using a CNN and a CNAN. By learning a human visual behavior in conjunction with spatial and temporal effects, it turned out the proposed model is able to learn the spatio-temporal sensitivity from a human perception point of view. Moreover, the temporal pooling technique using the CNAN predicted the temporal scoring behavior of humans. Through the rigorous simulations, we demonstrated that the predicted sensitivity maps agree with the HVS. The spatio-temporal sensitivity maps were robustly predicted against the various motion and distortion types. In addition, DeepVQA achieved the state-of-the-art correlations on LIVE and CSIQ databases. In the future, we plan to advance the proposed framework to NR-VQA, which is one of the most challenging problems.

Acknowledgment. This work was supported by Institute for Information & communications Technology Promotion through the Korea Government (MSIP) (No. 2016-0-00204, Development of mobile GPU hardware for photo-realistic real-time virtual reality).

References

1. Ninassi, A., Le Meur, O., Le Callet, P., Barba, D.: Considering temporal variations of spatial visual distortions in video quality assessment. IEEE J. Sel. Top. Signal Process. **3**(2), 253–265 (2009)
2. Bovik, A.C.: Automatic prediction of perceptual image and video quality. Proc. IEEE **101**(9), 2008–2024 (2013)
3. Kim, J., Lee, S.: Deep learning of human visual sensitivity in image quality assessment framework. In: Proceedings of IEEE Conference on Computer Vision and Pattern Recognition (CVPR) (2017)
4. Suchow, J.W., Alvarez, G.A.: Motion silences awareness of visual change. Curr. Biol. **21**(2), 140–143 (2011)
5. Fenimore, C., Libert, J.M., Roitman, P.: Mosquito noise in mpeg-compressed video: test patterns and metrics. In: Proceedings of SPIE the International Society For Optical Engineering, pp. 604–612. International Society for Optical Engineering (2000)
6. Jacquin, A., Okada, H., Crouch, P.: Content-adaptive postfiltering for very low bit rate video. In: Proceedings of Data Compression Conference, DCC 1997, pp. 111–120. IEEE (1997)
7. Saad, M.A., Bovik, A.C., Charrier, C.: Blind prediction of natural video quality. IEEE Trans. Image Process. **23**(3), 1352–1365 (2014)
8. Manasa, K., Channappayya, S.S.: An optical flow-based full reference video quality assessment algorithm. IEEE Trans. Image Process. **25**(6), 2480–2492 (2016)
9. Kim, T., Lee, S., Bovik, A.C.: Transfer function model of physiological mechanisms underlying temporal visual discomfort experienced when viewing stereoscopic 3D images. IEEE Trans. Image Process. **24**(11), 4335–4347 (2015)
10. Kim, J., Zeng, H., Ghadiyaram, D., Lee, S., Zhang, L., Bovik, A.C.: Deep convolutional neural models for picture-quality prediction: challenges and solutions to data-driven image quality assessment. IEEE Signal Process. Mag. **34**(6), 130–141 (2017)

11. Seshadrinathan, K., Soundararajan, R., Bovik, A.C., Cormack, L.K.: Study of subjective and objective quality assessment of video. IEEE Trans. Image Process. **19**(6), 1427–1441 (2010)
12. Park, J., Seshadrinathan, K., Lee, S., Bovik, A.C.: Video quality pooling adaptive to perceptual distortion severity. IEEE Trans. Image Process. **22**(2), 610–620 (2013)
13. Vinyals, O., Bengio, S., Kudlur, M.: Order matters: sequence to sequence for sets. arXiv preprint arXiv:1511.06391 (2015)
14. Yang, J., et al.: Neural aggregation network for video face recognition. In: Proceedings of IEEE Conference on Computer Vision and Pattern Recognition (CVPR), pp. 2492–2495
15. Graves, A., Wayne, G., Danihelka, I.: Neural turing machines. arXiv preprint arXiv:1410.5401 (2014)
16. Robson, J.: Spatial and temporal contrast-sensitivity functions of the visual system. JOSA **56**(8), 1141–1142 (1966)
17. Lee, S., Pattichis, M.S., Bovik, A.C.: Foveated video quality assessment. IEEE Trans. Multimed. **4**(1), 129–132 (2002)
18. Lee, S., Pattichis, M.S., Bovik, A.C.: Foveated video compression with optimal rate control. IEEE Trans. Image Process. **10**(7), 977–992 (2001)
19. Legge, G.E., Foley, J.M.: Contrast masking in human vision. JOSA **70**(12), 1458–1471 (1980)
20. Kim, H., Lee, S., Bovik, A.C.: Saliency prediction on stereoscopic videos. IEEE Trans. Image Process. **23**(4), 1476–1490 (2014)
21. Mittal, A., Saad, M.A., Bovik, A.C.: A completely blind video integrity oracle. IEEE Trans. Image Process. **25**(1), 289–300 (2016)
22. Le Callet, P., Viard-Gaudin, C., Barba, D.: A convolutional neural network approach for objective video quality assessment. IEEE Trans. Neural Netw. **17**(5), 1316–1327 (2006)
23. Kim, J., Nguyen, A.D., Lee, S.: Deep CNN-based blind image quality predictor. IEEE Trans. Neural Netw. Learn. Syst. **PP**(99), 1–14 (2018)
24. Chandler, D.M., Hemami, S.S.: VSNR: a wavelet-based visual signal-to-noise ratio for natural images. IEEE Trans. Image Process. **16**(9), 2284–2298 (2007)
25. Seshadrinathan, K., Bovik, A.C.: Motion tuned spatio-temporal quality assessment of natural videos. IEEE Trans. Image Process. **19**(2), 335–350 (2010)
26. Li, Y., Po, L.M., Cheung, C.H., Xu, X., Feng, L., Yuan, F., Cheung, K.W.: No-reference video quality assessment with 3D shearlet transform and convolutional neural networks. IEEE Trans. Circuits Syst. Video Technol. **26**(6), 1044–1057 (2016)
27. Daly, S.J.: Visible differences predictor: an algorithm for the assessment of image fidelity. In: Human Vision, Visual Processing, and Digital Display III, vol. 1666, pp. 2–16. International Society for Optics and Photonics (1992)
28. Kim, J., Lee, S.: Fully deep blind image quality predictor. IEEE J. Sel. Top. Signal Process. **11**(1), 206–220 (2017)
29. Oh, H., Ahn, S., Kim, J., Lee, S.: Blind deep S3D image quality evaluation via local to global feature aggregation. IEEE Trans. Image Process. **26**(10), 4923–4936 (2017)
30. Ye, P., Kumar, J., Kang, L., Doermann, D.: Unsupervised feature learning framework for no-reference image quality assessment. In: Proceedings of IEEE Conference on Computer Vision and Pattern Recognition (CVPR), pp. 1098–1105. IEEE (2012)

31. Laboratory of computational perception & image quality, Oklahoma State University, CSIQ video database. http://vision.okstate.edu/?loc=stmad
32. VQEG: Final report from the video quality experts group on the validation of objective models of video quality assessment, phase II
33. Wang, Z., Bovik, A.C., Sheikh, H.R., Simoncelli, E.P.: Image quality assessment: from error visibility to structural similarity. IEEE Trans. Image Process. **13**(4), 600–612 (2004)
34. Sheikh, H.R., Bovik, A.C.: Image information and visual quality. IEEE Trans. Image Process. **15**(2), 430–444 (2006)
35. Vu, P.V., Vu, C.T., Chandler, D.M.: A spatiotemporal most-apparent-distortion model for video quality assessment. In: 18th IEEE International Conference on Image Processing (ICIP), pp. 2505–2508. IEEE (2011)
36. Vu, P.V., Chandler, D.M.: ViS3: an algorithm for video quality assessment via analysis of spatial and spatiotemporal slices. J. Electron. Imaging **23**(1), 013016 (2014)

Semi-dense 3D Reconstruction
with a Stereo Event Camera

Yi Zhou[1,2](✉), Guillermo Gallego[3], Henri Rebecq[3], Laurent Kneip[4],
Hongdong Li[1,2], and Davide Scaramuzza[3]

[1] Australian National University, Canberra, Australia
yi.zhou@anu.edu.au
[2] Australian Centre for Robotic Vision, Brisbane, Australia
[3] Departments of Informatics and Neuroinformatics,
University of Zurich and ETH Zurich, Zurich, Switzerland
[4] School of Information Science and Technology,
ShanghaiTech University, Shanghai, China

Abstract. Event cameras are bio-inspired sensors that offer several advantages, such as low latency, high-speed and high dynamic range, to tackle challenging scenarios in computer vision. This paper presents a solution to the problem of 3D reconstruction from data captured by a stereo event-camera rig moving in a static scene, such as in the context of stereo Simultaneous Localization and Mapping. The proposed method consists of the optimization of an energy function designed to exploit small-baseline spatio-temporal consistency of events triggered across both stereo image planes. To improve the density of the reconstruction and to reduce the uncertainty of the estimation, a probabilistic depth-fusion strategy is also developed. The resulting method has no special requirements on either the motion of the stereo event-camera rig or on prior knowledge about the scene. Experiments demonstrate our method can deal with both texture-rich scenes as well as sparse scenes, outperforming state-of-the-art stereo methods based on event data image representations.

Multimedia Material

A supplemental video for this work is available at https://youtu.be/Qrnpj2FD1e4.

1   Introduction

Event cameras, such as the Dynamic Vision Sensor (DVS) [1], are novel devices that output pixel-wise intensity changes (called "events") asynchronously, at the

---

Electronic supplementary material The online version of this chapter (https://doi.org/10.1007/978-3-030-01246-5_15) contains supplementary material, which is available to authorized users.

© Springer Nature Switzerland AG 2018
V. Ferrari et al. (Eds.): ECCV 2018, LNCS 11205, pp. 242–258, 2018.
https://doi.org/10.1007/978-3-030-01246-5_15

time they occur. As opposed to standard cameras, they do not acquire entire image frames, nor do they operate at a fixed frame rate. This asynchronous and differential principle of operation reduces power and bandwidth requirements drastically. Endowed with microsecond temporal resolution, event cameras are able to capture high-speed motions, which would typically cause severe motion blur on standard cameras. In addition, event cameras have a very High Dynamic Range (HDR) (e.g., 140 dB compared to 60 dB of most standard cameras), which allows them to be used on a broad illumination range. Hence, event cameras open the door to tackle challenging scenarios that are inaccessible to standard cameras, such as high-speed and/or HDR tracking [2–8], control [9,10] and Simultaneous Localization and Mapping (SLAM) [11–16].

Because existing computer vision algorithms designed for standard cameras do not directly apply to event cameras, the main challenge in visual processing with these novel sensors is to devise specialized algorithms that can exploit the temporally asynchronous and spatially sparse nature of the data produced by event cameras to unlock their potential. Some preliminary works addressed this issue by combining event cameras with additional sensors, such as standard cameras [8,17,18] or depth sensors [17,19], to simplify the estimation task at hand. Although this approach obtained certain success, the capabilities of event cameras were not fully exploited since parts of such combined systems were limited by the lower dynamic range or slower devices. In this work, we tackle the problem of stereo 3D reconstruction for visual odometry (VO) or SLAM using event cameras alone. Our goal is to unlock the potential of event cameras by developing a method based on their working principle and using only events.

1.1 Related Work on Event-Based Depth Estimation

The majority of works on depth estimation with event cameras target the problem of "instantaneous" stereo, i.e., 3D reconstruction using events from a pair of synchronized cameras in stereo configuration (i.e., with a fixed baseline), during a very short time (ideally, on a per-event basis). Some of these works [20–22] follow the classical paradigm of solving stereo in two steps: epipolar matching followed by 3D point triangulation. Temporal coherence (e.g., simultaneity) of events across both left and right cameras is used to find matching events, and then standard triangulation [23] recovers depth. Other works, such as [24,25], extend cooperative stereo [26] to the case of event cameras. These methods are typically demonstrated in scenes with static cameras and few moving objects, so that event matches are easy to find due to uncluttered event data.

Some works [27,28] also target the problem of instantaneous stereo (depth maps produced using events over very short time intervals), but they use two non-simultaneous event cameras. These methods exploit a constrained hardware setup (two rotating event cameras with known motion) to either (i) recover intensity images on which conventional stereo is applied [27] or (ii) match events across cameras using temporal metrics and then use triangulation [28].

Recently, depth estimation with a *single* event camera has been shown in [11–14,29]. These methods recover a semi-dense 3D reconstruction of the scene by integrating information from the events of a moving camera over a longer time interval, and therefore, require information of the relative pose between the camera and the scene. Hence, these methods do not target the problem of instantaneous depth estimation but rather the problem of depth estimation for VO or SLAM.

Contribution. This paper is, to the authors' best knowledge, the first one to address the problem of non-instantaneous 3D reconstruction with a pair of event cameras in stereo configuration. Our approach is based on temporal coherence of events across left and right image planes. However, it differs from previous efforts (such as the instantaneous stereo methods [20–22, 27, 28]) in that: (i) we do not follow the classical paradigm of event matching plus triangulation, but rather a forward-projection approach that allows us to estimate depth without explicitly solving the event matching problem, (ii) we are able to handle sparse scenes (events generated by few objects) as well as cluttered scenes (events constantly generated everywhere in the image plane due to the motion of the camera), and (iii) we use camera pose information to integrate observations over time to produce semi-dense depth maps. Moreover, our method computes continuous depth values, as opposed to other methods, such as [11], which discretize the depth range.

Outline. Section 2 presents the 3D reconstruction problem considered and our solution, formulated as the minimization of an objective function that measures the temporal inconsistency of event time-surface maps across left and right image planes. Section 3 presents an approach to fuse multiple event-based 3D reconstructions into a single depth map. Section 4 evaluates our method on both synthetic and real event data, showing its good performance. Finally, Sect. 5 concludes the paper.

2   3D Reconstruction by Event Time-Surface Maps Energy Minimization

Our method is inspired by multi-view stereo pipelines for conventional cameras, such as DTAM [30], which aim at maximizing the photometric consistency through a number of narrow-baseline video frames. However, since event cameras do not output absolute intensity but rather intensity changes (the "events"), the direct photometric-consistency-based method cannot be readily applied. Instead, we exploit the fact that event cameras encode visual information in the form of microsecond-resolution timestamps of intensity changes.

For a stereo event camera, a detectable[1] 3D point in the overlapping field of view (FOV) of the cameras will generate an event on both left and right cameras. Ideally, these two events should spike simultaneously and their coordinates should be corresponding in terms of the epipolar geometry defined by both cameras. This property actually enables us to apply (and modify) an idea similar to

---

[1] A point at an intensity edge (i.e., non-homogeneous region of space), so that intensity changes (i.e., events) are generated when the point moves relative to the camera.

DTAM, simply by replacing the photometric consistency with the stereo temporal consistency. However, as shown in [31], stereo temporal consistency does not strictly hold at the pixel level because of signal latency and jitter effects. Hence, we define our stereo temporal consistency criterion by aggregating measurements over spatio-temporal neighborhoods, rather than by comparing the event timestamps at two individual pixels, as we show next.

2.1   Event Time-Surface Maps

We propose to apply patch-match to compare a pair of spike-history maps, in place of the photometric warping error as used in DTAM [30]. Specifically, to create two distinctive maps, we advocate the use of *Time-Surface* inspired by [32] for event-based pattern recognition. As illustrated in Fig. 1, the output of an event camera is a stream of events, where each event $e_k = (u_k, v_k, t_k, p_k)$ consists of the space-time coordinates where the intensity change of predefined size happened and the sign (polarity $p_k \in \{+1, -1\}$) of the change[2]. The time-surface map at time t is defined by applying an exponential decay kernel on the last spiking time t_{last} at each pixel coordinate $\mathbf{x} = (u, v)^T$:

$$T(\mathbf{x}, t) \doteq \exp\left(-\frac{t - t_{\text{last}}(\mathbf{x})}{\delta}\right), \tag{1}$$

where δ, the decay rate parameter, is a small constant number (e.g., 30 ms in our experiments). For convenient visualization and processing, (1) is further rescaled to the range [0, 255]. Our objective function is constructed on a set of time-surface maps (1) at different observation times $t = \{t_s\}$.

2.2   Problem Formulation

We follow a global energy minimization framework to estimate the inverse depth map $\mathcal{D}$ in the reference view (RV) from a number of stereo observations $s \in \mathcal{S}_{\text{RV}}$ nearby. A *stereo observation* at time t refers to a pair of time-surface maps created using (1), $(T_{\text{left}}(\cdot, t), T_{\text{right}}(\cdot, t))$. A stereo observation could be triggered by either a pose update or at a constant rate. For each pixel $\mathbf{x}$ in the reference view, its inverse depth $\rho^\star \doteq 1/z^\star$ is estimated by optimizing the objective function:

$$\rho^\star = \arg\min_\rho C(\mathbf{x}, \rho) \tag{2}$$

$$C(\mathbf{x}, \rho) \doteq \frac{1}{|\mathcal{S}_{\text{RV}}|} \sum_{s \in \mathcal{S}_{\text{RV}}} \|\tau_{\text{left}}^s(\mathbf{x}_1(\rho)) - \tau_{\text{right}}^s(\mathbf{x}_2(\rho))\|_2^2, \tag{3}$$

where $|\mathcal{S}_{\text{RV}}|$ denotes the number of involved neighboring stereo observations used for averaging. The function $\tau_{\text{left/right}}^s(\mathbf{x})$ returns the temporal information $T_{\text{left/right}}(\cdot, t)$ inside a $w \times w$ patch centered at image point $\mathbf{x}$. The residual

$$r_s(\rho) \doteq \|\tau_{\text{left}}^s(\mathbf{x}_1(\rho)) - \tau_{\text{right}}^s(\mathbf{x}_2(\rho))\|_2 \tag{4}$$

---

[2] Event polarity is not used, as [13] shows that it is not needed for 3D reconstruction.

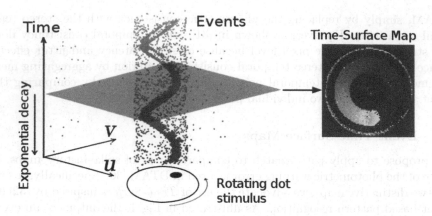

Fig. 1. Left: output of an event camera when viewing a rotating dot. Right: Time-surface map (1) at a time t, $\mathcal{T}(\mathbf{x}, t)$, which essentially measures how far in time (with respect to t) the last event spiked at each pixel $\mathbf{x} = (u, v)^T$. The brighter the color, the more recently the event was generated. Figure adapted from [33]. (Color figure online)

denotes the temporal difference in l_2 norm between patches centered at $\mathbf{x}_1$ and $\mathbf{x}_2$ in the left and right event cameras, respectively.

The geometry behind the proposed objective function is illustrated in Fig. 2. Since we assume the calibration (intrinsic and extrinsic parameters) as well as the pose of the left event camera T_{sr} at each observation are known (e.g., from a tracking algorithm such as [12,14]), the points $\mathbf{x}_1$ and $\mathbf{x}_2$ are given by $\mathbf{x}_1(\rho) = \pi(T_{sr}\pi^{-1}(\mathbf{x}, \rho))$ and $\mathbf{x}_2(\rho) = \pi(T_E T_{sr}\pi^{-1}(\mathbf{x}, \rho))$, respectively. The function $\pi : \mathbb{R}^3 \to \mathbb{R}^2$ projects a 3D point onto the camera's image plane, while its inverse function $\pi^{-1} : \mathbb{R}^2 \to \mathbb{R}^3$ back-projects a pixel into 3D space given the inverse depth ρ. T_E denotes the transformation from the left to the right event camera. Note that all event coordinates $\mathbf{x}$ are undistorted and rectified.

To verify that the proposed objective function (3) does lead to the optimum depth for a generic event in the reference view (Fig. 3(a)), a number of stereo observations from a real stereo event-camera sequence [34] have been created (Figs. 3(c) and (d)) and used to visualize the energy at the event location (Fig. 3(b)). The size of the patch is $w = 25$ pixels throughout the paper.

Note that our approach significantly departs from classical two-step event-processing methods [20–22] that solve the stereo matching problem first and then triangulate the 3D point, which is prone to errors due to the difficulty in establishing correct event matches during very short time intervals. These two-step approaches work in a "back-projection" fashion, mapping 2D event measurements to 3D space. Instead, our approach combines matching and triangulation in a single step, operating in a forward-projection manner (from 3D space to 2D event measurements). As shown in Fig. 2, an inverse depth hypothesis ρ yields a 3D point, $\pi^{-1}(\mathbf{x}, \rho)$, whose projection on both stereo image planes for all times "s" gives curves $\mathbf{x}_1^s(\rho)$ and $\mathbf{x}_2^s(\rho)$ that are compared in the objective

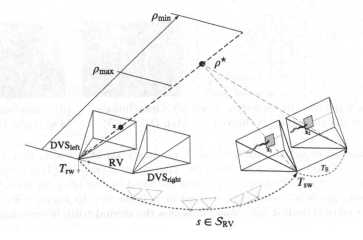

Fig. 2. Illustration of the geometry of the proposed problem and solution. The reference view (RV) is on the left, in which an event with coordinates $\mathbf{x}$ is back-projected into 3D space with a hypothetical inverse depth ρ. The optimal inverse depth ρ^*, lying inside the search interval $[\rho_{\min}, \rho_{\max}]$, corresponds to the real location of the 3D point which fulfills the temporal consistency in each neighboring stereo observation s.

function (3). Hence, an inverse depth hypothesis ρ establishes candidate stereo event matches, and the best matches are obtained once the objective function has been minimized with respect to ρ.

2.3 Inverse Depth Estimation

The proposed objective function (3) is optimized using non-linear least squares methods. The Gauss-Newton method is used here, which iteratively discovers the root of the necessary optimality condition

$$\frac{\partial C}{\partial \rho} = \frac{2}{|\mathcal{S}_{\mathrm{RV}}|} \sum_{s \in \mathcal{S}_{\mathrm{RV}}} r_s \frac{\partial r_s}{\partial \rho} = 0. \tag{5}$$

Substituting the linearization of r_s at ρ_k using the first order Taylor formula, $r_s(\rho_k + \Delta\rho) \approx r_s(\rho_k) + J_s(\rho_k)\Delta\rho$, in (5) we obtain

$$\sum_{s \in \mathcal{S}_{\mathrm{RV}}} J_s(r_s + J_s\Delta\rho) = 0, \tag{6}$$

where both, residual $r_s \equiv r_s(\rho_k)$ and Jacobian $J_s \equiv J_s(\rho_k)$, are scalars. Consequently the inverse depth ρ is iteratively updated by adding the increment

$$\Delta\rho = -\frac{\sum_{s \in \mathcal{S}_{\mathrm{RV}}} J_s r_s}{\sum_{s \in \mathcal{S}_{\mathrm{RV}}} J_s^2}. \tag{7}$$

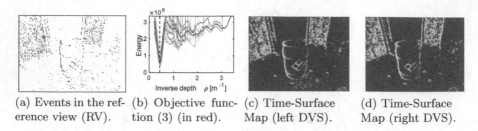

(a) Events in the ref- (b) Objective func- (c) Time-Surface (d) Time-Surface
erence view (RV).   tion (3) (in red).   Map (left DVS).   Map (right DVS).

Fig. 3. Proposed objective function. (a) A randomly selected event, at pixel $\mathbf{x}$, is marked by a red circle in the reference view. The energy $C(\mathbf{x}, \rho)$ in (3) is visualized in (b) as a function of ρ, with the thick red curve obtained by averaging the costs $C(\mathbf{x}_i, \rho)$ of neighboring pixels $\mathbf{x}_i$ in a patch centered at $\mathbf{x}$ (indicated by curves with random colors). The vertical dashed line (black) indicates the ground truth inverse depth. The time-surface maps of the left and the right event cameras at one of the observation times are shown in (c) and (d), respectively, where the patches for measuring the temporal residual are indicated in red. (Color figure online)

The Jacobian is computed by applying the chain rule,

$$
\begin{aligned}
J_s(\rho) &\doteq \frac{\partial}{\partial \rho} \|\mathcal{T}_{\text{left}}^s(\mathbf{x}_1(\rho)) - \mathcal{T}_{\text{right}}^s(\mathbf{x}_2(\rho))\|_2 \\
&= \frac{1}{\|\mathcal{T}_{\text{left}}^s - \mathcal{T}_{\text{right}}^s\|_2 + \epsilon} \left(\mathcal{T}_{\text{left}}^s - \mathcal{T}_{\text{right}}^s\right)_{1 \times w^2}^T \left(\frac{\partial \mathcal{T}_{\text{left}}^s}{\partial \rho} - \frac{\partial \mathcal{T}_{\text{right}}^s}{\partial \rho}\right)_{w^2 \times 1},
\end{aligned}
\tag{8}
$$

where, for simplicity, the pixel notation $\mathbf{x}_i(\rho)$ is omitted in the last equation. To avoid division by zero, a small number ϵ is added to the length of the residual vector. Actually, as shown by an investigation on the distribution of the temporal residual r_s in Sect. 3.1, the temporal residual is unlikely to be close to zero for valid stereo observations (i.e., patches with enough events). The derivative of the time-surface map with respect to the inverse depth is calculated by

$$
\frac{\partial \mathcal{T}^s}{\partial \rho} = \frac{\partial \mathcal{T}^s}{\partial \mathbf{x}} \frac{\partial \mathbf{x}}{\partial \rho} = \left(\frac{\partial \mathcal{T}^s}{\partial u}, \frac{\partial \mathcal{T}^s}{\partial v}\right)_{w^2 \times 2} \left(\frac{\partial u}{\partial \rho}, \frac{\partial v}{\partial \rho}\right)^T.
\tag{9}
$$

The computation of $\partial u / \partial \rho$ and $\partial v / \partial \rho$ is given in the supplementary material.

The overall procedure is summarized in Algorithm 1. The inputs of the algorithm are, respectively, the pixel coordinate $\mathbf{x}$ of an event in the RV, a set of stereo observations (time-surface maps) $\mathcal{T}_{\text{left/right}}^s$ ($s \in \mathcal{S}_{\text{RV}}$), the relative pose T_{sr} from the RV to each involved stereo observation s and the constant extrinsic parameters between both event cameras, T_{E}. The inverse depths of all events in the RV are estimated independently. Therefore, the computation is parallelizable. The basin of convergence is first localized by a coarse search over the range of plausible inverse depth values followed by a nonlinear refinement using the Gauss-Newton method. The coarse search step is selected to balance efficiency and accuracy when locating the basin of convergence, and is also based on our observation that the width of the basin is always bigger than 0.2 m^{-1} for the experiments carried out.

Algorithm 1. Inverse Depth Estimation at a Reference View (RV)

1: **Input**: pixel $\mathbf{x}$, stereo event observations $T_{\text{left}}^s, T_{\text{right}}^s$ and poses T_{sr}, T_{E}.
2: $\rho_0 \leftarrow \rho_{\text{initial}}$ (by coarse search over a range $[\rho_{\min}, \rho_{\max}]$).
3: **while** not converged **do**
4:     **for** each observation s **do**
5:         Compute $r_s(\rho_k)$ in (4).
6:         Compute $J_s(\rho_k)$ using (8).
7:     **end for**
8:     Update: $\rho_k \leftarrow \rho_k + \Delta\rho$, using (7).
9: **end while**
10: **return** Inverse depth ρ_k.

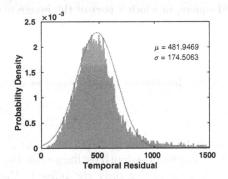

Fig. 4. Probability distribution (PDF) of the temporal residuals $\{r_i\}$: empirical (gray) and Gaussian fit $\mathcal{N}(\mu, \sigma^2)$ (red line). (Color figure online)

3   Semi-dense Reconstruction

The 3D reconstruction method presented in Sect. 2 produces a sparse depth map at the reference view (RV). To improve the density of the reconstruction while reducing the uncertainty of the estimated depth, we run the reconstruction method (Algorithm 1) on several RVs along time and fuse the results. To this end, the uncertainty of the inverse depth estimation is studied in this section. Based on the derived uncertainty, a fusion strategy is developed and is incrementally applied as sparse reconstructions of new RVs are obtained. Our final reconstruction approaches a semi-dense level as it reconstructs depth for all pixels that lie along edges.

3.1   Uncertainty of Inverse Depth Estimation

In the last iteration of Gauss-Newton's method, the inverse depth is updated by

$$\rho^\star \equiv \rho_k \leftarrow \rho_k + \Delta\rho(\mathbf{r}), \tag{10}$$

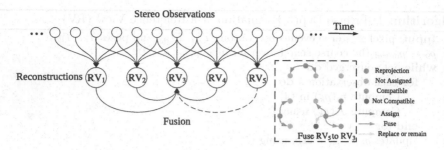

Fig. 5. Depth map fusion strategy. All stereo observations ($T^s_{\text{left}}, T^s_{\text{right}}$) are denoted by hollow circles and listed in chronological order. Neighboring RVs are fused into a chosen RV* (e.g., RV$_3$). Using the fusion from RV$_5$ to RV$_3$ as an example, the fusion rules are illustrated in the dashed square, in which a part of the image plane is visualized. The blue dots are the reprojections of 3D points in RV$_5$ on the image plane of RV$_3$. Gray dots represent unassigned pixels which will be assigned by blue dots within one pixel away. Pixels that have been assigned, e.g., the green ones (compatible with the blue ones) will be fused. Pixels that are not compatible (in red) will either remain or be replaced, depending on which distribution has the smallest uncertainty. (Color figure online)

where $\Delta\rho$ is a function of the residuals $\mathbf{r} \doteq \{r_1, r_2, \ldots, r_s \mid s \in \mathcal{S}_{RV}\}$ as defined in (7). The variance $\sigma^2_{\rho^*}$ of the inverse depth estimate can be derived using uncertainty propagation [35]. For simplicity, only the noise in the temporal residuals $\mathbf{r}$ is considered:

$$\sigma^2_{\rho^*} \approx \left(\frac{\partial \rho^*}{\partial \mathbf{r}}\right)^T (\sigma^2_r \mathrm{Id}) \frac{\partial \rho^*}{\partial \mathbf{r}} = \frac{\sigma^2_r}{\sum_{s \in \mathcal{S}_{RV}} J^2_s}. \tag{11}$$

The derivation of this equation can be found in the supplementary material. We determine σ_r empirically by investigating the distribution of the temporal residuals $\mathbf{r}$. Using the ground truth depth, we sample a large number of temporal residuals $\mathbf{r} = \{r_1, r_2, ..., r_n\}$. The variance σ^2_r is obtained by fitting a Gaussian distribution to the histogram of $\mathbf{r}$, as illustrated in Fig. 4.

3.2   Inverse Depth Fusion

To improve the density of the reconstruction, inverse depth estimates from multiple RVs are incrementally transferred to a selected reference view, RV*, and fused. Assuming the inverse depth of a pixel in RV$_i$ follows a distribution $\mathcal{N}(\rho_a, \sigma^2_a)$, its corresponding location in RV* is typically a non-integer coordinate $\mathbf{x}^f$, which will have an effect on the four neighboring pixels coordinates $\{\mathbf{x}^i_j\}^4_{j=1}$. Using $\mathbf{x}^i_1$ as an example, the fusion is performed based on the following rules:

1. Assign $\mathcal{N}(\rho_a, \sigma^2_a)$ to $\mathbf{x}^i_1$ if no previous distribution exists.
2. If there is an existing inverse depth distribution assigned at $\mathbf{x}^i_1$, e.g., $\mathcal{N}(\rho_b, \sigma^2_b)$, the compatibility between the two inverse depth hypotheses is checked to

decide whether they are fused. The compatibility is evaluated using the χ^2 test at [35]:

$$\frac{(\rho_a - \rho_b)^2}{\sigma_a^2} + \frac{(\rho_a - \rho_b)^2}{\sigma_b^2} < 5.99. \tag{12}$$

If the two hypotheses are compatible, they are fused into a single inverse depth distribution:

$$\mathcal{N}\left(\frac{\sigma_a^2 \rho_b + \sigma_b^2 \rho_a}{\sigma_a^2 + \sigma_b^2}, \frac{\sigma_a^2 \sigma_b^2}{\sigma_a^2 + \sigma_a^2}\right), \tag{13}$$

otherwise the distribution with the smallest variance remains.

An illustration of the fusion strategy is given in Fig. 5.

4   Experiments

The proposed stereo 3D reconstruction method is evaluated in this section. We first introduce the configuration of our stereo event-camera system and the datasets used in the experiments. Afterwards, both quantitative and qualitative evaluations are presented. Additionally, the depth fusion process is illustrated to highlight how it improves the density of the reconstruction while reducing depth uncertainty.

4.1   Stereo Event-Camera Setup

To evaluate our method, we use sequences from publicly available simulators [36] and datasets [34], and we also collect our own sequences using a stereo event-camera rig (Fig. 6). The stereo rig consists of two Dynamic and Active Pixel Vision Sensors (DAVIS) [37] of 240×180 pixel resolution, which are calibrated intrinsically and extrinsically[3] using *Kalibr* [38]. Since our algorithm is working on rectified and undistorted coordinates, the joint undistortion and rectification transformation are computed in advance.

As the stereo event-camera system moves, a new stereo observation $(\mathcal{T}_{\text{left}}^s, \mathcal{T}_{\text{right}}^s)$ is generated when a pose update is available. The generation consists of two steps. The first step is to generate a rectified event map by collecting all events that occurred within 10 ms (from the pose's updating time to the past), as shown in Fig. 3(a). The second step is to refresh the time-surface maps in both left and right event cameras, as shown in Figs. 3(c) and (d). One of the observations is selected as the RV. The rectified event map of the RV together with the rest of the observations are fed to the inverse depth estimation module (Algorithm 1). We use the rectified event map as a selection map, i.e., we estimate depth values only at the pixels with non-zero values in the rectified event map (as shown in Figs. 6(c) and (d)). As more and more RVs are reconstructed and fused together, the result becomes both more dense and more accurate.

---

[3] The DAVIS comprises both a frame camera and an event sensor (DVS) aligned perfectly on the same pixel array. Hence, we calibrate the stereo pair using standard methods on the intensity frames.

4.2   Results

The evaluation is performed on six sequences, including a synthetic sequence from the simulator [36], three sequences collected by ourselves (hand-held) and two sequences from [34] (with a stereo event camera mounted on a drone). A snapshot of each scene is given in the first column of Fig. 7. In the synthetic sequence, the stereo event-camera system looks orthogonally towards three frontal parallel planes while performing a pure translation. Our three sequences showcase typical office scenes with various office supplies. The stereo event-camera rig is hand-held and performs arbitrary 6-DOF motion, which is recorded by a motion-capture system with sub-millimeter accuracy. The other two sequences are collected in a large indoor environment using a drone [34], with pose information also from a motion-capture system. These two sequences are very challenging for two reasons: (*i*) a wide variety of structures such as chairs, barrels, a tripod on a cabinet, etc. can be found in this scene, and (*ii*) the drone undergoes relatively high-speed motions during data collection.

Cameras	DAVIS240
Width	240 pix
Height	180 pix
FOV	62.9°
Baseline	14.7 cm

(a) System informa-   (b) Stereo event-   (c) Event map on   (d) Event map on
tion.   camera rig.   the left camera.   the right camera.

Fig. 6. Left, (a) and (b): the stereo event-camera rig used in our experiment, consisting of two synchronized DAVIS [37] devices. Right, (c) and (d): rectified event maps at one time observation.

Quantitative evaluation on datasets with ground truth depth are given in Table 1, where we compare our method with two state-of-the-art instantaneous

Table 1. Quantitative evaluation on sequences with ground truth depth.

	Dataset	*simulation_3planes* [36]	*Indoor_flying1* [34]	*Indoor_flying3* [34]
	Depth range	2.76 m	4.96 m	5.74 m
Our method	Mean error	**0.03 m**	**0.13 m**	**0.33 m**
	Median error	**0.01 m**	**0.05 m**	0.11 m
	Relative error	**1.17%**	**2.65%**	**5.79%**
FCVF [39]	Mean error	0.05 m	0.99 m	1.03 m
	Median error	0.03 m	0.25 m	**0.11 m**
	Relative error	1.84%	20.8%	17.3%
SGM [40]	Mean error	0.08 m	0.93 m	1.19 m
	Median error	0.03 m	0.31 m	0.20 m
	Relative error	3.22%	18.7%	20.8%

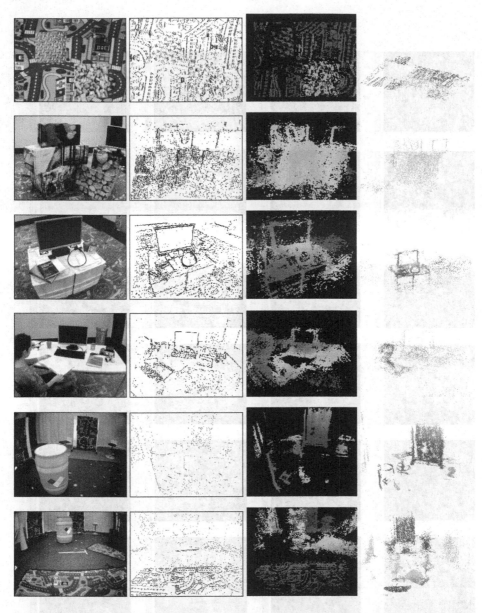

Fig. 7. Results of the proposed method on several datasets. Images on the first column are raw intensity frames (not rectified nor lens-distortion corrected). The second column shows the events (undistorted and rectified) in the left event camera of a reference view (RV). Semi-dense depth maps (after fusion with several neighboring RVs) are given in the third column, colored according to depth, from red (close) to blue (far). The fourth column visualizes the 3D point cloud of each sequence at a chosen perspective. No post-processing (such as regularization through median filtering [13]) was performed. (Color figure online)

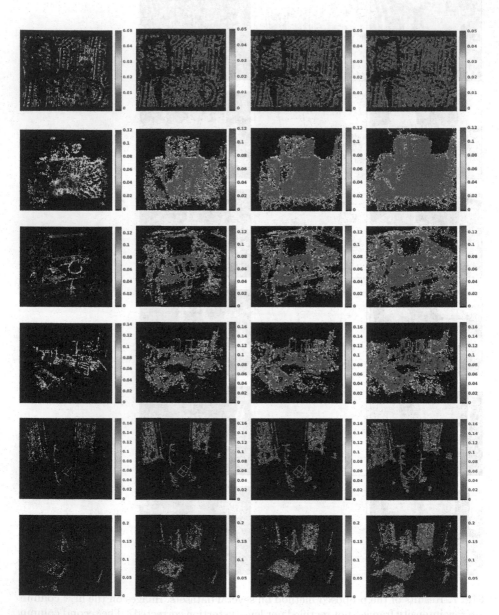

Fig. 8. Illustration of how the fusion strategy increasingly improves the density of the reconstruction while reducing depth uncertainty. The first column shows the uncertainty maps σ_ρ before the fusion. The second to the fourth columns report the uncertainty maps after fusing with 4, 8 and 16 neighboring estimations, respectively.

stereo matching methods, "Fast Cost-Volume Filtering" (FCVF) [39] and "Semi-Global Matching" (SGM) [40], working on pairs of time-surface images (as in Figs. 3(c) and (d)). We report the *mean* depth error, the *median* depth error and the relative error (defined as the *mean* depth error divided by the depth range of the scene [13]). In fairness to the comparison, the fully dense depth maps returned by FCVF and SGM are masked by the non-zero pixels in the time-surface images. Besides, the boundary of the depth maps are cropped considering the block size used in each implementation. The best results per sequence are highlighted in bold in Table 1. Our method outperforms the other two competitors on all sequences. Although FCVF and SGM also give satisfactory results on the synthetic sequence, they do not work well in more complicated scenarios in which the observations are either not dense enough, or the temporal consistency does not strictly hold in a single stereo observation.

Reconstruction results on all sequences are visualized in Fig. 7. Images on the first column are raw intensity frames from the DAVIS. They convey the appearance of the scenes but are not used by our algorithm. The second column shows rectified and undistorted event maps in the left event-camera of a RV. The number of the events depends on not only on the motion of the stereo rig but also on the amount of visual contrast in the scene. Semi-dense depth maps (after fusion with several neighboring RVs) are given in the third column, pseudo-colored from red (close) to blue (far). The last column visualizes the 3D point cloud of each sequence at a chosen perspective. Note that only points whose variance σ_ρ^2 is smaller than $0.8 \times (\sigma_\rho^{max})^2$ are visualized in 3D.

The reconstruction of the rectified events in one RV is sparse and, typically, full of noise. To show how the fusion strategy improves the density of the reconstruction as well as reduces the uncertainty, we additionally perform an experiment that visualizes the fusion process incrementally. As shown in Fig. 8, the first column visualizes the uncertainty maps before the fusion. The second to the fourth column demonstrates the uncertainty maps after fusing the result of a RV with its neighboring 4, 8 and 16 estimations, respectively. Hot colors refer to high uncertainty while cold colors mean low uncertainty. The result becomes increasingly dense and accurate as more and more RVs are fused. Note that the remaining highly uncertain estimates generally correspond to events that are caused by either noise or low-contrast patterns.

5 Conclusion

This paper has proposed a novel and effective solution to 3D reconstruction using a pair of temporally-synchronized event cameras in stereo configuration. This is, to the best of the authors' knowledge, the first one to address such a problem allowing stereo SLAM applications with event cameras. The proposed energy minimization method exploits spatio-temporal consistency of the events across cameras to achieve high accuracy (between 1% and 5% relative error), and it outperforms state-of-the-art stereo methods using the same spatio-temporal image representation of the event stream. Future work includes the development of a full stereo visual odometry system, by combining the proposed 3D reconstruction strategy with a stereo-camera pose tracker, in a parallel tracking and mapping fashion [14].

Acknowledgment. The research leading to these results is supported by the Australian Centre for Robotic Vision and the National Center of Competence in Research (NCCR) Robotics, through the Swiss National Science Foundation, the SNSF-ERC Starting Grant and the NCCR Ph.D. Exchange Scholarship Programme. Yi Zhou also acknowledges the financial support from the China Scholarship Council for his Ph.D. Scholarship No. 201406020098.

References

1. Lichtsteiner, P., Posch, C., Delbruck, T.: A 128 × 128 120 dB 15 μs latency asynchronous temporal contrast vision sensor. IEEE J. Solid-State Circuits **43**(2), 566–576 (2008). https://doi.org/10.1109/JSSC.2007.914337
2. Mueggler, E., Huber, B., Scaramuzza, D.: Event-based, 6-DOF pose tracking for high-speed maneuvers. In: IEEE/RSJ International Conference on Intelligent Robots and Systems (IROS), pp. 2761–2768 (2014).https://doi.org/10.1109/IROS.2014.6942940
3. Lagorce, X., Meyer, C., Ieng, S.H., Filliat, D., Benosman, R.: Asynchronous event-based multikernel algorithm for high-speed visual features tracking. IEEE Trans. Neural Netw. Learn. Syst. **26**(8), 1710–1720 (2015). https://doi.org/10.1109/TNNLS.2014.2352401
4. Zhu, A.Z., Atanasov, N., Daniilidis, K.: Event-based feature tracking with probabilistic data association. In: IEEE International Conference on Robotics and Automation (ICRA), pp. 4465–4470 (2017). https://doi.org/10.1109/ICRA.2017.7989517
5. Gallego, G., Lund, J.E.A., Mueggler, E., Rebecq, H., Delbruck, T., Scaramuzza, D.: Event-based, 6-DOF camera tracking from photometric depth maps. IEEE Trans. Pattern Anal. Mach. Intell. **40**(10), 2402–2412 (2018). https://doi.org/10.1109/TPAMI.2017.2658577
6. Gallego, G., Scaramuzza, D.: Accurate angular velocity estimation with an event camera. IEEE Robot. Autom. Lett. **2**, 632–639 (2017). https://doi.org/10.1109/LRA.2016.2647639
7. Mueggler, E., Gallego, G., Rebecq, H., Scaramuzza, D.: Continuous-time visual-inertial odometry with event cameras. IEEE Trans. Robot. (2018, to appear). https://doi.org/10.1109/TRO.2018.2858287
8. Gehrig, D., Rebecq, H., Gallego, G., Scaramuzza, D.: Asynchronous, photometric feature tracking using events and frames. In: European Conference on Computer Vision (ECCV) (2018, to appear). https://doi.org/10.1007/978-3-030-01258-8_46
9. Conradt, J., Cook, M., Berner, R., Lichtsteiner, P., Douglas, R.J., Delbruck, T.: A pencil balancing robot using a pair of AER dynamic vision sensors. In: IEEE International Symposium on Circuits and Systems (ISCAS), pp. 781–784 (2009). https://doi.org/10.1109/ISCAS.2009.5117867
10. Delbruck, T., Lang, M.: Robotic goalie with 3 ms reaction time at 4% CPU load using event-based dynamic vision sensor. Front. Neurosci. **7**, 223 (2013). https://doi.org/10.3389/fnins.2013.00223

11. Rebecq, H., Gallego, G., Scaramuzza, D.: EMVS: event-based multi-view stereo. In: British Machine Vision Conference (BMVC), September 2016. https://doi.org/ 10.5244/C.30.63

12. Kim, H., Leutenegger, S., Davison, A.J.: Real-time 3D reconstruction and 6-DOF tracking with an event camera. In: Leibe, B., Matas, J., Sebe, N., Welling, M. (eds.) ECCV 2016. LNCS, vol. 9910, pp. 349–364. Springer, Cham (2016). https://doi. org/10.1007/978-3-319-46466-4_21

13. Rebecq, H., Gallego, G., Mueggler, E., Scaramuzza, D.: EMVS: event-based multi-view stereo-3D reconstruction with an event camera in real-time. Int. J. Comput. Vis. 1–21 (2017). https://doi.org/10.1007/s11263-017-1050-6

14. Rebecq, H., Horstschäfer, T., Gallego, G., Scaramuzza, D.: EVO: a geometric approach to event-based 6-DOF parallel tracking and mapping in real-time. IEEE Robot. Autom. Lett. **2**, 593–600 (2017). https://doi.org/10.1109/LRA.2016. 2645143

15. Rebecq, H., Horstschaefer, T., Scaramuzza, D.: Real-time visual-inertial odometry for event cameras using keyframe-based nonlinear optimization. In: British Machine Vision Conference (BMVC), September 2017

16. Rosinol Vidal, A., Rebecq, H., Horstschaefer, T., Scaramuzza, D.: Ultimate SLAM? Combining events, images, and IMU for robust visual SLAM in HDR and high speed scenarios. IEEE Robot. Autom. Lett. **3**(2), 994–1001 (2018). https://doi. org/10.1109/LRA.2018.2793357

17. Censi, A., Scaramuzza, D.: Low-latency event-based visual odometry. In: IEEE International Conference on Robotics and Automation (ICRA), pp. 703–710 (2014). https://doi.org/10.1109/ICRA.2014.6906931

18. Kueng, B., Mueggler, E., Gallego, G., Scaramuzza, D.: Low-latency visual odometry using event-based feature tracks. In: IEEE/RSJ International Conference on Intelligent Robots and Systems (IROS), Daejeon, pp. 16–23, October 2016. https:// doi.org/10.1109/IROS.2016.7758089

19. Weikersdorfer, D., Adrian, D.B., Cremers, D., Conradt, J.: Event-based 3D SLAM with a depth-augmented dynamic vision sensor. In: IEEE International Conference on Robotics and Automation (ICRA), pp. 359–364, June 2014. https://doi.org/10. 1109/ICRA.2014.6906882

20. Kogler, J., Humenberger, M., Sulzbachner, C.: Event-based stereo matching approaches for frameless address event stereo data. In: Bebis, G. (ed.) ISVC 2011. LNCS, vol. 6938, pp. 674–685. Springer, Heidelberg (2011). https://doi.org/10. 1007/978-3-642-24028-7_62

21. Rogister, P., Benosman, R., Ieng, S.H., Lichtsteiner, P., Delbruck, T.: Asynchronous event-based binocular stereo matching. IEEE Trans. Neural Netw. Learn. Syst. **23**(2), 347–353 (2012). https://doi.org/10.1109/TNNLS.2011.2180025

22. Camunas-Mesa, L.A., Serrano-Gotarredona, T., Ieng, S.H., Benosman, R.B., Linares-Barranco, B.: On the use of orientation filters for 3D reconstruction in event-driven stereo vision. Front. Neurosci. **8**, 48 (2014). https://doi.org/10.3389/ fnins.2014.00048

23. Hartley, R., Zisserman, A.: Multiple View Geometry in Computer Vision, 2nd edn. Cambridge University Press, New York (2003). https://doi.org/10.1017/ CBO9780511811685

24. Piatkowska, E., Belbachir, A.N., Gelautz, M.: Asynchronous stereo vision for event-driven dynamic stereo sensor using an adaptive cooperative approach. In: International Conference on Computer Vision Workshops (ICCVW), pp. 45–50 (2013). https://doi.org/10.1109/ICCVW.2013.13

25. Osswald, M., Ieng, S.H., Benosman, R., Indiveri, G.: A spiking neural network model of 3D perception for event-based neuromorphic stereo vision systems. Sci. Rep. **7**, 1–12 (2017). https://doi.org/10.1038/srep40703. 40703
26. Marr, D., Poggio, T.: Cooperative computation of stereo disparity. Science **194**(4262), 283–287 (1976). https://doi.org/10.1126/science.968482
27. Schraml, S., Belbachir, A.N., Bischof, H.: An event-driven stereo system for real-time 3-D 360 panoramic vision. IEEE Trans. Ind. Electron. **63**(1), 418–428 (2016). https://doi.org/10.1109/tie.2015.2477265
28. Schraml, S., Belbachir, A.N., Bischof, H.: Event-driven stereo matching for real-time 3D panoramic vision. In: IEEE Conference on Computer Vision and Pattern Recognition (CVPR), pp. 466–474, June 2015. https://doi.org/10.1109/CVPR.2015.7298644
29. Gallego, G., Rebecq, H., Scaramuzza, D.: A unifying contrast maximization framework for event cameras, with applications to motion, depth, and optical flow estimation. In: IEEE Conference on Computer Vision and Pattern Recognition (CVPR), pp. 3867–3876 (2018). https://doi.org/10.1109/CVPR.2018.00407
30. Newcombe, R.A., Lovegrove, S.J., Davison, A.J.: DTAM: dense tracking and mapping in real-time. In: International Conference on Computer Vision (ICCV), pp. 2320–2327, November 2011. https://doi.org/10.1109/ICCV.2011.6126513
31. Benosman, R., Ieng, S.H., Rogister, P., Posch, C.: Asynchronous event-based Hebbian epipolar geometry. IEEE Trans. Neural Netw. **22**(11), 1723–1734 (2011). https://doi.org/10.1109/TNN.2011.2167239
32. Lagorce, X., Orchard, G., Gallupi, F., Shi, B.E., Benosman, R.: HOTS: a hierarchy of event-based time-surfaces for pattern recognition. IEEE Trans. Pattern Anal. Mach. Intell. **PP**(99), 1 (2016). https://doi.org/10.1109/TPAMI.2016.2574707
33. Liu, S.C., Delbruck, T.: Neuromorphic sensory systems. Curr. Opin. Neurobiol. **20**(3), 288–295 (2010). https://doi.org/10.1016/j.conb.2010.03.007
34. Zhu, A.Z., Thakur, D., Ozaslan, T., Pfrommer, B., Kumar, V., Daniilidis, K.: The multivehicle stereo event camera dataset: an event camera dataset for 3D perception. IEEE Robot. Autom. Lett. **3**(3), 2032–2039 (2018). https://doi.org/10.1109/lra.2018.2800793
35. Mur-Artal, R., Tardos, J.D.: Probabilistic semi-dense mapping from highly accurate feature-based monocular SLAM. In: Robotics: Science and Systems (RSS) (2015). https://doi.org/10.15607/RSS.2015.XI.041
36. Mueggler, E., Rebecq, H., Gallego, G., Delbruck, T., Scaramuzza, D.: The event-camera dataset and simulator: event-based data for pose estimation, visual odometry, and SLAM. Int. J. Robot. Res. **36**, 142–149 (2017). https://doi.org/10.1177/0278364917691115
37. Brandli, C., Berner, R., Yang, M., Liu, S.C., Delbruck, T.: A 240 × 180 130 dB 3 us latency global shutter spatiotemporal vision sensor. IEEE J. Solid-State Circuits **49**(10), 2333–2341 (2014). https://doi.org/10.1109/JSSC.2014.2342715
38. Furgale, P., Rehder, J., Siegwart, R.: Unified temporal and spatial calibration for multi-sensor systems. In: IEEE/RSJ International Conference on Intelligent Robots and Systems (IROS) (2013). https://doi.org/10.1109/IROS.2013.6696514
39. Hosni, A., Rhemann, C., Bleyer, M., Rother, C., Gelautz, M.: Fast cost-volume filtering for visual correspondence and beyond. IEEE Trans. Pattern Anal. Mach. Intell. **35**(2), 504–511 (2013). https://doi.org/10.1109/tpami.2012.156
40. Hirschmuller, H.: Stereo processing by semiglobal matching and mutual information. IEEE Trans. Pattern Anal. Mach. Intell. **30**(2), 328–341 (2008). https://doi.org/10.1109/tpami.2007.1166

Self-Calibrating Isometric Non-Rigid Structure-from-Motion

Shaifali Parashar[1]($\boxtimes$), Adrien Bartoli[1], and Daniel Pizarro[1,2]

[1] Institut Pascal - CNRS/Université Clermont Auvergne, Clermont-Ferrand, France
shaifali.parashar@gmail.com
[2] GEINTRA, Universidad de Alcalá, Alcalá de Henares, Spain
http://igt.ip.uca.fr/~ab/

Abstract. We present self-calibrating isometric non-rigid structure-from-motion (SCIso-NRSfM), the first method to reconstruct a non-rigid object from at least three monocular images with constant but unknown focal length. The majority of NRSfM methods using the perspective camera simply assume that the calibration is known. SCIso-NRSfM leverages the recent powerful differential approaches to NRSfM, based on formulating local polynomial constraints, where local means correspondence-wise. In NRSfM, the local shape may be solved from these constraints. In SCIso-NRSfM, the difficulty is to also solve for the focal length as a global variable. We propose to eliminate the shape using resultants, obtaining univariate polynomials for the focal length only, whose sum of squares can then be globally minimized. SCIso-NRSfM thus solves for the focal length by integrating the constraints for all correspondences and the whole image set. Once this is done, the local shape is easily recovered. Our experiments show that its performance is very close to the state-of-the-art methods that use a calibrated camera.

Keywords: NRSfM · Self-calibration · Uncalibrated camera
Differential geometry · Metric tensor · Christoffel symbols · Resultants

1 Introduction

Estimating the intrinsic camera parameters from images is known as camera self-calibration. In Structure-from-Motion (SfM), which is a mature technique for the 3D reconstruction of rigid objects from monocular images, the intrinsic parameters are required to achieve Euclidean 3D reconstruction [12]. SfM may use calibrated images directly [23,29] or uncalibrated images with self-calibration [22,26]. SfM was extended to handle non-rigid (deformable) objects in the last two decades with Non-Rigid Structure-from-Motion (NRSfM). While most recent SfM methods use the perspective camera, many early NRSfM methods [3,7,9,28,30,34] use a metric affine camera, namely the orthographic or weak-perspective camera. They handle uncalibrated images because these metric affine cameras only have a scale factor as intrinsic parameter, which couples

© Springer Nature Switzerland AG 2018
V. Ferrari et al. (Eds.): ECCV 2018, LNCS 11205, pp. 259–274, 2018.
https://doi.org/10.1007/978-3-030-01246-5_16

with the scale of the 3D structure in the reconstruction equations. However, the use of these metric affine cameras restricts the imaging conditions [12], which limits practical applicability. Concretely, the affine camera models do not capture the perspective effect and may thus be inaccurate. They may also yield flip ambiguities in the reconstruction. More recent NRSfM methods [5,6,17,18] use the perspective camera. They can thus cope with broader imaging conditions, are generally more accurate and do not suffer from the flip ambiguities. However, they assume that the camera is calibrated, which puts a different limit on their applicability. Two exceptions are [17,24], which assume that parts of the scene remain rigid. These rigid parts are used to self-calibrate the camera using an SfM method such as [20]. The estimated calibration is then used in a calibrated NRSfM method. Therefore [17,24] do not solve the problem of self-calibration in NRSfM strictly speaking but use a workaround based on a sensible but very strong assumption on the scene contents. Since there is a positive gain in choosing the perspective camera, self-calibrating NRSfM appears to be a natural and important problem to study.

We study self-calibrating NRSfM for isometrically deforming surfaces, widely used in recent work [4,5,18,24,28,33,34]. Isometry is one of the most intuitive deformation model and approximates the majority of real-life deformations. In order to deal with uncalibrated images, we use the common assumption that the camera has square pixels and a known principal point lying at the image center. Thus, the only intrinsic parameter which needs to be estimated is the focal length. Assuming that the focal length is constant, we propose a solution based on solving a univariate polynomial, modeling the contribution of $N \geq 3$ images in a least-squares fashion. Our method takes inspiration from a recent solution to isometric NRSfM [18]. This solution uses the image warps to constrain the differential 3D structure. The method uses advanced concepts from Riemannian geometry, namely the Metric Tensor (MT) and the Christoffel Symbols (CS). The MT represents the local surface structure and the CS expresses the rate of change of the MT. In addition, the method uses the concept of infinitesimal planarity, which is widely used in differential geometry. According to this assumption, the surface is planar at an infinitesimal level but maintains its curvature at the global level. The method arrives at Partial Differential Equations (PDEs) that can be converted to algebraic equations in two shape variables and solved locally. By locally we mean that the solution is obtained at each point correspondence independently. The two variables, related to the local 3D shape, are computed in [18] by minimizing the sum-of-squares of the algebraic equations using a computationally expensive polynomial optimization engine [13]. This local solution handles both wide and short baseline data and naturally copes with missing data and occlusions.

We introduce the focal length as an additional variable to the Riemannian framework of [18]. This leaves the CS unaltered but changes the MT. The reconstruction equations also change, containing the two local shape variables, similarly to [18], and a global variable representing the focal length. These equations are degree 5 polynomials, which means that the derivative of their sum-of-squares is a degree 9 polynomial in 3 variables, which is by far out of bounds for the existing polynomial optimization engines such as [13]. We propose a solution by segregating the global focal length from the local shape variables using the resultants. We obtain univariate polynomials in terms of the focal length. In spite of their high degree, they can be easily solved globally by minimizing their sum-of-squares using a standard root finding algorithm. This global formulation accumulates the local constraints for all correspondences and all images, making the focal length well-constrained and the solution stable. We finally use the focal length estimate to solve isometric NRSfM locally. Our solution improves on [18] by dropping the dependency on [13]. Concretely, it minimizes the sum-of-squares of univariate polynomials for each of the two shape variables, obtained using the resultant of the original multivariate reconstruction equations. Our experiments show that the focal length estimated by SCIso-NRSfM is close to the ground truth and the 3D reconstructed shape very close to calibrated NRSfM methods [5,18]. We also compare with the NRSfM methods [9,34] that use an orthographic camera and found that these are outperformed by SCIso-NRSfM.

2   State-of-the-Art and Contributions

Self-calibration has been extensively studied for SfM. It follows one of several possible scenarios where the camera intrinsics are partially constrained. The first solution [8] introduced the Kruppa equations, which use the epipolar geometry to draw constraints on the camera intrinsics. However, they suffer from singularities. Later, [21] proposed a stratified approach where a projective reconstruction is upgraded to affine using a modulus constraint, and further upgraded to Euclidean using linear constraints [11]. In contrast, a direct projective to metric upgrade was done by [14]. The most successful approach finds the explicit location of the absolute quadric using its dual [31]. It obtains a global solution to the fixed camera intrinsic scenario by solving algebraic equations. Based on this model, [20] proposed a linear algorithm to estimate a varying focal length.

Self-calibration was scarcely studied for deformable objects, partly because the subject is more recent than SfM and partly because it forms a less constrained problem. A related problem to NRSfM is Shape-from-Template (SfT) which uses a deformable 3D template and a single input image [1,25]. A solution to isometric SfT with focal length calibration was proposed in [2]. It works by solving for the focal length locally and using the median of these local solutions as final estimate. The local solutions were found to have a large spread across the input image. This is because locally the focal length is weakly constrained.

Self-calibration in NRSfM forms a difficult and open problem. First, the successful algebraic framework of the dual absolute quadric is based on the rigidity constraint and can thus not be borrowed from SfM. Second, the differential method for calibration in SfT showed signs of instabilities, even if SfT is a much more constrained problem than NRSfM. Our solution uses a differential framework in order to deal with deformations but estimates the focal length globally, by combining local constraints from all point correspondences and all images.

More precisely, we make the following main contributions. *(1)* We show how to form algebraic constraints for each point correspondence and image pair. These constraints depend on three variables related to the focal length and the local 3D shape and are not directly solvable. We show how to convert these constraints into easily solvable univariate polynomials. *(2)* We show how to form a numerically stable global solution to the focal length by integrating the local constraints over all points and images, and minimizing their sum-of-squares optimally. *(3)* We show how, given the estimated focal length, the local 3D shape may be recovered by minimizing the sum-of-squares of univariate polynomials. *(4)* We give an algorithm based solely on standard numerical tools.

3   Mathematical Background

Notation. Latin letters denote scalars and Greek letters denote functions. Bold Latin letters denote vectors and matrices. There are a few exceptions however, and $\mathbf{\Gamma}$, which denotes the CS matrix, is one of them. We use superscripts to index the $N \geq 3$ images. The reference image has index 1, without loss of generality. The other images have indexes $(j, r) \in \{2, \ldots, N\}$. We often drop the reference image index from the equations for the sake of clarity. For instance, the inverse depth function for image 1 will be defined as β^1 but often referred to as β. We use the subscript $i \in \{1, \ldots n\}$ to refer to a particular point correspondence, with n the total number of correspondences.

Surface and Camera Models. We model 3D surfaces as Riemannian manifolds. Figure 1 shows a surface $\mathcal{M}$ viewed in image $\mathcal{I}$. We use the perspective camera model Π. It takes as input the 3D point $\mathbf{Q} = \begin{pmatrix} x\ y\ z \end{pmatrix}^\top$ and outputs its normalized retinal coordinates $\mathbf{r} = \Pi(\mathbf{Q}) = \begin{pmatrix} \frac{x}{z}\ \frac{y}{z} \end{pmatrix}^\top$. We translate the image coordinates so that the principal point aligns with the origin. This allows the intrinsic parameter matrix $\mathbf{K}$ to be expressed in terms of the focal length f only, where $f > 0$ is expressed in px, meaning in number of pixels. The pixel coordinates $\mathbf{p} = \begin{pmatrix} u\ v \end{pmatrix}^\top$ are then related to the retinal coordinates as $\mathbf{r} = \begin{pmatrix} \frac{u}{f}\ \frac{v}{f} \end{pmatrix}^\top = \frac{\mathbf{p}}{f}$.

The image embedding ϕ is the 'inverse' of the projection Π for the points on $\mathcal{M}$. It maps the retinal coordinates $\mathbf{r}$ to the 3D point $\mathbf{Q}$ as:

$$\phi(\mathbf{r}) = \frac{1}{\beta(\mathbf{r})} \left(\mathbf{r}^\top\ 1 \right)^\top, \tag{1}$$

where $\beta(\mathbf{r})$ is the inverse-depth function. We omit the argument $\mathbf{r}$ in the subsequent use of $\phi(\mathbf{r})$, $\beta(\mathbf{r})$ and most other functions. We use ϕ to express the differential properties of the surface derived from the two concepts of Riemannian geometry, MT and CS, which we describe shortly.

Modeling NRSfM. We use a very similar model to [18], shown in Fig. 1. The goal of [18] was to solve for NRSfM with a calibrated camera but we also solve for the

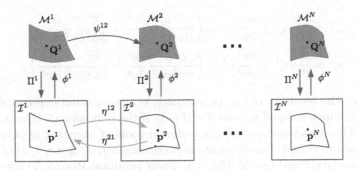

Fig. 1. Principal notations.

focal length. The model has N isometrically deforming surfaces $\mathcal{M}^1, \ldots, \mathcal{M}^N$ projected in the input images $\mathcal{I}^1, \ldots, \mathcal{I}^N$. The image warp η^{j1} represents the optic flow between $\mathcal{I}^j$ and $\mathcal{I}^1$. We have $\eta^{1j} = \left(\eta^{j1}\right)^{-1}$. We compute the warps from keypoint correspondences using [19]. The surfaces $\mathcal{M}^1$ and $\mathcal{M}^j$ are related by an isometric deformation function ψ^{1j}. Isometricity is the main constraint we use in SCIso-NRSfM.

Metric Tensor. Denoted $\mathbf{g}[\phi]$, the MT is a first-order differential quantity that describes physical surface properties such as lengths, angles and areas [16]. It can be derived from $\mathbf{J}_\phi$, the Jacobian of ϕ. Using ϕ from Eq. (1), $\mathbf{g}[\phi]$ is shown to be a 2×2 matrix given by:

$$\mathbf{g}[\phi] = \mathbf{J}_\phi^\top \mathbf{J}_\phi \text{ with } \mathbf{J}_\phi = \frac{1}{f\beta} \begin{pmatrix} 1 - u\zeta & -v\zeta & -f\zeta \\ -u\kappa & 1 - v\kappa & -f\kappa \end{pmatrix}^\top, \tag{2}$$

where we define the inverse-depth derivatives as $\beta_u = \frac{\partial \beta}{\partial u}$, $\beta_v = \frac{\partial \beta}{\partial v}$, and their ratio with the inverse-depth as $\zeta = \frac{\beta_u}{\beta}$, $\kappa = \frac{\beta_v}{\beta}$. For isometric surfaces, the MT is transferable across images using the first-order derivatives of the warps [18]:

$$\mathbf{g}[\phi^j] = \mathbf{J}_{\eta^{j1}}^\top \mathbf{g}[\phi^1] \mathbf{J}_{\eta^{j1}}. \tag{3}$$

Christoffel Symbols. Denoted $\mathbf{\Gamma}^u[\phi]$ and $\mathbf{\Gamma}^v[\phi]$, the CS are second-order differential quantities that describe the curvature of a surface [16]. They are defined as the rate of change of the MT. They usually have a very long and complex expression. This is however reduced using the infinitesimally planarity assumption, which allows one to neglect the second-order derivatives of the image embedding. This means that β in Eq. (1) is infinitesimally linear. Using ϕ from Eq. (1), $\mathbf{\Gamma}^u[\phi]$ and $\mathbf{\Gamma}^v[\phi]$ are shown to be 2×2 matrices given by:

$$\mathbf{\Gamma}^u[\phi] = -\begin{pmatrix} 2\zeta & \kappa \\ \kappa & 0 \end{pmatrix} \quad \mathbf{\Gamma}^v[\phi] = -\begin{pmatrix} 0 & \zeta \\ \zeta & 2\kappa \end{pmatrix}. \tag{4}$$

For isometric surfaces, the CS are transferable across images using the first- and second-order derivatives of the warps [18]:

$$\zeta^j = \frac{\partial u^1}{\partial u^2}\zeta^1 + \frac{\partial v^1}{\partial u^2}\kappa^1 - \left(\frac{\partial^2 u^1}{\partial u^2 \partial v^2}\frac{\partial v^2}{\partial u^1} + \frac{\partial^2 v^1}{\partial u^2 \partial v^2}\frac{\partial v^2}{\partial v^1}\right)$$

$$\kappa^j = \frac{\partial u^1}{\partial v^2}\zeta^1 + \frac{\partial v^1}{\partial v^2}\kappa^1 - \left(\frac{\partial^2 u^1}{\partial u^2 \partial v^2}\frac{\partial u^2}{\partial u^1} + \frac{\partial^2 v^1}{\partial u^2 \partial v^2}\frac{\partial u^2}{\partial v^1}\right). \tag{5}$$

Resultants. The resultant of two polynomials is a polynomial expression of their coefficients, which is equal to zero if and only if the polynomials have a common root [35]. This allows one to find the common roots of a system of polynomials. Consider as an example two bivariate polynomials $\alpha(t, u)$ and $\gamma(t, u)$ of degree l and m respectively and in variables t, u. Their resultant $\mathrm{Res}_t(\alpha, \gamma)$ with respect to t is a univariate polynomial in u. It is given as the determinant of the so-called Sylvester matrix $\mathbf{S}_t \in \mathbb{R}^{(l+m)\times(l+m)}$ as $\mathrm{Res}_t(\alpha, \gamma) = \det(\mathbf{S}_t)$. The elements of the Sylvester matrix depend on the coefficients of α, γ.

4   Self-Calibrating Isometric NRSfM

We first derive the reconstruction equations. These are constraints depending on two local shape variables and the focal length. We then show how these constraints can be optimized globally for just the focal length, and then locally for the shape.

4.1   The Reconstruction Equations

The reconstruction equations are built starting from the MT transfer Eq. (3). This equation involves the MT $\mathbf{g}[\phi^j]$, which is expressed in terms of the embedding's Jacobian $\mathbf{J}_{\phi^j}$ given by Eq. (2). The latter involves (ζ^j, κ^j), the ratios of inverse depth derivatives to inverse depth in image j. Because these are elements of the CS, we can express them in terms of the same ratios (ζ, κ) taken in image 1 using the CS transfer Eq. (5). We thus obtain a new expression of the MT $\mathbf{g}[\phi^j]$ depending on $(f, \beta^1, \beta^j, \zeta, \kappa)$. By substituting this expression in the MT transfer Eq. (3), we obtain a 2×2 matrix equation. Taking ratios, (β^1, β^j) vanish and we arrive at two independent algebraic PDEs $\mathcal{E}_{1,2}$ in (f, ζ, κ). These PDEs have coefficients (a_t^j, b_t^j) and are given by:

$$\mathcal{E}_1^j(f, \zeta, \kappa) = \sigma_7^j \zeta^3 + \sigma_5^j \zeta^2 + \sigma_3^j \zeta + \sigma_1^j \tag{6}$$

$$\mathcal{E}_2^j(f, \zeta, \kappa) = \sigma_8^j \zeta^3 + \sigma_6^j \zeta^2 + \sigma_4^j \zeta + \sigma_2^j, \tag{7}$$

with:

$$\sigma_1^j = a_{27}^j + a_{26}^j \kappa + a_{24}^j \kappa^2 + a_{21}^j \kappa^3 + s(a_{11}^j \kappa^3 + a_{14}^j \kappa^2 + a_{16}^j \kappa + a_{17}^j) + s^2(a_4^j \kappa^3 + a_7^j \kappa^2)$$

$$\sigma_2^j = b_{27}^j + b_{26}^j \kappa + b_{24}^j \kappa^2 + b_{21}^j \kappa^3 + s(b_{11}^j \kappa^3 + b_{14}^j \kappa^2 + b_{16}^j \kappa + b_{17}^j) + s^2(b_4^j \kappa^3 + b_7^j \kappa^2)$$

$$\sigma_3^j = a_{25}^j + a_{23}^j \kappa + a_{20}^j \kappa^2 + s(a_{10}^j \kappa^2 + a_{13}^j \kappa + a_{15}) + s^2(a_6^j \kappa + a_3^j \kappa^2)$$

$$\sigma_4^j = b_{25}^j + b_{23}^j \kappa + b_{20}^j \kappa^2 + s(b_{10}^j \kappa^2 + b_{13}^j \kappa + b_{15}) + s^2(b_6^j \kappa + b_3^j \kappa^2)$$

$$\sigma_5^j = a_{22}^j + a_{19}^j \kappa + s(a_{12}^j + a_9^j \kappa) + s^2(a_5^j + a_2^j \kappa) \quad \sigma_7^j = a_{18}^j + s a_8^j + s^2 a_1^j$$

$$\sigma_6^j = b_{22}^j + b_{19}^j \kappa + s(b_{12}^j + b_9^j \kappa) + s^2(b_5^j + b_2^j \kappa) \quad \sigma_8^j = b_{18}^j + s b_8^j + s^2 b_1^j \quad s = f^2.$$

The coefficients (a_t^j, b_t^j) directly depend on the derivatives of the warp η^{1j}. Choosing an image j, fixing a single point $\mathbf{r}$ and defining $k_1 = \zeta(\mathbf{r})$, $k_2 = \kappa(\mathbf{r})$, we obtain two algebraic equations $\mathcal{E}_{1,2}^j(f, k_1, k_2)$. For N images and a single point, we thus have a set of $2(N-1)$ polynomials $\mathfrak{E}_{12}(f, k_1, k_2) = \{\mathcal{E}_1^j(f, k_1, k_2), \mathcal{E}_2^j(f, k_1, k_2)\}_{j=2}^N$. Similar but simpler equations were obtained in [18] for a known focal length. These were then solved locally by minimizing their sum-of-squares using a computationally expensive polynomial optimization engine. This strategy cannot be used to estimate the focal length however, for two reasons. First, estimating the focal length locally would be extremely unstable. Second, the degree of the equations become prohibitive for the existing optimization engines. We next discuss our approach to obtain a global and tractable solution to f and a local solution to (k_1, k_2).

4.2 Solving for the Focal Length Globally

We show how to use the reconstruction equations $\mathfrak{E}_{12}(f, k_1, k_2)$ to find f globally. We use resultants to eliminate the dependency on (k_1, k_2), starting with k_1.

Eliminating k_1. The resultant of $\mathcal{E}_1^j, \mathcal{E}_2^j$ with respect to k_1 gives a new polynomial $\mathcal{E}_3^j$ depending on (f, k_2). Defining the Sylvester matrix $\mathbf{S}_{k_1} \in \mathbb{R}^{6\times6}$ as shown in Fig. 2 (left), we have:

$$\mathcal{E}_3^j(f, k_2) = \text{Res}_{k_1}(\mathcal{E}_1(f, k_1, k_2), \mathcal{E}_2(f, k_1, k_2), k_1) = \det(\mathbf{S}_{k_1})$$
$$= c_9^j k_2^9 + c_8^j k_2^8 + c_7^j k_2^7 + c_6^j k_2^6 + c_5^j k_2^5 + c_4^j k_2^4 + c_3^j k_2^3 + c_2^j k_2^2 + c_1^j k_2 + c_0^j, \tag{8}$$

where c_t^j are polynomials of degree 12 in $s = f^2$. Numerically, they are often of degree 3 or 4. For N images, we thus obtain $N - 1$ polynomial equations $\mathfrak{E}_3(f, k_2) = \{\mathcal{E}_3^j(f, k_2)\}_{j=2}^N$.

Eliminating k_2. We eliminate k_2 by evaluating the resultant of the equation for two image pairs, $(1, j)$ and $(1, r)$, in $\mathfrak{E}_3$. This gives a new polynomial equation $\mathcal{E}_4^{jr}$ depending on f only. Defining the Sylvester matrix $\mathbf{S}_{k_2} \in \mathbb{R}^{18\times18}$ as shown in Fig. 2 (right), we have:

$$\mathcal{E}_4^{jr}(f) = \text{Res}_{k_2}(\mathcal{E}_3^j, \mathcal{E}_3^r) = \det(\mathbf{S}_{k_2}). \tag{9}$$

For N images, we obtain $\frac{(N-1)(N-2)}{2}$ univariate polynomial equations $\mathfrak{E}_4(f) = \{\mathcal{E}_4^{jr}(f)\}_{j,r\in[2,N], j\neq r}$ of degree 216. Since c_t^j in Eq. (8) are numerically of degree 3 or 4, the degree of these polynomials lies between 54–72 instead of 216.

Solving for f. A globally optimal solution can be found by minimizing the sum-of-squares of the equation set $\mathfrak{E}_4$. For n points tracked over N images, we

$$
\begin{pmatrix}
\sigma_7^j & \sigma_5^j & \sigma_3^j & \sigma_1^j & 0 & 0 \\
0 & \sigma_7^j & \sigma_5^j & \sigma_3^j & \sigma_1^j & 0 \\
0 & 0 & \sigma_7^j & \sigma_5^j & \sigma_3^j & \sigma_1^j \\
\sigma_8^j & \sigma_6^j & \sigma_4^j & \sigma_2^j & 0 & 0 \\
0 & \sigma_8^j & \sigma_6^j & \sigma_4^j & \sigma_2^j & 0 \\
0 & 0 & \sigma_8^j & \sigma_6^j & \sigma_4^j & \sigma_2^j
\end{pmatrix}
$$

$$
\begin{pmatrix}
c_9^j & c_8^j & c_7^j & c_6^j & c_5^j & c_4^j & c_3^j & c_2^j & c_1^j & c_0^j & 0 & 0 & 0 & 0 & 0 & 0 & 0 & 0 & 0 \\
0 & c_9^j & c_8^j & c_7^j & c_6^j & c_5^j & c_4^j & c_3^j & c_2^j & c_1^j & c_0^j & 0 & 0 & 0 & 0 & 0 & 0 & 0 & 0 \\
0 & 0 & c_9^j & c_8^j & c_7^j & c_6^j & c_5^j & c_4^j & c_3^j & c_2^j & c_1^j & c_0^j & 0 & 0 & 0 & 0 & 0 & 0 & 0 \\
0 & 0 & 0 & c_9^j & c_8^j & c_7^j & c_6^j & c_5^j & c_4^j & c_3^j & c_2^j & c_1^j & c_0^j & 0 & 0 & 0 & 0 & 0 & 0 \\
0 & 0 & 0 & 0 & c_9^j & c_8^j & c_7^j & c_6^j & c_5^j & c_4^j & c_3^j & c_2^j & c_1^j & c_0^j & 0 & 0 & 0 & 0 & 0 \\
0 & 0 & 0 & 0 & 0 & c_9^j & c_8^j & c_7^j & c_6^j & c_5^j & c_4^j & c_3^j & c_2^j & c_1^j & c_0^j & 0 & 0 & 0 & 0 \\
0 & 0 & 0 & 0 & 0 & 0 & c_9^j & c_8^j & c_7^j & c_6^j & c_5^j & c_4^j & c_3^j & c_2^j & c_1^j & c_0^j & 0 & 0 & 0 \\
0 & 0 & 0 & 0 & 0 & 0 & 0 & c_9^j & c_8^j & c_7^j & c_6^j & c_5^j & c_4^j & c_3^j & c_2^j & c_1^j & c_0^j & 0 & 0 \\
0 & 0 & 0 & 0 & 0 & 0 & 0 & 0 & c_9^j & c_8^j & c_7^j & c_6^j & c_5^j & c_4^j & c_3^j & c_2^j & c_1^j & c_0^j & 0 \\
c_9^r & c_8^r & c_7^r & c_6^r & c_5^r & c_4^r & c_3^r & c_2^r & c_1^r & c_0^r & 0 & 0 & 0 & 0 & 0 & 0 & 0 & 0 & 0 \\
0 & c_9^r & c_8^r & c_7^r & c_6^r & c_5^r & c_4^r & c_3^r & c_2^r & c_1^r & c_0^r & 0 & 0 & 0 & 0 & 0 & 0 & 0 & 0 \\
0 & 0 & c_9^r & c_8^r & c_7^r & c_6^r & c_5^r & c_4^r & c_3^r & c_2^r & c_1^r & c_0^r & 0 & 0 & 0 & 0 & 0 & 0 & 0 \\
0 & 0 & 0 & c_9^r & c_8^r & c_7^r & c_6^r & c_5^r & c_4^r & c_3^r & c_2^r & c_1^r & c_0^r & 0 & 0 & 0 & 0 & 0 & 0 \\
0 & 0 & 0 & 0 & c_9^r & c_8^r & c_7^r & c_6^r & c_5^r & c_4^r & c_3^r & c_2^r & c_1^r & c_0^r & 0 & 0 & 0 & 0 & 0 \\
0 & 0 & 0 & 0 & 0 & c_9^r & c_8^r & c_7^r & c_6^r & c_5^r & c_4^r & c_3^r & c_2^r & c_1^r & c_0^r & 0 & 0 & 0 & 0 \\
0 & 0 & 0 & 0 & 0 & 0 & c_9^r & c_8^r & c_7^r & c_6^r & c_5^r & c_4^r & c_3^r & c_2^r & c_1^r & c_0^r & 0 & 0 & 0 \\
0 & 0 & 0 & 0 & 0 & 0 & 0 & c_9^r & c_8^r & c_7^r & c_6^r & c_5^r & c_4^r & c_3^r & c_2^r & c_1^r & c_0^r & 0 & 0 \\
0 & 0 & 0 & 0 & 0 & 0 & 0 & 0 & c_9^r & c_8^r & c_7^r & c_6^r & c_5^r & c_4^r & c_3^r & c_2^r & c_1^r & c_0^r & 0 \\
0 & 0 & 0 & 0 & 0 & 0 & 0 & 0 & c_9^r & c_8^r & c_7^r & c_6^r & c_5^r & c_4^r & c_3^r & c_2^r & c_1^r & c_0^r
\end{pmatrix}
$$

Fig. 2. The Sylvester matrices $\mathbf{S}_{k_1}$ (left) and $\mathbf{S}_{k_2}$ (right).

define the sum-of-squares cost as:

$$
C(f) = \sum_{i=1}^{n} \sum_{j=2}^{N} \sum_{\substack{r=2 \\ r \neq j}}^{N} \left(\mathcal{E}_4^{jr}(f) \right)^2. \tag{10}
$$

Using Fermat's interior extremum theorem, a local extrema of C occurs at the critical points, obtained by solving $\frac{\partial C}{\partial f}(f) = 0$. The set of critical points is given by $\mathfrak{F}_c = \{ f_c \mid \frac{\partial C}{\partial f}(f_c) = 0 \}$. In practice, the cost function C is a univariate polynomial of degree 108–144. We simply find the roots of its derivative polynomial to find $\mathfrak{F}_c$. The local minima are the critical points with a positive value of $\frac{\partial^2 C}{\partial f^2}$. Therefore the set of local minima $\mathfrak{F}_l \subset \mathfrak{F}_c$ is given by $\mathfrak{F}_l = \{ f_l \in \mathfrak{F}_c \mid \frac{\partial^2 C}{\partial f^2}(f_l) > 0 \}$. Finally, the globally optimal focal length is given by:

$$
\hat{f} = \arg \min_{f \in \mathfrak{F}_l} C(f). \tag{11}
$$

4.3   Solving for the Local Shape

We show how the local shape, represented by (k_1, k_2), can be solved for given an estimate $\hat{f}$ of the focal length, starting with k_2. Given $\hat{f}$, we have that $\mathfrak{E}_3(\hat{f}, k_2)$ forms a set of univariate polynomials in k_2. We find the optimal solution for k_2 by minimizing the sum-of-squares of these polynomials. For a point tracked over N images, the cost is:

$$C'(k_2) = \sum_{j=2}^{N} \left(\mathcal{E}_3^j(\hat{f}, k_2) \right)^2. \tag{12}$$

Because C' is a univariate polynomial, we find its minimum using the same process as described in the previous section for minimizing C. The optimal solution $\hat{k}_2$ is thus:

$$\hat{k}_2 = \arg \min_{k_2 \in \mathfrak{K}_2} C'(k_2) \text{ where } \mathfrak{K}_2 = \left\{ k_2 \,\middle|\, \frac{\partial C'}{\partial k_2}(k_2) = 0, \frac{\partial^2 C'}{\partial k_2^2}(k_2) > 0 \right\}. \tag{13}$$

Using $(\hat{f}, \hat{k}_2)$, we have that $\mathfrak{E}_{12}(\hat{f}, k_1, \hat{k}_2)$ forms a set of univariate polynomials in k_1. We find the optimal solution for k_1 by minimizing the sum-of-squares of these polynomials. For a point tracked over N images, the cost is:

$$C''(k_1) = \sum_{j=2}^{N} \left(\mathcal{E}_1(\hat{f}, k_1, \hat{k}_2) \right)^2 + \left(\mathcal{E}_2(\hat{f}, k_1, \hat{k}_2) \right)^2. \tag{14}$$

The optimal $\hat{k}_1$ is then:

$$\hat{k}_1 = \arg \min_{k_1 \in \mathfrak{K}_1} C''(k_1) \text{ where } \mathfrak{K}_1 = \left\{ k_1 \,\middle|\, \frac{\partial C''}{\partial k_1}(k_1) = 0, \frac{\partial^2 C''}{\partial k_1^2}(k_1) > 0 \right\}. \tag{15}$$

We arrive at an estimate $\left(\hat{k}_1, \hat{k}_2 \right)$ of the local shape for the reference image. By substituting this estimate in Eq. (5), we obtain an estimate $\left(\hat{k}_1^j, \hat{k}_2^j \right)$ of the local shape for the rest of the images.

5   Algorithm

We give our algorithm to solve SCIso-NRSfM. For numerical stability, as commonly done in SfM [12], the points' pixel coordinates are standardized using an isotropic scale factor mapping the image boundaries close to $[-1,1]^2$.

Inputs: Point correspondences $\{\mathbf{p}_i^j\}$ with visibility indicators $\{v_i^j\}$, $i \in [1,n]$, $j \in [1,N]$ ($v_i^j = 1$ means that the ith point is visible in the jth image)

(1) *Compute image warps* η^{j1}, $j \in [2, N]$. Use the points visible in the reference and jth images, meaning with indexes $\{i \in [1,n] \mid v_i^1 = v_i^j = 1\}$, to estimate the warp η^{j1} using [19].
(2) *Compute the optimal global solution to* f. Find $\hat{f}$ that minimizes C in Eq. (10).
(3) *Compute the optimal local shape* (k_1, k_2). Using the $\hat{f}$ obtained in the previous step, find $\hat{k}_2$ that minimizes C' in Eq. (12). Then, use $(\hat{f}, \hat{k}_2)$ to find $\hat{k}_1$ that minimizes C'' in Eq. (14).

(4) *Find normals and 3D points.* Find the Jacobian $\mathbf{J}_\phi$ in terms of $(\hat{k}_1, \hat{k}_2)$ using Eq. (2). Compute the surface normals $\hat{\mathbf{N}}_i^j$ by normalizing the cross-product of the Jacobians columns. Find the inverse depth β^{-1} by integrating the normals using the method in [18]. Apply the embedding ϕ from Eq. (1) to recover the points $\hat{\mathbf{Q}}_i^j$.

Outputs: Points $\{\hat{\mathbf{Q}}_i^j\}$, normals $\{\hat{\mathbf{N}}_i^j\}$, $i \in [1, n]$, $j \in [1, N]$, focal length $\hat{f}$.

6 Experiments

We tested SCIso-NRSfM (**SCIso**) on a synthetic *Cylinder* dataset [18] and two real datasets, namely *T-shirt* [4] and *Paper* [32] showing objects deforming isometrically. Since self-calibration has not yet been dealt within NRSfM, we compare SCIso-NRSfM with NRSfM methods that assume perspective projection and use calibrated data, **Pa17** [18] and **Ch17** [5]. Also, we compare against methods that assume orthographic projection and avoid the calibration, **Go11** [9] and **Vi12** [34]. For quantitative comparison, we measured the mean shape error (RMSE between computed and ground truth normals in degrees) and the 3D error (RMSE between computed and ground truth 3D points in mm).

Cylinder Dataset. This dataset contains randomly generated views of a cylindrical surface deforming isometrically. The cylindrical surface has a radius varying between 2 and 10. The image size is 640×480 px and the camera focal length is 540 px. The number of point correspondences is 400. We vary the number of images and correspondence noise. We compared all methods except **Go11**

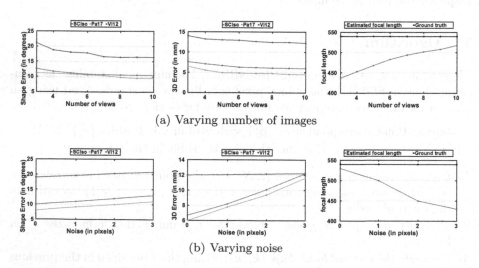

(a) Varying number of images

(b) Varying noise

Fig. 3. Results for the *Cylinder* dataset. Mean shape and 3D errors are shown against a varying number of images and noise level. The estimated and true focal lengths are also shown. Best viewed in color. (Color figure online)

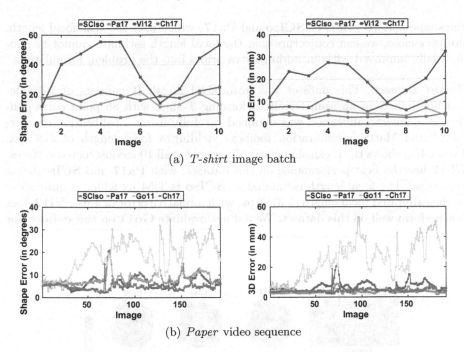

(a) *T-shirt* image batch

(b) *Paper* video sequence

Fig. 4. Results for the *T-shirt* and *Paper* datasets. Mean shape and 3D errors are shown. Best viewed in color. (Color figure online)

and **Ch17**. This is because **Go11** uses the low-rank model and requires a large number of images with short baseline and **Ch17** simply failed on this dataset. Figure 3a shows the mean shape and 3D errors for reconstructions performed with 3–10 images. The correspondence noise is chosen to follow a gaussian distribution with standard deviation of 1 px. The performance of **SCIso** is very similar to **Pa17** which solves NRSfM with a calibrated camera, which means using the true focal length, though **Pa17** performs slightly better. On increasing the number of images, all methods tend to obtain better results. The performance of **SCIso** and **Pa17** stabilizes with 5 images. However they yield a good reconstruction with 3 images as well. Therefore, they efficiently solve the minimal case. The estimation of focal length in **SCIso** improves with the number of images. For 8–10 images, it is very close to the true focal length. **Vi12** uses an orthographic camera model. Its performance is significantly worse than **SCIso** and **Pa17**.

Figure 3b shows the mean shape and 3D errors for reconstructions performed with 10 images by varying the noise between 0–3 px. The performance of **SCIso** is, again, very similar to **Pa17**, with **Pa17** performing slightly better. On increasing the noise, they both tend to degrade linearly. Interestingly, **Vi12** is barely affected by the noise in the tested range, however, its performance is consistently significantly worse than the other methods. The estimation of focal length in **SCIso** degrades with noise, though remaining reasonable. Interestingly, because the shape and 3D errors of **SCIso** and **Pa17**, which uses the true focal length, are very close, we can conjecture that the focal length estimate cannot be substantially improved without adding extra priors into the problem formulation.

T-shirt Dataset. This dataset was introduced in [4]. It consists of 10 wide-baseline images of an isometrically deforming T-shirt with 85 point correspondences. Camera calibration was obtained carefully using a calibration checkerboard and Matlab's calibration toolbox, yielding a focal length of 3780 px. Figure 4(a) shows the mean shape and 3D errors for all 10 reconstructed surfaces. **Ch17** has the best performance on this dataset, with **Pa17** and **SCIso** being very close. The focal length estimated by **SCIso** is 3954 px which is quite close to the calibrated focal length of 3780 px, with a relative error of 4.6%. **Vi12** does not perform well on this dataset. We did not evaluate **Go11** on this dataset, for the same reason as on the *Cylinder* dataset. Figure 5 shows the renderings of the error maps and textured reconstructed shape for two images.

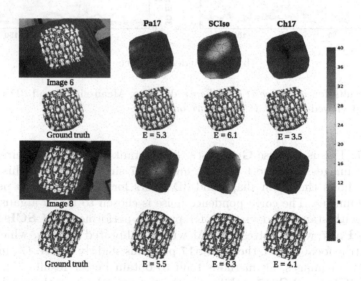

Fig. 5. Error maps and textured rendering of the reconstructed shape for two images of the *T-shirt* dataset. E is mean 3D error (in mm). Best viewed in color. (Color figure online)

Paper Dataset. This dataset was introduced in [32]. It consists of 191 images from a video sequence with 1500 point correspondences of a paper deforming isometrically. Camera calibration obtained from standard methods is provided, with a focal length of 528 px. Figure 4b shows the mean shape and 3D errors for all the 191 reconstructed surfaces. **Ch17** has the best performance on this dataset, with **Pa17** and **SCIso** being very close. The focal length estimated by **SCIso** using the first 10 images is 498 px, which is close to the actual focal length

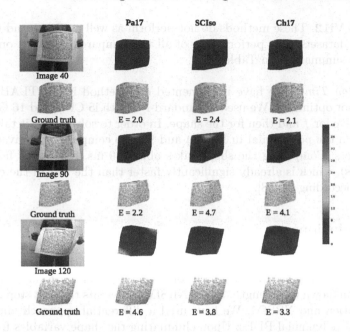

Fig. 6. Error maps and textured rendering of the reconstructed shape for three images of the *Paper* dataset. E is mean 3D error (in mm). Best viewed in color. (Color figure online)

of 528 px, with a relative error of 5.7%. **Go11** did not perform as well as the other methods. This may be explained by the fact that it uses an orthographic camera or because it is based on the low rank shape model. We could not evaluate **Vi12** on this dataset because of its prohibitive computation time. Figure 6 shows the renderings of the error maps and textured reconstructed shape for three images.

Summary of Experiments. We compared **SCIso** on a synthetic and two real datasets. We found it to be performing very closely to the current state-of-the-art NRSfM methods, namely **Pa17** and **Ch17**, that use a calibrated perspective camera. **SCIso** estimates the focal length to a good relative accuracy. We also compared with two NRSfM methods that use the orthographic camera, namely

Table 1. Summary of results on the *T-shirt* and *Paper* datasets. Es and Ep represent mean shape and 3D error respectively. %f denotes the relative error in focal length compared to the calibrated focal length serving as ground truth. xx represents values which could not be computed, as explained in the main text.

	SCIso			Pa17		Ch17		Go17		Vi12	
	Es	Ep	%f	Es	Ep	Es	Ep	Es	Ep	Es	Ep
T-shirt	19.1	8.9	4.6	15.8	4.7	6.1	3.5	xx	xx	37.8	20.6
Paper	9.6	7.1	5.7	6.2	3.8	4.8	4.3	18.6	24.7	xx	xx

Go11 and **Vi12**. These methods do not perform as well as **Pa17** and **Ch17** on the tested datasets. The performance of all the compared methods on the real datasets is summarized in Table 1.

Computation Time. We have implemented our method in MATLAB and the code was not optimized. We used a standard PC with i5 CPU and 16 GB RAM. We first solve for f and then for the shape. In order to solve for f, it takes about 76 s to form the polynomial in Eq. (9) and 90 s to compute its derivatives and find its roots. Computing the shape takes about 10 ms. It is much faster than Pa17 (1.5 s), which is already significantly faster than the rest of the compared methods, according to [18].

7   Conclusions

We have presented SCIso-NRSfM, a theory and an algorithm to reconstruct an isometrically deforming object from monocular uncalibrated images with constant but unknown focal length. SCIso-NRSfM represents the first step in joining self-calibration and NRSfM. We have used a differential approach and derived a system of polynomial PDEs. Upon eliminating the shape variables from these using resultants, we have then showed that the focal length could be recovered optimally by globally minimizing the constraints arising from all correspondences and all images in a single least-squares cost. Our experimental results have shown that SCIso-NRSfM compares very favorably to existing calibrated NRSfM algorithms against the number of images and correspondence noise, and recovers the focal length with a relative error of a few percents. They have also shown that SCIso-NRSfM works well for the minimal case of three images and improved with the number of images.

We finally give two possible lines of future research. First, in SfM, for rigid objects, there exist Critical Motion Sequences (CMS) [15, 27] in which case self-calibration cannot be resolved. These typically happen when the camera motion is not general enough, for instance when all optical axes intersect. The possible existence of CMS in SCIso-NRSfM is then a very natural question. In the deformable case however, the question must be addressed by considering the pose of the local surface with respect to the camera. In other words, there is not a unique pose for each image, but a continuously varying pose across the surface. This diversity seems to play in favor of dramatically reducing the chance of encountering a degenerate case in SCIso-NRSfM. Nonetheless, this is something we intend to thoroughly study in the near future. The second possible line of future research is to exploit SCIso-NRSfM in plane-based self-calibration. Almost all existing methods, such as [10], take as input a set of homographies relating the input images. It is well known that, when the observed plane is smaller in an image, the computed homography may be unstable. Interestingly, SCIso-NRSfM does not require homographies as inputs but uses the assumption of IP, which suggests that it forms differential constraints for infinitesimal planes. How these constraints relate to the absolute conic formalism now widely accepted in self-calibration and whether these constraints may aid plane-based self-calibration are profound questions which we indeed to study in the near future.

Acknowledgments. This research has received funding from the EU's FP7 through the ERC research grant 307483 FLEXABLE, the Spanish Ministry of Economy, Industry and Competitiveness under project ARTEMISA (TIN2016-80939- R) and the University of Alcalá, Spain under the project SEQUENCE (CCGP2017-EXP/048).

References

1. Bartoli, A., Gérard, Y., Chadebecq, F., Collins, T., Pizarro, D.: Shape-from-template. IEEE Trans. Pattern Anal. Mach. Intell. **37**(10), 2099–2118 (2015)
2. Bartoli, A., Pizarro, D., Collins, T.: A robust analytical solution to isometric shape-from-template with focal length calibration. In: ICCV (2013)
3. Bregler, C., Hertzmann, A., Biermann, H.: Recovering non-rigid 3D shape from image streams. In: CVPR (2000)
4. Chhatkuli, A., Pizarro, D., Bartoli, A.: Non-rigid shape-from-motion for isometric surfaces using infinitesimal planarity. In: BMVC (2014)
5. Chhatkuli, A., Pizarro, D., Collins, T., Bartoli, A.: Inextensible non-rigid structure-from-motion by second-order cone programming. IEEE Trans. Pattern Anal. Mach. Intell. 1 (2017)
6. Dai, Y., Li, H., He, M.: A simple prior-free method for non-rigid structure-from-motion factorization. Int. J. Comput. Vis. **107**(2), 101–122 (2014)
7. Del Bue, A., Smeraldi, F., Agapito, L.: Non-rigid structure from motion using non-parametric tracking and non-linear optimization. In: CVPRW (2004)
8. Faugeras, O.D., Luong, Q.-T., Maybank, S.J.: Camera self-calibration: theory and experiments. In: Sandini, G. (ed.) ECCV 1992. LNCS, vol. 588, pp. 321–334. Springer, Heidelberg (1992). https://doi.org/10.1007/3-540-55426-2_37
9. Gotardo, P., Martinez, A.: Kernel non-rigid structure from motion. In: ICCV (2011)
10. Gurdjos, P., Sturm, P.: Methods and geometry for plane-based self-calibration. In: CVPR (2003)
11. Hartley, R.I.: Self-calibration from multiple views with a rotating camera. In: Eklundh, J.-O. (ed.) ECCV 1994. LNCS, vol. 800, pp. 471–478. Springer, Heidelberg (1994). https://doi.org/10.1007/3-540-57956-7_52
12. Hartley, R.I., Zisserman, A.: Multiple View Geometry in Computer Vision. Cambridge University Press, New York (2000). ISBN: 0521623049
13. Henrion, D., Lasserre, J.B.: GloptiPoly: global optimization over polynomials with Matlab and SeDuMi. ACM Trans. Math. Softw. **29**(2), 165–194 (2003)
14. Heyden, A., Astrom, K.: Euclidean reconstruction from constant intrinsic parameters. In: ICPR (1996)
15. Kahl, F., Triggs, B., Astrom, A.: Critical motions for auto-calibration when some intrinsic parameters can vary. J. Math. Image Vis. **13**(2), 131–146 (2000)
16. Lee, J.: Riemannian manifolds : an introduction to curvature. Springer, New York (1997). https://doi.org/10.1007/b98852
17. Lladó, X., Del Bue, A., Agapito, L.: Non-rigid metric reconstruction from perspective cameras. Image Vis. Comput. **28**(9), 1339–1353 (2010)
18. Parashar, S., Pizarro, D., Bartoli, A.: Isometric non-rigid shape-from-motion with Riemannian geometry solved in linear time. IEEE Trans. Pattern Anal. Mach. Intell. (2017)

19. Pizarro, D., Khan, R., Bartoli, A.: Schwarps: locally projective image warps based on 2D schwarzian derivatives. Int. J. Comput. Vis. **119**(2), 93–109 (2016)
20. Pollefeys, M., Koch, R., Van Gool, L.: Self-calibration and metric reconstruction in spite of varying and unknown internal camera parameters. In: ICCV (1998)
21. Pollefeys, M., Van Gool, L.: Stratified self-calibration with the modulus constraint. IEEE Trans. Pattern Anal. Mach. Intell. **21**(8), 707–724 (1999)
22. Ramachandran, M., Veeraraghavan, A., Chellappa, R.: A fast bilinear structure from motion algorithm using a video sequence and inertial sensors. IEEE Trans. Pattern Anal. Mach. Intell. **33**(1), 186–193 (2011)
23. Ramalingam, S., Lodha, S., Sturm, P.: A generic structure-from-motion framework. Comput. Vis. Image Underst. **103**(1), 218–228 (2006)
24. Russell, C., Yu, R., Agapito, L.: Video pop-up: monocular 3D reconstruction of dynamic scenes. In: Fleet, D., Pajdla, T., Schiele, B., Tuytelaars, T. (eds.) ECCV 2014. LNCS, vol. 8695, pp. 583–598. Springer, Cham (2014). https://doi.org/10.1007/978-3-319-10584-0_38
25. Salzmann, M., Fua, P.: Linear local models for monocular reconstruction of deformable surfaces. IEEE Trans. Pattern Anal. Mach. Intell. **33**(5), 931–944 (2011)
26. Snavely, N., Seitz, S.M., Szeliski, R.: Modeling the world from internet photo collections. Int. J. Comput. Vis. **80**(1), 189–210 (2008)
27. Sturm, P.: Critical motion sequences for monocular self- calibration and uncalibrated Euclidean reconstruction. In: CVPR (1997)
28. Taylor, J., Jepson, A.D., Kutulakos, K.N.: Non-rigid structure from locally-rigid motion. In: CVPR (2010)
29. Tomasi, C., Kanade, T.: Shape and motion from image streams under orthography: a factorization method. Int. J. Comput. Vis. **9**(2), 137–154 (1992)
30. Torresani, L., Hertzmann, A., Bregler, C.: Nonrigid structure-from-motion: estimating shape and motion with hierarchical priors. IEEE Trans. Pattern Anal. Mach. Intell. **30**(5), 878–892 (2008)
31. Triggs, B.: Autocalibration and the absolute quadric. In: CVPR (1997)
32. Varol, A., Salzmann, M., Fua, P., Urtasun, R.: A constrained latent variable model. In: CVPR (2012)
33. Varol, A., Salzmann, M., Tola, E., Fua, P.: Template-free monocular reconstruction of deformable surfaces. In: ICCV (2009)
34. Vicente, S., Agapito, L.: Soft inextensibility constraints for template-free non-rigid reconstruction. In: Fitzgibbon, A., Lazebnik, S., Perona, P., Sato, Y., Schmid, C. (eds.) ECCV 2012. LNCS, vol. 7574, pp. 426–440. Springer, Heidelberg (2012). https://doi.org/10.1007/978-3-642-33712-3_31
35. Van der Waerden, B.L.: Modern Algebra. Springer, New York (2003)

Semi-supervised Deep Learning with Memory

Yanbei Chen[1($\boxtimes$)], Xiatian Zhu[2], and Shaogang Gong[1]

[1] Queen Mary University of London, London, UK
{yanbei.chen,s.gong}@qmul.ac.uk
[2] Vision Semantics Ltd., London, UK
eddy@visionsemantics.com

Abstract. We consider the semi-supervised multi-class classification problem of learning from sparse labelled and abundant unlabelled training data. To address this problem, existing semi-supervised deep learning methods often rely on the up-to-date "network-in-training" to formulate the semi-supervised learning objective. This ignores both the discriminative feature representation and the model inference uncertainty revealed by the network in the preceding learning iterations, referred to as the *memory* of model learning. In this work, we propose a novel Memory-Assisted Deep Neural Network (MA-DNN) capable of exploiting the memory of model learning to enable semi-supervised learning. Specifically, we introduce a memory mechanism into the network training process as an *assimilation-accommodation interaction* between the network and an external memory module. Experiments demonstrate the advantages of the proposed MA-DNN model over the state-of-the-art semi-supervised deep learning methods on three image classification benchmark datasets: SVHN, CIFAR10, and CIFAR100.

Keywords: Semi-supervised learning · Neural network with memory

1 Introduction

Semi-supervised learning (SSL) aims to boost the model performance by utilising the large amount of unlabelled data when only a limited amount of labelled data is available [4,37]. It is motivated that unlabelled data are available at large scale but labelled data are scarce due to high labelling costs. This learning scheme is useful and beneficial for many applications such as image search [6], web-page classification [2], document retrieval [21], genomics [29], and so forth. In the SSL literature, the most straightforward SSL algorithm is self-training where the target model is incrementally trained by additional self-labelled data given

---

Electronic supplementary material The online version of this chapter (https://doi.org/10.1007/978-3-030-01246-5_17) contains supplementary material, which is available to authorized users.

© Springer Nature Switzerland AG 2018
V. Ferrari et al. (Eds.): ECCV 2018, LNCS 11205, pp. 275–291, 2018.
https://doi.org/10.1007/978-3-030-01246-5_17

by the model's own predictions with high confidence [2,21,25]. This method is prone to error propagation in model learning due to wrong predictions of high confidence. Other common methods include Transductive SVM [3,10] and graph-based methods [1,39], which, however, are likely to suffer from poor scalability to large-scale unlabelled data due to inefficient optimisation.

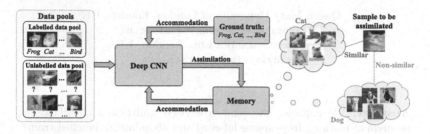

Fig. 1. Illustration of the memory-assisted semi-supervised deep learning framework that integrates a deep CNN with an external memory module trained concurrently. The memory module assimilates the incoming training data on-the-fly and generates an additional unsupervised memory loss to guide the network learning along with the standard supervised classification loss.

Recently, neural network based SSL methods [9,12,15,16,19,23,24,26,30,32, 35] start to dominate the progress due to the powerful representation-learning ability of deep neural networks. Most of these methods typically utilise the up-to-date in-training network to formulate the additional unsupervised penalty so as to enable semi-supervised learning. We consider that this kind of deep SSL scheme is sub-optimal provided that the memorising capacity of deep networks is often incomplete and insufficiently compartmentalised to represent knowledge accrued in the past learning iterations [34]. To effectively leverage such knowledge, we introduce a memory mechanism into the deep network training process to enable semi-supervised learning from small-sized labelled and large-sized unlabelled training data. In spirit of the Piaget's theory on human's ability of *continual learning* [7], we aim to design a SSL scheme that permits the deep model to additionally learn from its memory (*assimilation*) and adjust itself to fit optimally the incoming training data (*accommodation*) in an incremental manner. To this end, we formulate a novel memory-assisted semi-supervised deep learning framework: Memory-Assisted Deep Neural Network (MA-DNN) as illustrated in Fig. 1. MA-DNN is characterised by an assimilation-accommodation interaction between the network and an external memory module.

The key to our framework design is two-aspect: (1) the class-level discriminative feature representation and the network inference uncertainty are gradually accumulated in an external memory module; (2) this memorised information is utilised to assimilate the newly incoming image samples on-the-fly and generate an informative unsupervised memory loss to guide the network learning jointly with the supervised classification loss.

Our contribution is two-fold: (1) We propose to exploit the *memory* of model learning to enable semi-supervised deep learning from the sparse labelled and abundant unlabelled training data, whilst fully adopting the existing end-to-end training process. This is in contrast to most existing deep SSL methods that typically ignore the memory of model learning. (2) We formulate a novel *Memory-Assisted Deep Neural Network* (MA-DNN) characterised by a memory mechanism. We introduce an unsupervised memory loss compatible with the standard supervised classification loss to enable semi-supervised learning. Extensive comparative experiments demonstrate the advantages of our proposed MA-DNN model over a wide variety of state-of-the-art semi-supervised deep learning methods.

2   Related Works

Semi-supervised deep learning has recently gained increasing attraction due to the strong generalisation power of deep neural networks [12,14,15,19,24,30, 35]. A common strategy is to train the deep neural networks by simultaneously optimising a standard supervised classification loss on labelled samples along with an additional unsupervised loss term imposed on either unlabelled data [5,15,27] or both labelled and unlabelled data [14,19,24,35]. These additional loss terms are considered as *unsupervised* supervision signals, since ground-truth label is not necessarily required to derive the loss values. For example, Lee [15] utilises the cross-entropy loss computed on the pseudo labels (the classes with the maximum predicted probability given by the up-to-date network) of unlabelled samples as an additional supervision signal. Rasmus et al. [24] adopt the reconstruction loss between one clean forward propagation and one stochastically-corrupted forward propagation derived for the same sample. Miyato et al. [19] define the distributional smoothness against local random perturbation as an unsupervised penalty. Laine et al. [14] introduce an unsupervised L_2 loss to penalise the inconsistency between the network predictions and the temporally ensembled network predictions. Overall, the rationale of these SSL algorithms is to regularise the network by enforcing smooth and consistent classification boundaries that are robust to random perturbation [19,24]; or to enrich the supervision signals by exploiting the knowledge learned by the network, such as using the pseudo labels [15] or the temporally ensembled predictions [14].

Whilst sharing the generic spirit of introducing an unsupervised penalty, our method is unique in a number of fundamental ways: (i) Exploiting the memory of model learning: Instead of relying on the incomplete knowledge of a single up-to-date network to derive the additional loss [15], we employ a memory module to derive a memory loss based on the cumulative class-level feature representation and model inference uncertainty aggregated all through the preceding training iterations. (ii) Low computational cost: By utilising the memory mechanism, only one network forward propagation is required to compute the additional loss term for training the network, as opposed to more than one forward propagations required by other models [19,24]. (iii) Low consumption of memory footprint:

Instead of storing all the predictions of all training samples in a large mapped file [14], our online updated memory module consumes very limited memory footprint, therefore potentially more scalable to training data of larger scale.

Neural networks with memory are recently introduced to enable more powerful learning and reasoning ability for addressing several challenging tasks, such as question answering [18,31,34] and one-shot learning [11,28]. Augmenting a network with an external memory component is attractive due to its flexible capability of storing, abstracting and organising the past knowledge into a structural and addressable form. As earlier works, Weston et al. [34] propose Memory Networks, which integrate inference components with a memory component that can be read and written to remember supporting facts from the past for question answering. Kaiser et al. [11] propose a life-long memory module to record network activations of rare events for one-shot learning. Our work is conceptually inspired by these works, but it is the first attempt to explore the memory mechanism in semi-supervised deep learning. Besides the basic storage functionality, our memory module induces an assimilation-accommodation interaction to exploit the memory of model learning and generate an informative unsupervised memory loss that permits semi-supervised learning.

3   Memory-Assisted Deep Neural Network

We consider semi-supervised deep learning in the context of multi-class image classification. In this context, we have access to a limited amount of labelled image samples $\mathcal{D}_L = \{(I_{i,l}, y_{i,l})\}_i^{n_l}$ but an abundant amount of unlabelled image samples $\mathcal{D}_U = \{(I_{i,u})\}_i^{n_u}$, where $n_u \gg n_l$. Each unlabelled image is assumed to belong to one of the same K object categories (classes) $\mathcal{Y} = \{y_i\}_i^K$ as the labelled data, while their ground-truth labels are not available for training. The key objective of SSL is to enhance the model performance by learning from the labelled image data $\mathcal{D}_L$ and the additional unlabelled image data $\mathcal{D}_U$ simultaneously. To that end, we formulate a memory-assisted semi-supervised deep learning framework that integrates a deep neural network with a memory module, We call this *Memory-Assisted Deep Neural Network* (MA-DNN).

3.1   Approach Overview

The overall design of our MA-DNN architecture is depicted in Fig. 2. The proposed MA-DNN contains three parts: **(1)** A deep neural network (Sect. 3.2); **(2)** A memory module designed to record the memory of model learning (Sect. 3.3); and **(3)** An assimilation-accommodation interaction mechanism introduced for effectively exploiting the memory to facilitate the network optimisation in semi-supervised learning (Sect. 3.4).

3.2   Conventional Deep Neural Network

The proposed framework aims to work with existing standard deep neural networks. We select the Convolutional Neural Network (CNN) in this work due

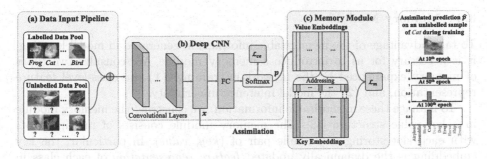

Fig. 2. An overview of Memory-Assisted Deep Neural Network (MA-DNN) for semi-supervised deep learning. During training, given **(a)** sparse labelled and abundant unlabelled training data, mini-batches of labelled/unlabelled data are feed-forward into **(b)** the deep CNN to obtain the up-to-date feature representation x and probabilistic prediction p for each sample. Given **(c)** the updated memory module, memory assimilation induces another multi-class prediction $\hat{p}$ (Eq. (4)) for each sample via key addressing and value reading. In accommodation, a memory loss $\mathcal{L}_m$ (Eq. (7)) is computed from $\hat{p}$ and employed as an additional supervision signal to guide the network learning jointly with the supervised classification loss. At test time, the memory module is no longer needed, so it does not affect the deployment efficiency.

to its powerful representation-learning capability for imagery data. To train a CNN for image classification, the supervised cross-entropy loss function is usually adopted. During training, given any training sample I, we feed-forward it through the up-to-date deep network to obtain a feature vector x and a multi-class probabilistic prediction vector p over all classes. Specifically, we predict the j-th class posterior probability of the labelled image sample I_i as

$$p(\boldsymbol{y}_j|\boldsymbol{x}_i) = \frac{\exp(\boldsymbol{W}_j^\top \boldsymbol{x}_i)}{\sum_{j=1}^{|\mathcal{Y}|} \exp(\boldsymbol{W}_j^\top \boldsymbol{x}_i)} \tag{1}$$

where x_i refers to the embedded deep feature representation of I_i extracted by the deep CNN, and W_j is the j-th class prediction function parameter. The cross-entropy loss on I_i against the ground-truth class label k is computed as

$$\mathcal{L}_{\text{ce}} = -\sum_{j=1}^{K} \mathbb{1}[\boldsymbol{y}_j = k]\log\Big(p(\boldsymbol{y}_j|\boldsymbol{x}_i)\Big) \tag{2}$$

Obviously, the cross-entropy loss function is restricted to learn from the labelled samples alone. To take advantage of the unlabelled training samples, a straightforward way is to utilise the predicted labels given by the up-to-date model in training. This, however, may be error-prone and unreliable given immature label estimations particularly at the beginning of model training. This presents a catch-22 problem. We overcome this problem by introducing a memory module into the network training process to progressively estimate more reliable predictions on the unlabelled data.

3.3   Memory Module

To take advantage of the memorisable information generated in model learning, it is necessary for us to introduce a memory module. We consider two types of memory experienced by the network-in-training: (1) the class-level feature representation, and (2) the model inference uncertainty.

To manage these memorisable information, we construct the memory module in a key-value structure [18]. The memory module consists of multiple slots with each slot storing a symbolic pair of (*key, value*). In particular, the key embedding is the dynamically updated *feature representation* of each class in the feature space. Utilising an univocal representation per class is based on the assumption that deep feature embeddings of each class can be gradually learned to distribute around its cluster centroid in the feature space [33]. Based on this assumption, the global feature distribution of all classes is represented by their cluster centroids in the feature space, whilst these cluster centroids are cumulatively updated as the key embeddings in a batch-wise manner. On the other hand, the value embedding records the similarly updated *multi-class probabilistic prediction* w.r.t. each class. Hence, each value embedding is the accumulated network predictions of samples from the same class that encodes the overall model inference uncertainty at the class level.

To represent the incrementally evolving feature space and the up-to-date overall model inference uncertainty, memory update is performed every iteration to accommodate the most recent updates of the network. We only utilise the labelled data for memory update, provided that unlabelled samples have uncertainty in class assignment and hence potentially induce the risk of error propagation. Formally, suppose there exist n_j labelled image samples $\{I_i\}$ from the j-th class ($j \in \{1, \cdots, K\}$) with their feature vectors and probabilistic predictions as $\{(x_i, p_i)\}_i^{n_j}$, the j-th memory slot (k_j, v_j) is cumulatively updated over all the training iterations as follows.

$$\begin{cases} k_j \leftarrow k_j - \eta \nabla k_j \\ v_j \leftarrow \dfrac{v_j - \eta \nabla v_j}{\sum_{i=1}^{K}(v_{j,i} - \eta \nabla v_{j,i})} \end{cases} \text{with} \begin{cases} \nabla k_j = \dfrac{\sum_{i=1}^{n_j}(k_j - x_i)}{1 + n_j} \\ \nabla v_j = \dfrac{\sum_{i=1}^{n_j}(v_j - p_i)}{1 + n_j} \end{cases} \quad (3)$$

where η denotes the learning rate (set to $\eta = 0.5$ in our experiments). The value embedding v_j is normalised to ensure its probability distribution nature. Along the training process, as the gradients $(\nabla k_j, \nabla v_j)$ progressively get smaller, the key and value embeddings will become more reliable to reflect the underlying feature structures and multi-class distributions. To begin the training process without imposing prior knowledge, we initialise all the key and value embeddings to $\mathbf{0}$ and $\frac{1}{K} \cdot \mathbf{1}$ (a uniform probabilistic distribution over K classes), respectively. This indicates the memorised information is fully discovered by the network during training, without any specific assumption on the problem settings, therefore potentially applicable to different semi-supervised image classification tasks.

3.4   The Assimilation-Accomodation Interaction

Given the updated memory of model learning, we further employ it to enable semi-supervised deep learning. This is achieved by introducing an assimilation-accomodation interaction mechanism with two operations executed every training iteration: (1) *Memory Assimilation*: Compute the memory prediction for each training sample by key addressing and value reading; (2) *Accommodation*: Compute the memory loss to formulate the final semi-supervised learning objective. We present the details of these operations in the following.

(1) Memory Assimilation. Given the forward propagated image representation x and network prediction p of the image I, memory assimilation induces another multi-class probabilistic prediction $\hat{p}$ based on the updated memory. We obtain this by *key addressing* and *value reading* [18]. Specifically, key addressing is to compute the addressing probability $w(m_i|I)$, i.e., the probabilistic assignment to each memory slot $m_i = (k_i, v_i)$, $i \in \{1, \cdots, K\}$, based on pairwise similarity w.r.t. each key embedding. In essence, $w(m_i|I)$ is the cluster assignment in the feature space. Given the addressing probabilities over all K memory slots, value reading is then applied to compute the memory prediction $\hat{p}$ by taking a weighted sum of all the value embeddings as follows.

$$\hat{p} = \sum_{i=1}^{K} w(m_i|I)\, v_i \tag{4}$$

According to label availability, we adopt two addressing strategies. The first is *position-based* addressing applied to labelled training samples. Formally, suppose the training sample I is labelled as the k-th class, the addressing probability is attained based on the position k as

$$w(m_i|I) = \begin{cases} 1, & i = k \\ 0, & i \neq k \end{cases} \tag{5}$$

The second is *content-based* addressing applied to unlabelled image samples. This strategy computes the addressing probability based on the pairwise similarity between the image sample I and the key embeddings k_i as

$$w(m_i|I) = \frac{e^{-\mathrm{dist}(x,k_i)}}{\sum_{j=1}^{K} e^{-\mathrm{dist}(x,k_j)}} \tag{6}$$

where x is the extracted feature vector of I and dist() denotes the Euclidean distance. Eq. (6) can be considered as a form of label propagation [38] based on the *cluster assumption* [35,36], in the sense that the probability mass is distributed according to proximity to each cluster centroid in the feature space. That is, probabilistic assignment is computed based on cluster membership.

(2) Accommodation. This operation provides the deep network with a memory loss to formulate the final semi-supervised learning objective such that the network can learn additionally from the unlabelled data. Specifically, we introduce a *memory loss* on each training sample x as follows.

$$\mathcal{L}_m = H(\hat{p}) + \max(\hat{p})D_{\mathrm{KL}}(p\|\hat{p}) \tag{7}$$

where $H()$ refers to the entropy measure; $\max()$ is the maximum function that returns the maximal value of the input vector; $D_{KL}()$ is the Kullback-Leibler (KL) divergence. Both $H()$ and $D_{KL}()$ can be computed without ground-truth labels and thus applicable to semi-supervised learning. The two loss terms in Eq. (7) are named as the Model Entropy (ME) loss and the Memory-Network Divergence (MND) loss, as explained below.

(i) The Model Entropy (ME) loss term $H(\hat{p})$ is formally computed as

$$H(\hat{p}) = -\sum_{j=1}^{K}\hat{p}(j)\log \hat{p}(j) \tag{8}$$

which quantifies the amount of information encoded in $\hat{p}$. From the information-theoretic perspective, the entropy reflects the overall model inference uncertainty. A high entropy on a *labelled* image sample indicates that $\hat{p}$ is an ambiguous multimodal probability distribution, which corresponds to the retrieved value embedding of a specific class. This indicates that the network cannot well distinguish between this class and the other classes, which is resulted from assigning inconsistent probabilistic predictions to image samples within the same class. On the other hand, a high entropy on an *unlabelled* sample suggests the severe class distribution overlap between different classes in the feature space. This is because the unlabelled sample cannot be assigned to a certain class with high probability. Therefore, minimising the model entropy H is equivalent to reducing class distribution overlap in the feature space and penalising inconsistent network predictions at the class level, which is essentially motivated by the *entropy minimisation* principle [8].

(ii) The Memory-Network Divergence (MND) loss term $D_{\mathrm{KL}}(p\|\hat{p})$ is computed between the network prediction p and the memory prediction $\hat{p}$ as follows.

$$D_{\mathrm{KL}}(p\|\hat{p}) = \sum_{j=1}^{K}p(j)\log \frac{p(j)}{\hat{p}(j)} \tag{9}$$

$D_{\mathrm{KL}}(p\|\hat{p})$ is a non-negative penalty that measures the discrepancy between two distributions: p and $\hat{p}$. It represents the additional information encoded in p compared to $\hat{p}$ in information theory. Minimising this KL divergence prevents the network prediction from overly deviating from the probabilistic distribution derived from the memory module. When $D_{\mathrm{KL}}(p\|\hat{p}) \to 0$, it indicates the network predictions match well with its memory predictions. Additionally, we also impose a dynamic weight: $\max(\hat{p})$, the maximum probability value of $\hat{p}$, to discount the importance of $D_{\mathrm{KL}}()$ when given an ambiguous memory prediction, i.e., a multimodal probability distribution. Hence, p is encouraged to match with $\hat{p}$ particularly when $\hat{p}$ corresponds to a confident memory prediction, i.e., a peaked probability distribution, where the peak corresponds to the assignment to a certain class with high probability.

The final **semi-supervised learning objective function** is formulated by merging Eqs. (7) and (2) as follows.

$$\mathcal{L} = \mathcal{L}_{ce} + \lambda \mathcal{L}_m \tag{10}$$

where λ is a hyper-parameter that is set to 1 to ensure equivalent importance of two loss terms during training.

3.5 Model Training

The proposed MA-DNN is trained by standard Stochastic Gradient Descent algorithm in an end-to-end manner. The algorithmic overview of model training is summarised in Algorithm 1.

Algorithm 1. Memory-Assisted Semi-Supervised Deep Learning.

Input: Labelled data $\mathcal{D}_L$ and unlabelled data $\mathcal{D}_U$.
Output: A deep CNN model for classification.
for $t = 1$ **to** *max_iter* **do**
    Sampling a mini-batch of labelled & unlabelled data.
    Network forward propagation (samples feed-forward).
    Memory update (Eq. (3)).
    Network supervised loss computation (Eq. (2)).
    Memory assimilation (Eq. (4)) and accommodation (Eq. (7)).
    Network update by back-propagation (Eq. (10)).
end for

---

4   Experiments

We validate the effectiveness of MA-DNN on three widely adopted image classification benchmark datasets, with comparison to other state-of-the-art methods in Sect. 4.2 and ablation studies in Sect. 4.2.

4.1   Evaluation on Semi-supervised Classification Benchmarks

Datasets. To evaluate our proposed MA-DNN, we select three widely adopted image classification benchmark datasets as detailed in the following.

(1) SVHN [20]: A Street View House Numbers dataset including 10 classes (0–9) of coloured digit images from Google Street View. The classification task is to recognise the central digit of each image. We use the format-2 version that provides cropped images sized at 32×32, and the standard 73,257/26,032 training/test data split.

(2) CIFAR10 [13]: A natural images dataset containing 50,000/10,000 training/test image samples from 10 object classes. Each class has 6,000 images with size 32 × 32.

(3) CIFAR100 [13]: A dataset (with same image size as CIFAR10) containing 50,000/10,000 training/test images from 100 more fine-grained classes with subtle inter-class visual discrepancy.

Experimental Protocol. Following the standard semi-supervised classification protocol [12,19,24,30], we randomly divide the training data into a small labelled set and a large unlabelled set. The number of labelled training images is 1,000/4,000/10,000 on SVHN/CIFAR10/CIFAR100 respectively, with the remaining 72,257/46,000/40,000 images as unlabelled training data. We adopt the common classification *error rate* as model performance measure, and report the average error rate over 10 random data splits.

Implementation Details. We adopt the same 10-layers CNN architecture as [14]. More implementation details are given in the supplementary material.

Comparison with State-of-the-art Methods. In Table 1, we compare our model to 11 state-of-the-art competitive methods with their reported results on SVHN, CIFAR10 and CIFAR100. Among all these methods, Mean Teacher is the only one that slightly outperforms our MA-DNN on the digit classification task. On the natural image classification tasks, our MA-DNN surpasses the best alternative (Temporal Ensembling) with a margin of 0.25% (12.16–11.91) and 2.83% (37.34–34.51) on CIFAR10 and CIFAR100 respectively. This indicates the performance superiority of the proposed MA-DNN in semi-supervised deep learning

Table 1. Evaluation on semi-supervised image classification benchmarks in comparison to state-of-the-art methods. **Metric:** Error rate (%) ± standard deviation, **lower is better.** "–" indicates no reported result. "*" indicates generative models.

Methods	SVHN [20]	CIFAR10 [13]	CIFAR100 [13]
DGM* [12]	36.02 ± 0.10	–	–
Γ-model [24]	–	20.40 ± 0.47	–
CatGAN* [30]	–	19.58 ± 0.58	–
VAT [19]	24.63	–	–
ADGM* [16]	22.86	–	–
SDGM* [16]	16.61 ± 0.24	–	–
ImpGAN* [27]	8.11 ± 1.3	18.63 ± 2.32	–
ALI* [5]	7.42 ± 0.65	17.99 ±1.62	–
Π-model [14]	4.82 ± 0.17	12.36 ± 0.31	39.19 ± 0.36
Temporal Ensembling [14]	4.42 ± 0.16	12.16 ± 0.24	37.34 ± 0.44
Mean Teacher [32]	**3.95 ± 0.19**	12.31 ± 0.28	–
MA-DNN (Ours)	4.21 ± 0.12	**11.91 ± 0.22**	**34.51 ± 0.61**

among various competitive semi-supervised learning algorithms. Additionally, it can also be observed that MA-DNN outperforms more significantly on the more challenging dataset CIFAR100 with more fine-grained semantic structures among more classes. This suggests that the memory loss derived from the memory of model learning can enhance more fine-grained class discrimination and separation to facilitate better semi-supervised learning. Therefore, MA-DNN is potentially more scalable than the other competitors on the image classification tasks that involve a larger number of classes.

Computational Costs. The per-batch distance computation complexity induced by memory assimilation and memory update is $\mathcal{O}(N_u K)$ and $\mathcal{O}(N_l)$ respectively, where K is the number of memory slots, N_l, N_u are the numbers of labelled and unlabelled samples in each mini-batch. For computational efficiency, all the memory operations are implemented as simple matrix manipulation on GPU with single floating point precision. Overall, MA-DNN is computationally efficient in a number of ways: (i) Only one network forward propagation is required to compute the additional supervision signal, as opposed to more than one forward propagations required by Γ-model, VAT, Π-model and Mean-Teacher. (ii) The consumption of memory footprint is limited. The memory size of the memory module in MA-DNN is only proportional to the number of classes; while Temporal Ensembling requires to store the predictions of all samples in a large mapped file with a memory size proportional to the number of training samples. (iii) Unlike generative models including DGM, CatGAN, ADGM, SDGM, ImpGAN, and ALI, our MA-DNN does not need to generate additional synthetic images during training, therefore resulting in more efficient model training.

4.2 Ablation Studies and Further Analysis

Effect of the Memory Loss. We evaluate the individual contribution of two loss terms in the memory loss formulation (Eq. (7)): (1) the Model Entropy (ME) (Eq. (8)), and (2) the Memory-Network Divergence (MND) (Eq. (9)). We measure the impact of each loss term by the *performance drop* when removing it from the memory loss formulation. Table 2 shows the evaluation results with comparison to the full memory loss formulation. We have the following observations: **(i)** Both loss terms bring positive effects to boost the model performance. The classification error rates increase when either of the two loss terms is eliminated. **(ii)** The MND term effectively enhances the model performance. Eliminating the MND term causes performance drop of 2.54% (6.75–4.21), 5.50% (17.41–11.91), 7.39% (41.90–34.51) on SVHN, CIFAR10, and CIFAR100 respectively. This indicates the effectiveness of encouraging the network predictions to be consistent with reliable memory predictions derived from the memory of model learning. **(iii)** The ME term is also effective. Eliminating the ME term causes performance drop of 0.38% (4.59–4.21), 0.72 % (12.63–11.91), 5.42% (39.93–34.51) on SVHN, CIFAR10, and CIFAR100 respectively. This suggests the benefit of penalising class distribution overlap and enhancing class separation, especially when the amount of classes increase – more classes are harder to be separated.

Table 2. Evaluation on the effect of individual memory loss terms. **Metric:** Error rate (%) ± standard deviation, **lower is better**. ME: Model Entropy; MND: Memory-Network Divergence.

Methods	SVHN [20]	CIFAR10 [13]	CIFAR100 [13]
Full (ME+MND)	**4.21 ± 0.12**	**11.91 ± 0.22**	**34.51 ± 0.61**
W/O ME	4.59 ± 0.11	12.63 ± 0.26	39.93 ± 0.34
W/O MND	6.75 ± 0.40	17.41 ± 0.15	41.90 ± 0.39

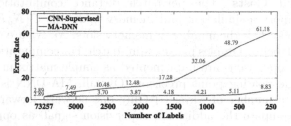

Fig. 3. Evaluation on the robustness of the MA-DNN on varying number of labelled training samples. **Metric:** Error rate, **lower is better**.

Overall, the evaluation in Table 2 demonstrates the complementary joint benefits of the two loss terms to improve the model performance in semi-supervised deep learning.

Labelled Training Sample Size. We evaluate the robustness of MA-DNN over varying numbers of labelled training samples. We conduct this evaluation on SVHN by varying the number of labelled samples from 73,257 (all training samples are labelled) to 250. As comparison, we adopt the supervised counterpart *CNN-Supervised* trained only using the same labelled data without the memory module. Figure 3 shows that as the size of labelled data decreases, the model performance of CNN-Supervised drops from 61.18% (given 73,257 labelled samples) to 2.89% (given 250 labelled samples), with a total performance drop of 58.29% in error rate. In contrast, the performance of MA-DNN degrades only by 5.94% (8.83–2.89). This indicates the proposed MA-DNN can effectively leverage additional unlabelled data to boost the model performance when both small-sized labelled and large-sized unlabelled training data are provided.

Evolution of the Memory Module. As aforementioned, the two types of class-level memorisable information recorded in the memory module is (1) the class-level feature representation (key embeddings), and (2) the model inference uncertainty (value embeddings). To understand how the memory module is updated during training, we visualise the evolution of the key embeddings and value embeddings in Figs. 4 and 5 and qualitatively analyse their effects as below.

	init	50th epoch	250th epoch	end
(a) labelled data				
(b) unlabelled data				
(c) test data				

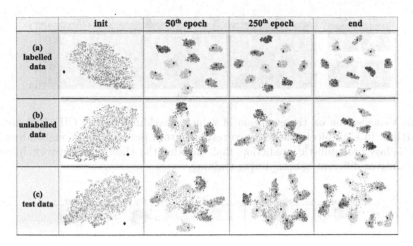

Fig. 4. Visualisation on the evolution of key embeddings (denoted as the *black dots*) and the multi-class data distribution (denoted as dots in colours) of (**a**) labelled data, (**b**) unlabelled data, (**c**) test data from CIFAR10 in the feature space during training. Data projection in 2-D space is attained by tSNE [17] based on the feature representation extracted on the *same* sets of data using the CNN at different training stages.

Effect of the Key Embeddings. As Fig. 4 shows, the key embeddings (denoted as the *black dots*) are essentially updated as the cluster centroids to capture the global manifold structure in the feature space. In particular, we have the following observations: (**i**) Fig. 4(a) shows that although the key embeddings are initialised as **0** without imposing prior knowledge, they are consistently updated to capture the underlying global manifold structure of the labelled data in the projected 2-D feature space, as seen at the $50/250^{th}$ epochs. (**ii**) Fig. 4(b) shows that there is severe class distribution overlap of the unlabelled data initially; however, such class distribution overlap tends to be gradually mitigated as the model is trained. (**iii**) Fig. 4(c) shows that the key embeddings also roughly capture the global manifold structure of the unseen test data, even though the network is not optimised to fit towards the test data distribution. Overall, these observations are in line with our motivation of recording the accumulatively updated cluster centroids as the key embeddings for deriving the probabilistic assignment on unlabelled samples based on the *cluster assumption*. Moreover, the evolution of unlabelled data distribution in Fig. 4(b) also qualitatively suggests that our memory loss serves to penalise the class distribution overlap and render the class decision boundaries to lie in the low density region. Note that the 2-D tSNE visualisation of high-dimensional data may not perfectly reflect the underlying structure of how classes are separated in the feature space.

Effect of the Value Embeddings. As Fig. 5 shows, the value embeddings essentially record the model inference uncertainty at the class level. At the initial training stages, the value embeddings reflect much higher inference uncertainty (multimodal distribution with higher entropy), but progressively reflect

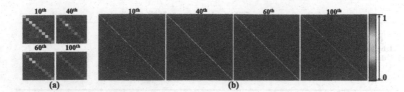

Fig. 5. Visualisation on the evolution of value embeddings on **(a)** CIFAR10 and **(b)** CIFAR100. In each block, each row corresponds to a per-class value embedding, i.e., a multi-class probabilistic prediction that encodes the class-level network inference uncertainty at different epochs during training.

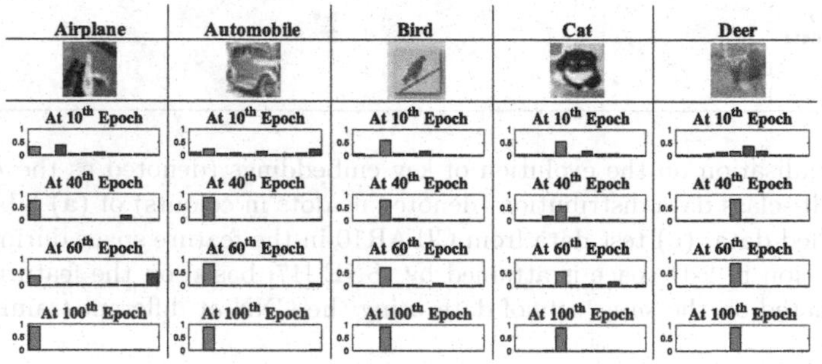

Fig. 6. Evolution of memory predictions of randomly selected *unlabelled* samples from CIFAR10. The *Red* bar corresponds to the *missing* ground-truth class. (Color figure online)

much lower inference uncertainty (peaked distribution with lower entropy) as the model is progressively trained. In fact, when removing the value embeddings, the probabilistic assignment on unlabelled samples can become particularly unreliable at the earlier training stages, which even leads to performance drops of 0.69/1.94/2.78% on SVHN/CIFAR10/CIFAR100 as verified in our experiments. Hence, the value embeddings can serve to reflect the class separation in the label space, and be utilised to smooth the probabilistic assignment with model inference uncertainty for deriving more reliable memory predictions.

Evolution of Memory Predictions. We visualise the evolution of memory predictions on the unlabelled samples from CIFAR10 at different training stages in Fig. 6. It can be observed that the memory predictions are progressively improving from more uncertain (ambiguous) to more confident on the unlabelled training samples. This not only demonstrates the good convergence property of the MA-DNN, but also indicates how the memory loss takes effect in model learning – (1) penalising class distribution overlap when given uncertain memory predictions at the earlier training stages while (2) encouraging the network predictions to be consistent with confident memory predictions, such that the unlabelled data is fitted optimally towards the underlying manifold structure.

5   Conclusions

In this work, we present a novel Memory-Assisted Deep Neural Network (MA-DNN) to enable semi-supervised deep learning on sparsely labelled and abundant unlabelled training data. The MA-DNN is established on the idea of exploiting the memory of model learning to more reliably and effectively learn from the unlabelled training data. In particular, we formulate a novel assimilation-accommodation interaction between the network and an external memory module capable of facilitating more effective semi-supervised deep learning by imposing a memory loss derived from the incrementally updated memory module. Extensive comparative evaluations on three semi-supervised image classification benchmark datasets validate the advantages of the proposed MA-DNN over a wide range of state-of-the-art methods. We also provide detailed ablation studies and further analysis to give insights on the model design and performance gains.

Acknowledgements. This work was partly supported by the China Scholarship Council, Vision Semantics Limited, the Royal Society Newton Advanced Fellowship Programme (NA150459) and Innovate UK Industrial Challenge Project on Developing and Commercialising Intelligent Video Analytics Solutions for Public Safety (98111-571149).

References

1. Blum, A., Lafferty, J., Rwebangira, M.R., Reddy, R.: Semi-supervised learning using randomized mincuts. In: International Conference on Machine Learning (2004)
2. Blum, A., Mitchell, T.: Combining labeled and unlabeled data with co-training. In: Proceedings of the Eleventh Annual Conference on Computational Learning Theory. ACM (1998)
3. Chapelle, O., Zien, A., Ghahramani, C.Z., et al.: Semi-supervised classification by low density separation. In: Tenth International Workshop on Artificial Intelligence and Statistics (2005)
4. Chapelle, O., Schlkopf, B., Zien, A.: Semi-supervised Learning. The MIT Press, Cambridge, MA (2010)
5. Dumoulin, V., et al.: Adversarially learned inference. In: International Conference on Learning Representation (2017)
6. Fergus, R., Weiss, Y., Torralba, A.: Semi-supervised learning in gigantic image collections. In: Advances in Neural Information Processing Systems (2009)
7. Ginsburg, H.P., Opper, S.: Piaget's Theory of Intellectual Development. Prentice-Hall Inc., Upper Saddle River (1988)
8. Grandvalet, Y., Bengio, Y.: Semi-supervised learning by entropy minimization. In: Advances in Neural Information Processing Systems (2005)
9. Haeusser, P., Mordvintsev, A., Cremers, D.: Learning by association-a versatile semi-supervised training method for neural networks. In: IEEE Conference on Computer Vision and Pattern Recognition (2017)
10. Joachims, T.: Transductive inference for text classification using support vector machines. In: International Conference on Machine Learning (1999)

11. Kaiser, Ł., Nachum, O., Roy, A., Bengio, S.: Learning to remember rare events. In: International Conference on Learning Representation (2017)
12. Kingma, D.P., Mohamed, S., Rezende, D.J., Welling, M.: Semi-supervised learning with deep generative models. In: Advances in Neural Information Processing Systems (2014)
13. Krizhevsky, A., Hinton, G.: Learning multiple layers of features from tiny images. Technical report, University of Toronto (2009)
14. Laine, S., Aila, T.: Temporal ensembling for semi-supervised learning. In: International Conference on Learning Representation (2017)
15. Lee, D.H.: Pseudo-label: The simple and efficient semi-supervised learning method for deep neural networks. In: ICML Workshop on Challenges in Representation Learning (2013)
16. Maaløe, L., Sønderby, C.K., Sønderby, S.K., Winther, O.: Auxiliary deep generative models. In: International Conference on Machine Learning (2016)
17. Maaten, L.V.D., Hinton, G.: Visualizing data using t-SNE. J. Mach. Learn. Res, 2579–2605 (2008)
18. Miller, A., Fisch, A., Dodge, J., Karimi, A.H., Bordes, A., Weston, J.: Key-value memory networks for directly reading documents. In: Proceedings of the 2016 Conference on Empirical Methods in Natural Language Processing (2016)
19. Miyato, T., Maeda, S.I., Koyama, M., Nakae, K., Ishii, S.: Distributional smoothing with virtual adversarial training. In: International Conference on Learning Representation (2016)
20. Netzer, Y., Wang, T., Coates, A., Bissacco, A., Wu, B., Ng, A.Y.: Reading digits in natural images with unsupervised feature learning. In: NIPS workshop on deep learning and unsupervised feature learning (2011)
21. Nigam, K., Ghani, R.: Analyzing the effectiveness and applicability of co-training. In: Proceedings of the ninth international conference on Information and knowledge management. ACM (2000)
22. Pereyra, G., Tucker, G., Chorowski, J., Kaiser, Ł., Hinton, G.: Regularizing neural networks by penalizing confident output distributions. In: International Conference on Learning Representation (2017)
23. Ranzato, M., Szummer, M.: Semi-supervised learning of compact document representations with deep networks. In: International Conference on Machine Learning (2008)
24. Rasmus, A., Berglund, M., Honkala, M., Valpola, H., Raiko, T.: Semi-supervised learning with ladder networks. In: Advances in Neural Information Processing Systems (2015)
25. Rosenberg, C., Hebert, M., Schneiderman, H.: Semi-supervised self-training of object detection models. In: Seventh IEEE Workshop on Applications of Computer Vision. Citeseer (2005)
26. Sajjadi, M., Javanmardi, M., Tasdizen, T.: Regularization with stochastic transformations and perturbations for deep semi-supervised learning. In: Advances in Neural Information Processing Systems, pp. 1163–1171 (2016)
27. Salimans, T., Goodfellow, I., Zaremba, W., Cheung, V., Radford, A., Chen, X.: Improved techniques for training gans. In: Advances in Neural Information Processing Systems (2016)
28. Santoro, A., Bartunov, S., Botvinick, M., Wierstra, D., Lillicrap, T.: Meta-learning with memory-augmented neural networks. In: International Conference on Machine Learning, pp. 1842–1850 (2016)
29. Shi, M., Zhang, B.: Semi-supervised learning improves gene expression-based prediction of cancer recurrence. Bioinformatics 27(21), 3017–3023 (2011)

30. Springenberg, J.T.: Unsupervised and semi-supervised learning with categorical generative adversarial networks. In: International Conference on Learning Representation (2016)
31. Sukhbaatar, S., Weston, J., Fergus, R., et al.: End-to-end memory networks. In: Advances in Neural Information Processing Systems (2015)
32. Tarvainen, A., Valpola, H.: Mean teachers are better role models: weight-averaged consistency targets improve semi-supervised deep learning results. In: Advances in Neural Information Processing Systems (2017)
33. Wen, Y., Zhang, K., Li, Z., Qiao, Y.: A discriminative feature learning approach for deep face recognition. In: Leibe, B., Matas, J., Sebe, N., Welling, M. (eds.) ECCV 2016. LNCS, vol. 9911, pp. 499–515. Springer, Cham (2016). https://doi.org/10.1007/978-3-319-46478-7_31
34. Weston, J., Chopra, S., Bordes, A.: Memory networks. In: International Conference on Learning Representation (2014)
35. Weston, J., Ratle, F., Mobahi, H., Collobert, R.: Deep learning via semi-supervised embedding. In: International Conference on Machine Learning (2008)
36. Zhou, D., Bousquet, O., Lal, T.N., Weston, J., Schölkopf, B.: Learning with local and global consistency. In: Advances in Neural Information Processing Systems (2004)
37. Zhu, X.: Semi-supervised learning literature survey. Comput. Sci. Univ. Wisconsin-Madison **2**(3), 4 (2006)
38. Zhu, X., Ghahramani, Z.: Learning from labeled and unlabeled data with label propagation. Technical Report CMU-CALD-02-107, Carnegie Mellon University (2002)
39. Zhu, X., Ghahramani, Z., Lafferty, J.D.: Semi-supervised learning using gaussian fields and harmonic functions. In: International Conference on Machine Learning (2003)

Deep Fundamental Matrix Estimation

René Ranftl[✉] and Vladlen Koltun

Intel Labs, Munich, Germany
ranftlr@gmail.com

Abstract. We present an approach to robust estimation of fundamental matrices from noisy data contaminated by outliers. The problem is cast as a series of weighted homogeneous least-squares problems, where robust weights are estimated using deep networks. The presented formulation acts directly on putative correspondences and thus fits into standard 3D vision pipelines that perform feature extraction, matching, and model fitting. The approach can be trained end-to-end and yields computationally efficient robust estimators. Our experiments indicate that the presented approach is able to train robust estimators that outperform classic approaches on real data by a significant margin.

1 Introduction

Deep learning has shown promising results on computer vision problems such as image categorization [20], image segmentation [24], and object detection [10]. Many problems that have been successfully tackled with deep learning share a common trait: The mapping from input to output is difficult to characterize by explicit mathematical modeling. This is especially true for the aforementioned applications, where even simple questions like what actually constitutes an object of a specific class cannot be answered in a simple way that lends itself to mathematical modeling [11]. Consequently, approaches such as deep learning, which are able to learn representations directly from large corpora of data are necessarily superior in these tasks.

On the other hand, certain computer vision problems, such as fundamental matrix estimation, can be defined in a precise mathematical way, provided that some assumptions are made about the data [12]. It is thus not surprising that these subfields have largely been spared by the recent surge in deep learning research.

However, being able to define a problem in a precise mathematical way doesn't necessarily mean that it can be easily solved. We argue that robust fundamental matrix estimation can be solved more accurately if the estimator can be adapted to the data at hand. For example, in an automotive scenario

---

Electronic supplementary material The online version of this chapter (https://doi.org/10.1007/978-3-030-01246-5_18) contains supplementary material, which is available to authorized users.

© Springer Nature Switzerland AG 2018
V. Ferrari et al. (Eds.): ECCV 2018, LNCS 11205, pp. 292–309, 2018.
https://doi.org/10.1007/978-3-030-01246-5_18

not all fundamental matrices are equally likely to occur. In fact, since the platform exhibits dominant forward or backward motion at all times, the space of fundamental matrices that can occur in this scenario is much smaller than the complete space of fundamental matrices. Another example is data that deviates from the common assumption of Gaussian inlier noise. Adapting model fitting approaches to different inlier noise distributions requires significant effort by an expert, but could be made much easier if the noise distribution can be learned from data.

In this work we present an approach that is able to learn a robust algorithm for fundamental matrix estimation from data. Our approach combines deep networks with a well-defined algorithmic structure and can be trained end-to-end. In contrast to naive deep learning approaches to this problem, our approach disentangles local motion estimation and geometric model fitting, leading to simplified training problems and interpretable estimation pipelines. As such it can act as a drop-in replacement for applications where the RANSAC [7] family of algorithms is commonly employed [27,35]. To achieve this, we formulate the robust estimation problem as a series of weighted homogeneous least-squares problems, where weights are estimated using deep networks.

Experiments on diverse real-world datasets indicate that the presented approach can significantly outperform RANSAC and its variants. Our experiments also show that estimators trained by the presented approach generalize across datasets. As a supporting result, we also show that the presented approach yields state-of-the-art accuracy in homography estimation.

2   Related Work

Robust fundamental matrix estimation, and more generally geometric model fitting, is a fundamental problem in computer vision that commonly arises in 3D processing tasks [12]. The common starting point is to first derive an estimator for outlier-free data. Various measures can then be taken to derive robust estimators that can deal with a certain amount of outliers.

Perhaps the most widely used approach for dealing with outliers is *RANdom SAmple Consensus* (RANSAC) [7], where one searches for a geometric model that has the most support in the form of inliers (defined based on some problem-specific point-to-model distance and a user-defined inlier threshold) using random sampling. There exists a vast amount of literature on variations of this basic idea [5,21,30,36,37,39]. What most of these works have in common is the general structure of the algorithm. First, a set of points is sampled and a model is estimated using a non-robust baseline estimator. Second, the model is scored by evaluating a robust scoring function on all points and the model is accepted as the current best guess if its score is better than all previously scored models. This process is repeated until some stopping criterion is reached. A common weakness that is shared by sampling-based approaches is their dependence on the minimum number of data points required to unambiguously define a model. As the size of the minimal set increases, the probability of sampling at least one outlier rises exponentially. Note that RANSAC has been integrated into a deep scene coordinate regression pipeline [3] for camera localization. This approach uses finite differences to backpropagate through the non-robust base estimator and inherits the basic weaknesses of RANSAC.

Another line of work adopts the basic idea of consensus set maximization, but tackles optimization using globally optimal methods [22,44]. Since the underlying optimization problem is NP-hard, these approaches are often prohibitively slow, degrading to exhaustive search in the worst case. While some progress has been made in speeding up globally optimal consensus set maximization [4], all known approaches are significantly slower than randomized algorithms and often lack the flexibility to tackle arbitrary geometric model fitting problems.

It is possible to directly robustify the base estimator using M-estimators [8,14,49,50]. This line of work is most closely related to the presented approach, as it usually leads to a series of weighted least-squares problems. The major weakness of these approaches is that they require careful initialization and/or continuation procedures. Moreover, these approaches typically implicitly assume that the inliers are subject to Gaussian noise, which may not always be the case. In contrast, the presented approach doesn't make any assumptions on the inlier noise distributions, nor does it require extensive care to initialize the optimization, as both are learned from data.

There has been growing interest in applying deep learning to 3D processing tasks. DeTone et al. learned a neural network to directly regress from a pair of input images to a homography [6]. This work was later extended with an image-based loss to allow unsupervised training [28]. Agrawal et al. [1] estimate ego-motion using a neural network as a pre-training step for high-level tasks. PoseNet [16,17] employs a convolutional network to estimate the pose of a given image for camera relocalization. The DeMoN architecture [41] provides, given two consecutive frames from a monocular camera, both an estimate of the depth of each pixel and an estimate of the motion between frames. A common characteristic of all these models is that they do not enforce the intrinsic structure of the problem, beyond their parametrization and training loss. As a consequence, a large amount of training data is needed and generalization performance is often a concern. A notable exception is the approach of Rocco et al. [31], which is modeled after the classical stages of feature extraction, matching, and model estimation. Note, however, that the model estimator again is a deep regressor that doesn't incorporate any geometric constraints.

In contrast to these works, our approach directly operates on putative matches, independently of how these matches were obtained. Keypoint detection and matching remain an independent step. As a consequence, our approach can be used as a drop-in replacement in pipelines where RANSAC and similar algorithms are currently employed. We argue that such a modular approach to tackling 3D processing using deep learning is highly desirable, given the lack of large-scale datasets in this domain. It is much easier to learn different subparts of 3D reconstruction systems, such as feature matching [34,45] and model estimation separately, as generating realistic training data for these subproblems becomes easier. Moreover, a modular approach leads to disentangled intermediate representations, which significantly enhances the interpretability of a pipeline.

Machine learning techniques have been applied to robustify and speed up optimization problems. Andrychowicz et al. [2] use neural networks to find update directions for gradient-descent algorithms. A framework to learn fixed-point iterations for point cloud registration is presented in [42]. These approaches are not directly applicable to fundamental matrix estimation, since gradient descent cannot be trivially applied.

3 Preliminaries

We refer to a single element of the input data of dimensionality d as a point $\mathbf{p}_i \in \mathbb{R}^d$. Let $\mathbf{P} \in \mathcal{P} = \mathbb{R}^{N \times d}$ be a collection of points of dimensionality d that contains N (not necessarily distinct) points. We use $(\mathbf{P})_i$ to refer to the i-th row of matrix $\mathbf{P}$. Note that points can be either points in some metric space, or in the case of fundamental matrix and homography estimation point correspondences (e.g., we have $\mathbf{p}_i \in \mathbb{R}^4$ in this case by concatenating the two image coordinates of putative correspondences $\tilde{\mathbf{p}}_i \leftrightarrow \tilde{\mathbf{p}}_i'$).

In many geometric model fitting problems a homogeneous least-squares optimization problem arises:

$$\underset{\mathbf{x}}{\text{minimize}} \quad \sum_{i=1}^{N} \|(\mathbf{A}(\mathbf{P}))_i \cdot \mathbf{x}\|^2 \tag{1}$$
$$\text{subject to} \quad \|\mathbf{x}\| = 1,$$

where $\mathbf{x} \in \mathbb{R}^{d'}$ defines the model parameters and $\mathbf{A} : \mathcal{P} \to \mathbb{R}^{kN \times d'}$ ($kN \geq d'$, $k > 0$) is a problem-specific mapping of the data points.

Note that (1) admits a closed-form solution. Popular examples of algorithms where optimization problems of this form arise are the eight-point algorithm for fundamental matrix estimation [13], the Direct Linear Transform (DLT) [12], and general total least-squares fitting.

Consider hyperplane fitting as a simple example. Let $(\mathbf{n}^\top, c)^\top$ specify a hyperplane with normal $\mathbf{n}$ and intercept c. The goal of hyperplane fitting is to infer $(\mathbf{n}^\top, c)^\top$ from a set of points $\mathbf{P}$. To fit a hyperplane in a total least-squares sense, we have

$$\mathbf{A}(\mathbf{P}) \in \mathbb{R}^{N \times d}, \qquad (\mathbf{A}(\mathbf{P}))_i = \mathbf{p}_i^\top - \frac{1}{N} \sum_{j=1}^{N} \mathbf{p}_j^\top. \tag{2}$$

Solving (1) with this definition allows us to extract the plane using the model extraction function $g(\mathbf{x})$ that maps $\mathbf{x}$ to the model parameters:

$$g(\mathbf{x}) = \left(\mathbf{x}^\top, -\mathbf{x} \cdot \frac{1}{N} \sum_{i=1}^{N} \mathbf{p}_i \right)^\top = (\mathbf{n}^\top, c)^\top. \tag{3}$$

If the data is free of outliers, the least-squares solution will be close to the true solution (depending on the inlier noise distribution and the specific form of the problem). However, in practical applications the data does usually contain outliers. (Even worse, there may be more outliers than inliers.) Solving the estimation problem in a least-squares sense will yield wrong estimates even in the presence of a single outlier.

Much work has gone into finding robust approaches to geometric model fitting [7,14,30,39]. One possible solution is to apply a robust loss function Φ to the residuals in (1). The resulting optimization problem does not admit a closed-form solution in general. A practical way to approximately solve the optimization problem is by solving a sequence of reweighted least-squares problems [38]:

$$\mathbf{x}^{j+1} = \arg\min_{\mathbf{x}: \|\mathbf{x}\|=1} \sum_{i=1}^{N} w(\mathbf{p}_i, \mathbf{x}^j) \|(\mathbf{A}(\mathbf{P}))_i \cdot \mathbf{x}\|^2, \tag{4}$$

where the exact form of the weights w depends on Φ and the geometric model at hand.

Coming back to the hyperplane fitting example, assume that $w(\mathbf{p}_i, \mathbf{x}^j) = w_i = 1$ if $\mathbf{p}_i$ is an inlier and $w(\mathbf{p}_i, \mathbf{x}^j) = w_i = 0$ otherwise. It is clear that given these weights, the correct model can be recovered in a single iteration of (4) by setting

$$(\mathbf{A}(\mathbf{P}))_i = \mathbf{p}_i^\top - \frac{\sum_{j=1}^{N} w_j \mathbf{p}_j^\top}{\sum_{j=1}^{N} w_j}, \qquad g(\mathbf{x}) = \left(\mathbf{x}^\top, -\mathbf{x} \cdot \frac{\sum_{j=1}^{N} w_j \mathbf{p}_j}{\sum_{j=1}^{N} w_j}\right)^\top. \tag{5}$$

Knowing the weights in advance is a chicken-and-egg problem. On the one hand, if we knew the true model we could trivially separate inliers from outliers. On the other hand, if we knew which points are inliers we could directly recover the correct model. In what follows, we will show that in many instances the weights can be estimated reasonably well using a deep network with appropriate structure.

4   Deep Model Fitting

Our approach is inspired by the structure of (4). It can be thought of as an iteratively reweighted least-squares algorithm (IRLS) with a complex, learned reweighting function. Since we are learning weights from data, we expect that our algorithm is able to outperform general purpose approaches whenever one or more of the following assumptions are true. (1) The input data admits regularity in the inlier and outlier distributions that can be learned. An example would be an outlier distribution that is approximately uniform and sufficiently dissimilar to the inlier noise distribution. This is a mild assumption that in fact has been exploited in sampling-based approaches previously [39]. (2) The problem has useful side information that can be integrated into the reweighting function. An example would be matching scores or keypoint geometry. (3) The output space is a subset of the full space of model parameters. An example would be fundamental matrix estimation for a camera mounted on a car or a wheeled robot.

We will show in our experimental evaluation that our approach indeed is able to outperform generic baselines if regularity is present in the data, while being competitive when there is no apparent regularity in the data.

In the following we adopt the general structure of algorithm (4), but do not assume a simple form of the weight function w. Instead we parametrize it using a deep network and learn the network weights from data such that the overall algorithm leads to accurate estimates. Our approach can be understood as a meta-algorithm that learns a complex and problem-dependent version of the IRLS algorithm with an unknown cost function. We show that this approach can be used to easily integrate side information into the problem, which can enhance and robustify the estimates.

Model Estimator. We first describe the fundamental building block of our app-roach, a version of (4) where the weights are parametrized by a deep network, and will discuss how the network can be trained end-to-end. We start by redefining the weight function as $w : \mathcal{P} \times \mathcal{S} \times \mathbb{R}^{d'} \to (\mathbb{R}_{>0})^N$, where $\mathbf{S} \in \mathcal{S} = \mathbb{R}^{N \times s}$ collects side information that may be available for each point. Note that this function is defined globally, thus individual points can influence each other. Since w can be a non-trivial function, we parametrize it by a deep network with weights $\boldsymbol{\theta}$. With this parametrization, a single step in algorithm (4) becomes

$$\mathbf{x}^{j+1} = \arg\min_{\mathbf{x}: \|\mathbf{x}\|=1} \sum_{i=1}^{N} (w(\mathbf{P}, \mathbf{S}, \mathbf{x}^j; \boldsymbol{\theta}))_i \|(\mathbf{A}(\mathbf{P}))_i \cdot \mathbf{x}\|^2. \tag{6}$$

The question is how to find a parametrization $\boldsymbol{\theta}$ that leads to robust and accurate estimates. We now drop the explicit dependence on the correspondences and side information for notational brevity and move to matrix form:

$$\mathbf{x}^{j+1} = \arg\min_{\mathbf{x}: \|\mathbf{x}\|=1} \|\mathbf{W}^j(\boldsymbol{\theta})\mathbf{A}\mathbf{x}\|^2, \tag{7}$$

where $(\mathbf{W}^j(\boldsymbol{\theta}))_{i,i} = \sqrt{w_i^j}$ collects the individual weights into a diagonal matrix.

Proposition 1. *Let $X = \mathbf{U}\boldsymbol{\Sigma}\mathbf{V}^\top$ denote the singular value decomposition (SVD) of a matrix X. The solution $\mathbf{x}^{j+1}$ of (7) is given by the right singular vector $\mathbf{v}_{d'}$ corresponding to the smallest singular value of the matrix $\mathbf{W}(\boldsymbol{\theta})\mathbf{A}$.*

This is a well-known fact as (7) is a homogeneous least-squares problem. For completeness, a derivation is given in supplementary material.

Proposition 1 implies that a solution to the model fitting problem is recovered as $g(f(\mathbf{W}(\boldsymbol{\theta})\mathbf{A}))$, where $f(X) = \mathbf{v}_{d'}$ and $g(\mathbf{x})$ is an appropriate function that maps from the SVD to the parameters of the geometric model. An example was already given in (5) for the case of hyperplane fitting. We will provide an example for fundamental matrix estimation in Sect. 5.

In order to learn the weights θ using gradient-based optimization, we need to be able to backpropagate the gradient through an SVD layer. Ionescu et al. [15] showed how this can be achieved using matrix calculus:

Proposition 2. *Assume that the singular vectors are ordered according to the magnitude of their singular values* $\mathbf{V} = (\mathbf{v}_1, \mathbf{v}_2, \ldots, \mathbf{v}_{d'})$ *such that* $\mathbf{v}_{d'}$ *is the singular vector corresponding to the smallest singular value. We need to backpropagate through* $g(f(X))$ *with* $f(X) = \mathbf{v}_{d'}$*. The gradient of* g *with respect to the input* X *is given by*

$$\frac{\partial g}{\partial X} = \mathbf{U}\left\{2\boldsymbol{\Sigma}\left(\mathbf{K}^{\top} \circ \left(\mathbf{V}^{\top}\frac{\partial g}{\partial \mathbf{v}_{d'}}\right)_{sym}\right)\right\}\mathbf{V}^{\top}, \tag{8}$$

where

$$\mathbf{K}_{ij} = \begin{cases} \frac{1}{\sigma_i^2 - \sigma_j^2}, & \text{if } i \neq j \\ 0, & \text{otherwise} \end{cases} \tag{9}$$

and σ_i *denotes the* i*-th singular value.*

The structure of the gradient (8) follows as a special case of the derivations in [15].

A schematic overview of the model estimator is shown in Fig. 1. The block takes as input the points $\mathbf{P}$ and a set of weights w. It constructs the matrix $\mathbf{W}(\theta)\mathbf{A}$ as a preprocessing step, applies a singular value decomposition, and then performs the model extraction step $g(\mathbf{x})$ that yields an estimate of the geometric model given the input weights. The estimated model can then be used to estimate a new set of weights, based on the input points, side information, and the residuals of the currently estimated model.

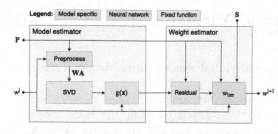

Fig. 1. Estimation module and network architecture. The estimation module is composed of two parts. Given input points and a weighting, a model is estimated using weighted least-squares. In the second stage a new set of weights is generated given the points, their residuals with respect to the previously estimated model, and possibly side information.

Table 1. Estimation module and network architecture. The network architecture of w_{init} and w_{iter}. A checkmark in column L-ReLU+IN indicates that a leaky ReLU followed by instance normalization is applied to the output of the layer.

Layer	# in	# out	L-ReLU+IN
1	–	64	✓
2	64	128	✓
3	128	1024	✓
4	1024	512	✓
5	512	256	✓
6	256	1	✗

Weight Estimator. To accurately estimate weights, the estimator needs to fulfill two requirements: It has to be equivariant to permutation of the input data and it has to be able to process an arbitrary number N of input points. The first requirement arises since the data presented to the weight estimator does not exhibit any natural ordering. Thus the function approximator needs to integrate global information in a way that is independent of the actual ordering of the input data points. The second requirement arises from the fact that in most applications we do not know the number of input points a priori.

To build a deep network that fulfills both requirements, we adopt the idea presented in [29] and [48] for processing unordered sets of points using deep networks. The key idea of these works is simple: In order to make a network equivariant to permutation of the input data, every operation in the network itself has to be equivariant to permutation. This is especially relevant for layers that operate across multiple data points. It can be shown that global average and max-pooling along dimension N fulfill this property. We adopt the general structure of [29] with a small modification: Instead of a single pooling layer that integrates global information, we perform instance normalization [40] after each layer:

$$(I(\mathbf{h}))_i = \frac{\mathbf{h}_i - \mu(\mathbf{h})}{\sqrt{\sigma^2(\mathbf{h}) + \epsilon}}, \tag{10}$$

where $\mathbf{h}_i$ is the feature vector corresponding to point i and the mean $\mu(\mathbf{h})$ as well as the variance $\sigma^2(\mathbf{h})$ are computed along dimension N. This operation integrates the distribution of global information across points and normalization into a single step. Since instance normalization is entirely composed of permutation equivariant operations, the overall network is equivariant to permutations of the input points. We found that this modification improves stability during training, especially in the high noise regime. A similar observation was made independently in concurrent work on essential matrix estimation [46]. We conjecture that for data with low signal-to-noise ratio, it is crucial to have multiple operations in the network that integrate data globally. This is in contrast to the original PointNet architecture [29], where a single global integration step in the form of a pooling layer is proposed.

An overview of the architecture is shown in Table 1. It consists of repeated application of a linear layer (acting independently for each point), followed by a leaky ReLU activation function [26] and the instance normalization module that enables global communication between points. In order to produce strictly positive weights, the error estimator is followed by a softmax. We experimented with different output activations and found that the softmax activation leads to initializations that are close to the least-squares estimate.

We define two networks: $w_{init}(\mathbf{P}, \mathbf{S})$ to compute an initial set of weights and a network $w_{iter}(\mathbf{P}, \mathbf{S}, \mathbf{r}, \mathbf{w}^j)$ to update the weights after a model estimation step, where $\mathbf{r}$ denotes the geometric residuals of the current estimate, $(\mathbf{r})_i = r(\mathbf{p}_i, g(\mathbf{x}^j))$.

Algorithm 1. Forward pass

1: Construct $\mathbf{A}(\mathbf{P})$
2: $w^0 \leftarrow \text{softmax}(w_{init}(\mathbf{P}, \mathbf{S}))$ ▷ Initial weights
3: **for** $j = 0$ **to** D **do**
4:     $\mathbf{X} \leftarrow \text{diag}(\mathbf{w}^j)\mathbf{A}$
5:     $\mathbf{U}, \mathbf{\Sigma}, \mathbf{V} \leftarrow \text{svd}(\mathbf{X})$
6:     Extract $\mathbf{x}^{j+1} = \mathbf{v}^{d'}$ from $\mathbf{V}$ ▷ Solution to (7)
7:     Compute residuals to construct $\mathbf{r}$ from $g(\mathbf{x}^{j+1})$
8:     $\mathbf{w}^{j+1} \leftarrow \text{softmax}(w_{iter}(\mathbf{P}, \mathbf{S}, \mathbf{r}, \mathbf{w}^j))$
9: **end for**
10: **return** $g(\mathbf{x}^D)$

Architecture. The complete architecture consists of an input weight estimator w_{init}, repeated application of the estimation module, and a geometric model estimator on the final weights. In practice we found that five consecutive estimation modules strike a good balance between accuracy and speed. An overview of a complete forward pass is shown in Algorithm 1.

We implement the network in PyTorch. In all applications that follow we use Adamax [18] with an initial learning rate of 10^{-3} and a batch size of 16. We reduce the learning rate every 10 epochs by a factor of 0.8 and train for a total of 100 epochs.

5   Fundamental Matrix Estimation

For a complete forward pass, the following problem-dependent components need to be specified: The preprocessing step $\mathbf{A}(\mathbf{P})$, the model extractor $g(\mathbf{x})$, and the residual $r(\mathbf{p}_i, \mathbf{x})$. Note that all of these quantities also need to be specified for RANSAC-type algorithms, since they specialize the general meta-algorithm to the specific problem instance. While our exposition focuses on fundamental matrix estimation, our approach can handle other types of problems that are based on homogeneous least-squares. We use homography estimation as an additional example. Note that other types of estimators which are not based on homogeneous least-squares could be integrated as long as they are differentiable. In addition we need to specify a training loss to be able to train the pipeline. We will show that the loss can be directly derived from the residual function r.

We perform robust fundamental matrix estimation based on the normalized 8-point algorithm [13]. We rescale all coordinates to the interval $[-1, 1]^2$ and define the preprocessing function

$$(\mathbf{A}(\mathbf{P}))_i = \text{vec}\left(\mathbf{T}\hat{\mathbf{p}}_i(\mathbf{T}'\hat{\mathbf{p}}'_i)^\top\right), \tag{11}$$

where $\hat{\mathbf{p}}_i = ((\mathbf{p}_i)_1, (\mathbf{p}_i)_2, 1)^\top$ and $\hat{\mathbf{p}}'_i = ((\mathbf{p}_i)_3, (\mathbf{p}_i)_4, 1)^\top$ are homogenous coordinates of the correspondences in the left and right image respectively, and $\mathbf{T}, \mathbf{T}'$

are normalization matrices that robustly center and scale the data [13] based on the estimated weights. We further define the model extractor as

$$g(\mathbf{x}) = \underset{\mathbf{F}:\ \det(\mathbf{F})=0}{\arg\min}\ \|\mathbf{F} - \mathbf{T}^\top(\mathbf{x})_{3\times3}\mathbf{T}'\|_F, \tag{12}$$

where $\mathbf{F}$ denotes the fundamental matrix. The model extractor explicitly enforces rank deficiency of the solution by projecting to the set of rank-deficient matrices. It is well-known that this projection can be carried out in closed formed by setting the smallest singular value of the full-rank solution to zero [13]. We use the symmetric epipolar distance as the residual function:

$$r(\mathbf{p}_i, \mathbf{F}) = \left|\hat{\mathbf{p}}_i^\top \mathbf{F}\hat{\mathbf{p}}_i'\right| \left(\frac{1}{\|\mathbf{F}^\top\hat{\mathbf{p}}_i\|_2} + \frac{1}{\|\mathbf{F}\hat{\mathbf{p}}_i'\|_2}\right). \tag{13}$$

Fundamental matrices cannot be easily compared directly due to their structure. We opt to compare them based on how they act on a given set of correspondences. To this end we generate virtual pairs of correspondences that are inliers to the groundtruth epipolar geometry by generating a grid of points in both images and reprojecting the points to the groundtruth epipolar lines. This results in virtual, noise-free inlier correspondences $\mathbf{p}_i^{gt}$ that can be used to define a geometrically meaningful loss. This can be understood as sampling the groundtruth epipolar geometry in image space. We define the training loss as

$$\mathcal{L} = \frac{1}{N_{gt}} \sum_{j=0}^{D} \sum_{i=1}^{N_{gt}} \min\left(r(\mathbf{p}_i^{gt}, g(\mathbf{x}^j)), \gamma\right). \tag{14}$$

Clamping the residuals ensures that hard problem instances in the training set do not dominate the training loss. We set $\gamma = 0.5$ for all experiments. Note that since the network admits interpretable intermediate representations, we attach a loss to all D intermediate results.

To facilitate efficient batch training, we constrain the number of keypoints per image pair to 1000, by randomly sampling a set of keypoints if the detected number is larger. We replicate random keypoints if the number of detected keypoints is smaller than 1000.

At test time we evaluate the estimated solution and perform a final, non-robust model fitting step to the 20 points with smallest residual error in order to correct for small inaccuracies in the estimated weights.

6   Experiments

In order to show that our approach is able to exploit regularity in data when it is present, while providing competitive performance on generic fundamental matrix estimation problems, we conduct experiments on datasets of varying regularity: (1) The Tanks and Temples dataset, which depicts images of medium-scale scenes taken from a hand-held camera [19]. This dataset presents a large-baseline scenario with generic camera extrinsics, but exhibits some regularity (particularly in the intrinsics) as all sequences in the dataset are acquired by two cameras. (2) The KITTI odometry dataset, which consists of consecutive frames in a driving scenario [9]. This datasets exhibits high regularity, with small baselines and epipolar geometries that are dominated by forward motion. (3) An unstructured SfM dataset, with images taken from community photo collections [43]. This dataset represents the most general case of fundamental matrix estimation, where image pairs are taken from arbitrary cameras over large baselines. We will show that our approach is still able to learn a robust estimator that performs as well as or better than classic sampling-based approaches in the most general case, while offering the possibility to specialize if regularity is present in the data.

Tanks and Temples. The Tanks and Temples dataset consists of medium-scale image sequences taken from a hand-held camera [19]. We use the sequences *Family*, *Francis*, *Horse*, and *Lighthouse* for training. We use *M60* for validation and evaluate on the three remaining 'Intermediate' sequences: *Panther*, *Playground*, and *Train*. (The train/val/test split was done in alphabetical order, by sequence name.) We reconstruct the sequences using the COLMAP SfM pipeline [35] to derive groundtruth camera poses and corresponding fundamental matrices. We use SIFT [25] to extract putative correspondences between all pairs of frames in a sequence and discard pairs which have less than 20 matches within one pixel of the groundtruth epipolar lines. The resulting dataset is composed of challenging wide-baseline pairs. An example is shown in Fig. 3 (rightmost column). Note that the SfM pipeline reasons globally about the consistency of 3D points and cameras, leading to accurate estimates with an average reprojection error below one pixel [35]. We generate two datasets: A default dataset were the correspondences were prefiltered using a ratio test with a cut-off of 0.8. Unless otherwise stated we train and test on this filtered dataset. The ratio test is a commonly employed technique in SIFT matching and can lead to greatly improved inlier ratios, but might lead to a sparse set of candidate correspondences. We generate a second significantly harder dataset without this pre-filtering step to test the robustness of our approach in the high noise regime.

Table 2. Performance on the Tanks and Temples dataset for different numbers of iterations D. $D = 5^*$ does not use any side information (the only inputs to the network are the x-y coordinates of the putative matches). *Direct reg.* is a network that directly regresses to the fundamental matrix.

	% Inliers	F-score	Mean	Median	Min	Max	Time [ms]
$D = 1$	42.30	44.80	3.45	1.00	0.08	1912.67	7
$D = 3$	44.91	47.25	1.98	0.82	0.08	566.70	18
$D = 5$	45.02	46.99	2.04	0.83	0.11	285.36	26
$D = 5^*$	44.60	46.42	2.23	0.84	0.10	391.64	26
Direct reg.	4.42	9.14	16.67	11.96	0.83	386.15	3

In a first experiment, we train our network with varying depths D and use the descriptor matching score as well as the ratio of best to second best match as side information. We report the average percentage of inliers (correspondences with epipolar distance below one pixel), the F1-score (where positives are defined as correspondences with an epipolar distance below one pixel with respect to the groundtruth epipolar line), and the mean and median epipolar distance to groundtruth matches. We additionally report the minimum and maximum errors incurred over the dataset. The results are summarized in Table 2. It can be observed that with a larger number of iterations, more accurate results are found. The setting $D = 1$ corresponds to only applying the neural network followed by a single weighted least-squares estimate. Using three steps of iterative refinement ($D = 3$) considerably improves the average inlier count as well as the overall accuracy. The network with five steps of iterative refinement ($D = 5$) performs comparably to three steps in most measures, but is more robust in the worst case. We thus use this architecture for all further evaluations.

We additionally evaluate the influence of side information. This is shown in the $D = 5^*$ setting, where only the locations of the putative correspondences are passed to the neural networks. Removing the side information leads to a small but noticeable drop in average accuracy. Finally, *Direct reg.* shows the result of an unstructured neural network that directly regresses from correspondences and side information to the coefficients of the fundamental matrix. The architecture resembles the $D = 1$ setting, with the weighted least-squares layer replaced by a pooling layer followed by three fully-connected layers. Details of the architecture can be found in the supplementary material. It can be seen that the unstructured network leads to considerably worse results. This highlights the importance of modeling the problem structure. We additionally report average execution times in milliseconds for the different architectures as measured on an NVIDIA Titan X GPU.

Table 3 compares our approach ($D = 5$) to RANSAC [7], Least Median of Squares (LMEDS) [32], MLESAC [39], and USAC [30]. Note that USAC is a state-of-the-art robust estimation pipeline. Similarly to our approach, it can leverage matching quality as additional side information to perform guided sampling. For fair comparison, we thus provide the matching scores (side information) to USAC. For RANSAC, LMEDS, and MLESAC we used the eight-point algorithm [13] as the base estimator, whereas USAC used the seven-point algorithm. For the baseline methods we performed a grid-search over hyperparameters on the training set.

As shown in Table 3, our approach outperforms all the baselines on both datasets. The difference is particularly striking on the dataset that does not include the ratio test. This datasets features very high outlier ratios (80%+), pushing the sampling-based approaches beyond their breakdown point in most cases. USAC and our approach perform considerably better than the other baselines on this dataset, which highlights the importance of using side information to guide the estimates.

Table 3. Results on the Tanks and Temples dataset. We evaluate two scenarios: moderate noise, where the putative correspondences were prefiltered using the ratio test, and high noise, without the ratio test. Our approach outperforms the baselines in both scenarios.

	Tanks and Temples – with ratio test				Tanks and Temples – without ratio test			
	% Inliers	F-score	Mean	Median	% Inliers	F-score	Mean	Median
RANSAC	42.61	42.99	**1.83**	1.09	2.98	10.99	122.14	79.28
LMEDS	42.96	40.57	2.41	1.14	1.57	4.78	120.63	108.72
MLESAC	41.89	42.39	2.04	1.08	2.13	8.28	131.11	93.04
USAC	42.76	43.55	3.72	1.24	4.45	23.55	46.32	8.52
Ours	**45.02**	**46.99**	2.04	**0.83**	**5.62**	**26.92**	**36.81**	**7.82**

Table 4. Results on the KITTI benchmark for different inlier thresholds. We evaluate a model that was trained on the KITTI training set as well as a model that was trained on Tanks and Temples, in order to show both ability to take advantage of regularities in the data and ability to learn an estimator that generalizes across datasets.

	@ 0.1px		@ 1px			
	% Inliers	F-score	% Inliers	F-score	Mean	Median
RANSAC	21.85	13.84	84.96	75.65	0.35	0.32
LMEDS	20.01	13.34	84.23	75.44	0.37	0.35
MLESAC	18.60	12.54	84.48	75.15	0.39	0.36
USAC	21.43	13.90	85.13	75.70	0.35	0.32
Ours tr. on T&T	21.00	13.31	84.81	75.08	0.39	0.33
Ours tr. on KITTI	**24.61**	**14.65**	**85.87**	**75.77**	**0.32**	**0.29**

KITTI Odometry Dataset. The KITTI odometry dataset [9] consists of 22 distinct driving sequences, eleven of which have publicly available groundtruth odometry. We follow the same protocol as on the previous dataset and use the ratio test to pre-filter the putative correspondences. We train our network on sequences *00* to *05* and use sequences *06* to *10* for testing.

Table 4 summarizes the results on this dataset. We show the results of two different models: One that was trained on the KITTI training set (*Ours tr. on KITTI*) and one that was trained on Tanks and Temples (*Ours tr. on T&T*). The results indicate that our approach is able to learn a model that is more accurate when specialized to the dataset. It is interesting to note that the model that was trained on the Tanks and Temples dataset generalizes to the KITTI dataset, even though the datasets are very different in terms of the camera geometry and the range of fundamental matrices that can occur. The model that was trained on Tanks and Temples performs comparably to the baseline

Table 5. Performance of fundamental matrix estimation on *Roman Forum*. This datasets exhibits a wide range of camera geometries and motions. Our approach leads to an estimator that is competitive with the baselines.

	@ *0.1px*		@ *1px*			
	% Inliers	F-score	% Inliers	F-score	Mean	Median
RANSAC	49.55	40.80	67.52	59.12	2.29	1.21
LMEDS	**51.74**	41.87	67.85	59.38	2.50	1.16
MLESAC	48.07	40.01	67.40	58.64	**1.45**	1.17
USAC	51.21	41.87	66.65	58.93	2.94	1.22
Ours	51.41	**43.28**	**68.31**	**60.67**	1.51	**1.02**

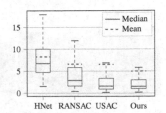

Fig. 2. Performance on the homography estimation task in terms of average corner error.

approaches, which indicates that a robust estimator that is applicable across datasets can be learned.

Community Photo Collections. We additionally show experiments on general community photo collection datasets [43]. This dataset admits no obvious regularity, with images taken from distinct cameras from a large variety of positions.

We use the sequence *Gendarmenmarkt* from this dataset for training, and use the sequence *Roman Forum* for testing. We reconstruct both sequences using COLMAP [35]. We randomly sample 10,000 image pairs from *Gendarmenmarkt* that contain at least 20 matches that are within 1 pixel of the groundtruth epipolar line to generate the training set. We randomly sample 1000 image pairs from *Roman Forum* to generate the test set. Table 5 summarizes the results on this dataset. It can be seen that our approach performs as well as or better than the baselines according to most measures. Since there is no apparent regularity in the data, this highlights the ability of our approach to learn a general-purpose estimator, while still being able to exploit regularity to its advantage if it is present in the data. We present qualitative results on this dataset in Fig. 3.

Homography Estimation. As a supporting contribution, we show that our approach leads to state-of-the-art results on the task of homography estimation. We use the DLT as a base estimator and provide exact expressions for $\mathbf{A}(\mathbf{P})$, $g(\mathbf{x})$, and the residuals in the supplementary material.

We follow the evaluation protocol defined in [6], which is based on the MS-COCO dataset [23]. For each image we extract random patches of size 256×256 pixels. We generate a groundtruth homography by perturbing the corners of the reference patch uniformly at random by up to 64 pixels. The inverse homography is used to warp the reference image and a second (warped) patch is extracted from the same location. We refer to [6] for further details on the dataset generation. We generate 10,000 training pairs and use ORB [33] and the Hamming distance for matching. We discard pairs with less than 100 matches and use a total of 500 points to allow batching. We use matching scores as side information and clamp the maximal residual in (14) to $\gamma = 64$.

Fig. 3. Image pairs from *Roman Forum* (first and second column) and *Tanks and Temples* (last column). Top row: First image with inliers (red) and outliers (blue). Bottom row: Epipolar lines of a random subset of inliers in the second image. We show the epipolar lines of our estimate (green) and of the groundtruth (blue). Images have been scaled for visualization. (Color figure online)

We compare our approach to a deep network for homography estimation [6] (HNet), RANSAC followed by a non-linear refinement stage, and USAC. To train the baseline network, we follow the exact protocol described in [6]. The test set consists of 1000 images from the MS-COCO test set that where generated in the same way as the training set with the exception that we do not discard pairs with less than 100 matches.

The results are summarized in Fig. 2. We report statistics of the average corner error of the estimated homographies. Note that our result of HNet is slightly better than what was reported by the authors (avg. error 8.0 pixels vs 9.2 pixels in [6]). Our approach outperforms both HNet and the SAC baselines.

7   Conclusion

We have presented a method for learning robust fundamental matrix estimators from data. Our experiments indicate that the learned estimators are robust and accurate on a variety of datasets. Our approach enables data-driven specialization of estimators to certain scenarios, such as ones encountered in autonomous driving. Our experiments indicate that general robust estimators that are competitive with the state of the art can be learned directly from data, alleviating the need for extensive modeling of error statistics.

We view the presented approach as a step towards modular SLAM and SfM systems that combine the power of deep networks with mathematically sound geometric modeling. In addition to the presented problem instances, our approach is directly applicable to other problems in multiple-view geometry that are based on the Direct Linear Transform, such as triangulation or the PnP problem [13]. Furthermore, the general scheme of the algorithm may be applicable to other problems where IRLS is employed [47].

References

1. Agrawal, P., Carreira, J., Malik, J.: Learning to see by moving. In: ICCV, pp. 37–45 (2015)
2. Andrychowicz, M., et al.: Learning to learn by gradient descent by gradient descent. In: NIPS, pp. 3981–3989 (2016)
3. Brachmann, E., et al.: DSAC - Differentiable RANSAC for camera localization. In: CVPR (2017)
4. Chin, T., Purkait, P., Eriksson, A.P., Suter, D.: Efficient globally optimal consensus maximisation with tree search. IEEE Trans. Pattern Anal. Mach. Intell. **39**(4), 758–772 (2017)
5. Chum, O., Matas, J.: Matching with PROSAC - progressive sample consensus. In: CVPR (2005)
6. DeTone, D., Malisiewicz, T., Rabinovich, A.: Deep image homography estimation (2016). arXiv:1606.03798
7. Fischler, M.A., Bolles, R.C.: Random sample consensus: a paradigm for model fitting with applications to image analysis and automated cartography. Commun. ACM **24**(6), 381–395 (1981)
8. Fitzgibbon, A.W.: Robust registration of 2D and 3D point sets. Image Vis. Comput. **21**(13–14), 1145–1153 (2003)
9. Geiger, A., Lenz, P., Urtasun, R.: Are we ready for autonomous driving? The KITTI vision benchmark suite. In: CVPR (2012)
10. Girshick, R., Donahue, J., Darrell, T., Malik, J.: Rich feature hierarchies for accurate object detection and semantic segmentation. In: CVPR (2014)
11. Grabner, H., Gall, J., Gool, L.J.V.: What makes a chair a chair? In: CVPR (2011)
12. Hartley, R., Zisserman, A.: Multiple View Geometry in Computer Vision. Cambridge University Press, Cambridge (2000)
13. Hartley, R.I.: In defense of the eight-point algorithm. IEEE Trans. Pattern Anal. Mach. Intell. **19**(6), 580–593 (1997)
14. Hoseinnezhad, R., Bab-Hadiashar, A.: An M-estimator for high breakdown robust estimation in computer vision. Comput. Vis. Image Underst. **115**(8), 1145–1156 (2011)
15. Ionescu, C., Vantzos, O., Sminchisescu, C.: Matrix backpropagation for deep networks with structured layers. In: ICCV (2015)
16. Kendall, A., Cipolla, R.: Geometric loss functions for camera pose regression with deep learning. In: CVPR (2017)
17. Kendall, A., Grimes, M., Cipolla, R.: PoseNet: A convolutional network for real-time 6-DOF camera relocalization. In: ICCV (2015)
18. Kingma, D.P., Ba, J.: Adam: A method for stochastic optimization. In: ICLR (2015)
19. Knapitsch, A., Park, J., Zhou, Q.Y., Koltun, V.: Tanks and temples: benchmarking large-scale scene reconstruction. ACM Trans. Graph. **36**(4), 78 (2017)
20. Krizhevsky, A., Sutskever, I., Hinton, G.E.: ImageNet classification with deep convolutional neural networks. In: NIPS (2012)

21. Lebeda, K., Matas, J., Chum, O.: Fixing the locally optimized RANSAC. In: BMVC (2012)
22. Li, H.: Consensus set maximization with guaranteed global optimality for robust geometry estimation. In: ICCV (2009)
23. Lin, T., et al.: Microsoft COCO: common objects in context. In: ECCV (2014)
24. Long, J., Shelhamer, E., Darrell, T.: Fully convolutional networks for semantic segmentation. In: CVPR (2015)
25. Lowe, D.G.: Distinctive image features from scale-invariant keypoints. Int. J. Comput. Vis. **60**(2), 91–110 (2004)
26. Maas, A.L., Hannun, A.Y., Ng, A.Y.: Rectifier nonlinearities improve neural network acoustic models. In: ICML Workshops (2013)
27. Mur-Artal, R., Montiel, J.M.M., Tardós, J.D.: ORB-SLAM: a versatile and accurate monocular SLAM system. IEEE Trans. Robot. **31**(5), 1147–1163 (2015)
28. Nguyen, T., Chen, S.W., Shivakumar, S.S., Taylor, C.J., Kumar, V.: Unsupervised deep homography: A fast and robust homography estimation model (2017). arXiv:1709.03966
29. Qi, C.R., Su, H., Mo, K., Guibas, L.J.: PointNet: Deep learning on point sets for 3D classification and segmentation. In: CVPR (2016)
30. Raguram, R., Chum, O., Pollefeys, M., Matas, J., Frahm, J.: USAC: a universal framework for random sample consensus. IEEE Trans. Pattern Anal. Mach. Intell. **35**(8), 2022–2038 (2013)
31. Rocco, I., Arandjelovic, R., Sivic, J.: Convolutional neural network architecture for geometric matching. In: CVPR (2017)
32. Rousseeuw, P.J.: Least median of squares regression. J. Am. Stat. Assoc. **79**(388), 871–880 (1984)
33. Rublee, E., Rabaud, V., Konolige, K., Bradski, G.R.: ORB: An efficient alternative to SIFT or SURF. In: ICCV (2011)
34. Savinov, N., Seki, A., Ladicky, L., Sattler, T., Pollefeys, M.: Quad-networks: unsupervised learning to rank for interest point detection. In: CVPR (2017)
35. Schönberger, J.L., Frahm, J.M.: Structure-from-motion revisited. In: CVPR (2016)
36. Tennakoon, R.B., Bab-Hadiashar, A., Cao, Z., Hoseinnezhad, R., Suter, D.: Robust model fitting using higher than minimal subset sampling. IEEE Trans. Pattern Anal. Mach. Intell. **38**(2), 350–362 (2016)
37. Torr, P.H.S.: Bayesian model estimation and selection for epipolar geometry and generic manifold fitting. Int. J. Comput. Vis. **50**(1), 35–61 (2002)
38. Torr, P.H.S., Murray, D.W.: The development and comparison of robust methods for estimating the fundamental matrix. Int. J. Comput. Vis. **24**(3), 271–300 (1997)
39. Torr, P.H.S., Zisserman, A.: MLESAC: a new robust estimator with application to estimating image geometry. Comput. Vis. Image Underst. **78**(1), 138–156 (2000)
40. Ulyanov, D., Vedaldi, A., Lempitsky, V.S.: Improved texture networks: maximizing quality and diversity in feed-forward stylization and texture synthesis. In: CVPR (2017)
41. Ummenhofer, B., Zhou, H., Uhrig, J., Mayer, N., Ilg, E., Dosovitskiy, A., Brox, T.: DeMoN: Depth and motion network for learning monocular stereo. In: CVPR (2017)
42. Vongkulbhisal, J., De la Torre, F., Costeira, J.P.: Discriminative optimization: theory and applications to point cloud registration. In: CVPR (2017)
43. Wilson, K., Snavely, N.: Robust global translations with 1DSfM. In: ECCV (2014)
44. Yang, J., Li, H., Jia, Y.: Optimal essential matrix estimation via inlier-set maximization. In: ECCV (2014)

45. Yi, K.M., Trulls, E., Lepetit, V., Fua, P.: LIFT: Learned invariant feature transform. In: ECCV (2016)
46. Yi, K.M., Trulls, E., Ono, Y., Lepetit, V., Salzmann, M., Fua, P.: Learning to find good correspondences. In: CVPR (2018)
47. Zach, C.: Robust bundle adjustment revisited. In: ECCV (2014)
48. Zaheer, M., Kottur, S., Ravanbakhsh, S., Póczos, B., Salakhutdinov, R., Smola, A.J.: Deep sets. In: NIPS (2017)
49. Zhang, Z.: Determining the epipolar geometry and its uncertainty: a review. Int. J. Comput. Vis. **27**(2), 161–195 (1998)
50. Zhou, Q., Park, J., Koltun, V.: Fast global registration. In: ECCV (2016)

TrackingNet: A Large-Scale Dataset and Benchmark for Object Tracking in the Wild

Matthias Müller, Adel Bibi, Silvio Giancola[✉], Salman Alsubaihi, and Bernard Ghanem

King Abdullah University of Science and Technology,
Thuwal, Kingdom of Saudi Arabia
{matthias.mueller.2,adel.bibi,silvio.giancola,
salman.alsubaihi,bernard.ghanem}@kaust.edu.sa
http://www.tracking-net.org

Abstract. Despite the numerous developments in object tracking, further improvement of current tracking algorithms is limited by small and mostly saturated datasets. As a matter of fact, data-hungry trackers based on deep-learning currently rely on object detection datasets due to the scarcity of dedicated large-scale tracking datasets. In this work, we present TrackingNet, the first large-scale dataset and benchmark for object tracking in the wild. We provide more than 30K videos with more than 14 million dense bounding box annotations. Our dataset covers a wide selection of object classes in broad and diverse context. By releasing such a large-scale dataset, we expect deep trackers to further improve and generalize. In addition, we introduce a new benchmark composed of 500 novel videos, modeled with a distribution similar to our training dataset. By sequestering the annotation of the test set and providing an online evaluation server, we provide a fair benchmark for future development of object trackers. Deep trackers fine-tuned on a fraction of our dataset improve their performance by up to 1.6% on OTB100 and up to 1.7% on TrackingNet Test. We provide an extensive benchmark on TrackingNet by evaluating more than 20 trackers. Our results suggest that object tracking in the wild is far from being solved.

Keywords: Object tracking · Dataset · Benchmark · Deep learning

This work was supported by the King Abdullah University of Science and Technology (KAUST) Office of Sponsored Research (OSR).
M. Müller, A. Bibi and S. Giancola—Equally contributed.

Electronic supplementary material The online version of this chapter (https:// doi.org/10.1007/978-3-030-01246-5_19) contains supplementary material, which is available to authorized users.

© Springer Nature Switzerland AG 2018
V. Ferrari et al. (Eds.): ECCV 2018, LNCS 11205, pp. 310–327, 2018.
https://doi.org/10.1007/978-3-030-01246-5_19

1   Introduction

Object tracking is a common task in computer vision, with a long history spanning decades [29,42,48]. Despite considerable progress in the field, object tracking remains a challenging task. Current trackers perform well on established datasets such as OTB [46,47] and VOT [21–26] benchmarks. However, most of these datasets are fairly small and do not fully represent the challenges faced when tracking objects *in the wild* (Fig. 1).

Fig. 1. Examples of tracking from our novel TrackingNet Test set.

Following the rise of deep learning in computer vision, the tracking community is currently embracing data-driven learning methods. Most trackers submitted to the annual challenge VOT17 [22] use deep features, while they were nonexistent in earlier versions VOT13 [25] and VOT14 [26]. In addition, nine out of the ten top-performing trackers in VOT17 [22] rely on deep features, outperforming the previous state-of-the-art trackers. However, the tracking community still lacks a dedicated large-scale dataset to train deep trackers. As a consequence, deep trackers are often restricted to using pretrained models from object classification [6] or use object detection datasets such as ImageNet Videos [40]. As an example of this, SiameseFC [2] and CFNet [43] show outstanding results by training specific Convolutional Neural Networks (CNNs) for tracking.

Since classical trackers rely on handcrafted features and because existing tracking datasets are small, there is currently no clear split between data used for training and testing. Recent benchmarks [22,33] now consider putting aside a sequestered test set to provide a fair comparison. Hence, it is common to see trackers developed and trained on the OTB [47] dataset before competing on VOT [24]. Note that VOT15 [23] is sampled from existing datasets like OTB100 [47] and ALOV300 [41], resulting in overlapping sequences (*e.g.* basketball, car, singer, *etc...*). Even though the redundancy is contained, one needs to be careful while selecting training video sequences, since training deep trackers on testing videos is not fair. As a result, there is usually not enough data to train deep networks for tracking and data from different fields are used to pre-train models, which is a limiting factor for certain architectures.

In this paper, we present TrackingNet, a large-scale object tracking dataset designed to train deep trackers. Our dataset has several advantages. First, the large training set enables the development of deep design specific for tracking. Second, the specificity of the dataset for object tracking enables novel architectures to focus on the temporal context between consecutive frames. Current large scale object detection datasets do not provide data densely annotated in time. Third, TrackingNet represents real-world scenarios by sampling over YouTube videos. As such, TrackingNet videos contain a rich distribution of object classes, which we enforce to be shared between training and testing. Last, we evaluate tracker performance on a segregated testing set with a similar distribution over object classes and motion. Trackers do not have access to the annotations of these videos but can obtain results and insights through an evaluation server.

Contributions. (i) We present TrackingNet, the first large-scale dataset for object tracking. We analyze the characteristics, attributes and uniqueness of TrackingNet when compared with other datasets (Sect. 3). (ii) We provide insights into different techniques to generate dense annotations from coarse ones. We show that most trackers can produce accurate and reliable dense annotations over 1 second-long intervals (Sect. 4). (iii) We provide an extended baseline for state-of-the-art trackers benchmarked on TrackingNet. We show that pretraining deep models on TrackingNet can improve their performance on other datasets by increasing their metrics by up to 1.7% (Sect. 5).

2   Related Work

In the following, we provide an overview of the various research on object tracking. The tasks in the field can be clustered between *multi-object tracking* [24,47] and *single-object tracking* [27,33]. The former focuses on multiple instance tracking of class-specific objects, relying on strong and fast object detection algorithms and association estimation between consecutive frames. The latter is the target of this work. It approaches the problem by *tracking-by-detection*, which consists of two main components: *model representation*, either generative [19,39] or discriminative [14,49], and *object search*, a trade-off between computational cost and dense sampling of the region of interest.

Correlation Filter Trackers. In recent years, correlation filter (CF) trackers [1,4,16,17] have emerged as the most common, fastest and most accurate category of trackers. CF trackers learn a filter at the first frame, which represents the object of interest. This filter localizes the target in successive frames before being updated. The main reason behind the impressive performance of CF trackers lies in the approximate dense sampling achieved by circularly shifting the target patch samples [17]. Also, the remarkable runtime performance is achieved by efficiently solving the underlying ridge regression problem in the Fourier domain [4]. Since the inception of CF trackers with single-channel features [4,17], they have been extended with kernels [16], multi-channel features [9] and scale adaptation [30]. In addition, many works enhance the original formulation by adapting the regression target [3], adding context [12,35], spatially regularizing the learned filters and learning continuous filters [10].

Deep Trackers. Beside the CF trackers that use deep features from object detection networks, few works explore more complete deep learning approaches. A first approach consists of learning generic features on a large-scale object detection dataset and successively fine-tuning domain-specific layers to be target-specific in an online fashion. MDNET [36] shows the success of such a method by winning the VOT15 [23] challenge. A second approach consists of training a fully convolutional network and using a feature map selection method to choose between shallow and deep layers during tracking [45]. The goal is to find a good trade-off between general semantic and more specific discriminative features, as well as, to remove noisy and irrelevant feature maps.

While both of these approaches achieve state-of-the-art results, their computation cost prohibits these algorithms from being deployed in real applications. A third approach consists of using Siamese networks that predict motion between consecutive frames. Such trackers are usually trained offline on a large-scale dataset using either deep regression [15] or a CNN matching function [2,13,43]. Due to their simple architecture and lack of online fine-tuning, only a forward pass has to be executed at test time. This results in very fast run-times (up to 100 fps on a GPU) while achieving competitive accuracy. However, since the model is not updated at test time, the accuracy highly depends on how well the training dataset captures appearance nuisances that occur while tracking various objects. Such approaches would benefit from a large-scale dataset like the one we propose in this paper.

Object Tracking Datasets. Numerous datasets are available for object tracking, the most common ones being OTB [47], VOT [24], ALOV300 [41] and TC128 [31] for single-object tracking and MOT [27,33] for multi-object tracking. **VIVID** [5] is an early attempt to build a tracking dataset for surveillance purposes. **OTB50** [46] and **OTB100** [47] provide 51 and 98 video sequences annotated with 11 different attributes and upright bounding boxes for each frame. **TC128** [31] comprises 129 videos, based on similar attributes and upright bounding boxes. **ALOV300** [41] comprises 314 videos sequences labelled with 14 attributes. **VOT** [24] proposes several challenges with up to 60 video sequences. It introduced rotated bounding boxes as well as extensive studies on object tracking annotations. **VOT-TIR** is a specific dataset from VOT focusing on Thermal InfraRed videos. **NUS PRO** [28] gathers an application-specific collection of 365 videos for people and rigid object tracking. **UAV123** and **UAV20L** [34] gather another application-specific collection of 123 videos and 20 long videos captured from a UAV or generated from a flight simulator. **NfS** [11] provides a set of 100 videos with high framerate, in an attempt to focus on fast motion. Table 1 provides a detailed overview of the most popular tracking datasets.

Table 1. Comparison of current datasets for object tracking.

Datasets	Nb Videos	Nb Annot.	Frame per Video	Nb Classes
VIVID [5]	9	16274	1808.2	-
TC128 [33]	129	55652	431.4	-
OTB50 [48]	51	29491	578.3	-
OTB100 [49]	98	58610	598.1	-
VOT16 [22]	60	21455	357.6	-
VOT17 [23]	60	21356	355.9	-
UAV20L [36]	20	58670	2933.5	-
UAV123 [36]	91	113476	1247.0	-
NUS PRO [29]	365	135305	370.7	-
ALOV300 [43]	314	151657	483.0	-
NfS [13]	100	383000	3830.0	-
MOT16 [35]	7	182326	845.6	-
MOT17 [35]	21	564228	845.6	-
TrackingNet (Train)	30132	14205677	471.4	27
TrackingNet (Test)	511	225589	441.5	27

Despite the availability of several datasets for object tracking, large scale datasets are necessary to train deep trackers. Therefore, current deep trackers rely on object detection datasets such as ImageNet Video [40] or Youtube-BoundingBoxes [38]. Those datasets provide object detection bounding boxes on videos, relatively sparse in time or at a low frame rate. Thus, they lack motion information about the object dynamics in consecutive frames. Still, they are widely used to pre-train deep trackers. They provide deep feature representation with object knowledge that can be transferred from detection to tracking.

3   TrackingNet

In this section, we introduce TrackingNet, a large-scale dataset for object tracking. TrackingNet assembles a total of 30,643 video segments with an average duration of 16.6s. All the 14,431,266 frames extracted from the 140 hours of visual content are annotated with a single upright bounding box. We provide a comparison with other tracking datasets in Table 1 and Fig. 2.

Our work attempts to bridge the gap between data-hungry deep trackers and scarcely-available large scale datasets. Our proposed tracking dataset is larger than the previous largest one by 2 orders of magnitude. We build TrackingNet to address object tracking in the wild. Therefore, the dataset copes with a large variety of frame rates, resolutions, context and object classes. In contrast with previous tracking datasets, TrackingNet is split between training and testing. We carefully select 30,132 training videos from Youtube-BoundingBoxes [38] and build a novel set of 511 testing videos with a distribution similar to the training set.

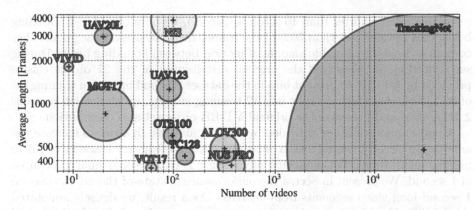

Fig. 2. Comparison of tracking datasets distributed across the number of videos and the average length of the videos. The size of circles is proportional to the number of annotated bounding boxes. Our dataset has the largest amount of videos and frames and the video length is still reasonable for short video tracking.

3.1   From YT-BB to TrackingNet Training Set

Youtube-BoundingBoxes (YT-BB) [38] is a large scale dataset for object detection. This dataset consists of approximately 380,000 video segments, annotated every second with upright bounding boxes. Those videos are gathered directly from YouTube, with a wide diversity in resolution, frame rate and duration.

Since YT-BB focuses on object detection, the object class is provided along with the bounding boxes. The dataset proposes a list of 23 object classes representative of the videos available on the YouTube platform. For the sake of tracking, we remove the object classes that lack motion by definition, in particular *potted plant* and *toilet*. Since the *person* class represents 25% of the annotations, we split it into 7 different classes based on their context. Overall, the distribution of the object classes in TrackingNet is shown in Fig. 3.

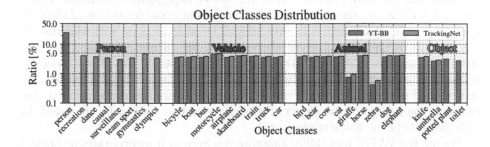

Fig. 3. Definition of object classes and macro classes.

To ensure decent quality in the videos for tracking purposes, we filtered out 90% of the videos based on attribute criteria. First, we avoid small segments by removing videos shorter than 15 seconds. Second, we only considered bounding boxes that covered less than 50% of the frame. Last, we preserve segments that contain at least a reasonable amount of motion between bounding boxes. During such filtering, we preserved the original distribution of the 21 object classes provided by YT-BB, to prevent bias in the dataset. We end up with a training set of 30,132 videos, which we split into 12 training subsets, each of which contains 2,511 videos and preserves the original YT-BB object classes distribution.

Coarse annotations are provided by YT-BB at 1 fps. In order to increase the annotation density, we rely on a mixture of state-of-the-art trackers to fill in missing annotations. We claim that any tracker is reliable on a small time lapse of 1 second. We present in Sect. 4 the performance of state-of-the-art trackers on 1 second-long video segments from OTB100. As a result, we densely annotated the 30,132 videos using a weighted average between a forward and a backward pass using the DCF tracker [16]. By doing so, we provide a densely annotated training dataset for object tracking, along with code for automatically downloading videos from YouTube and extracting the annotated frames.

3.2   From YT-CC to TrackingNet Testing Set

Alongside the training dataset, we compile a novel dataset for testing, which comprises 511 videos from YouTube with Creative Commons licence, namely YT-CC. We carefully select those videos to reflect the object class distribution from the training set. We ensure that those videos do not contain any copyrights, so they can be shared. We then used Amazon Mechanical Turk workers (Turkers) for annotating those videos. We annotate the first bounding boxes and define specific rules for the Turkers to carefully annotate the successive frames. We define the objects as in YT-BB for object detection, *i.e.* with the smallest bounding box fitting any visible part of the object to track.

Annotations should be defined in a deterministic way, using rules that are agreed upon and abided by during the annotation process. By defining the smallest upright bounding box around an object, we avoid any ambiguity. However, the bounding box may contain a large amount of background. For instance, the arm and the legs are always included for the *person* class, regardless of the person's pose. We argue that a tracker should be able to cope with deformable objects and to understand what it is tracking. In a similar fashion, the tails of animal are always included. In addition, the bounding box of an object is adjusted as a function of its visibility in the frame. Estimating the position of an occluded part of the object is not deterministic hence should be avoided. For instance, the handle of the object class *knife* could be hidden by the hand. In such cases, only the blade is annotated.

We use the VATIC tool [44] to annotate the frames. It incorporates an optical flow algorithm to guess the position of the next bounding boxes in successive frames. Turkers may annotate a non-tight bounding box around the object or rely on the optical flow to determine the bounding box location and size. To avoid such behavior, we visually inspect every single frame after each annotation round, rewarding good Turkers and rejecting bad annotations. We either restart the video annotation from scratch or ask Turkers to fine-tune previous results. With our supervision in the loop, we ensure the quality of our annotations after a few iterations, discourage bad annotators and incentivize the good ones.

3.3 Attributes

Successively, each video is annotated with a list of attributes defined in Table 2. 15 attributes are provided for our testing set, the first 5 are extracted automatically by analyzing the variation of the bounding boxes in time while the last 10 are manually checked by visually analyzing the 511 videos of our dataset. An overview of the attribute distribution is given in Fig. 4 and compared to OTB100 [47] and VOT17 [22].

Table 2. List and description of the 15 attributes that characterize videos in TrackingNet. **Top:** automatically estimated. **Bottom:** visually inspected.

Attr	Description
SV	Scale Variation: the ratio of bounding box area is outside the range $[0.5, 2]$ after 1s.
ARC	Aspect Ratio Change: the ratio of bounding box aspect ratio is outside the range $[0.5, 2]$ after 1s.
FM	Fast Motion: the motion of the ground truth bounding box is larger than the size of the bounding box.
LR	Low Resolution: at least one ground truth bounding box has less than 1000 pixels.
OV	Out-of-View: some portion of the target leaves the camera field of view.
IV	Illumination Variation: the illumination of the target changes significantly.
CM	Camera Motion: abrupt motion of the camera.
MB	Motion Blur: the target region is blurred due to the motion of target or camera.
BC	Background Clutter: the background near the target has similar appearance as the target.
SOB	Similar Object: there are objects of similar shape or same type near the target.
DEF	Deformation: non-rigid object deformation.
IPR	In-Plane Rotation: the target rotates in the image plane.
OPR	Out-of-Plane Rotation: the target rotates out of the image plane.
POC	Partial Occlusion: the target is partially occluded.
FOC	Full Occlusion: the target is fully occluded.

First, we claim to have better control over the number of frames per video in our dataset, with a more contained variation with respect to other datasets.

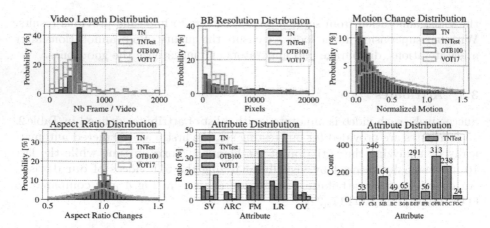

Fig. 4. (top to bottom, left to right): Distribution of the tracking videos in term of *Video length, BB Resolution, Motion Change, Scale Variation* and *attributes distribution* for the main tracking datasets.

We argue that such contained length diversity is more suitable for training with a constant batch size. Second, the distribution of the bounding box resolution is more diverse in TrackingNet, providing more diversity in the scale of the objects to track. Third, we show that challenges in OTB100 [47] and VOT17 [22] focus on objects with slightly larger motion, while TrackingNet shows a more natural motion distribution over the fastest moving instances in YT-BB. Similar conclusions can be drawn from the distribution of the aspect ratio change attribute. Fourth, more than 30% of the OTB100 instances have a constant aspect ratio, while VOT17 shows a flatter distribution. Once again, we argue that TrackingNet contains a more natural distribution of objects present in the wild. Last, we show statistics over the 15 attributes, which will be used to generate attribute specific tracking results in Sect. 5. Overall, we see that our sequestered testing set has an attribute distribution similar to that of our training set.

3.4   Evaluation

Annotation for the testing set should not be revealed to ensure a fair comparison between trackers. We thus evaluate the trackers through an online server. In a similar OTB100 fashion, we perform a One Pass Evaluation (OPE) and measure the success and precision of the trackers over the 511 videos. The success S is measured as the Intersection over Union (IoU) of the pixels between the ground truth bounding boxes (BB^{gt}) and the ones generated by the trackers (BB^{tr}). The trackers are ranked using the Area Under the Curve (AUC) measurement [47]. The precision P is usually measured as the distance in pixels between the centers C^{gt} and C^{tr} of the ground truth and the tracker bounding box, respectively. The trackers are ranked using this metric with a conventional threshold of 20 pixels.

Since the precision metric is sensitive to the resolution of the images and the size of the bounding boxes, we propose a third metric P_{norm}. We normalize the precision over the size of the ground truth bounding box, following Eq. 1. The trackers are then ranked using the AUC for normalized precision between 0 and 0.5. By substituting the original precision with the normalized one, we ensure the consistency of the metrics across different scales of objects to track. However, for bounding boxes with similar scale, success and normalized precision are very similar and show how far an annotation is from another. Nevertheless, we argue that they will differ in the case of different scales. For the sake of consistency, we provide results using precision, normalized precision and success.

$$S = \frac{|BB^{tr} \cap BB^{gt}|}{|BB^{tr} \cup BB^{gt}|} \qquad P = \|C^{tr} - C^{gt}\|_2$$
$$P_{norm} = \|W(C^{tr} - C^{gt})\|_2 \quad W = \mathrm{diag}(BB_x^{gt}, BB_y^{gt}) \tag{1}$$

4   Dataset Experiments

Since TrackingNet Training Set (~30K videos) is compiled from the YT-BB dataset, it is originally annotated with bounding boxes every second. While such sparse annotations might be satisfactory for some vision tasks, e.g. object classification and detection, deep network based trackers rely on learning the temporal evolution of bounding boxes over time. For instance, Siamese-like architectures [43,45] need to observe a large number of similar and dissimilar patches of the same object. Unfortunately, manually extending YT-BB is not feasible for such large number of frames. Thus, we have entertained the possibility of tracker-aided annotation to generate the missing dense bounding box annotations arising between the sparsely occurring original YT-BB ones. State-of-the-art trackers not only achieve impressive performance on standard tracking benchmarks, but they also perform well at high frame rates.

To assess such capability, we conducted four different experiments to decide which tracker would perform best in densely annotating OTB100 [47]. We chose among the following trackers: ECO [6], CSRDCF [32], BACF [12], SiameseFC [2], STAPLE$_{CA}$ [35], STAPLE [1], SRDCF [7], SAMF [30], CSK [17], KCF [18], DCF [18] and MOSSE [4]. To mimic the 1-second annotation in TrackingNet Training Set, we assume that all videos of OTB100 are captured at 30 fps and the OTB100 dataset is split into 1916 smaller sequences of 30 frames. We evaluate the previously highlighted trackers on the 1916 sequences of OTB100 by running them forward and backward through each sequence.

$$\mathbf{x}_{WG}^t = w_t \mathbf{x}_{FW}^t + (1 - w_t) \mathbf{x}_{BK}^t \tag{2}$$

The results of both the forward and backward passes are then combined by directly averaging the two results and by generating the convex combination (weighted average) according to Eq. 2, where $\mathbf{x}_{FW}^t$, $\mathbf{x}_{BK}^t$ and $\mathbf{x}_{WG}^t$ are the tracking results at frame t for the forward pass, backward pass, and the weighted average respectively. We tested the linear, quadratic, cubic and exponential decay combinations for the weight w_t. Note that the maximum sequence length is 30, thus $t \in [1, 30]$. The weighted average gives more weight to the results of the forward pass for frames closer to the first frame and vice versa. Figure 5 along with Table 3 show that most trackers perform almost equally well with the best performance upon using the weighted average strategy. Thereafter, since STAPLE$_{CA}$ [35] generates a reasonable accuracy with a frame rate of 30fps, we find it suitable for annotating the large training set in TrackingNet. We run STAPLE$_{CA}$ in both a forward and a backward pass where the results of both are later combined in a weighted average using a linear decay fashion as described in Eq. 2 using $w_t = (1 - t/30)$.

5   Tracking Benchmark

In our benchmark, we compare a large variety of tracking algorithms that cover all common tracking principles. The majority of current state-of-the-art algorithms are based on discriminative correlation filters with handcrafted or deep features. We select trackers to cover a large set of combinations of features and kernels. MOSSE [4], CSK [17], DCF [16], KCF [16] use simple features and do not adapt to scale variations. DSST [9], SAMF [30], and STA-PLE [1] use more sophisticated features like Colornames and try to compensate for scale variations. We also include trackers that propose some kind of general framework to improve upon correlation filter tracking. These include

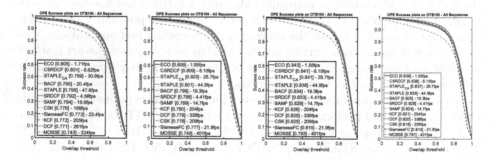

Fig. 5. Tracking results of 12 trackers on the OT100 dataset after splitting it into sequences of length 30 frames. **left to right:** forward pass, backward pass, linear and exponential decay average as in Eq. 2.

Table 3. Tracking results on the 1sec-long OTB100 dataset using different averaging.

OPE success	Forward	Backward	Average	Linear	Quadratic	Cubic	Exponential
Weight (w_t)	1	0	0.5	\multicolumn{3}{c}{$(1 - (t/30)^i)$}	$e^{-0.05t}$
ECO	0.805	0.809	0.824	**0.843**	0.833	0.838	0.839
DCF	0.771	0.779	0.799	**0.825**	0.813	0.820	0.820
STAPLE_CA	0.799	0.803	0.823	**0.841**	0.830	0.836	0.835

SRDCF [8], SAMF$_{AT}$ [30], STAPLE$_{CA}$ [35], BACF [12] and ECO-HC [6]. We include CFNet [43] and SiameseFC [2] to represent CNN matching trackers and MEEM [49] and DLSSVM [37] for structured SVM-based trackers. Last, we include some baseline trackers such as TLD [20], Struck [14], ASLA [19] and IVT [39] for reference. Table 4 summarizes the selected trackers along with their representation scheme, search method, runtime and a generic description.

Table 4. Evaluated Trackers. Representation: PI - Pixel Intensity, HOG - Histogram of Oriented Gradients, CN - Color Names, CH - Color Histogram, GK - Gaussian Kernel, K - Keypoints, BP - Binary Pattern, SSVM - Structured Support Vector Machine. Search: PF - Particle Filter, RS - Random Sampling, DS - Dense Sampling.

Tracker	Representation	Search	FPS	Venue
ASLA [19]	Sparse	PF	2.13	CVPR'12
IVT [39]	PCA	PF	11.7	IJCVIP'08
Struck [14]	SSVM, Haar	RS	16.4	ICCV'11
TLD [20]	BP	RS	22.9	PAMI'11
CSK [17]	PI, GK	DS	127	ECCV'12
DCF [16]	HOG	DS	175	PAMI'15
KCF [16]	HOG, GK	DS	119	PAMI'15
MOSSE [4]	PI	DS	223	CVPR'10
DSST [9]	PCA-HOG, PI	DS	11.9	BMVC'14
SAMF [30]	PI, HOG, CN, GK	DS	6.61	ECCVW'14
STAPLE [1]	HOG, CH	DS	22.1	CVPR'16
CSRDCF	HOG, CN, PI	DS	6.17	IJCV'18
SRDCF [8]	HOG	DS	3.17	ICCV'15
BACF [12]	HOG	DS	12.1	ICCV'17
ECO_HC [6]	HOG	DS	21.2	CVPR'17
SAMF_AT [30]	PI, HOG, CN, GK	DS	2.1	ECCV'16
STAPLE_CA [35]	HOG, CH	DS	15.9	CVPR'17
CFNET [43]	Deep	DS	10.7	CVPR'17
SiameseFC [2]	Deep	DS	11.6	ECCVW'16
MDNET [36]	Deep	RS	0.625	CVPR'16
ECO [6]	Deep	DS	4.16	CVPR'17
MEEM [49]	SSVM	RS	7.57	ECCV'14
DLSSVM [37]	SSVM	RS	5.59	CVPR'16

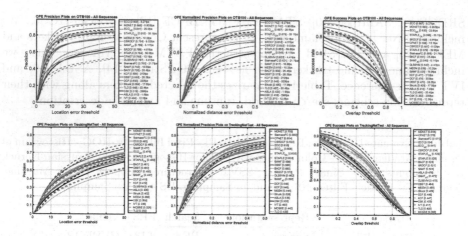

Fig. 6. Benchmark results on OTB100 (*top*) and on TrackingNet (*bottom*).

5.1   State-of-the-art Benchmark on TrackingNet

Figure 6 shows the results on the complete dataset. Note that the highest score for any tracker is about 60% success rate compared to around 90% on OTB. The top performing tracker is MDNET [36] that trains in an online fashion and is, as a result, able to adapt best. However, this comes at the cost of a very slow runtime. Next are CFNet [43] and SiameseFC [2] that benefit from being trained on a large-scale dataset (ImageNet Videos). However, as we show later, their performance can be further improved by using our training dataset.

5.2   Real-Time Tracking

For many real applications, tracking is not very useful if it cannot be done at real-time. Therefore, we conduct an experiment to evaluate how well trackers would perform in more realistic settings where frames are skipped if a tracker is too slow. We do this by subsampling the sequence based on each tracker's speed. Figure 7 shows the results of this experiment across the complete dataset. As expected, most trackers that run below real-time degrade. In the worst case,

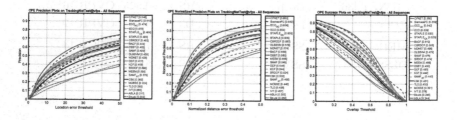

Fig. 7. Benchmark results on TrackingNet with variable frame rate (tracker fps).

this degradation can be as much as 50%, as is the case for Struck [14]. More recent trackers, in particular deep learning ones, are much less affected. CFNet [43] for example, does not degrade at all even though it only sees every third frame. This is probably due to the fact that it relies on a generic object matching function that was trained on a large-scale dataset.

5.3 Retraining on TrainingNet

We fine-tune SiameseFC [2] on a fraction of TrackingNet to show how our data can improve the tracking performance of deep-learning based trackers. The results are shown in Table 5. By training on only one of the twelve chunks (2511 videos) of our training dataset, we observe an increase in all the metrics on TrackingNet Test and OTB100. Fine-tuning using more chunks is expected to improve the performance even further.

Table 5. Fine-tuning results for SiameseFC on OTB100 and TrackingNet Test.

Benchmark	OTB100			TrackingNet Test		
Metric	Precision	Norm. Prec	Success	Precision	NormPrec	Success
SiameseFC (original)	0.765	0.621	0.569	0.533	0.663	0.571
SiameseFC (fine-tuned)	**0.781**	**0.632**	**0.576**	**0.543**	**0.673**	**0.581**

5.4 Attribute Specific Results

Each video in TrackingNet Test is annotated with 15 attributes described in Sect. 3. We evaluate all trackers per attribute to get insights about challenges facing state-of-the-art tracking algorithms. We show the most interesting results in Fig. 8 and refer the reader to the **supplementary material** for the remaining

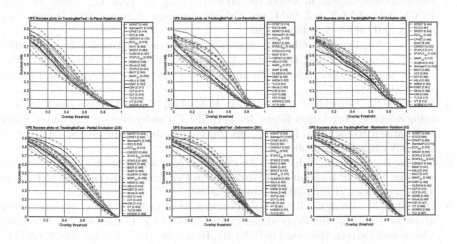

Fig. 8. Per-attribute results on TrackingNet Test.

attributes. We find that videos with in-plane rotation, low resolution targets, and full occlusion are consistently the most difficult. Trackers are least affected by illumination variation, partial occlusion, and object deformation.

6   Conclusion

In this work, we present TrackingNet, which is, to the best of our knowledge, the largest dataset for object tracking. We show how large-scale existing datasets for object detection can be leveraged for object tracking by a novel interpolation method. We also benchmark more than 20 tracking algorithms on this novel dataset and shed light on what attributes are especially difficult for current trackers. Lastly, we verify the usefulness of our large dataset in improving the performance of some deep learning based trackers.

In the future, we aim to extend the test set from 500 to 1000 videos. We plan to sample the extra 500 videos from different classes within the same category (*e.g.* tortoise/animal). This will allow for further evaluation in regards to generalization. After publication, we plan to release the training set with our interpolated annotations. We will also release the test sequences with initial bounding box annotations and the corresponding integration for the OTB toolkit. At the same time, we will publish our online evaluation server to allow researches to rank their tracking algorithms instantly.

References

1. Bertinetto, L., Valmadre, J., Golodetz, S., Miksik, O., Torr, P.H.: Staple: complementary learners for real-time tracking. In: Proceedings of the IEEE Conference on Computer Vision and Pattern Recognition, pp. 1401–1409 (2016)
2. Bertinetto, L., Valmadre, J., Henriques, J.F., Vedaldi, A., Torr, P.H.S.: Fully-convolutional siamese networks for object tracking. In: Hua, G., Jégou, H. (eds.) ECCV 2016. LNCS, vol. 9914, pp. 850–865. Springer, Cham (2016). https://doi.org/10.1007/978-3-319-48881-3_56
3. Bibi, A., Mueller, M., Ghanem, B.: Target response adaptation for correlation filter tracking. In: Leibe, B., Matas, J., Sebe, N., Welling, M. (eds.) ECCV 2016. LNCS, vol. 9910, pp. 419–433. Springer, Cham (2016). https://doi.org/10.1007/978-3-319-46466-4_25
4. Bolme, D.S., Beveridge, J.R., Draper, B.A., Lui, Y.M.: Visual object tracking using adaptive correlation filters. In: 2010 IEEE Conference on Computer Vision and Pattern Recognition (CVPR), pp. 2544–2550, June 2010. https://doi.org/10.1109/CVPR.2010.5539960
5. Collins, R., Zhou, X., Teh, S.K.: An open source tracking testbed and evaluation web site. In: IEEE International Workshop on Performance Evaluation of Tracking and Surveillance (PETS 2005), January 2005
6. Danelljan, M., Bhat, G., Khan, F.S., Felsberg, M.: ECO: efficient convolution operators for tracking. In: Proceedings of the 2017 IEEE Conference on Computer Vision and Pattern Recognition (CVPR), Honolulu, HI, USA, pp. 21–26 (2017)

7. Danelljan, M., Hager, G., Shahbaz Khan, F., Felsberg, M.: Learning spatially regularized correlation filters for visual tracking. In: Proceedings of the IEEE International Conference on Computer Vision, pp. 4310–4318 (2015)
8. Danelljan, M., Hager, G., Shahbaz Khan, F., Felsberg, M.: Learning spatially regularized correlation filters for visual tracking. In: The IEEE International Conference on Computer Vision (ICCV), December 2015
9. Danelljan, M., Hger, G., Shahbaz Khan, F., Felsberg, M.: Accurate scale estimation for robust visual tracking. In: Proceedings of the British Machine Vision Conference. BMVA Press (2014). https://doi.org/10.5244/C.28.65
10. Danelljan, M., Robinson, A., Shahbaz Khan, F., Felsberg, M.: Beyond correlation filters: learning continuous convolution operators for visual tracking. In: ECCV (2016)
11. Galoogahi, H.K., Fagg, A., Huang, C., Ramanan, D., Lucey, S.: Need for speed: a benchmark for higher frame rate object tracking. arXiv preprint arXiv:1703.05884 (2017)
12. Galoogahi, H.K., Fagg, A., Lucey, S.: Learning background-aware correlation filters for visual tracking. In: Proceedings of the 2017 IEEE Conference on Computer Vision and Pattern Recognition (CVPR), Honolulu, HI, USA, pp. 21–26 (2017)
13. Guo, Q., Feng, W., Zhou, C., Huang, R., Wan, L., Wang, S.: Learning dynamic Siamese network for visual object tracking. In: The IEEE International Conference on Computer Vision (ICCV), October 2017
14. Hare, S., Saffari, A., Torr, P.H.S.: Struck: structured output tracking with kernels. In: 2011 International Conference on Computer Vision, pp. 263–270. IEEE, November 2011. https://doi.org/10.1109/ICCV.2011.6126251
15. Held, D., Thrun, S., Savarese, S.: Learning to track at 100 FPS with deep regression networks. In: Leibe, B., Matas, J., Sebe, N., Welling, M. (eds.) ECCV 2016. LNCS, vol. 9905, pp. 749–765. Springer, Cham (2016). https://doi.org/10.1007/978-3-319-46448-0_45
16. Henriques, J.F., Caseiro, R., Martins, P., Batista, J.: High-speed tracking with kernelized correlation filters. In: IEEE Transactions on Pattern Analysis and Machine Intelligence (2015). https://doi.org/10.1109/TPAMI.2014.2345390
17. Henriques, J.F., Caseiro, R., Martins, P., Batista, J.: Exploiting the circulant structure of tracking-by-detection with kernels. In: Fitzgibbon, A., Lazebnik, S., Perona, P., Sato, Y., Schmid, C. (eds.) ECCV 2012. LNCS, vol. 7575, pp. 702–715. Springer, Heidelberg (2012). https://doi.org/10.1007/978-3-642-33765-9_50
18. Henriques, J.F., Caseiro, R., Martins, P., Batista, J.: High-speed tracking with kernelized correlation filters. IEEE Trans. Pattern Anal. Mach. Intell. 37(3), 583–596 (2015)
19. Jia, X., Lu, H., Yang, M.H.: Visual tracking via adaptive structural local sparse appearance model. In: 2012 IEEE Conference on Computer Vision and Pattern Recognition (CVPR), pp. 1822–1829, June 2012. https://doi.org/10.1109/CVPR.2012.6247880
20. Kalal, Z., Mikolajczyk, K., Matas, J.: Tracking-learning-detection. IEEE Trans. Pattern Anal. Mach. Intell. 34(7), 1409–1422 (2011). https://doi.org/10.1109/TPAMI.2011.239
21. Kristan, M.: The visual object tracking VOT2016 challenge results. In: Hua, G., Jégou, H. (eds.) ECCV 2016. LNCS, vol. 9914, pp. 777–823. Springer, Cham (2016). https://doi.org/10.1007/978-3-319-48881-3_54. http://www.springer.com/gp/book/9783319488806

22. Kristan, M., et al.: The visual object tracking vot2017 challenge results (2017). http://openaccess.thecvf.com/content_ICCV_2017_workshops/papers/w28/ Kristan_The_Visual_Object_ICCV_2017_paper.pdf
23. Kristan, M., et al.: The visual object tracking vot2015 challenge results. In: Visual Object Tracking Workshop 2015 at ICCV2015, December 2015
24. Kristan, M., et al.: A novel performance evaluation methodology for single-target trackers. IEEE Trans. Pattern Anal. Mach. Intell. **38**(11), 2137–2155 (2016). https://doi.org/10.1109/TPAMI.2016.2516982
25. Kristan, M.: The visual object tracking VOT2014 challenge results. In: Agapito, L., Bronstein, M.M., Rother, C. (eds.) ECCV 2014. LNCS, vol. 8926, pp. 191–217. Springer, Cham (2015). https://doi.org/10.1007/978-3-319-16181-5_14
26. Kristan, M.: The visual object tracking VOT2014 challenge results. In: Agapito, L., Bronstein, M.M., Rother, C. (eds.) ECCV 2014. LNCS, vol. 8926, pp. 191–217. Springer, Cham (2015). https://doi.org/10.1007/978-3-319-16181-5_14. http://www.votchallenge.net/vot2014/program.html
27. Leal-Taixé, L., Milan, A., Reid, I., Roth, S., Schindler, K.: Motchallenge 2015: towards a benchmark for multi-target tracking. arXiv preprint arXiv:1504.01942 (2015)
28. Li, A., Lin, M., Wu, Y., Yang, M.H., Yan, S.: NUS-PRO: a new visual tracking challenge. IEEE Trans. Pattern Anal. Mach. Intell. **38**(2), 335–349 (2016). https://doi.org/10.1109/TPAMI.2015.2417577
29. Li, X., Hu, W., Shen, C., Zhang, Z., Dick, A., Hengel, A.V.D.: A survey of appearance models in visual object tracking. ACM Trans. Intell. Syst. Technol. (TIST) **4**(4), 58 (2013)
30. Li, Y., Zhu, J.: A scale adaptive kernel correlation filter tracker with feature integration. In: Agapito, L., Bronstein, M.M., Rother, C. (eds.) ECCV 2014. LNCS, vol. 8926, pp. 254–265. Springer, Cham (2015). https://doi.org/10.1007/978-3-319-16181-5_18
31. Liang, P., Blasch, E., Ling, H.: Encoding color information for visual tracking: algorithms and benchmark. In: Image Processing, pp. 1–14. IEEE (2015). http://ieeexplore.ieee.org/xpls/abs_all.jsp?arnumber=7277070
32. Lukezic, A., Vojír, T., Zajc, L.C., Matas, J., Kristan, M.: Discriminative correlation filter with channel and spatial reliability. In: Proceedings of the IEEE Conference on Computer Vision and Pattern Recognition, vol. 2 (2017)
33. Milan, A., Leal-Taixé, L., Reid, I., Roth, S., Schindler, K.: MOT16: a benchmark for multi-object tracking, March 2016. arXiv:1603.00831 [cs], http://arxiv.org/abs/1603.00831, arXiv: 1603.00831
34. Mueller, M., Smith, N., Ghanem, B.: A benchmark and simulator for UAV tracking. In: Leibe, B., Matas, J., Sebe, N., Welling, M. (eds.) ECCV 2016. LNCS, vol. 9905, pp. 445–461. Springer, Cham (2016). https://doi.org/10.1007/978-3-319-46448-0_27
35. Mueller, M., Smith, N., Ghanem, B.: Context-aware correlation filter tracking. In: Proceedings of IEEE Conference on Computer Vision and Pattern Recognition (CVPR), pp. 1396–1404 (2017)
36. Nam, H., Han, B.: Learning multi-domain convolutional neural networks for visual tracking. In: The IEEE Conference on Computer Vision and Pattern Recognition (CVPR), June 2016
37. Ning, J., Yang, J., Jiang, S., Zhang, L., Yang, M.H.: Object tracking via dual linear structured SVM and explicit feature map. In: Proceedings of the IEEE Conference on Computer Vision and Pattern Recognition, pp. 4266–4274 (2016)

38. Real, E., Shlens, J., Mazzocchi, S., Pan, X., Vanhoucke, V.: Youtube-boundingboxes: a large high-precision human-annotated data set for object detection in video. In: 2017 IEEE Conference on Computer Vision and Pattern Recognition (CVPR), pp. 7464–7473. IEEE (2017)
39. Ross, D., Lim, J., Lin, R.S., Yang, M.H.: Incremental learning for robust visual tracking. Int. J. Comput. Vis. **77**(1–3), 125–141 (2008). https://doi.org/10.1007/s11263-007-0075-7
40. Russakovsky, O., et al.: Imagenet large scale visual recognition challenge. Int. J. Comput. Vis. **115**(3), 211–252 (2015)
41. Smeulders, A.W.M., Chu, D.M., Cucchiara, R., Calderara, S., Dehghan, A., Shah, M.: Visual tracking: an experimental survey. IEEE Trans. Pattern Anal. Mach. Intell. **36**(7), 1442–1468 (2014). https://doi.org/10.1109/TPAMI.2013.230
42. Smeulders, A.W., Chu, D.M., Cucchiara, R., Calderara, S., Dehghan, A., Shah, M.: Visual tracking: an experimental survey. IEEE Trans. Pattern Anal. Mach. Intell. **36**(7), 1442–1468 (2014)
43. Valmadre, J., Bertinetto, L., Henriques, J., Vedaldi, A., Torr, P.H.: End-to-end representation learning for correlation filter based tracking. In: 2017 IEEE Conference on Computer Vision and Pattern Recognition (CVPR), pp. 5000–5008. IEEE (2017)
44. Vondrick, C., Patterson, D., Ramanan, D.: Efficiently scaling up crowdsourced video annotation. Int. J. Comput. Vis. **101**(1), 184–204 (2013)
45. Wang, L., Ouyang, W., Wang, X., Lu, H.: Visual tracking with fully convolutional networks. In: 2015 IEEE International Conference on Computer Vision (ICCV), pp. 3119–3127, December 2015. https://doi.org/10.1109/ICCV.2015.357
46. Wu, Y., Lim, J., Yang, M.H.: Online object tracking: a benchmark. In: 2013 IEEE Conference on Computer vision and pattern recognition (CVPR), pp. 2411–2418. IEEE (2013)
47. Wu, Y., Lim, J., Yang, M.H.: Object tracking benchmark. IEEE Trans. Pattern Anal. Mach. Intell. **37**(9), 1834–1848 (2015)
48. Yilmaz, A., Javed, O., Shah, M.: Object tracking: a survey. ACM Comput. Surv. (CSUR) **38**(4), 13 (2006)
49. Zhang, J., Ma, S., Sclaroff, S.: MEEM: robust tracking via multiple experts using entropy minimization. In: Fleet, D., Pajdla, T., Schiele, B., Tuytelaars, T. (eds.) ECCV 2014. LNCS, vol. 8694, pp. 188–203. Springer, Cham (2014). https://doi.org/10.1007/978-3-319-10599-4_13

StarMap for Category-Agnostic Keypoint and Viewpoint Estimation

Xingyi Zhou[1](✉) , Arjun Karpur[1] , Linjie Luo[2] , and Qixing Huang[1]

[1] The University of Texas at Austin, Austin, USA
{zhouxy,akarpur,huangqx}@cs.utexas.edu
[2] Snap Inc., Venice, USA
linjie.luo@snap.com

Abstract. Semantic keypoints provide concise abstractions for a variety of visual understanding tasks. Existing methods define semantic keypoints separately for each category with a fixed number of semantic labels in fixed indices. As a result, this keypoint representation is infeasible when objects have a varying number of parts, e.g. chairs with varying number of legs. We propose a category-agnostic keypoint representation, which combines a multi-peak heatmap (StarMap) for all the keypoints and their corresponding features as 3D locations in the canonical viewpoint (CanViewFeature) defined for each instance. Our intuition is that the 3D locations of the keypoints in canonical object views contain rich semantic and compositional information. Using our flexible representation, we demonstrate competitive performance in keypoint detection and localization compared to category-specific state-of-the-art methods. Moreover, we show that when augmented with an additional depth channel (DepthMap) to lift the 2D keypoints to 3D, our representation can achieve state-of-the-art results in viewpoint estimation. Finally, we show that our category-agnostic keypoint representation can be generalized to novel categories.

Keywords: 3D vision · Category-agnostic · Keypoint estimation Viewpoint estimation · Pose estimation

1 Introduction

Semantic keypoints, such as joints on a human body or corners on a chair, provide concise abstractions of visual objects regarding their compositions, shapes, and poses. Accurate semantic keypoint detection forms the basis for many visual understanding tasks, including human pose estimation [4,22,25,51], hand pose estimation [46,52], viewpoint estimation [24,35], feature matching [15], fine-grained image classification [47], and 3D reconstruction [9,10,36,39].

Electronic supplementary material The online version of this chapter (https:// doi.org/10.1007/978-3-030-01246-5_20) contains supplementary material, which is available to authorized users.

© Springer Nature Switzerland AG 2018
V. Ferrari et al. (Eds.): ECCV 2018, LNCS 11205, pp. 328–345, 2018.
https://doi.org/10.1007/978-3-030-01246-5_20

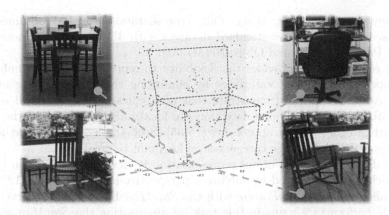

Fig. 1. Illustration of Canonical View Semantic Feature. It is shared across all object categories. We show 2 categories: chair (in blue) and table (in green). For the left frontal leg of chair on bottom left, it has (i) the same CanViewFeature with the same chair keypoint from a different viewpoint (bottom right), (ii) similar feature with another chair instance's corresponding keypoint (top right), and (iii) similar feature with left frontal leg from a table (top left). We *Can View* this feature in 3D space (middle). (Color figure online)

Existing methods define a fixed number of semantic keypoints for each object category in isolation [22, 24, 35, 40]. A standard approach is to allocate a heatmap channel for each keypoint. Or in other words, keypoints are inferred as separate heat maps according to their *encoding order*. This approach, however, is not suitable when objects have a varying number of parts, e.g. chairs with varying numbers of legs. The approach is even more limiting when we want to share and use keypoint labels of multiple different categories. In fact, keypoints of different categories do share rich compositional similarities. For instance, chairs and tables may share the same configuration of legs, and motorcycles and bicycles all contain wheels. Category-specific keypoint encodings fail to capture both the intra-category part variations and the inter-category part similarities.

In this paper, we propose a novel, category-agnostic keypoint representation. Our representation consists of two components: (1) a single channel, multi-peak heatmap, termed *StarMap*, for all keypoints of all objects; and (2) their respective feature (Fig. 1), termed *CanViewFeature*, which is defined as the 3D locations in a normalized canonical object view (or a world coordinte system). Specifically, StarMap combines the separate keypoint heat maps in previous approaches [24, 35] into a single heat map, and thus unifies the detection of different keypoints. CanViewFeature provides semantic discrimination between keypoints, i.e., through their locations in the normalized canonical object view. One intuition behind this representation is that the distribution of keypoints' 3D locations in the canonical object view encodes rich semantic and compositional information. For example, the locations of all legs are close to the ground, and they are below the seats. Our representation can be obtained via *supervised* training on any standard datasets with 3D viewpoint annotations, such as Pascal3D+ [42] and ObjectNet3D [41].

Our representation provides the flexibility to represent varying numbers of keypoints across different categories by eliminting the hard-encoding of keypoints. Additionally, we demonstrate that our representation can still achieve competitive results in keypoint detection and localization compared to the state-of-the-art category-specific approaches [15,35] (Sect. 4.2) by using simple nearest neighbor association on the category-level keypoint templates.

One direct application of our representation is viewpoint estimation [19,28, 35], which can be achieved by solving a perspective-n-points (PnP) [12] problem to align the *CanViewFeature* with the *StarMap*. Further, we observed considerable performance gains in this task by augmenting the *StarMap* with an additional depth channel (*DepthMap*) to lift the 2D image coordinates into 3D. We report state-of-the-art performance compared to previous viewpoint estimation methods [19,24,28,35] with ablation studies on each component. Finally, we show our method works well when applied to unseen categories. Full code is publicly available at https://github.com/xingyizhou/StarMap.

2   Related Works

Keypoint Estimation. Keypoint estimation, especially human joint estimation [4,22,31,33,49] and rigid object keypoint estimation [40,50], is a widely studied problem in computer vision. In the simplest case, a 2D/3D keypoint can be represented by a 2/3-dimension vector and learned by supervised regression. Toshev et al. [33] first trained a deep neural network for 2D human pose regression and Li et al. [13] extended this approach to 3D. Starting from Tompson et al. [32], the heatmap representation has dominated the 2D keypoint estimation community and has achieved great success in both 2D human pose estimation [22,38,44] and *single category* man-made object keypoint detection [39,40]. Recently, the heatmap representation has been generalized in various different directions. Cao et al. [4] and Newell et al. [21] extended the single peak heatmap (for single keypoint detection) to a multi-peak heatmap where each peak is one instance of a *specific type* of keypoint, enabling bottom-up, multi-person pose estimation. Pavlakos et al. [25] lifted the 2D pixel heatmap to a 3D voxel heatmap, resulting in an end-to-end 3D human pose estimation system. Tulsiani et al. [35] and Pavlakos et al. [24] stacked keypoint heatmaps from different object categories together for multi-category object keypoint estimation. Despite good performance gained by these approaches, they share a common limitation: each heatmap is only trained for a *specific keypoint type* from a specific object. Learning each keypoint individually not only ignores the intra-category variations or inter-category similarities, but also makes the representation inherently impossible to be generalized to unknown keypoint configurations for novel categories.

Viewpoint Estimation. Viewpoint estimation, i.e., estimating an object's orientation in a given frame, is a practical problem in computer vision and robotics [11,24]. It has been well explored by traditional techniques that solve for transformations between corresponding points in the world and image views; this is known as the Perspective-n-Point Problem [12,17]. Lately, viewpoint estimation accuracy and utility have been greatly improved in the deep learning era. Tulsiani et al. [35] introduced viewpoint estimation as a bin classification problem for each viewing angle (azimuth, elevation and in-plane rotation). Mousavian et al. [19] augmented the bin classification scheme by adding regression offsets within each bin so that predictions could be more fine-grained. Szeto et al. [29] used annotated keypoints as additional input to further improve bin classification. To combat scarcity of training data and generic features, Su et al. [28] proposed to synthesize images with known 3D viewpoint annotations and proposed a geometry-aware loss to further boost the estimation performance. Recently, Pavlakos et al. [24] proposed to use detected *semantic* keypoint followed by a PnP algorithm [12] to solve for the resulting viewpoint matrix and achieved state-of-the-art results. However, this method relies on category-specific keypoint annotation and is not generalizable. On the contrary, our approach is both accurate and category-agnostic, by utilizing category-agnostic keypoints.

General Keypoint Detection. There are several related concepts similar to our general semantic keypoint. The most well-known one is the SIFT descriptor [16], which aims to detect a large number of *interest* points based on local and *low level* image statistics. Also, the heatmap representation has been used in saliency detection [8] and visual attention [43], which detects a *region* of image which is "important" in the context. Similarly, Altwaijry et al. [1] used the heatmap representation to detect a set of points that is useful for feature matching. The key difference between our keypoint and the above concepts is that their keypoints do not contain semantic meanings and are not annotated by humans, making them less useful in high level vision tasks such as pose estimation.

To our best knowledge, we are the first to propose a category-agnostic keypoint representation and show that it is directly applicable to viewpoint estimation.

3   Approach

In this section, we describe our approach for learning a category-agnostic keypoint representation from a single RGB image. We begin with describing the representation in Sect. 3.1. We then introduce how to learn this representation in Sect. 3.2. Finally, we show a direct application of our representation in viewpoint estimation in Sect. 3.3.

3.1   Category-Agnostic Keypoint Representation

A desired general purpose keypoint representation should be both adaptive (i.e., should be able to represent different content of different visual objects) and semantically meaningful (i.e., should convey certain semantic information for downstream applications).

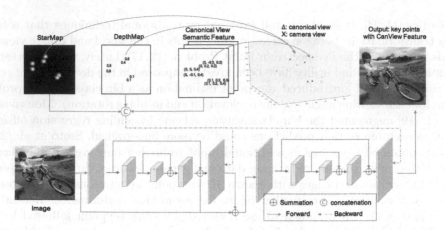

Fig. 2. Illustration of our framework. For an input image, our network predicts three component: StarMap, Canonical View Feature, and DepthMap. Varying number of keypoints are extracted at the peak location of StarMap and their Depth and CanViewFeature can be accessed at the corresponding channels.

So far the most widely used keypoint representation is the category specific stacked keypoint vector [33], which represents object keypoints by a $N \times D$ vector (N for number of keypoints and D for dimensions), or multi-channel heatmaps [22,32], which associate each channel with one specific keypoint on a specific object category, e.g., 16-channel heatmaps for human [22,32], 10-channel heatmaps for chair [40]. Although these representations are certainly semantically meaningful (e.g., the first channel of human heatmaps is the left ankle), it does not satisfy the adaptive property, e.g., chairs with legged bases and swivel bases cannot be learned together due to varying number of keypoints. As a result, they can not be considered as the same category based on their different keypoint configurations. To generalize heatmaps to multiple categories, a popular approach is to stack all heatmaps from all categories [24,35] (resulting in $\sum N_c$ output channels, where N_c is the number of keypoints of category c). In such a representation, keypoints from different objects are completely separated, e.g. seat corners from swivel chairs are irrelevant to seat corners from chairs. To merge keypoints from different objects, one has to establish consistent correspondences [48] between different keypoints across multiple categories, which is difficult or sometimes impossible.

In this paper, we introduce a hybrid representation that meets all desired properties. As illustrated in Fig. 2, our hybrid representation consists of three components, *StarMap*, *CanViewFeature* and *DepthMap*. In particular, StarMap specifies the image coordinates of keypoints where the number of keypoints can *vary* across different categories; CanViewFeature specifies the 3D locations of keypoints in a canonical coordinate system, which provide an identity for each keypoint; DepthMap lifts 2D keypoints into 3D. As we will see later, it enhances the performance of using this representation for the application of viewpoint estimation. Now we describe each component in more details.

StarMap. As shown in Fig. 2 (top left), StarMap is a single channel heatmap whose local maximums encode the image locations of the underlying points. It is motivated by the success of using one heatmap to encode occurrences of one keypoint on multiple persons [4,21]. In our setting, we generalize the idea to encode *all* keypoints of each object. This is in contrast to [4,21], which use multi-peak heatmaps to detect multiple *instances* of the *same* specific keypoint. In our implementation, given a heatmap, we extract the corresponding keypoints by detecting all local maximums, with respect to the 8-ring neighborhood whose values are above 0.05.

When comparing multi-channel heatmaps and a single channel heatmap, one intuition is that multi-channel heatmaps, which are category-specific and keypoint-specific representations, lead to better accuracy. However, as we will see later, using a single channel allows us to train the representation from bigger training data (multiple categories), leading to an overall better keypoint predictor. We also argue that a single-channel representation (1 channel vs 100+ channels on Pascal3D+ [42]) is favored when computational and memory resources are limited. On the other hand, *StarMap* alone does not provide the semantic meaning of each detected point. This drawback motivates the second component of our hybrid keypoint representation.

CanViewFeature. CanViewFeature collects the 3D locations of the keypoints in the canonical view. In our implementation, we allocate three channels for *CanViewFeature*. Specifically, after detecting a keypoint (peak) in *StarMap*, the values of these three channels at the corresponding pixel specify the 3D location in the canonical coordinate system. The design of *CanViewFeature* is motivated from recent works on embedding visual objects into latent spaces [30,37]. Such latent spaces provide a shared platform for comparing and linking different visual objects. Our representation shares the same abstract idea, yet we make the embedding *explicit* in 3D (where we *can view* the learned representation) and learnable in a *supervised* manner. This enables additional applications such as viewpoint estimation, as we will discuss later. When considering the space of keypoint configurations in the canonical space, it is easy to find that the feature is invariant to object pose and image appearance (scale, translation, rotation, lighting), little-variance to object shape (e.g., left frontal wheels from different cars are always in the left frontal area), and little variance to object category (e.g., frontal wheels from different categories are always in bottom frontal area).

Although *CanViewFeature* only provides 3D locations, we can leverage this to classify the keypoints, by using nearest neighbor association on the category-level keypoint templates.

DepthMap. *CanViewFeature* and *StarMap* are related to each other via a similarity transform (rotation, translation, scaling) and a perspective projection. It is certainly possible to solve a non-linear optimization problem to recover the underlying similarity transform. However, since the network predictions are not perfect, we found that this approach leads to sub-optimal results.

To stabilize this process and make the relation even simpler, we augment *StarMap* with one additional channel called *DepthMap*. The encoding is the same as *CanViewFeature*. More precisely, we first extract keypoints at peak locations and then access the corresponding pixels to obtain the depth values. When the camera intrinsic parameters are present, we use them to convert image coordinates and depth value into the true 3D location of the corresponding pixel. Otherwise, we assume weak-perspective projection, and directly use the image coordinates and depth value as an approximation of the underlying 3D location.

3.2 Learning Hybrid Keypoint Representation

Data Preparation. Training our hybrid representation requires annotations of 2D keypoints, their corresponding depths, and their corresponding 3D locations in the canonical view. We remark that such training data is feasible to obtain and publicly available [41,42]. 2D keypoint annotations per image are straightforward to retrieve [23] and thus widely available [2,3,14]. Also, annotating 3D keypoints of a CAD model [45] is not a hard task, given an interactive 3D UI such as MeshLab [5]. The canonical view of a CAD model is defined as the front view of an object with the largest 3D bounding box dimension scaled to $[-0.5, 0.5]$ (meaning it is zero centered). Note that just a few 3D CAD models need to be annotated for each category (about 10 per category), because keypoint configuration variation is orders of magnitude smaller than the image appearance variation. Given a collection of images and a small set of CAD models of the corresponding categories, a human annotator is asked to select the closest CAD model to the image's content, as done in Pascal3D+ and ObjectNet3D [41,42]. A coarse viewpoint is also annotated by manually dragging the selected CAD model to align the image appearance. In summary, all the annotations required to train our hybrid representation are relatively easy to acquire. We refer to [41,42] for more details on how to annotate such data.

We now describe how we calculate the depth annotation. Ideally, the transformation between the canonical view and image pixel coordinate is a full-perspective camera model:

$$s[u \ v \ 1]^T = \mathcal{A}[R|t][\overline{x} \ \overline{y} \ \overline{z} \ 1]^T, s.t., R^T R = I \tag{1}$$

where $\mathcal{A}$ describes intrinsic camera parameters, (u, v) is the 2D keypoint location in the image coordinate system, $(\overline{x}, \overline{y}, \overline{z})$ is the 3D location in canonical coordinate system. R, t, and s are the rotation matrix (i.e. viewpoint), translation vector, and scale factor, respectively. However, the camera intrinsic parameters are most likely unavailable in testing scenarios. In those cases, a weak-perspective camera model is often applied to *approximate* the 3D-to-2D transformation for keypoint estimation [24,49], by changing Eq. 1 to

$$s[u - c_x \ v - c_y \ d]^T = [R|t][\overline{x} \ \overline{y} \ \overline{z} \ 1]^T, s.t., R^T R = I \tag{2}$$

where (u, v) specifies the location of the keypoint, d is its associated depth, and (c_x, c_y) denotes the center of the image.

Letting $[x, y, z] = [R|t][\overline{x}, \overline{y}, \overline{z}, 1]^T$ be the transformed 3D keypoints in the metric space, we have $[u, v, d] = [x/s + c_x, y/s + c_y, z/s]$ (with unknown s), which transforms one point from the 3D metric space to the 2D pixel space with an augmented depth value d. In training, let N_c be the number of keypoints in category c. Both the viewpoint transformation matrix $[R|t]$ and the canonical points $\{\overline{x}_i, \overline{y}_i, \overline{z}_i\}_{i=1}^{N_c}$ are known, and we can calculate the rotated keypoints $\{x_i, y_i, z_i\}_{i=1}^{N_c}$. Moreover, the corresponding 2D keypoints $\{(u_i, v_i)\}_{i=1}^{N_c}$ are known, so we can simply solve the scale factor s by aligning the (u, v) and (x, y) plane bounding box size: $s = \frac{max(max_i(x_i) - min_i(x_i), max_i(y_i) - min_i(y_i))}{max(max_i(u_i) - min_i(u_i), max_i(v_i) - min_i(v_i))}$, which gives rise to the underlying depth value.

Network Training. As described above, we have full supervision for all of our 3 output components. Training is done as a supervised heatmap regression, i.e., we minimize the $L2$ distance between the output 5-channel heatmap and their ground truth. Note that for *CanViewFeature* and *DepthMap*, we only care about the output at peak locations. Following [20,21], we ignore the non-peak output locations rather than forcing them to be zero. This can be simply implemented by multiplying a mask matrix to both the network output and ground truth and then using a standard $L2$ loss.

Implementation Details. Our implementation is done in the PyTorch framework. We use a 2-stacks HourglassNetwork [22], which is the state-of-the-art architecture for 2D human pose estimation [2]. We trained our network using curriculum learning, i.e., we first train the network with only *StarMap* output for 90 epochs and then fine-tune the network with the *CanViewFeature* followed by *DepthMap* supervision for additional 90 epochs each. The whole training stages took about 2 days on one GTX 1080 TI GPU. All the hyper-parameters are set to the default values in the original Hourglass implementation [22].

3.3   Application in Viewpoint Estimation

The output of our approach (StarMap, DepthMap and CanViewFeature) can directly be used to estimate the viewpoint of the input image with respect to the canonical view (i.e., camera pose estimation). Specifically, Let $\mathbf{p}_i = (u_i - c_x, v_i - c_y, d_i)$ be the un-normalized 3D coordinate of keypoint p_i, where (c_x, c_y) is the image center. Let $\mathbf{q}_i$ be its counterpart in the canonical view. With $w_i \in [0, 1]$ we denote this keypoint's value on the heatmap, which indicates a confidence score. We solve for a similarity transformation between the image coordinate system and world coordinate system that is parameterized by a scalar $s \in \mathbb{R}^+$, a rotation $R \in SO(3)$, and a translation $\mathbf{t}$. This is done by minimizing the following objective function:

$$s^\star, R^\star, \mathbf{t}^\star = \operatorname*{argmin}_{s, R, \mathbf{t}} \sum_{i=1}^{N_I} w_i \| sR\mathbf{p}_i + \mathbf{t} - \mathbf{q}_i \|^2. \tag{3}$$

Note that (3) admits an explicit solution as described in [7], which we include here for completeness. The optimal rotation is given by

$$R^\star = U\mathrm{diag}(1, 1, \mathrm{sign}(M))V^T, \qquad M := \sum_{i=1}^{N_I} w_i(\mathbf{p}_i - \overline{\mathbf{p}})(\mathbf{q}_i - \overline{\mathbf{q}}) \qquad (4)$$

where $U\Sigma V^T = M$ is the SVD and $\overline{\mathbf{p}}, \overline{\mathbf{q}}$ are the mean of $\mathbf{p}_i, \mathbf{q}_i$.

4   Experiments

In this section, we perform experimental evaluations on the proposed hybrid keypoint representation. We begin with describing the experimental setup in Sect. 4.1. We then evaluate the accuracy of our keypoint detector and the application in viewpoint estimation in Sects. 4.2 and 4.3, respectively. We then present advanced analysis of our hybrid keypoint representation in Sect. 4.4. Finally, we show that our category-agnostic keypoint representation can be extended to novel categories in Sect. 4.5. Table 5 collect some qualitative results, and more results are deferred to the supplementary material.

4.1   Experimental Setup

We use Pascal3D+ [42] as our major evaluation benchmark. This dataset contains 12 man-made object categories with 2 K to 4 K images per category. We make use of the following annotations in our training: object bounding box, category-specific 2D keypoints (annotations from [3]), approximate 3D CAD model of the object, viewpoint of the image, and category-specific 3D keypoint annotations (corresponds with the 2D keypoint configuration) in the canonical coordinate system defined on each CAD model. Following [28,35], evaluation is done on the subset of the validation set that is non-truncated and non-occluded, which contains 2113 samples in total. As the evaluation protocols and baseline approaches vary across different tasks, we will describe them for each specific set of evaluations.

4.2   Keypoint Localization and Classification

We first evaluate our method on the keypoint estimation task, which specifies the locations of the predicted keypoints. Since keypoint locations alone do not carry the identities of each keypoint and cannot be used as identity-specific evaluation, we perform the evaluation by using two protocols – namely, with identification inferred from our learned CanViewFeature or with oracle assigned identification. Specifically, for the first protocol, for each category, we calculate the mean of the locations of each keypoint in the world coordinate system among all CAD models and use this as the *category-level* template. We then associate each keypoint with the ID of its nearest mean annotated keypoint in the template. For the second protocol, we assume a perfect ID assignment (or keypoint classification) by assigning the output keypoint ID as the closest annotation (in image coordinates). The second protocol can also be thought of as randomly perturbing the annotated keypoint order and picking the best one. Following the conventions [15,35], we use PCK($\alpha = 0.1$), or Percentage of Correct Keypoints, as the evaluation metric. PCK considers a keypoint to be correct if its $L2$ 2D pixel distance from the ground truth keypoint location is less than $0.1 \times max(h, w)$, where h and w are the object's bounding box dimensions.

Table 1. 2D Keypoint Localization Results. The results are shown in PCK($\alpha = 0.1$). Top: our result with nearest canonical feature as keypoint identification. Bottom: results with oracle keypoint identification.

PCK ($\alpha = 0.1$)	Aero	Bike	Boat	Bottle	Bus	Car	Chair	Table	Mbike	Sofa	Train	Tv	Mean
Long [15]	53.7	60.9	33.8	72.9	70.4	55.7	18.5	22.9	52.9	38.3	53.3	49.2	48.5
Tulsiani [35]	66.0	77.8	52.1	83.8	88.7	81.3	65.0	47.3	68.3	58.8	72.0	65.1	68.8
Pavlakos [24]	84.1	86.9	62.3	87.4	96.0	93.4	76.0	N/A	N/A	78.0	58.4	84.8	82.5
Ours	75.2	83.2	54.8	87.0	94.4	90.0	75.4	58.0	68.8	79.8	54.0	85.8	78.6
Pavlakos [24] Oracle Id	92.3	93.0	79.6	89.3	97.8	96.7	83.9	N/A	N/A	85.1	73.3	88.5	89.0
Ours Oracle Id	93.1	92.6	84.1	92.4	98.4	96.0	91.7	90.0	90.1	89.7	83.0	95.2	92.2

The keypoint localization and classification results are shown in Table 1. We show 3 state-of-the-art methods [15,24,35] for *category-specific* keypoint localization for comparison. The evaluation of [24] is done by ourselves based on their published model. For the first protocol, our result of 78.6% mean PCK($\alpha = 0.1$) is marginally better than the state-of-the-arts in 2014 [15,35], probably because we used a more up-to-date HourglassNetwork [22]. Our performance is slightly worse than [24], who uses the same Hourglass architecture but with stacked category-specific channels output ($\sum_c N_c$ output channels in total), which is expected. This is due to the error caused by incorrect keypoint ID association. We emphasize that all counterpart methods are category-specific, thus requiring ground truth object category as input while ours is general.

The second protocol (Bottom of Table 1) factors out the error caused by incorrect keypoint ID association. For a fair comparison, we also allow [24] to change its output order with the oracle nearest location (to eliminate the common left-right flip error [26]). We can see our score is 92.2%, which is 3.2% higher than that of Pavlakos et al [24]. This is quite encouraging since our approach is designed to be a general purpose keypoint predictor. This result shows that it is advantageous to train a unified network to predict keypoint locations, as this allows to train a single network with more relevant training data.

4.3 Viewpoint Estimation

Some qualitative results are shown in Table 5, and more results can be found in the supplementary material.

As a direct application, we evaluate our hybrid representation on the task of viewpoint estimation. The objective of viewpoint estimation is to predict the azimuth (a), elevation (e), and in-plane rotation (θ) of the image object with respect to the world coordinate system. In our experiment, we follow the conventions [28, 35] by measuring the angle between the predicted rotation vector and the ground truth rotation vector: $\Delta(R_{pred}, R_{gt}) = \frac{||logm(R_{pred}^T R_{gt})||_\mathcal{F}}{\sqrt{2}}$, where $R = R_Z(\theta)R_X(e - \pi/2)R_Z(-a)$ transforms the viewpoint representation (a, e, θ) into a rotation matrix. Here R_X, R_Y and R_Z are rotations along X, Y and Z axis, respectively.

We consider two metrics that are commonly applied in the literature [19, 24, 28, 35], namely, Median Error, which is the median of the rotation angle error, and Accuracy at θ, which is the percentage of keypoints whose error is less than θ. We use $\theta = \frac{\pi}{6}$, which is a default setting in the literature.

A popular approach for solving viewpoint estimation is to cast the problem as bin classification by discretiziing the space of (a, e, θ) [18, 19, 28, 35]. Since network architecture governs the performance of a neural network, we re-train the baseline models [35] with more modern network architectures [6]. We implemented a ResNet18 (**Res18-Specific**) with the same hyper-parameters as [35] (we also tried VGG [27] or ResNet50 [6] but observed very similar or worse performance).

We also want to remark that although viewpoint estimation itself is not a category-specific task, all the studied preview works have used a category-specific formulation, e.g., use *separate* last-layer bin classifiers for each category, resulting in $3 \times N_{categories} \times N_{bins}$ output units [34]. We also provide a general $3 \times N_{bins}$ viewpoint estimator as a baseline (**Res18-General**).

Table 2 compares our approach with previous techniques. Our method outperforms all previous methods and baselines in both testing metrics. Specifically with respect to MedErr, our approach achieved 10.4, which is lower than the prior state-of-the-art result reported in Mousavian et al [19]. In terms of $Acc_{\frac{\pi}{6}}$, our method outperforms the state-of-the-art result of Su et al [28]. This is a quite positive result, since [28] uses additional rendered images for training.

We further evaluate $Acc_{\frac{\pi}{18}}$, which assesses the percentage of very accurate predictions. In this case, we simply compare against our re-implemented Res18, which achieved similar results with other state-of-the-art techniques. As shown in Table 2, our approach is significantly better than Res18-General/Specific with respect to $Acc_{\frac{\pi}{18}}$. This shows the advantage of performing keypoint alignment for pose estimation.

Note that it is also possible to directly align CanViewFeature with StarMap for viewpoint estimation by a weak-perspective PnP [24] algorithm (**PnP** in Table 2). In this case, utilizing DepthMap outperforms the direct alignment by 8.1% in terms of $Acc_{\frac{\pi}{6}}$ and 1.75% in terms of $Acc_{\frac{\pi}{18}}$, respecctively. On one hand, this shows the usefulness of DepthMap, particularly when the prediction is noisy. On the other hand, the performance of both approaches becomes similar when the predictions are very accurate ($Acc_{\frac{\pi}{18}}$). This is expected since both approaches should output identical results when the predictions are perfect.

Table 2. Viewpoint Estimation on Pascal3D+ [42]. We compare our results with the state-of-the-arts and baselines. The results are shown in Median Error (lower better) and Accuracy (higher better).

	Aero	Bike	Boat	Bottle	Bus	Car	Chair	Table	Mbike	Sofa	Train	Tv	Mean
MedErr (Tulsiani [35])	13.8	17.7	21.3	12.9	5.8	9.1	14.8	15.2	14.7	13.7	8.7	15.4	13.6
MedErr (Pavlakos [24])	8.0	13.4	40.7	11.7	2.0	5.5	10.4	N/A	N/A	9.6	8.3	32.9	N/A
MedErr (Mousavian [19])	13.6	12.5	22.8	8.3	3.1	5.8	11.9	12.5	12.3	12.8	6.3	11.9	11.1
MedErr (Su [28])	15.4	14.8	25.6	9.3	3.6	6.0	9.7	10.8	16.7	9.5	6.1	12.6	11.7
MedErr (Mahendran [18])	14.2	18.7	27.2	9.5	3.0	6.9	15.8	14.4	16.4	10.7	6.6	14.3	13.1
MedErr (Res18-General)	14.3	16.7	26.9	13.2	5.8	8.8	17.7	26.7	15.7	14.4	8.8	16.2	13.3
MedErr (Res18-Specific)	14.7	15.8	25.6	13.1	5.7	8.6	16.3	18.1	15.1	13.8	8.2	14.1	12.8
MedErr (PnP)	9.5	14.0	43.6	9.9	3.3	6.6	11.4	64.9	14.3	11.5	7.7	21.8	11.2
MedErr (Ours)	10.1	14.5	30.0	9.1	3.1	6.5	11.0	23.7	14.1	11.1	7.4	13.0	**10.4**
$Acc\frac{\pi}{6}$ (Tulsiani [35])	0.81	0.77	0.59	0.93	0.98	0.89	0.80	0.62	0.88	0.82	0.80	0.80	0.8075
$Acc\frac{\pi}{6}$ (Pavlakos [24])	0.81	0.78	0.44	0.79	0.96	0.90	0.80	N/A	N/A	0.74	0.79	0.66	N/A
$Acc\frac{\pi}{6}$ (Mousavian [19])	0.78	0.83	0.57	0.93	0.94	0.90	0.80	0.68	0.86	0.82	0.82	0.85	0.8103
$Acc\frac{\pi}{6}$ (Su [28])	0.74	0.83	0.52	0.91	0.91	0.88	0.86	0.73	0.78	0.90	0.86	0.92	0.82
$Acc\frac{\pi}{6}$ (Res18-General)	0.79	0.75	0.53	0.90	0.96	0.93	0.62	0.57	0.85	0.82	0.81	0.77	0.7875
$Acc\frac{\pi}{6}$ (Res18-Specific)	0.79	0.77	0.54	0.93	0.95	0.93	0.75	0.57	0.84	0.79	0.81	0.84	0.8121
$Acc\frac{\pi}{6}$ (PnP)	0.80	0.70	0.37	0.88	0.94	0.86	0.76	0.48	0.80	0.92	0.74	0.57	0.7416
$Acc\frac{\pi}{6}$ (Ours)	0.82	0.86	0.50	0.92	0.97	0.92	0.79	0.62	0.88	0.92	0.77	0.83	**0.8225**
$Acc\frac{\pi}{18}$ (Res18-General)	0.28	0.18	0.17	0.27	0.82	0.61	0.23	0.33	0.18	0.15	0.61	0.27	0.3502
$Acc\frac{\pi}{18}$ (Res18-Specific)	0.29	0.21	0.21	0.30	0.86	0.62	0.28	0.33	0.21	0.18	0.59	0.30	0.3777
$Acc\frac{\pi}{18}$ (PnP)	0.52	0.36	0.13	0.50	0.83	0.65	0.48	0.29	0.31	0.44	0.61	0.27	0.4643
$Acc\frac{\pi}{18}$ (Ours)	0.49	0.34	0.14	0.56	0.89	0.68	0.45	0.29	0.28	0.46	0.58	0.37	**0.4818**

4.4   Analysis of Our Hybrid Keypoint Representation

Analysis of CanViewFeature. We use the ground-truth keypoint location, and compare their learned 3D locations for keypoint classification with popular point features used in the literature, namely, SIFT [16] and Conv5 of VGG [27]. For CanViewFeature, we still follow the same procedure of using nearest neighbor for keypoint classification. For SIFT and Conv5, a linear SVM is used to classify the keypoints [15].

Table 3 compares CanViewFeature with the two baseline approaches from [15]. We can see that CanViewFeature is significantly better than baseline

Table 3. Results for keypoint classification on Pascal3D+ Dataset [42]. We show keypoint classification accuracy of each category.

	Aero	Bike	Boat	Bottle	Bus	Car	Chair	Table	Mbike	Sofa	Train	Tv	Mean
SIFT [15]	35	54	41	76	68	47	39	69	49	52	74	78	57
Conv [15]	44	53	42	78	70	45	41	68	53	52	73	76	58
Ours	77	79	64	96	95	92	84	66	71	90	65	94	81

Table 4. Error analysis on Pascal3D+. We show results in Median Error and Accuracy.

	Aero	Bike	Boat	Bottle	Bus	Car	Chair	Table	Mbike	Sofa	Train	Tv	Mean
$MedErr$ (Ours)	10.1	14.5	30.0	9.1	3.1	6.5	11.0	23.7	14.1	11.1	7.4	13.0	10.43
$MedErr$ (GT Star)	9.2	13.3	31.3	8.2	3.1	5.7	10.7	78.2	13.8	10.1	7.0	13.4	9.92
$MedErr$ (GT Star+SCSF)	7.7	12.9	22.0	8.0	3.0	5.9	9.3	14.6	10.8	8.3	6.3	12.9	9.1
$MedErr$ (GT Star+Depth)	6.2	6.2	14.1	2.4	2.1	3.9	6.5	72.9	7.0	5.4	6.8	1.9	4.7
$Acc_{\frac{\pi}{6}}$ (Ours)	0.82	0.86	0.50	0.92	0.97	0.92	0.79	0.62	0.88	0.92	0.77	0.83	0.8225
$Acc_{\frac{\pi}{6}}$ (GT Star)	0.85	0.84	0.50	0.92	0.96	0.93	0.80	0.38	0.85	0.90	0.77	0.82	0.8211
$Acc_{\frac{\pi}{6}}$ (GT Star+SCSF)	0.86	0.84	0.63	0.95	0.99	0.95	0.88	0.62	0.84	0.92	0.88	0.85	0.8651
$Acc_{\frac{\pi}{6}}$ (GT Star+Depth)	0.86	0.93	0.63	0.95	0.97	0.91	0.82	0.38	0.87	0.92	0.84	0.93	0.8637

approaches. This shows the advantage of using a shared keypoint representation for training a general purpose keypoint detector.

Ablation Study on Representation Components. To better understand the importance of each component of our representation and whether they are well-trained, we provide error analysis by replacing each output component with its ground truth. To this end, we use viewpoint estimation as the task for evaluation, and Table 4 summarizes the results. Specifically, replacing StarMap with its ground truth does not provides much performance gains in both metrics, indicating that StarMap is fairly accurate. This is justified by the high keypoint accuracy reported in Sect. 4.2. Moreover, replacing either CanViewFeature or DepthMap with the underlying ground truth provides considerable performance gains in terms of $Acc_{\frac{\pi}{6}}$. In particular, using perfect DepthMap leads noticeable decrease in median error. This is expected since the general task of estimating pixel depth remains quite challenging.

4.5   Keypoint and Viewpoint Induction for Novel Categories

Our keypoint representation is category-agnostic and is free to be extended to novel object categories [34].

We note that Pascal3D+ [42] only contains 12 categories and it is hard to learn common inter-category information with such limited category samples. To further verify the generalization ability of our method, we used a newly published large scale 3D dataset, ObjectNet3D [41]. ObjectNet3D [41] has the

Table 5. Qualitative results of our full pipeline on Pascal3D+ [42] Dataset. 1st column: the input image; 2nd column: our predicted StarMap (shown on image); 3rd column: extracted keypoints after taking local maximum on StarMap, we show ground truth in large dots and prediction in small circled dots (The RGB color of the point encodes xyz coordinate for correspondence; 4th column: our predicted CanViewFeature (triangle) and their ground truth (circle); 5th column: our prediced 3D uvd coordinates, obtained by uv from StarMap and d from DepthMap; 6th column: rotated 3D point with our predicted viewpoint (cross) and ground truth viewpoint (triangle).

Input	StarMap	LocalMax.	CanViewFeat	Pred. 3D	Viewpoint

Table 6. Viewpoint estimation for novel categories results on ObjectNet3D+ [41]. We shown our results in $Acc_{\frac{\pi}{6}}$.

	Bed	Bookshelf	Calculator	Cellphone	Computer	Filing cabinet	Guitar	Iron	Knife
$Acc_{\frac{\pi}{6}}$ (Sup)	0.73	0.78	0.91	0.57	0.82	0.84	0.73	0.03	0.18
$Acc_{\frac{\pi}{6}}$ (Novel)	0.37	0.69	0.19	0.52	0.73	0.78	0.61	0.02	0.09
	Microwave	Pen	Pot	Rifle	Slipper	Stove	Toilet	Tub	Wheelchair
$Acc_{\frac{\pi}{6}}$ (Sup)	0.94	0.13	0.56	0.04	0.12	0.87	0.71	0.51	0.60
$Acc_{\frac{\pi}{6}}$ (Novel)	0.88	0.12	0.51	0.00	0.11	0.82	0.41	0.49	0.14

same annotations as Pascal3D+ [42] but with 100 categories. We evenly hold out 20 categories (every 5 categories sorted in the alphabetical order) from the training data and only used them for testing. Because Shoe and Door do not have keypoint annotation, we remove them from the testing set, resulting in 18 novel categories. Please refer to the supplementary for details on dataset details.

We compare the performance gap between including and withholding the 18 categories during training. The results are shown in Table 6. As expected, the viewpoint estimation accuracy of most categories drops. For some categories (Iron, Knife, Pen, Rifle, Slipper), both experiments fail (with accuracy lower than 20%). One explanation is that these 5 failed categories are small and narrow objects, whose annotations may not be accurate. For example, the keypoint annotations on ObjectNet3D [41] for small object are not always well-defined (see qualitative results in supplementary), e.g., Key and Spoon have dense keypoints annotation on their silhouette. For half of the 18 novel objects (bookshelf, cellphone, computer, filing cabinet, guitar, microwave, pot, stove, tub), the performance gap between including and withholding training data is less than 10%. This indicates that our representation is fairly general and can extend viewpoint estimation to novel categories.

Acknowledgement. We thank Shubham Tulsiani and Angela Lin for the helpful discussions.

References

1. Altwaijry, H., Veit, A., Belongie, S.J., Tech, C.: Learning to detect and match keypoints with deep architectures. In: BMVC (2016)
2. Andriluka, M., Pishchulin, L., Gehler, P., Schiele, B.: 2d human pose estimation: new benchmark and state of the art analysis. In: IEEE Conference on Computer Vision and Pattern Recognition (CVPR), June 2014
3. Bourdev, L., Maji, S., Brox, T., Malik, J.: Detecting people using mutually consistent poselet activations. In: Daniilidis, K., Maragos, P., Paragios, N. (eds.) ECCV 2010. LNCS, vol. 6316, pp. 168–181. Springer, Heidelberg (2010). https://doi.org/10.1007/978-3-642-15567-3_13
4. Cao, Z., Simon, T., Wei, S.E., Sheikh, Y.: Realtime multi-person 2d pose estimation using part affinity fields. In: CVPR, vol. 1, p. 7 (2017)

5. Cignoni, P., Callieri, M., Corsini, M., Dellepiane, M., Ganovelli, F., Ranzuglia, G.: MeshLab: an open-source mesh processing tool. In: Scarano, V., Chiara, R.D., Erra, U. (eds.) Eurographics Italian Chapter Conference, The Eurographics Association (2008). https://doi.org/10.2312/LocalChapterEvents/ItalChap/ItalianChapConf2008/129-136

6. He, K., Zhang, X., Ren, S., Sun, J.: Deep residual learning for image recognition. In: Proceedings of the IEEE Conference on Computer Vision and Pattern Recognition, pp. 770–778 (2016)

7. Horn, B.K.: Closed-form solution of absolute orientation using unit quaternions. JOSA A **4**(4), 629–642 (1987)

8. Huang, X., Shen, C., Boix, X., Zhao, Q.: Salicon: reducing the semantic gap in saliency prediction by adapting deep neural networks. In: ICCV (2015)

9. Kanazawa, A., Tulsiani, S., Efros, A.A., Malik, J.: Learning category-specific mesh reconstruction from image collections. arXiv (2018)

10. Kar, A., Tulsiani, S., Carreira, J., Malik, J.: Category-specific object reconstruction from a single image. In: Computer Vision and Pattern Regognition (CVPR) (2015)

11. Kendall, A., Grimes, M., Cipolla, R.: PoseNet: a convolutional network for real-time 6-DOF camera relocalization. In: 2015 IEEE International Conference on Computer Vision (ICCV), pp. 2938–2946. IEEE (2015)

12. Lepetit, V., Moreno-Noguer, F., Fua, P.: EPnP: an accurate O(n) solution to the PnP problem. Int. J. Comput. Vis. **81**(2), 155 (2009)

13. Li, S., Chan, A.B.: 3d human pose estimation from monocular images with deep convolutional neural network. In: Asian Conference on Computer Vision, pp. 332–347. Springer, Cham (2014)

14. Lin, T.-Y., et al.: Microsoft COCO: common objects in context. In: Fleet, D., Pajdla, T., Schiele, B., Tuytelaars, T. (eds.) ECCV 2014. LNCS, vol. 8693, pp. 740–755. Springer, Cham (2014). https://doi.org/10.1007/978-3-319-10602-1_48

15. Long, J.L., Zhang, N., Darrell, T.: Do convnets learn correspondence? In: Advances in Neural Information Processing Systems, pp. 1601–1609 (2014)

16. Lowe, D.G.: Distinctive image features from scale-invariant keypoints. Int. J. Comput. Vis. **60**(2), 91–110 (2004)

17. Lu, C.P., Hager, G.D., Mjolsness, E.: Fast and globally convergent pose estimation from video images. IEEE Trans. Pattern Anal. Mach. Intell. **22**(6), 610–622 (2000)

18. Mahendran, S., Ali, H., Vidal, R.: Joint object category and 3d pose estimation from 2d images. arXiv preprint arXiv:1711.07426 (2017)

19. Mousavian, A., Anguelov, D., Flynn, J., Košecká, J.: 3d bounding box estimation using deep learning and geometry. In: 2017 IEEE Conference on Computer Vision and Pattern Recognition (CVPR), pp. 5632–5640. IEEE (2017)

20. Newell, A., Deng, J.: Pixels to graphs by associative embedding. In: Advances in Neural Information Processing Systems. pp. 2168–2177 (2017)

21. Newell, A., Huang, Z., Deng, J.: Associative embedding: end-to-end learning for joint detection and grouping. In: Advances in Neural Information Processing Systems, pp. 2274–2284 (2017)

22. Newell, A., Yang, K., Deng, J.: Stacked Hourglass networks for human pose estimation. In: Leibe, B., Matas, J., Sebe, N., Welling, M. (eds.) ECCV 2016. LNCS, vol. 9912, pp. 483–499. Springer, Cham (2016). https://doi.org/10.1007/978-3-319-46484-8_29

23. Papadopoulos, D.P., Uijlings, J.R., Keller, F., Ferrari, V.: Extreme clicking for efficient object annotation. In: 2017 IEEE International Conference on Computer Vision (ICCV), pp. 4940–4949. IEEE (2017)

24. Pavlakos, G., Zhou, X., Chan, A., Derpanis, K.G., Daniilidis, K.: 6-DOF object pose from semantic keypoints. In: 2017 IEEE International Conference on Robotics and Automation (ICRA), pp. 2011–2018. IEEE (2017)
25. Pavlakos, G., Zhou, X., Derpanis, K.G., Daniilidis, K.: Coarse-to-fine volumetric prediction for single-image 3d human pose. In: 2017 IEEE Conference on Computer Vision and Pattern Recognition (CVPR), pp. 1263–1272. IEEE (2017)
26. Ronchi, M.R., Perona, P.: Benchmarking and error diagnosis in multi-instance pose estimation. In: The IEEE International Conference on Computer Vision (ICCV), October 2017
27. Simonyan, K., Zisserman, A.: Very deep convolutional networks for large-scale image recognition. arXiv preprint arXiv:1409.1556 (2014)
28. Su, H., Qi, C.R., Li, Y., Guibas, L.J.: Render for CNN: viewpoint estimation in images using CNNs trained with rendered 3d model views. In: Proceedings of the IEEE International Conference on Computer Vision, pp. 2686–2694 (2015)
29. Szeto, R., Corso, J.J.: Click here: human-localized keypoints as guidance for viewpoint estimation. arXiv preprint arXiv:1703.09859 (2017)
30. Taylor, J., Shotton, J., Sharp, T., Fitzgibbon, A.: The vitruvian manifold: inferring dense correspondences for one-shot human pose estimation. In: 2012 IEEE Conference on Computer Vision and Pattern Recognition (CVPR), pp. 103–110. IEEE (2012)
31. Tompson, J., Goroshin, R., Jain, A., LeCun, Y., Bregler, C.: Efficient object localization using convolutional networks. In: Proceedings of the IEEE Conference on Computer Vision and Pattern Recognition, pp. 648–656 (2015)
32. Tompson, J.J., Jain, A., LeCun, Y., Bregler, C.: Joint training of a convolutional network and a graphical model for human pose estimation. In: Advances in neural information processing systems. pp. 1799–1807 (2014)
33. Toshev, A., Szegedy, C.: Deeppose: human pose estimation via deep neural networks. In: Proceedings of the IEEE Conference on Computer Vision and Pattern Recognition, pp. 1653–1660 (2014)
34. Tulsiani, S., Carreira, J., Malik, J.: Pose induction for novel object categories. In: Proceedings of the IEEE International Conference on Computer Vision, pp. 64–72 (2015)
35. Tulsiani, S., Malik, J.: Viewpoints and keypoints. In: Proceedings of the IEEE Conference on Computer Vision and Pattern Recognition, pp. 1510–1519 (2015)
36. Tulsiani, S., Zhou, T., Efros, A.A., Malik, J.: Multi-view supervision for single-view reconstruction via differentiable ray consistency. In: Computer Vision and Pattern Regognition (CVPR) (2017)
37. Wei, L., Huang, Q., Ceylan, D., Vouga, E., Li, H.: Dense human body correspondences using convolutional networks. In: 2016 IEEE Conference on Computer Vision and Pattern Recognition, CVPR 2016, Las Vegas, NV, USA, June 27–30, pp. 1544–1553 (2016)
38. Wei, S.E., Ramakrishna, V., Kanade, T., Sheikh, Y.: Convolutional pose machines. In: Proceedings of the IEEE Conference on Computer Vision and Pattern Recognition, pp. 4724–4732 (2016)
39. Wu, J., Wang, Y., Xue, T., Sun, X., Freeman, W.T., Tenenbaum, J.B.: MarrNet: 3D shape reconstruction via 2.5D sketches. In: Advances In Neural Information Processing Systems (2017)
40. Wu, J., et al.: Single image 3D interpreter network. In: Leibe, B., Matas, J., Sebe, N., Welling, M. (eds.) ECCV 2016. LNCS, vol. 9910, pp. 365–382. Springer, Cham (2016). https://doi.org/10.1007/978-3-319-46466-4_22

41. Xiang, Y., et al.: ObjectNet3D: a large scale database for 3D object recognition. In: Leibe, B., Matas, J., Sebe, N., Welling, M. (eds.) ECCV 2016. LNCS, vol. 9912, pp. 160–176. Springer, Cham (2016). https://doi.org/10.1007/978-3-319-46484-8_10

42. Xiang, Y., Mottaghi, R., Savarese, S.: Beyond PASCAL: a benchmark for 3d object detection in the wild. In: 2014 IEEE Winter Conference on Applications of Computer Vision (WACV), pp. 75–82. IEEE (2014)

43. Xu, K., Ba, J., Kiros, R., Cho, K., Courville, A., Salakhudinov, R., Zemel, R., Bengio, Y.: Show, attend and tell: neural image caption generation with visual attention. In: International Conference on Machine Learning, pp. 2048–2057 (2015)

44. Yang, W., Li, S., Ouyang, W., Li, H., Wang, X.: Learning feature pyramids for human pose estimation. In: The IEEE International Conference on Computer Vision (ICCV), vol. 2 (2017)

45. Yi, L., et al.: A scalable active framework for region annotation in 3d shape collections. ACM Trans. Graph. (TOG) 35(6), 210 (2016)

46. Yuan, S., Garcia-Hernando, G., Stenger, B., Moon, G., Chang, J.Y., Lee, K.M., Molchanov, P., Kautz, J., Honari, S., Ge, L., et al.: 3d hand pose estimation: From current achievements to future goals. arXiv preprint arXiv:1712.03917 (2017)

47. Zhang, N., Donahue, J., Girshick, R., Darrell, T.: Part-based R-CNNs for fine-grained category detection. In: Fleet, D., Pajdla, T., Schiele, B., Tuytelaars, T. (eds.) ECCV 2014. LNCS, vol. 8689, pp. 834–849. Springer, Cham (2014). https://doi.org/10.1007/978-3-319-10590-1_54

48. Zhou, T., Krahenbuhl, P., Aubry, M., Huang, Q., Efros, A.A.: Learning dense correspondence via 3d-guided cycle consistency. In: Proceedings of the IEEE Conference on Computer Vision and Pattern Recognition, pp. 117–126 (2016)

49. Zhou, X., Huang, Q., Sun, X., Xue, X., Wei, Y.: Towards 3d human pose estimation in the wild: a weakly-supervised approach. In: The IEEE International Conference on Computer Vision (ICCV), October 2017

50. Zhou, X., Karpur, A., Gan, C., Luo, L., Huang, Q.: Unsupervised domain adaptation for 3d keypoint prediction from a single depth scan. arXiv preprint arXiv:1712.05765 (2017)

51. Zhou, X., Sun, X., Zhang, W., Liang, S., Wei, Y.: Deep kinematic pose regression. arXiv preprint arXiv:1609.05317 (2016)

52. Zhou, X., Wan, Q., Zhang, W., Xue, X., Wei, Y.: Model-based deep hand pose estimation. arXiv preprint arXiv:1606.06854 (2016)

Factorizable Net: An Efficient Subgraph-Based Framework for Scene Graph Generation

Yikang Li[1], Wanli Ouyang[2], Bolei Zhou[3], Jianping Shi[4], Chao Zhang[5], and Xiaogang Wang[1(✉)]

[1] The Chinese University of Hong Kong, Hong Kong, Hong Kong SAR, China
{ykli,xgwang}@ee.cuhk.edu.hk
[2] SenseTime Computer Vision Research Group,
The University of Sydney, Sydney, Australia
wanli.ouyang@sydney.edu.au
[3] MIT CSAIL, Cambridge, USA
bzhou@csail.mit.edu
[4] Sensetime Ltd., Beijing, China
shijianping@sensetime.com
[5] Samsung Telecommunication Research Institute, Beijing, China
c0502.zhang@samsung.com

Abstract. Generating scene graph to describe the object interactions inside an image gains increasing interests these years. However, most of the previous methods use complicated structures with slow inference speed or rely on the external data, which limits the usage of the model in real-life scenarios. To improve the efficiency of scene graph generation, we propose a subgraph-based connection graph to concisely represent the scene graph during the inference. A bottom-up clustering method is first used to factorize the entire graph into subgraphs, where each subgraph contains several objects and a subset of their relationships. By replacing the numerous relationship representations of the scene graph with fewer subgraph and object features, the computation in the intermediate stage is significantly reduced. In addition, spatial information is maintained by the subgraph features, which is leveraged by our proposed Spatial-weighted Message Passing (SMP) structure and Spatial-sensitive Relation Inference (SRI) module to facilitate the relationship recognition. On the recent Visual Relationship Detection and Visual Genome datasets, our method outperforms the state-of-the-art method in both accuracy and speed. Code has been made publicly available (https://github.com/yikang-li/FactorizableNet).

Keywords: Visual Relationship Detection · Scene graph generation
Scene understanding · Object interactions · Language and vision

---

Electronic supplementary material The online version of this chapter (https://doi.org/10.1007/978-3-030-01246-5_21) contains supplementary material, which is available to authorized users.

1   Introduction

Inferring the relations of the objects in images has drawn recent attentions in computer vision community on top of accurate object detection [6,28,34,35,37, 57,63]. Scene graph, as an abstraction of the objects and their pair-wise relationships, contains higher-level knowledge for scene understanding. Because of the structured description and enlarged semantic space of scene graphs, efficient scene graph generation will contribute to the downstream applications such as image retrieval [26,45] and visual question answering [33,38].

Currently, there are two approaches to generate scene graphs. The first approach adopts the two stage pipeline, which detects the objects first and then recognizes their pair-wise relationships [6,36,37,57,61]. The other approach is to jointly infer the objects and their relationships [34,35,57] based on the object region proposals. To generate a complete scene graph, both approaches should group the objects or object proposals into pairs and use the features of their union area (denoted as *phrase feature*), as the basic representation for predicate inference. Thus, the number of phrase features determines how fast the model performs. However, due to the number of combinations growing quadratically with that of objects, the problem will quickly get intractable as the number of objects grows. Employing fewer objects [35,57] or filtering the pairs with some simple criteria [6,34] could be a solution. But both sacrifice (the upper bound of) the model performance. As the most time-consuming part is the manipulations on the phrase feature, finding a more concise intermediate representation of the scene graph should be the key to solve the problem.

We observe that multiple phrase features can refer to some highly-overlapped regions, as shown by an example in Fig. 1. Prior to constructing different ⟨subject-object⟩ pairs, these features are of similar representations as they correspond to the same overlapped regions. Thus, a natural idea is to construct a shared representation for the phrase features of similar regions in the early stage. Then the shared representation is refined to learn a general representation of the are by passing the message from the connected objects. In the final stage, we can extract the required information from this shared representation to predict object relations by combining with different ⟨subject-object⟩ pairs. Based on this observation, we propose a subgraph-based scene graph generation approach, where the object pairs referring to the similar interacting regions are clustered into a subgraph and share the phrase representation (termed as *subgraph features*). In this pipeline, all the feature refining processes are done on the shared subgraph features. This design significantly reduces the number of the phrase features in the intermediate stage and speed up the model both in training and inference.

As different objects correspond to different parts of the shared subgraph regions, maintaining the spatial structure of the subgraph feature explicitly retains such connections and helps the subgraph features integrate more spatial information into the representations of the region. Therefore, 2-D feature maps are adopted to represent the subgraph features. And a spatial-weighted message passing (SMP) structure is introduced to employ the spatial correspondence

(person-wear-pants)

(pants-on-person)

(person-wear-helmet)

(helmet-on-person)

(person-play-snowboard)

(snowboard-under-person)

Fig. 1. Left: Selected objects; Middle: Relationships (*subject-predicate-object* triplets) are represented by phrase features in previous works [6,28,34,35,37,57,63]; Right: replacing the phrases with a concise subgraph representation, where relationships can be restored with subgraph features (green) and corresponding subject and object. (Color figure online)

between the objects and the subgraph region. Moreover, spatial information has been shown to be valuable in predicate recognition [6,36,61]. To leverage the such information, the Spatial-sensitive Relation Inference (SRI) module is designed. It fuses object feature pairs and subgraph features for the final relationship inference. Different from the previous works, which use object coordinates or the mask to extract the spatial features, our SRI could learn to extract the embedded spatial feature directly from the subgraph feature maps.

To summarize, we propose an efficient sub-graph based scene graph generation approach with following novelties: First, a bottom-up clustering method is proposed to factorize the image into subgraphs. By sharing the region representations within the subgraph, our method could significantly reduce the redundant computation and accelerate the inference speed. In addition, fewer representations allow us to use 2-D feature map to maintain the spatial information for subgraph regions. Second, a spatial weighted message passing (SMP) structure is proposed to pass message between object feature vectors and sub-graph feature maps. Third, a Spatial-sensitive Relation Inference (SRI) module is proposed to use the features from subject, object and subgraph representations for recognizing the relationship between objects. Experiments on Visual Relationship Detection [37] and Visual Genome [28] show our method outperforms the state-of-the-art method with significantly faster inference speed. Code has been made publicly available to facilitate further research.

2   Related Work

Visual Relationship has been investigated by numerous studies in the last decade. In the early stage, most of the works targeted on using specific types of visual relations, such as spatial relations [5,10,14,20,26,30] and actions (*i.e.* interactions between objects) [1,9,11,16,19,45,46,49,55,56,59]. In most of these studies, hand-crafted features were used in relationships or phrases detection and detection works and these works were mostly supposed to leveraging other tasks, such as object recognition [4,12,13,31,32,44,50,52,54], image classification and retrieval [17,39], scene understanding and generation [2,3,18,23,24,60,64], as well as text grounding [27,43,48]. However, in this paper, we focus on the higher-performed method dedicated to *generic* visual relationship detection task which is essentially different from works in the early stage.

In recent years, new methods are developed specifically for detecting visual relationships. An important series of methods [7,8,51] consider the *visual phrase* as an integrated whole, *i.e.* considering each distinct combination of object categories and relationship predicates as a distinct class. Such methods will become intractable when the number of such combinations becomes very large.

As an alternative paradigm, considering relationship predicates and object categories separately becomes more popular in recent works [36,41,62,63]. Generic visual relationship detection was first introduced as a visual task by Lu *et al.* in [37]. In this work, objects are detected first, and then the predicates between object pairs are recognized, where word embeddings of the object categories are employed as language prior for predicate recognition. Dai *et al.* proposed DR-Net to exploit the statistical dependencies between objects and their relationships for this task [6]. In this work, a CRF-like optimization process is adopted to refine the posterior probabilities iteratively [6]. Yu *et al.* presented a Linguistic Knowledge Distillation pipeline to employ the annotations and external corpus (*i.e.* wikipedia), where strong correlations between predicate and ⟨subject-object⟩ pairs are learned to regularize the training and provide extra cues for inference [61]. Plummer *et al.* designed a large collection of handcrafted linguistic and visual cues for visual relationship detection and constructed a pipeline to learn the weights for combining them [42]. Li *et al.* used the message passing structure among subject, object and predicate branches to model their dependencies [34].

The most related works are the methods proposed by Xu *et al.* [57] and Li *et al.* [35], both of which jointly detect the objects and recognize their relationships. In [57], the scene graph was constructed by refining the object and predicate features jointly in an iterative way. In [35], region caption was introduced as a higher-semantic-level task for scene graph generation, so the objects, pairwise relationships and region captions help the model learn representations from three different semantic levels. Our method differs in two aspects: (1) We propose a more concise graph to represent the connections between objects instead of enumerating every possible pair, which significantly reduces the computation complexity and allows us to use more object proposals; (2) Our model could learn to leverage the spatial information embedded in the subgraph feature maps to boost the relationship recognition. Experiments show that the proposed framework performs substantially better and faster in all different task settings.

3 Framework of the Factorizable Network

The overview of our proposed Factorizable Network (F-Net) is shown in Fig. 2. Detailed introductions to different components will be given in the following sections.

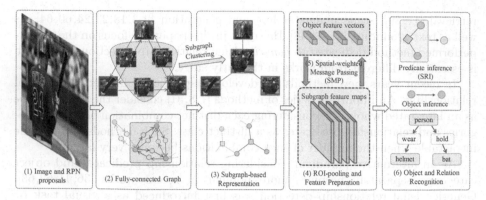

Fig. 2. Overview of our F-Net. (1) RPN is used for object region proposals, which shares the base CNN with other parts. (2) Given the region proposal, objects are grouped into pairs to build up a fully-connected graph, where every two objects are connected with two directed edges. (3) Edges which refer to similar phrase regions are merged into subgraphs, and a more concise connection graph is generated. (4) ROI-Pooling is employed to obtain the corresponding features (2-D feature maps for subgraph and feature vectors for objects). (5) Messages are passed between subgraph and object features along the factorized connection graph for feature refinement. (6) Objects are predicted from the object features and predicates are inferred based on the object features and the subgraph features. Green, red and yellow items refer to the subgraph, object and predicate respectively. (Color figure online)

The entire process can be summarized as the following steps: (1) generate object region proposals with Region Proposal Network (RPN) [47]; (2) group the object proposals into pairs and establish the fully-connected graph, where every two objects have two directed edges to indicate their relations; (3) cluster the fully-connected graph into several subgraphs and share the subgroup features for object pairs within the subgraph, then a factorized connection graph is obtained by treating each subgraph as a node; (4) ROI pools [15,21] the objects and subgraph features and transforms them into feature vectors and 2-D feature maps respectively; (5) jointly refine the object and subgraph features by passing message along the subgraph-based connection graph for better representations; (6) recognize the object categories with object features and their relations (predicates) by fusing the subgraph features and object feature pairs.

3.1 Object Region Proposal

Region Proposal Network [47] is adopted to generate object proposals. It shares the base convolution layers with our proposed F-Net. An auxiliary convolution layer is added after the shared layers. The anchors are generated by clustering the scales and ratios of ground truth bounding boxes in the training set [35].

3.2   Grouping Proposals into Fully-Connected Graph

As every two objects possibly have two relationships in opposite directions, we connect them with two directed edges (termed as phrases). A fully-connected graph is established, where every edge corresponds to a potential relationship (or *background*). Thus, N object proposals will have $N(N-1)$ candidate relations (yellow circles in Fig. 2 (2)). Empirically, more object proposals will bring higher recall and make it more likely to detect objects within the image and generate a more complete scene graph. However, large quantities of candidate relations may deteriorate the model inference speed. Therefore, we design an effective representations of all these relationships in the intermediate stage to adopt more object proposals.

3.3   Factorized Connection Graph Generation

By observing that many relations refer to overlapped regions (Fig. 1), we share the representations of the phrase region to reduce the number of the intermediate phrase representations as well as the computation cost. For any candidate relation, it corresponds to the union box of two objects (the minimum box containing the two boxes). Then we define its confidence score as the product of the scores of the two object proposals. With confidence scores and bounding box locations, non-maximum-suppression (NMS) [15] can be applied to suppress the number of the similar boxes and keep the bounding box with highest score as the representative. So these merged parts compose a subgraph and share an unified representation to describe their interactions. Consequently, we get a subgraph-based representation of the fully-connected graph: every subgraph contains several objects; every object belongs to several subgraphs; every candidate relation refers to one subgraph and two objects.

Discussion. In previous work, ViP-CNN [34] proposed a triplet NMS to pre-process the relationship candidates and remove some overlapped ones. However, it may falsely discard some possible pairs because only spatial information is considered. Differently, our method just proposes a concise representation of the fully-connect graph by sharing the intermediate representation. It does not prune the edges, but represent them in a different form. Every predicate will still be predicted in the final stage. Thus, it is no harm for the model potential to generate the full graph.

3.4   ROI-Pool the Subgraph and Object Features

After the clustering, we have two sets of proposals: objects and subgraphs. Then ROI-pooling [15,21] is used to generate corresponding features. Different from the prior art methods [35,57] which use feature vectors to represent the phrase features, we adopt 2-D feature maps to maintain the spatial information within the subgraph regions. As the subgraph feature is shared by several predicate inferences, 2-D feature map can learn more general representation of the region and its inherit spatial structure can help to identify the subject/object and their

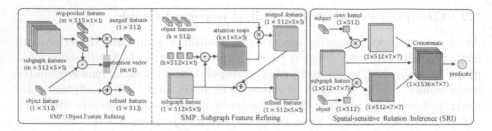

Fig. 3. Left: SMP structure for object/subgraph feature refining. Right: SRI Module for predicate recognition. Green, red and yellow refer to the subgraphs, objects and predicates respectively. $\odot$ denotes the dot product. $\oplus$ and $\otimes$ denote the element-wise sum and product. (Color figure online)

relations, especially the spatial relations. We continue employing the feature vector to represent the objects. Thus, after the pooling, 2-D convolution layers and fully-connected layers are used to transform the subgraph feature and object features respectively.

3.5 Feature Refining with Spatial-Weighted Message Passing

As object and subgraph features involve different semantic levels, where objects concentrate on the details and subgraph focus on their interactions, passing message between them could help to learn better representations by leveraging their complementary information. Thus, we design a spatial weighted message passing (SMP) structure to pass message between object feature vectors and subgraph feature maps (left part of Fig. 3). Messages passing from objects to subgraphs and from subgraphs to objects are two parallel processes. $\mathbf{o_i}$ denotes the object feature vector and $\mathbf{S_k}$ denotes the subgraph feature map.

Pass Message from Subgraphs to Objects. This process is to pass several 2-D feature maps to feature vectors. Since objects only require the general information about the subgraph regions instead of their spatial information, 2-D average pooling is directly adopted to pool the 2-D feature maps $\mathbf{S_k}$ into feature vectors $\mathbf{s_k}$. Because each object is connected to various number of subgraphs, we need first aggregate the subgraph features and then pass them to the target object nodes. Attention [58] across the subgraphs is employed to keep the scale aggregated features invariant to the number of input subgraphs and determine the importance of different subgraphs to the object:

$$\tilde{\mathbf{s}}_i = \sum_{\mathbf{S_k} \in \mathbb{S}_i} p_i(\mathbf{S}_k) \cdot \mathbf{s_k} \tag{1}$$

where $\mathbb{S}_i$ denotes the set of subgraphs connected to object i. $\tilde{\mathbf{s}}_i$ denotes aggregated subgraph features passed to object i. $\mathbf{s}_k$ denotes the feature vector average-pooled from the 2-D feature map $\mathbf{S}_k$. $p_i(\mathbf{S}_k)$ denotes the probability that $\mathbf{s}_k$ is passed to the target i-th object (attention vector in Fig. 3):

$$p_i(\mathbf{S}_k) = \frac{\exp\left(\mathbf{o}_i \cdot \mathrm{FC}^{(att\text{-}s)}\left(\mathrm{ReLU}\left(\mathbf{s}_k\right)\right)\right)}{\sum_{\mathbf{S}_k \in \mathbb{C}_i} \exp\left(\mathbf{o}_i \cdot \mathrm{FC}^{(att\text{-}s)}\left(\mathrm{ReLU}\left(\mathbf{s}_k\right)\right)\right)} \quad (2)$$

where $\mathrm{FC}^{(att\text{-}s)}$ transforms the feature $\mathbf{s}_k$ to the target domain of $\mathbf{o}_i$. ReLU denotes the Rectified Linear Unit layer [40].

After obtaining message features, the target object feature is refined as:

$$\hat{\mathbf{o}}_i = \mathbf{o}_i + \mathrm{FC}^{(s \to o)}\left(\mathrm{ReLU}\left(\tilde{\mathbf{s}}_i\right)\right) \quad (3)$$

where $\hat{\mathbf{o}}_i$ denotes the refined object feature. $\mathrm{FC}^{(s \to o)}$ denotes the fully-connected layer to transform merged subgraph features to the target object domain.

Pass Message from Objects to Subgraphs. Each subgraph connects to several objects, so this process is to pass several feature vectors to a 2-D feature map. Since different objects correspond to different regions of the subgraph features, when aggregating the object features, their weights should also depend on their locations:

$$\tilde{\mathbf{O}}_k(x,y) = \sum_{\mathbf{o}_i \in \mathbb{O}_k} \mathbf{P}_k(\mathbf{o}_i)(x,y) \cdot \mathbf{o}_i \quad (4)$$

where $\mathbb{O}_k$ denotes the set of objects contained in subgraph k. $\tilde{\mathbf{O}}_k(x,y)$ denotes aggregated object features to pass to subgraph k at location (x,y). $\mathbf{P}_k(\mathbf{o}_i)(x,y)$ denotes the probability map that the object feature $\mathbf{o}_i$ is passed to the k-th subgraph at location (x,y) (corresponding to the *attention maps* in Fig. 3):

$$\mathbf{P}_k(\mathbf{o}_i)(x,y) = \frac{\exp\left(\mathrm{FC}^{(att\text{-}o)}\left(\mathrm{ReLU}\left(\mathbf{o}_i\right)\right) \cdot \mathbf{S}_k(x,y)\right)}{\sum_{\mathbf{S}_k \in \mathbb{C}_i} \exp\left(\mathrm{FC}^{(att\text{-}o)}\left(\mathrm{ReLU}\left(\mathbf{o}_i\right)\right) \cdot \mathbf{S}_k(x,y)\right)} \quad (5)$$

where $\mathrm{FC}^{(att\text{-}o)}$ transforms $\mathbf{o}_i$ to the target domain of $\mathbf{S}_k(x,y)$. The probabilities are summed to 1 across all the objects at each location to normalize the scale of the message features. But there are no such constraints along the spatial dimensions. So different objects help to refine different parts of the subgraph features.

After the aggregation in Eq. 4, we get a feature map where the object features are aggregated with different weights at different locations. Then we can refine the subgraph features as:

$$\hat{\mathbf{S}}_k = \mathbf{S}_k + \mathrm{Conv}^{(o \to s)}\left(\mathrm{ReLU}\left(\tilde{\mathbf{O}}_k\right)\right) \quad (6)$$

where $\hat{\mathbf{S}}_i$ denotes the refined subgraph features. $\mathrm{Conv}^{(o \to s)}$ denotes the convolution layer to transform merged object messages to the target subgraph domain.
Discussion. Since subgraph features embed the interactions among several objects and objects are the basic elements of subgraphs, message passing between

object and subgraph features could: (1) help the object feature learn better representations by considering its interactions with other objects and introduce the contextual information; (2) refine different parts of subgraph features with corresponding object features. Different from the message passing in ISGG [57] and MSDN [35], our SMP (1) passes message between "points" (object vectors) and "2-D planes" (subgraph feature maps); (2) adopts attention scheme to merge different messages in a normalized scale. Besides, several SMP modules can be stacked to enhance the representation ability of the model.

3.6   Spatial-Sensitive Relation Inference

After the message passing, we have got refined representations of the objects $\mathbf{o}_i$ and subgraph regions $\mathbf{S}_k$. Object categories can be predicted directly with the object features. Because subgraph features may refer to several object pairs, we use the subject and object features along with their corresponding subgraph feature to predict their relationship:

$$\mathbf{p}^{\langle i,k,j \rangle} = \mathbf{f}\left(\mathbf{o}_i, \mathbf{S}_k, \mathbf{o}_j\right) \tag{7}$$

As different objects correspond to different regions of subgraph features, subject and object features work as the convolution kernels to extract the visual cues of their relationship from feature map.

$$\mathbf{S}_k^{(i)} = \mathrm{FC}\left(\mathrm{ReLU}\left(\mathbf{o}_i\right)\right) \otimes \mathrm{ReLU}\left(\mathbf{S}_k\right) \tag{8}$$

where $\mathbf{S}_k^{(i)}$ denotes the convolution result of subgraph feature map $\mathbf{S}_k$ with i-th object as convolution kernel. $\otimes$ denotes the convolution operation. As learning a convolution kernel needs large quantities of parameters, Group Convolution [29] is adopted. We set group numbers as the number of channels, so the group convolution can be reformulated as element-wise product.

Then we concatenate $\mathbf{S}_k^{(i)}$ and $\mathbf{S}_k^{(j)}$ with the subgraph feature $\mathbf{S}_k$ and predict the relationship directly with a fully-connected layer:

$$\mathbf{p}^{\langle i,k,j \rangle} = \mathrm{FC}^{(p)}\left(\mathrm{ReLU}\left(\left[\mathbf{S}_k^{(i)}; \mathbf{S}_k; \mathbf{S}_k^{(j)}\right]\right)\right) \tag{9}$$

where $\mathrm{FC}^{(p)}$ denotes the fully-connected layer for predicate recognition. $[\cdot]$ denotes the concatenation.

Bottleneck Layer. Directly predicting the convolution kernel leads to a lot of parameters to learn, which makes the model huge and hard to train. The number of parameters of $\mathrm{FC}^{(p)}$ equals:

$$\#\mathrm{FC}^{(p)} = C^{(p)} \times C \times W \times H \tag{10}$$

where $C^{(p)}$ denotes the number of predicate categories. C denotes the channel size. W and H denote the width and height of the feature map. Inspired by the bottleneck structure in [22], we introduce an additional 1×1 bottleneck convolution layer prior to $\text{FC}^{(p)}$ to reduce the number of channels (omitted in Fig. 3). After adding an bottleneck layer with channel size equalling to C', the parameter size gets:

$$\#\text{Conv}^{(bottleneck)} + \#\text{FC}^{(p)} = C \times C' + C^{(p)} \times C' \times W \times H \tag{11}$$

If we take $C' = C/2$, as $\#\text{Conv}^{(bottleneck)}$ is far less than $\#\text{FC}^{(p)}$, we almost half the number of parameters.

Discussion. In previous work, spatial features have been extracted from the coordinates of the bounding box or object masks [6,36,61]. Different from these methods, ours embeds the spatial information in the subgraph feature maps. Since $\text{FC}^{(p)}$ has different weights at different locations, it could learn to decide whether to leverage the spatial feature and how to use that by itself from the training data.

4 Experiments

In this section, implementation details of our proposed method and experiment settings will be introduced. Ablation studies will be done to show the effectiveness of different modules. We also compare our F-Net with state-of-the-art methods on both accuracy and testing speed.

4.1 Implementation Details

Model Details. ImageNet pretrained VGG16 [53] is adopted to initialize the base CNN, which is shared by RPN and F-Net. ROI-align [21] is used to generated 5×5 object and subgraph features. Two FC layers are used to transform the pooled object features to 512-dim feature vectors. Two 3×3 Conv layers are used to generate 512-dim subgraph feature maps. For SRI module, we use a 256-dim bottleneck layer to reduce the model size. All the newly introduced layers are randomly initialized.

Training Details. During training, we fix Conv_1 and Conv_2 of VGG16, and set the learning rate of the other convolution layers of VGG as 0.1 of the overall learning rate. Base learning rate is 0.01, and get multiplied by 0.1 every 3 epochs. RPN NMS threshold is set as 0.7. Subgraph clustering threshold is set as 0.5. For the training samples, 256 object proposals and 1024 predicates are sampled 50% foregrounds. There is no sampling for the subgraphs, so the subgraph connection maps are identical from training to testing. The RPN part is trained first, and then RPN, F-Net and base VGG part are jointly trained.

Inference Details. During testing phase, RPN NMS threshold and subgraph clustering threshold are set as 0.6 and 0.5 respectively. All the predicates (edges of fully-connected graph) will be predicted. Top-1 categories will be used as

Table 1. Dataset statistics. **VG-MSDN** and **VG-DR-Net** are two cleansed-version of raw Visual Genome dataset. **#Img** denotes the number of images. **#Rel** denotes the number of subject-predicate-object relation pairs. **#Object** and **#Predicate** denotes the number of object and predicate categories respectively.

Dataset	Training set		Testing set		#Object	#Predicate
	#Img	#Rel	#Img	#Rel		
VRD [37]	4,000	30,355	1,000	7,638	100	70
VG-MSDN [28,35]	46,164	507,296	10,000	111,396	150	50
VG-DR-Net [6,28]	67,086	798,906	8,995	26,499	399	24

the prediction for objects and relations. Predicated relationship triplets will be sorted in the descending order based on the products of their subject, object and predicate confidence probabilities. Inspired by Li *et al.* in [34], triplet NMS is adopted to remove the redundant predictions if the two triplets refer to the identical relationship.

4.2 Datasets

Two datasets are employed to evaluate our method, Visual Relationship Detection (VRD) [37] and Visual Genome [28]. VRD is a small benchmark dataset where most of the existing methods are evaluated. Compared to VRD, raw Visual Genome contains too many noisy labels, so dataset cleansing should be done to make it available for model training and evaluation. For fair comparison, we adopt two cleansed-version Visual Genome used in [35] and [6] and compare with their methods on corresponding datasets. Detailed statistics of the three datasets are shown in Table 1.

4.3 Evaluation Metrics

Models will be evaluated on two tasks, *Visual Phrase Detection (PhrDet)* and *Scene Graph Generation (SGGen)*. Visual Phrase Detection is to detect the ⟨subject-predicate-object⟩ phrases, which is tightly connected to the Dense Captioning [25]. Scene Graph Generation is to detect the objects within the image and recognize their pair-wise relationships. Both tasks recognize the ⟨subject-predicate-object⟩ triplets, but scene graph generation needs to localize both the subject and the object with at least 0.5 IOU (intersection over union) while visual phrase detection only requires one bounding box for the entire phrase.

Following [37], Top-K Recall (denoted as *Rec@K*) is used to evaluate how many labelled relationships are hit in the top K predictions. The reason why we use Recall instead of mean Average Precision (mAP) is that annotations of the relationships are not complete. mAP will falsely penalize the positive but unlabeled relations. In our experiments, *Rec@50* and *Rec@100* will be reported.

The testing speed of the model is also reported. Previously, only accuracy is reported in the papers. So lots of complicated structure and post-processing methods are used to enhance the Recall. As scene graph generation is getting closer to the practical applications and products, testing speed become a critical metric to evaluate the model. If not specified, testing speed is evaluated with Titan-X GPU.

4.4   Component Analysis

In this section, we perform several experiments to evaluate the effectiveness of different components of our F-Net (Table 2). All the experiments are performed on VG-MSDN [35] as it is larger than VRD [37] to eliminate overfitting and contains more predicate categories than VG-DR-Net [6].

Subgraph-Based Pipeline. For the baseline model 0, every relation candidate is represented by a phrase feature vector, and the predicates are predicted based on the concatenation of subject, object and phrase features. In comparison, model 1 and 2 adopt the subgraph-based presentation of the fully-connected graph with different numbers of object proposals. By comparing model 0 and 1, we can see that subgraph-based clustering could significantly speed up the model inference because of the fewer intermediate features. However, since most of the phrase features are approximated by the subgraph features, the accuracy of model 1 is slightly lower than that of model 0. However, the disadvantage of model 1 can be easily compensated by employing more object proposal as model 2 outperforms model 0 both in speed and accuracy by a large scale. Furthermore, model 1~6 are all faster than model 0, which proves the efficiency of our subgraph-based representations.

2-D Feature Map. From model 3, we start to use 2-D feature map to represent the subgraph features, which can maintain the spatial information within the subgraph regions. Compared to model 2, model 3 adopts 2-D representations of the subgraph features and use average-pooled subgraph features (concatenated with the subject and object feature) to predict the relationships. Since SRI is not used, the main difference is two 3×3 conv layers are used instead of FC layer to transform the subgraph features. Since we pool the subgraph regions to 5×5 feature maps, which is just the perceptual field of two 3×3 conv layers, therefore, model 3 has less parameters to learn and the spatial structure of the feature map could serve as a regularization. Therefore, compared to model 2, model 3 performs better.

Message Passing Between Objects and Subgraphs. When comparing Model 3 and 4, 2.02%~2.37% SGGen Recall increase is observed, which shows our proposed SMP could also help the model learn a better representation of the objects and the subgraph regions. With our proposed SMP, different parts of subgraph features can be refined by different objects, and object features can also get refined by receiving more information about their interactions with other

Table 2. Ablation studies of the proposed model. **PhrDet** denotes phrase detection task. **SGGen** denotes the scene graph generation task. **SubGraph** denotes whether to use Subgraph-based clustering strategy. **2-D** indicates whether we use 2-D feature map or feature vector to represent subgraph features. **#SMP** denotes the number of the Multimodal Message Passing structures (model 1 adopts the message passing in [35]). **#Boxes** denotes the number of object proposals we use during the testing. **SRI** denotes whether the SRI module is used (baseline method is average pooling the subgraph feature maps to vectors). **Speed** shows the time spent for one inference forward pass (second/image).

ID	SubGraph	#SMP	2-D	SRI	#Boxes	PhrDet		SGGen		Speed
						R@50	R@100	R@50	R@100	
0	-	0	-	-	64	16.92	21.04	8.52	10.81	0.65
1	✓	0	-	-	64	16.50	20.79	8.49	10.33	0.18
2	✓	0	-	-	200	18.71	22.77	9.73	12.02	0.20
3	✓	0	✓	-	200	19.09	22.88	9.90	12.08	0.32
4	✓	1	✓	-	200	20.48	25.69	11.62	14.55	0.42
5	✓	1	✓	✓	200	22.54	28.31	12.83	16.12	0.44
6	✓	2	✓	✓	200	22.84	28.57	13.06	16.47	0.55

object regions. Furthermore, when comparing model 5 and model 6, we can see that stacking more SMP modules can further improve the model performance as more complicated message paths are introduced. However, more SMP modules will deteriorate the testing speed, especially when we use feature maps to represent the subgraph features.

Spatial-Sensitive Relation Inference. From Eq. 9, Fully-Connected layer is used to predict the relationships from the 2-D feature map, so every point within the map will be assigned a location-specified weight and the SRI could learn to model the hidden spatial connections. Different from previous models that employing handcrafted spatial features like axises of the subject/object proposals, our model could not only improve the recognition accuracy of explicit spatial relationships like *above* and *below*, but also learn to extract the inherit spatial connection of other relationships. Experiment results of model 4 and 5 show the improvement brought by our proposed SRI module.

4.5   Comparison with Existing Methods

We compare our proposed F-Net with existing methods in Table 3. These methods can be roughly divided into two groups. One employs the two-stage pipeline, which is to detect the objects first and then recognize their relationships, including LP [37], DR-Net [6] and ILC [42]. Compared with these methods, our F-Net jointly recognizes the objects and their relationships, so the feature

Table 3. Comparison with existing methods on visual phrase detection (**PhrDet**) and scene graph generation(**SGGen**). **Speed** indicates the testing time spent on one image (second/image). Benchmark dataset, VRD [37], and two cleansed-version Visual Genome [6,28,35] are used for fair comparison.

Dataset	Model	PhrDet		SGGen		Speed
		Rec@50	Rec@100	Rec@50	Rec@100	
VRD [37]	LP [37]	16.17	17.03	13.86	14.70	1.18*
	ViP-CNN [34]	22.78	27.91	17.32	20.01	0.78
	DR-Net [6]	19.93	23.45	17.73	20.88	2.83
	ILC [42]	16.89	20.70	15.08	18.37	2.70**
	Ours Full:1-SMP	25.90	30.52	18.16	21.04	**0.45**
	Ours Full:2-SMP	**26.03**	**30.77**	**18.32**	**21.20**	0.55
VG-MSDN [28,35]	ISGG [57]	15.87	19.45	8.23	10.88	1.64
	MSDN [35]	19.95	24.93	10.72	14.22	3.56
	Ours-Full: 2-SMP	**22.84**	**28.57**	**13.06**	**16.47**	**0.55**
VG-DR-Net [6,28]	DR-Net [6]	23.95	27.57	**20.79**	23.76	2.83
	Ours-Full: 2-SMP	**26.91**	**32.63**	19.88	**23.95**	**0.55**

* Only consider the post-processing time given the CNN features and object detection results. ** As reported in [42], it takes about 45 min to test 1000 images on single K80 GPU.

level connections can be leveraged for better recognition. In addition, complicated post-processing stages introduced by these methods may reduce the inference speed and make it more difficult to implement with GPU or other high-performance hardware like FPGA. The other methods like ViP-CNN [34], ISGG [57], MSDN [35] adopt the similar pipeline to ours and propose different feature learning methods. Both ViP-CNN and ISGG used message passing to refine the object and predicate features. MSDN introduced an additional task, dense captioning, to improve scene graph generation. However, in these methods, each relationship is represented by an individual phrase feature. This leads to limited object proposals that are used to generate scene graph, as the number of relationships grows quadratically with that of the proposals. In comparison, our proposed subgraph-based pipeline significantly reduces the relationship representations by clustering them into subgraphs. Therefore, it allows us to use more object proposals to generate scene graph, and correspondingly, helps our model to perform better than these methods both in speed and accuracy.

5   Conclusion

This paper introduces an efficient scene graph generation model, Factorizable Network (F-Net). To tackle the problem of the quadratic combinations of possible relationships, a concise subgraph-based representation of the scene graph is introduced to reduce the number of intermediate representations during the inference. 2-D feature maps are used to maintain the spatial information within the subgraph region. Correspondingly, a Spatial-weighted Message Passing structure and a Spatial-sensitive Relation Inference module are designed to make use of the inherent spatial structure of the feature maps. Experiment results show that our model is significantly faster than the previous methods with better results.

Acknowledgement. This work is supported by Hong Kong Ph.D. Fellowship Scheme, SenseTime Group Limited, Samsung Telecommunication Research Institute, the General Research Fund sponsored by the Research Grants Council of Hong Kong (Project Nos. CUHK14213616, CUHK14206114, CUHK14205615, CUHK419412, CUHK14203015, CUHK14207814, CUHK14208417, CUHK14202217, and CUHK14239816), the Hong Kong Innovation and Technology Support Programme (No.ITS/121/15FX).

References

1. Antol, S., Zitnick, C.L., Parikh, D.: Zero-shot learning via visual abstraction. In: Fleet, D., Pajdla, T., Schiele, B., Tuytelaars, T. (eds.) ECCV 2014, Part IV. LNCS, vol. 8692, pp. 401–416. Springer, Cham (2014). https://doi.org/10.1007/978-3-319-10593-2_27
2. Berg, A.C., et al.: Understanding and predicting importance in images. In: CVPR (2012)
3. Chang, A., Savva, M., Manning, C.: Semantic parsing for text to 3D scene generation. In: ACL (2014)
4. Choi, M.J., Lim, J.J., Torralba, A., Willsky, A.S.: Exploiting hierarchical context on a large database of object categories. In: CVPR (2010)
5. Choi, W., Chao, Y.W., Pantofaru, C., Savarese, S.: Understanding indoor scenes using 3D geometric phrases. In: Proceedings of the IEEE Conference on Computer Vision and Pattern Recognition, pp. 33–40 (2013)
6. Dai, B., Zhang, Y., Lin, D.: Detecting visual relationships with deep relational networks. In: CVPR (2017)
7. Das, P., Xu, C., Doell, R.F., Corso, J.J.: A thousand frames in just a few words: lingual description of videos through latent topics and sparse object stitching. In: CVPR (2013)
8. Divvala, S.K., Farhadi, A., Guestrin, C.: Learning everything about anything: webly-supervised visual concept learning. In: CVPR (2014)
9. Elhoseiny, M., Cohen, S., Chang, W., Price, B.L., Elgammal, A.M.: Sherlock: scalable fact learning in images. In: AAAI (2017)
10. Elliott, D., Keller, F.: Image description using visual dependency representations. In: EMNLP (2013)
11. Farhadi, A., et al.: Every picture tells a story: generating sentences from images. In: Daniilidis, K., Maragos, P., Paragios, N. (eds.) ECCV 2010, Part IV. LNCS, vol. 6314, pp. 15–29. Springer, Heidelberg (2010). https://doi.org/10.1007/978-3-642-15561-1_2
12. Fidler, S., Leonardis, A.: Towards scalable representations of object categories: learning a hierarchy of parts. In: CVPR (2007)
13. Galleguillos, C., Belongie, S.: Context based object categorization: a critical survey. In: CVIU (2010)

14. Galleguillos, C., Rabinovich, A., Belongie, S.: Object categorization using co-occurrence, location and appearance. In: CVPR (2008)
15. Girshick, R.: Fast R-CNN. In: ICCV (2015)
16. Gkioxari, G., Girshick, R., Malik, J.: Contextual action recognition with R* CNN. In: ICCV (2015)
17. Gong, Y., Ke, Q., Isard, M., Lazebnik, S.: A multi-view embedding space for modeling internet images, tags, and their semantics. IJCV **106**, 210–233 (2014)
18. Gould, S., Rodgers, J., Cohen, D., Elidan, G., Koller, D.: Multi-class segmentation with relative location prior. IJCV **80**, 300–316 (2008)
19. Guadarrama, S., et al.: Youtube2text: recognizing and describing arbitrary activities using semantic hierarchies and zero-shot recognition. In: ICCV (2013)
20. Gupta, A., Davis, L.S.: Beyond nouns: exploiting prepositions and comparative adjectives for learning visual classifiers. In: Forsyth, D., Torr, P., Zisserman, A. (eds.) ECCV 2008, Part I. LNCS, vol. 5302, pp. 16–29. Springer, Heidelberg (2008). https://doi.org/10.1007/978-3-540-88682-2_3
21. He, K., Gkioxari, G., Dollár, P., Girshick, R.: Mask R-CNN. In: ICCV (2017)
22. He, K., Zhang, X., Ren, S., Sun, J.: Deep residual learning for image recognition (2015). arXiv preprint: arXiv:1512.03385
23. Hoiem, D., Efros, A.A., Hebert, M.: Putting objects in perspective. IJCV **80**, 3–15 (2008)
24. Izadinia, H., Sadeghi, F., Farhadi, A.: Incorporating scene context and object layout into appearance modeling. In: CVPR (2014)
25. Johnson, J., Karpathy, A., Fei-Fei, L.: Densecap: fully convolutional localization networks for dense captioning (2015). arXiv preprint: arXiv:1511.07571
26. Johnson, J., et al.: Image retrieval using scene graphs. In: CVPR (2015)
27. Karpathy, A., Joulin, A., Fei-Fei, L.F.: Deep fragment embeddings for bidirectional image sentence mapping. In: NIPS (2014)
28. Krishna, R., et al.: Visual genome: connecting language and vision using crowd-sourced dense image annotations. IJCV **123**, 32–73 (2017)
29. Krizhevsky, A., Sutskever, I., Hinton, G.E.: Imagenet classification with deep convolutional neural networks. In: NIPS, pp. 1097–1105 (2012)
30. Kulkarni, G., et al.: Baby talk: understanding and generating image descriptions. In: CVPR (2011)
31. Kumar, M.P., Koller, D.: Efficiently selecting regions for scene understanding. In: CVPR (2010)
32. Ladicky, L., Russell, C., Kohli, P., Torr, P.H.S.: Graph cut based inference with co-occurrence statistics. In: Daniilidis, K., Maragos, P., Paragios, N. (eds.) ECCV 2010, Part V. LNCS, vol. 6315, pp. 239–253. Springer, Heidelberg (2010). https://doi.org/10.1007/978-3-642-15555-0_18
33. Li, Y., et al.: Visual question generation as dual task of visual question answering. In: Proceedings of the IEEE Conference on Computer Vision and Pattern Recognition, pp. 6116–6124 (2018)
34. Li, Y., Ouyang, W., Wang, X., Tang, X.: ViP-CNN: visual phrase guided convolutional neural network. In: CVPR (2017)
35. Li, Y., Ouyang, W., Zhou, B., Wang, K., Wang, X.: Scene graph generation from objects, phrases and region captions. In: ICCV (2017)
36. Liao, W., Shuai, L., Rosenhahn, B., Yang, M.Y.: Natural language guided visual relationship detection (2017). arXiv preprint: arXiv:1711.06032

37. Lu, C., Krishna, R., Bernstein, M., Fei-Fei, L.: Visual relationship detection with language priors. In: Leibe, B., Matas, J., Sebe, N., Welling, M. (eds.) ECCV 2016, Part I. LNCS, vol. 9905, pp. 852–869. Springer, Cham (2016). https://doi.org/10.1007/978-3-319-46448-0_51
38. Lu, P., Li, H., Wei, Z., Wang, J., Wang, X.: Co-attending free-form regions and detections with multi-modal multiplicative feature embedding for visual question answering. In: AAAI (2018)
39. Mensink, T., Gavves, E., Snoek, C.G.: Costa: co-occurrence statistics for zero-shot classification. In: CVPR (2014)
40. Nair, V., Hinton, G.E.: Rectified linear units improve restricted Boltzmann machines. In: ICML (2010)
41. Peyre, J., Laptev, I., Schmid, C., Sivic, J.: Weakly-supervised learning of visual relations. In: ICCV (2017)
42. Plummer, B.A., Mallya, A., Cervantes, C.M., Hockenmaier, J., Lazebnik, S.: Phrase localization and visual relationship detection with comprehensive linguistic cues. In: ICCV (2017)
43. Plummer, B.A., Wang, L., Cervantes, C.M., Caicedo, J.C., Hockenmaier, J., Lazebnik, S.: Flickr30k entities: collecting region-to-phrase correspondences for richer image-to-sentence models. In: ICCV (2015)
44. Rabinovich, A., Vedaldi, A., Galleguillos, C., Wiewiora, E., Belongie, S.: Objects in context. In: ICCV (2007)
45. Ramanathan, V., et al.: Learning semantic relationships for better action retrieval in images. In: CVPR (2015)
46. Regneri, M., Rohrbach, M., Wetzel, D., Thater, S., Schiele, B., Pinkal, M.: Grounding action descriptions in videos. In: ACL (2013)
47. Ren, S., He, K., Girshick, R., Sun, J.: Faster R-CNN: towards real-time object detection with region proposal networks. In: NIPS (2015)
48. Rohrbach, A., Rohrbach, M., Hu, R., Darrell, T., Schiele, B.: Grounding of textual phrases in images by reconstruction (2015). arXiv preprint: arXiv:1511.03745
49. Rohrbach, M., Qiu, W., Titov, I., Thater, S., Pinkal, M., Schiele, B.: Translating video content to natural language descriptions. In: ICCV (2013)
50. Russell, B.C., Freeman, W.T., Efros, A.A., Sivic, J., Zisserman, A.: Using multiple segmentations to discover objects and their extent in image collections. In: CVPR (2006)
51. Sadeghi, M.A., Farhadi, A.: Recognition using visual phrases. In: CVPR (2011)
52. Salakhutdinov, R., Torralba, A., Tenenbaum, J.: Learning to share visual appearance for multiclass object detection. In: CVPR (2011)
53. Simonyan, K., Zisserman, A.: Very deep convolutional networks for large-scale image recognition (2014). arXiv preprint: arXiv:1409.1556
54. Sivic, J., Russell, B.C., Efros, A.A., Zisserman, A., Freeman, W.T.: Discovering objects and their location in images. In: ICCV (2005)
55. Thomason, J., Venugopalan, S., Guadarrama, S., Saenko, K., Mooney, R.: Integrating language and vision to generate natural language descriptions of videos in the wild. In: COLING (2014)
56. Xiong, Y., Zhu, K., Lin, D., Tang, X.: Recognize complex events from static images by fusing deep channels. In: CVPR (2015)
57. Xu, D., Zhu, Y., Choy, C.B., Fei-Fei, L.: Scene graph generation by iterative message passing. In: CVPR (2017)
58. Xu, K., et al.: Show, attend and tell: neural image caption generation with visual attention (2015). arXiv preprint: arXiv:1502.03044

59. Yao, B., Fei-Fei, L.: Grouplet: a structured image representation for recognizing human and object interactions. In: CVPR (2010)
60. Yao, J., Fidler, S., Urtasun, R.: Describing the scene as a whole: joint object detection, scene classification and semantic segmentation. In: CVPR (2012)
61. Yu, R., Li, A., Morariu, V.I., Davis, L.S.: Visual relationship detection with internal and external linguistic knowledge distillation. In: ICCV (2017)
62. Zhang, H., Kyaw, Z., Chang, S.F., Chua, T.S.: Visual translation embedding network for visual relation detection. In: CVPR (2017)
63. Zhuang, B., Liu, L., Shen, C., Reid, I.: Towards context-aware interaction recognition. In: ICCV (2017)
64. Zitnick, C.L., Parikh, D., Vanderwende, L.: Learning the visual interpretation of sentences. In: ICCV (2013)

Multi-fiber Networks for Video Recognition

Yunpeng Chen[1]([✉]), Yannis Kalantidis[2], Jianshu Li[1], Shuicheng Yan[1,3], and Jiashi Feng[1]

[1] National University of Singapore, Singapore, Singapore
{chenyunpeng,jianshu}@u.nus.edu,
{eleyans,elefjia}@nus.edu.sg
[2] Facebook Research, Menlo Park, USA
yannisk@fb.com
[3] Qihoo 360 AI Institute, Beijing, China

Abstract. In this paper, we aim to reduce the computational cost of spatio-temporal deep neural networks, making them run as fast as their 2D counterparts while preserving state-of-the-art accuracy on video recognition benchmarks. To this end, we present the novel *Multi-Fiber* architecture that slices a complex neural network into an ensemble of lightweight networks or *fibers* that run through the network. To facilitate information flow between fibers we further incorporate multiplexer modules and end up with an architecture that reduces the computational cost of 3D networks by an order of magnitude, while increasing recognition performance at the same time. Extensive experimental results show that our multi-fiber architecture significantly boosts the efficiency of existing convolution networks for both image and video recognition tasks, achieving state-of-the-art performance on UCF-101, HMDB-51 and Kinetics datasets. Our proposed model requires over $9\times$ and $13\times$ less computations than the I3D [1] and R(2+1)D [2] models, respectively, yet providing higher accuracy.

Keywords: Deep learning · Neural networks · Video · Classification Action recognition

1 Introduction

With the aid of deep convolutional neural networks, image understanding has achieved remarkable success in the past few years. Notable examples include residual networks [3] for image classification, FastRCNN [4] for object detection, and Deeplab [5] for semantic segmentation, to name a few. However, the progress of deep neural networks for video analysis still lags their image counterparts, mostly due to the extra computational cost and complexity of spatio-temporal inputs.

The temporal dimension of videos contains valuable motion information that needs to be incorporated for video recognition tasks. A popular and effective

© Springer Nature Switzerland AG 2018
V. Ferrari et al. (Eds.): ECCV 2018, LNCS 11205, pp. 364–380, 2018.
https://doi.org/10.1007/978-3-030-01246-5_22

way of reasoning spatio-temporally is to use spatio-temporal or 3D convolutions [6,7] in deep neural network architectures to learn video representations. A 3D convolution is an extension of the 2D (spatial) convolution, which has three-dimensional kernels that also convolve along the temporal dimension. The 3D convolution kernels can be used to build 3D CNNs (Convolutional Neural Networks) by simply replacing the 2D spatial convolution kernels. This keeps the model end-to-end trainable. State-of-the-art video understanding models, such as Res3D [7] and I3D [1] build their CNN models in this straightforward manner. They use multiple layers of 3D convolutions to learn robust video representations and achieve top accuracy on multiple datasets, albeit with high computational overheads. Although recent approaches use decomposed 3D convolutions [2,8] or group convolutions [9] to reduce the computational cost, the use of spatio-temporal models still remains prohibitive for practical large-scale applications. For example, regular 2D CNNs require around 10s GFLOPs for processing a single frame, while 3D CNNs currently require more than 100 GFLOPs for a single clip[1]. *We argue that a clip-based model should be able to highly outperform frame-based models at video recognition tasks for the same computational cost, given that it has the added capacity of reasoning spatio-temporally.*

In this work, we aim to substantially improve the efficiency of 3D CNNs while preserving their state-of-the-art accuracy on video recognition tasks. Instead of decomposing the 3D convolution filters as in [2,8], we focus on the other source of computational overhead for 3D CNNs, the large input tensors. We propose a sparsely connected architecture, the *Multi-Fiber* network, where each unit in the architecture is essentially composed of multiple *fibers*, *i.e.* lightweight 3D convolutional networks that are independent from each other as shown in Fig. 1(c). The overall network is thus sparsely connected and the computational cost is reduced by approximately N times, where N is the number of fibers used. To improve information flow across fibers, we further propose a lightweight multiplexer module, that redirects information between parallel fibers if needed and is attached at the head of each residual block. This way, with a minimal computational overhead, representations can be shared among multiple fibers, and the overall capacity of the model is increased.

Our main contributions can be summarized as follows:

(1) We propose a highly efficient multi-fiber architecture, verify its effectiveness by evaluating it 2D convolutional neural networks for image recognition and show that it can boost performance when embedded on common compact models.
(2) We extend the proposed architecture to spatio-temporal convolutional networks and propose the Multi-Fiber network (MF-Net) for learning robust video representations with significantly reduced computational cost, *i.e.* about an order of magnitude less than the current state-of-the-art 3D models.

---

[1] *E.g.* the popular ResNet-152 [3] and VGG-16 [10] models require 11 GFLOPs and 15 GFLOPs, respectively, for processing a frame, while I3D [1] and R(2+1)D-34 [2] require 108 GFLOPs and 152 GFLOPs, respectively.

(3) We evaluate our multi-fiber network on multiple video recognition benchmarks and outperform recent related methods with several times lower computational cost on the Kinetics, UCF-101 and HMDB51 datasets.

2 Related Work

When it comes to video models, the most successful approaches utilize deep learning and can be split into two major categories: models based on spatial or 2D convolutions and those that incorporate spatio-temporal or 3D convolutions.

The major advantage of adopting 2D CNN based methods is their computational efficiency. One of the most successful approaches in this category is the Two-stream Network [13] architecture. It is composed of two 2D CNNs, one working on frames and another on optical flow. Features from the two modalities are fused at the final stage and achieved high video recognition accuracy. Multiple approaches have extended or incorporated the two-stream model [14–17] and since they are built on 2D CNNs are very efficient, usually requiring less than 10 GFLOPS per frame. In a very interesting recent approach, CoViAR [18] further reduces computations to 4.2 GFLOPs per frame in average, by directly using the motion information from compressed frames and sharing motion features across frames. However, as these approaches rely on pre-computed motion features to capture temporal dependencies, they usually perform worse than 3D convolutional networks, especially when large video datasets are available for pre-training, such as Sports-1M [19] and Kinetics [20].

On the contrary, 3D convolution neural networks are naturally able to learn motion features from raw video frames in an end-to-end manner. Since they use 3D convolution kernels that model both spatial and temporal information, rather than 2D kernels which just model spatial information, more complex relations between motion and appearance can be learned and captured. C3D [7] is one of the early methods successfully applied to learning robust video features. It builds a VGG [10] alike structure but uses $3 \times 3 \times 3$ kernels to capture motion information. The Res3D [23] makes one step further by taking the advantage of residual connections to ease the learning process. Similarly, I3D [1] proposes to use the Inception Network [24] as the backbone network rather than residual networks to learn video representations. However, all of the methods suffer from high computational cost compared with regular 2D CNNs due to the newly added temporal dimension. Recently, S3D [8] and R(2+1)D [2] are proposed to use one $1 \times 3 \times 3$ convolution layer followed by another $3 \times 1 \times 1$ convolutional layer to approximate a full-rank 3D kernel to reduce the computations of a full-rank $3 \times 3 \times 3$ convolutional layer while achieving better precision. However, these methods still suffer from an order of magnitude more computational cost than their 2D competitors, which makes it difficult to train and deploy them in practical applications.

The idea of using spare connections to reduce the computational cost is similar to low-power networks built for mobile devices [25–27] as well as other recent approaches that try to sparsify parts of the network either through group convolutions [28] or through learning connectivity [29]. However, our proposed network

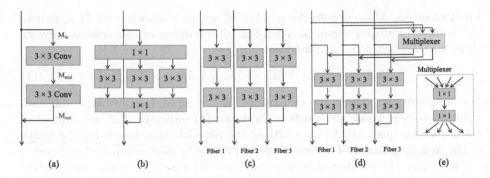

Fig. 1. From ResNet to multi-fiber. (a) A residual unit with two 3 × 3 convolution layers. (b) Conventional Multi-Path design, *e.g.* ResNeXt [28]. (c) The proposed multi-fiber design consisting of multiple separated lightweight residual units, called fibers. (d) The proposed multi-fiber architecture with a *multiplexer* for transferring information across separated fibers. (e) The architecture details of a multiplexer. It consists of two linear projection layers, one for dimension reduction and the other for dimension expansion.

is built for solving video recognition tasks and proposed different strategies that can also benefit existing low-power models, *e.g.* MobileNet-v2 [26]. We further discuss the differences of our architecture and compare against the most related and state-of-the-art methods in Sects. 3 and 4.

3 Multi-fiber Networks

The success of models that utilize spatio-temporal convolutions [1,2,7–9] suggests that it is crucial to have kernels spanning both the spatial and temporal dimensions. Spatio-temporal reasoning, however, comes at a cost: Both the convolutional kernels and the input-output tensors are multiple times larger.

In this section, we start by describing the basic module of our proposed model, *i.e.*, the multi-fiber unit. This unit can effectively reduce the number of connections within the network and enhance the model efficiency. It is generic and compatible with both 2D and 3D CNNs. For clearer illustration, we first demonstrate its effectiveness by embedding it into 2D convolutional architectures and evaluating its efficiency benefits for image recognition tasks. We then introduce its spatio-temporal 3D counterpart and discuss specific design choices for video recognition tasks.

3.1 The Multi-fiber Unit

The proposed multi-fiber unit is based on the highly modularized residual unit [3], which is easy to train and deploy. As shown in Fig. 1(a), the conventional residual unit uses two convolutional layers to learn features, which is straightforward but computationally expensive. To see this, let M_{in} denote the number of input channels, M_{mid} denote the number of middle channels, and M_{out} denote the number of output channels. Then the total number of connections between these two layers can be computed as

$$\# \text{ Connections} = M_{in} \times M_{mid} + M_{mid} \times M_{out}. \qquad (1)$$

For simplicity, we ignore the dimensions of the input feature maps and convolution kernels which are constant. Equation (1) indicates that the number of connections is quadratic to the width of the network, thus increasing the width of the unit by a factor of k would result in k^2 times more computational cost.

To reduce the number of connections that are essential to the overall computation cost, we propose to *slice* the complex residual unit into N parallel and separated paths (called *fibers*), each of which is isolated from the others, as shown in Fig. 1(c). In this way, the overall width of the unit remains the same, but the number of connections is reduced by a factor of N:

$$\begin{aligned}
\# \text{ Connections} &= N \times (M_{in}/N \times M_{mid}/N + M_{mid}/N \times M_{out}/N) \\
&= (M_{in} \times M_{mid} + M_{mid} \times M_{out})/N. \qquad (2)
\end{aligned}$$

We set $N = 16$ for all our experiments, unless otherwise stated. As we show experimentally in the following section, such a slicing strategy is intuitively simple yet effective. At the same time, however, slicing isolates each path from the others and blocks any information flow across them. This may result in limited learning capacity for data representations since one path cannot access and utilize the feature learned from the others. In order to recover part of the learning capacity, recent approaches that partially use slicing like ResNeXt [28], Xception [30] and MobileNet [25, 26] choose to only slice a small portion of layers and still use fully connected parts. The majority of layers (>60%) remains unsliced and dominates the computational cost, becoming the efficiency bottleneck. ResNeXt [28], for example, uses fully connected convolution layers at the beginning and end of each unit, and only slices the second layer as shown on Fig. 1(b). However, these unsliced layers dominate the computation cost and become the bottleneck. Different from only slicing a small portion of layers, we propose to slice the entire residual unit creating multiple fibers. To facilitate information flow, we further attach a lightweight bottleneck component we call the *multiplexer* that operates across fibers, in a residual manner.

The multiplexer acts as a router that redirects and amplifies features from all fibers. As shown in Fig. 1(e), the multiplexer first gathers features from all fibers using a 1×1 convolution layer, and then redirects them to specific fibers using the following 1×1 convolution layer. The reason for using two 1×1 layers instead of just one is to lower the computational overhead: we set the number of the first-layer output channels to be k times smaller than its input channels, so that the total cost would be reduced by a factor of $k/2$ compared with using a single 1×1 layer. The parameters within the multiplexer are randomly initialized and automatically adjusted by back-propagation end-to-end to maximize the performance gain for the given task. Batch normalization and ReLU nonlinearities are used before each layer. Figure 1(d) shows the full multi-fiber network, where the proposed multiplexer is attached at the beginning of the multi-fiber unit for routing features extracted from other paralleled fibers.

We note that, although the proposed multi-fiber architecture is motivated to reduce the number of connections for 3D CNNs to alleviate high computational cost, it is also applicable to 2D CNNs to further enhance efficiency of existing 2D architectures. To demonstrate this and verify effectiveness of the proposed architecture, we conduct several studies on 2D image classification tasks at first.

3.2 Justification of the Multi-fiber Architecture

We experimentally study the effectiveness of the proposed multi-fiber architecture by applying it on 2D CNNs for image classification and the ImageNet-1k dataset [31]. We use one of the most popular 2D CNN model, residual network (ResNet-18) [3], and the most computationally efficient ModelNet-v2 [26] as the backbone CNN in the following studies.

Our implementation is based on the code released by [32] using MXNet [33] on a cluster of 32 GPUs. The initial learning rate is set to 0.5 and decreases exponentially. We use a batch size of 1,024 and train the network for 360,000 iterations. As suggested by prior work [25], we use less data augmentations for obtaining better results. Since the above training strategy is different from the one used in our baseline methods [3,26], we report both our reproduced results and the reported results in their papers for fair comparison.

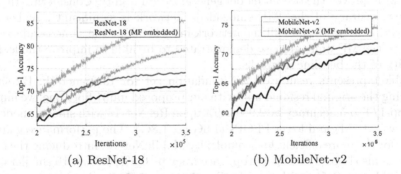

(a) ResNet-18   (b) MobileNet-v2

Fig. 2. Training and validation accuracy on the ImagaNet-1k dataset for (a) ResNet-18 and (b) MobileNet-v2 backbones respectively. The red lines stand for performance of the model with our proposed multi-fiber unit. The black lines show performance of our reproduced baseline model using exactly the same training settings as our method. The line thickness indicates results on the validation set (the ticker one) or the training set (the thinner one). (Color figure online)

The training curves in Fig. 2 plot the training and validation accuracy on ImageNet-1k during the last several iterations. One can observe that the network with our proposed Multi-fiber (MF) unit can consistently achieve higher training and validation accuracy than the baseline models, with the same number of

Table 1. Efficiency comparison on the ImageNet-1k validation set. "MF" stands for "multi-fiber unit", and Top-1/Top-5 accuracies are evaluated on a 224 × 224 single center crop [3]. "MF-Net" is our proposed network, with the architecture shown in Table 2. The ResNeXt row presents results for a ResNeXt-26 model of our design that has about the same number of FLOPS as MF-Net.

Model	Top-1 Acc.	Top-5 Acc.	#Params	FLOPs
ResNet-18 [3]	69.6%	89.2%	11.7 M	1.8 G
ResNet-18 (reproduced)	71.4%	90.2%	11.7 M	1.8 G
ResNet-18 (MF embedded)	74.3%	92.1%	9.6 M	1.6 G
ResNeXt-26 (8 × 16d)	72.8%	91.1%	6.3 M	1.1 G
ResNet-50 [3]	75.3%	92.2%	25.5 M	4.1 G
MobileNet-v2 (1.4) [26]	74.7%	–	6.9 M	585 M
MobileNet-v2 (1.4) (reproduced)	72.2%	90.8%	6.9 M	585 M
MobileNet-v2 (1.4) (MF embedded)	73.0%	91.1%	6.0 M	578 M
MF-Net ($N = 12$)	74.5%	92.0%	5.9 M	895 M
MF-Net ($N = 16$)	74.6%	92.0%	5.8 M	861 M
MF-Net ($N = 24$)	75.4%	92.5%	5.8 M	897 M
MF-Net ($N = 16$, w/o multiplexer)	70.2%	89.4%	4.5 M	600 M
MF-Net ($N = 16$, w/o multiplexer, deeper & wider)	71.0%	90.0%	6.4 M	897 M

iterations. Moreover, the resulted model has a smaller number of parameters and is more efficient (see Table 1). This demonstrates that embedding the proposed MF unit indeed helps reduce the model redundancy, accelerates the learning process and improves the overall model generalization ability. Considering the final training accuracy of the "MF embedded" network is significantly higher than the baseline networks and all the network models adopt the same regularization settings, the MF units are also demonstrated to be able to improve the learning capacity of the baseline networks.

Table 1 presents results on the validation set for Imagenet-1k. By simply replacing the original residual unit with our proposed multi-fiber one, we improve the Top-1/Top-5 accuracy by 2.9%/1.9% upon ResNet-18 with smaller model size (9.6M vs. 11.7M) and lower FLOPs (1.6G vs. 1.8G). The performance gain also stands for the more efficient low-complexity MobileNet-v2: introducing the multi-fiber unit also boosts its Top-1/Top-5 accuracy by 0.8%/0.3% with smaller model size (6.0M vs. 6.9M) and lower FLOPs (578M vs. 585M), clearly demonstrating its effectiveness. We note that our reproduced MobileNet-v2 has slightly lower accuracy than the reported one in [26] due to difference in the batch size, learning rate and update policy. But with the same training strategy, our reproduced ResNet-18 is 1.8% better than the reported one [3].

The two bottom sections of Table 1 further show ablation studies of our MF-Net, with respect to the number of fibers N and with/without the use of the multiplexer. As we see, increasing the number of fibers increases performance, while performance drops significantly when removing the multiplexer unit, demonstrating the importance of sharing information between fibers. Overall, we see

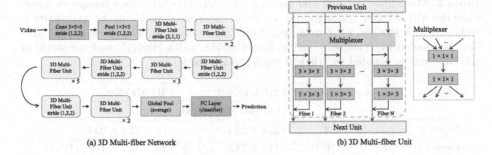

Fig. 3. Architecture of 3D multi-fiber network. (a) The overall architecture of 3D Multi-fiber Network. (b) The internal structure of each Multi-fiber Unit. Note that only the first 3 × 3 convolution layer has expanded on the 3rd temporal dimension for lower computational cost.

that our 2D multi-fiber network can perform as well as the much larger ResNet-50 [3], that has 25.5M parameters and requires 4.1 GFLOPS[2].

3.3 Spatio-Temporal Multi-fiber Networks

In this subsection, we extend out multi-fiber architecture to spatio-temporal inputs and present a new architecture for 3D convolutional networks and video recognition tasks. The design of our spatio-temporal multi-fiber network follows that of the "ResNet-34" [3] model, with a slightly different number of channels for lower GPU memory cost on processing videos. In particular, we reduce the number of channels in the first convolution layer, *i.e.* "Conv1", and increase the number of channels in the following layers, *i.e.* "Conv2-5", as shown in Table 2. This is because the feature maps in the first several layers have high resolutions and consume exponentially more GPU memory than the following layers for both training and testing.

The detailed network design is shown in Table 2, where we first design a 2D MF-Net and then "inflate" [1] its 2D convolutional kernels to 3D ones to build the 3D MF-Net. The 2D MF-Net is used as a pre-trained model for initializing the 3D MF-Net. Several recent works advocate separable convolution which uses two separate layers to replace one 3 × 3 layer [2,8]. Even though it may further reduce the computational cost and increase the accuracy, we do not use the separable convolution due to its high GPU memory consumption, considering video recognition application.

---

[2] It is worth noting that in terms of wall-clock time measured on our server, our MF-Net is only slightly (about 30%) faster than the highly optimized implementation of ResNet-50. We attribute this to the unoptimized implementation of group convolutions in CuDNN and foresee faster actual running times in the near future when group convolution computations are well optimized.

Table 2. Multi-fiber Network architecture. The "2D MF-Net" takes images as input, while the "3D MF-Net" takes frames, *i.e.* video clips, as input. Note, the complexity is evaluated with FLOPs, *i.e.* floating-point multiplication-adds. The stride of "3D MF-Net" is denoted by "(temporal stride, height stride, width stride)", and the stride of "2D MF-Net" is denoted by "(height stride, width stride)".

Layer	Repeat	#Channel	2D MF-Net		3D MF-Net	
			Output size	Stride	Output size	Stride
Input		3	224×224		$16 \times 224 \times 224$	
Conv1	1	16	112×112	(2,2)	$16 \times 112 \times 112$	(1,2,2)
MaxPool			56×56	(2,2)	$16 \times 56 \times 56$	(1,2,2)
Conv2	1	96	56×56	(1,1)	$8 \times 56 \times 56$	(2,1,1)
	2			(1,1)		(1,1,1)
Conv3	1	192	28×28	(2,2)	$8 \times 28 \times 28$	(1,2,2)
	3			(1,1)		(1,1,1)
Conv4	1	384	14×14	(2,2)	$8 \times 14 \times 14$	(1,2,2)
	5			(1,1)		(1,1,1)
Conv5	1	768	7×7	(2,2)	$8 \times 7 \times 7$	(1,2,2)
	2			(1,1)		(1,1,1)
AvgPooling			1×1		$1 \times 1 \times 1$	
FC			1000		400	
#Params			5.8 M		8.0 M	
FLOPs			861 M		11.1 G	

Figure 3 shows the inner structure of each 3D multi-fiber unit after the "inflation" from 2D to 3D. We note that all convolutional layers use 3D convolutions thus the input and output features contain an additional temporal dimension for preserving motion information.

4   Experiments

We evaluate the proposed multi-fiber network on three benchmark datasets, Kinetics [20], UCF-101 [34] and HMDB51 [35], and compare the results with other state-of-the-art models. All experiments are conducted using PyTorch [36] with input size of $16 \times 224 \times 224$ for both training and testing. Here 16 is the number of frames for each input clip. During testing, videos are resized to resolution 256×256, and we average clip predictions randomly sampled from the long video sequence to obtain the video predictions.

4.1   Video Classification with Motion Trained from Scratch

In this subsection, we study the effectiveness of the proposed model on learning video representations when motion features are trained from scratch. We use

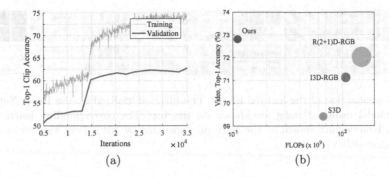

Fig. 4. Results on the Kinetics dataset (RGB Only). (a) The training and validation accuracy for multi-fiber network. (b) Efficiency comparison between different 3D convolutional networks. The area of each circle is proportional to the total parameter number of the model.

Table 3. Comparison on action recognition accuracy with state-of-the-arts on Kinetics. The complexity is measured using FLOPs, *i.e.* floating-point multiplication-adds. All results are only using RGB information, *i.e.* no optical flow. Results with citation numbers are copied from the respective papers.

Method	#Params	FLOPs	Top-1	Top-5
Two-Stream [1]	12 M	–	62.2%	–
ConvNet+LSTM [1]	9 M	–	63.3%	–
S3D [8]	8.8 M	66.4 G	69.4%	89.1%
I3D-RGB [1]	12.1 M	107.9 G	71.1%	89.3%
R(2+1)D-RGB [2]	63.6 M	152.4 G	72.0%	90.0%
MF-Net (Ours)	**8.0 M**	**11.1 G**	**72.8%**	**90.4%**

the large-scale Kinetics [20] benchmark dataset for evaluation, which consists of approximately 300, 000 videos from 400 action categories.

In this experiment, the 3D MF-Net model is initialized by inheriting parameters from a 2D one (see Sect. 3.3) pre-trained on the ImageNet-1k dataset. Then the 3D MF-Net is trained on Kinetics with an initial learning rate 0.1 which decays step-wisely with a factor 0.1. The weight decay is set to 0.0001 and we use SGD as the optimizer with a batch size 1, 024. We train the model on a cluster of 64 GPUs. Figure 4(a) shows the training and validation accuracy curves, from which we can see the network converges fast and the total training process only takes about 36,000 iterations.

Table 3 shows video action recognition results of different models trained on Kinetics. The models pre-trained on other large-scale video datasets, *e.g.* Sports-1M [19], using substantially more training videos are excluded in the table for fair comparison. As can be seen from the results, 3D based CNN models significantly

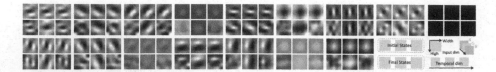

Fig. 5. Visualization of the learned filters. The filters initialized by the ImageNet pre-trained model using inflating are shown on the top. The corresponding learned 3D filters on Kinetics are shown at the bottom. (upscaled by 15x). Best viewed in color. (Color figure online)

improve the Top-1 accuracy upon 2D CNN based models. This performance gap is because 2D CNNs extract features from each frame separately and thus are incapable of modeling complex motion features from a sequence of raw frames even when LSTM is used, which limits their performance. On the other hand, 3D CNNs can learn motion features end-to-end from raw frames and thus are able to capture effective spatio-temporal information for video classification tasks. However, these 3D CNNs are computationally expensive compared 2D ones.

In contrast, our proposed MF-Net is more computationally efficient than existing 3D CNNs. Even with a moderate number of fibers, the computational overhead introduced by the temporal dimension is effectively compensated and our multi-fiber network only costs 11.1 GFLOPs, as low as regular 2D CNNs. Regarding performance and parameter efficiency, our proposed model achieves the highest Top-1/Top-5 accuracy and meanwhile it has the smallest model size. Compared with the best $R(2+1)D$-RGB, our model is over 13× faster with 8× less parameters, yet achieving 0.8% higher Top-1 accuracy. We note that the proposed model also costs the lowest GPU memory for both training and testing, benefiting from the optimized architecture mentioned in Sect. 3.3.

To get further insights into what our network learns, we visualize all 16 spatio-temporal kernels of the first convolutional layer in Fig. 5. Each 2-by-3 block corresponds to two $3 \times 3 \times 5 \times 5$ filters, with the top and bottom rows showing the filter before and after learning, respectively. As the filters are initialized from a 2D network pretrained on ImageNet and inflated in the temporal dimension, all three sub-kernels are identical in the beginning. After learning, however, we see filters evolving along the temporal dimension with diverse patterns, indicating that spatio-temporal features are learned effectively and embedded in these 3D kernels.

4.2 Video Classification with Fine-Tuned Models

In this experiment, we evaluate the generality and robustness of the proposed multi-fiber network by transferring the features learned on Kinetics to other datasets. We are interested in examining whether the proposed model can learn robust video representations that can generalize well to other datasets. We use the popular UCF-101 [34] and HMDB51 [35] as evaluation benchmarks.

The UCF-101 contains 13, 320 videos from 101 categories and the HMDB51 contains 6, 766 videos from 51 categories. Both are divided into 3 splits. We

Table 4. Action recognition accuracy on UCF-101 and HMDB51. The complexity is evaluated with FLOPs, *i.e.* floating-point multiplication-adds. The top part of the table refers to related methods based on 2D convolutions, while the lower part to methods utilizing spatio-temporal convolutions. Column "+OF" denotes the use of Optical Flow. FLOPs for computing optical flow are not considered.

Method	FLOPs	+OF	UCF-101	HMDB51
ResNet-50 [37]	3.8 G		82.3%	48.9%
ResNet-152 [37]	11.3 G		83.4%	46.7%
CoViAR [18]	4.2 G		90.4%	59.1%
Two-Stream [13]	3.3 G	✓	88.0%	59.4%
TSN [38]	3.8 G	✓	94.2%	69.4%
C3D [7]	38.5 G		82.3%	51.6%
Res3D [23]	19.3 G		85.8%	54.9%
ARTNet [16]	25.7 G		94.3%	70.9%
I3D-RGB [1]	107.9 G		95.6%	74.8%
R(2+1)D-RGB [2]	152.4 G		96.8%	74.5%
MF-Net (Ours)	**11.1 G**		96.0%	74.6%

follow experiment settings in [2,7,8,23] and report the averaged three-fold cross validation accuracy. For model training on both datasets, we use an initial learning rate 0.005 and decrease it for three times with a factor 0.1. The weight decay is set to 0.0001 and the momentum is set to 0.9 during the SGD optimization. All models are fine-tuned using 8 GPUs with a batch size of 128 clips.

Table 4 shows results of the multi-fiber network and comparison with state-of-the-art models. Consistent with above results, the multi-fiber network achieves the state-of-the-art accuracy with much lower computation cost. In particular, on the UCF-101 dataset, the proposed model achieves 96.0% Top-1 classification accuracy which is comparable with the sate-of-the-arts, but it is significantly more computationally efficient (11.1 vs. 152.4 GFLOPs). Compared with Res3D [23] which is also based on ResNet backbone and costs about 19.3 GFLOPs, the multi-fiber network achieves over 10% improvement in Top-1 accuracy (96.0% v.s. 85.8%) with 42% less computational cost.

Meanwhile, the proposed multi-fiber network also achieves the state-of-the-art accuracy on the HMDB51 dataset with significantly less computational cost. Compared with the 2D CNN based models that also only use RGB frames, our proposed model improves the accuracy by more than 15% (74.6% v.s. 59.1%). Even compared with the methods that using extra optical information, our proposed model still improves the accuracy by over 5%. This advantage partially benefits from richer motion features that learned from large-scale video pre-training datasets, while 2D CNNs cannot. Figure 6 shows the results in details. It is clear that our model provides an order of magnitude higher efficiency than previous state-of-the-arts in terms of FLOPs but still enjoys the high accuracy.

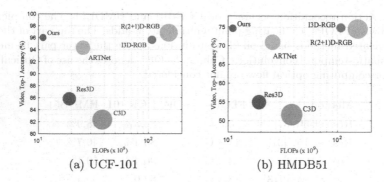

(a) UCF-101   (b) HMDB51

Fig. 6. Efficiency comparison between different methods. We use the area of each circle to show the total number of parameters for each model.

4.3 Discussion

The above experiments clearly demonstrate outstanding performance and efficiency of the proposed model. In this section, we discuss its potential limitations through success and failure case analysis on Kinetics.

We first study category-wise recognition accuracy. We calculate the accuracy for each category and sort them in a descending order, shown in Fig. 7(left). Among all 400 categories, we notice that 190 categories have an accuracy higher than 80% and 349 categories have an accuracy higher than 50%. Only 17 categories cannot be recognized well and have an accuracy lower than 30%. We list some examples along the spectrum in the right panel of Fig. 7. We find that in categories with highest accuracy there are either some specific objects/backgrounds clearly distinguishable from other categories or specific actions spanning long duration. On the contrary, categories with low accuracy usually do not display any distinguishing object and the target action usually lasts for a very short time within a long video.

To better understand success and failure cases, we visualize some of the video sequences in Fig. 8. The frames are evenly selected from the long video sequence.

Fig. 7. Statistical results on Kinetics validation dataset. Left: Accuracy distribution of the proposed model on the validation set of Kinetics. The category is sorted by accuracy in a descending order. Right: Selected categories and their accuracy.

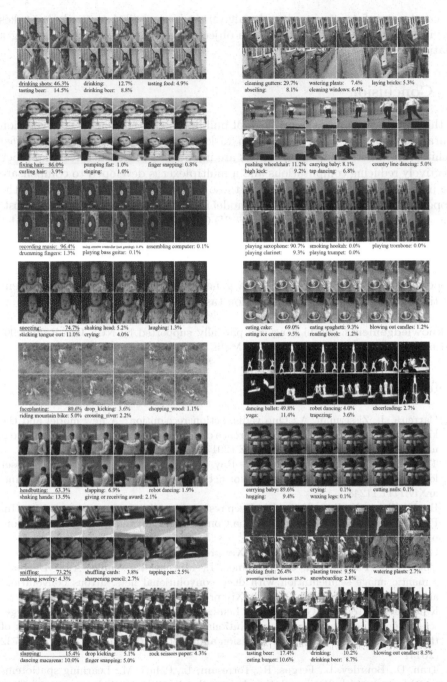

Fig. 8. Predictions made on the most difficult eight categories in Kinetics validation set. Left: Easy samples. Right: Hard samples. Top-5 confidence scores are shown below each video sequence. Underlines are used to emphasize correct prediction. Videos within the same row are from the same ground truth category.

As can be seen from the results, the algorithm is more likely to make mistakes on videos without any distinguishable object or containing an action lasting a relatively short period of time.

5   Conclusion

In this work, we address the problem of building highly efficient 3D convolution neural networks for video recognition tasks. We proposed a novel *multi-fiber* architecture, where sparse connections are introduced inside each residual block effectively reducing computations and a multiplexer is developed to compensate the information loss. Benefiting from these two novel architecture designs, the proposed model greatly reduces both model redundancy and computational cost. Compared with existing state-of-the-art 3D CNNs that usually consume an order of magnitude more computational resources than regular 2D CNNs, our proposed model costs significantly less resources yet achieves the state-of-the-art video recognition accuracy on Kinetics, UCF-101, HMDB51. We also showed that the proposed multi-fiber architecture is a generic method which can also benefit existing networks on image classification task.

Acknowledgements. Jiashi Feng was partially supported by NUS IDS R-263-000-C67-646, ECRA R-263-000-C87-133 and MOE Tier-II R-263-000-D17-112.

References

1. Carreira, J., Zisserman, A.: Quo vadis, action recognition? A new model and the kinetics dataset. In: 2017 IEEE Conference on Computer Vision and Pattern Recognition (CVPR), pp. 4724–4733. IEEE (2017)
2. Tran, D., Wang, H., Torresani, L., Ray, J., LeCun, Y., Paluri, M.: A closer look at spatiotemporal convolutions for action recognition (2017). arXiv preprint: arXiv:1711.11248
3. He, K., Zhang, X., Ren, S., Sun, J.: Deep residual learning for image recognition. In: Proceedings of the IEEE Conference on Computer Vision and Pattern Recognition, pp. 770–778 (2016)
4. Girshick, R.: Fast R-CNN (2015). arXiv preprint: arXiv:1504.08083
5. Chen, L.C., Papandreou, G., Kokkinos, I., Murphy, K., Yuille, A.L.: Deeplab: semantic image segmentation with deep convolutional nets, atrous convolution, and fully connected CRFs (2016). arXiv preprint: arXiv:1606.00915
6. Karpathy, A., Toderici, G., Shetty, S., Leung, T., Sukthankar, R., Fei-Fei, L.: Large-scale video classification with convolutional neural networks. In: Proceedings of the IEEE conference on Computer Vision and Pattern Recognition, pp. 1725–1732 (2014)
7. Tran, D., Bourdev, L., Fergus, R., Torresani, L., Paluri, M.: Learning spatiotemporal features with 3D convolutional networks. In: 2015 IEEE International Conference on Computer Vision (ICCV), pp. 4489–4497. IEEE (2015)
8. Xie, S., Sun, C., Huang, J., Tu, Z., Murphy, K.: Rethinking spatiotemporal feature learning for video understanding (2017). arXiv preprint: arXiv:1712.04851

9. Hara, K., Kataoka, H., Satoh, Y.: Can spatiotemporal 3D CNNs retrace the history of 2D CNNs and imagenet. In: Proceedings of the IEEE Conference on Computer Vision and Pattern Recognition, Salt Lake City, UT, USA, pp. 18–22 (2018)

10. Simonyan, K., Zisserman, A.: Very deep convolutional networks for large-scale image recognition (2014). arXiv preprint: arXiv:1409.1556

11. Shou, Z., Wang, D., Chang, S.F.: Temporal action localization in untrimmed videos via multi-stage CNNs. In: CVPR (2016)

12. Shou, Z., Chan, J., Zareian, A., Miyazawa, K., Chang, S.F.: CDC: convolutional-de-convolutional networks for precise temporal action localization in untrimmed videos. In: CVPR (2017)

13. Simonyan, K., Zisserman, A.: Two-stream convolutional networks for action recognition in videos. In: Advances in Neural Information Processing Systems, pp. 568–576 (2014)

14. Feichtenhofer, C., Pinz, A., Zisserman, A.: Convolutional two-stream network fusion for video action recognition. In: IEEE Conference on Computer Vision and Pattern Recognition (CVPR) (2016)

15. Ng, J.Y.H., Hausknecht, M., Vijayanarasimhan, S., Vinyals, O., Monga, R., Toderici, G.: Beyond short snippets: deep networks for video classification. In: 2015 IEEE Conference on Computer Vision and Pattern Recognition (CVPR), pp. 4694–4702. IEEE (2015)

16. Wang, L., Li, W., Li, W., Van Gool, L.: Appearance-and-relation networks for video classification (2017). arXiv preprint: arXiv:1711.09125

17. Tran, A., Cheong, L.F.: Two-stream flow-guided convolutional attention networks for action recognition. In: International Conference on Computer Vision (2017)

18. Wu, C.Y., Zaheer, M., Hu, H., Manmatha, R., Smola, A.J., Krähenbühl, P.: Compressed video action recognition (2017). arXiv preprint: arXiv:1712.00636

19. Karpathy, A., Toderici, G., Shetty, S., Leung, T., Sukthankar, R., Fei-Fei, L.: Large-scale video classification with convolutional neural networks. In: CVPR (2014)

20. Kay, W., et al.: The kinetics human action video dataset (2017). arXiv preprint: arXiv:1705.06950

21. Shou, Z., Gao, H., Zhang, L., Miyazawa, K., Chang, S.F.: Autoloc: weakly-supervised temporal action localization in untrimmed videos. In: Ferrari, V. (ed.) ECCV 2018, Part XVI. LNCS, vol. 11220, pp. 162–179. Springer, AG (2018)

22. Shou, Z.: Online detection of action start in untrimmed, streaming videos. In: Ferrari, V. et al. (eds.) ECCV 2018, Part III. LNCS, vol. 11207, pp. 551–568. Springer, AG (2018)

23. Tran, D., Ray, J., Shou, Z., Chang, S.F., Paluri, M.: Convnet architecture search for spatiotemporal feature learning (2017). arXiv preprint: arXiv:1708.05038

24. Szegedy, C., et al.: Going deeper with convolutions

25. Howard, A.G., et al.: Mobilenets: efficient convolutional neural networks for mobile vision applications (2017). arXiv preprint: arXiv:1704.04861

26. Sandler, M., Howard, A., Zhu, M., Zhmoginov, A., Chen, L.C.: Inverted residuals and linear bottlenecks: Mobile networks for classification, detection and segmentation (2018). arXiv preprint: arXiv:1801.04381

27. Zhang, X., Zhou, X., Lin, M., Sun, J.: Shufflenet: an extremely efficient convolutional neural network for mobile devices (2017). arXiv preprint: arXiv:1707.01083

28. Xie, S., Girshick, R., Dollár, P., Tu, Z., He, K.: Aggregated residual transformations for deep neural networks. In: 2017 IEEE Conference on Computer Vision and Pattern Recognition (CVPR), pp. 5987–5995. IEEE (2017)

29. Ahmed, K., Torresani, L.: Maskconnect: Connectivity learning by gradient descent. In: Ferrari, V., et al. (eds.) ECCV 2018, Part V. LNCS, vol. 11209, pp. 362–378. Springer, AG (2018)
30. Chollet, F.: Xception: deep learning with depthwise separable convolutions (2017). arXiv preprint: arXiv:1610.02357
31. Krizhevsky, A., Sutskever, I., Hinton, G.E.: Imagenet classification with deep convolutional neural networks. In: Advances in Neural Information Processing Systems, pp. 1097–1105 (2012)
32. Chen, Y., Li, J., Xiao, H., Jin, X., Yan, S., Feng, J.: Dual path networks. In: Advances in Neural Information Processing Systems, pp. 4470–4478 (2017)
33. Chen, T., et al.: Mxnet: a flexible and efficient machine learning library for heterogeneous distributed systems (2015). arXiv preprint: arXiv:1512.01274
34. Soomro, K., Zamir, A.R., Shah, M.: Ucf101: a dataset of 101 human actions classes from videos in the wild (2012). arXiv preprint: arXiv:1212.0402
35. Kuehne, H., Jhuang, H., Garrote, E., Poggio, T., Serre, T.: HMDB: a large video database for human motion recognition. In: 2011 IEEE International Conference on Computer Vision (ICCV), pp. 2556–2563. IEEE (2011)
36. Paszke, A., Gross, S., Chintala, S., Chanan, G.: Pytorch (2017)
37. Feichtenhofer, C., Pinz, A., Wildes, R.P.: Spatiotemporal multiplier networks for video action recognition. In: 2017 IEEE Conference on Computer Vision and Pattern Recognition (CVPR), pp. 7445–7454. IEEE (2017)
38. Wang, L., et al.: Temporal segment networks: towards good practices for deep action recognition. In: Leibe, B., Matas, J., Sebe, N., Welling, M. (eds.) ECCV 2016, Part VIII. LNCS, vol. 9912, pp. 20–36. Springer, Cham (2016). https://doi.org/10.1007/978-3-319-46484-8_2

Tackling 3D ToF Artifacts Through Learning and the FLAT Dataset

Qi Guo[1,2], Iuri Frosio[1(✉)], Orazio Gallo[1], Todd Zickler[2], and Jan Kautz[1]

[1] NVIDIA, Santa Clara, USA
ifrosio@nvidia.com
[2] Harvard SEAS, Cambridge, USA

Abstract. Scene motion, multiple reflections, and sensor noise introduce artifacts in the depth reconstruction performed by time-of-flight cameras. We propose a two-stage, deep-learning approach to address all of these sources of artifacts simultaneously. We also introduce FLAT, a synthetic dataset of 2000 ToF measurements that capture all of these nonidealities, and allows to simulate different camera hardware. Using the Kinect 2 camera as a baseline, we show improved reconstruction errors over state-of-the-art methods, on both simulated and real data.

Keywords: Time-of-Flight · MPI artifacts · Motion artifacts

1 Introduction

Depth estimation is central to several computer vision applications. Among the many existing strategies for extracting a scene's 3D information, Time-of-Flight (ToF) cameras are particularly popular due to their robustness and affordability.

ToF cameras leverage the relation between an object's distance from the sensor and the amount of time required for photons to travel to that object and back. In particular, Amplitude-Modulated Continuous-Wave (AMCW) cameras emit a periodic light signal and measure its phase delay upon return: the phase delay offers an estimate of the time of flight and, in turn, of depth. Any implementation of this approach requires several careful considerations.

First and foremost, the phase delay wraps at distances that correspond to multiples of the modulation period. A common approach is to combine information from different modulation frequencies: longer modulation periods extend the unambiguous range, while shorter periods allow resolving finer details. Using multiple frequencies, however, is not without consequences. The dynamic parts of the scene may be displaced between sequential measurements at different frequencies, causing depth estimation errors[1] that are particularly strong along the

---

[1] Some cameras use spatial multiplexing instead, and synchronize neighboring pixels with specific emission frequencies, thus sacrificing spatial resolution.

Electronic supplementary material The online version of this chapter (https://doi.org/10.1007/978-3-030-01246-5_23) contains supplementary material, which is available to authorized users.

© Springer Nature Switzerland AG 2018
V. Ferrari et al. (Eds.): ECCV 2018, LNCS 11205, pp. 381–396, 2018.
https://doi.org/10.1007/978-3-030-01246-5_23

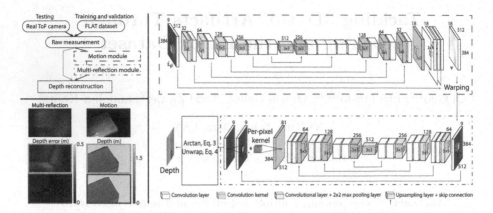

Fig. 1. The traditional ToF processing pipeline (green, libfreenect2 [1] as an example) and the proposed framework (red). The lower left panel shows artifacts generated by MPI and motion, that show up respectively as deformation close to corners and spikes or missing data close to the boundaries of moving objects in the traditional flowchart (green). These artifacts are greatly reduced by the proposed framework (red), which is based on the introduction of the motion and multi-reflection modules depicted in the right part. (Color figure online)

depth discontinuities. These artifacts can be identified and removed, at the cost of missing depth information at the corresponding pixels.

Another consideration is multi-path light transport. In addition to the direct emitter-object-sensor path, light may follow other paths and bounce multiple times before being recorded by one pixel. This phenomenon, called multiple-path interference (MPI), causes biased estimates of depth. Several methods attempt to attenuate the effects of MPI [2–6], some employing multiple modulation frequencies [2,3], which, as discussed above, can introduce motion artifacts. These could be reduced in theory by increasing the capture speed, but shorter exposure times may lead to a lower signal-to-noise ratio because of shot noise.

The delicate trade-offs between phase-unwrapping, motion, sensor noise, and MPI, have been studied in a variety of ways, with several methods attempting to attenuate the effects of the different sources of artifacts *independently*. To the best of our knowledge, however, there have been no attempts to tackle them jointly by learning, possibly because of the lack of large datasets.

We introduce a learning-based approach to tackle dynamic scenes, MPI, and shot noise *simultaneously*. Our two-stage architecture (Fig. 1) operates directly on the raw measurements of a multi-frequency ToF sensor, and produces improved measurements that are compatible with standard equations for phase-unwrapping and conversion to depth. The first stage is an encoder-decoder architecture [7] that attenuates motion artifacts by spatially warping the raw measurements onto a common 2D reference frame. This increases the number of pixels whose depth can be reliably estimated, especially near the boundaries of moving objects. The second stage is a kernel predicting network [8] that attenuates MPI and shot noise. Because ground truth depth for real-world scenes is difficult to capture, we introduce FLAT (Flexible, Large, Augmentable, ToF dataset), a synthetic dataset for training and evaluation, which allows to accurately simulate the raw measurements of different AMCW ToF cameras (including the Kinect 2) in the presence of MPI artifacts and shot noise; FLAT data can be augmented to approximate motion artifacts as well. Our contributions are:

(i) FLAT, a large, synthetic dataset of ToF measurements that simulates MPI, motion artifacts, shot noise, and different camera response functions.
(ii) A Deep Neural Network (DNN) architecture for attenuating motion, MPI, and shot noise artifacts that can be trained both in the raw measurement or depth domain.
(iii) A thorough validation, including an ablation study and a comparison with state-of-the-art algorithms for reducing MPI and motion artifacts.
(iv) A complete characterization of the Kinect 2 camera, including its camera response function and sensor noise characteristics.

Our DNN model, dataset and characterization of the Kinect 2 are available at http://research.nvidia.com/publication/2018-09_Tackling-3D-ToF.

2   Related Work

Several works separately reduce artifacts due to MPI, motion, or shot noise in AMCW ToF imaging. We group them into four categories.

Measurement Noise Reduction. Raw ToF measurements suffer from both systematic and random noise [9]. Systematic errors are often associated with imperfect sinusoidal modulations and can be reduced through calibration [9–11]. Shot noise and other types of random noise are typically addressed through bilateral filtering of the raw measurements, the depth map, or both sometimes using other images for guidance [12]. The performance of these approaches is generally satisfactory, and any system that intends to replace them, ours included, should not perform noticeably worse.

Motion Artifacts Reduction. Motion artifacts occur when objects move and ToF raw measurements are captured sequentially. Gottfried et al. [13] identify three ways to attenuate them: reduce the number of sequential measurements; detect and correct the regions affected by motion, both in the raw measurement domain and in the depth domain; or estimate the 2D motion fields between raw 2D measurement maps and apply corrective spatial warping. One way to detect affected pixels in raw measurements is by checking the *Plus* and *Minus* *rules* [14,15] that derive from physical constraints on the light measured in a static scene. After detection, pixels affected by motion blur can be corrected, for example, by interpolation [14]. Object motion also affects the frequency of reflected signals due to Doppler effect; however, to use the frequency shift to measure object motion requires a higher number of measurements and extensive processing [16].

Physics-Based MPI Reduction. Algorithms for recovering depth from ToF correlations usually assume the pure measurement of direct, single-bounce (emitter-surface-sensor) light paths. In practice, many photons bounce multiple times, causing "erroneous" measurements [2,10]. If multiple modulation frequencies are used, the problem can be tackled by processing the temporal change of each pixel of the raw measurements in the Fourier domain. For instance, in the absence of noise, K interfering paths can be resolved by $2K + 1$ frequency measurements [3]. Other techniques for the per-pixel temporal processing of raw ToF measurements include Prony's method, the matrix pencil method, orthogonal matching pursuit, EPIRIT/MUSIC, and atomic norm regularization [2]. Freedman et al. propose a real-time temporal processing technique that uses per-pixel optimization based on a light transport model with sparse and low-rank components [17]. Phasor Imaging exploits the fact that the effects of MPI are diminished at much higher modulation frequencies, and shows that simple temporal processing can succeed with as few as two such frequencies, albeit with a reduced unambiguous working range [18].

Learning-Based MPI Reduction. The difficulty of modeling MPI analytically makes machine learning an enticing alternative for its reduction. However, one obstacle is the lack of large, physically-accurate datasets for training, which are difficult to capture [19] and prohibitively expensive to simulate, until recently. Marco et al. use an encoder to learn a mapping from captured ToF measurements to a representation of (MPI-corrupted) depth, and then combine this with a limited number of simulated, direct-only ToF measurements to train a decoder that produces MPI-corrected depth maps [4]. Mutny et al. focus on corners of different materials and use a dataset of such corners to train a random forest with hand-crafted features [5]. A different strategy is taken by Son et al. who use a robotic arm and structured light system to capture ToF measurements with registered ground-truth depth [6]. They then train two neural networks to correct depth and refine edges through geodesic filtering.

We leverage the availability of computational power and advances in transient rendering [10,20] to synthesize a training dataset sufficiently large and diverse to explore a much larger class of learned models. In addition to physically-accurate MPI effects, the dataset provides realistic shot noise, supports augmentation with approximate motion models, and allows for efficient generation of raw measurements from AMCW ToF sensors with arbitrary modulation signals.

3   Time-of-Flight Camera Models

In this section we first review the theory of ToF reconstruction in the ideal case. We show that equations for depth reconstruction are differentiable, which allows for backpropagation. We then show the effect of MPI and motion on depth reconstruction, which helps framing the learning problem and defining the important factors for training. We leverage these elements to train a neural network, working in the domain of the raw measurements and before unwrapping, aimed at correcting these artifacts. The section is closed by an accurate characterization of the Kinect 2, which is our hardware testbed; this serves to produce accurate simulations for training and reduce the shift between synthetic and real data. All the math details for the section are in the Supplementary.

3.1   Ideal Camera Model

An AMCW ToF camera illuminates the scene with an amplitude-modulated, sinusoidal signal $g(t) = g_1\cos(\omega t) + g_0$, [16]. If camera and light source are co-located, and the scene static, the signal coming back to a pixel is

$$s\left(t\right) = \int_{-\infty}^{t} a(\tau)\cos(\omega t - 2\omega\tau)d\tau, \tag{1}$$

where $a(\tau)$ is the scene response function, i.e. the signal reaching the pixel at time τ. In an ideal scenario, the light is reflected once and the scene response is an impulse, $a(\tau) = a\delta(\tau - \tau_0)$. The travel time τ_0 directly translates to depth.

A *homodyne* ToF camera modulates the incident signal with a phase-delayed reference signal at the same frequency, $b\cos(\omega t - \psi)$. The exposure time of the camera is usually set to $T \gg 2\pi/\omega$. Simple trigonometry allows writing the raw correlation measurement $i_{\psi,\omega}$ as:

$$i_{\psi,\omega} = \int_{-T/2}^{T/2} s(t)b\cos\left(\omega t - \psi\right)dt \approx a(\tau_0)b\cos(\psi - 2\omega\tau_0) = af_{\psi,\omega}(\tau_0), \tag{2}$$

where we denote $f_{\psi,\omega}(\tau) = b\cos(\psi - 2\omega\tau)$ as the *camera function*. Using raw measurements captured at a single frequency ω and $K \geq 2$ phases $\boldsymbol{\psi} = (\psi_1, \ldots, \psi_K)$, the depth d can be recovered at each pixel as:

$$d = c/(2\omega)\ \arctan\left[(\sin\boldsymbol{\psi}\cdot\boldsymbol{i}_{\psi,\omega})/(\cos\boldsymbol{\psi}\cdot\boldsymbol{i}_{\psi,\omega})\right], \tag{3}$$

where $\boldsymbol{i}_{\psi,\omega}$ is the K-vector of per-phase measurements.

However, d wraps for depths larger than $\pi c/\omega$, and additional measurements at $L \geq 2$ different frequencies $\boldsymbol{\omega} = (\omega_1, \ldots, \omega_L)$ are required. Denoting the measurements at frequency ω_l as $\boldsymbol{i}_{\psi,\omega_l}$, an analytical expression for d was provided by Goshov and Solodkin [21] based on the Chinese remainder theorem:

$$d = \sum_{\boldsymbol{\omega}} A_l(\boldsymbol{\omega})\arctan\left[(\sin\boldsymbol{\psi}\cdot\boldsymbol{i}_{\psi,\omega_l})/(\cos\boldsymbol{\psi}\cdot\boldsymbol{i}_{\psi,\omega_l})\right] + B(\boldsymbol{\omega}), \tag{4}$$

where $\{A_l(\boldsymbol{\omega})\}_{l=1,\ldots,L}$ and $B(\boldsymbol{\omega})$ are constants. Based on Eq. 4, one can easily obtain the derivative $\partial d/\partial\boldsymbol{i}_{\psi,\omega_l}$, which makes it possible to backpropagate the error on d and to perform end-to-end training.

3.2   The Impact of Multiple Paths

In a realistic scenario, the signal that reaches the sensor is corrupted by multiple light paths that undergo different reflection events and have different path lengths. This means that the scene response $a(\tau)$ is not an impulse anymore, as it measures the arrival of the light reaching a pixel from all the possible light paths that connect it to the emitter. In this case, Eq. 2 becomes:

$$
\begin{aligned}
i_{\psi,\omega} &= \int_{-T/2}^{T/2} \left(\int_{-\infty}^{t} a(\tau)\cos(\omega t - 2\omega\tau)d\tau \right) b \cos(\omega t - \psi) \, dt \\
&\approx \int_{-\infty}^{t} a(\tau) b \cos(\psi - 2\omega\tau)d\tau = \int_{-\infty}^{t} a(\tau) f_{\psi,\omega}(\tau)d\tau.
\end{aligned}
\tag{5}
$$

When sinusoidal reference signals with different frequencies ω_l and phases ψ_k are measured sequentially, one obtains multiple channels of raw measurements. The multi-channel measurements at any pixel $i_{\psi,\omega}$ can be interpreted as a point in a multi-dimensional space, and while difficult to model analytically, there is structure in this space that can be exploited through learning.

In the ideal case of a single bounce, the set of all possible measurement vectors $i_{\psi,\omega}$ forms a "single-bounce measurement manifold" defined by Eq. 2. If only one frequency is used, measurements affected by MPI lie on the same manifold, and it is therefore impossible to identify and correct them. On the other hand, in the case of multiple frequencies, the manifold becomes a non-linear subspace, and MPI-affected vectors do not lie on it anymore. The MPI problem can then be recast as one of mapping real measurements, possibly affected by MPI, to the ideal one-bounce manifold, which is also the idea behind many existing approaches for MPI correction.

3.3   The Impact of Motion

Real scenes are rarely static. Because of the lateral and axial motion of objects with respect to the camera, sequential correlation measurements $i_{\psi,\omega}$ are misaligned. Moreover, the axial component of the motion also changes the scene response function $a(\tau)$: for example, even in the simple case of a single bounce, the term τ_0 in Eq. 2 changes with the axial motion of the object, whereas the measured intensity varies proportionally to the inverse-square of distance. In our indoor experimental setting we found both these phenomena to contribute significantly to the depth reconstruction error. Motion can even generate blur and Doppler within each raw correlation measurement, but we found these last effects negligible when compared to the previous ones.

3.4   Characterization of Kinect 2

The Kinect 2 is a well-documented, widely used ToF camera, with an open-source SDK (libfreenect2 [1]) that exposes raw correlation measurements and provides a baseline algorithm for benchmarking (indicated as LF2 in the following). We carefully characterize the camera functions, shot noise, vignetting, and per-pixel delay, to produce accurate simulations and mitigate the data shift between synthetic data from the FLAT dataset and real scenarios.

The Kinect 2 uses three modulation frequencies, each with three phases, for a total of nine camera functions $f_{\psi,\omega}(\tau)$. To calibrate the camera functions, we carefully align the optical axis to be normal to a Lambertian calibration plane. We place a light absorption tube in front of Kinect's light source to narrow down the beam emission angle and limit MPI. We translate the plane to known distances $\{d_j\}_{j=1...N}$ to obtain a series of raw measurements $\{i_{\psi,\omega}(d_j)\}_{j=1...N}$ that approximate $(d_j)^{-2} f_{\psi,\omega}(2d_j/c)$ up to a constant scale, for every pixel. After removing the squared-distance intensity decay $(d_j)^{-2}$, we have a series of observations of the camera functions $\{f_{\psi,\omega}(2d_j/c)\}$. Figure 2 shows three camera functions fitted by this method, parameterized as $b\cos(\psi - 2\omega\tau)$ (red and blue curve in Fig. 2), and $\max(\min(b_1\cos(\psi - 2\omega\tau), b_2), -b_2)$ (green curve in Fig. 2).

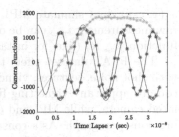

Fig. 2. Calibrated camera functions for Kinect 2; the points represent experimental data, the continuous line are the fitted camera functions. (Color figure online)

As for the shot noise, we assume each pixel to be independent from the others. We acquire data from 15 scenes; for each raw correlation measurement, we compute the per-pixel expected value as the average of 100 measurements. For any expected value, we collect the empirical distribution of the noisy samples in a lookup table, that is used to generate noisy data in simulation.

For the complete explanation of the calibration procedure, including vignetting and per-pixel time delay, we invite the reader to refer to the Supplementary, which also includes more experimental results.

4   The FLAT Dataset

An ideal dataset for training and validating ToF algorithms is large; allows simulating different camera response functions (like those in Sect. 3.4); allows including MPI, shot noise and motion; and exposes raw correlation measurements. We created the FLAT dataset with these principles in mind.

FLAT contains 2000 scene response functions, $\{a^j(\tau, x, y)\}_{j=1..2000}$, where we make the dependence on pixel (x, y) explicit. Each of these is computed through transient rendering [20], which simulates the irradiance received by the camera sensor at every time frame, after sending an impulse of light to the environment. The output of the renderer is a $n_\tau \times n_x \times n_y$ tensor, i.e. a discretized version of $a^j(\tau, x, y)$. The scenes in the dataset are generated from 70 object setups; each setup has 1 to 5 objects with lambertian surface and uniform albedo; their 3D models are from the Stanford 3D Scanning Repository [22] and the online collection [23]. We render each setup from approximately 30 point of views and orientations, at a spatial resolution of $(n_x = 424) \times (n_y = 512)$ pixels and for $n_\tau = 1000$ consecutive time intervals (each interval is $5e^{-11}$sec long); the horizontal field of view is $70°$ (corresponding to the Kinect 2 camera). Since bi-directional path tracing is used to sample and simulate each light ray,

$a^j(\tau, x, y)$ does simulate MPI. From the discretized version of $a^j(\tau, x, y)$, any raw measurement $i_{\psi,\omega}$ can be obtained as in Eq. 5, for any user-provided camera function $f_{\psi,\omega}(t)$ (like, for instance, the ones we estimated for Kinect 2).

The FLAT dataset offers the possibility to augment the raw measurement with shot noise, textures, vignetting, and motion. Within FLAT, we provide the code to apply any vignetting function and shot noise coherently with the simulated camera, while MPI and camera functions are handled as described in the previous paragraph. As a consequence, a physically correct simulation of different camera functions, MPI, vignetting, and shot noise is a computationally light task within FLAT. On the other hand, texture and motion are more expensive to render exactly. Since each scene in the FLAT dataset takes on the average 10 CPU hours to render, creating a large set of scenes with different textures and motions would require tens to hundreds of times longer. We handle this by providing tools to approximate texture and motion in real time (as specialized forms of data augmentation), while still providing a small testing set within FLAT with exact motion, texture, and rendering.

We approximate textures on the training data, by pixel-by-pixel multiplication of the rendered $i_{\psi,\omega}$ with texture maps from the CURET texture dataset [24]. This is an approximation that ignores the recursive impact that real textures have on MPI, but we have found that it is nonetheless useful as a form of data augmentation.

The FLAT dataset offers two different methods to augment the simulated raw measurements with approximate motion. To illustrate the first one, let us consider the Kinect 2, where nine correlation measurements of a static scene, $i_{\psi,\omega} = (i_{\psi_1,\omega_1}, \ldots, i_{\psi_9,\omega_9})$ are simulated. We generate a random 2D affine transform T and apply it to create a smooth motion as $i'_{\psi_j,\omega_j}(x, y) = i_{\psi_j,\omega_j}(T^{j-5}(x, y))$, where $T^n(x, y)$ is transforming (x, y) by T for n times, and $T^{-n}(T^n(x, y)) = (x, y)$. Notice that the first and last measurement will achieve the largest movement. To obtain a more complex movement, we simulate the motion of two or more objects with different affine transforms and composite the scene based on their depths. This approximate motion model is fast, but does not reproduce the MPI interaction between the objects in the scene. The second motion approximation method takes in input a rendered scene response function, $a(\tau, x, y)$. We generate then a random, 3D affine transformation and apply the corresponding displacement (v_x, v_y, v_z) to it, i.e., $a'(\tau, x, y) = a(\tau + v_z/c, x + v_x, y + v_y)$. Then we use Eq. 5 to compute one of the nine raw measurements. As in the previous method, the transform is applied multiple times to create a smooth motion between the nine measurements. This method is computationally more expensive compared to the previous one, but physically more accurate.

5   Network Architecture

We propose a two-module DNN (Fig. 1), to deal with MPI, motion, and shot noise in the domain of raw correlation measurements. We demonstrate the use of the modules on data from the Kinect 2. The two modules can be integrated

Table 1. Training specification.

Name	MOM + LF2	MOM-MRM + LF2*	MRM + LF2*
Training data	Motion, MPI	Motion, MPI	Static, MPI
Architecture	Encoder-Decoder	Encoder-Decoder-KPN (3 × 3 × 1)	KPN (1 × 1 × 9)
Depth reconstruction	LF2	LF2, no filter	LF2, no filter
Training loss	L2, Velocity	L2, Raw intensity	L2, Raw intensity
Fine tuning loss		L2, Depth	L2, Depth

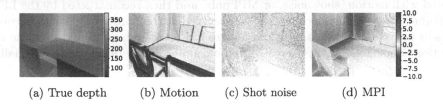

(a) True depth   (b) Motion   (c) Shot noise   (d) MPI

Fig. 3. Effect of non-idealities on the LF2 depth reconstruction error, in cm. (Color figure online)

into the LF2 [1] reconstruction pipeline, which is basically an implementation of Eq. 4 on Kinect 2. We leverage the differentiability of Eq. 4 to exploit, among other forms of training for the DNN, training using a loss function in the depth domain.

The first module (MOtion Module, MOM) is an encoder-decoder inspired by Flownet [7]. The aim of MOM is to output a velocity map to align the nine raw channels measured by Kinect2. Differently from the original design of Flownet, which computes the optical flow between two images in the same domain, MOM aligns raw correlation measurements taken with different camera functions, and therefore correlated, but visually different. Moreover, MOM takes in input nine misaligned channels and outputs eight optical flows at the same time, while Flownet deals with only one pair of images and one optical flow. The second module (Multi-Reflection Module, MRM) is based on a kernel-predicting network (KPN), that has been effectively used for burst denoising on shot noise [25]. MRM outputs nine spatially varying kernels for every pixel; each kernel is locally convolved with the input raw measurements, to produce a clean raw measurement by jointly removing shot and MPI noise on every channel.

Table 1 shows the details of different variations of the basic DNN architecture that we consider in our experiments. Notice that, when we use the MRM module, we modify the LF2 pipeline to remove bilateral filtering from it, because denoising is already performed by MRM; we indicate this variation of the LF2 pipeline as LF2*. The MOM-MRM (followed by LF2*) network inherits the encoder-decoder from MOM; training of MRM is performed with the output of MOM as input, the weights of MOM being fixed. We start training using the L2 error of the raw correlation measurements as loss. Then, we fine tune MRM using the L2 depth loss propagated through LF2*. Motion in the training data is generated using the first approximation method in the FLAT dataset. We also tried fine tuning using the second approximation, which is physically more accurate, obtaining similar results.

6   Experiments

To better illustrate the typical distribution of the artifacts introduced by motion, shot noise, and MPI, we show in Fig. 3 a scene from the FLAT dataset, rendered with motion, shot noise, or MPI only, and then reconstructed by the LF2 pipeline. Over/under shootings can be observed at the border of moving objects, where raw measurements from the foreground and the background mix due to motion. Shot noise in $i_{\psi,\omega}$ creates random noise in the depth map, especially in dark regions like background and image borders. MPI generates a low frequency noise in areas affected by light reflection, like the wall corner in Fig. 3.

6.1   MPI Correction

We first measure the effect of the MRM module on static scenes affected by MPI in the FLAT dataset, and compare it to LF2 [1], DToF [4], and Phasor [18], that are based respectively on multi-frequency, deep learning, and custom hardware. LF2 implements Eq. 4 on Kinect 2 and it constitutes our baseline to evaluate the improvement provided by our DNN on the same platform. DToF and Phasor require different sensor platforms than Kinect 2, but thanks to the flexibility of the FLAT dataset, we can simulate raw measurements using their specific modulation frequency and phase, and add the same level of noise for testing. As DToF and

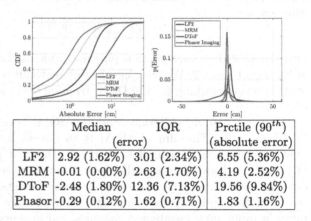

	Median	IQR	Prctile (90th)
	(error)		(absolute error)
LF2	2.92 (1.62%)	3.01 (2.34%)	6.55 (5.36%)
MRM	-0.01 (0.00%)	2.63 (1.70%)	4.19 (2.52%)
DToF	-2.48 (1.80%)	12.36 (7.13%)	19.56 (9.84%)
Phasor	-0.29 (0.12%)	1.62 (0.71%)	1.83 (1.16%)

Fig. 4. The upper left panel shows the CDF of the depth error for LF2, MRM, DToF, and Phasor, for simulated data from FLAT, affected by shot noise and MPI. The upper right panel shows the histogram of the error. All pixels whose real depth is in the [1.5 m, 5 m] range have been considered. Our MRM outperforms LF2 and DToF, and it comes much closer to the accuracy achieved using the MPI-dedicated, higher-frequency modulations of Phasor. The table shows corresponding median and Inter Quartile Range (IQR) of the depth error, and 90th percentile of the absolute error, in cm. The numbers in the brackets indicate the relative errors. (Color figure online)

Phasor do not mask unreliable output pixels (like LF2 does), and Phasor's working range is limited to [1.5 m, 5 m], we compare the depth error for all those pixels in this range only. Furthermore, as Phasor does not deal with shot noise, we apply a bilateral filter to remove noise from its output depth.

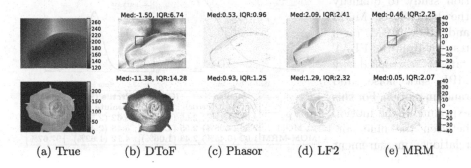

(a) True   (b) DToF   (c) Phasor   (d) LF2   (e) MRM

Fig. 5. Depth error for scenes from the FLAT dataset, corrupted by shot noise and MPI and reconstructed by DToF [10], Phasor Imaging [18], LF2 [1] and MRM, in cm. Errors are computed only in the unambiguous reconstruction range of Phasor Imaging, [1.5 m, 5 m]; no mask is used to remove unreliable pixels. The blue boxes in the first row show the receptive field for DToF and MRM. (Color figure online)

Results reported in Fig. 4 show that DToF produces the less accurate depth map. The median error of LF2 is biased because of the presence of MPI in the raw data—in fact, the LF2 pipeline does not include any mechanism to correct such non-ideality. This bias is effectively removed by MRM. Our method approaches the Phasor's accuracy, without requiring expensive hardware to create very high modulation frequencies (1063.3 MHz and 1034.1 MHz): MRM works with Kinect 2, which uses frequencies below 150 MHz. Figure 5 shows the results of typical scenes from the FLAT dataset, where Phasor and MRM outperform other methods in removing MPI. It is worth noticing that high frequency modulation signals, like those used in Phasor, are very susceptible to noise. In fact, we use a bilateral filter to reduce the effect of shot noise on the output of Phasor. Although this effectively reduces random noise, any misalignment on raw correlation measurements (like the one occurring in case of motion) creates a systematic noise that cannot be eliminated by bilateral filtering, which dramatically reduces the accuracy of Phasor (Fig. 7c). Our MRM appears much more reliable in this situation (Fig. 7e).

The case of a real scene of a corner, acquired in static conditions with a Kinect 2, is depicted in Fig. 8. The ground truth shape of the scene could be estimated by checkerboard calibration applied to each of the three planes of the corner. This figure shows that MRM can significantly reduce MPI artifacts (compared to LF2) not only in simulation, but also in realistic conditions.

6.2   Motion Artifact Correction and Ablation Study

We perform an ablation study to quantify the benefits of MOM and MOM-MRM, on a test set from the FLAT dataset corrupted by MPI, shot noise, and random motion. For this experiment, the motion between the nine correlations measurement is fully simulated by moving the objects in 3D space. This allows testing the MOM and MOM-MRM on simulated raw correlation measurements affected by a real motion field, even if the modules are trained on approximated motion data. We compare depth reconstruction through LF2, MOM, and MOM-MRM, each using the same masking method provided by LF2 to eliminate unreliable pixels, like those along misaligned object boundaries due to motion. The density (i.e., percentage of reconstructed pixels) reported in Fig. 6 is therefore representative of how well objects boundaries are re-aligned by MOM. The depth accuracy is slightly higher for MOM compared to LF2, but the main advantage for MOM is a reduction of the unreliable pixels, as density increases from 93.56% to 95.50%. Red boxes in Fig. 9 demonstrate in simulation how introducing the MOM module can reduce the presence of holes in the reconstructed scene, especially close to object boundaries. The introduction of the MRM module further increases the density and reduces the bias in the depth error caused by MPI. Also this effect is clearly visible in the green boxes in Fig. 9, where the introduction of the MRM module leads to the reduction of the MPI artifact in the corner of the room.

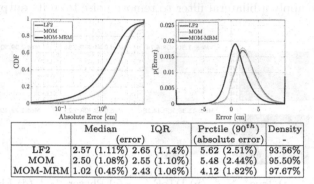

	Median (error)	IQR	Prctile (90th) (absolute error)	Density -
LF2	2.57 (1.11%)	2.65 (1.14%)	5.62 (2.51%)	93.56%
MOM	2.50 (1.08%)	2.55 (1.10%)	5.48 (2.44%)	95.50%
MOM-MRM	1.02 (0.45%)	2.43 (1.06%)	4.12 (1.82%)	97.67%

Fig. 6. The upper left panel shows the CDF of the depth error for LF2, MOM and MOM-MRM, for simulated data from the FLAT dataset, affected by shot noise, MPI, and motion. The upper right panel shows the histogram of the error. Only those pixels that have been reconstructed contribute to the statistics. The table shows the corresponding reconstruction errors (median, 90th percentile, and Inter Quartile Range (IQR), in cm). The numbers in the brackets indicate the relative errors. (Color figure online)

6.3   Putting Everything Together

Figure 7 shows a simulation from the FLAT dataset, where the scene has been corrupted by shot noise, MPI, and a small motion (an average of 10 pixels between the first and last raw correlation measurements). Phasor imaging cannot produce a reliable depth map in this case: even a small motion changes the measured phase significantly, because of the fast modulation frequency. MRM still outperforms LF2, reducing the MPI, whereas the architecture trained to

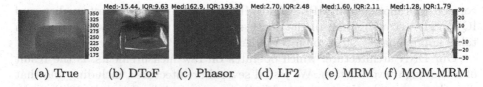

(a) True   (b) DToF   (c) Phasor   (d) LF2   (e) MRM   (f) MOM-MRM

Fig. 7. Depth error for different reconstruction methods and a simulated scene from FLAT, corrupted by shot noise, MPI, and small motion. Units in cm. (Color figure online)

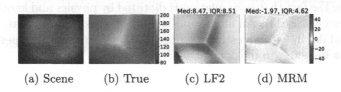

(a) Scene   (b) True   (c) LF2   (d) MRM

Fig. 8. A real scene of a corner captured by a Kinect 2 (a) with ground truth depth (b) and depth errors for LF2 (c), and MRM (d). MPI artifacts show up as lobes close to the corner in LF2, and are reduced by MRM. Units in cm. (Color figure online)

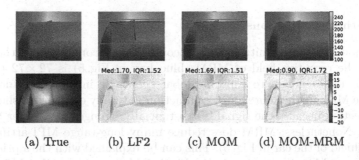

(a) True   (b) LF2   (c) MOM   (d) MOM-MRM

Fig. 9. A simulated scene from FLAT, corrupted by shot noise, MPI, and motion. The upper row shows the depth maps. The lower left panel is the intensity image, other panels in the row are depth errors. MOM aligns object boundaries and allows a more dense reconstruction (red boxes in b, c). MRM mostly corrects MPI artifacts in the smooth areas (green boxes in c, d). Units in cm. (Color figure online)

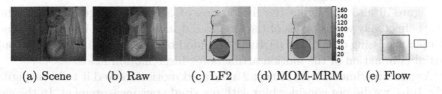

(a) Scene   (b) Raw   (c) LF2   (d) MOM-MRM   (e) Flow

Fig. 10. Panel (a) shows the average of nine raw correlation measurements acquired by Kinect 2, with a moving ball (blue box); panel (b) shows one of the raw measurements. Our method (d) reduces the motion artifacts compared to LF2 (c). The optical flow generated from MOM is shown in panel (e). The red box highlights the reflective hand bar with specular reflections; if not masked out, our method fails on these pixels. Units in cm. (Color figure online)

correct both motion and MPI, MOM-MRM, performs best (lowest median and IQR). The reconstruction of the depth scene using the MOM-MRM approach takes approximately 90 ms on a NVIDIA TitanV GPU.

Our DNN architecture, which operates on raw measurements, is the result of a thorough investigation. We tested several architectures, including one that directly outputs depth as suggested in the recent work by Su et al. [26], but the reconstruction error was consistently larger than that of the proposed DNN. We believe this is due to the fact a DNN that outputs the depth directly would be forced to learn the non-linear mapping from raw measurements to depth, instead of leveraging the fact that such relation is dictated by physics and known (see the inverse-tangent of Eq. 4). An additional benefit of working in the raw domain is that, beyond depth, we can estimates uncertainty as in the LF2 pipeline, which is useful, for instance, to mask out bad depth values.

Figure 10 shows an example of a real scene with moving objects (ball in the blue box), captured by Kinect 2. Notice that Fig. 10a is blurred as it averages nine raw measurements, whereas each individual raw measurement is still sharp, as in Fig. 10b. Coherently with simulations, the main effect of MOM is the reduction of the holes close to the boundaries of the moving object.

6.4   Method Limitations

Our method has some limitations that could be overcome with further development. The receptive field of MRM (blue box in Fig. 5) is 72×72 pixels, in theory not large enough to capture global geometric information and correct long-range MPI; furthermore, our loss function naturally emphasizes short-range MPI correction because the signal is substantially stronger for shorter traveling distances. Nonetheless, MRM does reduce many long-range MPI artifacts (see the windshield of the car in Fig. 5). This can be explained with the a priori information about object appearance learned by MRM, or assuming that MRM learns to project measurements corrupted by long-range MPI onto the single-bounce manifold (details in the Supplementary).

Another limitation is that FLAT only includes diffuse materials. Therefore MRM cannot reconstruct surfaces with strong specular reflections, as the door handle (red box) in Fig. 10.

Figure 10 also highlights the limitations of MOM for large motions: while MOM effectively warps pixels of the foreground moving object, it is not designed to inpaint missing data of the partially occluded background. This results in only partial elimination of the motion artifacts for large motion fields.

As our experiments with Kinect 2 and rapid motion showed it to be negligible (Fig. 10b), we did not consider blur within a single raw measurement. In the case motion blur becomes significant for other platforms, approximate blur can be easily included when simulating measurements from FLAT.

Lastly, our method assumes constant ambient light (as in typical indoor conditions) to model the camera noise. Characterizing the noise induced by ambient light separately may lead to a more accurate noise model.

7 Conclusion

Motion, MPI and shot noise can significantly affect the accuracy of depth reconstruction in ToF imaging. We have shown that deep learning can be used to reduce motion and MPI artifacts jointly, on an off-the-shelf ToF camera, in the domain of raw correlation measurements. We demonstrated the effectiveness of our MOM and MRM modules through an ablation study, and reported results on both synthetic and real data. Alternative methods to tackle these artifacts are still to be explored; we believe that our flexible FLAT dataset represents a helpful instrument along this research line.

References

1. Xiang, L., et al.: libfreenect2: Release 0.2, April 2016
2. Bhandari, A., Raskar, R.: Signal processing for time-of-flight imaging sensors: an introduction to inverse problems in computational 3-D imaging. IEEE Signal Process. Mag. **33**, 45–58 (2016)
3. Feigin, M., Bhandari, A., Izadi, S., Rhemann, C., Schmidt, M., Raskar, R.: Resolving multipath interference in kinect: an inverse problem approach. Sensors **16**, 3419–3427 (2016)
4. Marco, J., et al.: DeepToF: off-the-shelf real-time correction of multipath interference in time-of-flight imaging. ACM Trans. Graph. (SIGGRAPH ASIA) **36**, 219 (2017)
5. Mutny, M., Nair, R., Gottfried, J.: Learning the correction for multi-path deviations in time-of-flight cameras. arXiv preprint arXiv:1512.04077 (2015)
6. Son, K., Liu, M., Taguchi, Y.: Automatic learning to remove multipath distortions in time-of-flight range images for a robotic arm setup. arXiv preprint arXiv:1601.01750 (2016)
7. Dosovitskiy, A. et al.: Flownet: learning optical flow with convolutional networks. In: Proceedings of the IEEE International Conference on Computer Vision (ICCV) (2015)
8. Bako, S., et al.: Kernel-predicting convolutional networks for denoising monte carlo renderings. ACM Trans. Graph. (SIGGRAPH) **36**, 97 (2017)
9. Jung, J., Lee, J.-Y., Kweon, I.S.: Noise aware depth denoising for a time-of-flight camera. In: Korea-Japan Joint Workshop on Frontiers of Computer Vision (2014)
10. Jarabo, A., Masia, B., Marco, J., Gutierrez, D.: Recent advances in transient imaging: A computer graphics and vision perspective. Vis. Inform. **1**, 65–79 (2017)
11. Ferstl, D., Reinbacher, C., Riegler, G., Rüther, M., Bischof, H.: Learning depth calibration of time-of-flight cameras. In: Proceedings of the British Machine Vision Conference (BMVC) (2015)
12. Lenzen, F., et al.: Denoising strategies for time-of-flight data. In: Grzegorzek, M., Theobalt, C., Koch, R., Kolb, A. (eds.) Time-of-Flight and Depth Imaging. Sensors, Algorithms, and Applications. LNCS, vol. 8200, pp. 25–45. Springer, Heidelberg (2013). https://doi.org/10.1007/978-3-642-44964-2_2
13. Gottfried, J.M., Nair, R., Meister, S., Garbe, C.S., Kondermann, D.: Time of flight motion compensation revisited. In: IEEE International Conference on Image Processing (ICIP), (2014)
14. Lee, S.: Time-of-flight depth camera motion blur detection and deblurring. IEEE Signal Process. Lett. **21**, 663–666 (2014)

15. Hansard, M., Lee, S., Choi, O., Horaud, R.: Time-of-Flight Cameras: Principles Methods and Applications. Springer Publishing Company, London (2012). https://doi.org/10.1007/978-1-4471-4658-2
16. Heide, F., Heidrich, W., Hullin, M., Wetzstein, G.: Doppler time-of-flight imaging. ACM Trans. Graph. (SIGGRAPH) **34**, 36 (2015)
17. Freedman, D., Krupka, E., Smolin, Y., Leichter, I., Schmidt, M.: SRA: fast removal of general multipath for tof sensors. arXiv preprint arXiv:1403.5919 (2014)
18. Gupta, M., Nayar, S.K., Hullin, M.B., Martin, J.: Phasor imaging: A generalization of correlation-based time-of-flight imaging. ACM Trans. Graph. **34**, 156 (2015)
19. Nair, R., et al.: Ground truth for evaluating time of flight imaging. In: Grzegorzek, M., Theobalt, C., Koch, R., Kolb, A. (eds.) Time-of-Flight and Depth Imaging. Sensors, Algorithms, and Applications. LNCS, vol. 8200, pp. 52–74. Springer, Heidelberg (2013). https://doi.org/10.1007/978-3-642-44964-2_4
20. Jarabo, A., Marco, J., Muñoz, A., Buisan, R., Jarosz, W., Gutierrez, D.: A framework for transient rendering. ACM Trans. Graph. (SIGGRAPH ASIA) **33**, 177 (2014)
21. Gushov, V., Solodkin, Y.N.: Automatic processing of fringe patterns in integer interferometers. Opt. Lasers Eng. **14**, 311–324 (1991)
22. Curless, B., Levoy, M.: A volumetric method for building complex models from range images. In: Proceedings of the 23rd Annual Conference on Computer Graphics and Interactive Techniques, pp. 303–312. ACM (1996)
23. Burkardt, J.: Obj files: A 3D object format (2016). https://people.sc.fsu.edu/jburkardt/data/obj/obj.html
24. Dana, K.J., Van Ginneken, B., Nayar, S.K., Koenderink, J.J.: Reflectance and texture of real-world surfaces. ACM Trans. Graph. (TOG) **18**, 1–34 (1999)
25. Mildenhall, B., Barron, J.T., Chen, J., Sharlet, D., Ng, R., Carroll, R.: Burst denoising with kernel prediction networks. In: Proceedings of the IEEE Conference on Computer Vision and Pattern Recognition (CVPR) (2018)
26. Su, S., Heide, F., Wetzstein, G., Heidrich, W.: Deep end-to-end time-of-flight imaging. In: The IEEE Conference on Computer Vision and Pattern Recognition (CVPR), June 2018

Zero-Shot Object Detection

Ankan Bansal[1]([⊠]), Karan Sikka[2], Gaurav Sharma[3], Rama Chellappa[1],
and Ajay Divakaran[2]

[1] University of Maryland, College Park, MD, USA
{ankan,rama}@umiacs.umd.edu
[2] SRI International, Princeton, NJ, USA
{karan.sikka,ajay.divakaran}@sri.com
[3] NEC Labs America, Cupertino, CA, USA
grv@nec-labs.com

Abstract. We introduce and tackle the problem of zero-shot object detection (ZSD), which aims to detect object classes which are not observed during training. We work with a challenging set of object classes, not restricting ourselves to similar and/or fine-grained categories as in prior works on zero-shot classification. We present a principled approach by first adapting visual-semantic embeddings for ZSD. We then discuss the problems associated with selecting a background class and motivate two background-aware approaches for learning robust detectors. One of these models uses a fixed background class and the other is based on iterative latent assignments. We also outline the challenge associated with using a limited number of training classes and propose a solution based on dense sampling of the semantic label space using auxiliary data with a large number of categories. We propose novel splits of two standard detection datasets – MSCOCO and VisualGenome, and present extensive empirical results in both the traditional and generalized zero-shot settings to highlight the benefits of the proposed methods. We provide useful insights into the algorithm and conclude by posing some open questions to encourage further research.

1 Introduction

Humans can effortlessly make a mental model of an object using only textual description, while machine recognition systems, until not very long ago, needed to be shown visual examples of every category of interest. Recently, some work has been done on *zero-shot* classification using textual descriptions [53], leveraging progress made on both visual representations [51] and semantic text embeddings [21,34,39]. In zero-shot classification, at training time visual examples are provided for some visual classes but during testing the model is expected to recognize instances of classes which were not seen, with the constraint that the new classes are semantically related to the training classes.

A. Bansal—Most of the work was done when AB was an intern at SRI International.

© Springer Nature Switzerland AG 2018
V. Ferrari et al. (Eds.): ECCV 2018, LNCS 11205, pp. 397–414, 2018.
https://doi.org/10.1007/978-3-030-01246-5_24

This problem is solved within the framework of transfer learning [13,40], where visual models for seen classes are transferred to the unknown classes by exploiting semantic relationships between the two. For example, as shown in Fig. 1, the semantic similarities between classes "hand" and "arm" are used to detect an instance of a related (unseen) class "shoulder". While such a setting has been used for object classification, object detection has remained mostly in the fully supervised setting as it is much more challenging. In comparison to object classification, which aims to predict the class label of an object in an image, object detection aims at predicting bounding box locations for multiple objects in an image. While classification can rely heavily on contextual cues, e.g. airplane co-occurring with clouds, detection needs to exactly localize the object of interest and can potentially be degraded by contextual correlations [56]. Furthermore, object detection requires learning additional invariance to appearance, occlusion, viewpoint, aspect ratio etc. in order to precisely delineate a bounding box [19].

In the past few years, several CNN-based object detection methods have been proposed. Early methods [16,17] started with an object proposal generation step and classified each object proposal as belonging to a class from a fixed set of categories. More recent methods either generate proposals inside a CNN [46], or have implicit regions directly in the image or feature maps [32,44]. These methods achieved significant performance improvements on small datasets which contain tens to a few hundreds of object categories [8,30]. However, the problem of detecting a large number of classes of objects has not received sufficient attention. This is mainly due to the lack of available annotated data as getting bounding box annotations for thousands of categories of objects is an expensive process. Scaling supervised detection to the level of classification (tens to hundreds of thousands of classes) is infeasible due to prohibitively large annotations costs. Recent works have tried to avoid such annotations, e.g. [45] proposed an object detection method that can detect several thousand object classes by using available (image-level) class annotations as weak supervision for object detection. Zero-shot learning has been shown to be effective in situations where there is a lack of annotated data [12,14,31,38,53,54,59,60]. Most prior works on zero-shot learning have addressed the classification problem [5–7,11,20,23,26,27,37,41,43,50,52], using semantic word-embeddings [11,23] or attributes [12,27,28,59] as a bridge between seen and unseen classes.

In the present work, we introduce and study the challenging problem of *zero-shot detection* for diverse and general object categories. This problem is difficult owing to the multiple challenges involved with detection, as well as those with operating in a zero-shot setting. Compared to fully supervised object detection, zero-shot detection has many differences, notably the following. While in the fully supervised case a background class is added to better discriminate between objects (e.g. car, person) and background (e.g. sky, wall, road), the meaning of "background" is not clear for zero-shot detection, as it could involve both background "stuff" as well as objects from unannotated/unseen classes. This leads to non-trivial practical problems for zero-shot detection. We propose two ways to address this problem: one using a fixed background class and the other using a

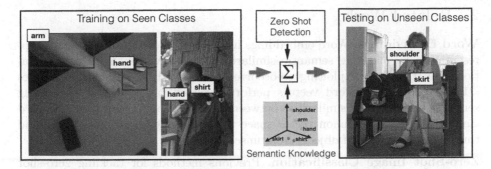

Fig. 1. We highlight the task of zero-shot object detection where objects "arm", "hand", and "shirt" are observed (seen) during training, but "skirt", and "shoulder" are not. These unseen classes are localized by our approach that leverages semantic relationships between seen and unseen classes along with the proposed zero-shot detection framework. The example has been generated by our model.

large open vocabulary for differentiating different background regions. We start with a standard zero-shot classification architecture [13] and adapt it for zero-shot object detection. This architecture is based on embedding both images and class labels into a common vector space. In order to include information from background regions, following supervised object detection, we first try to associate the background image regions into a single background class embedding. However, this method can be improved by using a latent assignment based alternating algorithm which associates the background boxes to potentially different classes belonging to a large open vocabulary. Since most object detection benchmark datasets usually have a few hundred classes, the label space can be sparsely populated. We show that dense sampling of the class label space by using additional data improves zero-shot detection. Along with these two enhancements, we provide qualitative and quantitative results to provide insights into the success as well as failure cases of the zero-shot detection algorithms, that point us to novel directions towards solving this challenging problem.

To summarize, the main contributions of this paper are: (i) we introduce the problem of zero-shot object detection (ZSD) in real world settings and present a baseline method for ZSD that follows existing work on zero-shot image classification using multimodal semantic embeddings and fully supervised object detection; (ii) we discuss some challenges associated with incorporating information from background regions and propose two methods for training background-aware detectors; (iii) we examine the problem with sparse sampling of classes during training and propose a solution which densely samples training classes using additional data; and (iv) we provide extensive experimental and ablation studies in traditional and generalized zero-shot settings to highlight the benefits and shortcomings of the proposed methods and provide useful insights which point to future research directions.

2 Related Work

Word Embeddings. Word embeddings map words to a continuous vector representation by encoding semantic similarity between words. Such representations are trained by exploiting co-occurrences in words in large text corpuses [21,34,35,39]. These word vectors perform well on tasks such as measuring semantic and syntactic similarities between words. In this work we use the word embeddings as the common vector space for both images and class labels and thus enable detection of objects from unseen categories.

Zero-Shot Image Classification. Previous methods for tackling zero-shot classification used attributes, like shape, color, pose or geographical information as additional sources of information [10,26,27]. More recent approaches have used multimodal embeddings to learn a compatibility function between an image vector and class label embeddings [1,2]. In [52], the authors augment the bilinear compatibility model by adding latent variables. The deep visual-semantic embedding model [11] used labeled image data and semantic information from unannotated text data to classify previously unseen image categories. We follow a similar methodology of using labeled object bounding boxes and semantic information in the form of unsupervised word embeddings to detect novel object categories. For a more compehensive overview of zero-shot classification, we refer the reader to the detailed survey by Fu et al. [13].

Object Detection. Early object detection approaches involved getting object proposals for each image and classifying those object proposals using an image classification CNN [16,17,46,55]. More recent approaches use a single pass through a deep convolution network without the need for object region proposals [32,44]. Recently, Redmon et al. [45] introduced an object detector which can scale upto 9000 object categories using both bounding box and image-level annotations. Unlike this setting, we work in a more challenging setting and do not observe any labels for the test object classes during training. We build our detection framework on an approach similar to the proposal-based approaches mentioned above.

Multi-modal Learning. Using multiple modalities as additional sources of information has been shown to improve performance on several computer vision and machine learning tasks. These methods can be used for cross-modal retrieval tasks [9], or for transferring classifiers between modalities. Recently, [4] used images, text, and sound for generating deep discriminative representations which are shared across the three modalities. Similarly, [58] used images and text descriptions for better natural language based visual entity localization. In [18], the authors used a shared vision and language representation space to obtain image-region and word descriptors that can be shared across multiple vision and language domains. Our work also uses multi-modal learning for building a robust object detector for unseen classes. Another related work is by Li et al. [28], which learns object-specific attributes to classify, segment, and predict novel objects. The problem proposed here differs considerably from this in detecting a large set of objects in unconstrained settings and does not rely on using attributes.

Comparison with Recent Works on ZSD. After completion of this work, we found two parallel works by Zhu et al. [61] and Rahman et al. [42] that target a similar problem. Zhu et al. focus on a different problem of generating object proposals for unseen objects. Rahman et al. [42] propose a loss formulation that combines max-margin learning and a semantic clustering loss. Their aim is to separate individual classes and reduce the noise in semantic vectors. A key difference between our work and Rahman et al. is the choice of evaluation datasets. Rahman et al. use the ILSVRC-2017 detection dataset [47] for training and evaluation. This dataset is more constrained in comparison to the ones used in our work (MSCOCO and VisualGenome) because it contains only about one object per image on an average. We would also like to note that due to a relatively simpler test setting, Rahman et al. does not consider the corrruption of the background class by unseen classes as done in this work and by Zhu et al.

3 Approach

We first outline our baseline zero-shot detection framework that adapts prior work on zero-shot learning for the current task. Since this approach does not consider the diversity of the background objects during training, we then present an approach for training a background-aware detector with a fixed background class. We highlight some possible limitations of this approach and propose a latent assignment based background-aware model. Finally, we describe our method for densely sampling labels using additional data, which improves generalization.

3.1 Baseline Zero-Shot Detection (ZSD)

We denote the set of all classes as $\mathcal{C} = \mathcal{S} \cup \mathcal{U} \cup \mathcal{O}$, where $\mathcal{S}$ denotes the set of seen (train) classes, $\mathcal{U}$ the set of unseen (test) classes, and $\mathcal{O}$ the set of classes that are neither part of seen or unseen classes. Note that our methods do not require a pre-defined test set. We fix the unseen classes here just for quantitative evaluation. We work in a zero-shot setting for object detection where, during training we are provided with labeled bounding boxes that belong to the seen classes only, while during testing we detect objects from unseen classes. We denote an image as $I \in \mathbb{R}^{M \times N \times 3}$, provided bounding boxes as $b_i \in \mathbb{N}^4$, and their associated labels as $y_i \in \mathcal{S}$. We extract deep features from a given bounding box obtained from an arbitrary region proposal method. We denote extracted deep features for each box b_i as $\phi(b_i) \in \mathbb{R}^{D_1}$. We use semantic embeddings to capture the relationships between seen and unseen classes and thus transfer a model trained on the seen classes to the unseen classes as described later. We denote the semantic embeddings for different class labels as $w_j \in \mathbb{R}^{D_2}$, which can be obtained from pre-trained word embedding models such as Glove [39] or fastText [21]. Our approach is based on visual-semantic embeddings where both image and text features are embedded in the same metric space [11,50]. We project features from the bounding box to the semantic embedding space itself via a linear projection,

$$\psi_i = W_p \phi(b_i) \tag{1}$$

where, $W_p \in \mathbb{R}^{D_2 \times D_1}$ is a projection matrix and ψ_i is the projected feature. We use the common embedding space to compute a similarity measure between a projected bounding box feature ψ_i and a class embedding w_j for class label y_j as the cosine similarity S_{ij} between the two vectors. We train the projection by using a max-margin loss which enforces the constraint that the matching score of a bounding box with its true class should be higher than that with other classes. We define loss for a training sample b_i with class label y_i as,

$$\mathcal{L}(b_i, y_i, \theta) = \sum_{j \in \mathcal{S}, j \neq i} \max(0, m - S_{ii} + S_{ij}) \tag{2}$$

where θ refers to the parameters of the deep CNN and the projection matrix, and m is the margin. We also add an additional reconstruction loss to $\mathcal{L}$, as suggested by Kodirov et al. [23], to regularize the semantic embeddings. In particular, we use the projected box features to reconstruct the original deep features and calculate the reconstruction loss as the squared $L2$-distance between the reconstructed feature and the original deep feature. During test we predict the label $(\hat{y}_i)$ for a bounding box (b_i) by finding its nearest class based on the similarity scores with different class embeddings, i.e.

$$\hat{y}_i = \arg\max_{j \in \mathcal{U}} S_{ij} \tag{3}$$

It is common for object detection approaches to include a background class to learn a robust detector that can effectively discriminate between foreground objects and background objects. This helps in eliminating bounding box proposals which clearly do not contain any object of interest. We refer to these models as background-aware detectors. However, selecting a background for zero-shot detection is a non-trivial problem as we do not know if a given background box includes background "stuff" in the classical sense e.g. sky, ground etc. or an instance of an unseen object class. We thus train our first (baseline) model only on bounding boxes that contain seen classes.

3.2 Background-Aware Zero-Shot Detection

While background boxes usually lead to improvements in detection performance for current object detection methods, for ZSD to decide which background bounding boxes to use is not straight-forward. We outline two approaches for extending the baseline ZSD model by incorporating information from background boxes during training.

Statically Assigned Background (SB) Based Zero-Shot Detection. Our first background-aware model follows as a natural extension of using a fixed background class in standard object detectors to our embedding framework. We accomplish this by adding a fixed vector for the background class in our embedding space. Such 'statically-assigned' background modeling in ZSD, while providing a way to incorporate background information, has some limitations. First, we are working with the structure imposed by the semantic text embeddings that represent each class by a vector relative to other semantically related classes. In such a case it is difficult to learn a projection that can map all the diverse background appearances, which surely belong to semantically varied classes, to a single embedding vector representing one monolithic background class. Second, even if we are able to learn such a projection function, the model might not work well during testing. It can map any unseen class to the single vector corresponding to the background, as it has learned to map everything, which is not from seen classes, to the singleton background class.

Latent Assignment Based (LAB) Zero-Shot Detection. We solve the problems above by spreading the background boxes over the embedding space by using an Expectation Maximization (EM)-like algorithm. We do so by assigning multiple (latent) classes to the background objects and thus covering a wider range of visual concepts. This is reminiscent of semi-supervised learning algorithms [48]; we have annotated objects for seen classes and unlabeled boxes for the rest of the image regions. At a higher level we encode the knowledge that a background box does not belong to the set of seen classes ($\mathcal{S}$), and could potentially belong to a number of different classes from a large vocabulary set, referred to as background set and denoted as $\mathcal{O}$.

We first train a baseline ZSD model on boxes that belong to the seen classes. We then follow an iterative EM-like training procedure (Algorithm 1), where, in the first of two alternating steps, we assign labels to some randomly sampled background boxes in the training set as classes in $\mathcal{O}$ using our trained model with equation 3. In the second step, we re-train our detection model with the boxes, labeled as above, included. In the next iteration, we repeat the first step for another part of background boxes and retrain our model with the new training data. This proposed approach is also related to open-vocabulary learning where we are not restricted by a fixed set of classes [20,57], and to latent-variable based classification models e.g. [49].

3.3   Densely Sampled Embedding Space (DSES)

The ZSD method, described above, relies on learning a common embedding space that aligns object features with label embeddings. A practical problem in learning such a model with small datasets is that there are only a small number of seen classes, which results in a sparse sampling of the embedding space during training. This is problematic particularly for recognizing unseen classes which, by definition, lie in parts of the embedding space that do not have training examples. As a result the method may not converge towards the right alignment between visual and text modalities. To alleviate this issue, we propose to augment the training procedure with additional data from external sources that contain boxes belonging to classes other than unseen classes, $y_i \in \mathcal{C} - \mathcal{U}$. In other words, we aim to have a dense sampling of the space of object classes during training to improve the alignment of the embedding spaces. We show empirically that, because the extra data being used is from diverse external sources and is distinct from seen and unseen classes, it improves the baseline method.

Algorithm 1. LAB algorithm

Given: `annoData` (annotated data), `bgData` (background/unannotated data), $\mathcal{C}$ (set of all classes), $\mathcal{S}$ (seen classes), $\mathcal{U}$ (unseen classes), $\mathcal{O}$ (background set), `initModel` (pre-trained network)

`currModel` ← train(`initModel`, `annoData`)

for $i = 1$ to `niters` do

    `currBgData` ← ϕ

    for b in `bgData` do

        // distribute background boxes over open vocabulary minus seen classes

        b_{new} ←predict(b, `currModel`, $\mathcal{O}$)

        // $\mathcal{O} = \mathcal{C} \setminus (\mathcal{S} \cup \mathcal{U})$

        `currBgData` ← `currBgData` $\cup \{b_{new}\}$

    `currAnnoData` ← `annoData` $\cup$ `currBgData`

    `currModel`←train(`currModel`,`currAnnoData`)

return `currModel`

---

4 Experiments

We first describe the challenging public datasets we use to validate the proposed approaches, and give the procedure for creating the novel training and test splits[1]. We then discuss the implementation details and the evaluation protocol. Thereafter, we give the empirical performance for different models followed by some ablation studies and qualitative results to provide insights into the methods.

MSCOCO [30] We use training images from the 2014 training set and randomly sample images for testing from the validation set.

VisualGenome (VG) [25] We remove non-visual classes from the dataset; use images from part-1 of the dataset for training, and randomly sample images from part-2 for testing.

OpenImages (OI) [24] We use this dataset for densely sampling the label space as described in Sect. 3.3. It contains about 1.5 million images containing 3.7 million bounding boxes that span 545 object categories.

Procedure for Creating Train and Test Splits: For dividing the classes into seen (train) and unseen (test) classes, we use a procedure similar to [3]. We begin with word-vector embeddings for all classes and cluster them into K clusters using cosine similarity between the word-vectors as the metric. We randomly select 80% classes from each cluster and assign these to the set of seen classes. We assign the remaining 20% classes from each cluster to the test set. We set the number of clusters to 10 and 20 for MSCOCO and VisualGenome respectively. Out of all the available classes, we consider only those which have a synset associated with them in the WordNet hierarchy [36] and also have a word vector available. This gives us 48 training classes and 17 test classes for

---

[1] Visit http://ankan.umiacs.io/zsd.html.

MSCOCO and 478 training classes and 130 test classes for VisualGenome. For MSCOCO, to avoid taking unseen categories as background boxes, we remove all images from the training set which contain any object from unseen categories. However, we can not do this for VG because the large number of test categories and dense labeling results in most images being eliminated from the training set. After creating the splits we have 73,774 training and 6,608 test images for MSCOCO, and 54,913 training and 7,788 test images for VG.

4.1 Implementation Details

Preparing Datasets for Training: We first obtain bounding box proposals for each image in the training set. We construct the training datasets by assigning each proposal a class label from seen classes or the "background" class based on its IoU (Intersection over Union) with a ground truth bounding box. Since, majority of the proposals belong to background, we only include a part of the background boxes. Any proposal with $0 < \text{IoU} < 0.2$ with a ground truth bounding box is included as a background box in the training set. Apart from these, we also include a few randomly selected background boxes with $\text{IoU} = 0$ with any ground truth bounding boxes. Any proposal with an $\text{IoU} > 0.5$ with a ground-truth box is assigned to the class of the ground-truth box. Finally, we get 1.4 million training boxes for MSCOCO and 5.8 million training boxes for VG. We use these boxes for training the two background aware models. As previously mentioned, we only use boxes belonging to seen classes for training the baseline ZSD model. In this case, we have 0.67 million training boxes for MSCOCO and about 2.6 million training boxes for VG. We train our model on these training sets and test them on the test sets as described above.

Baseline ZSD Model: We build our ZSD model on the RCNN framework that first extracts region proposals, warps them, and then classifies them. We use the Edge-Boxes method [62] with its default parameters for generating region proposals and then warp them to an image of size 224×224. We use the (pre-trained) Inception-ResNet v2 model [51] as our base CNN for computing deep features. We project image features from a proposal box to the 300 dimensional semantic text space by adding a fully-connected layer on the last layer of the CNN. We use the Adam optimizer [22] with a starting learning rate of 10^{-3} for the projection matrix and 10^{-5} for the lower layers. The complete network, including the projection layer, is first pre-trained on the MSCOCO dataset with the test classes removed for different models and datasets. For each algorithm, we perform end-to-end training while keeping the word embeddings fixed. The margin for ranking loss was set to 1 and the reconstruction loss was added to max-margin loss after multiplying it by a factor of 10^{-3}. We provide algorithm specific details below.

Static Background Based ZSD: In this case, we include the background boxes obtained as described above in the training set. The single background class is assigned a fixed label vector $[1, \dots, 0]$ (this fixed background vector was chosen so as to have norm one similar to the other class embeddings).

LAB: We first create a vocabulary ($\mathcal{C}$) which contains all the words for which we have word-vectors and synsets in the WordNet hierarchy [36]. We then remove any label from seen and unseen classes from this set. The size of the vocabulary was about 82 K for VG and about 180 K for MSCOCO. In the first iteration, we use our baseline ZSD model to obtain labels from the vocabulary set for some of the background boxes. We add these boxes with the newly assigned labels to the training set for the next iteration (see Algorithm 1). We fine-tune the model from the previous iteration using this new training set for about one epoch. During our experiments we iterate over this process five times. Our starting learning rates were the same as above and we decreased them by a factor of 10 after every 2 iterations.

Dense Sampling of the Semantic Space: To increase the label density, we use additional data from OI to augment the training sets for both VG and MSCOCO. We remove all our test classes from OI and add the boxes from remaining classes to the training sets. This led to an addition of 238 classes to VG and 330 classes to MSCOCO during training. This increases the number of training bounding boxes for VG to 3.3 million and to 1 million for MSCOCO.

4.2 Evaluation Protocol

During evaluation we use Edge-Boxes for extracting proposals for each image and select only those proposals that have a proposal score (given by Edge-Boxes) greater than 0.07. This threshold was set based on trade-offs between performance and evaluation time. We pass these proposals through the base CNN and obtain a score for each test class as outlined in Sect. 3.1. We apply greedy non-maximal suppression [17] on all the scored boxes for each test class independently and reject boxes that have an IoU greater than 0.4 with a higher scoring box. We use recall as the main evaluation metric for detection instead of the commonly used mean average precision (mAP). This is because, for large-scale crowd-sourced datasets such as VG, it is often difficult to exhaustively label bounding box annotations for all instances of an object. Recall has also been used in prior work on detecting visual relationships [33] where it is infeasible to annotate all possible instances. The traditional mAP metric is sensitive to missing annotations and will count such detections as false positives. We define Recall@K as the recall when only the top K detections (based on prediction score) are selected from an image. A predicted bounding box is marked as true positive only if it has an IoU overlap greater than a certain threshold t with a ground truth bounding box and no other higher confidence predicted bounding box has been assigned to the same ground truth box. Otherwise it is marked as a false positive. For MSCOCO we also report the mAP since all object instances in MSCOCO are annotated.

4.3 Quantitative Results

We present extensive results (Recall@100) for different algorithms on MSCOCO and VG datasets in Table 1 for three different IoU overlap thresholds. We also

Table 1. $|\mathcal{S}|$, $|\mathcal{U}|$, and $|\mathcal{O}|$ refer to the number of seen, unseen and the average number of active background classes considered during training respectively. BG-aware means background-aware representations. This table shows Recall@100 performance for the proposed zero-shot detection approaches (see Sect. 3) on the two datasets at different IoU overlap thresholds with the ground-truth boxes. The numbers in parentheses are mean average precision (mAP) values for MSCOCO. The number of test (unseen) classes for MSCOCO and VisualGenome are 17 and 130 respectively.

ZSD Method	BG-aware	#classes			MSCOCO IoU			#classes			Visual Genome IoU		
		$|\mathcal{S}|$	$|\mathcal{U}|$	$|\mathcal{O}|$	0.4	0.5	0.6	$|\mathcal{S}|$	$|\mathcal{U}|$	$|\mathcal{O}|$	0.4	0.5	0.6
Baseline		48	17	0	34.36	22.14 (0.32)	11.31	478	130	0	8.19	5.19	2.63
SB	✓	48	17	1	34.46	24.39 (0.70)	12.55	478	130	1	6.06	4.09	2.43
DSES		378	17	0	**40.23**	**27.19** (0.54)	**13.63**	716	130	0	7.78	4.75	2.34
LAB	✓	48	17	343	31.86	20.52 (0.27)	9.98	478	130	1673	**8.43**	**5.40**	**2.74**

show the number of seen, unseen, and background classes for each case. During our discussion we report Recall@100 at a threshold of IoU ≥ 0.5 unless specified otherwise.

On the VG dataset the baseline model achieves 5.19% recall and the static background (SB) model achieves a recall of 4.09%. This marked decline in performance is because all the background boxes are being mapped to a single vector. In VG some of these background boxes might actually belong to the seen (train) or unseen (test) categories. This leads to the SB model learning sub-optimal visual embeddings. However, for MSCOCO we observe that the SB model increases the recall to 24.39% from the 22.14% achieved by the baseline model. This is because we remove all images that contain any object from unseen classes from the training set for MSCOCO. This precludes the possibility of having any background boxes belonging to the test classes in the training set. As a result, the SB model is not corrupted by non-background objects and is thus more robust than the baseline.

When we densely sample the embedding space and augment the training classes with additional data, the recall for MSCOCO increases significantly from 22.14% (for baseline) to 27.19%. This shows that dense sampling is beneficial for predicting unseen classes that lie in sparsely sampled parts of the embedding space. With dense sampling, the number of train classes in MSCOCO are expanded by a factor of 7.8 to 378. In contrast, VG a priori has a large set of seen classes (478 versus 48 in MSCOCO), and the classes expand only by a factor of 1.5 (716) when using DSES. As a result dense sampling is not able to improve the embedding space obtained by the initial set of categories. In such scenarios it might be beneficial to use more sophisticated methods for sampling additional classes that are not represented well in the training set [15,29,40].

The latent assignment based (LAB) method outperforms the baseline, SB, and DSES on VG. It achieves a recall of 5.40% compared to 5.19%, 4.09% and 4.75% achieved by baseline, SB, and DSES respectively. The consistent improvement across all IoUs compared to SB, that uses a static background, confirms the benefits of spreading background objects over the embedding space. However, LAB gives a lower performance compared to the baseline for MSCOCO (20.52% by LAB versus 22.14% by baseline). This is not surprising since the iterations for LAB initialize with a larger set of seen classes for VG as compared to MSCOCO, resulting in an embedding that covers a wider spectrum of visual space. As a result, LAB is able to effectively spread the background boxes over a larger set of classes for VG leading to better detections. On the other hand, for MSCOCO a sparsely sampled embedding space restricts the coverage of visual concepts leading to the background boxes being mapped to a few visual categories. We also see this empirically in the average number of background classes (set $\mathcal{O}$) assigned to the background boxes during iterations for LAB, which were 1673 for VG versus 343 for MSCOCO. In the remainder of the paper we focus on LAB method for VG and SB for MSCOCO due to their appropriateness for the respective datasets.

We observe that the relative class-wise performance trends are similar to object detection methods, such as Faster RCNN[2] trained on fully supervised data. For example, classes such as "bus" and "elephant" are amongst the best performing while "scissors" and "umbrella" rank amongst the worst in performance. In addition to these general trends, we also discover some interesting findings due to the zero-shot nature of the problem. For example, the class "cat", which generally performs well with standard object detectors, did not perform well with SB. This results from having an insufficient number of semantically related categories for this class in the training set which does not allow the model to effectively capture the appearance of class "cat" during testing. For such cases we find dense sampling to be useful during training. The class "cat" is one of the top performing categories with DSES. Based on such cases we infer that for ZSD the performance is both a function of appearance characteristics of the class as well as its relationship to the seen classes. For VG, the best performing classes, such as "laptop", "car", "building", "chair", seem to have well defined appearance characteristics compared to bad performing classes, such as "gravel", "vent", "garden", which seem to be more of "stuff" than "things". We also observe that the model is unable to capture any true positive for the class "zebra" and is instead detecting instances of "zebra" as either "cattle" or "horse". This is because the model associates a "zebra" with a "giraffe", which is close in the semantic space. The model is able to adapt the detector for the class "giraffe" to the class "zebra" but fails to infer additional knowledge needed for a successful detector that a zebra differs from a giraffe in having white stripes, lower height, and has a body structure similar to a horse. Finally, we also observe that compared to the baseline, LAB achieves similar or better performance on 104 of 130 classes on VG. While for MSCOCO, SB and DSES achieve better or similar performance on 12 and 13 classes respectively out of 17 classes, highlighting the advantages of the proposed models.

---

[2] http://cocodataset.org/#detections-leaderboard.

4.4 Generalized Zero-Shot Detection (GZSD)

The generalized zero-shot learning setting is more realistic than the previously discussed zero-shot setting [53] because both seen and unseen classes are present during evaluation. This is more challenging than ZSD because it removes the prior knowledge that the objects at test time belong to unseen classes only. We use a simple novelty detection step which does not need extra supervision. Given a test bounding box, b_i, we first find the most probable train and test classes (see (3)) ($\hat{y}_i^s$ and $\hat{y}_i^u$ respectively) and the corresponding similarity scores (s_i and u_i). As the novelty detection step, we check if u_i is greater than some threshold n_t. We assign the given bounding box to class $\hat{y}_i^u$ if $u_i \geq n_t$, otherwise to $\hat{y}_i^s$. For MSCOCO, DSES gives the best performance in the GZSD setting too. At $n_t = 0.2$, DSES achieves a Recall@100 of 15.02% for seen classes and 15.32% for unseen classes (harmonic mean (HM) 15.17% [53]) at $IoU \geq 0.5$ compared to 14.54% and 10.57% (HM 12.24%) for the LAB model and 16.93% and 8.91% (HM 11.67%) for baseline.

4.5 Ablation Studies

We compare results when considering different number, K, of high-confidence detections. We define $K = All$ as the scenario where we consider all boxes returned by the detector with a confidence score greater than the threshold for evaluation. We compare LAB and the SB models for VG and MSCOCO respectively, with the corresponding baseline models in Table 2.

Table 2. Ablation studies on background-aware approaches for ZSD. We highlight results where the performance is higher for background-aware approaches compared to the corresponding baseline. For MSCOCO, the values in parentheses are mAP values.

	MSCOCO						VisualGenome					
	Baseline			SB			Baseline			LAB		
K↓ IoU→	0.3	0.4	0.5	0.3	0.4	0.5	0.3	0.4	0.5	0.3	0.4	0.5
All	47.91	37.86	24.47 (0.22)	43.79	35.58	**25.12** (0.64)	13.88	9.98	6.45	12.75	9.61	6.22
100	43.62	34.36	22.14 (0.32)	42.22	**34.46**	24.39 (0.70)	11.34	8.19	5.19	11.20	**8.43**	**5.40**
80	41.69	32.64	21.01 (0.38)	41.47	**33.98**	24.01 (0.72)	10.41	7.55	4.75	**10.45**	**7.86**	**5.06**
50	36.19	27.37	17.05 (0.50)	**39.82**	**32.6**	**23.16** (0.81)	7.98	5.79	3.68	**8.54**	**6.44**	**4.14**

The difference in performance between the cases $K = All$ and $K = 100$ is small, in general, for the background-aware algorithms unlike the baseline. For example, on MSCOCO the recall for SB falls by an average (across IoUs) of 1.14% points, compared to a fall of 3.37% for the baseline. This trend continues further down to $K = 80$ and $K = 50$ with a gradual decline in performance as K decreases. This shows that the high confidence detections produced by our model are of high quality.

We observe that the background-aware models give better quality detections compared to baselines. The Recall@K for the corresponding background-aware models are better than the baseline at lower K and higher IoU threshold values for both datasets. This region represents higher quality detections. This shows that incorporating knowledge from background regions is an important factor for improving detection quality and performance for ZSD.

4.6 Qualitative Results

Figure 2 shows output detections by the background aware models, i.e. LAB on VisualGenome (first two rows) and SB on MSCOCO (last row). Blue boxes show correct detections and red boxes show false positives. These examples confirm that the proposed models are able to detect unseen classes without observing any samples during training. Further, the models are able to successfully detect multiple objects in real-world images with background clutter. For example, in the image taken in an office (1st row 3rd column), the model is able to detect object classes such as "writing", "chair", "cars". It is also interesting to note that our approach understands and detects "stuff" classes such as "vegetation", and "floor". As discussed in Sect. 4.3, we have shown a failure case "zebra", that results from having limited information regarding the fine-grained differences between seen and unseen classes.

Fig. 2. This figure shows some detections made by the background-aware methods. We have used Latent Assignment Based model for VisualGenome (rows 1–2) and the Static Background model (row 3) for MSCOCO. Reasonable detections are shown in blue and two failure cases in red. (Color figure online)

5 Discussion and Conclusion

We used visual-semantic embeddings for ZSD and addressed the problems associated with the framework which are specific for ZSD. We proposed two background-aware approaches; the first one uses a fixed background class while the second iteratively assigns background boxes to classes in a latent variable framework. We also proposed to improve the sampling density of the semantic label space using auxiliary data. We proposed novel splits of two challenging public datasets, MSCOCO and VisualGenome, and gave extensive quantitative and qualitative results to validate the methods proposed.

Some of the limitations of the presented work, and areas for future work, are as follows. It is important to incorporate some lexical ontology information ("is a" and "is part of" relationships) during training and testing for learning models on large vocabularies. Most current object detection frameworks ignore the hierarchical nature of object classes. For example, a "cat" object should incur a lower loss when predicted as "animal" vs. when predicted as "vehicle". Although a few works have tried to address this issue [18,44], we believe further work in this direction would be beneficial for zero-shot detection. We also feel that additional work is needed to generalize bounding-box regression and hard-negative mining for new objects.

Acknowledgements. This project is sponsored by the Air Force Research Laboratory (AFRL) and Defense Advanced Research Projects Agency (DARPA) under the contract number USAF/AFMC AFRL FA8750-16-C-0158. **Disclaimer**: The views, opinions, and/or findings expressed are those of the author(s) and should not be interpreted as representing the official views or policies of the Department of Defense or the U.S. Government.

The work of AB and RC is supported by the Intelligence Advanced Research Projects Activity (IARPA) via Department of Interior/Interior Business Center (DOI/IBC) contract number D17PC00345. The U.S. Government is authorized to reproduce and distribute reprints for Governmental purposes not withstanding any copyright annotation thereon. **Disclaimer**: The views and conclusions contained herein are those of the authors and should not be interpreted as necessarily representing the official policies or endorsements, either expressed or implied of IARPA, DOI/IBC or the U.S. Government.

We would like to thank the reviewers for their valuable comments and suggestions.

References

1. Akata, Z., Perronnin, F., Harchaoui, Z., Schmid, C.: Label-embedding for attribute-based classification. In: CVPR, pp. 819–826. IEEE (2013)
2. Akata, Z., Reed, S., Walter, D., Lee, H., Schiele, B.: Evaluation of output embeddings for fine-grained image classification. In: CVPR, pp. 2927–2936. IEEE (2015)
3. Anne Hendricks, L., Venugopalan, S., Rohrbach, M., Mooney, R., Saenko, K., Darrell, T., Mao, J., Huang, J., Toshev, A., Camburu, O., et al.: Deep compositional captioning: Describing novel object categories without paired training data. In: CVPR, pp. 1–10. IEEE (2016)

4. Aytar, Y., Vondrick, C., Torralba, A.: See, hear, and read: Deep aligned representations. arXiv preprint arXiv:1706.00932 (2017)
5. Bendale, A., Boult, T.E.: Towards open set deep networks. In: CVPR, pp. 1563–1572. IEEE (2016)
6. Changpinyo, S., Chao, W.L., Gong, B., Sha, F.: Synthesized classifiers for zero-shot learning. In: CVPR, pp. 5327–5336. IEEE (2016)
7. Elhoseiny, M., Saleh, B., Elgammal, A.: Write a classifier: Zero-shot learning using purely textual descriptions. In: CVPR, pp. 2584–2591. IEEE (2013)
8. Everingham, M., Van Gool, L., Williams, C.K., Winn, J., Zisserman, A.: The pascal visual object classes (voc) challenge. IJCV **88**(2), 303–338 (2010)
9. Faghri, F., Fleet, D.J., Kiros, J.R., Fidler, S.: Vse++: Improved visual-semantic embeddings. arXiv preprint arXiv:1707.05612 (2017)
10. Ferrari, V., Marin-Jimenez, M., Zisserman, A.: Pose search: retrieving people using their pose. In: CVPR, pp. 1–8. IEEE (2009)
11. Frome, A., Corrado, G.S., Shlens, J., Bengio, S., Dean, J., Mikolov, T.: Devise: A deep visual-semantic embedding model. In: NIPS, pp. 2121–2129 (2013)
12. Fu, Y., Hospedales, T.M., Xiang, T., Gong, S.: Attribute learning for understanding unstructured social activity. In: Fitzgibbon, A., Lazebnik, S., Perona, P., Sato, Y., Schmid, C. (eds.) ECCV 2012, Part IV. LNCS, vol. 7575, pp. 530–543. Springer, Heidelberg (2012). https://doi.org/10.1007/978-3-642-33765-9_38
13. Fu, Y., Xiang, T., Jiang, Y.G., Xue, X., Sigal, L., Gong, S.: Recent advances in zero-shot recognition. arXiv preprint arXiv:1710.04837 (2017)
14. Fu, Y., Yang, Y., Hospedales, T., Xiang, T., Gong, S.: Transductive multi-label zero-shot learning. arXiv preprint arXiv:1503.07790 (2015)
15. Gavves, S., Mensink, T., Tommasi, T., Snoek, C., Tuytelaars, T.: Active transfer learning with zero-shot priors: reusing past datasets for future tasks. In: ICCV, pp. 2731–2739. IEEE (2015)
16. Girshick, R.: Fast R-CNN. In: ICCV, pp. 1440–1448. IEEE (2015)
17. Girshick, R., Donahue, J., Darrell, T., Malik, J.: Region-based convolutional networks for accurate object detection and segmentation. TPAMI **38**(1), 142–158 (2016)
18. Gupta, T., Shih, K., Singh, S., Hoiem, D.: Aligned image-word representations improve inductive transfer across vision-language tasks. arXiv preprint arXiv:1704.00260 (2017)
19. Hoiem, D., Chodpathumwan, Y., Dai, Q.: Diagnosing error in object detectors. In: Fitzgibbon, A., Lazebnik, S., Perona, P., Sato, Y., Schmid, C. (eds.) ECCV 2012, Part III. LNCS, vol. 7574, pp. 340–353. Springer, Heidelberg (2012). https://doi.org/10.1007/978-3-642-33712-3_25
20. Jain, L.P., Scheirer, W.J., Boult, T.E.: Multi-class open set recognition using probability of inclusion. In: Fleet, D., Pajdla, T., Schiele, B., Tuytelaars, T. (eds.) ECCV 2014, Part III. LNCS, vol. 8691, pp. 393–409. Springer, Cham (2014). https://doi.org/10.1007/978-3-319-10578-9_26
21. Joulin, A., Grave, E., Bojanowski, P., Mikolov, T.: Bag of tricks for efficient text classification. arXiv preprint arXiv:1607.01759 (2016)
22. Kingma, D., Ba, J.: Adam: A method for stochastic optimization. arXiv preprint arXiv:1412.6980 (2014)
23. Kodirov, E., Xiang, T., Gong, S.: Semantic autoencoder for zero-shot learning. arXiv preprint arXiv:1704.08345 (2017)
24. Krasin, I., et al.: Openimages: A public dataset for large-scale multi-label and multi-class image classification. Dataset https://github.com/openimages (2017)

25. Krishna, R., et al.: Visual genome: Connecting language and vision using crowd-sourced dense image annotations. arXiv preprint arXiv:1602.07332 (2016)
26. Lampert, C.H., Nickisch, H., Harmeling, S.: Learning to detect unseen object classes by between-class attribute transfer. In: CVPR, pp. 951–958. IEEE (2009)
27. Lampert, C.H., Nickisch, H., Harmeling, S.: Attribute-based classification for zero-shot visual object categorization. TPAMI **36**(3), 453–465 (2014)
28. Li, Z., Gavves, E., Mensink, T., Snoek, C.G.M.: Attributes make sense on segmented objects. In: Fleet, D., Pajdla, T., Schiele, B., Tuytelaars, T. (eds.) ECCV 2014, Part VI. LNCS, vol. 8694, pp. 350–365. Springer, Cham (2014). https://doi.org/10.1007/978-3-319-10599-4_23
29. Lim, J.J., Salakhutdinov, R.R., Torralba, A.: Transfer learning by borrowing examples for multiclass object detection. In: NIPS, pp. 118–126 (2011)
30. Lin, T.-Y., Maire, M., Belongie, S., Hays, J., Perona, P., Ramanan, D., Dollár, P., Zitnick, C.L.: Microsoft COCO: common objects in context. In: Fleet, D., Pajdla, T., Schiele, B., Tuytelaars, T. (eds.) ECCV 2014, Part V. LNCS, vol. 8693, pp. 740–755. Springer, Cham (2014). https://doi.org/10.1007/978-3-319-10602-1_48
31. Liu, J., Kuipers, B., Savarese, S.: Recognizing human actions by attributes. In: CVPR, pp. 3337–3344. IEEE (2011)
32. Liu, W., Anguelov, D., Erhan, D., Szegedy, C., Reed, S., Fu, C.-Y., Berg, A.C.: SSD: single shot multibox detector. In: Leibe, B., Matas, J., Sebe, N., Welling, M. (eds.) ECCV 2016, Part I. LNCS, vol. 9905, pp. 21–37. Springer, Cham (2016). https://doi.org/10.1007/978-3-319-46448-0_2
33. Lu, C., Krishna, R., Bernstein, M., Fei-Fei, L.: Visual relationship detection with language priors. In: Leibe, B., Matas, J., Sebe, N., Welling, M. (eds.) ECCV 2016, Part I. LNCS, vol. 9905, pp. 852–869. Springer, Cham (2016). https://doi.org/10.1007/978-3-319-46448-0_51
34. Mikolov, T., Chen, K., Corrado, G., Dean, J.: Efficient estimation of word representations in vector space. arXiv preprint arXiv:1301.3781 (2013)
35. Mikolov, T., Sutskever, I., Chen, K., Corrado, G.S., Dean, J.: Distributed representations of words and phrases and their compositionality. In: NIPS, pp. 3111–3119 (2013)
36. Miller, G.A.: Wordnet: a lexical database for english. Commun. ACM **38**(11), 39–41 (1995)
37. Norouzi, M., Mikolov, T., Bengio, S., Singer, Y., Shlens, J., Frome, A., Corrado, G.S., Dean, J.: Zero-shot learning by convex combination of semantic embeddings. arXiv preprint arXiv:1312.5650 (2013)
38. Parikh, D., Kovashka, A., Parkash, A., Grauman, K.: Relative attributes for enhanced human-machine communication. In: AAAI (2012)
39. Pennington, J., Socher, R., Manning, C.D.: Glove: global vectors for word representation. EMNLP **14**, 1532–1543 (2014)
40. Qi, G.J., Aggarwal, C., Rui, Y., Tian, Q., Chang, S., Huang, T.: Towards cross-category knowledge propagation for learning visual concepts. In: CVPR, pp. 897–904. IEEE (2011)
41. Qiao, R., Liu, L., Shen, C., Hengel, A.v.d.: Visually aligned word embeddings for improving zero-shot learning. arXiv preprint arXiv:1707.05427 (2017)
42. Rahman, S., Khan, S., Porikli, F.: Zero-shot object detection: Learning to simultaneously recognize and localize novel concepts. arXiv preprint arXiv:1803.06049 (2018)
43. Rahman, S., Khan, S.H., Porikli, F.: A unified approach for conventional zero-shot, generalized zero-shot and few-shot learning. arXiv preprint arXiv:1706.08653 (2017)

44. Redmon, J., Divvala, S., Girshick, R., Farhadi, A.: You only look once: Unified, real-time object detection. In: CVPR, pp. 779–788. IEEE (2016)
45. Redmon, J., Farhadi, A.: Yolo9000: better, faster, stronger. arXiv preprint arXiv:1612.08242 (2016)
46. Ren, S., He, K., Girshick, R., Sun, J.: Faster R-CNN: Towards real-time object detection with region proposal networks. In: NIPS, pp. 91–99 (2015)
47. Russakovsky, O., Deng, J., Su, H., Krause, J., Satheesh, S., Ma, S., Huang, Z., Karpathy, A., Khosla, A., Bernstein, M.: Imagenet large scale visual recognition challenge. Int. J. Comput. Vis. **115**(3), 211–252 (2015)
48. Seeger, M.: Learning with labeled and unlabeled data. Technical report (2000)
49. Sharma, G., Jurie, F., Schmid, C.: Expanded parts model for semantic description of humans in still images. TPAMI **39**(1), 87–101 (2017)
50. Socher, R., Ganjoo, M., Manning, C.D., Ng, A.: Zero-shot learning through cross-modal transfer. In: NIPS, pp. 935–943 (2013)
51. Szegedy, C., Ioffe, S., Vanhoucke, V., Alemi, A.A.: Inception-v4, inception-ResNet and the impact of residual connections on learning. In: AAAI, pp. 4278–4284 (2017)
52. Xian, Y., Akata, Z., Sharma, G., Nguyen, Q., Hein, M., Schiele, B.: Latent embeddings for zero-shot classification. In: CVPR, pp. 69–77. IEEE (2016)
53. Xian, Y., Lampert, C.H., Schiele, B., Akata, Z.: Zero-shot learning-a comprehensive evaluation of the good, the bad and the ugly. arXiv preprint arXiv:1707.00600 (2017)
54. Xu, B., Fu, Y., Jiang, Y.G., Li, B., Sigal, L.: Heterogeneous knowledge transfer in video emotion recognition, attribution and summarization. TPAMI **9**, 255–270 (2016)
55. Xu, H., Lv, X., Wang, X., Ren, Z., Bodla, N., Chellappa, R.: Deep regionlets for object detection. CoRR abs/1712.02408 (2017)
56. Yu, R., Chen, X., Morariu, V.I., Davis, L.S.: The role of context selection in object detection. arXiv preprint arXiv:1609.02948 (2016)
57. Zhang, H., Shang, X., Yang, W., Xu, H., Luan, H., Chua, T.S.: Online collaborative learning for open-vocabulary visual classifiers. In: CVPR, pp. 2809–2817. IEEE (2016)
58. Zhang, Y., Yuan, L., Guo, Y., He, Z., Huang, I.A., Lee, H.: Discriminative bimodal networks for visual localization and detection with natural language queries. arXiv preprint arXiv:1704.03944 (2017)
59. Zhang, Z., Saligrama, V.: Zero-shot learning via joint latent similarity embedding. In: CVPR, pp. 6034–6042. IEEE (2016)
60. Zhang, Z., Saligrama, V.: Zero-shot recognition via structured prediction. In: Leibe, B., Matas, J., Sebe, N., Welling, M. (eds.) ECCV 2016, Part VII. LNCS, vol. 9911, pp. 533–548. Springer, Cham (2016). https://doi.org/10.1007/978-3-319-46478-7_33
61. Zhu, P., Wang, H., Bolukbasi, T., Saligrama, V.: Zero-shot detection. arXiv preprint arXiv:1803.07113 (2018)
62. Zitnick, C.L., Dollár, P.: Edge boxes: locating object proposals from edges. In: Fleet, D., Pajdla, T., Schiele, B., Tuytelaars, T. (eds.) ECCV 2014, Part V. LNCS, vol. 8693, pp. 391–405. Springer, Cham (2014). https://doi.org/10.1007/978-3-319-10602-1_26

A Modulation Module for Multi-task Learning with Applications in Image Retrieval

Xiangyun Zhao[1], Haoxiang Li[2(✉)], Xiaohui Shen[3], Xiaodan Liang[4], and Ying Wu[1]

[1] EECS Department, Northwestern University, Evanston, USA
[2] AIBee, Palo Alto, USA
hxli@aibee.com
[3] Bytedance AI Lab, Beijing, China
[4] Carnegie Mellon University, Pittsburgh, USA

Abstract. Multi-task learning has been widely adopted in many computer vision tasks to improve overall computation efficiency or boost the performance of individual tasks, under the assumption that those tasks are correlated and complementary to each other. However, the relationships between the tasks are complicated in practice, especially when the number of involved tasks scales up. When two tasks are of weak relevance, they may compete or even distract each other during joint training of shared parameters, and as a consequence undermine the learning of all the tasks. This will raise *destructive interference* which decreases learning efficiency of shared parameters and lead to low quality loss local optimum w.r.t. shared parameters. To address the this problem, we propose a general modulation module, which can be inserted into any convolutional neural network architecture, to encourage the coupling and feature sharing of relevant tasks while disentangling the learning of irrelevant tasks with minor parameters addition. Equipped with this module, gradient directions from different tasks can be enforced to be consistent for those shared parameters, which benefits multi-task joint training. The module is end-to-end learnable without ad-hoc design for specific tasks, and can naturally handle many tasks at the same time. We apply our approach on two retrieval tasks, face retrieval on the CelebA dataset [12] and product retrieval on the UT-Zappos50K dataset [34,35], and demonstrate its advantage over other multi-task learning methods in both accuracy and storage efficiency.

1 Introduction

Multi-task learning aims to improve learning efficiency and boost the performance of individual tasks by jointly learning multiple tasks at the same time.

Part of the work is done when Xiangyun Zhao was an intern at Adobe Research advised by Haoxiang Li and Xiaohui Shen.

© Springer Nature Switzerland AG 2018
V. Ferrari et al. (Eds.): ECCV 2018, LNCS 11205, pp. 415–432, 2018.
https://doi.org/10.1007/978-3-030-01246-5_25

With the recent prevalence of deep learning-based approaches in various computer vision tasks, multi-task learning is often implemented as parameter sharing in certain intermediate layers in a unified convolutional neural network architecture [19,33]. However, such feature sharing only works when the tasks are correlated and complementary to each other. When two tasks are irrelevant, they may provide competing or even contradicting gradient directions during feature learning. For example, learning to predict face attributes of "Open Mouth" and "Young" can lead to discrepant gradient directions for the examples in Fig. 1. Because the network is supervised to produce nearby embeddings in one task but faraway embeddings in the other task, the shared parameters get conflicting training signals. It is analogous to the *destructive interference* problem in Physics where two waves of equal frequency and opposite phases cancel each other. It would make the joint training much more difficult and negatively impact the performance of all the tasks.

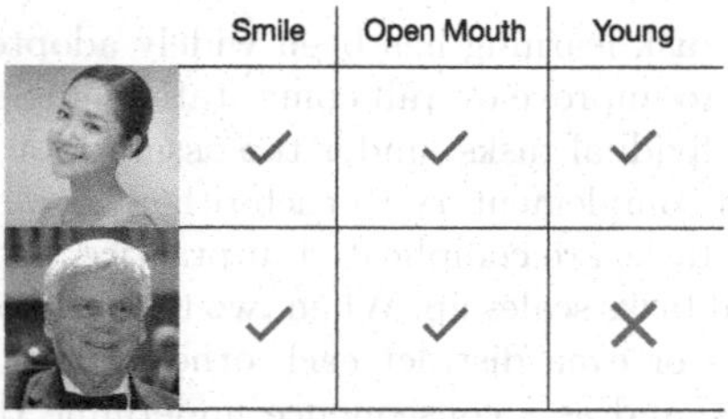

Fig. 1. Conflicting training signals in multi-task learning: when jointly learning discriminative features for multiple face attributes, some samples may introduce conflicting training signals in updating shared model parameters, such as "Smile" vs. "Young".

Although this problem is rarely identified in the literature, many of the existing methods are in fact designed to mitigate *destructive interference* in multi-task learning. For example, in the popular multi-branch neural network architecture and its variants, the task-specific branches are designed carefully with the prior knowledge regarding the relationships of certain tasks [8,18,20]. By doing this, people expect less conflicting training signals to the shared parameters. Nevertheless, it is difficult to generalize those specific designs to other tasks where the relationships may vary, or to scale up to more tasks such as classifying more than 20 facial attributes at the same time, where the task relationships become more complicated and less well studied.

To overcome these limitations, we propose a novel modulation module, which can be inserted into arbitrary network architecture and learned through end-to-end training. It can encourage correlated tasks to share more features, and at the same time disentangle the feature learning of irrelevant tasks. In back-propagation of the training signals, it modulates the gradient directions from different tasks to be more consistent for those shared parameters; in the feed-forward pass, it modulates the features towards task-specific feature spaces. Since it does not require prior knowledge of the relationships of the tasks, it can be applied to various multi-task learning problems, and handle many tasks at the same time. One related work is [24] which try to increase model capacity without a proportional increase in computation.

To validate the effectiveness of the proposed approach, we apply the modulation module in a neural network to learn the feature embedding of multiple attributes, and evaluate the learned feature representations on diverse retrieval tasks. In particular, we first propose a joint training framework with several embedded modulation modules for the learning of multiple face attributes, and evaluate the attribute-specific face retrieval results on the CelebA dataset. In addition, we provide thorough analysis on the task relationships and the capability of the proposed module in promoting correlated tasks while decoupling unrelated tasks. Experimental results show that the advantage of our approach is more significant with more tasks involved, showing its generalization capability to larger-scale multi-task learning problems. Compared with existing multi-task learning methods, the proposed module learns improved task-specific features and supports a compact model for scalability. We further apply the proposed approach in product retrieval on the UT-Zappos50K dataset, and demonstrate its superiority over other state-of-the-art methods.

Overall, the contributions of this work are four-fold:

- We address the *destructive interference* problem of unrelated tasks in multi-task learning, which is rarely discussed in previous work.
- We propose a novel modulation module that is general and end-to-end learnable, to adaptively couple correlated tasks while decoupling unrelated ones during feature learning.
- With minor task-specific overhead, our method supports scalable multi-task learning without manually grouping of tasks.
- We apply the module to the feature learning of multiple attributes, and demonstrate its effectiveness on retrieval tasks, especially on large-scale problems (e.g., as many as 20 attributes are jointly learned).

2   Related Work

2.1   Multi-task Learning

It has been observed in many prior works that jointly learning of multiple correlated tasks can help improve the performance of each of them, for example, learning face detection with face alignment [19,37], learning object detection with segmentation [2,4], and learning semantic segmentation with depth estimation [15,29]. While these works mainly study what related tasks can be jointly learned in order to mutually benefit each other, we instead investigate a proper joint training scheme given any tasks without assumption on their relationships.

A number of research efforts have been devoted to exploiting the correlations among related tasks for joint training. For example, Jou et al. [8] propose the Deep Cross Residual Learning to introduce the cross-residuals connections as a form of network regularization for better network generalization. Misra et al. [14] propose the Cross-stitch Networks to combine the activations from multiple task-specific networks for better joint training. Kokkinos et al. [9] propose UberNet to jointly learn low-, mid-, and high-level vision tasks by branching out task-specific paths from different stages in a deep CNN.

Most multi-task learning frameworks, if not all, involve parameters shared across tasks and task-specific parameters. In joint learning beyond similar tasks, it is desirable to automatically discover what and how to share between tasks. Recent works along this line include Lu et al. [13], who propose to automatically discover a neural network design to group similar tasks together; Yang et al. [32], who model this problem as tensor factorization to learn how to share knowledge across tasks; and Veit et al. [26], who propose to share all neural network layers but masking the final image features differently conditioned on the attributes/tasks.

Compared to these existing works, in this paper, we explicitly identify the problem of *destructive interference* and propose a metric to quantify it. Our observation further confirms its correlation to the quality of learned features. Moreover, our proposed module is end-to-end learnable and flexible to be inserted anywhere into an existing network architecture. Hence, our method can further enhance the structure learned with the algorithm from Lu et al. [13] to improve its suboptimal within-group branches. When compared with the tensor factorization by Yang et al. [32], our module is lightweight, easy to train, and with a small and accountable overhead to include additional tasks. Condition similar networks [26] shares this desirable scalability feature with our method in storage efficiency. However, as they do not account for the *destructive interference* problem in layers other than the final feature layer, we empirically observe that their method does not scale-up well in accuracy for many tasks (See Sect. 4.2).

2.2 Image Retrieval

In this work, we evaluate our method with applications on image retrieval. Image retrieval has been widely studied in computer vision [7,16,17,25,27,28]. We do not study the efficiency problem in image retrieval as in many prior works [7,11,16,28]. Instead, we focus on learning discriminative task-specific image features for accurate retrieval.

Essentially, our method is related to how discriminative image features can be extracted. In the era of deep learning, feature extraction is a very important and fundamental research direction. From the early pioneering AlexNet [10] to recent seminal ResNet [5] and DenseNet [6], the effectiveness and efficiency of neural networks have been largely improved. This line of research focuses on designing better neural network architectures, which is independent of our method. By design, our algorithm can potentially benefit from better backbone architectures.

Another important related research area is metric learning [21,23,30,31], which mostly focuses on designing an optimization objective to find a metric to maximize the inter-class distance while minimizing the intra-class distance. They are often equivalent to learning a discriminative subspace or feature embedding.

Some of them have been introduced into deep learning as the loss function for better feature learning [3,22]. Our method is by design agnostic to the loss function, and we can potentially benefit from more sophisticated loss functions to learn more discriminative image feature for all tasks. In our experiment, we use triplet loss [22] due to its simplicity.

3   Our Method

In this section, we first identify the *destructive interference* problem in sharing features for multi-task learning and then present the technical details of our modulation module to resolve this problem.

3.1   Destructive Interference

Despite that a multi-task neural network can have many variants which involve the learning of different task combinations, the fundamental technique is to share intermediate network parameters for different tasks, and jointly train with all supervision signals from different tasks by gradient descent methods. One issue raised from this common scheme is that two irrelevant or weakly relevant tasks may drag gradients propagated from different tasks in conflicting or even opposite directions. Thus, learning the shared parameters can suffer from the well-known *destructive interference* problem.

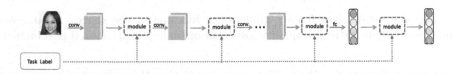

Fig. 2. A neural network fully modulated by our proposed modules: in testing, the network takes inputs as the image and task label to extract discriminative image features for the specified task.

Formally, we denote θ as the parameters of a neural network F over different tasks, I as its input, and $f = F(I|\theta)$ as its output. The update of θ follows its gradient:

$$\nabla\theta = \frac{\partial L}{\partial f}\frac{\partial f}{\partial \theta}, \tag{1}$$

where L is the loss function.

In multi-task learning, θ will be updated by gradients from different tasks. Essentially, $\frac{\partial L}{\partial f}$ directs the learning of θ. In common cases, a discriminative loss generally encourages f_i and f_j to be similar for images I_i and I_j from the same class. However, the relationship of I_i and I_j can change in multi-task learning, even flip in different tasks. When training all these tasks, the update directions of θ may be conflicting, which is the namely *destructive interference* problem.

Table 1. Accuracy and UCR Comparison on three face attribute-based retrieval tasks (See Sect. 4.1 for details): the comparison empirically support our analysis of the *destructive interference* problem and the assumption that reasonable task-specific modulation parameters can be learned from data

	smile Acc.	open mouth Acc.	young Acc.	smile/young UCR	smile/open-mouth UCR
smile + young + open mouth(a)	84.71%	74.73 %	71.6%	-	-
smile + young(b)	83.85%	-	74.71%	22.1%	-
smile + open mouth(c)	91.72%	92.65%	-	-	43.71%
Three Independent Networks(d)	93.32%	94.40%	84.90%	-	-
With Proposed Modulation(e)	94.03%	95.31%	86.20%	**50.63%**	**52.77%**
With Proposed Modulation + Reg(f)	**94.94%**	**95.58%**	**87.75%**	-	-

More specifically, given a mini-batch of training samples from task t and t', $\nabla\theta = \nabla\theta_t + \nabla\theta_{t'}$, where $\nabla\theta_{t/t'}$ denotes gradients from samples of task t/t'. Gradients from two tasks are negatively impacting the learning of each other, when

$$A_{t,t'} = sign(\langle \nabla\theta_t, \nabla\theta_{t'} \rangle) = -1. \tag{2}$$

The *destructive interference* hinders the learning of the shared parameters and essentially leads to low quality loss local optimum w.r.t. shared parameters.

Empirical Evidence. We validate our assumption through a toy experiment on jointly learning of multiple attribute-based face retrieval tasks. More details on the experimental settings can be found in Sect. 4.1.

Intuitively, the attribute *smile* is related to attribute *open mouth* but irrelevant to attribute *young*[1]. As shown in Table 1, when we share all the parameters of the neural network across different tasks, the results degrade when jointly training the tasks compared with training three independent task-specific networks. The degradation when jointly training *smile* and *young* is much more significant than the one when jointly training *smile* and *open mouth*. That is because there are always some conflicting gradients from some training samples even if two tasks are correlated, and apparently when the two tasks are with weak relevance, the conflicts become more frequent, making the joint training ineffective.

To further understand how the learning leads to the above results, we follow Eq. 2 to quantitatively estimate the compatibility of task pairs by looking at the ratio of mini-batches with $A_{t,t'} > 0$ in one training epoch. So we define this ratio

---

[1] Here the attribute refers to its estimation from a given face image.

as Update Compliance Ratio(UCR) which measures the consistence of two tasks. The larger the UCR is, the more consistent the two tasks are in joint training. As shown in Table 1, in joint learning of *smile* and *open mouth* we observe higher compatibility compared with joint learning of *smile* and *young*, which explains the accuracy discrepancy from (b) to (c) in Table 1. Comparing (e) with (b) and (c), the accuracy improvement is accompanied with UCR improvement which explains how the proposed module improves the overall performance. With our proposed method introduced as following, we observe increased UCR for both task pairs.

3.2   A Modulation Module

Most multi-task learning frameworks involve task-specific parameters and shared parameters. Here we introduce a modulation module as a generic framework to add task-specific parameters and link it to alleviation of *destructive interference*.

More specifically, we propose to modulate the feature maps with task-specific projection matrix $\mathbf{W}_t$ for task t. As illustrated in Fig. 2, this module maintains the feature map size to keep it compatible with layers downwards in the network architecture. Following we will discuss how this design affects the back-propagation and feed-forward pass.

Back-Propagation. In back-propagation, *destructive interference* happens when gradients from two tasks t and t' over the shared parameters θ have components in conflicting directions, i.e., $\langle \nabla \theta_t, \nabla \theta_{t'} \rangle < 0$. It can be simply derived that the proposed modulation over feature maps is equivalent to modulating shared parameters with task-specific masks $\mathbf{M}_{t/t'}$. With the proposed modulation, the update to θ is now $\mathbf{M}_t \nabla \theta_t + \mathbf{M}_{t'} \nabla \theta_{t'}$. Since the task-specific masks/projection matrices are learnable, we observe that the training process will naturally mitigate the *destructive interference* by reducing the average across-task gradient angles $\langle \mathbf{M}_t \nabla \theta_t, \mathbf{M}_{t'} \nabla \theta_{t'} \rangle$, which is observed to result in better local optimum of shared parameters.

Feed-Forward Pass. Given feature map x with size $M \times N \times C$ and the modulation projection matrix $\mathbf{W}$, we have

$$x' = \mathbf{W}_t \times x, \tag{3}$$

which is the input to the next layer.

A full projection matrix would require $\mathbf{W}_t$ of size $MNC \times MNC$, which is infeasible in practice and the modulation would degenerate to completely separated branches with a full project matrix. Therefore, we firstly simplify the W_t to have shared elements within each channel. Formally, $\mathbf{W} = \{w_{i,j}\}, \{i,j\} \in \{1, \ldots, C\}$

$$x'_{mni} = \sum_{j=1}^{C} x_{mnj} * w_{i,j}, \tag{4}$$

where x'_{mni}, x_{mni} and w_{ij} denote elements from input, output feature maps and W_t respectively. We ignore the subscription t for simplicity. Here $\mathbf{W}$ is in fact a channel-wise projection matrix.

We can further reduce the computation by simplifying the $\mathbf{W}_t$ to be a channel-wise scaling vector $\mathbf{W}_t$ with size C as illustrated in Fig. 2.

Formally, $\mathbf{W} = \{w_c\}, c \in \{1, \dots, C\}$.

$$x'_{mnc} = x_{mnc} * w_c, \tag{5}$$

where x'_{mnc} and x_{mnc} denotes elements from input and output feature maps respectively.

Compared with the channel-wise scaling vector design, we observe empirically the overall improvement from the channel-wise projection matrix design is marginal, hence we will mainly discuss and evaluate the simpler channel-wise scaling vector option. This module can be easily implemented by adding task specific linear transformations as shown in Fig. 3.

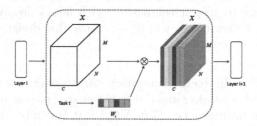

Fig. 3. Structure of the proposed Modulation Module which adapts features via learned weights with respect to each task. This module can be inserted between any layers and maintain the network structure.

3.3 Training

The modulation parameters $\mathbf{W}_t$ are learned together with the neural network parameters through back-propagation. In this paper, we use triplet loss [22] as the objective for optimization. More specifically, given a set of triplets from different tasks $(I_a, I_p, I_n, t) \in \mathbf{T}$,

$$L = \sum_{\mathbf{T}} [\|f_a - f_p\|^2 + \alpha - \|f_a - f_n\|^2)]_+ \tag{6}$$

$$f_{a,p,n} = F(I_{a,p,n}|\theta, \mathbf{W}_t)), \tag{7}$$

where α is the expected distance margin between positive pair and negative pair, I_a is the anchor sample, I_p is the positive sample, I_n is the negative sample and t is the task.

When training the Neural Network with a discriminative loss, we argue that by introducing the Modulation module into the neural network, it will learn to leverage the additional knobs to decouple unrelated tasks and couple related ones to minimize the training loss. In the toy experiment shown in Table 1, we primarily show that our method can surpass fully independent learning. The reduced ratios of conflicting mini-batches in training as shown in Table 1 also validate our design.

The learned $\mathbf{W}_*$ capture the relationship of tasks implicitly. We obtained $\mathbf{W}_s$, $\mathbf{W}_y$ and $\mathbf{W}_o$ for *smile, young, open-mouth* respectively. Then the element-wise difference between $\mathbf{W}_s$ and $\mathbf{W}_o$, $\nabla\mathbf{W}_{s,o}$, and the difference between $\mathbf{W}_s$ and $\mathbf{W}_y$, $\nabla\mathbf{W}_{s,y}$, are obtained to measure their relevancy. The mean and variance of $\nabla\mathbf{W}_{s,o}$ is 0.18 and 0.03 while the mean and variance of $\nabla\mathbf{W}_{s,y}$ is 0.24 and 0.047.

We further empirically validate this assumption by introducing an additional regularization loss to encode human prior knowledge on the tasks' relevancy. We assume the learned $\mathbf{W}$ for *smile* would be more similar to the one for *open mouth* compared with the one for *young*. We regularize the pairs of relevant tasks to have similar task-specific $\mathbf{W}$s with

$$L_a = max(0, \|\mathbf{W}_i - \mathbf{W}_j\|^2 + \beta - \|\mathbf{W}_i - \mathbf{W}_k\|^2), \tag{8}$$

where β is the expected margin, i, j, k denotes three tasks, and task pair (i, j) is considered more relevant compared to task pair (i, k). L_a is weighted by a hyper-parameter λ and combined with the above triplet loss over samples in training.

As shown in Table 1, the accuracy of our method augmented with this regularization loss is better but the gap is only marginal. This suggests that without encoding prior knowledge through the loss, the learned $\mathbf{W}$s may implicitly capture task relationships in a similar way. On the other hand, it is impractical to manually define all pairwise relationships when the number of tasks scales up, hence we ignore this regularization loss in our large-scale experiments.

4   Experiments

In the experiments, we evaluate the performance of our approach on the face retrieval and product retrieval tasks.

4.1   Setup

In both retrieval settings, we define a task as retrieval based on a certain attribute of either face or product. Both datasets have the per-image annotation for each attribute. To quantitatively evaluate the methods under the retrieval setting, we randomly sample image triplets from their testing sets as our benchmarks. Each triplet consists of an anchor sample I_a, a positive sample I_p, and a negative sample I_n. Given a triplet, we retrieve one sample from I_p and I_n with I_a and consider it a success if I_p is preferred. In our method, we extract discriminative features with the proposed network and measure image pair distance by their

Table 2. Our Basic Neural Network Architecture: Conv-Pool-ResnetBlock stands for a 3×3 conv-layer followed by a stride 2 pooling layer and a standard residual block consist of 2 3×3 conv-layers.

Name	Operation	Output Size
conv1	3×3 convolution	$148 \times 148 \times 32$
block2	Conv-Pool-ResnetBlock	$73 \times 73 \times 64$
block3	Conv-Pool-ResnetBlock	$35 \times 35 \times 128$
block4	Conv-Pool-ResnetBlock	$16 \times 16 \times 128$
block5	Conv-Pool-ResnetBlock	$7 \times 7 \times 128$
fc	Fully-Connected	256

euclidean distance of features. The accuracy metric is the ratio of successfully retrieved triplets.

Unless stated otherwise, we use the neural network architecture in Table 2 for our method, our re-implementation of other state-of-the-art methods, and our baseline methods.

We add the proposed Modulation modules to all layers from block4 to the final layer and use ADAGRAD [1] for optimization in training with learning rate 0.01. We uniformly initialize the parameters in all added modules to be 1. We use the batch size of 180 for 20 tasks and 168 for 7 tasks joint training. In each mini-batch, we evenly sample triplets for all tasks. Our method generally converges after 40 epochs.

4.2   Face Retrieval

Dataset. We use Celeb-A dataset [12] for the face retrieval experiment. Celeb-A consists of more than 200,000 face images with binary annotations on 40 face attributes related to age, expression, decoration, etc. We select 20 attributes more related to face appearance and ignore attributes around decoration such as eyeglasses and hat for our experiments. We also report the results on 40 attributes to verify the effectiveness on 40 attributes.

We randomly sampled 30000 triplets for training and 10000 triplets for testing for each task. Our basic network architecture is shown in Table 2. We augment it by inserting our gradient modulation modules and train from scratch.

Results. We report our evaluation of the following methods in Table 3:

- Ours: we insert the proposed Modulation modules to the block4, block5, and fc layers to the network in Table 2 and jointly train it with all training triplets from 20 tasks;
- Conditional Similarity Network (CSN) from Veit et al. [26]: we follow the open-sourced implementation from the authors to replace the network architecture with ours and jointly train it with all training triplets from 20 tasks;

- Independent Task-specific Network (ITN): in this strong baseline we train 20 task-specific neural networks with training triplets from each task independently;
- Single Fully-shared Network (FSN): we train one network with all training triplets.

Table 3. Accuracy comparison on the joint training of 20 face attributes: with far fewer parameters, our method achieves best mean accuracy over the 20 tasks compared with the competing methods.

Methods:	Ours	CSN	ITN	FSN	IB-256	IB-25	Only mask
Average Accuracy	**84.86%**	72.81%	84.61%	69.4%	83.69%	75.47%	76.32%
Number of Baseline Parameters	3 M	3 M	3 M	3 M	3 M	3 M	3 M
Number of additional Parameters	10 k	3 k	51 M	0	1.3 M	128 k	10 k
smile	**93.77%**	75.59%	93.32%	78.83%	92.76%	82.91%	87.64%
shadow	**94.67%**	92.83%	92.25%	85.39%	92.83%	88.02%	86.41%
bald	**91.83%**	87.80%	90.70%	81.79%	89.47%	78.11%	88.42%
are-eyebrows	78.36%	63.94%	**79.60%**	66.19%	76.84%	66.00%	72.10%
chubby	**90.2%**	85.32%	87.29%	79.06%	88.66%	82.79%	85.39%
double-chin	**91.45%**	85.61%	89.57%	81.15%	89.92%	83.08%	87.19%
high-cheekbone	88.53%	71.25%	**88.93%**	74.57%	87.25%	76.53%	82.80%
goatee	**94.47%**	90.66%	94.06%	83.48%	94.17%	84.68%	91.52%
mustache	**93.41%**	89.21%	93.23%	82.40%	93.21%	87.52%	89.89%
no-beard	**93.84%**	82.35%	93.69%	80.52%	93.98%	86.51%	85.69%
sideburns	95.27%	90.95%	94.88%	86.20%	95.04%	88.81%	91.85%
bangs	**90.22%**	71.91%	89.96%	69.96%	89.13%	78.75%	80.34%
straight-hair	72.98%	63.31%	**73.24%**	61.70%	71.98%	62.33%	65.47%
wavy-hair	**76.59%**	59.34%	76.10%	59.49%	75.62%	64.04%	65.11%
receding-hairline	**87.33%**	75.63%	86.93%	72.02%	86.24%	80.17%	79.94%
bags-eyes	85.90%	76.39%	**85.93%**	72.39%	84.64%	76.01%	82.05%
bushy-eyebrows	**88.73%**	79.22%	88.32%	74.52%	88.44%	80.50%	80.50%
young	84.87%	60.61%	**84.90%**	61.55%	83.48%	73.05%	66.23%
oval-face	**72.21%**	64.33%	71.52%	63.54%	70.16%	62.10%	65.10%
mouth-open	**94.59%**	87.32%	94.40%	72.71%	92.22%	89.03%	86.59%

Table 4. Comparison of UCR between different tasks on joint training of seven face attributes with our method (red) and the fully shared network baseline (black): we quantitatively demonstrate the mitigation of *destructive interference* with our method.

	smile	ovalface	shadow	bald	arc-eyebrows	big-lips	big-nose
smile	-	51.56/48.47	67.70/26.33	67.82/32.30	52.32/45.40	54.83/49.49	58.72/45.25
ovalface	51.56/48.47	-	67.36/26.94	64.99/35.29	57.86/50.13	57.74/49.32	54.98/46.64
shadow	67.70/26.33	67.36/26.94	-	91.67/30.54	66.87/26.48	72.51/28.25	69.90/29.99
bald	67.82/32.30	64.99/35.29	91.67/30.54	-	61.74/31.67	67.60/36.22	72.66/41.04
arc-eyebrows	52.32/45.40	57.86/50.13	66.87/26.48	61.74/31.67	-	58.86/51.13	50.34/41.43
big-lips	54.83/46.49	57.74/49.32	72.51/28.25	67.70/36.22	58.86/51.13	-	55.20/46.84
big-nose	58.72/45.25	54.98/46.64	69.90/29.99	72.66/41.04	50.34/41.43	55.20/46.84	-

- Independent Branch 256 (IB-256): based on shared parameters, we add task-specific branch with feature size 256.
- Independent Branch 25 (IB-25): based on shared parameters, we add task-specific branch with feature size 25.
- Only-mask: our network is pretrained from the independent branch model, the shared parameters are fixed and only the module parameters are learned.

Table 5. Ablation Study of our method: with more layers modulated by the proposed method, performance generally improves; channel-wise projection module is marginally better than the default channel-wise scaling vector design.

Face Attributes:	smile	ovalface	shadow	bald	arc-eyebrows	big-lips	big-nose	Average Accuracy
Single Fully-shared Network	78.39%	64.39%	79.55%	77.62%	69.17%	61.71%	68.88%	71.38%
Independent Task-specific Networks	93.32%	71.52%	92.25%	90.70%	79.60%	**67.35%**	84.35%	82.72%
CSN	91.39%	68.41%	92.51%	**90.79%**	77.53%	65.79%	82.03%	81.20%
Ours (from block5)	93.35%	70.47%	90.44%	88.79%	77.12%	66.36%	83.84%	81.48%
Ours (from block4)	93.69%	71.44%	92.06%	90.66%	**80.00%**	67.15%	84.26%	82.75%
Ours (from block3)	93.83%	71.04%	**93.28%**	90.66%	79.76%	67.53%	**84.76%**	**82.98%**
Ours (from block2)	**94.11%**	71.94%	92.5%	90.70%	78.66%	66.36%	84.10%	82.62%
channel-wise projection (from block4)	**94.10%**	**71.98%**	92.69%	90.58%	78.95%	66.78%	84.48%	82.79%

Single Fully-shared network and CSN severely suffer from the *destructive interference* as shown in Table 3. Note when jointly training only 7 tasks, CSN performs much better than the fully-shared network and similarly to fully shared network with additional parameters as shown in Table 5. However, it does not scale up to handle as many as 20 tasks. Since the majority of the parameters are naively shared across tasks until the last layer, CSN still suffers from *destructive interference*.

We then compare our methods with Independent Branch methods. Independent Branch methods naively add task specific branches above the shared parameters. The branching for IB-25 and IB256 begins at the end of the baseline model in Table 2, i.e., different attributes have different branches after the FC layer. As illustrated in Table 3, our method clearly outperforms them with much fewer task-specific parameters. Regarding the number of additional parameters, we observe that to approximate accuracy of our method, this baseline needs about 1.3 M task-specific parameters, which is 100 times of ours. The comparison indicates that our module is more efficient in leveraging additional parameters budget.

Table 6. Accuracy Comparison on joint training of 4 product retrieval tasks on UT-Zappos50k: our method significantly outperforms others.

Tasks	Class	Closure	Gender	Heel	Average Accuracy
Single Fully-shared Network	78.95%	80.33%	69.22%	73.35%	75.46%
Independent Task-specific Networks	92.01%	89.12%	79.10%	85.97%	86.61%
CSN [26]	93.06%	89.37%	78.09	86.42%	86.73%
Ours	**93.34%**	**90.57%**	**79.50%**	**89.27%**	**88.17%**

Compared with the independently trained task-specific networks, our method achieves slightly better average accuracy with almost 20 times fewer parameters. Notably, our method achieves obvious improvement for both face shape related attributes (*chubby, double chin*) and all three beard related attributes (*goatee, mustache, sideburns*), which demonstrates that the proposed method does not only decouple unrelated tasks but also adaptively couples related tasks to improve their learning. We show some example retrieval results in Fig. 4.

We reported the Update Compliance Ratio (UCR) comparison in Table 4. Our method significantly improves the UCR in the joint training for all task pairs. This indicates that the proposed module is effective in alleviating the *destructive interference* by leading the gradients over shared parameters from different tasks to be more consistent.

To further validate that the source of improvement is from better shared parameters instead of simply additional task specific parameters. We keep our shared parameters fixed as the ones trained with the strong baseline IB-256 and only make the modulation modules trainable. As reported in the last column in Table 3, the results are not as good as our full pipeline, which suggests that the proposed modules improved the learning of shared parameters. To validate the effectiveness of our method on 40 attributes, we evaluate our method on 40 attributes and obtain average 85.75% which is significant better than 78.22% of our baseline IB-25 which has same network complexity but with independent branches.

Ablation Study. In Table 5, we evaluate how the performance evolves when we insert more Modulation modules into the network. By adding proposed modules to all layers after block$N$, $N = 5, 4, 3, 2$, we observe that the performance generally increases with more layers modulated. This is well-aligned with our intuition that with gradients modulated in more layers, the destructive inference problem gets solved better. Because early layers in the neural networks generally learn primitive filters [36] shared across a broad spectrum of tasks, shared parameters may not suffer from conflicting updates. Hence the performance improvement saturates eventually.

We also experiment with channel-wise projection matrix instead of channel-wise scaling vector in the proposed modules as introduced in Sect. 3.2. We observe marginal improvement with the more complicated module, as shown in the last row of Table 5. This suggests that potentially with more parameters being modulated, the overall performance improves at the cost of additional task-specific parameters. It also shows that the proposed channel-wise scaling vector design is a cost-effective choice.

4.3 Product Retrieval

Dataset. We use UT-Zappos50K dataset [34, 35] for the product retrieval experiment. UT-Zappos50K is a large shoe dataset consisting of more than 50,000 catalog images collected from the web. The datasets are richly annotated and we can retrieve shoes based on their type, suggested gender, height of their heel, and the closing mechanism. We jointly learn these 4 tasks in our experiment. We follow the same training, validation, and testing set splits as Veit et al. [26] to sample triplets.

Results. As shown in Table 6, our method is significantly better than all other competing methods. Because CSN manually initializes the 1-dimensional mask for each attribute to be non-overlapping, their method does not exploit their correlation well when two tasks are correlated. We argue that naively sharing features for all tasks may hinder the further improvement of CSN due to gradient discrepancy among different tasks. In our method, proposed modules are inserted in the network and the correlation of different tasks are effectively exploited. Especially for *heel* task, our method obtains a nearly 3 point gain over CSN. Note that because our network architecture is much simpler than the one used by Veit et al. [26] and does not pre-train on ImageNet. The numbers are generally not compatible to those reported in their paper.

5 Discussion

5.1 General Applicability

In this paper, we mainly discuss multi-task learning with application in image retrieval in which each task has similar network structure and loss functions.

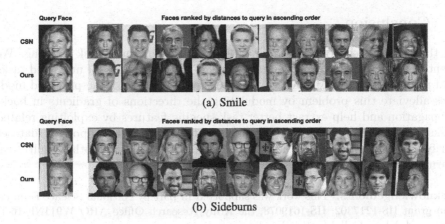

Fig. 4. Example face retrieval results in two tasks: using models jointly trained for 20 face attributes with CSN and our method respectively. Some incorrectly ranked faces are highlighted in red. (Color figure online)

By design the proposed module is not limited to a specific loss and should be applicable to handle different tasks and different loss functions.

In general multi-task learning, each task may have its specifically designed network architecture and own loss, such as face detection and face alignment [19,37], learning object detection and segmentation [2,4], learning semantic segmentation and depth estimation [15,29]. The signals from different tasks could be explicitly conflicting as well and lead to severe *destructive interference* especially when the number of jointly learned tasks scale up. When such severe *destructive interference* happens, the proposed module could be added to modulate the update directions as well as task-specific features. We leave it as our future work to validate this assumption through experiments.

5.2 Speed and Memory Size Trade-off

Similar to a multi-branch architecture and arguably most multi-task learning frameworks, our method shares the problem of runtime speed and memory size trade-off in inference. One can either choose to keep all task-specific feature maps in memory to finish all the predictions in a single pass or iteratively feed-forward through the network from the shared feature maps to keep a tight memory footprint. However, we should highlight that our method can achieve better accuracy with a more compact model in storage. Either a single pass inference or iterative inference could be feasible with our method. Since most computations happen in the early stage in inference, with the proposed modules, our method only added 15% overhead in feed-forward time. The feature maps after block4 are much smaller than the ones in the early stages, so the increased memory footprint would be sustainable for 20 tasks too.

6   Conclusion

In this paper, we propose a Modulation module for multi-task learning. We identify the *destructive interference* problem in joint learning of unrelated tasks and propose to quantify it with Update Compliance Ratio. The proposed modules alleviate this problem by modulating the directions of gradients in backpropagation and help extract better task-specific features by exploiting related tasks. Extensive experiments on CelebA dataset and UT-Zappos50K dataset verify the effectiveness and advantage of our approach over other multi-task learning methods.

Acknowledgements. This work was supported in part by National Science Foundation grant IIS-1217302, IIS-1619078, the Army Research Office ARO W911NF-16-1-0138, and Adobe Collaboration Funding.

References

1. Duchi, J., Hazan, E., Singer, Y.: Adaptive subgradient methods for online learning and stochastic optimization. J. Mach. Learn. Res. **12**, 2121–2159 (2011)
2. Girshick, R., Donahue, J., Darrell, T., Malik, J.: Rich feature hierarchies for accurate object detection and semantic segmentation. In: Computer Vision and Pattern Recognition (2014)
3. Hadsell, R., Chopra, S., LeCun, Y.: Dimensionality reduction by learning an invariant mapping. In: 2006 IEEE Computer Society Conference on Computer Vision and Pattern Recognition, vol. 2, pp. 1735–1742. IEEE (2006)
4. He, K., Gkioxari, G., Dollar, P., Girshick, R.: Mask R-CNN. In: The IEEE International Conference on Computer Vision (ICCV), October 2017
5. He, K., Zhang, X., Ren, S., Sun, J.: Deep residual learning for image recognition. In: Proceedings of the IEEE Conference on Computer Vision and Pattern Recognition, pp. 770–778 (2016)
6. Huang, G., Liu, Z., van der Maaten, L., Weinberger, K.Q.: Densely connected convolutional networks. In: The IEEE Conference on Computer Vision and Pattern Recognition (CVPR), July 2017
7. Jegou, H., Douze, M., Schmid, C.: Product quantization for nearest neighbor search. IEEE Trans. Pattern Anal. Mach. Intell. **33**(1), 117–128 (2011)
8. Jou, B., Chang, S.F.: Deep cross residual learning for multitask visual recognition. In: Proceedings of the 2016 ACM on Multimedia Conference, pp. 998–1007. ACM (2016)
9. Kokkinos, I.: Ubernet: training a universal convolutional neural network for low-, mid-, and high-level vision using diverse datasets and limited memory. In: 2017 IEEE Conference on Computer Vision and Pattern Recognition (CVPR) (2017)
10. Krizhevsky, A., Sutskever, I., Hinton, G.E.: Imagenet classification with deep convolutional neural networks. In: Advances in Neural Information Processing Systems, pp. 1097–1105 (2012)
11. Lin, K., Yang, H.F., Hsiao, J.H., Chen, C.S.: Deep learning of binary hash codes for fast image retrieval. In: The IEEE Conference on Computer Vision and Pattern Recognition (CVPR) Workshops, June 2015
12. Liu, Z., Luo, P., Wang, X., Tang, X.: Deep learning face attributes in the wild. In: Proceedings of International Conference on Computer Vision (ICCV) (2015)

13. Lu, Y., et al.: Fully-adaptive feature sharing in multi-task networks with applications in person attribute classification. In: The IEEE Conference on Computer Vision and Pattern Recognition (CVPR), July 2017
14. Misra, I., Shrivastava, A., Gupta, A., Hebert, M.: Cross-stitch networks for multi-task learning. In: Proceedings of the IEEE Conference on Computer Vision and Pattern Recognition, pp. 3994–4003 (2016)
15. Mousavian, A., Pirsiavash, H., Košecká, J.: Joint semantic segmentation and depth estimation with deep convolutional networks. In: 2016 Fourth International Conference on 3D Vision (3DV), pp. 611–619. IEEE (2016)
16. Perronnin, F., Liu, Y., Sánchez, J., Poirier, H.: Large-scale image retrieval with compressed fisher vectors. In: 2010 IEEE Conference on Computer Vision and Pattern Recognition (CVPR), pp. 3384–3391. IEEE (2010)
17. Philbin, J., Chum, O., Isard, M., Sivic, J., Zisserman, A.: Object retrieval with large vocabularies and fast spatial matching. In: IEEE Conference on Computer Vision and Pattern Recognition, CVPR 2007, pp. 1–8. IEEE (2007)
18. Ranjan, R., Patel, V.M., Chellappa, R.: Hyperface: a deep multi-task learning framework for face detection, landmark localization, pose estimation, and gender recognition. arXiv preprint arXiv:1603.01249 (2016)
19. Ranjan, R., Sankaranarayanan, S., Castillo, C.D., Chellappa, R.: An all-in-one convolutional neural network for face analysis. In: 2017 12th IEEE International Conference on Automatic Face & Gesture Recognition (FG 2017), pp. 17–24. IEEE (2017)
20. Rothe, R., Timofte, R., Van Gool, L.: Dex: deep expectation of apparent age from a single image. In: Proceedings of the IEEE International Conference on Computer Vision Workshops, pp. 10–15 (2015)
21. Schapire, R.E., Singer, Y.: Boostexter: a boosting-based system for text categorization. Mach. Learn. **39**(2–3), 135–168 (2000)
22. Schroff, F., Kalenichenko, D., Philbin, J.: Facenet: a unified embedding for face recognition and clustering. In: Proceedings of the IEEE Conference on Computer Vision and Pattern Recognition, pp. 815–823 (2015)
23. Schultz, M., Joachims, T.: Learning a distance metric from relative comparisons. In: Advances in Neural Information Processing Systems, pp. 41–48 (2004)
24. Shazeer, N., et al.: Outrageously large neural networks: the sparsely-gated mixture-of-experts layer. arXiv preprint arXiv:1701.06538 (2017)
25. Shen, X., Lin, Z., Brandt, J., Avidan, S., Wu, Y.: Object retrieval and localization with spatially-constrained similarity measure and k-NN re-ranking. In: 2012 IEEE Conference on Computer Vision and Pattern Recognition (CVPR), pp. 3013–3020. IEEE (2012)
26. Veit, A., Belongie, S., Karaletsos, T.: Conditional similarity networks. In: Computer Vision and Pattern Recognition (CVPR) (2017)
27. Wan, J., et al.: Deep learning for content-based image retrieval: a comprehensive study. In: Proceedings of the 22nd ACM International Conference on Multimedia, pp. 157–166. ACM (2014)
28. Wang, J., Kumar, S., Chang, S.F.: Semi-supervised hashing for scalable image retrieval. In: 2010 IEEE Conference on Computer Vision and Pattern Recognition (CVPR), pp. 3424–3431. IEEE (2010)
29. Wang, P., et al.: Towards unified depth and semantic prediction from a single image. In: Proceedings of the IEEE Conference on Computer Vision and Pattern Recognition, pp. 2800–2809 (2015)
30. Weinberger, K.Q., Saul, L.K.: Distance metric learning for large margin nearest neighbor classification. J. Mach. Learn. Res. **10**, 207–244 (2009)

31. Xing, E.P., Jordan, M.I., Russell, S.J., Ng, A.Y.: Distance metric learning with application to clustering with side-information. In: Advances in Neural Information Processing Systems, pp. 521–528 (2003)
32. Yang, Y., Hospedales, T.M.: Deep multi-task representation learning: a tensor factorisation approach. CoRR abs/1605.06391 (2016)
33. Yin, X., Liu, X.: Multi-task convolutional neural network for face recognition. arXiv preprint arXiv:1702.04710 (2017)
34. Yu, A., Grauman, K.: Fine-grained visual comparisons with local learning. In: Computer Vision and Pattern Recognition (CVPR), June 2014
35. Yu, A., Grauman, K.: Semantic jitter: dense supervision for visual comparisons via synthetic images. In: International Conference on Computer Vision (ICCV), October 2017
36. Zeiler, M.D., Fergus, R.: Visualizing and understanding convolutional networks. In: Fleet, D., Pajdla, T., Schiele, B., Tuytelaars, T. (eds.) ECCV 2014. LNCS, vol. 8689, pp. 818–833. Springer, Cham (2014). https://doi.org/10.1007/978-3-319-10590-1_53
37. Zhang, K., Zhang, Z., Li, Z., Qiao, Y.: Joint face detection and alignment using multitask cascaded convolutional networks. IEEE Signal Process. Lett. 23(10), 1499–1503 (2016)

Fast and Accurate Intrinsic Symmetry Detection

Rajendra Nagar$^{(\boxtimes)}$ and Shanmuganathan Raman

Electrical Engineering, Indian Institute of Technology Gandhinagar,
Gandhinagar, India
{rajendra.nagar,shanmuga}@iitgn.ac.in

Abstract. In computer vision and graphics, various types of symmetries
are extensively studied since symmetry present in objects is a fundamental cue for understanding the shape and the structure of objects. In
this work, we detect the intrinsic reflective symmetry in triangle meshes
where we have to find the intrinsically symmetric point for each point of
the shape. We establish correspondences between functions defined on
the shapes by extending the functional map framework and then recover
the point-to-point correspondences. Previous approaches using the functional map for this task find the functional correspondences matrix by
solving a non-linear optimization problem which makes them slow. In this
work, we propose a closed form solution for this matrix which makes our
approach faster. We find the closed-form solution based on our following
results. If the given shape is intrinsically symmetric, then the shortest
length geodesic between two intrinsically symmetric points is also intrinsically symmetric. If an eigenfunction of the Laplace-Beltrami operator
for the given shape is an even (odd) function, then its restriction on the
shortest length geodesic between two intrinsically symmetric points is
also an even (odd) function. The sign of a low-frequency eigenfunction
is the same on the neighboring points. Our method is invariant to the
ordering of the eigenfunctions and has the least time complexity. We
achieve the best performance on the SCAPE dataset and comparable
performance with the state-of-the-art methods on the TOSCA dataset.

Keywords: Intrinsic symmetry · Functional map · Eigenfunction

1 Introduction

The importance of various types of symmetry is evident while solving problems such as shape segmentation, mesh repairing, shape matching, retrieving
the normal forms of 3D models [12,30,60], inverse procedural modeling [31],
shape recognition [14], shape understanding [34], shape completion [47,49], and

---

Electronic supplementary material The online version of this chapter (https://
doi.org/10.1007/978-3-030-01246-5_26) contains supplementary material, which is
available to authorized users.

© Springer Nature Switzerland AG 2018
V. Ferrari et al. (Eds.): ECCV 2018, LNCS 11205, pp. 433–450, 2018.
https://doi.org/10.1007/978-3-030-01246-5_26

shape editing [10,15,20,33,54,55]. The problem of detecting intrinsic symmetry is shown to be an NP-hard problem since it amounts to finding an intrinsically symmetric point for each point [37]. However, correspondences between the intrinsically symmetric points completely characterize the intrinsic symmetry of a shape since the intrinsic symmetry is a non-rigid transformation which can not be represented a matrix as opposed to the extrinsic symmetry which can be represented by a matrix [16]. We exploit the functional map approach that finds correspondences between functions instead of points [36]. Then, the point-to-point correspondences can be recovered in $O(n \log(n))$, where n is the number of vertices. We extend this framework for the detection of intrinsic symmetry. The functional map framework has already been used for detecting intrinsic symmetry in previous works [24,52]. The main task in these approaches was to determine the functional correspondence matrix which transforms a function to its intrinsic image. Various constraints have been enforced on this matrix. It is not known yet, how many constraints are sufficient. Further, they solved a non-linear optimization problem to estimate the functional correspondence matrix which makes the method slow. For the intrinsic symmetry detection problem, we show that the functional correspondences matrix is a diagonal matrix and a diagonal entry is $+1$ (-1), if the corresponding eigenfunction is an even (odd) function. This closed-form solution makes our method faster.

We determine if a particular eigenfunction is even or odd based on our following result. An eigenfunction is an even (odd) function if its restriction to the shortest length geodesic between two intrinsically symmetric points is an even (odd) function. Therefore, we need to find a few accurate pairs of intrinsically symmetric points which we find using our following results. If we directly pair points based on the similarity between their heat kernel signatures [48], we may get false pairs. For example, a pair of points on the tip of the index finger and the tip of the ring finger of the same hand of a human model. The reason is that, if two neighboring points are subjected to the same strength heat sources, then their heat diffusion processes will also be similar because of the very small sizes of the fingers with respect to the body size. However, we observer that the sign of a low-frequency eigenfunction on the neighboring points is the same. Hence, we put high penalty for pairing two points if signs of first few low-frequency eigenfunctions are the same for both the points. The models of the benchmark datasets are obtained by applying an imperfect isometry, so the theory only holds approximately. Furthermore, some of the triangles may not be Delaunay triangles. Therefore, we may not get accurate correspondences using the original eigenfunctions. Hence, we transform the original eigenfunctions to make them near perfect even or odd functions. Following are our main contributions.

1. We propose a novel approach to find a few accurate pairs of intrinsically symmetric points based on the following property of eigenfunctions: the signs of low-frequency eigenfunction on neighboring points are the same.
2. We propose a novel and efficient approach for finding the functional correspondence matrix. We prove that the functional matrix for the intrinsic symmetry

detection problem is a diagonal matrix and a diagonal entry is +1 (−1) if the corresponding eigenfunction is an even (odd) function.

3. We propose a novel approach to determine the sign of an eigenfunction by showing that, if a manifold contains intrinsic symmetry and an eigenfunction is an even (odd) function, then its restriction to the shortest length geodesic between any two intrinsically symmetric points is an even (odd) function.

4. We transform the eigenfunctions to make them more invariant to self-isometry.

2   Related Works

Reflective symmetry detection methods are categorized by the types of the input data and the reflective symmetry present in the input data. The input data can be a digital image, point cloud, triangle mesh, etc. The main types of reflective symmetries are extrinsic and intrinsic. The well known methods for detecting the extrinsic symmetry are [21,26,28,29,40,45–47,51] and for detecting the intrinsic symmetry are [5,6,13,17,18,22,27,37,38,41,41,42,44,45,53,56,58,60]. Furthermore, the intrinsic symmetry can be characterized as global and partial intrinsic symmetry. Our method finds global and partial intrinsic symmetry in triangle meshes. We discuss only the relevant works and suggest the readers to follow the excellent state-of-the-art report in [32] and the survey in [25].

Ovsjanikov et al. detected intrinsic symmetry using the global point signature (GPS) [37]. The main claim was that the GPS embedding transforms the problem from intrinsic to extrinsic symmetry detection. They showed that the GPS embedding was robust to the topological noises. They found pairs of symmetric points by comparing the GPS of one point to the signed-GPS of the other point. The time complexity of determining the sign (even or odd) of an eigenfunction is $O(n \log(n))$ since they compared GPSs of all the possible pairs. Furthermore, the time complexity of the overall method is $O(k^3 n \log(n))$ excluding the computation of eigenfunctions, where k is the number of eigenfunctions used. We propose a more efficient method which takes $(O(kn \log(n)))$ for detecting intrinsic symmetry. Furthermore, we observe that the approach by [37] is sensitive to the sign flip and eigenfunction ordering. Whereas, our method is independent of sign flip and ordering since we determine the sign of each eigenfunction independently from the others. Mitra et al. used a voting based approach to detect intrinsic symmetry and then applied transformation in the voting space to deform the input model to have perfect extrinsic symmetry [30]. Xu et al. used a generalized voting scheme to find the partial intrinsic symmetry curve without explicitly finding the intrinsically symmetric point for each point [57]. Xu et al. efficiently found pairs of intrinsically symmetric points using a voting based approach [56]. They factored out symmetry based on the scale of symmetry. However, they needed to tune a parameter depending on how much the input shape is distorted [56]. The methods by Zheng et al. [13,60] also used voting approach. These voting based methods do not utilize spatial coherency. Therefore, they may produce pairs of intrinsically symmetric points which may not be spatially continuous. Furthermore, they may have high complexity due to a large number of possible pairs for the voting.

In [41], the authors proposed a non-convex optimization framework to accurately detect full and partial symmetries of 3D models. However, the initialization severely affects the performance, and the complexity also is very high. Lipman *et al.* efficiently found the pairs of intrinsically symmetric points in point clouds and triangle meshes using the novel symmetry factored embedding technique [23]. However, their main bottleneck is the time complexity which is $O(n^{2.5} \log(n))$. Kim *et al.* used anti-Möbius transformation to accurately find intrinsically symmetric pairs of points [16]. They first find a sparse set of pairs of intrinsically symmetric points. Then, they transform intrinsic symmetry into extrinsic symmetry using the Möbius transform. However, they required $O(n^2)$ space for mid-edge flattening and $O(|\mathcal{S}|^4)$ for finding the anti-Möbius transformation, where $\mathcal{S}$ is the set of symmetry invariant points. Furthermore, false pairs in the first step may severely affect the overall performance.

3   Intrinsic Symmetry Detection

3.1   Background

Let $\mathcal{M}$ be a compact and connected 2-manifold representing the input shape. Let $L^2(\mathcal{M}) = \{f : \mathcal{M} \to \mathbb{R} | \langle f, f \rangle_{\mathcal{M}} = \int_{\mathcal{M}} f^2(x)dx < \infty\}$ be the space of square integrable functions defined on $\mathcal{M}$. The Laplace-Beltrami operator on a shape $\mathcal{M}$ is defined as $\Delta_{\mathcal{M}} f = -\text{div}_{\mathcal{M}}(\nabla_{\mathcal{M}} f)$ and admits an eigenvalue decomposition $\Delta_{\mathcal{M}} \phi_i(x) = \lambda_i \phi_i(x), \forall x \in \mathcal{M}$. Here, $0 = \lambda_1 \leq \lambda_2 \leq \dots$ are the eigenvalues and $\phi_1, \phi_2, \dots$ are the corresponding eigenfunctions. The eigenfunctions $\phi_1, \phi_2, \dots$ form a basis for the space $L^2(\mathcal{M})$. Therefore, any function $f \in L^2(\mathcal{M})$ can be represented as $f(x) = \sum_{i=1}^{\infty} \langle f, \phi_i \rangle_{\mathcal{M}} \phi_i(x), \forall x \in \mathcal{M}$. The functional map framework was first proposed in [36] for establishing point-to-point dense correspondence between two isometric shapes. The main idea was to establish correspondences between the functions, defined on the shapes, rather than the points. This idea reduced the time complexity to $O(n \log n)$. Let $\mathcal{M}$ and $\mathcal{N}$ be two shapes. Let $T_f : L^2(\mathcal{N}) \to L^2(\mathcal{M})$ be a linear mapping between functions defined on these shapes. That is, if $g : \mathcal{N} \to \mathbb{R}$ and $f : \mathcal{M} \to \mathbb{R}$ are two corresponding functions then $T_f(g) = f$. The mapping T_f is represented by a matrix $\mathbf{C} \in \mathbb{R}^{k \times k}$ such that $\mathbf{b} = \mathbf{Ca}$, where $\mathbf{a} = \begin{bmatrix} a_1 & a_2 & \dots & a_k \end{bmatrix}^{\top}$ and $\mathbf{b} = \begin{bmatrix} b_1 & b_2 & \dots & b_k \end{bmatrix}^{\top}$ are the representations of the functions g and f in the truncated bases $\{\phi_i^{\mathcal{N}}\}_{i=1}^{k}$ and $\{\phi_i^{\mathcal{M}}\}_{i=1}^{k}$, respectively. Therefore, the main goal is to find the matrix $\mathbf{C}$ which completely characterizes the dense correspondence between the two shapes.

3.2   Functional Maps for Intrinsic Symmetry Detection

We extend the functional map framework for detecting the intrinsic symmetry which can be thought of as a shape correspondence problem where we have to find the correspondences between the points of the same shape rather than the points on the two different shapes. The functional map framework is applicable for two isometric shapes also. Therefore, we can use it to detect the intrinsic symmetry since a symmetric shape is a self-isometric shape [37]. The intrinsic symmetry $T_{\mathrm{p}} : \mathcal{M} \to \mathcal{M}$ of $\mathcal{M}$ is defined as follows. If the points $x \in \mathcal{M}$ and $y \in \mathcal{M}$ are intrinsically symmetric, then $T_{\mathrm{p}}(x) = y$ and $T_{\mathrm{p}}(y) = x$. We first find the mapping between the functions and then use it to find the correspondences between the intrinsically symmetric points. Let us consider the space $L^2(\mathcal{M})$ and let $T : L^2(\mathcal{M}) \to L^2(\mathcal{M})$ be a functional map which maps the functions defined on the same shape. Then, this functional map T completely characterizes the intrinsic symmetry T_{p} if $T(g) = f$ and $T(f) = g$, where $f, g \in L^2(\mathcal{M})$ are intrinsically symmetric functions, i.e. $f \circ T_{\mathrm{p}}(x) = g(x)$, $g \circ T_{\mathrm{p}}(x) = f(x), \forall x \in \mathcal{M}$. Therefore, our goal is to find the matrix $\mathbf{C}$ which characterizes the functional mapping T for the intrinsic symmetry detection problem. For the problem of finding correspondences between two shapes, various constraints have been imposed on the matrix $\mathbf{C}$. Then, the matrix $\mathbf{C}$ was the optimal solution of an optimization problem. However, we show that a closed form solution exists for the matrix $\mathbf{C}$ for the problem of detecting the intrinsic symmetry, which we state as follows.

Theorem 1. *Let $T : L^2(\mathcal{M}) \to L^2(\mathcal{M})$ be a mapping between the functions defined on a shape $\mathcal{M}$ and T characterizes the intrinsic symmetry T_p of $\mathcal{M}$, i.e. $T(g) = f, T(f) = g$, $\forall f, g \in L^2(\mathcal{M})$ such that $f \circ T_p(x) = g(x)$, $g \circ T_p(x) = f(x), \forall x \in \mathcal{M}$. Then, the matrix $\mathbf{C}$ representing T is a diagonal matrix. $\mathbf{C}_{i,i} = +1$, if $\langle T(\phi_i), \phi_i \rangle_{\mathcal{M}} = +1$, and $\mathbf{C}_{i,i} = -1$, if $\langle T(\phi_i), \phi_i \rangle_{\mathcal{M}} = -1$.*

Proof. The functions f, g belong to the space $L^2(\mathcal{M})$. We can represent f and g as $f(x) = \sum_{i=1}^{\infty} b_i \phi_i(x)$ and $g(x) = \sum_{i=1}^{\infty} a_i \phi_i(x)$. Since T is a linear mapping, we have $T(f) = T\left(\sum_{i=1}^{\infty} b_i \phi_i(x)\right) = \sum_{i=1}^{\infty} b_i T(\phi_i(x))$. Since $T(\phi_i(x))$ is also a function in the space $L^2(\mathcal{M})$, it can be represented in the basis $\{\phi_i\}_{i=1}^{\infty}$ as $T(\phi_i(x)) = \sum_{j=1}^{\infty} c_{ij} \phi_j(x)$, where $c_{ij} = \langle T(\phi_i), \phi_j \rangle_{\mathcal{M}}$. Therefore, we have that $T(f) = \sum_{j=1}^{\infty} \sum_{i=1}^{\infty} c_{ij} b_i \phi_j(x)$. Since $T(f) = g$, it follows that $\sum_{j=1}^{\infty} \sum_{i=1}^{\infty} c_{ij} b_i \phi_j(x) = \sum_{j=1}^{\infty} a_j \phi_j(x)$. Therefore, $a_j = \sum_{i=1}^{\infty} c_{ij} b_i$. Equivalently, we can write it as $\mathbf{a} = \mathbf{C}\mathbf{b}$, where $\mathbf{C}_{i,j} = c_{ij} = \langle T(\phi_i), \phi_j \rangle_{\mathcal{M}}$. According to [37], the eigenfunctions (corresponding to the non-repeating eigenvalues) are self-isometry invariant with sign ambiguity i.e. $\phi_i \circ T_{\mathrm{p}}(x) = \pm \phi_i(x)$, $\forall x \in \mathcal{M}$. Furthermore, the functional map T completely characterizes the intrinsic symmetry. Therefore, $T(\phi_i) = +\phi_i$, if $\phi_i \circ T_{\mathrm{p}}(x) = \phi_i(x)$, and $T(\phi_i) = -\phi_i$, if $\phi_i \circ T_{\mathrm{p}}(x) = -\phi_i(x), \forall x \in \mathcal{M}$. Since the eigenfunctions $\phi_1, \phi_2, \ldots$ form an orthogonal basis for the space $L^2(\mathcal{M})$, we have that $\langle \pm \phi_i, \phi_j \rangle_{\mathcal{M}} = 0$ if $i \neq j$. Therefore, $\mathbf{C}_{i,j} = \langle T(\phi_i), \phi_j \rangle_{\mathcal{M}} = \langle \pm \phi_i, \phi_j \rangle_{\mathcal{M}}$. Therefore, $\mathbf{C}_{i,j} = 0$, if $i \neq j$. Hence, the matrix $\mathbf{C}$ is a diagonal matrix. Furthermore, $\mathbf{C}_{i,i} = +1$, if $\langle T(\phi_i), \phi_i \rangle_{\mathcal{M}} = +1$, and $\mathbf{C}_{i,i} = -1$, if $\langle T(\phi_i), \phi_i \rangle_{\mathcal{M}} = -1$. □

Therefore, the problem of determining whether $\mathbf{C}_{i,i} = +1$ or $\mathbf{C}_{i,i} = -1$ is equivalent to determining whether $\phi_i \circ T_{\mathrm{p}}(x) = +\phi_i(x)$ or $\phi_i \circ T_{\mathrm{p}}(x) = -\phi_i(x)$, $\forall x \in \mathcal{M}$. It is observed that if $\phi_i \circ T_{\mathrm{p}} = +\phi_i$ then ϕ_i is a symmetric or an even function and if $\phi_i \circ T_{\mathrm{p}} = -\phi_i$, then ϕ_i is an anti-symmetric or an odd function in the intrinsic sense. We can not apply the definition of the vector space here, since the domain of the eigenfunctions is not a vector space. A function $f : \mathbb{R}^2 \to \mathbb{R}$ is an even function, if $f(-\mathbf{x}) = f(\mathbf{x}), \forall \mathbf{x} \in \mathbb{R}^2$. This definition is not valid for the functions defined on the manifolds, since if $x \in \mathcal{M}$, then it may not always be true that $-x \in \mathcal{M}$. However, we generalize the following property of vector spaces to the manifolds to determine the sign of eigenfunctions. Let $f : \mathbb{R}^2 \to \mathbb{R}$ be a function symmetric on $\mathbb{R}^2$ and $\ell = \{\mathbf{x} : \mathbf{x} = t\mathbf{x}_1 + (1 - t)\mathbf{x}_2, t \in [0,1]\}$ be the line segment joining the mirror symmetric points $\mathbf{x}_1$ and $\mathbf{x}_2$. Then, it is trivial to show that the restriction $f_\ell : \ell \to \mathbb{R}$ of the function f on the set ℓ is also symmetric. Here, we also observe that the set $\mathbb{R}^2$ is symmetric about any of its coordinate axes and the set ℓ is also symmetric. We formally generalize these results on manifolds as follows.

Theorem 2. *Let $\mathcal{M}$ be a compact and connected 2-manifold. Let there exist a self-isometry $T_p : \mathcal{M} \to \mathcal{M}$ on $\mathcal{M}$. Let $x, y \in \mathcal{M}$ be two points which are intrinsically symmetric, i.e., $T_p(x) = y$ and $T_p(y) = x$. Let $\gamma(t) : [0,1] \to \mathcal{M}$ be the shortest length geodesic curve between the points x and y such that $\gamma(0) = x$ and $\gamma(1) = y$. Then, $T_p(\gamma(t)) = \gamma(1 - t)$ and $T_p(\gamma(1 - t)) = \gamma(t), \forall t \in [0,1]$.*

Proof. Let $\beta(t) = T_\mathrm{p}(\gamma(t))$. We have to show that $\beta(t) = \gamma(1 - t)$. Since T_p is an isometry, according to (Proposition 16.3, [11], Chap. 3, p. 91 [35]) T_p maps a shortest length geodesic on $\mathcal{M}$ to a shortest length geodesic on $\mathcal{M}$. Therefore, $\beta(t)$ is also a shortest length geodesic. Now, we have $\beta(0) = T_\mathrm{p}(\gamma(0)) = T_\mathrm{p}(x) = y$ and $\beta(1) = T_\mathrm{p}(\gamma(1)) = T_\mathrm{p}(y) = x$. Therefore, $\beta(t)$ is the shortest length geodesic between the points x and y such that $\beta(0) = y$ and $\beta(1) = x$. Since there can only be a single shortest length geodesic curve between two points (except continuous symmetry, like sphere), both the geodesics $\gamma(t)$ and $\beta(t)$ trace the same path. However, their start and end points are flipped. Therefore, $\beta(t) = \gamma(1 - t) \Rightarrow T_\mathrm{p}(\gamma(t)) = \gamma(1 - t)$. Since the self-isometry is an involution, i.e. $T_\mathrm{p} \circ T_\mathrm{p}(x) = x, \forall x \in \mathcal{M}$, we have $\gamma(t) = T_\mathrm{p} \circ T_\mathrm{p}(\gamma(t)) = T_\mathrm{p}(T_\mathrm{p}(\gamma(t))) = T_\mathrm{p}(\gamma(1 - t)) \Rightarrow T_\mathrm{p}(\gamma(1 - t)) = \gamma(t)$. $\square$

The intuitive is that if a shape is intrinsically symmetric, then the shortest length geodesic curve between any two intrinsically symmetric points is also intrinsically symmetric. This result helps us to determine the sign of the eigenfunctions of the Laplace-Beltrami operator. First, we show that the result $\phi_i \circ T_p(x) = \pm\phi_i(x) \ \forall x \in \mathcal{M}$ holds true if we restrict the eigenfunctions on the shortest length geodesic curve between the intrinsically symmetric points. The restriction of ϕ_i on a curve $\gamma(t)$ is defined as $\phi_i \circ \gamma(t) : [0,1] \to \mathbb{R}$. Since, $\phi_i \circ T_\mathrm{p} = \pm\phi_i, \forall i$ such that i-th eigenvalue is non repeating, each eigenfunction is always either an even (sign= $+1$) or an odd (sign= -1) function. Hence, if restriction of the eigenfunction ϕ_i on the shortest length geodesic between the intrinsically symmetric points has sign $+1$ (-1), then the sign of ϕ_i is also $+1$ (-1).

Proposition 1. *Let $x, y \in \mathcal{M}$ be two intrinsically symmetric points and $\gamma(t) : [0,1] \to \mathcal{M}$ be the shortest length geodesic curve between the points x and y. Then, $\phi_i \circ \gamma(t) = \pm\phi_i \circ \gamma(1 - t), \forall t \in [0,1]$.*

Proof. Using Theorem 2, we proceed as $\phi_i(\gamma(t)) = \phi_i(T_p(\gamma(1-t))) = (\phi_i \circ T_p)(\gamma(1-t))$. We know that $\phi_i \circ T_p = \pm\phi_i$. Hence, $\phi_i(\gamma(t)) = \pm\phi_i(\gamma(1-t))$. $\square$

We apply the above result to find whether an eigenfunction is even or odd as follows. We first determine a set of candidate pairs of intrinsically symmetric points. Then we find the shortest length geodesic curve between each pair. Then, for each eigenfunction ϕ_i, we determine if the restricted eigenfunction $\phi_i \circ \gamma(t)$ is an even or an odd function for each pair.

3.3   Computation of Eigenfunction of Laplace-Beltrami Operator

Let $\mathcal{T} = (\mathcal{V}, \mathcal{F}, \mathcal{E})$ be a triangle mesh, where $\mathcal{V}$ is the set of n vertices, $\mathcal{F}$ is the set of faces, and $\mathcal{E}$ is the set of edges. We follow the method in [39] to find the eigenvalues and the corresponding eigenvectors of the Laplace-Beltrami operator in the discrete settings. The discrete Laplace-Beltrami operator is defined by the matrix $\mathbf{L} = -\mathbf{A}^{-1}\mathbf{M}$. Both $\mathbf{M}$ and $\mathbf{A}$ are of size $n \times n$ and are defined as follows.

$$\mathbf{M}_{j,j'} = \begin{cases} \frac{\cot(\alpha_{jj'}) + \cot(\beta_{jj'})}{2} & \text{if } (j,j') \in \mathcal{E} \\ -\sum_{j'' \neq j} \mathbf{M}_{j,j''} & \text{if } j = j' \\ 0 & \text{if } (j,j') \notin \mathcal{E}, \end{cases}$$

$\mathbf{A} = \text{diag}(a_1, a_2, \ldots, a_n)$, and, $a_j = \frac{1}{3}\sum_{j', j'':(j,j',j'') \in \mathcal{F}} a_{jj'j''}$ (the area of the shaded region in the inset figure). Here, $a_{jj'j''}$ is the area of the face (j, j', j''). In the discrete settings, we denote eigenfunctions by $\phi_i, i \in [k]$, and are the solutions of the generalized eigen-problem $\mathbf{M}\phi_i = -\lambda_i\mathbf{A}\phi_i$. Here, $[k] = \{1, 2, \ldots, k\}$. We denote the value of ϕ_i at the j-th point or vertex by $\phi_i(x_j)$.

3.4   Detecting Pairs of Intrinsically Symmetric Points

In order to detect the intrinsic symmetry, according to Theorem 1, we need to find the matrix $\mathbf{C}$ defined as $\mathbf{C}_{i,i'} = 0$, if $i \neq i'$, $\mathbf{C}_{i,i} = +1$, if ϕ_i is an even function, and $\mathbf{C}_{i,i} = -1$, if ϕ_i is an odd function. According to Proposition 1, the eigenfunction ϕ_i is an even function (odd) if its restriction on the shortest length geodesic between intrinsically symmetric points is also an even function (odd). Therefore, our first task is to find a few accurate candidate pairs of intrinsically symmetric points.

We find the heat kernel signature (HKS) feature points [48] on the given mesh $\mathcal{T}$. HKS feature points are the local maxima of the function $\sum_{i=1}^k e^{-\lambda_i t_h}\phi_i^2(x_j)$ defined on the shape $\mathcal{T}$ for all vertices $x_j, j \in [n]$. We use $k = 13$ for our experiments. Let $\{x_j\}_{j \in \mathcal{I}}$ be the set of HKS feature points, where, $\mathcal{I} \subset [n]$, and $|\mathcal{I}| = d$. We set $t_h = \frac{4\ln 10}{\lambda_2}$ as defined in [48]. To find the pairs of intrinsically symmetric points, we do not directly match the HKS descriptors. The reason is that this strategy may fail very frequently. In Fig. 1(a), we show the detected HKS feature points and the pairs detected by direct matching of their HKS descriptors on the Kids model [9]. In Fig. 1(b), we show the zoomed

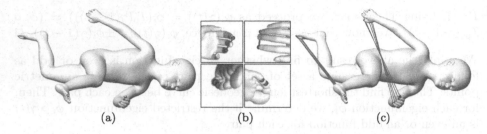

(a)   (b)   (c)

Fig. 1. Direct HKS matching vs. restricted HKS matching. (a)–(b) Pairs of intrinsically symmetric points using HKS similarity. It suffers from the fact that if two neighboring points are subjected to a same strength heat source, then their heat diffusions will be similar. (c) Pairs obtained by restricted HKS matching. We observe that the sign of low frequency eigenfunctions on two neighboring points is the same. Therefore, we assign a high cost for pairing two points having the same vectors of signs of eigenfunctions.

pairs of symmetric points on the feet and the hands for better visualization. We observe that the tips of two fingers of the same hand got paired. The reason behind getting such matches is that if two neighboring points are subjected to a same strength heat source, then their heat diffusion processes will be similar. Therefore, their HKS descriptors will be similar. Hence, we have to assign a high cost for pairing two neighboring points. Furthermore, determining if two points are neighbors requires us to find the geodesic distance between each possible pair. This can be a costly process since there can be a large number of possible pairs. We propose a fast approach to determine if two points are neighbors based on the following observation.

Observation 1. *Let x_j and $x_{j'}$ be any two neighboring points in $\mathcal{T}$. Then, $\mathbf{s}_j = \mathbf{s}_{j'}$ for low frequency eigenfunctions, i.e., for small k.*

Here, $\mathbf{s}_j$ and $\mathbf{s}_{j'}$ are the j-th and j'-th columns of the matrix $\mathbf{S} = \begin{bmatrix} \mathbf{s}_1 \ \mathbf{s}_2 \ \ldots \ \mathbf{s}_d \end{bmatrix} \in \{-1, +1\}^{k \times d}$. The i-th element of the vector $\mathbf{s}_j$ is the sign of the i-th eigenfunction on the j-th point of the set $\{x_j\}_{j \in \mathcal{I}}$. We give an intuitive understanding of this observation based on the nodal domains of the eigenfunctions. The nodal set of the eigenfunction ϕ_i is the set $\mathcal{B}_i = \{x \in \mathcal{M} : \phi_i(x) = 0\}$. A nodal domain is a component in the set $\mathcal{M} \backslash \mathcal{B}_i$. The set $\mathcal{M} \backslash \mathcal{B}_i$ is the collection of components or segments on the shape which are separated by the set $\mathcal{B}_i$. The value of the eigenfunction ϕ_i in any of its nodal domain is either positive or negative [43,59]. Therefore, if two points lie in the same nodal domain, then the eigenfunction ϕ_i will have the same sign on both the points. Now, the neighborliness of two points depends on the size or the area of the nodal domain. According to the Courant's nodal domain theorem, the number of nodal domains of ϕ_i is less than i [59]. Therefore, the size of the nodal domains remains significantly large for low frequency eigenfunctions. Hence, neighboring points remain in the same nodal domain for all the low frequency eigenfunctions. Therefore, the sign of all low frequency eigenfunctions remains the same on neighboring points.

We choose eigenfunctions corresponding to the first 13 lowest eigenvalues and corresponding eigenvectors for our experiment.

Hence, we assign a high cost for pairing the points x_j and $x_{j'}$, if their sign vectors $\mathbf{s}_j$ and $\mathbf{s}_{j'}$ are the same. Let $\mathbf{H} = \begin{bmatrix} \mathbf{h}_1 \ \mathbf{h}_2 \ \dots \ \mathbf{h}_d \end{bmatrix} \in \mathbb{R}^{h \times d}$ be the heat kernel signatures matrix of the detected d HKS feature points, where we choose $h = 50$ steps. We define the affinity matrix $\mathbf{W} \in \mathbb{R}^{d \times d}$ such that $\mathbf{W}_{j,j'} = \|\mathbf{h}_j - \mathbf{h}_{j'}\|_2 + q\psi(\|\mathbf{s}_j - \mathbf{s}_{j'}\|_2), \forall (j, j') \in [d] \times [d], j \neq j'$ and $\mathbf{W}_{j,j} = q, \forall j \in [d]$. Here $\psi(t) = 0$, if $t > 0$ and $\psi(t) = 1$, if $t = 0$, and q is any large positive constant. We now pair these points such that if $x_{j'}$ is intrinsically symmetric point of the point x_j, then x_j should be the intrinsically symmetric point of the point $x_{j'}$. We achieve this by representing the matching by a matrix $\mathbf{\Pi} \in \{0, 1\}^{d \times d}$, where $\mathbf{\Pi}_{j,j'} = 1$ and $\mathbf{\Pi}_{j',j} = 1$, if the points x_j and $x_{j'}$ form a pair and 0, otherwise. Now, we enforce the constraints $\mathbf{\Pi}\mathbf{1} = \mathbf{1}$ and $\mathbf{\Pi}^\top\mathbf{1} = \mathbf{1}$ to achieve one-to-one matching, where $\mathbf{1}$ is a vector of size d with all elements equal to 1. We get many points which can not be paired. Therefore, we cap the number of pairs by c which we represent by the constraint $\mathbf{1}^\top\mathbf{\Pi}\mathbf{1} = 2c$. Further, to make it feasible, we modify the one-to-one matching constraints to $\mathbf{\Pi}\mathbf{1} \leq \mathbf{1}$ and $\mathbf{\Pi}^\top\mathbf{1} \leq \mathbf{1}$. Now, we frame the problem of pairing the points in the below optimization problem.

$$\min_{\mathbf{\Pi} \in \{0,1\}^{d \times d}} \sum_{j=1}^{d} \sum_{j'=1}^{d} \mathbf{\Pi}_{j,j'} \mathbf{W}_{j,j'}, \text{ subject to } \mathbf{\Pi}\mathbf{1} \leq \mathbf{1}, \ \mathbf{\Pi}^\top\mathbf{1} \leq \mathbf{1}, \ \mathbf{1}^\top\mathbf{\Pi}\mathbf{1} = 2c. \quad (1)$$

We note that, problem (1) is equivalent to the below linear assignment problem.

$$\min_{\boldsymbol{\pi} \in \{0,1\}^{d^2 \times 1}} \text{vec}(\mathbf{W})^\top \boldsymbol{\pi}, \text{ subject to } \mathbf{C}_1\boldsymbol{\pi} \leq \mathbf{1}, \ \mathbf{C}_2\boldsymbol{\pi} \leq \mathbf{1}, \ \mathbf{c}_3^\top\boldsymbol{\pi} = 2c. \quad (2)$$

Here, the vector $\boldsymbol{\pi} = \text{vec}(\mathbf{\Pi})$, $\mathbf{C}_2 = \mathbf{1}^\top \otimes \mathbf{I}$, $\mathbf{c}_3$ is the vector of size $d^2 \times 1$ with all elements equal to 1, and $\mathbf{I}$ is the identity matrix of size $d \times d$. The matrix $\mathbf{C}_1$ is $d \times d^2$ matrix and defined such that the j-th row is the circular shift, by jd elements on the right, of the row vector of size $1 \times d^2$ with the first d elements equal to 1 and the last $d^2 - d$ elements equal to 0. The time complexity of this problem is exponential in the number of variables. However, the size of our problem is very small. In all our experiments $d \leq 25$. We use the MATLAB function `intlinprog` to solve this problem which takes $\approx 0.03\,\text{s}$.

3.5 Determining the Sign of Eigenfunctions

Proposition 1 states that the eigenfunction ϕ_i is an even (odd) function, if its restriction $\phi_i \circ \gamma_j(t) : [0, 1] \to \mathbb{R}$ on the shortest length geodesic $\gamma_j(t)$ between any two intrinsically symmetric points x_j and $x_{j'}$ is an even (odd) function. Let $\{(x_j, x_{j'})\}_{j=1}^{c}$, be the set of detected pairs of intrinsically symmetric points. We find the shortest length geodesic curve between two intrinsically symmetric points using [50] with approximate setting (Dijkstra's algorithm), since the exact geodesic curve may not pass through the vertices of the mesh which may require us to perform interpolation for calculating the values of $\phi_i \circ \gamma_j(t)$ for

$\gamma_j(t) \notin \mathcal{V}$. Let $\mathbf{p}_{ij}$ be the restriction (vector of size equal to the number of vertices in the geodesic) of the eigenfunction ϕ_i on the shortest length geodesic curve between the intrinsically symmetric points x_j and $x_{j'}$. Then, the sign s_i of eigenfunction ϕ_i is equal to $+1$, if $\sum_{j=1}^{c} \mathbf{p}_{ij}^{\top}\texttt{flip}(\mathbf{p}_{ij}) > 0$ and equal to -1, if $\sum_{j=1}^{c} \mathbf{p}_{ij}^{\top}\texttt{flip}(\mathbf{p}_{ij}) < 0$. We do not consider the eigenfunction ϕ_i if $\sum_{j=1}^{c} \mathbf{p}_{ij}^{\top}\texttt{flip}(\mathbf{p}_{ij}) = 0$. Equivalently, we define the diagonal entries of the functional correspondence matrix $\mathbf{C}$ as $\mathbf{C}_{i,i} = s_i$. In Fig. 2(a) and (c), we show the eigenfunctions ϕ_2 and ϕ_3, respectively, with the geodesic curves for two pairs of detected intrinsically symmetric points on a shape from Kids dataset [9]. In Fig. 2(b) and (d), we show the functions $\phi_i \circ \gamma_j(t)$ for $i = 2, 3$ and $j = 1, 2$. We observe that $\mathbf{C}_{2,2} = -1$ and $\mathbf{C}_{3,3} = +1$.

One can directly use the values of an eigenfunction on the intrinsically symmetric points to find the sign instead of checking it on the geodesic between these points. However, this approach could be sensitive to the noise. If the value of an eigenfunction at the feature point has changed due to noise, then the point-based method will fail. Whereas, it is less likely that due to the noise the value of an eigenfunction will be changed at all the points on the geodesic. Our geodesic based method will detect the sign correctly due to averaging of signs.

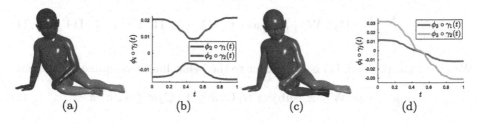

(a)   (b)   (c)   (d)

Fig. 2. (a)–(b): The eigenfunction ϕ_2 on the Kids model which is an even function and its restrictions $\phi_2 \circ \gamma_j(t)$, $j = 1, 2$, shown in red and blue colors (on hands and feet), which are also even functions. (c)–(d): The eigenfunction ϕ_3 on the Kids model which is an odd function and its restrictions $\phi_3 \circ \gamma_j(t)$, $j = 1, 2$, shown in purple and orange colors (on hands and feet), which are also odd functions. (Color figure online)

3.6   Correcting the Eigenfunctions

The models of the benchmark datasets are obtained by applying an imperfect isometry, so the theory only holds approximately. Furthermore, some of the triangles may not be Delaunay triangles and the eigenfunctions are sensitive to the change in the triangulation of the mesh. Therefore, all the eigenfunctions may not be perfectly even or odd which may give the erroneous symmetry detected in Sect. 3.7. Consider Fig. 3(a), where the eigenfunction ϕ_{10} is not perfectly even on the legs. We transform the eigenfunctions such that they preserve the pairs of intrinsically symmetric functions. We extend the framework in [19]. Let $\mathbf{\Phi} = [\phi_1\ \phi_2 \cdots \phi_k] \in \mathbb{R}^{n \times k}$, and $\mathbf{D} = \text{diag}(\lambda_1, \lambda_2, \ldots, \lambda_k) \in \mathbb{R}^{k \times k}$. Let $\mathbf{\Phi}\mathbf{R}$ be the transformed basis obtained by applying the linear operator $\mathbf{R}$ on the basis $\mathbf{\Phi}$. Then, we impose the constraints $\mathbf{R}^{\top}\mathbf{D}\mathbf{R} = \mathbf{D}$ and $\text{off}(\mathbf{R}^{\top}\mathbf{D}\mathbf{R}) = 0$ so that the new eigenfunctions admit to the original eigenfunction decomposition problem as proposed in [19], where $\text{off}(\mathbf{M}) = \sum_j \sum_{j':j'\neq j} \mathbf{M}_{j,j'}^2$ for any matrix $\mathbf{M}$.

Now, let $f_j, g_j : \mathcal{M} \to \mathbb{R}$ be two functions such that f_j and g_j are intrinsic images of each other. That is, $f_j \circ T_p(x) = g_j(x)$ and $g_j \circ T_p(x) = f_j(x)$ are equivalent. Let $\mathbf{f}_j \in \mathbb{R}^n$ and $\mathbf{g}_j \in \mathbb{R}^n$ be the discrete versions of f_j and g_j, respectively. Let $\mathbf{R}^\top \mathbf{\Phi}^\top \mathbf{f}_j$ and $\mathbf{R}^\top \mathbf{\Phi}^\top \mathbf{g}_j$ be the representations of the functions $\mathbf{f}_j$ and $\mathbf{g}_j$ in the transformed basis $\mathbf{\Phi R}$, respectively. We want the transformed basis $\mathbf{\Phi R}$ such that $\mathbf{R}^\top \mathbf{\Phi}^\top \mathbf{f}_j = \mathbf{C} \mathbf{R}^\top \mathbf{\Phi}^\top \mathbf{g}_j$. Let $\mathbf{F} = \begin{bmatrix} \mathbf{f}_1 \cdots \mathbf{f}_c \mid \mathbf{g}_1 \cdots \mathbf{g}_c \end{bmatrix} \in \mathbb{R}^{n \times 2c}$ and $\mathbf{G} = \begin{bmatrix} \mathbf{g}_1 \cdots \mathbf{g}_c \mid \mathbf{f}_1 \cdots \mathbf{f}_c \end{bmatrix} \in \mathbb{R}^{n \times 2c}$ be the matrices representing $2c$ (bidirectional) pairs of intrinsically symmetric functions. We formulate the below optimization framework to find the transformation matrix $\mathbf{R}$.

$$\min_{\mathbf{R}} \text{off}(\mathbf{R}^\top \mathbf{D R}) + \|\mathbf{R}^\top \mathbf{D R} - \mathbf{D}\|_F^2$$

$$\text{subject to } \mathbf{R}^\top \mathbf{\Phi}^\top \mathbf{F} = \mathbf{C} \mathbf{R}^\top \mathbf{\Phi}^\top \mathbf{G}, \ \mathbf{R}^\top \mathbf{R} = \mathbf{I}, \det(\mathbf{R}) = +1, \mathbf{R} \in \mathbb{R}^{k \times k}. \quad (3)$$

Here, $\mathbf{R}^\top \mathbf{R} = \mathbf{I}$ follows from the fact that the transformed basis $\mathbf{\Phi R}$ is an orthogonal basis. Here, the set $\{\mathbf{R} \in \mathbb{R}^{k \times k} : \mathbf{R}^\top \mathbf{R} = \mathbf{I}, \det(\mathbf{R}) = +1\}$ is the special orthogonal group $\mathcal{SO}(k)$. Hence, we solve the below optimization problem.

$$\min_{\mathbf{R} \in \mathcal{SO}(k)} \text{off}(\mathbf{R}^\top \mathbf{D R}) + \|\mathbf{R}^\top \mathbf{D R} - \mathbf{D}\|_F^2 + \mu \|\mathbf{R}^\top \mathbf{\Phi}^\top \mathbf{F} - \mathbf{C} \mathbf{R}^\top \mathbf{\Phi}^\top \mathbf{G}\|_F^2. \quad (4)$$

We use the Riemannian-trust-region method, proposed in [1,2], to solve this optimization problem. We use the `manopt` toolbox [7] for this purpose. We provide the Riemannian gradient and Hessian of this cost function in the supplementary material. We empirically found the optimal μ to be equal to 1 in our experiments. We choose the functions $\mathbf{f}_j$ and $\mathbf{g}_j$ such that, $\mathbf{f}_j = 1$ at the point x_j and 0 everywhere else, and $\mathbf{g}_j = 1$ at the point $x_{j'}$ and 0 everywhere else. Here, x_j and $x_{j'}$ are intrinsically symmetric points. In Fig. 3(a) and (b), we show the effect of correction on (ϕ_{10}). We observe that ϕ_{10}, which was not perfectly symmetric on the legs and the belly, becomes more symmetric. The large

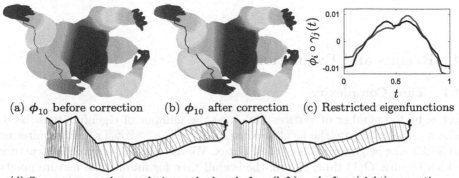

(a) ϕ_{10} before correction   (b) ϕ_{10} after correction   (c) Restricted eigenfunctions

(d) Symmetry on the geodesic on the legs before (left) and after (right) correction.

Fig. 3. Visualization of the eigenfunction correction.

blue patch on the belly also got moved to center which was more towards left before correction. Here, the value of eigenfunction is color encoded, more blue implies more negative and more yellow implies more positive. In Fig. 3(c), we show the restriction of ϕ_{10} on the geodesic between the two symmetric points which becomes more symmetric after the correction.

3.7   Dense Intrinsically Symmetric Correspondence

Let $\mathbf{f}_j$ be the function such that $\mathbf{f}_j = 1$ at x_j and 0 elsewhere. Similarly, let $\mathbf{g}_{j'}$ be the function such that $\mathbf{g}_{j'} = 1$ at $x_{j'}$ and 0 elsewhere. Let $\mathbf{R}^\top \mathbf{\Phi}^\top \mathbf{f}_j$ and $\mathbf{R}^\top \mathbf{\Phi}^\top \mathbf{g}_{j'}$ be their basis representation. Then, if the point x_j and $x_{j'}$ are intrinsically symmetric then $\mathbf{R}^\top \mathbf{\Phi}^\top \mathbf{f}_j = \mathbf{C}\mathbf{R}^\top \mathbf{\Phi}^\top \mathbf{g}_{j'}$. Which is equivalent to $\mathbf{R}^\top \mathbf{\Phi}^\top \mathbf{F} = \mathbf{C}\mathbf{R}^\top \mathbf{\Phi}^\top \mathbf{G}$ if we consider all points. Now, if $\mathbf{F}$ is equal to the identity matrix of size $n \times n$, then $\mathbf{G}_{j,j'} = 1$, if point x_j and $x_{j'}$ form a pair of intrinsically symmetric points, and 0 otherwise. Now following [36], the intrinsically symmetric point of x_j is the nearest neighbor of the j-th column of the matrix $\mathbf{R}^\top \mathbf{\Phi}^\top$ among the columns of the matrix $\mathbf{C}\mathbf{R}^\top \mathbf{\Phi}^\top$. The obtained correspondences are continuous as shown in [36]. Our method is invariant to the ordering of the eigenfunction since the sign of ϕ_i and $\mathbf{C}_{i,i}$ only depend on the eigenfunction ϕ_i. In Fig. 3(d), we show the detected symmetry on a geodesic on legs before and after correction.

Table 1. The total time for computing intrinsic symmetry for the methods MT [16], BIM[17], OFM [24], GRS [52], and the proposed approach on the SCAPE dataset [3].

	MT	BIM	OFM	GRS	Our
Time (min)	-	360	60	24	8

Table 2. The correspondence rates and mesh rates for the methods MT [16], BIM [17], OFM [24], GRS [52], and the proposed approach on the SCAPE dataset [3].

	MT	BIM	OFM	GRS	Our
Corr rate (%)	82.0	84.8	91.7	94.5	**97.5**
Mesh rate (%)	71.8	76.1	97.2	98.6	**100**

4   Results and Evaluation

4.1   Time Complexity

Let n be the number of vertices and k be the number of eigenfunctions used. The feature points are the local maximums of $\sum_{i=1}^{k} e^{-\lambda_i t_h} \phi_i^2(x_j)$. It requires us to find 2-ring neighborhoods of each vertex. We use the half-edge data structure which requires $O(1)$ time. Hence, the overall time for finding the feature points is $O(n)$. The optimization problem in Eq. (4) takes $O(nk^2)$ when solved using Riemannian trust region method. We use the ANN library [4] to find the nearest neighbor for each column of the matrix $\mathbf{R}^\top \mathbf{\Phi}^\top \in \mathbb{R}^{k \times n}$ among the columns of

Table 3. The correspondence rates and mesh rates for the methods MT [16], BIM [17], OFM [24], GRP [52], and the proposed approach on the TOSCA dataset [8].

	Corr rate (%)					Mesh Rate (%)				
	MT	BIM	OFM	GRS	Our	MT	BIM	OFM	GRS	Our
Cat	66.0	93.7	90.9	**96.5**	95.6	54.6	90.9	90.9	100	100
Centaur	92.0	**100**	96.0	92.0	**100**	100	100	100	100	100
David	82.0	**97.4**	94.8	92.5	**96.2**	57.1	100	100	100	100
Dog	91.0	**100**	93.2	97.4	**98.8**	88.9	100	88.9	100	100
Horse	92.0	97.1	95.2	**99.4**	97.3	100	100	87.5	100	100
Michael	87.0	**98.9**	94.6	91.4	**96.5**	75	100	100	100	100
Victoria	83.0	**98.3**	98.7	95.5	96.2	63.6	100	100	100	100
Wolf	100	100	100	**100**	**100**	100	100	100	100	100
Gorilla	-	98.9	98.9	**100**	**100**	-	100	100	100	100
Average	85.0	**98.0**	95.1	94.5	**97.8**	76	98.7	92.6	**100**	100

the matrix $\mathbf{CR}^{\top}\mathbf{\Phi}^{\top} \in \mathbb{R}^{k \times n}$ which takes time $O(kn\log(n))$. Hence, the time complexity is $O(kn\log(n)) + O(n) + O(nk^2) \approx O(kn\log(n))$, since $k << n$. In our experiments $k = 13$ (empirical) and $n \approx 15000$. The time complexity of computing the k smallest eigenvalues and corresponding eigenvectors of symmetric matrix is $O(n^2 k)$ which is common to all spectral decomposition based methods.

4.2   Comparison

Evaluation Metrics. We use the following evaluation metrics to compare the results of our method to that of the state-of-the-art methods as defined in [16]. **Correspondence rate**: Let $(x_j, x_{j'}^{\mathrm{g}})$ be the ground truth correspondence and $(x_j, x_{j'}^{\mathrm{e}})$ be the estimated correspondence, then the correspondence $(x_j, x_{j'}^{\mathrm{e}})$ is called true positive if the geodesic distance between the points $x_{j'}^{\mathrm{g}}$ and $x_{j'}^{\mathrm{e}}$ is less than $\sqrt{area(\mathcal{T})/20\pi}$ as used in [16]. The correspondence rate is the fraction of true positive correspondences in the total estimated correspondences. **Mesh rate**: The mesh rate is the fraction of shapes for which the correspondence rate is more than 75% in the total shapes as used in [16]. **Time Complexity**: Total time required for computing symmetry for each shape in the given dataset. **Datasets.** We evaluate our approach on the SCAPE [3] and TOSCA [8] datasets. The SCAPE dataset contains 71 models. Each model in SCAPE dataset contains 12500 vertices and 24998 faces. The TOSCA dataset contains 80 models. On an average 20 ground truth intrinsically symmetric correspondences provided for each model in the datasets SCAPE and TOSCA. In the Fig. 4, we show a few results of the proposed approach on both the datasets. We have only shown the sparsely detected correspondences for better visualization.

Comparison Methods. We compare the results of our approach on the datasets SCAPE and TOSCA with the four methods Möbius transformation

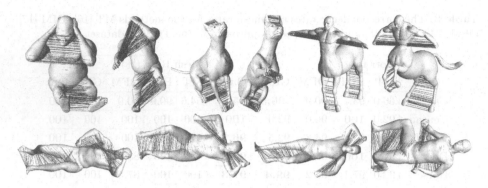

Fig. 4. Results of our approach on the TOSCA [8] (first row) and the SCAPE [3] (second row) datasets. Detected correspondences (sparse) are shown in blue color. Correspondences in red color are the ones detected in Sect. 3.4.

voting (MT) [16], Blended Intrinsic Maps (BIM) [17], Properly Constrained Orthogonal Functional Map (OFM) [24], and Group Representation of Symmetries (GRS) [52].

Discussions on the Comparison. In Table 1, we present the total time required for detecting the intrinsic symmetry in all the models of the TOSCA dataset for all the methods. We observe that our method is the fastest method on the TOSCA dataset. Our method takes around 6 s for each model whereas the method BIM takes around 270 s, the method OFM takes around 45 s, and the method GRS takes around 18 s. Our method takes 4.2 min to compute intrinsic symmetry in all the models of the SCAPE dataset. The possible reasons for our faster computation include finding the correspondence matrix using a closed form solution and determining the sign of eigenfunctions by computing the approximate shortest length geodesic curves between two intrinsically symmetric points. In Tables 2 and 3, we present the correspondence rate (Corr rate) and the mesh rate for all the methods for all the models of the SCAPE and the TOSCA datasets, respectively. The mesh rate for our method is equal to 100% and the correspondence rate is equal to 97.8% which is very close to the state-of-the-art correspondence rate 98% of the method [17]. However, the average computation time for each mesh is around 270 s for the method [17], whereas it is around 6 s for our method. We achieve the state-of-the-art performance on the SCAPE dataset.

Effect of Holes. In Fig. 5, we show the detected intrinsic symmetry in the partial model from the SHREC16 [9] dataset. Here, the partial shape is obtained by making holes in the original shape such that it contains 90% area of the main shape. We observe that our method is invariant to significant holes.

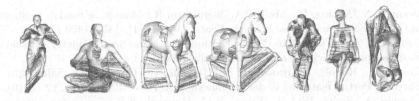

Fig. 5. Partial intrinsic symmetry detection results on the dataset SHREC16 [9].

5 Conclusions

We have presented a fast and an accurate algorithm for detecting intrinsic symmetry in triangle meshes. We showed that the functional correspondence matrix is diagonal and a diagonal entry is $+1$ (-1) if the corresponding eigenfunction is even (odd). We showed that the restriction of an even (odd) eigenfunction on the shortest length geodesic between any two intrinsically symmetric points also is an even (odd) function. This result has helped us to derive a closed form solution to find diagonal entries of this matrix. We achieved state-of-the-art performance on the SCAPE dataset and second best on the TOSCA dataset. We achieved the best time complexity. Furthermore, our approach is invariant to the ordering of eigenfunctions and robust to the presence of holes in the input mesh. Our method is limited to the intrinsic reflective symmetry. It can not find the other types of symmetries such as rotational symmetry. We would like to extend our approach to more general symmetries. Our approach may fail to detect intrinsic symmetry in non-connected manifolds. As future work, we would like to extend the functional map to detect intrinsic symmetries in non-connected manifolds.

Acknowledgment. R. Nagar was supported by the TCS research Scholarship.

References

1. Absil, P.A., Baker, C.G., Gallivan, K.A.: Trust-region methods on riemannian manifolds. Found. Comput. Math. **7**(3), 303–330 (2007)
2. Absil, P.A., Mahony, R., Sepulchre, R.: Optimization Algorithms on Matrix Manifolds. Princeton University Press, Princeton (2009)
3. Anguelov, D., Srinivasan, P., Koller, D., Thrun, S., Rodgers, J., Davis, J.: Scape: shape completion and animation of people. In: ACM Transactions on Graphics (TOG), vol. 24, pp. 408–416. ACM (2005)
4. Arya, S., Mount, D.M., Netanyahu, N.S., Silverman, R., Wu, A.Y.: An optimal algorithm for approximate nearest neighbor searching fixed dimensions. J. ACM (JACM) **45**(6), 891–923 (1998)
5. Berner, A., Bokeloh, M., Wand, M., Schilling, A., Seidel, H.P.: Generalized intrinsic symmetry detection (2009)
6. Berner, A., Wand, M., Mitra, N.J., Mewes, D., Seidel, H.P.: Shape analysis with subspace symmetries. In: Computer Graphics Forum, vol. 30, pp. 277–286. Wiley Online Library (2011)

7. Boumal, N., Mishra, B., Absil, P.A., Sepulchre, R.: Manopt, a matlab toolbox for optimization on manifolds. J. Mach. Learn. Res. **15**(1), 1455–1459 (2014)
8. Bronstein, A.M., Bronstein, M.M., Kimmel, R.: Numerical geometry of non-rigid shapes. Springer Science & Business Media (2008)
9. Cosmo, L., Rodolà, E., Bronstein, M., Torsello, A., Cremers, D., Sahillioglu, Y.: Shrec16: Partial matching of deformable shapes. Proc. 3DOR **2**(9), 12 (2016)
10. Dessein, A., Smith, W.A.P., Wilson, R.C., Hancock, E.R.: Symmetry-aware mesh segmentation into uniform overlapping patches. In: Computer Graphics Forum, vol. 36, pp. 95–107. Wiley Online Library (2017)
11. Gallier, J., Quaintance, J.: Notes on differential geometry and Lie groups. University of Pennsylvania (2018)
12. Ghosh, D., Amenta, N., Kazhdan, M.: Closed-form blending of local symmetries. In: Computer Graphics Forum, vol. 29, pp. 1681–1688. Wiley Online Library (2010)
13. Jiang, W., Xu, K., Cheng, Z.Q., Zhang, H.: Skeleton-based intrinsic symmetry detection on point clouds. Graph. Models **75**(4), 177–188 (2013)
14. Kazhdan, M., Funkhouser, T., Rusinkiewicz, S.: Symmetry descriptors and 3D shape matching. In: Proceedings of the 2004 Eurographics/ACM SIGGRAPH Symposium on Geometry Processing, pp. 115–123. ACM (2004)
15. Kerber, J., Bokeloh, M., Wand, M., Seidel, H.P.: Scalable symmetry detection for urban scenes. In: Computer Graphics Forum, vol. 32, pp. 3–15. Wiley Online Library (2013)
16. Kim, V.G., Lipman, Y., Chen, X., Funkhouser, T.: Möbius transformations for global intrinsic symmetry analysis. In: Computer Graphics Forum, vol. 29, pp. 1689–1700. Wiley Online Library (2010)
17. Kim, V.G., Lipman, Y., Funkhouser, T.: Blended intrinsic maps. In: ACM Transactions on Graphics (TOG), vol. 30, p. 79. ACM (2011)
18. Korman, S., Litman, R., Avidan, S., Bronstein, A.M.: Probably approximately symmetric: Fast 3d symmetry detection with global guarantees. CoRR abs 1403, 2 (2014)
19. Kovnatsky, A., Bronstein, M.M., Bronstein, A.M., Glashoff, K., Kimmel, R.: Coupled quasi-harmonic bases. In: Computer Graphics Forum, vol. 32, pp. 439–448. Wiley Online Library (2013)
20. Kurz, C., et al.: Symmetry-aware template deformation and fitting. In: Computer Graphics Forum, vol. 33, pp. 205–219. Wiley Online Library (2014)
21. Li, B., Johan, H., Ye, Y., Lu, Y.: Efficient 3D reflection symmetry detection: a view-based approach. Graph. Models **83**, 2–14 (2016)
22. Li, C., Wand, M., Wu, X., Seidel, H.P.: Approximate 3D partial symmetry detection using co-occurrence analysis. In: 2015 International Conference on 3D Vision (3DV), pp. 425–433. IEEE (2015)
23. Lipman, Y., Chen, X., Daubechies, I., Funkhouser, T.: Symmetry factored embedding and distance. In: ACM Transactions on Graphics (TOG), vol. 29, p. 103. ACM (2010)
24. Liu, X., Li, S., Liu, R., Wang, J., Wang, H., Cao, J.: Properly constrained orthonormal functional maps for intrinsic symmetries. Comput. Graph. **46**, 198–208 (2015)
25. Liu, Y., Hel-Or, H., Kaplan, C.S., Van Gool, L., et al.: Computational symmetry in computer vision and computer graphics. Found. Trends Comput. Graph. Vis. **5**(1–2), 1–195 (2010)
26. Loy, G., Eklundh, J.-O.: Detecting symmetry and symmetric constellations of features. In: Leonardis, A., Bischof, H., Pinz, A. (eds.) ECCV 2006. LNCS, vol. 3952, pp. 508–521. Springer, Heidelberg (2006). https://doi.org/10.1007/11744047_39

27. Lukáč, M., et al.: Nautilus: recovering regional symmetry transformations for image editing. ACM Trans. Graph. (TOG) **36**(4), 108 (2017)
28. Martinet, A., Soler, C., Holzschuch, N., Sillion, F.X.: Accurate detection of symmetries in 3D shapes. ACM Trans. Graph. (TOG) **25**(2), 439–464 (2006)
29. Mitra, N.J., Guibas, L.J., Pauly, M.: Partial and approximate symmetry detection for 3D geometry. ACM Trans. Graph. (TOG) **25**(3), 560–568 (2006)
30. Mitra, N.J., Guibas, L.J., Pauly, M.: Symmetrization. In: ACM Transactions on Graphics (TOG), vol. 26, p. 63. ACM (2007)
31. Mitra, N.J., Pauly, M.: Symmetry for architectural design. Advances in Architectural Geometry, pp. 13–16 (2008)
32. Mitra, N.J., Pauly, M., Wand, M., Ceylan, D.: Symmetry in 3D geometry: extraction and applications. In: Computer Graphics Forum, vol. 32, pp. 1–23. Wiley Online Library (2013)
33. Mitra, N.J.,Wand, M., Zhang, H., Cohen-Or, D., Kim, V., Huang, Q.X.: Structure-aware shape processing. In: ACM SIGGRAPH 2014 Courses, p. 13. ACM (2014)
34. Mitra, N.J., Yang, Y., Yan, D., Li, W., Agrawala, M.: Illustrating how mechanical assemblies work. ACM Trans. Graph. **29**, 58 (2010)
35. O'neill, B.: Semi-Riemannian geometry with applications to relativity, vol. 103. Academic press (1983)
36. Ovsjanikov, M., Ben-Chen, M., Solomon, J., Butscher, A., Guibas, L.: Functional maps: a flexible representation of maps between shapes. ACM Trans. Graph. (TOG) **31**(4), 30 (2012)
37. Ovsjanikov, M., Sun, J., Guibas, L.: Global intrinsic symmetries of shapes. In: Computer Graphics Forum, vol. 27, pp. 1341–1348. Wiley Online Library (2008)
38. Panozzo, D., Lipman, Y., Puppo, E., Zorin, D.: Fields on symmetric surfaces. ACM Trans. Graph. (TOG) **31**(4), 111 (2012)
39. Pinkall, U., Polthier, K.: Computing discrete minimal surfaces and their conjugates. Exp. Math. **2**(1), 15–36 (1993)
40. Podolak, J., Shilane, P., Golovinskiy, A., Rusinkiewicz, S., Funkhouser, T.: A planar-reflective symmetry transform for 3D shapes. ACM Trans. Graph. (TOG) **25**(3), 549–559 (2006)
41. Raviv, D., Bronstein, A.M., Bronstein, M.M., Kimmel, R.: Full and partial symmetries of non-rigid shapes. Int. J. Comput. Vis. **89**(1), 18–39 (2010)
42. Raviv, D., Bronstein, A.M., Bronstein, M.M., Kimmel, R., Sapiro, G.: Diffusion symmetries of non-rigid shapes. In: Proceedings of the 3DPVT, vol. 2. Citeseer (2010)
43. Reuter, M., Biasotti, S., Giorgi, D., Patanè, G., Spagnuolo, M.: Discrete laplace-beltrami operators for shape analysis and segmentation. Comput. Graph. **33**(3), 381–390 (2009)
44. Shehu, A., Brunton, A., Wuhrer, S., Wand, M.: Characterization of partial intrinsic symmetries. In: Agapito, L., Bronstein, M.M., Rother, C. (eds.) ECCV 2014. LNCS, vol. 8928, pp. 267–282. Springer, Cham (2015). https://doi.org/10.1007/978-3-319-16220-1_19
45. Shi, Z., Alliez, P., Desbrun, M., Bao, H., Huang, J.: Symmetry and orbit detection via lie-algebra voting. In: Computer Graphics Forum, vol. 35, pp. 217–227. Wiley Online Library (2016)
46. Sipiran, I., Gregor, R., Schreck, T.: Approximate symmetry detection in partial 3D meshes. In: Computer Graphics Forum, vol. 33, pp. 131–140. Wiley Online Library (2014)

47. Speciale, P., Oswald, M.R., Cohen, A., Pollefeys, M.: A symmetry prior for convex variational 3D reconstruction. In: Leibe, B., Matas, J., Sebe, N., Welling, M. (eds.) ECCV 2016. LNCS, vol. 9912, pp. 313–328. Springer, Cham (2016). https://doi.org/10.1007/978-3-319-46484-8_19

48. Sun, J., Ovsjanikov, M., Guibas, L.: A concise and provably informative multi-scale signature based on heat diffusion. In: Computer Graphics Forum, vol. 28, pp. 1383–1392. Wiley Online Library (2009)

49. Sung, M., Kim, V.G., Angst, R., Guibas, L.: Data-driven structural priors for shape completion. ACM Trans. Graph. (TOG) 34(6), 175 (2015)

50. Surazhsky, V., Surazhsky, T., Kirsanov, D., Gortler, S.J., Hoppe, H.: Fast exact and approximate geodesics on meshes. In: ACM Transactions on Graphics (TOG), vol. 24, pp. 553–560. ACM (2005)

51. Thomas, D.M., Natarajan, V.: Detecting symmetry in scalar fields using augmented extremum graphs. IEEE Trans. Vis. Comput. Graph. 19(12), 2663–2672 (2013)

52. Wang, H., Huang, H.: Group representation of global intrinsic symmetries. In: Computer Graphics Forum, vol. 36, pp. 51–61. Wiley Online Library (2017)

53. Wang, Y., et al.: Symmetry hierarchy of man-made objects. In: Computer Graphics Forum, vol. 30, pp. 287–296. Wiley Online Library (2011)

54. Wu, X., Wand, M., Hildebrandt, K., Kohli, P., Seidel, H.P.: Real-time symmetry-preserving deformation. In: Computer Graphics Forum, vol. 33, pp. 229–238. Wiley Online Library (2014)

55. Xiao, C., Jin, L., Nie, Y., Wang, R., Sun, H., Ma, K.L.: Content-aware model resizing with symmetry-preservation. Vis. Comput. 31(2), 155–167 (2015)

56. Xu, K., et al.: Multi-scale partial intrinsic symmetry detection. ACM Trans. Graph. (TOG) 31(6), 181 (2012)

57. Xu, K., et al.: Partial intrinsic reflectional symmetry of 3D shapes. In: ACM Transactions on Graphics (TOG), vol. 28, p. 138. ACM (2009)

58. Yoshiyasu, Y., Yoshida, E., Guibas, L.: Symmetry aware embedding for shape correspondence. Comput. Graph. 60, 9–22 (2016)

59. Zelditch, S.: Eigenfunctions and nodal sets. Surv. Differ. Geom. 18(1), 237–308 (2013)

60. Zheng, Q., et al.: Skeleton-intrinsic symmetrization of shapes. In: Computer Graphics Forum, vol. 34, pp. 275–286. Wiley Online Library (2015)

Objects that Sound

Relja Arandjelović[1]([⊠]) and Andrew Zisserman[1,2]

[1] DeepMind, London, UK
relja@google.com
[2] VGG, Department of Engineering Science, University of Oxford, Oxford, UK

Abstract. In this paper our objectives are, first, networks that can embed audio and visual inputs into a common space that is suitable for cross-modal retrieval; and second, a network that can localize the object that sounds in an image, given the audio signal. We achieve both these objectives by training from unlabelled video using only *audio-visual correspondence* (AVC) as the objective function. This is a form of cross-modal self-supervision from video.

To this end, we design new network architectures that can be trained for cross-modal retrieval and localizing the sound source in an image, by using the AVC task. We make the following contributions: (i) show that audio and visual embeddings can be learnt that enable both within-mode (*e.g.* audio-to-audio) and between-mode retrieval; (ii) explore various architectures for the AVC task, including those for the visual stream that ingest a single image, or multiple images, or a single image and multi-frame optical flow; (iii) show that the semantic object that sounds within an image can be localized (using only the sound, no motion or flow information); and (iv) give a cautionary tale on how to avoid undesirable shortcuts in the data preparation.

1 Introduction

There has been a recent surge of interest in cross-modal learning from images and audio [1–4]. One reason for this surge is the availability of virtually unlimited training material in the form of videos (*e.g.* from YouTube) that can provide both an image stream and a (synchronized) audio stream, and this cross-modal information can be used to train deep networks. Cross-modal learning itself has a long history in computer vision, principally in the form of images and text [5–7]. Although audio and text share the fact that they are both sequential in nature, the challenges of using audio to partner images are significantly different to those of using text. Text is much closer to a semantic annotation than audio. With text, *e.g.* in the form of a provided caption of an image, the concepts (such as 'a dog') are directly available and the problem is then to provide a correspondence between the noun 'dog' and a spatial region in the image [5,8]. Whereas, for audio, obtaining the semantics is less direct, and has more in common with image classification, in that the concept dog is not directly available from the signal but requires something like a ConvNet to obtain it (think of classifying

© Springer Nature Switzerland AG 2018
V. Ferrari et al. (Eds.): ECCV 2018, LNCS 11205, pp. 451–466, 2018.
https://doi.org/10.1007/978-3-030-01246-5_27

(a) Input image with sound   (b) Where is the sound?

Fig. 1. Where is the sound? Given an input image and sound clip, our method learns, without a single labelled example, to localize the object that makes the sound.

an image as to whether it contains a dog or not, and classifying an audio clip as to whether it contains the sound of a dog or not).

In this paper our interest is in cross-modal learning from images and audio [1–4,9–12]. In particular, we use unlabelled video as our source material, and employ *audio-visual correspondence* (AVC) as the training objective [4]. In brief, given an input pair of a video frame and 1 s of audio, the AVC task requires the network to decide whether they are in correspondence or not. The labels for the positives (matching) and negatives (mismatched) pairs are obtained directly, as videos provide an automatic alignment between the visual and the audio streams – frame and audio coming from the same time in a video are positives, while frame and audio coming from different videos are negatives. As the labels are constructed directly from the data itself, this is an example of "self-supervision" [13–22], a subclass of unsupervised methods.

The AVC task stimulates the learnt visual and audio representations to be both discriminative, to distinguish between matched and mismatched pairs, and semantically meaningful. The latter is the case because the only way for a network to solve the task is if it learns to classify semantic concepts in both modalities, and then judge whether the two concepts correspond. Recall that the visual network only sees a single frame of video and therefore it cannot learn to cheat by exploiting motion information.

In this paper we propose two networks that enable new functionalities: in Sect. 3 we propose a network architecture that produces *embeddings* directly suitable for cross-modal retrieval; in Sect. 4 we design a network and a learning procedure capable of *localizing* the sound source, *i.e.* answering the basic question – "Which object in an image is making the sound?". An example is shown in Fig. 1. Both of these are trained from scratch with no labels whatsoever, using the same unsupervised audio-visual correspondence task (AVC).

2 Dataset

Throughout the paper we use the publicly available AudioSet dataset [23]. It consists of 10 s clips from YouTube with an emphasis on audio events, and video-level audio class labels (potentially more than 1 per video) are available, but are noisy; the labels are organized in an ontology. To make the dataset more manageable and interesting for our purposes, we filter it for sounds of musical instruments, singing and tools, yielding 110 audio classes (the full list is given in the appendix [24], removing uninteresting classes like breathing, sine wave, sound effect, infrasound, silence, *etc.* The videos are challenging as many are of poor quality, the audio source is not always visible, and the audio stream can be artificially inserted on top of the video, *e.g.* it is often the case that a video is compiled of a musical piece and an album cover, text naming the song, still frame of the musician, or even completely unrelated visual motifs like a landscape, *etc.* The dataset already comes with a public train-test split, and we randomly split the public training set into training and validation sets in 90%–10% proportions. The final *AudioSet-Instruments* dataset contains 263k, 30k and 4.3k 10 s clips in the train, val and test splits, respectively.

We re-emphasise that no labels whatsoever are used for any of our methods since we treat the dataset purely as a collection of label-less videos. Labels are only used for quantitative evaluation purposes, *e.g.* to evaluate the quality of our unsupervised cross-modal retrieval (Sect. 3.1).

3   Cross-Modal Retrieval

In this section we describe a network architecture capable of learning good visual and audio embeddings from scratch and without labels. Furthermore, the two embeddings are aligned in order to enable querying across modalities, *e.g.* using an image to search for related sounds.

The *Audio-Visual Embedding Network (AVE-Net)* is designed explicitly to facilitate cross-modal retrieval. The input image and 1 s of audio (represented as a log-spectrogram) are processed by vision and audio subnetworks (Figs. 2a and b), respectively, followed by feature fusion whose goal is to determine whether the image and the audio correspond under the AVC task. The architecture is shown in full detail in Fig. 2c. To enforce feature alignment, the AVE-Net computes the correspondence score as a function of the Euclidean distance between the normalized visual and audio embeddings. This information bottleneck, the single scalar value that summarizes whether the image and the audio correspond, forces the two embeddings to be aligned. Furthermore, the use of the Euclidean distance during training is crucial as it makes the features "aware" of the distance metric, therefore making them amenable to retrieval [26].

The two subnetworks produce a 128-D L2 normalized embedding for each of the modalities. The Euclidean distance between the two 128-D features is computed, and this single scalar is passed through a tiny FC, which scales and shifts the distance to calibrate it for the subsequent softmax. The bias of the FC essentially learns the threshold on the distance above which the two features are deemed not to correspond.

Relation to Previous Works. The L^3-Net introduced in [4] and shown in Fig. 2d, was also trained using the AVC task. However, the L^3-Net audio and visual

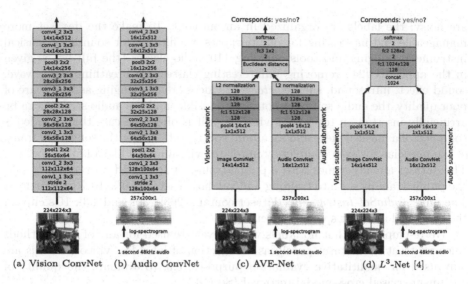

(a) Vision ConvNet   (b) Audio ConvNet   (c) AVE-Net   (d) L^3-Net [4]

Fig. 2. ConvNet architectures. Each blocks represents a single layer with text providing more information – first row: layer name and optional kernel size, second row: output feature map size. Each convolutional layer is followed by batch normalization [25] and a ReLU nonlinearity, and the first fully connected layer (fc1) is followed by ReLU. All pool layers perform max pooling and their strides are equal to the kernel sizes. (a) and (b) show the vision and audio ConvNets which perform initial feature extraction from the image and audio inputs, respectively. (c) Our AVE-Net is designed to produce aligned vision and audio embeddings as the only information, a single scalar, used to decide whether the two inputs correspond is the Euclidean distance between the embeddings. (d) In contrast, the L^3-Net [4] architecture combines the two modalities by concatenation and a couple of fully connected layers which produce the corresponds or not classification scores.

features are inadequate for cross-modal retrieval (as will be shown in the results of Sect. 3.1) as they are not aligned in any way – the fusion is performed by concatenating the features and the correspondence score is computed only *after* the fully connected layers. In contrast, the AVE-Net moves the fully connected layers into the vision and audio subnetworks and directly optimizes the features for cross-modal retrieval.

The training bears resemblance to metric learning via the contrastive loss [27], but (i) unlike contrastive loss which requires tuning of the margin hyper-parameter, ours is parameter-free, and (ii) it explicitly computes the corresponds-or-not output, thus making it directly comparable to the L^3-Net while contrastive loss would require another hyper-parameter for the distance threshold. Wang *et al.* [28] also train a network for cross-modal retrieval but use a triplet loss which also contains the margin hyper-parameter, they use pretrained networks, and consider different modalities (image-text) with fully supervised correspondence labels. In concurrent work, Hong *et al.* [29] use a similar technique with pretrained networks and triplet loss for joint embedding of music and video. Recent work of [12] also trains networks for cross-modal retrieval, but uses an ImageNet pretrained network as a teacher. In our case, we train the entire network from scratch.

3.1 Evaluation and Results

The architectures are trained on the AudioSet-Instruments train-val set, and evaluated on the AudioSet-Instruments test set described in Sect. 2. Implementation details are given below in Sect. 3.3.

On the audio-visual correspondence task, AVE-Net achieves an accuracy of 81.9%, beating slightly the L^3-Net which gets 80.8%. However, AVC performance is not the ultimate goal since the task is only used as a proxy for learning good embeddings, so the real test of interest here is the retrieval performance.

To evaluate the intra-modal (e.g. image-to-image) and cross-modal retrieval, we use the AudioSet-Instruments test dataset. A single frame and surrounding 1s of audio are sampled randomly from each test video to form the retrieval database. All combinations of image/audio as query and image/audio as database are tested, e.g. audio-to-image uses the *audio* embedding as the query vector to search the database of visual embeddings, answering the question "Which image could make this sound?"; and image-to-image uses the *visual* embedding as the query vector to search the same database.

Evaluation Metric. The performance of a retrieval system is assessed using a standard measure – the normalized discounted cumulative gain (nDCG). It measures the quality of the ranked list of the top k retrieved items (we use $k = 30$ throughout) normalized to the $[0, 1]$ range, where 1 signifies a perfect ranking in which items are sorted in a non-increasing relevance-to-query order. For details on the definition of the relevance, refer to the appendix [24]. Each item in the test dataset is used as a query and the average nDCG@30 is reported as the final retrieval performance. Recall that the labels are noisy, and note that we only extract a single frame/1s audio per video and can therefore miss the relevant event, so the ideal nDCG of 1 is highly unlikely to be achievable.

Baselines. We compare to the L^3-Net as it is also trained in an unsupervised manner, and we train it using an identical procedure and training data to our method. As the L^3-Net is expected not to work for cross-modal retrieval since the representation are not aligned in any way, we also test the L^3-Net representations aligned with CCA as a baseline. In addition, vision features extracted from the last hidden layer of the VGG-16 network trained in a fully-supervised manner on ImageNet [30] are evaluated as well. For cross-modal retrieval, the VGG16-ImageNet visual features are aligned with the L^3-Net audio features using CCA, which is a strong baseline as the vision features are fully-supervised while the audio features are state-of-the-art [4]. Note that the vanilla L^3-Net produces 512-D representations, while VGG16 yields a 4096-D visual descriptor. For computational reasons, and for fair comparison with our AVE-Net which produces 128-D embeddings, all CCA-based methods use 128 components. For all cases the representations are L2-normalized as we found this to significantly improve the performance; note that AVE-Net includes L2-normalization in the architecture and therefore the re-normalization is redundant.

Table 1. Cross-modal and intra-modal retrieval. Comparison of our method with unsupervised and supervised baselines in terms of the average nDCG@30 on the AudioSet-Instruments test set. The columns headers denote the modalities of the query and the database, respectively, where *im* stands for *image* and *aud* for *audio*. Our AVE-Net beats all baselines convincingly.

Method	im-im	im-aud	aud-im	aud-aud
Random chance	.407	.407	.407	.407
L^3-Net [4]	.567	.418	.385	.653
L^3-Net with CCA	.578	.531	.560	.649
VGG16-ImageNet [30]	.600	–	–	–
VGG16-ImageNet + L^3-Audio CCA	.493	.458	.464	.618
AVE-Net	**.604**	**.561**	**.587**	**.665**

Results. The nDCG@30 for all combinations of query-database modalities is shown in Table 1. For intra-modal retrieval (image-image, audio-audio) our AVE-Net is better than all baselines including slightly beating VGG16-ImageNet for image-image, which was trained in a fully supervised manner on another task. It is interesting to note that our network has never seen same-modality pairs during training, so it has not been trained explicitly for image-image and audio-audio retrieval. However, intra-modal retrieval works because of transitivity – an image of a violin is close in feature space to the sound of a violin, which is in turn close to other images of violins. Note that despite learning essentially the same information on the same task and training data as the L^3-Net, our AVE-Net outperforms the L^3-Net because it is Euclidean distance "aware", *i.e.* it has been designed and trained with retrieval in mind.

For cross-modal retrieval (image-audio, audio-image), AVE-Net beats all baselines, verifying that our unsupervised training is effective. The L^3-Net representations are clearly not aligned across modalities as their cross-modal retrieval performance is on the level of random chance. The L^3-Net features aligned with CCA form a strong baseline, but the benefits of directly training our network for alignment are apparent. It is interesting that aligning vision features trained on ImageNet with state-of-the-art L^3-Net audio features using CCA performs worse than other methods, demonstrating a case for unsupervised learning from a more varied dataset, as it is not sufficient to just use ImageNet-pretrained networks as black-box feature extractors.

Figure 3 shows some qualitative retrieval results, illustrating the efficacy of our approach. The system generally does retrieve relevant items from the database, while making reasonable mistakes such as confusing the sound of a zither with an acoustic guitar.

Fig. 3. Cross-modal and intra-modal retrieval. Each column shows one query and retrieved results. Purely for visualization purposes, as it is hard to display sound, the frame of the video that is aligned with the sound is shown instead of the actual sound form. The sound icon or lack of it indicates the audio or vision modality, respectively. For example, the last column illustrates query by image into an audio database, thus answering the question "Which sounds are the most plausible for this query image?" Note that many audio retrieval items are indeed correct despite the fact that their corresponding frames are unrelated – e.g. the audio of the blue image with white text does contain drums – this is just an artefact of how noisy real-world YouTube videos are.

3.2   Extending the AVE-Net to Multiple Frames

It is also interesting to investigate whether using information from multiple frames can help solving the AVC task. For these results only, we evaluate two modifications to the architecture from Fig. 2a to handle a different visual input – multiple frames (AVE+MF) and optical flow (AVE+OF). For conciseness, the details of the architectures are explained in the appendix [24], but the overall idea is that for AVE+MF we input 25 frames and convert convolution layers from 2D to 3D, while for AVE+OF we combine information from a single frame and 10 frames of optical flow using a two-stream network in the style of [31].

The performance of the AVE+MF and AVE+OF networks on the AVC task are 84.7% and 84.9%, respectively, compared to our single input image network's 81.9%. However, when evaluated on retrieval, they fail to provide a boost, e.g. the AVE+OF network achieves 0.608, 0.558, 0.588, and 0.665 for im-im, im-aud, aud-im and aud-aud, respectively; this is comparable to the performance of the vanilla AVE-Net that uses a single frame as input (Table 1). One explanation of this underwhelming result is that, as is the case with most unsupervised approaches, the performance on the training objective is not necessarily in perfect correlation with the quality of learnt features and their performance on the task of interest. More specifically, the AVE+MF and AVE+OF could be using the motion information available at input to solve the AVC task more easily by exploiting some lower-level information (*e.g.* changes in the motion could be correlated with changes in sound, such as when seeing the fingers playing a guitar or flute), which in turn provides less incentive for the network to learn good semantic embeddings. For this reason, a single frame input is used for all other experiments.

3.3   Preventing Shortcuts and Implementation

Preventing Shortcuts. Deep neural networks are notorious for finding subtle data shortcuts to exploit in order to "cheat" and thus not learn to solve the task in the desired manner; an example is the misuse of chromatic aberration in [14] to solve the relative-position task. To prevent such behaviour, we found it important to carefully implement the sampling of AVC negative pairs to be as similar as possible to the sampling of positive pairs. In detail, a positive pair is generated by sampling a random video, picking a random frame in that video, and then picking a 1 s audio with the frame at its mid-point. It is tempting to generate a negative pair by randomly sampling two different videos and picking a random frame from one and a random 1 s audio clip from the other. However, this produces a slight statistical difference between positive and negative audio samples, in that the mid-point of the positives is always aligned with a frame and is thus at a multiple of 0.04 s (the video frame rate is 25 fps), while negatives have no such restrictions. This allows a shortcut as it appears the network is able to learn to recognize audio samples taken at multiples of 0.04 s, therefore distinguishing positives from negatives. It probably does so by exploiting low-level artefacts of MPEG encoding and/or audio resampling. Therefore, with this naive implementation of negative pair generation the network has less incentive to strongly learn semantically meaningful information.

To prevent this from happening, the audio for the negative pair is also sampled only from multiples of 0.04 s. Without shortcut prevention, the AVE-Net achieves an artificially high accuracy of 87.6% on the AVC task, compared to 81.9% with the proper sampling safety mechanism in place, but the performance of the network without shortcut prevention on the retrieval task is consistently 1–2% worse. Note that, for fairness, we train the L^3-Net with shortcut prevention as well.

The L^3-Net training in [4] does not encounter this problem due to performing additional data augmentation by randomly misaligning the audio and the frame by up to 1 s for both positives and negatives. We apply this augmentation as well, but our observation is important to keep in mind for future unsupervised approaches where exact alignment might be required, such as audio-visual synchronization.

Implementation Details. We follow the same setup and implementation details as in [4]. Namely, the input frame is a 224 × 224 colour image, while the 1 s of audio is resampled at 48 kHz, converted into a log-spectrogram (window length 0.01 s and half-window overlap) and treated as a 257 × 200 greyscale image. Standard data augmentation is used – random cropping, horizontal flipping and brightness and saturation jittering for vision, and random clip-level amplitude jittering for audio. The network is trained with cross-entropy loss for the binary classification task – whether the image and the audio correspond or not – using the Adam optimizer [32], weight decay 10^{-5}, and learning rate obtained by grid search. Training is done using 16 GPUs in parallel with synchronous updates implemented in TensorFlow, where each worker processes a 128-element batch, thus making the effective batch size 2048.

Note that the only small differences from the setup of [4] are that: (i) We use a stride of 2 pixels in the first convolutional layers as we found it to not affect the performance while yielding a 4× speedup and saving in GPU memory, thus enabling the use of 4× larger batches (the extra factor of 2× is through use of a better GPU); and (ii) We use a learning rate schedule in the style of [33] where the learning rate is decreased by 6% every 16 epochs. With this setup we are able to fully reproduce the L^3-Net results of [4], achieving even slightly better performance (+0.5% on the ESC-50 classification benchmark [34]), probably due to the improved learning rate schedule and the use of larger batches.

4   Localizing Objects that Sound

A system which understands the audio-visual world should associate appearance of an object with the sound it makes, and thus be able to answer "where is the object that is making the sound?" Here we outline an architecture and a training procedure for learning to localize the sounding object, while still operating in the scenario where there is no supervision, neither on the object location level nor on their identities. We again make use of the AVC task, and show that by designing the network appropriately, it is possible to learn to localize sounding objects in this extremely challenging label-less scenario.

In contrast to the standard AVC task where the goal is to learn a single embedding of the entire image which explains the sound, the goal in sound localization is to find regions of the image which explain the sound, while other regions should not be correlated with it and belong to the background. To operationalize this, we formulate the problem in the Multiple Instance Learning (MIL) framework [35]. Namely, local region-level image descriptors are extracted on a spatial grid and a similarity score is computed between the audio embedding and each of the vision descriptors. For the goal of finding regions which correlate well with the sound, the maximal similarity score is used as the measure of the image-audio agreement. The network is then trained in the same manner as for the AVC task, *i.e.* predicting whether the image and the audio correspond. For corresponding pairs, the method encourages one region to respond highly and therefore localize the object, while for mismatched pairs the maximal score

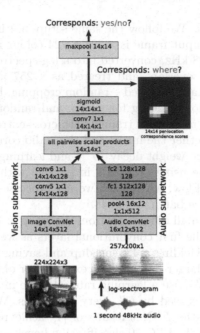

Fig. 4. Audio-Visual Object Localization (AVOL-Net). The notation and some building blocks are shared with Fig. 2. The audio subnetwork is the same as in AVE-Net (Fig. 2c). The vision network, instead of globally pooling the feature tensor, continues to operate at the 14×14 resolution, with relevant FCs (vision-fc1, vision-fc2, fc3) converted into their "fully convolutional" equivalents (*i.e.* 1×1 convolutions conv5, conv6, conv7). The similarities between the audio and all vision embeddings reveal the location of the object that makes the sound, while the maximal similarity is used as the correspondence score.

should be low thus making the entire score map low, indicating, as desired, there is no object which makes the input sound. In essence, the audio representation forms a filter which "looks" for relevant image patches in a similar manner to an attention mechanism.

Our *Audio-Visual Object Localization Network (AVOL-Net)* is depicted in Fig. 4. Compared to the AVE-Net (Fig. 2c), the vision subnetwork does not pool conv4_2 features but keeps operating on the 14×14 resolution. To enable this, the two fully connected layers fc1 and fc2 of the vision subnetwork are converted to 1×1 convolutions conv5 and conv6. Feature normalization is removed to enable features to have a low response on background regions. Similarities between each of the 14×14 128-D visual descriptors and the single 128-D audio descriptor are computed via a scalar product, producing a 14×14 similarity score map. Similarly to the AVE-Net, the scores are calibrated using a tiny 1×1 convolution (fc3 converted to be "fully convolutional"), followed by a sigmoid which produces the localization output in the form of the image-audio correspondence score for each spatial location. Max pooling over all spatial locations is performed to obtain the final correspondence score, which is then used for training on the AVC task using the logistic loss.

Relation to Previous Works. While usually hinting at object localization, previous cross-modal works fall short from achieving this goal. Harwath *et al.* [2] demonstrate localizing objects in the audio domain of a spoken text, but do not design their network for localization. In [4], the network, trained from scratch, internally learns object detectors, but has never been demonstrated to be able to answer the question "Where is the object that is making the sound?", nor, unlike our approach, was it trained with this ability in mind. Rather, their heatmaps are produced by examining responses of its various neurons given *only* the input image. The output is computed *completely independently of the sound* and therefore cannot answer "Where is the object that is making the sound?".

Our approach has similarities with [36,37] who used max and average pooling, respectively, to learn object detectors without bounding box annotations in the single visual modality setting, but use ImageNet pretrained networks and image-level labels. The MIL-based approach also has connections with attention mechanisms as it can be viewed as "infinitely hard" attention [8,38]. Note that we do not use information from multiple audio channels which could aid localization [39] because (i) this setup generally requires known calibration of the multi-microphone rig which is unknown for unconstrained YouTube videos, (ii) the number of channels changes across videos, (iii) quality of audio on YouTube varies significantly while localization methods based on multi-microphone information are prone to noise and reverberation, and (iv) we desire that our system learns to detect semantic concepts rather than localize by "cheating" through accessing multi-microphone information. Finally, a similar technique to ours appears in the concurrent work of [40], while later works of [41,42] are also relevant.

4.1 Evaluation and Results

First, the accuracy of the localization network (AVOL-Net) on the AVC task is the same as that of the AVE-Net embedding network in Sect. 3, which is encouraging as it means that switching to the MIL setup does not cause a loss in accuracy and the ability to detect semantic concepts in the two modalities.

The ability of the network to localize the object(s) that sound is demonstrated in Fig. 5. It is able to detect a wide range of objects in different viewpoints and scales, and under challenging imaging conditions. A more detailed discussion including the analysis of some failure cases is available in the figure caption. As expected from an unsupervised method, it is not necessarily the case that it detects the entire object but can focus only on specific discriminative parts such as the interface between the hands and the piano keyboard. This interacts with the more philosophical question of what is an object and what is it that is making the sound – the body of the piano and its strings, the keyboard, the fingers on the keyboard, the whole human together with the instrument, or the entire orchestra? How should a gramophone or a radio be handled by the system, as they can produce arbitrary sounds?

From the impressive results in Fig. 5, one question that comes to mind is whether the network is simply detecting the salient object in the image, which

Fig. 5. What is making the sound? Localization output of the AVOL-Net on the unseen test data; see Fig. 1 and https://goo.gl/JVsJ7P for more. Recall that the network sees a single frame and therefore cannot "cheat" by using motion information. Each pair of images shows the input frame (left) and the localization output for the input frame and 1 s of audio around it, overlaid over the frame (right). Note the wide range of detectable objects, such as keyboards, accordions, drums, harps, guitars, violins, xylophones, people's mouths, saxophones, etc. Sounding objects are detected despite significant clutter and variations in lighting, scale and viewpoint. It is also possible to detect multiple relevant objects: two violins, two people singing, and an orchestra. The final row shows failure cases, where the first two likely reflects the noise in the training data as many videos contain just music sheets or text overlaid with music playing, in columns 3–4 the network probably just detects the salient parts of the scene, while in columns 5–6 it fails to detect the sounding objects.

is not the desired behaviour. To test this hypothesis we can provide mismatched frame and audio pairs as inputs to interrogate the network to answer "what would make this sound?", and check if salient objects are still highlighted regardless of the irrelevant sound. Figure 6 shows that this is indeed not the case, as when, for example, drums are played on top of an image of a violin, the localization map is empty. In contrast, when another violin is played, the network highlights the violin. Furthermore, to completely reject the saliency hypothesis – in the case of an image depicting a piano and a flute, it is possible to play a flute sound and the network will pick the flute, while if a piano is played, the piano is highlighted in the image. Therefore, the network has truly learnt to disentangle multiple objects in an image and maintain a discriminative embedding for each of them.

To evaluate the localization performance quantitatively, 500 clips are sampled randomly from the validation data and the middle frame annotated with the localization of the instrument producing the sound. We then compare two

Fig. 6. What would make this sound? Similarly to Fig. 5, the AVOL-Net localization output is shown given an input image frame and 1 s of audio. However, here the frame and audio are mismatched. Each triplet of images shows the (left) input audio, (middle) input frame, and (right) localization output overlaid over the frame. Purely for visualization purposes, as it is hard to display sound, the frame of the video that is aligned with the sound is shown instead of the actual sound form (left). On the example of the first triplet: (left) flute sound illustrated by an image of a flute, (middle) image of a piano and a flute, (right) the flute from the middle image is highlighted as our network successfully answers the question "What in the piano-flute image would make a flute sound?" In each row the input frame is fixed while the input audio varies, showing that object localization does depend on the sound and therefore our system is not just detecting salient objects in the scene but is achieving the original goal – localizing the object that sounds.

methods of predicting the localization (as in [36]): first, a baseline method that always predicts the center of the image; second, the mode of the AVOL-Net heatmap produced by inputting the sound of the clip. The baseline achieves 57.2%, whilst AVOL-Net achieves 81.7%. This demonstrates that the AVOL-NET is not simply highlighting the salient object at the center of the image. Failure cases are mainly due to the problems with the AudioSet dataset described in Sect. 2. Note, it is necessary to annotate the data, rather than using a standard benchmark, since datasets such as PASCAL VOC, COCO, DAVIS, KITTI, do not contain musical instruments. This also means that off-the-shelf object detectors for instruments are not available, so could not be used to annotate AudioSet frames with bounding boxes.

Finally, Fig. 7 shows the localization results on videos. Note that each video frame and surrounding audio are processed completely independently, so no motion information is used, nor is there any temporal smoothing. The results reiterate the ability of the system to detect an object under a variety of poses, and to highlight different objects depending on the varying audio context. Please see YouTube playlist https://goo.gl/JVsJ7P for more video results.

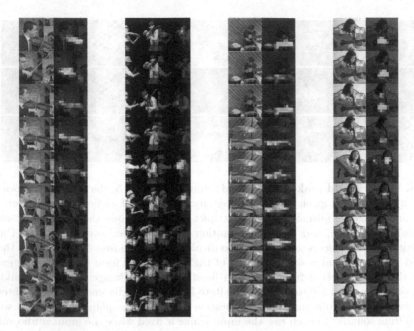

Fig. 7. What is making the sound? The visualization is the same as for Fig. 5 but here each column contains frames from a single video, taken 1 s apart. The frames are processed completely independently, motion information is not used, nor there is any temporal smoothing. Our method reliably detects the sounding object across varying poses (columns 1–2), and shots (column 3). Furthermore, it is able to switch between objects that are making the sound such as interleaved speech and guitar during a guitar lesson (column 4).

5   Conclusions and Future Work

We have demonstrated that the unsupervised audio-visual correspondence task enables, with appropriate network design, two entirely new functionalities to be learnt: cross-modal retrieval, and semantic based localization of objects that sound. The AVE-Net was shown to perform cross-modal retrieval even better than supervised baselines, while the AVOL-Net exhibits impressive object localization capabilities. Potential improvements could include modifying the AVOL-Net to have an explicit soft attention mechanism, rather than the max-pooling used currently.

Acknowledgements. We thank Carl Doersch for useful insights regarding preventing shortcuts.

References

1. Aytar, Y., Vondrick, C., Torralba, A.: SoundNet: learning sound representations from unlabeled video. In: NIPS (2016)
2. Harwath, D., Torralba, A., Glass, J.R.: Unsupervised learning of spoken language with visual context. In: NIPS (2016)
3. Owens, A., Wu, J., McDermott, J.H., Freeman, W.T., Torralba, A.: Ambient sound provides supervision for visual learning. In: Leibe, B., Matas, J., Sebe, N., Welling, M. (eds.) ECCV 2016. LNCS, vol. 9905, pp. 801–816. Springer, Cham (2016). https://doi.org/10.1007/978-3-319-46448-0_48
4. Arandjelović, R., Zisserman, A.: Look, listen and learn. In: Proceedings of ICCV (2017)
5. Barnard, K., Duygulu, P., de Freitas, N., Forsyth, D., Blei, D., Jordan, M.: Matching words and pictures. JMLR **3**, 1107–1135 (2003)
6. Duygulu, P., Barnard, K., de Freitas, J.F.G., Forsyth, D.A.: Object recognition as machine translation: learning a lexicon for a fixed image vocabulary. In: Heyden, A., Sparr, G., Nielsen, M., Johansen, P. (eds.) ECCV 2002. LNCS, vol. 2353, pp. 97–112. Springer, Heidelberg (2002). https://doi.org/10.1007/3-540-47979-1_7
7. Frome, A., et al.: Devise: a deep visual-semantic embedding model. In: NIPS (2013)
8. Xu, K., et al.: Show, attend and tell: neural image caption generation with visual attention. arXiv preprint arXiv:1502.03044 (2015)
9. de Sa, V.R.: Learning classification from unlabelled data. In: NIPS (1994)
10. Kidron, E., Schechner, Y.Y., Elad, M.: Pixels that sound. In: Proceedings of CVPR (2005)
11. Owens, A., Isola, P., McDermott, J.H., Torralba, A., Adelson, E.H., Freeman, W.T.: Visually indicated sounds. In: Proceedings of CVPR, pp. 2405–2413 (2016)
12. Aytar, Y., Vondrick, C., Torralba, A.: See, hear, and read: deep aligned representations. CoRR abs/1706.00932 (2017)
13. Dosovitskiy, A., Springenberg, J.T., Riedmiller, M., Brox, T.: Discriminative unsupervised feature learning with convolutional neural networks. In: NIPS (2014)
14. Doersch, C., Gupta, A., Efros, A.A.: Unsupervised visual representation learning by context prediction. In: Proceedings of CVPR (2015)
15. Agrawal, P., Carreira, J., Malik, J.: Learning to see by moving. In: Proceedings of ICCV (2015)
16. Wang, X., Gupta, A.: Unsupervised learning of visual representations using videos. In: Proceedings of ICCV, pp. 2794–2802 (2015)
17. Zhang, R., Isola, P., Efros, A.A.: Colorful image colorization. In: Leibe, B., Matas, J., Sebe, N., Welling, M. (eds.) ECCV 2016. LNCS, vol. 9907, pp. 649–666. Springer, Cham (2016). https://doi.org/10.1007/978-3-319-46487-9_40
18. Misra, I., Zitnick, C.L., Hebert, M.: Shuffle and learn: unsupervised learning using temporal order verification. In: Leibe, B., Matas, J., Sebe, N., Welling, M. (eds.) ECCV 2016. LNCS, vol. 9905, pp. 527–544. Springer, Cham (2016). https://doi.org/10.1007/978-3-319-46448-0_32
19. Pathak, D., Krähenbühl, P., Donahue, J., Darrell, T., Efros, A.A.: Context encoders: feature learning by inpainting. In: Proceedings of CVPR, pp. 2536–2544 (2016)
20. Noroozi, M., Favaro, P.: Unsupervised learning of visual representations by solving jigsaw puzzles. In: Leibe, B., Matas, J., Sebe, N., Welling, M. (eds.) ECCV 2016. LNCS, vol. 9910, pp. 69–84. Springer, Cham (2016). https://doi.org/10.1007/978-3-319-46466-4_5

21. Fernando, B., Bilen, H., Gavves, E., Gould, S.: Self-supervised video representation learning with odd-one-out networks. In: Proceedings of ICCV (2017)
22. Doersch, C., Zisserman, A.: Multi-task self-supervised visual learning. In: Proceedings of ICCV (2017)
23. Gemmeke, J.F., et al.: Audio set: an ontology and human-labeled dataset for audio events. In: ICASSP (2017)
24. Arandjelović, R., Zisserman, A.: Objects that sound. CoRR abs/1712.06651 (2017)
25. Ioffe, S., Szegedy, C.: Batch normalization: accelerating deep network training by reducing internal covariate shift. In: Proceedings of ICML (2015)
26. Arandjelović, R., Gronat, P., Torii, A., Pajdla, T., Sivic, J.: NetVLAD: CNN architecture for weakly supervised place recognition. In: IEEE PAMI (2017)
27. Chopra, S., Hadsell, R., LeCun, Y.: Learning a similarity metric discriminatively, with application to face verification. In: Proceedings of CVPR, vol. 1, pp. 539–546. IEEE (2005)
28. Wang, L., Li, Y., Lazebnik, S.: Learning deep structure-preserving image-text embeddings. In: Proceedings of CVPR (2016)
29. Hong, S., Im, W., S. Yang, H.: CBVMR: content-based video-music retrieval using soft intra-modal structure constraint. In: ACM ICMR (2018)
30. Simonyan, K., Zisserman, A.: Very deep convolutional networks for large-scale image recognition. In: International Conference on Learning Representations (2015)
31. Simonyan, K., Zisserman, A.: Two-stream convolutional networks for action recognition in videos. In: NIPS (2014)
32. Kingma, D.P., Ba, J.: Adam: a method for stochastic optimization. In: Proceedings of ICLR (2015)
33. Szegedy, C., et al.: Going deeper with convolutions. In: Proceedings of CVPR (2015)
34. Piczak, K.J.: ESC: dataset for environmental sound classification. In: Proceedings of ACMM (2015)
35. Dietterich, T.G., Lathrop, R.H., Lozano-Perez, T.: Solving the multiple instance problem with axis-parallel rectangles. Artif. Intell. 89(1–2), 31–71 (1997)
36. Oquab, M., Bottou, L., Laptev, I., Sivic, J.: Is object localization for free? - Weakly-supervised learning with convolutional neural networks. In: Proceedings of CVPR (2015)
37. Zhou, B., Khosla, A., Lapedriza, A., Oliva, A., Torralba, A.: Learning deep features for discriminative localization. In: Proceedings of CVPR (2016)
38. Bahdanau, D., Cho, K., Bengio, Y.: Neural machine translation by jointly learning to align and translate. In: Proceedings of ICLR (2015)
39. Shivappa, S.T., Rao, B.D., Trivedi, M.M.: Audio-visual fusion and tracking with multilevel iterative decoding: framework and experimental evaluation. IEEE J. Sel. Top. Signal Process. 4(5), 882–894 (2010)
40. Senocak, A., Oh, T.H., Kim, J., Yang, M.H., Kweon, I.S.: On learning association of sound source and visual scenes. In: Proceedings of CVPR (2018)
41. Zhao, H., Gan, C., Rouditchenko, A., Vondrick, C., McDermott, J., Torralba, A.: The sound of pixels. In: Ferrari, (eds.) ECCV 2018, Part I. LNCS, vol. 11205, pp. 587–604. Springer, Cham (2018)
42. Owens, A., Efros, A.A.: Audio-visual scene analysis with self-supervised multisensory features. In: Proceedings of ECCV (2018, to appear)

Deblurring Natural Image Using Super-Gaussian Fields

Yuhang Liu[1] , Wenyong Dong[1]([✉]), Dong Gong[2], Lei Zhang[2],
and Qinfeng Shi[2]

[1] Computer School, Wuhan University, Hubei, China
{liuyuhang,dwy}@whu.edu.cn
[2] School of Computer Science, The University of Adelaide, Adelaide, Australia
{dong.gong,lei.zhang,javen.shi}@adelaide.edu.au

Abstract. Blind image deblurring is a challenging problem due to its
ill-posed nature, of which the success is closely related to a proper image
prior. Although a large number of sparsity-based priors, such as the
sparse gradient prior, have been successfully applied for blind image
deblurring, they inherently suffer from several drawbacks, limiting their
applications. Existing sparsity-based priors are usually rooted in modeling the response of images to some specific filters (e.g., image gradients), which are insufficient to capture the complicated image structures.
Moreover, the traditional sparse priors or regularizations model the filter response (e.g., image gradients) independently and thus fail to depict
the long-range correlation among them. To address the above issues,
we present a novel image prior for image deblurring based on a Super-
Gaussian field model with adaptive structures. Instead of modeling the
response of the fixed short-term filters, the proposed Super-Gaussian
fields capture the complicated structures in natural images by integrating potentials on all cliques (e.g., centring at each pixel) into a joint
probabilistic distribution. Considering that the fixed filters in different
scales are impractical for the coarse-to-fine framework of image deblurring, we define each potential function as a super-Gaussian distribution.
Through this definition, the partition function, the curse for traditional
MRFs, can be theoretically ignored, and all model parameters of the proposed Super-Gaussian fields can be data-adaptively learned and inferred
from the blurred observation with a variational framework. Extensive
experiments on both blind deblurring and non-blind deblurring demonstrate the effectiveness of the proposed method.

1 Introduction

Image deblurring involves the estimation of a sharp image when given a blurred
observation. Generally, this problem can be formalized as follows:

$$\mathbf{y} = \mathbf{k} \otimes \mathbf{x} + \mathbf{n}, \tag{1}$$

Electronic supplementary material The online version of this chapter (https://
doi.org/10.1007/978-3-030-01246-5_28) contains supplementary material, which is
available to authorized users.

© Springer Nature Switzerland AG 2018
V. Ferrari et al. (Eds.): ECCV 2018, LNCS 11205, pp. 467–484, 2018.
https://doi.org/10.1007/978-3-030-01246-5_28

where the blurred image **y** is generated by convolving the latent image **x** with a blur kernel **k**, $\otimes$ denotes the convolution operator, and **n** denotes the noise corruption. When the kernel **k** is unknown, the problem is termed blind image deblurring (BID), and conversely, the non-blind image deblurring (NBID). It has been shown that both of these two problems are highly ill-posed. Thus, to obtain meaningful solutions, appropriate priors on latent image **x** is necessary.

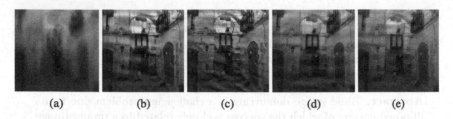

    (a)   (b)   (c)   (d)   (e)

Fig. 1. Deblurring results (and PSNR values) of a challenging example from [1]. From left to right: Blurred image (22.386), Cho and Lee [2] (22.611), Xu and Jia [3] (22.782), Pan et al. [4] (26.259), Ours (27.5427).

It has been found that the statistics of image response to specific filters can well depict the underlying structures as priors. One of the most representative examples is the sparse character in natural gradient domain, which conveys the response of an image to some basic filters, e.g., $[-1,1]$, and represents the locally spatial coherence of natural images. Inspired by this, extensive prevailing methods [5–13] have developed various sparse priors or regularizations to emphasize the sparsity on the latent images in gradient domain for deblurring. A brief review will be introduced in Sect. 2. Although these methods have made such remarkable progress, their performance still need to be improved to satisfy the requirement of real applications, especially when handling some challenging cases. This is caused by two aspects of inherent limitations in these prior models. (1) Image gradient only records the response of the image to several basic filters, which are insufficient to capture structures more complicated than local coherence. In general, those complicated structures often benefit recovering more details in the deblurred results. (2) Most of existing sparse priors (e.g., Laplace prior) or regularizations (e.g., ℓ_p norm, $0 \le p \le 1$) model the gradient on each pixel independently, and thus fails to depict the long-range correlation among pixels, such as non-local similarity or even more complex correlation. Failure to consider such kind of correlation often results in some unnatural artifacts in the deblurred results, as shown in Fig. 1.

To simultaneously address these two problems, we propose to establish an appropriate image prior with the high order Markov random fields (MRFs) model. This is motivated by the two advantages of MRFs. First, MRFs can learn an ensemble of filters to determine the statistic distribution of images, which is sufficient to capture the complicated image structures. Second, MRFs integrates the potential defined on each clique (i.e., centering at each pixel) into a probabilistic joint distribution, which is able to capture the long-range correlation among pixels potentially.

However, traditional MRFs models (e.g., Fields of experts (FoE) [14]) cannot be directly embedded into the commonly used BID framework which estimates the blur kernel in a coarse-to-fine scheme. Due to the intractable partition function, those models often learn parameters from an external image database, which results in the response of the latent image to those learned filters distributing differently across various scales and thus failing to be well depicted by the same MRFs model. For example, the learned filters lead to a heavy-tailed sparse distribution on the fine-scale while a Gaussian distribution on the coarse scale. That is one of the inherent reasons for why MRFs model is rarely employed for BID.

To overcome this difficulty, we propose a novel MRFs based image prior, termed super-Gaussian fields (SGF), where each potential is defined as a super-Gaussian distribution. By doing this, the partition function, the curse for traditional MRFs, can be theoretically ignored during parameter learning. With this advantage, the proposed MRF model can be seamlessly integrated into the coarse-to-fine framework, and all model parameters, as well as the latent image, can be data-adaptively learned and inferred from the blurred observation with a variational framework. Compared with prevailing deblurring methods on extensive experiments, the proposed method shows obvious superiority under both BID and NBID settings.

2   Related Work

2.1   Blind Image Deblurring

Due to the pioneering work of Fergus et al. [5] that imposes sparsity on image in the gradient spaces, sparse priors have attracted attention [5–13]. For example, a mixture of Gaussian models is early used to chase the sparsity due to its excellent approximate capability [5,6]. A total variation model is employed since it can encourage gradient sparsity [7,8]. A student-t prior is utilized to impose the sparsity [9]. A super-Gaussian model is introduced to represent a general sparse prior [10]. Those priors are limited by the fact that they are related to the l_1-norm. To relax the limitation, many the l_p-norm (where $p < 1$) based priors are introduced to impose sparsity on image [11–13]. For example, Krishnan et al. [11] propose a normalized sparsity prior (l_1/l_2). Xu et al. [12] propose a new sparse l_0 approximation. Ge et al. [13] introduce a spike-and-slab prior that corresponds to the l_0-norm. However, all those priors are limited by the fact that they assume the coefficients in the gradient spaces are mutually independent.

Besides the above mentioned sparse priors, a family of blind deblurring approaches explicitly exploits the structure of edges to estimate the blur kernel [2,3,15–19]. Joshi et al. [16] and Cho et al. [15] rely on restoring edges from the blurry image. However, they fail to estimate the blur kernel with large size. To remedy it, Cho and Lee [2] alternately recover sharp edges and the blur kernel in a coarse-to-fine fashion. Xu and Jia [3] further develop this work. However, these approaches heavily rely on empirical image filters. To avoid it, Sun et al. [17] explore the edges of natural images using learned patch prior. Lai et al. [18] predict the edges by learned prior. Zhou and Komodakis [19] detect edges using a high-level scene-specific prior. All those priors only explore the local patch in the latent image but neglect the global characters.

Rather than exploiting edges, there are many other priors. Komodakis and Paragios [20] explore the quantized version of the sharp image by a discrete MRF prior. Their MRF prior is different with the proposed SG-FoE prior that is a continuous MRF prior. Michaeli and Irani [21] seek sharp image by the recurrence of small image patches. Gong et al. [22,23] hire a subset of the image gradients for kernel estimation. Pan et al. [4] and Yan et al. [24] explore dark and bright pixels for BID, respectively. Besides, deep learning based methods have been adopted recently [25,26].

2.2 High-Order MRFs for Image Modeling

Since gradient filters only model the statistics of first derivatives in the image structure, high-order MRF generalizes traditional based-gradient pairwise MRF models, e.g., cluster sparsity field [27], by defining linear filters on large maximal cliques. Based on the Hammersley-Clifford theorem [28], high-order MRF can give the general form to model image as follows:

$$p(\mathbf{x}; \Theta) = \frac{1}{Z(\Theta)} \prod_{c \in C} \prod_{j=1}^{J} \phi(\mathbf{J}_j \mathbf{x}_c), \tag{2}$$

where C are the maximal cliques, $\mathbf{x}_c$ are the pixels of clique c, $\mathbf{J}_j$ are the linear filters and $j = 1, ..., J$, $Z(\Theta)$ is the partition function with parameters Θ that depend on ϕ and $\mathbf{J}_j$, ϕ are the potentials. In contrast to previous high-order MRF in which the model parameters are hand-defined, FoE [14], a class of high-order MRF, can learn the model parameters from an external database, and hence has attracted high attention in image denoising [29,30], NBID [31] and image super resolution [32].

3   Image Modeling with Super-Gaussian Fields

In this section, we first figure out the reason why traditional high-order MRFs models cannot be directly embedded into the coarse-to-fine deblurring framework. To this end, we comprehensively investigate a typical high-order MRF model, Gaussian scale mixture-FoE model (GSM-FoE) [29], and finally find out its inherent limitation. Then, we propose a super-Gaussian Fields based image prior model and analyze its properties.

3.1   Blind Image Deblurring with GSM-FoE

According to [29], GSM-FoE follows the general MRFs form in (2) and defines each potential with GSM as follows:

$$\phi(\mathbf{J}_j\mathbf{x}_c; \alpha_{j,k}) = \sum\nolimits_{k=1}^{K} \alpha_{j,k}\mathcal{N}(\mathbf{J}_j\mathbf{x}_c; 0, \eta_j/s_k), \qquad (3)$$

where $\mathcal{N}(\mathbf{J}_j\mathbf{x}_c; 0, \eta_j/s_k)$ denotes the Gaussian probability density function with zero mean and variance η_j/s_k. s_k and $\alpha_{j,k}$ denote the scale and weight parameters, respectively. It has been shown that GSM-FoE can well depict the sparse and wide heavy-tailed distributions [29]. Similar as most previous MRFs models, the partition function $Z(\Theta)$ for GSM-FoE is generally intractable since it requires integrating over all possible images. However, evaluating $Z(\Theta)$ is necessitated to learn all the model parameters, e.g., $\{\mathbf{J}_j\}$ and $\{\alpha_{j,k}\}$ (η_j and s_k are generally constant). To sidestep this difficulty, most MRFs models including GSM-FoE turn to learn model parameters by maximizing the likelihood in (2) on an external image database [14,29,30], and then apply the learned model in the following applications, e.g., image denoising, super-resolution etc.

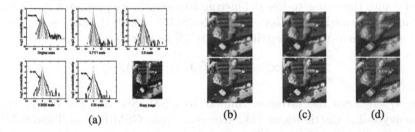

Fig. 2. (a) The 8 distributions with different colors of outputs by applying the 8 learned filters from [29] to the sharp image (the bottom right in (a)) at different scales. The 0.7171, 0.5, 0.3536 and 0.25 denote different downsampling rates. (b)–(d) The top: Blurred images with different kernel size (Successively, 13×13, 19×19, 27×27). The bottom: Corresponding deblurred images using GSM-FoE.

However, the pre-learned GSM-FoE cannot be directly employed to BID. This is because of that BID commonly adopts a coarse-to-fine framework, while the responses of the latent image to these learned filters in the pre-learned GSM-FoE often express different distributions across various scales and thus fails to be well fitted by the same GSM-FoE prior. To illustrate this point clearly, we apply the learned filters in GSM-FoE to an example image and show the responses of an image across various scales in Fig. 2a. We can find that the response obtained in the fine scale (e.g., the original scale) exhibits obvious sparsity as well as heavy tails, while the response obtained in more coarse scales (e.g., 0.3536 and 0.25, the down-sampling rates) exhibits a Gaussian-like distribution. Thus, the Gaussian-like response in coarse scale cannot be well fitted by the GSM-FoE which prefers to fitting sparse and heavy-tailed distribution. A similar observation is also reported in [29]. To further demonstrate the negative effect of such kind of distribution mismatch on BID, we embed the pre-learned GSM-FoE prior into the Bayesian MMSE framework introduced in the following Sect. 4.1 to deal with an example image blurred with different kernel sizes. The deblurred results are shown in Fig. 2b–d. Generally, a blurred image with larger kernel size requires deblurring at the coarser scale. For example, deblurring image with 13×13 kernel requires deblurring at 0.5 scale and obtains a good result, since the filter response exhibits sparsity and heavy tails at 0.5 scale shown as in Fig. 2a. However, deblurring image with 19×19 kernel obtains an unsatisfactory result, since it requires deblurring at 0.3536 scale where the filter response mismatches the sparse and heavy-tailed distribution depicted by GSM-FoE shown as Fig. 2a. In addition, more artifacts are generated in the deblurred results when the kernel size is 27×27, since it requires deblurring at 0.25 scale which produces more serious distribution mismatch.

3.2   Super-Gaussian Fields

To overcome the distribution mismatch problem of pre-learned MRFs model and embed it into the coarse-to-fine deblurring framework, we propose a novel MRFs prior model, termed super-Gaussian fields (SGF), which defines each potential in (2) as a super-Gaussian distribution [10,33] as follows:

$$\phi(\mathbf{J}_j \mathbf{x}_c) = \max_{\gamma_{j,c} \geq 0} \mathcal{N}(\mathbf{J}_j \mathbf{x}_c; 0, \gamma_{j,c}), \tag{4}$$

where $\gamma_{j,c}$ denotes the variance. Similar to GSM, SG also can depict sparse and heavy-tailed distributions [33]. Different from GSM-FoE and most MRFs models, the partition function in super-Gaussian fields can be ignored during parameter learning. More importantly, with such an advantage, it is possible to learn its model parameters directly from the blurred observation in each scale, and thus the proposed super-Gaussian fields can be seamlessly embedded into the coarse-to-fine deblurring framework. In the following, we give the theoretical results to ignore the partition function in details.

Property 1. The potential ϕ of SGF is related to $\mathbf{J}_j$ and $\mathbf{x}_c$, but not $\gamma_{j,c}$. Hence, the partition function $Z(\Theta)$ of SGF just depends on the linear filters $\mathbf{J}_j$.

Proof. As shown in (4), $\gamma_{j,c}$ can be determined by $\mathbf{J}_j$ and $\mathbf{x}_c$. Hence, the potential ϕ in (4) is related to only $\mathbf{J}_j$ and $\mathbf{x}_c$. Furthermore, because $Z(\Theta) = \int \prod_{c \in C} \prod_{j=1}^{J} \phi(\mathbf{J}_j \mathbf{x}_c) d\mathbf{x}$, the partition function $Z(\Theta)$ just depends on the linear filters $\mathbf{J}_j$ once the integral is done. Namely, $\Theta = \{\mathbf{J}_j | j = 1, ..., J\}$.

Property 2. Given any set of J orthonormal vectors $\{\mathbf{V}_{\mathbf{J}_j}\}, \{\mathbf{V}_{\mathbf{J}_j'}\}$, $\mathbf{V}_{\mathbf{J}_j}$ denote the vectored version of the linear filters $\mathbf{J}_j$ ($\mathbf{V}_{\mathbf{J}_j}$ is the vector formed through the concatenation of vectors of $\mathbf{J}_j$), for the partition function of SGF: $Z(\{\mathbf{V}_{\mathbf{J}_j}\}) = Z(\{\mathbf{V}_{\mathbf{J}_j'}\})$.

To proof Property 2, we first introduce the following theory,

Theorem 1 *([30]).   Let $E(\mathbf{V}_{\mathbf{J}_j}^T \mathbf{T_x})$ be an arbitrary function of $\mathbf{V}_{\mathbf{J}_j}^T \mathbf{T_x}$ and define $Z(\mathbf{V}) = \int e^{-\sum_j E(\mathbf{V}_{\mathbf{J}_j}^T \mathbf{T_x})} d\mathbf{x}$, where $\mathbf{T_x}$ denotes the Toeplitz (convolution) matrix (e.g., $\mathbf{J}_j \otimes \mathbf{x} = \mathbf{V}_{\mathbf{J}_j}^T \mathbf{T_x}$.) with $\mathbf{x}$. Then $Z(\mathbf{V}) = Z(\mathbf{V}')$ for any set of J orthonormal vectors $\{\mathbf{V}_{\mathbf{J}_j}\}, \{\mathbf{V}'_{\mathbf{J}_j}\}$.*

Proof (to Property 2). Since the partition function $Z(\Theta)$ of SGF just depends on the linear filters $\{\mathbf{J}_{\mathbf{J}_j}\}$ as mentioned in Property 1 and the potential ϕ in (4) also perfectly meets the form of $E(\mathbf{V}_{\mathbf{J}_j}^T \mathbf{T_x})$ in Theorem 1, it is easy to proof Property 2.

Based on Property 1, we do not need to evaluate the partition function $Z(\Theta)$ of SGF to straightforward update $\gamma_{j,c}$, since $Z(\Theta)$ do not depend on $\gamma_{j,c}$. Further, based on Property 2, we can also do not need evaluate $Z(\Theta)$ of SGF to update $\mathbf{J}_j$, if we limit updating $\mathbf{J}_j$ in the orthonormal space.

4   Image Deblurring with the Proposed SGF

In this section, we first propose a iterative method with SGF to handle BID in an coarse-to-fine scheme. We then show how to extend the proposed to non-blind image deblurring and non-uniform blind image deblurring.

4.1   Blind Image Deblurring with SGF

Based on the proposed SGF, namely (2) and (4), we propose a novel approach for BID in this section. In contrast to some existing methods which can only estimate the blur kernel, our approach can simultaneously recover latent image and the blur kernel. We will further discuss it in Sect. 4.2.

Recovering Latent Image. Given the blur kernel, a conventional approach to recover latent image is Maximum a Posteriori (MAP) estimation. However, MAP favors the no-blur solution due to the influence of image size [34]. To overcome it, we introduce Bayesian MMSE to recover latent image. MMSE can eliminate the influence by integration on image as follows [35]:

$$\hat{\mathbf{x}} = \arg\min_{\tilde{\mathbf{x}}} \int \|\tilde{\mathbf{x}} - \mathbf{x}\|^2 p(\mathbf{x}|\mathbf{y}, \mathbf{k}, \mathbf{J}_j, \gamma_{j,c}) d\mathbf{x} = E(\mathbf{x}|\mathbf{y}, \mathbf{k}, \mathbf{J}_j, \gamma_{j,c}), \qquad (5)$$

which is equal to the mean of the posterior distribution $p(\mathbf{x}|\mathbf{y}, \mathbf{k}, \mathbf{J}_j, \gamma_{j,c})$. Computing the posterior distribution is general intractable. Conventional approaches that resort to sum-product belief propagation or sampling algorithms often face with high computational cost. To reduce the computational burden, we use a variational posterior distribution $q(\mathbf{x})$ to approximate the true posterior distribution $p(\mathbf{x}|\mathbf{y}, \mathbf{k}, \mathbf{J}_j, \gamma_{j,c})$. The variational posterior $q(\mathbf{x})$ can be found by minimizing the Kullback-Leibler divergence $KL(q(\mathbf{x})|p(\mathbf{x}|\mathbf{y},\mathbf{k},\mathbf{J}_j,\gamma_{j,c}))$. This optimization is equivalent to the maximization of the lower bound of the free energy:

$$\max_{q(\mathbf{x}),\mathbf{k},\mathbf{J}_j,\gamma_{j,c}} F = \max_{q(\mathbf{x}),\mathbf{k},\mathbf{J}_j,\gamma_{j,c}} \int q(\mathbf{x}) \log p(\mathbf{x},\mathbf{y}|\mathbf{k},\mathbf{J}_j,\gamma_{j,c}) d\mathbf{x} - \int q(\mathbf{x}) \log q(\mathbf{x}) d\mathbf{x}. \quad (6)$$

Normally, $p(\mathbf{x},\mathbf{y}|\mathbf{k},\mathbf{J}_j,\gamma_{j,c})$ in (6) should be equivalent to $p(\mathbf{y}|\mathbf{x},\mathbf{k},\mathbf{J}_j,\gamma_{j,c})p(\mathbf{x})$. We empirically introduce a weight parameter λ to regularize the influences of prior and likelihood similar to [14,29]. In this case, $p(\mathbf{x},\mathbf{y}|\mathbf{k},\mathbf{J}_j,\gamma_{j,c}) = p(\mathbf{y}|\mathbf{x},\mathbf{k},\mathbf{J}_j,\gamma_{j,c})p(\mathbf{x})^\lambda$. Without loss of generality, we assume that the noise in (1) obeys i.i.d. Gaussian distribution with zero mean and δ^2 variance.

Inferring $q(\mathbf{x})$: Setting the partial differential of (6) with respect to $q(\mathbf{x})$ to zero and omitting the details of derivation, we obtain:

$$-\log q(\mathbf{x}) = \frac{1}{2}\mathbf{x}^T\mathbf{A}\mathbf{x} - \mathbf{b}^T\mathbf{x}, \quad (7)$$

with $\mathbf{A} = \delta^{-2}\mathbf{T}_\mathbf{k}^T\mathbf{T}_\mathbf{k} + \sum_j \lambda\mathbf{T}_{\mathbf{J}_j}^T\mathbf{W}_j\mathbf{T}_{\mathbf{J}_j}$, $\mathbf{b} = \delta^{-2}\mathbf{T}_\mathbf{k}^T\mathbf{y}$, where the image $\mathbf{x}$ is vectored here, $\mathbf{W}_j$ denote the diagonal matrices with $\mathbf{W}_j(i,i) = \gamma_{j,c}^{-1}$ where i is the index over image pixels and corresponds to the center of clique c, $\mathbf{T}_\mathbf{k}$ and $\mathbf{T}_{\mathbf{J}_j}$ denote the Toeplitz (convolution) matrix with the filter $\mathbf{k}$ and $\mathbf{J}_j$, respectively. Similar to [6,10], to reduce computational burden, the mean $\langle\mathbf{x}\rangle$ of $q(\mathbf{x})$ can be found by the linear system $\mathbf{A}\langle\mathbf{x}\rangle = \mathbf{b}$, where $\langle*\rangle$ refers to the expectation of $*$, and the covariance $\mathbf{A}^{-1}$ of $q(\mathbf{x})$ that will be used in (9) is approximated by inverting only the diagonals of $\mathbf{A}$.

Learning $\mathbf{J}_j$: Although $\mathbf{J}_j$ is related to the intractable partition function $Z(\Theta)$, based on Property 2, we can limit learning $\mathbf{J}_j$ in the orthonormal space where $Z(\{\mathbf{J}_j\})$ is constant. For that, we can easily define a set $\{\mathbf{B}_j\}$ and then consider all possible rotations of a single basis set of filters $\mathbf{B}_j$. That is, if we use $\mathbf{B}$ to denote a matrix whose j-th column is $\mathbf{B}_j$ and $\mathbf{R}$ to denote any orthogonal matrix, then $Z(\mathbf{B}) = Z(\mathbf{R}\mathbf{B})$. Consequently, we can give the solution of updating $\mathbf{J}_j$ by maximizing (6) under the condition that $\mathbf{R}$ is any orthogonal matrix as follows:

$$\mathbf{R}_j = eig\min(\mathbf{B}^T\langle\mathbf{T}_\mathbf{x}\mathbf{W}_j\mathbf{T}_\mathbf{x}^T\rangle\mathbf{B}), \quad \mathbf{V}_{\mathbf{J}_j} = \mathbf{B}\mathbf{R}_j, \quad (8)$$

where $eig\min(*)$ denotes the eigenvector of $*$ with minimal eigenvalue, $\mathbf{T}_\mathbf{x}$ denotes the Toeplitz (convolution) matrix with $\mathbf{x}$. We require that $\mathbf{R}_j$ be orthogonal to the previous columns $\mathbf{R}_1, \mathbf{R}_2, ..., \mathbf{R}_{j-1}$.

Learning $\gamma_{j,c}$: By contrast to updating $\mathbf{J}_j$, updating $\gamma_{j,c}$ is more straightforward because $Z(\Theta)$ is not related to $\gamma_{j,c}$ as mentioned in Property 1. We can easy give the solution of updating $\gamma_{j,c}$ by setting the partial differential of (6) with respect to $\gamma_{j,c}$ to zero, as follows:

$$\gamma_{j,c} = \langle(\mathbf{J}_j\mathbf{x}_c)^2\rangle. \quad (9)$$

Learning δ^2: Learning δ^2 is easy performed by setting the partial differential of (6) with respect to δ^2 to zero. However, this way is problematic because BID is a underdetermined problem where the size of the sharp image $\mathbf{x}$ is larger than that of the blurred image $\mathbf{y}$. We introduce the hyper-parameter d to remedy it similar to [36] as follows:

$$\delta^2 = \frac{\langle(\mathbf{y} - \mathbf{k} \otimes \mathbf{x})^2\rangle}{n} + d, \tag{10}$$

where n is the size of image.

Recovering the Blur Kernel. Similar to existing approaches [6,12,17], given $\langle\mathbf{x}\rangle$, we obtain the blur kernel estimation by solving

$$\min_{\mathbf{k}} \|\nabla\mathbf{x} \otimes \mathbf{k} - \nabla\mathbf{y}\|_2^2 + \beta\|\mathbf{k}\|_2^2, \tag{11}$$

where $\nabla\mathbf{x}$ and $\nabla\mathbf{y}$ denote the latent image $\langle\mathbf{x}\rangle$ and the blurred image $\mathbf{y}$ in the gradient spaces, respectively. To speed up computation, FFT is used as derived in [2]. After obtaining $\mathbf{k}$, we set the negative elements of $\mathbf{k}$ to 0, and normalize $\mathbf{k}$. The proposed approach is implemented in a coarse-to-fine manner similar to state-of-the-art methods. Algorithm 1 shows the pseudo-code of the propose approach.

Algorithm 1. Pseudo-code of the propose approach

Input: Blurred image $\mathbf{y}$
Output: The blur kernel $\mathbf{k}$
1: Initialize: $\mathbf{k}, \mathbf{x}, \mathbf{J}_j, \mathbf{B}, \delta^2, \gamma_{j,c}, \lambda, \beta$ and d
2: **while** stopping criterion is not satisfied **do**
3:     Inferring latent image $\mathbf{x}$, learning filters $\mathbf{J}_j$ and variances $\gamma_{j,c}$ by (7)–(9)
4:     Update for blur kernel $\mathbf{k}$ by (11)
5:     Learning for noise δ^2 by (10)
6: **end while**

4.2 Extension to Other Deblurring Problems

In this section, we extent the above method to handle the other two deblurring problems, namely the non-uniform Blind deblurring and the non-blind deblurring.

Non-uniform Blind Deblurring. The proposed approach can be extended to handle the non-uniform blind deblurring where the blur kernel varies across spatial domain [37,38]. Generally, the non-uniform blind deblurring problem can be formulated as [37]:

$$\mathbf{V_y} = \mathbf{D}\mathbf{V_x} + \mathbf{V_n}, \quad \text{or} \quad \mathbf{V_y} = \mathbf{E}\mathbf{V_k} + \mathbf{V_n}, \tag{12}$$

where $\mathbf{V_y}$, $\mathbf{V_x}$ and $\mathbf{V_n}$ denote the vectored forms of $\mathbf{y}$, $\mathbf{x}$ and $\mathbf{n}$ in (1). $\mathbf{D}$ is a large sparse matrix, where each row contains a local blur filter acting on $\mathbf{V_x}$ to generate a blurry pixel and each column of $\mathbf{E}$ contains a projectively transformed copy of the sharp image when $\mathbf{V_x}$ is known. $\mathbf{V_k}$ is the weight vector which satisfies $\mathbf{V}_{kt} \geq 0$ and $\sum_t \mathbf{V}_{kt} = 1$. Based on (12), the proposed approach can handle the non-uniform blind deblurring problem by alternatively solving the following problems:

$$\max_{q(\mathbf{V_x}),\mathbf{D},\mathbf{J}_j,\gamma_{j,c}} \int q(\mathbf{V_x}) \log q(\mathbf{V_x}) d\mathbf{V_x} - \int q(\mathbf{V_x}) \log p(\mathbf{V_x}, \mathbf{V_y} | \mathbf{D}, \mathbf{J}_j, \gamma_{j,c}) d\mathbf{V_x},$$
(13)

$$\min_{\mathbf{V_k}} \|\nabla \mathbf{E}\mathbf{V_k} - \mathbf{V}_{\nabla y}\|_2^2 + \beta \|\mathbf{V_k}\|_1.$$
(14)

Here, (14) employs l_1-norm to encourage a sparse kernel as [37]. The optimal $q(\mathbf{V_x})$ in (13) can be computed by using formulas similar to (7)–(9) in which $\mathbf{k}$ is replaced by $\mathbf{D}$. In addition, the efficient filter flow [39] is adopted to accelerate the implementation of the proposed approach.

Non-blind Image Deblurring. Similar as most of previous non-blind image deblurring, the proposed approach can handle non-blind image deblurring by (7)–(9) with the kernel $\mathbf{k}$ given beforehand.

5   Analysis

In this part, we demonstrate two properties of the proposed SGF in image deblurring. *(1) The learned filters in SGF are sparse-promoting.* As mentioned in (8),

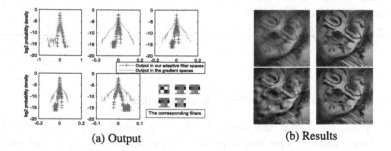

(a) Output   (b) Results

Fig. 3. Comparison of the outputs in the gradient spaces and our adaptive filter spaces at different scales. (a) The distributions of the filter outputs of sharp image (The top right in (b)) in gradient spaces and our adaptive spaces (by using filters corresponding to the bottom right in (a)) at different scales. From top to bottom and from left to right: the original, 0.7171 (sampling rate), 0.5, 0.3536, 0.25 scales. The bottom right is our final obtained filters corresponding to the different scales. (b) From top to bottom, from left to right: blurred image, sharp image, estimated latent images with basic filters and our adaptive filters.

the filters in SGF are estimated as the eigenvector of $\langle \mathbf{T_x W}_j \mathbf{T_x^T} \rangle$ with minimal eigenvalue, viz., the filters are the singular vector $\langle \mathbf{T_x}(\mathbf{W}_j)^{\frac{1}{2}} \rangle$ with minimal singular value. This implies that the proposed method seeks filters $\mathbf{J}_j$ which lead to $\mathbf{V}_{\mathbf{J}_j}^T \mathbf{T_x}(\mathbf{W}_j)^{\frac{1}{2}}$ being sparse as possible. $\mathbf{V_{J}}_j$ denotes the vectorized $\mathbf{J}_j$. Since $(\mathbf{W}_j)^{\frac{1}{2}}$ is a diagonal matrix which only scales each column of $\mathbf{T_x}$, the sparsity of $\mathbf{V}_{\mathbf{J}_j}^T \mathbf{T_x}(\mathbf{W}_j)^{\frac{1}{2}}$ is mainly determined by $\mathbf{V}_{\mathbf{J}_j}^T \mathbf{T_x}$. Consequently, the proposed approach seeks filters $\mathbf{J}_j$ which lead to the corresponding response $\mathbf{V_{J}}_j \mathbf{T_x}$ of the latent image being as sparse as possible. This can be further illustrated by the visual results in Fig. 3(a) where the distribution of image response to these learned filters are plotted. *(2) These filters $\mathbf{J}_j$s learned in each scales are more powerful than the basic filters for image gradient which are extensively adopted in previous methods.* To illustrate this point, we compare the response of the latent image to these learned filters with image gradient in Fig. 3(a). It can be seen that those learned filters lead to more sparse response than that on gradients. With these two group of filters, we recover the latent image with the proposed approach. The corresponding deblurred results are shown in Fig. 3(b). We can find that these learned filters lead to more clear and sharp results. These results demonstrate that those learned filters are more powerful than the basic filters for image gradient.

6   Experiments

In this section, we illustrate the capabilities of the proposed method for blind, non-blind and non-uniform image deblurring. We first evaluate its performance for blind image deblurring on three datasets and some real images. Then, we evaluate its performance for non-blind image deblurring. Finally, we report results on blurred images undergoing non-uniform blur kernel.

Experimental Setting: In all experiments unless especially mentioned, we set $\delta^2 = 0.002$, $\beta = 20$, $\gamma_{j,c} = 1e^{-3}$ and $d = 1e^{-4}$. To initialize the filters $\mathbf{J}_j$, we first downsample all images (grayscale) from the dataset [40] to reduce noise, then train 8 3×3 filters $\mathbf{J}_j$ on the downsampling images using the method proposed in [29] as the initialization. λ is set as $1/8$. To initialize basis set $\mathbf{B}$, we use the shifted versions of the whitening filter whose power spectrum equals the mean power spectrum of $\mathbf{J}_j$ as suggested in [30]. We use the proposed non-blind approach in Sect. 4.2 to give the final sharp image unless otherwise mentioned. We implement the proposed method in Matlab and evaluate the performance on an Intel Core i7 CPU with 8 GB of RAM. Our implementation processes images of 255×255 pixels in about 27 s.

6.1   Experiments on Blind Image Deblurring

Dataset from Levin et al. [41]: The proposed method is first applied to a widely used dataset [41], which consists of 32 blurred images, corresponding to

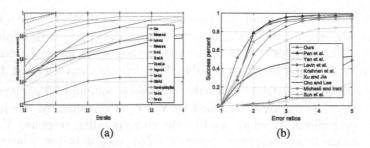

Fig. 4. Quantitative evaluations on dataset [41] (a) and dataset [17] (b).

4 ground truth images and 8 motion blur kernels. We compare it with state-of-the-art approaches [2–7,11,12,17,21,24]. To further verify the performance of GSM-FoE, we implement GSM-FoE for BID by integrating the pre-learned GSM-FoE prior into the Bayesian MMSE framework introduced in the following Sect. 4.1. We also verify the performance of the proposed method without updating filters to illustrate the necessity to update filters. For the fair comparison, after estimating blur kernels using different approaches, we use the nonblind deconvolution algorithm [42] with the same parameters in [6] to reconstruct the final latent image. The deconvolution error ratio, which measures the ratio between the Sum of Squared Distance (SSD) deconvolution error with the estimated and correct kernels, is used to evaluate the performance of different methods above. Figure 4a shows the cumulative curve of error ratio. The results shows that the proposed method obtains the best performance in terms of success percent 100% under error ratio 2. More detailed results can be found in supplementary material.

Dataset from Sun et al. [17]: In a second set of experiments we use dataset from [17], which contains 640 images synthesized by blurring 80 natural images with 8 motion blur kernels borrowed from [41]. For fair comparison, we use the non-blind deconvolution algorithm of Zoran and Weiss [43] to obtain the final latent image as suggested in [17]. We compare the proposed approach with [2, 3,6,11,17,21]. Figure 4b shows the cumulative curves of error ratio. Our results are visually competitive with others.

Dataset from Köhler et al. [1]: We further implement the proposed method on dataset, which is blurred by space-varying blur, borrowed from [1]. Although real images often exhibit spatially varying blur kernel, many approaches that assume shift-invariant blur kernel can perform well. We compare the proposed approach with [2–5,11,38,44,45]. The peak-signal-to-noise ratio (PSNR) is used to evaluate their performance. Figure 5 shows the PSNRs of different approaches above. We can see that our results are superior to the state-of-the-art approaches.

Comparison of the Proposed Approach, Pan et al. [4] and Yan et al. [24]: Recently, the method in [4] based on dark channel prior shows state-of-the-art results. As shown in Figs. 4a and 5, the proposed method performs on par

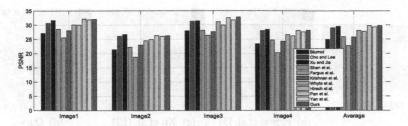

Fig. 5. Quantitative evaluations on Dataset [1]. Our results are competitive.

with the method in [4] on datasets Levin et al. [41] and Köhler et al. [1]. On the other hand, the method in [4] fails to handle blurred images which do not satisfy the condition of the dark channel prior, e.g., images with sky patches [46]. To a certain extent, Yan et al. [24] alleviate the limitation of the dark channel prior with bright pixels. However, the methods in Yan et al. [24] is still affected by complex brightness, as shown in Fig. 6.

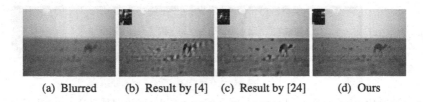

    (a) Blurred   (b) Result by [4] (c) Result by [24]   (d) Ours

Fig. 6. A challenging example with sky patches.

Real Images: We further test the proposed method using two real natural images. In Fig. 7 we show two comparisons on real photos with unknown camera shakes. For blurred image (a), Xu et al. [12] and the proposed method produce high-quality images. Further, for the blurred image (e), the proposed method produces sharper edges around the texts than Xu and Jia [3] and Sun et al. [17].

6.2   Experiments on Non-blind Image Deblurring

We also use the dataset from [41] to verify the performance of the proposed approach on non-blind image deblurring where the blur kernel is given by reference to [41]. Here, we set $\delta^2 = 1e^{-4}$ and the remaining parameters are initialized as mentioned above. We compare the proposed method against Levin et al. [42] with the same parameters in [6], Krishnan and Fergus [47], Zoran and Weiss [43] and Schmidt et al. [31]. Schmidt et al. [31] and the proposed method are based on high-order MRFs. The difference is that Schmidt et al. [31] use GSM-FoE model but we use the proposed SGF. The SSD is also used to evaluate the performance of different methods.

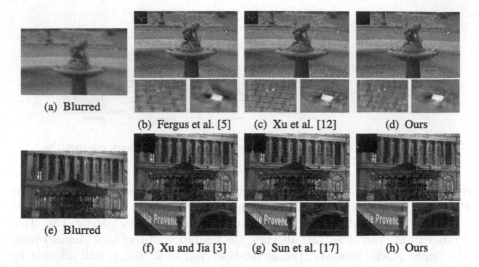

(a) Blurred

(b) Fergus et al. [5]   (c) Xu et al. [12]   (d) Ours

(e) Blurred

(f) Xu and Jia [3]   (g) Sun et al. [17]   (h) Ours

Fig. 7. Two example images with unknown camera shake from [3,5].

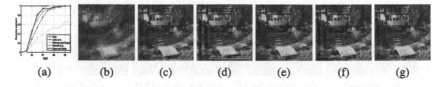

(a)   (b)   (c)   (d)   (e)   (f)   (g)

Fig. 8. Quantitative and qualitative evaluation on dataset [41]. (a) Cumulative histograms of SSD. (b)–(h) show a challenging example. From left to right: Blurred SSD:574.38, Levin et al. [42] SSD:73.51, Krishnan and Fergus [47] SSD:182.41, Zoran and Weiss [43] SSD:64.03, Schmidt et al. [31] SSD:64.35, Ours SSD:44.61.

Figure 8 shows the cumulative curve of SSD and deblurred results by different approaches on a challenging example. We can see that Zoran and Weiss [43] and the proposed produce competitive results. Additionally, as shown in Table 1, compared with Zoran and Weiss [43], the proposed method obtains lower the average SSD and less run time. Further, compared with GSM-FoE based Schmidt et al. [31], our SG-FoE acquires better results and requires more less run time.

6.3   Experiments on Non-uniform Image Deblurring

In the last experiment, we evaluate the performance of the proposed approach on blurred images with non-uniform blur kernel. β in (14) is set as 0.01 for non-uniform deblurring. Again, initializing $\gamma_{j,c} = 1e^{-3}$, $\mathbf{J}_j$, λ and B are the same as blind deblurring. We compare the proposed method with Whyte et al. [37] and Xu et al. [12]. Figure 9 shows two real natural images with non-uniform blur kernel and deblurred results. The proposed method generates images with fewer artifacts and more details.

Table 1. Average SSD and run time on dataset [41].

	Levin et al. [42]	Zoran and Weiss [43]	Schmidt et al. [31]	Krishnan and Fergus [47]	Ours
Average SSD	30.20	24.60	25.43	82.35	**21.77**
Time (s)	109	3093	>10000	6	485

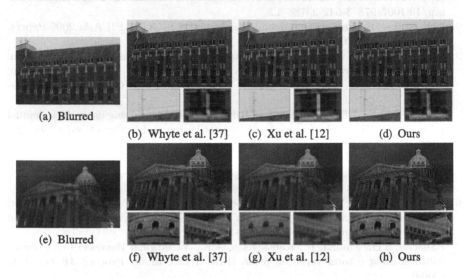

(a) Blurred

(b) Whyte et al. [37]   (c) Xu et al. [12]   (d) Ours

(e) Blurred

(f) Whyte et al. [37]   (g) Xu et al. [12]   (h) Ours

Fig. 9. Non-uniform blind deblurring results.

7 Conclusions

To capture the complicated image structures for image deblurring, we analyze the reason why traditional high-order MRFs model fails to handle BID in a coarse-to-fine scheme. To overcome this problem, we propose a novel supper-Gaussian fields model. This model contains two exciting properties, Property 1 and Property 2 introduced in Sect. 3.1, so that the partition function can be theoretically ignored during parameter learning. With this advantage, the proposed MRF model has been integrated into blind, non-blind and non-uniform blind image deblurring framework. Extensive experiments demonstrate the effectiveness of the proposed method. In contrast to previous fixed gradient based approaches, the proposed method explores sparsity in adaptive sparse-promoting filter spaces so that it dramatically performs well. It is interesting to exploit adaptive sparse-promoting filter spaces by other methods for BID in the future.

Acknowledgements. This work is in part supported by National Natural Science Foundation of China (No. 61672024, 61170305 and 60873114) and Australian Research Council grants (DP140102270 and DP160100703). Yuhang has been supported by a scholarship from the China Scholarship Council.

References

1. Köhler, R., Hirsch, M., Mohler, B., Schölkopf, B., Harmeling, S.: Recording and playback of camera shake: benchmarking blind deconvolution with a real-world database. In: Fitzgibbon, A., Lazebnik, S., Perona, P., Sato, Y., Schmid, C. (eds.) ECCV 2012. LNCS, vol. 7578, pp. 27–40. Springer, Heidelberg (2012). https://doi.org/10.1007/978-3-642-33786-4_3
2. Cho, S., Lee, S.: Fast motion deblurring. In: ACM SIGGRAPH Asia 2009 Papers, pp. 145:1–145:8 (2009)
3. Xu, L., Jia, J.: Two-phase kernel estimation for robust motion deblurring. In: Daniilidis, K., Maragos, P., Paragios, N. (eds.) ECCV 2010. LNCS, vol. 6311, pp. 157–170. Springer, Heidelberg (2010). https://doi.org/10.1007/978-3-642-15549-9_12
4. Pan, J., Sun, D., Pfister, H., Yang, M.H.: Blind image deblurring using dark channel prior. In: The IEEE Conference on Computer Vision and Pattern Recognition, pp. 1628–1636 (2016)
5. Fergus, R., Singh, B., Hertzmann, A., Roweis, S.T., Freeman, W.T.: Removing camera shake from a single photograph. ACM Trans. Graph. 25(25), 787–794 (2006)
6. Levin, A., Weiss, Y., Durand, F., Freeman, W.T.: Efficient marginal likelihood optimization in blind deconvolution. In: The IEEE Conference on Computer Vision and Pattern Recognition, pp. 2657–2664 (2011)
7. Babacan, S.D., Molina, R., Katsaggelos, A.K.: Variational Bayesian blind deconvolution using a total variation prior. IEEE Trans. Image Process. 18(1), 12–26 (2009)
8. Perrone, D., Favaro, P.: Total variation blind deconvolution: the devil is in the details. In: The IEEE Conference on Computer Vision and Pattern Recognition, pp. 2909–2916 (2014)
9. Tzikas, D., Likas, A., Galatsanos, N.: Variational Bayesian blind image deconvolution with student-T priors. In: IEEE International Conference on Image Processing, pp. 109–112 (2007)
10. Babacan, S.D., Molina, R., Do, M.N., Katsaggelos, A.K.: Bayesian blind deconvolution with general sparse image priors. In: Fitzgibbon, A., Lazebnik, S., Perona, P., Sato, Y., Schmid, C. (eds.) ECCV 2012. LNCS, vol. 7577, pp. 341–355. Springer, Heidelberg (2012). https://doi.org/10.1007/978-3-642-33783-3_25
11. Krishnan, D., Tay, T., Fergus, R.: Blind deconvolution using a normalized sparsity measure. In: The IEEE Conference on Computer Vision and Pattern Recognition, pp. 233–240. IEEE (2011)
12. Xu, L., Zheng, S., Jia, J.: Unnatural l0 sparse representation for natural image deblurring. In: The IEEE Conference on Computer Vision and Pattern Recognition, pp. 1107–1114 (2013)
13. Ge, D., Idier, J., Carpentier, E.L.: Enhanced sampling schemes for MCMC based blind Bernoulli Gaussian deconvolution. Signal Process. 91(4), 759–772 (2009)
14. Roth, S., Black, M.J.: Fields of experts. Int. J. Comput. Vis. 82(2), 205 (2009)
15. Cho, T.S., Paris, S., Horn, B.K.P., Freeman, W.T.: Blur kernel estimation using the radon transform. In: The IEEE Conference on Computer Vision and Pattern Recognition, pp. 241–248 (2011)
16. Joshi, N., Szeliski, R., Kriegman, D.J.: PSF estimation using sharp edge prediction. In: The IEEE Conference on Computer Vision and Pattern Recognition, pp. 1–8 (2008)

17. Sun, L., Cho, S., Wang, J., Hays, J.: Edge-based blur kernel estimation using patch priors. In: IEEE International Conference on Computational Photography, pp. 1–8 (2013)
18. Lai, W.S., Ding, J.J., Lin, Y.Y., Chuang, Y.Y.: Blur kernel estimation using normalized color-line priors. In: The IEEE Conference on Computer Vision and Pattern Recognition, pp. 64–72 (2015)
19. Zhou, Y., Komodakis, N.: A MAP-estimation framework for blind deblurring using high-level edge priors. In: Fleet, D., Pajdla, T., Schiele, B., Tuytelaars, T. (eds.) ECCV 2014. LNCS, vol. 8690, pp. 142–157. Springer, Cham (2014). https://doi.org/10.1007/978-3-319-10605-2_10
20. Komodakis, N., Paragios, N.: MRF-based blind image deconvolution. In: Lee, K.M., Matsushita, Y., Rehg, J.M., Hu, Z. (eds.) ACCV 2012. LNCS, vol. 7726, pp. 361–374. Springer, Heidelberg (2013). https://doi.org/10.1007/978-3-642-37431-9_28
21. Michaeli, T., Irani, M.: Blind deblurring using internal patch recurrence. In: Fleet, D., Pajdla, T., Schiele, B., Tuytelaars, T. (eds.) ECCV 2014. LNCS, vol. 8691, pp. 783–798. Springer, Cham (2014). https://doi.org/10.1007/978-3-319-10578-9_51
22. Gong, D., Tan, M., Zhang, Y., Hengel, A.V.D., Shi, Q.: Blind image deconvolution by automatic gradient activation. In: The IEEE Conference on Computer Vision and Pattern Recognition, pp. 1827–1836 (2016)
23. Gong, D., Tan, M., Zhang, Y., van den Hengel, A., Shi, Q.: Self-paced kernel estimation for robust blind image deblurring. In: International Conference on Computer Vision, pp. 1661–1670 (2017)
24. Yan, Y., Ren, W., Guo, Y., Wang, R., Cao, X.: Image deblurring via extreme channels prior. In: The IEEE Conference on Computer Vision and Pattern Recognition, pp. 6978–6986 (2017)
25. Nimisha, T., Singh, A.K., Rajagopalan, A.: Blur-invariant deep learning for blind-deblurring. In: The IEEE International Conference on Computer Vision, vol. 2 (2017)
26. Xu, X., Pan, J., Zhang, Y.J., Yang, M.H.: Motion blur kernel estimation via deep learning. IEEE Trans. Image Process. 27(1), 194–205 (2018)
27. Zhang, L., Wei, W., Zhang, Y., Shen, C., van den Hengel, A., Shi, Q.: Cluster sparsity field: an internal hyperspectral imagery prior for reconstruction. Int. J. Comput. Vis. 126(8), 797–821 (2018)
28. Besag, J.: Spatial interaction and the statistical analysis of lattice systems. J. R. Stat. Soc. Ser. B (Methodological) 36(2), 192–236 (1974)
29. Schmidt, U., Gao, Q., Roth, S.: A generative perspective on MRFs in low-level vision. In: The IEEE Conference on Computer Vision and Pattern Recognition, pp. 1751–1758 (2010)
30. Weiss, Y., Freeman, W.T.: What makes a good model of natural images? In: The IEEE Conference on Computer Vision and Pattern Recognition, pp. 1–8 (2007)
31. Schmidt, U., Schelten, K., Roth, S.: Bayesian deblurring with integrated noise estimation. In: The IEEE Conference on Computer Vision and Pattern Recognition, pp. 2625–2632 (2011)
32. Zhang, H., Zhang, Y., Li, H., Huang, T.S.: Generative Bayesian image super resolution with natural image prior. IEEE Trans. Image Process. 21(9), 4054–4067 (2012)
33. Palmer, J.A., Wipf, D.P., Kreutz-Delgado, K., Rao, B.D.: Variational EM algorithms for non-Gaussian latent variable models. In: Advances in Neural Information Processing Systems, pp. 1059–1066 (2005)
34. Levin, A., Weiss, Y., Durand, F., Freeman, W.T.: Understanding blind deconvolution algorithms. IEEE Trans. Pattern Anal. Mach. Intell. 33(12), 2354 (2011)

35. Murphy, K.P.: Machine Learning: A Probabilistic Perspective. MIT Press, Cambridge (2012)
36. Wipf, D., Zhang, H.: Revisiting Bayesian blind deconvolution. J. Mach. Learn. Res. **15**(1), 3595–3634 (2014)
37. Whyte, O., Sivic, J., Zisserman, A., Ponce, J.: Non-uniform deblurring for shaken images. Int. J. Comput. Vis. **98**(2), 168–186 (2012)
38. Hirsch, M., Schuler, C.J., Harmeling, S., Scholkopf, B.: Fast removal of non-uniform camera shake. In: International Conference on Computer Vision, pp. 463–470 (2011)
39. Hirsch, M., Sra, S., Scholkopf, B., Harmeling, S.: Efficient filter flow for space-variant multiframe blind deconvolution. In: The IEEE Conference on Computer Vision and Pattern Recognition, pp. 607–614 (2010)
40. Martin, D.R., Fowlkes, C., Tal, D., Malik, J.: A database of human segmented natural images and its application to evaluating segmentation algorithms and measuring ecological statistics. In: Proceedings of the International Conference on Computer Vision, vol. 2, no. 11, pp. 416–423 (2002)
41. Levin, A., Weiss, Y., Durand, F., Freeman, W.T.: Understanding and evaluating blind deconvolution algorithms. In: The IEEE Conference on Computer Vision and Pattern Recognition, pp. 1964–1971 (2009)
42. Levin, A., Fergus, R., Durand, F., Freeman, W.T.: Image and depth from a conventional camera with a coded aperture. ACM Trans. Graph. **26**(3), 70 (2007)
43. Zoran, D., Weiss, Y.: From learning models of natural image patches to whole image restoration. In: IEEE International Conference on Computer Vision, pp. 479–486 (2011)
44. Shan, Q., Jia, J., Agarwala, A.: High-quality motion deblurring from a single image. ACM Trans. Graph. **27**(3), 15–19 (2008)
45. Whyte, O., Sivic, J., Zisserman, A.: Deblurring shaken and partially saturated images. Int. J. Comput. Vis. **110**(2), 185–201 (2014)
46. He, K., Sun, J., Tang, X.: Single image haze removal using dark channel prior. IEEE Trans. Pattern Anal. Mach. Intell. **33**(12), 2341–2353 (2011)
47. Krishnan, D., Fergus, R.: Fast image deconvolution using hyper-Laplacian priors. In: Advances in Neural Information Processing Systems, pp. 1033–1041 (2009)

Question-Guided Hybrid Convolution for Visual Question Answering

Peng Gao[1], Hongsheng Li[1(✉)], Shuang Li[1], Pan Lu[1], Yikang Li[1],
Steven C. H. Hoi[2], and Xiaogang Wang[1]

[1] CUHK-SenseTime Joint Lab, The Chinese University of Hong Kong,
Sha Tin, Hong Kong
{penggao,hsli,sli,plu,ykli,xgwang}@ee.cuhk.edu.hk
[2] School of Information Systems,
Singapore Management Univeristy, Singapore, Singapore
chhoi@smu.edu.sg

Abstract. In this paper, we propose a novel Question-Guided Hybrid Convolution (QGHC) network for Visual Question Answering (VQA). Most state-of-the-art VQA methods fuse the high-level textual and visual features from the neural network and abandon the visual spatial information when learning multi-modal features. To address these problems, question-guided kernels generated from the input question are designed to convolute with visual features for capturing the textual and visual relationship in the early stage. The question-guided convolution can tightly couple the textual and visual information but also introduce more parameters when learning kernels. We apply the group convolution, which consists of question-independent kernels and question-dependent kernels, to reduce the parameter size and alleviate over-fitting. The hybrid convolution can generate discriminative multi-modal features with fewer parameters. The proposed approach is also complementary to existing bilinear pooling fusion and attention based VQA methods. By integrating with them, our method could further boost the performance. Experiments on VQA datasets validate the effectiveness of QGHC.

Keywords: VQA · Dynamic parameter prediction
Group convolution

1 Introduction

Convolution Neural Networks (CNN) and Recurrent Neural Networks (RNN) have shown great success in vision and language tasks [12,39,46]. Recently, CNN and RNN are jointly trained for learning feature representations for multi-modal tasks, including image captioning [3,4], text-to-image retrieval [5,34], and Visual Question Answering (VQA) [6,26,40]. Among the vision-language tasks, VQA is one of the most challenging problems. Instead of embedding images and their textual descriptions into the same feature subspace as in the text-image matching

© Springer Nature Switzerland AG 2018
V. Ferrari et al. (Eds.): ECCV 2018, LNCS 11205, pp. 485–501, 2018.
https://doi.org/10.1007/978-3-030-01246-5_29

problem [7, 8, 27], VQA requires algorithms to answer natural language questions about the visual contents. The methods are thus designed to understand both the questions and the image contents to reason the underlying truth.

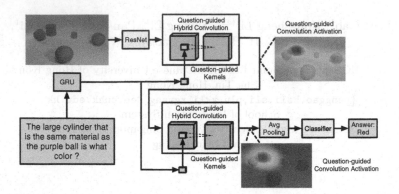

Fig. 1. Illustration of using multiple Question-guided Hybrid Convolution modules for VQA. Question-guided kernels are predicted by the input question and convoluted with visual features. Visualization of the question-guided convolution activations show they gradually focus on the regions corresponding to the correct answer.

To infer the answer based on the input image and question, it is important to fuse the information from both modalities to create joint representations. Answers could be predicted by learning classifiers on the joint features. Early VQA methods [9] fuse textual and visual information by feature concatenation. State-of-the-art feature fusion methods, such as Multimodal Compact Bilinear pooling (MCB) [10], utilize bilinear pooling to learn multi-model features.

However, the above type of methods have main limitations. The multi-modal features are fused in the latter model stage and the spatial information from visual features gets lost before feature fusion. The visual features are usually obtained by averaging the output of the last pooling layer and represented as 1-d vectors. But such operation abandons the spatial information of input images. In addition, the textual and visual relationship is modeled only on the topmost layers and misses details from the low-level and mid-level layers.

To solve these problems, we propose a feature fusion scheme that generates multi-modal features by applying question-guided convolutions on the visual features (see Fig. 1). The mid-level visual features and language features are first learned independently using CNN and RNN. The visual features are designed to keep the spatial information. And then a series of kernels are generated based on the language features to convolve with the visual features. Our model tightly couples the multi-modal features in an early stage to better capture the spatial information before feature fusion. One problem induced by the question-guided kernels is that the large number of parameters make it hard to train the model. Directly predicting "full" convolutional filters requires estimating thousands of parameters (*e.g.* 256 number of 3×3 filters convolve with the 256-channel input feature map). This is memory-inefficient and time-consuming, and does not result in satisfactory performances (as shown in our experiments).

Motivated by the group convolution [1,13,14], we decompose large convolution kernels into group kernels, each of which works on a small number of input feature maps. In addition, only a portion of such group convolution kernels (*question-dependent kernels*) are predicted by RNN and the remaining kernels (*question-independent kernels*) are freely learned via back-propagation. Both question-dependent and question-independent kernels are shown to be important, and we name the proposed operation as *Question-guided Hybrid Convolution (QGHC)*. The visual and language features are deeply fused to generate discriminative multi-modal features. The spatial relations between the input image and question could be well captured by the question-guided convolution. Our experiments on VQA datasets validate the effectiveness of our approach and show advantages of the proposed feature fusion over the state-of-the-arts.

Our contributions can be summarized in threefold. (1) We propose a novel multi-modal feature fusion method based on question-guided convolution kernels. The relative visual regions have high response to the input question and spatial information could be well captured by encoding such connection in the QGHC model. The QGHC explores deep multi-modal relationships which benefits the visual question reasoning. (2) To achieve memory efficiency and robust performance in the question-guided convolution, we propose the group convolution to learn kernel parameters. The question-dependent kernels model the relationship of visual and textual information while the question-independent kernels reduce parameter size and alleviate over-fitting. (3) Extensive experiments and ablation studies on the public datasets show the effectiveness of the proposed QGHC and each individual component. Our approach outperforms the state-of-the-art methods using much fewer parameters.

2   Related Work

Bilinear Pooling for VQA. Solving the VQA problem requires the algorithms to understand the relation between images and questions. It is important to obtain discriminative multi-modal features for accurate answer prediction. Early methods utilize feature concatenation [9] for multi-modal feature fusion [15,27,34]. Recently, bilinear pooling methods are introduced for VQA to capture high-level interactions between visual and textual features. Multimodal Compact Bilinear Pooling (MCB) [10] projects the language and visual features into a higher dimensional space and convolves them in the Fast Fourier Transform space. In Multimodal Low-rank Bilinear (MLB) [11], the weighting tensor for bilinear pooling is approximated by three weight matrices, which enforces the rank of the weighting tensor to be low-rank. The multi-modal features are obtained as the Hadamard product of the linear-projected visual and language features. Ben-younes *et al* [12] propose the Multimodal Tucker Fusion (MUTAN), which unifies MCB and MLB into the same framework . The weights are decomposed according to the Tucker decomposition. MUTAN achieves better performance than MLB and MCB with fewer parameters.

Attention Mechanisms in Language and VQA Tasks. The attention mechanisms [17,41] are originally proposed for solving language-related tasks [16]. Xu *et al* [17] introduce an attention mechanism for image captioning, which shows that the attention maps could be adaptively generated for predicting captioning words. Based on [17], Yang *et al* [18] propose to stack multiple attention layers so that each layer can focus on different regions adaptively. In [19], a co-attention mechanism is proposed. The model generates question attention and spatial attention masks so that salient words and regions could be jointly selected for more effective feature fusion. Similarly, Lu *et al* [20] employ a co-attention mechanism to simultaneously learn free-form and detection-based image regions related to the input question. In MCB [10], MLB [11], and MUTAN [12], attention mechanisms are adopted to partially recover the spatial information from the input image. Question-guided attention methods [17,21] are proposed to generate attention maps from the question.

Dynamic Network. Network parameters could be dynamically predicted across different modalities. Our approach is mostly related to methods in this direction. In [22], language are used to predict parameters of a fully-connected (FC) layer for learning visual features. However, the predicted fully-connected layer cannot capture spatial information of the image. To avoid introducing too many parameters, they predict only a small portion of parameters using a hashing function. However, this strategy introduces redundancy because the FC parameters only contain a small amount of training parameters. In [23], language is used to modulate the mean and variance parameters of the Batch Normalization layers in the visual CNN. However, learning the interactions between two modalities by predicting the BN parameters has limited learning capacity. We conduct comparisons with [22,23]. Our proposed method shows favorable performance. We notice that [24] use language-guided convolution for object tracking. However, they predict all the parameters which is difficult to train.

Group Convolution in Deep Neural Networks. Recent research found that the combination of depth-wise convolution and channel shuffle with group convolution could reduce the number of parameters in CNN without hindering the final performance. Motivated by Xception [13], ResNeXt [14], and ShuffleNet [25], we decompose the visual CNN kernels into several groups. By shuffling parameters among different groups, our model can reduce the number of predicted parameters and improve the answering accuracy simultaneously. Note that for existing CNN methods with group convolution, the convolutional parameters are solely learned via back-propagation. In contrast, our QGHC consists of question-dependent kernels that are predicted based on language features and question-independent kernels that are freely updated.

3   Visual Question Answering with Question-Guided Hybrid Convolution

ImageQA systems take an image and a question as inputs and output the predicted answer for the question. ImageQA algorithms mostly rely on deep learning models and design effective approaches to fuse the multi-modal features for answering questions. Instead of fusing the textual and visual information in high level layers, such as feature concatenation in the last layer, we propose a novel multi-modal feature fusion method, named Question-guided Hybrid Convolution (QGHC). Our approach couples the textual-visual features in early layers for better capturing textual-visual relationships. It learns question-guided convolution kernels and reserves the visual spatial information before feature fusion, and thus achieves accurate results. The overview of our method is illustrated in Fig. 1. The network predicts convolution kernels based on the question features, and then convolve them with visual feature maps. We stack multiple question-guided hybrid convolution modules, an average pooling layer, and a classifier layer together. The output of the language-guided convolution is the fused textual-visual features maps which used for answering questions. To improve the memory efficiency and experimental accuracy, we utilize the group convolution to predict a portion of convolution kernels based on the question features.

3.1   Problem Formulation

Most state-of-the-art VQA methods rely on deep neural networks for learning discriminative features of the input image I and question q. Usually, Convolutional Neural Networks (CNN) are adopted for learning visual features, while Recurrent Neural Networks (RNN) (*e.g.*, Long Short-Term Memory (LSTM) or Gated Recurrent Unit (GRU)) encode the input question, *i.e.*,

$$f_v = \text{CNN}(I; \theta_v), \tag{1}$$
$$f_q = \text{RNN}(q; \theta_q), \tag{2}$$

where f_v and f_q represent visual features and question features respectively.

Conventional ImageQA systems focus on designing robust feature fusion functions to generate multi-modal image-question features for answer prediction. Most state-of-the-art feature fusion methods fuse 1-d visual and language feature vectors in a symmetric way to generate the multi-modal representations. The 1-d visual features are usually generated by the deep neural networks (*e.g.*, GoogleNet and ResNet) with a global average pooling layer. Such visual features f_v and the later fused textual-visual features abandon spatial information of the input image and thus less robust to spatial variations.

3.2   Question-Guided Hybrid Convolution (QGHC) for Multi-modal Feature Fusion

To fully utilize the spatial information of the input image, we propose Language-guided Hybrid Convolution for feature fusion. Unlike bilinear pooling methods that treat visual and textual features in a symmetric way, our approach performs the convolution on visual feature maps and the convolution kernels are predicted based on the question features which can be formulated as:

$$f_{v+q} = \text{CNN}_p(I; \tilde{\theta}_v(f_q)), \tag{3}$$

where CNN_p is the output before the last pooling layer, $\tilde{\theta}_v(f_q)$ denotes the convolutional kernels predicted based on the question feature $f_q \in \mathbb{R}^d$, and the convolution on visual feature maps with the predicted kernels $\tilde{\theta}_v(q)$ results in the multi-modal feature maps f_{v+q}.

However, the naive solution of directly predicting "full" convolutional kernels is memory-inefficient and time-consuming. Mapping the question features to generate full CNN kernels contains a huge number of learnable parameters. In our model, we use the fully-connected layer to learn the question-guided convolutional kernels. To predict a commonly used $3 \times 3 \times 256 \times 256$ kernel from a 2000-d question feature vector, the FC layer for learning the mapping generates 117 million parameters, which is hard to learn and causes over-fitting on existing VQA datasets. In our experiments, we validate that the performance of the naive solution is even worse than the simple feature concatenation.

To mitigate the problem, we propose to predict parameters of group convolution kernels. The group convolution divides the input feature maps into several groups along the channel dimension, and thus each group has a reduced number of channels for convolution. Outputs of convolution with each group are then concatenated in the channel dimension to produce the output feature maps. In addition, we classify the convolution kernels into dynamically-predicted kernels and freely-updated kernels. The dynamic kernels are question-dependent, which are predicted based on the question feature vector f_q. The freely-updated kernels are question-independent. They are trained as conventional convolution kernels via back-propagation. The dynamically-predicted kernels fuse the textual and visual information in early model stage which better capture the multi-model relationships. The freely-updated kernels reduce the parameter size and ensure the model can be trained efficiently. By shuffling parameters among these two kinds of kernels, our model can achieve both the accuracy and efficiency. During the testing phase, the dynamic kernels are decided by the questions while the freely updated kernels are fixed for all input image-question pairs.

Formally, we substitute Eq. (3) with the proposed QGHC for VQA,

$$f_{v+q} = \text{CNN}_g\left(I; \tilde{\theta}_v(f_q), \theta_v\right), \tag{4}$$

$$\hat{a} = \text{MLP}(f_{v+q}), \tag{5}$$

where CNN_g denotes a group convolution network with dynamically-predicted kernels $\tilde{\theta}_v(f_q)$ and freely-updated kernels θ_v. The output of the CNN f_{v+q} fuses the textual and visual information and infers the final answers. MLP is a multi-layer perception module and $\hat{a}$ is the predicted answers.

The freely-updated kernels can capture pre-trained image patterns and we fix them during the testing stage. The dynamically-predicted kernels are dependent on the input questions and capture the question-image relationships. Our model fuses the textual and visual information in early model stage by the convolution operation. The spatial information between two modalities is well preserved which leads to more accurate results than previous feature concatenation strategies. The combination of the dynamic and freely-updated kernels is crucial important in keeping both the accuracy and efficiency and shows promising results in our experiments.

3.3   QGHC Module

We stack multiple QGHC modules to better capture the interactions between the input image and question. Inspired by ResNet [28] and ResNeXt [14], our QGHC module consists of a series of 1×1, 3×3, and 1×1 convolutions.

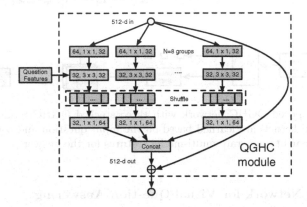

Fig. 2. Network structure of our QGHC module with $N = 8$ and $C_i = C_o = 512$. The question features are used to learn n convolution groups in the 3×3 convolution layer (the yellow block). A group shuffling layer is utilized to share the textual information from question-guided kernels to the whole network. (Color figure online)

As shown in Fig. 2, the module is designed similarly to the ShffuleNet [25] module with group convolution and identity shortcuts. The C_i-channel input feature maps are first equally divided into N groups (paths). Each of the N groups then goes through 3 stages of convolutions and outputs C_o/N-d feature maps. For each group, the first convolution is a 1×1 convolution that outputs $C_i/2N$-channel feature maps. The second 3×3 convolution outputs $C_i/2N$-channel feature maps, and the final 1×1 convolution outputs C_o/N-channel feature maps. We add a group shuffling layer after the 3×3 convolution layer to make features between different groups interact with each other and keep the advantages of both the dynamically-predicted kernels and freely-updated kernels. The output of C_o/N-channel feature maps for the N groups are then concatenated together along the channel dimension. For the shortcut connection, a 1×1 convolution transforms the input feature maps to C_o-d features, which are added with the output feature maps. Batch Normalization and ReLU are performed after each convolutional operation except for the last one, where ReLU is performed after the addition with the shortcut.

The 3×3 group convolution is guided by the input questions. We randomly select n group kernels. Their parameters are predicted based on the question features. Those kernel weights are question-dependent and are used to capture location-sensitive question-image interactions. The remaining $N - n$ group kernels have freely-updated kernels. They are updated via back-propagation in the training stage and are fixed for all images during testing. These kernels capture the pre-trained image patterns or image-question patterns. They are constant to the input questions and images.

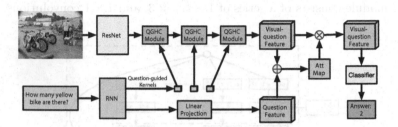

Fig. 3. The proposed QGHC network with three stacked QGHC modules for VQA. Question-guided kernels are learned based on the input question and convoluted with visual feature maps to generate multi-modal features for the answer prediction.

3.4   QGHC Network for Visual Question Answering

The network structure for our QGHC network is illustrated in Fig. 3. The ResNet [28] is first pre-trained on the ImageNet to extract mid-level visual features. The question features are generated by a language RNN model.

The visual feature maps are then send to three QGHC modules with $N = 8$ groups and $C_o = 512$. The output of the QGHC modules f_{v+q} has the same spatial sizes with the input feature maps. A global average pooling is applied to the final feature maps to generate the final multi-modal feature representation for predicting the most likely answer $\hat{a}$.

To learn the dynamic convolution kernels in the QGHC modules, the question feature f_q is transformed by two FC layers with a ReLU activation in between. The two FC layers first project the question to a 9216-d vector. The 3×3 question-dependent kernel weights of the three QGHC modules are obtained by reshaping the learned parameters into $3 \times 3 \times 32 \times 32$. However, directly training the proposed network with both dynamically-predicted kernels and freely-updated kernels is non-trivial. The dynamic kernel parameters are the output of the ReLU non-linear function with different magnitudes compared with the freely-updated kernel parameters. We adopt the Weight Normalization [29] to balance the weights between the two types of 3×3 kernels, which stabilizes the training of the network.

3.5 QGHC Network with Bilinear Pooling and Attention

Our proposed QGHC network is also complementary with the existing bilinear pooling fusion methods and the attention mechanism.

To combine with the MLB fusion scheme [11], the multi-modal features extracted from the global average pooling layer could be fused with the RNN question features again using a MLB. The fused features could be used to predict the final answers. The second stage fusion of textual and visual features brings a further improvement on the answering accuracy in our experiments.

We also apply an attention model to better capture the spatial information. The original global average pooling layer is thus replaced by the attention map. To weight more on locations of interest, a weighting map is learned by attention mechanism. A 1×1 convolution following a spatial Softmax function generates the attention weighting map. The final multi-modal features is the weighted summation of features at all the locations. The output feature maps from the last QGHC module are added with the linearly transformed question features. The attention mechanism is shown as the green rectangles in Fig. 3.

4 Experiments

We test our proposed approach and compare it with the state-of-the-arts on two public datasets, the CLEVR dataset [30] and VQA dataset [6].

Table 1. Ablation studies of our proposed QGHC network on the VQA dataset. QD and QI stands for question-dependent and -independent kernels.

Model	Parameter size		val
	QD weights	QI weights	All
QGHC	5.4M	0.9M	59.24
QGHC-1	1.8M	0.3M	58.88
QGHC-2	3.6M	0.6M	59.04
QGHC-4	7.2M	1.2M	59.13
QGHC-1/2	1.3M	0.7M	58.78
QGHC-group 4	8.7M	2.1M	59.01
QGHC-group 16	1.3 M	0.15M	58.22
QGHC-w/o shuffle	5.4M	0.9M	58.92
QGHC-1-naive	471M	0M	55.32
QGHC-1-full	117M	0.2M	57.01
QGHC-1-group	14M	0.03M	58.41
QGHC+concat	-	-	59.80
QGHC+MUTAN	-	-	60.13
QGHC+att.	-	-	60.64

4.1   VQA Dataset

Data and Experimental Setup. The VQA dataset is built from 204,721 MS-COCO images with human annotated questions and answers. On average, each image has 3 questions and 10 answers for each question. The dataset is divided into three splits: training (82,783 images), validation (40,504 images) and testing (81,434 images). A testing subset named *test-dev* with 25% samples can be evaluated multiple times a day. We follow the setup of previous methods and perform ablation studies on the testing subset. Our experiments focus on the open-ended task, which predict the correct answer in the free-form language expressions. If the predicted answer appears more than 3 times in the ground truth answers, the predicted answer would be considered as correct.

Our models have the same setting when comparing with the state-of-the-art methods. The compared methods follow their original setup. For the proposed approach, images are resized to 448×448. The $14 \times 14 \times 2048$ visual features are learned by an ImageNet pre-trained ResNet-152, and the question is encoded to a 2400-d feature vector by the skip-thought [31] using GRU. The candidate questions are selected as the most frequent 2,000 answers in the training and validation sets. The model is trained using the ADAM optimizer with an initial learning rate of 10^{-4}. For results on the validation set, only the training set is used for training. For results on test-dev, we follow the setup of previous methods, both the training and validation data are used for training.

Ablation Studies on the VQA Dataset. We conduct ablation studies to investigate factors that influence the final performance of our proposed QGHC network. The results are shown in Table 1. Our default QGHC network (denoted as *QGHC*) has a visual ResNet-152 followed by three consecutive QGHC modules. Each QGHC module has a 1×1 stage-1 convolution with freely-updated kernels, a 3×3 stage-2 convolution with both dynamically-predicted kernels and freely-updated kernels, and another 1×1 convolution stage with freely-updated kernels (see Fig. 2). Each of these three stage convolutions has 8 groups. They have 32, 32, and 64 output channels respectively.

We first investigate the influence of the number of QGHC modules and the number of convolution channels. We list the results of different number of QGHC modules in Table 1. *QGHC-1*, *QGHC-2*, *QGHC-4* represent 1, 2, and 4 QGHC modules respectively. As shown in Table 1, the parameter size improves as the number of QGHC increases but there is no further improvement when stacking more than 3 QGHC modules. We therefore keep 3 QGHC modules in our model. We also test halving the numbers of output channels of the three group convolutions to 16, 16, and 32 (denoted as *QGHC-1/2*). The results show that halving the number of channels only slightly decreases the final accuracy.

We then test different group numbers. We change the group number from 8 to 4 (*QGHC-group 4*) and 16 (*QGHC-group 16*). Our proposed method is not sensitive to the group number of the convolutions and the model with 8 groups achieves the best performance. We also investigate the influence of the group shuffling layer. Removing the group shuffling layer (denoted as *QGHC-w/o shuffle*) decreases the accuracy by 0.32% compared with our model. The shuffling layer makes features between different groups interact with each other and is helpful to the final results.

For different QGHC module structures, we first test a naive solution. The QGHC module is implemented as a single 3×3 "full" convolution without groups. Its parameters are all dynamically predicted by question features (denoted as *QGHC-1-naive*). We then convert the single 3×3 full convolution to a series of 1×1, 3×3, 1×1 full convolutions with residual connection between the input and output feature maps (denoted as *QGHC-1-full*), where the 3×3 convolution kernels arc all dynamically predicted by the question features. The improvement of QGHC-1-full over QGHC-1-naive demonstrates the advantages of the residual structure. Based on QGHC-1-full, we convert all the full convolutions to group convolutions with 8 groups (denoted as *QGHC-1-group*). The results outperforms QGHC-1-full, which show the effectiveness of the group convolution. However, the accuracy is still inferior to our proposed QGHC-1 with hybrid convolution. The results demonstrate that the question-guided kernels can help better fuse the textual and visual features and achieve robust answering performance.

Finally, we test the combination of our method with different additional components. (1) The multi-modal features are concatenated with the question features, and then fed into the FC layer for answer prediction. (denoted as *QGHC+concat*). It results in a marginal improvement in the final accuracy. (2) We use MUTAN [12] to fuse our QGHC-generated multi-modal features with question features again for answer prediction (denoted as *QGHC+MUTAN*). It has better results than QGHC+concat. (3) The attention is also added to QGHC following the descriptions in Sect. 3.5 (denoted as *QGHC+att.*).

Comparison with State-of-the-Art Methods. QGHC fuses multi-modal features in an efficient way. The output feature maps of our QGHC module utilize the textual information to guide the learning of visual features and outperform state-of-the-art feature fusion methods. In this section, we compare our proposed approach (without using the attention module) with state-of-the-arts. The results on the VQA dataset are shown in Table 2. We compare our proposed approach with multi-modal feature concatenation methods including MCB [10], MLB [11], and MUTAN [12]. Our feature fusion is performed before the spatial pooling and can better capture the spatial information than previous methods. Since MUTAN can be combined with MLB (denoted as MUTAN+MLB) to further improve the overall performance.

Attention mechanism is widely utilized in VQA algorithms for associating words with image regions. Our method can be combined with attention models for predicting more accurate answers. In Sect. 3.5, we adopt a simple attention implementation. More complex attention mechanisms, such as hierachical attention [19] and stacked attention [18] can also be combined with our approach. The results in Table 3 list the answering accuracies on the VQA dataset of different state-of-the-art methods with attention mechanism.

Table 2. Comparisons of question answering accuracy of the proposed approach and the state-of-the-art methods on the VQA dataset without using the attention mechanism.

Model	#parameters	test-dev				val
		Y/N	Number	Other	All	All
Concat [32]	-	79.25	36.18	46.69	58.91	56.92
MCB [10]	32M	80.81	35.91	46.43	59.40	57.39
MLB [11]	7.7M	82.02	36.61	46.65	60.08	57.91
MUTAN [12]	4.9M	81.45	37.32	47.17	60.17	58.16
MUTAN+MLB [12]	17.5M	82.29	37.27	48.23	61.02	58.76
MFB [33]	-	81.80	36.70	51.20	62.20	-
DPPNet [22]	-	80.71	37.23	41.69	57.22	-
QGHC-1	2.1M	-	-	-	-	58.88
QGHC	5.4M	82.39	**37.36**	53.24	63.48	59.24
QGHC+concat	-	82.54	36.94	**54.00**	63.86	59.80
QGHC+MUTAN	-	**82.96**	37.16	53.88	**64.00**	**60.13**

Table 3. Comparisons of question answering accuracy of the proposed approach and the state-of-the-art methods on the VQA dataset with the attention mechanism.

Model	test-dev				test-std
	Y/N	Number	Other	All	All
SMem [17]	80.90	37.30	43.10	58.00	58.20
NMN [35]	81.20	38.00	44.00	58.60	58.70
SAN [18]	79.30	36.60	46.10	58.70	58.90
MRN [36]	80.81	35.91	46.43	59.40	57.39
DNMN [37]	81.10	38.60	45.40	59.40	59.40
MHieCoAtt [19]	79.70	38.70	51.70	61.80	62.10
MODERN [23]	81.38	36.06	51.64	62.16	-
RAU [38]	81.90	39.00	53.00	63.30	63.20
MCB+Att [10]	82.20	37.70	54.80	64.20	-
DAN [42]	83.00	39.10	53.90	64.30	64.20
MFB+Att [33]	82.50	38.30	55.20	64.60	-
EENMN [43]	-	-	-	64.90	-
MLB+Att [11]	**84.02**	37.90	54.77	65.08	65.07
MFB+CoAtt [33]	83.20	**38.80**	55.50	65.10	-
QGHC+Att+Concat	83.54	38.06	**57.10**	**65.89**	**65.90**

We also compare our method with dynamic parameter prediction methods. DPPNet [22] (Table 2) and MODERN [23] (Table 3) are two state-of-the-art dynamic learning methods. Compared with DPPNet(VGG) and MODERN(ResNet-152), QGHC improves the performance by 6.78% and 3.73% respectively on the test-dev subset, which demonstrates the effectiveness of our QGHC model.

4.2 CLEVR Dataset

The CLEVR dataset [30] is proposed to test the reasoning ability of VQA tasks, such as counting, comparing, and logical reasoning. Questions and images from CLEVR are generated by a simulation engine that randomly combines 3D objects. This dataset contains 699,989 training questions, 149,991 validation questions, and 149,988 test questions.

Experimental Setting. In our proposed model, the image is resized to 224 × 224. The question is first embedded to a 300-d vector through a FC layer followed by a ReLU non-linear function, and then input into a 2-layer LSTM with 256 hidden states to generate textual features. Our QGHC network contains three QGHC modules for fusing multi-modal information. All parameters are learned from scratch and trained in an end-to-end manner. The network is trained using the ADAM optimizer with the learning rate 5×10^{-4} and batch size 64. All the results are reported on the validation subset.

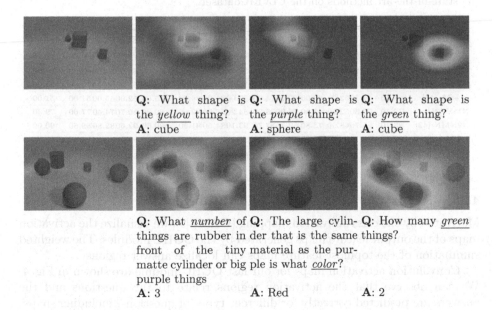

Q: What shape is the *yellow* thing?
A: cube

Q: What shape is the *purple* thing?
A: sphere

Q: What shape is the *green* thing?
A: cube

Q: What *number* of things are rubber in front of the matte cylinder or big purple things
A: 3

Q: The large cylinder that is the same tiny material as the purple is what *color*?
A: Red

Q: How many *green* things?
A: 2

Fig. 4. Visualization of answer activation maps generate by the QGHC.

Comparison with State-of-the-Arts. We compare our model with the following methods. *CNN-LSTM* [6] encodes images and questions using CNN and LSTM respectively. The encoded image features and question features are concatenated and then passed through a MLP to predict the final answers. *Multimodal Compact Bilinear Pooling (MCB)* [10] fuses textual and visual feature by compact bilinear pooling which captures the high level interaction between images and questions. *Stacked Attention (SA)* [18] adopts multiple attention models to refine the fusion results and utilizes linear transformations to obtain the attention maps. MCB and SA could be combined with the above CNN-LSTM method. *Neural Module Network (NMN)* [35] propose a sentence parsing method and a dynamic neural network. However, sentence parsing might fail in practice and lead to bad network structure. *End-to-end Neural Module Network (N2NMN)* [43] learns to parse the question and predicts the answer distribution using dynamic network structure.

The results of different methods on the CLEVR dataset are shown in Table 4. The multi-modal concatenation (CNN-LSTM) does not perform well, since it cannot model the complex interactions between images and questions. Stacked Attention (+SA) can improve the results since it utilizes the spatial information from input images. Our QGHC model still outperforms +SA by 17.40%. For the N2NMN, it parses the input question to dynamically predict the network structure. Our proposed method outperforms it by 2.20%.

Table 4. Comparisons of question answering accuracy of the proposed approach and the state-of-the-art methods on the CLVER dataset.

Model	Overall	Exist	Count	Compare integers			Query attribute				Compare attribute			
				Equal	Less	More	Size	Color	Material	Shape	Size	Color	Material	Shape
Human [44]	92.60	96.60	86.70	79.00	87.00	91.00	97.00	95.00	94.00	94.00	94.00	98.00	96.00	96.00
CNN-LSTM [6]	52.30	65.20	43.70	57.00	72.00	69.00	59.00	32.00	58.00	48.00	54.00	54.00	51.00	53.00
+MCB [10]	51.40	63.40	42.10	57.00	71.00	68.00	59.00	32.00	57.00	48.00	51.00	52.00	50.00	51.00
+SA [18]	68.50	71.10	52.2	60.00	82.00	74.00	87.00	81.00	88.00	85.00	52.00	55.00	51.00	51.00
NMN [35]	72.10	79.30	52.50	61.20	77.90	75.20	84.20	68.90	82.60	80.20	80.70	74.40	77.60	79.30
N2NMN [43]	83.70	85.70	68.50	73.80	89.70	87.70	93.10	84.50	91.50	90.60	92.60	82.80	89.60	90.00
FiLM [45]	97.7	99.1	94.3	96.8			99.1				99.1			
QGHC(ours)	86.30	78.10	91.17	67.30	87.14	83.28	93.65	87.86	86.75	90.70	86.24	87.24	86.75	86.93

4.3   Visualization of Question-Guided Convolution

Motivated by the class activation mapping (CAM) [9], we visualize the activation maps of the output feature maps generated by the QGHC modules. The weighted summation of the topmost feature maps can localize answer regions.

Convolution activation maps for our last QGHC module are shown in Fig. 4. We can observe that the activation regions relate to the questions and the answers are predicted correctly for different types of questions, including shape, color, and number. In addition, we also visualize the activation maps of different QGHC modules by training an answer prediction FC layer for each of them. As examples shown in Fig. 1, the QGHC gradually focus on the correct regions.

5   Conclusion

In this paper, we propose a question-guided hybrid convolution for learning discriminative multi-modal feature representations. Our approach fully utilizes the spatial information and is able to capture complex relations between the image and question. By introducing the question-guided group convolution kernels with both dynamically-predicted and freely-updated kernels, the proposed QGHC network shows strong capability on solving the visual question answering problem. The proposed approach is complementary with existing feature fusion methods and attention mechanisms. Extensive experiments demonstrate the effectiveness of our QGHC network and its individual components.

Acknowledgement. This work is supported by SenseTime Group Limited, the General Research Fund sponsored by the Research Grants Council of Hong Kong (Nos. CUHK14213616, CUHK14206114, CUHK14205615, CUHK14203015, CUHK14239816, CUHK419412, CUHK14207814, CUHK14208417, CUHK14202217), the Hong Kong Innovation and Technology Support Program (No.ITS/121/15FX), the National Research Foundation, Prime Minister's Office, Singapore under its International Research Centres in Singapore Funding Initiative.

References

1. Krizhevsky, A., Sutskever, I., Hinton, G.E.: Imagenet classification with deep convolutional neural networks. In: Advances in neural information processing systems, pp. 1097–1105 (2012)
2. Sutskever, I., Vinyals, O., Le, Q.V.: Sequence to sequence learning with neural networks. In: Advances in neural information processing systems, pp. 3104–3112 (2014)
3. Li, Y., Ouyang, W., Zhou, B., Wang, K., Wang, X.: Scene graph generation from objects, phrases and region captions. In: Proceedings of the IEEE Conference on Computer Vision and Pattern Recognition, pp. 1261–1270 (2017)
4. Xu, K., et al.: Show, attend and tell: Neural image caption generation with visual attention. In: International Conference on Machine Learning, pp. 2048–2057 (2015)
5. Hu, R., Xu, H., Rohrbach, M., Feng, J., Saenko, K., Darrell, T.: Natural language object retrieval. In: Proceedings of the IEEE Conference on Computer Vision and Pattern Recognition, pp. 4555–4564 (2016)
6. Antol, S., et al.: VQA: visual question answering. In: Proceedings of the IEEE International Conference on Computer Vision pp. 2425–2433 (2015)
7. Frome, A., Corrado, G.S., Shlens, J., Bengio, S., Dean, J., Mikolov, T., et al.: DeViSE: a deep visual-semantic embedding model. In: Advances in neural information processing systems, pp. 2121–2129 (2013)
8. Reed, S., Akata, Z., Lee, H., Schiele, B.: Learning deep representations of fine-grained visual descriptions. In: Proceedings of the IEEE Conference on Computer Vision and Pattern Recognition, pp. 49–58 (2016)
9. Zhou, B., Tian, Y., Sukhbaatar, S., Szlam, A., Fergus, R.: Simple baseline for visual question answering. arXiv preprint arXiv:1512.02167 (2015)
10. Fukui, A., Park, D.H., Yang, D., Rohrbach, A., Darrell, T., Rohrbach, M.: Multimodal compact bilinear pooling for visual question answering and visual grounding. arXiv preprint arXiv:1606.01847 (2016)

11. Kim, J.H., On, K.W., Kim, J., Ha, J.W., Zhang, B.T.: Hadamard product for low-rank bilinear pooling. arXiv preprint arXiv:1610.04325 (2016)
12. Ben-younes, H., Cadene, R., Cord, M., Thome, N.: MUTAN: Multimodal tucker fusion for visual question answering. arXiv preprint arXiv:1705.06676 (2017)
13. Chollet, F.: Xception: deep learning with depthwise separable convolutions. arXiv preprint arXiv:1610.02357 (2016)
14. Xie, S., Girshick, R., Dollár, P., Tu, Z., He, K.: Aggregated residual transformations for deep neural networks. arXiv preprint arXiv:1611.05431 (2016)
15. Lin, T.Y., RoyChowdhury, A., Maji, S.: Bilinear CNN models for fine-grained visual recognition. In: Proceedings of the IEEE International Conference on Computer Vision, pp. 1449–1457 (2015)
16. Bahdanau, D., Cho, K., Bengio, Y.: Neural machine translation by jointly learning to align and translate. arXiv preprint arXiv:1409.0473 (2014)
17. Xu, H., Saenko, K.: Ask, attend and answer: exploring question-guided spatial attention for visual question answering. In: Leibe, B., Matas, J., Sebe, N., Welling, M. (eds.) ECCV 2016. LNCS, vol. 9911, pp. 451–466. Springer, Cham (2016). https://doi.org/10.1007/978-3-319-46478-7_28
18. Yang, Z., He, X., Gao, J., Deng, L., Smola, A.: Stacked attention networks for image question answering. In: Proceedings of the IEEE Conference on Computer Vision and Pattern Recognition, pp. 21–29 (2016)
19. Lu, J., Yang, J., Batra, D., Parikh, D.: Hierarchical question-image co-attention for visual question answering. In: Advances In Neural Information Processing Systems, pp. 289–297 (2016)
20. Lu, P., Li, H., Zhang, W., Wang, J., Wang, X.: Co-attending free-form regions and detections with multi-modal multiplicative feature embedding for visual question answering. In: Proceedings of AAAI, pp. 7218–7225 (2018)
21. Chen, K., Wang, J., Chen, L.C., Gao, H., Xu, W., Nevatia, R.: ABC-CNN: an attention based convolutional neural network for visual question answering. arXiv preprint arXiv:1511.05960 (2015)
22. Noh, H., Hongsuck Seo, P., Han, B.: Image question answering using convolutional neural network with dynamic parameter prediction. In: Proceedings of the IEEE Conference on Computer Vision and Pattern Recognition, pp. 30–38 (2016)
23. de Vries, H., Strub, F., Mary, J., Larochelle, H., Pietquin, O., Courville, A.: Modulating early visual processing by language. arXiv preprint arXiv:1707.00683 (2017)
24. Li, Z., Tao, R., Gavves, E., Snoek, C.G., Smeulders, A., et al.: Tracking by natural language specification. In: Proceedings of the IEEE Conference on Computer Vision and Pattern Recognition, pp. 6495–6503 (2017)
25. Zhang, X., Zhou, X., Lin, M., Sun, J.: ShuffleNet: an extremely efficient convolutional neural network for mobile devices. arXiv preprint arXiv:1707.01083 (2017)
26. Li, Y., et al.: Visual question generation as dual task of visual question answering. In: Proceedings of the IEEE Conference on Computer Vision and Pattern Recognition, pp. 6116–6124 (2018)
27. Li, S., Xiao, T., Li, H., Yang, W., Wang, X.: Identity-aware textual-visual matching with latent co-attention. In: IEEE International Conference on Computer Vision (2017)
28. He, K., Zhang, X., Ren, S., Sun, J.: Deep residual learning for image recognition. In: Proceedings of the IEEE conference on computer vision and pattern recognition, pp. 770–778 (2016)
29. Salimans, T., Kingma, D.P.: Weight normalization: a simple reparameterization to accelerate training of deep neural networks. In: Advances in Neural Information Processing Systems, pp. 901–909 (2016)

30. Johnson, J., Hariharan, B., van der Maaten, L., Fei-Fei, L., Zitnick, C.L., Girshick, R.: CLEVR: a diagnostic dataset for compositional language and elementary visual reasoning. arXiv preprint arXiv:1612.06890 (2016)
31. Kiros, R., et al.: Skip-thought vectors. In: Advances in neural information processing systems, pp. 3294–3302 (2015)
32. Zhou, B., Khosla, A., Lapedriza, A., Oliva, A., Torralba, A.: Learning deep features for discriminative localization. In: Proceedings of the IEEE Conference on Computer Vision and Pattern Recognition, pp. 2921–2929 (2016)
33. Yu, Z., Yu, J., Fan, J., Tao, D.: Multi-modal factorized bilinear pooling with co-attention learning for visual question answering
34. Li, S., Xiao, T., Li, H., Zhou, B., Yue, D., Wang, X.: Person search with natural language description. In: IEEE Conference on Computer Vision and Pattern Recognition (2017)
35. Andreas, J., Rohrbach, M., Darrell, T., Klein, D.: Neural module networks. In: Proceedings of the IEEE Conference on Computer Vision and Pattern Recognition, pp. 39–48 (2016)
36. Kim, J.H., et al.: Multimodal residual learning for visual QA. In: Advances in Neural Information Processing Systems, pp. 361–369 (2016)
37. Andreas, J., Rohrbach, M., Darrell, T., Klein, D.: Learning to compose neural networks for question answering. In: Proceedings of NAACL-HLT, pp. 1545–1554 (2016)
38. Noh, H., Han, B.: Training recurrent answering units with joint loss minimization for VQA. arXiv preprint arXiv:1606.03647 (2016)
39. Li, Y., Ouyang, W., Wang, X., Tang, X.: ViP-CNN: Visual phrase guided convolutional neural network. In: CVPR (2017)
40. Lu, P., Ji, L., Zhang, W., Duan, N., Zhou, M., Wang, J.: R-VQA: learning visual relation facts with semantic attention for visual question answering. In: Proceedings of SIGKDD (2018)
41. Li, S., Bak, S., Carr, P., Wang, X.: Diversity regularized spatiotemporal attention for video-based person re-identification. In: IEEE Conference on Computer Vision and Pattern Recognition (2018)
42. Nam, H., Ha, J.W., Kim, J.: Dual attention networks for multimodal reasoning and matching. arXiv preprint arXiv:1611.00471 (2016)
43. Hu, R., Andreas, J., Rohrbach, M., Darrell, T., Saenko, K.: Learning to reason: end-to-end module networks for visual question answering. arXiv preprint arXiv:1704.05526 (2017)
44. Johnson, J., et al.: Inferring and executing programs for visual reasoning. In: ICCV (2017)
45. Perez, E., Strub, F., De Vries, H., Dumoulin, V., Courville, A.: Film: visual reasoning with a general conditioning layer. arXiv preprint arXiv:1709.07871 (2017)
46. Li, Y., Ouyang, W., Zhou, B., Shi, J., Zhang, C., Wang, X.: Factorizable net: an efficient subgraph-based framework for scene graph generation. In: ECCV (2018)

Geometric Constrained Joint Lane Segmentation and Lane Boundary Detection

Jie Zhang, Yi Xu[✉], Bingbing Ni, and Zhenyu Duan

SJTU-UCLA Joint Center for Machine Perception and Inference,
Shanghai Jiao Tong University, Shanghai 200240, China
{a135b920,xuyi,nibingbing,ol7650}@sjtu.edu.cn

Abstract. Lane detection is playing an indispensable role in advanced driver assistance systems. The existing approaches for lane detection can be categorized as lane area segmentation and lane boundary detection. Most of these methods abandon a great quantity of complementary information, such as geometric priors, when exploiting the lane area and the lane boundaries alternatively. In this paper, we establish a multiple-task learning framework to segment lane areas and detect lane boundaries simultaneously. The main contributions of the proposed framework are highlighted in two facets: (1) We put forward a multiple-task learning framework with mutually interlinked sub-structures between lane segmentation and lane boundary detection to improve overall performance. (2) A novel loss function is proposed with two geometric constraints considered, as assumed that the lane boundary is predicted as the outer contour of the lane area while the lane area is predicted as the area integration result within the lane boundary lines. With an end-to-end training process, these improvements extremely enhance the robustness and accuracy of our approach on several metrics. The proposed framework is evaluated on KITTI dataset, CULane dataset and RVD dataset. Compared with the state of the arts, our approach achieves the best performance on the metrics and a robust detection in varied traffic scenes.

Keywords: Lane segmentation · Semantic segmentation

1 Introduction

Trajectory planning [20] of autonomous driving is an challenging task in the field of computer vision. Lane area segmentation is a crucial issue in trajectory planning which classifies different lanes and generates definite driving areas.

Texture-based approaches are proposed in the early works. Texture features from different color spaces are aggregated to enhance the robustness of lane detection [3,22,24]. Generally, there are homogeneous regions in the lane area, so it is difficult to establish distinguishable feature descriptors for these regions.

Without adequate texture information to rely on, the supplement of lane boundaries is critical to precise detection of lane area. Traditional approaches

© Springer Nature Switzerland AG 2018
V. Ferrari et al. (Eds.): ECCV 2018, LNCS 11205, pp. 502–518, 2018.
https://doi.org/10.1007/978-3-030-01246-5_30

extract boundary information to tackle the problem of homogeneous regions in lane areas, where the high-pass filters are dominantly used [4,7,12,18]. With boundary information extracted, final lane areas are sketched by lane boundaries [9]. However, boundary information is frequently missing due to occlusions and dashing markers. Severely, surrounding shadows and vehicles often introduce irrelevant information that withers the detection performance. In recent years, fully convolutional neural networks (FCN) are put forward [6,10,23,25], where contextual features are self-learned with an encoder-decoder structure to enhance lane segmentation. FCN has achieved much better performance than traditional approaches [3,22,24]. Under ill-defined conditions, it is hard for FCN to effectively provide a significant, unique representation of lane areas.

In fact, there exists a geometric relationship between a lane area and its boundaries: lane areas always lie between lane boundaries, while a lane boundary consists of the outer contour of the lane area. To make use of this relationship, some prior models are advanced through a sequential processing strategy [2,30,35]. Some models extract lane boundaries to greatly reduce the search range for lane detection [8]. Given the lane boundaries, segmentation algorithms are applied to the bounded regions to refine lane labels. Reversely, some models segment lane areas first. Boundary information is then extracted by high-pass filters around segmented lane areas with a tolerance range [2,35]. However, these models treated lane area segmentation and lane boundary detection as two separate subprocesses, which share no information with each other, leading to a loss of geometrical dependency. Moreover, extremely poor performance could happen when the first sub-process is severely interfered by outliers.

To address abovementioned problems, we are motivated to provide a unified solution of lane area segmentation and lane boundary detection with a multi-task learning framework. Rather than simply fuse outputs of different tasks at final decision stage, we apply one shared encoder to the neural network for integrating complementary information of two tasks. Due to the lack of priors and loss of information, single-task approaches cannot achieve desired performance. Additionally, a novel structure called link encoder is appended, which can implicitly extract interrelationship information between lane area and its boundaries. Therefore, the flowed information between two tasks refines the performance for each other. At the classifier layer, the result is generated by the superposition of such a refinement over the original output. As shown in Fig. 1, segmentation is interfered severely by outliers and it is unable to recover from error segmentation. In our approach, when lane area segmentation fails to segment hard examples, the other task of lane boundary detection with a good performance could provide valid features and recover the segmentation task from failure. It is the same vice versa. Furthermore, two geometric prior constraints are proposed in our model to regularize the problem of lane detection into well-posed formulation. Given lane boundary detection, we predict the lane area as the area integration result with the lane boundaries as the upper bound and the lower bound. Given extracted lane areas, lane boundaries are predicted as the outer contours. The differences between the prediction results and the ground truth are then formulated as two loss terms to emphasize geometric priors during model training. The geometric constraints are differentiable due to pixel-wise convolution. The overall network is capable of joint-training as an end-to-end implementation. Experimental results on benchmarks demonstrate that our approach outperforms other state-of-art approaches under several metrics.

2   Related Work

Traditional methods of lane segmentation dominantly utilize pixel-level and super-pixel level features. Among the pixel-level features [2,3,15,33], color features robust to shadow interference are extracted for lane segmentation using region growing [3]. Texture features from varied color space are described by histogram peaks and temporal filter responses, then lane areas are generated within flat regions [15]. Alon et al. compute dominant edges based on pixel-wise gradient map and form them as the lane boundaries [33]. With the guidance of these boundaries, a color-based region growing is followed to generate lane areas. Valente et al. [2] extract pixel-level color features and classify them into lane areas first. Then boundaries are introduced to constrain the refinement of lane areas. To handle outlier situations, super-pixel features are preferably used. Li et al. [22] train an AdaBoost classifier with super-pixel color features extracted by Orthogonal Matching Pursuit algorithm to enhance lane detection.

With the development of deep learning methods, semantic segmentation has got impressive results [5,23,27]. Several modified single-task networks are proposed, focusing on embedding extra knowledge into networks [6,10]. Gao et al. [10] advance contour priors and location priors to segment lane region elaborately. Due to the lack of priors and loss of information, multi-task approaches are proposed to tackle this problem by introducing more surrounding constraints. Oliveira et al. [25] train a joint classification, detection and semantic segmentation network with a shared encoder. With a joint-training manner, the final lane area is generated by better features containing more surrounding details. However, inherent connections are not mined between multiple outputs, making it difficult to explain the mechanism behind the network structure.

Plenty of works utilize high-pass filters for boundary detection [4,12]. Haloi et al. [12] combine responses from 2nd- and 4th-order filters to obtain lane boundary features with adaptive thresholding. Aly et al. filter inverse perspective mapping (IPM) image with 2D Gaussian kernels [4]. Kortli et al. [18] and Bergasa et al. [7] detect edges with a canny kernel and the Otsu method.

However, the precision of lane boundary detection suffers from illumination variations, noises and cluttered background. Some deep learning techniques are developed to improve the performance. Overfeat detector is proposed to integrate recognition, localization and detection using convolution [29]. Later, Huval et al. [14] modify Overfeat structure to handle lane boundary detection and vehicle detection at the same time. However, these methods are sensitive to surrounding objects. So, Li et al. [21] feed the features extracted by convolution layers into a recurrent neuron layer as a sequence, where the spatial continuity constraint is used to regularize the result of lane detection. Kim et al. [16] propose a simpler but effective network structure. They finetune the network with a pretrained VGG network to generate detection results. These approaches require extra data for sufficient pretraining, and they are sensitive to cluttered background.

Fig. 1. Reciprocal constraints with geometric relation. **Left:** With an image input, traditional methods generate a binary segmentation mask for lane areas (green) or lane boundaries (red), which are severely affected by outlier situations. **Right:** Our approach introduces a geometric constraint into a multi-task network, which is capable to restore the missing lane area and lane boundaries (blue) mutually. (Color figure online)

3 Methodology

3.1 Overview of Multi-task Framework

For human perception, lane area is always inseparable from the judgment of its boundaries. However, the existing lane detection methods dominantly rely on a single-task network to independently train lane segmentation and lane boundary detection, completely ignoring the inherent geometric constraints between two tasks. Simple multi-task networks like MultiNet [32] are developed to combine tasks together, such as classification, detection and segmentation, without investigating the inherent relationship between tasks. There are two major problems in these state-of-the-art methods: the loss of interrelationship between multiple training tasks and the lack of geometric priors for well-posed formulation. As a result, they are always stuck in detection failure on hard examples.

Inspired by this observation, we propose a multi-task learning framework to provide a unified solution of lane segmentation and lane boundary detection. The network architecture is illustrated in Fig. 2, which consists of an encoder network and a decoder network, as a kind of fully convolutional network (FCN). Rather than conducting segmentation and detection with two separate networks, the proposed framework conducts two tasks with one shared encoder network and two separated decoders. To classify pixels into binary labels, each decoder is followed by a sigmoid classifier. Specifically, each decoder is connected to a link encoder to stream complementary information between two tasks and thus the features of two decoders could be reciprocally refined.

To achieve well-posed formulation of the multi-task learning framework, we propose a novel loss function by introducing the inherent geometric priors between tasks, as assumed that the lane boundary is predicted as the outer

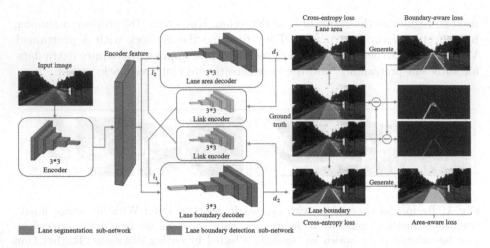

Fig. 2. The proposed multi-task framework. Input images are fed into a shared encoder, which extracts the critical features for lane segmentation and lane boundary detection. Two inter-link encoders connected to each decoder provide complementary information for tasks. The overall performance is enhanced by introducing a structure loss, assuming that the lane boundary is predicted as the outer contour of the lane area while the lane area is predicted as the area integration result within the lane boundaries.

contour of the lane area while the lane area is predicted as the area integration result within the lane boundaries. These geometric priors are critical to find a consistent solution of lane segmentation and lane boundary detection. With an end-to-end training process, these improvements extremely enhance the robustness and accuracy of our approach on several metrics

3.2   Critical Feature Extraction Using a Shared Encoder

To illustrate the activated regions by encoders of lane segmentation and lane boundary detection in a single task learning framework respectively, we visualize each activation map using a heat map. As shown in Fig. 3, the lanes with the similar textures are all emphasized by lane segmentation [19], which incurs the ambiguity problem of lane detection. Also, some background regions are activated. In contrast, the edges in background incur a more severe outlier problem for lane boundary detection.

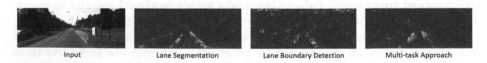

Fig. 3. Activation map of encoders. Activation maps are generated from final convolution layers of encoders. Pixel color indicates task-related saliency with respect to input images. (Color figure online)

A shared encoder is proposed to greatly reduce the ambiguity problem and outliers, because the features critical to the performance improvement of both tasks have been emphasized during network training process. As compared in Fig. 3, a clearer lane extraction is obtained while using the shared encoder.

3.3   Complementary Feature Extraction Using an Inter-link Encoder

The shared encoder puts much attention to the features critical to the overall performance. However, some important features for one task might be suppressed once they are not so critical in the other task. For example, lane area segmentation puts much emphasis on the fine-grained texture features for accurate pixel-wise label, while lane boundary detection prefers edge-like features.

Fig. 4. Top: Original image and FP+FN area (red) generated by the initial network. **Bottom:** The image of absolute difference before and after the refinements by inter-link encoders. As noted from the heat maps, the initial false positive results are effectively suppressed and the originally missed lane pixels are well restored, as emphasized in warm color. (Color figure online)

An inter-link encoder is put forward to stream complementary information between two tasks and thus the features of two decoders could be reciprocally refined. As shown in Fig. 2, decoders initially receive the feature f and output preliminary results as the inputs of inter-link encoders. Then these decoders generate final results with the refined features, where features f are complemented with inter-link encoders outputs l_1 and l_2 using simple concatenation. Thus decoders actually do forward pass twice. These refined features enhance the representation of lanes. It is expected to improve the performance of lane segmentation and lane boundary detection in a unified way.

At the first row in Fig. 4, segmentation results are generated without inter-link encoders, where the red regions indicate false positive and false negative results. The bottom row shows absolute difference image before and after refinements from inter-link encoders, where pixels are highlighted using heat map to indicate the absolute difference of segmentation confidence. As emphasized with warm color, with addition information provided by inter-link encoders, it is notable that the originally false positive results are then effectively suppressed, and the originally missed lane pixels are well restored.

3.4   Geometry Constrained Structure Loss

Boundary Aware Loss for Lane Area Segmentation. With cross-entropy set up as a loss function for lane area segmentation, it results in groups of pixels with false labels due to high ambiguity. We introduce a boundary-aware loss for lane area segmentation, assuming that there exists a consistency between the boundaries of segmented lane areas with the ground truth of lane boundaries.

Fig. 5. Boundary-aware loss and area-aware loss. **Left:** An illustration of our boundary-aware loss. The blue area indicates boundary inconsistency. **Right:** An illustration of our area-aware loss. Different intensities in prediction areas indicate different prediction confidence. The difference between restored area and ground truth indicates the area aware loss. (Color figure online)

It is noted that a slight deviation of lane boundaries from ground truth could produce an extremely large loss with pixel-wise comparison, as illustrated in Fig. 5. Therefore, we employ IoU loss [26] to measure boundary inconsistency. Accordingly a slight deviation would results in a small IoU loss, which ensures convergence. Let $\mathcal{I}$ denote the set of pixels in the image. For every pixel p in the pixel set $\mathcal{I}$, y_p corresponds to its output probability. And $g = \{0, 1\}^{M \times N}$ is the ground truth for the set $\mathcal{I}$. Here, M and N are the height and width of the image. By masking lane segmentation results with the lane area bounded by the ground truth of lane boundaries, our boundary-aware loss l_{ba} can be defined as:

$$\text{IoU} = \frac{\sum_{p \in \mathcal{I}} (y_p \times g_p)}{\sum_{p \in \mathcal{I}} (y_p + g_p - y_p \times g_p)}, \tag{1}$$

$$l_{ba} = 1 - IoU, \tag{2}$$

where $\times$ denotes a pixel-wise multiplication.

Two consistency constraints are imposed to enhance the results of lane segmentation. The cross entropy loss term l_{lce} measures the consistency between the segmented area and its ground truth. Additionally, the loss term l_{ba} measures the consistency between the boundaries of the segmented area and the lane boundary ground truth. Correspondingly, the loss function l_{lt} to measure the total error of lane segmentation is updated as:

$$l_{lt} = l_{lce} + \lambda_1 \times l_{ba}, \tag{3}$$

where λ_1 is a constant for balancing two losses. Here we set λ_1 as 0.5. With only pixel-wise linear calculation involved, l_{ba} is fully differentiable.

Area-aware Loss for Lane Boundary. Compared with lane area segmentation, lane boundary detection suffers more from the higher missing rate due to the lower Signal Noise Ratio around boundaries. Motivated by the geometric prior that the lane area is the area integration result with lane boundaries as the upper and lower bounds, an area-aware loss is proposed to measure the difference between the lane area restored from detected lane boundary and lane area ground truth.

Our area-aware loss function is expressed as:

$$l_{aa} = \sum_{\mathcal{G}(p)=1} [1 - I_r(p)], \tag{4}$$

where $\mathcal{G}$ is the pixel-wise label set of lane area ground truth, and $\mathcal{G}(p) = 1$ denotes that pixel p belongs to the lane area, and $I_r(p)$ is the calculated probability of pixel p belonging to the restored lane area. The loss function l_{mt} to measure the error of lane boundary detection is defined as

$$l_{mt} = l_{mce} + \lambda_2 \times l_{aa}, \tag{5}$$

where l_{mce} is the cross-entropy loss measuring the consistency between the detected lane boundary and its ground truth in a complementary way.

Pixels with strong spatial correlation always present similar intensity distribution, therefore we estimate pixel intensities in the restored lane area directly from the closest pixels on lane boundaries. Denote pixels of two boundary lane boundaries as pixel set $\mathcal{B}$. For pixel p between lane boundary ground truth, its probability belonging to lane area is equal to the probability of the closest pixel on lane boundaries, which is computed as:

$$I_r(p) = \frac{1}{n} \sum_{j=1}^{n} I_b(v_j), \tag{6}$$

$$v_j = \arg \min_{m_i} [d(p, m_i)] \quad m_i \in \mathcal{B}, \tag{7}$$

where $d(x, y)$ is the Euclidean distance between pixels x and y, $I_b(v)$ is the pixel probability in boundary detection map.

Computing the restored lane area from Eqs. 6 and 7, we reform the loss function l_{aa} as:

$$l_{aa} = \sum_{\mathcal{G}(p)=1} [1 - I_r(p)] = \sum_{\mathcal{G}(p)=1} \left\{ 1 - \frac{1}{n} \sum_{j=1}^{n} I_b\{\arg \min_{m_i} [d(p, m_i)]\} \right\} \quad m_i \in \mathcal{B}, \tag{8}$$

Thus, the integrated loss function is finally formulated as below:

$$l = l_{lce} + \lambda_1 \times l_{ba} + l_{mce} + \lambda_2 \times l_{aa}. \tag{9}$$

3.5 Training Details

Our framework is designed to be fully-convolutional and differentiable, thus it could be trained in an end-to-end manner. In this section, we mainly focus on implementation details of training process.

The shared encoder network is initialized by ImageNet [28] with VGG structure [31]. First, we start with training single lane segmentation subnetwork. Secondly, we turn to both subnetworks of lane area segmentation and boundary detection, which is trained without inter-link encoder structure. Finally, our multi-task learning framework is overall retrained with inter-link encoders added.

We concatenate an all-zero tensor to the output of the shared encoder, so that the input feature dimension of decoders remains the same during the iterative training procedure. The overall framework utilizes a batch normalization with the batch size of 3. To avoid overfitting, a dropout layer [13] is adopted with a rate of 0.2. We use the Adam optimizer [17] and pretrain the lane segmentation and lane boundary detection subnetworks with a learning rate of 10^{-3}. For multi-task framework training process, learning rate is set as 10^{-4} until convergence.

4 Experiment

We evaluate our approach on two lane segmentation datasets: KITTI dataset [11], Road-Vehicle dataset (RVD) [8] and CULane dataset [34]. Approaches are coded and evaluated by Tensorflow [1]. Processing time is evaluated on GeForce GTX TITAN with $160 * 320$ input images.

4.1 Dataset and Evaluation

The KITTI dataset contains 289 training images and 290 testing images, including four subsets of road scenes: urban marked road (UM), urban multiple marked road (UMM), urban unmarked road (UU) and URBAN ROAD (the union of the former three). UM is defined as marked roads with two lanes, while UMM consists of the roads with multiple lanes. UU stands for roads without lane markings and contains one lane only.

The RVD dataset contains more than 10 h of traffic scenarios with multiple sensors under different weather and road conditions, including highway scenes, night scenes and rain scenes. There are over 10,000 manually labeled images in this dataset, which are divided into different scenes with respect to surrounding conditions such as weather and illumination.

The CULane dataset contains 133,235 images extracted from 55 h of traffic videos, which is divided into 88,880 images for training set, 9,675 for validation set and 34,680 for testing set. The test set is split into 8 subsets based on their scenes to demonstrate the robustness of different network structures. This newly released dataset contains lane boundary ground truth only, so we generate lane area ground truth according to bounded areas of lane boundaries.

To evaluate lane segmentation results, we follow the classical pixel-wise segmentation metrics with precision (P), recall (R), F1-measure and IoU score. The metrics with the removal of foreshortening effects are not considerd, because inverse perspective mapping incurs distortions in the ground truth.

For lane boundary detection, we evaluate the performance with a pixel-wise metric. On KITTI dataset, when the distance of detected lane boundary and ground truth is smaller than a threshold (1.5% of image diagonal), the detected lane boundary is regarded as a true positive (TP). While on the CULane dataset, we follow its metric for fair comparison. When the IoU of detected lane boundary and ground truth is larger than 0.5 threshold, the detected boundary is regarded as a true positive (TP) [34]. The same for all the methods for comparison. The final results are evaluated with precision (P), recall (R) and F1-measure.

4.2   Results and Discussion

Our experiments are designed as two parts. First, we compare our lane area segmentation approach with state-of-the-art methods on KITTI, CULane and RVD dataset. Then, to demonstrate the effectiveness of our multi-task structure, lane boundary detection results are evaluated on KITTI and CULane dataset.

Lane Segmentation Results on KITTI. The proposed network is first compared with state-of-the-art approaches (including the SegNet [5], the U-Net [27] and the Up-Conv-Poly [25]) on KITTI dataset. Table 1 shows the overall results. Compared with the baseline approach [5], our methods are superior to it. Joint-training improves performance even without an inter-link encoder and structure loss functions. Benefited from the investigation of inherent inter-relationship between tasks, our multi-task framework obtains a better feature representation than a single-task network and boosts performance further.

Table 1. Lane segmentation results on URBAN_ROAD KITTI dataset. 'multi-task', 'loss', 'link' and 'link+loss' denote networks without losses or link structure, with losses only, with link structure only and with both losses and link structure.

Method	Runtime (ms)	F1	P	R	IoU
SegNet [5]	19.43	0.894	0.899	0.889	0.808
U-Net [27]	16.92	0.909	0.875	**0.945**	0.833
Up-Conv-Poly [25]	11.27	0.921	0.921	0.922	0.854
Ours (multi-task)	34.70	0.920	0.911	0.929	0.852
Ours (loss)	34.70	0.925	0.917	0.933	0.861
Ours (inter-link)	41.28	0.927	0.925	0.930	0.865
Ours (inter-link+loss)	41.28	**0.933**	**0.936**	0.930	**0.874**

Note that our approach also outperforms U-Net and Up-Conv-Poly with a gain of 4.1% and 2.0% on IoU score. Both approaches connect encoder layers with decoder layers, which make decoders receive the same scale information from encoders directly. Our multi-task network better captures the dependency of geometric structure of lanes and markers. We also evaluate approaches on several different traffic scenes in Table 2. Results show that our approach is robust to scenario changes.

Table 2. Lane segmentation results on KITTI subsets(UM/UMM/UU)

Method	UM lane				UMM lane				UU lane			
	F1	P	R	IoU	F1	P	R	IoU	F1	P	R	IoU
SegNet [5]	0.926	0.920	0.933	0.863	0.927	0.905	0.950	0.864	0.859	0.905	0.817	0.752
U-Net [27]	0.924	0.876	**0.977**	0.859	0.929	0.877	**0.988**	0.867	0.904	0.907	0.902	0.826
Up-Conv-Poly [25]	0.936	0.929	0.944	0.881	0.953	0.943	0.963	0.910	0.918	0.936	0.901	0.849
Ours (Multi-task)	0.932	0.913	0.951	0.872	0.953	0.932	0.974	0.910	0.919	0.933	0.906	0.850
Ours (Loss)	0.950	0.940	0.961	0.906	0.952	0.932	0.972	0.908	0.922	0.927	**0.917**	0.855
Ours (Link)	0.948	0.942	0.954	0.901	0.958	0.947	0.970	0.926	0.921	0.932	0.911	0.855
Ours (Link+Loss)	**0.954**	**0.957**	0.951	**0.912**	**0.962**	**0.957**	0.967	**0.927**	**0.931**	**0.947**	0.916	**0.871**

We study the influence of inter-link encoders and structure loss functions in our model. Note that we achieve 86.1% IoU score on our structure-loss-only approach and 86.5% IoU score in our inter-link-only approach. With inter-link encoders and losses added, our final approach (link+loss) achieves 87.4% on IoU and 93.3% on F1-measure. The individually applied structure loss and inter-link encoders play a crucial role in promoting segmentation results. Figure 7 shows some lane area segmentation results obtained by our approach, Up-Conv-Net and U-Net approaches on the KITTI dataset. Our approach effectively handles hard cases such as vanishing boundaries on the first two columns of Fig. 7.

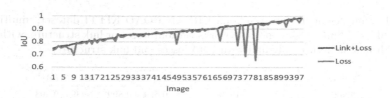

Fig. 6. The IoU metric evaluated with a single image in KITTI dataset. The blue line is our approach with structure loss functions while the orange line is our approach without structure loss. (Color figure online)

To demonstrate the efficiency of structure loss, our approaches with and without structure loss are evaluated by several examples of single images in Fig. 6. We randomly pick 100 images in KITTI dataset and calculate the IoU score for both approaches. The evaluation results reveal that, the introduction of structure loss structure loss presents higher robustness to disturbance.

Lane Segmentation Results on CULane Dataset. We also evaluate lane segmentation on a newly published CULane dataset. The test set is divided into 8 different scenes: Arrow, Crowded, Curve, Dazzle light, Night, No line, Normal and Shadow. The overall performance is also shown in the last column.

Experiment results are shown in Table 3. It is significant that our method outperforms state-of-the-art methods on all 8 subsets and achieves 90.2% F1-measure and 82.4% IoU on the overall dataset, demonstrating that our method is more robust to handle various traffic scenes than state-of-the-art methods. Also, our method achieves a remarkable improvement on 4 subsets (Arrow, Crowd, Shadow and Normal). This is because our method could capture lane boundary structure from cluttered backgrounds. The well-extracted boundary features provide complementary information to effectively suppress error segmentation.

Table 3. Lane segmentation results on CULane dataset

Method	Arrow		Crowd		Curve		Dazzle light		Night	
	F1	IoU	F1	IoU	F1	IoU	F1	IoU	F1	IoU
U-Net [27]	0.909	0.832	0.906	0.828	0.865	0.763	0.873	0.775	0.875	0.779
SegNet [5]	0.906	0.829	0.899	0.818	0.846	0.733	0.867	0.765	0.847	0.735
Up-Conv-Poly [25]	0.899	0.816	0.903	0.823	0.864	0.761	0.886	0.796	0.871	0.772
Ours	**0.922**	**0.856**	**0.913**	**0.841**	**0.868**	**0.765**	**0.891**	**0.803**	**0.876**	**0.781**

Method	No line		Normal		Shadow		Total	
	F1	IoU	F1	IoU	F1	IoU	F1	IoU
U-Net [27]	0.802	0.671	0.934	0.887	0.825	0.703	0.892	0.810
SegNet [5]	0.800	0.668	0.932	0.873	0.835	0.711	0.883	0.794
Up-Conv-Poly [25]	0.813	0.685	0.935	0.878	0.832	0.711	0.892	0.807
Ours	**0.814**	**0.686**	**0.949**	**0.903**	**0.872**	**0.774**	**0.902**	**0.824**

Lane Segmentation Results on RVD Dataset. Furthermore, we evaluate lane segmentation on the RVD dataset. As mentioned in 4.1, this dataset contains three different scenes: Highway, Night and Rainy & Snowy Day. Besides SegNet, U-Net and Up-Conv-Poly, we evaluate the performance of CMA method [8].

Table 4. Lane segmentation results on RVD dataset

Method	Highway				Night				Rainy & Snowy Day			
	F1	P	R	IoU	F1	P	R	IoU	F1	P	R	IoU
U-Net [27]	0.972	0.972	0.973	0.947	0.946	0.915	0.980	0.898	0.971	0.963	0.979	0.944
SegNet [5]	0.978	0.969	0.987	0.957	0.968	0.962	0.975	0.940	0.971	0.965	0.978	0.944
Up-Conv-Poly [25]	0.979	0.977	0.982	0.960	0.974	0.972	0.977	0.950	0.971	**0.979**	0.963	0.944
CMA [8]	0.989	**0.989**	0.989	/	0.976	0.976	0.977	/	0.974	0.968	0.980	/
Ours	**0.990**	0.987	**0.992**	**0.979**	**0.988**	**0.989**	**0.987**	**0.981**	**0.977**	0.973	**0.981**	**0.956**

Overall results are presented in Table 4. Note that CMA only extracts end-points of two lane boundaries to segment lane area. It enforces a rigid geometric assumption, and thus fails to segment curve lanes. In contrast, the geometric priors introduced in our network are more applicable in various scenes, achieving a significant improvement over all the metrics. Although the performance on Highway is similar due to clear background, we dramatically improve the performance in other scenes, especially in night scenarios. With a better representation of boundary information and geometry constraints, illumination variation and image degradation are well-handled by our approach.

Lane Boundary Detection Results. In addition to lane segmentation, we also evaluate the effectiveness of lane boundary detection on KITTI and CULane dataset. We test several approaches with manually labeled lane boundary ground truth, and present the performance of SegNet [5], SegNet-Ego-Lane [16] and SCNN [34]. We also report our approach only with the cross-entropy loss to emphasize the effectiveness of structure loss function on KITTI dataset. Some lane boundary detection results are also shown in Fig. 7.

The results on KITTI dataset are provided in Table 5. As for precision, Seg-Net yields slightly better than us. However, SegNet has a extremely low recall rate, which indicates that SegNet misses plenty of true positives. Our approach achieves the highest recall rate than other approaches, as well as the F1 measure.

Fig. 7. Lane area segmentation and lane boundary detection results on KITTI dataset. Green corresponds to true positives, blue to false positives and red to false negatives. (Color figure online)

Table 5. Lane boundary results on KITTI dataset

Method	F1	P	R
SegNet [5]	0.691	**0.865**	0.575
SegNet-Ego-Lane [16]	0.522	0.411	0.714
Ours (inter-link)	0.788	0.806	0.771
Ours (inter-link+loss)	**0.831**	0.838	**0.824**

Table 6. Lane boundary results on CULane dataset (F1-measure)

Method	Normal	Crowded	Night	No line	Shadow	Arrow	Dazzle light	Curve	Total
SegNet [5]	0.792	0.617	0.496	0.145	0.294	0.710	0.389	0.456	0.572
SegNet-Ego-Lane [16]	0.754	0.620	0.578	0.177	0.310	0.714	0.476	0.430	0.584
SCNN [34]	0.883	0.753	0.686	**0.365**	0.593	0.821	0.531	0.594	0.720
Ours	**0.897**	**0.765**	**0.687**	0.351	**0.655**	**0.822**	**0.674**	**0.632**	**0.731**

The ablation analysis of our approaches indicates that the lane area-aware loss function dramatically improves the performance of lane boundary detection. We gain 3.2% on precision, 5.3% on recall and 4.3% on F1 measure.

The results on CULane dataset are shown in Table 6. Note that our method outperforms state-of-the-art methods on 7 subsets. State-of-the-art methods have worse performance mainly due to the image degradation and the missing of lane boundaries. As for the image degradation problem, our subnetwork is able to extracts better boundary features with our area-aware loss. So we dramatically improve performance on Night, Dazzle Light and Shadow subsets, where image quality is affected severely by illumination conditions. For unseen lane boundary problem, it is extremely difficult to extract enough boundary features for boundary detection. Although SCNN introduces context information for boundary detection, various scenes contain extremely different context information, resulting in inaccuracy of lane detection results. Meanwhile, our inter-link structure utilizes more robust geometric relationship between lane areas and boundaries, which constrains each other for better performance.

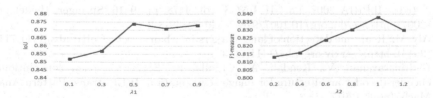

Fig. 8. Parameters λ_1 and λ_2 validation experiments on KITTI

4.3 Parameter Study

To choose optimal parameters λ_1 and λ_2, parameter study is performed on 10-fold cross validation set. The performance of different λ_1 values is compared by IoU score of lane area segmentation while λ_2 performance are evaluated by F1-measure of lane boundary detection. The final results are shown in Fig. 8, where both parameters are chosen at regular intervals. Although λ_1 larger than 0.5 achieves similar IoU score, the experiment shows large λ_1 is sensitive to hyperparameters. So λ_1 is set to 0.5. And λ_2 is set to 1.0 for the best performance.

5 Conclusion

We propose a multi-task learning framework to jointly address the problems of lane segmentation and lane boundary detection. In this framework, a shared encoder and an inter-link encoder structure are proposed, whose benefits for the boost of detection precision have been proved by experiments. In addition, we come up with two novel loss functions which are established to be applicable to a more general traffic scene. The proposed method is compared with state-of-the-art ones on KITTI and RVD dataset, and shows a leading performance.

Acknowledgement. This work was supported by National Science Foundation of China 61671298 and STCSM 17511105400, 18DZ2270700. This work was supported by SJTU-UCLA Joint Center for Machine Perception and Inference. The work was also partially supported by NSFC (U1611461, 61502301, 61521062), China's Thousand Youth Talents Plan, the 111 project B07022 and MoE Key Lab of Artificial Intelligence, AI Institute, Shanghai Jiao Tong University, China.

References

1. Abadi, M., et a.: TensorFlow: Large-scale machine learning on heterogeneous systems (2015). http://tensorflow.org/
2. Alon, Y., Ferencz, A., Shashua, A.: Off-road path following using region classification and geometric projection constraints. In: 2006 IEEE Computer Society Conference on Computer Vision and Pattern Recognition (CVPR 2006), New York, NY, USA, pp. 689–696, 17–22 June 2006. https://doi.org/10.1109/CVPR.2006.213
3. Álvarez, J.M., López, A.M., Baldrich, R.: Shadow resistant road segmentation from a mobile monocular system. In: Martí, J., Benedí, J.M., Mendonça, A.M., Serrat, J. (eds.) IbPRIA 2007, Part II. LNCS, vol. 4478, pp. 9–16. Springer, Heidelberg (2007). https://doi.org/10.1007/978-3-540-72849-8_2
4. Aly, M.: Real time detection of lane markers in urban streets. CoRR abs/1411.7113 (2014). http://arxiv.org/abs/1411.7113
5. Badrinarayanan, V., Kendall, A., Cipolla, R.: SegNet: a deep convolutional encoder-decoder architecture for image segmentation. IEEE Trans. Pattern Anal. Mach. Intell. (2017)
6. Barnes, D., Maddern, W., Posner, I.: Find your own way: weakly-supervised segmentation of path proposals for urban autonomy. In: 2017 IEEE International Conference on Robotics and Automation, ICRA 2017, Singapore, Singapore, pp. 203–210, May 29–June 3 2017. https://doi.org/10.1109/ICRA.2017.7989025

7. Bergasa, L.M., Almeria, D., Almazán, J., Torres, J.J.Y., Arroyo, R.: DriveSafe: An app for alerting inattentive drivers and scoring driving behaviors. In: 2014 IEEE Intelligent Vehicles Symposium Proceedings, Dearborn, MI, USA, pp. 240–245, 8–11 June 2014. https://doi.org/10.1109/IVS.2014.6856461

8. Chen, S., Zhang, S., Shang, J., Chen, B., Zheng, N.: Brain inspired cognitive model with attention for self-driving cars. CoRR abs/1702.05596 (2017). http://arxiv.org/abs/1702.05596

9. Fischler, M.A., Bolles, R.C.: Random sample consensus: a paradigm for model fitting with applications to image analysis and automated cartography. Commun. ACM **24**(6), 381–395 (1981). https://doi.org/10.1145/358669.358692

10. Gao, J., Wang, Q., Yuan, Y.: Embedding structured contour and location prior in siamesed fully convolutional networks for road detection. In: 2017 IEEE International Conference on Robotics and Automation, ICRA 2017, Singapore, Singapore, pp. 219–224 29 May–3 June 2017. https://doi.org/10.1109/ICRA.2017.7989027

11. Geiger, A., Lenz, P., Stiller, C., Urtasun, R.: Vision meets robotics: the KITTI dataset. Int. J. Robot. Res. **32**(11), 1231–1237 (2013). https://doi.org/10.1177/0278364913491297

12. Haloi, M., Jayagopi, D.B.: Vehicle local position estimation system. CoRR abs/1503.06648 (2015). http://arxiv.org/abs/1503.06648

13. Hinton, G.E., Srivastava, N., Krizhevsky, A., Sutskever, I., Salakhutdinov, R.: Improving neural networks by preventing co-adaptation of feature detectors. CoRR abs/1207.0580 (2012). http://arxiv.org/abs/1207.0580

14. Huval, B., et al.: An empirical evaluation of deep learning on highway driving. CoRR abs/1504.01716 (2015). http://arxiv.org/abs/1504.01716

15. Katramados, I., Crumpler, S., Breckon, T.P.: Real-time traversable surface detection by colour space fusion and temporal analysis. In: Fritz, M., Schiele, B., Piater, J.H. (eds.) ICVS 2009. LNCS, vol. 5815, pp. 265–274. Springer, Heidelberg (2009). https://doi.org/10.1007/978-3-642-04667-4_27

16. Kim, J., Park, C.: End-to-end ego lane estimation based on sequential transfer learning for self-driving cars. In: 2017 IEEE Conference on Computer Vision and Pattern Recognition Workshops, CVPR Workshops, Honolulu, HI, USA, pp. 1194–1202, 21–26 July 2017. https://doi.org/10.1109/CVPRW.2017.158

17. Kingma, D.P., Ba, J.: Adam: A method for stochastic optimization. CoRR abs/1412.6980 (2014). http://arxiv.org/abs/1412.6980

18. Kortli, Y., Marzougui, M., Bouallegue, B., Bose, J.S.C., Rodrigues, P., Atri, M.: A novel illumination-invariant lane detection system. In: 2017 2nd International Conference on Anti-Cyber Crimes (ICACC), pp. 166–171, March 2017

19. Kotikalapudi, R., contributors: keras-vis (2017). https://github.com/raghakot/keras-vis

20. Levinson, J., et al.: Towards fully autonomous driving: systems and algorithms. In: 2011 IEEE Intelligent Vehicles Symposium (IV), Baden-Baden, Germany, pp. 163–168, 5–9 June 2011

21. Li, J., Mei, X., Prokhorov, D.V., Tao, D.: Deep neural network for structural prediction and lane detection in traffic scene. IEEE Trans. Neural Netw. Learn. Syst. **28**(3), 690–703 (2017). https://doi.org/10.1109/TNNLS.2016.2522428

22. Li, J., Jin, L., Fei, S., Ma, J.: Robust urban road image segmentation. In: Proceedings of the 11th World Congress on Intelligent Control and Automation, pp. 2923–2928, June 2014

23. Long, J., Shelhamer, E., Darrell, T.: Fully convolutional networks for semantic segmentation. CoRR abs/1411.4038 (2014). http://arxiv.org/abs/1411.4038

24. Lu, K., Li, J., An, X., He, H.: A hierarchical approach for road detection. In: 2014 IEEE International Conference on Robotics and Automation, ICRA 2014, Hong Kong, China, pp. 517–522, 31 May–7 June 2014. https://doi.org/10.1109/ICRA.2014.6906904

25. Oliveira, G.L., Burgard, W., Brox, T.: Efficient deep models for monocular road segmentation. In: 2016 IEEE/RSJ International Conference on Intelligent Robots and Systems, IROS 2016, Daejeon, South Korea, pp. 4885–4891, 9–14 October 2016. https://doi.org/10.1109/IROS.2016.7759717

26. Rahman, M.A., Wang, Y.: Optimizing intersection-over-union in deep neural networks for image segmentation. In: Bebis, G. (ed.) ISVC 2016. LNCS, vol. 10072, pp. 234–244. Springer, Cham (2016). https://doi.org/10.1007/978-3-319-50835-1_22

27. Ronneberger, O., Fischer, P., Brox, T.: U-Net: convolutional networks for biomedical image segmentation. In: Navab, N., Hornegger, J., Wells, W.M., Frangi, A.F. (eds.) MICCAI 2015. LNCS, vol. 9351, pp. 234–241. Springer, Cham (2015). https://doi.org/10.1007/978-3-319-24574-4_28. http://lmb.informatik.uni-freiburg.de/Publications/2015/RFB15a. arXiv:1505.04597 [cs.CV]

28. Russakovsky, O., et al.: ImageNet large scale visual recognition challenge. Int. J. Comput. Vision (IJCV) 115(3), 211–252 (2015)

29. Sermanet, P., Eigen, D., Zhang, X., Mathieu, M., Fergus, R., LeCun, Y.: OverFeat: integrated recognition, localization and detection using convolutional networks. CoRR abs/1312.6229 (2013). http://arxiv.org/abs/1312.6229

30. Simonyan, K., Vedaldi, A., Zisserman, A.: Deep inside convolutional networks: visualising image classification models and saliency maps. CoRR abs/1312.6034 (2013). http://arxiv.org/abs/1312.6034

31. Simonyan, K., Zisserman, A.: Very deep convolutional networks for large-scale image recognition. CoRR abs/1409.1556 (2014). http://arxiv.org/abs/1409.1556

32. Teichmann, M., Weber, M., Zöllner, J.M., Cipolla, R., Urtasun, R.: MultiNet: real-time joint semantic reasoning for autonomous driving. CoRR abs/1612.07695 (2016). http://arxiv.org/abs/1612.07695

33. Valente, M., Stanciulescu, B.: Real-time method for general road segmentation. In: IEEE Intelligent Vehicles Symposium, IV 2017, Los Angeles, CA, USA, pp. 443–447, 11–14 June 2017. https://doi.org/10.1109/IVS.2017.7995758

34. Pan, X., Shi, J., Luo, P., Wang, X., Tang, X.: Spatial as deep: Spatial CNN for traffic scene understanding. In: AAAI Conference on Artificial Intelligence (AAAI), February 2018

35. Zhang, G., Zheng, N., Cui, C., Yang, G.: An efficient road detection method in noisy urban environment. In: Intelligent Vehicles Symposium, pp. 556–561 (2009)

Unpaired Image Captioning
by Language Pivoting

Jiuxiang Gu[1]([✉]), Shafiq Joty[2], Jianfei Cai[2], and Gang Wang[3]

[1] ROSE Lab, Nanyang Technological University, Singapore, Singapore
jgu004@ntu.edu.sg
[2] SCSE, Nanyang Technological University, Singapore, Singapore
{srjoty,asjfcai}@ntu.edu.sg
[3] Alibaba AI Labs, Hangzhou, China
gangwang6@gmail.com

Abstract. Image captioning is a multimodal task involving computer vision and natural language processing, where the goal is to learn a mapping from the image to its natural language description. In general, the mapping function is learned from a training set of image-caption pairs. However, for some language, large scale image-caption paired corpus might not be available. We present an approach to this unpaired image captioning problem by language pivoting. Our method can effectively capture the characteristics of an image captioner from the pivot language (Chinese) and align it to the target language (English) using another pivot-target (Chinese-English) sentence parallel corpus. We evaluate our method on two image-to-English benchmark datasets: MSCOCO and Flickr30K. Quantitative comparisons against several baseline approaches demonstrate the effectiveness of our method.

Keywords: Image captioning · Unpaired learning

1 Introduction

Recent several years have witnessed unprecedented advancements in automatic image caption generation. This progress can be attributed *(i)* to the invention of novel deep learning framework that learns to generate natural language descriptions of images in an end-to-end fashion, and *(ii)* to the availability of large annotated corpora of images paired with captions such as MSCOCO [30] to train these models. The dominant methods are based on an encoder-decoder framework, which uses a deep convolutional neural network (CNN) to encode the image into a feature vector, and then use a recurrent neural network (RNN) to generate the caption from the encoded vector [27,29,44]. More recently, approaches of using attention mechanisms and reinforcement learning have dominated the MSCOCO captioning leaderboard [1,18,39].

Despite the impressive results achieved by the deep learning framework, one performance bottleneck is the availability of large paired datasets because neural image captioning models are generally *annotation-hungry* requiring a large

© Springer Nature Switzerland AG 2018
V. Ferrari et al. (Eds.): ECCV 2018, LNCS 11205, pp. 519–535, 2018.
https://doi.org/10.1007/978-3-030-01246-5_31

amount of annotated image-caption pairs to achieve effective results [19]. However, in many applications and languages, such large-scale annotations are not readily available, and are expensive and slow to acquire. In these scenarios, unsupervised methods that can generate captions from unpaired data or semi-supervised methods that can exploit paired annotations from other domains or languages are highly desirable [5]. In this paper, we pursue the later research avenue, where we assume that we have access to image-caption paired instances in one language (Chinese), and our goal is to transfer this knowledge to a target language (English) for which we do not have such image-caption paired datasets. We also assume that we have access to a separate source-target (Chinese-English) parallel corpus to help us with the transformation. In other words, we wish to use the source language (Chinese) as a pivot language to bridge the gap between an input image and a caption in the target language (English).

The concept of using a pivot language as an intermediary language has been studied previously in machine translation (MT) to translate between a resource-rich language and a resource-scarce language [6,25,42,46]. The translation task in this strategy is performed in two steps. A source-to-pivot MT system first translates a source sentence into the pivot language, which is in turn translated to the target language using a pivot-to-target MT system. Although related, image captioning with the help of a pivot language is fundamentally different from MT, since it involves putting together two different tasks – captioning and translation. In addition, the pivot-based *pipelined* approach to MT suffers from two major problems when it comes to image captioning. First, the conventional pivot-based MT methods assume that the datasets for source-to-pivot and pivot-to-target translations come from the same (or similar) domain(s) with similar styles and word distributions. However, as it comes to image captioning, captions in the pivot language (Chinese) and sentences in the (Chinese-English) parallel corpus are quite different in styles and word distributions. For instance, MSCOCO captioning dataset mostly consists of images of a large scene with object instances (nouns), whereas language parallel corpora are more generic. Second, the errors made in the source-to-pivot translation get propagated to the pivot-to-target translation module in the pipelined approach.

In this paper, we present an approach that can effectively capture the characteristics of an image captioner from the source language and align it to the target language using another source-target parallel corpus. More specifically, our pivot-based image captioning framework comprises an image captioner *image-to-pivot*, an encoder-decoder model that learns to describe images in the pivot language, and a *pivot-to-target* translation model, another encoder-decoder model that translates the sentence in pivot language to the target language, and these two models are trained on two separate datasets. We tackle the variations in writing styles and word distributions in the two datasets by adapting the language translation model to the captioning task. This is achieved by adapting both the encoder and the decoder of the pivot-to-target translation model. In particular, we regularize the word embeddings of the encoder (of pivot language) and the decoder (of target language) models to make them similar to image captions.

We also introduce a joint training algorithm to connect the two models and enable them to interact with each other during training. We use AIC-ICC [47] and AIC-MT [47] as the training datasets and two datasets (MSCOCO and Flickr30K [37]) as the validation datasets. The results show that our approach yields substantial gains over the baseline methods on the validation datasets.

2 Background

Image Caption Generation. Image caption generation is a fundamental problem of automatically generating natural language descriptions of images. Motivated by the recent advances in deep neural networks [13,20] and the release of large scale datasets [30,37,47], many studies [15,17,18,22,24,45,48,50,52] have used neural networks to generate image descriptions. Inspired by the success of encoder-decoder framework for neural machine translation (NMT) [1,9], many researchers have proposed to use such a framework for image caption generation [18,44]. One representative work in this direction is the method proposed by Vinyals *et al.* [44]. They encode the image with a CNN and use a Long Short-Term Memory (LSTM) network as the decoder, and the decoder is trained to maximize the log-likelihood estimation of the target captions. After that, many approaches have been proposed to improve such encoder-decoder framework. One of the most commonly used approaches is the attention mechanism [18,49]. Xu *et al.* [49] use the attention mechanisms to incorporate the spatial attention on convolutional features of an image into decoder. Another improvement is to leverage the high-level visual attributes to enhance the sentence decoder [31,51,52]. Recently, Gu *et al.* [19] propose a CNN-based image captioning model, which can explore both long-term and temporal information in word sequences for caption generation.

Exposure bias and loss-evaluation mismatch have been the major problems in sequence prediction tasks [38]. Exposure bias happens when a model is trained to predict a word given the previous ground-truth words but uses its own generated words during inference. The schedule sampling approach proposed in [2] can mitigate the exposure bias by selecting between the ground-truth words and the machine generated words according to the scheduled probability in training. Recently, the loss-evaluation mismatch problem has been well-addressed in sequence prediction tasks [18,32,38,39]. Rennie *et al.* [39] address both exposure bias and loss-evaluation problems with a self-critical learning, which utilizes the inference mode as the baseline in training. Gu *et al.* [18] propose a coarse-to-fine learning approach which simultaneously solves the multi-stage training problem as well as the exposure bias issue. The most closely related to our approach is [22]. However, they construct a multilingual parallel dataset based on MSCOCO image corpus, while in our paper, we do not have such a multilingual corpus.

Neural Machine Translation. Neural machine translation is an approach that directly models the conditional probability of translating a sentence in source language into a sentence in target language. A natural choice to model such a decomposition is to use RNN-based models [1,23,26,34,40]. Recently, researchers have tried to improve the translation performance by introducing the attention mechanism [10,26,35,41]. The attention-based translation model proposed by Kalchbrenner et al. [26] is an early attempt to train the end-to-end NMT model. Luong et al. [33] extend the basic encoder-decoder framework to multiple encoders and decoders. However, large-scale parallel corpora are usually not easy to obtain for some language pairs. This is unfortunate because NMT usually needs a large amount of data to train. As a result, improving NMT on resource-scarce language pairs has attracted much attention [16,55].

Recently, many works have been done in the area of pivot strategies of NMT [3,11,14,25,42,46,53]. Pivot-based approach introduces a third language, named pivot language for which there exist source-pivot and pivot-target parallel corpora. The translation of pivot-based approaches can be divided into two steps: the sentence in the source language is first translated into a sentence in the pivot language, which is then translated to a sentence in the target language. However, such pivot-based approach has a major problem that the errors made in the source-to-pivot model will be forwarded to the pivot-to-target model. Recently, Cheng et al. [7] introduce an autoencoder to reconstruct monolingual corpora. They further improve it in [8], in which they propose a joint training approach for pivot-based NMT.

3   Unpaired Image Captioning

Let $D_{i,x} = \{(i,x)^{(n_i)}\}_{n_i=0}^{N_i-1}$ denote the dataset with N_i image-caption pairs, and $D_{x,y} = \{(x,y)^{(n_x)}\}_{n_x=0}^{N_x-1}$ denote the translation dataset with N_x source-target sentence pairs. For notational simplicity, we use i to denote an image instance as well as the image modality. Similarly, we use x to represent a source sentence as well as a source/pivot language (Chinese), and y to represent a target sentence and a target language (English). Our ultimate goal is to learn a mapping function to describe an image i with a caption y. Formally,

$$y \sim \arg\max_{y} \{P(y|i; \theta_{i \to y})\} \tag{1}$$

where $\theta_{i \to y}$ are the model parameters to be learned in the absence of any paired data, $i^{(n_i)} \not\leftrightarrow y^{(n_y)}$. We use the pivot language x to learn the mapping: $i \xrightarrow{\theta_{i \to x}} x \xrightarrow{\theta_{x \to y}} y$. Note that image-to-pivot ($D_{i,x}$) and pivot-to-target ($D_{x,y}$) in our setting are two distinct datasets with possibly no common elements.

Figure 1 illustrates our pivot-based image captioning approach. We have an image captioning model $P(x|i; \theta_{i \to x})$ to generate a caption in the pivot language from an image and a NMT model $P(y|x; \theta_{x \to y})$ to translate this caption into the target language. In addition, we have an autoencoder in the target language $P(\hat{y}|\hat{y}; \theta_{\hat{y} \to \hat{y}})$ that guides the target language decoder to produce caption-like sentences. We train these components jointly so that they interact with each other. During inference, given an unseen image i to be described, we use the joint decoder:

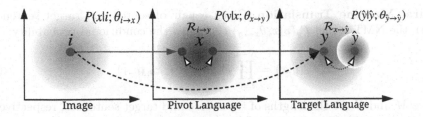

Fig. 1. Pictorial depiction of our pivot-based unpaired image captioning setting. Here, i, x, y, and $\hat{y}$ denote source image, pivot language sentence, target language sentence, and ground truth captions in target language, respectively. We use a dashed line to denote that there is no parallel corpus available for the pair. Solid lines with arrows represent decoding directions. Dashed lines inside a language (circle) denote stylistic and distributional differences between caption and translation data.

$$y \sim \arg\max_{y} \left\{ P(y|i; \theta_{i \to x}, \theta_{x \to y}) \right\} \tag{2}$$

In the following, we first give an overview of neural methods for image captioning and machine translation using paired (parallel) data. Then, we present our approach that extends these standard models for unpaired image captioning with a pivot language.

3.1 Encoder-Decoder Models for Image Captioning and Machine Translation

Standard Image Captioning. For image captioning in the paired setting, the goal is to generate a caption $\tilde{x}$ from an image i such that $\tilde{x}$ is as similar to the ground truth caption x. We use $P_x(x|i; \theta_{i \to x})$ to denote a standard encoder-decoder based image captioning model with $\theta_{i \to x}$ being the parameters. We first encode the given image to the image features v with a CNN-based image encoder: $v = \text{CNN}(i)$. Then, we predict the image description x from the global image feature v. The training objective is to maximize the probability of the ground truth caption words given the image:

$$\tilde{\theta}_{i \to x} = \arg\max_{\theta_{i \to x}} \left\{ \mathcal{L}_{i \to x} \right\} \tag{3}$$

$$= \arg\max_{\theta_{i \to x}} \left\{ \sum_{n_i=0}^{N_i-1} \sum_{t=0}^{M^{(n_i)}-1} \log P_x(x_t^{(n_i)} | x_{0:t-1}^{(n_i)}, i^{(n_i)}; \theta_{i \to x}) \right\} \tag{4}$$

where N_i is the number of image-caption pairs, $M^{(n_i)}$ is the length of the caption $x^{(n_i)}$, x_t denotes a word in the caption, and $P_x(x_t^{(n_i)} | x_{0:t-1}^{(n_i)}, i^{(n_i)})$ corresponds to the activation of the Softmax layer. The decoded word is drawn from:

$$x_t \sim \arg\max_{\mathcal{V}_{i \to x}^x} P(x_t | x_{0:t-1}; i) \tag{5}$$

where $\mathcal{V}_{i \to x}^x$ is the vocabulary of words in the image-caption dataset $D_{i,x}$.

Neural Machine Translation. Given a pair of source and target sentences (x, y), the NMT model $P_y(y|x; \theta_{x \to y})$ computes the conditional probability:

$$P_y(y|x) = \prod_{t=0}^{N-1} P(y_t|y_{0:t-1}; x_{0:M-1}) \tag{6}$$

where M and N are the lengths of the source and target sentences, respectively. The maximum-likelihood training objective of the model can be expressed as:

$$\tilde{\theta}_{x \to y} = \arg\max_{\theta_{x \to y}} \left\{ \mathcal{L}_{x \to y} \right\} \tag{7}$$

$$= \arg\max_{\theta_{x \to y}} \left\{ \sum_{n_x=0}^{N_x-1} \sum_{t=0}^{N^{(n_x)}-1} \log P_y(y_t^{(n_x)}|y_{0:t-1}^{(n_x)}; x^{(n_x)}; \theta_{x \to y}) \right\} \tag{8}$$

During inference we calculate the probability of the next symbol given the source sentence encoding and the decoded target sequence so far, and draw the word from the dictionary according to the maximum probability:

$$y_t \sim \arg\max_{\mathcal{V}_{x \to y}^y} P(y_t|y_{0:t-1}; x_{0:M-1}) \tag{9}$$

where $\mathcal{V}_{x \to y}^y$ is the vocabulary of the target language in the translation dataset $D_{x,y}$.

Unpaired Image Captioning by Language Pivoting. In the unpaired setting, our goal is to generate a description y in the target language for an image i without any pair information. We assume, there is a second language x called "pivot" for which we have (separate) image-pivot and pivot-target paired datasets. The image-to-target model in the pivot-based setting can be decomposed into two sub-models by treating the pivot sentence as a latent variable:

$$P(y|i; \theta_{i \to x}, \theta_{x \to y}) = \sum_x P_x(x|i; \theta_{i \to x}) P_y(y|x; \theta_{x \to y}) \tag{10}$$

where $P_x(x|i; \theta_{i \to x})$ and $P_y(y|x; \theta_{x \to y})$ are the image captioning and NMT models, respectively. Due to the exponential search space in the pivot language, we approximate the captioning process with two steps. The first step translates the image i into a pivot language sentence $\tilde{x}$. Then, the pivot language sentence is translated to a target language sentence $\tilde{y}$. To learn such a pivot-based model, a simple approach is to combine the two loss functions in Eqs. (3) and (7) as follows:

$$\mathcal{J}_{i \to x, x \to y} = \mathcal{L}_{i \to x} + \mathcal{L}_{x \to y} \tag{11}$$

During inference, the decoding decision is given by:

$$\tilde{x} = \arg\max_x \left\{ P_x(x|i; \tilde{\theta}_{i \to x}) \right\} \tag{12}$$

$$\tilde{y} = \arg\max_y \left\{ P_y(y|\tilde{x}; \tilde{\theta}_{x \to y}) \right\} \tag{13}$$

where $\tilde{x}$ is the image description generated from i in the pivot language, $\tilde{y}$ is the translation of $\tilde{x}$, and $\tilde{\theta}_{i \rightarrow x}$ and $\tilde{\theta}_{x \rightarrow y}$ are the learned model parameters.

However, this *pipelined* approach to image caption generation in the target language suffers from couple of key limitations. First, image captioning and machine translation are two different tasks. The image-to-pivot and pivot-to-target models are quite different in terms of vocabulary and parameter space because they are trained on two possibly unrelated datasets. Image captions contain description of objects in a given scene, whereas machine translation data is more generic, in our case containing news event descriptions, movie subtitles, and conversational texts. They are two different domains with differences in writing styles and word distributions. As a result, the captions generated by the pipeline approach may not be similar to human-authored captions. Figure 1 distinguishes between the two domains of pivot and target sentences: caption domain and translation domain (see second and third circles). The second limitation is that the errors made by the image-to-pivot captioning model get propagated to the pivot-to-target translation model.

To overcome the limitations of the pivot-based caption generation, we propose to reduce the discrepancy between the image-to-pivot and pivot-to-target models, and to train them jointly so that they learn better models by interacting with each other during training. Figure 2 illustrates our approach. The two models share some common aspects that we can exploit to connect them as we describe below.

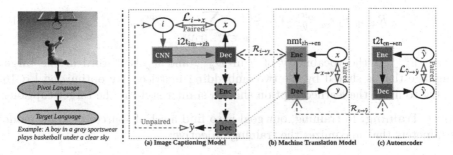

Fig. 2. Illustration of our image captioning model with pivot language. The image captioning model first transforms an image into latent pivot sentences, from which our machine translation model generates the target caption.

Connecting Image-to-Pivot and Pivot-to-Target. One way to connect the two models is to share the corresponding embedding matrices by defining a common embedding matrix for the decoder of image-to-pivot and the encoder of pivot-to-target. However, since the caption and translation domains are different, their word embeddings should also be different. Therefore, rather than having a common embedding matrix, we add a regularizer $\mathcal{R}_{i \rightarrow y}$ that attempts to bring the input embeddings of the NMT model close to the output embeddings of image captioning model by minimizing their l_2 distance. Formally,

$$\mathcal{R}_{i \to y}(\theta_{i \to x}^{w_x}, \theta_{x \to y}^{w_x}) = - \sum_{w_x \in \mathcal{V}_{i \to x}^x \cap \mathcal{V}_{x \to y}^x} ||\theta_{i \to x}^{w_x} - \theta_{x \to y}^{w_x}||_2 \tag{14}$$

where w_x is a word in the pivot language that is shared by the two embedding matrices, and $\theta_{i \to x}^{w_x} \in \mathbb{R}^d$ denotes the vector representation of w_x in the source-to-pivot model, and $\theta_{x \to y}^{w_x} \in \mathbb{R}^d$ denotes the vector representation of w_x in the pivot-to-target model. Note that, here we adapt $\theta_{x \to y}^{w_x}$ towards $\theta_{i \to x}^{w_x}$, that is, $\theta_{i \to x}^{w_x}$ is already a learned model and kept fixed during adaptation.

Adapting the encoder embeddings of the NMT model does not guarantee that the decoder of the model will produce caption-like sentences. For this, we need to also adapt the decoder embeddings of the NMT model to the caption data. We first use the target-target parallel corpus $D_{\hat{y}, \hat{y}} = \{(\hat{y}^{(n_{\hat{y}})}, \hat{y}^{(n_{\hat{y}})})\}_{n_{\hat{y}}=0}^{N_{\hat{y}}-1}$ to train an autoencoder $P(\hat{y}|\hat{y}; \theta_{\hat{y} \to \hat{y}})$, where $\theta_{\hat{y} \to \hat{y}}$ are the parameters of the autoencoder. The maximum-likelihood training objective of autoencoder can be expressed as:

$$\tilde{\theta}_{\hat{y} \to \hat{y}} = \arg \max_{\theta_{\hat{y} \to \hat{y}}} \{\mathcal{L}_{\hat{y} \to \hat{y}}\} \tag{15}$$

where $\mathcal{L}_{\hat{y} \to \hat{y}}$ is the cross-entropy (XE) loss. The autoencoder then "teaches" the decoder of the translation model $P(y|x; \theta_{x \to y})$ to learn similar word representations. This is again achieved by minimizing the l_2 distance between two vectors:

$$\mathcal{R}_{x \to \hat{y}}(\theta_{x \to y}^{w_y}, \theta_{\hat{y} \to \hat{y}}^{w_y}) = - \sum_{w_y \in \mathcal{V}_{x \to y}^y \cap \mathcal{V}_{\hat{y} \to \hat{y}}^y} ||\theta_{x \to y}^{w_y} - \theta_{\hat{y} \to \hat{y}}^{w_y}||_2 \tag{16}$$

where $\mathcal{V}_{\hat{y} \to \hat{y}}^y$ is the vocabulary of y in $D_{\hat{y}, \hat{y}}$, and w_y is a word in the target language that is shared by the two embedding matrices. By optimizing Eq. 16, we try to make the learned caption share a similar style as the target captions.

Joint Training. In training, our goal is to find a set of source-to-target model parameters that maximizes the training objective:

$$\mathcal{J}_{i \to x, x \to y, y \to \hat{y}} = \mathcal{L}_{i \to x} + \mathcal{L}_{x \to y} + \mathcal{L}_{\hat{y} \to \hat{y}} + \lambda \mathcal{R}_{i \to x, x \to y, y \to \hat{y}} \tag{17}$$

$$\mathcal{R}_{i \to x, x \to y, y \to \hat{y}} = \mathcal{R}_{i \to y}(\theta_{i \to x}^{w_x}, \theta_{x \to y}^{w_x}) + \mathcal{R}_{x \to \hat{y}}(\theta_{x \to y}^{w_y}, \theta_{\hat{y} \to \hat{y}}^{w_y}) \tag{18}$$

where λ is the hyper-parameter used to balance the preference between the loss terms and the connection terms. Since both the captioner $P_x(x|i; \theta_{i \to x})$ and the translator $P_y(y|x; \theta_{x \to y})$ have large vocabulary sizes (see Table 1), it is hard to train the joint model with an initial random policy. Thus, in practice, we pre-train the captioner, translator and autoencoder first, and then jointly optimize them with Eq. (17).

4 Experiments

Datasets. In our experiments, we choose the two independent datasets used from AI Challenger (AIC) [47]: AIC Image Chinese Captioning (AIC-ICC) and AIC Chinese-English Machine Translation (AIC-MT), as the training datasets, while using MSCOCO and Flickr30K English captioning datasets as the test datasets. Table 1 shows the statistics of the datasets used in our experiments.

Table 1. Statistics of the datasets used in our experiments, where "im" denotes the image, "zh" denotes Chinese, and "en" denotes English.

	Dataset	Lang.	Source		Target	
			# Image/Sent.	Vocab. size	# Sent.	Vocab. size
Training	AIC-ICC	im → zh	240 K	–	1,200 K	4,461
	AIC-MT	zh → en	10,000 K	50,004	10,000 K	50,004
Testing	MSCOCO	im → en	123 K	–	615 K	9,487
	Flickr30K	im → en	30 K	–	150 K	7,000

Training Datasets. For image-to-Chinese captioning training, we follow the settings in AIC-ICC [47] and take 210,000 images for training and 30,000 images for model validation. Each image contains five reference Chinese captions, and each of the captions contains most of the common daily scenes in which a person usually appears. We use the *"Jieba"*[1], a Chinese text segmentation module, for word segmentation. We truncate all the captions longer than 16 tokens and prune the vocabulary by dropping words with a frequency less than 5, resulting in a vocabulary size of 4,461 words.

We take Chinese as the pivot language and learn a Chinese-to-English translation model on AIC-MT. AIC-MT consists of 10,000K Chinese-English parallel sentences, and the English sentences are extracted from English learning websites and movie subtitles. We reserve 4 K sentence pairs for validation and 4 K sentence pairs for testing. During preprocessing, we remove the empty lines and retain sentence pairs with no more than 50 words. We prune the vocabulary and end up with a vocabulary of size 50,004 words including special Begin-of-Sentence (BOS) and End-of-Sentence (EOS) tokens. To guide the target decoder to generate caption-like sentences, an autoencoder is also trained with the target image descriptions extracted from MSCOCO. In our training, we extract 60,000 image descriptions from the MSCOCO training split, and randomly sort these samples.

Validation Datasets. We validate the effectiveness of our method on MSCOCO and Flickr30K datasets. The images in MSCOCO typically contain multiple objects with significant contextual information. Likewise, each image in MSCOCO also has five reference description, and most of these descriptions

---

[1] https://github.com/fxsjy/jieba.

are depicting humans participating in various activities. We use the same test splits as that in [27]. For MSCOCO, we use 5,000 images for validation and 5,000 images for testing, and for Flickr30K, we use 1,000 images for testing.

4.1 Implementation Details

Architecture. As can be seen in Fig. 2, we have three models used in our image captioner. The first model i2t$_{im \to zh}$ learns to generate the Chinese caption x from a given image i. It is a standard CNN-RNN architecture [44], where word outputted from the previous time step is taken as the input for the current time step. For each image, we encoder it with ResNet-101 [21], and then apply average pooling to get a vector of dimensions 2,048. After that, we map the image features through a linear projection and get a vector of dimensions 512. The decoder is implemented based on an LSTM network. The dimensions of the LSTM hidden states and word embedding are fixed to 512 for all of the models discussed in this paper. Each sentence starts with a special BOS token, and ends with an EOS token.

The second model nmt$_{zh \to en}$ learns to translate the Chinese sentence x to the English sentence y. It has three components: a sentence encoder, a sentence decoder, and an attention module. The words in the pivot language are first mapped to word vectors and then fed into a bidirectional LSTM network. The decoder predicts the target language words based on the encoded vector of the source sentence as well as its previous outputs. The encoder and the decoder are connected through an attention module which allows the decoder to focus on different regions of the source sentence during decoding.

The third model t2t$_{en \to en}$ learns to produce the caption-style English sentence $\hat{y}$. It is essentially an autoencoder trained on a set of image descriptions extracted from MSCOCO, where the encoder and the decoder are based on one-layer LSTM network. The encoder reads the whole sentence as input and the decoder is to reconstruct the input sentence.

Training Setting. All the modules are randomly initialized before training except the image CNN, for which we use a pre-trained model on ImageNet. We first independently train the image Chinese captioner, the Chinese-to-English translator, and the autoencoder with the cross-entropy loss on AIC-ICC, AIC-MT, and MSCOCO corpus, respectively. During this stage, we use Adam [28] algorithm to do model updating with a mini-batch size of 100. The initial learning rate is $4e^{-4}$, and the momentum is 0.9. The best models are selected according to the validation scores, which are then used for the subsequent joint training. Specifically, we combine the just trained models with the connection terms, and conduct a joint training with Eq. (17). We set the hyper-parameter λ to 1.0, and train the joint model using Adam optimizer with a mini-batch size of 64 and an initial learning rate of $2e^{-4}$. Weight decay and dropout are applied in this training phase to prevent over-fitting.

Testing setting. During testing, the output image description is first formed by drawing words in pivot language from i2t$_{im \to zh}$ until an EOS token is reached,

Table 2. Performance comparisons on AIC-ICC. The results of i2t$_{im \to zh}$ are achieved via beam search.

Image Chinese captioning					
Approach	B@1	B@2	B@3	B@4	CIDEr
i2t$_{im \to zh}$	**77.8**	**65.9**	**55.5**	**46.6**	**144.2**
AIC-I2T [47]	76.5	64.8	54.7	46.1	142.5

Table 3. Performance comparisons on AIC-MT test dataset. Note that our nmt$_{zh \to en}$ model uses beam search.

Chinese-to-English Translation		
Approach	Accuracy	Perplexity
nmt$_{zh \to en}$	55.0	8.9
Google Translation	**57.8**	–

and then translated with nmt$_{zh \to en}$ to the target language. Here we use beam search for the two inference procedures. Beam search is an efficient decoding method for RNN-based models, which keeps the top-k hypotheses at each time step, and considers them as the candidates to generate a new top-k hypotheses at the next time step. We set a fixed beam search size of $k = 5$ for i2t$_{im \to zh}$ and $k = 10$ for nmt$_{zh \to en}$. We evaluate the quality of the generated image descriptions with the standard evaluation metrics: BLEU [36], METEOR [12], and CIDEr [43]. Since BLEU aims to assess how similar two sentences are, we also evaluate the diversity of the generated sentence with Self-BLEU [54], which takes one sentence as the hypothesis and the others as the reference, and then calculates BLEU score for every generated sentence. The final Self-BLEU score is defined as the average BLEU scores of the sentences.

4.2 Quantitative Analysis

Results of Image Chinese Captioning. Table 2 shows the comparison results on the AIC-ICC validation set, where B@n is short for BLEU-n. We compare our i2t$_{im \to zh}$ model with the baseline [47] (named AIC-I2T). Both AIC-I2T and our image caption model (i2t$_{im \to zh}$) are trained with cross-entropy loss. We can see that our model outperforms the baseline in all the metrics. This might be due to different implementation details, e.g., AIC-I2T utilizes Inception-v3 for the image CNN while we use ResNet-101.

Results of Chinese-to-English Translation. Table 3 provides the comparison between our attention-based machine translator with the online Google translator on AIC-MT test split. We use the "googletrans"[2], a free Python tool that provides Google translator API. The perplexity value in the second column is the geometric mean of the inverse probability for each predicted word. Our attention-based NMT model (nmt$_{zh \to en}$) is trained on AIC-MT training set. We can see that our model is slightly worse than online Google translation in accuracy. This not surprising considering that Google's translator is trained on much larger datasets with more vocabulary coverage, and it is a more complex system that ensembles multiple NMT models.

---

[2] https://pypi.python.org/pypi/googletrans

Results of Unpaired Image English Captioning. Table 4 shows the comparisons among different variants of our method on MSCOCO dataset. Our upper bound is achieved by an image captioning model i2t$_{im\rightarrow en}$ that is trained with paired English captions. i2t$_{im\rightarrow en}$ shares the same architecture as i2t$_{im\rightarrow zh}$, except that they have different vocabulary sizes. The lower bound is achieved by pipelinining i2t$_{im\rightarrow zh}$ and nmt$_{zh\rightarrow en}$. In the pipeline setting, these two models are trained on AIC-ICC and AIC-MT, respectively. We also report the results of our implementation of FC-2K [39], which adopts a similar architecture.

Table 4. Results of unpaired image-to-English captioning on MSCOCO 5K and Flickr30K 1K test splits, where M is short for METEOR.

Approach	Lang.	B@1	B@2	B@3	B@4	M	CIDEr
MSCOCO							
i2t$_{im\rightarrow en}$ (Upper bound, XE Loss)	en	73.2	56.3	42.0	31.2	25.3	95.1
FC-2K [39] (ResNet101, XE Loss)	en	–	–	–	29.6	25.2	94.0
i2t$_{im\rightarrow zh}$ + nmt$_{zh\rightarrow en}$ ($\mathcal{R}_{i\rightarrow x,x\rightarrow y,y\rightarrow \hat{y}}$)	en	**46.2**	**24.0**	**11.2**	**5.4**	13.2	**17.7**
i2t$_{im\rightarrow zh}$ + nmt$_{zh\rightarrow en}$ ($\mathcal{R}_{i\rightarrow x,x\rightarrow y}$)	en	45.5	23.6	11.0	5.3	13.1	17.3
i2t$_{im\rightarrow zh}$ + nmt$_{zh\rightarrow en}$ (Lower bound)	en	42.0	20.6	9.5	3.9	12.0	12.3
i2t$_{im\rightarrow zh}$ + Online Google translation	en	42.2	21.8	10.7	5.3	**14.5**	17.0
Flickr30K							
i2t$_{im\rightarrow en}$ (Upper bound, XE Loss)	en	63.1	43.8	30.2	20.7	17.7	40.1
i2t$_{im\rightarrow zh}$ + nmt$_{zh\rightarrow en}$ ($\mathcal{R}_{i\rightarrow x,x\rightarrow y,y\rightarrow \hat{y}}$)	en	**49.7**	**27.8**	**14.8**	**7.9**	13.6	**16.2**
i2t$_{im\rightarrow zh}$ + nmt$_{zh\rightarrow en}$ ($\mathcal{R}_{i\rightarrow x,x\rightarrow y}$)	en	48.7	26.1	12.8	6.4	13.0	14.9
i2t$_{im\rightarrow zh}$ + nmt$_{zh\rightarrow en}$ (Lower bound)	en	45.9	25.2	13.1	6.9	12.5	13.9
i2t$_{im\rightarrow zh}$ + Online Google Translation	en	46.2	25.4	13.9	7.7	**14.4**	15.8

For unpaired image-to-English captioning, our method with the connection term on pivot language ($\mathcal{R}^{w_x}_{i\rightarrow x,x\rightarrow y}$) outperforms the method of combining i2t$_{im\rightarrow zh}$ with online Google translation in terms of B@n and CIDEr metrics, while obtaining significant improvements over the lower bound. This demonstrates the effectiveness of the connection term on the pivot language. Moreover, by adding the connection term on the target language, our model with the two connection terms ($\mathcal{R}_{i\rightarrow x,x\rightarrow y,y\rightarrow \hat{y}}$) further improves the performance. This suggests that a small corpus in the target domain is able to make the decoder to generate image descriptions that are more like captions. The connection terms help to bridge the word representations of the two different domains. The captions generated by Google translator have higher METEOR. We speculate the following reasons. First, Google Translator generates longer captions than ours. Since METEOR computes the score not only on the basis of n-gram precision but also of uni-gram recall, its default parameters favor longer translations than other metrics [4]. Second, in addition to exact word matching, METEOR considers matching of word stems and synonyms. Since Google translator is trained on a much larger corpus than ours, it generates more synonymous words. Table 4 also shows the results of unpaired image English captioning on Flickr30K, where we can draw similar conclusions.

We further evaluate the diversity of the generated image descriptions using Self-BLEU metric. Table 5 shows the detailed Self-BLEU scores. It can be seen that our method generates image descriptions with the highest diversity, compared with the upper and lower bounds. For better comparison, we also calculate the Self-BLEU scores calculated on ground truth captions.

Table 5. Self-BLEU scores on MSCOCO 5K test split. Note that lower Self-BLEU scores imply higher diversity of the image descriptions.

Approach	Lang.	Self-B@2	Self-B@3	Self-B@4	Self-B@5
i2t$_{im \to en}$ (GT Captions)	en	85.0	67.8	49.1	34.4
i2t$_{im \to en}$ (Upper bound)	en	99.0	97.5	94.6	90.7
i2t$_{im \to zh}$ + nmt$_{zh \to en}$ ($\mathcal{R}_{i \to x, x \to y, y \to \hat{y}}$)	en	**95.6**	**91.7**	**86.5**	**80.2**
i2t$_{im \to zh}$ + nmt$_{zh \to en}$ (Lower bound)	en	98.1	95.9	92.3	87.6

We also conduct a human evaluation of the generated captions for different models as well as the ground truth captions. A total number of 12 evaluators of different educational background were invited, and a total of 1.2 K samples were randomly selected from the test split for the user study. Particularly, we measure the caption quality from two aspects: *relevant* and *resemble*. The *relevant* metric indicates whether the caption is correct according to the image content. The *resemble* metric assesses to what extent the systems produce captions that resemble human-authored captions. The evaluators assessed the quality in 5 grades: 1-very poor, 2-poor, 3-barely acceptable, 4-good, 5-very good. Each evaluator assessed randomly chosen 100 images. The results presented in Table 6 demonstrate that our approach can generate relevant and human understandable image captions as the paired (Upper bound) approach.

Table 6. Evaluation results of user assessment on MSCOCO 1.2 test split.

Approach	i2t$_{im \to zh}$ + nmt$_{zh \to en}$ ($\mathcal{R}_{i \to x, x \to y, y \to \hat{y}}$)	Upper bound	Ground-truth
Relevant	3.81	3.99	4.68
Resemble	3.78	4.05	4.48

4.3   Qualitative Results

We provide some captioning examples in Fig. 3 for a better understanding of our model. We show in different color the generated captions for several images by the three models along with the ground truth (GT) captions. From these exemplary results, we can see that, compared with the paired model i2t$_{im\to en}$, our pivot-based unpaired model i2t$_{im\to zh\to en}(\mathcal{R}_{i\to x,x\to y,y\to\hat{y}})$ often generates more diverse captions; thanks to the additional translation data. At the same time, our model can generate caption-like sentences by bridging the gap between the datasets and by joint training of the model components. For example, with the detected people in the first image, our model generates the sentence with *"a bunch of people in sports suits"*, which is more diverse than the sentence with *"a group of baseball players"* generated by the paired model.

Fig. 3. Examples of the generated sentences on MSCOCO test images, where i2t$_{im\to zh}$ is the image captioner trained on AIC-ICC, i2t$_{im\to en}$ is the image captioner trained on MSCOCO, i2t$_{im\to zh\to en}$ $(\mathcal{R}_{i\to x,x\to y,y\to\hat{y}})$ and i2t$_{im\to zh\to en}$ $(\mathcal{R}_{i\to x,x\to y})$ are our proposed models for unpaired image captioning, and GT stands for ground truth caption.

5   Conclusion

In this paper, we have proposed an approach to unpaired image captioning with the help of a pivot language. Our method couples an image-to-pivot captioning model with a pivot-to-target NMT model in a joint learning framework. The coupling is done by adapting the word representations in the encoder and the decoder of the NMT model to produce caption-like sentences. Empirical evaluation demonstrates that our method consistently outperforms the baseline methods on MSCOCO and Flickr30K image captioning datasets. In our future work, we plan to explore the idea of 'back-translation' to create pseudo Chinese-English translation data for English captions, and adapt our decoder language model by training on this pseudo dataset.

Acknowledgments. This research was carried out at the Rapid-Rich Object Search (ROSE) Lab at the Nanyang Technological University, Singapore. The ROSE Lab is supported by the National Research Foundation, Singapore, and the Infocomm Media Development Authority, Singapore. We gratefully acknowledge the support of NVIDIA AI Tech Center (NVAITC) for our research at NTU ROSE Lab, Singapore.

References

1. Bahdanau, D., Cho, K., Bengio, Y.: Neural machine translation by jointly learning to align and translate. In: ICLR (2015)
2. Bengio, S., Vinyals, O., Jaitly, N., Shazeer, N.: Scheduled sampling for sequence prediction with recurrent neural networks. In: NIPS, pp. 1171–1179 (2015)
3. Bertoldi, N., Barbaiani, M., Federico, M., Cattoni, R.: Phrase-based statistical machine translation with pivot languages. In: IWSLT, pp. 143–149 (2008)
4. Cer, D., Manning, C.D., Jurafsky, D.: The best lexical metric for phrase-based statistical mt system optimization. In: NAACL, pp. 555–563 (2010)
5. Chen, T.H., Liao, Y.H., Chuang, C.Y., Hsu, W.T., Fu, J., Sun, M.: Show, adapt and tell: adversarial training of cross-domain image captioner. In: ICCV, pp. 521–530 (2017)
6. Chen, Y., Liu, Y., Li, V.O.: Zero-resource neural machine translation with multi-agent communication game. In: AAAI, pp. 5086–5093 (2018)
7. Cheng, Y., et al.: Semi-supervised learning for neural machine translation. In: ACL, pp. 1965–1974 (2016)
8. Cheng, Y., Yang, Q., Liu, Y., Sun, M., Xu, W.: Joint training for pivot-based neural machine translation. In: IJCAI, pp. 3974–3980 (2017)
9. Cho, K., et al.: Learning phrase representations using rnn encoder-decoder for statistical machine translation, pp. 1724–1734 (2014)
10. Cohn, T., Hoang, C.D.V., Vymolova, E., Yao, K., Dyer, C., Haffari, G.: Incorporating structural alignment biases into an attentional neural translation model. In: ACL, pp. 876–885 (2016)
11. Cohn, T., Lapata, M.: Machine translation by triangulation: making effective use of multi-parallel corpora. In: ACL, pp. 728–735 (2007)
12. Denkowski, M., Lavie, A.: Meteor universal: language specific translation evaluation for any target language. In: ACL, pp. 376–380 (2014)
13. Ding, H., Jiang, X., Shuai, B., Liu, A.Q., Wang, G.: Context contrasted feature and gated multi-scale aggregation for scene segmentation. In: CVPR, pp. 2393–2402 (2018)
14. El Kholy, A., Habash, N., Leusch, G., Matusov, E., Sawaf, H.: Language independent connectivity strength features for phrase pivot statistical machine translation. In: ACL, pp. 412–418 (2013)
15. Fang, H., et al.: From captions to visual concepts and back. In: CVPR, pp. 1473–1482 (2015)
16. Firat, O., Sankaran, B., Al-Onaizan, Y., Vural, F.T.Y., Cho, K.: Zero-resource translation with multi-lingual neural machine translation. In: EMNLP, pp. 268–277 (2016)
17. Gu, J., Cai, J., Joty, S., Niu, L., Wang, G.: Look, imagine and match: improving textual-visual cross-modal retrieval with generative models. In: CVPR, pp. 7181–7189 (2018)
18. Gu, J., Cai, J., Wang, G., Chen, T.: Stack-captioning: coarse-to-fine learning for image captioning. In: AAAI, pp. 6837–6844 (2018)
19. Gu, J., Wang, G., Cai, J., Chen, T.: An empirical study of language CNN for image captioning. In: ICCV, pp. 1222–1231 (2017)
20. Gu, J.: Recent advances in convolutional neural networks. Pattern Recognit. 77, 354–377 (2017)
21. He, K., Zhang, X., Ren, S., Sun, J.: Deep residual learning for image recognition. In: CVPR, pp. 770–778 (2016)

22. Hitschler, J., Schamoni, S., Riezler, S.: Multimodal pivots for image caption translation. In: ACL, pp. 2399–2409 (2016)
23. Jean, S., Cho, K., Memisevic, R., Bengio, Y.: On using very large target vocabulary for neural machine translation. In: ACL, pp. 1–10 (2015)
24. Jia, X., Gavves, E., Fernando, B., Tuytelaars, T.: Guiding long-short term memory for image caption generation. In: ICCV, pp. 2407–2415 (2015)
25. Johnson, M., et al.: Google's multilingual neural machine translation system: enabling zero-shot translation. In: TACL, pp. 339–352 (2016)
26. Kalchbrenner, N., Blunsom, P.: Recurrent continuous translation models. In: EMNLP, pp. 1700–1709 (2013)
27. Karpathy, A., Fei-Fei, L.: Deep visual-semantic alignments for generating image descriptions. In: CVPR, pp. 3128–3137 (2015)
28. Kingma, D., Ba, J.: Adam: a method for stochastic optimization. In: ICLR (2015)
29. Kulkarni, G., et al.: Baby talk: understanding and generating image descriptions. In: CVPR, pp. 1601–1608 (2011)
30. Lin, T.-Y., et al.: Microsoft COCO: common objects in context. In: Fleet, D., Pajdla, T., Schiele, B., Tuytelaars, T. (eds.) ECCV 2014. LNCS, vol. 8693, pp. 740–755. Springer, Cham (2014). https://doi.org/10.1007/978-3-319-10602-1_48
31. Liu, C., Sun, F., Wang, C., Wang, F., Yuille, A.: MAT: a multimodal attentive translator for image captioning. In: IJCAI, pp. 4033–4039 (2017)
32. Liu, S., Zhu, Z., Ye, N., Guadarrama, S., Murphy, K.: Improved image captioning via policy gradient optimization of spider. In: ICCV, pp. 873–881 (2017)
33. Luong, M.T., Le, Q.V., Sutskever, I., Vinyals, O., Kaiser, L.: Multi-task sequence to sequence learning. In: ICLR (2016)
34. Luong, M.T., Sutskever, I., Le, Q.V., Vinyals, O., Zaremba, W.: Addressing the rare word problem in neural machine translation. In: ACL, pp. 11–19 (2015)
35. Mi, H., Sankaran, B., Wang, Z., Ittycheriah, A.: Coverage embedding models for neural machine translation. In: EMNLP, pp. 955–960 (2016)
36. Papineni, K., Roukos, S., Ward, T., Zhu, W.J.: BLEU: a method for automatic evaluation of machine translation. In: ACL, pp. 311–318 (2002)
37. Plummer, B.A., Wang, L., Cervantes, C.M., Caicedo, J.C., Hockenmaier, J., Lazebnik, S.: Flickr30k entities: collecting region-to-phrase correspondences for richer image-to-sentence models. In: ICCV, pp. 2641–2649 (2015)
38. Ranzato, M., Chopra, S., Auli, M., Zaremba, W.: Sequence level training with recurrent neural networks. In: ICLR (2016)
39. Rennie, S.J., Marcheret, E., Mroueh, Y., Ross, J., Goel, V.: Self-critical sequence training for image captioning. In: CVPR, pp. 7008–7024 (2017)
40. Sutskever, I., Vinyals, O., Le, Q.V.: Sequence to sequence learning with neural networks. In: NIPS, pp. 3104–3112 (2014)
41. Tu, Z., Lu, Z., Liu, Y., Liu, X., Li, H.: Modeling coverage for neural machine translation. In: ACL, pp. 76–85 (2016)
42. Utiyama, M., Isahara, H.: A comparison of pivot methods for phrase-based statistical machine translation. In: NAACL, pp. 484–491 (2007)
43. Vedantam, R., Lawrence Zitnick, C., Parikh, D.: CIDEr: Consensus-based image description evaluation. In: CVPR, pp. 4566–4575 (2015)
44. Vinyals, O., Toshev, A., Bengio, S., Erhan, D.: Show and tell: a neural image caption generator. In: CVPR, pp. 3156–3164 (2015)
45. Vinyals, O., Toshev, A., Bengio, S., Erhan, D.: Show and tell: lessons learned from the 2015 MSCOCO image captioning challenge. In: PAMI, pp. 652–663 (2017)
46. Wu, H., Wang, H.: Pivot language approach for phrase-based statistical machine translation. Mach. Transl. 21, 165–181 (2007)

47. Wu, J., et al.: AI challenger: a large-scale dataset for going deeper in image understanding. arXiv preprint arXiv:1711.06475 (2017)
48. Wu, Q., Shen, C., Liu, L., Dick, A., Hengel, A.V.D.: What value do explicit high level concepts have in vision to language problems? In: CVPR, pp. 203–212 (2016)
49. Xu, K., et al.: Show, attend and tell: neural image caption generation with visual attention. In: ICML, pp. 2048–2057 (2015)
50. Yang, X., Zhang, H., Cai, J.: Shuffle-then-assemble: learning object-agnostic visual relationship features. In: ECCV (2018)
51. Yao, T., Pan, Y., Li, Y., Qiu, Z., Mei, T.: Boosting image captioning with attributes. In: ICCV, pp. 22–29 (2017)
52. You, Q., Jin, H., Wang, Z., Fang, C., Luo, J.: Image captioning with semantic attention. In: CVPR, pp. 4651–4659 (2016)
53. Zahabi, S.T., Bakhshaei, S., Khadivi, S.: Using context vectors in improving a machine translation system with bridge language. In: ACL, pp. 318–322 (2013)
54. Zhu, Y., et al.: Texygen: a benchmarking platform for text generation models. In: SIGIR, pp. 1097–1100 (2018)
55. Zoph, B., Yuret, D., May, J., Knight, K.: Transfer learning for low-resource neural machine translation. In: EMNLP, pp. 1568–1575 (2016)

Efficient Uncertainty Estimation
for Semantic Segmentation in Videos

Po-Yu Huang[1]($\boxtimes$), Wan-Ting Hsu[1]($\boxtimes$), Chun-Yueh Chiu[1]($\boxtimes$),
Ting-Fan Wu[2]($\boxtimes$), and Min Sun[1]($\boxtimes$)

[1] National Tsing Hua University, Taipei, Taiwan
andy11330@gmail.com, cindyemail0720@gmail.com,
chiupick86@gapp.nthu.edu.tw,sunmin@ee.nthu.edu.tw
[2] Umbo Computer Vision, Taipei, Taiwan
tingfan.wu@umbocv.com

Abstract. Uncertainty estimation in deep learning becomes more important recently. A deep learning model can't be applied in real applications if we don't know whether the model is certain about the decision or not. Some literature proposes the Bayesian neural network which can estimate the uncertainty by Monte Carlo Dropout (MC dropout). However, MC dropout needs to forward the model N times which results in N times slower. For real-time applications such as a self-driving car system, which needs to obtain the prediction and the uncertainty as fast as possible, so that MC dropout becomes impractical. In this work, we propose the region-based temporal aggregation (RTA) method which leverages the temporal information in videos to simulate the sampling procedure. Our RTA method with Tiramisu backbone is **10x** faster than the MC dropout with Tiramisu backbone ($N = 5$). Furthermore, the uncertainty estimation obtained by our RTA method is comparable to MC dropout's uncertainty estimation on pixel-level and frame-level metrics.

Keywords: Uncertainty · Segmentation · Video · Efficient

1 Introduction

Nowadays, deep learning has become a powerful tool in various applications. The uncertainty estimation in deep learning has got more attention as well. Some applications need not only the prediction of the model but also the confidence of this prediction. For instance, in the biomedical field, the confidence of cancer diagnosis is essential for doctors to make the decision. For self-driving car system to avoid accidents, the model should know what situation haven't seen before and then return to human control. There are some methods of uncertainty estimation [2,11,20] for deep learning have been proposed, but most of them need to sample several times, which is harmful to real-time applications. Slow inference of uncertainty estimation is an important issue before applying on real-time applications.

© Springer Nature Switzerland AG 2018
V. Ferrari et al. (Eds.): ECCV 2018, LNCS 11205, pp. 536–552, 2018.
https://doi.org/10.1007/978-3-030-01246-5_32

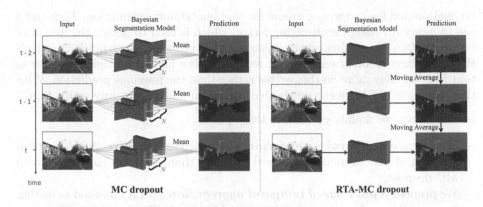

Fig. 1. Comparison of MC dropout and TA-MC/RTA-MC dropout. Left: MC dropout samples N times for every frame, which cause N times slower. Right: TA-MC/RTA-MC dropout aggregates previous output into final prediction and uncertainty. For every frame, TA-MC/RTA-MC dropout only needs to calculate segmentation model and optical flow once.

In general, neural networks can only generate prediction instead of uncertainty. Lack of uncertainty estimation is a shortcoming of neural networks. Bayesian neural networks [7,25] solve this problem by modeling the posterior of networks weights. But they often increase computation cost and the number of model parameters. Recently, Gal et al. [10] propose dropout as an approximation technique without increasing parameters which is easy to implement called MC dropout. Though MC dropout is useful and powerful, the inference is very slow because it needs to perform N (e.g., $N = 50$) stochastic forward pass through the network and average the results to obtain the prediction and uncertainty. Therefore, our work proposed utilizing video's temporal information to speed up the inference and also maintain the performance.

For video segmentation, we can make good use of the temporal information based on the properties of video continuity. We propose two main methods called *temporal aggregation (TA)* and *region-based temporal aggregation (RTA)*. For static objects in videos, calculating the average output of N consecutive frames has the same effect as utilizing MC dropout with N samples. Hence, we propose *TA* method that approximates the sampling procedure of MC dropout by calculating the moving average of the outputs in consecutive frames (see Fig. 1). To obtain the correct aggregation for moving objects in videos, we utilize optical flow to catch the flow of each pixel in the frame and aggregate each pixel's output depending on the flow. This *TA* method can also be used to calculate any kinds of uncertainty estimation function, i.e, *Entropy*, *Bald*. In this way, we can speed up MC dropout 10 times. The specific speed up rate is depend on backbone model. For larger backbone, our method can speed up even more. Furthermore, we designed *RTA* based on *TA*. For some objects with large displacements in videos, the large shift of pixels might result in poor flow estimation and lead to wrong prediction and uncertainty estimation. Thus, *RTA* can dynamically assign multiplying factor, which is used to decide the weight of incoming data, depending on the reconstruction error for every pixel. For pixels that have large reconstruction error, we shall assign higher multiplying factor so that they will rely more on themselves rather than the previous prediction. With the benefits of *RTA*, we can get better prediction and uncertainty estimation.

In this paper, we mainly contribute three points:

- We propose **temporal aggregation (TA)** method to solve the slow speed problem of MC dropout. We speed up more than 10 times comparing with MC dropout.
- We propose **region-based temporal aggregation (RTA)** method to further improve the performance of *TA* by considering the flow accuracy. With our *RTA* method, we get comparable accuracy in video segmentation on CamVid dataset with only less than 2% drop on mean IoU metric.
- We obtain nice uncertainty estimation which is evaluated in pixel-level and frame-level metric. Our uncertainty estimation even outperforms MC dropout on frame-level metrics.

2   Related Work

First, We will introduce uncertainty estimation methods in Sect. 2.1. Next, some important segmentation models will be mentioned in Sect. 2.2. Finally, we introduce some works leverage the temporal information in the video.

2.1   Uncertainty Estimation

Uncertainty is an important issue for some current decision-making tasks, i.e., self-driving car, drone, robotics. We can just blindly assume that the prediction of the model is accurate but sometimes the truth is not. To really understand what a model doesn't know is a critical issue nowadays. It helps us to know how much we can trust the prediction of the model. However, the majority of the segmentation works cannot generate a probabilistic output with a measure of model uncertainty.

Bayesian neural networks [7, 25] is a well-known method that model uncertainty in neural networks. They turn deep learning model into a probabilistic model by learning the distribution over networks weights. Bayesian neural network's prediction is hard to obtain. Variational inference [12] is often used to approximate the posterior of the model. Blundell et al. [2] model a Gaussian distribution over weights in the neural networks rather than having a single fixed value, however, each weight should contain mean and variance to represent a Gaussian distribution that doubles the number of parameters. Recently, Gal et al. [10, 11, 20] use dropout as an approximation of variational inference. When testing time, they keep dropping neurons, which can be interpreted as adding a Bernoulli distribution over the weights. This technique called MC dropout that has been successfully used in camera relocalisation [21] and segmentation [20]. However, it still needs to sample model many times to estimate uncertainty. In this work, we propose leveraging video temporal information to speed up the MC dropout sampling process.

2.2 Semantic Segmentation

Semantic image segmentation that uses convolutional neural networks has achieved several breakthroughs in recent years. It is a pixel-wise labeling task that classifies every pixel into defined class. Long et al. [24], popularize CNN architectures for dense predictions without any fully connected layers. This method allowed segmentation maps to be generated for an image of any size and was also much faster compared to the patch classification approach. Ronneberger et al. [30] propose U-net, which is an encoder-decoder architecture that focuses on improving more accurate boundaries. Howard et al. [15] combined the ideas of MobileNets Depthwise Separable Convolutions with UNet to build a high speed, low parameter Semantic Segmentation model. PSP-Net [34] uses ResNet as the backbone and utilizes global information from pyramid layers to provide more accurate semantics. DeepLab [5] replaced fully connected CRF(conditional random field) to the last layer of CNN for improving the performance. In this work, we select Bayesian SegNet [1] and Tiramusi [18] to demonstrate our idea. Both methods are encoder-decoder architecture. Tiramisu is the state-of-the-art of CamVid dataset.

2.3 Leverage Temporal Information

Previously, some works make use of superpixels [4,13], patches [8,29], object proposal [28], optical flow [17,27] as temporal information to reduce the computational complexity. Furthermore, video segmentation has gained significant improvement based on temporal information. Among all these temporal information, the most recent works heavily rely on optical flow. Srivastava et al. [33] use the image in one stream, and optical flow in the other stream to recognize actions in the video. Simonyan et al. [32] simultaneously predict pixel-wise object segmentation and optical flow in videos. Cheng et al. [6] emphasize temporal information at the frame level instead of the final box level to improve detection accuracy. To enhance the reference feature map, they utilize optical flow network the work of Zhu et al. [35] to estimate the motions between nearby frames and the reference frame. They then aggregate feature maps warping from nearby frames to the reference frame according to the flow motion. Briefly speaking, all these works utilize optical flow appropriately in video tasks. To the best of our knowledge, we are the first work that uses optical flow as temporal information to speed up uncertainty estimation.

3 Method

We first give a brief introduction of Bayesian neural networks with Monte Carlo dropout (MC) in Sect. 3.1. Next, we introduce our temporal aggregation Monte

Carlo dropout (TA-MC) in Sect. 3.2. Finally, we propose a region-based temporal aggregation Monte Carlo dropout (RTA-MC) which can further improve both the accuracy and uncertainty estimation in Sect. 3.3.

3.1   Preliminary: Bayesian Neural Network with MC Dropout

Bayesian neural networks are probabilistic models that do not learn a set of deterministic parameters but a distribution over those parameters. It aims to learn the posterior distribution of the neural network's weights W given training data X and Y.

The posterior distribution, which is denoted as $p(W|X,Y)$, usually cannot be evaluated analytically. Variational inference is often used to approximate the posterior distribution. Given an approximating distribution over the network's weights, $q(W)$, we minimize the Kullback-Leibler (KL) divergence between $p(W|X,Y)$ and $q(W)$.

$$KL(q(W) \parallel p(W|X,Y))$$ (1)

Dropout variational inference is a useful technique for approximating posterior distribution. Dropout can be viewed as using the Bernoulli distribution as the approximation distribution $q(W)$. At testing time, the prediction can be approximated by sampling model N times which is referred as Monte Carlo dropout (MC).

$$p(y^*|x^*,X,Y) \approx \frac{1}{N}\sum_{n=1}^{N} p(y^*|x^*,\hat{\omega}_n)$$ (2)

The uncertainty of the classification can be obtained by several functions:

(a) Entropy [31]:

$$H[y|x,X,Y] = -\sum_{c} p(y = c|x,X,Y) \log p(y = c|x,X,Y)$$ (3)

(b) BALD [14]:

$$I[y,\omega|x,X,Y] = H[y|x,X,Y] - E_{p(\omega|X,Y)}[H[y|x,\omega]]$$ (4)

(c) Variation ratio [9]:

$$\text{variation-ratio}[x] = 1 - \max_{y} p(y|x,X,Y)$$ (5)

(d) Mean standard deviation (Mean STD) [19,20]:

$$\sigma_c = \sqrt{E_{q(\omega)}\left[p(y = c|x,\omega)^2\right] - E_{q(\omega)}\left[p(y = c|x,\omega)\right]^2}$$ (6)

$$\sigma(x) = \frac{1}{c}\sum_{c} \sigma_c$$ (7)

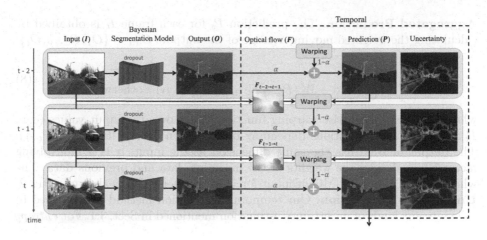

Fig. 2. The process of our temporal aggregation MC dropout (TA-MC) for video segmentation. Every time step Bayesian segmentation model sample one output and calculate optical flow. To average the incoming output, we warp the previous prediction depend on optical flow. Final prediction is weighted sum with multiplying factor α

Bayesian neural networks with MC dropout can obtain better performance and uncertainty estimation. However, it requires to sample N times (e.g., $N = 50$) for predicting each image, which is N times slower than the original network. For real-time applications such as self-driving cars, which needs to obtain the prediction and uncertainty estimation as fast as possible, so that MC dropout becomes impractical. In this work, we propose temporal aggregation MC dropout to speed up the MC dropout process.

3.2 Temporal Aggregation MC Dropout (TA-MC)

Our temporal aggregation MC dropout (TA-MC) method utilizes the temporal property in videos. Since a video contains consecutive frames, same objects may appear in many different frames and thus will be forwarded by the Bayesian model repeatedly. If a video contains static frames (i.e., a static scene observed by a static camera), the average output of N consecutive frames is the same as MC dropout with N samples. For video segmentation, though the frames are not static (i.e., the objects in the scene and the camera are both moving), the consecutive frames are still similar. The objects are often shifted slightly in the next frame. Hence, by warping each pixel to the new position in the next frame, we can aggregate the outputs of the pixels in consecutive frames correctly.

Notations. Given a video $V = \{I_1, I_2, ..., I_t, ..., I_T\}$ where I_t is the tth frame and T is the length of the video, the outputs of the Bayesian neural network are denoted as $O = \{O_1, O_2, ..., O_t, ..., O_T\}$. Note that O are the outputs without MC sampling, which means each frame is forwarded by Bayesian model (with dropout) for only one time. To get the aggregated predictions, we calculate the optical flow between consecutive frames $F = \{F_{1\to2}, F_{2\to3}, ..., F_{T-1\to T}\}$ where $F_{t\to t+1}$ indicates the optical flow from frame I_t to frame I_{t+1}.

Aggregated Prediction. The prediction P_t for each frame I_t is obtained by calculating the weighted moving average of the outputs $O_{1:t} = \{O_1, O_2, ..., O_t\}$:

$$P_t = \begin{cases} O_t & \text{if } t = 1, \\ O_t \times \alpha + W\left(P_{t-1}, F_{t-1 \to t}\right) \times (1 - \alpha) & \text{otherwise,} \end{cases} \tag{8}$$

where $W\left(\cdot\right)$ is a pixel-wise warping function that moves the input values (e.g., P_{t-1}) to their new positions depending on the given optical flow (e.g., F_{t-1}). The output of $W(\cdot)$ has the same dimension as the input. α is a multiplying factor which decides the weights of the incoming data and previous data. The whole system of our TA-MC dropout for video segmentation is shown in Fig. 2.
Uncertainty Estimation. Our temporal aggregation method can be used to calculate any kinds of uncertainty estimation mentioned in Sect. 3.1. For *entropy* and *variation ratio*, the uncertainty can be simply derived from aggregated prediction P_t, while *BALD* and *Mean STD* encounter other expectation that needed to be aggregated. *BALD* needs to aggregate $E_{p(\omega|X,Y)}\left[H\left[y|x,\omega\right]\right]$ and *Mean STD* needs to aggregate $E_{q(\omega)}\left[p\left(y = c|x,\omega\right)\right]^2$.

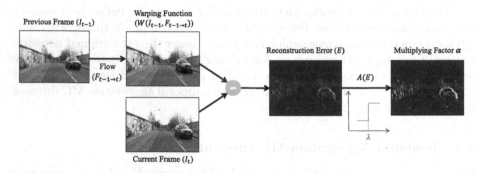

Fig. 3. Region-based temporal aggregation (RTA). We design a step function to acquire dynamic multiplying factor α for improving the TA method. For regions that have wrong optical flow estimation (i.e., the reconstruction error is greater than a threshold λ), we use a larger multiplying factor to let the pixels rely more on itself rather than the previous predictions. See more detailed in Sect. 3.3.

3.3   Region-Based Temporal Aggregation MC Dropout (RTA-MC)

Our TA-MC dropout works for most of the case; however, when the optical flow estimation is wrong, it will cause the uncertainty estimation inaccurate. For some regions that contain fast moving objects or occlusion, the optical flow may not be accurate. Bad flow estimation results in calculating moving average on the wrong patch and thus getting wrong prediction and uncertainty for those pixels. To solve this problem, we propose the region-based temporal aggregation (RTA) that can dynamically assign different multiplying factor (α in Eq. 8) for every pixel depending on its reconstruction error.

The reconstruction error E of warping I_{t-1} to I_t is derived from the pixel-wise difference of the warped frame $W\left(I_{t-1}, F_{t-1 \to t}\right)$ and I_t.

$$E = \left| I_t - W\left(I_{t-1}, F_{t-1 \to t}\right) \right|. \tag{9}$$

where E is a matrix contains pixel-wise reconstruction error and $E_{ij} \in [0, 255]$. For a pixel that has large reconstruction error, we will give it a higher multiplying factor α_{err} since the optical flow may be inaccurate and thus the prediction should rely more on itself rather than the previous predictions. We design a decision function $A\left(E\right)$ that decides α for every pixel depending on the reconstruction error (see Fig. 3).

$$\alpha_{ij} = A\left(E_{ij}\right) = \begin{cases} \alpha_{acc} & \text{if } E_{ij} \leq \lambda, \\ \alpha_{err} & \text{otherwise,} \end{cases} \tag{10}$$
$$\alpha = \{\alpha_{ij}\}_{ij}$$

where α_{ij} is the multiplying factor for the pixel in position (i, j). $A(\cdot)$ is a step function with a threshold λ which is a hyper-parameter deciding whether the optical flow has bad estimation or not. α_{acc} and α_{error} are also hyper-parameters which indicate the multiplying factor for good flow estimation and bad flow estimation, respectively. α_{err} should be higher than α_{acc} (e.g., $\alpha_{acc} = 0.2$ and $\alpha_{err} = 0.7$). Then, we simply replace α in Eq. 8 with α in Eq. 10 to obtain our region-based temporal aggregation MC dropout (RTA-MC). By applying our RTA method, the mismatch aggregation will be attenuated and can further improve the prediction and the uncertainty estimation.

4   Experiment

In this section, we describe the dataset that used for the video segmentation in Sect. 4.1 and our implementation details in Sect. 4.2. Next, we compare our TA-MC dropout and RTA-MC dropout with MC dropout in several different aspects. First, in Sect. 4.3, we compare the performance of video segmentation and the inference time. Second, in Sect. 4.4, we show that our methods can obtain comparable uncertainty estimation.

4.1   Dataset

CamVid [3] is a road scene segmentation dataset which contains four 30 Hz videos. The frames are labeled every 1 s, and each pixel is labeled into 11 classes such as sky, building, road, car, etc. There are total 701 labeled frames split into 367 training frames, 101 validation frames and 233 test frames. All frames are resized to 360×480 pixels in our experiments.

Table 1. Performance test on CamVid dataset. Upper three rows are comparisons of SegNet backbone; Lower four rows are comparisons of Tiramisu backbone. Both comparisons show that our methods can speed up more than 10x with only 1–2For fairly comparison, we reduce the Tiramisu MC sample time to N=5 to get the same accuracy as our methods. In this situation, our methods are still 10x faster.

Method	Building	Tree	Sky	Car	Sign-Symbol	Road	Pedestrian	Fence	Column-Pole	Side-walk	Bicyclist	Class avg.	Global avg.	Mean IoU	Inference Time (s)	Speed Up Ratio
SegNet MC (N=50)	88.9	88.7	95.0	89.0	49.4	95.8	73.5	51.4	43.3	93.2	57.0	75.0	90.6	63.7	2.00	1
SegNet TA-MC	88.6	89.7	94.5	88.2	48.1	95.3	70.7	44.7	36.4	94.1	52.7	73.0	90.3	62.1	0.18	10.97
SegNet RTA-MC	88.4	89.3	94.9	88.9	48.7	95.4	73.0	45.6	41.4	94.0	51.6	73.7	90.4	62.5	0.18	10.97
Tiramisu MC (N=50)	89.7	87.2	95.6	84.9	58.4	95.1	82.5	54.1	49.6	84.6	52.3	75.8	89.8	64.0	11.72	1
Tiramisu MC (N=5)	88.7	86.6	95.4	83.7	58.4	94.6	80.6	52.0	49.2	84.0	55.0	75.3	89.2	62.4	1.17	10.00
Tiramisu TA-MC	90.3	87.4	94.8	84.2	55.8	94.5	79.2	51.3	40.6	85.6	46.7	73.8	89.6	62.3	0.37	31.58
Tiramisu RTA-MC	90.1	87.1	94.9	84.1	56.7	94.7	79.2	48.1	42.2	85.4	49.8	73.9	89.5	62.4	0.37	31.58

4.2   Implementation Details

We apply the Bayesian SegNet model [20] and Tiramisu model [18] to demonstrate our TA and RTA method. We train both models by the same setting in the original paper. We set α in Eq. 8 for TA-MC dropout to 0.2. For RTA-MC dropout, we use threshold λ as 10 to determine whether the flow estimation is wrong. Note that the reconstruction error of flow is in the range of $[0, 255]$ and the average error is about 2. Hence, we choose the threshold λ slightly higher than the average error. α_{acc} and α_{err} in Eq. 10 are set to 0.2 and 0.7, respectively. We use FlowNet 2.0 [16] for our optical flow estimation. We implement all methods in Pytorch [26] framework and experiment on GTX 1080 for time measurement.

4.3   Results of Video Segmentation

We compare MC dropout with our TA-MC dropout and RTA-MC dropout on CamVid dataset by two models. We first show the performance of the video segmentation on several different metrics: (1) pixel-wise classification accuracy on every class, (2) class average accuracy (class avg.), (3) overall pixel-wise classification accuracy (global avg.), (4) mean intersection over union (mean IoU) and (5) inference time. The results are shown in Table 1. For SegNet, Our

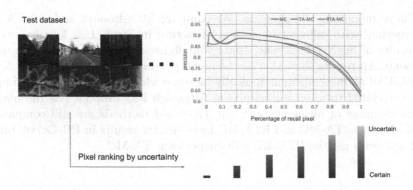

Fig. 4. Ation of the Pixel-level metric Precision-Recall curve. First, calculate the uncertainty map of all test data. Then rank all pixels by uncertainty value. The horExplanizontal axis is the percentage of recall pixel which means we keep how many percentages of most certain pixels to calculate precision. The vertical axis is the mIoU.

TA-MC dropout can reach comparable accuracy, and the RTA-MC dropout further improves the performance with only 1.2% drop on mean IoU metric. For Tiramisu, our methods also can reach comparable accuracy.

In the case of comparable accuracy, our method can further speed up the inference time. Since our methods only need to forward one time for each frame; while MC dropout needs to sample N times. For SegNet, we can obtain almost 11 times speed up. Note that our TA-MC dropout and RTA-MC dropout can perform the same speed as the only difference between them is the multiplying factor (α in Eq. 8) which doesn't affect the speed. The inference time of the RTA-MC dropout mainly contains the inference time of the Bayesian SegNet model and the FlowNet 2.0 model which are 0.04 seconds and 0.13 s, respectively. FlowNet 2.0 model takes 70% of the whole inference time. If we use the bigger segmentation model, we can get a better improvement in the speed. Therefore, we use Tiramisu model which is the state-of-the-art model in CamVid but 6x slower than SegNet to show better speed up ratio. For Tiramisu, Our method can achieve 31x faster than MC dropout sample 50 times. To fairly compare inference time, we reduce the MC dropout sample time to 5 times. The accuracy becomes the same as our methods. In this case, our methods are still 10x faster than MC dropout. This table shows that in the same accuracy level, our methods can speed up inference time 10x.

4.4   Results of Uncertainty Estimation

We evaluate the uncertainty estimation in pixel-level and frame-level metrics.
Pixel-level Metric. The pixel-level evaluation is inspired by Precision-Recall Curve metric in [22]. This curve shows the accuracy of the remained pixels as removing pixels with uncertainty larger than different percentile thresholds. Detail explanation is in Fig. 4. A reliable uncertainty estimation should let the

PR-Curve monotonically decrease. We compare MC dropout and our TA and RTA method with different uncertainty function in Fig. 5. Left four figures are the results of SegNet backbone. Right four figures are the results of Tiramisu backbone. All results show that as the recall percentage drop from 1 to 0.5, the mean IoU of all methods monotonically increase which means the uncertain pixels is correlated to misclassified pixels. Although MC dropout has the highest accuracy almost at all percentage, our TA-based methods are still comparable to MC dropout. TA-MC and RTA-MC have similar results in PR-Curve, but at the frame-level metric, RTA-MC will outperform TA-MC.

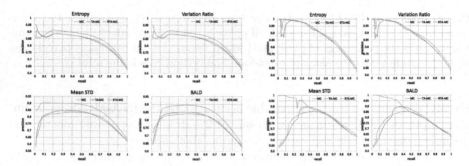

Fig. 5. Pixel-level precision-recall curves. Left four figures are the results of SegNet backbone. Right four figures are the results of Tiramisu backbone. We use mean IoU as the precision metric. We show the comparison of MC dropout, TA-MC dropout and RTA-MC dropout on four different uncertainty estimation methods. Our methods achieve comparable results especially when using *Entropy* and *Variation Ratio* as the uncertainty estimation functions.

Frame-level Metric. Pixel-level metric is good to evaluate the uncertainty estimation. However, pixel-wise uncertainty estimation is hard to leverage in real applications. For example, active learning system wants to find which frame is valuable to be labeled rather than decides which pixel should be labeled. Here, we propose frame-level uncertainty metrics to show that our uncertainty estimation can work well and faster in real applications. The procedure is shown on Fig. 6. First, frames are ranked by the error of prediction as the ground truth ranking sequence. Then, we rank frames by the uncertainty estimation and evaluate the uncertainty ranking sequence by two metrics: **Kendall tau** [23] and **Ranking IoU**. Kendall tau is a well-known ranking metric measures how the ranking sequence is similar to the ground truth sequence. The value is bounded in 1 (fully identical sequence) and −1 (fully different sequence). Table 2 shows the comparison of Kendall tau by SegNet and Tiramisu backbone. Though Table 2 shows that the highest scores appears in *Mean STD* and *BALD*, RTA-MC outperforms MC in *Entropy* and *Variation Ratio*. It also shows that RTA-MC improves frame-level ranking compare to TA-MC. It is attributed to the decision

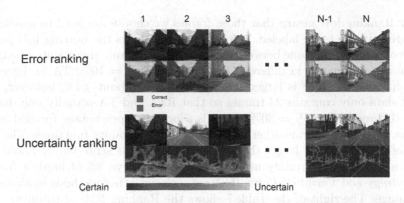

Fig. 6. Explanation of frame-level metric. First, calculate the error rate of each test data frame by looking at the ground truth to get the error ranking sequence. Second, calculate the frame uncertainty of all test data to get the uncertainty ranking sequence. Then measure the similarity between two sequences by Kendall tau and Ranking IOU.

Table 2. Comparison of Kendall tau. For both backbone, the result shows that RTA-MC has the highest value in *Entropy* and *Variation Ratio*. For overall performance, RTA-MC is comparable to MC dropout.

Method	Entropy	Variation ratio	Mean STD	BALD
SegNet MC	0.647	0.668	**0.677**	**0.671**
SegNet TA-MC	0.626	0.631	0.540	0.527
SegNet RTA-MC	**0.662**	**0.674**	0.627	0.620
Tiramisu MC	0.636	0.653	0.659	**0.647**
Tiramisu TA-MC	0.660	0.674	**0.663**	0.626
Tiramisu RTA-MC	**0.664**	**0.678**	0.635	0.612

function $A(E)$ which reduces the uncertainty value of pixels with wrong flow estimation which harm the frame-level uncertainty. Kendall tau compares the whole sequence similarity, but real applications pay more attention on higher ranking similarity than whole ranking. Therefore, we define a novel frame-level ranking metric called Ranking IoU. Given a percentage of frame P_f to retrieve, we retrieve frames depend on error $G(P_f) = \{g_1, g_2, ..., g_m, ..., g_M\}$ and uncertainty $U(P_f) = \{u_1, u_2, ..., u_m, ..., u_M\}$. The ranking IoU is:

$$\text{Ranking IoU} = \frac{G(P_f) \cap U(P_f)}{G(P_f) \cup U(P_f)} \tag{11}$$

Larger Ranking IoU means that those frames we choose are hard to predict, so they are valuable to be labeled. Left of the Fig. 7 shows the ranking IoU performance of SegNet backbone between different methods and uncertainty functions. We show performance in different P_f. In column $P_f = 10\%$, TA in *Variation Ratio* has 52.2% which is larger than RTA's 47.8% about 4.4%; however, 10% of test data only contains 23 frames so that RTA and TA actually only have 1 frame difference. For $P_f = 30\%$ which is a practical percentage for real applications, RTA outperforms other methods in all uncertainty functions. The best score of RTA 69.6% is larger than MC dropout's best score 66.7% about 3%, which means our uncertainty method can more retrieve 3% of hardest frames. For *Entropy* and *Variation Ratio*, RTA outperforms other methods in almost all percentage. The right of the Table 7 shows the Ranking IOU of tiramisu backbone. The results are similar to SegNet backbone that for *Entropy* and *Variation Ratio*, RTA outperforms other methods. Table 2 and Fig 7 indicate that RTA can generate high-quality uncertainty. Figure 8 shows the visualization of prediction, uncertainty, and error. It shows that RTA's uncertainty quality is comparable to MC dropout and the large uncertainty pixels are correlated to the misclassified pixels.

Metric	Method	Percentage				Metric	Method	Percentage			
		10%	30%	50%	70%			10%	30%	50%	70%
	MC	47.8	59.4	72.4	85.2		MC	34.8	60.9	70.7	**86.4**
Entropy	TA	47.8	65.2	69.8	85.8	Entropy	TA	**47.8**	**63.8**	71.6	84.6
	RTA	47.8	**66.7**	**73.3**	**88.9**		RTA	47.8	63.8	**74.1**	86.4
	MC	47.8	62.3	74.1	85.2		MC	34.8	60.9	74.1	86.4
Variation Ratio	TA	**52.2**	63.8	70.7	85.2	Variation Ratio	TA	47.8	**65.2**	72.4	85.8
	RTA	47.8	**65.2**	**76.7**	**88.3**		RTA	**52.1**	65.2	**75.9**	**87.7**
	MC	**52.2**	66.7	**71.6**	**86.4**		MC	30.4	63.8	**76.7**	**86.4**
Mean STD	TA	43.5	65.2	65.5	74.1	Mean STD	TA	**47.8**	**75.4**	74.1	82.0
	RTA	43.5	**69.6**	69.8	82.7		RTA	43.4	68.1	73.3	82.1
	MC	**47.8**	66.7	**71.6**	**87.7**		MC	30.4	62.3	72.4	**86.4**
BALD	TA	43.5	62.3	64.7	74.1	BALD	TA	43.5	**71.0**	**71.6**	80.2
	RTA	43.5	**69.6**	67.2	82.1		RTA	**47.8**	66.7	**71.6**	80.9

Fig. 7. Ranking IoU. Left table is the result of SegNet backbone. Right table is the result of Tiramisu backbone. For retrieving 30%, 50% and 70% of frames RTA-MC have the highest score by using Variation ratio.

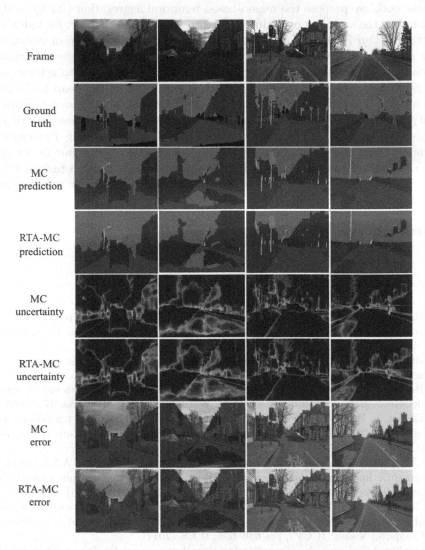

Fig. 8. Results comparison on CamVid dataset(MC dropout v.s RTA-MC dropout). The top row is the input image, with the ground truth shown in the second row. The third row and fourth row show the segmentation prediction of MC dropout and RTA-MC respectively. Its corresponding uncertainty map is also shown in the fifth and sixth row where the more brighter space represents higher uncertainty. We even show the error in the last two rows where the red space represents the wrong prediction, and the tiffany-blue space represents correct prediction. (Color figure online)

5   Conclusions

In this work, we propose the region-based temporal aggregation (RTA) method to simulate the sampling procedure of Monte Carlo (MC) dropout for video segmentation. Our RTA method utilizes the temporal information from videos and only needs to sample one time to generate the prediction and the uncertainty for each frame. Compared to using general MC dropout, RTA can achieve similar performance on CamVid dataset with only 1.2% drop on mean IoU metric and incredibly speed up the inference process 10.97 times. Moreover, the uncertainty obtained by the RTA method is also comparable on pixel-level metric and even outperforms MC dropout on frame-level metric when using *Entropy* and *Variation Ratio* as the uncertainty estimation function. With our faster approach, we expect to extend our method on instance segmentation task in future work. In real-time applications, it's more important to obtain the instance-level uncertainty more precisely.

Acknowledgment. We thank Umbo CV, MediaTek, MOST 107-2634-F-007-007 for their support.

References

1. Badrinarayanan, V., Kendall, A., Cipolla, R.: SegNet: a deep convolutional encoder-decoder architecture for image segmentation. IEEE Trans. Pattern Anal. Mach. Intell. **39**(12), 2481–2495 (2017)
2. Blundell, C., Cornebise, J., Kavukcuoglu, K., Wierstra, D.: Weight uncertainty in neural networks. arXiv preprint arXiv:1505.05424 (2015)
3. Brostow, G.J., Fauqueur, J., Cipolla, R.: Semantic object classes in video: a high-definition ground truth database. Pattern Recognit. Lett. **30**(2), 88–97 (2009)
4. Chang, J., Wei, D., Fisher III, J.W.: A video representation using temporal superpixels. In: 2013 IEEE Conference on Computer Vision and Pattern Recognition (CVPR), pp. 2051–2058. IEEE (2013)
5. Chen, L.C., Papandreou, G., Kokkinos, I., Murphy, K., Yuille, A.L.: DeepLab: semantic image segmentation with deep convolutional nets, atrous convolution, and fully connected CRFs. arXiv preprint arXiv:1606.00915 (2016)
6. Cheng, J., Tsai, Y.H., Wang, S., Yang, M.H.: SegFlow: joint learning for video object segmentation and optical flow. In: 2017 IEEE International Conference on Computer Vision (ICCV), pp. 686–695. IEEE (2017)
7. Denker, J.S., Lecun, Y.: Transforming neural-net output levels to probability distributions. In: Advances in Neural Information Processing Systems, pp. 853–859 (1991)
8. Fan, Q., Zhong, F., Lischinski, D., Cohen-Or, D., Chen, B.: JumpCut: non-successive mask transfer and interpolation for video cutout. ACM Trans. Graph. **34**(6), 195 (2015)
9. Freeman, L.C.: Elementary Applied Statistics for Students in Behavioral Science. Wiley, New York (1965)
10. Gal, Y., Ghahramani, Z.: Dropout as a Bayesian approximation: representing model uncertainty in deep learning. In: 33rd International Conference on Machine Learning, ICML 2016, vol. 3, pp. 1651–1660 (2016)

11. Gal, Y., Ghahramani, Z.: Bayesian convolutional neural networks with Bernoulli approximate variational inference. arXiv preprint arXiv:1506.02158 (2015)
12. Graves, A.: Practical variational inference for neural networks. In: Advances in Neural Information Processing Systems, pp. 2348–2356 (2011)
13. Grundmann, M., Kwatra, V., Han, M., Essa, I.: Efficient hierarchical graph-based video segmentation. In: Computer Vision and Pattern Recognition (CVPR), pp. 2141–2148. IEEE (2010)
14. Houlsby, N., Huszár, F., Ghahramani, Z., Lengyel, M.: Bayesian active learning for classification and preference learning. arXiv preprint arXiv:1112.5745 (2011)
15. Howard, A.G., et al.: MobileNets: efficient convolutional neural networks for mobile vision applications. arXiv preprint arXiv:1704.04861 (2017)
16. Ilg, E., Mayer, N., Saikia, T., Keuper, M., Dosovitskiy, A., Brox, T.: FlowNet 2.0: evolution of optical flow estimation with deep networks. In: IEEE Conference on Computer Vision and Pattern Recognition (CVPR), vol. 2 (2017)
17. Jang, W.D., Kim, C.S.: Online video object segmentation via convolutional trident network. In: Proceedings of the IEEE Conference on Computer Vision and Pattern Recognition, pp. 5849–5858 (2017)
18. Jégou, S., Drozdzal, M., Vazquez, D., Romero, A., Bengio, Y.: The one hundred layers Tiramisu: fully convolutional denseNets for semantic segmentation. In: 2017 IEEE Conference on Computer Vision and Pattern Recognition Workshops (CVPRW), pp. 1175–1183. IEEE (2017)
19. Kampffmeyer, M., Salberg, A.B., Jenssen, R.: Semantic segmentation of small objects and modeling of uncertainty in urban remote sensing images using deep convolutional neural networks. In: 2016 IEEE Conference on Computer Vision and Pattern Recognition Workshops (CVPRW), pp. 680–688. IEEE (2016)
20. Kendall, A., Badrinarayanan, V., Cipolla, R.: Bayesian SegNet: model uncertainty in deep convolutional encoder-decoder architectures for scene understanding. arXiv preprint arXiv:1511.02680 (2015)
21. Kendall, A., Cipolla, R.: Modelling uncertainty in deep learning for camera relocalization. In: 2016 IEEE International Conference on Robotics and Automation (ICRA), pp. 4762–4769. IEEE (2016)
22. Kendall, A., Gal, Y.: What uncertainties do we need in Bayesian deep learning for computer vision? In: Advances in Neural Information Processing Systems, pp. 5580–5590 (2017)
23. Kendall, M.: A new measure of rank correlation. Biometrika 30, 81–93 (1938)
24. Long, J., Shelhamer, E., Darrell, T.: Fully convolutional networks for semantic segmentation. In: Proceedings of the IEEE Conference on Computer Vision and Pattern Recognition, pp. 3431–3440 (2015)
25. MacKay, D.J.: A practical Bayesian framework for backpropagation networks. Neural Comput. 4(3), 448–472 (1992)
26. Paszke, A., et al.: Automatic differentiation in PyTorch (2017)
27. Perazzi, F., Khoreva, A., Benenson, R., Schiele, B., Sorkine-Hornung, A.: Learning video object segmentation from static images. In: Computer Vision and Pattern Recognition (2017)
28. Perazzi, F., Wang, O., Gross, M., Sorkine-Hornung, A.: Fully connected object proposals for video segmentation. In: Proceedings of the IEEE International Conference on Computer Vision, pp. 3227–3234 (2015)
29. Ramakanth, S.A., Babu, R.V.: SeamSeg: video object segmentation using patch seams. In: CVPR, vol. 2, p. 5 (2014)

30. Ronneberger, O., Fischer, P., Brox, T.: U-Net: convolutional networks for biomedical image segmentation. In: Navab, N., Hornegger, J., Wells, W.M., Frangi, A.F. (eds.) MICCAI 2015. LNCS, vol. 9351, pp. 234–241. Springer, Cham (2015). https://doi.org/10.1007/978-3-319-24574-4_28
31. Shannon, C.E.: A mathematical theory of communication. ACM SIGMOBILE Mob. Comput. Commun. Rev. **5**(1), 3–55 (2001)
32. Simonyan, K., Zisserman, A.: Two-stream convolutional networks for action recognition in videos. In: Advances in Neural Information Processing Systems, pp. 568–576 (2014)
33. Srivastava, N., Hinton, G., Krizhevsky, A., Sutskever, I., Salakhutdinov, R.: Dropout: a simple way to prevent neural networks from overfitting. J. Mach. Learn. Res. **15**(1), 1929–1958 (2014)
34. Zhao, H., Shi, J., Qi, X., Wang, X., Jia, J.: Pyramid scene parsing network. In: IEEE Conference on Computer Vision and Pattern Recognition (CVPR), pp. 2881–2890 (2017)
35. Zhu, X., Wang, Y., Dai, J., Yuan, L., Wei, Y.: Flow-guided feature aggregation for video object detection. arXiv preprint arXiv:1703.10025 (2017)

Person Search by Multi-Scale Matching

Xu Lan[1]([✉]), Xiatian Zhu[2], and Shaogang Gong[1]

[1] Queen Mary University of London, London, UK
{x.lan, s.gong}@qmul.ac.uk
[2] Vision Semantics Ltd., London, UK
eddy@visionsemantics.com

Abstract. We consider the problem of person search in unconstrained scene images. Existing methods usually focus on improving the person detection accuracy to mitigate negative effects imposed by misalignment, mis-detections, and false alarms resulted from noisy people auto-detection. In contrast to previous studies, we show that sufficiently reliable person instance cropping is achievable by slightly improved state-of-the-art deep learning object detectors (e.g. Faster-RCNN), and the under-studied multi-scale matching problem in person search is a more severe barrier. In this work, we address this multi-scale person search challenge by proposing a *Cross-Level Semantic Alignment* (CLSA) deep learning approach capable of learning more discriminative identity feature representations in a unified end-to-end model. This is realised by exploiting the in-network feature pyramid structure of a deep neural network enhanced by a novel cross pyramid-level semantic alignment loss function. This favourably eliminates the need for constructing a computationally expensive image pyramid and a complex multi-branch network architecture. Extensive experiments show the modelling advantages and performance superiority of CLSA over the state-of-the-art person search and multi-scale matching methods on two large person search benchmarking datasets: CUHK-SYSU and PRW.

Keywords: Person search · Person detection and re-identification
Multi-scale matching · Feature pyramid · Image pyramid
Semantic alignment

1 Introduction

Person search aims to find a probe person in a gallery of whole unconstrained scene images [41]. It is an extended form of person re-identification (re-id) [12] by additionally considering the requirement of automatically detecting people in the scene images besides matching the identity classes. Unlike the conventional person re-id problem assuming the gallery images as either manually cropped or carefully filtered auto-detected bounding boxes [2,3,15,20,24,25,37,39,40,44], person search deals with raw unrefined detections with many false cropping and unknown degrees of misalignment. This yields a more challenging matching

© Springer Nature Switzerland AG 2018
V. Ferrari et al. (Eds.): ECCV 2018, LNCS 11205, pp. 553–569, 2018.
https://doi.org/10.1007/978-3-030-01246-5_33

problem especially in the process of person re-id. Moreover, auto-detected person boxes often vary more significantly in scale (resolution) than the conventional person re-id benchmarks (Fig. 1(b)), due to the inherent uncontrolled distances between persons and cameras (Fig. 1(a)). It is therefore intrinsically a *multi-scale matching* problem. However, this problem is currently under-studied in person search [28,41,47].

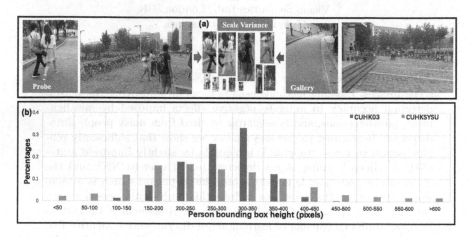

Fig. 1. Illustration of the intrinsic multi-scale matching challenge in person search. (a) Auto-detected person bounding boxes vary significantly in scale. (b) The person scale distribution of CUHK-SYSU (person search benchmark) covers a much wider range than manually refined CUHK-03 (person re-id benchmark).

In this work, we aim to address the multi-scale matching problem in person search. We show that this is a significant factor in improving the model matching performance, given the arbitrary and unknown size changes of persons in auto-detected bounding boxes. However, existing methods [28,41,47] focus on the person detection and localisation in scene images, which turns out not to be a severe bottleneck for the overall search performance as indicated in our experiments. For example, using the ground-truth person bounding boxes only brings a Rank-1 gain of 1.5% alongside employing ResNet-50 [14] for person search on the CUHK-SYSU benchmark [41]. In contrast, with the same ResNet-50 model, our proposed multi-scale matching learning improves the person search Rank-1 rate by 6.0% on the same benchmark (Fig. 6).

We make three **contributions** in this study: **(1)** We identify the multi-scale matching problem in person search – an element missing in the literature but found to be significant for improving the model performance. **(2)** We formulate a *Cross-Level Semantic Alignment* (CLSA) deep learning approach to addressing the multi-scale matching challenge. This is based on learning an end-to-end in-network feature pyramid representation with superior robustness in coping with variable scales of auto-detected person bounding boxes. **(3)** We improve the

Faster-RCNN model for more reliable person localisation in uncontrolled scenes, facilitating the overall search performance. Extensive experiments on two benchmarks CUHK-SYSU [41] and PRW [47] show the person search advantages of the proposed CLSA over state-of-the-art methods, improving the best competitor by 7.3% on CUHK-SYSU and 11.9% on PRW in Rank-1 accuracy.

2 Related Work

Person Search. Person search is a recently introduced problem of matching a probe person bounding box against a set of gallery whole scene images [41,47]. This is challenging due to the uncontrolled false alarms, mis-detections, and misalignment emerging in the auto-detection process. In the literature, there are only a handful of person search works [28,41,47]. Xiao et al. [41] propose a joint detection and re-id deep learning model for seeking their complementary benefits. Zheng et al. [47] study the effect of person detection on the identity matching performance. Liu et al. [28] consider recursively search refinement to more accurately locate the target person in the scene. While existing methods focus on detection enhancement, we show that by a state-of-the-art deep learning object detector with small improvements, person localisation is not a big limitation. Instead, the multi-scale matching problem turns out a more severe challenge in person search. In other words, solving the multi-scale problem is likely to bring more performance gain than improving person detection (Fig. 6(c)).

Person Re-Identification. Person search is essentially an extension of the conventional person re-id problem [12] with an additional requirement of automatic person detection in the scenes. Given the manual construction nature of re-id datasets, the scale diversity of gallery images tends to be restricted. It is simply harder for humans to verify and label the person identity of small bounding boxes, therefore leading to the selection and labelling bias towards large boxes (Fig. 1(b)). Consequently, the intrinsic multi-scale matching challenge is *artificially* suppressed in re-id benchmarks, hence losing the opportunity to test the real-world model robustness. Existing re-id methods can mostly afford to ignore the problem of multi-scale person bounding boxes in algorithm design. Whilst extensive efforts have be made to solving the re-id problem [3,5–7,17,20,22–25,36–40,46,48], there are only limited works considering multi-scale matching [5,29]. Beyond all these existing methods, our CLSA is designed specially to explore the in-network feature pyramid in deep learning for more effectively solving the under-studied multi-scale challenge in person search.

3 Cross-Level Semantic Alignment for Person Search

We want to establish a person search system capable of automatically detecting and matching persons in unconstrained scenes with any probe person. With the arbitrary distances between people and cameras in public space, person images are inherently captured at varying scales and resolutions. This raises the multi-scale matching challenge. To overcome this problem, we formulate a Cross-Level

Semantic Alignment (CLSA) deep learning approach. An overview of the CLSA is illustrated in Fig. 2. The CLSA contains two components: (1) Person detection which locates all person instances in the gallery scene images for facilitating the subsequent identity matching. (2) Person re-identification which matches the probe image against a large number of arbitrary scale gallery person bounding boxes (the key component of CLSA). We provide the component details below.

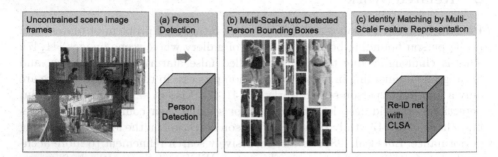

Fig. 2. Overview of the proposed multi-scale learning person search framework. (a) Person detection for cropping people from the whole scene images at (b) varying scales (resolutions). (c) Person identity matching is then conducted by a re-id model.

3.1   Person Detection

As a pre-processing step, person detection is important in order to achieve accurate search [41,47]. We adopt the Faster-RCNN model [35] as the CLSA detection component, due to its strong capability of detecting varying sized objects in unconstrained scenes. To further enhance person detection performance and efficiency, we introduce a number of design improvement on the original model. **(1)** Instead of using the conventional RoI (Region of Interest) pooling layer, we crop and resize the region feature maps to 14×14 in pixel, and further max-pool them to 7×7 for gaining better efficiency [4]. **(2)** After pre-training the backbone ResNet-50 net on ImageNet-1K, we fix the 1st building-block (the 1st 4 layers) in fine-tuning on the target person search data. This allows to preserve the shared low-level features learned from larger sized source data whilst simultaneously adapting the model to target data. **(3)** We keep and exploit all sized proposals for reducing the mis-detection rate at extreme scales in uncontrolled scenes before the Non-Maximum Suppression (NMS) operation. In deployment, we consider all detection boxes scored above 0.5, rather than extracting a fixed number of boxes from each scene image [47]. This is because the gallery scene images may contain varying (unknown in priori) number of people.

3.2   Multi-Scale Matching by Cross-Level Semantic Alignment

Given auto-detected person bounding boxes at arbitrary scales from the gallery scene images, we aim to build a person identity search model robust for multi-scale matching. To this end, we explore the seminal image/feature pyramid concept [1,8,21,31]. Our motivation is that a single-scale feature representation blurs salient and discriminative information at different scales useful in person identity matching; And a pyramid representation allows to be "scale-invariant" (more "scale insensitive") in the sense that a scale change in matching images is counteracted by a scale shift within the feature pyramid.

Build-In Feature Pyramid. We investigate the multi-scale feature representation learning in deep Convolutional Neural Network (CNN) to exploit the built-in feature pyramid structure formed on a single input image scale. Although CNN features have shown to be more robust to variance in image scale, pyramids are still effective in seeking more accurate detection and recognition results [27].

For the CNN architecture, we adopt the state-of-the-art ResNet-50 [14] as the backbone network (Fig. 3) of the identity matching component. In this study, we particularly leverage the feature pyramid hierarchy with low-to-high levels of semantics from bottom to top layers, automatically established in model learning optimisation [43]. Given the block-wise net structure in ResNet-50, we build a computationally efficient K-levels feature pyramid using the last conv layer of top-K ($K = 3$ in our experiments) blocks. The deepest layer of each block is supposed to have the most semantic features.

Nonetheless, it is not straightforward to exploit the ResNet-50 feature hierarchy. This is because the build-in pyramid has large semantic gaps across levels due to the distinct depths of layers. The features from lower layers are less discriminative for person matching therefore likely hurt the overall representational capacity if applied jointly with those from higher layers.

Cross-Level Semantic Alignment. To address the aforementioned problems, we improve the in-network feature pyramid by introducing a Cross-Level Semantic Alignment (CLSA) learning mechanism. The aim is to achieve a feature pyramid with all levels encoding the desired high-level person identity semantics. Formally, to train our person identity matching model, we adopt the softmax Cross-Entropy (CE) loss function to optimise an identity classification task. The CE loss on a training person bounding box $(\boldsymbol{I}, y)$ is computed as:

$$\mathcal{L}_{\text{ce}} = -\log\Big(\frac{\exp(\boldsymbol{W}_y^\top \boldsymbol{x})}{\sum_{i=1}^{|\mathcal{Y}|} \exp(\boldsymbol{W}_i^\top \boldsymbol{x})}\Big) \tag{1}$$

where $\boldsymbol{x}$ specifies the feature vector of $\boldsymbol{I}$ by the last layer, $\mathcal{Y}$ the training identity class space, and $\boldsymbol{W}_y$ the y-th ($y \in \mathcal{Y}$) class prediction function parameters.

In our case, $\boldsymbol{x}$ is the top pyramid level, also denoted as $\boldsymbol{x}^K$. For anyone of the top-K ResNet blocks, we obtain $\boldsymbol{x}$ by applying an average pooling layer and a FC layer on the output feature maps (Fig. 3(b)). Consider the different feature scale distributions across layers [30], we further normalise $\boldsymbol{x}$ by batch normalisation and ReLU non-linearity. In this way, we compute the feature representations for all K pyramid layers $\{\boldsymbol{x}^1, \cdots, \boldsymbol{x}^K\}$.

Recall that we aim to render all levels of feature representations identity semantic. To this end, we first project each of these features $\{\boldsymbol{x}^1, \cdots, \boldsymbol{x}^K\}$ by a

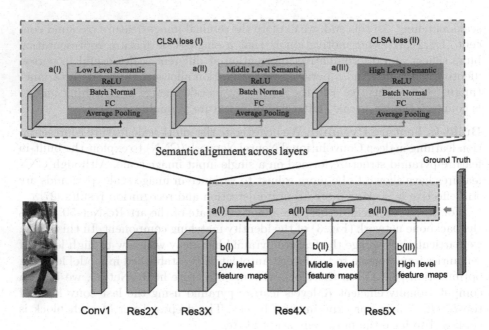

Fig. 3. Overview of the proposed Cross-Level Semantic Alignment (CLSA) approach in a ResNet-50 based implementation.

FC layer into the identity semantic space with the same dimension as $\mathcal{Y}$. The resulted semantic class probability vectors are denoted as $\{\boldsymbol{p}^1, \cdots, \boldsymbol{p}^K\}$ with $\boldsymbol{p}^k = [p_1^k, \cdots, p_{|\mathcal{Y}|}^k]$, $k \in \{1, \cdots, K\}$. To transfer the strongest semantics from the top (K-th) pyramid level to a lower (s-th) level, we introduce a Kullback-Leibler divergence based Cross-Level Semantic Alignment (CLSA) loss formulation inspired by knowledge distillation [16]:

$$\mathcal{L}_{\text{clsa}}(s) = \sum_{j=1}^{|\mathcal{Y}|} \tilde{p}_j^K \log \frac{\tilde{p}_j^K}{\tilde{p}_j^s}. \tag{2}$$

where $\tilde{p}_j^k$ is a *softened* per-class prediction semantic score obtained by

$$\tilde{p}_j^k = \frac{\exp(p_j^k/T)}{\sum_{j=1}^{|\mathcal{Y}|} \exp(p_j^k/T)}, \tag{3}$$

where the temperature parameter T controls the softening degree (higher values meaning more softened predictions). We set T = 3 following the suggestion in [16]. To enable end-to-end deep learning, we add this CLSA loss on top of the conventional CE loss (Eq. (1)):

$$\mathcal{L} = \mathcal{L}_{\text{ce}} + T^2 \sum_{s=1}^{K-1} \mathcal{L}_{\text{clsa}}(s) \tag{4}$$

where T^2 serves as a weighting parameter between the two loss terms.

Identity Matching by CLSA Feature Pyramid. In deployment, we first compute a CLSA feature pyramid by forward propagating any given person bounding box image. We then concatenate the feature vectors of all pyramid levels as the final representation for person re-id matching.

Remarks. The CLSA is similar in spirit to a few person re-id matching methods [5,29]. However, these methods adopt the image pyramid scheme, in contrast to the CLSA leveraging the in-network feature pyramid on a single image scale therefore more efficient. The FPN model [27] also exploits the build-in pyramid. The CLSA differs from FPN in a number of fundamental ways: (1) FPN focuses on object detection and segmentation, whilst CLSA aims to address fine-grained identity recognition and matching. (2) FPN additionally performs feature map unsampling hence less efficient than CLSA. (3) CLSA performs semantic alignment and transfer in the low-dimensional class space, in comparison to more expensive FPN's feature alignment. We will evaluate and compare these multi-scale learning methods against CLSA in our experiments (Table 4).

4   Experiments

Datasets. To evaluate the CLSA, we selected two person search benchmarks: CUHK-SYSU [41] and PRW [47]. We adopted the standard evaluation setting as summarised in Table 1. In particular, the CUHK-SYSU dataset contains 18,184 scene images, 8,432 labelled person IDs, and 96,143 annotated person bounding boxes. Each probe person appears in two or more scene gallery images captured from different locations. The training set has 11,206 images and 5,532 probe persons. Within the testing set, the probe set includes 2,900 person bounding boxes and the gallery contains a total of 6,978 whole scene images. The PRW dataset provides a total of 11,816 video frames and 43,110 person bounding boxes. The training set has 482 different IDs from 5,704 frames. The testing set contains 2,057 probe people along with a gallery of 6,112 scene images. In terms of bounding box scale, CUHK-SYSU and PRW range from 37×13 to 793×297, and 58×21 to 777×574, respectively. This shows the two person search datasets present the intrinsic multi-scale challenge. Example images are shown in Fig. 4.

Performance Metrics. For person detection, a person box is considered as correct if overlapping with the ground truth over 50% [41,47]. For person identity matching or re-id, we adopted the Cumulative Matching Characteristic (CMC) and mean Average Precision (mAP). The CMC is computed on each individual rank k as the probe cumulative percentage of truth matches appearing at ranks $\leq k$. The mAP measures the recall of multiple truth matches, computed by first computing the area under the Precision-Recall curve for each probe, then calculating the mean of Average Precision over all probes [46].

Implementation Details. We adopted the Pytorch framework [33] to conduct all the following experiments. For training the person detector component, we

Fig. 4. Example probe person and unconstrained scene images on (a) CUHK-SYSU [41] and (b) PRW [47]. Green bounding box: the ground truth probe person in the scene. ✓: Contain the probe person. ✗: Not contain the probe person.

Table 1. Evaluation setting, data statistics, and person bounding box scale of the CUHK-SYSU and PRW benchmarks. Bbox: Bounding box.

Dataset	Images	**Bbox scale**	IDs	Bbox Scale	ID Split		Bbox Split	
					Train	Test	Train	Test
CUHK-SYSU	18,184	96,143	8,432	37 × 13−793 × 297	5,532	2,900	55,272	40,871
PRW	11,816	43,110	932	58 × 21−777 × 574	482	450	18,048	25,062

adopted the SGD algorithm with the momentum set to 0.9, the weight decay to 0.0001, the iteration to 110,000, and the batch size to 256. We initialised the learning rate at 0.001, with a decay factor of 10 at every 30,000 iterations. For training the identity matching component, we used both annotated and detected (over 50% Intersection over Union (IoU) with the annotated and sharing the identity labels) boxes as [47]. We set the momentum to 0.9, the weight decay to 0.00001, the batch size to 64, and the epoch to 100. The initial learning rate was set at 0.01, and decayed by 10 at every 40 epochs. All person bounding boxes were resized to 256 × 128 pixels. To construct the in-network feature pyramid, we utilised the top 3 (Res3x, Res4x, Res5x) blocks in our final model implementation, i.e. $K = 3$ in Eq. (4). We also evaluated other pyramid constructing ways in the component analysis (Sect. 4.3).

4.1   Comparisons to State-Of-The-Art Person Search Methods

We compared the proposed CLSA method with two groups of existing person search approaches: (1) Three most recent state-of-the-art methods (NPSM [28], OIM [41], CWS [47]); and (2) Five popular person detectors (DPM [10], ACF [9], CCF [42], LDCF [32], and R-CNN [11]) with hand-crafted (BoW [46], LOMO [26],

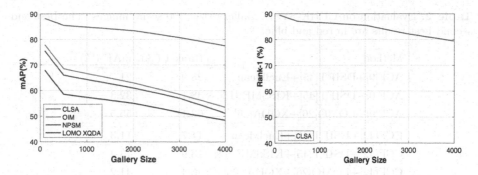

Fig. 5. Model scalability evaluation over different gallery search sizes on CUHK-SYSU.

DenseSIFT-ColorHist (DSIFT) [45]) or deep learning (IDNet [41]) features based re-id metric learning methods (KISSME [18], XQDA [26]).

Evaluation on CUHK-SYSU. Table 2 reports the person search performance on CUHK-SYSU with the standard gallery size of 100 scene images. It is clear that the CLSA significantly outperforms all other competitors. For instance, the CLSA surpasses the top-2 alternative models NPSM and OIM (both are end-to-end deep learning models) by 7.3% (88.5-81.2) and 9.8% (88.5-78.7) in Rank-1, 9.3% (87.2-77.9) and 11.7% (87.2-75.5) in mAP, respectively. The performance margin of CLSA against other non-deep-learning methods is even larger, due to that these models rely on less discriminative hand-crafted features without the modelling advantage of jointly learning stronger representation and matching metric model. This shows the overall performance superiority of the CLSA over current state-of-the-art methods, thanks to the joint contributions of improved person detection model (see more details below) and the proposed multi-scale deep feature representation learning mechanism.

To evaluate the model efficiency, we conducted a person search test among 100 gallery images on CUHK-SYSU. We deployed a desktop with a Nvidia Titan X GPU. Applying CLSA, OIM, and NPSM takes 1.2, 0.8, and 120 s, respectively. This indicates that the performance advantages of our CLSA do not sacrifice the model efficiency.

To test the model performance scalability, we further evaluated top-3 methods under varying gallery sizes in the range from 100 to 4,000 (the whole test gallery set). We observed in Fig. 5 that all methods degrade the performance given larger gallery search pools. When increasing the gallery size from 100 to 4,000, the mAP performance of NPSM drops from 77.9% to 53.0%, i.e. −24.9% degradation (no reported Rank-1 results). In comparison, the CLSA is more robust against the gallery size, with mAP/Rank-1 drop at −9.7% (77.5-87.2) and −9.1% (79.4-88.5). This is primarily because more distracting people are involved in the identity matching process, presenting more challenging tasks. Importantly, the performance gain of CLSA over other competitors becomes even higher at larger search scales, desirable in real-world applications. This

Table 2. Evaluation on CUHK-SYSU. Gallery size: 100 scene images. The best and second-best results are in red and blue.

Method	Rank-1 (%)	mAP (%)
ACF[9]+DSIFT[45]+Euclidean	25.9	21.7
ACF[9]+DSIFT[45]+KISSME [18]	38.1	32.3
ACF[9]+LOMO[26]+XQDA[26]	63.1	55.5
CCF[42]+DSIFT[45]+Euclidean	11.7	11.3
CCF[42]+DSIFT[45]+KISSME [18]	13.9	13.4
CCF[42]+LOMO[26]+XQDA [26]	46.4	41.2
CCF[42]+IDNet[41]	57.1	50.9
CNN[35]+DSIFT[45]+Euclidean	39.4	34.5
CNN[35]+DSIFT[45]+KISSME [18]	53.6	47.8
CNN[35]+LOMO[26]+XQDA [26]	74.1	68.9
CNN[35]+IDNet[41]	74.8	68.6
OIM[41]	78.7	75.5
NPSM[28]	81.2	77.9
CLSA	88.5	87.2

indicates the superior deployment scalability and robustness of CLSA over existing methods in tackling a large scale person search problem, further showing the importance of solving the previously ignored multi-scale matching challenge given auto-detected noisy bounding boxes in person search.

Evaluation on PRW. We further evaluated the CLSA against 11 existing competitors on the PRW dataset under the benchmarking setting with 11,816 gallery scene images. Overall, we observed similar performance comparisons with the state-of-the-art methods as on CUHK-SYSU. In particular, the CLSA is still the best person search performer with significant accuracy margins over other alternative methods, surpassing the second-best model NPSM by 11.9% (65.0-53.1) and 14.5% (38.7-24.2) in Rank-1 and mAP, respectively. This consistently suggests the model design advantages of CLSA over existing person search methods in a different video surveillance scenario.

4.2   Comparisons to Alternative Multi-Scale Learning Methods

Apart from existing person search methods, we further evaluated the effectiveness of CLSA by comparing with the in-network feature pyramid (baseline) and four state-of-the-art multi-scale deep learning approaches including DeepMu [34], MST [13], DPFL [5], and FPN [27] on the CUHK-SYSU benchmark. We used the standard 100 sized gallery setting in this test. For all compared methods, we utilised the same person detection model and the same backbone identity match-

Table 3. Evaluation on PRW. The best and second-best results are in red and blue.

Method	Rank-1 (%)	mAP (%)
ACF-Alex[9]+LOMO[26]+XQDA[26]	30.6	10.3
ACF-Alex[9]+IDE$_{det}$[47]	43.6	17.5
ACF-Alex[9]+IDE$_{det}$[47]+CWS[47]	45.2	17.8
DPM-Alex[10]+LOMO[26]+XQDA[26]	34.1	13.0
DPM-Alex[10]+IDE$_{det}$[47]	47.4	20.3
DPM-Alex[10]+IDE$_{det}$[47]+CWS[47]	48.3	20.5
LDCF[32]+LOMO[26]+XQDA [26]	31.1	11.0
LDCF[32]+IDE$_{det}$[47]	44.6	18.3
LDCF[32]+IDE$_{det}$[47]+CWS[47]	45.5	18.3
OIM[41]	49.9	21.3
NPSM[28]	53.1	24.2
CLSA	65.0	38.7

Table 4. Evaluating different multi-scale deep learning methods on CUHK-SYSU in the standard 100 sized gallery setting. FLOPs: FLoating point OPerations.

Method	Rank-1 (%)	mAP (%)	FLOPs ($\times 10^9$)
ResNet-50	82.5	81.6	**2.678**
In-Network Pyramid	81.1	80.2	**2.678**
DeepMu [34]	78.3	75.8	-
MST [13]	82.7	81.9	8.034
DPFL [5]	84.7	83.8	5.400
FPN [27]	85.5	85.0	4.519
CLSA	**88.5**	**87.2**	2.680

ing network (except DeepMu that exploits a specially proposed CNN architecture) as the CLSA for fair comparison.

Table 4 shows that the proposed CLSA is more effective than other multi-scale learning algorithms in person search. In particular, we have these observations: **(1)** The in-network feature pyramid decreases the overall performance as compared to using the standard ResNet-50 features (no pyramid) by a margin of 1.4% (82.5-81.1) in Rank-1 and 1.4% (81.6-80.2) in mAP. This verifies our hypothesis that directly applying the CNN feature hierarchy may harm the model performance due to the intrinsic semantic discrepancy across different pyramid levels. **(2)** CLSA improves the baseline in-network feature pyramid by a gain of 7.4% (88.5-81.1) in Rank-1 and 7.0% (87.2-80.2) in mAP. This indicates the exact effectiveness of the proposed cross-level semantic alignment mechanism in enhancing the person identity matching capability of the CNN feature representation in an end-to-end learning manner. (3) Three ResNet-50 based competitors all bring about person search performance improvement although less significant than the CLSA. This collectively suggests the importance of addressing the multi-scale matching problem in person search. (4) For model computational efficiency in FLOPs (FLoating point OPerations) per bounding box, CLSA has the least (a marginal) cost increase compared to other state-of-the-art multi-scale learning methods. This shows the superior cost-effectiveness of CLSA over alternative methods in addition to its accuracy advantages.

4.3 Further Analysis and Discussions

Effect of Person Detection. We analysed the effect of person detection on the person search performance using the CUHK-SYSU benchmark. We started with the three customised components of Faster-RCNN (Sect. 3.1). Table 5 shows that: (1) The region proposal resizing and max-pool operation does not hurt the model performance. In effect, this is a replacement of ROI pooling. In the context of an average pooling to 1×1 feature map followed, such a design remains the capability of detecting small objects therefore imposing no negative effect. (2) Freezing the first block's parameters in fine-tuning detector helps due to the commonality of source and target domain data in low-level feature patterns. (3) Using all sized proposals improves the result. It is worthy noting this does not reduce the model efficiency, because only top 256 boxes per image are remained after the Non-Maximum Suppression operation, similar to the conventional case of selecting larger proposals. There are an average of 6.04 bounding boxes per image on CUHK-SYSU.

Table 5. Detection model component analysis on CUHK-SYSU.

	Full		No resize & max-pool		Not fix 1st block		Not all sized proposals	
Metric (%)	Rank-1	mAP	Rank-1	mAP	Rank-1	mAP	Rank-1	mAP
CLSA	**88.5**	87.2	88.3	**87.3**	87.7	86.8	87.9	86.9

We then evaluated the holistic person detection performance with comparison to other two detection models (ACF [9] and CCF [42]). For person detection, it is shown in Fig. 6(a) that the precision performance of both ACF and CCF drops quickly when increasing the recall rate, whilst our improved Faster-RCNN remains more stable. This shows the effectiveness of deep learning detectors along additional model improvement from our CLSA. This is consistent with the results in Tables 2 and 3 that the CLSA outperforms ACF or CCF based methods by 20+% in both rank-1 and mAP.

We further tested the person search effect of our detection model by comparing with the results based on ground-truth bounding boxes. It is found in Fig. 6(b) with perfect person detection, the CLSA gives only a gain of 0.9%

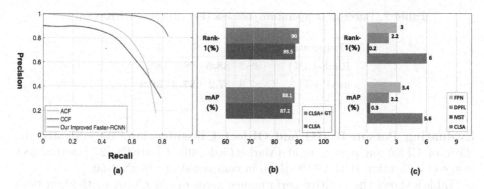

Fig. 6. Evaluation of person detection on CUHK-SYSU in the standard 100 sized gallery setting. **(a)** Person detection precision-recall performance. **(b)** The person search performance of the CLSA based on auto-detected *or* ground-truth person bounding box images. **(c)** Person detection *versus* multi-scale learning on the effect of person search performance.

(88.1-87.2) in mAP and 1.5% (90.0-88.5) in Rank-1. This indicates that the person detection component is not necessarily a major performance bottleneck in person search, thanks to modern object detection models. On the other hand, Table 4 also shows that addressing the multi-scale challenge is more critical for the overall model performance on person search, e.g. CLSA brings a performance boost of 6.0% (88.5-82.5%) in Rank-1 and 5.6% (87.2-81.6) in mAP over the baseline network ResNet-50.

Effect of Feature Pyramid. We evaluated the performance effect of feature pyramid of CLSA on CUHK-SYSU. Recall that the in-network feature pyramid construction is based on the selection of ResNet blocks (see Sect. 3.2 and Fig. 3). We tested three block selection schemes: 5-4, 5-4-3 (used in the final CLSA solution), and 5-4-3-2. Table 6 shows that a three-level pyramid is the optimal. It also suggests that performing semantic alignment directly with elementary features such as those extracted from the Res2X block may degrade the overall representation benefit in the pyramid, due to the hard-to-bridge semantic gap.

Table 6. Effect of in-network feature pyramid construction on CUHK-SYSU.

Blocks Selection	5-4	5-4-3	5-4-3-2
Rank-1 (%)	87.3	**88.5**	85.3
mAP (%)	86.2	**87.2**	84.3

Effect of Temperature Softness. We evaluated the impact of the temperature parameter setting in Eq. (3) in the range from 1 to 7. Table 7 shows that this parameter is not sensitive with the best value as 3.

Table 7. Effect of temperature softness (Eq. (3)) on CUHK-SYSU.

Temperature T	1	3	5	7
Rank-1 (%)	88.3	**88.5**	88.3	88.1
mAP (%)	87.0	87.2	**87.3**	86.9

Evaluating Person Re-ID and Object Classification. We evaluated the effect of CLSA on person re-id (Market1501 [46], CUHK03 [23]) and object image classification (CIFAR100 [19]), in comparison to ResNet-50.

Table 8 shows the positive performance gains of our CLSA method on both tasks. For example, the CLSA improves person re-id by 3.5% (88.9-85.4) in Rank-1 and 4.5% (73.1-68.6) in mAP on Market-1501. This gain is smaller than that on the same source video based PRW (see Table 3), due to the potential reason that person bounding boxes of Market-1501 have been manually processed with limited and artificial scale variations. Moreover, our method also benefits the CIFAR object classification with a 1.5% (76.2-74.7) top-1 rate gain. These observations suggest the consistent and problem-general advantages of our model in addition to person search in unconstrained scene images.

Table 8. Evaluating the CLSA on re-id and object classification benchmarks.

Dataset	Market-1501 [46]		CUHK03 [23]		Dataset	CIFAR100 [19]
Metric (%)	Rank-1	mAP	Rank-1	mAP	Metric (%)	Top-1 rate
ResNet-50	85.4	68.6	48.8	47.5	ResNet-110	74.7
CLSA	**88.9**	**73.1**	**52.3**	**50.9**	CLSA	**76.2**

5   Conclusion

In this work, we present a novel *Cross-Level Semantic Alignment* (CLSA) deep learning framework for person search in unconstrained scene images. In contrast to existing person search methods that focus on improving the people detection performance, our experiments show that solving the multi-scale matching challenge is instead more significant for improving the person search results. To solve this under-studied cross-scale person search challenge, we propose an end-to-end CLSA deep learning method by constructing an in-network feature pyramid structural representation and enhancing its representational power with a semantic alignment learning loss function. This is designed specially to make all feature pyramidal levels identity discriminative therefore leading to a more effective hierarchical representation for matching person images with large and unconstrained scale variations. Extensive comparative evaluations have been conducted on two large person search benchmarking datasets CUHK-SYSU and

PRW. The results validate the performance superiority and advantages of the proposed CLSA model over a variety of state-of-the-art person search, person re-id and multi-scale learning methods. We also provide comprehensive in-depth CLSA component evaluation and analysis to give the insights on model performance gain and design considerations. In addition, we further validate the more general performance advantages of the CLSA method on the person re-identification and object categorisation tasks.

Acknowledgements. This work was partly supported by the China Scholarship Council, Vision Semantics Limited, the Royal Society Newton Advanced Fellowship Programme (NA150459), and Innovate UK Industrial Challenge Project on Developing and Commercialising Intelligent Video Analytics Solutions for Public Safety (98111-571149).

References

1. Adelson, E.H., Anderson, C.H., Bergen, J.R., Burt, P.J., Ogden, J.M.: Pyramid methods in image processing. RCA Eng. **29**(6), 33–41 (1984)
2. Chang, X., Hospedales, T.M., Xiang, T.: Multi-level factorisation net for person re-identification. In: IEEE Conference on Computer Vision and Pattern Recognition, vol. 1, p. 2 (2018)
3. Chen, W., Chen, X., Zhang, J., Huang, K.: Beyond triplet loss: a deep quadruplet network for person re-identification. In: Proceedings of the IEEE Conference on Computer Vision and Pattern Recognition (CVPR), vol. 2 (2017)
4. Chen, X., Gupta, A.: An implementation of faster RCNN with study for region sampling. arXiv (2017)
5. Chen, Y., Zhu, X., Gong, S.: Person re-identification by deep learning multi-scale representations. In: Workshop of IEEE International Conference on Computer Vision, pp. 2590–2600 (2017)
6. Chen, Y.C., Zhu, X., Zheng, W.S., Lai, J.H.: Person re-identification by camera correlation aware feature augmentation. IEEE Trans. Pattern Anal. Mach. Intell. **40**(2), 392–408 (2018)
7. Cheng, D., Gong, Y., Zhou, S., Wang, J., Zheng, N.: Person re-identification by multi-channel parts-based CNN with improved triplet loss function. In: Proceedings of the IEEE Conference on Computer Vision and Pattern Recognition (CVPR), pp. 1335–1344 (2016)
8. Dalal, N., Triggs, B.: Histograms of oriented gradients for human detection. In: IEEE Conference on Computer Vision and Pattern Recognition (2005)
9. Dollár, P., Appel, R., Belongie, S., Perona, P.: Fast feature pyramids for object detection. IEEE Trans. Pattern Anal. Mach. Intell. **36**(8), 1532–1545 (2014)
10. Felzenszwalb, P.F., Girshick, R.B., McAllester, D., Ramanan, D.: Object detection with discriminatively trained part-based models. IEEE Trans. Pattern Anal. Mach. Intell. **32**(9), 1627–1645 (2010)
11. Girshick, R., Donahue, J., Darrell, T., Malik, J.: Rich feature hierarchies for accurate object detection and semantic segmentation. In: IEEE Conference on Computer Vision and Pattern Recognition, pp. 580–587 (2014)
12. Gong, S., Cristani, M., Yan, S., Loy, C.C.: Person Re-Identification. Springer, London (2014). https://doi.org/10.1007/978-1-4471-6296-4

13. He, K., Zhang, X., Ren, S., Sun, J.: Spatial pyramid pooling in deep convolutional networks for visual recognition. In: European Conference on Computer Vision, pp. 346–361 (2014)
14. He, K., Zhang, X., Ren, S., Sun, J.: Deep residual learning for image recognition. In: IEEE Conference on Computer Vision and Pattern Recognition, pp. 770–778 (2016)
15. Hermans, A., Beyer, L., Leibe, B.: In defense of the triplet loss for person re-identification. arXiv (2017)
16. Hinton, G., Vinyals, O., Dean, J.: Distilling the knowledge in a neural network. arXiv (2015)
17. Jiao, J., Zheng, W.S., Wu, A., Zhu, X., Gong, S.: Deep low-resolution person re-identification. In: AAAI Conference on Artificial Intelligence (2018)
18. Koestinger, M., Hirzer, M., Wohlhart, P., Roth, P.M., Bischof, H.: Large scale metric learning from equivalence constraints. In: IEEE Conference on Computer Vision and Pattern Recognition, pp. 2288–2295 (2012)
19. Krizhevsky, A., Hinton, G.: Learning multiple layers of features from tiny images. Technical report, University of Toronto (2009)
20. Lan, X., Wang, H., Gong, S., Zhu, X.: Deep reinforcement learning attention selection for person re-identification. arXiv (2017)
21. Lazebnik, S., Schmid, C., Ponce, J.: Beyond bags of features: spatial pyramid matching for recognizing natural scene categories. In: IEEE Conference on Computer Vision and Pattern Recognition (2006)
22. Li, M., Zhu, X., Gong, S.: Unsupervised person re-identification by deep learning tracklet association. In: European Conference on Computer Vision (2018)
23. Li, W., Zhao, R., Xiao, T., Wang, X.: Deepreid: Deep filter pairing neural network for person re-identification. In: CVPR (2014)
24. Li, W., Zhu, X., Gong, S.: Person re-identification by deep joint learning of multi-loss classification. arXiv (2017)
25. Li, W., Zhu, X., Gong, S.: Harmonious attention network for person re-identification. In: IEEE Conference on Computer Vision and Pattern Recognition (2018)
26. Liao, S., Hu, Y., Zhu, X., Li, S.Z.: Person re-identification by local maximal occurrence representation and metric learning. In: IEEE International Conference on Computer Vision, pp. 2197–2206 (2015)
27. Lin, T.Y., Dollár, P., Girshick, R., He, K., Hariharan, B., Belongie, S.: Feature pyramid networks for object detection. In: IEEE Conference on Computer Vision and Pattern Recognition (2017)
28. Liu, H., et al.: Neural person search machines. In: IEEE International Conference on Computer Vision (2017)
29. Liu, J., et al.: Multi-scale triplet CNN for person re-identification. In: Proceedings of the 2016 ACM on Multimedia Conference, pp. 192–196. ACM (2016)
30. Liu, W., Rabinovich, A., Berg, A.C.: Parsenet: looking wider to see better. arXiv (2015)
31. Lowe, D.G.: Distinctive image features from scale-invariant keypoints. Int. J. Comput. Vis. 60(2), 91–110 (2004)
32. Nam, W., Dollár, P., Han, J.H.: Local decorrelation for improved pedestrian detection. In: Advances in Neural Information Processing Systems, pp. 424–432 (2014)
33. Paszke, A., Gross, S., Chintala, S., Chanan, G.: Pytorch (2017)
34. Qian, X., Fu, Y., Jiang, Y.G., Xiang, T., Xue, X.: Multi-scale deep learning architectures for person re-identification. In: IEEE International Conference on Computer Vision (2017)

35. Ren, S., He, K., Girshick, R., Sun, J.: Faster R-CNN: towards real-time object detection with region proposal networks. In: Advances in Neural Information Processing Systems, pp. 91–99 (2015)
36. Wang, H., Gong, S., Zhu, X., Xiang, T.: Human-in-the-loop person re-identification. In: Leibe, B., Matas, J., Sebe, N., Welling, M. (eds.) ECCV 2016. LNCS, vol. 9908, pp. 405–422. Springer, Cham (2016). https://doi.org/10.1007/978-3-319-46493-0_25
37. Wang, H., Zhu, X., Gong, S., Xiang, T.: Person re-identification in identity regression space. Int. J. Comput. Vis. (2018)
38. Wang, J., Zhu, X., Gong, S., Li, W.: Transferable joint attribute-identity deep learning for unsupervised person re-identification. In: IEEE Conference on Computer Vision and Pattern Recognition (2018)
39. Wang, T., Gong, S., Zhu, X., Wang, S.: Person re-identification by video ranking. In: Fleet, D., Pajdla, T., Schiele, B., Tuytelaars, T. (eds.) ECCV 2014. LNCS, vol. 8692, pp. 688–703. Springer, Cham (2014). https://doi.org/10.1007/978-3-319-10593-2_45
40. Xiao, T., Li, H., Ouyang, W., Wang, X.: Learning deep feature representations with domain guided dropout for person re-identification. In: IEEE Conference on Computer Vision and Pattern Recognition, pp. 1249–1258 (2016)
41. Xiao, T., Li, S., Wang, B., Lin, L., Wang, X.: Joint detection and identification feature learning for person search. In: IEEE Conference on Computer Vision and Pattern Recognition, pp. 3376–3385 (2017)
42. Yang, B., Yan, J., Lei, Z., Li, S.Z.: Convolutional channel features. In: IEEE International Conference on Computer Vision, pp. 82–90 (2015)
43. Zeiler, M.D., Fergus, R.: Visualizing and understanding convolutional networks. In: Fleet, D., Pajdla, T., Schiele, B., Tuytelaars, T. (eds.) ECCV 2014. LNCS, vol. 8689, pp. 818–833. Springer, Cham (2014). https://doi.org/10.1007/978-3-319-10590-1_53
44. Zhang, Y., Xiang, T., Hospedales, T.M., Lu, H.: Deep mutual learning. In: IEEE Conference on Computer Vision and Pattern Recognition (2018)
45. Zhao, R., Ouyang, W., Wang, X.: Unsupervised salience learning for person re-identification. In: IEEE Conference on Computer Vision and Pattern Recognition, pp. 3586–3593 (2013)
46. Zheng, L., Shen, L., Tian, L., Wang, S., Wang, J., Tian, Q.: Scalable person re-identification: a benchmark. In: IEEE International Conference on Computer Vision, pp. 1116–1124 (2015)
47. Zheng, L., Zhang, H., Sun, S., Chandraker, M., Tian, Q.: Person re-identification in the wild. arXiv (2017)
48. Zhu, X., Wu, B., Huang, D., Zheng, W.S.: Fast openworld person re-identification. IEEE Trans. Image Process. (2017)

A Hybrid Model for Identity Obfuscation by Face Replacement

Qianru Sun$^{(\boxtimes)}$, Ayush Tewari, Weipeng Xu, Mario Fritz,
Christian Theobalt, and Bernt Schiele

Max Planck Institute for Informatics,
Saarland Informatics Campus, Saarbrücken, Germany
{qsun,atewari,wxu,mfritz,theobalt,schiele}@mpi-inf.mpg.de

Abstract. As more and more personal photos are shared and tagged in social media, avoiding privacy risks such as unintended recognition, becomes increasingly challenging. We propose a new hybrid approach to obfuscate identities in photos by head replacement. Our approach combines state of the art parametric face synthesis with latest advances in Generative Adversarial Networks (GAN) for data-driven image synthesis. On the one hand, the parametric part of our method gives us control over the facial parameters and allows for explicit manipulation of the identity. On the other hand, the data-driven aspects allow for adding fine details and overall realism as well as seamless blending into the scene context. In our experiments we show highly realistic output of our system that improves over the previous state of the art in obfuscation rate while preserving a higher similarity to the original image content.

1 Introduction

Visual data is shared publicly at unprecedented scales through social media. At the same time, however, advanced image retrieval and face recognition algorithms, enabled by deep neural networks and large-scale training datasets, allow to index and recognize privacy relevant information more reliably than ever. To address this exploding privacy threat, methods for reliable identity obfuscation are crucial. Ideally, such a method should not only effectively hide the identity information but also preserve the realism of the visual data, i.e., make obfuscated people look realistic.

Existing techniques for identity obfuscation have evolved from simply covering the face with often unpleasant occluders, such as black boxes or mosaics, to more advanced methods that produce natural images [1–3]. These methods either perturb the imagery in an imperceptible way to confuse specific recognition algorithms [2,3], or substantially modify the appearance of the people in

---

Electronic supplementary material The online version of this chapter (https://doi.org/10.1007/978-3-030-01246-5_34) contains supplementary material, which is available to authorized users.

© Springer Nature Switzerland AG 2018
V. Ferrari et al. (Eds.): ECCV 2018, LNCS 11205, pp. 570–586, 2018.
https://doi.org/10.1007/978-3-030-01246-5_34

the images, thus making them unrecognizable even for generic recognition algorithms and humans [1]. Among the latter category, recent work [1] leverages a generative adversarial network (GAN) to inpaint the head region conditioned on facial landmarks. It achieves state-of-the-art performance in terms of both recognition rate and image quality. However, due to the lack of controllability of the image generation process, the results of such a purely data-driven method inevitably exhibit artifacts by inpainting faces of unfitting face pose, expression or implausible shape. In contrast, parametric face models [4] give us complete control of facial attributes and have demonstrated compelling results for applications such as face reconstruction, expression transfer and visual dubbing [4–6]. Importantly, using a parametric face model allows to control the identify of a person as well as to preserve attributes such as face pose and expression by rendering and blending an altered face over the original image. However, this naive face replacement yields unsatisfactory results, since (1) fine level details cannot be synthesized by the model, (2) imperfect blending leads to unnatural output images and (3) only the face region is obfuscated while the larger head and hair regions, which also contain a lot of identity information, remain untouched.

In this paper, we propose a novel approach that combines a data-driven method and a parametric face model, and therefore leverages the best of two worlds. To this end, we disentangle and solve our problem in two stages (see Fig. 1): In the first stage, we replace the face region in the image with a rendered face of a different identity. To this end we replace the identity related component of the original person in the parameter vector of the face model while preserving attributes of original facial expression. In the second stage, a GAN is trained to synthesize the complete head image given the rendered face and an obfuscated region around the head as conditional inputs. In this stage, the missing region in the input is inpainted and fine grained details are added, resulting in a photo-realistic output image. Our qualitative and quantitative evaluations show that our approach significantly outperforms the baseline methods on publicly available datasets with both lower recognition rate and higher image quality.

2   Related Work

Identity Obfuscation. Blurring the face region or covering it with occluders, such as a mosaic or a black bar, are still the predominant techniques for visual identity obfuscation in photos and videos. The performance of these methods in concealing identity against machine recognition systems has been studied in [7,8]. They show that these simple techniques not only introduce unpleasant artifacts, but also become less effective due to the improvement of CNN-based recognition methods. Hiding the identity information while preserving the photorealism of images is still an unsolved problem. Only a few works have attempted to tackle this problem.

For *target-specific* obfuscations, Sharif et al. [3] and Oh et al. [2] used *adversarial example* based methods which perturb the imagery in an imperceptible manner aiming to confuse specific machine recognition systems. Their obfuscation patterns are invisible to humans and the obfuscation performance is strong. However, obfuscation can only be guaranteed for target-specific recognizers.

To confuse *target-generic* machine recognizers and even human recognizers, Brkic et al. [9] generated full body images that overlay with the target person masks. However, synthesized persons with uniform poses do not match scene context which leads to blending artifacts in final images. The recent work of [1] inpaints fake head images conditioned on the context and blends generated heads with diverse poses into varied background and body poses in social media photos. While achieving state-of-the-art performance in terms of both recognition rate and image quality, the results of such a purely data-driven method inevitably exhibits artifacts like the change of attributes such as face poses and expressions.

Parametric Face Models. Blanz and Vetter [10] learn an affine parametric 3D Morphable Model (3DMM) of face geometry and texture from 200 high-quality scans. Higher-quality models have been constructed using more scans [11], or by using information from in-the-wild images [12,13]. Such parametric models can act as strong regularizers for 3D face reconstruction problems, and have been widely used in optimization based [5,12,14–17] and learning-based [18–23] settings. Recently, a model-based face autoencoder (MoFA) has been introduced [4] which combines a trainable CNN encoder with an expert-designed differentiable rendering layer as decoder, which allows for end-to-end training on real images. We use such an architecture and extend it to reconstruct faces from images where the face region is blacked out or blurred for obfuscation. We also utilize the semantics of the parameters of the 3DMM by replacing the identity-specific parameters to synthesize overlaid faces with different identities. While the reconstructions obtained using parametric face models are impressive, they are limited to the low-dimensional subspace of the models. Many high-frequency details are not captured and the face region does not blend well with the surroundings in overlaid 3DMM renderings. Some reconstruction methods go beyond the low-dimensional parametric models [6,16,17,19,21,24] to capture more detail, but most lack parametric control of the captured high-frequency details.

Image Inpainting and Refinement. We propose a GAN based method in the second stage to refine the rendered 3DMM face pixels for higher realism as well as to inpaint the obfuscated head pixels around the rendered face. In [25,26], rendered images are modified to be more realistic by means of adversarial training. The generated data works well for specific tasks such as gaze estimation and hand pose estimation, with good results on real images. Yeh et al. [27] and Pathak et al. [28] have used GANs to synthesize missing content conditioned on image context. Both of these approaches assume strong appearance similarity or connection between the missing parts and their contexts. Sun et al. [1] inpainted head pixels conditioned on facial landmarks. Our method, conditioned on parametric face model renderings, gives us control to change the identity of the generated face while also synthesizing more photo-realistic results.

3 Face Replacement Framework

We propose a novel face replacement approach for identity obfuscation that combines a data-driven method with a parametric face model.

Our approach consists of two stages (see Fig. 1). Experimenting on different modalities of input results in different levels of obfuscation[1]. In the first stage, we can not only render a reconstructed face on the basis of a parametric face model (3DMM), but can also replace the face region in the image with the rendered face of a different identity. In the second stage, a GAN is trained to synthesize the complete head image given the rendered face and a further obfuscated image around the face as conditional inputs. The obfuscation here protects the identity information contained in the ears, hair, etc. In this stage, the obfuscated region is inpainted with realistic content and fine grain details missing in the rendered 3DMM are added, resulting in a photo-realistic output image.

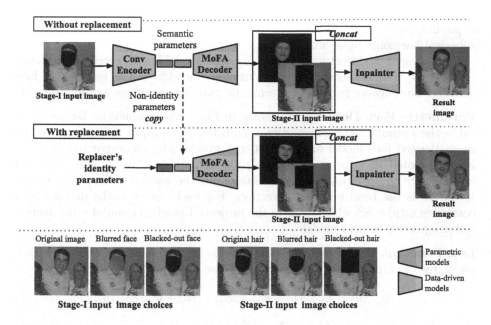

Fig. 1. Our obfuscation method based on data-driven deep models and parametric face models. The bottom row shows the input image choices for stage-I and stage-II. Different input combination results in different levels of obfuscation.

3.1 Stage-I: Face Replacement

Stage-I of our approach reconstructs 3D faces from the input images using a parametric face model. We train a convolutional encoder to regress the model's

---

[1] Stage-I input image choices: *Original image, Blurred face* and *Blacked-out face.* Stage-II input image choices: *Original hair, Blurred hair* and *Blacked-out hair.*

semantic parameters from the input. This allows us to render a synthetic face reconstructed from a person and also gives us the control to modify its rendered identity based on the parameter vector.

Semantic Parameters. We denote the set of all semantic parameters as $p = (\alpha, \beta, \delta, \phi, \gamma)$, $|p| = 257$. These parameters describe the full appearance of the face. We use an affine parametric 3D face model to represent our reconstructions. α and β represent the shape and reflectance of the face, and correspond to the identity of the person. These parameters are the coefficients of the PCA vectors constructed from 200 high-quality face scans [10]. δ are the coefficients of the expression basis vectors computed using PCA on selected blend shapes of [29,30]. We use 80 α, 80 β and 64 δ parameters. Together, they define the per-vertex position and reflectance of the face mesh represented in the topology used by [13]. In addition, we also estimate the rigid pose (ϕ) of the face and the scene illumination (γ). Rigid pose is parametrized with 6 parameters corresponding to a $3D$ translation vector and Euler angles for the rotation. Scene illumination is parameterized using 27 parameters corresponding to the first 3 bands of the spherical harmonic basis functions [31].

Our stage-I architecture is based on the Model-based Face Autoencoder (MoFA) [4] and consists of a convolutional encoder and a parametric face decoder. The encoder regresses the semantic parameters p given an input image[2].

Parametric Face Decoder. As shown in Fig. 1, the parametric face decoder takes the output of the convolutional encoder, p, as input and generates the reconstructed face model and its rendered image. The reconstructed face can be represented as $v_i(p) \in \mathbb{R}^3$ and $c_i(p) \in \mathbb{R}^3$, $\forall i \in [1, N]$, where $v_i(p)$ and $c_i(p)$ denote the position in camera space and the shaded color of the vertex i, and N is the total number of vertices. For each vertex i, the decoder also computes $u_i(p) \in \mathbb{R}^2$ which denotes the projected pixel location of $v_i(p)$ using a full perspective camera model.

Loss Function. Our auto-encoder in stage-I is trained using a loss function that compares the input image to the output of the decoder as

$$E_{loss}(p) = E_{land}(p) + w_{photo}E_{photo}(p) + w_{reg}E_{reg}(p). \tag{1}$$

Here, $E_{land}(p)$ is a landmark alignment term which measures the distance between 66 fiducial landmarks [13] in the input image with the corresponding landmarks on the output of the parametric decoder,

$$E_{land}(p) = \sum_{i=1}^{66} ||l_i - u_x(p)||_2^2. \tag{2}$$

l_i is the ith landmark's image position and x is the index of the corresponding landmark vertex on the face mesh. Image landmarks are computed using the dlib

---

[2] We use AlexNet [32] as the encoder.

toolkit [33]. $E_{photo}(p)$ is a photometric alignment term which measures the per-vertex appearance difference between the reconstruction and the input image,

$$E_{photo}(p) = \sum_{i \in V} ||I(u_i(p)) - c_i(p)||_2. \qquad (3)$$

V is the set of visible vertices and I is the image for the current training iteration. $E_{reg}(p)$ is a Tikhonov style statistical regularizer which prevents degenerate reconstructions by penalizing parameters far away from their mean,

$$E_{reg}(p) = \sum_{i=1}^{80} \frac{\alpha_i}{(\sigma_s)_i} + w_e \sum_{i=1}^{64} \frac{\delta_i}{(\sigma_e)_i} + w_r \sum_{i=1}^{80} \frac{\beta_i}{(\sigma_r)_i}. \qquad (4)$$

σ_s, σ_e, σ_r are the standard deviations of the shape, expression and reflectance vectors respectively. Please refer to [4,13] for more details on the face model and the loss function. Since the loss function $E_{loss}(p)$ is differentiable, we can back-propagate the gradients to the convolutional encoder, enabling self-supervised learning of the network.

Replacement of Identity Parameters. The controllable semantic parameters of the face model have the advantage that we can modify them after face reconstruction. Note that the shape and reflectance parameters α and β of the face model depend on the identity of the person [10,20]. We propose to modify these parameters (referred to as identity parameters from now on) and render synthetic overlaid faces with different identities, while keeping all other dimensions fixed. While all face model dimensions could be modified we want to avoid unfitting facial attributes. For example, changing all dimensions of the reflectance parameters can lead to misaligned skin color between the rendered face and the body. To alleviate this problem, we keep the first, third and fourth dimensions of β, which control the global skin tone of the face, fixed.

After obtaining the semantic parameters on all our training set (over 2k different identities), we first cluster the identity parameters into 15 different identity clusters with the respective cluster means as representatives. We then replace the identity parameters of the current test image with the parameters of the cluster that is either closest (`Replacer1`), at middle distance (`Replacer8`) or furthest away (`Replacer15`) to evaluate different levels of obfuscation (Fig. 2). Note that each test image has its own `Replacers`.

Input Image Obfuscation. In addition to replacing the identity parameters, we also optionally allow additional obfuscation by blurring or blacking out the face region in the input image for Stage-I (the face region is determined by reconstructing the face from the original image). These obfuscation strategies force the Stage-I network to predict the semantic parameters only using the context information (Fig. 3), thus reducing the extent of facial identity information captured in the reconstructions. We train networks for these strategies using the full body images with the obfuscated face region as input while using the original

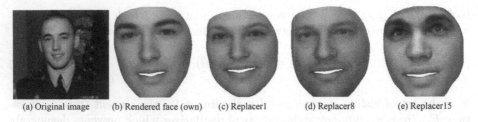

(a) Original image   (b) Rendered face (own)   (c) Replacer1   (d) Replacer8   (e) Replacer15

Fig. 2. Replacement of identity parameters in Stage-I allows us to generate faces with different identities.

Blacked-out face   Rendered face   Aligned face   Blurred face   Rendered face   Aligned face

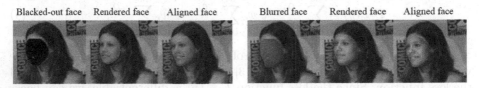

Fig. 3. Stage-I output: If the face in the input image is blacked out or blurred, our network can still predict reasonable parametric reconstructions which align to the contour of the face region. The appearance is also well estimated from the context information. The results are further aligned using an optimization-based strategy.

unmodified images in the loss function $E_{loss}(p)^3$. This approach gives us results which preserve the boundary of the face region and the skin color of the person even for such obfuscated input images (Fig. 3). The rigid pose and appearance of the face is also nicely estimated.

In addition to reducing the identity information in the rendered face, the Stage-I network also removes the expression information when faces in the input images are blurred or blacked out. To better align our reconstructions with the input images without adding any identity-specific information, we further refine only the rigid pose and expression estimates of the reconstructions. We minimize part of the energy term in (1) after initializing all parameters with the predictions of our network.

$$p^* = \underset{p}{\operatorname{argmin}} \, E_{refine}(p) \tag{5}$$

$$E_{refine}(p) = E_{land}(p) + w_{reg} E_{reg}(p) \tag{6}$$

Note that only ϕ and δ are optimized during refinement. We use 10 non-linear iterations of a Gauss-Newton optimizer to minimize this energy. As can be seen in Fig. 3, this optimization strategy significantly improves the alignment between the reconstructions and the input images. Note that input image obfuscation can be combined with identity replacement to further change the identity of the rendered face.

---

[3] If the input image is not obfuscated in Stage-I, we directly use the pre-trained coarse model of [13] to get the parameters and the rendered face.

The output of stage-I is the shaded rendering of the face reconstruction. The synthetic face lacks high-frequency details and does not blend perfectly with the image as the expressiveness of the parametric model is limited. Stage-II enhances this result and provides further obfuscation by removing/reducing the context information from the full head region.

3.2 Stage-II: Inpainting

Stage-II is conditioned on the rendered face image from Stage-I and an obfuscated region around the head to inpaint a realistic image. There are two objectives for this inpainter: (1) inpainting the blurred/blacked-out hair pixels in the head region; (2) modifying the rendered face pixels to add fine details and realism to match the surrounding image context. The architecture is composed of a convolutional generator G and discriminator D, and is optimized by L1 loss and adversarial loss.

Input. For the generator G, RGB channels of both the obfuscated image I and the rendered face from Stage-I F are concatenated as input. For the discriminator D, we take the inpainted image as *fake* and the original image as *real*. Then, we feed the (*fake, real*) pairs into the discriminator. We use the whole body image instead of just the head region in order to generate natural transitions between the head and the surrounding regions including body and background, especially for the case of obfuscated input.

Head Generator (G) and Discriminator (D). The head generator G is a "U-Net"-based architecture [34], i.e. Convolutional Auto-encoder with skip connections between encoder and decoder[4], following [1,35,36]. It generates a natural head image given both the surrounding context and the rendered face. The architecture of the discriminator D is the same as in DCGAN [37].

Loss Function. We use L1 reconstruction loss plus adversarial loss, named $\mathcal{L}^G$, to optimize the generator and the adversarial loss, named $\mathcal{L}^D$, to optimize the discriminator. For the generator, we use the head-masked L1 loss such that the optimizer focuses more on the appearance of the targeted head region,

$$\mathcal{L}^G = \mathcal{L}_{bce}(D(G(I,F)),1) + \lambda \|(G(I,F) - I_O) \odot M_h\|_1, \qquad (7)$$

where M_h is the head mask (from the annotated bounding box), I_O denotes the original image and $\mathcal{L}_{bce}$ is the binary cross-entropy loss. λ controls the importance of the L1 term[5]. Then, for the discriminator, we have the following losses:

$$\mathcal{L}^D = \mathcal{L}_{adv}^D = \mathcal{L}_{bce}(D(I_O),1) + \mathcal{L}_{bce}(D(G(I,F)),0). \qquad (8)$$

---

[4] Network architectures and hyper-parameters are given in supplementary materials.
[5] When λ is too small, the adversarial loss dominates the training and it is more likely to generate artifacts; when λ is too big, the generator mainly uses the L1 loss and generates blurry results.

We also tried to add a de-identification loss derived from verification models [38], in order to change the identity of the person in the generated image. However, this has a conflicting objective with the L1 loss and we were not able to find a good trade-off between them.

Figure 4 shows the effect of our inpainter. In (a) when the original hair image is given, the inpainter refines the rendered face pixels to match surroundings, e.g., the face skin becomes more realistic in the bottom image. In (b), (c), the inpainter not only refines the face pixels but also generates the blurred/missing head pixels based on the context.

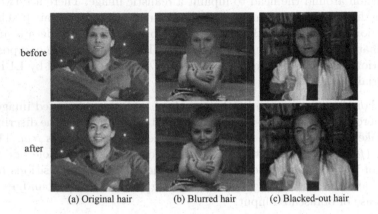

before

after

(a) Original hair   (b) Blurred hair   (c) Blacked-out hair

Fig. 4. Visualization results before and after inpainting. On the top row, rendered faces are overlayed onto the color images for better comparison of details.

4   Recognizers

Identity obfuscation in this paper is target-generic: it is designed to work against any recognizer, be it machine or human. In this paper, we use both recognizers to test our approach.

4.1   Machine Recognizers

We use an automatic recognizer `naeil` [39], the state-of-the-art for person recognition in social media images [1,40]. In contrast to typical person recognizers, `naeil` also uses body and scene context cues for recognition. It has thus proven to be relatively immune to common obfuscation techniques like blacking-out or blurring the head region [7].

We first train feature extractors over head and body regions, and then train SVM identity classifiers on those features. We can concatenate features from multiple regions (e.g. head+body) to make use of multiple cues. In our work, we use GoogleNet features from `head` and `head+body` for evaluation. We have also verified that the obfuscation results show similar trends against AlexNet-based analogues (see supplementary materials).

4.2 Human Recognizers

We also conduct human recognition experiments to evaluate the obfuscation effectiveness in a perceptual way. Given an original head image and the head images inpainted by variants of our method and results of other methods, we ask users to recognize the original person from the inpainted ones, and to also choose the farthest one in terms of identity. Users are guided to focus on identity recognition rather than the image quality. For each method, we calculate the percentage of times its results were chosen as the farthest identity (higher number implies better obfuscation performance).

5 Experiments

An obfuscation method should not only effectively hide the identity information but also produce photo-realistic results. Therefore, we evaluate our results on the basis of recognition rate and visual realism. We also study the impact of different levels of obfuscation yielded from different input modalities at two stages.

5.1 Dataset

Our obfuscation method needs to be evaluated on realistic social media photos. PIPA dataset [41] is the largest social media dataset (37,107 Flickr images with 2,356 annotated individuals), which shows people in diverse events, activities and social relations [42]. In total, 63,188 person instances are annotated with head bounding boxes from which we create head masks. We split the PIPA dataset into a training set and a test set without overlapping identities, following [1]. In the training set, there are 2,099 identities, 46,576 instances and in the test set 257 identities, 5,175 instances. We further prune images with strong profile or back of the head views from both sets following [1], resulting in 23,884 training and 1,084 test images. As our pipeline takes a fixed-size input ($256 \times 256 \times 3$), we normalize the image size of the dataset. To this end, we crop and zero-pad the images so that the face appears in the top middle block of a 3×4 grid in the entire image. Details of our crop method are given in supplementary materials.

5.2 Input Modalities

Our method allows 18 different combinations of input modalities, which is a combination of 3 types of face modalities, 3 types of hair modalities and the choice of modifying the face identity parameters (default replacer is `Replacer15`). Note that, only 17 of them are valid for obfuscation, since the combination of original face and hair aims to reconstruct the original image. Due to space limitations, we compare a representative subset, as shown in Table 1. The complete results can be found in the supplementary material.

In order to blur the face and hair regions in the input images, we use the same Gaussian kernel as in [1,7]. Note that in contrast to those methods, our reconstructed face model provides the segmentation of the face region allowing us to precisely blur the face or hair region.

5.3   Results

In this section, we evaluate the proposed hybrid approach with different input modalities in terms of the realism of images and the obfuscation performance.

Image Realism. We evaluate the quality of the inpainted images compared to the ground truth (original) images using Structure Similarity Score (SSIM) [43]. During training, the body parts are not obfuscated, so we report the mask-SSIM [1,35] for the head region only (SSIM scores are in supplementary materials). This score measures how close the inpainted head is to the original head.

The SSIM metric is not applicable when using a `Replacer`, as ground truth images are not available. Therefore, we conduct a human perceptual study (HPS) on Amazon Mechanical Turk (AMT) following [1,35]. For each method, we show 55 real and 55 inpainted images in a random order to 20 users, who are asked to answer whether the image looks real or fake within 1s.

Obfuscation Performance. Obfuscation evaluation is to measure how well our methods can fool automatic person recognizers as well as humans. We have defined machine recognizers and human recognizers in Sect. 4.

For machine recognizers, we report the average recognition rates for 1,084 test images in Table 1. For human recognition, we randomly choose 45 instances then ask recognizers to verify the identity, given the original image as reference, from the obfuscated images of six representative methods: two methods in [1] and four methods indexed by **v9-v12**, see the last column of Table 1.

Comparison to the State-of-the-Art. In Table 1, we report quantitative evaluation results on different input modalities and in comparison to [1]. We also implement the exact same models of [1] on our cropped data for fair comparisons. We also compare the visual quality of our results with [1], see Fig. 5.

Our best obfuscation rate is achieved by **v12**. The most comparable method in [1] is *Blackhead+PDMDec*, where the input is an image with a fully blacked-out head and the landmarks are generated by *PDMDec*. Comparing **v12** with it, we achieve 2.6% lower recognition rate (2.6% higher for confusing machine recognizers) using **head** features. Our method does even better (15.3% higher) in fooling human recognizers. In addition, our method has clearly higher image quality in terms of HPS, 0.33 vs. 0.15 [1]. Figure 5 shows that our method generates more natural images in terms of consistent skin colors, proper head poses and vivid face expressions.

Parametric Model Versus GAN. For the ablation study of our hybrid model, we replace the parametric model in Stage-I with a GAN. We use the same architecture as the stage-II network of [1], but without the landmark channel. This is inspired by the regional completion method using GANs [44]. We consider two comparison scenarios: when the input face is blacked-out (indexed by **v13**), we compare with **v8**; when the head is blacked-out (indexed by **v14**), we compare with **v9**. We observe that **v13** results in a lower mask-SSIM score of 0.80 (**v8** has 0.85) with the same recognition rate of 64.4%. This means that the GAN generates lower-quality images without performing better obfuscation. **v14** has

Table 1. Quantitative results comparing with the state-of-the-art methods [1]. Image quality: Mask-SSIM and HPS scores (both the higher, the better). Obfuscation effectiveness: recognition rates of machine recognizers (lower is better) and confusion rates of human recognizers (higher is better). **v*** simply represents the method in that row.

Obfuscation method			Evaluation				
Stage-I	Stage-II		Image quality		Machine		Human
	Hair	Rendered face	Mask-SSIM	HPS	head	body+head	confusion
Original	-	-	1.00	0.93	85.6%	88.3%	
[1]	Blackhead+Detect		0.41	0.19	10.1%	21.4%	-
[1]	Blackhead	PDMDec.	0.20	0.11	5.6%	17.4%	-
[1], our crop	Blackhead+Detect		0.43	0.34	12.7%	24.0%	4.1%
[1], our crop	Blackhead+PDMDec.		0.23	0.15	9.7%	19.7%	20.1%
v1, Original	Overlay-No-Inpainting		0.75	0.58	66.9%	68.9%	
v2, Original	Original	Own	0.87	0.71	70.8%	71.5%	-
v3, Original	Original	Replacer15	-	0.49	47.6%	57.4%	-
v4, Blurred	Original	Own	0.86	0.59	59.9%	65.2%	-
v5, Blurred	Original	Replacer15	-	0.41	26.3%	41.7%	-
v6, Blurred	Blurred	Own	0.55	0.55	25.8%	38.0%	-
v7, Blurred	Blurred	Replacer15	-	0.40	12.7%	29.3%	-
v8, Blacked	Original	Own	0.85	0.60	59.3%	64.4%	-
v9, Blacked	Blacked	Own	0.47	0.41	14.2%	25.7%	2.9%
v10, Blacked	Blacked	Replacer1	-	0.45	11.8%	23.5%	6.2%
v11, Blacked	Blacked	Replacer8	-	0.39	9.3%	22.4%	31.3%
v12, Blacked	Blacked	Replacer15	-	0.33	**7.1%**	**18.1%**	**35.4%**

a lower recognition rate of 19.7% vs. **v9**'s 25.7%, but its mask-SSIM (image quality) is only 0.23, 0.24 lower than **v9**'s 0.47. If we make use of face replacement (only applicable when using our parametric model-based approach), we are able to achieve a lower recognition rate of 18.1%, sacrificing only 0.08 in terms of image quality (see HPS of **v9** and **v12** in Table 1).

Analysis of Different Face/Hair Modalities. Table 1 shows that different modalities of the input yield different levels of obfuscation and image quality. In general, the image quality is roughly correlated to the recognition rate. With higher level of modification to an image, the identity will be more effectively obfuscated, but the image quality will also deteriorate accordingly. However, we can observe that the recognition rate drops quicker than the image quality.

It is worth noting that when there is no inpainting on the rendered faces (**v1**), HPS score is 0.58, 0.13 lower than **v2**, verifying that rendered faces are less realistic than inpainted ones. Not surprisingly, the best image quality is achieved by **v2** which aims to reconstruct the original image without obfuscation. On top of that, when we use blurred faces in Stage-I (**v4**), the machine recognition rate (`head`) drops from 70.8% to 59.9%. This indicates that blurring the face region indeed partially conceals the identity information.

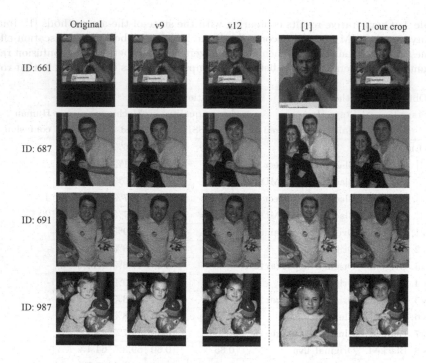

Fig. 5. Result images by methods **v9** and **v12**, compared to original images and the results of the *Blackhead* scenario using *PDMDec* landmarks in [1]. Note that the image scale difference with [1] is because of different cropping methods.

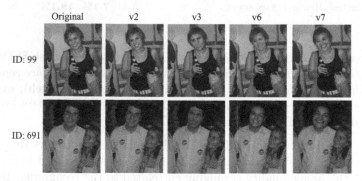

Fig. 6. Result images of methods **v2**, **v3**, **v6** and **v7**, compared to the original images.

When we blur the hair region (**v6**), the recognition rate sharply drops to 25.8%, which implies that the region around the face contains a large amount of identity information. When we remove all information from the face and hair regions (**v9**), we get an even lower recognition rate of 14.2%.

Face Replacement is of Great Effectiveness. We can see from Table 1 that replacing the face parameters with those of another identity is an effective way of hiding the identity information. Regardless of the face and hair input modalities, the obfuscation performances on both recognizers are significantly improved using `Replacer15` rendered faces than using `Own` rendered faces. Replacing faces from close to far identities also has an obvious impact on the obfuscation effectiveness. From **v10** to **v12** in Table 1, we can see using `Replacer8` yields clearly better obfuscation than the `Replacer1`, e.g., obfuscation for humans gets 25.1% improvement. This is further evidenced by the comparison between the `Replacer15` and `Replacer1`. Visually, Figs. 6 and 5 show that replacing the face parameters indeed makes the faces very different.

Trade-off Between Image Quality and Obfuscation. Figure 7 shows the machine recognition rate vs. image quality plots for different obfuscation methods (some are not in Table 1 but in supplementary materials). Points on the curves from left to right are the results of using *Blacked-out*, *Blurred* and *Original* hair inputs for stage-II.

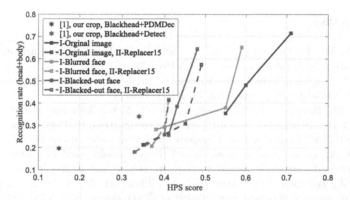

Fig. 7. Scatter curves of different obfuscation methods. HPS scores change along X-axis for different obfuscation levels (*Blacked-out, Blurred, Original*) on hair regions.

This figure allows users to select the method with the highest image quality given a specified obfuscation threshold. For example, if a user would like to take the risk of 30% recognizability at most, the highest image quality he/she can get is about 0.45, corresponding to the middle point on the blue dashed line (the method of *Original image, Blurred hair*, `Replacer15`). On the other hand, if a user requires the image quality to be at least 0.30, the best obfuscation possible corresponds to the first point of the red dashed line (the method of *Blacked-out face, Blacked-out hair*, `Replacer15`). The global coverage of these plots show the selection constrains, such as when a user strictly controls the privacy leaking rate under 20%, there are only two applicable methods: *Blackhead+PDMDec* [1] (image quality is only 0.15) and ours (*Blacked-out face, Blacked-out hair*, `Replacer15`) where the image quality is higher at 0.33.

6   Conclusion

We have introduced a new hybrid approach to obfuscate identities in photos by head replacement. Thanks to the combination of a parametric face model reconstruction and rendering, and the GAN-based data-driven image synthesis, our method gives us complete control over the facial parameters for explicit manipulation of the identity, and allows for photo-realistic image synthesis. The images synthesized by our method confuse not only the machine recognition systems but also humans. Our experimental results have demonstrated output of our system that improves over the previous state of the art in obfuscation rate while generating obfuscated images of much higher visual realism.

Acknowledgments. This research was supported in part by German Research Foundation (DFG CRC 1223) and the ERC Starting Grant CapReal (335545). We thank Dr. Florian Bernard for the helpful discussions.

References

1. Sun, Q., Ma, L., Oh, S.J., Gool, L.V., Schiele, B., Fritz, M.: Natural and effective obfuscation by head inpainting. In: CVPR (2018)
2. Oh, S.J., Fritz, M., Schiele, B.: Adversarial image perturbation for privacy protection - a game theory perspective. In: ICCV (2017)
3. Sharif, M., Bhagavatula, S., Bauer, L., Reiter, M.K.: Accessorize to a crime: Real and stealthy attacks on state-of-the-art face recognition. In: Proceedings of the 2016 ACM SIGSAC Conference on Computer and Communications Security (2016)
4. Tewari, A., et al.: MoFA: model-based deep convolutional face autoencoder for unsupervised monocular reconstruction. In: ICCV, vol. 2 (2017)
5. Thies, J., Zollhöfer, M., Stamminger, M., Theobalt, C., Nießner, M.: Face2Face: real-time face capture and reenactment of RGB videos. In: CVPR (2016)
6. Garrido, P., et al.: Reconstruction of personalized 3D face rigs from monocular video. ACM Trans. Graph. **35**(3), 28:1–28:15 (2016). (Presented at SIGGRAPH 2016)
7. Oh, S.J., Benenson, R., Fritz, M., Schiele, B.: Faceless person recognition: privacy implications in social media. In: Leibe, B., Matas, J., Sebe, N., Welling, M. (eds.) ECCV 2016. LNCS, vol. 9907, pp. 19–35. Springer, Cham (2016). https://doi.org/10.1007/978-3-319-46487-9_2
8. McPherson, R., Shokri, R., Shmatikov, V.: Defeating image obfuscation with deep learning. arXiv:1609.00408 (2016)
9. Brkic, K., Sikiric, I., Hrkac, T., Kalafatic, Z.: I know that person: generative full body and face de-identification of people in images. In: CVPR Workshops, pp. 1319–1328 (2017)
10. Blanz, V., Vetter, T.: A morphable model for the synthesis of 3D faces. In: SIGGRAPH. ACM Press/Addison-Wesley Publishing Co., pp. 187–194 (1999)
11. Booth, J., Roussos, A., Zafeiriou, S., Ponniah, A., Dunaway, D.: A 3D morphable model learnt from 10,000 faces. In: CVPR (2016)
12. Booth, J., Antonakos, E., Ploumpis, S., Trigeorgis, G., Panagakis, Y., Zafeiriou, S.: 3D face morphable model "in-the-wild". In: CVPR (2017)

13. Tewari, A., et al.: Self-supervised multi-level face model learning for monocular reconstruction at over 250 hz. In: CVPR (2018)
14. Roth, J., Tong, Y., Liu, X.: Adaptive 3D face reconstruction from unconstrained photo collections. IEEE Trans. Pattern Anal. Mach. Intell. **39**(11), 2127–2141 (2017)
15. Romdhani, S., Vetter, T.: Estimating 3D shape and texture using pixel intensity, edges, specular highlights, texture constraints and a prior. In: CVPR (2005)
16. Garrido, P., Valgaxerts, L., Wu, C., Theobalt, C.: Reconstructing detailed dynamic face geometry from monocular video. ACM Trans. Graph. **32**, 158:1–158:10 (2013). (Proceedings of SIGGRAPH Asia 2013)
17. Shi, F., Wu, H.T., Tong, X., Chai, J.: Automatic acquisition of high-fidelity facial performances using monocular videos. ACM Trans. Graph. (TOG) **33**(6), 222 (2014)
18. Richardson, E., Sela, M., Kimmel, R.: 3D face reconstruction by learning from synthetic data. In: 3DV (2016)
19. Sela, M., Richardson, E., Kimmel, R.: Unrestricted facial geometry reconstruction using image-to-image translation. In: ICCV (2017)
20. Tran, A.T., Hassner, T., Masi, I., Medioni, G.G.: Regressing robust and discriminative 3D morphable models with a very deep neural network. In: CVPR (2017)
21. Richardson, E., Sela, M., Or-El, R., Kimmel, R.: Learning detailed face reconstruction from a single image. In: CVPR (2017)
22. Dou, P., Shah, S.K., Kakadiaris, I.A.: End-to-end 3D face reconstruction with deep neural networks. In: CVPR (2017)
23. Kim, H., Zollöfer, M., Tewari, A., Thies, J., Richardt, C., Christian, T.: InverseFaceNet: Deep Single-Shot Inverse Face Rendering From A Single Image. arXiv:1703.10956 (2017)
24. Cao, C., Bradley, D., Zhou, K., Beeler, T.: Real-time high-fidelity facial performance capture. ACM Trans. Graph. **34**(4), 46:1–46:9 (2015)
25. Shrivastava, A., Pfister, T., Tuzel, O., Susskind, J., Wang, W., Webb, R.: Learning from simulated and unsupervised images through adversarial training. In: CVPR, pp. 2242–2251 (2017)
26. Mueller, F., et al.: Ganerated hands for real-time 3D hand tracking from monocular RGB. In: CVPR (2018)
27. Yeh, R., Chen, C., Lim, T., Hasegawa-Johnson, M., Do, M.N.: Semantic image inpainting with perceptual and contextual losses. arXiv:1607.07539 (2016)
28. Pathak, D., Krähenbühl, P., Donahue, J., Darrell, T., Efros, A.A.: Context encoders: feature learning by inpainting. In: CVPR (2016)
29. Alexander, O., Rogers, M., Lambeth, W., Chiang, M., Debevec, P.: The Digital Emily Project: photoreal facial modeling and animation. In: ACM SIGGRAPH Courses, pp. 12:1–12:15. ACM (2009)
30. Cao, C., Weng, Y., Zhou, S., Tong, Y., Zhou, K.: Facewarehouse: a 3D facial expression database for visual computing. IEEE Trans. Vis. Comput. Graph. **20**(3), 413–425 (2014)
31. Ramamoorthi, R., Hanrahan, P.: A signal-processing framework for inverse rendering. In: SIGGRAPH, pp. 117–128. ACM (2001)
32. Krizhevsky, A., Sutskever, I., Hinton, G.E.: ImageNet classification with deep convolutional neural networks. In: NIPS, pp. 1097–1105 (2012)
33. King, D.E.: Dlib-ml: a machine learning toolkit. J. Mach. Learn. Res. **10**, 1755–1758 (2009)

34. Ronneberger, O., Fischer, P., Brox, T.: U-Net: convolutional networks for biomedical image segmentation. In: Navab, N., Hornegger, J., Wells, W.M., Frangi, A.F. (eds.) MICCAI 2015. LNCS, vol. 9351, pp. 234–241. Springer, Cham (2015). https://doi.org/10.1007/978-3-319-24574-4_28

35. Ma, L., Jia, X., Sun, Q., Schiele, B., Tuytelaars, T., Gool, L.V.: Pose guided person image generation. In: NIPS, pp. 405–415 (2017)

36. Ma, L., Sun, Q., Georgoulis, S., Gool, L.V., Schiele, B., Fritz, M.: Disentangled person image generation. In: CVPR (2018)

37. Radford, A., Metz, L., Chintala, S.: Unsupervised representation learning with deep convolutional generative adversarial networks. In: ICLR (2016)

38. Mirjalili, V., Raschka, S., Namboodiri, A.M., Ross, A.: Semi-adversarial networks: convolutional autoencoders for imparting privacy to face images. In: 2018 International Conference on Biometrics, ICB 2018, Gold Coast, Australia, 20–23 February 2018, pp. 82–89 (2018)

39. Oh, S.J., Benenson, R., Fritz, M., Schiele, B.: Person recognition in personal photo collections. In: ICCV (2015)

40. Oh, S.J., Benenson, R., Fritz, M., Schiele, B.: Person recognition in social media photos. arXiv:1710.03224 (2017)

41. Zhang, N., Paluri, M., Taigman, Y., Fergus, R., Bourdev, L.D.: Beyond frontal faces: Improving person recognition using multiple cues. In: CVPR (2015)

42. Sun, Q., Schiele, B., Fritz, M.: A domain based approach to social relation recognition. In: CVPR (2017)

43. Wang, Z., Bovik, A.C., Sheikh, H.R., Simoncelli, E.P.: Image quality assessment: from error visibility to structural similarity. IEEE Trans. Image Process. **13**(4), 600–612 (2004)

44. Iizuka, S., Simo-Serra, E., Ishikawa, H.: Globally and locally consistent image completion. ACM Trans. Graph. **36**(4), 107:1–107:14 (2017)

The Sound of Pixels

Hang Zhao[1]([⊠]), Chuang Gan[1,2], Andrew Rouditchenko[1], Carl Vondrick[1,3],
Josh McDermott[1], and Antonio Torralba[1]

[1] Massachusetts Institute of Technology, Cambridge, USA
{hangzhao,roudi,jhm,torralba}@mit.edu
[2] MIT-IBM Watson AI Lab, Cambridge, USA
ganchuang1990@gmail.com
[3] Columbia University, New York City, USA
cvondrick@gmail.com

Abstract. We introduce PixelPlayer, a system that, by leveraging large
amounts of unlabeled videos, learns to locate image regions which produce sounds and separate the input sounds into a set of components that
represents the sound from each pixel. Our approach capitalizes on the
natural synchronization of the visual and audio modalities to learn models that jointly parse sounds and images, without requiring additional
manual supervision. Experimental results on a newly collected MUSIC
dataset show that our proposed Mix-and-Separate framework outperforms several baselines on source separation. Qualitative results suggest
our model learns to ground sounds in vision, enabling applications such
as independently adjusting the volume of sound sources.

Keywords: Cross-modal learning · Sound separation and localization

1 Introduction

The world generates a rich source of visual and auditory signals. Our visual
and auditory systems are able to recognize objects in the world, segment image
regions covered by the objects, and isolate sounds produced by objects. While
auditory scene analysis [5] is widely studied in the fields of environmental sound
recognition [18,26] and source separation [4,6,9,41,42,52], the natural synchronization between vision and sound can provide a rich supervisory signal for
grounding sounds in vision [17,21,28]. Training systems to recognize objects
from vision or sound typically requires large amounts of supervision. In this
paper, however, we leverage joint audio-visual learning to discover objects that
produce sound in the world without manual supervision [1,30,36].

We show that by working with both auditory and visual information, we can
learn in an unsupervised way to recognize objects from their visual appearance
or the sound they make, to localize objects in images, and to separate the audio
component coming from each object. We introduce a new system called PixelPlayer. Given an input video, PixelPlayer jointly separates the accompanying

© Springer Nature Switzerland AG 2018
V. Ferrari et al. (Eds.): ECCV 2018, LNCS 11205, pp. 587–604, 2018.
https://doi.org/10.1007/978-3-030-01246-5_35

audio into components and spatially localizes them in the video. PixelPlayer enables us to listen to the sound originating from each pixel in the video.

Figure 1 shows a working example of PixelPlayer (check the project website[1] for sample videos and interactive demos). In this example, the system has been trained with a large number of videos containing people playing instruments in different combinations, including solos and duets. No label is provided on what instruments are present in each video, where they are located, and how they sound. During test time, the input (Fig. 1a) is a video of several instruments played together containing the visual frames $I(x, y, t)$, and the mono audio $S(t)$. PixelPlayer performs audio-visual source separation and localization, splitting the input sound signal to estimate output sound components $S_{out}(x, y, t)$, each one corresponding to the sound coming from a spatial location (x, y) in the video frame. As an illustration, Fig. 1c shows the recovered audio signals for 11 example pixels. The flat blue lines correspond to pixels that are considered as silent by the system. The non-silent signals correspond to the sounds coming from each individual instrument. Figure 1d shows the estimated sound energy, or volume of the audio signal from each pixel. Note that the system correctly detects that the sounds are coming from the two instruments and not from the background. Figure 1e shows how pixels are clustered according to their component sound signals. The same color is assigned to pixels that generate very similar sounds.

The capability to incorporate sound into vision will have a large impact on a range of applications involving the recognition and manipulation of video. PixelPlayer's ability to separate and locate sounds sources will allow more isolated

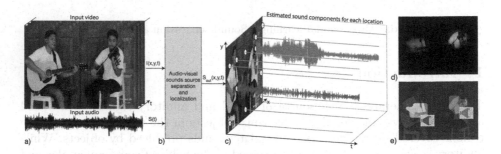

Fig. 1. PixelPlayer localizes sound sources in a video and separates the audio into its components without supervision. The figure shows: (a) The input video frames $I(x, y, t)$, and the video mono sound signal $S(t)$. (b) The system estimates the output sound signals $S_{out}(x, y, t)$ by separating the input sound. Each output component corresponds to the sound coming from a spatial location (x, y) in the video. (c) Component audio waveforms at 11 example locations; straight lines indicate silence. (d) The system's estimation of the sound energy (or volume) of each pixel. (e) Clustering of sound components in the pixel space. The same color is assigned to pixels with similar sounds. As an example application of clustering, PixelPlayer would enable the independent volume control of different sound sources in videos.

---

[1] http://sound-of-pixels.csail.mit.edu.

processing of the sound coming from each object and will aid auditory recognition. Our system could also facilitate sound editing in videos, enabling, for instance, volume adjustments for specific objects or removal of the audio from particular sources.

Concurrent to this work, there are papers [11,29] at the same conference that also show the power of combining vision and audio to decompose sounds into components. [11] shows how person appearance could help solving the cocktail party problem in speech domain. [29] demonstrates an audio-visual system that separates on-screen sound vs. background sounds not visible in the video.

This paper is presented as follows. In Sect. 2, we first review related work in both the vision and sound communities. In Sect. 3, we present our system that leverages cross-modal context as a supervisory signal. In Sect. 4, we describe a new dataset for visual-audio grounding. In Sect. 5, we present several experiments to analyze our model. Subjective evaluations are presented in Sect. 6.

2   Related Work

Our work relates mainly to the fields of sound source separation, visual-audio cross-modal learning, and self-supervised learning, which will be briefly discussed in this section.

Sound Source Separation. Sound source separation, also known as the "cocktail party problem" [14,25], is a classic problem in engineering and perception. Classical approaches include signal processing methods such as Non-negative Matrix Factorization (NMF) [8,40,42]. More recently, deep learning methods have gained popularity [7,45]. Sound source separation methods enable applications ranging from music/vocal separation [39], to speech separation and enhancement [12,16,27]. Our problem differs from classic sound source separation problems because we want to separate sounds into visually and spatially grounded components.

Learning Visual-Audio Correspondence. Recent work in computer vision has explored the relationship between vision and sound. One line of work has developed models for generating sound from silent videos [30,51]. The correspondence between vision and sound has also been leveraged for learning representations. For example, [31] used audio to supervise visual representations, [3,18] used vision to supervise audio representations, and [1] used sound and vision to jointly supervise each other. In work related to our paper, people studied how to localize sounds in vision according to motion [19] or semantic cues [2,37], however they do not separate multiple sounds from a mixed signal.

Self-Supervised Learning. Our work builds off efforts to learn perceptual models that are "self-supervised" by leveraging natural contextual signals in images [10,22,24,33,38], videos [13,20,32,43,44,46], and even radio signals [48]. These approaches utilize the power of supervised learning while not requiring manual annotations, instead deriving supervisory signals from the structure in natural data. Our model is similarly self-supervised, but uses self-supervision to learn to separate and ground sound in vision.

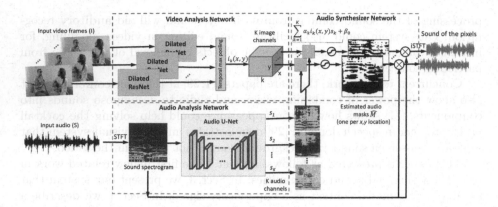

Fig. 2. Procedure to generate the sound of a pixel: pixel-level visual features are extracted by temporal max-pooling over the output of a dilated ResNet applied to T frames. The input audio spectrogram is passed through a U-Net whose output is K audio channels. The sound of each pixel is computed by an audio synthesizer network. The audio synthesizer network outputs a mask to be applied to the input spectrogram that will select the spectral components associated with the pixel. Finally, inverse STFT is applied to the spectrogram computed for each pixel to produce the final sound.

3   Audio-Visual Source Separation and Localization

In this section, we introduce the model architectures of PixelPlayer, and the proposed Mix-and-Separate training framework that learns to separate sound according to vision.

3.1   Model Architectures

Our model is composed of a video analysis network, an audio analysis network, and an audio synthesizer network, as shown in Fig. 2.

Video Analysis Network. The video analysis network extracts visual features from video frames. Its choice can be an arbitrary architecture used for visual classification tasks. Here we use a dilated variation of the ResNet-18 model [15] which will be described in detail in the experiment section. For an input video of size T×H×W×3, the ResNet model extracts per-frame features with size T×(H/16)×(W/16)×K. After `temporal pooling` and `sigmoid` activation, we obtain a visual feature $i_k(x, y)$ for each pixel with size K.

Audio Analysis Network. The audio analysis network takes the form of a U-Net [35] architecture, which splits the input sound into K components s_k, $k = (1, ..., K)$. We empirically found that working with audio spectrograms gives better performance than using raw waveforms, so the network described in this paper uses the Time-Frequency (T-F) representation of sound. First, a Short-Time Fourier Transform (STFT) is applied on the input mixture sound to obtain its spectrogram. Then the magnitude of spectrogram is transformed into log-frequency scale (analyzed in Sect. 5), and fed into the U-Net which yields K feature maps containing features of different components of the input sound.

Audio Synthesizer Network. The synthesizer network finally predicts the predicted sound by taking pixel-level visual feature $i_k(x, y)$ and audio feature s_k. The output sound spectrogram is generated by vision-based spectrogram masking technique. Specifically, a mask $M(x, y)$ that could separate the sound of the pixel from the input is estimated, and multiplied with the input spectrogram. Finally, to get the waveform of the prediction, we combine the predicted magnitude of spectrogram with the phase of input spectrogram, and use inverse STFT for recovery.

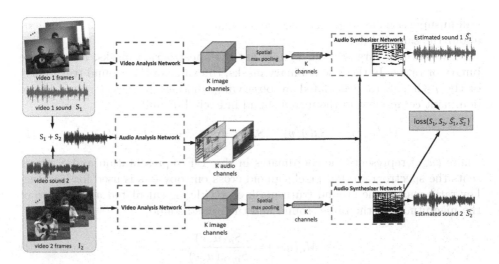

Fig. 3. Training pipeline of our proposed Mix-and-Separate framework in the case of mixing two videos ($N = 2$). The dashed boxes represent the modules detailed in Fig. 2. The audio signals from the two videos are added together to generate an input mixture with known constituent source signals. The network is trained to separate the audio source signals conditioned on corresponding video frames; its output is an estimate of both sound signals. Note that we do not assume that each video contains a single source of sound. Moreover, no annotations are provided. The system thus learns to separate individual sources without traditional supervision.

3.2   Mix-and-Separate Framework for Self-supervised Training

The idea of the Mix-and-Separate training procedure is to artificially create a complex auditory scene and then solve the auditory scene analysis problem of separating and grounding sounds. Leveraging the fact that audio signals are approximately additive, we mix sounds from different videos to generate a complex audio input signal. The learning objective of the model is to separate a sound source of interest conditioned on the visual input associated with it.

Concretely, to generate a complex audio input, we randomly sample N videos $\{I_n, S_n\}$ from the training dataset, where $n = (1, ..., N)$. I_n and S_n represent the visual frames and audio of the n-th video, respectively. The input sound mixture is created through linear combinations of the audio inputs as $S_{mix} = \sum_{n=1}^{N} S_n$. The model f learns to estimate the sounds in each video $\hat{S}_n$ given the audio mixture and the visual of the corresponding video $\hat{S}_n = f(S_{mix}, I_n)$.

Figure 3 shows the training framework in the case of $N = 2$. The training phase differs from the testing phase in that (1) we sample multiple videos randomly from the training set, mix the sample audios and target to recover each of them given their corresponding visual input; (2) video-level visual features are obtained by spatial-temporal max pooling instead of pixel-level features. Note that although we have clear targets to learn in the training process, it is still unsupervised as we do not use the data labels and do not make assumptions about the sampled data.

The learning target in our system are the spectrogram masks, they can be binary or ratios. In the case of binary masks, the value of the ground truth mask of the n-th video is calculated by observing whether the target sound is the dominant component in the mixed sound in each T-F unit,

$$M_n(u, v) = [\![S_n(u, v) \geq S_m(u, v)]\!], \quad \forall m = (1, ..., N), \tag{1}$$

where (u, v) represents the coordinates in the T-F representation and S represents the spectrogram. Per-pixel sigmoid cross entropy loss is used for learning. For ratio masks, the ground truth mask of a video is calculated as the ratio of the magnitudes of the target sound and the mixed sound,

$$M_n(u, v) = \frac{S_n(u, v)}{S_{mix}(u, v)}. \tag{2}$$

In this case, per-pixel $L1$ loss [47] is used for training. Note that the values of the ground truth mask do not necessarily stay within $[0, 1]$ because of interference.

4   MUSIC Dataset

The most commonly used videos with audio-visual correspondence are musical recordings, so we introduce a musical instrument video dataset for the proposed task, called MUSIC (Multimodal Sources of Instrument Combinations) dataset.

We retrieved the MUSIC videos from YouTube by keyword query. During the search, we added keywords such as "cover" to find more videos that were not post-processed or edited.

MUSIC dataset has 714 untrimmed videos of musical solos and duets, some sample videos are shown in Fig. 4. The dataset spans 11 instrument categories:

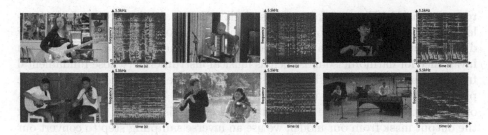

Fig. 4. Example frames and associated sounds from our video dataset. The top row shows videos of solos and the bottom row shows videos of duets. The sounds are displayed in the time-frequency domain as spectrograms, with frequency on a log scale.

Fig. 5. Dataset Statistics: (a) Shows the distribution of video categories. There are 565 videos of solos and 149 videos of duets. (b) Shows the distribution of video durations. The average duration is about 2 min.

accordion, acoustic guitar, cello, clarinet, erhu, flute, saxophone, trumpet, tuba, violin and xylophone. Figure 5 shows the dataset statistics.

Statistics reveal that due to the natural distribution of videos, duet performances are less balanced than the solo performances. For example, there are almost no videos of tuba and violin duets, while there are many videos of guitar and violin duets.

5 Experiments

5.1 Audio Data Processing

There are several steps we take before feeding the audio data into our model. To speed up computation, we sub-sampled the audio signals to 11 kHz, such that the highest signal frequency preserved is 5.5 kHz. This preserves the most perceptually important frequencies of instruments and only slightly degrades the overall audio quality. Each audio sample is approximately 6 s, randomly cropped from the untrimmed videos during training. An STFT with a window size of 1022 and a hop length of 256 is computed on the audio samples, resulting in a 512×256 Time-Frequency (T-F) representation of the sound. We further re-sample this signal on a log-frequency scale to obtain a 256×256 T-F representation. This step is similar to the common practice of using a Mel-Frequency scale, *e.g.* in speech recognition [23]. The log-frequency scale has the dual advantages of (1) similarity to the frequency decomposition of the human auditory system (frequency discrimination is better in absolute terms at low frequencies) and (2) translation invariance for harmonic sounds such as musical instruments (whose fundamental frequency and higher order harmonics translate on the log-frequency scale as the pitch changes), fitting well to a ConvNet framework. The log magnitude values of T-F units are used as the input to the audio analysis network. After obtaining the output mask from our model, we use an inverse sampling step to convert our mask back to linear frequency scale with size 512×256, which can be applied on the input spectrogram. We finally perform an inverse STFT to obtain the recovered signal.

5.2 Model Configurations

In all the experiments, we use a variant of the ResNet-18 model for the video analysis network, with the following modifications made: (1) removing the last `average pooling` layer and `fc` layer; (2) removing the stride of the last residual block, and making the convolution layers in this block to have a dilation of 2; (3) adding a last 3×3 convolution layer with K output channels. For each video sample, it takes T frames with size $224 \times 224 \times 3$ as input, and outputs a feature of size K after `spatiotemporal max pooling`.

The audio analysis network is modified from U-Net. It has 7 convolutions (or down-convolutions) and 7 de-convolutions (or up-convolution) with skip connections in between. It takes an audio spectrogram with size $256 \times 256 \times 1$, and outputs K feature maps of size $256 \times 256 \times K$.

The audio synthesizer takes the outputs from video and audio analysis networks, fuses them with a weighted summation, and outputs a mask that will be applied on the spectrogram. The audio synthesizer is a linear layer which has very few trainable parameters (K weights $+1$ bias). It could be designed to have more complex computations, but we choose the simple operation in this work to show interpretable intermediate representations, which will be shown in Sect. 5.6.

Our best model takes 3 frames as visual input, and uses the number of feature channels $K = 16$.

5.3 Implementation Details

Our goal in the model training is to learn on natural videos (with both solos and duets), evaluate quantitatively on the validation set, and finally solve the source separation and localization problem on the natural videos with mixtures. Therefore, we split our MUSIC dataset into 500 videos for training, 130 videos for validation, and 84 videos for testing. Among them, 500 training videos contain both solos and duets, the validation set only contains solos, and the test set only contains duets.

During training, we randomly sample $N = 2$ videos from our MUSIC dataset, which can be solos, duets, or silent background. Silent videos are made by pairing silent audio waveforms randomly with images from the ADE dataset [50] which contains images of natural environments. This technique regularizes the model better in localizing objects that sound by introducing more silent videos. To recap, the input audio mixture could contain 0 to 4 instruments. We also experimented with combining more sounds, but that made the task more challenging and the model did not learn better.

In the optimization process, we use a SGD optimizer with momentum 0.9. We set the learning rate of the audio analysis network and the audio synthesizer both as 0.001, and the learning rate of the video analysis network as 0.0001 since we adopt a pre-trained CNN model on ImageNet.

5.4   Sound Separation Performance

To evaluate the performance of our model, we also use the Mix-and-Separate process to make a validation set of synthetic mixture audios and the separation is evaluated.

Figure 6 shows qualitative results of our best model, which predicts binary masks that apply on the mixture spectrogram. The first row shows one frame per sampled videos that we mix together, the second row shows the spectrogram (in log frequency scale) of the audio mixture, which is the actual input to the audio analysis network. The third and fourth rows show ground truth masks and the predicted masks, which are the targets and output of our model. The fifth and sixth rows show the ground truth spectrogram and predicted spectrogram after applying masks on the input spectrogram. We could observe that even with the complex patterns in the mixed spectrogram, our model can "segment" the target instrument components out successfully.

Table 1. Model performances of baselines and different variations of our proposed model, evaluated in NSDR/SIR/SAR. Binary masking in log frequency scale performs best in most metrics.

	NMF [42]	DeepConvSep [7]	Spectral regression	Ratio mask		Binary mask	
				Linear scale	Log scale	Linear scale	Log scale
NSDR	3.14	6.12	5.12	6.67	8.56	6.94	**8.87**
SIR	6.70	8.38	7.72	12.85	13.75	12.87	**15.02**
SAR	10.10	11.02	10.43	13.87	**14.19**	11.12	12.28

To quantify the performance of the proposed model, we use the following metrics: the Normalized Signal-to-Distortion Ratio (NSDR), Signal-to-Interference Ratio (SIR), and Signal-to-Artifact Ratio (SAR) on the validation set of our synthetic videos. The NSDR is defined as the difference in SDR of the separated signals compared with the ground truth signals and the SDR of the mixture

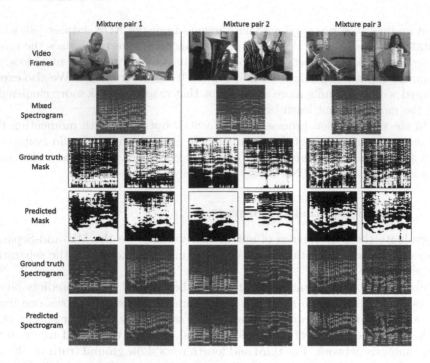

Fig. 6. Qualitative results on vision-guided source separation on synthetic audio mixtures. This experiment is performed only for quantitative model evaluation.

signals compared with the ground truth signals. This represents the improvement of using the separated signal compared with using the mixture as each separated source. The results reported in this paper were obtained by using the open-source `mir_eval` [34] library.

Results are shown in Table 1. Among all the models, baseline approaches NMF [42] and DeepConvSep [7] use audio and ground-truth labels to do source separation. All variants of our model use the same architecture we described, and take both visual and sound input for learning. Spectral Regression refers to the model that directly regresses output spectrogram values given an input mixture spectrogram, instead of outputting spectrogram mask values. From the numbers in the table, we can conclude that (1) masking based approaches are generally better than direct regression; (2) working in the log frequency scale performs better than in the linear frequency scale; (3) binary masking based method achieves similar performance as ratio masking.

Meanwhile, we found that the NSDR/SIR/SAR metrics are not the best metrics for evaluating perceptual separation quality, so in Sect. 6 we further conduct user studies on the audio separation quality.

5.5 Visual Grounding of Sounds

As the title of paper indicates, we are fundamentally solving two problems: localization and separation of sounds.

Sound Localization. The first problem is related to the spatial grounding question, "which pixels are making sounds?" This is answered in Fig. 7: for natural videos in the dataset, we calculate the sound energy (or volume) of each pixel in the image, and plot their distributions in heatmaps. As can be seen, the model accurately localizes the sounding instruments.

Fig. 7. "Which pixels are making sounds?" Energy distribution of sound in pixel space. Overlaid heatmaps show the volumes from each pixel.

Clustering of Sounds. The second problem is related to a further question: "what sounds do these pixels make?" In order to answer this, we visualize the sound each pixel makes in images in the following way: for each pixel in a video frame, we take the feature of its sound, namely the vectorized log spectrogram magnitudes, and project them onto 3D RGB space using PCA for visualization purposes. Results are shown in Fig. 8, different instruments and the background in the same video frame have different color embeddings, indicating different sounds that they make.

Fig. 8. "What sounds do these pixels make?" Clustering of sound in space. Overlaid colormap shows different audio features with different colors. (Color figure online)

Discriminative Channel Activations. Given our model could separate sounds of different instruments, we explore its channel activations for different categories. For validation samples of each category, we find the strongest activated channel, and then sort them to generate a confusion matrix. Figure 9 shows the (a) visual and (b) audio confusion matrices from our best model. If we simply evaluate classification by assigning one category to one channel, the accuracy is 46.2% for vision and 68.9% for audio. Note that no learning is involved here, we expect much higher performance by using a linear classifier. This experiment demonstrates that the model has implicitly learned to discriminate instruments visually and auditorily.

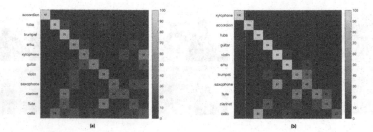

Fig. 9. (a) Visual and (b) audio confusion matrices by sorting channel activations with respect to ground truth category labels.

In a similar fashion, we evaluate object localization performance of the video analysis network based on the channel activations. To generate a bounding box from the channel activation map, we follow [49] to threshold the map. We first segment the regions of which the value is above 20% of the max value of the activation map, and then take the bounding box that covers the largest connected component in the segmentation map. Localization accuracy under different intersection over union (IoU) criterion are shown in Table 2.

Table 2. Object localization performance of the learned video analysis network.

IoU threshold	0.3	0.4	0.5
Accuracy(%)	66.10	47.92	32.43

5.6   Visual-Audio Corresponding Activations

As our proposed model is a form of self-supervised learning and is designed such that both visual and audio networks learn to activate simultaneously on the same channel, we further explore the representations learned by the model. Specifically, we look at the K channel activations of the video analysis network before `max pooling`, and their corresponding channel activations of the audio analysis network. The model has learned to detect important features of specific objects across the individual channels. In Fig. 10 we show the top activated videos of channel 6, 11 and 14. These channels have emerged as violin, guitar and xylophone detectors respectively, in both visual and audio domains. Channel 6 responds strongly to the visual appearance of violin and to the higher order harmonics in violin sounds. Channel 11 responds to guitars and the low frequency region in sounds. And channel 14 responds to the visual appearance of xylophone and to the brief, pulse-like patterns in the spectrogram domain. For other channels, some of them also detect specific instruments while others just detect specific features of instruments.

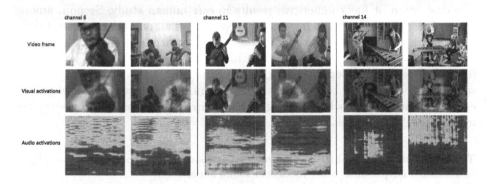

Fig. 10. Visualizations of corresponding channel activations. Channel 6 has emerged as a violin detector, responding strongly to the presence of violins in the video frames and to the high order harmonics in the spectrogram, which are colored brighter in the spectrogram of the figure. Likewise, channel 11 and 14 seems to detect the visual and auditory characteristics of guitars and xylophones.

6   Subjective Evaluations

The objective and quantitative evaluations in Sect. 5.4 are mainly performed on the synthetic mixture videos, the performance on the natural videos needs to be further investigated. On the other hand, the popular NSDR/SIR/SAR metrics used are not closely related to perceptual quality. Therefore we conducted crowd-sourced subjective evaluations as a complementary evaluation. Two studies are conducted on Amazon Mechanical Turk (AMT) by human raters, a sound separation quality evaluation and a visual-audio correspondence evaluation.

6.1   Sound Separation Quality

For the sound separation evaluation, we used a subset of the solos from the dataset as ground truth. We prepared the outputs of the baseline NMF model and the outputs of our models, including spectral regression, ratio masking and binary masking, all in log frequency scale. For each model, we take 256 audio outputs from the same set for evaluation and each audio is evaluated by 3 independent AMT workers. Audio samples are randomly presented to the workers, and the following question is asked: "Which sound do you hear? 1. A, 2. B, 3. Both, or 4. None of them". Here A and B are replaced by their mixture sources, e.g. A=clarinet, B=flute.

Subjective evaluation results are shown in Table 3. We show the percentages of workers who heard only the correct solo instrument (Correct), who heard only the incorrect solo instrument (Wrong), who heard both of the instruments (Both), and who heard neither of the instruments (None). First, we observe that although the NMF baseline did not have good NSDR numbers in the quantitative evaluation, it has competitive results in our human study. Second, among our models, the binary masking model outperforms all other models by a margin, showing its advantage in separation as a classification model. The binary masking model gives the highest correct rate, lowest error rate, and lowest confusion (percentage of Both), indicating that the binary model performs source separation perceptively better than the other models. It is worth noticing that even the ground truth solos do not give 100% correct rate, which represents the upper bound of performance.

Table 3. Subjective evaluation of sound separation performance. Binary masking-based model outperforms other models in sound separation.

Model	Correct(%)	Wrong(%)	Both(%)	None(%)
NMF	45.70	15.23	21.35	17.71
Spectral regression	18.23	15.36	64.45	1.95
Ratio mask	39.19	19.53	27.73	13.54
Binary mask	**59.11**	11.59	18.10	11.20
Ground truth solo	70.31	16.02	7.68	5.99

6.2 Visual-Sound Correspondence Evaluations

The second study focuses on the evaluation of the visual-sound correspondence problem. For a pixel-sound pair, we ask the binary question: "Is the sound coming from this pixel?" For this task, we only evaluate our models for comparison as the task requires visual input, so audio-only baselines are not applicable. We select 256 pixel positions (50% on instruments and 50% on background objects) to generate corresponding sounds with different models, and get the percentage of Yes responses from the workers, which tells the percentage of pixels with good source separation and localization, results are shown in Table 4. This evaluation also demonstrates that the binary masking-based model gives the best performance in the vision-related source separation problem.

Table 4. Subjective evaluation of visual-sound correspondence. Binary masking-based model best relates vision and sound.

Model	Yes(%)
Spectral regression	39.06
Ratio mask	54.68
Binary mask	67.58

7   Conclusions

In this paper, we introduced PixelPlayer, a system that learns from unlabeled videos to separate input sounds and also locate them in the visual input. Quantitative results, qualitative results, and subjective user studies demonstrate the effectiveness of our cross-modal learning system. We expect our work can open up new research avenues for understanding the problem of sound source separation using both visual and auditory signals.

Acknowledgement. This work was supported by NSF grant IIS-1524817. We thank Adria Recasens, Yu Zhang and Xue Feng for insightful discussions.

References

1. Arandjelovic, R., Zisserman, A.: Look, listen and learn. In: 2017 IEEE International Conference on Computer Vision (ICCV), pp. 609–617. IEEE (2017)
2. Arandjelović, R., Zisserman, A.: Objects that sound (2017). arXiv preprint arXiv:1712.06651
3. Aytar, Y., Vondrick, C., Torralba, A.: Soundnet: learning sound representations from unlabeled video. In: Advances in Neural Information Processing Systems, pp. 892–900 (2016)
4. Belouchrani, A., Abed-Meraim, K., Cardoso, J.F., Moulines, E.: A blind source separation technique using second-order statistics. IEEE Trans. Sig. Process. **45**(2), 434–444 (1997)
5. Bregman, A.S.: Auditory Scene Analysis: The Perceptual Organization of Sound. MIT Press, Cambridge (1994)
6. Cardoso, J.F.: Infomax and maximum likelihood for blind source separation. IEEE Sig. Process. Lett. **4**(4), 112–114 (1997)
7. Chandna, P., Miron, M., Janer, J., Gómez, E.: Monoaural audio source separation using deep convolutional neural networks. In: Tichavský, P., Babaie-Zadeh, M., Michel, O.J.J., Thirion-Moreau, N. (eds.) LVA/ICA 2017. LNCS, vol. 10169, pp. 258–266. Springer, Cham (2017). https://doi.org/10.1007/978-3-319-53547-0_25
8. Cichocki, A., Zdunek, R., Phan, A.H., Amari, S.I.: Nonnegative Matrix and Tensor Factorizations: Applications to Exploratory Multi-Way Data Analysis and Blind Source Separation. Wiley, Chichester (2009)
9. Comon, P., Jutten, C.: Handbook of Blind Source Separation: Independent Component Analysis and Applications. Academic Press, San Diego (2010)

10. Doersch, C., Gupta, A., Efros, A.A.: Unsupervised visual representation learning by context prediction. In: Proceedings of the IEEE International Conference on Computer Vision, pp. 1422–1430 (2015)
11. Ephrat, A., et al.: Looking to listen at the cocktail party: a speaker-independent audio-visual model for speech separation (2018). arXiv preprint arXiv:1804.03619
12. Gabbay, A., Ephrat, A., Halperin, T., Peleg, S.: Seeing through noise: speaker separation and enhancement using visually-derived speech (2017). arXiv preprint arXiv:1708.06767
13. Gan, C., Gong, B., Liu, K., Su, H., Guibas, L.J.: Geometry-guided CNN for self-supervised video representation learning (2018)
14. Haykin, S., Chen, Z.: The cocktail party problem. Neural Comput. **17**(9), 1875–1902 (2005)
15. He, K., Zhang, X., Ren, S., Sun, J.: Deep residual learning for image recognition. In: Proceedings of the IEEE Conference on Computer Vision and Pattern Recognition, pp. 770–778 (2016)
16. Hershey, J.R., Chen, Z., Le Roux, J., Watanabe, S.: Deep clustering: discriminative embeddings for segmentation and separation. In: 2016 IEEE International Conference on Acoustics, Speech and Signal Processing (ICASSP), pp. 31–35. IEEE (2016)
17. Hershey, J.R., Movellan, J.R.: Audio vision: using audio-visual synchrony to locate sounds. In: Solla, S.A., Leen, T.K., Müller, K. (eds.) Advances in Neural Information Processing Systems, vol. 12, pp. 813–819. MIT Press (2000). http://papers.nips.cc/paper/1686-audio-vision-using-audio-visual-synchrony-to-locate-sounds.pdf
18. Hershey, S., Chaudhuri, S., Ellis, D.P., Gemmeke, J.F., Jansen, A., Moore, R.C., Plakal, M., Platt, D., Saurous, R.A., Seybold, B., et al.: Cnn architectures for large-scale audio classification. In: 2017 IEEE International Conference on Acoustics, Speech and Signal Processing (ICASSP), pp. 131–135. IEEE (2017)
19. Izadinia, H., Saleemi, I., Shah, M.: Multimodal analysis for identification and segmentation of moving-sounding objects. IEEE Trans. Multimed. **15**(2), 378–390 (2013)
20. Jayaraman, D., Grauman, K.: Learning image representations tied to ego-motion. In: Proceedings of the IEEE International Conference on Computer Vision, pp. 1413–1421 (2015)
21. Kidron, E., Schechner, Y.Y., Elad, M.: Pixels that sound. In: Proceedings of the 2005 IEEE Computer Society Conference on Computer Vision and Pattern Recognition (CVPR 2005), vol. 1, pp. 88–95. IEEE Computer Society, Washington (2005). https://doi.org/10.1109/CVPR.2005.274
22. Larsson, G., Maire, M., Shakhnarovich, G.: Colorization as a proxy task for visual understanding. In: CVPR, vol. 2, p. 8 (2017)
23. Logan, B.: Mel frequency cepstral coefficients for music modeling. Int. Soc. Music Inf. Retrieval **270**, 1–11 (2000)
24. Ma, W.C., Chu, H., Zhou, B., Urtasun, R., Torralba, A.: Single image intrinsic decomposition without a single intrinsic image. In: Ferrari, V., et al. (eds.) ECCV 2018, Part XIV. LNCS, vol. 11205, pp. 211–229. Springer, Cham (2018)
25. McDermott, J.H.: The cocktail party problem. Curr. Biol. **19**(22), R1024–R1027 (2009)
26. Mesaros, A., Heittola, T., Diment, A., Elizalde, B., Ankit Shah, E.A.: Dcase 2017 challenge setup: tasks, datasets and baseline system. In: DCASE 2017 - Workshop on Detection and Classification of Acoustic Scenes and Events (2017)

27. Nagrani, A., Albanie, S., Zisserman, A.: Seeing voices and hearing faces: cross-modal biometric matching (2018). arXiv preprint arXiv:1804.00326
28. Ngiam, J., Khosla, A., Kim, M., Nam, J., Lee, H., Ng, A.Y.: Multimodal deep learning. In: Proceedings of the 28th International Conference on International Conference on Machine Learning, ICML 2011, pp. 689–696 (2011)
29. Owens, A., Efros, A.A.: Audio-visual scene analysis with self-supervised multisensory features (2018). arXiv preprint arXiv:1804.03641
30. Owens, A., Isola, P., McDermott, J., Torralba, A., Adelson, E.H., Freeman, W.T.: Visually indicated sounds. In: Proceedings of the IEEE Conference on Computer Vision and Pattern Recognition, pp. 2405–2413 (2016)
31. Owens, A., Wu, J., McDermott, J.H., Freeman, W.T., Torralba, A.: Ambient sound provides supervision for visual learning. In: Leibe, B., Matas, J., Sebe, N., Welling, M. (eds.) ECCV 2016. LNCS, vol. 9905, pp. 801–816. Springer, Cham (2016). https://doi.org/10.1007/978-3-319-46448-0_48
32. Pathak, D., Girshick, R., Dollár, P., Darrell, T., Hariharan, B.: Learning features by watching objects move. In: Proceedings of CVPR, vol. 2 (2017)
33. Pathak, D., Krahenbuhl, P., Donahue, J., Darrell, T., Efros, A.A.: Context encoders: feature learning by inpainting. In: Proceedings of the IEEE Conference on Computer Vision and Pattern Recognition, pp. 2536–2544 (2016)
34. Raffel, C., et al.: mir_eval: a transparent implementation of common mir metrics. In: Proceedings of the 15th International Society for Music Information Retrieval Conference, ISMIR. Citeseer (2014)
35. Ronneberger, O., Fischer, P., Brox, T.: U-Net: convolutional networks for biomedical image segmentation. In: Navab, N., Hornegger, J., Wells, W.M., Frangi, A.F. (eds.) MICCAI 2015. LNCS, vol. 9351, pp. 234–241. Springer, Cham (2015). https://doi.org/10.1007/978-3-319-24574-4_28
36. de Sa, V.R.: Learning classification with unlabeled data. In: Advances in Neural Information Processing Systems, pp. 112–119 (1993)
37. Senocak, A., Oh, T.H., Kim, J., Yang, M.H., Kweon, I.S.: Learning to localize sound source in visual scenes (2018). arXiv preprint arXiv:1803.03849
38. Shu, Z., Yumer, E., Hadap, S., Sunkavalli, K., Shechtman, E., Samaras, D.: Neural face editing with intrinsic image disentangling (2017). arXiv preprint arXiv:1704.04131
39. Simpson, A.J.R., Roma, G., Plumbley, M.D.: Deep karaoke: extracting vocals from musical mixtures using a convolutional deep neural network. In: Vincent, E., Yeredor, A., Koldovský, Z., Tichavský, P. (eds.) LVA/ICA 2015. LNCS, vol. 9237, pp. 429–436. Springer, Cham (2015). https://doi.org/10.1007/978-3-319-22482-4_50
40. Smaragdis, P., Brown, J.C.: Non-negative matrix factorization for polyphonic music transcription. In: 2003 IEEE Workshop on Applications of Signal Processing to Audio and Acoustics, pp. 177–180. IEEE (2003)
41. Vincent, E., Gribonval, R., Févotte, C.: Performance measurement in blind audio source separation. IEEE Trans. Audio Speech Lang. Process. **14**(4), 1462–1469 (2006)
42. Virtanen, T.: Monaural sound source separation by nonnegative matrix factorization with temporal continuity and sparseness criteria. IEEE Trans. Audio Speech Lang. Process. **15**(3), 1066–1074 (2007)
43. Vondrick, C., Pirsiavash, H., Torralba, A.: Generating videos with scene dynamics. In: Advances in Neural Information Processing Systems, pp. 613–621 (2016)
44. Vondrick, C., Shrivastava, A., Fathi, A., Guadarrama, S., Murphy, K.: Tracking emerges by colorizing videos (2018). arXiv preprint arXiv:1806.09594

45. Wang, D., Chen, J.: Supervised speech separation based on deep learning: an overview (2017). arXiv preprint arXiv:1708.07524
46. Wang, X., Gupta, A.: Unsupervised learning of visual representations using videos. In: ICCV, pp. 2794–2802 (2015)
47. Zhao, H., Gallo, O., Frosio, I., Kautz, J.: Loss functions for image restoration with neural networks. IEEE Trans. Comput. Imaging **3**(1), 47–57 (2017)
48. Zhao, M., et al.: Through-wall human pose estimation using radio signals. In: Proceedings of the IEEE Conference on Computer Vision and Pattern Recognition, pp. 7356–7365 (2018)
49. Zhou, B., Khosla, A., Lapedriza, A., Oliva, A., Torralba, A.: Learning deep features for discriminative localization. In: Proceedings of the IEEE Conference on Computer Vision and Pattern Recognition, pp. 2921–2929 (2016)
50. Zhou, B., Zhao, H., Puig, X., Fidler, S., Barriuso, A., Torralba, A.: Scene parsing through ADE20K dataset. In: Proceedings of CVPR (2017)
51. Zhou, Y., Wang, Z., Fang, C., Bui, T., Berg, T.L.: Visual to sound: Generating natural sound for videos in the wild (2017). arXiv preprint arXiv:1712.01393
52. Zibulevsky, M., Pearlmutter, B.A.: Blind source separation by sparse decomposition in a signal dictionary. Neural Comput. **13**(4), 863–882 (2001)

Adaptive Affinity Fields for Semantic Segmentation

Tsung-Wei Ke(✉)🆔, Jyh-Jing Hwang(✉)🆔, Ziwei Liu(✉)🆔,
and Stella X. Yu(✉)🆔

UC Berkeley/ICSI, Berkeley, USA
{twke,jyh,zwliu,stellayu}@berkeley.edu

Abstract. Semantic segmentation has made much progress with increasingly powerful pixel-wise classifiers and incorporating structural priors via Conditional Random Fields (CRF) or Generative Adversarial Networks (GAN). We propose a simpler alternative that learns to verify the spatial structure of segmentation *during training only*. Unlike existing approaches that enforce semantic labels on individual pixels and match labels between neighbouring pixels, we propose the concept of *Adaptive Affinity Fields* (AAF) to capture and *match the semantic relations* between neighbouring pixels in the label space. We use *adversarial learning* to select the optimal affinity field size for each semantic category. It is formulated as a *minimax* problem, optimizing our segmentation neural network in a best worst-case learning scenario. AAF is versatile for representing structures as a collection of pixel-centric relations, easier to train than GAN and more efficient than CRF without run-time inference. Our extensive evaluations on PASCAL VOC 2012, Cityscapes, and GTA5 datasets demonstrate its above-par segmentation performance and robust generalization across domains.

Keywords: Semantic segmentation · Affinity field Adversarial learning

1 Introduction

Semantic segmentation of an image refers to the challenging task of assigning each pixel a categorical label, e.g., *motorcycle* or *person*. Segmentation performance is often measured in a pixel-wise fashion, in terms of mean Intersection over Union (mIoU) across categories between the ground-truth (Fig. 1b) and the predicted label map (Fig. 1c).

Much progress has been made on segmentation with convolutional neural nets (CNN), mostly due to increasingly powerful pixel-wise classifiers, *e.g.*, VGG-16 [21,32] and ResNet [14,33], with the convolutional filters optimized by minimizing the average pixel-wise classification error over the image.

T.-W Ke and J.-J Hwang—Equal contributors. Jyh-Jing is a visiting student from the University of Pennsylvania.

© Springer Nature Switzerland AG 2018
V. Ferrari et al. (Eds.): ECCV 2018, LNCS 11205, pp. 605–621, 2018.
https://doi.org/10.1007/978-3-030-01246-5_36

| (a) Image | (b) Ground Truth | (c) Softmax | (d) Affinity | (e) AAF |

Fig. 1. We propose new pairwise pixel loss functions that capture the spatial structure of segmentation. Given an image (**a**), the task is to predict the ground-truth labeling (**b**). When a deep neural net is trained with conventional softmax cross-entropy loss on individual pixels, the predicted segmentation (**c**) is often based on visual appearance and oblivious of the spatial structure of each semantic class. Our work imposes an additional pairwise pixel label affinity loss (**d**), matching the label relations among neighbouring pixels between the prediction and the ground-truth. We also learn the neighbourhood size for each semantic class, and our adaptive affinity fields result (**e**) picks out both large bicycle shields and thin spokes of round wheels.

Even with big training data and with deeper and more complex network architectures, pixel-wise classification based approaches fundamentally lack the spatial discrimination power when foreground pixels and background pixels are close or mixed together: Segmentation is poor when the visual evidence for the foreground is weak, *e.g.*,glass motorcycle shields, or when the spatial structure is small, *e.g.*,thin radial spokes of all the wheels (Fig. 1c).

There have been two main lines of efforts at incorporating structural reasoning into semantic segmentation: Conditional Random Field (CRF) methods [15,37] and Generative Adversarial Network (GAN) methods [12,22].

1. CRF enforces label consistency between pixels measured by the similarity in visual appearance (*e.g.*,raw pixel value). An optimal labeling is solved via message passing algorithms [8,20]. CRF is employed either as a post-processing step [6,15], or as a plug-in module inside deep neural networks [19, 37]. Aside from its time-consuming iterative inference routine, CRF is also sensitive to visual appearance changes.
2. GAN is a recent alternative for imposing structural regularity in the neural network output. Specifically, the predicted label map is tested by a discriminator network on whether it resembles ground truth label maps in the training set. GAN is notoriously hard to train, particularly prone to model instability and mode collapses [27].

We propose a simpler approach, by learning to verify the spatial structure of segmentation *during training only*. Instead of enforcing semantic labels on individual pixels and matching labels between neighbouring pixels using CRF or GAN, we propose the concept of *Adaptive Affinity Fields (AAF)* to capture and match the relations between neighbouring pixels in the label space. How the semantic label of each pixel is related to those of neighboring pixels, *e.g.*,whether they are *same or different*, provides a distributed and pixel-centric description of semantic relations in the space and collectively they describe *Motorcycle wheels are round with thin radial spokes*. We develop new affinity field matching loss functions to learn a CNN that automatically outputs a segmentation respectful of spatial structures and small details.

The pairwise pixel affinity idea has deep roots in perceptual organization, where local affinity fields have been used to characterize the intrinsic geometric structures in early vision [26], the grouping cues between pixels for image segmentation via spectral graph partitioning [31], and the object hypothesis for non-additive score verification in object recognition at the run time [1].

Technically, affinity fields at different neighbourhood sizes encode structural relations at different ranges. Matching the affinity fields at a fixed size would not work well for all semantic categories, e.g.,thin structures are needed for *persons* seen at a distance whereas large structures are for *cows* seen close-up.

One straightforward solution is to search over a list of possible affinity field sizes, and pick the one that yields the minimal affinity matching loss. However, such a practice would result in selecting trivial sizes which are readily satisfied. For example, for large uniform semantic regions, the optimal affinity field size would be the smallest neighbourhood size of 1, and any pixel-wise classification would already get them right without any additional loss terms in the label space.

We propose *adversarial learning* for size-adapted affinity field matching. Intuitively, we select the right size by pushing the affinity field matching with different sizes to the extreme: Minimizing the affinity loss should be hard enough to have a real impact on learning, yet it should still be easy enough for the network to actually improve segmentation towards the ground-truth, *i.e.,*a best worst-case learning scenario. Specifically, we formulate our AAF as a *minimax* problem where we simultaneously *maximize* the affinity errors over multiple kernel sizes and *minimize* the overall matching loss. Consequently, our adversarial network learns to assign a smaller affinity field size to *person* than to *cow*, as the person category contains finer structures than the cow category.

Our AAF has a few appealing properties over existing approaches (Table 1).

Table 1. Key differences between our method and other popular structure modeling approaches, namely CRF [15] and GAN [12]. The performance (% mIoU) is reported with PSPNet [36] architecture on the Cityscapes [10] validation set.

Method	Structure guidance	Training	Run-time inference	Performance
CRF [15]	Input image	Medium	Yes	76.53
GAN [12]	Ground-truth labels	Hard	no	76.20
Our AAF	Label affinity	Easy	no	**79.24**

1. It provides a **versatile representation** that encodes spatial structural information in distributed, pixel-centric relations.
2. It is **easier to train** than GAN and **more efficient** than CRF, as AAF only impacts network learning during training, requiring no extra parameters or inference processes during testing.

3. It is **more generalizable to visual domain changes**, as AAF operates on the label relations not on the pixel values, capturing desired intrinsic geometric regularities despite of visual appearance variations.

We demonstrate its effectiveness and efficiency with extensive evaluations on Cityscapes [10] and PASCAL VOC 2012 [11] datasets, along with its remarkable generalization performance when our learned networks are applied to the GTA5 dataset [28].

2   Related Works

Most methods treat semantic segmentation as a pixel-wise classification task, and those that model structural correlations provide a small gain at a large computational cost.

Semantic Segmentation. Since the introduction of fully convolutional networks for semantic segmentation [21], deeper [16,33,36] and wider [25,29,34] network architectures have been explored, drastically improving the performance on benchmarks such as PASCAL VOC [11]. For example, Wu et al.[33] achieved higher segmentation accuracy by replacing backbone networks with more powerful ResNet [14], whereas Yu et al.[34] tackled fine-detailed segmentation using atrous convolutions. While the performance gain in terms of mIoU is impressive, these pixel-wise classification based approaches fundamentally lack the spatial discrimination power when foreground and background pixels are close or mixed together, resulting in unnatural artifacts in Fig. 1c.

Structure Modeling. Image segmentation has highly correlated outputs among the pixels. Formulating it as an independent pixel labeling problem not only makes the pixel-level classification unnecessarily hard, but also leads to artifacts and spatially incoherent results. Several ways to incorporate structure information into segmentation have been investigated [4,8,15,17,19,24,37]. For example, Chen et al.[6] utilized denseCRF [15] as post-processing to refine the final segmentation results. Zheng et al.[37] and Liu et al.[19] further made the CRF module differentiable within the deep neural network. Pairwise low-level image cues, such as grouping affinity [18,23] and contour cues [3,5], have also been used to encode structures. However, these methods are sensitive to visual appearance changes, or require expensive iterative inference procedures.

Our work provides another perspective to structure modeling by matching the relations between neighbouring pixels in the label space. Our segmentation network learns to verify the spatial structure of segmentation only during training; once it is trained, it is ready for deployment without run-time inference.

3   Our Approach: Adaptive Affinity Fields

We first briefly revisit the classic pixel-wise cross-entropy loss commonly used in semantic segmentation. The drawbacks of pixel-wise supervision lead to our concept of region-wise supervision. We then describe our region-wise supervision through affinity fields, and introduce an adversarial process that learns an adaptive affinity kernel size for each category. We summarize the overall AAF architecture in Fig. 2.

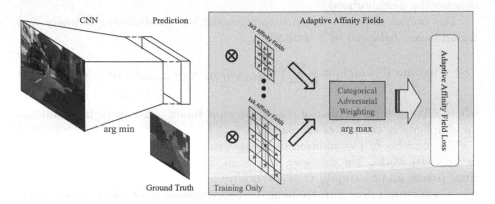

Fig. 2. Method overview: Learning semantic segmentation with adaptive affinity fields. The adaptive affinity fields consist of two parts: the affinity field loss with multiple kernel sizes and corresponding categorical adversarial weightings. Note that the adaptive affinity fields are only introduced during training and there is no extra computation during inference.

3.1   From Pixel-Wise Supervision to Region-Wise Supervision

Pixel-wise cross-entropy loss is most often used in CNNs for semantic segmentation [6,21]. It penalizes pixel-wise predictions independently and is known as a form of *unary supervision*. It implicitly assumes that the relationships between pixels can be learned as the effective receptive field increases with deeper layers. Given predicted categorical probability $\hat{y}_i(l)$ at pixel i w.r.t.its ground truth categorical label l, the total loss is the average of cross-entropy loss at pixel i:

$$\mathcal{L}^i_{\text{unary}} = \mathcal{L}^i_{\text{cross-entropy}} = -\log \hat{y}_i(l). \tag{1}$$

Such a unary loss does not take the semantic label correlation and scene structure into account. The objects in different categories interact with each other in a certain pattern. For example, cars are usually on the road while pedestrians on the sidewalk; buildings are surrounded by the sky but never on top of it. Also, some shapes of a certain category occur more frequently, such as rectangles in trains, circles in bikes, and straight vertical lines in poles. This kind of inter-class and inner-class pixel relationships are informative and can be integrated into learning as structure reasoning. We are thus inspired to propose an additional region-wise loss to impose penalties on inconsistent unary predictions and encourage the network to learn such intrinsic pixel relationships.

Region-wise supervision extends its pixel-wise counterpart from independent pixels to neighborhoods of pixels, *i.e.,*, the region-wise loss considers a patch of predictions and ground truth jointly. Such region-wise supervision $\mathcal{L}_{\text{region}}$ involves designing a specific loss function for a patch of predictions $\mathcal{N}(\hat{y}_i)$ and corresponding patch of ground truth $\mathcal{N}(y_i)$ centered at pixel i, where $\mathcal{N}(\cdot)$ denotes the neighborhood.

The overall objective is hence to minimize the combination of unary and region losses, balanced by a constant λ:

$$S^* = \operatorname*{argmin}_{S} \mathcal{L} = \operatorname*{argmin}_{S} \frac{1}{n} \sum_i \Big(\mathcal{L}_{\text{unary}}^i(\hat{y}_i, y_i) + \lambda \mathcal{L}_{\text{region}}^i\big(\mathcal{N}(\hat{y}_i), \mathcal{N}(y_i)\big) \Big), \quad (2)$$

where n is the total number of pixels. We omit index i and averaging notations for simplicity in the rest of the paper.

The benefits of the addition of region-wise supervision have been explored in previous works. For example, Luc *et al.*[22] exploited GAN [12] as structural priors, and Mostajabi *et al.*[24] pre-trained an additional auto-encoder to inject structure priors into training the segmentation network. However, their approaches require much hyper-parameter tuning and are prone to overfitting, resulting in very small gains over strong baseline models. Please see Table 1 for a comparison.

3.2   Affinity Field Loss Function

Our affinity field loss function overcome these drawbacks and is a flexible region-wise supervision approach that is also easy to optimize.

The use of pairwise pixel affinity has a long history in image segmentation [31,35]. The grouping relationships between neighbouring pixels are derived from the image and represented by a graph, where a node denotes a pixel and a weighted edge between two nodes captures the similarity between two pixels. Image segmentation then becomes a graph partitioning problem, where all the nodes are divided into disjoint sets, with maximal weighted edges within the sets and minimal weighted edges between the sets.

We define pairwise pixel affinity based not on the image, but on ground-truth label map. There are two types of label relationships between a pair of pixels: whether their labels are the same or different. If pixel i and its neighbor j have the same categorical label, we impose a grouping force which encourages network predictions at i and j to be similar. Otherwise, we impose a separating force which pushes apart their label predictions. These two forces are illustrated in Fig. 3 left.

Specifically, we define a pairwise affinity loss based on KL divergence between binary classification probabilities, consistent with the cross-entropy loss for the unary label prediction term. For pixel i and its neighbour j, depending on whether two pixels belong to the same category c in the ground-truth label map y, we define a non-boundary term $\mathcal{L}_{\text{affinity}}^{i\bar{b}c}$ for the grouping force and an boundary term $\mathcal{L}_{\text{affinity}}^{ibc}$ for the separating force in the prediction map $\hat{y}$:

$$\mathcal{L}_{\text{affinity}}^{ic} = \begin{cases} \mathcal{L}_{\text{affinity}}^{ibc} = D_{KL}(\hat{y}_j(c)||\hat{y}_i(c)) & \text{if } y_i(c) = y_j(c) \\ \mathcal{L}_{\text{affinity}}^{ibc} = \max\{0, m - D_{KL}(\hat{y}_j(c)||\hat{y}_i(c))\} & \text{otherwise} \end{cases} \quad (3)$$

$D_{KL}(\cdot)$ is the Kullback-Leibler divergence between two Bernoulli distributions P and Q with parameters p and q respectively: $D_{KL}(P||Q) = p \log \frac{p}{q} + \bar{p} \log \frac{\bar{p}}{\bar{q}}$ for the binary distribution $[p, 1-p]$ and $[q, 1-q]$, where $p, q \in [0, 1]$. For simplicity, we abbreviate the notation as $D_{KL}(p||q)$. $\hat{y}_j(c)$ denotes the prediction probability of j in class c. The overall loss is the average of $\mathcal{L}_{\text{affinity}}^{ic}$ over all categories and pixels.

Discussion 1. Our affinity loss encourages similar network predictions on two pixels of the same ground-truth label, regardless of what their actual labels are. The collection of such pairwise bonds inside a segment ensure that all the pixels achieve the same label. On the other hand, our affinity loss pushes network predictions apart on two pixels of different ground-truth labels, again regardless of what their actual labels are. The collection of such pairwise repulsion help create clear segmentation boundaries.

Discussion 2. Our affinity loss may appear similar to CRF [15] on the pairwise grouping or separating forces between pixels. However, a crucial difference is that CRF models require iterative inference to find a solution, whereas our affinity loss only impacts the network training with pairwise supervision. A similar perspective is metric learning with contrastive loss [9], commonly used in face identification tasks. Our affinity loss works better for segmentation tasks, because it penalizes the network predictions directly, and our pairwise supervision is *in addition to* and *consistent with* the conventional unary supervision.

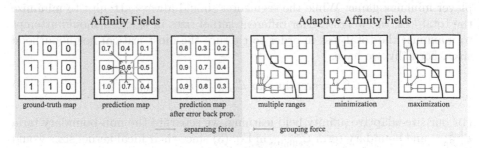

Fig. 3. Left: Our affinity field loss separates predicted probabilities across the boundary and unifies them within the segment. **Right:** The affinity fields can be defined over multiple ranges. Minimizing the affinity loss over different ranges results in trivial solutions which are readily satisfied. Our size-adaptive affinity field loss is achieved with adversarial learning: Maximizing the affinity loss over different kernel sizes selects the most critical range for imposing pairwise relationships in the label space, and our goal is to minimize this maximal loss – i.e., use the best worst case scenario for most effective training.

3.3   Adaptive Kernel Sizes from Adversarial Learning

Region-wise supervision often requires a preset kernel size for CNNs, where pairwise pixel relationships are measured in the same fashion across all pixel locations. However, we cannot expect one kernel size fits all categories, since the ideal kernel size for each category varies with the average object size and the object shape complexity.

We propose a size-adaptive affinity field loss function, optimizing the weights over a set of affinity field sizes for each category in the loop:

$$\mathcal{L}_{\text{multiscale}} = \sum_c \sum_k w_{ck} \mathcal{L}_{\text{region}}^{ck} \quad \text{s.t.} \sum_k w_{ck} = 1 \quad \text{and} \quad w_{ck} \geq 0 \qquad (4)$$

where $\mathcal{L}_{\text{region}}^{ck}$ is a region loss defined in Eq. (2), yet operating on a specific class channel c with kernel size $k \times k$ with a corresponding weighting w_{ck}.

If we just minimize the affinity loss with size weighting w included, w would likely fall into a trivial solution. As illustrated in Fig. 3 right, the affinity loss would be minimum if the smallest kernels are highly weighted for non-boundary terms and the largest kernels for boundary terms, since nearby pixels are more likely to belong to the same object and far-away pixels to different objects. Unary predictions based on the image would naturally have such statistics, nullifying any potential effect from our pairwise affinity supervision.

To optimize the size weighting without trivializing the affinity loss, we need to push the selection of kernel sizes to the extreme. Intuitively, we need to enforce pixels in the same segment to have the same label prediction as far as possible, and likewise to enforce pixels in different segments to have different predictions as close as possible. We use the best worst case scenario for most effective training.

We formulate the adaptive kernel size selection process as optimizing a two-player minimax game: While the segmenter should always attempt to minimize the total loss, the weighting for different kernel sizes in the loss should attempt to maximize the total loss in order to capture the most critical neighbourhood sizes. Formally, we have:

$$S^* = \underset{S}{\text{argmin}} \max_{w} \mathcal{L}_{\text{unary}} + \mathcal{L}_{\text{multiscale}}. \qquad (5)$$

For our size-adaptive affinity field learning, we separate the non-boundary term $\mathcal{L}_{\text{affinity}}^{\bar{b}ck}$ and boundary term $\mathcal{L}_{\text{affinity}}^{bck}$ in Eq. (3) since their ideal kernel sizes would be different. Our adaptive affinity field (AAF) loss becomes:

$$S^* = \underset{S}{\text{argmin}} \max_{w} \mathcal{L}_{\text{unary}} + \mathcal{L}_{\text{AAF}}, \qquad (6)$$

$$\mathcal{L}_{\text{AAF}} = \sum_c \sum_k (w_{\bar{b}ck} \mathcal{L}_{\text{affinity}}^{\bar{b}ck} + w_{bck} \mathcal{L}_{\text{affinity}}^{bck}), \qquad (7)$$

$$\text{s.t.} \sum_k w_{\bar{b}ck} = \sum_k w_{bck} = 1 \text{ and } w_{\bar{b}ck}, w_{bck} \geq 0.$$

4   Experimental Setup

4.1   Datasets

We compare our proposed affinity fields and AAF with other competing methods on the PASCAL VOC 2012 [11] and Cityscapes [10] datasets.

PASCAL VOC 2012. PASCAL VOC 2012 [11] segmentation dataset contains 20 object categories and one background class. Following the procedure of [6, 21,36], we use augmented data with the annotations of [13], resulting in 10,582, 1,449, and 1,456 images for training, validation and testing.

Cityscapes. Cityscapes [10] is a dataset for semantic urban street scene understanding. 5000 high quality pixel-level finely annotated images are divided into training, validation, and testing sets with 2975, 500, and 1525 images, respectively. It defines 19 categories containing flat, human, vehicle, construction, object, nature, *etc.*

4.2   Evaluation Metrics

All existing semantic segmentation works adopt **pixel-wise mIoU** [21] as their metric. To fully examine the effectiveness of our AAF on fine structures in particular, we also evaluate all the models using **instance-wise mIoU** and **boundary detection metrics**.

Instance-Wise mIoU. Since the pixel-wise mIoU metric is often biased toward large objects, we introduce the instance-wise mIoU to alleviate the bias, which allow us to evaluate fairly the performance on smaller objects. The per category instance-wise mIoU is formulated as $\hat{U}_c = \frac{\sum_x n_{c,x} \times U_{c,x}}{\sum_x n_{c,x}}$, where $n_{c,x}$ and $U_{c,x}$ are the number of instances and IoU of class c in image x, respectively.

Boundary Detection Metrics. We compute semantic boundaries using the semantic predictions and benchmark the results using the standard benchmark for contour detection proposed by [2], which summarizes the results by precision, recall, and f-measure.

4.3   Methods of Comparison

We briefly describe other popular methods that are used for comparison in our experiments, namely, GAN's adversarial learning [12], contrastive loss [9], and CRF [15].

GAN's Adversarial Learning. We investigate a popular framework, the Generative Adversarial Networks (GAN) [12]. The discriminator D in GAN works as injecting priors for region structures. The adversarial loss is formulated as

$$\mathcal{L}^i_{\text{adversarial}} = \log D(\mathcal{N}(y_i)) + \log(1 - D(\mathcal{N}(\hat{y}_i))). \tag{8}$$

We simultaneously train the segmentation network S to minimize log $(1 - D(\mathcal{N}(\hat{y}_i)))$ and the discriminator to maximize $\mathcal{L}_{\text{adversarial}}$.

Pixel Embedding. We study the region-wise supervision over feature map, which is implemented by imposing the contrastive loss [9] on the last convolutional layer before the softmax layer. The contrastive loss is formulated as

$$\mathcal{L}^i_{\text{contrast}} = \begin{cases} \mathcal{L}^{i\bar{e}}_{\text{contrast}} = \|f_j - f_i\|^2_2 & \text{if } y_i(c) = y_j(c) \\ \mathcal{L}^{ie}_{\text{contrast}} = \max\{0, m - \|f_j - f_i\|^2_2\} & \text{otherwise,} \end{cases} \quad (9)$$

where f_i denotes L_2-normalized feature vector at pixel i, and m is set to 0.2.

CRF-Based Processing. We follow [6]'s implementation by post-processing the prediction with dense-CRF [15]. We set bi_w to 1, bi_xy_std to 40, bi_rgb_std to 3, pos_w to 1, and pos_xy_std to 1 for all experiments. It is worth mentioning that CRF takes additional 40 s to generate the final results on Cityscapes, while our proposed methods introduce no inference overhead.

4.4   Implementation Details

Our implementation follows the ones of base architectures, which are PSPNet [36] in most cases or FCN [21]. We use the poly learning rate policy where the current learning rate equals the base one multiplied by $(1 - \frac{\text{iter}}{\text{max\_iter}})^{0.9}$. We set the base learning rate as 0.001. The training iterations for all experiments is 30 K on VOC dataset and 90 K on Cityscapes dataset while the performance can be further improved by increasing the iteration number. Momentum and weight decay are set to 0.9 and 0.0005, respectively. For data augmentation, we adopt random mirroring and random resizing between 0.5 and 2 for all datasets. We do not upscale the logits (prediction map) back to the input image resolution, instead, we follow [6]'s setting by downsampling the ground-truth labels for training ($output\_stride = 8$).

PSPNet [36] shows that larger "cropsize" and "batchsize" can yield better performance. In their implementation, "cropsize" can be up to 720 × 720 and "batchsize" to 16 using 16 GPUs. To speed up the experiments for validation on VOC, we downsize "cropsize" to 336 × 336 and "batchsize" to 8 so that a single GTX Titan X GPU is sufficient for training. We set "cropsize" to 480 × 480 during inference. For testing on PASCAL VOC 2012 and all experiments on Cityscapes dataset, we use 4-GPUs to train the network. On VOC dataset, we set the "batchsize" to 16 and set "cropsize" to 480 × 480. On Cityscaeps, we set the "batchsize" to 8 and "cropsize" to 720 × 720. For inference, we boost the performance by averaging scores from left-right flipped and multi-scale inputs ($scales = \{0.5, 0.75, 1, 1.25, 1.5, 1.75\}$).

For affinity fields and AAF, λ is set to 1.0 and margin m is set to 3.0. We use ResNet101 [14] as the backbone network and initialize the models with weights pre-trained on ImageNet [30].

5   Experimental Results

We benchmark our proposed methods on two datasets, PASCAL VOC 2012 [11] and Cityscapes [10]. All methods are evaluated by three metrics: mIoU, instance-wise mIoU and boundary detection recall. We include some visual examples to demonstrate the effectiveness of our proposed methods in Fig. 5.

5.1   Pixel-Level Evaluation

Validation Results. For training on PASCAL VOC 2012 [11], we first train on *train_aug* for 30 K iterations and then fine-tune on *train* for another 30 K iterations with base learning rate as 0.0001. For Cityscapes [10], we only train on finely annotated images for 90 K iterations. We summarize the mIoU results on validation set in Tables 2 and 3, respectively.

With FCN [21] as base architecture, the affinity field loss and AAF improve the performance by 2.16% and 3.04% on VOC and by 1.88% and 2.37% on Cityscapes. With PSPNet [36] as the base architecture, the results also improves consistently: GAN loss, embedding contrastive loss, affinity field loss and AAF improve the mean IoU by 0.62%, 1.24%, 1.68% and 2.27% on VOC; affinity field loss and AAF improve by 2.00% and 2.52% on Cityscapes. It is worth noting that large improvements over PSPNet on VOC are mostly in categories with fine structures, such as "bike", "chair", "person", and "plant".

Testing Results. On PASCAL VOC 2012, the training procedure for PSPNet and AAF is the same as follows: We first train the networks on *train_aug* and then fine-tune on *train_val*. We report the testing results on VOC 2012 and

Table 2. Per-class results on Pascal VOC 2012 validation set. Gray colored background denotes using FCN as the base architecture.

Method	aero	bike	bird	boat	bottle	bus	car	cat	chair	cow	table	dog	horse	mbike	person	plant	sheep	sofa	train	tv	mIoU
FCN	86.95	59.25	85.18	70.33	73.92	78.86	82.30	85.64	33.57	69.34	27.41	78.04	71.45	70.45	85.54	57.42	71.55	32.48	74.91	59.10	68.91
PSPNet	92.56	66.70	91.10	76.52	80.88	94.43	88.49	93.14	38.87	89.33	62.77	86.44	89.72	88.36	87.48	56.95	91.77	46.23	88.59	77.14	80.12
Affinity	88.66	59.25	87.85	72.19	76.36	80.65	80.74	87.82	35.38	73.45	30.17	79.84	68.15	73.52	87.96	53.95	75.46	37.15	76.62	73.42	71.07
AAF	88.15	67.83	87.06	72.05	76.45	85.43	80.58	88.33	35.47	72.76	31.55	79.68	67.01	77.96	88.20	50.31	73.16	42.71	78.14	73.87	71.95
GAN	92.36	65.94	91.80	76.35	77.70	95.39	89.21	93.30	43.35	89.25	61.81	86.93	91.28	87.43	87.21	68.15	90.64	49.64	88.79	73.83	80.74
Emb.	91.28	69.50	92.62	77.60	78.74	95.03	89.57	93.67	43.21	88.76	62.47	86.68	91.28	88.47	87.44	69.21	91.53	52.17	89.30	74.60	81.36
Affinity	91.52	**74.74**	92.09	78.17	80.73	95.70	89.52	92.83	43.29	89.21	60.33	87.50	90.96	88.77	88.88	**71.00**	88.54	50.61	89.64	78.22	81.80
AAF	92.97	73.68	92.49	80.51	79.73	96.15	90.92	93.42	**45.11**	89.00	62.87	87.97	91.32	90.28	**89.30**	69.05	88.92	**52.81**	89.05	78.91	**82.39**

Table 3. Per-class results on Cityscapes validation set. Gray colored background denotes using FCN as the base architecture.

Method	road	swalk	build.	wall	fence	pole	tlight	tsign	veg.	terrain	sky	person	rider	car	truck	bus	train	mbike	bike	mIoU
FCN	97.31	79.28	89.52	38.08	48.63	49.70	59.37	69.94	90.86	56.58	92.38	75.91	46.24	92.26	50.41	64.51	39.73	54.91	73.07	66.77
PSPNet	97.96	83.89	92.22	57.24	59.31	58.89	68.39	77.07	92.18	63.71	94.42	81.80	63.11	94.85	73.54	84.82	67.42	69.34	77.42	76.72
Affinity	97.52	80.90	90.42	40.45	49.81	55.97	63.92	73.37	91.49	59.01	93.30	78.17	52.16	92.85	52.53	65.78	39.28	52.88	74.53	68.65
AAF	97.58	81.19	90.50	42.30	50.34	57.47	65.39	74.83	91.54	59.25	93.11	78.65	52.98	93.15	53.10	67.58	38.40	51.57	74.80	69.14
CRF	97.96	83.82	92.14	57.16	59.28	57.48	67.71	76.61	92.09	63.67	94.35	81.62	62.98	94.81	73.59	84.81	67.49	69.22	77.28	76.53
GAN	97.95	83.59	92.01	56.92	60.17	58.63	68.37	77.36	92.28	62.70	94.42	81.59	62.27	94.94	78.09	82.79	56.75	69.19	77.78	76.20
Affinity	98.08	85.58	92.60	58.33	61.45	**66.80**	**74.19**	81.29	92.90	65.34	94.87	84.00	65.84	95.50	76.84	85.80	64.19	72.32	79.83	78.72
AAF	98.18	85.35	92.86	58.87	61.48	66.64	74.00	80.98	92.95	65.31	94.91	**84.27**	**66.98**	95.51	79.39	87.06	67.80	72.91	80.19	**79.24**

Cityscapes in Tables 4 and 5, respectively. Our re-trained PSPnet does not reach the same performance as originally reported in the paper because we do not bootstrap the performance by fine-tuning on hard examples (like "bike" images), as pointed out in [7]. We demonstrate that our proposed AAF achieve 82.17% and 79.07% mIoU, which is better than the PSPNet by 1.54% and 2.77% and competitive to the state-of-the-art performance.

Table 4. Per-class results on Pascal VOC 2012 testing set.

Method	aero	bike	bird	boat	bottle	bus	car	cat	chair	cow	table	dog	horse	mbike	person	plant	sheep	sofa	train	tv	mIoU
PSPNet	94.01	68.08	88.80	64.87	75.87	95.60	89.59	93.15	37.96	88.20	72.58	89.96	93.30	87.52	86.65	61.90	87.05	60.81	87.13	74.65	80.63
AAF	91.25	**72.90**	90.69	68.22	77.73	95.55	90.70	94.66	**40.90**	89.53	72.63	91.64	94.07	88.33	**88.84**	**67.26**	92.88	62.62	85.22	74.02	**82.17**

Table 5. Per-class results on Cityscapes test set.

Method	road	swalk	build.	wall	fence	pole	tlight	tsign	veg.	terrain	sky	person	rider	car	truck	bus	train	mbike	bike	mIoU
PSPNet	98.33	84.21	92.14	49.67	55.81	57.62	69.01	74.17	92.70	70.86	95.08	84.21	66.58	95.28	73.52	80.59	70.54	65.54	73.73	76.30
AAF	98.53	85.56	93.04	53.81	58.96	**65.93**	75.02	78.42	93.68	72.44	95.58	86.43	70.51	95.88	73.91	82.68	76.86	68.69	76.40	**79.07**

5.2   Instance-Level Evaluation

We measure the instance-wise mIoU on VOC and Cityscapes validation set as summarized in Tables 6 and 7, respectively In instance-wise mIoU, our AAF is higher than base architecture by 3.94% on VOC and 2.94% on Cityscapes. The improvements on fine-structured categories are more prominent. For example, the "bottle" is improved by 12.89% on VOC, "pole" and "tlight" is improved by 9.51% and 9.04% on Cityscapes.

Table 6. Per-class instance-wise IoU results on Pascal VOC 2012 validation set.

Method	aero	bike	bird	boat	bottle	bus	car	cat	chair	cow	table	dog	horse	mbike	person	plant	sheep	sofa	train	tv	mIoU
PSPNet	87.54	53.08	83.53	76.95	45.13	87.68	68.77	89.01	39.26	88.78	51.49	88.88	84.41	85.95	77.60	48.68	86.25	54.18	88.25	66.11	73.60
Affinity	89.42	61.72	84.64	79.86	57.57	88.81	71.74	88.91	44.78	89.55	52.55	91.22	86.12	87.40	81.10	58.33	85.15	60.61	88.47	68.86	76.73
AAF	89.76	**61.74**	84.40	**81.87**	**58.04**	89.03	**73.68**	90.46	**46.67**	89.65	**55.63**	91.33	85.85	88.36	**81.93**	**59.84**	84.52	**62.67**	89.35	68.80	**77.54**

Table 7. Per-class instance-wise IOU results on Cityscapes validation set.

Method	road	swalk	build.	wall	fence	pole	tlight	tsign	veg.	terrain	sky	person	rider	car	truck	bus	train	mbike	bike	mIoU
PSPNet	97.64	78.23	88.36	34.48	42.00	51.68	50.71	68.29	89.65	40.14	86.63	78.35	75.91	92.09	87.28	90.85	62.74	85.33	73.02	72.28
Affinity	97.73	80.51	89.32	38.21	45.89	**61.31**	**59.75**	73.41	90.62	43.22	88.20	81.18	**80.29**	93.24	89.60	94.10	50.69	84.76	75.59	74.61
AAF	97.86	80.40	89.44	38.38	46.33	61.19	**59.75**	73.55	90.63	42.51	88.48	**81.27**	80.08	93.18	89.47	93.73	60.74	86.40	75.84	**75.22**

5.3   Boundary-Level Evaluation

Next, we analyze quantitatively the improvements of boundary localization. We include the boundary recall on VOC in Table 8 and Cityscapes in Table 9. We omit the precision table due to smaller performance difference. The overall boundary recall is improved by 7.9% and 8.0% on VOC and Cityscapes, respectively. It is worth noting that the boundary recall is improved for every category. This result demonstrates that boundaries of all categories can all benefit from affinity fields and AAF. Among all, the improvements on categories with complicated boundaries, such as "bike", "bird", "boat", "chair", "person", and "plant" are significant on VOC. On Cityscapes, objects with thin structures are improved most, such as "pole", "tlight", "tsign", "person", "rider", and "bike".

Table 8. Per-class boundary recall results on Pascal VOC 2012 validation set.

Method	aero	bike	bird	boat	bottle	bus	car	cat	chair	cow	table	dog	horse	mbike	person	plant	sheep	sofa	train	tv	mean
PSPNet	.694	.420	.658	.417	.624	.626	.562	.667	.297	.587	.279	.667	.608	.513	.554	.235	.547	.413	.551	.512	.527
Affinity	.745	**.573**	.708	.524	.693	.678	.627	.690	**.455**	.620	.383	.732	.655	.602	**.648**	**.370**	.583	.546	.609	**.635**	**.610**
AAF	.746	.559	.704	.524	.684	.675	.622	.701	.441	.612	.391	.728	.653	.595	.647	.355	.580	.547	.608	.628	.606

Table 9. Per-class boundary recall results on Cityscapes validation set.

Method	road	swalk	build.	wall	fence	pole	tlight	tsign	veg.	terrain	sky	person	rider	car	truck	bus	train	mbike	bike	mean
PSPNet	.458	.771	.584	.480	.537	.587	.649	.687	.650	.589	.587	.733	.631	.812	.577	.734	.569	.550	.697	.625
Affinity	.484	.826	.686	.532	.632	**.760**	**.769**	**.780**	.754	.663	.655	**.814**	**.748**	.852	.627	.792	.589	.651	.798	**.706**
AAF	.482	.826	.685	.533	.643	.756	.768	.780	.753	.645	.653	**.814**	.746	.851	.644	.789	.590	.642	**.801**	.705

5.4 Adaptive Affinity Field Size Analysis

We further analyze our proposed AAF methods on: (1) optimal affinity field size for each category, and (2) effective combinations of affinity field sizes.

Optimal Adaptive Affinity Field Size. We conduct experiments on VOC with our proposed AAF on three $k \times k$ kernel sizes where $k = 3, 5, 7$. We report the optimal adaptive kernel size on the contour term calculated as $k_c^e = \sum_k w_{eck} \times k$, and summarized in Fig. 4. As shown, "person" and "dog" benefit from smaller kernel size (3.1 and 3.4), while "cow" and "plant" from larger kernel size (4.6 and 4.5). We display some image patches with the corresponding effective receptive field size.

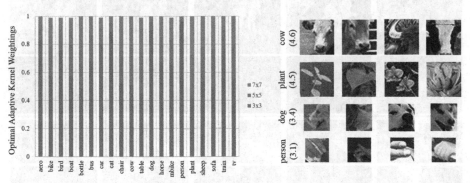

Fig. 4. Left: The optimal weightings for different kernel sizes of the edge term in AAF for each category on PASCAL VOC 2012 validation set. **Right:** Visualization of image patches with corresponding effective receptive field sizes, suggesting how kernel sizes capture the shape complexity in critical regions of different categories.

Combinations of Affinity Field Sizes. We explore the effectiveness of different selections of $k \times k$ kernels, where $k \in \{3, 5, 7\}$, for AAF. Summarized in Table 10, we observe that combinations of 3×3 and 5×5 kernels have the optimal performance.

Table 10. Per-category IOU results of AAF with different combinations of kernel sizes k on VOC 2012 validation set. '✓' denotes the inclusion of respective kernel size as opposed to '×'.

$k=3$	$k=5$	$k=7$	aero	bike	bird	boat	bottle	bus	car	cat	chair	cow	table	dog	horse	mbike	person	plant	sheep	sofa	train	tv	mIoU
✓	×	×	89.02	68.86	90.05	73.52	77.87	94.04	86.94	91.04	40.85	85.82	54.08	84.31	89.12	84.91	86.72	67.52	85.56	52.55	87.60	73.78	79.00
✓	✓	×	90.19	68.48	89.87	76.91	77.56	93.84	89.08	91.45	40.67	85.82	57.23	85.33	89.77	85.97	86.93	65.68	85.12	52.22	87.25	74.07	79.45
✓	✓	✓	89.45	68.46	90.44	75.82	77.03	94.09	88.01	91.42	38.67	85.98	56.16	84.32	89.22	84.98	87.09	67.35	87.15	55.20	88.22	73.30	79.40

5.5 Generalizability

We further investigate the robustness of our proposed methods on different domains. We train the networks on the Cityscapes dataset [10] and test them on another dataset, Grand Theft Auto V (GTA5) [28] as shown in Fig. 5. The GTA5 dataset is generated from the photo-realistic computer game–*Grand Theft*

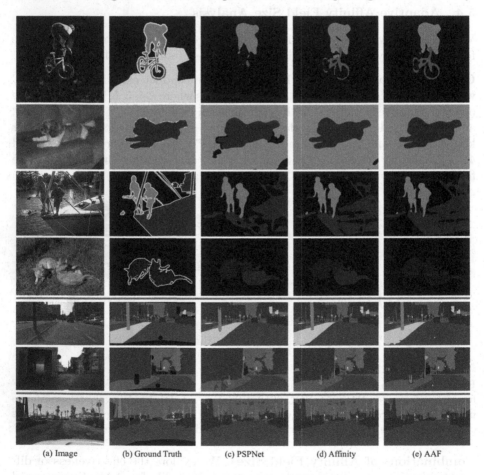

(a) Image   (b) Ground Truth   (c) PSPNet   (d) Affinity   (e) AAF

Fig. 5. Visual quality comparisons on the VOC 2012 [11] validation set (the first four rows), Cityscapes [10] validation set (the middle two rows) and GTA5 [28] part 1 (the bottom row): (a) image, (b) ground truth, (c) PSPNet [36], (d) affinity fields, and (e) adaptive affinity fields (AAF).

Table 11. Per-class results on GTA5 Part 1.

Method	road	swalk	build.	wall	fence	pole	tlight	tsign	veg.	terrain	sky	person	rider	car	truck	bus	train	mbike	bike	mIoU	pix. acc
PSPNet	61.79	34.26	37.30	13.31	18.52	26.51	31.64	17.51	55.00	8.57	82.47	42.73	49.78	69.25	34.31	18.21	25.00	33.14	6.86	35.06	68.78
Affinity	75.26	30.34	44.10	12.91	20.19	29.78	31.50	23.98	64.25	11.83	74.32	48.28	49.12	67.39	25.76	23.82	20.29	41.48	5.63	**36.86**	75.13
AAF	83.07	27.82	51.16	10.41	18.76	28.58	31.74	24.98	61.38	12.25	70.65	50.53	48.06	53.35	26.80	20.97	24.50	39.56	9.37	36.52	**78.28**

Auto V [28], which consists of 24,966 images with densely labelled segmentation maps compatible with Cityscapes. We test on GTA5 Part 1 (2,500 images). We summarize the performance in Table 11. It is shown that without fine-tuning, our proposed AAF outperforms the PSPNet [36] baseline model by 9.5% in mean pixel accuracy and 1.46% in mIoU, which demonstrates the robustness of our proposed methods against appearance variations.

6 Summary

We propose adaptive affinity fields (AAF) for semantic segmentation, which incorporate geometric regularities into segmentation models, and learn local relations with adaptive ranges through adversarial training. Compared to other alternatives, our AAF model is (1) effective (encoding rich structural relations), (2) efficient (introducing no inference overhead), and (3) robust (not sensitive to domain changes). Our approach achieves competitive performance on standard benchmarks and also generalizes well on unseen data. It provides a novel perspective towards structure modeling in deep learning.

References

1. Amir, A., Lindenbaum, M.: Grouping-based nonadditive verification. IEEE Trans. Pattern Anal. Mach. Intell. **20**(2), 186–192 (1998)
2. Arbelaez, P., Maire, M., Fowlkes, C., Malik, J.: Contour detection and hierarchical image segmentation. IEEE Trans. Pattern Anal. Mach. Intell. **33**(5), 898–916 (2011)
3. Bertasius, G., Shi, J., Torresani, L.: Semantic segmentation with boundary neural fields. In: CVPR (2016)
4. Bertasius, G., Torresani, L., Yu, S.X., Shi, J.: Convolutional random walk networks for semantic image segmentation. In: CVPR (2017)
5. Chen, L.C., Barron, J.T., Papandreou, G., Murphy, K., Yuille, A.L.: Semantic image segmentation with task-specific edge detection using cnns and a discriminatively trained domain transform. In: CVPR (2016)
6. Chen, L.C., Papandreou, G., Kokkinos, I., Murphy, K., Yuille, A.L.: Deeplab: semantic image segmentation with deep convolutional nets, atrous convolution, and fully connected crfs (2016). arXiv preprint arXiv:1606.00915
7. Chen, L.C., Papandreou, G., Schroff, F., Adam, H.: Rethinking atrous convolution for semantic image segmentation (2017). arXiv preprint arXiv:1706.05587
8. Chen, L.C., Schwing, A., Yuille, A., Urtasun, R.: Learning deep structured models. In: ICML (2015)

9. Chopra, S., Hadsell, R., LeCun, Y.: Learning a similarity metric discriminatively, with application to face verification. In: CVPR (2005)
10. Cordts, M., Omran, M., Ramos, S., Rehfeld, T., Enzweiler, M., Benenson, R., Franke, U., Roth, S., Schiele, B.: The cityscapes dataset for semantic urban scene understanding. In: CVPR (2016)
11. Everingham, M., Van Gool, L., Williams, C.K., Winn, J., Zisserman, A.: The pascal visual object classes (VOC) challenge. Int. J. Comput. Vis. **88**, 303–338 (2010)
12. Goodfellow, I., Pouget-Abadie, J., Mirza, M., Xu, B., Warde-Farley, D., Ozair, S., Courville, A., Bengio, Y.: Generative adversarial nets. In: NIPS (2014)
13. Hariharan, B., Arbeláez, P., Bourdev, L., Maji, S., Malik, J.: Semantic contours from inverse detectors. In: ICCV (2011)
14. He, K., Zhang, X., Ren, S., Sun, J.: Deep residual learning for image recognition. In: CVPR (2016)
15. Krähenbühl, P., Koltun, V.: Efficient inference in fully connected CRFS with gaussian edge potentials. In: NIPS (2011)
16. Li, X., Liu, Z., Luo, P., Loy, C.C., Tang, X.: Not all pixels are equal: difficulty-aware semantic segmentation via deep layer cascade. In: CVPR (2017)
17. Lin, G., Shen, C., van den Hengel, A., Reid, I.: Efficient piecewise training of deep structured models for semantic segmentation. In: CVPR (2016)
18. Liu, S., De Mello, S., Gu, J., Zhong, G., Yang, M.H., Kautz, J.: Learning affinity via spatial propagation networks. In: NIPS (2017)
19. Liu, Z., Li, X., Luo, P., Loy, C.C., Tang, X.: Semantic image segmentation via deep parsing network. In: CVPR (2015)
20. Liu, Z., Li, X., Luo, P., Loy, C.C., Tang, X.: Deep learning markov random field for semantic segmentation. IEEE Trans. Pattern Anal. Mach. Intell. **40**, 1814–1828 (2017)
21. Long, J., Shelhamer, E., Darrell, T.: Fully convolutional networks for semantic segmentation. In: CVPR (2015)
22. Luc, P., Couprie, C., Chintala, S., Verbeek, J.: Semantic segmentation using adversarial networks. NIPS Workshop (2016)
23. Maire, M., Narihira, T., Yu, S.X.: Affinity CNN: learning pixel-centric pairwise relations for figure/ground embedding. In: CVPR (2016)
24. Mostajabi, M., Maire, M., Shakhnarovich, G.: Regularizing deep networks by modeling and predicting label structure. In: Proceedings of the IEEE Conference on Computer Vision and Pattern Recognition, pp. 5629–5638 (2018)
25. Noh, H., Hong, S., Han, B.: Learning deconvolution network for semantic segmentation. In: CVPR (2015)
26. Poggio, T.: Early vision: from computational structure to algorithms and parallel hardware. Comput. Vis. Graph. Image Process. **31**(2), 139–155 (1985)
27. Radford, A., Metz, L., Chintala, S.: Unsupervised representation learning with deep convolutional generative adversarial networks (2015). arXiv preprint arXiv:1511.06434
28. Richter, Stephan R., Vineet, Vibhav, Roth, Stefan, Koltun, Vladlen: Playing for data: ground truth from computer games. In: Leibe, Bastian, Matas, Jiri, Sebe, Nicu, Welling, Max (eds.) ECCV 2016. LNCS, vol. 9906, pp. 102–118. Springer, Cham (2016). https://doi.org/10.1007/978-3-319-46475-6_7
29. Ronneberger, Olaf, Fischer, Philipp, Brox, Thomas: U-Net: convolutional networks for biomedical image segmentation. In: Navab, Nassir, Hornegger, Joachim, Wells, William M., Frangi, Alejandro F. (eds.) MICCAI 2015. LNCS, vol. 9351, pp. 234–241. Springer, Cham (2015). https://doi.org/10.1007/978-3-319-24574-4_28

30. Russakovsky, O., Deng, J., Su, H., Krause, J., Satheesh, S., Ma, S., Huang, Z., Karpathy, A., Khosla, A., Bernstein, M., Berg, A.C., Fei-Fei, L.: Imagenet large scale visual recognition challenge. Int. J. Comput. Vis. **115**, 211–252 (2015)
31. Shi, J., Malik, J.: Normalized cuts and image segmentation. IEEE Trans. Pattern Anal. Mach. Intell. **22**(8), 888–905 (2000)
32. Simonyan, K., Zisserman, A.: Very deep convolutional networks for large-scale image recognition (2014). arXiv preprint arXiv:1409.1556
33. Wu, Z., Shen, C., Hengel, A.V.D.: High-performance semantic segmentation using very deep fully convolutional networks (2016). arXiv preprint arXiv:1604.04339
34. Yu, F., Koltun, V.: Multi-scale context aggregation by dilated convolutions. In: ICLR (2016)
35. Yu, S.X., Shi, J.: Multiclass spectral clustering. In: ICCV (2003)
36. Zhao, H., Shi, J., Qi, X., Wang, X., Jia, J.: Pyramid scene parsing network. In: CVPR (2017)
37. Zheng, S., et al.: Conditional random fields as recurrent neural networks. In: ICCV (2015)

ReenactGAN: Learning to Reenact Faces via Boundary Transfer

Wayne Wu[1]([✉])[ID], Yunxuan Zhang[1][ID], Cheng Li[1][ID], Chen Qian[1][ID], and Chen Change Loy[2][ID]

[1] SenseTime Research, Beijing, China
{wuwenyan,zhangyunxuan,chengli,qianchen}@sensetime.com
[2] Nanyang Technological University, Singapore, Singapore
ccloy@ntu.edu.sg

Abstract. We present a novel learning-based framework for face reenactment. The proposed method, known as ReenactGAN, is capable of transferring facial movements and expressions from an arbitrary person's monocular video input to a target person's video. Instead of performing a direct transfer in the pixel space, which could result in structural artifacts, we first map the source face onto a boundary latent space. A transformer is subsequently used to adapt the source face's boundary to the target's boundary. Finally, a target-specific decoder is used to generate the reenacted target face. Thanks to the effective and reliable boundary-based transfer, our method can perform photo-realistic face reenactment. In addition, ReenactGAN is appealing in that the whole reenactment process is purely feed-forward, and thus the reenactment process can run in real-time (30 FPS on one GTX 1080 GPU). Dataset and model are publicly available on our project page (Project Page: https://wywu.github.io/projects/ReenactGAN/ReenactGAN.html).

Keywords: Face reenactment · Face generation · Face alignment
GAN

1 Introduction

Face reenactment aims at transferring one source person's facial expression and movements to another target person's face. Faithful photo-realistic facial reenactment finds a wide range of applications, including film production, video conferencing, and augmented reality (*e.g.*, virtual YouTuber). Thanks to the increasingly accurate and reliable 3D facial model fitting [2,9] and landmarks detection [6,19,39,50–52,60,61] techniques on RGB-D and RGB

W. Wu and Y. Zhang—This work was done during an internship at SenseTime Research.

Electronic supplementary material The online version of this chapter (https://doi.org/10.1007/978-3-030-01246-5_37) contains supplementary material, which is available to authorized users.

© Springer Nature Switzerland AG 2018
V. Ferrari et al. (Eds.): ECCV 2018, LNCS 11205, pp. 622–638, 2018.
https://doi.org/10.1007/978-3-030-01246-5_37

cameras in recent years, many impressive face reenactment methods are proposed [3,18,32,34,35,41]. Most existing approaches represent face as a predefined parametric 3D model. These methods typically involve tracking and optimization to fit a source video into a restrictive set of facial poses and expression parametric space, and then render the manipulated target output. In general, optimization-based methods can handle background regions better, compared to feed-forward based method that can only support pixels generation around the face. Nevertheless, a pre-defined parametric 3D model can hardly capture all subtle movements of the human face. In addition, these works require large efforts and delicacy designs of complex parametric fitting. Considering the algorithmic complexity of these approaches, few of them are open-sourced.

The emergence of Generative Adversarial Network (GAN) based approaches, *e.g.*, Pix2Pix [15] and CycleGAN [57], offers an appealing and succinct alternative for face reenactment. Nonetheless, despite the success of GAN in many image-to-image transfer applications [15,27,57], training a pure learning-based method for face reenactment is *non-trivial*: (1) Face images are captured under very different poses, expressions and lighting conditions. Thus learning a direct face-to-face mapping based on limited samples but covering all variances is hard. A conventional state-of-the-art GAN such as CycleGAN would generate unnatural images in extreme conditions such as large pose, or fail on unseen images, as shown in Fig. 1. (2) No pairwise data is available as we can hardly match diverse expressions given an arbitrary set of source and target videos. (3) We wish to perform *many-to-one* mapping, *i.e.*, reenact a specific target with just a single model given any source faces. This scenario violates the assumption of CycleGAN since an inverse mapping (one-to-many) does not exist.

Fig. 1. The proposed ReenactGAN is capable of manipulating a target face in a video by transferring movements and facial expressions from an arbitrary person's video. In contrast to CycleGAN [57], ReenactGAN can comfortably support the reenactment of large facial movements. CycleGAN is infeasible to transfer unseen data as shown in the last three columns.

To address the first two challenges, we are required to define a space or medium that allows an effective and robust transfer of facial movement and expressions. Inspired by previous facial model fitting approaches, we propose the use of facial contours or boundaries as a compact medium to capture facial geometric variances. Specifically, we map a source face into a latent boundary space, which we wish facial movement and expressions are faithfully kept. We then adapt the space to the specific target person and decode for the appearance.

Introducing facial boundaries as the latent space is beneficial for face reenactment. *Firstly*, the mapping between face images and the facial boundary space relates to the well-studied face alignment problem. Thanks to contemporary facial landmark detection methods [6,19,50,61], face boundaries can be obtained accurately and robustly under large poses, diverse expressions and extreme lighting conditions. This is a unique advantage that is not available in direct raw pixels-based mapping. *Secondly*, transferring diverse expression with unpaired data is simplified. The availability of large-scale face alignment training sets provides high-quality paired training data that consist face images and the corresponding boundaries. Learning without paired data only happens in the well-defined boundary space, whilst the input face encoding and target face decoding processes can fully leverage the power of pairwise face alignment data.

Our final challenge is to resolve the *many-to-one* mapping problem. We address this problem by formulating a GAN-based transformer to adapt the boundary space of input face to the target face. To ensure the quality of transformation, we constrain the process with a cycle loss, an adversarial loss, and a shape loss in the PCA space. With the target-specific transformer, we can reenact a target face based on images or videos from arbitrary sources. Overall, the proposed **ReenactGAN** hinges on three components: (1) an encoder to encode an input face into a latent boundary space, (2) a target-specific transformer to adapt an arbitrary source boundary space to that of a specific target, and (3) a target-specific decoder, which decodes the latent space to the target face. ReenactGAN is easy to re-implement and distribute since each component in the framework is a feed-forward network, and the only training material is source-target videos and a facial alignment training set.

We summarize our contributions as follows:

- We introduce the notion of 'boundary latent space' for face reenactment. We found that facial boundaries hold sufficient geometric information to reenact a face with rich expressions but being relatively 'identity-agnostic' in comparison to direct mapping with raw pixels. Importantly, the boundary space is more robust to challenging poses, expressions and lighting conditions.
- Based on the notion of boundary latent space, we propose a novel learning-based face reenactment framework. All components are feed-forward. In contrast to traditional model-based methods, the proposed ReenactGAN is easier to train and implement.

– We introduce target-specific transformers in the latent space to achieve many-to-one face reenactment, which is otherwise impossible using a conventional GAN-based image-to-image transfer method.

2   Related Work

Face Reenactment: Most of the existing studies can be categorized as a 'model-based' approach. These methods typically consist of three steps: (1) Face capturing, *e.g.* tracking face templates [41], using optical flow as appearance and velocity measurements to match the face in the database [22], or employing either RGB [4] or RGB-D camera [34] to capture face movements. Recent advances of facial landmark detection methods [5,51] enable us to effectively track input's facial component like eyes and mouth. (2) Once the facial movement is captured, many studies will subsequently to fit the movement in a parametric space or model, including head pose [41,44], eye gaze [36,44], or PCA coefficients over 3D model bases [35] and even detail 3D face meshes [48]. (3) Once a model is fitted, the next step is to re-render a new video. Garrido *et al.* [8] directly retrieves similar pose to the source from the target video, and render new video through morphing. A similar strategy is employed in [35] to optimize the inner-mouth generation process. Retrieval-based methods are arguably low in computational efficiency [35,40]. Recently, CycleGAN provides a new feasible solution for face reenactment. To our best knowledge, although there are no published peer-reviewed papers in the literature, some interesting work was released or demonstrated in the community [16,47,53]. In contrast to the CycleGAN that can only handle a single source person and one target, our framework aims at solving the harder many-to-one problem, which permits more practical usages.

Generative Adversarial Network (GAN) and CycleGAN: Generative Adversarial Networks (GAN) [10] has been extensively used and extended for image generation including facial images. By employing the adversarial loss, one can map a low-dimensional noise vector input [10], a fashion design coding [59], an unrealistic rendered facial image [28] or a text description [54] to a realistic image. Zhu *et al.* [57] has shown that by adding a cycle consistency loss, CycleGAN achieves impressive results in learning the transformation function between two domains. Recently, Mueller *et al.* [27] leveraged a geometric consistency loss to preserve hand pose based on CycleGAN. Our method is different in directly taking image-to-image translation on the geometric latent space rather than adding an auxiliary geometric constraint. Xu *et al.* [53] applied CycleGAN to learn the transformation between a specific person pair. They added specific discriminators on different facial components to enhance the performance of each local part. In contrast to [53], our ReenactGAN first maps all faces into a boundary latent space and then decodes it to each specific person. With the proposed target-specific transformer, each decoder can reenact arbitrary person to a specific target based on the adapted boundary space, thus achieving many-to-one reenactment efficiently and conveniently. Introducing the boundary space also improves facial action consistency and the robustness for extreme poses.

3   Face Reenactment via Boundary Transfer

The proposed framework, ReenactGAN, is depicted in Fig. 2. ReenactGAN can be divided into three components: a boundary encoder, a target-specific many-to-one transformer, and a target-specific decoder. Each component is a feed-forward network. In the test phase, a query face will be forwardly passed through each component. The remainder of this section will be organized as follows: Sect. 3.1 presents the encoder, decoder, and the joint reconstruction loss; Sect. 3.2 describes the boundary latent layer; Sect. 3.3 explains the details of the target-specific many-to-one transformer.

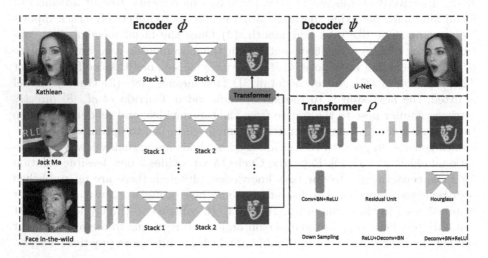

Fig. 2. The framework of ReenactGAN: There are three main components, all of which are feed-forward networks. In the test phase, an encoder ϕ encodes an image x into the boundary space b. A transformer ρ adapts an arbitrary face's boundary into the target's. A decoder ψ decodes the adapted boundary $\rho(b)$ to a target's face t.

3.1   Encoder and Decoder

Our goal is to find a function pair: an encoder $\phi : \mathcal{X} \to \mathcal{B}$ and a target-specific decoder $\psi_{\mathcal{T}} : \mathcal{B} \to \mathcal{X}$, where $\mathcal{X}$ represents faces at the raw pixel space, and $\mathcal{B}$ denotes the boundary space. The encoder maps a face $x \in \mathcal{X}$ into a latent space $b \in \mathcal{B}$. The target-specific decoder decodes a latent boundary b back to a specific person's face $t \in \mathcal{T} \subset \mathcal{X}$. We design our encoder and decoder following the state-of-the-art Pix2Pix approach [15] to synthesize photo-realistic faces. Specifically, we adopt a combined loss widely used in generation tasks [21,30,45]:

$$L(\psi \cdot \phi, \theta) = L_{\text{GAN}}(\psi \cdot \phi, \theta) + L_{\ell_1}(\psi \cdot \phi) + L_{\text{feat}}(\psi \cdot \phi). \tag{1}$$

Without the loss of generality, we denote $\psi_{\mathcal{T}}$ as ψ. The first term L_{GAN} is an adversarial loss, which employs a discriminator θ to distinguish the real sample t

and the reconstructed sample $\psi \cdot \phi(t)$. The second term L_{ℓ_1} is an L1 reconstruction loss. The third term L_{feat} measures the L2 distance between relu2_2 and relu3_3 features of the VGG-16 [31] network. The combination of these three losses is widely used for image reconstruction to generate sharp and realistic outputs. It is noteworthy that our target-specific decoder ψ_T does not forcefully decode B back to the full face space X. Instead, each target-specific decoder only focuses on one target person's face subset T such that high-quality specific-person synthesis can be achieved. This notion is shown in Fig. 3. To achieve this goal, we collect a set of target's faces $\{t_1, \ldots, t_N\} \in T$ during the training stage to train the ψ_T. The encoder ϕ is shared and all $\{\psi.\}$ and ϕ are jointly trained.

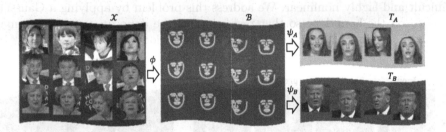

Fig. 3. An illustration of encoding and decoding process: We first encode all faces into a latent boundary space B. Then for each target T, we have a specific-decoder ψ_T to decode latent boundary to the corresponding face $t \in T \subset B$.

The loss in Eq. (1) effectively train the pair of ψ, ϕ, which allows us to map face images into the latent space B, and vice versa. Our next challenge is to bridge the gap between the source boundary space and the target boundary space. We discuss the challenges and our solution in the next section.

3.2 Boundary Latent Space

Recall that Eq. (1) only facilitates the mapping between the pixel space X and latent space B. In this section, we discuss how to design the latent space B. We hope that the latent space could satisfy two properties. Firstly, B should be sensitive to facial expression but less so on identity. In particular, assuming two faces x_1, x_2 with different identities but the same expression, they should be mapped to a nearby location in the the the boundary space B. Secondly, B should encompass rich structural information to support the decoding process for appearance.

To this end, we design the latent space as a stack of K boundary heatmaps, $\{M_i\}_{i=1}^{K}$, each of which represents the contour of a specific facial part, e.g., upper left eyelid and nose bridge. Each heatmap maintains sufficient spatial resolution of 64×64 to retain the structural information of a face. Some examples of heatmaps (projected to a single map for visualization) are shown in Fig. 3. As can be observed, the boundary heatmaps are appealing in that they are not affected by background clutter, lighting, and facial textures. In comparison to the raw pixels space, faces with the same expression are naturally closer to each other in this boundary space.

To constrain the learning of this latent space, during the training of encoder ϕ and decoder ψ, we add a L1 loss between the encoder output, $\phi(x)$, and its associated ground-truth boundary heatmaps $\{M_i\}$. We prepare the ground-truth boundary heatmaps by exploiting existing facial landmark datasets [20,50]. Specifically, each face image is defined with a set of P landmarks represented as $\mathcal{S}$. The subset of landmarks corresponding to the i-th facial part, denoted by $S_i \subset \mathcal{S}$, is firstly interpolated to get a dense boundary line. We then set points on the line to 1 and others as 0. Note that this form of sparse binary heatmap would cause problem since regressing to a single value point at the boundary is difficult and highly nonlinear. We address this problem by applying a Gaussian smooth on the boundary so that regression can be done on a confidence map located in the immediate vicinity of the boundary location.

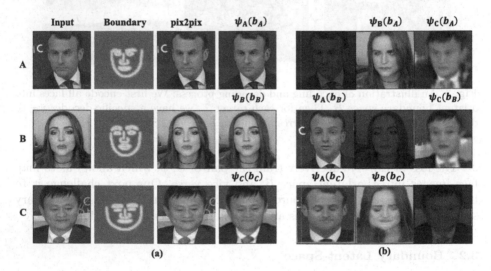

Fig. 4. (a) Face reconstruction with and without boundary latent space. From left to right: 1. Raw image input; 2. Boundary map used for latent supervision; 3. Pix2Pix's reconstruction results without boundary latent space; 4. Reconstruction results with boundary latent space. (b) Face reenactment without boundary transformer. We apply a target-specific decoder using other's boundary as input. Here no adaptation is made on the boundary for a specific target, therefore failures can be seen if face boundaries do not match well with the decoder.

In Fig. 4(a), we compare the reconstruction quality of faces with and without using the boundary latent space. Reconstruction not using the latent space is equivalent to Pix2Pix [15]. As can be seen from the third and fourth columns, introducing boundary latent space do not affect the reconstruction quality, justifying the stability of the learned boundary space. Figure 4(b) shows some preliminary results of applying target-specific decoder, such as ψ of Emmanuel Macron

(A), with boundary heatmaps of Jack Ma (C) or Kathleen (B) as input (see the last row). When two faces share a similar shape, *e.g.*, persons A and B, the reenactment is satisfactory. However, when the face shape differs, a decoder would suffer in decoding a mismatched boundary input causing artifacts in its generated image. The observation motivates the need of the boundary transformer, which we will discuss in the next section.

We wish to point out that facial boundaries are by no means the only medium to serve as the latent space. We believe any medium that could faithfully represent facial expression and movement, yet near-identity-agnostic can be used here. Facial boundaries are chosen here as we have access to public large-scale landmark dataset for constraining the learning of the space. Other medium such as facial expression space and densely annotated coordinates [11,12] is applicable if large datasets are available to constrain the learning of the space.

3.3   Boundary Transformer

As shown in Fig. 4(b), applying a target-specific decoder on the boundary heatmaps of other person may lead to severe artifacts when there is a large structural gap between the face shapes of the source and target. We address this problem through target-specific transformers, ρ_T. The design of ρ_T aims to bridge the gap between an arbitrary people's and the target's boundary space, so as to transfer an arbitrary boundary into a specific target. Formally, it maps $\phi(\mathcal{X})$ to $\phi(\mathcal{T})$.

The learning of this transformer can be formulated in the CycleGAN framework [57] since $\phi(\mathcal{X})$ and $\phi(\mathcal{T})$ are unpaired (they are obtained from videos of different persons). Nevertheless, as shown in Fig. 3, $\mathcal{T}$ is only a subset of $\mathcal{X}$, finding the inverse mapping from $\phi(\mathcal{T})$ to $\phi(\mathcal{X})$ is problematic since the mapping from an arbitrary people to one may exist, but the inverse is a multivalued function that cannot be easily solved by a feed-forward network.

Recall that ρ_T reduce the full set $\mathcal{B}$ to a subset $\mathcal{B}_T$. If we only consider one ρ_T, its inverse is multi-valued, and it is infeasible to establish the cycle consistency. However, if we consider multiple target-transformers at the same time

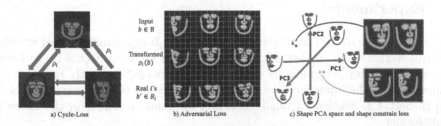

a) Cycle-Loss   b) Adversarial Loss   c) Shape PCA space and shape constrain loss

Fig. 5. Transformer's loss: (a) For each person we maintain a transformer. We enforce all transformers to satisfy the rule of cyclic consistency. (b) For each person we also have a discriminator C_i to predict if a boundary map belongs to him/her. (c) We constrain the input and output of each transformer to be close in PCA subspace.

and modify the cyclic loss of [57], we can circumvent the aforementioned issue. Let's assume that we have several training data of several targets, $\{\mathcal{T}_1, \ldots, \mathcal{T}_N\}$, where $\mathcal{T}_i \subset \mathcal{X}$. For brevity, we denote the image of one target's face in the boundary space $\phi(\mathcal{T}_i)$ as $\mathcal{B}_i \subset \mathcal{B}$. We hope to train a series of transformers, which can transform $\mathcal{B}$ to each $\mathcal{B}_i$. As illustrated in Fig. 5, the loss of for training the transformers consists of three terms:

$$L(\{\rho.\}, \{C.\}) = L_{\text{cycle}} + L_{\text{GAN}} + L_{\text{shape}}, \tag{2}$$

where $\{\rho.\}$ is the set of transformers and $\{C.\}$ is the set of corresponding discriminators in the adversarial learning notion.

The first term is a loss that constrains the cycle consistency. Specifically, we let $b_i \in \mathcal{B}_i$ and we sample an arbitrary transformer ρ_j, where $j \neq i$. With this term we wish to define a loss such that $\rho_j(b_i)$ belongs to $\mathcal{B}_j$ and $\rho_i \cdot \rho_j(b_i)$ equals to b_i. The loss can be written as

$$L_{\text{cycle}} = \mathbb{E}_{i \neq j} \left[\| \rho_i \cdot \rho_j(b_i) - b_i \| \right]. \tag{3}$$

The second term defines the vanilla GAN loss. We train a discriminator C_i for each target person. The responsibility of a discriminator is to distinguish one target's real pose from transformed pseudo poses. The loss is defined as

$$L_{\text{GAN}}(\{\rho.\}, \{C.\}) = \sum_i \left(\mathbb{E}_{b_i \in \mathcal{B}_i} \log C_i(b_i) + \mathbb{E}_{b' \in \mathcal{B}} \log(1 - C_i \cdot \rho_i(b)) \right). \tag{4}$$

The third term is a shape constrain loss that encourages a transformed boundary to better follow its source. The loss is defined between the input and output of a transformer. Specifically, we first use a fully-connected layer to map the shape latent b to a vector. We then compress the vector via PCA and only keep the first M coefficients that capture the rough motion of the head. We denote this linear process as the function R and define the shape constraint loss as

$$L_{\text{shape}} = \mathbb{E}_{b \in \mathcal{B}, i \in 1, \ldots, N} \left[R(b) - R \cdot \rho_i(b) \right]. \tag{5}$$

4   Experiments

We evaluate face reenactment from two aspects: (1) Image quality – after we show the qualitative result in Sect. 4.1, we report a user study in Sect. 4.2. (2) Facial action consistency – to measure if the generated output correctly captures the expressions in the input face, we compare the response of facial action units [7, 25] in Sect. 4.3. Section 4.4 finally provides an ablation study on the losses of transformer.

Celebrity Video Dataset: For $\{\mathcal{T}_1, \ldots, \mathcal{T}_N\}$, we collect five celebrities' videos from YouTube, namely Donald Trump, Emmanuel Macron, Theresa May, Jack Ma and Kathleen. The average length is 30 min. These celebrities have quite different facial characteristics thus the videos are well-suited for robustness evaluation. All of the 200K faces are annotated with 98-landmarks using a semi-automatic methodology, in which each face is annotated by a state-of-the-art facial landmark detection method [50] followed by additional manual correction. The Celebrity Video Dataset (CelebV) are available on our project page.

Boundary Estimation Dataset: We combine two face alignment datasets to generate the ground truth of boundary heatmaps. The first one is WFLW [50] dataset, which provides 10000 photos with 98 annotated landmarks on each face. WFLW dataset enables us to generate 14 contours including nose bridge, right upper eyebrow, left upper eyebrow, *etc.* The second dataset is Helen [20], we use the annotation protocol of Helen [20] for the nose boundary. These two types of protocol are fused and then used to generate the ground truth of boundary heatmaps as discussed in Sect. 3.2. Finally, 15 ground truth boundary heatmaps are obtained for the training of Encoder.

Pre-processing: The faces were detected by Faster R-CNN [29], tracked by KCF tracker [13]. Faces belong to irrelevant people are removed by DeepFace [33] from the training set. Each face was normalized to a mean shape with rigid transformation and cropped to 256×256.

Training Details: Encoder is trained on 7500 faces of WFLW Dataset and then fine-tuned on CelebV Dataset, while Transformer and Decoder are both trained only on CelebV Dataset. Due to the limited space, we report the network architecture and training details in our supplementary material.

4.1   Qualitative Comparisons with State-of-the-arts

We compare ReenactGAN with two state-of-the-art methods. (1) CycleGAN: since there is no commonly accepted CycleGAN-based implementation for face reenactment, we implement our own based on [57]. (2) Face2Face [35]: Face2Face is not open-sourced. Comparisons are thus limited by our attempts to crop images/videos from its released YouTube demo.

Figure 6 compares our method with the two state-of-the-art methods. All three methods work well for frontal faces. By contrast, the proposed method works well on profile faces (Fig. 6(a)), while being more effective in transferring expressions of unseen people to the target (Fig. 6(b)). It is observed that the vanilla CycleGAN performs poorly on hair generation. We believe that this issue may be solved by increasing the power of discriminator [53]. Our method does not suffer from the same problem, by encoding into the boundary latent space, the hair information will be first excluded, then be rendered by the decoder. On the other hand, in contrast to Face2Face that only alters the appearance of inner-face, our model can additionally track the global head pose from the source video (Fig. 6(c)).

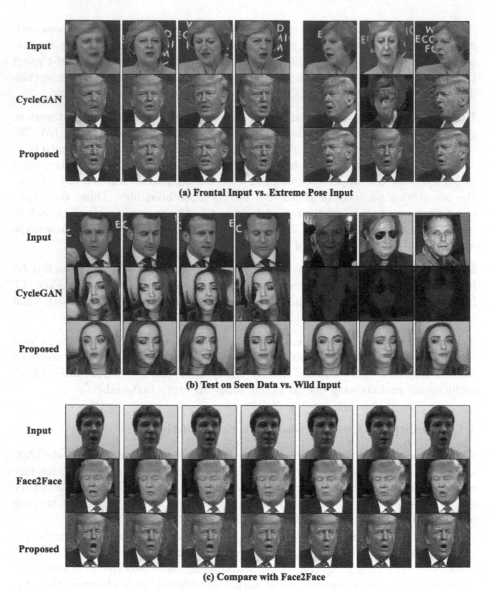

(a) Frontal Input vs. Extreme Pose Input

(b) Test on Seen Data vs. Wild Input

(c) Compare with Face2Face

Fig. 6. Qualitative comparison with state-of-the-arts: We compare ReenactGAN with a GAN-based method - CycleGAN [57] and model-based approach Face2Face [35]. In the second case we tried wild inputs that a model has never seen. Vanilla CycleGAN fails because it only learns the transformation between one source person and one target.

4.2   A User Study on Face Reenactment Quality

We are curious about several questions: does the image has a sound quality, sharp and clear? Does the image contain strange artificial textures? Does the expression of the image look real? We are also interested in another question: during the training of CycleGAN [57], the model has already 'seen' some data. How good does it work on the unseen wild data?

To answer these questions, rather than taking general image quality assessment methods [23,24,46] or perceptual loss [58] for evaluation, we perform a user study since human observation is more direct and reasonable for the validation of perceptual realism. We ask 30 volunteers to compare the quality between two generated photos. Specifically, we follow the protocol presented in [15,55], in which each comparison is limited to 10 seconds. After numerous comparisons, we determine the score of each faces via TrueSkill algorithm [14] (an offline generalization of Elo-Rating). To avoid biases caused by photo contents (*e.g.*, one may perceive a photo that is more attractive as to have a better quality or may consider a frontal face as lower quality), we prepare our comparisons to have the same pose and similar expression.

We measure the quality among seven different settings: (1) Ground Truth, a.k.a $t \in \mathcal{T}$; (2) Reconstruction result of the ground truth, $\psi_{\mathcal{T}} \cdot \phi(t)$; (3) Seen data with ReenactGAN, $\psi_{\mathcal{T}} \cdot \rho_{\mathcal{T}} \cdot \phi(t')$, which $t' \in \mathcal{T}' \neq \mathcal{T}$; (4) Unseen data with ReenactGAN, $\psi_{\mathcal{T}} \cdot \rho_{\mathcal{T}} \cdot \phi(x')$, which $x' \in \mathcal{X}_{Test}$, also x' does not belong to any trained target identity; (5) Seen data without transformer, $\psi_{\mathcal{T}} \cdot \phi(t')$; (6) Unseen data without transformer $\psi_{\mathcal{T}} \cdot \phi(x')$; (7) Seen data with CycleGAN.

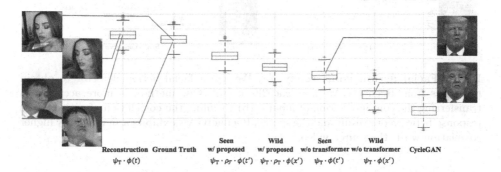

Fig. 7. **User study:** We compare the quality among the real video and 6 different groups of generated result. Then we computing their quality score via TrueSkill and visualize the statistic.

We prepared 180 groups of results for this user study. For each group, we first picked a face in the target set. We then retrieved the most similar pose in-the-wild from both input set and source training set, and generated six results using different models. In each group, the full $C_7^2 = 21$ comparisons were evaluated. Then we used TrueSkill [14] algorithm to compute the score of each image. It is evident from Fig. 7 that the proposed method outperforms CycleGAN in this user study. The transformer plays a crucial role in the reenactment. Unseen wild data will cause a performance drop but ReenactGAN can handle this challenge well. Interestingly, we found that $\psi_{\mathcal{T}} \cdot \phi$ would inpaint the occluded facial part, and thus volunteers sometimes marked the reconstructed result to have a better quality over the ground truth.

4.3   Facial Action Consistency

Besides image quality, we propose an interesting way to measure the effectiveness of face reenactment methods on transferring facial expressions. We borrow the notion of facial action units (AU) [1,17,37,38,42,43,49,56]. Specifically, we train an action unit detector on DISFA [26] dataset, which provides 12 kinds of facial action units. We use 98 facial landmarks as input to train a MLP for each action unit. The reason why we only use facial landmarks as input is to prevent overfitting on this relatively small dataset. The 5-fold cross-validation accuracy is averagely 55.2% on DISFA [26], which is competitive with the state-of-the-art method (58.4% [49], the random guess is 8.3%).

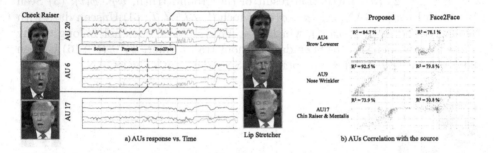

Fig. 8. Facial action consistency: (a) We use a facial action detector to obtain responses from ReenactGAN and Face2Face [35]. Our method is more accurate in transferring the contour motion of mouth. (b) Profiling the correlation of action unit's response between our result and the source, ReenactGAN exhibits a significantly higher correlation w.r.t. the source video.

To compare with Face2Face [35], we first collect its demo video[3] as input, then reenact it to Trump. The result is compared with [35]'s result on Trump. We apply our facial AU detectors on the input video and two resulting videos, respectively from Face2Face and ReenactGAN.

In Fig. 8(a) we show the response of three AUs over the time. Comparing the first two rows, the proposed method exhibits more synchronized response with the source input and yields higher AU scores. We also compute three typical AUs response correlations between the input and each output in Fig. 8(b). ReenactGAN records significantly higher correlations against the baseline. The full comparison will be presented in the supplementary material.

---

[3] https://www.youtube.com/watch?v=ohmajJTcpNk

4.4 Ablation Study on Boundary Transformer

In Sect. 3.2 we mentioned that by merely compose the encoder and a target-specific decoder, $\psi_T \cdot \phi$, one can already roughly reenact a source face to the target, as long as their face shapes adhere. Figure 9(a) provide a more detailed qualitative comparisons on the results with and without the transformer. Without the transformer, decoder sometimes generates blurred (row 2, 4) results or images with severe textural artifacts (row 3).

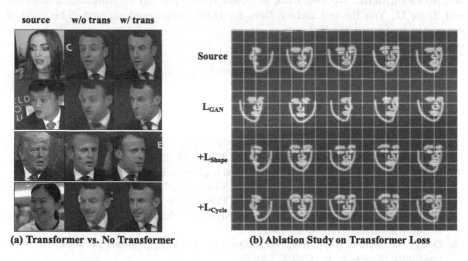

source	w/o trans	w/ trans

(a) Transformer vs. No Transformer   (b) Ablation Study on Transformer Loss

Fig. 9. Ablation study on boundary transformer: (a) Comparing the results of ReenactGAN with and without the transformer. (b) The effect of adding different loss terms to the transformer loss in Eq. (2).

In another experiment, we study the role of each term in the loss function (Eq. (2)). Figure 9(b) shows the adherence of facial boundary given the source, when we sequentially add a loss term to the transformer loss. By adding shape constraint, the transformed poses track the source's pose better than applying the GAN loss alone. By adding the cycle loss, we can further refine the result. A careful inspection of the last two rows reveals that the cycle loss helps to improve the generation of eyes and mouth regions.

5 Conclusion and Discussion

We have presented a learning-based method, ReenactGAN, for photo-realistic face reenactment. Our method is novel in that we take a radically different approach to transfer source person to the target. Specifically, we bridge the source and target domains by introducing a boundary latent space. Our extensive qualitative and quantitative experiments showed that this boundary space is effective to reenact faces with accurate expressions and good quality. The many-to-one transformer also effectively extends the capability of the decoder. The trained model can comfortably handle faces from unseen people. Some improvements are feasible and obvious: (1) We can introduce facial component discriminators to enhance the generation on each facial part. (2) We may compress multiple target's decoders into one network, which is more efficient. (3) It will be interesting to investigate learning-based reenactment between faces of human and non-human (animal or cartoon characters).

Acknowledgment. We would like to thank Kwan-Yee Lin for insightful discussion, and Tong Li, Yue He and Lichen Zhou for their exceptional support. This work is supported by SenseTime Research.

References

1. Bartlett, M.S., Littlewort, G., Frank, M.G., Lainscsek, C., Fasel, I.R., Movellan, J.R.: Automatic recognition of facial actions in spontaneous expressions. J. Multimedia **1**(6), 22–35 (2006)
2. Cao, C., Weng, Y., Lin, S., Zhou, K.: 3D shape regression for real-time facial animation. ACM Trans. Graph. (TOG) **32**(4), 41 (2013)
3. Cheng, Y.T., et al.: 3D-model-based face replacement in video. ACM (2009)
4. Dale, K., Sunkavalli, K., Johnson, M.K., Vlasic, D., Matusik, W., Pfister, H.: Video face replacement. ACM Trans. Graph. (TOG) **30**(6), 1–10 (2011)
5. Deng, J., Trigeorgis, G., Zhou, Y., Zafeiriou, S.: Joint multi-view face alignment in the wild arXiv:1708.06023 (2017)
6. Dong, X., Yan, Y., Ouyang, W., Yang, Y.: Style aggregated network for facial landmark detection. In: CVPR (2018)
7. Ekman, P., Friesen, W., Hager, J.: Facial Action Coding System (FACS): Manual. A Human Face (2002)
8. Garrido, P., Valgaerts, L., Rehmsen, O., Thormahlen, T., Perez, P., Theobalt, C.: Automatic face reenactment. In: CVPR (2014)
9. Garrido, P., et al.: VDub: modifying face video of actors for plausible visual alignment to a dubbed audio track. In: Computer Graphics Forum, vol. 34, pp. 193–204. Wiley Online Library (2015)
10. Goodfellow, I.J., et al.: Generative adversarial networks. In: NIPS, vol. 3, pp. 2672–2680 (2014)
11. Güler, R.A., Neverova, N., Kokkinos, I.: Densepose: Dense human pose estimation in the wild. In: CVPR (2018)
12. Güler, R.A., Trigeorgis, G., Antonakos, E., Snape, P., Zafeiriou, S., Kokkinos, I.: DenseReg: fully convolutional dense shape regression in-the-wild. In: CVPR (2017)
13. Henriques, J.F., Caseiro, R., Martins, P., Batista, J.: High-speed tracking with kernelized correlation filters. IEEE Trans. Pattern Anal. Mach. Intell. (TPAMI) **37**(3), 583–596 (2015)
14. Herbrich, R., Minka, T., Graepel, T.: TrueSkill^{tm}: a bayesian skill rating system. In: NIPS (2006)
15. Isola, P., Zhu, J.Y., Zhou, T., Efros, A.A.: Image-to-image translation with conditional adversarial networks. In: CVPR (2017)
16. Jin, X., Qi, Y., Wu, S.: Cyclegan face-off arXiv:1712.03451 (2017)
17. Kapoor, A., Picard, R.W.: Multimodal affect recognition in learning environments. In: MM (2005)

18. Kim, H., et al.: Deep video portraits. In: SIGGRAPH (2018)
19. Kumar, A., Chellappa, R.: Disentangling 3D pose in a dendritic CNN for uncon-
    strained 2D face alignment. In: CVPR (2018)
20. Le, V., Brandt, J., Lin, Z., Bourdev, L., Huang, T.S.: Interactive facial feature
    localization. In: Fitzgibbon, A., Lazebnik, S., Perona, P., Sato, Y., Schmid, C.
    (eds.) ECCV 2012. LNCS, vol. 7574, pp. 679–692. Springer, Heidelberg (2012).
    https://doi.org/10.1007/978-3-642-33712-3_49
21. Ledig, C., et al.: Photo-realistic single image super-resolution using a generative
    adversarial network. In: CVPR (2017)
22. Li, K., Xu, F., Wang, J., Dai, Q., Liu, Y.: A data-driven approach for facial expres-
    sion synthesis in video. In: CVPR (2012)
23. Lin, K.Y., Wang, G.: Hallucinated-IQA: no-reference image quality assessment via
    adversarial learning. In: CVPR (2018)
24. Lin, K.Y., Wang, G.: Self-supervised deep multiple choice learning network for
    blind image quality assessment. In: BMVC (2018)
25. Mahoor, M.H., Cadavid, S., Messinger, D.S., Cohn, J.F.: A framework for auto-
    mated measurement of the intensity of non-posed facial action units. In: CVPR
    (2009)
26. Mavadati, S.M., Mahoor, M.H., Bartlett, K., Trinh, P., Cohn, J.F.: DISFA: a spon-
    taneous facial action intensity database. IEEE Trans. Affect. Comput. (TAC) 4(2),
    151–160 (2013)
27. Mueller, F., et al.: GANerated hands for real-time 3D hand tracking from monoc-
    ular RGB. In: CVPR (2018)
28. Nguyen, A., Yosinski, J., Bengio, Y., Dosovitskiy, A., Clune, J.: Plug & play
    generative networks: conditional iterative generation of images in latent space
    arXiv:1612.00005 (2016)
29. Ren, S., He, K., Girshick, R.B., Sun, J.: Faster R-CNN: towards real-time object
    detection with region proposal networks. In: NIPS (2015)
30. Sajjadi, M.S.M., Scholkopf, B., Hirsch, M.: Enhancenet: single image super-
    resolution through automated texture synthesis. In: ICCV (2017)
31. Simonyan, K., Zisserman, A.: Very deep convolutional networks for large-scale
    image recognition, vol. abs/1409.1556 (2014)
32. Suwajanakorn, S., Seitz, S.M., Kemelmacher-Shlizerman, I.: What makes tom
    hanks look like tom hanks. In: ICCV (2015)
33. Taigman, Y., Yang, M., Ranzato, M., Wolf, L.: DeepFace: closing the gap to human-
    level performance in face verification. In: CVPR (2014)
34. Thies, J., Zollhöfer, M., Nießner, M., Valgaerts, L., Stamminger, M., Theobalt, C.:
    Real-time expression transfer for facial reenactment. ACM Trans. Graph. (TOG)
    34(6), 183 (2015)
35. Thies, J., Zollhöfer, M., Stamminger, M., Theobalt, C., Nießner, M.: Face2Face:
    real-time face capture and reenactment of RGB videos. In: CVPR (2016)
36. Thies, J., Zollhöfer, M., Stamminger, M., Theobalt, C., Nießner, M.: Facevr:
    Real-time facial reenactment and eye gaze control in virtual reality. CoRR
    abs/1610.03151 (2016)
37. Tong, Y., Liao, W., Ji, Q.: Facial action unit recognition by exploiting their
    dynamic and semantic relationships. IEEE Trans. Pattern Anal. Mach. Intell.
    (TPAMI) 29(10), 1683–1699 (2007)
38. Tran, D.L., Walecki, R., Rudovic, O., Eleftheriadis, S., Schuller, B.W., Pantic, M.:
    Deepcoder: semi-parametric variational autoencoders for automatic facial action
    coding. In: ICCV (2017)

39. Trigeorgis, G., Snape, P., Nicolaou, M.A., Antonakos, E., Zafeiriou, S.: Mnemonic descent method: a recurrent process applied for end-to-end face alignment. In: CVPR (2016)
40. Upchurch, P., Gardner, J., Bala, K., Pless, R., Snavely, N., Weinberger, K.Q.: Deep feature interpolation for image content changes. arXiv:1611.05507 (2016)
41. Vlasic, D., Brand, M., Pfister, H., Popović, J.: Face transfer with multilinear models. ACM Trans. Graph. (TOG) 24(3), 426–433 (2005)
42. Walecki, R., Rudovic, O., Pavlovic, V., Pantic, M.: Copula ordinal regression for joint estimation of facial action unit intensity. In: CVPR (2016)
43. Walecki, R., Rudovic, O., Pavlovic, V., Schuller, B.W., Pantic, M.: Deep structured learning for facial action unit intensity estimation. In: CVPR (2017)
44. Wang, C., Shi, F., Xia, S., Chai, J.: Realtime 3D eye gaze animation using a single RGB camera. ACM Trans. Graph. (TOG) 35(4), 118 (2016)
45. Wang, T., Liu, M., Zhu, J., Tao, A., Kautz, J., Catanzaro, B.: High-resolution image synthesis and semantic manipulation with conditional GANs. In: CVPR (2018)
46. Wang, Z., Bovik, A.C., Sheikh, H.R., Simoncelli, E.P.: Image quality assessment: from error visibility to structural similarity. IEEE Trans. Image Process. (TIP) 13(4), 600–612 (2004)
47. Wei, T.: Cyclegan face-off (2017). https://www.youtube.com/watch?v=Fea4k Zq0oFQ
48. Wu, C., et al.: Model-based teeth reconstruction. ACM Trans. Graph. (TOG) 35(6), 220 (2016)
49. Wu, S., Wang, S., Pan, B., Ji, Q.: Deep facial action unit recognition from partially labeled data. In: ICCV (2017)
50. Wu, W., Qian, C., Yang, S., Wang, Q., Cai, Y., Zhou, Q.: Look at boundary: a boundary-aware face alignment algorithm. In: CVPR (2018)
51. Wu, W., Yang, S.: Leveraging intra and inter-dataset variations for robust face alignment. In: CVPR Workshop (2017)
52. Xiao, S., Feng, J., Xing, J., Lai, H., Yan, S., Kassim, A.: Robust facial landmark detection via recurrent attentive-refinement networks. In: Leibe, B., Matas, J., Sebe, N., Welling, M. (eds.) ECCV 2016. LNCS, vol. 9905, pp. 57–72. Springer, Cham (2016). https://doi.org/10.1007/978-3-319-46448-0_4
53. Xu, R., Zhou, Z., Zhang, W., Yu, Y.: Face transfer with generative adversarial network arXiv:1710.06090 (2017)
54. Zhang, H., et al.: StackGAN: text to photo-realistic image synthesis with stacked generative adversarial networks. In: ICCV (2017)
55. Zhang, Y., Liu, L., Li, C., Loy, C.C.: Quantifying facial age by posterior of age comparisons. In: BMVC (2017)
56. Zhao, K., Chu, W., Zhang, H.: Deep region and multi-label learning for facial action unit detection. In: CVPR (2016)
57. Zhu, J.Y., Park, T., Isola, P., Efros, A.A.: Unpaired image-to-image translation using cycle-consistent adversarial networkss. In: ICCV (2017)
58. Zhu, J., et al.: Toward multimodal image-to-image translation. In: NIPS (2017)
59. Zhu, S., Fidler, S., Urtasun, R., Lin, D., Loy, C.C.: Be your own Prada: fashion synthesis with structural coherence. In: ICCV (2017)
60. Zhu, S., Li, C., Change Loy, C., Tang, X.: Face alignment by coarse-to-fine shape searching. In: CVPR (2015)
61. Zhu, S., Li, C., Loy, C.C., Tang, X.: Unconstrained face alignment via cascaded compositional learning. In: CVPR (2016)

Learning to Anonymize Faces for Privacy Preserving Action Detection

Zhongzheng Ren[1,2]($\boxtimes$) (ID), Yong Jae Lee[1,2] (ID), and Michael S. Ryoo[1] (ID)

[1] EgoVid Inc., Daejeon, South Korea
mryoo@egovid.com
[2] University of California, Davis, Davis, USA
{zzren,yongjaelee}@ucdavis.edu

Abstract. There is an increasing concern in computer vision devices invading users' privacy by recording unwanted videos. On the one hand, we want the camera systems to recognize important events and assist human daily lives by understanding its videos, but on the other hand we want to ensure that they do not intrude people's privacy. In this paper, we propose a new principled approach for learning a video *face anonymizer*. We use an adversarial training setting in which two competing systems fight: (1) a video anonymizer that modifies the original video to remove privacy-sensitive information while still trying to maximize spatial action detection performance, and (2) a discriminator that tries to extract privacy-sensitive information from the anonymized videos. The end result is a video anonymizer that performs pixel-level modifications to anonymize each person's face, with minimal effect on action detection performance. We experimentally confirm the benefits of our approach compared to conventional hand-crafted anonymization methods including masking, blurring, and noise adding. Code, demo, and more results can be found on our project page https://jason718.github.io/project/privacy/main.html.

1 Introduction

Computer vision technology is enabling automatic understanding of large-scale visual data and is becoming a crucial component of many societal applications with ubiquitous cameras. For instance, cities are adopting networked camera systems for policing and intelligent resource allocation, individuals are recording their lives using wearable devices, and service robots at homes and public places are becoming increasingly popular.

Simultaneously, there is an increasing concern in these systems invading the privacy of their users; in particular, from unwanted video recording. On the one hand, we want the camera systems to recognize important events and assist human daily lives by understanding its videos, but on the other hand we want to ensure that they do not intrude the people's privacy. Most computer vision algorithms require loading high resolution images/videos that can contain privacy-sensitive data to CPU/GPU memory to enable visual recognition. They sometimes even require network access to high computing power servers,

© Springer Nature Switzerland AG 2018
V. Ferrari et al. (Eds.): ECCV 2018, LNCS 11205, pp. 639–655, 2018.
https://doi.org/10.1007/978-3-030-01246-5_38

Identity: Alex   Identity: ???
Action: Brush Teeth   Action: Brush Teeth

Fig. 1. Imagine the following scenario: you would like a personal assistant that can alert you when your adorable child Alex performs undesirable actions, such as eating mom's make-up or drinking dirty water out of curiosity. However, you do not want your personal assistant to record Alex's face, because you are concerned about his privacy information since the camera could potentially be hacked. Ideally, we would like a face anonymizer that can preserve Alex's privacy (i.e., make his face no longer recognizable as Alex) while at the same time unaltering his actions. In this paper, our goal is to create such a system. (Real experimental results.)

sending potentially privacy-sensitive images/videos. All these create a potential risk of one's private visual data being snatched by someone else. In the worst case, the users are under the risk of being monitored by a hacker if their cameras/robots at home are cracked. There can also be hidden backdoors installed by the manufacturer, guaranteeing their access to cameras at one's home.

To address these concerns, we need a principled way to 'anonymize' one's videos. Existing anonymization methods include extreme downsampling [38] or image masking, as well as more advanced image processing techniques using image segmentation [4]. Although such techniques remove scene details in the images/videos in an attempt to protect privacy, they are based on heuristics rather than being learned, and there is no guarantee that they are optimal for privacy-protection. Moreover, they can hurt the ensuing visual recognition performance due to loss of information [38]. Thus, a key challenge is creating an approach that can simultaneously anonymize videos, while ensuring that the anonymization does not negatively affect recognition performance; see Fig. 1.

In this paper, we propose a novel principled approach for *learning* the video anonymizer. We use an adversarial training strategy; i.e., we model the learning process as a fight between two competing systems: (1) a video anonymizer that modifies the original video to remove privacy-sensitive information while preserving scene understanding performance, and (2) a discriminator that extracts privacy-sensitive information from such anonymized videos. We use human face identity as the representative private information—since face is one of the strongest cues to infer a person's identity—and use action detection as the representative scene understanding task.

To implement our idea, we use a multi-task extension of the generative adversarial network (GAN) [11] formulation. Our face anonymizer serves as the generator and modifies the face pixels in video frames to minimize face identification accuracy. Our face identifier serves as the discriminator, and tries to maximize face identification accuracy in spite of the modifications. The activity detection model serves as another component to favor modifications that lead to maximal activity detection. We experimentally confirm the benefits of our approach for privacy-preserving action detection on the DALY [52] and JHMDB [19] datasets compared to conventional hand-crafted anonymization methods including masking, blurring, and noise adding.

Finally, although outside the scope of this work, the idea is that once we have the learned anonymizer, we could apply it to various applications including surveillance, smart-home cameras, and robots, by designing an embedded chipset responsible for the anonymization at the hardware-level. This would allow the images/videos to lose the identity information before they get loaded to the processors or sent to the network for recognition.

2   Related Work

Privacy-Preserving Recognition. There are very few research studies on human action recognition that preserve identity information. The objective is to remove the identity information of people appearing in 'testing' videos (which is a bit different from protecting privacy of people in training data [1,57]), while still enabling reliable recognition from such identity-removed videos.

Ryoo *et al.* [38] worked on learning of efficient low resolution video transforms to classify actions from extreme low resolution videos. Chen *et al.* [7] extended [50] for low resolution videos, designing a two-stream version of it. Ryoo *et al.* [37] further studied the method of learning a better representation space for such very low resolution (e.g., 16×12) videos. All these previous works relied on video downsampling techniques which are hand-crafted and thus not guaranteed to be optimal for privacy-preserving action recognition. Indeed, the low resolution recognition performances of these works were much lower than the state-of-the-art on high resolution videos, particularly for large-scale video datasets. Jourabloo *et al.* [21] de-identify faces while preserving facial attributes by fusing faces with similar attributes. It achieves impressive results on grayscale facial pictures with attribute annotations. However, it is specific to the facial attribute setting and is not applicable to more general privacy-sensitive tasks such as action recognition.

Action Detection. Action recognition has a long research history [2]. In the past several years, CNN models have obtained particularly successful results. This includes two-stream CNNs [8,43] and 3-D XYT convolutional models [6,47] for action classification, as well as models for temporal action detection [33,42].

Our paper is related to spatial action detection from videos, which is the task of localizing actions (with bounding boxes) in each video frame and categorizing them. Recent state-of-the-art spatial action detectors are modified from object detection CNNs models. Gkioxari and Malik [10] extend the R-CNN [9] framework to a two-stream variant which takes RGB and flow as input. Wein-zaepfel *et al.* [51] improved this method by introducing tracking-by-detection to get temporal results. Two-stream Faster R-CNN [35] was then introduced by [32,39]. Singh *et al.* [44] modified the SSD [25] detector to achieve real-time action localization. In this work, we use Faster RCNN [35] as our frame-level action detector.

Face Recognition. Face recognition is a well-studied problem [23,59]. Recent deep learning methods and large-scale annotated datasets have dramatically increased the performance on this task [26,27,41,45,46,53]. Some approaches treat it as a multi-class classification problem and use a vanilla softmax function [45,46]. Wen *et al.* [53] introduce the "center loss" and combine it with the softmax loss to jointly minimize intra-class feature distance while maximizing inter-class distance. The state-of-the-art approach of [41] uses the triplet loss with hard instance mining but it requires 200 millions training images. Recent work [26,27] demonstrate strong performance by combining metric learning with classification. In this work, we use [26] as our face recognition module.

Network Attacking. Our work is also closely related to the problem of network attacking. Existing CNN based classifiers are easily fooled [5,12,28,30,54] even when the input images are perturbed in an unnoticeable way to human eyes. Correspondingly, there is also a line of work studying defense methods [12,31,55]. Our work is similar to network attacking methods since our modified images need to attack a face identifier. However, the difference is that we want to dramatically change the content, so that the identity is unrecognizable (even for humans), while also optimizing it for action recognition.

Generative Adversarial Networks (GANs). GANs [11] have been proposed to generate realistic images in an unsupervised manner. Since then, numerous works [3,34,40] have studied ways to improve training of GANs to generate high-quality and high-resolution images. It is currently the most dominant generative model and the key to its success is the adversarial loss, which forces the generated data distribution to be indistinguishable from the real one. GANs have been generalized and applied to various vision tasks such as image-to-image translation [16], super resolution [24], domain adaptation [36], and object detection [49]. Recent work uses GANs to suppress user information in video features for privacy [17], but it only focused on feature extraction without considering modification of actual pixels in image data. In this paper, we extend the GAN formulation to learn an explicit *face modifier* to anonymize each person's face without hurting action detection performance. Also, compared to image-to-image translation, style transfer, and domain adaptation works, our network does not require a target domain to borrow the visual style or content from.

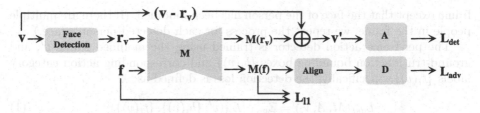

Fig. 2. Our network architecture for privacy-preserving action detection. We simultaneously train a face modifier M whose job is to alter the input face (f or r_v) so that its identity no longer matches that of the true identity, and an action detector A whose job is to learn to accurately detect actions in videos in spite of the modifications. The face classifier D acts as an adversary and ensures that the modified face is non-trivial. See text for details. (Gray blobs are not learned during training.)

3 Approach

Given a set of training videos V and face images F, our goal is to learn a face modifier that anonymizes each person in the video frames and images (i.e., so that they cannot be correctly recognized by a face recognition system) while simultaneously training an action detector that can detect each person's action in spite of the modification. We formulate the problem as a multi-task learning objective. The overall framework is depicted in Fig. 2. There are three major learnable components: the modifier M which takes a face image as input and anonymizes it, an action detector A which detects the actions of the people in each video frame, and a face classifier D that classifies the identity of each face.

There are two main advantages in using both videos and images for training. First, we can leverage existing large-scale labeled face datasets to learn identity information. Second, we can train our model on action detection datasets that do not have any identity annotations. In other words, we do not need to create a new specific dataset to train our model, but instead can leverage the (disparate) datasets that were created for face recognition and action detection without any additional annotations.

We next introduce the loss functions and then explain the training procedure. The implementation details are given at the end.

3.1 Formulation

Our loss for training the model consists of three parts: an adversarial classification loss for identity modification; an action detection loss for training the action detector; and an L1 loss to encourage each generated image to preserve as much structure (pose, brightness, etc.) of the original unmodified face as possible.

Action Detection Loss. Given an input frame from video dataset $v \in V$, we first apply a face detector to get face region r_v. We then feed r_v into the modifier M and replace r_v with the resulting modified image $M(r_v)$ in the original frame to get $v' = v - r_v + M(r_v)$. In other words, the frame is identical to the original frame except that the face of the person has been modified. (If there are multiple people in the frame, we repeat the process for each detected person's face.)

The per-frame action detector is trained using the modified frame v', and ground-truth action bounding boxes $\{b_i(v)\}$ and corresponding action category labels $\{t_i(v)\}$. Specifically, the detection loss is defined as:

$$L_{det}(M, A, V) = \mathbb{E}_{v \sim V}[L_A(v', \{b_i(v)\}, \{t_i(v)\})] \tag{1}$$

where L_A is the sum of the four losses in Faster-RCNN [36]: RPN classification and regression, and Fast-RCNN classification and regression. We choose Faster-RCNN as it is one of the state-of-the-art object detection frameworks that has previously been used for spatial action detection successfully (e.g., [32,39]).

Adversarial Classification. Using a state-of-the-art face classifier, we can easily achieve high face verification accuracy [26,27]. In particular, we use the face classifier formulation of [26] to be the target discriminator for our setting. In order to fool it, our modifier M needs to generate a very different-looking person. Simultaneously, the face classifier D should continuously be optimized with respect to the anonymized faces $M(f)$, so that it can correctly identify the face despite any modifications. Our D is initialized with pre-trained parameters learned from large-scale face datasets.

We use an adversarial loss to model this two-player game [11]. Specifically, during training, we take turns updating M and D. Here, we denote the input image from the face dataset as $f \in F$ and the corresponding identity label as $i_f \in I$. The loss is expressed as:

$$L_{adv}(M, D, F) = -\mathbb{E}_{(f \sim F, i_f \sim I)}[L_D(M(f), i_f)] - \mathbb{E}_{(f \sim F, i_f \sim I)}[L_D(f, i_f)]. \tag{2}$$

Here the classification loss L_D is the angular softmax loss [26], which has been shown to be better than vanilla softmax via its incorporation of a metric learning objective. When updating M this loss is minimized, while when updating D it is maximized. This simultaneously enforces a good modifier to be learned that can fool the face classifier (i.e., make it classify the modified face with the wrong identity), while the face classifier also becomes more robust in dealing with the modifications to correctly classify the face despite the modifications. Furthermore, we optimize D for face classification using both the modified images $M(f)$ and the original images f. We find that this leads to the modifier producing faces that look very different from the original faces, as we show in the experiments.

Photorealistic Loss. We use an L1 loss to encourage the modified image to preserve the basic structure (pose, brightness, etc.) of the original picture. The L1 loss was previously used in image translation work [16,60] to force visual similarity between a generated image and the input image. Although this loss does not directly contribute to our goal of privacy-preserving action detection, we add it because we want the modified image to retain enough scene/action information that can also be recognizable by a human observer. At the same time since we want to ensure enough modification so that the person's identity

Algorithm 1. Privacy Preserving Action Detection

Input: Video frames V and action labels; Face images F and identity labels; Face classifier D; Training iteration T_1, T_2

Output: Face modifier M; Privacy preserving action detector A

1: **for** $t = 1$ to T_1 **do**
2:      $M(f) \rightarrow f'$ // Face modification
3:      $\arg\max_D L_{adv}(M, D, F)$ // Update D
4:      $det\_face(v) \rightarrow r_v$ // Face detection
5:      **if** $\#faces\_in\_frame > 0$ // Video frame modification
6:          $M(r_v) \rightarrow r'_v, (v - r_v) + r'_v \rightarrow v'$
7:      **else**   // No Faces to modify
8:          $v \rightarrow v'$
9:      $\arg\min_{M,A} L_{det}(M, A, V) + L_{adv}(M, D, F) + \lambda L_{l1}(M, F)$ // Update M, A
10: **for** $\tau = 1$ to T_2 **do**
11:      $\arg\min_A L_{det}(M, A, V)$ // Freeze M, D; Update A

is no longer recognizable, we use a weight λ and set its value to be relatively small to avoid making the modified image look too similar to the original one:

$$L_{l1}(M, F) = \mathbb{E}_{f \sim F}[\lambda \|M(f) - f\|_1] \tag{3}$$

Full Objective. Our full objective is:

$$L(M, D, A, V, F) = L_{det}(M, A, V) + L_{adv}(M, D, F) + L_{l1}(M, F) \tag{4}$$

We aim to solve:

$$\arg\min_{M,A} \max_D L(M, D, A, V, F) \tag{5}$$

Our algorithm's pseudo code for learning is shown in Algorithm 1. There are two things to note: (1) if there are no frontal faces in a frame (due to occlusion or if the person is facing away from the camera), we use the original, unmodified frame to train the action detector; (2) During training, we update the face classifier, modifier, and action detector iteratively. Therefore, the input image to the action detector keeps changing, which can make its optimization difficult and unstable. To overcome this, once the loss terms for the modifier and face classifier converge, we fix the modifier and face classifier and only fine-tune the action detector. A similar training procedure is used for our baseline approaches in Sect. 5, with the only difference being the modification procedure.

4   Implementation

Face Detection. We use SSH [29] face detector to detect faces in our video dataset, which produces high recall but with some false positives. Therefore, we keep the detections with probability greater than 0.8 and feed the rest into the MTCNN [58] face detector to remove false positives by using it as a binary classifier. After these two steps, we get a clean and highly-accurate set of face bounding boxes.

Face Modification. We adapt the architecture for our modifier from Johnson *et al.* [20], which has demonstrated impressive image translation performance on various datasets by Zhu *et al.* [60]. We use the 9 residual blocks network and instance normalization [48]. The input images are upsampled or sampled to 256 × 256 via bilinear interpolation.

Spatial Action Detection. We use Faster-RCNN [35] with ResNet-101 [14] as the backbone network for action detection and train it end-to-end. Images are resized so that the shorter length is 340 pixels for JHMDB and 600 × 800 pixels for DALY following Gu *et al.* [13].

Face Identity Classification. We use the SphereFace-20 [26] network, which combines metric learning and classification to learn a discriminative identity classifier. We use the CASIA-WebFace pretrained [56] model for initialization. The input face images are aligned and cropped using facial keypoints. We use a differentiable non-parametric grid generator and sampler for cropping (similar to the warping procedure in Spatial Transformer Networks [18] except there are no learnable parameters) to make our whole network end-to-end trainable.

Training Details. We use the Adam solver [22], with momentum parameters $\beta_1 = 0.5$, $\beta_2 = 0.999$. A learning rate of 0.001 for Faster RCNN, 0.0003 for face modifier and face classifier. We train the entire network for 12 epochs and drop the learning rate by $\frac{1}{10}$ after the seventh epoch.

5   Results

In this section, we first provide details on the evaluation metrics and datasets, and then explain the baseline methods. We then evaluate our method's performance both quantitatively and qualitatively. In addition, we conduct a user study to verify whether the modified photos can fool human subjects. Finally, we perform ablation studies to dissect the contribution of each model component.

5.1   Metrics and Datasets

Action Detection. We measure detection performance using the standard mean Average Precision (mAP) metric. The IoU threshold δ is set to 0.5 when measuring spatial localization. We use two datasets: DALY [52] and JHMDB (split1) [19], as they contain a number of actions that involve the face area and thus are good testbeds for our joint face anonymization and action detection model. For example, some of the action classes have similar body movement and hand motions near the head (taking photos, phoning, brushing hair) or mouth (drinking, brushing teeth, playing harmonica, applying make up on lips).

Face Recognition. Following previous works [26,27], we measure face recognition performance by training our model on face classification and evaluating on binary face verification. CASIA-WebFace [56] is used for training and the input images are aligned and cropped using the facial keypoints estimated by MTCNN [58]. During testing, we extract the features after the last fully-connected layer and then compute cosine similarity for face verification on LFW [15], one of the most popular face datasets for this task. Note that here our motivation is not to create a new face recognition model but rather to use an established method as an adversary for our adversarial setting.

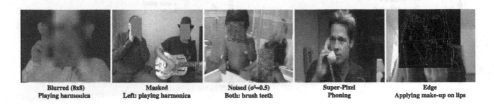

| Blurred (8x8) | Masked | Noised (σ^2=0.5) | Super-Pixel | Edge |
| Playing harmonica | Left: playing harmonica | Both: brush teeth | Phoning | Applying make-up on lips |

Fig. 3. Baseline modification examples. Although these methods largely conceal the true identity, they can also be detrimental to action detection performance especially if the action involves the facial region. (Zoom in for details, better viewed in pdf.)

5.2   Baselines

One straightforward and brute force solution to address privacy concerns is to detect faces and modify them using simple image processing methods such as blurring, masking, and additive noise, etc. To explore whether they are viable solutions, we use several of them as our baselines and evaluate their performance on both action detection and face recognition. For action detection, the detected face boxes are enlarged by 1.6× to ensure that they include most of the head region, and then are modified. This enlargement also helps the video face region r_v be more similar to the face image f, which has some background context (see examples in Fig. 5 top).

We want to ensure that the baseline face anonymization methods are strong enough to preserve privacy (i.e., make the original face identity unrecognizable to humans). With this motivation, we implemented the following methods: (1) **Un-anonymized**: no protection is applied; (2) **Blur**: following Ryoo et al. [38], we downsample the face region to extreme low-resolution ($8 \times 8, 16 \times 16, 24 \times 24$) and then upsample back; (3) **Masked**: the faces are masked out; (4) **Noise**: strong Gaussian noise is added ($\sigma^2 = 0.1, 0.3, 0.5$); (5) **Super-pixel**: following [4], we use superpixels and replace each pixel's RGB value with its superpixel's mean RGB value; (6) **Edge**: following [4], face regions are replaced by their corresponding edge map. Example modifications are shown in Fig. 3.

Figure 4 shows action detection accuracy (y-axis) vs. face verification error (x-axis) for the baselines, with JHMDB results on left and DALY results on right. As expected, the baselines greatly increase face recognition error (and thus improving anonymization) compared to the original un-anonymized frames. However, at the same time, they also harm action detection performance on both DALY and JHMDB. These results indicate that simple image processing methods are double-edged swords; although they may be able to protect privacy (to varying degrees), the protection comes with the negative consequence of poor action recognition performance.

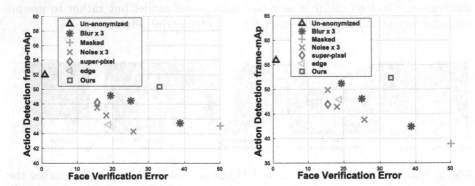

Fig. 4. x-axis is face verification error and y-axis is action detection mAP. The closer a model's performance is to the top-right corner, the better. **Left:** JHMDB; **Right:** DALY. (Color figure online)

5.3   Quantitative Results

Overall Performance. Fig. 4 also shows ours results indicated by the **red square** maker. Our method simultaneously optimizes on both tasks and achieves better results compared to the baselines. As two extreme one-sided solutions, the 'Un-anonymized' (top-left) and 'Masked' (bottom-right) baselines can only address either action detection or face verification. Our action detection results are significantly better than others while being quite close to the un-anonymized detection results. For face verification, our method is only worse than two baselines (8 × 8 down-sampling and masking) but outperforms the others.

Per Class Accuracy. As described earlier, there are certain actions that are more influenced by face modification. Therefore, we next investigate per-class detection results to closely analyze such cases. As shown in Table 1, we find that our model boosts action detection accuracy with a bigger margin compared to the baselines if the actions are 'drinking', 'phoning', 'playing harmonica', and 'taking photos or videos'. This result makes sense since these actions involve the face areas and our approach best preserves the original pictures' semantics. Our model only marginally improves over or performs worse for 'cleaning floor', 'cleaning windows', 'ironing' because these actions have almost nothing to do with faces. Overall, these results indicate that our model modifies each face in a way that ensures high action detection performance.

Table 1. Action detection accuracy on DALY. 'Lip', 'Brush', 'Floor', 'Window', 'Drink', 'Fold', 'Iron', 'Phone', 'Harmonica', 'Photo', denote category 'applying make-up on lips', 'brushing teeth', 'cleaning floor', 'cleaning windows', 'drinking', 'folding textile', 'ironing', 'phoning', 'playing harmonica', 'taking photos or videos'.

Action	Lip	Brush	Floor	Window	Drink	Fold	Iron	Phone	Harmonica	Photo	mAP
Un-anonymized	92.30	51.26	76.73	27.87	31.23	32.67	75.30	51.50	73.91	55.74	56.85
Blur(8 × 8)	84.31	17.87	79.39	27.77	6.60	28.68	71.69	28.40	31.13	48.09	42.39
Blur(16 × 16)	82.07	32.40	79.53	32.14	10.74	31.35	74.91	36.97	48.37	52.51	48.10
Blur(24 × 24)	**92.08**	**39.84**	79.93	31.77	15.23	34.96	74.65	46.33	51.78	53.09	51.97
Noise($\sigma^2 = 0.1$)	87.71	31.37	78.41	31.87	12.41	34.80	76.50	42.37	50.14	53.48	49.91
Noise($\sigma^2 = 0.3$)	87.64	24.98	78.59	**32.68**	8.34	35.33	74.96	40.12	36.01	45.42	46.47
Noise($\sigma^2 = 0.5$)	83.63	21.45	**81.32**	29.59	7.43	29.08	77.97	33.93	27.35	46.35	43.81
Masked	67.06	15.19	78.86	26.58	6.59	25.53	72.95	27.79	21.32	46.76	38.86
Edge	80.30	29.46	78.02	30.51	10.31	32.64	**79.15**	35.15	54.69	49.62	47.99
Super-pixel	79.47	26.09	80.82	32.22	11.46	**35.29**	77.70	30.30	42.18	53.68	46.92
Ours	89.20	33.08	77.12	32.56	**22.93**	33.86	77.07	**46.52**	**55.32**	**55.54**	**52.32**

5.4 Qualitative Results

Same picture before and after modification. We next show examples of pictures before and after modification in Fig. 5. The first four rows show images from the face dataset, while the bottom two rows show images from the video dataset. Overall, we can see that our modifier generates realistic pictures that change the person's identity. Importantly, the basic structure (pose, clothing, background) and the actions (brushing teeth, playing harmonica, putting makeup on lips) are preserved, showing the contribution of the $L1$ and action detection losses.

To change the person's identity, our network tends to focus more on local details. For example, in the first row, our model changes the gender; in the third row, the hair style (baldness and color) is changed; in the fourth row, facial details like nose, eye glasses, and eyebrow get modified. We can make the same observation for the video frame results: the two teeth brushing teenagers become older; the ethnicity of the woman who is putting makeup on her lips changes.

Different modified pictures of the same person. Here we explore how our model modifies different face images of the same person. This is to answer whether our model first recognizes the person and then systematically changes his/her identity, or whether it changes the identity in a more stochastic manner.

Figure 6 shows the results. The set of original images (prior to modification; not shown here) in each row all have the same identity. The first four rows show modified images of: Jackie Chan, Leonardo DiCaprio, Serena Williams, and Vladimir Putin. The bottom two rows show different modified frames of the same person in the same video. Given the consistency in the modifications for the same person (i.e., the modified faces look similar), it appears that our model is recognizing the identity of the person and systematically modifying it to generate a new identity. This result is surprising because there is nothing in our objective that forces the model to do this; one hypothesis is that this happens

Fig. 5. The same image before and after anonymization. The picture on the left of each pair is the original image, and the one on the right is the modified image. The first four rows are from the face dataset; the bottom two are from the video dataset.

because we are using gradient ascent to maximize face classification error and it is an easier optimization to reshape the face identity manifold in a systematic way compared to perturbing each face instance separately.

5.5   User Study

We conducted a very simple user study to investigate how well our modifier can fool humans. We designed three questions: (Q1) We sample a pair of modified images from the testing set and ask our subjects whether the pair corresponds to

Fig. 6. Anonymized images. Top: different modified pictures of the same person; Bottom: different modified frames in the same video.

the same person. We collect 12 positive pairs and 12 negative pairs. (Q2) We use our model to modify 16 famous celebrities in LFW (who are not in our training data) and ask our subjects to name them or say 'no idea'. (Q3) We display a set of modified images, and ask our subjects if they think this technology is good enough to protect their own privacy.

In total, we collected 400 answers from 10 different subjects. The overall accuracy for Q1 is 53.3%, which is close to random guessing (50%). For Q2, among the celebrities they know, our subjects could only name 19.75% of them correctly based on the modified images. Finally for Q3, all subjects except 2 responded that they felt their identity information would be protected if they were to use this technology.

5.6   Ablation Study

Does the face classifier remain accurate? During the training process, we observed that the generator (i.e., modifier) tends to "win" over the discriminator (i.e., face classifier). This raises the concern that our face classifier may no longer be robust enough to correctly classify an unmodified face. To answer this, we take the trained face classifier and evaluate it on the original un-anonymized LFW faces. The classifier's features produce 94.75% verification accuracy. On modified LFW faces, they only achieve 66.95%. This shows that the classifier can still accurately recognize the original faces despite being "fooled" by the modified faces.

Gradient ascent or use random label when optimizing M? Inspired by existing network attacking works [5,12,28,30,54], we can also optimize our modifier so that it fools the classifier to classify the modified image as a random face category. (In our approach, as shown in Algorithm 1, we instead perform gradient ascent to maximize classification loss.) In practice, we find that random negative sample optimization produces much worse results where the resulting generated faces have obvious artifacts and lose too much detail.

One possible explanation for this is that the optimization for this baseline is much harder compared to gradient ascent (i.e., maximizing classification error for the correct identity). Here, the optimization target keeps changing randomly during training, which leads to the entire network suffering from mode collapse. Thus, it simply produces a consistent blur regardless of the original identity. In contrast, gradient ascent makes the modified image still look like a face, only with a different identity.

6   Conclusion

We presented a novel approach to learn a face anonymizer and activity detector using an adversarial learning formulation. Our experiments quantitatively and qualitatively demonstrate that the learned anonymizer confuses both humans and machines in face identification while producing reliable action detection.

Acknowledgements. This research was conducted as a part of EgoVid Inc.'s research activity on privacy-preserving computer vision, and was supported in part by the Technology development Program (S2557960) funded by the Ministry of SMEs and Startups (MSS, Korea), and NSF IIS-1748387. We thank all the subjects who participated in our user study. We also thank Chongruo Wu, Fanyi Xiao, Krishna Kumar Singh, and Maheen Rashid for their valuable discussions.

References

1. Abadi, M., et al.: Deep learning with differential privacy. In: ACM Conference on Computer and Communications Security (CCS) (2016)
2. Aggarwal, J.K., Ryoo, M.S.: Human activity analysis: a review. ACM Comput. Surv. **43**, 16 (2011)
3. Arjovsky, M., Chintala, S., Bottou, L.: Wasserstein generative adversarial networks. In: ICML (2017)
4. Butler, D.J., Huang, J., Roesner, F., Cakmak, M.: The privacy-utility tradeoff for remotely teleoperated robots. In: ACM/IEEE International Conference on Human-Robot Interaction (HRI) (2015)
5. Carlini, N., Wagner, D.A.: Towards evaluating the robustness of neural networks. In: IEEE Symposium on Security and Privacy (2017)
6. Carreira, J., Zisserman, A.: Quo Vadis, Action recognition? A new model and the kinetics dataset. In: CVPR (2017)
7. Chen, J., Wu, J., Konrad, J., Ishwar, P.: Semi-coupled two-stream fusion convnets for action recognition at extremely low resolutions. In: WACV (2017)
8. Feichtenhofer, C., Pinz, A., Zisserman, A.: Convolutional two-stream network fusion for video action recognition. In: CVPR (2016)
9. Girshick, R.B., Donahue, J., Darrell, T., Malik, J.: Rich feature hierarchies for accurate object detection and semantic segmentation. In: CVPR (2014)
10. Gkioxari, G., Malik, J.: Finding action tubes. In: CVPR (2015)
11. Goodfellow, I., et al.: Generative adversarial nets. In: NIPS (2014)
12. Goodfellow, I.J., Shlens, J., Szegedy, C.: Explaining and harnessing adversarial examples. In: ICLR (2015)
13. Gu, C., et al.: AVA: a video dataset of spatio-temporally localized atomic visual actions. In: CVPR (2018)
14. He, K., Zhang, X., Ren, S., Sun, J.: Deep residual learning for image recognition. In: CVPR (2016)
15. Huang, G.B., Ramesh, M., Berg, T., Learned-Miller, E.: Labeled faces in the wild: a database for studying face recognition in unconstrained environments. Technical report 07–49, University of Massachusetts, Amherst, October 2007
16. Isola, P., Zhu, J.Y., Zhou, T., Efros, A.A.: Image-to-image translation with conditional adversarial networks. In: CVPR (2017)
17. Iwasawa, Y., Nakayama, K., Yairi, I., Matsuo, Y.: Privacy issues regarding the application of DNNs to activity-recognition using wearables and its countermeasures by use of adversarial training. In: IJCAI (2017)
18. Jaderberg, M., Simonyan, K., Zisserman, A., Kavukcuoglu, K.: Spatial transformer networks. In: NIPS (2015)
19. Jhuang, H., Gall, J., Zuffi, S., Schmid, C., Black, M.J.: Towards understanding action recognition. In: International Conference on Computer Vision (ICCV), pp. 3192–3199 (2013)
20. Johnson, J., Alahi, A., Fei-Fei, L.: Perceptual losses for real-time style transfer and super-resolution. In: Leibe, B., Matas, J., Sebe, N., Welling, M. (eds.) ECCV 2016. LNCS, vol. 9906, pp. 694–711. Springer, Cham (2016). https://doi.org/10.1007/978-3-319-46475-6_43
21. Jourabloo, A., Yin, X., Liu, X.: Attribute preserved face de-identification. In: IAPR International Conference on Biometrics (2015)
22. Kingma, D.P., Ba, J.: Adam: a method for stochastic optimization. CoRR abs/1412.6980 (2014)

23. Learned-Miller, E., Huang, G.B., RoyChowdhury, A., Li, H., Hua, G.: Labeled faces in the wild: a survey. In: Kawulok, M., Celebi, M.E., Smolka, B. (eds.) Advances in Face Detection and Facial Image Analysis, pp. 189–248. Springer, Cham (2016). https://doi.org/10.1007/978-3-319-25958-1_8

24. Ledig, C., et al.: Photo-realistic single image super-resolution using a generative adversarial network. CoRR (2016)

25. Liu, W., et al.: SSD: single shot multibox detector. In: Leibe, B., Matas, J., Sebe, N., Welling, M. (eds.) ECCV 2016. LNCS, vol. 9905, pp. 21–37. Springer, Cham (2016). https://doi.org/10.1007/978-3-319-46448-0_2

26. Liu, W., Wen, Y., Yu, Z., Li, M., Raj, B., Song, L.: Sphereface: deep hypersphere embedding for face recognition. In: CVPR (2017)

27. Liu, W., Wen, Y., Yu, Z., Yang, M.: Large-margin softmax loss for convolutional neural networks. In: ICML (2016)

28. Moosavi-Dezfooli, S., Fawzi, A., Fawzi, O., Frossard, P.: Universal adversarial perturbations. In: CVPR (2017)

29. Najibi, M., Samangouei, P., Chellappa, R., Davis, L.: SSH: single stage headless face detector. In: ICCV (2017)

30. Papernot, N., McDaniel, P.D., Goodfellow, I.J.: Transferability in machine learning: from phenomena to black-box attacks using adversarial samples. CoRR abs/1605.07277 (2016)

31. Papernot, N., McDaniel, P.D., Wu, X., Jha, S., Swami, A.: Distillation as a defense to adversarial perturbations against deep neural networks. In: IEEE Symposium on Security and Privacy (2016)

32. Peng, X., Schmid, C.: Multi-region two-stream R-CNN for action detection. In: Leibe, B., Matas, J., Sebe, N., Welling, M. (eds.) ECCV 2016. LNCS, vol. 9908, pp. 744–759. Springer, Cham (2016). https://doi.org/10.1007/978-3-319-46493-0_45

33. Piergiovanni, A., Ryoo, M.S.: Learning latent super-events to detect multiple activities in videos. In: CVPR (2018)

34. Radford, A., Metz, L., Chintala, S.: Unsupervised representation learning with deep convolutional generative adversarial networks. In: ICLR (2016)

35. Ren, S., He, K., Girshick, R., Sun, J.: Faster R-CNN: towards real-time object detection with region proposal networks. TPAMI **39**, 1137–1149 (2016)

36. Ren, Z., Lee, Y.J.: Cross-domain self-supervised multi-task feature learning using synthetic imagery. In: CVPR (2018)

37. Ryoo, M.S., Kim, K., Yang, H.J.: Extreme low resolution activity recognition with multi-siamese embedding learning. In: AAAI (2018)

38. Ryoo, M.S., Rothrock, B., Fleming, C.: Privacy-preserving egocentric activity recognition from extreme low resolution. In: AAAI (2017)

39. Saha, S., Singh, G., Sapienza, M., Torr, P.H., Cuzzolin, F.: Deep learning for detecting multiple space-time action tubes in videos. In: BMVC (2016)

40. Salimans, T., Goodfellow, I.J., Zaremba, W., Cheung, V., Radford, A., Chen, X.: Improved techniques for training GANs. In: NIPS (2016)

41. Schroff, F., Kalenichenko, D., Philbin, J.: Facenet: A unified embedding for face recognition and clustering. In: CVPR (2015)

42. Sigurdsson, G.A., Varol, G., Wang, X., Farhadi, A., Laptev, I., Gupta, A.: Hollywood in homes: crowdsourcing data collection for activity understanding. In: Leibe, B., Matas, J., Sebe, N., Welling, M. (eds.) ECCV 2016. LNCS, vol. 9905, pp. 510–526. Springer, Cham (2016). https://doi.org/10.1007/978-3-319-46448-0_31

43. Simonyan, K., Zisserman, A.: Two-stream convolutional networks for action recognition in videos. In: NIPS (2014)

44. Singh, G., Saha, S., Sapienza, M., Torr, P., Cuzzolin, F.: Online real time multiple spatiotemporal action localisation and prediction on a single platform. In: ICCV (2017)

45. Sun, Y., Wang, X., Tang, X.: Deep learning face representation from predicting 10,000 classes. In: CVPR (2014)

46. Taigman, Y., Yang, M., Ranzato, M., Wolf, L.: DeepFace: closing the gap to human-level performance in face verification. In: CVPR (2014)

47. Tran, D., Bourdev, L.D., Fergus, R., Torresani, L., Paluri, M.: C3D: generic features for video analysis. CoRR, abs/1412.0767 (2014)

48. Ulyanov, D., Vedaldi, A., Lempitsky, V.S.: Instance normalization: the missing ingredient for fast stylization. CoRR abs/1607.08022 (2016)

49. Wang, X., Shrivastava, A., Gupta, A.: A-fast-RCNN: hard positive generation via adversary for object detection. In: CVPR (2017)

50. Wang, Z., Chang, S., Yang, Y., Liu, D., Huang, T.S.: Studying very low resolution recognition using deep networks. In: CVPR (2016)

51. Weinzaepfel, P., Harchaoui, Z., Schmid, C.: Learning to track for spatio-temporal action localization. In: ICCV (2015)

52. Weinzaepfel, P., Martin, X., Schmid, C.: Human action localization with sparse spatial supervision. arXiv preprint arXiv:1605.05197 (2016)

53. Wen, Y., Zhang, K., Li, Z., Qiao, Y.: A discriminative feature learning approach for deep face recognition. In: Leibe, B., Matas, J., Sebe, N., Welling, M. (eds.) ECCV 2016. LNCS, vol. 9911, pp. 499–515. Springer, Cham (2016). https://doi.org/10.1007/978-3-319-46478-7_31

54. Xiao, C., Zhu, J., Li, B., He, W., Liu, M., Song, D.: Spatially transformed adversarial examples. In: ICLR (2018)

55. Xu, W., Evans, D., Qi, Y.: Feature squeezing: detecting adversarial examples in deep neural networks. CoRR abs/1704.01155 (2017)

56. Yi, D., Lei, Z., Liao, S., Li, S.Z.: Learning face representation from scratch. CoRR abs/1411.7923 (2014)

57. Yonetani, R., Boddeti, V.N., Kitani, K.M., Sato, Y.: Privacy-preserving visual learning using doubly permuted homomorphic encryption. In: ICCV (2017)

58. Zhang, K., Zhang, Z., Li, Z., Qiao, Y.: Joint face detection and alignment using multitask cascaded convolutional networks. IEEE Sig. Process. Lett. 23, 1499–1503 (2016)

59. Zhao, W., Chellappa, R., Phillips, P.J., Rosenfeld, A.: Face recognition: a literature survey. ACM Comput. Surv. 35, 399–458 (2003)

60. Zhu, J.Y., Park, T., Isola, P., Efros, A.A.: Unpaired image-to-image translation using cycle-consistent adversarial networks. In: ICCV (2017)

Joint Person Segmentation and Identification in Synchronized First- and Third-Person Videos

Mingze Xu[✉], Chenyou Fan, Yuchen Wang, Michael S. Ryoo,
and David J. Crandall

School of Informatics, Computing, and Engineering, Indiana University,
Bloomington, IN 47408, USA
{mx6,fan6,wang617,mryoo,djcran}@indiana.edu

Abstract. In a world of pervasive cameras, public spaces are often captured from multiple perspectives by cameras of different types, both fixed and mobile. An important problem is to organize these heterogeneous collections of videos by finding connections between them, such as identifying correspondences between the people appearing in the videos and the people holding or wearing the cameras. In this paper, we wish to solve two specific problems: (1) given two or more synchronized third-person videos of a scene, produce a pixel-level segmentation of each visible person and identify corresponding people across different views (i.e., determine who in camera A corresponds with whom in camera B), and (2) given one or more synchronized third-person videos as well as a first-person video taken by a mobile or wearable camera, segment and identify the camera wearer in the third-person videos. Unlike previous work which requires ground truth bounding boxes to estimate the correspondences, we perform person segmentation and identification jointly. We find that solving these two problems simultaneously is mutually beneficial, because better fine-grained segmentation allows us to better perform matching across views, and information from multiple views helps us perform more accurate segmentation. We evaluate our approach on two challenging datasets of interacting people captured from multiple wearable cameras, and show that our proposed method performs significantly better than the state-of-the-art on both person segmentation and identification.

Keyword: Synchronized first- and third-person cameras

1 Introduction

There will be an estimated 45 *billion* cameras on Earth by 2022—more than five times the number of people [25]! In a world with so many cameras, it will be commonplace for a scene to be simultaneously recorded by multiple cameras of different types. For example, a busy city street may be recorded by not only fixed surveillance cameras, but also by mobile cameras on smartphones, laptops,

© Springer Nature Switzerland AG 2018
V. Ferrari et al. (Eds.): ECCV 2018, LNCS 11205, pp. 656–672, 2018.
https://doi.org/10.1007/978-3-030-01246-5_39

tablets, self-driving cars, and even wearable devices like GoPro [1] and Snap Spectacles [2]. As cameras continue to multiply, new techniques will be needed to organize and make sense of these weakly-structured collections of video. For example, a key problem in many applications is to detect, identify, and track people. Combining data from multiple cameras could significantly improve performance on this and other scene understanding problems, since evidence from multiple viewpoints could help resolve ambiguities caused by occlusion, perspective distortion, etc. However, integrating evidence across heterogeneous cameras in unconstrained dynamic environments is a challenge, especially for wearable and mobile devices where the camera is moving unpredictably.

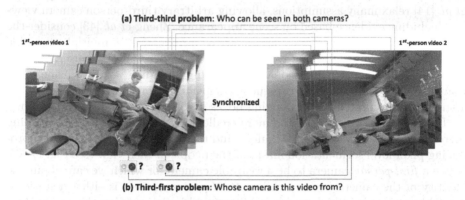

Fig. 1. Two or more people move around an environment while wearing cameras. We are interested in two specific, related problems: (a) given one or more synchronized third-person videos of a scene, segment all the visible people and identify corresponding people across the different videos; and (b) given one or more synchronized third-person videos of a scene as well as a video that was taken by a wearable first-person camera, identify and segment the person who was wearing the camera in the third-person videos.

For example, consider a law enforcement scenario in which multiple police officers chase a suspect through a crowded square. Body-worn police cameras (which nearly 95% of U.S. police departments use or plan to deploy [24]) record events from the officers' perspectives. Investigators later want to reconstruct the incident by combining the first-person wearable camera videos with third-person views from surveillance cameras and civilian smartphone videos uploaded to social media. In any given frame of any given camera, they may want to identify: (1) fine-grained, pixel-level segmentation masks for all people of interest, including both the suspect and the officers (e.g., for activity or action recognition), (2) the instances in which one of the camera wearers (officers) was visible in another camera's view, and (3) instances of the same person appearing in different views at the same time. The scene is complex and crowded, requiring fine-grained segmentation masks to separate individual people (since frequent occlusions would cause bounding boxes to overlap). The wearable camera videos are particularly challenging because the cameras themselves are moving rapidly.

While person tracking and (re-)identification are well-studied in computer vision [37,44], only recently have they been considered in challenging scenarios of heterogeneous first-person and traditional cameras. Ardeshir and Borji [4] consider the case of several people moving around while wearing cameras, and try to match each of these first-person views to one of the people appearing in a third-person, overhead view of the scene. This is challenging because the camera wearer is never seen in their own wearable video, so he or she must be identified by matching their motion from a third-person perspective with the first-person visual changes that are induced by their movements. That paper's approach is applicable in closed settings with overhead cameras (e.g., a museum), but not in unconstrained environments such as our law enforcement example. Fan *et al.* [14] relax many assumptions, allowing arbitrary third-person camera views and including evidence based on scene appearance. Zheng *et al.* [43] consider the distinct problem of identifying the same person appearing in multiple wearable camera videos (but not trying to identify the camera wearers themselves). But these techniques identify individual people using bounding boxes, which are too coarse in crowded scenes with frequent occlusions. Moreover, these techniques assume that accurate oracle bounding boxes are available (even at test time).

In this paper, we consider the more challenging problem of not only finding correspondences between people in first- and third-person cameras, but also producing pixel-level segmentation masks of the people in each view (see Fig. 1). We define a *first-person* camera to be a wearable camera for which we care about the identity of the camera wearer, while a *third-person* camera is either a static *or* wearable camera for which we are *not* interested in determining the wearer. Our hypothesis is that simultaneous segmentation and matching is mutually beneficial: segmentation helps refine matching by producing finer-grained appearance features (compared to bounding boxes), which are important in crowded scenes with many occlusions, while matching helps locate a person of interest and produce better segmentation masks, which in turn help in tasks like activity and action recognition. We show that previous work [14] is a special case of ours, since we can naturally handle their first- and third-person cases. We evaluate on two publicly available datasets augmented with pixel-level annotations, showing that we achieve significantly better results than numerous baselines.

2   Related Work

We are not aware of work on joint person segmentation and identification in first- and third-person cameras, so we draw inspiration from several related problems.

Object Segmentation in Images and Videos. Deep learning has achieved state-of-the-art performance on semantic image segmentation [5,9,27,28,42], typically using fully convolutional networks (FCNs) that extract low-resolution features and then up-sample. Other approaches [18,26,30,31] are based on region proposals, inspired by R-CNNs [16,32] for object detection. For example, Mask R-CNNs [18] separately predict object masks and their class labels, avoiding competition among classes and improving performance for overlapped instances.

For object segmentation in video [7,20–22,38,39], most methods assume that the object mask in the first frame is known (during both training and testing) and the task is to propagate them to subsequent frames. Khoreva *et al.* [29] propose guided instance segmentation that uses the object mask from the previous frame to predict the next one. The network is pre-trained (off-line) on static images and fine-tuned (on-line) on the first frame's annotations for specific objects of interest. We follow a similar formulation, except that we incorporate both appearance and optical flow in a two-stream network, helping to better update the object mask across time. Our work is also inspired by the pixel-level Siamese matching network of Yoon *et al.* [41] that segments and identifies objects, even those not seen during training. We extend to multiple cameras by using object instances across multiple synchronized videos to learn variations and correspondences in appearance across views. Cheng *et al.* [10] propose a two-stream network which outputs segmentation and optical flow simultaneously, where segmentation focuses on objectness and optical flow exploits motion. Inspired by their observation that segmentation and optical flow benefit each other, we propose a novel architecture that jointly performs person segmentation and identification.

Co-segmentation. Our work is related to co-segmentation of objects appearing in multiple images [33] or videos [8,11,15,17,34]. Several methods use Markov Random Fields with a regularized difference of feature histograms, for example, by assuming a Gaussian prior on the objectness appearance [33] or computing sum squared differences [6]. Chiu *et al.* [11] use distance-dependent Chinese Restaurant Processes as priors on both appearance and motion for unsupervised (not semantic) co-segmentation. Fu *et al.* [15] address video co-segmentation as CRF inference on an object co-selection graph, but segmentation candidates are computed only by a category-independent method [13] and are not refined from information across multiple videos. Guo *et al.* [17] perform iterative constrained clustering using seed superpixels and pairwise constraints, and refine the segmentation with a multi-class MRF. Most of these methods assume that either a target object appears in all videos or that videos contain at least one common target object, and none apply deep learning. To the best of our knowledge, ours is the first paper to propose a deep learning approach to co-segmentation in videos, and is applicable both to single and multiple camera scenarios.

First-Person Cameras. Ardeshir and Borji [4] match a set of first-person videos to a set of people appearing in a top-view video using graph matching, but assume there are multiple first-person cameras sharing the same field of view at any time and only consider third-person cameras that are overhead. Fan *et al.* [14] identify a first-person camera wearer in a third-person video using a two-stream semi-Siamese network that incorporates spatial and temporal information from both views, and learns a joint embedding space from first- and third-person matches. Zheng *et al.* [43] identify people appearing in multiple wearable camera videos (but do not identify the camera wearers themselves).

The above work assumes that the people have been detected with accurate bounding boxes in both training *and test* datasets. We build on these methods, proposing a novel architecture that simultaneously segments and identifies camera wearers and others. We find that segmenting and identifying are mutually beneficial; in the law scenario described above with crowded scenes and occluded people, for example, fine-grained segmentation masks are needed to accurately extract visual features specific to any given person, while identity information from multiple views helps accurately segment the person in any individual view.

3   Our Approach

Given two or more videos taken from a set of cameras (potentially both static and wearable cameras), we wish to segment each person appearing in these videos, identify matches between segments that correspond to the same person across different views, and identify the segments that correspond to the wearer of each first-person camera. The main idea is that despite having very different perspectives, synchronized cameras recording the same environment should be capturing some of the same people and background objects. This overlap permits finding similarities and correspondences among these videos in both visual and motion domains, as long as differences caused by differing viewpoints are ignored. Unlike prior work [14] which assumes a ground truth bounding box is available for each person in each frame, we perform segmentation and matching simultaneously. We hypothesize that these two tasks are mutually beneficial: person segmentations provide more accurate information than coarse bounding boxes for people matching, while people's appearance and motion from different perspectives produce better segmentation masks.

More concretely, we formulate our problem as two separate tasks. The *third-third problem* is to segment each person and find person correspondences across different views captured from a pair of third-person cameras. The *third-first problem* is to segment and identify the camera wearer of a given first-person video in third-person videos. We first introduce a basic network architecture for both problems: a two-stream fully convolutional network (FCN) that estimates a segmentation mask for each person using the current RGB frame, stacked optical flow fields, and segmentation result of the previous frame (which we call the *pre-mask*) (Sect. 3.1). We then introduce a Siamese network for each of our two problems, that incorporates the FCN and allows person segmentation and identification to benefit each other (Sect. 3.2). Finally we describe our loss used for segmentation and distance metric learning (Sect. 3.3).

3.1   Two-Stream FCN Network

We use FCN8s [28] as the basis of our framework but with several important modifications. We chose FCN8s due to their effectiveness and compactness, although other architectures such as DeepLabv3+ [9] and Mask R-CNN [18] could be easily used. Figure 2 presents our novel architecture. To take advantage of video and incorporate evidence from both appearance and motion, we expand FCN8s to a two-stream architecture, where a *visual stream* receives RGB frames (top of Fig. 2) and a *motion stream* receives stacked optical flow fields (bottom).

This design is inspired by Simonyan and Zisserman [35], although their network was proposed for a completely different problem (action recognition from a single static camera). To jointly consider both spatial and temporal information, we use "early" fusion to concatenate features at levels pool3, pool4, and pool5 (middle of Fig. 2). Following FCN8s to incorporate "coarse, high level information with fine, low level information" [28] for more accurate segmentation, we combine the fused features from these different levels.

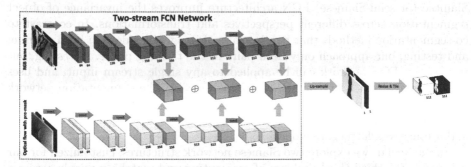

Fig. 2. Visualization of our two-stream FCN network. We feed RGB frames with pre-masks to the visual stream (top, dark grey) and stacked optical flow fields with pre-mask to the motion stream (bottom, light grey). The spatial and temporal features at pool3, pool4, and pool5 are fused to predict the segmentation of the target person. We downsample the extracted features of the softmax layer by 16, then tile the background and foreground channels by 512, separately.

However, in contrast to Long *et al.*'s FCN8s, our two-stream FCN targets instance segmentation: we want to segment specific people, not just all instances of the "person" class. We address this with an instance-by-instance strategy in both training and test, in which we only consider a single person at a time. In order to guide the network to segment a specific person among the many that may appear in a frame, we append that person's binary pre-mask (without any semantic information) to the input of each stream as an additional channel. This pre-mask provides a rough estimate of the person's location and his or her approximate shape in the current frame. In training, our network is pre-trained by taking ground truth pre-masks as inputs, and then fine-tuned with estimated masks from the previous frame. In testing, we assume that we have a (possibly quite coarse) segmentation of each person in the first frame and propagate this mask forward by evaluating each subsequent unlabeled frame in sequence. A pixel-level classification loss function is used to guide learning (Sect. 3.3).

3.2 Siamese Networks

The network in the last section learns to estimate the segmentation mask of a specific person across frames of video. We now use this network in a Siamese structure with a contrastive loss to match person instances across different third- and first-person views. The main idea behind our Siamese networks is to learn an embedding space such that features captured by different cameras from different perspectives are close together only if they actually belong to the same person—i.e., so that a person's appearance features are invariant to camera viewpoint. The Siamese formulation allows us to simultaneously learn the viewpoint-invariant embedding space for matching identities and the pixel-wise segmentation network described above in an end-to-end fashion. Moreover, our Siamese (or semi-Siamese) FCN architecture improves the invariance of object segmentation across different perspectives and transformations. In contrast to co-segmentation methods that require pairs of images or videos in both training and testing, our approach only need pairs in the training phase. In testing, our two-stream FCN network can be applied to any single stream input, and uses the embedding space to match with others. To allow the segmentation network to receive arbitrary sizes of inputs, our contrastive loss function is generalized to a 3D representation space, with a Euclidean distance for positive exemplars and a hinge loss for negative ones.

In particular, we explore two Siamese network structures, customized for our two tasks: the third-third problem of segmenting and matching people across a pair of cameras, and the third-first problem of segmenting a person of interest and identifying if he or she is the wearer of a first-person camera. The third-third problem considers a more general case in which the cameras may be static or may be wearable, but they are all viewing a person of interest from a third-person viewpoint; we thus use a full-Siamese network that shares all convolution layers in the FCN branch and the embedding layers. In contrast, the third-first problem must match feature representations from different perspectives (identifying how a camera wearer's ego-motion visible in a first-person view correlates with that same motion's appearance from a third-person view). As in [14], our third-first network is formulated in a semi-Siamese structure, where separate shallow layers capture different low-level features while deeper ones are shared.

Third-Third Network. Figure 3 shows the architecture of our third-third network, which segments and matches people in common from a pair of third-person camera views. We use a Siamese structure with two branches of the FCN network from Fig. 2 (and discussed in Sect. 3.1), where all corresponding convolution layers are shared. The Siamese branch is thus encouraged to learn relationships between people's appearance in different views by optimizing a generalized embedding space. The key idea is that despite being captured from very different perspectives, the same person in synchronized videos should have some correspondences in both visual and motion domains.

In more detail, given an RGB frame and optical flow fields (appended with the pre-mask of the person of interest) as inputs, each of size $W \times H$, the FCN branch estimates a binary-valued person segmentation mask of the same size. The Siamese branch is then appended to the pool5 layer of both visual and motion streams with an input size of $512 \times W' \times H'$, where $W' = \frac{W}{16}$ and $H' = \frac{H}{16}$, for matching. To obtain more accurate representations for each

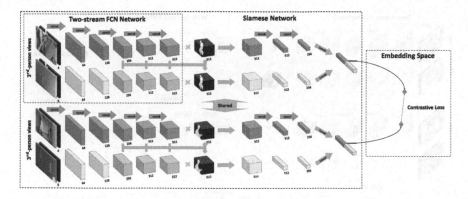

Fig. 3. Our third-third network segments and identifies the people in common across different videos. The network is composed of two FCN branches with a Siamese structure, where all convolution layers (shown in the same color) are shared. (Color figure online)

"target" person, we re-weight the spatial and temporal features by multiplying them with the confidence outputs of the FCN branch. To emphasize the pixel positions belonging to the person while retaining some contextual information, we use soft attention maps after the softmax layer rather than the estimated segmentation mask. We first resize the soft attention of the foreground from $1 \times W \times H$ to $1 \times W' \times H'$ and tile it to $512 \times W' \times H'$ to fit the size of `pool5` outputs. For both visual and motion streams, we multiply this resized confidence map with the features, which gives a higher score to the person's pixels and a low score to the background. By "cropping out" the region corresponding to a person from the feature maps, the match across two views should receive a higher correspondence. This correspondence will also back-propagate its confidence to improve segmentation. Finally, the re-weighted spatial and temporal features are concatenated together for matching each person instance.

Third-First Network. Figure 4 shows the architecture of our third-first network, the goal of which is to segment a first-person camera wearer in third-person videos and to recognize the correspondence between the first-person view and its representation in third-person videos. To be specific, given a first-person video, our network must decide which, if anyone, of the people appearing in a third-person video is the wearer of this first-person camera, and to estimate the wearer's segmentation. In contrast to the third-third network which has two FCN branches focusing on the same task (person segmentation), the second branch of the third-first network receives the first-person videos as inputs and is designed to extract the wearer's ego-motion and the visual information of the background, which hopefully also provides constraints for the segmentation. We thus propose a semi-Siamese network to learn the first- and third-person distance metric, where the first-person branch has a similar structure to the FCN but without the up-sampling layers or the segmentation loss. The structure

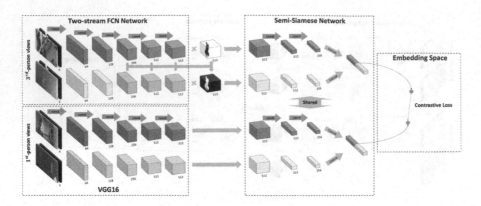

Fig. 4. Our third-first network segments and identifies the first-person camera wearer in third-person videos. The network is formulated in a semi-Siamese structure where only convolution layers of the embedding space (shown in the same color) are shared. (Color figure online)

of the Siamese branch is similar to that of the third-third network, but with a different re-weighting method: we multiply the spatial features with the soft attention of the background but the temporal features with the soft attention of the foreground. We do this because camera wearers do not appear in their own first-person videos (with occasional exceptions of arms or hands), but the backgrounds reflect some similarities between different perspectives; meanwhile, motion features of camera wearers in third-person videos is related to the ego-motion in first-person videos. The re-weighted appearance and motion features are then concatenated after several convolution operations, as discussed above.

3.3 Loss Functions

We propose two loss functions for joint segmentation and distance metric optimization for a batch of N training exemplars. First, *sigmoid cross entropy loss* compares a predicted segmentation mask to ground truth,

$$L_{seg} = -\sum_i^N \sum_w^W \sum_h^H \left(S_{i,w,h} \cdot \log \hat{S}_{i,w,h} + (1 - S_{i,w,h}) \cdot \log(1 - \hat{S}_{i,w,h}) \right), \quad (1)$$

where $\hat{S}_i \in \{0,1\}^{W \times H}$ is the predicted segmentation mask of exemplar i and $S_i \in \{0,1\}^{W \times H}$ is the corresponding ground truth mask. Second, *generalized contrastive loss* encourages low distances between positive exemplars (pairs of corresponding people) and high distances between negative ones,

$$L_{siam} = \sum_i^N \sum_c^C \sum_w^{W''} \sum_h^{H''} y_i \, ||a_{i,c,w,h} - b_{i,c,w,h}||^2$$
$$+ (1 - y_i) \max(m - ||a_{i,c,w,h} - b_{i,c,w,h}||, 0)^2, \quad (2)$$

where m is a constant, a_i and b_i are two features corresponding to exemplar i, and y_i is 1 if i is a correct correspondence and 0 otherwise. This loss enables our model to learn an embedding space for arbitrary input sizes.

4   Experiments

We test our third-third and third-first networks on joint person segmentation and identification in two datasets of synchronized first- and third-person videos, collected by two different authors. We primarily evaluate on the publicly available IU ShareView dataset [14], consisting of 9 sets of two 5–10 min first-person videos. Each set contains 3–4 participants performing a variety of everyday activities (shaking hands, chatting, eating, etc.) in one of six indoor environments. Each person in each frame is annotated with a ground truth bounding box and a unique person ID. To evaluate our methods on person segmentation, we manually augmented a subset of the dataset with pixel-level person annotations, for a total of 1,277 labeled frames containing 2,654 annotated person instances. We computed optical flow fields for all videos using FlowNet2.0 [19].

Since adjacent frames are typically highly correlated, we split the training and test datasets at the video level, with 6 video sets used for training (875 annotated frames) and 3 sets for testing (402 annotated frames). In each set of videos, there are 3–4 participants, two of which wear first-person cameras. Note that a first-person camera never sees its own wearer, so the people not wearing cameras are the ones who are in common across the first-person videos. Since our approach uses sequences of contiguous frames and pairs of instances (either a pair of two people or a pair of one person and one camera view), we divide each video set into several short sequences, each with 10–15 consecutive frames. More specifically, in training we create 484 positive and 1,452 negative pairs for the third-third problem, and 865 positive and 1,241 negative pairs for the third-first problem (about a 1:3 ratio). In testing, each problem has 10 sequences of pairs of videos, and each video has 20 consecutive frames (about 4 s). Thus we have about 400 annotated test frames for evaluating matching, and about 1,000 person instances for evaluating segmentation (since every frame has 2–3 people).

We also evaluate our models on a subset of UTokyo Ego-Surf [40], which contains 8 diverse groups of first-person videos recorded synchronously during face-to-face conversations in both indoor and outdoor environments. Limited by the size of the dataset (only 3 available pairs of short videos including 3–4 participants), we use it only for testing, and still train on IU ShareView. As before, we manually created pixel-level person annotations for 10 sequences of pairs of videos, each with 20 consecutive frames.

4.1   Evaluation Protocol

We implemented our networks in PyTorch [3], and performed all experiments on a single Nvidia Titan X Pascal GPU.

Training. Our training process consisted of two stages: (a) optimizing only the FCN branch supervised by the pixel-level classifier for providing imperfect but reasonable soft attentions, and (b) optimizing the joint model (either the third-third or third-first network) based on the person segmentation and identification tasks, simultaneously. Our two-stream FCN network is built on VGG16 [36], and we initialized both visual and motion streams using weights pre-trained on ImageNet [12]. The FCN branch was then optimized with an instance-by-instance strategy, which only considers one particular person of interest at a time, and uses the ground truth pre-mask as an additional channel to indicate which person the network should focus on. We used stochastic gradient descent (SGD) with fixed learning rate 10^{-4}, momentum 0.9, weight decay 0.0005, and batch size 25. Learning was terminated after 30 epochs. Our joint model was then initialized with the weights of the pre-trained FCN and fine-tuned by considering pairs of instances as inputs for person segmentation and identification. We again used SGD optimization but with learning rate 10^{-5}. For the first 20 epochs, we froze the weights of the FCN branch, and optimized the Siamese branch to make the contrastive loss converge to a "reasonable" range (not too large to destroy the soft attention). We then started the joint learning process, and terminated after *another* 40 epochs.

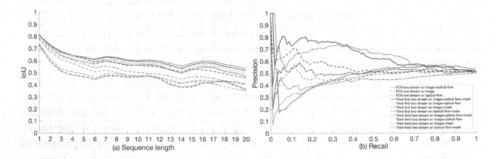

Fig. 5. IoU and precision-recall curves of our models on IU ShareView dataset [14]

Testing. In contrast to training, which requires pairs of videos as inputs, our joint model can be applied to an individual stream, where each video frame is processed to simultaneously estimate each person's segmentation and extract corresponding features for matching between different streams. In testing, all possible pairs of instances are considered as candidate matches: each pair contains either two people from different videos in the third-third problem, or a first-person camera view and a person appearing in a third-person video in the third-first problem. Unlike methods that require a pair of instances as input, our approach only needs to process each person and camera view once.

4.2   Evaluation

For both third-first and third-third problems, we evaluate our method with two tasks: person (1) segmentation and (2) identification across multiple cameras.

Person Segmentation is evaluated in terms of *intersection over union (IoU)* between the estimated segmentation maps and the ground truth. This is measured over each video in the test dataset by applying our models to each frame. Our model sequentially takes the segmentation results from the previous frame (the pre-mask) as input to guide the segmentation of the next frame. In the evaluation, the ground segmentation mask of the first (and only the first) video frame is assumed to be available.

Person Identification is evaluated with *Mean average precision (mAP)* and *Accuracy (ACC)*, each of which takes a different view of the problem. mAP treats people matching as a retrieval problem: given all possible pairs of person instances from two different cameras (i.e., two person instances from different third-person videos in the third-third problem *or* one person instance from third-person video and one first-person video in the third-first problem), we wish to retrieve all pairs corresponding to the same person. ACC evaluates whether the single best match for a given candidate is correct: for every person instance in each view, the classifier is forced to choose a single matching instance in all other views, and we calculate the percentage of matches that are correct. This setting is the same to the one used in Fan *et al.* [14], except that their task is significantly easier because they assume person ground-truth bounding boxes are available during both training and testing, whereas our approach must infer the person's position (as well as segmentation mask) automatically.

4.3   Experimental Results

Baselines. To characterize the difficulty of segmentation in this dataset, we first test several baselines, shown in Table 1 for IU ShareView. Copy First simply propagates the ground truth segmentation mask from the first frame to all following frames in the sequence. In a completely static scenes with no motion, the IoU of Copy First should be 100.0, but our dataset includes frequent motion of both the wearable cameras and people, and thus shows a relatively low IoU of 41.9. A second baseline consisting of a single-stream FCN using only image information achieves somewhat better IoU of 47.1, while a third baseline consisting of a single-stream FCN using only optical flow achieves 50.9. A two-stream baseline FCN that combines both visual and motion performs significantly better than either one-stream network, achieving IoU of 57.3.

Our Models. We next test our approach that jointly performs segmentation with person instance matching. On segmentation, our full model produces an IoU of 62.7 for the third-third scenario and 61.9 for third-first, compared to 57.3 for the two-stream baseline that performs only segmentation. Figure 5(a) reports more detailed analysis of the segmentation performance (Y-axis) based on the length of video sequences (X-axis), and shows that our approach is still able to predict reasonable results on long videos. To permit a fair comparison across models, both the one- and two-stream FCNs were optimized with the same hyper-parameters (discussed in Sect. 4.1). Table 1 also presents results on person instance matching on IU ShareView. We achieved mAP scores of 49.0 and 65.2 on the third-third and third-first problems, respectively, and ACCs of 55.5 and 73.1. We compare these results with the state-of-the-art method of Fan *et al.* [14]. Their task is to match first-person camera views to camera wearers in *static* third-person video, so we extend it to our third-third and third-first problems by re-implementing their best model using VGG16 [36] (instead of AlexNet [23]) and training on our new, augmented dataset. The results show that our joint model outperforms in both third-third (mAP of 49.0 vs. 44.2) and third-first (mAP of 65.2 vs. 64.1) problems. This is likely due to learning a more accurate embedding space, with the help of jointly learning to perform segmentation. More importantly, our approach is able to obtain more accurate feature representations from people's pixel-level locations rather than simply relying on rough bounding boxes. Figure 5(b) compares the precision-recall curves of the different techniques for person matching.

Table 1. Experimental results of our models on IU ShareView dataset [14]

Network architecture					Evaluation		
	Backbone	Streams		Re-weighting	Segmentation	Identification	
		Image	Optical flow		IoU	mAP	ACC
Baselines	Copy first			-	41.9	-	-
	FCN	X		-	47.1	-	-
	FCN		X	-	50.9	-	-
	FCN	X	X	-	57.3	-	-
Third-third	VGG	X	X	Bounding box [14]	-	44.2	40.1
	FCN	X		Soft attention	49.3	44.3	44.5
	FCN		X	Soft attention	54.1	48.4	46.2
	FCN	X	X	W/o	60.6	45.6	48.9
	FCN	X	X	Soft attention	**62.7**	**49.0**	**55.5**
Third-first	VGG	X	X	Bounding box [14]	-	64.1	50.6
	FCN	X		Soft attention	47.4	51.4	52.7
	FCN		X	Soft attention	58.9	55.1	53.1
	FCN	X	X	W/o	59.8	64.0	61.7
	FCN	X	X	Soft attention	**61.9**	**65.2**	**73.1**

UTokyo Ego-Surf Dataset. We also test our models on our subset of UTokyo Ego-Surf (without retraining), and Table 2 summarizes the results. Though performing worse than on the IU ShareView dataset on which they were trained, the models still give reasonable results, indicating robustness even though the datasets are recorded by different cameras (Xiaoyi Yi vs. Panasonic HX-A500) and scenarios (indoor vs. outdoor).

Table 2. Experimental results of our models on UTokyo Ego-Surf dataset [40]

Network architecture				Evaluation		
	Backbone	*Streams*		Re-weighting	*Segmentation*	*Identification*
		Image	Optical flow		IoU	mAP	ACC
Third-third	FCN	X	X	W/o	42.1	43.8	36.7
	FCN	X	X	Soft attention	**43.0**	**45.5**	**42.0**
Third-first	FCN	X	X	W/o	41.4	45.2	44.0
	FCN	X	X	Soft attention	**43.6**	**52.0**	**55.2**

Ablation Studies. We also test simpler variants of our technique. To evaluate our re-weighting method that incorporates estimated soft attention maps, we tried *not* re-weighting the spatial and temporal features and simply using `pool5` layer outputs. We also compare with the results of [14], which uses ground truth bounding boxes to "crop out" regions of interest. As shown in Tables 1 and 2, using re-weighting with soft attention not only outperforms for the matching task but also generates better segmentation maps. Our ablation study also tested the relative contribution of each of our motion and visual feature streams. As shown in Table 1, our dual-stream approach performs significantly better than either single-stream optical flow or visual information on both the third-third and third-first problems, evaluated on both segmentation and matching (Fig. 6).

Fig. 6. Sample results of the third-third and third-first problems, where two videos of each sample are from two synchronized wearable cameras. The color of person segmentation masks and camera views indicates the correspondences across different cameras. (Color figure online)

5   Conclusion

We presented a novel fully convolutional network (FCN) with Siamese and semi-Siamese structures for joint person instance segmentation and identification. We also prepared a new, challenging dataset with person pixel-level annotations and correspondences in multiple first- and third-person cameras. Our results demonstrated the effectiveness and robustness of our approach on joint person segmentation and identification. The results suggested that jointly inferring pixel-level segmentation maps and correspondences of people helps perform each individual task more accurately, and that incorporating both visual and motion information works better than either individually.

Although our results are encouraging, our techniques have limitations and raise opportunities for future work. First, the joint models assume people appear in every frame of the video, so that our approach will treat someone who disappears from the scene and then re-enters as a new person instance. While this assumption is reasonable for the relatively short video sequences we consider here, future work could easily add a re-identification module to recognize people who have appeared in previous frames. Second, the joint models perform a FCN forward pass for every individual person in each frame; future work could explore sharing computation costs to improve the efficiency of our method, especially for real-time applications. Lastly, we plan to further evaluate our approach on larger datasets including more diverse scenarios.

Acknowledgments. This work was supported by the National Science Foundation (CAREER IIS-1253549), and the IU Office of the Vice Provost for Research, the College of Arts and Sciences, and the School of Informatics, Computing, and Engineering through the Emerging Areas of Research Project "Learning: Brains, Machines, and Children." We would like to thank Sven Bambach for assisting with dataset collection, and Katherine Spoon and Anthony Tai for suggestions on our paper draft.

References

1. http://www.gopro.com/
2. http://www.spectacles.com/
3. http://pytorch.org/
4. Ardeshir, S., Borji, A.: Ego2Top: matching viewers in egocentric and top-view videos. In: Leibe, B., Matas, J., Sebe, N., Welling, M. (eds.) ECCV 2016. LNCS, vol. 9909, pp. 253–268. Springer, Cham (2016). https://doi.org/10.1007/978-3-319-46454-1_16
5. Badrinarayanan, V., Kendall, A., Cipolla, R.: SegNet: a deep convolutional encoder-decoder architecture for image segmentation. arXiv:1511.00561 (2015)
6. Batra, D., Kowdle, A., Parikh, D., Luo, J., Chen, T.: iCoseg: interactive cosegmentation with intelligent scribble guidance. In: CVPR (2010)
7. Caelles, S., Maninis, K.K., Pont-Tuset, J., Leal-Taixé, L., Cremers, D., Van Gool, L.: One-shot video object segmentation. In: CVPR (2017)
8. Chen, D.J., Chen, H.T., Chang, L.W.: Video object cosegmentation. In: ACMMM (2012)
9. Chen, L.C., Zhu, Y., Papandreou, G., Schroff, F., Adam, H.: Encoder-decoder with atrous separable convolution for semantic image segmentation. arXiv:1802.02611 (2018)
10. Cheng, J., Tsai, Y.H., Wang, S., Yang, M.H.: SegFlow: joint learning for video object segmentation and optical flow. In: ICCV (2017)

11. Chiu, W.C., Fritz, M.: Multi-class video co-segmentation with a generative multi-video model. In: CVPR (2013)
12. Deng, J., Dong, W., Socher, R., Li, L.J., Li, K., Fei-Fei, L.: ImageNet: a large-scale hierarchical image database. In: CVPR (2009)
13. Endres, I., Hoiem, D.: Category independent object proposals. In: Daniilidis, K., Maragos, P., Paragios, N. (eds.) ECCV 2010. LNCS, vol. 6315, pp. 575–588. Springer, Heidelberg (2010). https://doi.org/10.1007/978-3-642-15555-0_42
14. Fan, C., et al.: Identifying first-person camera wearers in third-person videos. In: CVPR (2017)
15. Fu, H., Xu, D., Zhang, B., Lin, S.: Object-based multiple foreground video co-segmentation. In: CVPR (2014)
16. Girshick, R.: Fast R-CNN. In: CVPR (2015)
17. Guo, J., Cheong, L.F., Tan, R.T., Zhou, S.Z.: Consistent foreground co-segmentation. In: ACCV (2014)
18. He, K., Gkioxari, G., Dollár, P., Girshick, R.: Mask R-CNN. arXiv:1703.06870 (2017)
19. Ilg, E., Mayer, N., Saikia, T., Keuper, M., Dosovitskiy, A., Brox, T.: FlowNet 2.0: evolution of optical flow estimation with deep networks. In: CVPR (2017)
20. Jang, W.D., Kim, C.S.: Online video object segmentation via convolutional trident network. In: CVPR (2017)
21. Jun Koh, Y., Kim, C.S.: Primary object segmentation in videos based on region augmentation and reduction. In: CVPR (2017)
22. Khoreva, A., Perazzi, F., Benenson, R., Schiele, B., Sorkine-Hornung, A.: Learning video object segmentation from static images. arXiv:1612.02646 (2016)
23. Krizhevsky, A., Sutskever, I., Hinton, G.E.: Imagenet classification with deep convolutional neural networks. In: NIPS (2012)
24. Lafayette Group: Survey of technology needs - body worn cameras. Technical report (2015)
25. LDV Capital: 45 billion cameras by 2022 fuel business opportunities. Technical report (2017)
26. Li, Y., Qi, H., Dai, J., Ji, X., Wei, Y.: Fully convolutional instance-aware semantic segmentation. arXiv:1611.07709 (2016)
27. Lin, G., Milan, A., Shen, C., Reid, I.: RefineNet: multi-path refinement networks for high-resolution semantic segmentation. In: CVPR (2017)
28. Long, J., Shelhamer, E., Darrell, T.: Fully convolutional networks for semantic segmentation. In: CVPR (2015)
29. Perazzi, F., Khoreva, A., Benenson, R., Schiele, B., Sorkine-Hornung, A.: Learning video object segmentation from static images. In: CVPR (2017)
30. Pinheiro, P.O., Collobert, R., Dollár, P.: Learning to segment object candidates. In: NIPS (2015)
31. Pinheiro, P.O., Lin, T.-Y., Collobert, R., Dollár, P.: Learning to refine object segments. In: Leibe, B., Matas, J., Sebe, N., Welling, M. (eds.) ECCV 2016. LNCS, vol. 9905, pp. 75–91. Springer, Cham (2016). https://doi.org/10.1007/978-3-319-46448-0_5
32. Ren, S., He, K., Girshick, R., Sun, J.: Faster R-CNN: towards real-time object detection with region proposal networks. In: NIPS (2015)
33. Rother, C., Minka, T., Blake, A., Kolmogorov, V.: Cosegmentation of image pairs by histogram matching-incorporating a global constraint into MRFs. In: CVPR (2006)

34. Rubio, J.C., Serrat, J., López, A.: Video co-segmentation. In: Lee, K.M., Matsushita, Y., Rehg, J.M., Hu, Z. (eds.) ACCV 2012. LNCS, vol. 7725, pp. 13–24. Springer, Heidelberg (2013). https://doi.org/10.1007/978-3-642-37444-9_2

35. Simonyan, K., Zisserman, A.: Two-stream convolutional networks for action recognition in videos. In: NIPS (2014)

36. Simonyan, K., Zisserman, A.: Very deep convolutional networks for large-scale image recognition. arXiv:1409.1556 (2014)

37. Smeulders, A.W.M., Chu, D.M., Cucchiara, R., Calderara, S., Dehghan, A., Shah, M.: Visual tracking: an experimental survey. PAMI 36, 1442–1468 (2014)

38. Tokmakov, P., Alahari, K., Schmid, C.: Learning video object segmentation with visual memory. arXiv:1704.05737 (2017)

39. Voigtlaender, P., Leibe, B.: Online adaptation of convolutional neural networks for video object segmentation. arXiv:1706.09364 (2017)

40. Yonetani, R., Kitani, K.M., Sato, Y.: Ego-surfing first-person videos. In: CVPR (2015)

41. Yoon, J.S., Rameau, F., Kim, J., Lee, S., Shin, S., Kweon, I.S.: Pixel-level matching for video object segmentation using convolutional neural networks. arXiv:1708.05137 (2017)

42. Zhao, H., Shi, J., Qi, X., Wang, X., Jia, J.: Pyramid scene parsing network. arXiv:1612.01105 (2016)

43. Zheng, K., et al.: Learning view-invariant features for person identification in temporally synchronized videos taken by wearable cameras. In: ICCV (2017)

44. Zheng, L., Yang, Y., Hauptmann, A.G.: Person re-identification: past, present and future. arXiv:1610.02984 (2016)

Neural Graph Matching Networks for Fewshot 3D Action Recognition

Michelle Guo[1]([✉]) [iD], Edward Chou[1] [iD], De-An Huang[1] [iD], Shuran Song[2] [iD],
Serena Yeung[1] [iD], and Li Fei-Fei[1] [iD]

[1] Computer Science Department, Stanford University, Stanford, USA
mguo95@cs.stanford.edu
[2] Computer Science Department, Princeton University, Princeton, USA

Abstract. We propose Neural Graph Matching (NGM) Networks, a
novel framework that can learn to recognize a previous unseen 3D action
class with only a few examples. We achieve this by leveraging the inherent
structure of 3D data through a graphical representation. This allows
us to modularize our model and lead to strong data-efficiency in few-
shot learning. More specifically, NGM Networks jointly learn a graph
generator and a graph matching metric function in an end-to-end fashion
to directly optimize the few-shot learning objective. We evaluate NGM
on two 3D action recognition datasets, CAD-120 and PiGraphs, and
show that learning to generate and match graphs both lead to significant
improvement of few-shot 3D action recognition over the holistic baselines.

1 Introduction

Recent availability of commodity depth sensors has provided new ways to capture
3D data, but labeled depth datasets are scarce, making it difficult to transfer
the success of deep learning techniques from the RGB domain [1,2]. This is
especially true for videos, where the difficulty and cost of labelling has already
been a roadblock for collecting RGB video datasets [3,4]. One possible approach
is to use self-supervised [5,6] or unsupervised learning [7] for learning a 3D data
representation that serves as an efficient model initialization for the tasks of
interest. While such methods have been successfully applied to RGB-D action
recognition [5] and 3D scene labeling [7], we argue that it does not fully utilize
the labeled 3D datasets that are readily available [8–11].

In this work, we introduce *few-shot learning* [12] to 3D action recognition,
where the model is explicitly trained to deal with scarce training data for previously unseen classes. This is in contrast to representation learning approaches,
where the model is not informed with the task of interest. While recent works
have addressed few-shot learning in the RGB domain [12–14], adapting these

---

Electronic supplementary material The online version of this chapter (https://
doi.org/10.1007/978-3-030-01246-5_40) contains supplementary material, which is
available to authorized users.

© Springer Nature Switzerland AG 2018
V. Ferrari et al. (Eds.): ECCV 2018, LNCS 11205, pp. 673–689, 2018.
https://doi.org/10.1007/978-3-030-01246-5_40

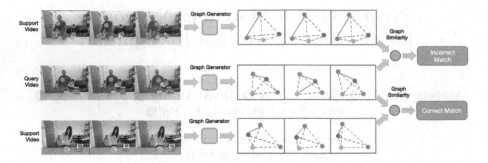

Fig. 1. The proposed Neural Graph Matching Networks is able to recognize a previously unseen action class with only a few examples. We achieve this by leveraging the spatial information inherent in the 3D data. As shown in the figure, the query video (middle) is visually similar to the video of a different class (top), which can confuse holistic approaches. However, NGM is able to leverage the graphical representation and match the query to the video with the correct class (bottom).

method to the 3D space is a non-trivial task. Unlike the images, where effective RGB representations exist (i.e., ImageNet [15] pretrained CNN), its counterpart in 3D video is still an open research problem [16–18]. As we will show in our experiments, direct application of few-shot learning to the existing 3D representation does not lead to effective generalization to novel classes.

Our key observation to resolve this challenge is that there is inherent structure in 3D data that can be naturally leveraged to provide modularity for our representation, and thus lead to more effective few-shot learning. Modularity and compositionality has been shown to be effective for improving data efficiency in visual question answering [19–21]. As shown in Fig. 1, visually diverse actions of the same class can be correlated by their underlying structure.

With these insights, we propose Neural Graph Matching (NGM) Networks, a novel graph-based approach that learns to generate and match graphs for few-shot 3D action recognition. NGM consists of two stages that can be trained jointly in an end-to-end fashion. The first stage is graph generation, where we leverage the 3D spatial information of the environment captured by the 3D data to generate the intermediate graphical representation, or the *interaction graph.* For each action, the graph uses nodes to represent physical entities in a 3D scene (e.g. body parts, objects) and edges to represent the interactions between the entities (e.g. touch, gaze) [22]. This graphical structure allows us to better model both the spatial relationship between human and objects and to capture the temporal evolution of videos, while also using stronger data efficiency in the few-shot setting. The second stage is graph matching, where we learn on the graph-based matching function as a metric to enable few-shot training on the generated interaction graph. In this way, NGM automatically learns in an end-to-end fashion both the graphical representation of the 3D environment and the graph matching metric function that are best suited for few-shot learning of novel 3D action classes. This is in contrast to holistic-based approaches [16–18,23],

Fig. 2. CAD-120 Point Clouds. We evaluate NGM on the CAD-120 dataset, which contains RGB-D videos of everyday actions. We visualize single point cloud frames where each point is the 3-D projected (x_i, y_i, z_i) of the corresponding depth frame.

where the high-dimensional input is directly mapped to a feature representation without explicitly leveraging any spatial information captured by the 3D data. For example, PointNet [18] processes permutation and geometric invariant point clouds, holistically processing the scene's point-representation.

We evaluate few-shot learning of Neural Graph Matching Networks on two 3D action datasets: CAD-120 [9] (Fig. 2) and PiGraphs [22]. We show that when there is only a single example available, NGM is able to outperform the holistic baseline up to 20% by explicitly leveraging 3D spatial information. In addition, we show that the proposed end-to-end framework is able to learn meaningful graph generations and matching metrics that perform significantly better than heuristically generated edges.

To summarize our main contributions, we: (i) introduce the few-shot learning task for 3D action recognition to address the challenge of scarce training data compared to 2D; (ii) propose the use of graphical representations to explicitly leverage the spatial information in 3D data; (iii) present Neural Graph Matching Networks, a novel framework that learns to jointly generate and match the graphical representation in an end-to-end fashion, which leads to stronger data efficiency for 3D few-shot learning.

2   Related Work

Few-shot Learning. Few-shot learning and similar concepts have been examined thoroughly in past literature. Many of these works cover the use of holistic based approaches [12–14,24–26]. Vinyals et al. [12] uses matching networks to perform one-shot learning, casting set-to-set test labels for unobserved classes using k-nearest neighbors with cosine distance. Snell et al. [14] carries along this approach using euclidean distance and creating a prototypical representation of each class. Both approaches use a holistic approach, where raw input and label pairs which are fed into the network without leveraging structural data. Also, both works use a fixed similarity metric in that only certain distance computations are used for the K-NN classification. Further works have introduced other techniques for learned similarity metrics. Santoro et al. [26] explores the topic of relational reasoning, where a module learns a relation between two objects within the relation network using MLPs and synaptic weights.

3D Action Recognition. Traditional 3D action recognition approaches rely on hand-crafted features, such as HON4D [27] and HOPC [28] to capture the spatial-temporal information. One dominant alternative is the skeleton based approaches [29,30], where the video is represented as a sequence of joint positions. Recent 3D action recognition approaches utilize skeletal pose or temporal features that are typically fed into a combination of convolutional and recurrent networks [31–33]. Part-aware LSTMs have been explored for RGB-D action recognition; however the focus there is on nodes instead of graphs. While most 3D action recognition approaches are designed for supervised learning, addressing 3D action recognition for the few-shot setting has been relatively unexplored.

Modularity and Compositionality. Modular approaches have been shown important for data efficiency in visual understanding. One example is the visual question answering problem [20,21]. Our work is tied to compositionality, where a set of entities and there interactions are used to describe the action. Ikizler et al. [34] describes an approach of breaking down movements per body part to compose a larger activity description task. Gu et al. [35] outlines a distinct approach towards compositionality, using action primitives to describe an action instead of body parts. Other representations include: *scene graphs* for objects and relationships in a 2D scene [36], and *interaction graphs* [22] to model 3D data for scene synthesis.

Deep Learning on Graphs. A few works learn on graph node embeddings over a single large graph [37–39]. This is similar to word embeddings learned in natural language processing models (e.g., word2vec [40]). However, in this work, we must process multiple different graphs representing various action video examples. Related to our work on graph processing are graph neural networks (GNNs), which are capable of processing arbitrary graphs. GNNs have been used to model a variety of structural data, including molecular fingerprints, citation networks, and knowledge graphs [41,42]. GNNs has also been used to model relationships between images for few-shot image classification [43].

3   Problem Formulation

3.1   Fewshot-Learning

We first formulate the few-shot learning problem following the definitions in previous works [12,14]. In contrast to standard classification problem, the classes are split into two types in few-shot learning. Let $\mathcal{C} = \{1,...K\}$ be the set of all classes, which is split into sets: $\mathcal{C}_{train}$, the training classes that have sufficient data for few-shot learning, and $\mathcal{C}_{test}$, the novel or unseen classes that have only a few labeled data. A k-shot N-way classification in few-shot learning means that we have N novel classes (*i.e.*, $|\mathcal{C}_{test}| = N$), and each novel class has k examples.

The success of recent few-shot learning approaches [12–14,24–26] relies on transferring the representation learned in the training classes $\mathcal{C}_{train}$ to the novel classes $\mathcal{C}_{test}$ for improved data efficiency. In other words, the few-shot learning problem can be formulated as learning a metric function $\phi(x_i, x_j)$ for two input examples x_i and x_j from $\mathcal{C}_{train}$, which can generalize to novel classes $\mathcal{C}_{test}$ so that $\phi(x_i, x_j)$ is small for data points in the same class, while larger and more distant for data from different classes. One naive approach for learning $\phi(\cdot, \cdot)$ is to directly apply supervised training on $\mathcal{C}_{train}$, which directly minimizes the intra-class distance while maximizing the inter-class distance. However, it has been shown that a better approach is to employ "episodic training" that simulates the few-shot setting to learn $\phi(x_i, x_j)$ in $\mathcal{C}_{train}$ [12]. This leads to stronger generalization to novel classes $\mathcal{C}_{test}$.

3.2 Graph-Based Few-Shot Learning

Our work follows the few-shot learning setup, and introduces it to 3D action recognition (see Fig. 8 in Supplementary). The key challenge is that, unlike the image counterpart, the form of the metric function $\phi(\cdot, \cdot)$ is still a critical research problem. We argue that direct application of holistic approaches, such as PointNet [18], does not fully utilize the spatial information in the 3D data. Image processing and proposing and segmenting arbitrary objects remains a challenge [44], while the extra dimension in 3D data allows us to better model the relationships between human and objects. Thus, our primary contribution is to explicitly leverage the spatial information with graphical representation. Formally, our Neural Graph Matching Networks can be seen as decomposing the metric function as:

$$\phi(x_i, x_j) = \phi_{GM}(g(x_i), g(x_j)), \tag{1}$$

where $g(\cdot)$ is our graph generator that obtains the interaction graph from the input, and $\phi_{GM}(\cdot, \cdot)$ is the graph matching network we learn jointly with the generator to directly optimize for few-shot learning.

4 Methods

We have formulated few-shot learning as learning the metric function $\phi(\cdot, \cdot)$ from the training classes $\mathcal{C}_{train}$, and the goal is to learn to generalize to $\mathcal{C}_{test}$ for few-shot classification. The primary contribution of our work is to explicitly leverage the 3D information by decomposing the metric into $\phi(x_i, x_j) = \phi_{GM}(g(x_i), g(x_j))$, the graph matching metric ϕ_{GM}, and the graph generator $g(\cdot)$. This decomposition allows us to better leverage spatial information that is inherent in the 3D data, and leads to stronger generalization for few-shot learning. An overview of our method is shown in Fig. 3. We first discuss our graph learning approach in Sect. 4.1, followed by the graph matching method in Sect. 4.2. Finally, we show how the combination of the two can be trained in a end-to-end fashion in Sect. 4.3.

4.1 Graph Generation

Our key insight is that 3D data contains inherent spatial structure which can be encoded in graphical form to improve data-efficiency of few-shot learning. The challenge is that we aim to achieve graph generation without graph supervision

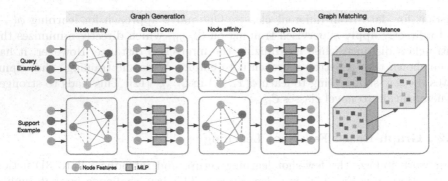

Fig. 3. Overview of Neural Graph Matching (NGM) Networks. NGM consists of two parts: graph generation and the graph matching metric, which are jointly optimized for few-shot learning. In graph generation, we utilize graph convolution to generation node features that take the contextual information into account. For the graph matching metric, we propose *graph tensor* as the graph representation that allow us to combine information in both the graph structure and the continuous node representation.

and annotation. One naive approach is to use heuristics based approaches and hard-code the graph generation process. However, such heuristics can easily be affected by noise, and it is not guaranteed to be beneficial to our few-shot learning problem. We address the challenge by formulating the graph generation as a differentiable process, which can be trained jointly with our graph matching metric to directly optimize for the few-shot objective.

We use the *interaction graph* as our graphical representation, which is composed of nodes that represent physical entities in a 3D scene (e.g. body parts, objects) as well as edges that represent interactions between the entities (e.g. touch, gaze) [22]. Given a set of node categories C and a set of node relationships E, an interaction graph $G_{i,t}$ representing a video frame $x_{i,t}$ is a tuple $(N_{i,t}, E_{i,t})$ where $N_{i,t} = \{n_1, ..., n_n\}$ is the set of nodes with each $n_j \in C$, and E is the set of undirected edges of the form (n_j, e, n_k), where $n_j, n_k \in N$ and $e \in E$.

Node Construction. Nodes of an interaction graph can be obtained using either human annotated object and pose detections, or any pretrained object or pose detector. Each node contains associated features $\rho_{i,t}$, which can be extracted from the raw pixels of the image (e.g. 3D position).

Edge Learning. In contrast to node construction, which are well-studied problems in the object and pose detection space, edge learning to capture the relationship between objects in the scene is still an on-going research area [45]. In contrast to previous works that use fully supervised learning for the edges [45], we learn the edge generation jointly with our graph matching metric for few-shot learning. It is thus important for the edge learning process to be differentiable. This expands the semantics of our learned interaction graph edges beyond predefined heuristics (e.g. contact, gaze) [22]. Given two nodes x_i, x_j from the graph, we define the edge strength $A_{i,j}$ between the nodes as:

$$A_{i,j} = \psi(x_i, x_j) = \text{MLP}_{edge}(|f(x_i) - f(x_j)|), \qquad (2)$$

where $f(\cdot)$ is the feature representation of the node, and $\text{MLP}_{edge}(\cdot)$ is a multilayer perceptron. Taking the absolute difference between the features instead of concatenating them ensures that the operation satisfy the symmetry property [43]. Thus, $f(\cdot)$ plays an important role for the quality of our edges. It is important that $f(\cdot)$ also depends on the graph structure, and is not applied independently for each node, as the same object can have very different relationships with others depending on different context. When making cereal, the node for bowl should be closely related to hand, while the relationship shouldn't exist when the action is just opening the microwave. We thus update the node feature representation with neighboring node's representation using graph convolution networks [42] to make $f(\cdot)$ also depend on the adjacency matrix. We update them iteratively:

$$f^{(k+1)}(x_i) = \sigma((D^{(k)})^{-\frac{1}{2}} A_i^{(k)} (D^{(k)})^{-\frac{1}{2}} f^{(k)}(x_i) W_{edge}), \qquad (3)$$

$$A_{i,j}^{(k)} = \text{MLP}_{edge}(|f^{(k)}(x_i) - f^{(k)}(x_j)|), \qquad (4)$$

where $D_{i,i}^{(k)} = \sum_j A_{j,i}^{(k)}$ is the diagonal node degree matrix, and W_{edge} is the trainable matrix for feature representation. We use the initial node feature from node construction as $f^{(0)}(\cdot)$. In this case, our generated edges would depend on the structure of the graph depending on the context. Note that we keep the continuous edge strength in the adjacency matrix A to preserve the learned edge as a differentiable inputs for our graph matching metric function. This allows us to train the graph generation to directly optimize few-shot generalization.

4.2 Graph Matching

We have discussed how we generate the interaction graph as the graphical representation to explicitly leverage the spatial information inherent in the 3D input. As discussed in Sect. 3, we formulate the few-shot learning $\phi(x_i, x_j) = \phi_{GM}(g(x_i), g(x_j))$ as learning jointly the graph generation $g(\cdot)$ and graph matching ϕ_{GM}. Now we discuss the graph matching metric ϕ_{GM}.

In contrast to classical *exact graph matching* problem [46], where there is an isomorphic relationship between the two comparing graphs, our data-driven graphs can have varying number of nodes. This is called the *inexact graph matching* [47], and has been important for image segmentation and processing [48]. However, classical inexact graph matching usually abstracts away from the node representation or feature, which does not fully utilize the input information in our case. For example, even when the node for hand is close to an object, the corresponding action still depends on other context in the input, and cannot be solely captured by the graph structure.

On the other extreme is recent approaches that aims to learn a *graph embedding* [49] as a single vector representation capturing all the information in the graph. While it is possible to include the edge information through approaches like graph neural networks [42,50], 3D action recognition often requires us to keep fine-grained information. For example, when an action is interacting with cluttered objects, it is important that we explicitly model their relationships.

We thus propose to use *graph tensor* as the graph matching representation. A graph tensor $\mathbf{T} \in \mathbb{R}^{|C| \times |C| \times d}$ is a three dimensional tensor, where $|C|$ is the number of node types, and d the dimension of the node feature. We define:

$$\mathbf{T}_{m,m,:} = \sum_{c(i)=m} \hat{f}(x_i), \text{ and } \mathbf{T}_{m,k,:} = \sum_{c(i)=m,c(j)=k} \hat{\psi}(x_i, x_j) \text{ for } i \neq j, \quad (5)$$

where $c(i)$ is the node type of node i, $\hat{f}(\cdot)$ the node matching feature, and $\psi(\cdot, \cdot)$ the edge feature for matching. For the node matching feature we reuse the weights W_{edge} from graph generation and define:

$$\hat{f}(x_i) = \sigma(\tilde{D}^{-\frac{1}{2}} A_i \tilde{D}^{-\frac{1}{2}} f(x_i) W_{edge}), \quad (6)$$

where A is the final adjacency matrix from node generation, and $f(\cdot)$ is the corresponding final node feature. For the edge matching feature, we reuse the node affinity from Eq. 2: $\psi(\cdot, \cdot) = \hat{\psi}(\cdot, \cdot)$. For two interaction graphs G_i and G_j, we thus define the graph matching metric as:

$$\phi_{GM}(G_i, G_j) = ||\mathbf{T}(G_i) - \mathbf{T}(G_j)||^2, \quad (7)$$

the distance between the corresponding graph tensors. Here we overload the notation $\mathbf{T}$, where now $\mathbf{T}(G)$ is the graph tensor of graph G. One implicit assumption of our method is that we assume the availability of the node type classifier $c(\cdot)$ for aggregating and matching the nodes of the same type. Node type in this case can be human joint or object class. This resolves the node correspondence and simplifies the graph matching problem.

In the few-shot setting, we hope to learn a deep graph matching metric between a query graph generated from query and support graphs generated from the support examples in each action class. We follow the prototypical networks [14], and define the prototypical graph tensor of a class k as $\mathbf{T}_k = \frac{1}{N} \sum_{c(i)=k} \mathbf{T}_i$ the average of graph tensor of all the support graphs.

To predict the action class for a given query example x_i, we compare the query's graph tensor with the prototypical graph tensor of each class k:

$$p(y = k|x_i) = \frac{\exp(-||\mathbf{T}(g(x_i)), \mathbf{T}_k||^2)}{\sum_{k'} \exp(-||\mathbf{T}(g(x_i)), \mathbf{T}_{k'}||^2)} = \frac{\exp(-\phi_{GM}(x_i, \mathbf{x}_k))}{\sum_{k'} \exp(-\phi_{GM}(x_i, \mathbf{x}_{k'}))}, \quad (8)$$

where $\mathbf{x}_k$ is the synthetic prototype for type k for interpretation.

4.3 Learning and Optimization

Learning is performed by minimizing the negative log-probability of the true class k via stochastic gradient descent:

$$J = -\log p(y = k|x_i) = \frac{\exp(-\phi_{GM}(x_i, \mathbf{x}_k))}{\sum_{k'} \exp(-\phi_{GM}(x_i, \mathbf{x}_{k'}))} \quad (9)$$

We use *episode-based* training [12] to simulate the few-shot setting at training to directly optimize for generalization to unseen novel classes.

Note that the proposed Neural Graph Matching Networks is end-to-end trainable from the input x. We have defined neural graph matching as:

$$\phi_{GM}(x_i, x_j) = \|\mathbf{T}(g(x_i)) - \mathbf{T}(g(x_j))\|^2. \tag{10}$$

From Eqs. 3 and 4, we can see that both the output feature and adjacency matrix are differentiable for graph generator $g(\cdot)$. From Eq. 5, both the node matching feature $\hat{f}(\cdot)$ and the edge matching feature $\hat{\psi}(\cdot)$ are differentiable. In this case, we are able to train the loss in Eq. 9 directly from the input with episode-based training. This allows us to jointly learn the optimized graph and the corresponding graph matching metric for few-shot learning.

5 Experiments

In this work, our goal is few-shot 3D action recognition, where the model is able to classify novel classes with only a few training examples. Instead of directly applying a holistic approach as used in the image space, we propose to use an interaction graph as the intermediate representation to explicitly leverage the inherent spatial information in 3D data. Our experiments aim to answer the following questions: (1) How does NGM's graphical representation approach compare with holistic methods such as PointNet [18] for few-shot 3D action learning? (2) How important are learnable edges for capturing node interaction beyond heuristics (*e.g.,* distance)? (3) How does the proposed *graph tensor* representation for learning graph matching function compare with alternatives such inexact graph matching and graph embedding? We answer the questions by comparing NGM with state-of-the-art 3D representations [10,18], and conduct extensive ablation studies on the design choices of our model.

5.1 Datasets

We use two 3D action dataset with varieties of human-object interactions, where there exists challenging fine-grained actions to recognize. This is ideal for evaluating few-shot 3D action recognition. Because most existing few-shot approaches rely on the principle of transferring knowledge from seen classes to unseen classes, it is important for the seen and unseen classes to be related. At the same time, the actions should still be fine-grained to have challenges for proper evaluation.

CAD-120. We use CAD-120, a RGB-D video dataset containing over 60,000 video frames of activity performed by 4 subjects (Fig. 2). We focus on evaluating the sub-activity labels (*e.g.,* reaching, moving, placing) and their combination with objects in the scene (*e.g.,* bowl, milk, and microwave). These fine-grained interactions with the objects make the classification challenging in few-shot setting. In addition, as the subjects are only given high-level instruction of the

Table 1. Few-Shot Action Recognition Results. We compare our method to baseline holistic methods and baseline part-based methods.

Model	CAD-120		PiGraphs	
	1-shot	5-shot	1-shot	5-shot
PointNet [18]	57.2	69.1	60.6	82.5
P-LSTM [10]	60.5	68.1	66.6	71.7
S-RNN [51]	65.4	85.4	–	–
NGM w/o Edges	66.1	85.0	75.9	71.1
NGM	**78.5**	**91.1**	**80.2**	**88.3**

action, there can be real-world execution varieties in the videos. For our experiments, we split the dataset into 20 training and 10 testing classes.

PiGraphs. We use the PiGraphs dataset [22], which uses RGB-D sensors to capture common activities, annotated as sets of verb-noun pairs such as `use-laptop`, `lie-bed`, and `look-whiteboard`. Annotations also include verb-noun pair compositions, resulting in action classes such as `stand-floor+write-whiteboard` and `sit-chair+look-monitor+type-keyboard`. The dataset contains reconstructed 3D indoor environments, which is ideal for understanding 3D human-object interaction. In addition, the dataset comes with voxel annotation that is not available in the CAD-120 dataset. We utilize the *iGraphs* from the original PiGraphs dataset as our heuristic-derived baseline. We used 32 training and 10 testing classes for our experiments.

For both datasets, nodes were derived from object locations in the dataset. We note that node locations can easily be extracted using a state-of-the-art object detector, but our work is primarily focused on the problem of generating and learning node *relationships*.

5.2 Evaluating 3D Action Representation for Few-Shot Learning

We now evaluate the representations for few-shot 3D action learning and analyze the importance of explicit graphical structure learning. We compare our method to three baselines:

PointNet. PointNet [18] utilizes permutation invariant operators and directly consumes the point cloud as input. This approach has achieved state-of-the-art results on 3D classification and semantic segmentation. We select this baseline as the representative holistic approach without explicitly leveraging the spatial information, and aim to capture the action classification by learning from the whole scene. For a fair comparison, in addition to the point coordinates and RGB values, we also concatenate the detected object type of each point as input to the PointNet.

P-LSTM. Part-aware LSTM (P-LSTM) [10] is an important skeleton based 3D action recognition approach that has been widely used. Unlike PointNet,

Fig. 4. We show the prediction of our model (green label) and P-LSTM [10] (red label) on the CAD-120 dataset. Each action example is represented by three frames (start, middle, end) of the action clip. The graph is overlaid on each frame, where yellow dots are nodes, and green lines are edges. Our graph based approach is able to correctly predict the action class while raw input data can be confusing the PLSTM. (Color figure online)

P-LSTM implicity allows the emergence of structure in the LSTM cell. However, this structure is not explicitly required as in our Neural Graph Matching. In addition to the human joint location, we also feed in the object locations to P-LSTM for a fair comparison.

NGM w/o Edges. We compare our own ablation model without edges as a baseline. In this case, neither the graph learning in graph generation (Sect. 4.1) nor the graph tensor in graph matching (Sect. 4.2) would be possible. In this case, the model is reduced a graph embedding model without passing messages between nodes. We choose this baseline to show the importance of learning both the edges and the graph matching tensor.

Results. The 1-shot and 5-shot action recognition results on both the CAD-120 and the PiGraphs datasets are shown in Table 1. It can be seen that NGM significantly outperforms the baselines on both datasets. We can see that, without enough training data in few-shot learning, holistic representation like Point-Net cannot learn effective features for classification. On the other hand, while P-LSTM and S-RNN are effective for supervised action recognition, without enough data, the hidden states of these recurrent neural networks are unable to capture the structure of the video. In contrast to the baseline, NGM explicitly leverages the interaction graph as the graphical representation, and uses graph tensor in the graph matching stage to compare not only the vector representation

Table 2. Graph Learning Ablation Study. We assess the effect of our edge learning. We compare having no edges, heuristic-defined edges, and our learned edges.

Edges	CAD-120		PiGraphs	
	1-shot	5-shot	1-shot	5-shot
None	66.1	85.0	75.9	82.5
Human-Object	74.9	89.7	75.5	71.3
Proximity	77.2	88.1	–	–
Learned	**78.5**	**91.1**	**80.2**	**88.3**

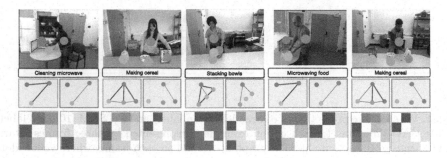

Fig. 5. CAD-120 Graph Learning Results. We show five examples of generated graph (green) compared with the heuristic-defined graph (red) in the middle row. Top row shows the corresponding frame, and bottom row shows the adjacency matrix. It can be seen that NGM generates node relationships that are important to understand the action but not captured in the heuristic edges. For example, NGM automatically generates the edge between human and the microwave in the *cleaning microwave* action. (Color figure online)

of nodes, but also the structure of the graph through edge matching feature. It is important to note that the performance of "NGM w/o Edges" is significantly lower than our full model. This shows that learning the structure and relationship between objects/nodes in the scene plays an important role for generalizing few-shot learning to novel classes. For comparison, fully supervised results for PiGraphs and CAD-120 are 94.7% and 93.7%. The higher performance in the fully supervised setting demonstrates few-shot learning is more challenging than fully supervised learning on these datasets. In the following sections, we will discuss more thorough analysis of each component of our model.

Qualitative Results. We show qualitative results comparing P-LSTM model (red label) to NGM (green label) in Fig. 4. In particular, P-LSTM has difficulty capturing the specific interaction with an object (e.g. placing vs. reaching milk, opening vs. reaching medicine box). In addition, for action sequences where the human is interacting with multiple objects, P-LSTM does not always correctly predict the correct object relevant for the interaction (e.g., placing milk vs. box, reaching bowl vs. microwave). From the graphs shown in Fig. 4, we can see that

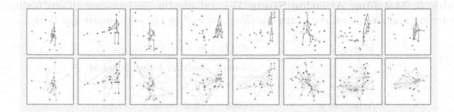

Fig. 6. Comparison of our heuristic graph (top) and our generated graph (bottom). In contrast to the heuristic edges which only contain human joints and immediate objects in contact, our learned edges is able to incorporate further context of the action. While not hand-crafted, the learned edges is still able to capture that this is a human-centered problem and center the edges around the human. (Color figure online)

the explicit modeling of the evolution of graphs over time is a useful signal for predicting the correct action. For instance, in the case of *reaching medicine box*, the graph begins with no edges, then creates an edge between the human and the medicine box at later timesteps to represent "reaching".

5.3   Evaluating Edge Learning

Graph Learning is Important. We have shown in Sect. 5.2 that explicitly learning the object/human relationships through edges plays an important role to the success of our method. We now analyze the effect of different edge generation approaches. In addition to "NGM no Edge" (shown as "None" in this section), we consider two heuristics for generating the edges: The first is "Proximity", where we add an edge between two nodes if the 3D locations are close. The second is "Human-Object", which is similar to "Proximity", but we only add the edge if it is between a human joint and a object. The motivation is that it can focus the model on the human-object interaction that are important to understanding the action. The results are shown in Table 2. It can be seen that both of the heuristics can improve over the "None" baseline, but the proposed edge learning approach still performs the best. Inherently, heuristically-defined graphs are sensitive to noise in node location and constrained by hand-crafted rules that are challenging to generalize. For instance, if a human is close to an unrelated object, a proximity-based edge generator would naively create an undesired edge relationship between the human and the object. The forced mixing of unrelated node features such as in this case can affect performance.

Qualitative Results. In contrast to heuristic edge generation techniques, NGM automatically discovers the important node relationships by optimizing the graph structure for the few-shot learning objective, leading to better prediction performance. NGM has the freedom to learn edge semantics beyond specific hand-designed criteria (e.g., proximity) for node linking. We visualize learned edges in Figs. 5 and 6. NGM-learned graphs (green) contain node relationships that are not captured in heuristic-defined graphs (red).

Table 3. Matching Ablation Study. We evaluate the performance of our features matching and our graph structure matching, as well as the combination of both.

Match	CAD-120		PiGraphs	
	1-shot	5-shot	1-shot	5-shot
Features	61.1	78.3	77.8	74.1
Adjacency	60.5	78.2	78.3	74.1
Adjacency & Features	**78.5**	**91.1**	**80.2**	**88.3**

Cleaning microwave in Fig. 5 links the human node with a cleaning cloth, while NGM additionally links the human with the microwave, even placing stronger weight on the human-microwave than the human-cloth edge, showing that this relationship is critical to predicting the action class. In *making cereal*, we see that the heuristic graph links a naive edge between the human and the cereal. NGM also predicts this edge, but also learned the relevance of the milk jug and the bowl for the cereal-making action, despite the human not being in contact with these objects.

We similarly visualize our learned node relationships on the PiGraphs dataset in Fig. 6, in comparison to the heuristic graphs. The heuristic graph (Top) mainly captures the human skeleton and the immediate objects in contact with skeleton joints. Such a representation is akin to several existing methods on pose-based action recognition methods [29, 30]. In contrast, our learned graph captures far more complex relationships in the scene that are directly optimal for predicting the corresponding action class. Our learned edges tend to center towards the human, which is intuitive given that the PiGraphs dataset is focused on human-centric interactions. However, the edges do not contain the human skeleton edges, suggesting that edges between human joints may not actually be crucial to the classification of action scenes.

5.4 Evaluating Graph Matching Representation

In contrast to classical graph matching [47] and graph embeddings [42], our proposed *graph tensor* in Sect. 4.2 combines both the node representation along with the graph structure to our matching function. We now analyze the importance of combining the continuous feature with the graph structure. The results are shown in Table 3. It can be seen that having only the node representation or the graph structure cannot fully represent the graph for few-shot learning. This shows that there exists complementary information in the holistic graph embedding and the structural adjacency matrix, and the proposed graph tensor is able to leverage and combine both information.

6 Conclusion

We presented Neural Graph Matching (NGM) Networks, a novel few-shot learning framework that leverage the inherent spatial information in 3D through a graphical intermediate representation. NGM consists of two parts: a graph generator, and a graph matching metric, which can be jointly trained in an end-to-end fashion to directly optimize for the few-shot learning objective. We demonstrate that this leads to stronger generalization to unseen classes with only a few-example when compared to both holistic and heuristic-defined approaches.

References

1. Krizhevsky, A., Sutskever, I., Hinton, G.E.: ImageNet classification with deep convolutional neural networks. In: NIPS (2012)
2. He, K., Zhang, X., Ren, S., Sun, J.: Deep residual learning for image recognition. In: CVPR (2016)
3. Caba Heilbron, F., Escorcia, V., Ghanem, B., Carlos Niebles, J.: ActivityNet: a large-scale video benchmark for human activity understanding, pp. 961–970 (2015)
4. Karpathy, A., Toderici, G., Shetty, S., Leung, T., Sukthankar, R., Fei-Fei, L.: Large-scale video classification with convolutional neural networks. In: CVPR (2014)
5. Luo, Z., Peng, B., Huang, D.A., Alahi, A., Fei-Fei, L.: Unsupervised learning of long-term motion dynamics for videos. In: CVPR (2017)
6. Misra, I., Zitnick, C.L., Hebert, M.: Shuffle and learn: unsupervised learning using temporal order verification. In: Leibe, B., Matas, J., Sebe, N., Welling, M. (eds.) ECCV 2016. LNCS, vol. 9905, pp. 527–544. Springer, Cham (2016). https://doi.org/10.1007/978-3-319-46448-0_32
7. Lai, K., Bo, L., Fox, D.: Unsupervised feature learning for 3D scene labeling. In: ICRA (2014)
8. Chang, A.X., et al.: ShapeNet: an information-rich 3D model repository. arXiv preprint arXiv:1512.03012 (2015)
9. Koppula, H.S., Gupta, R., Saxena, A.: Learning human activities and object affordances from RGB-D videos. Int. J. Robot. Res. **32**, 951–970 (2013)
10. Shahroudy, A., Liu, J., Ng, T.T., Wang, G.: NTU RGB+ D: a large scale dataset for 3D human activity analysis. In: CVPR (2016)
11. Song, S., Lichtenberg, S.P., Xiao, J.: SUN RGB-D: a RGB-D scene understanding benchmark suite. In: CVPR (2015)
12. Vinyals, O., Blundell, C., Lillicrap, T., Wierstra, D., et al.: Matching networks for one shot learning. In: Advances in Neural Information Processing Systems, pp. 3630–3638 (2016)
13. Garcia, V., Bruna, J.: Few-shot learning with graph neural networks. In: ICLR (2018)
14. Snell, J., Swersky, K., Zemel, R.S.: Prototypical networks for few-shot learning. arXiv preprint arXiv:1703.05175 (2017)
15. Deng, J., Dong, W., Socher, R., Li, L.J., Li, K., Fei-Fei, L.: ImageNet: a large-scale hierarchical image database. In: CVPR (2009)
16. Masci, J., Boscaini, D., Bronstein, M., Vandergheynst, P.: Geodesic convolutional neural networks on riemannian manifolds. In: ICCV Workshops (2015)
17. Wu, Z., et al.: 3D ShapeNets: a deep representation for volumetric shapes. In: CVPR (2015)
18. Qi, C.R., Su, H., Mo, K., Guibas, L.J.: PointNet: deep learning on point sets for 3D classification and segmentation. arXiv preprint arXiv:1612.00593 (2016)
19. Andreas, J., Rohrbach, M., Darrell, T., Klein, D.: Neural module networks. In: Proceedings of the IEEE Conference on Computer Vision and Pattern Recognition, pp. 39–48 (2016)

20. Johnson, J., et al.: Inferring and executing programs for visual reasoning. arXiv preprint arXiv:1705.03633 (2017)
21. Hu, R., Andreas, J., Rohrbach, M., Darrell, T., Saenko, K.: Learning to reason: end-to-end module networks for visual question answering. CoRR, abs/1704.05526 3 (2017)
22. Savva, M., Chang, A.X., Hanrahan, P., Fisher, M., Nießner, M.: PiGraphs: learning interaction snapshots from observations. ACM Trans. Graph. (TOG) 35(4), 139 (2016)
23. Qi, C.R., Su, H., Mo, K., Guibas, L.J.: PointNet: deep learning on point sets for 3D classification and segmentation. In: CVPR (2017)
24. Ravi, S., Larochelle, H.: Optimization as a model for few-shot learning (2016)
25. Santoro, A., Bartunov, S., Botvinick, M., Wierstra, D., Lillicrap, T.: Meta-learning with memory-augmented neural networks. In: ICML (2016)
26. Santoro, A., Raposo, D., Barrett, D.G., Malinowski, M., Pascanu, R., Battaglia, P., Lillicrap, T.: A simple neural network module for relational reasoning. arXiv preprint arXiv:1706.01427 (2017)
27. Oreifej, O., Liu, Z.: HON4D: histogram of oriented 4D normals for activity recognition from depth sequences. In: CVPR (2013)
28. Rahmani, H., Mahmood, A., Huynh, D.Q., Mian, A.: HOPC: histogram of oriented principal components of 3D pointclouds for action recognition. In: Fleet, D., Pajdla, T., Schiele, B., Tuytelaars, T. (eds.) ECCV 2014. LNCS, vol. 8690, pp. 742–757. Springer, Cham (2014). https://doi.org/10.1007/978-3-319-10605-2_48
29. Wang, J., Liu, Z., Wu, Y., Yuan, J.: Mining actionlet ensemble for action recognition with depth cameras. In: CVPR (2012)
30. Vemulapalli, R., Arrate, F., Chellappa, R.: Human action recognition by representing 3D skeletons as points in a lie group. In: CVPR (2014)
31. Li, C., Wang, P., Wang, S., Hou, Y., Li, W.: Skeleton-based action recognition using LSTM and CNN. arXiv preprint arXiv:1707.02356 (2017)
32. Liu, M., Chen, C., Meng, F.M., Liu, H.: 3D action recognition using multi-temporal skeleton visualization. In: CVPR 2017, p. 391 (2017)
33. Yan, S., Xiong, Y., Lin, D.: Spatial temporal graph convolutional networks for skeleton-based action recognition. arXiv preprint arXiv:1801.07455 (2018)
34. Ikizler, N., Forsyth, D.A.: Searching for complex human activities with no visual examples. Int. J. Comput. Vis. 80, 337–357 (2008)
35. Gu, C., et al.: AVA: a video dataset of spatio-temporally localized atomic visual actions. CoRR, CoRR:1705.08421 (2017)
36. Johnson, J., et al.: Image retrieval using scene graphs. In: Proceedings of the IEEE Conference on Computer Vision and Pattern Recognition, pp. 3668–3678 (2015)
37. Perozzi, B., Al-Rfou, R., Skiena, S.: DeepWalk: Online learning of social representations. In: Proceedings of the 20th ACM SIGKDD International Conference on Knowledge Discovery and Data Mining, pp. 701–710. ACM (2014)
38. Tang, J., Qu, M., Wang, M., Zhang, M., Yan, J., Mei, Q.: LINE: large-scale information network embedding. In: Proceedings of the 24th International Conference on World Wide Web, pp. 1067–1077. International World Wide Web Conferences Steering Committee (2015)
39. Grover, A., Leskovec, J.: node2vec: scalable feature learning for networks. In: Proceedings of the 22nd ACM SIGKDD International Conference on Knowledge Discovery and Data Mining, pp. 855–864. ACM (2016)
40. Mikolov, T., Sutskever, I., Chen, K., Corrado, G.S., Dean, J.: Distributed representations of words and phrases and their compositionality. In: Advances in Neural Information Processing Systems, pp. 3111–3119 (2013)

41. Kearnes, S., McCloskey, K., Berndl, M., Pande, V., Riley, P.: Molecular graph convolutions: moving beyond fingerprints. J. Comput. Aided Mol. Des. **30**(8), 595–608 (2016)
42. Kipf, T.N., Welling, M.: Semi-supervised classification with graph convolutional networks. arXiv preprint arXiv:1609.02907 (2016)
43. Garcia, V., Bruna, J.: Few-shot learning with graph neural networks. arXiv preprint arXiv:1711.04043 (2017)
44. He, K., Gkioxari, G., Dollár, P., Girshick, R.: Mask R-CNN. In: ICCV (2017)
45. Lu, C., Krishna, R., Bernstein, M., Fei-Fei, L.: Visual relationship detection with language priors. In: Leibe, B., Matas, J., Sebe, N., Welling, M. (eds.) ECCV 2016. LNCS, vol. 9905, pp. 852–869. Springer, Cham (2016). https://doi.org/10.1007/978-3-319-46448-0_51
46. Ullmann, J.R.: An algorithm for subgraph isomorphism. J. ACM (JACM) **23**(1), 31–42 (1976)
47. Riesen, K., Jiang, X., Bunke, H.: Exact and inexact graph matching: Methodology and applications. In: Aggarwal, C., Wang, H. (eds.) Managing and Mining Graph Data, pp. 217–247. Springer, Boston (2010)
48. Morrison, P., Zou, J.J.: Inexact graph matching using a hierarchy of matching processes. Comput. Vis. Media **1**(4), 291–307 (2015)
49. Cai, H., Zheng, V.W., Chang, K.: A comprehensive survey of graph embedding: problems, techniques and applications. IEEE Trans. Knowl. Data Eng. (2018)
50. Defferrard, M., Bresson, X., Vandergheynst, P.: Convolutional neural networks on graphs with fast localized spectral filtering. In: NIPS, pp. 3844–3852 (2016)
51. Jain, A., Zamir, A.R., Savarese, S., Saxena, A.: Structural-RNN: deep learning on spatio-temporal graphs. In: Proceedings of the IEEE Conference on Computer Vision and Pattern Recognition, pp. 5308–5317 (2016)

Graph R-CNN for Scene Graph Generation

Jianwei Yang[1](✉) [iD], Jiasen Lu[1], Stefan Lee[1], Dhruv Batra[1,2],
and Devi Parikh[1,2]

[1] Georgia Institute of Technology, Atlanta, USA
{jw2yang,jiasenlu,steflee,dbatra,parikh}@gatech.edu
[2] Facebook AI Research, Menlo Park, USA

Abstract. We propose a novel scene graph generation model called
Graph R-CNN, that is both effective and efficient at detecting objects
and their relations in images. Our model contains a Relation Proposal
Network (RePN) that efficiently deals with the quadratic number of
potential relations between objects in an image. We also propose an
attentional Graph Convolutional Network (aGCN) that effectively captures contextual information between objects and relations. Finally, we
introduce a new evaluation metric that is more holistic and realistic than
existing metrics. We report state-of-the-art performance on scene graph
generation as evaluated using both existing and our proposed metrics.

Keywords: Graph R-CNN · Scene graph generation
Relation proposal network · Attentional graph convolutional network

1 Introduction

Visual scene understanding has traditionally focused on identifying *objects in
images* – learning to predict their presence (*i.e.* image classification [9,15,34])
and spatial extent (*i.e.* object detection [7,22,31] or segmentation [21]). These
object-centric techniques have matured significantly in recent years, however,
representing scenes as collections of objects fails to capture relationships which
may be essential for scene understanding.

A recent work [12] has instead proposed representing visual scenes as graphs
containing objects, their attributes, and the relationships between them. These
scene graphs form an interpretable structured representation of the image that
can support higher-level visual intelligence tasks such as captioning [24,39],
visual question answering [1,11,35,37–39], and image-grounded dialog [3]. While
scene graph representations hold tremendous promise, extracting scene graphs
from images – efficiently and accurately – is challenging. The natural approach
of considering every pair of nodes (objects) as a potential edge (relationship) –
essentially reasoning over fully-connected graphs – is often effective in modeling

---

J. Yang and J. Lu – Equal contribution

© Springer Nature Switzerland AG 2018
V. Ferrari et al. (Eds.): ECCV 2018, LNCS 11205, pp. 690–706, 2018.
https://doi.org/10.1007/978-3-030-01246-5_41

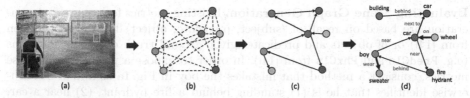

Fig. 1. Given an image (a), our proposed approach first extracts a set of objects visible in the scene and considers possible relationships between all nodes (b). Then it prunes unlikely relationships using a learned measure of 'relatedness', producing a sparser candidate graph structure (c). Finally, an attentional graph convolution network is applied to integrate global context and update object node and relationship edge labels.

contextual relationships but scales poorly (quadratically) with the number of objects, quickly becoming impractical. The naive fix of randomly sub-sampling edges to be considered is more efficient but not as effective since the distribution of interactions between objects is far from random – take Fig. 1(a) as an example, it is much more likely for a 'car' and 'wheel' to have a relationship than a 'wheel' and 'building'. Furthermore, the types of relationships that typically occur between objects are also highly dependent on those objects.

Graph R-CNN. In this work, we propose a new framework, Graph R-CNN, for scene graph generation which effectively leverages object-relationship regularities through two mechanisms to intelligently sparsify and reason over candidate scene graphs. Our model can be factorized into three logical stages: (1) object node extraction, (2) relationship edge pruning, and (3) graph context integration, which are depicted in Fig. 1. In the object node extraction stage, we utilize a standard object detection pipeline [32]. This results in a set of localized object regions as shown in Fig. 1b. We introduce two important novelties in the rest of the pipeline to incorporate the real-world regularities in object relationships discussed above. First, we introduce a relation proposal network (RePN) that learns to efficiently compute *relatedness scores* between object pairs which are used to intelligently prune unlikely scene graph connections (as opposed to random pruning in prior work). A sparse post-pruning graph is shown in Fig. 1c. Second, given the resulting sparsely connected scene graph candidate, we apply an attentional graph convolution network (aGCN) to propagate higher-order context throughout the graph – updating each object and relationship representation based on its neighbors. In contrast to existing work, we predict per-node edge attentions, enabling our approach to learn to modulate information flow across unreliable or unlikely edges. We show refined graph labels and edge attentions (proportional to edge width) in Fig. 1d.

To validate our approach, we compare our performance with existing methods on the Visual Genome [14] dataset and find that our approach achieves an absolute gain of 5.0 on Recall@50 for scene graph generation [40]. We also perform extensive model ablations and quantify the impact of our modeling choices.

Evaluating Scene Graph Generation. Existing metrics for scene graph generation are based on recall of ⟨subject, predicate, object⟩ triplets (e.g. SGGen from [14]) or of objects and predicates given ground truth object localizations (e.g. PredCls and PhrCls from [14]). In order to expose a problem with these metrics, consider a method that mistakes the boy in Fig. 1a as a man but otherwise identifies that he is (1) standing behind a fire hydrant, (2) near a car, and (3) wearing a sweater. Under the triplet-based metrics, this minor error (boy vs man) would be heavily penalized despite most of the boy's relationships being correctly identified. Metrics that provide ground-truth regions side-step this problem by focusing strictly on relationship prediction but cannot accurately reflect the test-time performance of the entire scene graph generation system.

To address this mismatch, we introduce a novel evaluation metric (SGGen+) that more holistically evaluates the performance of scene graph generation with respect to objects, attributes (if any), and relationships. Our proposed metric SGGen+ computes the total recall for singleton entities (objects and predicates), pair entries ⟨object, attribute⟩ (if any), and triplet entities ⟨subject, predicate, object⟩. We report results on existing methods under this new metric and find our approach also outperforms the state-of-the-art significantly. More importantly, this new metric provides a more robust and holistic measure of similarity between generated and ground-truth scene graphs.

Summary of Contributions. Concretely, this work addresses the scene graph generation problem by introducing a novel model (Graph R-CNN), which can leverage object-relationship regularities, and proposes a more holistic evaluation metric (SGGen+) for scene graph generation. We benchmark our model against existing approaches on standard metrics and this new measure – outperforming existing approaches.

2   Related Work

Contextual Reasoning and Scene Graphs. The idea of using context to improve scene understanding has a long history in computer vision [16,27,28,30]. More recently, inspired by representations studied by the graphics community, Johnson et al.[12] introduced the problem of extracting scene graphs from images, which generalizes the task of object detection [6,7,22,31,32] to also detecting relationships and attributes of objects.

Scene Graph Generation. A number of approaches have been proposed for the detection of both objects and their relationships [2,17–19,23,26,29,40,42–44,46]. Though most of these works point out that reasoning over a quadratic number of relationships in the scene graph is intractable, each resorted to heuristic methods like random sampling to address this problem. Our work is the first to introduce a trainable relationship proposal network (RePN) that learns to prune unlikely relationship edges from the graph without sacrificing efficacy. RePN provides high-quality relationship candidates, which we find improves overall scene graph generation performance.

Most scene graph generation methods also include some mechanisms for context propagation and reasoning over a candidate scene graph in order to refine the final labeling. In [40], Xu *et al.*decomposed the problem into two sub-graphs – one for objects and one for relationships – and performed message passing. Similarly, in [17], the authors propose two message-passing strategies (parallel and sequential) for propagating information between objects and relationships. Dai *et al.*[2] address model the scene graph generation process as inference on a conditional random field (CRF). Newell *et al.* [26] proposed to directly generate scene graphs from image pixels without the use of object detector based on associative graph embeddings. In our work, we develop a novel attentional graph convolutional network (aGCN) to update node and relationship representations by propagating context between nodes in candidate scene graphs – operating both on visual and semantic features. While similar in function to the message-passing based approach above, aGCN is highly efficient and can learn to place attention on reliable edges and dampen the influence of unlikely ones.

A number of previous approaches have noted the strong regularities in scene graph generation which motivate our approach. In [23], Lu *et al.* integrates semantic priors from language to improve the detection of meaningful relationships between objects. Likewise, Li *et al.* [18] demonstrated that region captions can also provide useful context for scene graph generation. Most related to our motivation, Zeller *et al.*[42] formalize the notion of motifs (*i.e.*, regularly occurring graph structures) and examine their prevalence in the Visual Genome dataset [14]. The authors also propose a surprisingly strong baseline which directly uses frequency priors to predict relationships – explicitly integrating regularities in the graph structure.

Relationship Proposals. Our Relationship Proposal Network (RePN) is inspired and relates strongly to the region proposal network (RPN) of faster R-CNN [32] used in object detection. Our RePN is also similar in spirit to the recently-proposed relationship proposal network (Rel-PN) [45]. There are a number of subtle differences between these approaches. The Rel-PN model independently predicts proposals for subject, objects and predicates, and then re-scores all valid triples, while our RePN generates relations conditioned on objects, allowing it to learn object-pair relationship biases. Moreover, their approach is class agnostic and has not been used for scene graph generation.

Graph Convolutional Networks (GCNs). GCNs were first proposed in [13] in the context of semi-supervised learning. GCNs decompose complicated computation over graph data into a series of localized operations (typically only involving neighboring nodes) for each node at each time step. The structure and edge strengths are typically fixed prior to the computation. For completeness, we note that an upcoming publication [36] has concurrently and independently developed a similar GCN attention mechanism (as aGCN) and shown its effectiveness in other (non-computer vision) contexts.

3   Approach

In this work, we model scene graphs as graphs consisting of image regions, relationships, and their labellings. More formally, let I denote an image, V be a set of nodes corresponding to localized object regions in I, $E \in \binom{V}{2}$ denote the relationships (or edges) between objects, and O and R denote object and relationship labels respectively. Thus, the goal is to build a model for $P(S = (V, E, O, R)|I)$. In this work, we factorize the scene graph generation process into three parts:

$$P(\mathcal{S}|\boldsymbol{I}) = \overbrace{P(\boldsymbol{V}|\boldsymbol{I})}^{\substack{\text{Object Region}\\\text{Proposal}}} \underbrace{P(\boldsymbol{E}|\boldsymbol{V}, \boldsymbol{I})}_{\substack{\text{Relationship}\\\text{Proposal}}} \overbrace{P(\boldsymbol{R}, \boldsymbol{O}|\boldsymbol{V}, \boldsymbol{E}, \boldsymbol{I})}^{\text{Graph Labeling}} \tag{1}$$

which separates graph construction (nodes and edges) from graph labeling. The intuition behind this factorization is straightforward. First, the object region proposal $P(\boldsymbol{V}|\boldsymbol{I})$ is typically modeled using an off-the-shelf object detection system such as [32] to produce candidate regions. Notably, existing methods typically model the second relationship proposal term $P(\boldsymbol{E}|\boldsymbol{V}, \boldsymbol{I})$ as a uniform random sampling of potential edges between vertices $\boldsymbol{V}$. In contrast, we propose a relationship proposal network (RePN) to directly model $P(\boldsymbol{E}|\boldsymbol{V}, \boldsymbol{I})$ – making our approach the first that allows for learning the entire generation process end-to-end. Finally, the graph labeling process $P(\boldsymbol{R}, \boldsymbol{O}|\boldsymbol{V}, \boldsymbol{E}, \boldsymbol{I})$ is typically treated as an iterative refinement process [2,17,40]. A brief pipeline is shown in Fig. 2.

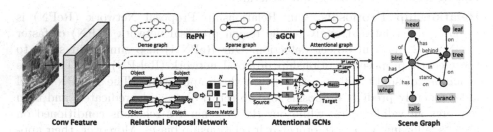

Fig. 2. The pipeline of our proposed Graph R-CNN framework. Given an image, our model first uses RPN to propose object regions, and then prunes the connections between object regions through our relation proposal network (RePN). Attentional GCN is then applied to integrate contextual information from neighboring nodes in the graph. Finally, the scene graph is obtained on the right side.

In the following, we discuss the components of our proposed Graph R-CNN model corresponding to each of the terms in Eq. 1. First, we discuss our use of Faster R-CNN [32] for node generation in Sect. 3.1. Then in Sect. 3.2 we introduce our novel relation proposal network architecture to intelligently generate edges. Finally, in Sect. 3.3 we present our graph convolutional network [13] with learned attention to adaptively integrate global context for graph labeling.

3.1   Object Proposals

In our approach, we use the Faster R-CNN [32] framework to extract a set of n object proposals from an input image. Each object proposal i is associated with a spatial region $r_i^o = [x_i, y_i, w_i, h_i]$, a pooled feature vector x_i^o, and an initial estimated label distribution p_i^o over classes $C=\{1, \ldots, k\}$. We denote the collection of these vectors for all n proposals as the matrices $R^o \in \mathbb{R}^{n \times 4}$, $X^o \in \mathbb{R}^{n \times d}$, and $P^o \in \mathbb{R}^{n \times |C|}$ respectively.

3.2   Relation Proposal Network

Given the n proposed object nodes from the previous step, there are $O(n^2)$ possible connections between them; however, as previously discussed, most object pairs are unlikely to have relationships due to regularities in real-world object interactions. To model these regularities, we introduce a relation proposal network (RePN) which learns to efficiently estimate the *relatedness* of an object pair. By pruning edges corresponding to unlikely relations, the RePN can efficiently sparsify the candidate scene graph – retaining likely edges and suppressing noise introduced from unlikely ones.

In this paper, we exploit the estimated class distributions (P^o) to infer relatedness – essentially learning soft class-relationships priors. This choice aligns well with our intuition that certain classes are relatively unlikely to interact compared with some other classes. Concretely, given initial object classification distributions P^o, we score all $n * (n - 1)$ directional pairs $\{p_i^o, p_j^o | i \neq j\}$, computing the relatedness as $s_{ij} = f(p_i^o, p_j^o)$ where $f(\cdot, \cdot)$ is a learned relatedness function. One straightforward implementation of $f(\cdot, \cdot)$ could be passing the concatenation $[p_i^o, p_j^o]$ as input to a multi-layer perceptron which outputs the score. However, this approach would consume a great deal of memory and computation given the quadratic number of object pairs. To avoid this, we instead consider an asymmetric kernel function:

$$f(p_i^o, p_j^o) = \langle \Phi(p_i^o), \Psi(p_j^o) \rangle, i \neq j \qquad (2)$$

where $\Phi(\cdot)$ and $\Psi(\cdot)$ are projection functions for subjects and objects in the relationships respectively[1]. This decomposition allows the score matrix $S = \{s_{ij}\}^{n \times n}$ to be computed *with only two projection processes for X^o followed by a matrix multiplication*. We use two multi-layer perceptrons (MLPs) with identical architecture (but different parameters) for $\Phi(\cdot)$ and $\Psi(\cdot)$. We also apply a sigmoid function element-wise to S such that all relatedness scores range from 0 to 1.

After obtaining the score matrix for all object pairs, we sort the scores in descending order and choose top K pairs. We then apply non-maximal suppression (NMS) to filter out object pairs that have significant overlap with others.

---

[1] We distinguish between the first and last object in a relationship as subject and object respectively, that is, ⟨subject, relationship, object⟩.

Each relationship has a pair of bounding boxes, and the combination order matters. We compute the overlap between two object pairs $\{u, v\}$ and $\{p, q\}$ as:

$$IoU(\{u, v\}, \{p, q\}) = \frac{I(r_u^o, r_p^o) + I(r_v^o, r_q^o)}{U(r_u^o, r_p^o) + U(r_v^o, r_q^o)} \quad (3)$$

where operator I computes the intersection area between two boxes and U the union area. The remaining m object pairs are considered as candidates having meaningful relationships E. With E, we obtain a graph $\mathcal{G} = (V, E)$, which is much sparser than the original fully connected graph. Along with the edges proposed for the graph, we get the visual representations $X^r = \{x_1^r, ..., x_m^r\}$ for all m relationships by extracting features from the union box of each object pair.

3.3   Attentional GCN

To integrate contextual information informed by the graph structure, we propose an attentional graph convolutional network (aGCN). Before we describe our proposed aGCN, let us briefly recap a 'vanilla' GCN in which each node i has a representation $z_i \in \mathbb{R}^d$, as proposed in [13]. Briefly, for a target node i in the graph, the representations of its neighboring nodes $\{z_j \mid j \in \mathcal{N}(i)\}$ are first transformed via a learned linear transformation W. Then, these transformed representations are gathered with predetermined weights α, followed by a non-linear function σ (ReLU [25]). This layer-wise propagation can be written as:

$$z_i^{(l+1)} = \sigma \left(z_i^{(l)} + \sum_{j \in \mathcal{N}(i)} \alpha_{ij} W z_j^{(l)} \right) \quad (4)$$

or equivalently we can collect node representations into a matrix $Z \in \mathbb{R}^{d \times Tn}$

$$z_i^{(l+1)} = \sigma \left(W Z^{(l)} \alpha_i \right) \quad (5)$$

for $\alpha_i \in [0, 1]^n$ with 0 entries for nodes not neighboring i and $\alpha_{ii} = 1$. In conventional GCN, the connections in the graph are known and coefficient vector α_i are preset based on the symmetrically normalized adjacency matrix of features.

In this paper, we extend the conventional GCN to an attentional version, which we refer to as aGCN, by learning to adjust α. To predict attention from node features, we learn a 2-layer MLP over concatenated node features and compute a softmax over the resulting scores. The attention for node i is

$$u_{ij} = w_h^T \sigma(W_a[z_i^{(l)}, z_j^{(l)}]) \quad (6)$$

$$\alpha_i = \text{softmax}(u_i), \quad (7)$$

where w_h and W_a are learned parameters and $[\cdot, \cdot]$ is the concatenation operation. By definition, we set $\alpha_{ii} = 1$ and $\alpha_{ij} = 0 \ \forall j \notin \mathcal{N}(i)$. As attention is a function of node features, each iteration results in altered attentions which affects successive iterations.

aGCN for Scene Graph Generation. Recall that from the previous sections we have a set of N object regions and m relationships. From these, we construct a graph G with nodes corresponding to object and relationship proposals. We insert edges between relation nodes and their associated objects. We also add skip-connect edges directly between all object nodes. These connections allow information to flow directly between object nodes. Recent work has shown that reasoning about object correlation can improve detection performance [10]. We apply aGCN to this graph to update object and relationship representations based on global context.

Note that our graph captures a number of different types of connections (*i.e.* object $\leftrightarrow$ relationship, relationship $\leftrightarrow$ subject and object $\leftrightarrow$ object). In addition, the information flow across each connection may be asymmetric (the informativeness of subject on relationship might be quite different from relationship to subject). We learn different transformations for each type and ordering – denoting the linear transform from node type a to node type b as W^{ab} with s=subjects, o=objects, and r=relationships. Using the same notation as in Eq. 5 and writing object and relationship features as Z^o and Z^r, we write the representation update for object nodes as

$$z_i^o = \sigma(\overbrace{W^{\text{skip}}Z^o\boldsymbol{\alpha}^{\text{skip}}}^{\substack{\text{Message from}\\\text{Other Objects}}} + \overbrace{W^{sr}Z^r\boldsymbol{\alpha}^{sr} + W^{or}Z^r\boldsymbol{\alpha}^{or}}^{\substack{\text{Messages from}\\\text{Neighboring Relationships}}}) \qquad (8)$$

with $\boldsymbol{\alpha}_{ii}^{\text{skip}}$=1 and similarly for relationship nodes as

$$z_i^r = \sigma(z_i^r + \underbrace{W^{rs}Z^o\boldsymbol{\alpha}^{rs} + W^{ro}Z^o\boldsymbol{\alpha}^{ro}}_{\text{Messages from Neighboring Objects}}). \qquad (9)$$

where $\boldsymbol{\alpha}$ are computed at each iteration as in Eq. 7.

One open choice is how to initialize the object and relationship node representations z which could potentially be set to any intermediate feature representation or even the pre-softmax output corresponding to class labels. In practice, we run both a visual and semantic aGCN computation – one with visual features and the other using pre-softmax outputs. In this way, we can reason about both lower-level visual details (*i.e.* two people are likely talking if they are facing one another) as well as higher-level semantic co-occurrences (*i.e.* cars have wheels). Further, we set the attention in the semantic aGCN to be that of the visual aGCN – effectively modulating the flow of semantic information based on visual cues. This also enforces that real-world objects and relationships represented in both graphs interact with others in the same manner.

3.4   Loss Function

In Graph R-CNN, we factorize the scene graph generation process into three sub-processes: $P(R, O|V, E, I)$, $P(E|V, I)$, $P(V|I)$, which were described above. During training, each of these sub-processes are trained with supervision. For $P(V|I)$, we use the same loss as used in RPN, which consists of a binary cross entropy loss on proposals and a regression loss for anchors. For $P(E|V, I)$, we use another binary cross entropy loss on the relation proposals. For the final scene graph generation $P(R, O|V, E, I)$, two multi-class cross entropy losses are used for object classification and predicate classification.

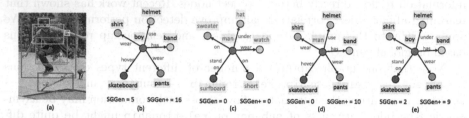

Fig. 3. A example to demonstrate the difference between SGGen and SGGen+. Given the input image (a), its ground truth scene graph is depicted in (b). (c)–(e) are three generated scene graphs. For clarity, we merely show the connections with *boy*. At the bottom of each graph, we compare the number of correct predictions for two metrics.

4   Evaluating Scene Graph Generation

Scene graph generation is naturally a structured prediction problem over attributed graphs, and how to correctly and efficiently evaluate predictions is an under-examined problem in prior work on scene graph generation. We note that graph similarity based on minimum graph edit distance has been well-studied in graph theory [5]; however, computing exact solution is NP-complete and approximation APX-hard [20].

Prior work has circumvented these issues by evaluating scene graph generation under a simple triplet-recall based metric introduced in [40]. Under this metric which we will refer to as SGGen, the ground truth scene graph is represented as a set of ⟨object, relationship, subject⟩ triplets and recall is computed via exact match. That is to say, a triplet is considered 'matched' in a generated scene graph if all three elements have been correctly labeled, and both object and subject nodes have been properly localized (*i.e.*, bounding box IoU >0.5). While simple to compute, this metric results in some unintuitive notions of similarity that we demonstrate in Fig. 3.

Figure 3a shows an input image overlaid with bounding box localizations of correspondingly colored nodes in the ground truth scene graph shown in (b). (c), (d), and (e) present erroneously labeled scene graphs corresponding to these same localizations. Even a casual examination of (c) and (d) yields the stark difference in their accuracy – while (d) has merely mislabeled the boy as a man, (c) has failed to accurately predict even a single node or relationship! Despite these differences, neither recalls a single complete triplet and are both scored identically under SGGen (*i.e.*, 0).

To address this issue, we propose a new metric called SGGen+ as the augmentation of SGGen. SGGen+ not only considers the triplets in the graph, but also the singletons (object and predicate). The computation of SGGen+ can be formulated as:

$$Recall = \frac{C(O) + C(P) + C(T)}{N} \tag{10}$$

where $C(\cdot)$ is a counting operation, and hence $C(O)$ is the number of object nodes correctly localized and recognized; $C(P)$ is for predicate. Since the location of predicate depends on the location of subject and object, only if both subject and object are correctly localized and the predicate is correctly recognized, we will count it as one. $C(T)$ is for triplet, which is the same as SGGen. Here, N is the number of entries (the sum of number of objects, predicates and relationships) in the ground truth graph. In Fig. 3, using our SGGen+, the recall for graph (c) is still 0, since all predictions are wrong. However, the recall for graph (d) is not 0 anymore since most of the object and all predicate predictions are correct, except for one wrong prediction for the red node. Based on our new metric, we can obtain a much comprehensive measurement of scene graph similarity.

5   Experiments

Recently, there are some inconsistencies in existing work on scene graph generation in terms of data preprocessing, data split, and evaluation. This makes it difficult to systematically benchmark progress and cleanly compare numbers across papers. So we first clarify the details of our experimental settings.

Datasets. There are a number of splits of the Visual Genome dataset that have been used in the scene graph generation literature [18,40,45]. The most commonly used is the one proposed in [40]. Hence, in our experiments, we follow their preprocessing strategy and dataset split. After preprocessing, the dataset is split into training and test sets, which contains 75,651 images and 32,422 images, respectively. In this dataset, the top-frequent 150 object classes and 50 relation classes are selected. Each image has around 11.5 objects and 6.2 relationships in the scene graph.

Training. For training, multiple strategies have been used in literature. In [18, 26,40], the authors used two-stage training, where the object detector is pre-trained, followed by the joint training of the whole scene graph generation model. To be consistent with previous work [18,40], we also adopt the two-stage training – we first train the object detector and then train the whole model jointly until convergence.

Metrics. We use four metrics for evaluating scene graph generation, including three previously used metrics and our proposed SGGen+ metric:

- **Predicate Classification (PredCls):** The performance for recognizing the relation between two objects given the ground truth locations.
- **Phrase Classification (PhrCls):** The performance for recognizing two object categories and their relation given the ground truth locations.

- **Scene Graph Generation (SGGen):** The performance for detecting objects (IoU > 0.5) *and* recognizing the relations between object pairs.
- **Comprehensive Scene Graph Generation (SGGen+):** Besides the triplets counted by SGGen, it considers the singletons and pairs (if any), as described earlier.

Evaluation. In our experiments, we multiply the classification scores for subjects, objects and their relationships, then sort them in descending order. Based on this order, we compute the recall at top 50 and top 100, respectively. Another difference in existing literature in the evaluation protocol is w.r.t. the PhrCls and PredCls metrics. Some previous works [18,26] used different models to evaluate along different metrics. However, such a comparison is unfair since the models could be trained to overfit the respective metrics. For meaningful evaluation, we evaluate a single model – the one obtained after joint training – across all metrics.

5.1   Implementation Details

We use Faster R-CNN [32] associated with VGG16 [33] as the backbone based on the PyTorch re-implementation [41]. During training, the number of proposals from RPN is 256. For each proposal, we perform ROI Align [8] pooling, to get a 7×7 response map, which is then fed to a two-layer MLP to obtain each proposal's representation. In RePN, the projection functions $\Phi(\cdot)$ and $\Psi(\cdot)$ are simply two-layer MLPs. During training, we sample 128 object pairs from the quadratic number of candidates. We then obtain the union of boxes of the two objects and extract a representation for the union. The threshold for box-pair NMS is 0.7. In aGCN, to obtain the attention for one node pair, we first project the object/predicate features into 256-d and then concatenate them into 512-d, which is then fed to a two-layer MLP with a 1-d output. For aGCN, we use two aGCN layers at the feature level and semantic level, respectively. The attention on the graph is updated in each aGCN layer at the feature level, which is then fixed and sent to the aGCN at the semantic level.

Training. As mentioned, we perform stage-wise training – we first pretrain Faster R-CNN for object detection, and then fix the parameters in the backbone to train the scene graph generation model. SGD is used as the optimizer, with initial learning rate 1e−2 for both training stages.

5.2   Analysis on New Metric

We first quantitatively demonstrate the difference between our proposed metric SGGen+ and SGGen. We compare them by perturbing ground truth scene graphs. We consider assigning random incorrect labels to objects; perturbing objects 1) without relationships, 2) with relationships, and 3) both. We vary the fraction of nodes which are perturbed among {20%, 50%, 100%}. Recall is reported for both metrics. As shown in Table 1, SGGen is completely insensitive to the perturbation of objects without relationships (staying at 100 consistently) since it only considers relationship triplets. Note that there are on average 50.1% objects without relationships in the dataset, which SGGen omits. On the other hand, SGGen is overly sensitive to label errors on objects with relationships (reporting 54.1 at only 20% perturbation where the overall scene graph is still quite accurate). Note that even at 100% perturbation the object localizations and relationships are still correct such that SGGen+ provides a non-zero score, unlike SGGen which considers the graph entirely wrong. Overall, we hope this analysis demonstrates that SCGen+ is more comprehensive compared to SCGen.

Table 1. Comparisons between SGGen and SGGen+ under different perturbations.

Perturb Type	none	w/o relationship			w/ relationship			both		
Perturb Ratio	0%	20%	50%	100%	20%	50%	100%	20%	50%	100%
SGGen	100.0	100.0	100.0	100.0	54.1	22.1	0.0	62.2	24.2	0.0
SGGen+	100.0	94.5	89.1	76.8	84.3	69.6	47.9	80.1	56.6	22.8

5.3 Quantitative Comparison

We compare our Graph R-CNN with recent proposed methods, including Iterative Message Passing (IMP) [40], Multi-level scene Description Network (MSDN) [18]. Furthermore, we evaluate the neural motif frequency baseline proposed in [42]. Note that previous methods often use slightly different pre-training procedures or data split or extra supervisions. For a fair comparison and to control for such orthogonal variations, we reimplemented IMP, MSDN and frequency baseline in our codebase. Then, we re-train IMP and MSDN based on our backbone – specifically, we used the same pre-trained object detector, and then jointly train the scene graph generator until convergence. We denote these as IMP† and MSDN†. Using the same pre-trained object detector, we report the neural motif frequency baseline in [42] as NM-Freq†.

Table 2. Comparison on Visual Genome test set [14]. We reimplemented IMP [40] and MSDN [18] using the same object detection backbone for fair comparison.

Method	SGGen+		SGGen		PhrCls		PredCls	
	R@50	R@100	R@50	R@100	R@50	R@100	R@50	R@100
IMP [40]	-	-	3.4	4.2	21.7	24.4	44.8	53.0
MSDN [18]	-	-	7.7	10.5	19.3	21.8	63.1	66.4
Pixel2Graph [26]	-	-	9.7	11.3	26.5	30.0	68.0	75.2
IMP† [40]	25.6	27.7	6.4	8.0	20.6	22.4	40.8	45.2
MSDN† [18]	25.8	28.2	7.0	9.1	27.6	29.9	53.2	57.9
NM-Freq† [42]	26.4	27.8	6.9	9.1	23.8	27.2	41.8	48.8
Graph R-CNN (Us)	**28.5**	**35.9**	**11.4**	**13.7**	**29.6**	**31.6**	**54.2**	**59.1**

We report the scene graph generation performance in Table 2. The top three rows are numbers reported in the original paper, and the bottom four rows are the numbers from our re-implementations. First, we note that our re-implementations of IMP and MSDN (IMP† and MSDN†) result in performance that is close to or better than the originally reported numbers under some metrics (but not all), which establishes that the takeaway messages next are indeed due to our proposed architectural choices – relation proposal network and attentional GCNs. Next, we notice that Graph R-CNN outperforms IMP† and MSDN†. This indicates that our proposed Graph R-CNN model is more effective to extract the scene graph from images. Our approach also outperforms the frequency baseline on all metrics, demonstrating that our model has not just learned simple co-occurrence statistics from training data, but rather also captures context in individual images. More comprehensively, we compare with IMP and MSDN on the efficiency over training and inference. IMP uses 2.15× while MSDN uses 1.86× our method. During inference, IMP is 3.27× while MSDN is 3.80× slower than our Graph R-CNN. This is mainly due to the simplified architecture design (especially the aGCN for context propagation) in our model.

5.4   Ablation Study

In Graph R-CNN, we proposed two novel modules – relation proposal network (RePN) and attentional GCNs (aGCN). In this sub-section, we perform ablation studies to get a clear sense of how these different components affect the final performance. The left-most columns in Table 3 indicate whether or not we used

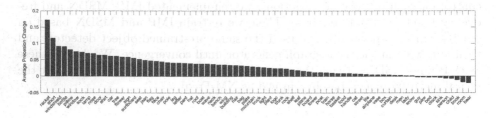

Fig. 4. Per category object detection performance change after adding RePN.

Table 3. Ablation studies on Graph R-CNN. We report the performance based on four scene graph generation metrics and the object detection performance in mAP@0.5.

RePN	GCN	aGCN	Detection	SGGen+		SGGen		PhrCls		PredCls	
			mAP@0.5	R@50	R@100	R@50	R@100	R@50	R@100	R@50	R@100
-	-	-	20.4	25.9	27.9	6.1	7.9	17.8	19.9	33.5	38.4
✓	-	-	**23.6**	27.6	34.8	8.7	11.1	18.3	20.4	34.5	39.5
✓	✓	-	23.4	28.1	35.3	10.8	13.4	27.2	29.5	52.3	57.2
✓	-	✓	23.0	**28.5**	**35.9**	**11.4**	**13.7**	**29.4**	**31.6**	**54.2**	**59.1**

RePN, GCN, and attentional GCN (aGCN) in our approach. The results are reported in the remaining columns of Table 3. We also report object detection performance mAP@0.5 following Pascal VOC's metric [4].

In Table 3, we find RePN boosts SGGen and SGGen+ significantly. This indicates that our RePN can effectively prune the spurious connections between objects to achieve high recall for the correct relationships. We also notice it improves object detection significantly. In Fig. 4 we show the per category object detection performance change when RePN is added. For visual clarity, we dropped every other column when producing the plot. We can see that almost all object categories improve after adding RePN. Interestingly, we find the detection performance on categories like *racket, short, windshield, bottle* are most significantly improved. Note that many of these classes are smaller objects that have strong relationships with other objects, e.g. rackets are often carried by people. Evaluating PhrCls and PredCls involves using the ground truth object locations. Since the number of objects in images (typically <25) is much less than the number of object proposals (64), the number of relation pairs is already very small. As a result, RePN has less effect on these two metrics.

By adding the aGCNs into our model, the performance is further improved. These improvements demonstrate that the aGCN in our Graph R-CNN can capture meaningful context across the graph. We also compare the performance of our model with and without attention. We see that by adding attention on top of GCNs, the performance is higher. This indicates that controlling the extent to which contextual information flows through the edges is important. These results align with our intuitions mentioned in the introduction. Figure 5 shows generated scene graphs for test images. With RePN and aGCN, our model is able to generate higher recall scene graphs. The green ellipsoids shows the correct relationship predictions in the generated scene graph.

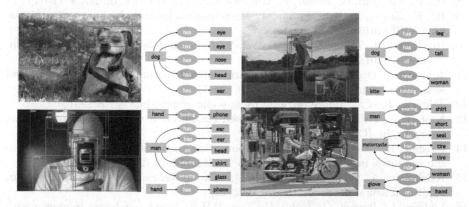

Fig. 5. Qualitative results from Graph R-CNN. In images, blue and orange bounding boxes are ground truths and correct predictions, respectively. In scene graphs, blue ellipsoids are ground truth relationships while green ones denote correct predictions.

6   Conclusion

In this work, we introduce a new model for scene graph generation – Graph R-CNN. Our model includes a relation proposal network (RePN) that efficiently and intelligently prunes out pairs of objects that are unlikely to be related, and an attentional graph convolutational network (aGCN) that effectively propagates contextual information across the graph. We also introdce a novel scene graph generation evaluation metric (SGGen+) that is more fine-grained and realistic than existing metrics. Our approach outperforms existing methods for scene graph generation, as evaluated using existing metrics and our proposed metric.

Acknowledgements. This work was supported in part by NSF, AFRL, DARPA, Siemens, Google, Amazon, ONR YIPs and ONR Grants N00014-16-1-{2713,2793}.

References

1. Antol, S., et al.: VQA: visual question answering. In: ICCV, pp. 2425–2433 (2015)
2. Dai, B., Zhang, Y., Lin, D.: Detecting visual relationships with deep relational networks. In: CVPR (2017)
3. Das, A., et al.: Visual dialog. In: CVPR (2017)
4. Everingham, M., Van Gool, L., Williams, C., Winn, J., Zisserman, A.: The Pascal visual object classes challenge 2012 results, vol. 5 (2012). http://www.pascal-network.org/challenges/VOC/voc2012/workshop/index.html
5. Gao, X., Xiao, B., Tao, D., Li, X.: A survey of graph edit distance. Pattern Anal. Appl. **13**(1), 113–129 (2010)
6. Girshick, R.: Fast R-CNN. In: CVPR (2015)
7. Girshick, R., Donahue, J., Darrell, T., Malik, J.: Rich feature hierarchies for accurate object detection and semantic segmentation. In: CVPR (2014)
8. He, K., Gkioxari, G., Dollár, P., Girshick, R.: Mask R-CNN. In: ICCV (2017)
9. He, K., Zhang, X., Ren, S., Sun, J.: Deep residual learning for image recognition. In: CVPR (2016)
10. Hu, H., Gu, J., Zhang, Z., Dai, J., Wei, Y.: Relation networks for object detection. In: CVPR (2018)
11. Johnson, J., et al.: CLEVR: a diagnostic dataset for compositional language and elementary visual reasoning. In: CVPR (2017)
12. Johnson, J., et al.: Image retrieval using scene graphs. In: CVPR (2015)
13. Kipf, T.N., Welling, M.: Semi-supervised classification with graph convolutional networks. In: ICLR (2017)
14. Krishna, R., et al.: Visual genome: Connecting language and vision using crowd-sourced dense image annotations. IJCV **123**(1), 32–73 (2017)
15. Krizhevsky, A., Sutskever, I., Hinton, G.E.: ImageNet classification with deep convolutional neural networks. In: NIPS (2012)
16. Ladicky, L., Russell, C., Kohli, P., Torr, P.H.S.: Graph cut based inference with co-occurrence statistics. In: Daniilidis, K., Maragos, P., Paragios, N. (eds.) ECCV 2010. LNCS, vol. 6315, pp. 239–253. Springer, Heidelberg (2010). https://doi.org/10.1007/978-3-642-15555-0_18
17. Li, Y., Ouyang, W., Wang, X.: ViP-CNN: a visual phrase reasoning convolutional neural network for visual relationship detection. In: CVPR (2017)

18. Li, Y., Ouyang, W., Zhou, B., Wang, K., Wang, X.: Scene graph generation from objects, phrases and region captions. In: ICCV (2017)
19. Liang, X., Lee, L., Xing, E.P.: Deep variation-structured reinforcement learning for visual relationship and attribute detection. In: CVPR (2017)
20. Lin, C.-L.: Hardness of approximating graph transformation problem. In: Du, D.-Z., Zhang, X.-S. (eds.) ISAAC 1994. LNCS, vol. 834, pp. 74–82. Springer, Heidelberg (1994). https://doi.org/10.1007/3-540-58325-4_168
21. Lin, T.Y., Dollár, P., Girshick, R., He, K., Hariharan, B., Belongie, S.: Feature pyramid networks for object detection. In: CVPR (2017)
22. Liu, W., et al.: SSD: single shot multibox detector. In: Leibe, B., Matas, J., Sebe, N., Welling, M. (eds.) ECCV 2016. LNCS, vol. 9905, pp. 21–37. Springer, Cham (2016). https://doi.org/10.1007/978-3-319-46448-0_2
23. Lu, C., Krishna, R., Bernstein, M., Fei-Fei, L.: Visual relationship detection with language priors. In: Leibe, B., Matas, J., Sebe, N., Welling, M. (eds.) ECCV 2016. LNCS, vol. 9905, pp. 852–869. Springer, Cham (2016). https://doi.org/10.1007/978-3-319-46448-0_51
24. Lu, J., Yang, J., Batra, D., Parikh, D.: Neural baby talk. In: CVPR (2018)
25. Nair, V., Hinton, G.E.: Rectified linear units improve restricted Boltzmann machines. In: ICML (2010)
26. Newell, A., Deng, J.: Pixels to graphs by associative embedding. In: NIPS (2017)
27. Oliva, A., Torralba, A.: The role of context in object recognition. Trends Cogn. Sci. **11**(12), 520–527 (2007)
28. Parikh, D., Zitnick, C.L., Chen, T.: From appearance to context-based recognition: Dense labeling in small images. In: CVPR (2008)
29. Peyre, J., Laptev, I., Schmid, C., Sivic, J.: Weakly-supervised learning of visual relations. In: ICCV (2017)
30. Rabinovich, A., Vedaldi, A., Galleguillos, C., Wiewiora, E., Belongie, S.: Objects in context. In: ICCV (2007)
31. Redmon, J., Divvala, S., Girshick, R., Farhadi, A.: You only look once: unified, real-time object detection. In: CVPR (2016)
32. Ren, S., He, K., Girshick, R., Sun, J.: Faster r-cnn: Towards real-time object detection with region proposal networks. In: NIPS (2015)
33. Simonyan, K., Zisserman, A.: Very deep convolutional networks for large-scale image recognition. arXiv preprint arXiv:1409.1556 (2014)
34. Szegedy, C., et al.: Going deeper with convolutions. In: CVPR (2015)
35. Teney, D., Liu, L., Hengel, A.V.d.: Graph-structured representations for visual question answering. In: CVPR (2017)
36. Veličković, P., Cucurull, G., Casanova, A., Romero, A., Liò, P., Bengio, Y.: Graph attention networks. In: ICLR (2018)
37. Wang, P., Wu, Q., Shen, C., Dick, A., van den Hengel, A.: FVQA: fact-based visual question answering. In: PAMI (2017)
38. Wang, P., Wu, Q., Shen, C., van den Hengel, A.: The VQA-machine: learning how to use existing vision algorithms to answer new questions. In: CVPR (2017)
39. Wu, Q., Shen, C., Wang, P., Dick, A., van den Hengel, A.: Image captioning and visual question answering based on attributes and external knowledge. In: PAMI (2017)
40. Xu, D., Zhu, Y., Choy, C.B., Fei-Fei, L.: Scene graph generation by iterative message passing. In: CVPR (2017)
41. Yang, J., Lu, J., Batra, D., Parikh, D.: A faster Pytorch implementation of faster R-CNN (2017). https://github.com/jwyang/faster-rcnn.pytorch

42. Zellers, R., Yatskar, M., Thomson, S., Choi, Y.: Neural motifs: Scene graph parsing with global context. In: CVPR (2018)
43. Zhang, H., Kyaw, Z., Chang, S.F., Chua, T.S.: Visual translation embedding network for visual relation detection. In: CVPR (2017)
44. Zhang, H., Kyaw, Z., Yu, J., Chang, S.F.: Ppr-fcn: weakly supervised visual relation detection via parallel pairwise r-fcn (2017)
45. Zhang, J., Elhoseiny, M., Cohen, S., Chang, W., Elgammal, A.: Relationship proposal networks. In: CVPR (2017)
46. Zhuang, B., Liu, L., Shen, C., Reid, I.: Towards context-aware interaction recognition for visual relationship detection. In: ICCV (2017)

Deep Cross-Modal Projection Learning for Image-Text Matching

Ying Zhang[iD] and Huchuan Lu[✉][iD]

Dalian University of Technology, Dalian, China
zyd10907@mail.dlut.edu.cn, lhchuan@dlut.edu.cn

Abstract. The key point of image-text matching is how to accurately measure the similarity between visual and textual inputs. Despite the great progress of associating the deep cross-modal embeddings with the bi-directional ranking loss, developing the strategies for mining useful triplets and selecting appropriate margins remains a challenge in real applications. In this paper, we propose a cross-modal projection matching (CMPM) loss and a cross-modal projection classification (CMPC) loss for learning discriminative image-text embeddings. The CMPM loss minimizes the KL divergence between the projection compatibility distributions and the normalized matching distributions defined with all the positive and negative samples in a mini-batch. The CMPC loss attempts to categorize the vector projection of representations from one modality onto another with the improved norm-softmax loss, for further enhancing the feature compactness of each class. Extensive analysis and experiments on multiple datasets demonstrate the superiority of the proposed approach.

Keywords: Image-text matching · Cross-modal projection Joint embedding learning · Deep learning

1 Introduction

Exploring the relationship between image and natural language has recently attracted great interest among researchers, due to its great importance in various applications, such as bi-directional image and text retrieval [22,44], natural language object retrieval [10], image captioning [35,43], and visual question answering (VQA) [1,18]. A critical task for these applications is to measure the similarity between visual data and textual descriptions. Existing deep learning approaches either attempts to learn joint embeddings [21,39,40,44] for image and text in a shared latent space, or build a similarity learning network [11,15,16,22,40] to compute the matching score for image-text pairs. The joint embedding learning based methods have shown great potential in learning discriminative cross-modal representations and computation efficiency at the test stage.

© Springer Nature Switzerland AG 2018
V. Ferrari et al. (Eds.): ECCV 2018, LNCS 11205, pp. 707–723, 2018.
https://doi.org/10.1007/978-3-030-01246-5_42

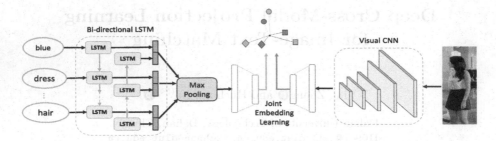

Fig. 1. Deep image-text embedding learning

Generally, the joint embedding learning framework for image-text matching adopts the two-branch [21,39,40,44] architecture (as shown in Fig. 1), where one branch extracts the image features and the other one encodes the text representations, and then the discriminative cross-modal embeddings are learned with designed objective functions. The most commonly used functions include canonical correlation analysis (CCA) [44], and bi-directional ranking loss [21,39,40]. Compared with CCA based methods, the bi-directional ranking loss produces better stability and performance [40] and is being more and more widely used in cross-modal matching [21,39]. Nevertheless, it suffers from sampling useful triplets and selecting appropriate margins in real applications.

Despite the great success of these deep learning techniques in matching image and text with only the pair correspondence, some recent works [15,16,28] explore more effective cross-modal matching algorithms with identity-level annotations. These research efforts demonstrated that the discrimination ability of the learned image-text embeddings can be greatly enhanced via introducing category classification loss as either auxiliary task [28] or pre-trained initialization [15,16]. Consider the fact that independent classification may not fully exploit the identity information for cross-modal feature learning, [15] developed the Cross-Modal Cross-Entropy (CMCE) loss which employs the cross-modal sample-to-identity affinity for category prediction, whereas this strategy requires to allocate additional identity feature buffer, which could bring large memory consumption when there are large number of subjects.

To address these problems, we propose a cross-modal projection matching (CMPM) loss and a cross-modal projection classification (CMPC) loss, which introduces the cross-modal feature projection operation for learning discriminative image-text embeddings. The CMPM loss attempts to minimize the KL divergence between projection compatibility distributions and the normalized matching distributions, in order to increase the variance between unmatched samples and the association between the matched ones. The CMPM loss function does not need to select specific triplets or tune the margin parameter, and exhibits great stability with various batch size. For the assistant classification task with identity labels, the CMPC loss attempts to classify the vector projection of the features from one modality onto the matched features from another modality, instead of independently categorizing the original features.

Extensive experiments and analysis demonstrate the superiority of the proposed approach for efficiently learning discriminative image-text embeddings.

2 Related Work

2.1 Deep Image-Text Matching

Most existing approaches for matching image and text based on deep learning can be roughly divided into two categories: (1) joint embedding learning [15,21, 39,40,44] and (2) pairwise similarity learning [11,15,22,28,40].

Joint embedding learning aims to find a joint latent space under which the embeddings of images and texts can be directly compared. This type of approaches usually associate features from two modalities with correlation loss [44], and the bi-directional ranking loss [21,39,40]. The deep canonical correlation analysis (DCCA) [44] aims to learn nonlinear transformations of two views of data with the deep networks such that the resulting representations are highly linearly correlated, while the major caveat of DCCA is the eigenvalue problem brought by unstable covariance estimation in each mini-batch [23,40]. The bi-directional ranking loss [21,39,40] extends the triplet loss [29], which requires the distance between matched samples to be smaller than unmatched ones by a margin for image-to-text and text-to-image ranking. Whereas the bi-directional ranking loss inherits the disadvantage of selecting negative samples and margins from the triplet loss.

Pairwise similarity learning focus on designing a similarity network which predicts the matching score for image-text pairs. Apart from the efforts [40] to measure the global similarity between image and text, many of the research works [11,15,22,26,28] attempt to maximize the alignments between image regions and textual fragments. However, this strategy may lack efficiency involving preparing all the image-text pairs to predict the matching score at the test stage.

For image-text matching with identity-level annotations, Reed et al. [28] proposed to learn discriminative image-text joint embeddings with the indication of class labels, and collected two datasets of fine-grained visual descriptions, while [16] attempted to search persons with language description under the assistance of identity classification. As an improvement, Li et al. [15] developed a two-stage learning strategy for textual-visual matching. Stage-1 pre-trains the network with the cross-modal cross-entropy (CMCE) loss under the supervision of identity labels, and stage-2 retrains the network with latent co-attention restriction under the supervision of pairwise labels.

2.2 Discriminative Feature Learning

Recent years have witnessed the advance of deep neural networks for learning discriminative features, which has great importance in many visual tasks, such as face recognition [19,20,29,32,41], face verification [33,37], and person re-identification [2,8,42]. Intuitively, discriminative features should be able to maximize both the inter-class separability and the intra-class compactness.

As the most widely used supervision loss for learning strong representations, cross-entropy loss (or softmax loss) [32,33,42] has achieved significant success in various applications. Nevertheless, many research works have been focusing on improvements to generate more discriminative features. Wen *et al.* [41] proposed the center loss to assist the softmax loss for face recognition, where the distance between samples and the corresponding class centres are minimized to improve the intra-class compactness. Liu *et al.* developed the L-softmax [20] which introduces the angular margin into softmax loss for further increasing the feature separability, and refined it to A-softmax [19] by adding the normalization of the classification weights. It is notable that the A/L-softmax imposes feature discriminativeness by incorporating the angular margin to achieve remarkable results in face recognition. However, the strong restriction of angular and weights makes models difficult to converge [3,36,38] in real applications, especially when the training data has too many subjects. Ranjan *et al.* [27] proposed to normalize the features to strengthen the verification signal and better model the difficult samples. Wang *et al.* [37] modified the softmax loss by normalizing both the features and the classification weights, which achieves performance improvements with much easier implementation.

On the other hand, deep metric learning gains increasing popularity by learning general distance metrics, under which the distance between relevant samples are smaller than that of irrelevant ones. Hadsell *et al.* [5] proposed the contrastive loss to minimize the distance between similar points and restrict the distance between dissimilar points to be smaller than a margin. Schroff *et al.* [29] designed the triplet loss to encourage a relative distance constraint between matched face pairs and unmatched ones, and it has proved effective for matching pedestrians from different cameras in [8]. Recently, quadruplet loss [2] added a negative pair constrain to the triplet loss such that the intra-class variations and inter-class similarities are further reduced. It also introduced the adaptive margin to compute distance penalization and select negative samples.

Unfortunately, there are two main challenges when applying the above loss functions: sampling useful data units (i.e. positive and negative pairs, triplets, or quadruplets) and determining appropriate margins. Generating all possible triplets would result in heavy computation and slower convergence [29] while sampling the hardest negatives may cause the network to converge to a bad local optimum [29,31]. [29] proposed to choose semi-hard negative samples from within a mini-batch online, while this strategy requires large batch size to select useful negative samples. Song *et al.* [31] optimized the smoothed upper bound of the original triplet loss and utilized all the negative samples within a mini-batch, and Sohn *et al.* [30] proposed the N-pair loss in the form of multi-class softmax loss with the request of carefully selected imposter examples. To avoid highly-sensitive parameters, the Histogram loss [34] is developed to estimate the similarity distributions of all the positive and negative pairs in a mini-batch and then minimize the probability that a random negative pair has a higher similarity than a random positive pair, under which the large batch size is preferred to achieve better performance. Nevertheless, these modifications for learning embeddings to preserve the association relationship of samples are specifically designed for single-modal applications, and may not readily adapt to the cross-modal matching problems.

3   The Proposed Algorithm

3.1   Network Architecture

The framework of our proposed method is shown in Fig. 1. We can see that the image-text matching architecture consists of three components: a visual CNN to extract image features, a bi-directional LSTM (Bi-LSTM) to encode text features, and a joint learning module for associating the cross-modal representations.

Given a sentence, we apply basic tokenizing and split it into words, and then sequentially process them with a Bi-LSTM. The hidden states of forward and backward directions are concatenated, and the initial text representations are obtained with max-pooling strategy. For an image, we employ MobileNet [9] and extract its initial feature from the last pooling layer. In the association module, the extracted image and text features are embedded into a shared latent space, where the compatibility between matched features and the variance between unmatched samples are maximized.

In this paper, we focus on learning the discriminative features in the association module, and describe the proposed cross-modal projection matching (CMPM) and cross-modal projection classification (CMPC) loss function in the following sections.

3.2   Cross-Modal Projection Matching

We introduce a novel image-text matching loss termed as Cross-Modal Projection Matching (CMPM), which incorporates the cross-modal projection into KL divergence to associate the representations across different modalities.

Given a mini-batch with n image and text samples, for each image x_i the image-text pairs are constructed as $\{(x_i, z_j), y_{i,j}\}_{j=1}^n$, where $y_{i,j} = 1$ means that (x_i, z_j) is a matched pair, while $y_{i,j} = 0$ indicates the unmatched ones. The probability of matching x_i to z_j is defined as

$$p_{i,j} = \frac{\exp(x_i^\top \bar{z}_j)}{\sum_{k=1}^n \exp(x_i^\top \bar{z}_k)} \quad s.t. \ \bar{z}_j = \frac{z_j}{\|z_j\|} \tag{1}$$

where $\bar{z}_j$ denotes the normalized text feature. Geometrically $x_i^\top \bar{z}_j$ represents the scalar projection image feature x_i onto text feature z_j and $p_{i,j}$ can be viewed as the percent of scalar projection of (x_i, z_j) among all pairs $\{(x_i, z_j)\}_{j=1}^n$ in a mini batch. Figure 2(a) shows the geometrical explanation of the cross-modal projection. We can see that the more similar image feature to text feature, the

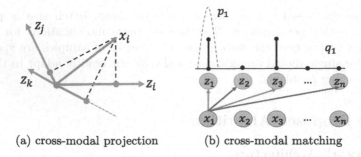

(a) cross-modal projection   (b) cross-modal matching

Fig. 2. Interpretation of cross-modal projection and matching. (a) The image feature x_i is projected onto different text directions, and the scalar projection of x_i onto the matched text z_i is larger than that of unmatched text z_j and z_k. (b) For the image x_1 with z_1 and z_3 as matched candidates (green arrowed line) in a mini-batch, and the other texts as unmatched samples (red arrowed line), the CMPM loss attempts to find a distribution p_1 having low probability where the true matching distribution q_1 has low probability (Color figure online)

larger the scalar projection would be. Note that the scalar projection can be negative if the two vectors lie in opposite directions, such as $x_i^\top \bar{z}_k$ shown in the figure.

Considering the fact that there might be more than one matched text samples for x_i in a mini-batch, we normalize the true matching probability of (x_i, z_j) as

$$q_{i,j} = \frac{y_{i,j}}{\sum_{k=1}^{n} y_{i,k}} \tag{2}$$

The matching loss of associating x_i with correctly matched text samples is defined as

$$\mathcal{L}_i = \sum_{j=1}^{n} p_{i,j} \log \frac{p_{i,j}}{q_{i,j}+\epsilon} \tag{3}$$

where ϵ is a small number to avoid numerical problems, and the matching loss from image to text in a mini-batch is computed by

$$\mathcal{L}_{i2t} = \frac{1}{n} \sum_{i=1}^{n} \mathcal{L}_i \tag{4}$$

Note that Eq. 3 actually represents the KL divergence from distribution q_i to p_i, and minimizing $KL(p_i \| q_i)$ attempts to select a p_i that has low probability where q_i has low probability [4]. Figure 2(b) illustrates the proposed matching loss with a mini-batch data, we can see that the true matching distribution q_1 for image x_1 has multiple modes with more than one matched text candidates in the mini batch, and the proposed matching loss attempts to select a single mode distribution p_1 to avoid putting probability mass in the low-probability areas between modes of q_1, such that the compatibility of the unmatched image-text pairs are minimized while the relevance of the matched pairs are maximized. Note that given an image, all the positive and negative text candidates in a mini-batch are taken into consideration for computing the matching loss, getting rid of the dedicated sampling procedures in traditional bi-directional ranking loss.

It might raise the concerns about using $KL(\boldsymbol{q}_i \| \boldsymbol{p}_i)$ to maximize the compatibility of matched pairs for learning discriminative embeddings. As explained in [4], $KL(\boldsymbol{q}_i \| \boldsymbol{p}_i)$ would try to find $\boldsymbol{p}_i$ as a blur mode, towards generating high probability where $\boldsymbol{q}_i$ has high probability. This may cause difficulties for distinguishing matched and unmatched pairs when there are multiple positive pairs in a mini-batch. The advantages of $KL(\boldsymbol{p}_i \| \boldsymbol{q}_i)$ over $KL(\boldsymbol{q}_i \| \boldsymbol{p}_i)$ will be further demonstrated in experiments.

In image-text embedding learning, the matching loss is often computed in two directions [21,39,40]: the image-to-text matching loss requires the matched text to be closer to the image than unmatched ones, and in verse the text-to-image matching loss constrains the related text to rank before unrelated ones. Similarly, the matching loss $\mathcal{L}_{t2i}$ from text to image can be formulated by exchanging $\boldsymbol{x}$ and $\boldsymbol{z}$ in Eqs. 1–4, and the bi-directional CMPM loss is calculated by

$$\mathcal{L}_{cmpm} = \mathcal{L}_{i2t} + \mathcal{L}_{t2i} \tag{5}$$

3.3 Cross-Modal Projection Classification

For image-text matching with identity-level annotations, the classification loss applied to each modality helps to learn more discriminative features. However, the matching relationships of image-text pairs may not be sufficiently exploited in separate classification tasks. In this section, we develop a novel classification function where the cross-modal projection is integrated into the norm-softmax loss to further enhance the compactness of the matched embeddings.

Norm-Softmax. First we revisit the traditional softmax loss by looking into the decision criteria of softmax classifiers. Given the extracted image features $\mathcal{X} = \{\boldsymbol{x}_i\}_{i=1}^{N}$ from visual CNN, text features $\mathcal{Z} = \{\boldsymbol{z}_i\}_{i=1}^{N}$ from Bi-LSTM, and the label set $\mathcal{Y} = \{y_i\}_{i=1}^{N}$ from M classes, the original softmax loss for classifying images can be computed as

$$\mathcal{L}_{softmax} = \frac{1}{N} \sum_i -log(\frac{exp(\boldsymbol{W}_{y_i}^{\top} \boldsymbol{x}_i + b_{y_i})}{\sum_j exp(\boldsymbol{W}_j^{\top} \boldsymbol{x}_i + b_j)}) \tag{6}$$

where y_i indicates the label of $\boldsymbol{x}_i$, $\boldsymbol{W}_{y_i}$ and $\boldsymbol{W}_j$ represent the y_i-th and j-th column of weight matrix $\boldsymbol{W}$, and b_{y_i} and b_j respectively denote the y_i-th and j-th element of bias vector $\boldsymbol{b}$.

To improve the discriminative ability of the image feature $\boldsymbol{x}_i$ during classification, we impose weight normalization on the softmax loss as with [19,37], and reformulate Eq. 6 as

$$\mathcal{L}_{image} = \frac{1}{N} \sum_i -log(\frac{exp(\boldsymbol{W}_{y_i}^{\top} \boldsymbol{x}_i)}{\sum_j exp(\boldsymbol{W}_j^{\top} \boldsymbol{x}_i)}) \quad s.t. \ \|\boldsymbol{W}_j\| = 1 \tag{7}$$

Compared with the original softmax loss, the norm-softmax loss normalizes all the weight vectors into the same length in order to reduce the impact of weight magnitude in distinguishing different samples. Here we omit the bias b for simplifying analysis and in fact found it makes no difference as with [19, 20].

The intuitive explanation of the norm-softmax loss is shown in Fig. 3. We can see that, for the original softmax, the classification results depends on $\|W_k\| \|x\| \cos(\theta_k), (k = 1, 2)$, where θ_k indicates the angle between x and W_k. For the norm-softmax, all the weight vectors are normalized into the same length, and the classification results can be only depended on $\|x\| \cos(\theta_k)$. This restriction encourages the feature x to distribute more compactly along the weight vector in order to be correctly classified.

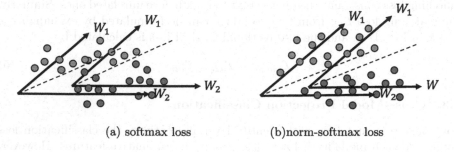

(a) softmax loss   (b)norm-softmax loss

Fig. 3. Geometric interpretation of softmax and norm-softmax

Cross-Modal Projection. In this paper, we attempt to classify the projection of image features onto the corresponding text features instead of categorizing the original feature representations. The cross-modal projection integrates the image-text similarity into classification and thus strengthens the association within matched pairs.

By incorporating the cross-modal projection into the norm-softmax, we can reformulated Eq. 7 as

$$\mathcal{L}_{ipt} = \frac{1}{N} \sum_i -log(\frac{exp(W_{y_i}^\top \hat{x}_i)}{\sum_j exp(W_j^\top \hat{x}_i)}) \quad s.t. \ \|W_j\| = r, \ \hat{x}_i = x_i^\top \bar{z}_i \cdot \bar{z}_i \quad (8)$$

where $\hat{x}_i$ denotes the vector projection of image feature x_i onto normalized text feature $\bar{z}_i$. Intuitively, all the matched text samples needs to lie in the direction of W_{y_i} for the image feature x_i to project onto, in order to promote correct categorization. The text classification loss function can be written as

$$\mathcal{L}_{tpi} = \frac{1}{N} \sum_i -log(\frac{exp(W_{y_i}^\top \hat{z}_i)}{\sum_j exp(W_j^\top \hat{z}_i)}) \quad s.t. \ \|W_j\| = r, \ \hat{z}_i = z_i^\top \bar{x}_i \cdot \bar{x}_i \quad (9)$$

The final CMPC loss can be calculated with

$$\mathcal{L}_{cmpc} = \mathcal{L}_{ipt} + \mathcal{L}_{tpi} \quad (10)$$

3.4 Objective Functions

For matching tasks with only pairwise correspondence, we can utilize the proposed CMPM loss for learning discriminative image-text embeddings. If identity labels are available, we adopt the joint of the proposed CMPM loss and CMPC loss for more accurately associating the cross-modal representations. The overall objective function is formulated as

$$\mathcal{L} = \mathcal{L}_{cmpm} + \mathcal{L}_{cmpc} \tag{11}$$

At the test stage, given an image and text, we first extract the image feature x and text feature z with the visual CNN and Bi-LSTM network, respectively. Then the cosine distance between x and z is computed for image-to-text and text-to-image retrieval evaluation.

4 Experiments

4.1 Datasets and Settings

Datasets. Five datasets are used in our experiments. The *Flickr30K* [45] dataset contains 31,783 images with each one annotated by five text descriptions. We adopt the data split in [12] to use 29,783 images for training, 1,000 images for validation, and 1,000 images for testing. The *MSCOCO* [17] dataset consists of 12,3287 images and each one is also described by five sentences. Following the protocol of [12], we split the data into 82,783 training, 30,504 validation, and 5,000 test images, and report the evaluation results on both 5 K and 1K (5 fold) test images. The *CUHK-PEDES* [16] dataset contains 40,206 pedestrian images of 13,003 identities, with each image described by two textual descriptions. The dataset is split into 11,003 training identities with 34,054 images, 1000 validation persons with 3,078 images and 1000 test individuals with 3,074 images. The *Caltech-UCSD Birds (CUB)* [28] dataset consists of 11,788 bird images from 200 different categories. Each image is labelled with 10 visual descriptions. The dataset is split into 100 training, 50 validation and 50 test categories. The *Oxford-102 Flowers (Flowers)* [28] dataset contains 8,189 flower images of 102 different categories, and each image has 10 textual descriptions. The data splits provide 62 training, 20 validation, and 20 test categories.

Evaluation Metrics. We adopt Recall@K (K = 1, 5, 10) [12] and AP@50 [28] for retrieval evaluation. Recall@K (or R@K) indicates the percentage of the queries where at least one ground-truth is retrieved among the top-K results, and AP@50 represents the percent of top-50 scoring images whose class matches that of the text query, averaged over all the test classes.

Implementation Details. All the models are implemented in TensorFlow with a NVIDIA GEFORCE GTX 1080 GPU. For all the datasets, we use

MobileNet [9] and Bi-LSTM for learning visual and textual features, respectively. The adam optimizer [13] is employed for optimization with $lr = 0.0002$. For Flickr30K and MSCOCO, we also report the results with ResNet-152 [7] as image feature extractor, where we start training with $lr = 0.0002$ for 15 epochs with fixed image encoder and then training the whole model with $lr = 0.00002$ for 30 epochs.

Table 1. Comparison of bi-directional retrieval results (R@K(%)) on Flickr30K

Method	Image-to-Text			Text-to-Image		
	R@1	R@5	R@10	R@1	R@5	R@10
DCCA [44]	16.7	39.3	52.9	12.6	31.0	43.0
DVSA [12]	22.2	48.2	61.4	15.2	37.7	50.5
m-CNN [22]	33.6	64.1	74.9	26.2	56.3	69.6
VQA-A [18]	33.9	62.5	74.5	24.9	52.6	64.8
DSPE [39]	40.3	68.9	79.9	29.7	60.1	72.1
sm-LSTM [11]	42.5	71.9	81.5	30.2	60.4	72.3
RRF-Net [21]	47.6	77.4	87.1	35.4	68.3	79.9
DAN [26]	**55.0**	**81.8**	**89.0**	**39.4**	**69.2**	**79.1**
CMPM (MobileNet)	37.1	65.8	76.3	29.1	56.3	67.7
CMPM+CMPC (MobileNet)	40.3	66.9	76.7	30.4	58.2	68.5
CMPM (ResNet-152)	48.3	75.6	84.5	35.7	63.6	74.1
CMPM+CMPC (ResNet-152)	49.6	76.8	86.1	37.3	65.7	75.5

4.2 Results on the Flickr30K Dataset

We summarize the comparison of retrieval results on the Filckr30K dataset in Table 1. We can see that with MobileNet as image encoder, the proposed CMPM loss achieves competitive results of R@1 = 37.1% for image-to-text retrieval, and R@1 = 29.1% for text-to-image retrieval. The performance can be improved to 48.3% and 35.7% respectively by employing ResNet-152 as with RRF-Net [21] and DAN [26]. We also explore the assistant effect of the CMPC loss by training the classifiers single category per image, and we observe that the retrieval results can be further improved by around 1.3%, demonstrating the effectiveness of cross-modal projection learning for image-text matching.

4.3 Results on the MSCOCO Dataset

We compare the proposed approach with state-of-the-art methods on the MS-COCO dataset in Table 2. We can see that for 1K test images the proposed CMPM loss achieves R@1 = 56.1% and 44.6% with image and text as quires, respectively. For 5K test images the algorithm achieves R@1 = 31.1% and 22.9%, outperforming the second best by 7.0% and 5.3%, which further verifies the superiority of the proposed loss functions.

Table 2. Comparison of bi-directional retrieval results (R@K(%)) on MSCOCO

Method	Image-to-Text			Text-to-Image		
	R@1	R@5	R@10	R@1	R@5	R@10
1K test images						
DVSA [12]	38.4	69.9	80.5	27.4	60.2	74.8
GMM-FV [14]	39.4	67.9	80.9	25.1	59.8	76.6
m-CNN [22]	42.8	73.1	84.1	32.6	68.6	82.8
VQA-A [18]	50.5	80.1	89.7	37.0	70.9	82.9
DSPE [39]	50.1	79.7	89.2	39.6	75.2	86.9
sm-LSTM [11]	53.2	83.1	91.5	40.7	75.8	87.4
RRF-Net [21]	**56.4**	85.3	91.5	43.9	78.1	88.6
CMPM (MobileNet)	51.4	80.8	89.8	40.9	73.9	85.2
CMPM+CMPC (MobileNet)	52.9	83.8	92.1	41.3	74.6	85.9
CMPM (ResNet-152)	56.1	**86.3**	**92.9**	**44.6**	**78.8**	**89.0**
5K test images						
DVSA [12]	16.5	39.2	52.0	10.7	29.6	42.2
GMM-FV [14]	17.3	39.0	50.2	10.8	28.3	40.1
VQA-A [18]	23.5	50.7	63.6	16.7	40.5	53.8
CMPM (MobileNet)	23.9	51.5	65.4	18.9	43.8	56.9
CMPM+CMPC (MobileNet)	24.6	52.3	66.4	19.1	44.6	58.4
CMPM (ResNet-152)	**31.1**	**60.7**	**73.9**	**22.9**	**50.2**	**63.8**

Table 3. Comparison of text-to-image retrieval results (R@K(%)) on CUHK-PEDES

Method	Text-to-Image	
	R@1	R@10
deeper LSTM Q+norm I [1]	17.19	57.82
iBOWIMG [46]	8.00	30.56
NeuralTalk [35]	13.66	41.72
Word CNN-RNN [28]	10.48	36.66
GNA-RNN [16]	19.05	53.64
GMM+HGLMM [14]	15.03	42.27
Latent Co-attention [15]	25.94	60.48
CMPM	**44.02**	**77.00**
CMPM+CMPC	**49.37**	**79.27**

4.4   Results on the CUHK-PEDES Dataset

Table 3 compares the proposed method against existing approaches on the CUHK-PEDES dataset. We can see that the proposed CMPM loss achieves 44.02% of R@1 and 77.00% of R@10, outperforming the second best performer [15] by a large margin. When we add the CMPC loss supervised by the identity-level annotations, the text-to-image retrieval performance is further improved to 49.37% for R@1 and 79.27% for R@10. This illustrates the effectiveness of the CMPM loss for person search applications, and the promotion effect of the CMPC loss when the category labels are available in real applications.

4.5   Results on the CUB and Flowers Dataset

The comparison of image-to-text and text-to-image retrieval results on the CUB and Flowers dataset is shown in Table 4. Consider that the bi-directional losses are implemented in our approach, we choose the symmetric results [15] of the existing methods for fair comparison. We can see that the proposed algorithm outperforms the state-of-the-art, achieving 64.3% of R@1 for image-to-text retrieval and 67.9% of AP@50 for text-to-image retrieval on CUB, and reporting the best R@1 of 68.90% for image-to-text retrieval and the second best AP@50 of 69.70% for text-to-image retrieval on Flowers.

Table 4. Comparison of image-to-text (R@K(%)) and text-to-image (AP@K(%)) retrieval results on the CUB and Flowers dataset

Method	CUB		Flowers	
	Image-to-Text	Text-to-Image	Image-to-Text	Text-to-Image
	R@1	AP@50	R@1	AP@50
Bow [6]	44.1	39.6	57.7	57.3
Word2Vec [25]	38.6	33.5	54.2	52.1
Word CNN [28]	51.0	43.3	60.7	56.3
Word CNN-RNN [28]	56.8	48.7	65.6	59.6
GMM+HGLMM [14]	36.5	35.6	54.8	52.8
Triplet [15]	52.5	52.4	64.3	64.9
Latent Co-attention [15]	61.5	57.6	68.4	**70.1**
CMPM	**62.1**	**64.6**	66.1	67.7
CMPM+CMPC	**64.3**	**67.9**	**68.9**	69.7

5   Ablation Studies

To investigate the effect of each component of the proposed CMPM and CMPC loss, we perform a series of ablation studies on the CUHK-PEDES dataset. We conduct further comparative experiments in three aspects: comparison of the CMPM loss with other matching losses under various batch size, impact of cross-modal projection and weight normalization for the CMPC loss, and the cross-modal feature distribution learned with different losses.

5.1 Analysis of Cross-Modal Matching

Table 5 compares the proposed CMPM loss with the commonly used bi-directional ranking (Bi-rank) loss [21,39,40], the most similar N-pair loss [30], and Histogram Loss [34] with different batch size on the CUHK-PEDES dataset. We add the image-to-text retrieval evaluation for more comprehensive analysis of learned embeddings, since good cross-modal embeddings should be able to perform bi-directional matching tasks. Note that all the loss functions are implemented in the bi-directional mode and the triplets are online sampled.

Table 5. R@1 (%) comparison of cross-modal matching functions with different batch size on the CUHK-PEDES dataset

Matching Loss	Text-to-Image				Image-to-Text			
	16	32	64	128	16	32	64	128
Bi-rank [21]	31.11	37.85	42.11	41.42	32.56	41.28	47.46	46.88
Histogram [34]	14.68	19.20	21.70	21.31	4.78	13.53	13.04	2.88
N-pair [30]	34.57	45.55	45.68	39.33	17.66	13.66	12.07	10.83
$KL(q_i\|p_i)$	42.58	43.81	41.89	36.06	41.87	38.81	22.35	19.97
CMPM	42.28	43.42	44.02	42.43	51.95	52.09	51.98	48.67

From the table we can see that the previous matching loss fluctuates greatly when the batch size varies between 16 and 128. The bi-directional ranking loss depends on larger batch size to generate comparative matching accuracies, due to the negative sampling requirements [29]. The Histogram loss [34] performs much worse than other methods for cross-modal matching. The N-pair loss [30] produce better text-to-image retrieval results with moderate batch size, while the image-to-text matching performance are much worse. This might due to the scalar gap of image and text embeddings from different networks. The $KL(q_i\|p_i)$ discussed in Sect. 3.2 generates satisfying results when the batch size is small, while deteriorates with larger batch size of 128. This further verifies the analysis that, when there are more positive pairs in larger mini batches, the inappropriate KL direction blurring the multiple modes could cause ambiguities for image-text matching. In contrast, the proposed CMPM loss produces much more stable matching results with different batch size (R@1 remains above 42% for text-to-image retrieval), and the advantages are more obvious when the batch size are too small or too large, exhibiting great superiority and broad applicability.

5.2 Analysis of Cross-Modal Classification

Table 6 illustrates the impact of the softmax loss, weight normalization (normW) and cross-modal projection (CMP) in image-text embedding learning on the CUHK-PEDES dataset. We can see that adding the supervision loss indeed

Table 6. R@1 (%) comparison of different components of the cross-modal projection learning on the CUHK-PEDES dataset

Matching CMPM	Classification			Text-to-Image		Image-to-Text	
	softmax	normW	CMP	R@1	R@10	R@1	R@10
✓	✗	✗	✗	44.02	77.00	51.98	87.02
✓	✓	✗	✗	45.38	78.43	55.14	89.30
✓	✓	✓	✗	47.12	78.38	56.51	90.50
✓	✓	✗	✓	46.95	79.40	55.82	89.17
✓	✓	✓	✓	49.37	79.45	57.71	91.28
✗	✓	✗	✓	16.93	40.90	17.63	43.98
✗	✓	✓	✓	42.25	73.29	50.72	85.95

improves the matching performance, while the original softmax loss offers limited assistance. By adding the weight normalization, the R@1 rates are increased from 45.38% to 47.12% for image-to-text retrieval, and 55.14% to 56.51% for text-to-image retrieval. The cross-modal projection further improves the bi-directional retrieval results by 2.25% and 1.20%. We also notice that the CMPC loss alone achieves competitive results for image-text matching and weight normalization brings significant improvements. This indicates the effectiveness of weight normalization and cross-modal projection in learning discriminative cross-modal representations.

5.3 Feature Visualization

To better understand the effect of the proposed cross-modal matching loss and cross-modal classification loss for learning discriminative image-text embeddings, we show the t-SNE [24] visualization the test feature distribution learned

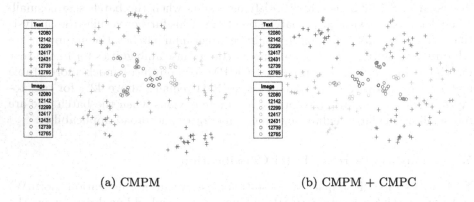

(a) CMPM   (b) CMPM + CMPC

Fig. 4. Comparison of feature distribution learned with the proposed approach using the CMPM loss and CMPM+CMPC loss on the CUHK-PEDES dataset. From Fig. 4(a) we can see that the CMPM loss learns image-text embeddings distributed along radial spokes, where the image and text features from the same class approximately lie in the same direction. This type of angular distribution is consistent with the traditional softmax loss [19], and therefore the added CMPC loss naturally improves the compactness of the features along each spoke as shown in Fig. 4(b). We can also observe that the radius of image feature areas is smaller than text features, which indicates the scalar gap brought by different networks (i.e., the CNN network for image and Bi-LSTM for text). In experiments we obtain the average length (value of ℓ_2 norm) of 52.62 for image features and 128.92 for text features. The cross-modal distribution shows the importance of feature normalization in cross-modal projection for bridging the scalar gap in image-text embedding learning.

6   Conclusions

In this paper, we proposed a novel cross-modal projection matching loss (CMPM) and cross-modal projection classification (CMPC) loss, for learning deep discriminative image-text embeddings. The CMPM loss utilize the KL divergence to minimize the compatibility score of the unmatched image-text pairs while maximizing the relevance between the matched ones. It shows great stability and superiority for associating image and text under various batch size, without triplet sampling and margin selection that hampers the traditional bi-directional ranking loss. The CMPC loss incorporates the matching relationship into the auxiliary classification task, which further enhances the representation compactness of each category. In the future, we will work on how to better interact the matching task and classification task in identity-aware matching problems.

Acknowledgements. This work was supported by the Natural Science Foundation of China under Grant 61725202, 61751212, 61771088, 61632006 and 91538201.

References

1. Antol, S., et al.: VQA: visual question answering. In: ICCV, pp. 2425–2433 (2015)
2. Chen, W., Chen, X., Zhang, J., Huang, K.: Beyond triplet loss: a deep quadruplet network for person re-identification. In: CVPR, pp. 1320–1329 (2017)
3. Deng, J., Guo, J., Zafeiriou, S.: ArcFace: additive angular margin loss for deep face recognition. arXiv: 1801.07698 (2018)
4. Goodfellow, I., Bengio, Y., Courville, A.: Deep Learning. MIT Press (2016). http://www.deeplearningbook.org
5. Hadsell, R., Chopra, S., LeCun, Y.: Dimensionality reduction by learning an invariant mapping. In: CVPR, pp. 1735–1742 (2006)
6. Harris, Z.S.: Distributional structure. Word **10**(2–3), 146–162 (1954)
7. He, K., Zhang, X., Ren, S., Sun, J.: Deep residual learning for image recognition. In: CVPR, pp. 770–778 (2016)

8. Hermans, A., Beyer, L., Leibe, B.: In defense of the triplet loss for person re-identification. arXiv: 1703.07737 (2017)
9. Howard, A.G., et al.: MobileNets: efficient convolutional neural networks for mobile vision applications. arXiv: 1704.04861 (2017)
10. Hu, R., Xu, H., Rohrbach, M., Feng, J., Saenko, K., Darrell, T.: Natural language object retrieval. In: CVPR, pp. 4555–4564 (2016)
11. Huang, Y., Wang, W., Wang, L.: Instance-aware image and sentence matching with selective multimodal LSTM. In: CVPR, pp. 7254–7262 (2017)
12. Karpathy, A., Li, F.: Deep visual-semantic alignments for generating image descriptions. In: CVPR, pp. 3128–3137 (2015)
13. Kingma, D.P., Ba, J.: Adam: a method for stochastic optimization. arXiv: 1412.6980 (2014)
14. Klein, B., Lev, G., Sadeh, G., Wolf, L.: Associating neural word embeddings with deep image representations using fisher vectors. In: CVPR, pp. 4437–4446 (2015)
15. Li, S., Xiao, T., Li, H., Yang, W., Wang, X.: Identity-aware textual-visual matching with latent co-attention. In: ICCV, pp. 1908–1917 (2017)
16. Li, S., Xiao, T., Li, H., Zhou, B., Yue, D., Wang, X.: Person search with natural language description. In: CVPR, pp. 5187–5196 (2017)
17. Lin, T.-Y., et al.: Microsoft COCO: common objects in context. In: Fleet, D., Pajdla, T., Schiele, B., Tuytelaars, T. (eds.) ECCV 2014. LNCS, vol. 8693, pp. 740–755. Springer, Cham (2014). https://doi.org/10.1007/978-3-319-10602-1_48
18. Lin, X., Parikh, D.: Leveraging visual question answering for image-caption ranking. In: Leibe, B., Matas, J., Sebe, N., Welling, M. (eds.) ECCV 2016. LNCS, vol. 9906, pp. 261–277. Springer, Cham (2016). https://doi.org/10.1007/978-3-319-46475-6_17
19. Liu, W., Wen, Y., Yu, Z., Li, M., Raj, B., Song, L.: SphereFace: deep hypersphere embedding for face recognition. In: CVPR, pp. 6738–6746 (2017)
20. Liu, W., Wen, Y., Yu, Z., Yang, M.: Large-margin softmax loss for convolutional neural networks. In: ICML, pp. 507–516 (2016)
21. Liu, Y., Guo, Y., Bakker, E.M., Lew, M.S.: Learning a recurrent residual fusion network for multimodal matching. In: ICCV, pp. 4127–4136 (2017)
22. Ma, L., Lu, Z., Shang, L., Li, H.: Multimodal convolutional neural networks for matching image and sentence. In: ICCV, pp. 2623–2631 (2015)
23. Ma, Z., Lu, Y., Foster, D.P.: Finding linear structure in large datasets with scalable canonical correlation analysis. In: ICML, pp. 169–178 (2015)
24. van der Maaten, L.: Accelerating t-SNE using tree-based algorithms. J. Mach. Learn. Res. 15(1), 3221–3245 (2014)
25. Mikolov, T., Sutskever, I., Chen, K., Corrado, G.S., Dean, J.: Distributed representations of words and phrases and their compositionality. In: NIPS, pp. 3111–3119 (2013)
26. Nam, H., Ha, J., Kim, J.: Dual attention networks for multimodal reasoning and matching. In: CVPR, pp. 2156–2164 (2017)
27. Ranjan, R., Castillo, C.D., Chellappa, R.: L2-constrained softmax loss for discriminative face verification. arXiv: 1703.09507 (2017)
28. Reed, S.E., Akata, Z., Lee, H., Schiele, B.: Learning deep representations of fine-grained visual descriptions. In: CVPR, pp. 49–58 (2016)
29. Schroff, F., Kalenichenko, D., Philbin, J.: FaceNet: a unified embedding for face recognition and clustering. In: CVPR, pp. 815–823 (2015)
30. Sohn, K.: Improved deep metric learning with multi-class N-pair loss objective. In: NIPS, pp. 1849–1857 (2016)

31. Song, H.O., Xiang, Y., Jegelka, S., Savarese, S.: Deep metric learning via lifted structured feature embedding. In: CVPR, pp. 4004–4012 (2016)
32. Sun, Y., Wang, X., Tang, X.: Deep learning face representation from predicting 10, 000 classes. In: CVPR, pp. 1891–1898 (2014)
33. Taigman, Y., Yang, M., Ranzato, M., Wolf, L.: DeepFace: closing the gap to human-level performance in face verification. In: CVPR, pp. 1701–1708 (2014)
34. Ustinova, E., Lempitsky, V.S.: Learning deep embeddings with histogram loss. In: NIPS, pp. 4170–4178 (2016)
35. Vinyals, O., Toshev, A., Bengio, S., Erhan, D.: Show and tell: lessons learned from the 2015 MSCOCO image captioning challenge. PAMI $39(4)$, 652–663 (2017)
36. Wang, F., Liu, W., Liu, H., Cheng, J.: Additive margin softmax for face verification. arXiv: 1801.05599 (2018)
37. Wang, F., Xiang, X., Cheng, J., Yuille, A.L.: NormFace: L_2 hypersphere embedding for face verification. arXiv: 1704.06369 (2017)
38. Wang, H., Wang, Y., Zhou, Z., Ji, X., Li, Z., Gong, D., Zhou, J., Liu, W.: CosFace: large margin cosine loss for deep face recognition. arXiv: 1801.09414 (2018)
39. Wang, L., Li, Y., Lazebnik, S.: Learning deep structure-preserving image-text embeddings. In: CVPR, pp. 5005–5013 (2016)
40. Wang, L., Li, Y., Lazebnik, S.: Learning two-branch neural networks for image-text matching tasks. arXiv: 1704.03470 (2017)
41. Wen, Y., Zhang, K., Li, Z., Qiao, Y.: A discriminative feature learning approach for deep face recognition. In: Leibe, B., Matas, J., Sebe, N., Welling, M. (eds.) ECCV 2016. LNCS, vol. 9911, pp. 499–515. Springer, Cham (2016). https://doi.org/10.1007/978-3-319-46478-7_31
42. Xiao, T., Li, H., Ouyang, W., Wang, X.: Learning deep feature representations with domain guided dropout for person re-identification. In: CVPR, pp. 1249–1258 (2016)
43. Xu, K., et al.: Show, attend and tell: Neural image caption generation with visual attention. In: ICML, pp. 2048–2057 (2015)
44. Yan, F., Mikolajczyk, K.: Deep correlation for matching images and text. In: CVPR, pp. 3441–3450 (2015)
45. Young, P., Lai, A., Hodosh, M., Hockenmaier, J.: From image descriptions to visual denotations: new similarity metrics for semantic inference over event descriptions. TACL 2, 67–78 (2014)
46. Zhou, B., Tian, Y., Sukhbaatar, S., Szlam, A., Fergus, R.: Simple baseline for visual question answering. arXiv: 1512.02167 (2015)

ShapeStacks: Learning Vision-Based Physical Intuition for Generalised Object Stacking

Oliver Groth[✉], Fabian B. Fuchs, Ingmar Posner, and Andrea Vedaldi

Department of Engineering, University of Oxford, Oxford, UK
{ogroth,fabian,ingmar,vedaldi}@robots.ox.ac.uk

Abstract. Physical intuition is pivotal for intelligent agents to perform complex tasks. In this paper we investigate the passive acquisition of an intuitive understanding of physical principles as well as the active utilisation of this intuition in the context of generalised object stacking. To this end, we provide *ShapeStacks* (Source code & data are available at http://shapestacks.robots.ox.ac.uk): a simulation-based dataset featuring 20,000 stack configurations composed of a variety of elementary geometric primitives richly annotated regarding semantics and structural stability. We train visual classifiers for binary stability prediction on the ShapeStacks data and scrutinise their learned physical intuition. Due to the richness of the training data our approach also generalises favourably to real-world scenarios achieving state-of-the-art stability prediction on a publicly available benchmark of block towers. We then leverage the physical intuition learned by our model to actively construct stable stacks and observe the emergence of an intuitive notion of *stackability* - an inherent object affordance - induced by the active stacking task. Our approach performs well exceeding the stack height observed during training and even manages to counterbalance initially unstable structures.

Keywords: Intuitive physics · Stability prediction · Object stacking

1 Introduction

Research in cognitive science [8,14] highlights how the ability of humans to manipulate the environment depends strongly on our ability to intuitively understand its physics from visual observations. Intuitive physics may be just as important for autonomous agents to effectively and efficiently perform complex tasks such as object stacking or (dis-)assembly - and even the creation and use of tools. Central to these deliberations is an understanding of the physical properties of objects in the context of how they are meant to be used. Such object *affordances* are typically pre-defined given knowledge of the task at hand [11,12]. In contrast, we posit that relevant affordances do not need to be specified a priori but can be learned in a task-driven manner.

© Springer Nature Switzerland AG 2018
V. Ferrari et al. (Eds.): ECCV 2018, LNCS 11205, pp. 724–739, 2018.
https://doi.org/10.1007/978-3-030-01246-5_43

Inspired by recent work in computer vision [15,23] and robotics [6,17,25] we consider the task of *object stacking* and the problem of learning – from passive visual observations – its intuitive physical principles. By leveraging the model's acquired intuitions, we are able to utilise the passive observation in an active manipulation task as outlined in Fig. 1, which sets us apart from prior art in both scope and reach.

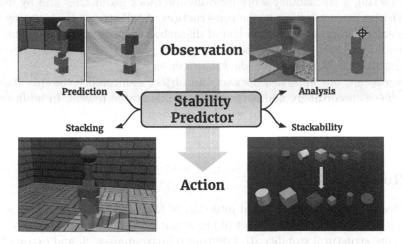

Fig. 1. We present a visual classifier which is trained on stacks of diverse shapes to distinguish between stable and unstable structures. We demonstrate that the implicit knowledge captured by the predictor can be utilised to detect structural instabilities, infer the *stackability* (utility with regard to stacking) of objects and guide a simulated stacking process solely from visual cues.

Firstly, we argue that in order for agents to perform complex tasks they need to be able to interact with a variety of different object types. We therefore investigate the stacking problem using a broader set of geometric primitives than found in related works. To this end we introduce *ShapeStacks*, a simulation-based dataset specifically created to enable exploration of stackability of a variety of objects. Furthermore, *ShapeStacks* is, to the best of our knowledge, the first such dataset with annotations of the mechanical points of failure of stacks, which are inferred by formally analysing the underlying physics. This makes *ShapeStacks* the most rigorous and complete publicly available dataset in this space.

Secondly, based on the *ShapeStacks* dataset, we extend the investigation of stability prediction presented in [15,23] to include stacks containing multiple object geometries. This allows for a more rigorous qualitative and quantitative evaluation of system performance. For example, our work, for the first time, quantifies if a model trained for stability prediction correctly localizes the underlying stability violations. We demonstrate that our model based on *ShapeStacks* outperforms the baseline by Lerer et al. [15] and performs commensurately with the current state-of-the-art [23] on real-world image data without requiring a physics engine during test time.

Lastly, in order to investigate our main hypothesis – namely that meaningful affordances emerge from representations learned by performing concrete tasks – our work goes beyond the passive assessment of stacked towers as stable or unstable and actively performs stacking. In particular, we argue that, through the passive task of stability prediction, our system implicitly learns to assess the *stackability* of the individual object geometries involved. We demonstrate this by extracting a stackability score for different block geometries and by using it to prioritise piece selection in the construction of tall stacks. By inserting noise in the actual stacking process in lieu of disturbances present in real agents (e.g. motor and perception noise as well as contact physics) we demonstrate that a more intuitive notion of object *stackability* emerges.

As a result, our approach discovers an object's suitability towards stacking, ranks pieces accordingly and successfully builds stable towers. In addition, we show that our model is able to stabilise previously unstable structures by the addition of counterweights, arguably by developing an intuitive understanding of *counterbalancing*.

2   Related Work

The idea of vision-based physical intuition is firmly rooted in cognitive science where it is a long standing subject of investigation [14]. Humans are very apt at predicting structural stability [1], inferring relative masses [8] and extrapolating trajectories of moving objects [14]. Although the exact workings of human physical intuition remain elusive, it has recently gained increasing traction in the machine learning, computer vision and robotics communities. The combination of powerful deep learning models and physics simulators yielded encouraging results in predicting the movement of objects on inclined surfaces [24] and the dynamics of ball collision [2,3,5].

While some prior work on intuitive physics assumed direct access to physical parameters, such as position and velocity, several authors have considered learning physics from visual observations instead. Examples include reasoning about support relations [7,10] and their geometric affordances and inferring forces in *Newtonian* image understanding [18]. Our aim is similar in that we learn the affordance of *stackability* – an object's utility towards stacking – from visual observation. Importantly, however, in our work affordances are not specified *a priori*, but emerge by passively predicting the stability of object stacks.

The latter is related to several recent works in stability prediction. Lerer et al. [15] pioneered the area by demonstrating feed-forward stability prediction of stacks from simulated and real images, releasing a collection of the latter as a public benchmark. Wu et al. [23] proposed more sophisticated predictors based on re-rendering an observed scene and using a physics engine to compute stability, outperforming [15] on their real-world data. In contrast, our approach achieves performance commensurate to [23] while using only efficient feed forward prediction as in [15].

The problem of structural stability is also well studied in the robotics community, especially in the context of manipulation tasks. Early work implements rule-based approaches with rudimentary visual perception for the game of Jenga [21] or the safe deconstruction of object piles [19]. More recently, advances in 3D perception and physical simulation have been exploited to stack irregular objects like stones [6].

The experimental setup of Li et al. [16,17] is related to ours in that a stability predictor is trained for Kappla blocks in simulation which is then applied to guide stacking with a robotic arm. Our work is set apart from [16,17] in that we are considering a variety of object geometries as well as more challenging stack configurations. Furthermore, [16,17] do not consider object affordances.

More recently, Zhu et al. [25] show that an end-to-end approach with an end-effector in the loop can be used to learn visuo-motor skills sufficient to stack two blocks on top of one another – both in simulation and in the real world. Their work can be seen as complementary to ours, focusing on the end-effector actuation during stacking while we concentrate on the visual feedback loop and the emerging object affordances.

3   The ShapeStacks Dataset

In this section we describe the *ShapeStacks* dataset, starting from an overview of its contents (Sect. 3.1) followed by an analysis of the physics of stacking (Sect. 3.2). The latter is required to explain the design of *ShapeStacks* as well as to precisely define some of its physical data annotations. The full dataset including simulation descriptions and data generation scripts is publicly available.

3.1   Dataset Content

ShapeStacks is a large collection of 20,000 simulated block-stacking scenarios. The selection of the scenarios emphasizes diversity by featuring multiple geometries, degrees of structural complexity and types of structural stability violations, as shown in Fig. 2.

A detailed summary of the dataset content is provided in Table 1. Each scenario is a single-stranded stack of cubes, cuboids, cylinders and spheres, all with varying dimensions, proportions and colours. The 20,000 scenarios are split roughly evenly among scenarios that contain only cubes (for comparing to related work on stability prediction [15,23], and scenarios containing cuboids, cylinders and spheres (abbrev. CCS). Stacks have variable heights, from two to six objects, with the majority built up to a height of three. Each scenario can either be stable or unstable. This is determined by running a physics simulation with the given scenario as starting condition[1]. For every stack height, we provide an equal amount of stable and unstable scenarios. Furthermore, unstable scenarios are evenly divided into the two different instability types (cf. Sect. 3.2).

---

[1] We only report and release scenarios where the simulation outcome aligns with the physical derivation. Scenarios which behave differently due to imprecisions of the simulator are discarded.

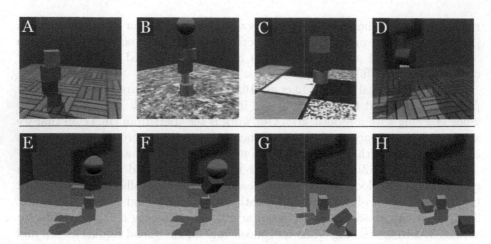

Fig. 2. Different scenarios from the ShapeStacks data set. (A) - (D) depict initial stack setups: (A) stable, rectified tower of cubes, (B) stable tower where multiple objects counterbalance each other; some recorded images are cropped purposefully to include the difficulty of partial observability, (C) stable, but visually challenging scenario due to colours and textures, (D) violation of planar-surface-principle (VPSF). (E) - (H) show the simulation of an unstable, collapsing tower due to a centre of mass violation (VCOM).

Scenarios are split into train (~70%), validation (~15%), and test (~15%) sets. Each scenario is rendered with a randomised set of background textures, object colours and lighting conditions. We record every scenario from 16 different camera angles and save RGB images of a resolution of 224 × 224 pixels.

Table 1. *ShapeStacks* contents. On the left, we present the number of scenarios and recorded images in both subsets of the dataset. *CCS* consists of cuboids, cylinders and spheres of varying size while *Cubes* only features regular blocks. On the right, we report the rendering and annotation details. See Sect. 3.2 for the derivation of the stability violation types *VCOM* and *VPSF*.

Stack height	CCS (# Scenarios)			Cubes (# Scenarios)			Rendering & Annotation
	Train	Val	Test	Train	Val	Test	**Rendering** ✓224 × 224 RGB
$h = 2$	1,340	286	286	1,680	360	360	**Randomised Scenes** ✓25 Background Textures
$h = 3$	2,464	528	528	1,680	360	360	✓6 Object Colours
$h = 4$	1,716	368	368	1,558	332	332	✓5 Lighting Conditions
$h = 5$	678	144	144	1,274	272	272	**Annotation** ✓0/1 Stability
$h = 6$	194	40	40	1,030	220	220	✓VCOM & VPSF
# Scenarios	6,392	1,366	1,366	7,222	1,544	1,544	✓Scene Semantics
# Images	102,272	21,856	21,856	115,552	24,704	24,704	

Every recorded image carries a binary stability label. Also, every image is aligned with a segmentation map relating the different parts of the image to their semantics with regard to stability. The segmentation map annotates the object which violates the stability of the tower, the first object to fall during the collapse and the base and top of the tower.

3.2   The Mechanics of Stacking

While our goal is to study intuitive physics and the emergence of object affordances, we argue that a precise understanding of the physical properties of the scenarios is essential to control data generation as well as to evaluate models.

In this paper, we restrict our attention to *single-stranded stacks*: each object S rests on top of another object S' or the ground plane and no two objects are at the same level. That is, we exclude structures such as arches, multiple columns, forks, etc. We also assume that all objects are *convex*, so that a straight line between any two points of the object is fully contained within it.

In order to determine the stability of a stack, we must use the notion of *Centre of Mass* (CoM). Let $\mathbf{p} = (x, y, z) \in S_i \subset \mathbb{R}^3$ be a point contained within the rigid body S_i. If m is the mass of the object and if the material is homogeneous with density ρ, then its CoM is given by $\mathbf{r}_i = \rho \int_{S_i} \mathbf{p} \, dx \, dy \, dz / m$.

We now study the stability of an object on top of another and then generalize the result to a full stack. For that, it is useful to refer to the topmost two blocks in Fig. 3. Assume that the rigid body S_4 is immersed in a uniform gravity field acting in the negative direction of the z axis. Furthermore, assume that S_4 is resting on a horizontal surface (in this case S_3) such that all of its contact points are contained in a horizontal plane π and $A \subset \pi$ denotes the convex hull of such points. Then S_4 is stable if, and only if, the projection of its CoM $\mathbf{r}_4$ on π is contained in A [22], which we write as $\mathrm{Proj}_\pi(\mathbf{r}_4) \in A$. If S_4 rests in a stable position on S_3, the combination of (S_3, S_4) can be seen as a rigid body with CoM $\mathbf{r}_3^4$. We can then check the stability of the entity (S_4, S_3) with respect to S_2. Proceeding iteratively for every object from top to bottom of the stack results in the following lemma illustrated in Fig. 3:

Lemma 1. *Let $S_1, \ldots, S_n$ be a collection of convex rigid bodies forming a single-stranded tower resting on a flat ground plane S_0. Let $m_1, \ldots, m_n$ be the masses of the objects and $\mathbf{r}_1, \ldots, \mathbf{r}_n$ their centres of mass. Furthermore, let A_i be the contact surface between object S_{i-1} and S_i and let $\pi_i \subset A_i$ be the plane containing it. Assume that π is parallel to the xy plane, which in turn is orthogonal to gravity. Then, if the objects are initially at rest, the tower is stable if, and only if,*

$$\forall i = 1, \ldots, n-1: \quad \mathrm{Proj}_{\pi_i}(\mathbf{r}_{i+1}^n) \in A_i, \quad \mathbf{r}_{i+1}^n = \frac{\sum_{j=i+1}^n m_j \mathbf{r}_j}{\sum_{j=i+1}^n m_j} \tag{1}$$

where $\mathbf{r}_{i+1}^n$ is the overall CoM of the topmost $n - i$ blocks.

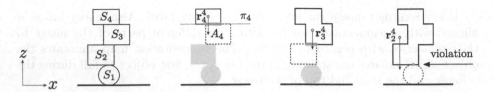

Fig. 3. Centre of Mass criterion. The stability of a stack can be tested by considering sub-stacks sequentially, from top to bottom. For stability, the projection of the CoM of each sub-stack must lie within the contact surface with the block supporting it. As shown on the right, a cylindrical or spherical object offers an infinitesimally small contact surface which does not afford stability.

This lemma can be used to assess the stability of a stack by checking the CoM condition from top to bottom for every interface A_i. Note that what is important is not the centre of mass of the individual blocks, but that of the part of the tower above each surface A_i. Thus it is possible to construct a stable stack that has apparent CoM violations for individual blocks, but that is overall stable due to the counter-balancing effect of the other blocks on top. Importantly, this allows for complex stacks that cannot be constructed in a bottom-up manner by placing only one object at a time.

We specifically distinguish between two types of instabilities. The first is *violation of the planar surface criterion* (VPSF). This is caused by an object stacked on top of a curved surface which violates Eq. (1) due to the infinitesimally small contact area. It is worth noting that this depends on the shape of the objects and not on the relative object positioning. The second type of instability is called *violation of the centre of mass criterion* (VCOM), and comprises violations of Eq. (1) that depend instead on the positioning of the objects in the stack. For each unstable scenario we introduce either a VPSF or a VCOM violation for exactly one contact area A_i.

For dataset construction, Lemma 1 thus allows us to tightly control which stability violation occurs in each simulated scenario and to mark in each image which object it is attributable to (cf. Fig. 4).

4   Stability Prediction

In this section, we construct models that can predict the stability of a stack from RGB images alone. We learn these models from passive observations of stable and unstable stacks. Specifically, our vision-based stability classifier is trained to distinguish between stable and unstable towers (Sect. 4.1) and validated by demonstrating state-of-the-art performance on both simulated and real data. We also quantify how reliably the models can localise the mechanical stability violations present in the unstable stacks (Sect. 4.2).

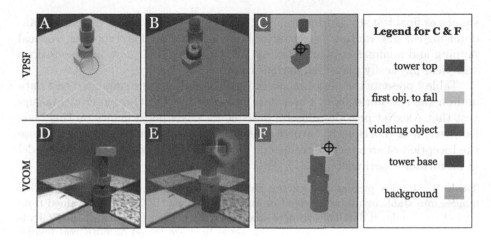

Fig. 4. Attention visualisation obtained via an occlusion study. A Gaussian blur is applied in a sliding window manner to the image (A, D), the increase (red)/decrease (blue) in the predicted stability is shown as a heatmap in (B, E), and the latter is compared to ground-truth segmentation maps in (C, F). The centres of attention are compared to the respective segmentation maps (C) and (F) and indeed correlate with the respective violation sites as indicated by the cross hairs. (Color figure online)

4.1   Training the Stability Predictor

We train a visual classifier for the task of predicting whether a shape stack is stable or not using images[2] from the *ShapeStacks* dataset, annotated with binary stability labels.

To this end we investigate the use of two neural network architectures commonly used for image-based classification: AlexNet [13] and Inception v4 [20]. In both cases we optimise the network parameters θ given our dataset $D = \{(x^{(1)}, y^{(1)}), \ldots, (x^{(m)}, y^{(m)})\}$ of images $x^{(i)}$ and stability labels $y^{(i)}$ by minimising the following logistic regression loss:

$$L(\theta; D) = -\sum_{i=1}^{m} y^{(i)} \log \left(\frac{1}{1 + e^{-f(x^{(i)};\theta)}} \right) + (1 - y^{(i)}) \log \left(1 - \frac{1}{1 + e^{-f(x^{(i)};\theta)}} \right) \quad (2)$$

The unscaled logit output of the CNNs is denoted by $f(x; \theta)$ and the label values are $y = 0$ for stable and $y = 1$ for unstable images. Inception v4 and AlexNet are both trained using the RMSProp optimiser [9] with solver hyperparameters as reported in [20] for 80 epochs.

We use the two different subsets of *ShapeStacks* during training (cf. Table 1), each one containing an equal amount of stable and unstable images. Both types of violations (VCOM and VPSF, cf. Sect. 3.2) are evenly represented among unstable images. We also reserve a set of 46,560 images featuring stacks of all

---

[2] We only use still images of initial stack configurations and no images depicting collapses from later time points in the simulations.

shapes as final test set. During training, we augment the training images by randomising colours, varying aspect-ratios, and applying random cropping, vertical flipping and minimal in-plane rotation. We ensure that all data augmentations still yield physically plausible, upright towers.

Table 2 presents the performance of the classifiers on our simulated test data and on the real-world block tower data provided by [15]. Our experiments suggest that AlexNet provides a useful baseline for CNN performance on this task. However, it is consistently outperformed by the Inception network. We choose the Inception v4 architecture trained on ShapeStacks data as the reference model in all further experiments.

Table 2. Stability prediction accuracy given as the percentage of correctly classified images into stable or unstable. AlexNet and Inception v4 (INCPv4) are trained from scratch on simulated data consisting of stacks featuring either cubes or CCS. INCPv4-IMGN is pre-trained on ImageNet [4]. All algorithms are tested on both *real* images from [15] and *simulated* images from our *ShapeStacks* test split featuring all shapes.

	AlexNet		INCPv4-IMGN		**INCPv4**		Physnet	VDA
	Cubes	CCS	Cubes	CCS	Cubes	CCS	[15]	[23]
Simulated	60.5%	58.8%	76.2%	**84.9%**	77.7%	**84.9%**	N/A^4	N/A^4
Real [15]	65.5%	52.5%	73.2%	64.9%	74.7%	66.3%	66.7%	**75%**
Simulated Examples					Real Examples			

As expected, both models perform best on the real-world data when only trained on cubes as the real-world images also only show stacks of cubes. Best performance is reached for both models on the combined ShapeStacks test data (featuring all shapes) when training is also performed on multiple object types. However, it is surprising how well the Inception network generalises from cubes to other structures suggesting that it learned an intuition about the CoM principle (Sect. 3.2) which is also applicable to more complex shapes.

On real images, Inception v4, trained from scratch on our dataset, outperforms the baseline from Lerer et al. [15] and is on par with the more complex visual de-animation approach by Wu et al. [23], which translates the observed images into a physical state and checks stability with a physics engine. We attribute this to the richness of the *ShapeStacks* dataset as well as to our data augmentation scheme, which results in a visually and structurally diverse set of stacks and hence affords good generalisation.

4.2   Instability Localisation

In order to probe whether the network grounds its stability prediction on sound mechanical principles we examine its ability to localise mechanical points of failure. Our approach is similar to that of [15] though owing to the annotations included in the *ShapeStacks* dataset we are able to conduct a quantitative analysis on 1,500 randomly sampled images from the test set by comparing the network's attention maps with the corresponding ground truth stability segmentation maps (cf. Fig. 4).

Specifically, we compute the attention maps by conducting an occlusion study whereby images are blurred using a Gaussian filter with a standard deviation of 30 pixels applied in a sliding window manner with stride 8 and a patch size of 14×14 pixels. To avoid creating object-like occlusion artefacts, the blurred patch does not have rigid boundaries but gradually fades into the image (cf. Fig. 4A and D). The patched images are given as an input to the stability classifier and the predicted stability scores are aggregated in a map (cf. Fig. 4B and E).

We then check whether the maximiser of the attention map is contained within the object responsible for stability violation (cf. Fig. 4C and F) and report results in Table 3. In 79.9% of all unstable cases, the network focuses on the violation region, which we define as the smallest rectangle enclosing the violating object and the first object to fall.

For VPSF instabilities, the network attends to the violating, curved object with a likelihood of 52.1%. For VCOM instabilities, the network's main focus still remains on the violating object but is also spread out to the unsupported upper part of the tower (*First Object to Fall + Tower Top*) in 38.1% of the cases, which is in line with the physics governing VCOM instabilities (cf. Eq. (1)).

Table 3. The fraction of times the network attends image areas with specific physical meaning (cf. Fig. 4). 1,500 images were analysed with an Inception v4 network trained on the CCS data (cf. Sect. 4.1). The first row is aggregated over all instability types and the second and third rows offer a breakdown for the CoM (VCOM) and planar surface violations (VPSF), respectively. The fourth row lists the fractions of the areas occupied with the respective label across the segmentation maps of all unstable scenarios and serves as a reference point of how likely it is to focus on a specific area just by random chance. Likewise, the fifth row reports random chance attention within the tower.

	Violating object	First Obj. to fall	Violation area	Tower base	Tower top	Background
VCOM &VPSF	38.9%	29.3%	79.9%	5.9%	5.5%	20.4%
VCOM	32.7%	30.8%	76.5%	6.5%	7.3%	22.7%
VPSF	52.1%	26.3%	87.1%	4.6%	1.7%	15.4%
Random chance	1.6%	1.9%	4.9%	1.7%	1.8%	93.0%
Random in tower	19.3%	22.9%	59.0%	20.5%	21.7%	14.5%

5 Stacking and Stackability

So far, we have focussed on predicting the stability of stacks. However, it is not clear whether the models we learned understand the geometric affordances needed for actively building new stacks. Here, we answer this question by considering three active stacking tasks. The first one is to estimate the *stackability* of different objects and prioritise them while stacking (Sect. 5.1). The second is to accurately estimate the optimal placement of blocks on a stack through visual feedback (Sect. 5.2). The third is to counter-balance an unstable structure by placing an additional object on top (Sect. 5.3). All tasks show encouraging performance indicating that models do indeed acquire actionable physical knowledge from passive stability prediction.

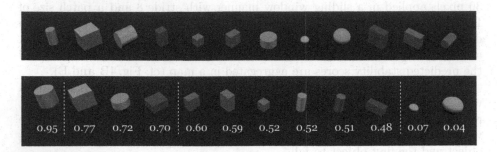

Fig. 5. *Top row*: An unordered set of objects with random orientations. *Bottom row*: objects sorted from most stackable (left) to least stackable (right). Every object is oriented in the way which affords best *stackability* according to our network. The scores allow for division between different stability categories as visualised with white vertical lines.

5.1   Stackability

Different object shapes intrinsically have different stacking potential: While a cuboid can serve as a solid base in every orientation, a cylinder can only support objects when placed upright and a sphere is never a good choice as a supporting object. If an agent is given a set of blocks to stack, it can use an understanding of such affordances to prioritise objects, placing the most stable ones at the bottom of the stack. We define *stackability* of an object (i.e. its utility with regard to stack construction) by answering the question: "How well can this object support the others in my set?" Next, we show how to answer this question quantitatively using our learned stability predictor.

Given a set of objects, we compute their relative stackability scores as follows: Each object is placed on the ground as if it were the base of the stack using one of its discrete orientations[3]. Then, all other objects are systematically placed on top of the base object, one at a time, in all of their respective orientations. An image of the resulting combination is generated and assessed for stability using our predictor. Positions for the top objects are sampled within a defined radius around the base object via simulated annealing and the maximum stability score

---

[3] Cuboids afford three discrete orientations, one for each of its three distinct faces (considering symmetry). Cylinders afford two orientations (upright and sideways) and spheres afford only one orientation due to their radial symmetry.

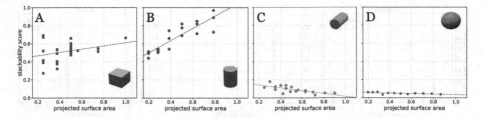

Fig. 6. Correlation of the *stackability* score with the projected surface area for different object classes. The projected surface area is calculated by projecting the object onto the x-y-plane. Spheres and lying cylinders are given very low *stackability* scores. Upright cylinders and cuboids are generally more stackable as the projected surface area grows.

is recorded. The stackability score of the base object is then estimated as the average maximum stability achieved by all the other objects as they are placed on top of it. We also add random perturbations to the base position, with the idea of reflecting stackability robustness in the estimated score.

Stackability can then be used to rank objects' shapes and orientations based on how well they can be expected to support other objects, as illustrated in Fig. 5. We also examine the model's understanding of stackability quantitatively in Fig. 6 computing scores over all object classes with varying volumes and aspect ratios. We generally find that the model ranks shapes in a sensible manner, preferring to stack on the largest face of cuboids, then on upright cylinders, and reject spheres as generally unsuitable for stacking. The results suggest that the suitability of different geometries to stacking is implicitly learned by stability prediction.

5.2   Stacking Shapes in Simulation

Next, we investigate the ability of the stability predictor to not only order objects in an active stacking scenario, but also to accurately position them in stable configurations. To do so, we design three stacking scenarios involving different shape types: cubes, cuboids and CCS. In each scenario, the method is given a pool of 12 different object shapes and sizes to stack with the goal of building as tall a tower as possible. Every scenario is observed from six cameras (cf. Fig. 8D) which move upwards as the stack grows to guarantee full coverage of the process at any time. At the beginning of every stacking episode, background textures, object colors and scene lights are randomised. Then the stack order and best orientation for each objects are computed according to the stackability score (cf. Sect. 5.1).

The stacking process commences with the first object being placed at the scene centre. The object at place r in the stacking queue is always spawned at a fixed height h_r above the current tower trunk and candidate positions are sampled in the x-y-plane at $z = h_r$ according to the simulated annealing process described in Sect. 5.1. If no stable position is identified for a particular object

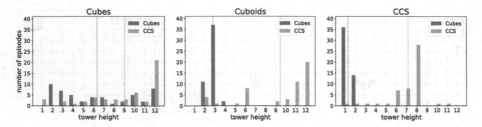

Fig. 7. Stacking performance. The height of the bars indicate how often the algorithm built a tower with the respective number of objects before it fell over. The mean tower height is indicated with a vertical dashed line. (Color figure online)

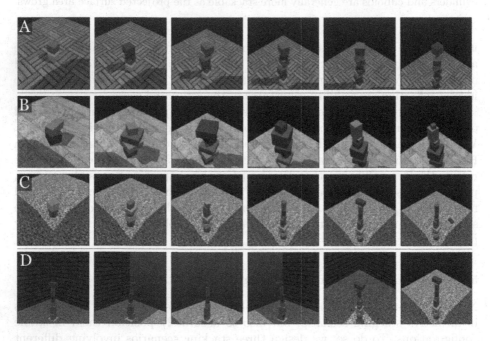

Fig. 8. Three examples of stacking attempts. In (A) and (B), the algorithm successfully stacked up cubes and cuboids to the maximum height of 12. In C, the algorithm placed the 10th object in a way that violates Eq. (1). In (D), the images obtained from the different camera angles are shown for the failed stacking attempt in (C).

(i.e. logistic regression score < 0.5), it is put aside and disregarded for the rest of the process. The process is iterated until the placement of an object results in the collapse of the stack or no more objects are available.

In Fig. 7, we report achieved stack heights for two differently trained models in the three scenarios with cubes, cuboids and CCS, respectively. For each stacking episode, the algorithm is given a pool of 12 randomised objects. However, CCS scenarios always include exactly two spheres, so the maximum achievable height in this case is 11. We compare two stability predictors: One trained on

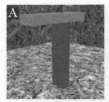

Object	Success Rate
Cube	76%
Cuboid	94%
Cylinder	72%
Sphere	98%

Fig. 9. Counterbalancing unstable structures. A: frozen, unstable stack; B: collapsing tower; C: successful placement of a counterweight that prevents collapse. Right: success rates for different counterweight types aggregated over 50 episodes.

cubes only (blue bars) and one trained on CSS objects (orange bars). The CCS stability predictor clearly outperforms the one trained on cubes only in all three scenarios. In fact, the cubes predictor only manages perform decently on cube stacking and largely fails when confronted with varied shapes highlighting the importance of training on a diverse shape set.

5.3   Balancing Unstable Structures

In the final task, we present our model with an unstable stack, freeze it such that it does not collapse, and then ask the algorithm to place an additional object on top to counter-balance the instability. This is a subtle task that requires the model to understand the concept of counterbalancing and cannot be solved by simply centering a block on top of the one below. Figure 9 shows that our algorithm successfully solves this task with high probability in an "unstable T scenario" for different types of counterweight objects.

6   Conclusions

We investigate the acquisition of physical intuition and geometric affordances in the context of vision-based, generalised object stacking. To that end, we construct the *ShapeStacks* dataset featuring diverse stacks of shapes with detailed annotations of mechanical stability violations and release it publicly. We train a visual stability predictor on ShapeStacks which performs commensurately with state-of-the-art on simulated and real world images. Our model also correctly localises structural instabilities, yields an intuitive notion about the stackability of objects and successfully guides a simulated stacking process solely based on visual cues. Our results suggest that an intuitive understanding about physical principles and geometric affordances can be acquired from visual observation and effectively utilised in manipulation tasks.

Acknowledgement. This research was funded by the European Research Council under grant ERC 677195-IDIU and the EPSRC AIMS Centre for Doctoral Training at Oxford University.

References

1. Battaglia, P.W., Hamrick, J.B., Tenenbaum, J.B.: Simulation as an engine of physical scene understanding. Proc. Natl. Acad. Sci. **110**(45), 18327–18332 (2013). https://doi.org/10.1073/pnas.1306572110. http://www.pnas.org/cgi/doi/10.1073/pnas.1306572110
2. Battaglia, P., Pascanu, R., Lai, M., Rezende, D.J., et al.: Interaction networks for learning about objects, relations and physics. In: Advances in Neural Information Processing Systems, pp. 4502–4510 (2016)
3. Chang, M.B., Ullman, T., Torralba, A., Tenenbaum, J.B.: A compositional object-based approach to learning physical dynamics, pp. 1–15 (2016). http://arxiv.org/abs/1612.00341
4. Deng, J., Dong, W., Socher, R., Li, L.J., Li, K., Fei-Fei, L.: ImageNet: a large-scale hierarchical image database. In: IEEE Conference on Computer Vision and Pattern Recognition, CVPR 2009, pp. 248–255. IEEE (2009)
5. Fragkiadaki, K., Agrawal, P., Levine, S., Malik, J.: Learning visual predictive models of physics for playing billiards, pp. 1–12 (2015). http://arxiv.org/abs/1511.07404
6. Furrer, F., et al.: Autonomous robotic stone stacking with online next best object target pose planning. In: Proceedings - IEEE International Conference on Robotics and Automation, pp. 2350–2356 (2017). https://doi.org/10.1109/ICRA.2017.7989272
7. Gupta, A., Efros, A.A., Hebert, M.: Blocks world revisited: image understanding using qualitative geometry and mechanics. In: Daniilidis, K., Maragos, P., Paragios, N. (eds.) ECCV 2010. LNCS, vol. 6314, pp. 482–496. Springer, Heidelberg (2010). https://doi.org/10.1007/978-3-642-15561-1_35
8. Hamrick, J.B., Battaglia, P.W., Griffiths, T.L., Tenenbaum, J.B.: Inferring mass in complex scenes by mental simulation. Cognition **157** (2016). https://doi.org/10.1016/j.cognition.2016.08.012
9. Hinton, G., Srivastava, N., Swersky, K.: Coursera, neural networks for machine learning, lecture 6e (2014). http://www.cs.toronto.edu/~tijmen/csc321/slides/lecture_slides_lec6.pdf
10. Jia, Z., Gallagher, A.C., Saxena, A., Chen, T.: 3D reasoning from blocks to stability. IEEE Trans. Pattern Anal. Mach. Intell. **37**(5), 905–918 (2015). https://doi.org/10.1109/TPAMI.2014.2359435
11. Kjellström, H., Romero, J., Kragić, D.: Visual object-action recognition: inferring object affordances from human demonstration. Comput. Vis. Image Underst. **115**(1), 81–90 (2011). https://doi.org/10.1016/j.cviu.2010.08.002
12. Koppula, H.S., Saxena, A.: Anticipating human activities using object affordances for reactive robotic response. IEEE Trans. Pattern Anal. Mach. Intell. **38**(1), 14–29 (2016). https://doi.org/10.1109/TPAMI.2015.2430335
13. Krizhevsky, A., Sutskever, I., Hinton, G.E.: ImageNet classification with deep convolutional neural networks. In: Advances in Neural Information Processing Systems, pp. 1–9 (2012). https://doi.org/10.1016/j.protcy.2014.09.007
14. Kubricht, J.R., Holyoak, K.J., Lu, H.: Intuitive physics: current research and controversies. Trends Cogn. Sci. **21**(10), 749–759 (2017). https://doi.org/10.1016/j.tics.2017.06.002
15. Lerer, A., Gross, S., Fergus, R.: Learning physical intuition of block towers by example. In: Proceedings of the 33rd International Conference on International Conference on Machine Learning - Volume 48, ICML 2016, pp. 430–438. JMLR.org (2016). http://dl.acm.org/citation.cfm?id=3045390.3045437

16. Li, W., Azimi, S., Leonardis, A., Fritz, M.: To fall or not to fall: a visual approach to physical stability prediction. arXiv preprint arXiv:1604.00066 (2016)
17. Li, W., Leonardis, A., Fritz, M.: Visual stability prediction for robotic manipulation. In: Proceedings - IEEE International Conference on Robotics and Automation, pp. 2606–2613 (2017). https://doi.org/10.1109/ICRA.2017.7989304
18. Mottaghi, R., Bagherinezhad, H., Rastegari, M., Farhadi, A.: Newtonian image understanding: unfolding the dynamics of objects in static images. In: 2016 IEEE Conference on Computer Vision and Pattern Recognition (CVPR) (2016). https://doi.org/10.1109/CVPR.2016.383
19. Ornan, O., Degani, A.: Toward autonomous disassembling of randomly piled objects with minimal perturbation. IEEE International Conference on Intelligent Robots and Systems, pp. 4983–4989 (2013). https://doi.org/10.1109/IROS.2013.6697076
20. Szegedy, C., Ioffe, S., Vanhoucke, V., Alemi, A.A.: Inception-v4, inception-ResNet and the impact of residual connections on learning. In: AAAI, vol. 4, p. 12 (2017)
21. Wang, J., Rogers, P., Parker, L., Brooks, D., Stilman, M.: Robot Jenga: autonomous and strategic block extraction. In: 2009 IEEE/RSJ International Conference on Intelligent Robots and Systems, IROS 2009, pp. 5248–5253 (2009). https://doi.org/10.1109/IROS.2009.5354303
22. Wieber, P.B.: On the stability of walking systems. In: Proceedings of the Third IARP International Workshop on Humanoid and Human Friendly Robotics, pp. 1–7 (2002). https://doi.org/10.1088/0264-9381/12/2/003
23. Wu, J., Lu, E., Kohli, P., Freeman, W.T., Tenenbaum, J.B.: Learning to see physics via visual de-animation. In: Advances in Neural Information Processing Systems (NIPS) (2017)
24. Wu, J., Yildirim, I., Lim, J., Freeman, W., Tenenbaum, J.: Galileo: perceiving physical object properties by integrating a physics engine with deep learning. In: Advances in Neural Information Processing Systems 28 (NIPS 2015), pp. 1–9 (2015)
25. Zhu, Y., et al.: Reinforcement and imitation learning for diverse visuomotor skills. CoRR abs/1802.09564 (2018). http://arxiv.org/abs/1802.09564

Inner Space Preserving Generative Pose Machine

Shuangjun Liu and Sarah Ostadabbas[(⊠)]

Augmented Cognition Lab, Electrical and Computer Engineering Department,
Northeastern University, Boston, USA
{shuliu,ostadabbas}@ece.neu.edu
http://www.northeastern.edu/ostadabbas/

Abstract. Image-based generative methods, such as generative adversarial networks (GANs) have already been able to generate realistic images with much context control, specially when they are conditioned. However, most successful frameworks share a common procedure which performs an image-to-image translation with pose of figures in the image untouched. When the objective is reposing a figure in an image while preserving the rest of the image, the state-of-the-art mainly assumes a single rigid body with simple background and limited pose shift, which can hardly be extended to the images under normal settings. In this paper, we introduce an image "inner space" preserving model that assigns an interpretable low-dimensional pose descriptor (LDPD) to an articulated figure in the image. Figure reposing is then generated by passing the LDPD and the original image through multi-stage augmented hourglass networks in a conditional GAN structure, called inner space preserving generative pose machine (ISP-GPM). We evaluated ISP-GPM on reposing human figures, which are highly articulated with versatile variations. Test of a state-of-the-art pose estimator on our reposed dataset gave an accuracy over 80% on PCK0.5 metric. The results also elucidated that our ISP-GPM is able to preserve the background with high accuracy while reasonably recovering the area blocked by the figure to be reposed.

Keywords: conditional Generative adversarial networks (cGANS)
Inner space preserving · Generative pose models · Articulated bodies

1 Introduction

Photographs are important because they seem to capture so much: in the right photograph we can almost feel the sunlight, smell the ocean breeze, and see the fluttering of the birds. And yet, none of this information is actually present in a

Electronic supplementary material The online version of this chapter (https://doi.org/10.1007/978-3-030-01246-5_44) contains supplementary material, which is available to authorized users.

© Springer Nature Switzerland AG 2018
V. Ferrari et al. (Eds.): ECCV 2018, LNCS 11205, pp. 740–759, 2018.
https://doi.org/10.1007/978-3-030-01246-5_44

two-dimensional image. Our human knowledge and prior experience allow us to recreate "much" of the world state (i.e. its inner space) and even fill in missing portions of occluded objects in an image since the manifold of *probable* world states has a lower dimension than the world state space.

Like humans, deep networks can use context and learned "knowledge" to fill in missing elements. But more than that, if trained properly, they can modify (repose) a portion of the inner space while preserving the rest, allowing us to significantly change portions of the image. In this paper, we present a novel deep learning based generative model that takes an image and pose specification and creates a similar image in which a target element is reposed. In Fig. 1, we reposed a human figure a number of different ways based on a single painting by the early 20th century painter, Thomas Eakins.

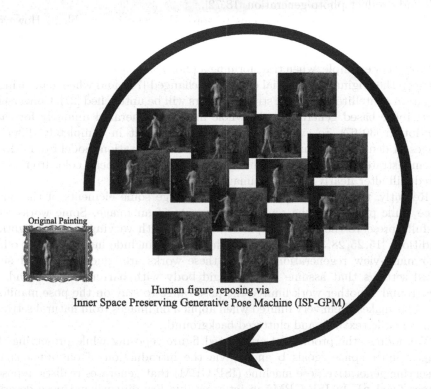

Original Painting

Human figure reposing via
Inner Space Preserving Generative Pose Machine (ISP-GPM)

Fig. 1. Inner space preserving reposing of one of Thomas Eakins' paintings: William Rush Carving His Allegorical Figure of the Schuylkill River, 1908.

In reposing a figure there are three goals: (a) the output image should look like a realistic image in the style of the source image, (b) the figure should be in the specified pose, and (c) the rest of the image should be as similar to the original as possible. Generative adversarial networks (GANs) [23], are the "classic" approach to solving the first goal by generating novel images that match a certain style. More recently, other approaches have been developed that merge deep learning and probabilistic models including the variational autoencoder (VAE) to generate realistic images [7,16,35,37,48,52,57,70,73].

The second goal, putting the figure in the correct pose, requires a more controlled generation approach. Much of the work in this area is based around conditional GANs (cGAN) [42] or conditional VAE (cVAE) [35,62]. The contextual information can be supplied in a variety of ways. Many of these algorithms generate based on semantic meaning, which could be class labels, attributes, or text descriptors [22,47,54,65,67]. Others are conditioned on an image often called as image-to-image translation [70]. The success of image-to-image translation is seen in many tasks including colorization [26,36,73], semantic image segmentation [11–13,19,24,38,43,45,49,58], texture transfer [17], outdoor photo generation with specific attributes [34,60], scene generation with semantic layout [30], and product photo generation [18,72].

At a superficial level, this seems to solve the reposing problem. However, these existing approaches generally either focus on preserving the image (goal c) or generating an entirely novel image based on the contextual image (goal b), but not both. For example, when transforming a photo of a face to a sketch, the result will keep the original face spatial contour unchanged [70], and when generating a map from a satellite photo, the street contours will be untouched [27]. Conversely, in attribute based generation, the whole image is generated uniquely for each description [30,67], so even minor changes will result in completely different images. A demo case from an attribute based bird generation model from [54,56] is demonstrated in Fig. 2, in which only changing a bird's head color from black to red will alter nearly the entire image.[1]

Recently, there have been attempts to change some elements of the inner space while preserving the remaining elements of an image. Some works successfully preserve the object graphical identities with varying poses or lighting conditions [15,25,28,32,33,40,41,68]. These works include human face or office chair multi-view regeneration. Yet, all these works are conducted under simplified settings that assume a single rigid body with barren textures and no background. Another work limited the pose range to stay on the pose manifold [68]. This makes them very limited when applied on images from natural settings with versatile textures and cluttered background.

We address the problem of articulated figure reposing while preserving the image's inner space (goals b and c) via the introduction of our inner space preserving generative pose machine (ISP-GPM) that generates realistic reposed images (goal a). In ISP-GPM, an interpretable low-dimensional pose descriptor (LDPD) is assigned to the specified figure in the 2D image domain. Altering LDPD causes figure to be reposed. For image regeneration, we used stack of augmented hourglass networks in a cGAN framework, conditioned on both LDPD and the original image. We replaced hourglass network original downsampling mechanism by pure convolutional layers to maximize the "inner space" preservation between the original and reposed images. Furthermore, we extended the

---

[1] For this experiment, the random term was set to zero to rule out differences due to the input.

(a)   (b)

Fig. 2. Generated bird figures from work presented in [56] with captions as: (a) this bird has a *black* head, a pointy orange beak, and yellow body, (b) this bird has a *red* head, a pointy orange beak, and yellow body. (Color figure online)

"pose" concept to a more general format which is no longer a simple rotation of a single rigid body, but instead the relative relationship between all the physical entities present in an image and its background. We push the boundary to an extreme case—a highly articulated object (i.e. human body) against a naturalistic background (code available at [2]). A direct outcome of ISP-GPM is that by altering the pose state in an image, we can achieve unlimited generative reinterpretation of the original world, which ultimately leads to a one-shot ISP data augmentation.

2   Related Work

Pose altering is very common in our physical world. If we take photographs of a dynamic articulated object over time, they can hardly be the same. These images share a strong similarity due to having a relatively static background with only differences caused by changes in the object's pose states. We can perceive these differences since the pose information is partially reflected in these images. However, the true "reposing" actually happens in the 3D space and the 2D mapping is just a simple projection afterwards. This fact inspired 3D rendering engines such as Blender, Maya, or 3DS Max to simulate the physical world in (semi)exact dimensions at graphical level, synthesize 3D objects in it, repose the object in 3D, and then finally render a 2D image from the reposed object using a virtual camera [37]. Following this pipeline, there are recent attempts to generate synthesized human images [51,61,63]. SCAPE method parameterizes the human body shapes into a generalized template using dense 3D scans of a person in multiple poses [5]. Authors in [11] mapped the photographs of clothing into SCAPE model to boost human 3D pose dataset. Physical rendering and real textures are combined in [64] to generate a synthetic human dataset. However, these methods inevitably require sophisticated 3D rendering engines and avatar data is needed either from full 3D scanning with special equipment or generated from generalized templates [5,39], which means such data is not easily accessible or extendable to novel figures.

Image-based generative methods, such as GANs and VAEs have already been able to generate realistic images with much context control, specially when they are conditioned [7,27,54]. There are also works addressing pose issue of rigid (e.g. chair [14]) or single (e.g. face [68]) objects. An autoencoder structure to capture shift or rotation changes is employed in [35], which successfully regenerates images of 2D digits and 3D graphics rendered images with pose shift. Deep convolutional inverse graphics network (IGN) [33] learns interpretable representation of images including out-of-plane rotations and lighting variations to generate face and chairs from different view points. Based on IGN concept, Yang employed a recurrent network to apply out-of-plane rotations to human faces and 3D chairs to generate new images [68]. In [15], authors built a convolutional neural network (CNN) model for chair view rendering, which can interpolate between given viewpoints to generate missing ones or invent new chair styles by interpolating between chairs from the training set. By incorporating 3D morphable model into a GAN structure, the authors in [71] proposed a framework which can generate face frontalization in the wild with less training data. These works as a matter of fact in a sense preserve the inner space information with the target identity unchanged. However, most are limited to a single rigid body with simple or no background, and are inadequate to deal with complex articulated objects such as human body in a realistic background setting.

In the last couple of years, there have been a few image-based generative models proposed for human body reposing. In [54,56], by localizing exact body parts, human figures were synthesized with provided attributes. However, though pose information is provided exactly, the appearance are randomly sampled under attribute context. Lassner and colleagues in [37] generated vivid human figures with varying poses and clothing textures by sampling from a given set of attributes. A direct result of sampling based method is a strong coupling effect between different identities in the image, in which the pose state cannot get altered without the image inner space change.

In this paper, we focus on the same pose and reposing topics but extend them to a more general format of highly articulated object with versatile background under realistic/wild settings. We are going to preserve the original inner space of the image, while altering the pose of the an specific figure in the image. Instead of applying a large domain shift on an image such as changing the day to night, or the summer to winter, we aim to model a pose shift caused by a movement in the 3D physical world, while the inner space of the world stays identical to its version before this movement. Inspired by this idea, we present our inner space preserving generative pose machine (ISP-GPM), in which rather than attribute based sampling, we focus on specific image instances.

3   World State and Inner Space of an Image

"No man ever steps in the same river twice" quoted from Heraclitus.

Our world is dynamically changing. Taking one step forward, raising hand a little bit, moving our head to the side, all these tiny motions make us visually different from a moment ago. These changes are also dependably reflected in the photographs taken from us. In most cases, for a short period of time, we can assume such changes are purely caused by pose shift instead of characteristic changes of all related entities. Let's simply call the partial world captured by an image "the world". If we model the world by a set of rigid bodies, for a single rigid body without background (the assumption in the most of the state-of-the-art), the world state can be described by appearance term α and the pose state β of the rigid body as $W_s = \{\alpha, \beta\}$ and the reposing process is conduced by altering β to a target pose $\hat{\beta}$. However, real world can hardly be described by a simple rigid body, but clustered articulated rigid bodies and background. In this case, we formulate the world state as:

$$W_s = \{\alpha_i, \beta_i, \phi(i,j) | i, j \in N\}. \tag{1}$$

where, N stands for the total number of rigid bodies in the world and $\phi(i,j)$ stands for the constraints between two rigid bodies. For example, a human has N (depending on the granularity of the template that we choose) articulated limbs in which the joints between them follow the biomechanical constraints of the body. A pure reposing process in physical world should keep the α_i terms unchanged. However, in imaging process, only part of the α_i information is preserved as α_i^{in} with $\alpha_i = \alpha_i^{in} + \alpha_i^{out}$, where α_i^{out} stands for the missing information in the image with respect to the physical world. We assume each image can partially preserved the physical world information and we call this partially preserved world state the "inner space". If α_i^{in} and $\phi(i,j)$ term are preserved during figure i reposing, we call this process "inner space preserving".

Another assumption is that in the majority of cases, the foreground (F) and the background (B) should be decoupled in the image, which means if figure $i \in F$ and figure $j \in B$, the $\phi(i,j)$ is empty or vice versa. This means if a bird with black head and yellow body is the foreground, the identical bird can be in different backgrounds such as on a tree or in the sky. However, strong coupling between foreground and background is often seen in attribute-based models as shown in Fig. 2. Instead, we designed our generative pose machine to reflect: (1) inner space preserving, and (2) foreground and background decoupling.

4   ISP-GPM: Inner Space Preserving Generative Pose Machine

The ISP-GPM addresses the extensive pose transformation of articulated figures in an image through the following process: given an image with specified figure and its interpretable low-dimensional pose descriptor (LDPD), ISP-GPM outputs a reposed figure with original image inner space preserved (see Fig. 3). The key components of the ISP-GPM are: (1) a CNN interface converter to make the LDPD compatible with the first convolutional layer of the ISP-GPM interface, and (2) a generative pose machine to generate reposed figures using the regression structure of hourglass networks when stacked in a cGAN framework in order to force the pose descriptor into the regenerated images.

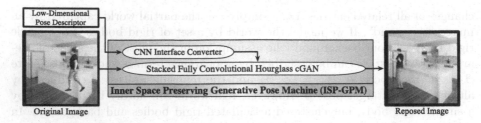

Fig. 3. An overview of the Inner Space Preserving Generative Pose Machine (ISP-GPM) framework.

4.1   CNN Interface Converter

We employed an LDPD in the 2D image domain, which in the majority of the human pose dataset such as Max Planck institute informatics (MPII) [3] and Leeds sports pose (LSP) [29] is defined as the vector of 2D joint position coordinates. To make this descriptor compatible with the convolutional layer interface of ISP-GPM, we need a CNN interface converter. The most straight forward converter could simply set the joint point in the image, similar to the work described in [56]. As human body can be represented by a connected graph [4,8], more specifically a tree structure, in this work we further appended the edge information into our converter. Assume human pose to be represented by 2D locations of its N joints. Let's use N channel maps to hold this information as joint map, J_{Map}. For each joint i with coordinates (x_i, y_i), if joint i's parent joint exists, we are going to draw a line from (x_i, y_i) to its parent location in channel i of J_{Map}. In generating J_{Map}s, the draw operation is conducted by image libraries such as OpenCV [10].

4.2   Stacked Fully Convolutional Hourglass cGAN

Many previous works have proved the effectiveness of multi-stage estimation structure in human pose estimation, such as 2016 revolutionary work of convolutional pose machine [66]. As an inverse operation to regenerate figures of humans, we employed a similar multi-stage structure. Furthermore, human pose can be described in a multi-scale fashion, starting from simple joint description to sophisticated clothing textures on each body part, which inspired the use of an hourglass model with a stacked regression structure [44]. However, instead of pose estimation or segmentation, for human reposing problem, more detailed information needs to be preserved in both encoding and decoding phases of the hourglass network. Therefore, we replaced hourglass network's max pooling and the nearest upsampling modules by pure convolutional layers to maximize the information preservation. The skip structure of the original hourglass network is also preserved to let more original high frequency parts pass through. Original hourglass is designed for image regression purpose. In our case, we augment hourglass original design by introducing structure losses [27], which penalize the joint configuration of the output. We forced the pose into the generated image by employing a cGAN mechanism.

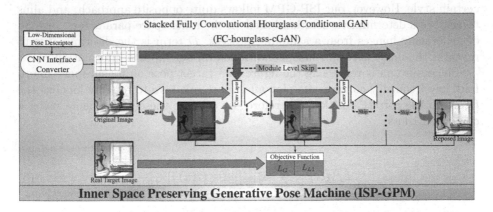

Fig. 4. Inside the stacked FC-hourglass-cGAN part of the ISP-GPM. Blue arrows stand for the image flow, yellow arrows for the hourglass feature maps, and green arrows for J_{Map} flow. (Color figure online)

An overview of our stacked fully convolutional hourglass cGAN (FC-hourglass-cGAN) is shown in Fig. 4, where we employed a dual skip mechanism, a module level skip as well as the inner module level skips. Each FC-hourglass employs a encoder-decoder like structure [6,44,46]. Stacked FC-hourglass plays the generator role in our design, while another convolutional net plays the discriminator role. We employed an intermediate supervision mechanism similar to [44], however the supervision is conducted by both L1 loss and generator loss, as described in the following section.

4.3 Stacked Generator and Discriminator Losses

Due to the ISP-GPM stacked structure, the generator loss comes from all intermediate stages to the final one. The loss for generator is then computed as:

$$L_G(G, D) = \mathbb{E}_{u,v}[\log D(u, v)] + \sum_{i=1}^{N_{stk}} \mathbb{E}_u[\log(1 - D(u, G(u)[i]))]. \tag{2}$$

where, u stands for the combined input of J_{Map} and the original image, and v is the target reposed image. G is stacked FC-hourglass that acts as the generator role, N_{stk} stands for the total number of stacks in the generator G, and D is the discriminator part of the cGAN. Different from commonly used generator, our G gives multiple output according to the stack number. $G(u)[i]$ stands for the i-th output conditioned on u. Another difference from traditional cGAN design is that we do not include the random term z as it is common in most

GAN based models [22,23,42,47,62,67]. The particular reason to have this term in traditional GAN based model is to introduce higher variation into the sampling process. The main reason behind introducing randomness in GAN is to capture a probabilistic distribution which generates *novel* images that match a certain style. However, our ISP-GPM follows quite opposite approach, and aims to achieve a deterministic solution based on the inner space parameters, instead of generating images from a sampling process. D term is the discriminator to reveal if the input is real or fake, conditioned on our input u information.

Since our aim is regressing the figure to a target pose on its subspace manifold, low frequency components play an import role here to roughly localize the figure to the correct position. Therefore, we capture these components using a classical L1 loss:

$$L_{L1}(G) = \sum_{i=1}^{N_{stk}} \mathbb{E}_{u,v}[|||v - G(u)[i]||_1].$$
(3)

We used a weighted term λ to balance the importance of L1 and G losses in our target objective function:

$$L_{obj}^* = \arg \min_G \max_D L_G(G, D) + \lambda L_{L1}(G).$$
(4)

5   Model Evaluation

To illustrate our inner space preserving concept and the performance of the proposed ISP-GPM, we chose a specific figure as our reposing target, the human body, due to the following rationale. First and foremost, human body is a highly articulated object with over 14 components depending on the defined limb granularity. Secondly, human pose estimation and tracking is a well-studied topic [9,20,50,53,59,66] as it is highly needed in abundant applications such as pedestrian detection, surveillance, self-driving cars, human-machine interaction, healthcare, etc. Lastly, several open-source datasets are available including MPII [3], BUFFY [21], LSP [29], FLIC [59], and SURREAL [64], which can facilitate deep learning-based model training and wide range of test samples for model evaluation.

5.1   Dataset Description

Although well-known datasets for human pose estimation [3,29,59] exist, few of them can satisfy our reposing purpose. As mentioned in Sect. 3, we aim at preserving the inner space of the original image before figure reposing. Therefor, we need pairs of images with the same α term but varying β term, which means identical background and human. The majority of the existing datasets are collected from different people individually with no connections between images, so they have varying α and β. A better option is extracting images from consecutive frames of a video. However, not many labelled video datasets from human are available. Motion capture system can facilitate auto labeling process, but they focus on the pose data without specifically augmenting the appearance α, such that "the same person may appear under more than one subject number" as they mentioned in [1]. The motion capture marks are also uncommon in images taken from natural settings. Another issue with daily video clips is that the background is unconstrained as it could be dynamic caused by camera motion or other independent entities in the background. Although, our framework can handle such cases by expanding world state in Eq. (1) to accommodate several dynamic figures in the scene, in this paper, we focus on a case with images from a human as the figure of interest in a static yet busy background.

Alternatively, we shift our attention to the synthesized datasets of human poses with perfect joint labeling and background control. We employed SUR-REAL (Synthetic hUmans foR REAL tasks) dataset of synthesized humans with various appearance textures and background [64]. All pose data are originated from the Carnegie Mellon University motion capture (mocap) dataset [1]. The total number of video clips for training is 54265 with combined different overlap settings [64]. Another group of 504 clips are used for model evaluation. One major issue of using SURREAL to suit our purpose is that the human subjects are not always shown in the video since it employs a fixed camera setting and the subjects are faithfully driven by the motion capture data. We filtered the SURREAL dataset to get rid of the frames without the human in them and also the clips with too short duration such as 1 frame clips.

5.2   ISP-GPM Implementation

Our pipeline was implemented in Torch with environment settings of CUDA8.0, CUDNN 5 with NVIDIA GeForce GTX 1080-Ti. Our implementation builds on the architecture of the original hourglass [44,64]. Discriminator net follows the design in [27]. Adams optimizer with $\beta 1 = 0.5$ and learning rate of 0.0002 was employed during training [31]. We used 3 stacked hourglass with input resolution of 128×128. In each hourglass, 5 convolutions configuration is employed with lowest resolution of 4×4. There are skip layers at all scale levels.

We used the weighted sum loss during generator training with more emphasis on L1 loss to give priority to the major structure generation instead of textures. We set $\lambda = 100$ in Eq. (4) as we observed transparency in the resultant image if we give a small λ. Our input is set to $128 \times 128 \times 3$ due to the memory limitations. The pose data is 16×2 vector to indicate 16 key point positions of human body as defined in SURREAL dataset [64]. In training session, we employed a batch size of 3, epoch number of 5000, and conduct 50 epochs for each test.

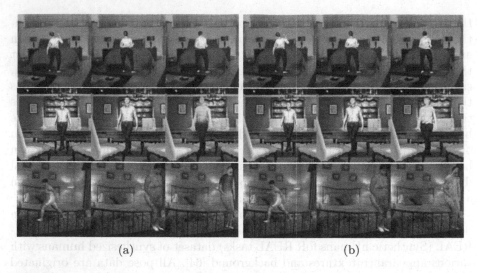

(a)   (b)

Fig. 5. Inner space preserving human reposing with different downsampling layers: (a) downsampled with max pooling, and (b) downsampled with convolution layers. First column is the input image, second column is the ground truth image of the target pose, last column is the generated image from ISP-GPM.

5.3   ISP-GPM with Different Configurations

To compare the quality of the resultant reposed images between ISP-GPMs with different model configurations, we fixed the input image to be the first frame of each test clip and the 60th or the last frame as the target pose image.

Downsampling Strategies: We first compared the quality of the reposing when fully convolution (FC) layers vs. max pooling downsampling is used in the stacked hourglass network. To make a clear comparison, we chose same test case for different model configurations and presented the input images, ground truth and generated images in Fig. 5. Each row shows a test example. Columns from left to right stand for the input image, ground truth and generated result. With the given two examples, it is clear that the max pooling is prone to the blurriness, while the FC configuration outputs more detailed textures. However, the last row of Fig. 5 uncovers that FC configuration is more likely to result in abnormal colors when compared to the max pooling configuration. This is expectable since the max pooling prefers to preserve the local information of an area.

Discriminator Layer: Inspired by [27], we employed the discriminator layer with different patch sizes to test its performance. Patch sizes can be tuned by altering the discriminator layer numbers to cover patches with different sizes. In this experiment, all the configurations we chose can effectively generate human

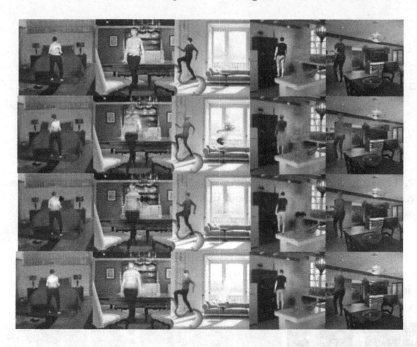

Fig. 6. Reposed human figure under different network configurations: 1st to 3rd row with two to four layers discriminator network and 4th row without discriminator but only L1 loss.

contours at indicated position but only differs in the image quality. So we only show the outcomes by changing the discriminator layer from two to four as depicted in 1st to 3rd row of Fig. 6, respectively. The figure's last row shows the output without discriminator layer. We discover that the discriminator did help in texture generation, however larger patches in contrast will result in strong artifacts as shown in 2nd and 3rd row of Fig. 6. In the case with no discriminator and only L1 loss, the output is obviously prone to blurriness which is consistent with findings from previous works [27,35,48]. We believe larger patch takes higher level structure information into consideration, however the local textures on the generated human can provides better visual quality, as seen in the 1st row of Fig. 6) with two layers discriminator.

To better illustrate the discriminator's role during training session, we recorded loss of each component during training with different network configurations as shown in Fig. 7. Model without discriminator are only shown in Fig. 7a. Though model without discriminator shows better performance on L1 metric, it does not always yield good looking images as it prefers to pick median values among possible colors to achieve better L1. There are a common trend that all G loss increase as training went on and the final G loss is even stronger than initial state. By observing the training process, we found out it is a process that the original human start fading away while the target posed human reveals

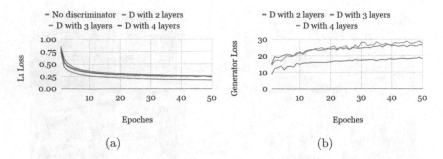

Fig. 7. Losses during training for different network configurations: (a) L1 loss, (b) Generator loss. Note that model without discriminator only shows in L1 loss.

itself gradually. Indeed, no matter how strong the generator is, its output cannot be as real as original one. So, at the beginning the generated image will be more likely to fool the discriminator as it keeps much of the real image information with less artifact.

Fig. 8. Image quality comparison of the generative models for human figures presented by (a) Lassner [37], (b) Reed [56], and (c) our ISP-GPM.

5.4 Comparison with the State-of-the-Art

There are few works focusing on human image generation via generative models, including Reed's [55,56] and Lassner's [37]. We compared the outputs of our ISP-GPM model with these works as shown in Fig. 8 (excluding [55] since the code is not provided). We omitted the input images in Fig. 8 and only displayed the reposed ones to provide a direct visual comparison with other methods.

Figure 8 shows that Lassner's [37] method preserves the best texture information in the generated images. However, there are three aspects in Lassner's that need to be noted. First of all, their generation process is more like a random sampling process from the human image manifold. Secondly, to condition this model on pose, SMPL model is needed for silhouette generation, which inevitably takes advantages of a 3D engine. Thirdly, they can generate humans with vivid background, however it is like a direct mask overlapping process with fully observed background images in advance [37]. In our ISP-GPM, both human and background are generated and merged in the same pipeline. Our pose information is a low-dimensional pose descriptor that can be generated manually. Additionally, both human and background are only partially observed due to human facing direction and the occlusion caused by the human in the scene. As for [56], the work is not an ISP model, as illustrated by an example earlier in Fig. 2.

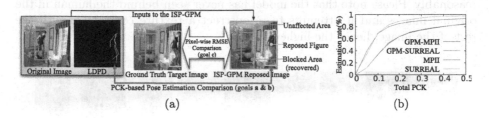

(a)   (b)

Fig. 9. (a) ISP quantitative evaluation schematic, (b) Pose estimation accuracy comparison tested on MPII, SURREAL, and our ISP-GPM datasets.

5.5 Quantitative Evaluation

To jointly evaluate goals **a** and **b**, we *hypothesized* that if the generated reposed images are realistic enough with specified pose, their pose should be recognizable by a pose recognition model trained on real-world images. We employed a high performance pose estimation model with a convolutional network architecture [44], to compare the estimated pose in the reposed synthetic image against the LDPD assigned to it in the input. We selected 100 images from both *MPII Human Pose* and *SURREAL* datasets in continuous order to avoid possible cherry picking. We selected the 20th frame of random video sequences to repose original images to form re-rendered ISP-GPM version datasets, namely MPII-GPM and SURREAL-GPM with joint labels compatible with the MPII joint definition. Please note that to synthesize the reposed images, we used ISP-GPM model with three layers discriminator and L1 loss as described in Sect. 5.3.

We used probability of correct keypoint (PCK) criteria for pose estimation performance evaluation, which is the measure of joint localization accuracy [69]. The average pose estimation rates (over 12 body joints) tested on MPII-GPM and SURREAL-GPM datasets are shown in Fig. 9b and compared with the pose estimator accuracy [44] tested on 100 images from original MPII and SURREAL datasets. These results illustrate that a well-trained pose estimator model is able to recognize the pose of our reposed images with over 80% accuracy on PCK0.5 metric. Therefore, ISP-GPM not only reposes the human figure accurately, but also makes it realistic enough to fool a state-of-the-art pose detection model to take its parts as human limbs.

With respect to goal **c**, we tested the inner space preserving ability in two folds: (1) the background of the reposed image (i.e. the unaffected area) should stay as similar as possible to the original image, and (2) the blocked area by the figure in original pose should be recovered with respect to the context. To test (1), we blocked out the affected areas where the figure of interest occupies in original and target images and computed the pixel-wise mean RMSE between the unaffected area of both images (**RMSE = 0.050 ± 0.001**). To evaluate (2), we compared the recovered blocked area with the ground truth target image (**RMSE = 0.172 ± 0.010**). These results elucidate that our ISP-GPM is able to preserve the background with high accuracy while recovering the blocked area reasonably. Please note that the model has never seen behind the human in the original images and it attempts to reconstruct a texture compatible with the rest of the image, hence the higher RMSE.

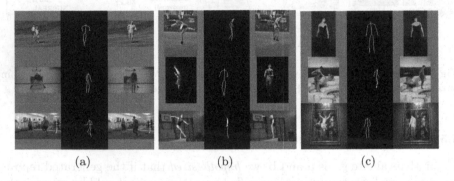

(a)   (b)   (c)

Fig. 10. ISP reposing of human figures: (a) MPII dataset [3], (b) LSP dataset [29] and (c) art works in the following order, Madame X (1884)–John Singer Sargent, Silver Favourites (1903)–Lawrence Alma-Tadema, Saint Sebastian Tended–Saint Irene and her Maid-Bernardo Strozzi.

6   ISP-GPM in Real World

To better illustrate the capability of ISP-GPM, we applied it on real world images from well-known datasets, MPII [3] and LSP [29]. As there is no ground truth to illustrate the target pose, we visualized the LDPD into a skeleton image by connecting the joints according to their kinematic relationships. ISP reposed images of MPII [3] and LSP [29] are shown in Fig. 10a and b, respectively. Each sample shows input image, visualized skeleton, and the generated image from left to right.

Arts are originated from real world and we believe when created, they also preserved inner space of an imagined world by the artist. So, we also applied our ISP-GPM on the arts inspired by human figures including paintings and sculptures. They are either from publicly accessible websites or art works in museums captured by a regular smartphone camera. The ISP reposing results are shown in Fig. 10c. From results of the real world images, the promising performance of ISP-GPM is apparent. However, there are still failure cases such as the residue of the original human that the network is unable to fully erased or the loss of the detailed texture and shape information.

References

1. CMU Graphics Lab Motion Capture Database (2018). http://mocap.cs.cmu.edu/info.php
2. ISP-GPM code (2018). http://www.northeastern.edu/ostadabbas/2018/07/23/inner-space-preserving-generative-pose-machine/
3. Andriluka, M., Pishchulin, L., Gehler, P., Schiele, B.: 2D human pose estimation: new benchmark and state of the art analysis. In: Proceedings of the IEEE Conference on Computer Vision and Pattern Recognition, pp. 3686–3693 (2014)
4. Andriluka, M., Roth, S., Schiele, B.: Pictorial structures revisited: people detection and articulated pose estimation. In: IEEE Conference on Computer Vision and Pattern Recognition, CVPR 2009, pp. 1014–1021 (2009)
5. Anguelov, D., Srinivasan, P., Koller, D., Thrun, S., Rodgers, J., Davis, J.: SCAPE: shape completion and animation of people. ACM Trans. Graph. (TOG) 24(3), 408–416 (2005)
6. Badrinarayanan, V., Kendall, A., Cipolla, R.: SegNet: a deep convolutional encoder-decoder architecture for image segmentation. IEEE Trans. Pattern Anal. Mach. Intell. 39(12), 2481–2495 (2017)
7. Bao, J., Chen, D., Wen, F., Li, H., Hua, G.: CVAE-GAN: fine-grained image generation through asymmetric training. CoRR, abs/1703.10155, 5 (2017)
8. Bergtholdt, M., Kappes, J., Schmidt, S., Schnörr, C.: A study of parts-based object class detection using complete graphs. Int. J. Comput. Vis. 87(1–2), 93 (2010)
9. Bourdev, L., Malik, J.: Poselets: body part detectors trained using 3D human pose annotations. In: 2009 IEEE 12th International Conference on Computer Vision, pp. 1365–1372 (2009)
10. Bradski, G., Kaehler, A.: OpenCV. Dr. Dobb's J. Softw. Tools 3 (2000)
11. Chen, L.C., Papandreou, G., Kokkinos, I., Murphy, K., Yuille, A.L.: DeepLab: semantic image segmentation with deep convolutional nets, atrous convolution, and fully connected CRFs. IEEE Trans. Pattern Anal. Mach. Intell. 40(4), 834–848 (2018)
12. Ciresan, D., Giusti, A., Gambardella, L.M., Schmidhuber, J.: Deep neural networks segment neuronal membranes in electron microscopy images. In: Advances in Neural Information Processing Systems, pp. 2843–2851 (2012)
13. Dai, J., He, K., Sun, J.: Convolutional feature masking for joint object and stuff segmentation. In: Proceedings of the IEEE Conference on Computer Vision and Pattern Recognition, pp. 3992–4000 (2015)
14. Dosovitskiy, A., Brox, T.: Generating images with perceptual similarity metrics based on deep networks. In: Advances in Neural Information Processing Systems, pp. 658–666 (2016)
15. Dosovitskiy, A., Springenberg, J.T., Brox, T.: Learning to generate chairs with convolutional neural networks. In: 2015 IEEE Conference on Computer Vision and Pattern Recognition (CVPR), pp. 1538–1546 (2015)
16. Dosovitskiy, A., Springenberg, J.T., Tatarchenko, M., Brox, T.: Learning to generate chairs, tables and cars with convolutional networks. IEEE Trans. Pattern Anal. Mach. Intell. 39(4), 692–705 (2017)
17. Efros, A.A., Freeman, W.T.: Image quilting for texture synthesis and transfer. In: Proceedings of the 28th Annual Conference on Computer Graphics and Interactive Techniques, pp. 341–346 (2001)
18. Eitz, M., Hays, J., Alexa, M.: How do humans sketch objects? ACM Trans. Graph. 31(4), 44–1 (2012)

19. Farabet, C., Couprie, C., Najman, L., LeCun, Y.: Learning hierarchical features for scene labeling. IEEE Trans. Pattern Anal. Mach. Intell. **35**(8), 1915–1929 (2013)
20. Felzenszwalb, P., McAllester, D., Ramanan, D.: A discriminatively trained, multiscale, deformable part model. In: IEEE Conference on Computer Vision and Pattern Recognition, CVPR 2008, pp. 1–8 (2008)
21. Ferrari, V., Marin-Jimenez, M., Zisserman, A.: Progressive search space reduction for human pose estimation. In: IEEE Conference on Computer Vision and Pattern Recognition, CVPR 2008, pp. 1–8 (2008)
22. Gauthier, J.: Conditional generative adversarial nets for convolutional face generation. Class Project for Stanford CS231N: Convolutional Neural Networks for Visual Recognition, Winter semester **2014**(5), 2 (2014)
23. Goodfellow, I., et al.: Generative adversarial nets. In: Advances in Neural Information Processing Systems, pp. 2672–2680 (2014)
24. Hariharan, B., Arbeláez, P., Girshick, R., Malik, J.: Simultaneous detection and segmentation. In: Fleet, D., Pajdla, T., Schiele, B., Tuytelaars, T. (eds.) ECCV 2014. LNCS, vol. 8695, pp. 297–312. Springer, Cham (2014). https://doi.org/10.1007/978-3-319-10584-0_20
25. Hinton, G.E., Krizhevsky, A., Wang, S.D.: Transforming auto-encoders. In: Honkela, T., Duch, W., Girolami, M., Kaski, S. (eds.) ICANN 2011. LNCS, vol. 6791, pp. 44–51. Springer, Heidelberg (2011). https://doi.org/10.1007/978-3-642-21735-7_6
26. Iizuka, S., Simo-Serra, E., Ishikawa, H.: Let there be color!: joint end-to-end learning of global and local image priors for automatic image colorization with simultaneous classification. ACM Trans. Graph. (TOG) **35**(4), 110 (2016)
27. Isola, P., Zhu, J.Y., Zhou, T., Efros, A.A.: Image-to-image translation with conditional adversarial networks. arXiv preprint (2017)
28. Jampani, V., Nowozin, S., Loper, M., Gehler, P.V.: The informed sampler: a discriminative approach to Bayesian inference in generative computer vision models. Comput. Vis. Image Underst. **136**, 32–44 (2015)
29. Johnson, S., Everingham, M.: Clustered pose and nonlinear appearance models for human pose estimation. In: Proceedings of the British Machine Vision Conference (2010). https://doi.org/10.5244/C.24.12
30. Karacan, L., Akata, Z., Erdem, A., Erdem, E.: Learning to generate images of outdoor scenes from attributes and semantic layouts. arXiv preprint arXiv:1612.00215 (2016)
31. Kinga, D., Adam, J.B.: A method for stochastic optimization. In: International Conference on Learning Representations (ICLR), vol. 5 (2015)
32. Kulkarni, T.D., Mansinghka, V.K., Kohli, P., Tenenbaum, J.B.: Inverse graphics with probabilistic CAD models. arXiv preprint arXiv:1407.1339 (2014)
33. Kulkarni, T.D., Whitney, W.F., Kohli, P., Tenenbaum, J.: Deep convolutional inverse graphics network. In: Advances in Neural Information Processing Systems, pp. 2539–2547 (2015)
34. Laffont, P.Y., Ren, Z., Tao, X., Qian, C., Hays, J.: Transient attributes for high-level understanding and editing of outdoor scenes. ACM Trans. Graph. (TOG) **33**(4), 149 (2014)
35. Larsen, A.B.L., Sønderby, S.K., Larochelle, H., Winther, O.: Autoencoding beyond pixels using a learned similarity metric. In: International Conference on Machine Learning, pp. 1558–1566 (2016)

36. Larsson, G., Maire, M., Shakhnarovich, G.: Learning representations for automatic colorization. In: Leibe, B., Matas, J., Sebe, N., Welling, M. (eds.) ECCV 2016. LNCS, vol. 9908, pp. 577–593. Springer, Cham (2016). https://doi.org/10.1007/978-3-319-46493-0_35

37. Lassner, C., Pons-Moll, G., Gehler, P.V.: A generative model of people in clothing. arXiv preprint arXiv:1705.04098 (2017)

38. Long, J., Shelhamer, E., Darrell, T.: Fully convolutional networks for semantic segmentation. In: Proceedings of the IEEE Conference on Computer Vision and Pattern Recognition, pp. 3431–3440 (2015)

39. Loper, M., Mahmood, N., Romero, J., Pons-Moll, G., Black, M.J.: SMPL: a skinned multi-person linear model. ACM Trans. Graph. (TOG) 34(6), 248 (2015)

40. Loper, M.M., Black, M.J.: OpenDR: an approximate differentiable renderer. In: Fleet, D., Pajdla, T., Schiele, B., Tuytelaars, T. (eds.) ECCV 2014. LNCS, vol. 8695, pp. 154–169. Springer, Cham (2014). https://doi.org/10.1007/978-3-319-10584-0_11

41. Michalski, V., Memisevic, R., Konda, K.: Modeling deep temporal dependencies with recurrent grammar cells. In: Advances in Neural Information Processing Systems, pp. 1925–1933 (2014)

42. Mirza, M., Osindero, S.: Conditional generative adversarial nets. arXiv preprint arXiv:1411.1784 (2014)

43. Mostajabi, M., Yadollahpour, P., Shakhnarovich, G.: Feedforward semantic segmentation with zoom-out features. In: Proceedings of the IEEE Conference on Computer Vision and Pattern Recognition, pp. 3376–3385 (2015)

44. Newell, A., Yang, K., Deng, J.: Stacked hourglass networks for human pose estimation. In: Leibe, B., Matas, J., Sebe, N., Welling, M. (eds.) ECCV 2016. LNCS, vol. 9912, pp. 483–499. Springer, Cham (2016). https://doi.org/10.1007/978-3-319-46484-8_29

45. Ning, F., Delhomme, D., LeCun, Y., Piano, F., Bottou, L., Barbano, P.E.: Toward automatic phenotyping of developing embryos from videos. IEEE Trans. Image Process. 14(9), 1360–1371 (2005)

46. Noh, H., Hong, S., Han, B.: Learning deconvolution network for semantic segmentation. In: Proceedings of the IEEE International Conference on Computer Vision, pp. 1520–1528 (2015)

47. Odena, A., Olah, C., Shlens, J.: Conditional image synthesis with auxiliary classifier GANs. arXiv preprint arXiv:1610.09585 (2016)

48. Pathak, D., Krahenbuhl, P., Donahue, J., Darrell, T., Efros, A.A.: Context encoders: feature learning by inpainting. In: Proceedings of the IEEE Conference on Computer Vision and Pattern Recognition, pp. 2536–2544 (2016)

49. Pinheiro, P., Collobert, R.: Recurrent convolutional neural networks for scene labeling. In: International Conference on Machine Learning, pp. 82–90 (2014)

50. Pishchulin, L., Andriluka, M., Gehler, P., Schiele, B.: Strong appearance and expressive spatial models for human pose estimation. In: 2013 IEEE International Conference on Computer Vision (ICCV), pp. 3487–3494 (2013)

51. Pons-Moll, G., Taylor, J., Shotton, J., Hertzmann, A., Fitzgibbon, A.: Metric regression forests for human pose estimation. In: BMVC (2013)

52. Radford, A., Metz, L., Chintala, S.: Unsupervised representation learning with deep convolutional generative adversarial networks. arXiv preprint arXiv:1511.06434 (2015)

53. Ramanan, D.: Learning to parse images of articulated bodies. In: Advances in Neural Information Processing Systems, pp. 1129–1136 (2007)

54. Reed, S., Akata, Z., Yan, X., Logeswaran, L., Schiele, B., Lee, H.: Generative adversarial text to image synthesis. In: Proceedings of the 33rd International Conference on International Conference on Machine Learning-Volume 48, pp. 1060–1069 (2016)
55. Reed, S., van den Oord, A., Kalchbrenner, N., Bapst, V., Botvinick, M., de Freitas, N.: Generating interpretable images with controllable structure. In: ICLR (2017)
56. Reed, S.E., Akata, Z., Mohan, S., Tenka, S., Schiele, B., Lee, H.: Learning what and where to draw. In: Advances in Neural Information Processing Systems, pp. 217–225 (2016)
57. Rezende, D.J., Mohamed, S., Wierstra, D.: Stochastic backpropagation and approximate inference in deep generative models. In: International Conference on Machine Learning, pp. 1278–1286 (2014)
58. Ronneberger, O., Fischer, P., Brox, T.: U-Net: convolutional networks for biomedical image segmentation. In: Navab, N., Hornegger, J., Wells, W.M., Frangi, A.F. (eds.) MICCAI 2015. LNCS, vol. 9351, pp. 234–241. Springer, Cham (2015). https://doi.org/10.1007/978-3-319-24574-4_28
59. Sapp, B., Taskar, B.: MODEC: multimodal decomposable models for human pose estimation. In: 2013 IEEE Conference on Computer Vision and Pattern Recognition (CVPR), pp. 3674–3681 (2013)
60. Shih, Y., Paris, S., Durand, F., Freeman, W.T.: Data-driven hallucination of different times of day from a single outdoor photo. ACM Trans. Graph. (TOG) 32(6), 200 (2013)
61. Shotton, J., et al.: Real-time human pose recognition in parts from single depth images. In: 2011 IEEE Conference on Computer Vision and Pattern Recognition (CVPR), pp. 1297–1304 (2011)
62. Sohn, K., Lee, H., Yan, X.: Learning structured output representation using deep conditional generative models. In: Advances in Neural Information Processing Systems, pp. 3483–3491 (2015)
63. Taylor, J., Shotton, J., Sharp, T., Fitzgibbon, A.: The vitruvian manifold: inferring dense correspondences for one-shot human pose estimation. In: 2012 IEEE Conference on Computer Vision and Pattern Recognition (CVPR), pp. 103–110 (2012)
64. Varol, G., et al.: Learning from synthetic humans. In: 2017 IEEE Conference on Computer Vision and Pattern Recognition (CVPR 2017) (2017)
65. Walker, J., Doersch, C., Gupta, A., Hebert, M.: An uncertain future: forecasting from static images using variational autoencoders. In: Leibe, B., Matas, J., Sebe, N., Welling, M. (eds.) ECCV 2016. LNCS, vol. 9911, pp. 835–851. Springer, Cham (2016). https://doi.org/10.1007/978-3-319-46478-7_51
66. Wei, S.E., Ramakrishna, V., Kanade, T., Sheikh, Y.: Convolutional pose machines. In: Proceedings of the IEEE Conference on Computer Vision and Pattern Recognition, pp. 4724–4732 (2016)
67. Yan, X., Yang, J., Sohn, K., Lee, H.: Attribute2Image: conditional image generation from visual attributes. In: Leibe, B., Matas, J., Sebe, N., Welling, M. (eds.) ECCV 2016. LNCS, vol. 9908, pp. 776–791. Springer, Cham (2016). https://doi.org/10.1007/978-3-319-46493-0_47
68. Yang, J., Reed, S.E., Yang, M.H., Lee, H.: Weakly-supervised disentangling with recurrent transformations for 3D view synthesis. In: Advances in Neural Information Processing Systems, pp. 1099–1107 (2015)
69. Yang, Y., Ramanan, D.: Articulated human detection with flexible mixtures of parts. IEEE Trans. Pattern Anal. Mach. Intell. 35(12), 2878–2890 (2013)
70. Yi, Z., Zhang, H.R., Tan, P., Gong, M.: DualGAN: unsupervised dual learning for image-to-image translation. In: ICCV, pp. 2868–2876 (2017)

71. Yin, X., Yu, X., Sohn, K., Liu, X., Chandraker, M.: Towards large-pose face frontal-ization in the wild. arXiv preprint arXiv:1704.06244 (2017)
72. Yoo, D., Kim, N., Park, S., Paek, A.S., Kweon, I.S.: Pixel-level domain transfer. In: Leibe, B., Matas, J., Sebe, N., Welling, M. (eds.) ECCV 2016. LNCS, vol. 9912, pp. 517–532. Springer, Cham (2016). https://doi.org/10.1007/978-3-319-46484-8_31
73. Zhang, R., Isola, P., Efros, A.A.: Colorful image colorization. In: Leibe, B., Matas, J., Sebe, N., Welling, M. (eds.) ECCV 2016. LNCS, vol. 9907, pp. 649–666. Springer, Cham (2016). https://doi.org/10.1007/978-3-319-46487-9_40

Attention-Based Ensemble for Deep Metric Learning

Wonsik Kim, Bhavya Goyal, Kunal Chawla, Jungmin Lee,
and Keunjoo Kwon[✉]

Samsung Research, Samsung Electronics, Seoul, Korea
{wonsik16.kim,bhavya.goyal,kunal.chawla,
jm411.lee,keunjoo.kwon}@samsung.com

Abstract. Deep metric learning aims to learn an embedding function, modeled as deep neural network. This embedding function usually puts semantically similar images close while dissimilar images far from each other in the learned embedding space. Recently, ensemble has been applied to deep metric learning to yield state-of-the-art results. As one important aspect of ensemble, the learners should be diverse in their feature embeddings. To this end, we propose an attention-based ensemble, which uses multiple attention masks, so that each learner can attend to different parts of the object. We also propose a divergence loss, which encourages diversity among the learners. The proposed method is applied to the standard benchmarks of deep metric learning and experimental results show that it outperforms the state-of-the-art methods by a significant margin on image retrieval tasks.

Keywords: Attention · Ensemble · Deep metric learning

1 Introduction

Deep metric learning has been actively researched recently. In deep metric learning, feature embedding function is modeled as a deep neural network. This feature embedding function embeds input images into feature embedding space with a certain desired condition. In this condition, the feature embeddings of similar images are required to be close to each other while those of dissimilar images are required to be far from each other. To satisfy this condition, many loss functions based on the distances between embeddings have been proposed [3,4,6,14,25,27–29,33,37]. Deep metric learning has been successfully applied in image retrieval task on popular benchmarks such as CARS-196 [13], CUB-200-2011 [35], Stanford online products [29], and in-shop clothes retrieval [18] datasets.

Electronic supplementary material The online version of this chapter (https:// doi.org/10.1007/978-3-030-01246-5_45) contains supplementary material, which is available to authorized users.

© Springer Nature Switzerland AG 2018
V. Ferrari et al. (Eds.): ECCV 2018, LNCS 11205, pp. 760–777, 2018.
https://doi.org/10.1007/978-3-030-01246-5_45

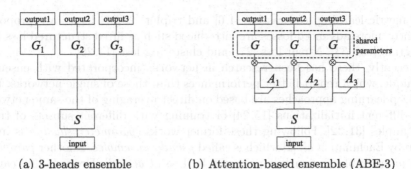

Fig. 1. Difference between M-heads ensemble and attention-based ensemble. Both assume shared parameters for bottom layers (S). (a) In M-heads ensemble, different feature embedding functions are trained for different learners (G_1, G_2, G_3). (b) In attention-based ensemble, single feature embedding function (G) is trained while each learner learns different attention modules (A_1, A_2, A_3)

Ensemble is a widely used technique of training multiple learners to get a combined model, which performs better than individual models. For deep metric learning, ensemble concatenates the feature embeddings learned by multiple learners which often leads to better embedding space under given constraints on the distances between image pairs. The keys to success in ensemble are high performance of individual learners as well as diversity among learners. To achieve this objective, different methods have been proposed [22,39]. However, there has not been much research on optimal architecture to yield diversity of feature embeddings in deep metric learning.

Our contribution is to propose a novel framework to encourage diversity in feature embeddings. To this end, we design an architecture which has multiple attention modules for multiple learners. By attending to different locations for different learners, diverse feature embedding functions are trained. They are regularized with divergence loss which aims to differentiate the feature embeddings from different learners. Equipped with it, we present M-way attention-based ensemble (ABE-M) which learns feature embedding with M diverse attention masks. The proposed architecture is represented in Fig. 1(b). We compare our model to our M-heads ensemble baseline [16], in which different feature embedding functions are trained for different learners (Fig. 1(a)), and experimentally demonstrate that the proposed ABE-M shows significantly better results with less number of parameters.

2   Related Works

Deep Metric Learning and Ensemble. The aim of the deep metric learning is to find an embedding function $f : \mathcal{X} \to \mathcal{Y}$ which maps samples x from a data space $\mathcal{X}$ to a feature embedding space $\mathcal{Y}$ so that $f(x_i)$ and $f(x_j)$ are closer in some metric when x_i and x_j are semantically similar. To achieve this goal, in deep metric learning, contrastive [4,6] and triplet [25,37] losses are proposed. Recently, more advanced losses are introduced such as lifted structured loss [29], histogram loss [33], N-pair loss [27], and clustering loss [14,28].

Recently, there has been research in networks incorporated with ensemble technique, which report better performances than those of single networks. Earlier deep learning approaches are based on direct averaging of the same networks with different initializations [15,24] or training with different subsets of training samples [31,32]. Following these former works, *parameter sharing* is introduced by Bachman *et al.* [2] which is called *pseudo-ensembles*. Another *parameter sharing* ensemble approach is proposed by Lee *et al.* [16]. Dropout [30] can be interpreted as an ensemble approach which takes exponential number of networks with high correlation. In addition to dropout, Veit *et al.* [34] state that *residual networks* behave like ensembles of relatively shallow networks. Recently the ensemble technique has been applied in deep metric learning as well. Yuan *et al.* [39] propose to ensemble a set of models with different complexities in cascaded manner. They train deeply supervised cascaded networks using easier examples through earlier layers of the networks while harder examples are further exploited in later layers. Opitz *et al.* [22] use online gradient boosting to train each learner in ensemble. They try to reduce correlation among learners using re-weighting of training samples. Opitz *et al.* [21] propose an efficient averaging strategy with a novel *DivLoss* which encourages diversity of individual learners.

Attention Mechanism. Attention mechanism has been used in various computer vision problems. Earlier researches utilize RNN architectures for attention modeling [1,19,26]. These RNN based attention models solve classification tasks using object parts detection by sequentially selecting attention regions from images and then learning feature representations for each part. Besides RNN approaches, Liu *et al.* [17] propose *fully convolutional attention networks*, which adopts hard attention from a region generator. And Zhao *et al.* [40] propose *diversified visual attention networks*, which uses different scaling or cropping of input images for different attention masks. However, our ABE-M is able to learn diverse attention masks without relying on a region generator. In addition, ABE-M uses soft attention, therefore, the parameter update is straightforward by backpropagation in a fully gradient-based way while previous approaches in [1,17,19,26,40] use hard attention which requires policy gradient estimation.

Jaderberg *et al.* [11] propose spatial transformer networks which models attention mechanism using parameterized image transformations. Unlike aforementioned approaches, their model is differentiable and thus can be trained in a fully gradient-based way. However, their attention is limited to a set of predefined and parameterized transformations which could not yield arbitrary attention masks.

3 Attention-Based Ensemble

3.1 Deep Metric Learning

Let $f : \mathcal{X} \to \mathcal{Y}$ be an isometric embedding function between metric spaces $\mathcal{X}$ and $\mathcal{Y}$ where $\mathcal{X}$ is a $N_{\mathcal{X}}$ dimensional metric space with an unknown metric function $d_{\mathcal{X}}$ and $\mathcal{Y}$ is a $N_{\mathcal{Y}}$ dimensional metric space with a known metric function $d_{\mathcal{Y}}$. For example, $\mathcal{Y}$ could be a Euclidean space with Euclidean distance or the unit sphere in a Euclidean space with angular distance.

Our goal is to approximate f with a deep neural network from a dataset $\mathcal{D} = \{(x^{(1)}, x^{(2)}, d_{\mathcal{X}}(x^{(1)}, x^{(2)}))|x^{(1)}, x^{(2)} \in \mathcal{X}\}$ which are samples from $\mathcal{X}$. In case we cannot get the samples of metric $d_{\mathcal{X}}$, we consider the label information from the dataset with labels as the relative constraint of the metric $d_{\mathcal{X}}$. For example, from a dataset $\mathcal{D}_{\mathcal{C}} = \{(x, c)|x \in \mathcal{X}, c \in \mathcal{C}\}$ where $\mathcal{C}$ is the set of labels, for $(x_i, c_i), (x_j, c_j) \in \mathcal{D}_{\mathcal{C}}$ the contrastive metric constraint could be defined as the following:

$$\begin{cases} d_{\mathcal{X}}(x_i, x_j) = 0, & \text{if } c_i = c_j; \\ d_{\mathcal{X}}(x_i, x_j) > m_c, & \text{if } c_i \neq c_j, \end{cases} \tag{1}$$

where m_c is an arbitrary margin. The triplet metric constraint for (x_i, c_i), $(x_j, c_j), (x_k, c_k) \in \mathcal{D}_{\mathcal{C}}$ could be defined as the following:

$$d_{\mathcal{X}}(x_i, x_j) + m_t < d_{\mathcal{X}}(x_i, x_k), \quad c_i = c_j \text{ and } c_i \neq c_k, \tag{2}$$

where m_t is a margin. Note that these metric constraints are some choices of how to model $d_{\mathcal{X}}$, not those of how to model f.

An embedding function f is isometric or distance preserving embedding if for every $x_i, x_j \in \mathcal{X}$ one has $d_{\mathcal{X}}(x_i, x_j) = d_{\mathcal{Y}}(f(x_i), f(x_j))$. In order to have an isometric embedding function f, we optimize f so that the points embedded into $\mathcal{Y}$ produce exactly the same metric or obey the same metric constraint of $d_{\mathcal{X}}$.

3.2 Ensemble for Deep Metric Learning

A classical ensemble for deep metric learning could be the method to average the metric of multiple embedding functions. We define the ensemble metric function d_{ensemble} for deep metric learning as the following:

$$d_{\text{ensemble},(f_1,\dots,f_M)}(x_i, x_j) = \frac{1}{M} \sum_{m=1}^{M} d_{\mathcal{Y}}(f_m(x_i), f_m(x_j)), \tag{3}$$

where f_m is an independently trained embedding function and we call it a learner.

In addition to the classical ensemble, we can consider the ensemble of two-step embedding function. Consider a function $s : \mathcal{X} \to \mathcal{Z}$ which is an isometric embedding function between metric spaces $\mathcal{X}$ and $\mathcal{Z}$ where $\mathcal{X}$ is a $N_{\mathcal{X}}$ dimensional metric space with an unknown metric function $d_{\mathcal{X}}$ and $\mathcal{Z}$ is a $N_{\mathcal{Z}}$ dimensional metric space with an unknown metric function $d_{\mathcal{Z}}$. And we consider the isometric embedding $g : \mathcal{Z} \to \mathcal{Y}$ where $\mathcal{Y}$ is a $N_{\mathcal{Y}}$ dimensional metric space with a known metric function $d_{\mathcal{Y}}$. If we combine them into one function $b(x) = g(s(x)), x \in \mathcal{X}$, the combined function is also an isometric embedding $b : \mathcal{X} \to \mathcal{Y}$ between metric spaces $\mathcal{X}$ and $\mathcal{Y}$.

Like the parameter sharing ensemble [16], with the independently trained multiple g_m and a single s, we can get multiple embedding functions $b_m : \mathcal{X} \to \mathcal{Y}$ as the following:

$$b_m(x) = g_m(s(x)). \tag{4}$$

We are interested in another case where there are multiple embedding functions $b_m : \mathcal{X} \to \mathcal{Y}$ with multiple s_m and a single g as the following:

$$b_m(x) = g(s_m(x)). \tag{5}$$

Note that a point in $\mathcal{X}$ can be embedded into multiple points in $\mathcal{Y}$ by multiple learners. In Eq. (5), s_m does not have to preserve the label information while it only has to preserve the metric. In other words, a point with a label could be mapped to multiple locations in $\mathcal{Z}$ by multiple s_m and finally would be mapped to multiple locations in $\mathcal{Y}$. If this were the ensemble of classification models where g approximates the distribution of the labels, all s_m should be label preserving functions because the outputs of s_m become the inputs of one classification model g.

For the embedding function of Eq. (5), we want to make s_m attends to the diverse aspects of data x in $\mathcal{X}$ while maintaining a single embedding function g which disentangles the complex manifold $\mathcal{Z}$ into Euclidean space. By exploiting the fact that a point x in $\mathcal{X}$ can be mapped to multiple locations in $\mathcal{Y}$, we can encourage each s_m to map x into distinctive points z_m in $\mathcal{Z}$. Given an isometric embedding $g : \mathcal{Z} \to \mathcal{Y}$, if we enforce y_m in $\mathcal{Y}$ mapped from x to be far from each other, z_m in $\mathcal{Z}$ mapped from x will be far from each other as well. Note that we cannot apply this divergence constraint to z_m because metric d_z in $\mathcal{Z}$ is unknown. We train each b_m to be isometric function between $\mathcal{X}$ and $\mathcal{Y}$ while applying the divergence constraint among y_m in $\mathcal{Y}$. If we apply the divergence constraint to classical ensemble models or multihead ensemble models, they do not necessarily induce the diversity because each f_m or g_m could arbitrarily compose different metric spaces in $\mathcal{Y}$ (Refer to experimental results in Sect. 6.2). With the attention-based ensemble, union of metric spaces by multiple s_m is mapped by a single embedding function g.

3.3   Attention-Based Ensemble Model

As one implementation of Eq. (5), we propose the attention-based ensemble model which is mainly composed of two parts: feature extraction module $F(x)$ and attention module $A(x)$. For the feature extraction, we assume a general multi-layer perceptron model as the following:

$$F(x) = h_l(h_{l-1}(\cdots(h_2(h_1(x))))) \tag{6}$$

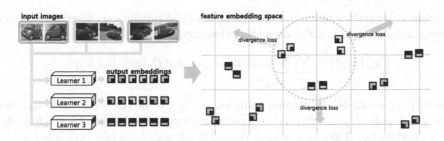

Fig. 2. Illustration of feature embedding space and divergence loss. Different car brands are represented as different colors: red, green and blue. Feature embeddings of each learner are depicted as a square with different mask patterns. Divergence loss pulls apart the feature embeddings of different learners using same input (Color figure online)

We break it into two parts with a branching point at i, $S(\cdot)$ includes h_l, $h_{l-1}, \ldots, h_{i+1}$, and $G(\cdot)$ includes $h_i, h_{i-1}, \ldots, h_1$. We call $S(\cdot)$ a spatial feature extractor and $G(\cdot)$ a global feature embedding function with respect to the output of each function. For attention module, we also assume a general multi-layer perceptron model which outputs a three dimensional blob with channel, width, and height as an attention mask. Each element in the attention masks is assumed to have a value from 0 to 1. Given aforementioned two modules, the combined embedding function $B_m(x)$ for the learner m is defined as the following:

$$B_m(x) = G(S(x) \circ A_m(S(x))),\tag{7}$$

where $\circ$ denotes element-wise product (Fig. 1(b)).

Note that, same feature extraction module is shared across different learners while individual learners have their own attention module $A_m(\cdot)$. The attention function $A_m(S(x))$ outputs an attention mask with same size as output of $S(x)$. This attention mask is applied to the output feature of $S(x)$ with an element-wise product. Attended feature output of $S(x) \circ A_m(S(x))$ is then fed into global feature embedding function $G(\cdot)$ to generate an embedding feature vector. If all the elements in the attention mask are 1, the model $B_m(x)$ is reduced to a conventional multi-layer perceptron model.

3.4 Loss

The loss for training aforementioned attention model is defined as:

$$L(\{(x_i, c_i)\}) = \sum_m L_{\text{metric},(m)}(\{(x_i, c_i)\}) + \lambda_{\text{div}} L_{\text{div}}(\{x_i\}),\tag{8}$$

where $\{(x_i, c_i)\}$ is a set of all training samples and labels, $L_{\text{metric},(m)}(\cdot)$ is the loss for the isometric embedding for the m-th learner, $L_{\text{div}}(\cdot)$ is regularizing term for diversifying the feature embedding of each learner $B_m(x)$ and λ_{div} is the weighting parameter to control the strength of the regularizer. More specifically, divergence loss L_{div} is defined as the following:

$$L_{\text{div}}(\{x_i\}) = \sum_i \sum_{p,q} \max(0, m_{\text{div}} - d_{\mathcal{Y}}(B_p(x_i), B_q(x_i))^2), \tag{9}$$

where $\{x_i\}$ is set of all training samples, $d_{\mathcal{Y}}$ is the metric in $\mathcal{Y}$ and m_{div} is a margin. A pair $(B_p(x_i), B_q(x_i))$ represents feature embeddings of a single image embedded by two different learners. We call it self pair from now on while positive and negative pairs refer to pairs of feature embeddings with same labels and different labels, respectively.

The divergence loss encourages each learner to attend to the different part of the input image by increasing the distance between the points embedded by the input image (Fig. 2). Since the learners share the same functional module to extract features, the only differentiating part is the attention module. Note that our proposed loss is not directly applied to the attention masks. In other words, the attention masks among the learners may overlap. And also it is possible to have the attention masks some of which focus on small region while other focus on larger region including small one.

4   Implementation

We perform all our experiments using GoogLeNet [32] as the base architecture. As shown in Fig. 3, we use the output of max pooling layer following the `inception(3b)` block as our spatial feature extractor $S(\cdot)$ and remaining network as our global feature embedding function $G(\cdot)$. In our implementation, we simplify attention module $A_m(\cdot)$ as $A'_m(C(\cdot))$ where $C(\cdot)$ consists of `inception(4a)` to `inception(4e)` from GoogLeNet, which is shared among all M learners and $A'_m(\cdot)$ consists of a convolution layer of 480 kernels of size 1×1 to match the output of $S(\cdot)$ for the element-wise product. This is for efficiency in terms of memory and computation time. Since $C(\cdot)$ is shared across different learners, forward and backward propagation time, memory usage, and number of parameters are decreased compared to having separate $A_m(\cdot)$ for each learner (without any shared part). Our preliminary experiments showed no performance drop with this choice of implementation.

We study the effects of different branching points and depth of attention module in Sect. 6.3. We use contrastive loss [3,4,6] as our distance metric loss function which is defined as the following:

$$L_{\text{metric},(m)}(\{(x_i, c_i)\}) = \frac{1}{N} \sum_{i,j} (1 - y_{i,j})[m_c - D^2_{m,i,j}]_+ + y_{i,j} D^2_{m,i,j},$$
$$D_{m,i,j} = d_{\mathcal{Y}}(B_m(x_i), B_m(x_j)), \tag{10}$$

where $\{(x_i, c_i)\}$ is set of all training samples and corresponding labels, N is the number of training sets, $y_{i,j}$ is a binary indicator of whether or not the label c_i is equal to c_j, $d_{\mathcal{Y}}$ is the euclidean distance, $[\cdot]_+$ denotes the hinge function

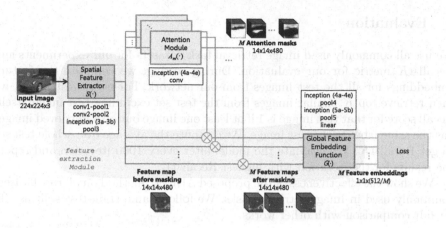

Fig. 3. The implementation of attention-based ensemble (ABE-M) using GoogLeNet

$\max(0, \cdot)$ and m_c is the margin for contrastive loss. Both of margins m_c and m_{div} (in Eq. 8) is set to 1.

We implement the proposed ABE-M method using caffe [12] framework. During training, the network is initialized from a pre-trained network on ImageNet ILSVRC dataset [24]. The final layer of the network and the convolution layer of attention module are randomly initialized as proposed by Glorot *et al.* [5]. For optimizer, we use stochastic gradient descent with momentum optimizer with momentum as 0.9, and we select the base learning rate by tuning on validation set of the dataset.

We follow earlier works [29,38] for preprocessing and unless stated otherwise, we use the input image size of 224×224. All training and testing images are scaled such that their longer side is 256, keeping the aspect ratio fixed, and padding the shorter side to get 256×256 images. During training, we randomly crop images to 224×224 and then randomly flip horizontally. During testing, we use the center crop. We subtract the channel-wise mean of ImageNet dataset from the images. For training and testing images of cropped datasets, we follow the approach in [38]. For CARS-196 [13] cropped dataset, 256×256 scaled cropped images are used; while for CUB-200-2011 [35] cropped dataset, 256×256 scaled cropped images with fixed aspect ratio and shorter side padded are used.

We run our experiments on nVidia Tesla M40 GPU (24GBs GPU memory), which limits our batch size to 64 for ABE-8 model. Unless stated otherwise, we use the batch size of 64 for our experiments. We sample our mini-batches by first randomly sampling 32 images and then positive pairs for first 16 images and negative pairs for next 16 images, thus making the mini-batch of size 64. Unless mentioned otherwise, we report the results of our method using embedding size of 512. This makes the embedding size for individual learners to be $512/M$.

5   Evaluation

We use all commonly used image retrieval task datasets for our experiments and Recall@K metric for our evaluation. During testing, we compute the feature embeddings for all the test images from our network. For every test image, we then retrieve top K similar images from the test set excluding test image itself. Recall score for that test image is 1 if at least one image out of K retrieved images has the same label as the test image. We compute the average over whole test set to get Recall@K. We evaluate the model after every 1000 iteration and report the results for the iteration with highest Recall@1.

We show the effectiveness of the proposed ABE-M method on all the datasets commonly used in image retrieval tasks. We follow same train-test split as [29] for fair comparison with other works.

- **CARS-196** [13] dataset contains images of 196 different classes of cars and is primarily used for our experiments. The dataset is split into 8,144 training images and 8,041 testing images (98 classes in both).
- **CUB-200-2011** [35] dataset consists of 11,788 images of 200 different bird species. We use the first 100 classes for training (5,864 images) and the remaining 100 classes for testing (5,924 images).
- **Stanford online products (SOP)** [29] dataset has 22,634 classes with 120,053 product images. 11,318 classes are used for training (59,551 images) while other 11,316 classes are for testing (60,502 images).
- **In-shop clothes retrieval** [18] dataset contains 11,735 classes of clothing items with 54,642 images. Following similar protocol as [29], we use 3,997 classes for training (25,882 images) and other 3,985 classes for testing (28,760 images). The test set is partitioned into the query set of 3,985 classes (14,218 images) and the retrieval database set of 3,985 classes (12,612 images).

Since CARS-196 and CUB-200-2011 datasets consist of bounding boxes too, we report the results using original images and cropped images both for fair comparison.

6   Experiments

6.1   Comparison of ABE-M with M-heads

To show the effectiveness of our ABE-M method, we first compare the performance of ABE-M and M-heads ensemble (Fig. 1(a)) with varying ensemble embedding sizes (denoted with superscript) on CARS-196 dataset. As show in Table 1 and Fig. 4, our method outperforms M-heads ensemble by a significant margin. The number of model parameters for ABE-M is much less compared to M-heads ensemble as the global feature extractor $G(\cdot)$ is shared among learners. But, ABE-M requires higher flops because of extra computation of attention modules. This difference becomes increasingly insignificant with increasing values of M.

Table 1. Recall@K(%) comparison with baseline on CARS-196. Superscript denotes ensemble embedding size

K	Ensemble				Individual Learners				params	flops
	1	2	4	8	1	2	4	8	($\times 10^7$)	($\times 10^9$)
1-head^{512}	67.2	77.4	85.3	90.7	-	-	-	–	0.65	1.58
2-heads^{512}	73.3	82.5	88.6	93.0	$70.2 \pm {.03}$	$79.8 \pm {.52}$	$86.7 \pm {.01}$	$91.9 \pm {.37}$	1.18	2.25
4-heads^{512}	76.6	84.2	89.3	93.2	$70.4 \pm {.80}$	$79.9 \pm {.38}$	$86.5 \pm {.43}$	$91.4 \pm {.42}$	2.24	3.60
8-heads^{512}	76.1	84.3	90.3	93.9	$68.3 \pm {.39}$	$78.5 \pm {.39}$	$86.0 \pm {.37}$	$91.3 \pm {.31}$	4.36	6.28
ABE-1^{512}	67.3	77.3	85.3	90.9	-	-	-	-	0.97	2.21
ABE-2^{512}	76.8	84.9	90.2	94.0	$70.9 \pm {.58}$	$80.3 \pm {.04}$	$87.1 \pm {.07}$	$92.2 \pm {.20}$	0.98	2.96
ABE-4^{512}	<u>82.5</u>	<u>89.1</u>	<u>93.0</u>	<u>95.5</u>	$74.4 \pm {.51}$	$83.1 \pm {.47}$	$89.1 \pm {.34}$	$93.2 \pm {.36}$	1.05	4.46
ABE-8^{512}	**85.2**	**90.5**	**93.9**	**96.1**	$75.0 \pm {.39}$	$83.4 \pm {.24}$	$89.2 \pm {.31}$	$93.2 \pm {.24}$	1.20	7.46
ABE-1^{64}	65.9	76.5	83.7	89.3	-	-	-	-	0.92	2.21
ABE-2^{128}	75.5	84.0	89.4	93.6	$68.6 \pm {.38}$	$78.8 \pm {.38}$	$85.7 \pm {.43}$	$91.3 \pm {.16}$	0.96	2.96
ABE-4^{256}	81.8	88.5	92.4	95.1	$72.3 \pm {.68}$	$81.4 \pm {.45}$	$87.9 \pm {.23}$	$92.3 \pm {.13}$	1.04	4.46

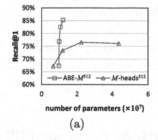
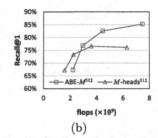

Fig. 4. Recall@1 comparison with baseline on CARS-196 as a function of (a) number of parameters and (b) flops. Both of ABE-M and M-heads has embedding size of 512

ABE-1 contains only one attention module and hence is not an ensemble and does not use divergence loss. ABE-1 performs similar to 1-head. We also report the performance of individual learners of the ensemble. From Table 1, we can see that the performance of ABE-M^{512} ensemble is increasing with increasing M. The performance of individual learners is also increasing with increasing M despite the decrease in embedding size of individual learners ($512/M$). The same increase is not seen for the case of M-heads. Further, we can refer to ABE-1^{64}, ABE-2^{128}, ABE-4^{256} and ABE-8^{512}, where all individual learners have embedding size 64. We can see a clear increase in recall of individual learners with increasing values of M.

6.2 Effects of Divergence Loss

ABE-M Without Divergence Loss. To analyze the effectiveness of divergence loss in ABE-M, we conduct experiments without divergence loss on

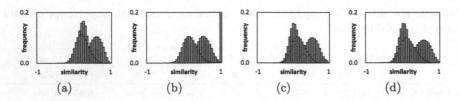

(a)   (b)   (c)   (d)

Fig. 5. Histograms of cosine similarity of positive (blue), negative (red), self (green) pairs trained with different methods. Self pair refers to the pair of feature embeddings from different learners using same image. (a) Attention-based ensemble (ABE-8) using proposed loss, (b) attention-based ensemble (ABE-8) without divergence loss, (c) 8-heads ensemble, (d) 8-heads ensemble with divergence loss. In the case of attention-based ensemble, divergence loss is necessary for each learner to be trained to produce different features by attending to different locations. Without divergence loss, one can see all learners learn very similar embedding. Meanwhile, in the case of M-heads ensemble, there is no effect of applying divergence loss. (Color figure online)

Table 2. Recall@K(%) comparison in ABE-M ensemble without divergence loss L_{div} on CARS-196

K	Ensemble				Individual learners			
	1	2	4	8	1	2	4	8
ABE-8^{512}	85.2	90.5	93.9	96.1	75.0 $\pm$ 0.39	83.4 $\pm$ 0.24	89.2 $\pm$ 0.31	93.2 $\pm$ 0.24
ABE-8^{512} without L_{div}	69.7	78.8	86.2	91.5	69.5 $\pm$ 0.11	78.8 $\pm$ 0.14	86.1 $\pm$ 0.15	91.5 $\pm$ 0.09

CARS-196 and show the results in Table 2. As we can see, ABE-M without divergence loss performs similar to its individual learners whereas there is significant gain in ensemble performance of ABE-M compared to its individual learners.

We also calculate the cosine similarity between positive, negative, and self pairs, and plot in Fig. 5. With divergence loss (Fig. 5(a)), all learners learn diverse embedding function which leads to decrease in cosine similarity of self pairs. Without divergence loss (Fig. 5(b)), all learners converge to very similar embedding function so that the cosine similarity of self pairs is close to 1. This could be because all learners end up learning similar attention masks which leads to similar embeddings for all of them.

We visualize the learned attention masks of ABE-8 on CARS-196 in Fig. 6. Due to the space limitation, results from only three learners out of eight and three channels out of 480 are illustrated. The figure shows that different learners are attending to different parts for the same channel. Qualitatively, our proposed loss successfully diversify the attention masks produced by different learners. They are attending to different parts of the car such as upper part, bottom part, roof, tires, lights and so on. In 350th channel, for instance, learner 1 is focusing on bottom part of car, learner 2 on roof and learner 3 on upper part including roof. At the bottom of Fig. 6, the mean of the attention masks across all channels

input images

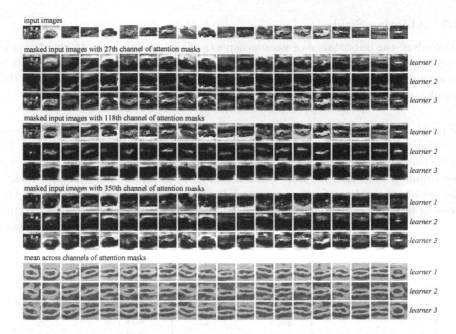

Fig. 6. The attention masks learned by each learner of ABE-8 on CARS-196. Due to the space limitation, results from only three learners out of eight and three channels out of 480 are illustrated. Each column shows the result of different input images. Different learners attend to different parts of the car such as upper part, bottom part, roof, tires, lights and so on

shows that the learned embedding function focuses more on object areas than the background.

Divergence Loss in M-heads. We show the result of experiments of 8-heads ensemble with divergence loss in Table 3. We can see that the divergence loss does not improve the performance in 8-heads. From Fig. 5(c), we can notice that cosine similarities of self pairs are close to zero for M-heads. Figure 5(d) shows that the divergence loss does not affect the cosine similarity of self pairs significantly. As mentioned in Sect. 3.2, we hypothesize this is because each of $G_m(\cdot)$ could arbitrarily compose different metric spaces in $\mathcal{Y}$.

Table 3. Recall@$K(\%)$ comparison in M-heads ensemble with divergence loss L_{div} on CARS-196

K	1	2	4	8
8-heads	76.1	84.3	90.3	93.9
8-heads with L_{div}	76.0	84.6	89.7	93.5

6.3   Ablation Study

To analyze the importance of various aspects of our model, we performed experiments on CARS-196 dataset of ABE-8 model, varying a few hyperparameters at a time and keeping others fixed. (More ablation study can be found in the supplementary material.)

Sensitivity to Depth of Attention Module. We demonstrate the effect of depth of attention module by changing the number of inception blocks in it. To make sure that we can take the element wise product of the attention mask with the input of attention module, the dimension of attention mask should match the input dimension of attention module. Because of this we remove all the pooling layers in our attention module. Figure 7(a) shows Recall@1 with varying number of inception blocks in attention module starting from 1 (`inception(4a)`) to 7 (`inception(4a) to inception(5b)`) in GoogLeNet. We can see that the attention module with 5 inception blocks (`inception(4a) to inception(4e)`) performs the best.

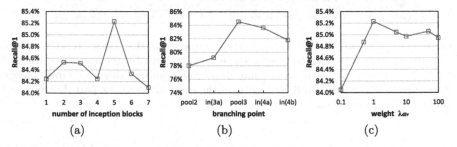

Fig. 7. Recall@1 while varying hyperparameters and architectures: (a) number of inception blocks used for attention module $A_k(\cdot)$, (b) branching point of attention module, and (c) weight λ_{div}. Here, `inception(3a)` is abbreviated as `in(3a)`

Sensitivity to Branching Point of Attention Module. The branching point of the attention module is where we split the network between spatial feature extractor $S(\cdot)$ and global feature embedding function $G(\cdot)$. To analyze the choice of branching point of the attention module, we keep the number of inception blocks in attention module same (*i.e.* 5) and change branching points from `pool2` to `inception(4b)`. From Fig. 7, we see that `pool3` performs the best with our architecture.

We carry out this experiment with batch size 40 for all the branching points. For ABE-M model, the memory requirement for the $G(\cdot)$ is M times compared to the individual learner. Since early branching point increases the depth of $G(\cdot)$ while decreasing the depth for $S(\cdot)$, it would consequently increase the memory requirement of the whole network. Due to the memory constraints of GPU, we started the experiments from branching points `pool2` and adjusted the batch size.

Table 4. Recall@K(%) score on CUB-200-2011 and CARS-196

K	CUB-200-2011				CARS-196			
	1	2	4	8	1	2	4	8
Contrastive[128] [29]	26.4	37.7	49.8	62.3	21.7	32.3	46.1	58.9
LiftedStruct[128] [29]	47.2	58.9	70.2	80.2	49.0	60.3	72.1	81.5
N-Pairs[64] [27]	51.0	63.3	74.3	83.2	71.1	79.7	86.5	91.6
Clustering[64] [28]	48.2	61.4	71.8	81.9	58.1	70.6	80.3	87.8
Proxy NCA[64] [20] (See footnote 1)	49.2	61.9	67.9	72.4	73.2	82.4	86.4	87.8
Smart Mining[64] [7]	49.8	62.3	74.1	83.3	64.7	76.2	84.2	90.2
Margin[128] [38] (See footnote 1)	**63.6**	**74.4**	**83.1**	**90.0**	79.6	86.5	91.9	95.1
HDC[384] [39]	53.6	65.7	77.0	85.6	73.7	83.2	89.5	93.8
Angular Loss[512] [36]	54.7	66.3	76.0	83.9	71.4	81.4	87.5	92.1
A-Bier[512] [23]	57.5	68.7	78.3	86.2	82.0	89.0	_93.2_	**96.1**
ABE-2[384]	55.9	68.1	77.4	85.7	77.2	85.1	90.5	94.2
ABE-4[384]	57.8	69.0	78.8	86.5	82.2	88.6	92.6	95.6
ABE-8[384]	60.2	71.4	_80.5_	_87.7_	_83.8_	_89.7_	_93.2_	95.5
ABE-2[512]	55.7	67.9	78.3	85.5	76.8	84.9	90.2	94.0
ABE-4[512]	57.9	69.3	79.5	86.9	82.5	89.1	93.0	95.5
ABE-8[512]	_60.6_	_71.5_	79.8	87.4	**85.2**	**90.5**	**94.0**	**96.1**

Sensitivity to λ_{div}. Figure 7 shows the effect of λ_{div} on Recall@K for ABE-M model. We can see that $\lambda_{\text{div}} = 1$ performs the best and lower values degrades the performance quickly.

6.4   Comparison with State of the Art

We compare the results of our approach with current state-of-the-art techniques. Our model performs the best on all the major benchmarks for image retrieval. Tables 4, 6 and 7 compare the results with previous methods such as Lifted-Struct [29], HDC [39], Margin[1] [38], BIER [22], and A-BIER [22] on CARS-196 [13], CUB-200-2011 [35], SOP [29], and in-shop clothes retrieval [18] datasets. Results on the cropped datasets are listed in Table 5.

---

[1] All compared methods use GoogLeNet architecture except Margin which uses ResNet-50 [8] and Proxy-NCA uses IncpeptionBN [10].

Table 5. Recall@K(%) score on CUB-200-2011 (cropped) and CARS-196 (cropped)

K	CUB-200-2011				CARS-196			
	1	2	4	8	1	2	4	8
PDDM + Triplet[128] [9]	50.9	62.1	73.2	82.5	46.4	58.2	70.3	80.1
PDDM + Quadruplet[128] [9]	58.3	69.2	79.0	88.4	57.4	68.6	80.1	89.4
HDC[384] [39]	60.7	72.4	81.9	89.2	83.8	89.8	93.6	96.2
Margin[128] [38] (See footnote 1)	63.9	75.3	84.4	90.6	86.9	92.7	95.6	97.6
A-BIER[512] [23]	65.5	75.8	83.9	90.2	90.3	94.1	_96.8_	_97.9_
ABE-2[512]	64.9	76.2	84.2	90.0	88.2	92.8	95.6	97.3
ABE-4[512]	_68.0_	_77.8_	_86.3_	_92.1_	_91.6_	_95.1_	_96.8_	97.8
ABE-8[512]	**70.6**	**79.8**	**86.9**	**92.2**	**93.0**	**95.9**	**97.5**	**98.5**

Table 6. Recall@K(%) score on Stanford online products dataset (SOP)

K	1	10	100	1000
Contrastive[128] [29]	42.0	58.2	73.8	89.1
LiftedStruct[512] [29]	62.1	79.8	91.3	97.4
N-Pairs[512] [27]	67.7	83.8	93.0	97.8
Clustering[64] [28]	67.0	83.7	93.2	-
Proxy NCA[64] [20] (See footnote 1)	73.7	-	-	-
Margin[128] [38] (See footnote 1)	72.7	86.2	93.8	98.0
HDC[384] [39]	69.5	84.4	92.8	97.7
A-Bier[512] [23]	74.2	86.9	94.0	97.8
ABE-2[512]	75.4	88.0	94.7	**98.2**
ABE-4[512]	_75.9_	_88.3_	_94.8_	**98.2**
ABE-8[512]	**76.3**	**88.4**	**94.8**	**98.2**

Table 7. Recall@K(%) score on in-shop clothes retrieval dataset

K	1	10	20	30	40	50
FasionNet+Joints[4096] [18]	41.0	64.0	68.0	71.0	73.0	73.5
FasionNet+Poselets[4096] [18]	42.0	65.0	70.0	72.0	72.0	75.0
FasionNet[4096] [18]	53.0	73.0	76.0	77.0	79.0	80.0
HDC[384] [39]	62.1	84.9	89.0	91.2	92.3	93.1
A-BIER[512] [23]	83.1	95.1	96.9	97.5	97.8	98.0
ABE-2[512]	85.2	96.0	97.2	97.8	98.2	98.4
ABE-4[512]	_86.7_	_96.4_	_97.6_	_98.0_	_98.4_	_98.6_
ABE-8[512]	**87.3**	**96.7**	**97.9**	**98.2**	**98.5**	**98.7**

7 Conclusion

In this work, we present a new framework for ensemble in the domain of deep metric learning. It uses attention-based architecture that attends to parts of the image. We use multiple such attention-based learners for our ensemble. Since ensemble benefits from diverse learners, we further introduce a divergence loss to diversify the feature embeddings learned by each learner. The divergence loss encourages that the attended parts of the image for each learner are different. Experimental results demonstrate that the divergence loss not only increases the performance of ensemble but also increases each individual learners' performance compared to the baseline. We demonstrate that our method outperforms the current state-of-the-art techniques by significant margin on several image retrieval benchmarks including CARS-196 [13], CUB-200-2011 [35], SOP [29], and in-shop clothes retrieval [18] datasets.

References

1. Ba, J., Mnih, V., Kavukcuoglu, K.: Multiple object recognition with visual attention. In: International Conference on Learning Representations (2015)
2. Bachman, P., Alsharif, O., Precup, D.: Learning with pseudo-ensembles. In: Advances in Neural Information Processing Systems (2014)
3. Bell, S., Bala, K.: Learning visual similarity for product design with convolutional neural networks. Graphics **34**(4), 98 (2015)
4. Chopra, S., Hadsell, R., LeCun, Y.: Learning a similarity metric discriminatively, with application to face verification. In: Computer Vision and Pattern Recognition (2005)
5. Glorot, X., Bengio, Y.: Understanding the difficulty of training deep feedforward neural networks. In: International Conference on Artificial Intelligence and Statistics (2010)
6. Hadsell, R., Chopra, S., LeCun, Y.: Dimensionality reduction by learning an invariant mapping. In: Computer Vision and Pattern Recognition (2006)
7. Harwood, B., VijayKumarB., G., Carneiro, G., Reid, I.D., Drummond, T.: Smart mining for deep metric learning. In: International Conference on Computer Vision (2017)
8. He, K., Zhang, X., Ren, S., Sun, J.: Deep residual learning for image recognition. In: Computer Vision and Pattern Recognition (2016)
9. Huang, C., Loy, C.C., Tang, X.: Local similarity-aware deep feature embedding. In: Advances in Neural Information Processing Systems (2016)
10. Ioffe, S., Szegedy, C.: Batch normalization: accelerating deep network training by reducing internal covariate shift. In: International Conference on Machine Learning (2015)
11. Jaderberg, M., Simonyan, K., Zisserman, A., Kavukcuoglu, K.: Spatial transformer networks. In: Advances in Neural Information Processing Systems (2015)
12. Jia, Y., et al.: Caffe: convolutional architecture for fast feature embedding. In: International Conference on Multimedia (2014)
13. Krause, J., Stark, M., Deng, J., Fei-Fei, L.: 3D object representations for fine-grained categorization. In: Workshop on 3D Representation and Recognition (2013)

14. Law, M.T., Urtasun, R., Zemel, R.S.: Deep spectral clustering learning. In: International Conference on Machine Learning (2017)
15. Lee, C.Y., Xie, S., Gallagher, P., Zhang, Z., Tu, Z.: Deeply-supervised nets. In: Artificial Intelligence and Statistics (2015)
16. Lee, S., Purushwalkam, S., Cogswell, M., Crandall, D., Batra, D.: Why M heads are better than one: training a diverse ensemble of deep networks. arXiv preprint arXiv:1511.06314 (2015)
17. Liu, X., Xia, T., Wang, J., Lin, Y.: Fully convolutional attention localization networks: efficient attention localization for fine-grained recognition. arXiv preprint arXiv:1603.06765 (2016)
18. Liu, Z., Luo, P., Qiu, S., Wang, X., Tang, X.: DeepFashion: powering robust clothes recognition and retrieval with rich annotations. In: Computer Vision and Pattern Recognition (2016)
19. Mnih, V., Heess, N., Graves, A., et al.: Recurrent models of visual attention. In: Advances in Neural Information Processing Systems (2014)
20. Movshovitz-Attias, Y., Toshev, A., Leung, T.K., Ioffe, S., Singh, S.: No fuss distance metric learning using proxies. In: International Conference on Computer Vision (2017)
21. Opitz, M., Possegger, H., Bischof, H.: Efficient model averaging for deep neural networks. In: Asian Conference on Computer Vision (2016)
22. Opitz, M., Waltner, G., Possegger, H., Bischof, H.: BIER-boosting independent embeddings robustly. In: International Conference on Computer Vision (2017)
23. Opitz, M., Waltner, G., Possegger, H., Bischof, H.: Deep metric learning with BIER: boosting independent embeddings robustly. arXiv preprint arXiv:1801.04815 (2018)
24. Russakovsky, O., Deng, J., Su, H., Krause, J., Satheesh, S., Ma, S., Huang, Z., Karpathy, A., Khosla, A., Bernstein, M.: Imagenet large scale visual recognition challenge. Int. J. Comput. Vis. **115**(3), 211–252 (2015)
25. Schroff, F., Kalenichenko, D., Philbin, J.: Facenet: A unified embedding for face recognition and clustering. In: Computer Vision and Pattern Recognition (2015)
26. Sermanet, P., Frome, A., Real, E.: Attention for fine-grained categorization. In: International Conference on Learning Representations Workshop (2015)
27. Sohn, K.: Improved deep metric learning with multi-class N-pair loss objective. In: Advances in Neural Information Processing Systems (2016)
28. Song, H.O., Jegelka, S., Rathod, V., Murphy, K.: Deep metric learning via facility location. In: Computer Vision and Pattern Recognition (2017)
29. Song, H.O., Xiang, Y., Jegelka, S., Savarese, S.: Deep metric learning via lifted structured feature embedding. In: Computer Vision and Pattern Recognition (2016)
30. Srivastava, N., Hinton, G., Krizhevsky, A., Sutskever, I., Salakhutdinov, R.: Dropout: a simple way to prevent neural networks from overfitting. J. Mach. Learn. Res. **15**(1), 1929–1958 (2014)
31. Sutskever, I., Vinyals, O., Le, Q.V.: Sequence to sequence learning with neural networks. In: Advances in Neural Information Processing Systems (2014)
32. Szegedy, C., et al.: Going deeper with convolutions. In: Computer Vision and Pattern Recognition (2015)
33. Ustinova, E., Lempitsky, V.: Learning deep embeddings with histogram loss. In: Advances in Neural Information Processing Systems (2016)
34. Veit, A., Wilber, M.J., Belongie, S.: Residual networks behave like ensembles of relatively shallow networks. In: Advances in Neural Information Processing Systems (2016)

35. Wah, C., Branson, S., Welinder, P., Perona, P., Belongie, S.: The Caltech-UCSD Birds-200-2011 dataset. Technical report CNS-TR-2011-001, California Institute of Technology (2011)
36. Wang, J., Zhou, F., Wen, S., Liu, X., Lin, Y.: Deep metric learning with angular loss. In: International Conference on Computer Vision (2017)
37. Weinberger, K.Q., Saul, L.K.: Distance metric learning for large margin nearest neighbor classification. J. Mach. Learn. Res. **10**(2), 207–244 (2009)
38. Wu, C.Y., Manmatha, R., Smola, A.J., Krähenbühl, P.: Sampling matters in deep embedding learning. In: International Conference on Computer Vision (2017)
39. Yuan, Y., Yang, K., Zhang, C.: Hard-aware deeply cascaded embedding. In: International Conference on Computer Vision (2017)
40. Zhao, B., Wu, X., Feng, J., Peng, Q., Yan, S.: Diversified visual attention networks for fine-grained object classification. Multimedia **19**(6), 1245–1256 (2017)

Learning Compression from Limited Unlabeled Data

Xiangyu He[1,2] and Jian Cheng[1,2,3](✉)

[1] National Laboratory of Pattern Recognition, Institute of Automation, Chinese Academy of Sciences, Beijing, China
{xiangyu.he,jcheng}@nlpr.ia.ac.cn
[2] University of Chinese Academy of Sciences, Beijing, China
[3] Center for Excellence in Brain Science and Intelligence Technology, Beijing, China

Abstract. Convolutional neural networks (CNNs) have dramatically advanced the state-of-art in a number of domains. However, most models are both computation and memory intensive, which arouse the interest of network compression. While existing compression methods achieve good performance, they suffer from three limitations: (1) the inevitable retraining with enormous labeled data; (2) the massive GPU hours for retraining; (3) the training tricks for model compression. Especially the requirement of retraining on original datasets makes it difficult to apply in many real-world scenarios, where training data is not publicly available. In this paper, we reveal that re-normalization is the practical and effective way to alleviate the above limitations. Through quantization or pruning, most methods may compress a large number of parameters but ignore the core role in performance degradation, which is the Gaussian conjugate prior induced by batch normalization. By employing the re-estimated statistics in batch normalization, we significantly improve the accuracy of compressed CNNs. Extensive experiments on ImageNet show it outperforms baselines by a large margin and is comparable to label-based methods. Besides, the fine-tuning process takes less than 5 min on CPU, using 1000 unlabeled images.

Keywords: Deep neural networks · Label-free network compression

1 Introduction

Convolutional neural networks (CNNs) have achieved impressive performances in many challenging problems [15,24], and even surpass human-level for certain tasks such as ImageNet classification [16]. As CNN-based recognition systems [3] continue to grow, it is critical to improve inference efficiency while maintaining accuracy [5].

Since network compression introduces efficient approximations to CNNs and compressed models require less memory and fewer operations, parameter quantization [8,18,30], pruning [11,13] and low-rank [33,38] representations have

© Springer Nature Switzerland AG 2018
V. Ferrari et al. (Eds.): ECCV 2018, LNCS 11205, pp. 778–795, 2018.
https://doi.org/10.1007/978-3-030-01246-5_46

become a topic of interest in the deep learning community. Especially quantization, with the boom of AI chips, will be the workhorse in industry. While these techniques have driven advances in power efficiency, they still face a considerable accuracy loss under low-bit or highly sparse compression. Retraining on the original dataset is usually inevitable. Unfortunately, the retraining process needs a sufficiently large open training dataset which is inaccessible for many real-world applications, such as medical diagnosis [9], drug discovery and toxicology [1]. Therefore, it is imperative to avoid retraining or require no training data.

In this work, we alleviate the accuracy degradation in direct network compression through label-free fine-tuning. For network quantization, which comprises two primary components: weight quantization and feature map quantization. Intuitively, the quantization error determines the performance loss. Therefore, we propose the Quasi-Lloyd-Max algorithm to minimize the weight quantization error. To further improve the accuracy of compressed networks, we explore the reason of feature map distortion. In light of Bayesian networks, we reveal that statistic shift of batch normalization results in the accuracy degradation of direct compression. When network parameters misfit approximate Gaussian distribution, the prior assumption of mean and variance should mismatch the corrupted features. By employing the re-estimated statistics in batch normalization, the performance of compressed CNNs can be rapidly recovered. Extensive experiments on 4-bit quantization and pruning demonstrate the robustness of this viewpoint.

Compared with conventional label-based compression methods, the main contributions of this paper are as follows:

- We reveal the hidden factor why direct network compression results in performance degradation, and prove that 4-bit or sparse representation remains capable of original tasks without retraining.
- A Quasi-Lloyd-Max algorithm is proposed to minimize the weight quantization error on 4-bit networks.
- The fine-tuning time decreases from days (GPU) to minutes (CPU), by using limited unlabeled data.

2   Related Work

The redundant parameters of deep neural networks induce inefficient computation and large memory footprint. Most compression approaches can be viewed as the regularization techniques to solve these problems. Recently, along with the existence of TPU [22] and low precision BLAS [10], parameter fixed-point representation has frequently been discussed. Traditional hash-based vector quantization, such as HashNet [2], may not directly benefit from customized hardware. In contrast, 8-8-bit structures get TensorRT [27] or TPU [22] support easily. Bit-oriented methods with potential $64\times$ acceleration, such as BC [7], FFN [34], BNN [6] and XNOR-Net [30], compress DNNs to extreme 1 bit ($\sim32\times$ compression), while suffering an irreversible accuracy loss. INQ [39] shows the reasonable performance of 2^n framework; nevertheless, plenty of labeled data is required for retraining.

For low-rank representation, early studies share the same starting point: using matrix low-rank approximation to reduce the computation. Conventional network structures with regular filters and large feature maps are friendly to matrix decomposition. Generalized Singular Vector Decomposition [38], Tucker Decomposition [23] and Tensor Block Term Decomposition [33,35] are widely used on AlexNet [24], VGG-16 [31] and GoogleNet [32]. At the cost of negligible loss in accuracy, they gain several times acceleration with a certain amount of compression. Very recently, MobileNet [17] with channel-wise convolution shows the potential capability to extract distinguishing features within limited parameters. Most notably, this network structure is identical to the decomposed matrix, which invalidates the current decomposition methods. Similar problems still arise in ResNet [16] with 1×1 filters.

Weight pruning benefits from Sparse GEneral Matrix Multiplication (Sparse GEMM) and highly optimized hardware design [14]. Combining with clustering and Huffman coding [13], promising compression results without accuracy loss were reported. The problem is hundreds [11] or even thousands [14] of retraining epochs are time-consuming, and is still heavily reliant on labeled datasets.

By using feature map fitting, [4,36] implicitly learn from the well-trained networks through the Euclidean distance between feature maps of full-precision and compressed networks. Nevertheless, deeper network structures and imbalanced class samples would be the nightmare to hand-tuned layer by layer analysis.

3   Weight Quantization

Since quantization has been the mainstream compression technique in industry, we first review the cause of quantization, then discuss three hardware-friendly quantizers under different metrics. The scheme with least accuracy loss is adopted in further feature map recovery.

3.1   Cause

In early research, [12,19] show that it is possible to train deep neural networks using 16-bit fixed-point numbers. Fixed-point computation with high speed and low power consumption is much more friendly to embedded devices. The small circuits would allow for the configuration of more arithmetic units. Besides, the low-bit data representation minimizes the memory footprint, which reduces the data transmission time for the customized device like FPGA [12,13,25].

3.2 ℓ_2 Norm Metric

Since customized hardware units have fully supported fixed-point multiplication and addition, quantizing float numbers to their nearest fixed-point representations by *shift* and *carry* operations can easily accelerate inference time. Suppose the fixed-point number is represented as $[I_{bit} : F_{bit}]$, and the Integer part plus the Fraction part yields the real number. Mathematically this problem, dubbed round-to-nearest, can be stated as follows,

$$\mathbf{Q}^* = \arg\min_{\mathbf{Q}} \; J(\mathbf{Q}) = \|\mathbf{W} - \mathbf{Q}\|_2^2$$

$$s.t. \; \mathbf{Q}_i \in \{-2^I/2, -2^I/2 + 2^{-F}, \dots 0, \dots, 2^I/2 - 2^{-F}\}$$

where $\mathbf{Q}$ is forced to fit the large number in $\mathbf{W}$. This metric minimizes the loss function at the cost of small numbers and becomes much more sensitive to outliers. That is, large numbers determine the bit-width selection of I_{bit} and F_{bit}. To partly solve this problem, a scaling factor $\alpha \in \mathbb{R}$ is introduced,

$$\alpha^*, \mathbf{Q}^* = \arg\min_{\alpha > 0, \mathbf{Q}} \; J(\alpha, \mathbf{Q}) = \|\mathbf{W} - \alpha\mathbf{Q}\|_2^2$$

It has been proved that scaling factor could dramatically enlarge the domain of values [30]. Although the function is convex in each variable only, they are not convex in each variable together. It is infeasible to solve $J(\alpha, \mathbf{Q})$ in the sense of finding global minima, especially under the discrete constraint. However, it is possible to find local minima using iterative numerical optimization. Consider the following problem,

$$\alpha^*, \; \mathbf{Q}^* = \arg\min_{\alpha > 0} \; (\alpha^2 \mathbf{Q}^T\mathbf{Q} - 2\alpha\mathbf{Q}^T\mathbf{W} + c), \tag{1}$$

where $\mathbf{Q}$ corresponds to a set of fixed-point numbers and $c = \sum_i \mathbf{W}_i^2$ is an α and $\mathbf{Q}$ independent constant. Thus, for any given $\mathbf{Q}$, the optimal α is

$$\alpha^* = \frac{\mathbf{Q}^T\mathbf{W}}{\mathbf{Q}^T\mathbf{Q}}. \tag{2}$$

By substituting α^* into (1), the optimization problem leads to the partial derivatives $\frac{\partial J(\alpha, \mathbf{Q})}{\partial \mathbf{Q}}$. Setting it to zero, then project the solution to given discrete space

$$\mathbf{Q}^* \approx \mathbf{Fix}(\mathbf{W}/\alpha^*). \tag{3}$$

Algorithm 1 iteratively updates α^* and $\mathbf{Q}^*$ through quantizer $\mathbf{Fix}(\cdot)$, such as round-to-nearest, 2^n (i.e., quantized to nearest power of 2) or uniform quantization (i.e., quantized to nearest quantization interval endpoints). Following the iterative update rule, the Euclidean distance between $\mathbf{W}$ and $\alpha\mathbf{Q}$ is optimized in each iteration.

3.3   Discrete Entropy Metric

Similar to the squared Euclidean distance (ℓ_2) which is the canonical example of a Bregman distance, another useful measure is the generalized Kullback-Leibler divergence (KL) generated by the convex function $\sum_i p_i \ln p_i$. In this case,

$$\alpha^*, \mathbf{Q}^* = \arg\min_{\alpha > 0, \mathbf{Q}} \; D(\alpha\mathbf{Q}\|\mathbf{W}) = \sum_i (|\mathbf{W}_i| \ln \frac{\mathbf{W}_i}{\alpha\mathbf{Q}_i} - |\mathbf{W}_i| + \alpha|\mathbf{Q}_i|)$$

$$s.t. \; \alpha > 0, \; \mathbf{Q}_i \in \{\pm 2^0\Delta, \pm 2^1\Delta, \dots, \pm 2^{k-1}\Delta\}$$

Algorithm 1. Quasi-Lloyd-Max Algorithm.

Require: Full precision weights $\mathbf{W}$, metric $J(\cdot)$ (ℓ_2, KL, etc.) and quantizer $\mathbf{Fix}(\cdot)$.
Ensure: Updated $\widetilde{\mathbf{W}} \approx \alpha^*\mathbf{Q}^*$ and fixed-point $\mathbf{Q}^*$.
1: **for** k^{th} filter in l^{th} layer **do**
2:      $\alpha_{l,k} \leftarrow$ Initialize parameters
3:      **repeat**
4:          $\alpha_{l,k}^*, \mathbf{Q}_{l,k}^* \leftarrow \arg\min\limits_{\alpha,\mathbf{Q}} J\left(\alpha_{l,k}, \mathbf{Q}_{l,k}\right)$; {Fix α, solve $\mathbf{Q}$; Fix $\mathbf{Q}$, solve α}
5:          swap($\alpha_{l,k}, \alpha_{l,k}^*$);
6:      **until** convergence of parameters $\alpha_{l,k}$
7:      $\mathbf{Y}_l \leftarrow \widetilde{\mathbf{W}}_l * \widetilde{\mathbf{X}}_l \approx \alpha_l^*(\mathbf{Q}_l^* \circledast \widetilde{\mathbf{X}}_l)$; {low-bit convolution + cblas_sscal}
8:      $\widetilde{\mathbf{X}}_{l+1} \leftarrow \psi(\mathbf{Y}_l)$; {ReLU + INT 8-bit quantization}
9: **end for**

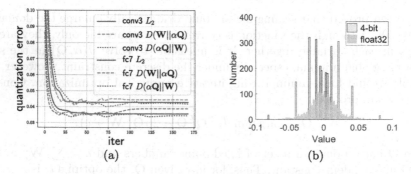

(a)   (b)

Fig. 1. (a) Quasi-Lloyd-Max convergence comparsion of different metrics. The Euclidean distance between $\mathbf{W}$ and $\alpha\mathbf{Q}$ is reported. (b) The distributions of quantized 4-bit (2^n quantization) and full-precision weights of the third convolution layer (some bars get merged for clearness)

where Δ corresponds to the minimum value of 2^n in k-bit quantization. Like ℓ_2 norm metric, this loss function is also lower bounded by zero.

Consider the function of $D(\alpha\mathbf{Q}||\mathbf{W})$ to be differentiated partially with respect to the elements of $\mathbf{Q}$, which is

$$\frac{\partial D_{(\alpha\mathbf{Q}||\mathbf{W})}}{\partial \mathbf{Q}_i} = -\frac{|\mathbf{W}_i|}{\mathbf{Q}_i} + \alpha \cdot sgn(\mathbf{Q}_i). \tag{4}$$

With fixed α, similarly we have

$$\frac{\partial D_{(\alpha\mathbf{Q}||\mathbf{W})}}{\partial \alpha} = -\frac{1}{\alpha}\sum_i |\mathbf{W}_i| + \sum_i |\mathbf{Q}_i|. \tag{5}$$

By setting both equations to zero, we obtain a pair of local minima of KL Divergence. Hence, the solutions to $D(\alpha\mathbf{Q}||\mathbf{W})$ are $\alpha^* = \frac{\sum_i |\mathbf{W}_i|}{\sum_i |\mathbf{Q}_i^*|}$ and $\mathbf{Q}^* = \mathbf{Fix}(\frac{\mathbf{W}}{\alpha^*})$ through Quasi-Lloyd-Max iterations.

In mathematics, generalized Kullback-Leibler Divergence is similar to a metric, but satisfies neither the triangle inequality nor symmetry. We further test

$D(\mathbf{W}||\alpha\mathbf{Q})$ as a weight quantization loss on AlexNet, shown in Fig. 1(b). Following the same procedure, we obtain

$$\frac{\partial D_{(\mathbf{W}||\alpha\mathbf{Q})}}{\partial \alpha} = \sum_i |\mathbf{Q}_i| \ln\alpha + \sum_i |\mathbf{Q}_i|(\ln\frac{|\mathbf{Q_i}|}{|\mathbf{W}_i|}) \tag{6}$$

$$\frac{\partial D_{(\mathbf{W}||\alpha\mathbf{Q})}}{\partial \mathbf{Q}_i} = \alpha \cdot sgn(\mathbf{Q}_i) \cdot \ln\frac{\alpha\mathbf{Q_i}}{\mathbf{W_i}}. \tag{7}$$

In this case, $\alpha^* = \exp(\frac{\sum_i |\mathbf{Q}_i^*| \ln\frac{|\mathbf{W}_i|}{|\mathbf{Q}_i^*|}}{\sum_i |\mathbf{Q}_i^*|})$ and $\mathbf{Q}^*$ remains the same as Eq. (4).

Taking the third convolution layer and the second fully connected layer of AlexNet as examples, Fig. 1(a) shows the convergence under different metrics. In our evaluations, all metrics converge in the first few iterations and obtain nearly the same quantization error. Since ℓ_2 yields more steady convergence speed, we evaluate the accuracy of different quantizer under ℓ_2 norm metric. As listed in Table 1 (whole network quantization except the first layer), 2^n outperforms other quantizers by a large margin; thus we follow this setting in the next experiments.

Table 1. Quantizer comparsion of 4-bit Weights and 8-bit activations (ℓ_2 Norm)

Models		Round-to-nearest	Uniform	2^n	Full-precision
AlexNet	Top-1	48.32	43.12	**58.66**	60.43
	Top-5	72.93	67.73	**81.17**	82.47
ResNet-18	Top-1	45.92	50.18	**55.76**	69.08
	Top-5	71.33	75.63	**79.75**	89.03
ResNet-50	Top-1	54.61	55.99	**68.14**	75.30
	Top-5	77.98	79.00	**87.98**	92.11

3.4 Feature-Based Metric

In general, feature map extracted from input data is more crucial than weights in computer vision tasks. To fit the output features rather than pre-trained weights would further improve the performance [36]. Taking full-precision features $\mathbf{Y}$ and quantized input activations $\widetilde{\mathbf{X}}$ into account, we obtain the multi-objective optimization problem:

$$\alpha^*, \mathbf{Q}^* = \arg\min_{\alpha>0,\mathbf{Q}} ||\mathbf{W} - \alpha\mathbf{Q}||_2^2 + \lambda||\mathbf{Y} - \alpha\widetilde{\mathbf{X}}\mathbf{Q}^T||_2^2. \tag{8}$$

With $\lambda = 0$, Eq. (8) degrades to ℓ_2 metric. For large λ, feature map fitting becomes more crucial. This problem could be solved by Quasi-Lloyd-Max in a similar way. The closed-form solutions of each step are

$$\alpha^* = \frac{\lambda \sum_{i=1}^{m} \mathbf{Q}^T \widetilde{\mathbf{X}}_i^T \mathbf{Y}_i + \mathbf{Q}^T \mathbf{W}}{\lambda \sum_{i=1}^{m} \mathbf{Q}^T \widetilde{\mathbf{X}}_i^T \widetilde{\mathbf{X}}_i \mathbf{Q} + \mathbf{Q}^T \mathbf{Q}} \tag{9}$$

$$(\alpha^* \lambda \sum_{i=1}^{m} \widetilde{\mathbf{X}}_i^T \widetilde{\mathbf{X}}_i + \alpha^* \mathbf{I})\mathbf{Q} = \lambda \sum_{i=1}^{m} \widetilde{\mathbf{X}}_i^T \mathbf{Y}_i + \mathbf{W}, \tag{10}$$

where $\mathbf{I}$ corresponding to $n \times n$ unit matrix and m refers to m smaples. If $\widetilde{\mathbf{X}}_i^T \widetilde{\mathbf{X}}_i$ is symmetric positive definite, then by using *modified Cholesky decomposition*, one may simplify Eq.(10) as $\alpha^*(\lambda \sum_i \widetilde{\mathbf{X}}_i^T \widetilde{\mathbf{X}}_i + \mathbf{I}) = \mathbf{LDL}^T$, where L is a lower triangular matrix with unit diagonal elements and D is a diagonal matrix with positive elements on the diagonal. To solve $\mathbf{LDL}^T \mathbf{x} = \mathbf{y}$, we only need to address $\mathbf{Lx}' = \mathbf{y}$ and $\mathbf{DL}^T \mathbf{x} = \mathbf{x}'$, which is faster and with better numerical stability.

However, given limited unlabeled data, there is no global measurement to facilitate the selection of λ. In our experiments, the iterative numerical approximation to solve $\mathbf{Q}$ can be hugely affected by the different settings. Hence, the explicit feature-map based method is deprecated in our further evaluations. Compared with various metrics, Table 2 shows that the ℓ_2 norm could better reflect the weight fitting error.

Table 2. Metric Comparsion of Direct 4-bit 2^n Weight Quantization

Models		ℓ_2 Norm	$D_{(\mathbf{W}\|\alpha\mathbf{Q})}$	$D_{(\alpha\mathbf{Q})\|\mathbf{W}}$	Fmap-based
AlexNet	Top-1	**58.90**	56.30	57.59	–
	Top-5	**81.43**	79.40	80.26	–

4   Feature Recovery

To further improve the performance of compressed networks, we focus on the "Gaussian-like" feature distribution. From a Bayesian perspective, the conjugate prior induced by batch normalization results in the performance gap between full-precision network and post hoc compression. Therefore, we can use batch normalization to refine a well-trained network with low-bit or sparse representation.

4.1   Bayesian Networks

The methodology of CNNs is to find the maximum a posteriori (MAP) weights given a training dataset ($\mathbf{D}$) and a prior distribution $p(\mathcal{W})$ over model parameters $\mathcal{W}$. Suppose that $\mathbf{D}$ consists of N batch samples $\{(x_i, y_i)_{i=1:N}\}$, then $p(\mathcal{W}|\mathbf{D}) = \frac{p(\mathbf{D}|\mathcal{W})p(\mathcal{W})}{p(\mathbf{D})}$. Due to the difficulty in calculating $p(\mathbf{D})$, it is common to approximate $p(\mathcal{W}|\mathbf{D})$ using a variational distribution $q_\tau(\mathcal{W})$. By optimizing the variational parameters τ so that the Kullback-Leiber (KL) divergence is minimized:

$$\mathcal{L}(\tau) = -\mathbb{E}_{q_\tau(\mathcal{W})}[\log p(\mathbf{D}|\mathcal{W})] + KL(q_\tau(\mathcal{W})\|p(\mathcal{W})) \qquad (11)$$

$$= -\int_{\mathcal{W}} q_\tau(\mathcal{W})\log p(\mathbf{D}|\mathcal{W})d\mathcal{W} + KL(q_\tau(\mathcal{W})\|p(\mathcal{W})). \qquad (12)$$

Equation (13) is known as the evidence-lower-bound (ELBO), assuming i.i.d. observation noise.

In practice, a Monte Carlo integration is usually employed to estimate the expectation term $\mathbb{E}_{q_\tau(\mathcal{W})}[\log p(\mathbf{D}|\mathcal{W})]$. Using weight samples $\hat{\mathcal{W}}^i \sim q_\tau(\mathcal{W})$ for each batch i, leads to the following approximation:

$$\mathcal{L}(\tau) := -\frac{1}{N}\sum_{i=1}^{N}\log p(\mathbf{D}|\hat{\mathcal{W}}^i) + KL(q_\tau(\mathcal{W})\|p(\mathcal{W})) \qquad (13)$$

$$:= \underbrace{-\frac{1}{N}\sum_{i=1}^{N}\log p(\mathbf{y}_i|\mathbf{x}_i, \hat{\mathcal{W}}^i)}_{negative\ log-likelihood} + \underbrace{KL(q_\tau(\mathcal{W})\|p(\mathcal{W}))}_{KL\ divergence}. \qquad (14)$$

Especially, for batch normalization parameters $\{\mu_B, \sigma_B\} \in \mathcal{W}$, we regard the inference at training time as a stochastic process, estimated mean and variance based on samples in a mini-batch are two stochastic variables. Assume i.i.d. M samples where $\mathbf{z}_i = \overline{Wx} \sim \mathcal{N}(\mu, \sigma^2)$ and $\mu_i = \frac{1}{M}\sum_{k=1}^{M}\mathbf{z}_k$. By using central limit theorem (CLT) for sufficient random sampling through SGD, we have $\mu_B \sim \mathcal{N}(\mu, \frac{\sigma^2}{M})$. Due to $\mathbb{E}[(\mathbf{z}_i - \mu)^2] = \sigma^2$, similarly we obtain $\sigma_B^2 \sim \mathcal{N}(\sigma^2, \frac{\mathbb{E}[(\mathbf{z}_i-\mu)^4]-\sigma^4}{M})$.

4.2   KL Divergence and Weight Regularization

Probabilistically, $p(\mathbf{D}|\mathcal{W}) = \prod_{i=1}^{N}p(\mathbf{y}_i|\mathbf{x}_i, \mathcal{W})$, the posterior $p(\mathbf{y}_i|\mathbf{x}_i, \mathcal{W})$ expresses a predictive distribution generated by a parameteric model $\mathcal{W}$, e.g., the cross-entropy criterion for multi-classification. The negative loglikelihood defines $\mathcal{L}$ as follows:

$$\mathcal{L}(\mathbf{y}) = -\frac{1}{N}\sum_{i=1}^{N}\log p(\mathbf{y}_i|\mathbf{x}_i, \mathcal{W}) + \frac{\lambda}{2}\|\boldsymbol{\omega}\|_2^2. \qquad (15)$$

where $\boldsymbol{\omega}$ is learnable parameters such as weights, and $\mathcal{W}$ also includes random parameters such as μ_B, σ_B.

Since both $\mathcal{L}(\tau)$ and $\mathcal{L}(\mathbf{y})$ are solved by gradient descent, the second terms of Eqs. (15) and (17) illustrate the connection between KL divergence (i.e., $p(\mathcal{W})$) w.r.t the estimated distribution $q_\tau(\mathcal{W})$) and weight regularization:

$$\frac{\partial KL(q_\tau(\mathcal{W})\|p(\mathcal{W}))}{\partial\boldsymbol{\omega}} = \frac{\partial\frac{\lambda}{2}\boldsymbol{\omega}^T\boldsymbol{\omega}}{\partial\boldsymbol{\omega}}. \qquad (16)$$

The regularization term can be viewed as a log-prior distribution over weights, such as Gaussian derived from ℓ_2 norm. Under the constraint of low-bit or sparsity, the penalty term introduces different priors (e.g., spike-and-slab in pruning) which hugely affect the approximation to $p(\mathcal{W})$. We now describe how weight compression corrupts batch normalization parameters.

For random variables in batch normalization, the KL divergence between approximation $\mathcal{N}(\mu_q, \sigma_q^2)$ and true distribution $\mathcal{N}(\mu_p, \sigma_p^2)$ can be calculated using:

$$KL(q(\mathcal{W})\|p(\mathcal{W})) = \frac{(\mu_q - \mu_p)^2}{2\sigma_p^2} + \log \frac{\sigma_p}{\sigma_q} + \frac{\sigma_q^2}{2\sigma_p^2} - \frac{1}{2}.$$

Since μ_p, σ_p won't change during training, which is independent to ω, thus $\mu_p' = \sigma_p' = 0$, and then $\frac{\partial KL}{\partial \omega} = \frac{(\mu_q - \mu_p)\mu_q'}{\sigma_p^2} + \frac{(\sigma_q^2 - \sigma_p^2)\sigma_q'}{\sigma_q \sigma_p^2}$. The optimal approximation $\mu_q \rightarrow \mu_p$, $\sigma_q^2 \rightarrow \sigma_p^2$ reaches its limit when regularization term solved by SGD (partial derivative is zero). When we compress the well-trained networks, the weight regularization has changed implicitly, in another word, former estimations should introduce a great bias. Fortunately, as proved in Sect. 4.2, the expectations of μ_q and σ_q^2 converge to the real distribution parameters, then it is possible to renew the distorted features through re-estimation.

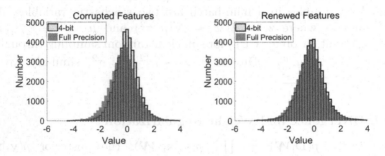

Fig. 2. Feature distribution comparsion for AlexNet 5th batch-normalization layer

4.3   Renew Distorted Features

While it is impractical to update weights through inference on unlabeled data, re-estimation on $\mu_\mathbf{B}$ and $\sigma_\mathbf{B}$ is still feasible. From [21], the mean and variance of activations holds that

$$\mathbb{E}[\tilde{x}] := \mathbb{E}[\tilde{\mu}_\mathbf{B}] \tag{17}$$

$$Var[\tilde{x}] := \frac{m}{m-1}\mathbb{E}[\tilde{\sigma}_\mathbf{B}^2], \tag{18}$$

where $\mathbb{E}(\tilde{\mu}) = \frac{1}{m}\sum_{i=1}^m \tilde{x}_i$ and $\mathbb{E}(\tilde{\sigma}^2) = \frac{1}{m}\sum_{i=1}^m (\tilde{x}_i - \tilde{\mu})^2$.

In Bayesian theory, if the posterior distribution is in the same probability distribution family as the prior, then the prior is called a conjugate prior for the likelihood function. Especially, Gaussian distribution is a conjugate prior for the likelihood that is also Gaussian. In this case, we have shown that batch normalization parameters obey normal distribution and combine the empirical observations that output feature of batch normalization is "more Gaussian" [20,21], one may derive that convolution, or inner-product layer tends to be a Gaussian likelihood. Thus, after compression, by choosing a new Gaussian prior (i.e., re-normalization or re-estimation), it will be more likely that the posterior distribution is also Gaussian:

$$P_{Gaussian} \propto P_{likelihood} \times P_{normal}.$$

Since batch normalization is commonly employed after convolution, the distribution of distorted features can be directly renewed. After the re-normalization, Fig. 2 shows that the distribution has been restored. Nevertheless, interpreting compressed networks as a likelihood function is a weak approximation. The performance of extremely quantized networks, such as binary or ternary, will not be improved since the corruption of likelihood function. In those cases, retraining on the original dataset is somehow inevitable.

5   Experiments

In this section, we verify the effectiveness of proposed methods on ImageNet dataset (ILSVRC 2012). Generally speaking, training-free quantization or pruning on deep neural networks is challenging, but we achieve much closer accuracy to full precision networks. We implement weight pruning and low-bit quantization on three representative CNNs: AlexNet [30], ResNet-18 [16] and MobileNet [17]. Besides, we also evaluate on ResNet-50 [16] to examine the validity of re-normalization on deeper network structures. All images are resized to have 256 pixel at short dimension and then a central crop of 224×224 is selected for re-normalization and evaluation. No data augmentation was used for all experiments.

5.1   Network Quantization

8-bit quantization with few samples or, ideally, without input data is becoming the workhorse in industry. As shown in Table 3, our 8-8-bit has reached the comparable accuracy with the full precision network. To achieve higher efficiency on embedded devices, we prove that even 4-bit weights could reach approximately 32-bit level. Using the same 4-bit weights in Sect. 3.2, we re-normalize those models on 1 K images randomly selected from ILSVRC 2012 training dataset without label information.

As shown in Table 4, the performance of 4-8-bit network (except the first layer) was hugely improved from direct quantization. Compared with Nvidia

Table 3. Results of 8-8-bit (whole network weights & features 8-bit) quantization on ILSVRC2012 validation dataset. Round-to-nearest with ℓ_2 metric was adopted in 8-bit weights. For 8-bit feature maps, we just quantize float numbers to nearest fixed-points

Models		Our baseline	Our Gap	TensorRT Baseline	TensorRT[27] Gap
AlexNet	Top-1	60.43	**+0.50**	57.08	−0.08
	Top-5	82.47	**+0.29**	80.06	−0.08
ResNet-18	Top-1	69.08	−0.08	–	–
	Top-5	89.03	−0.06	–	–
ResNet-50	Top-1	75.30	−0.27	73.23	**−0.20**
	Top-5	92.11	−0.02	91.18	−0.03

Table 4. Final Performance of Network 2^n Quantization. Accuracy loss corresponding to full precision network is reported (4-bit Weights & 8-bit Activations)

Models		Baseline	w/o ReNorm	w/ ReNorm
AlexNet	Top-1	60.43	−1.77	**−0.39**
	Top-5	82.47	−1.30	**-0.20**
ResNet-18	Top-1	69.08	-13.21	-1.83
	Top-5	89.03	−9.28	**−1.01**
ResNet-50	Top-1	75.30	−7.16	−2.14
	Top-5	92.11	−4.13	**−0.99**
MobileNet	Top-1	70.81	−70.80	−9.75
	Top-5	89.85	−89.82	−6.37

TenorRT, 1250 images were used to update the parameters of 8-bit networks; we need 1000 images to learn 4-bit quantization. Results on AlexNet, ResNet-18, and ResNet-50 show the steady performance improvements, which have nearly approached the 32-bit level. MobileNet, with channel-wise convolution layers, is far more challenging to quantize. After straightforward 4-bit weight quantization, the accuracy dropped to nearly zero. This delicate network structure is equivalent to the low-rank representation of Tensor Block Term Decomposition [33]. For this reason, channel-wise convolution with little redundancy is naturally difficult to compress. Since the runtime speed of 8-bit MobileNet on CPU has already only 31 ms (Tensorflow 1.1.0), 4-bit could be a trade-off between even higher speed and lower accuracy.

Table 5 further shows the comparison between accuracy and learning cost. Our 4-8-bit is still competitive with retraining methods. In some cases, 4-8-bit even outperforms some label-based counterparts on AlexNet. For 4-4-bit, slightly different from Sect. 3.2, we quantize features to nearest 2^n (without scale) during the process of re-normalization.

Compared with the 8-8-bit framework, 4-8-bit achieves not only 2× model compression but higher runtime speed. Low bit-width enables more fixed-point

Table 5. Quantization comparison for AlexNet and ResNet-18. Top-1 and Top-5 gap to the corresponding full-precision network is reported. Label-based retraining methods are marked as "+Label". The bit width before and after "+" is for weight and activation respectively. Not reported retraining epoch was shown as "*". "~ 0" requires no backward propagation

AlexNet				
Bit Precision	Method	Top-1 gap	Top-5 gap	Epochs
8 + 8	DoREFA [40]	−2.90	–	* + Label
	Going Deeper [29]	−0.88	−1.06	∼0
	Ours	**+0.50**	**+0.29**	**∼ 0**
5 + 32	INQ [39]	+0.15	+0.23	∼8 + Label
4 + 4	WQ [28]	−1.2	−1.1	∼6 + Label
4 + 8	Ours	−0.39	−0.20	∼0
5 + 4	LogQuant [26]	–	−3.20	*
4 + 4	Ours	-3.24	-2.13	∼0
ResNet-18				
4 + 32	INQ [39]	**+0.62**	**+0.32**	∼8 + Label
4 + 8	Ours	−1.83	−1.01	**∼ 0**

multiplications at the same clock frequency of the chip. This could provide dramatic data-level parallelism to achieve higher speedup. Besides, retraining methods can still benefit from feature map recovery. 3-8-bit AlexNet with +25.43% Top-1 and +26.86% Top-5 improvement yields 50.69% (Top-1) and 74.87% (Top-5) accuracy. This result provides a better starting point for retraining 3-bit networks.

5.2 Weight Pruning

To further verify the conclusion in Sect. 4.2, we apply network pruning (based on absolute value) to well-trained parameters. Figure 3(a) shows the trade-off between compression rate and accuracy. Within one iteration, i.e., using 1 K images, we recover the performance to the practical level (solid line in Fig. 3(a)). This steady performance improvement not only appeared in network quantization but also in weight pruning.

Since AlexNet with over-parameterized inner-product layers is the typical network structure to examine the effectiveness of pruning approach, we compare the typical pruning approach [14] with ours on compression rate. As listed in Table 6, our method even pruned more parameters on two layers, especially Fc1 with most parameters in AlexNet. The overall compression rate of FC was still very close. Considering the training cost of both methods, ours has a significant advantage of high-efficiency. Due to the accuracy loss under high compression rate, we show the trade-off between training cost and performance in Table 7.

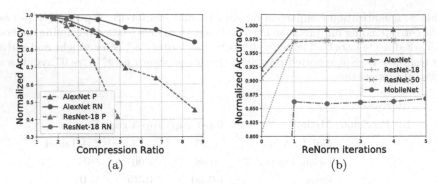

Fig. 3. (a) Normalized accuracy of the compressed networks under different compression rate. "1" indicates original network precision. The performance of direct pruning and re-normalized network are shown as "P" and "RN". We stop pruning when the accuracy drops to 0.85 (normalized). (b) Normalized accuracy changes over re-normalization iterations. 1K different images were used in each iteration

In our experiments, deeper networks, such as ResNet-50, and lightweight structures, such as MobileNet, obtain the same results. For 3× pruning, MobileNet achieves +53.82% Top-5 improvement to 78.43%, with 43% convolution layer and 7.3% fully connected layer parameters. ResNet-50 yields +6.92% Top-5 improvement to 90.00%, with 35% convolution layer and 10% fully connected layer parameters. The performance improvements are consistent in all our experiments, indicating that better performance becomes available by higher performance network.

Table 6. Model Sparsity Comparsion on AlexNet

Layer	$\frac{|w \neq 0|}{|w|}\%$ [14]	Total.%	$\frac{|w \neq 0|}{|w|}\%$ (Ours)	Total.%
Conv1	~84%	~37%	**63.1%**	48.6%
Conv2	~38%		42.1%	
Conv3	~35%		49.8%	
Conv4	~37%		50.0%	
Conv5	~37%		49.0%	
Fc1	~9%	~10%	**7.6%**	12.6%
Fc2	~9%		14.5%	
Fc3	~25%		52.4%	
10,000 iterations			**1** iteration	
120W labeled images			**1K unlabeled** images	

Table 7. The comparsion for different compressed models with the number of training epochs and the final compression rate. "*" indicates the not reported training epoch. Label-based retraining methods are marked as "+Label"

Methods	Top-1	Epochs	Compression	Parameters
Dynamic Surgery [11]	56.91	~140 + Label	**17.7×**	**3.48**M
Fastfood-32-AD [37]	**58.07**	* + Label	2×	32.8M
Fastfood-16-AD [37]	57.10	* + Label	3.7×	16.4M
Han et al. [14]	57.23	≥960 + Label	9×	6.7M
Naive Cut [14]	42.82	0	4.4×	13.8M
Ours	55.28	~ 0	6.73×	9.26M

5.3   Time Consumption

As listed in Table 8, most networks take only a few minutes to refine the distorted features, and as illustrated in Fig. 3(b), using more images has almost no contribution to the final accuracy. Setting batch size to 1K is just a trade-off between memory size and the sampling error of $\mathbb{E}(\hat{x})$ and $Var(\hat{x})$. By using large memory GPU, the whole process may take only a few seconds. This should lead to reduced time consumption of several orders of magnitudes. We believed that learning time speedup with limited unlabeled data is far more practical in real-world applications since slightly accuracy loss is unnoticeable to customers.

Table 8. Time consumption of feature recovery (1 batch = 1K images), evaluated on Intel Xeon CPU E5-2680 v4 @2.40 GHz x2

	AlexNet	ResNet-18	ResNet-50	MobileNet
1 batch	64s	172s	295s	197s

6   Conclusion

In this paper, we analyze the compression loss from Bayesian perspective and prove that batch normalization statistics misfit is one of the crucial reason for the performance loss. By using the proposed Quasi-Lloyd-Max and re-normalization, we quantize 4-bit networks to nearly full-precision level without retraining. In the experiments of network pruning, we further prove the robustness of this theorem. Our learning process is much more efficient than existing methods since considerably less data are required. In conclusion, we partly solve the real-world challenge of learning from limited unlabeled data to compress deep neural networks, which could be applied in a wide range of applications.

Acknowledgements. This work was supported in part by National Natural Science Foundation of China (No. 61332016), the Strategic Priority Research Program of Chinese Academy of Science, Grant No. XDBS01000000.

References

1. Burbidge, R., Trotter, M.W.B., Buxton, B.F., Holden, S.B.: Drug design by machine learning: support vector machines for pharmaceutical data analysis. Comput. Chem. **26**(1), 5–14 (2002)
2. Chen, W., Wilson, J.T., Tyree, S., Weinberger, K.Q., Chen, Y.: Compressing neural networks with the hashing trick. In: Bach, F.R., Blei, D.M. (eds.) Proceedings of the 32nd International Conference on Machine Learning, ICML 2015, Lille, France, 6–11 July 2015, pp. 2285–2294. JMLR.org (2015). http://jmlr.org/proceedings/papers/v37/chenc15.html
3. Chen, X., Kundu, K., Zhang, Z., Ma, H., Fidler, S., Urtasun, R.: Monocular 3D object detection for autonomous driving. In: 2016 IEEE Conference on Computer Vision and Pattern Recognition, CVPR 2016, Las Vegas, NV, USA, 27–30 June 2016, pp. 2147–2156. IEEE Computer Society (2016)
4. Cheng, J., Wu, J., Leng, C., Wang, Y., Hu, Q.: Quantized CNN: A unified approach to accelerate and compress convolutional networks. IEEE Trans. Neural Netw. Learn. Syst., 1–14 (2017)
5. Cheng, J., Wang, P., Li, G., Hu, Q., Lu, H.: Recent advances in efficient computation of deep convolutional neural networks. Front. IT EE **19**(1), 64–77 (2018). https://doi.org/10.1631/FITEE.1700789
6. Courbariaux, M., Bengio, Y.: BinaryNet: training deep neural networks with weights and activations constrained to +1 or -1. arXiv abs/1602.02830 (2016)
7. Courbariaux, M., Bengio, Y., David, J.: Binaryconnect: Training deep neural networks with binary weights during propagations. In: Cortes, C., Lawrence, N.D., Lee, D.D., Sugiyama, M., Garnett, R. (eds.) Advances in Neural Information Processing Systems 28: Annual Conference on Neural Information Processing Systems 2015, 7–12 December 2015, Montreal, Quebec, Canada, pp. 3123–3131. Curran Associates, Inc. (2015). http://papers.nips.cc/paper/5647-binaryconnect-training-deep-neural-networks-with-binary-weights-during-propagations
8. Dettmers, T.: 8-bit approximations for parallelism in deep learning. arXiv abs/1511.04561 (2015)
9. Djuric, U., Zadeh, G., Aldape, K., Diamandis, P.: Precision histology: how deep learning is poised to revitalize histomorphology for personalized cancer care. NPJ Precis. Oncol. **1**, 22 (2017)
10. Group, G.: gemmlowp: a small self-contained low-precision GEMM library (2016). https://github.com/google/gemmlowp
11. Guo, Y., Yao, A., Chen, Y.: Dynamic network surgery for efficient DNNs. In: Lee, D.D., Sugiyama, M., von Luxburg, U., Guyon, I., Garnett, R. (eds.) Advances in Neural Information Processing Systems 29: Annual Conference on Neural Information Processing Systems 2016, 5–10 December 2016, Barcelona, Spain, pp. 1379–1387. Curran Associates, Inc. (2016). http://papers.nips.cc/paper/6165-dynamic-network-surgery-for-efficient-dnns

12. Gupta, S., Agrawal, A., Gopalakrishnan, K., Narayanan, P.: Deep learning with limited numerical precision. In: Bach, F.R., Blei, D.M. (eds.) Proceedings of the 32nd International Conference on Machine Learning, ICML 2015, Lille, France, 6–11 July 2015, pp. 1737–1746. JMLR.org (2015). http://jmlr.org/proceedings/papers/v37/gupta15.html

13. Han, S., Mao, H., Dally, W.J.: Deep compression: compressing deep neural network with pruning, trained quantization and huffman coding. arXiv abs/1510.00149 (2015)

14. Han, S., Pool, J., Tran, J., Dally, W.J.: Learning both weights and connections for efficient neural network. In: Cortes, C., Lawrence, N.D., Lee, D.D., Sugiyama, M., Garnett, R. (eds.) Advances in Neural Information Processing Systems 28: Annual Conference on Neural Information Processing Systems 2015, 7–12 December 2015, Montreal, Quebec, Canada. pp. 1135–1143. Curran Associates, Inc. (2015). http://papers.nips.cc/paper/5784-learning-both-weights-and-connections-for-efficient-neural-network

15. He, K., Gkioxari, G., Dollár, P., Girshick, R.B.: Mask R-CNN. In: IEEE International Conference on Computer Vision, ICCV 2017, Venice, Italy, 22–29 October 2017. pp. 2980–2988. IEEE Computer Society (2017). https://doi.org/10.1109/ICCV.2017.322

16. He, K., Zhang, X., Ren, S., Sun, J.: Deep residual learning for image recognition. In: 2016 IEEE Conference on Computer Vision and Pattern Recognition, CVPR 2016, Las Vegas, NV, USA, 27–30 June 2016, pp. 770–778. IEEE Computer Society (2016)

17. Howard, A.G., et al.: MobileNets: efficient convolutional neural networks for mobile vision applications. arXiv abs/1704.04861 (2017)

18. Hu, Q., Wang, P., Cheng, J.: From hashing to CNNs: training binary weight networks via hashing. In: McIlraith, S.A., Weinberger, K.Q. (eds.) Proceedings of the Thirty-Second AAAI Conference on Artificial Intelligence, New Orleans, Louisiana, USA, 2–7 February 2018. AAAI Press (2018). https://www.aaai.org/ocs/index.php/AAAI/AAAI18/paper/view/16466

19. Hwang, K., Sung, W.: Fixed-point feedforward deep neural network design using weights +1, 0, and -1. In: 2014 IEEE Workshop on Signal Processing Systems, SiPS 2014, Belfast, United Kingdom, 20–22 October 2014, pp. 174–179. IEEE (2014), https://doi.org/10.1109/SiPS.2014.6986082

20. Hyvärinen, A., Oja, E.: Independent component analysis: algorithms and applications. Neural Netw. 13(4-5), 411–430 (2000). https://doi.org/10.1016/S0893-6080(00)00026-5

21. Ioffe, S., Szegedy, C.: Batch normalization: Accelerating deep network training by reducing internal covariate shift. In: Bach, F.R., Blei, D.M. (eds.) Proceedings of the 32nd International Conference on Machine Learning, ICML 2015, Lille, France, 6–11 July 2015. pp. 448–456. JMLR.org (2015). http://jmlr.org/proceedings/papers/v37/ioffe15.html

22. Jouppi, N.P., et al.: In-datacenter performance analysis of a tensor processing unit. arXiv abs/1704.04760 (2017)

23. Kim, Y., Park, E., Yoo, S., Choi, T., Yang, L., Shin, D.: Compression of deep convolutional neural networks for fast and low power mobile applications. arXiv abs/1511.06530 (2015)

24. Krizhevsky, A., Sutskever, I., Hinton, G.E.: Imagenet classification with deep convolutional neural networks. In: Bartlett, P.L., Pereira, F.C.N., Burges, C.J.C., Bottou, L., Weinberger, K.Q. (eds.) Advances in Neural Information Processing Systems 25: 26th Annual Conference on Neural Information Processing Systems 2012. Proceedings of a meeting held 3–6 December 2012, Lake Tahoe, Nevada, United States, pp. 1106–1114. Curran Associates, Inc. (2012). http://papers.nips.cc/paper/4824-imagenet-classification-with-deep-convolutional-neural-networks

25. Li, G., Li, F., Zhao, T., Cheng, J.: Block convolution: towards memory-efficient inference of large-scale CNNs on FPGA. In: 2018 Design, Automation & Test in Europe Conference & Exhibition, DATE 2018, Dresden, Germany, 19–23 March 2018, pp. 1163–1166. IEEE (2018)

26. Miyashita, D., Lee, E.H., Murmann, B.: Convolutional neural networks using logarithmic data representation. arXiv abs/1603.01025 (2016)

27. NVIDIA: 8-bit inference with tensorrt (2017). http://on-demand.gputechconf.com/gtc/2017/presentation/s7310-8-bit-inference-with-tensorrt.pdf

28. Park, E., Ahn, J., Yoo, S.: Weighted-entropy-based quantization for deep neural networks. In: 2017 IEEE Conference on Computer Vision and Pattern Recognition, CVPR 2017, Honolulu, HI, USA, 21–26 July 2017, pp. 7197–7205. IEEE Computer Society (2017)

29. Qiu, J., et al.: Going deeper with embedded FPGA platform for convolutional neural network. In: Chen, D., Greene, J.W. (eds.) Proceedings of the 2016 ACM/SIGDA International Symposium on Field-Programmable Gate Arrays, Monterey, CA, USA, 21–23 February 2016, pp. 26–35. ACM (2016)

30. Rastegari, M., Ordonez, V., Redmon, J., Farhadi, A.: XNOR-Net: ImageNet classification using binary convolutional neural networks. In: Leibe, B., Matas, J., Sebe, N., Welling, M. (eds.) ECCV 2016. LNCS, vol. 9908, pp. 525–542. Springer, Cham (2016). https://doi.org/10.1007/978-3-319-46493-0_32

31. Simonyan, K., Zisserman, A.: Very deep convolutional networks for large-scale image recognition. arXiv abs/1409.1556 (2014)

32. Szegedy, C., et al.: Going deeper with convolutions. In: IEEE Conference on Computer Vision and Pattern Recognition, CVPR 2015, Boston, MA, USA, 7–12 June 2015, pp. 1–9. IEEE Computer Society (2015)

33. Wang, P., Cheng, J.: Accelerating convolutional neural networks for mobile applications. In: Hanjalic, A., et al. (eds.) Proceedings of the 2016 ACM Conference on Multimedia Conference, MM 2016, Amsterdam, The Netherlands, 15–19 October 2016, pp. 541–545. ACM (2016)

34. Wang, P., Cheng, J.: Fixed-point factorized networks. In: 2017 IEEE Conference on Computer Vision and Pattern Recognition, CVPR 2017, Honolulu, HI, USA, 21–26 July 2017, pp. 3966–3974. IEEE Computer Society (2017)

35. Wang, P., Hu, Q., Fang, Z., Zhao, C., Cheng, J.: DeepSearch: a fast image search framework for mobile devices. TOMCCAP 14(1), 6:1–6:22 (2018)

36. Wu, J., Leng, C., Wang, Y., Hu, Q., Cheng, J.: Quantized convolutional neural networks for mobile devices. In: 2016 IEEE Conference on Computer Vision and Pattern Recognition, CVPR 2016, Las Vegas, NV, USA, 27–30 June 2016, pp. 4820–4828. IEEE Computer Society (2016)

37. Yang, Z., et al.: Deep fried convnets. In: 2015 IEEE International Conference on Computer Vision, ICCV 2015, Santiago, Chile, 7–13 December 2015, pp. 1476–1483. IEEE Computer Society (2015)

38. Zhang, X., Zou, J., Ming, X., He, K., Sun, J.: Efficient and accurate approximations of nonlinear convolutional networks. In: IEEE Conference on Computer Vision and Pattern Recognition, CVPR 2015, Boston, MA, USA, 7–12 June 2015, pp. 1984–1992. IEEE Computer Society (2015)
39. Zhou, A., Yao, A., Guo, Y., Xu, L., Chen, Y.: Incremental network quantization: towards lossless CNNs with low-precision weights. arXiv abs/1702.03044 (2017)
40. Zhou, S., Ni, Z., Zhou, X., Wen, H., Wu, Y., Zou, Y.: DoReFa-Net: training low bitwidth convolutional neural networks with low bitwidth gradients. arXiv abs/1606.06160 (2016)

Discriminative Region Proposal Adversarial Networks for High-Quality Image-to-Image Translation

Chao Wang(iD), Haiyong Zheng(✉)(iD), Zhibin Yu(iD), Ziqiang Zheng(iD),
Zhaorui Gu(iD), and Bing Zheng(iD)

Ocean University of China, Qingdao 266100, China
chaowangplus@gmail.com,
{zhenghaiyong,yuzhibin,guzhaorui,bingzh}@ouc.edu.cn,
zhengziqiang@stu.ouc.edu.cn
http://vision.ouc.edu.cn

Abstract. Image-to-image translation has been made much progress with embracing Generative Adversarial Networks (GANs). However, it's still very challenging for translation tasks that require high quality, especially at high-resolution and photorealism. In this paper, we present Discriminative Region Proposal Adversarial Networks (DRPAN) for high-quality image-to-image translation. We decompose the procedure of image-to-image translation task into three iterated steps, first is to generate an image with global structure but some local artifacts (via GAN), second is using our DRPnet to propose the most fake region from the generated image, and third is to implement "image inpainting" on the most fake region for more realistic result through a reviser, so that the system (DRPAN) can be gradually optimized to synthesize images with more attention on the most artifact local part. Experiments on a variety of image-to-image translation tasks and datasets validate that our method outperforms state-of-the-arts for producing high-quality translation results in terms of both human perceptual studies and automatic quantitative measures.

Keywords: GAN · DRPAN · Image-to-image translation

1 Introduction

From the aspect of human visual perception, why we consider a synthesized image as fake is often because it contains local artifacts. Although it looks like real at the first glance, we can still easily distinguish the fake from the real

Electronic supplementary material The online version of this chapter (https://doi.org/10.1007/978-3-030-01246-5_47) contains supplementary material, which is available to authorized users.

© Springer Nature Switzerland AG 2018
V. Ferrari et al. (Eds.): ECCV 2018, LNCS 11205, pp. 796–812, 2018.
https://doi.org/10.1007/978-3-030-01246-5_47

by gazing for only about 1000 ms [5]. Human being has the ability to draw a realistic scene from coarse structure to fine detail, that is, we usually get the global structure of a scene while focus on the detail of an object and understand how it is associated with surroundings. Under this intuition, our goal of this work is to develop an image-to-image translation system for high-quality image synthesis with clear structure and vivid details.

Many efforts have been made to develop an automatic image-to-image translation system. The straightforward approach was to optimize on pixel-wise space with L1 or L2 loss [9,23]. However, both of them suffer from blur problem. So some works added adversarial loss for generating more sharp images in both spatial and spectral dimensions [14]. Except for the GAN loss, perceptual loss has been used in image-to-image translation tasks, but it was limited to a pre-training deep model and the training datasets [37]. Although we have a variety of losses to evaluate the discrepancy between real image and generated image, using GAN for image-to-image translation still encounters with the artifacts and unsmooth color distribution problems, and it is even hard to generate high-resolution photo-realistic images because of the high dimension distribution [26].

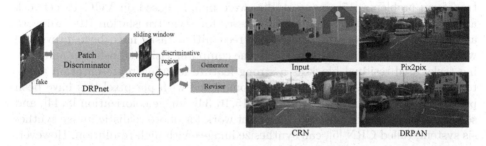

Fig. 1. Left: Our Discriminative Region Proposal network (DRPnet). **Right**: Synthesized samples compared with previous works on Cityscapes validation dataset [6]. The regions within red window show obvious artifacts or deformation. Our method can synthesize images with clear structure and vivid details. (Color figure online)

So, how could we solve this problem intuitively? We decompose the procedure of image-to-image translation task into three iterated steps, first is to generate an image with global structure but some local artifacts (via GAN), second is to propose the most fake region from the generated image (using our DRPnet shown in Fig. 1), and third is to implement "image inpainting" on the most fake region for more realistic result, so that the system (our DRPAN) can be gradually optimized to synthesize images with more attention on the most artifact local part. Inspired by this motivation, we develop a framework based on patch-wise discriminator to predict the discriminative score map and use sliding windows to find the most artificial region. Then the proposed discriminative region will be used to mask the corresponding real sample and output as "masked fake". Finally, we propose a reviser to distinguish the real from the masked fake for producing realistic details and serve as auxiliaries for generator to synthesize high-quality translation results. The reviser will critic on the fake image iteratively with different regions. We provide a weighted parameter to balance the contribution of the patch discriminator and our reviser for different levels of translation tasks. Using this proposed DRPAN, we can synthesize high-quality images with high-resolution and photo-reality details but less artifacts.

The main contribution of the study is threefold: first, we design the mechanism to explore patch-based discriminators for producing discriminative region; second, we propose the reviser for GANs to provide constructive revisions for generator which usually are missed by patch discriminator; third, we build a DRPAN model as a general-purpose solution for high-quality image-to-image translation tasks on different levels. The code of this paper is available at https://github. com/godisboy/DRPAN.

2   Related Works

Feed-Forward Based Approach. Deep Convolutional Neural Networks (CNNs) have been performed well on many computer vision tasks. For style transform problems [15], many studies were mainly based on VGG-16 network architecture [20] and used perceptual losses for style translation [10]. Network architectures that work well on object recognition tasks have been proved to work well on generative models, *e.g.*, some computer vision translation and editing tasks used residual block as a strong feature learning representation architecture [19,22]. Feed-forward CNNs accompanied with per-pixel loss have been presented for image super-resolution [9,15,16,34], image colorization [8,44], and semantic segmentation [4,23,31]. A recent work for photo realistic image synthesis system, called CRN [5], can synthesize images with high resolution. However, the images synthesized by feed-forward based approach usually become smooth too much rather than realistic, *i.e.*, not sharp enough in details. Besides, these methods are limited to be applied to other image-to-image translation tasks.

GAN Based Approach. GANs [11] introduced an unsupervised method to learn real data distribution. And DCGAN [29] firstly used CNNs to train generative adversarial networks which was hard to be deployed in other tasks before. Then, CNNs were extensively used for designing GAN architectures. Towards stable training of GAN, WGAN [1] replaced Jensen-Shannon divergence by Wasserstein distance as the optimization metric, and recently a variety of more stable alternatives have been proposed [12,18,28]. Wang and Gupta [38] combined structured GAN with style GAN to learn to generate natural indoor scenes. Reed *et al.* [30] used text as conditional input to synthesize images with semantic variation. Pathak *et al.* [27] proposed context encoders for image inpainting accompanied by adversarial loss. Li *et al.* [21] trained GANs with a combination of reconstruction loss, two adversarial losses and a semantic parsing loss for face completion. Nguyen *et al.* [25] presented Plus and Play Generative Networks for high-resolution and photo-realistic image generation with the resolution of 227×227 images. Isola *et al.* explored [14] conditional GANs for a variety of image-to-image translation problems. ID-CGAN [43] combined conditional GANs with perceptual loss for single image de-raining and de-snowing. Considering that the paired images are less and hard to collect, some works proposed unpaired or unsupervised translation frameworks [17,40,46]. But it limits to the similarity of translation between source domain A and target domain B.

PatchGAN was firstly used in neural style transfer with CNNs based on patch feature inputs [20]. Pix2pix [14] showed that a full ImageGAN does not show quality improvement compared with a low 70×70 patch discriminator which has less parameters and needs low computing resource. SimGAN [35] used patch based score map for real image synthesis tasks and mapped a full image to a probability map. Our method explores PatchGAN to a unified discriminative region proposal network model for deciding where and how to synthesize via a reviser. We show that this approach can improve translation results on high-quality, especially at high-resolution and photo-reality.

3   Method

Our image-to-image translation model, called Discriminative Region Proposal Adversarial Networks (DRPAN), is composed of three components: a generator, a discriminator, and a reviser. The discriminator explores PatchGAN to construct Discriminative Region Proposal network (DRPnet, see Fig. 1) to find and extract the discriminative region for producing masked fake sample, while the reviser adopts CNN to distinguish the real from the masked fake to provide constructive revisions for generator. The overall network architecture and data flow are illustrated in Fig. 2.

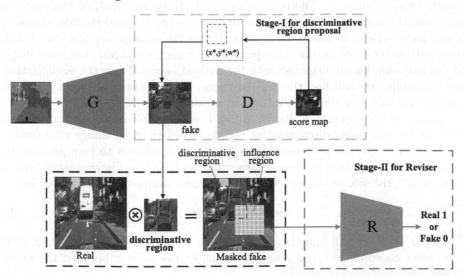

Fig. 2. The overall network architecture and data flow of our proposed Discriminative Region Proposal Adversarial Networks (DRPAN), which is composed of three components: a generator, a discriminator, and a reviser, and is a unified model for image-to-image translation tasks.

Figure 3 shows our process of how to improve the quality of synthesized image. It can be seen that, as our DRPAN continues to train, the discriminative region for masked fake images (right) varies so that the quality of synthesized images (left) are improved with brighter score map (the first and the last). Besides, although it is hard to distinguish the synthesized sample from the real sample after many epochs, our DRPAN can still revise the generator to optimize the synthesized result in the details for high quality.

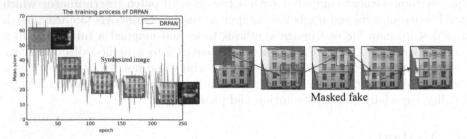

Fig. 3. The training process of DRPAN on facades dataset [36]. **Left**: The plotting curve shows mean value of score map on synthesized samples. **Right**: Step by step synthesis on different discriminative regions.

3.1 DRPAN

We first suggest that patch-based discriminators produce meaningful score maps, which may have applications beyond image synthesis. Figure 4 shows the output results of score map on different quality levels (fake and real) of images by a pre-trained PatchGAN. It can be seen that, the score maps of the fake samples, which have obvious artifacts and shape deformation on some regions, are almost dark with lower score on the corresponding regions; in contrast, the score maps of the real samples are brightest with the highest scores. From the visualization of score maps, we can find the darkest region for proposing the discriminative region that indicates the remarkable fake region.

Based on the observation shown in Fig. 4, we explore patch discriminator to DRPnet for producing discriminative region. Given an input image with resolution $w_i \times w_i$, and it is processed by the patch discriminator to be a probability score map with size $w_s \times w_s$. Suppose we want to obtain the discriminative region at $w^* \times w^*$, the size of sliding window w for score map can be calculated by

$$w = w^* \times w_s / w_i. \tag{1}$$

Then our DRPnet will find the discriminative square patch on score map with the center coordinates (x_c, y_c) and length w, so the scale τ between the input image and output score map is

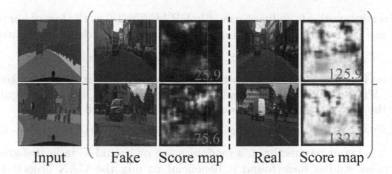

Input   Fake   Score map   Real   Score map

Fig. 4. The output results of score map on different quality levels (fake and real) of images by a pre-trained PatchGAN. The darkest regions on score maps mean the lowest quality, indicating that patch-based discriminators can be explored for discriminative region proposal.

$$\tau = \frac{w_i - w*}{w_s - w}. \tag{2}$$

The center coordinates (x_c^*, y_c^*) of discriminative region will be calculated by

$$\begin{cases} x_c^* = \tau \times x_c, \\ y_c^* = \tau \times y_c. \end{cases} \tag{3}$$

Finally, the discriminative region d_r produced by DRPnet can be expressed as

$$d_r = F_{\text{DRPnet}}(x_c^*, y_c^*, w^*). \tag{4}$$

Instead of only optimizing the independent local regions, we consider the relationship between fake discriminative region and real surrounding influence regions, so that it can connect the fake to the real for providing constructive revisions to generator. The influence region is defined as the region which is connected to the "most fake regions" and has semantic and spatial relationship with the content in it (e.g., the wheel is often below the car window). For this purpose, we mask the corresponding real sample using the fake discriminative region to make masked fake sample, and then design a reviser using CNN to distinguish real from masked fake to optimize the generator for synthesizing high-quality images. The reviser we proposed can also be used for other GANs to improve the quality of generated samples.

3.2 Objective

For image-to-image translation tasks, we not only want to generate the realistic samples, but also desire diversity with different conditional inputs. The original GANs suffer from instability and mode collapse problems [1,2]. So some recent works [1,12,28] improved the training of GAN. To stably train our DRPAN with high-diversity synthesis ability, we modify DRAGAN [18] as the loss of our reviser R, and use the original objective function for training Patch Discriminator.

$$\mathcal{L}_D(G, D_p) = \mathbb{E}_y[\log D_p(x, y)] + \mathbb{E}_{x,z}[\log(1 - D_p(x, G(x, z)))]. \tag{5}$$

For reviser R, to distinguish between the very similar real and masked fake $y_{\mathrm{mask}} = M(G(x, z))$ ($M(\cdot)$ represents the mask operation), we add a regularization to the loss of reviser as the penalty, which is expressed as

$$\mathcal{L}_R(G, R) = \mathbb{E}_y[\log R(x, y)] + \mathbb{E}_{x,z}[\log(1 - R(x, y_{\mathrm{mask}}))] + \alpha \mathbb{E}_{x,\delta}[\|\|\nabla_x R(x + \delta)\| - 1]^2, \tag{6}$$

where α is hyper parameter, δ is random noise on x, and ∇ indicates gradient.

Previous studies have found it beneficial to mix the GAN objective with a more traditional loss, such as L2 and L1 distance [14,35]. Considering that L1 distance encourages less blurring than L2 [14], we provide extra L1 loss for regularization on the whole input image and the local discriminative region to generator, which is defined as

$$\mathcal{L}_{L_1}(G) = \beta \mathbb{E}_{x,y,z}[\|y - G(x, z)\|_1] + \gamma \mathbb{E}_{d_r, y_r, z}[\|y_r - F_{\mathrm{DRPnet}}(G(x, z))\|_1], \tag{7}$$

where β and γ are hyper parameters, d_r is the discriminative region, and y_r represents the region on the real image corresponding to the discriminative region on the synthesized image. Then the total loss of generator can be expressed as

$$\mathcal{L}_G(G, D_p, R) = -\mathbb{E}_{x,z}[\log(1 - D_p(x, G(x, z)))] - \mathbb{E}_{x,z}[\log(1 - R(x, y_{\mathrm{mask}}))] + \mathcal{L}_{L_1}(G). \tag{8}$$

Our proposed model totally contains a generator G, a patch discriminator D_p for DRPnet, and a reviser R. G will be optimized by D_p, R and L_1. And our full objective function is

$$L(G, D_p, R) = (1 - \lambda)\mathcal{L}_D(G, D_p) + \lambda\mathcal{L}_R(G, R) + \mathcal{L}_{L_1}(G), \tag{9}$$

where λ is a hyper parameter to balance $\mathcal{L}_D$ and $\mathcal{L}_R$.

3.3   Network Architecture

For our generator, we use architecture based on [19] which has convincing power for single image super-resolution. We adopt convolution and fractionally convolution blocks for down and up sampling respectively, and 9 residual blocks [46] for task learning. Each layer uses Batch Normalization [13] and ReLU [24] as activation function. For patch discriminator, we mainly implement with 70×70 Patch-GAN [14,20]. The DRPAN reviser is a discriminator modified on DCGAN [29] that has a global view on the whole input. At the end of both discriminator and reviser, we adopt Sigmoid as activation function to output probability.

4   Experiments

To evaluate the performance of our proposed method on image-to-image translation tasks, we deploy a variety of experiments about different levels of translation tasks to compare our method with state-of-the-arts. And for different tasks, we also use different evaluation metrics including human perceptual studies and automatic quantitative measures.

4.1 Evaluation Metrics

Image Quality Evaluation. PSNR, SSIM [39] and VIF [33] are some of the most popular evaluation metrics in low-level computer vision tasks such as deblurring, dehazing and image restoration. So for de-raining and aerial to maps tasks, we adopt PSNR, SSIM, VIF and RECO [3] to qualify the performance of results.

Image Segmentation Evaluation Metrics. We use standard metrics from Cityscapes benchmark [6] to evaluate real to semantic labels task on Cityscapes dataset, including per-pixel accuracy, per-class accuracy, and Class IOU.

Amazon Mechanical Turk (AMT). AMT [14,40,46] is adopted in many tasks as a gold metric to evaluate how real the synthesized images, and we use it as evaluation metric for semantic labels to photo and maps to aerial tasks.

FCN-8s Score. The intuition of using an off-the-shelf classifiers for automatic quantitative measurement is that if the generated images are realistic, classifiers trained on real images will be able to classify the synthesized image correctly as well [14]. We use the FCN-8s score [23] to evaluate semantic labels to real task on Cityscapes dataset. The FCN-8s model trained on Cityscapes segmentation tasks is taken from [14].

4.2 Why DRPAN?

To study the influence of DRPAN for revising synthesis and different situations of loss between proposed region and real region. We set an experiments which start from a pre-trained PatchGAN and continue for several training pipelines: continue training with PatchGAN; continue training with PatchGAN and L1 loss of discriminative and real region; continue training with PatchGAN and reviser.

We argue that the PatchD is efficient to discover the most fake or real region (Fig. 4) from the image but is limited to improve these regions with fine details for that PatchD is hard to capture the high dimension distribution. In this case, we propose a DRPnet (explore the strength of PatchD) for discriminative region proposal and design a reviser to gradually remove visual artifacts, and thus reduce it to lower dimension estimation problem. This can be seen as a "top-down" procedure which is different from other gradually "bottom-up" image generation method [42]. Figure 5 shows the necessity of our proposed DRPAN for high-quality image-to-image translation, which illustrates that continue training PatchD is no help to reduce artifacts even with a L1 loss for balance, and DRPAN with only L1 loss can smooth the artifacts but not very sharp in details, while DRPAN with reviser exceeds the PatchD's performance with less visual artifacts. The combination of reviser and L1 loss can reduce these artifacts ignored by PatchD. We also find that fake-mask operation can improve the fluency of whole image in certain samples (*e.g.*, the connection between door and wall). So DRPAN with fake-mask is implemented in the following experiments.

Input	PatchD	PatchD	Fake region L1 loss	Fake region Reviser	Fake region Reviser+L1 loss	Fake-mask Reviser+L1 loss

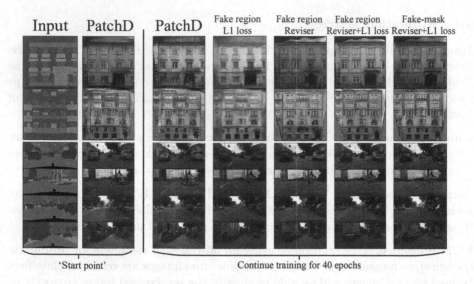

'Start point'   Continue training for 40 epochs

Fig. 5. Different methods with various losses produce different quality of results. The second column is the start point of comparison trained by PatchD, and all other models are continued trained for 40 epochs more. These experiments validate the necessary of our DRPnet for discriminative region proposal, our reviser for optimizing generator, and our fake-mask operation for improving synthesis.

4.3 Low Level Translation

We first apply our model on two low level translation tasks which are only related to the appearance translation of images, for example, in de-raining task we don't need change the content and texture of the input sample. So we set $\lambda = 1$ in Eq. 9 for image synthesis using only reviser.

Single Image De-raining. We trained and tested our DRPAN model on single image de-raining task using the procedure as same as [43], and evaluated the results by both qualitative and quantitative metrics. Figure 6 shows the qualitative results of our DRPAN with different sizes of discriminative region compared to ID-CGAN [43], and DRPAN outperforms ID-CGAN with not only more effective de-raining but also more vivid color and clear details. Table 1 reports the corresponding quantitative results evaluated by PSNR, SSIM, VIF, and RECO metrics, and the best results (in bold font) are achieved all by our DRPAN.

Bw to Color. We trained our DRPAN model for image colorization task on ImageNet [7], and tested on ImageNet val dataset with an example shown in Fig. 7. Our DRPAN can produce compelling colorization results compared with classification with class rebalancing [44]. In addition, we run AMT evaluation for colorization (Table 2). Our method fooled participants on 27.8% which is competitive with the full method from [44].

Input | ID-CGAN | DRPAN(16) | DRPAN(32) | DRPAN(64) | DRPAN(128)

Fig. 6. Example results of our DRPAN with different sizes of discriminative region compared to ID-CGAN [43] on single image de-raining task.

Table 1. Quantitative comparison of our DRPAN (with different sizes of discriminative region) with ID-CGAN [43] and PAN [37] on image de-raining. DRPAN performs best (in bold font) evaluated by PSNR, SSIM, VIF, and RECO metrics

Method metrics	L2+ CGAN	ID-CGAN [43]	PAN [37]	DRPAN (w/o mask)	DRPAN (128)	DRPAN (64)	DRPAN (32)	DRPAN (16)
PSNR	22.19	22.91	23.35	25.51	25.87	25.76	25.92	**26.20**
SSIM	0.8083	0.8198	0.8303	0.8688	0.8714	0.8765	**0.8788**	0.8712
VIF	0.3640	0.3885	0.4050	0.4923	0.4818	0.4962	**0.5001**	0.4783
RECO	–	–	–	0.9670	1.0770	**1.1072**	1.1067	1.0875

4.4   Real to Abstract Translation

We then implement our proposed DRPAN on two tasks of real to abstract translation which requires many-to-one abstraction ability.

Real to Semantic Labels. For real to semantic labels task, we tested our DRPAN model on two of the most used datasets: Cityscapes and facades. Figure 8 shows the qualitative results of our DRPAN compared to Pix2pix [14] on Cityscapes dataset for translating real to semantic labels, and DRPAN can synthesize more realistic results that are closer to ground truth than Pix2pix, meanwhile, the quantitative results in Table 3 can also tell this in terms of per-pixel accuracy, per-class accuracy, and Class IOU.

Table 2. AMT "real vs fake" test on colorization

Method	% Turkers labeled real
L2 regression	23.4%
Classification	**29.7%**
DRPAN	27.8%

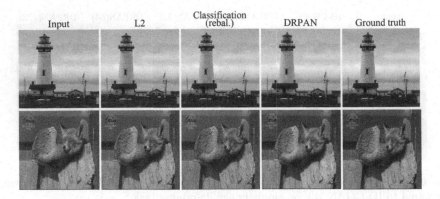

Fig. 7. Example results of our DRPAN compared to L2 regression [44] and Classification (rebal.) [44] on image colorization task.

Aerial to Maps. We also applied our DRPAN on aerial photo to maps task, and the experiment was implemented using paired images with 512 × 512 resolution [14]. The top row of Fig. 9 shows the qualitative results of our DRPAN compared to Pix2pix [14], indicating that our DRPAN can correctly translate the motorway on aerial photo into the orange line on the map while Pix2pix can't.

4.5 Abstract to Real Translation

Besides, we also demonstrate our proposed DRPAN on several abstract to real tasks that can translate one to many: semantic labels to photo, maps to aerial, edge to real, and sketch to real.

Semantic Labels to Real. For semantic labels to real task, the translation model aims to synthesize real world images from semantic labels. CGAN based works fail to capture the details in the real world and suffer from deformation and blur problems. CNN based methods such as CRN can synthesize high-resolution

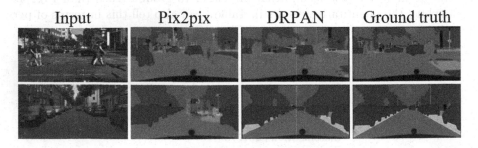

Fig. 8. Example results of our DRPAN compared to Pix2pix [14] on real to semantic labels task.

| Input | Pix2pix | DRPAN | Ground truth |

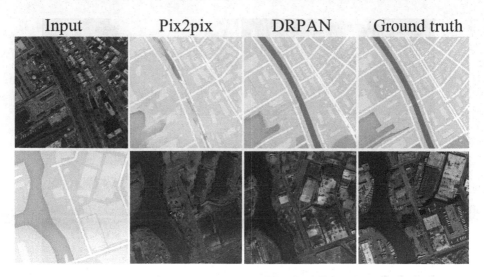

Fig. 9. Example results of our DRPAN compared to Pix2pix [14] on aerial to maps (top) and maps to aerial (bottom) tasks.

but smooth rather than realistic results. Figure 10 shows qualitative comparison of results, from which it can be seen that our DRPAN can synthesize the most realistic results with high-quality (more clear and less distorted while high resolution) compared to Pix2pix [14] and CRN [5].

The evaluation of GAN is still a challenging problem. Many works [14,32, 38,44] used off-the-shelf classifiers as automatic measures of synthesized images. Table 4 reports performance evaluation on segmentation of FCN-8s model, and our DRPAN exceeds Pix2pix [14] by 10% on per-pixel accuracy and also achieves highest performance on per-class accuracy and Class IOU.

Maps to Aerial. As opposed to aerial to maps task, we also tested our DRPAN on maps to aerial task, and the qualitative results are shown in the bottom row of Fig. 9, which clearly demonstrates that our DRPAN can synthesize higher quality aerial photos than Pix2pix [14].

Human Perceptual Validation. We assess the performance of abstract to real on semantic labels to photo and maps to aerial by AMT. For fake against real study, we followed the perceptual study protocol from [14], and collected data of each algorithm from 30 participants. Each participant has 1000 ms to look one sample. We also compared how realistic the synthesized images between different algorithms. Table 5 illustrates that images synthesized by DRPAN are ranked more realistic than state-of-the-arts (DRPAN 18.2% > CRN 9.4% > StackGAN-like 6.8% > Pix2pix 5.3%), moreover, compared to Pix2pix [14], StackGAN-like [42] and CRN [5], images synthesized by DRPAN are ranked more realistic by 91.2%, 84.6% and 75.7% respectively. Table 6 reports the comparison on maps to aerial task and our DRPAN fooled participants on 39.0% over 18.7% of Pix2pix and 26.8% of CycleGAN [46] respectively.

Fig. 10. Example results of our DRPAN compared to Pix2pix [14] and CRN [5] on semantic labels to real task with 512 × 512 resolution.

Table 3. Quantitative comparison of our DRPAN with Pix2pix [14] on real to semantic labels task (Cityscapes dataset)

Model	Per-pixel acc.	Per-class acc.	Class IOU
L1+U-Net [14]	0.86	0.42	0.35
Pix2pix [14]	0.83	0.36	0.29
DRPAN (w/o fake-mask)	**0.86**	**0.48**	**0.39**
DRPAN	**0.88**	**0.52**	**0.43**

Table 4. Quantitative comparison of our DRPAN with other models on semantic labels to real task (Cityscapes dataset) by FCN-8s score

Model	Per-pixel acc.	Per-class acc.	Class IOU
L1+CGAN [14]	0.63	0.21	0.16
CRN	0.69	0.21	**0.20**
DRPAN (w/o fake-mask)	**0.72**	**0.22**	0.19
DRPAN	**0.73**	**0.24**	0.19
Ground truth	0.80	0.26	0.21

Edges to Real and Sketch to Real. For the edge to real and sketch to real tasks, previous works often encounter with two problems [14]: one is that it's easy to generate artifacts and artificial color distribution in regions when the input

Table 5. AMT real vs. fake results test on Cityscapes semantic labels to photo task

Model	% Turkers labeled real
Pix2pix [14]	5.3%
StackGAN-like [42]	6.8%
CRN [5]	9.4%
DRPAN (w/o fake-mask)	**14.3%**
DRPAN	**18.2%**
	% Turkers labeled more realistic
DRPAN vs. Pix2pix [14]	**91.2%**
DRPAN vs. StackGAN-like	**84.6%**
DRPAN vs. CRN [5]	**75.7%**

Table 6. AMT real vs. fake results test on maps to aerial task

Model	% Turkers labeled real
Pix2pix [14]	25.2%
DRPAN (w/o fake-mask)	31.7%
DRPAN	**33.4%**

such as edge is sparse; the other is that it's difficult to deal with unusual inputs like sketch. We tested our DRPAN model on UT Zappos50k dataset [41] and edge to handbag dataset [45]. Figure 11 shows that our model can also handle these two problems well.

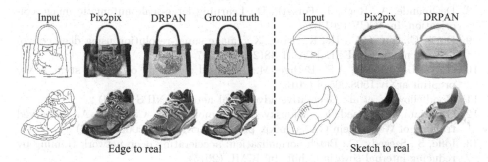

Fig. 11. Example results of our DRPAN compared to Pix2pix [14] on edge to real (left) and sketch to real (right) tasks.

5   Conclusions

We propose Discriminative Region Proposal Adversarial Networks (DRPAN) towards high-resolution and photo-reality image-to-image translation. Human perceptual studies and automatic quantitative measures validate the performance of our proposed DRPAN against the state-of-the-arts for synthesizing high-quality results. We hope it can be explored for discriminative feature learning and other computer vision tasks in the future.

Acknowledgments. This work was supported by the National Natural Science Foundation of China under Grants 61771440 and 41776113, and Qingdao Municipal Science and Technology Program under Grant 17-1-1-5-jch.

References

1. Arjovsky, M., Chintala, S., Bottou, L.: Wasserstein GAN. In: ICML (2017)
2. Arora, S., Ge, R., Liang, Y., Ma, T., Zhang, Y.: Generalization and equilibrium in generative adversarial nets (GANs). arXiv preprint arXiv:1703.00573 (2017)
3. Baroncini, V., Capodiferro, L., Di Claudio, E.D., Jacovitti, G.: The polar edge coherence: a quasi blind metric for video quality assessment. In: ESPC (2009)
4. Chen, L., Papandreou, G., Kokkinos, I., Murphy, K., Yuille, A.L.: Semantic image segmentation with deep convolutional nets and fully connected CRFs. In: ICLR (2015)
5. Chen, Q., Koltun, V.: Photographic image synthesis with cascaded refinement networks. In: ICCV (2017)
6. Cordts, M., et al.: The Cityscapes dataset for semantic urban scene understanding. In: CVPR (2016)
7. Deng, J., Dong, W., Socher, R., Li, L.J., Li, K., Fei-Fei, L.: ImageNet: a large-scale hierarchical image database. In: CVPR (2009)
8. Deshpande, A., Rock, J., Forsyth, D.: Learning large-scale automatic image colorization. In: ICCV (2015)
9. Dong, C., Loy, C.C., He, K., Tang, X.: Image super-resolution using deep convolutional networks. IEEE TPAMI **38**(2), 295–307 (2016)
10. Gatys, L.A., Ecker, A.S., Bethge, M.: A neural algorithm of artistic style. arXiv preprint arXiv:1508.06576 (2015)
11. Goodfellow, I., et al.: Generative adversarial nets. In: NIPS (2014)
12. Gulrajani, I., Ahmed, F., Arjovsky, M., Dumoulin, V., Courville, A.: Improved training of Wasserstein GANs. arXiv preprint arXiv:1704.00028 (2017)
13. Ioffe, S., Szegedy, C.: Batch normalization: accelerating deep network training by reducing internal covariate shift. In: ICML (2015)
14. Isola, P., Zhu, J.Y., Zhou, T., Efros, A.A.: Image-to-image translation with conditional adversarial networks. In: CVPR (2017)
15. Johnson, J., Alahi, A., Fei-Fei, L.: Perceptual losses for real-time style transfer and super-resolution. In: Leibe, B., Matas, J., Sebe, N., Welling, M. (eds.) ECCV 2016. LNCS, vol. 9906, pp. 694–711. Springer, Cham (2016). https://doi.org/10.1007/978-3-319-46475-6_43
16. Kim, J., Lee, J.K., Lee, K.M.: Accurate image super-resolution using very deep convolutional networks. In: CVPR (2016)

17. Kim, T., Cha, M., Kim, H., Lee, J., Kim, J.: Learning to discover cross-domain relations with generative adversarial networks. arXiv preprint arXiv:1703.05192 (2017)

18. Kodali, N., Abernethy, J., Hays, J., Kira, Z.: How to train your DRAGAN. arXiv preprint arXiv:1705.07215 (2017)

19. Ledig, C., et al.: Photo-realistic single image super-resolution using a generative adversarial network. In: CVPR (2017)

20. Li, C., Wand, M.: Precomputed real-time texture synthesis with Markovian generative adversarial networks. In: Leibe, B., Matas, J., Sebe, N., Welling, M. (eds.) ECCV 2016. LNCS, vol. 9907, pp. 702–716. Springer, Cham (2016). https://doi.org/10.1007/978-3-319-46487-9_43

21. Li, Y., Liu, S., Yang, J., Yang, M.H.: Generative face completion. In: CVPR (2017)

22. Lin, G., Milan, A., Shen, C., Reid, I.: RefineNet: multi-path refinement networks for high-resolution semantic segmentation. In: CVPR (2017)

23. Long, J., Shelhamer, E., Darrell, T.: Fully convolutional networks for semantic segmentation. In: CVPR (2015)

24. Nair, V., Hinton, G.E.: Rectified linear units improve restricted Boltzmann machines. In: ICML (2010)

25. Nguyen, A., Clune, J., Bengio, Y., Dosovitskiy, A., Yosinski, J.: Plug & play generative networks: conditional iterative generation of images in latent space. In: CVPR (2017)

26. Odena, A., Olah, C., Shlens, J.: Conditional image synthesis with auxiliary classifier GANs. In: ICLR (2016)

27. Pathak, D., Krahenbuhl, P., Donahue, J., Darrell, T., Efros, A.A.: Context encoders: feature learning by inpainting. In: CVPR (2016)

28. Qi, G.J.: Loss-sensitive generative adversarial networks on Lipschitz densities. arXiv preprint arXiv:1701.06264 (2017)

29. Radford, A., Metz, L., Chintala, S.: Unsupervised representation learning with deep convolutional generative adversarial networks. In: ICLR (2016)

30. Reed, S., Akata, Z., Yan, X., Logeswaran, L., Schiele, B., Lee, H.: Generative adversarial text to image synthesis. In: ICML (2016)

31. Ronneberger, O., Fischer, P., Brox, T.: U-Net: convolutional networks for biomedical image segmentation. In: Navab, N., Hornegger, J., Wells, W.M., Frangi, A.F. (eds.) MICCAI 2015. LNCS, vol. 9351, pp. 234–241. Springer, Cham (2015). https://doi.org/10.1007/978-3-319-24574-4_28

32. Salimans, T., Goodfellow, I., Zaremba, W., Cheung, V., Radford, A., Chen, X.: Improved techniques for training GANs. In: NIPS (2016)

33. Sheikh, H.R., Bovik, A.C.: Image information and visual quality. IEEE TIP **15**(2), 430–444 (2006)

34. Shi, W., et al.: Real-time single image and video super-resolution using an efficient sub-pixel convolutional neural network. In: CVPR (2016)

35. Shrivastava, A., Pfister, T., Tuzel, O., Susskind, J., Wang, W., Webb, R.: Learning from simulated and unsupervised images through adversarial training. In: CVPR (2017)

36. Tyleček, R., Šára, R.: Spatial pattern templates for recognition of objects with regular structure. In: Weickert, J., Hein, M., Schiele, B. (eds.) GCPR 2013. LNCS, vol. 8142, pp. 364–374. Springer, Heidelberg (2013). https://doi.org/10.1007/978-3-642-40602-7_39

37. Wang, C., Xu, C., Wang, C., Tao, D.: Perceptual adversarial networks for image-to-image transformation. In: IJCAI (2017)

38. Wang, X., Gupta, A.: Generative image modeling using style and structure adversarial networks. In: Leibe, B., Matas, J., Sebe, N., Welling, M. (eds.) ECCV 2016. LNCS, vol. 9908, pp. 318–335. Springer, Cham (2016). https://doi.org/10.1007/978-3-319-46493-0_20
39. Wang, Z., Bovik, A.C., Sheikh, H.R., Simoncelli, E.P.: Image quality assessment: from error visibility to structural similarity. IEEE TIP **13**(4), 600–612 (2004)
40. Yi, Z., Zhang, H., Tan, P., Gong, M.: DualGAN: unsupervised dual learning for image-to-image translation. In: ICCV (2017)
41. Yu, A., Grauman, K.: Fine-grained visual comparisons with local learning. In: CVPR (2014)
42. Zhang, H., et al.: StackGAN: text to photo-realistic image synthesis with stacked generative adversarial networks. In: ICCV (2017)
43. Zhang, H., Sindagi, V., Patel, V.M.: Image de-raining using a conditional generative adversarial network. In: CVPR (2017)
44. Zhang, R., Isola, P., Efros, A.A.: Colorful image colorization. In: Leibe, B., Matas, J., Sebe, N., Welling, M. (eds.) ECCV 2016. LNCS, vol. 9907, pp. 649–666. Springer, Cham (2016). https://doi.org/10.1007/978-3-319-46487-9_40
45. Zhu, J.-Y., Krähenbühl, P., Shechtman, E., Efros, A.A.: Generative visual manipulation on the natural image manifold. In: Leibe, B., Matas, J., Sebe, N., Welling, M. (eds.) ECCV 2016. LNCS, vol. 9909, pp. 597–613. Springer, Cham (2016). https://doi.org/10.1007/978-3-319-46454-1_36
46. Zhu, J., Park, T., Isola, P., Efros, A.A.: Unpaired image-to-image translation using cycle-consistent adversarial networks. In: ICCV (2017)

Unsupervised Video Object Segmentation Using Motion Saliency-Guided Spatio-Temporal Propagation

Yuan-Ting Hu[1]([⊠]), Jia-Bin Huang[2], and Alexander G. Schwing[1]

[1] University of Illinois at Urbana-Champaign, Champaign, USA
{ythu2,aschwing}@illinois.edu
[2] Virginia Tech, Blacksburg, USA
jbhuang@vt.edu

Abstract. Unsupervised video segmentation plays an important role in a wide variety of applications from object identification to compression. However, to date, fast motion, motion blur and occlusions pose significant challenges. To address these challenges for unsupervised video segmentation, we develop a novel saliency estimation technique as well as a novel neighborhood graph, based on optical flow and edge cues. Our approach leads to significantly better initial foreground-background estimates and their robust as well as accurate diffusion across time. We evaluate our proposed algorithm on the challenging DAVIS, SegTrack v2 and FBMS-59 datasets. Despite the usage of only a standard edge detector trained on 200 images, our method achieves state-of-the-art results outperforming deep learning based methods in the unsupervised setting. We even demonstrate competitive results comparable to deep learning based methods in the semi-supervised setting on the DAVIS dataset.

1 Introduction

Unsupervised foreground-background video object segmentation of complex scenes is a challenging problem which has many applications in areas such as object identification, security, and video compression. It is therefore not surprising that many efforts have been devoted to developing efficient techniques that are able to effectively separate foreground from background, even in complex videos.

In complex videos, cluttered backgrounds, deforming shapes, and fast motion are major challenges. In addition, in the unsupervised setting, algorithms have to automatically discover foreground regions in the video. To this end, classical video object segmentation techniques [6,9,11,18,22,23,46,50,58] often

---

Electronic supplementary material The online version of this chapter (https://doi.org/10.1007/978-3-030-01246-5_48) contains supplementary material, which is available to authorized users.

© Springer Nature Switzerland AG 2018
V. Ferrari et al. (Eds.): ECCV 2018, LNCS 11205, pp. 813–830, 2018.
https://doi.org/10.1007/978-3-030-01246-5_48

Fig. 1. Video object segmentation in challenging scenarios. Given an input video, our algorithm produces accurate segmentation of the foreground object *without any manual annotations*. Our method is capable of handling unconstrained videos that span a wide variety of situations including occlusion (BUS), non-ridge deformation (DANCE-JUMP), and dynamic background (KITE-SURF).

assume rigid background motion models and incorporate a scene prior, two assumptions which are restrictive in practice. Trajectory based methods, such as [5, 8, 12, 15, 45], require selection of clusters or a matrix rank, which may not be intuitive. Graphical model based approaches [2, 16, 24, 51, 52, 54] estimate the foreground regions using a probabilistic formulation. However, for computational efficiency, the constructed graph usually contains only local connections, both spatially and temporally, reducing the ability to consider long-term spatial and temporal coherence patterns. To address this concern, diffusion based methods [35], *e.g.*, [13, 55], propagate an initial foreground-background estimate more globally. While promising results are shown, diffusion based formulations rely heavily on the initialization as well as an accurate neighborhood graph encoding the semantic distance between pixels or superpixels.

Therefore, in this paper, we develop (1) a new initialization technique and (2) a more robust neighborhood graph. Our initialization technique is based on the intuition that the optical flow on the boundary of an image differs significantly from the moving direction of the object of interest. Our robust neighborhood graph is built upon accurate edge detection and flow cues.

We highlight the performance of our proposed approach in Fig. 1 using three challenging video sequences. Note the fine details that our approach is able to segment despite the fact that our method is unsupervised. Due to accurate initial estimates and a more consistent neighborhood graph, we found our method to be robust to different parameter choices. Quantitatively, our initialization technique and neighborhood graph result in significant improvements for unsupervised foreground-background video segmentation when compared to the current state-of-the-art. On the recently released DAVIS dataset [42], our unsupervised non-deep learning based segmentation technique outperforms current state-of-the-art methods by more than 1.3% in the unsupervised setting. Our method also achieves competitive performance compared with deep net based techniques in the semi-supervised setting.

2   Related Work

The past decade has seen the rapid development in video object segmentation [17,19,20,25,31–33,38,40,44,51,52,57]. Given different degrees of human interaction, these methods model inter- and intra-frame relationship of the pixels or superpixels to determine the foreground-background labeling of the observed scene. Subsequently, we classify the literature into four areas based on the degree of human involvement and discuss the relationship between video object and video motion segmentation.

Unsupervised Video Object Segmentation: Fully automatic approaches for video object segmentation have been explored recently [7,13,30,31,39,40,57,59], and no manual annotation is required in this setting. Unsupervised foreground segmentation discovery can be achieved by motion analysis [13,40], trajectory clustering [39], or object proposal ranking [31,57]. Our approach computes motion saliency in a given video based on boundary similarity of motion cues. In contrast, Faktor and Irani [13] find motion salient regions by extracting dominant motion. Subsequently they obtain the saliency scores by computing the motion difference with respect to the detected dominant motion. Papazoglou and Ferrari [40] identify salient regions by finding the motion boundary based on optical flow and computing inside-outside maps to detect the object of interest.

Recently, deep learning based methods [25,48,49] were also used to address unsupervised video segmentation. Although these methods do not require the ground truth of the first frame of the video (unsupervised as opposed to semi-supervised), they need a sufficient amount of labeled data to train the models. In contrast, our approach works effectively in the unsupervised setting and does not require training data beyond the one used to obtain an accurate edge detector.

Tracking-Based Video Object Segmentation: In this setting, the user annotation is reduced to only one mask for the first frame of the video [4,17,24,36,41, 51,52]. These approaches track the foreground object and propagate the segmentation results to successive frames by incorporating cues such as motion [51,52] and supervoxel consistency [24]. Again, our approach differs in that we don't consider any human labels.

Interactive Video Object Segmentation: Interactive video object segmentation allows users to annotate the foreground segments in key frames to generate impressive results by propagating the user-specified masks across the entire video [14,24,34,38,44]. Price *et al.* [44] further combine multiple features, of which the weights are automatically selected and learned from user inputs. Fan *et al.* [14] tackle interactive segmentation by enabling bi-directional propagation of the masks between non-successive frames. Our approach differs in that the proposed method does not require any human interaction.

Video Motion Segmentation: Video motion segmentation [5] aims to segment a video based on motion cues, while video object segmentation aims at segmenting the foreground based on objects. The objective function differs: for motion segmentation, clustering based methods [5,29,32,39] are predominant and group point trajectories. In contrast, for video object segmentation, a binary labeling formulation is typically applied as we show next by describing our approach.

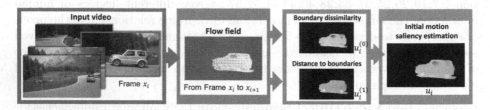

Fig. 2. Motion saliency estimation. Given an input video, we compute the flow field for each frame. We detect the saliency score based on the flow vector by calculating a boundary dissimilarity map $u^{(0)}$ and a distance map $u^{(1)}$ indicating the distance of each pixel to the boundaries. We use minimum barrier distance to measure the distance. The motion saliency estimation is computed by averaging the boundary dissimilarity map and the distance map.

3   Unsupervised Video Object Segmentation

The two most important ingredients for unsupervised video object segmentation are the initial saliency estimate as well as a good assessment of the neighborhood relation of pixels or superpixels. For initial saliency prediction in unsupervised video object segmentation we describe a novel method comparing the motion at a pixel to the boundary motion. Intuitively, boundary pixels largely correspond to background and pixels with a similar motion are likely background too. To construct a meaningful neighborhood relation between pixels we assess flow and appearance cues. We provide details for both contributions after describing an overview of our unsupervised video object segmentation approach.

Method Overview: Our method uses a diffusion mechanism for unsupervised video segmentation. Hence, the approach distributes an initial foreground saliency estimate over the F frames x_i, $i \in \{1, \ldots, F\}$, of a video $x = (x_1, \ldots, x_F)$. To this end, we partition each frame into a set of nodes using superpixels, and estimate and encode their semantic relationship within and across frames using a global neighborhood graph. Specifically, we represent the global neighborhood graph by a weighted row-stochastic adjacency matrix

$G \in \mathbb{R}^{N \times N}$, where N is the total number of nodes in the video. Diffusion of the initial foreground saliency estimates $v^0 \in \mathbb{R}^N$ for each node is performed by repeated matrix multiplication of the current node estimate with the adjacency matrix G, i.e., for the t-th diffusion step $v^t = Gv^{t-1}$.

With the adjacency matrix G and initialization v^0 being the only inputs to the algorithm, it is obvious that they are of crucial importance for diffusion based unsupervised video segmentation. We focus on both points in the following and develop first a new saliency estimation of v^0 before discussing construction of the neighborhood graph G.

3.1 Saliency Estimation

For unsupervised video object segmentation, we propose to estimate the motion saliency by leveraging a boundary condition. Since we are dealing with video, motion is one of the most important cues for identifying moving foreground objects. In general, the motion of the foreground object differs from background motion. But importantly, the background region is often connected to the boundary of the image. While the latter assumption is commonly employed for *image saliency* detection, it has not been exploited for *motion saliency* estimation. To obtain the initial saliency estimate v^0 defined over superpixels, we average the pixelwise motion saliency results u over the spatial support of each superpixel. We subsequently describe our developed procedure for foreground saliency estimation, taking advantage of the boundary condition. The proposed motion saliency detection is summarized in Fig. 2.

Conventional motion saliency estimation techniques for video object segmentation are based on either background subtraction [6], trajectory clustering [5], or motion separation [13]. Background subtraction techniques typically assume a static camera, which is not applicable for complex videos. Trajectory clustering groups points with similar trajectories, which is sensitive to non-rigid transformation. Motion separation detects background by finding the dominant motion and subsequently calculates the difference in magnitude and/or orientation between the motion at each pixel, and the dominant motion. The larger the difference, the more likely the pixel to be foreground. Again, complex motion poses challenges, making it hard to separate foreground from background.

In contrast, we propose to use the boundary condition that is commonly used for *image saliency* detection [53,56] to support *motion saliency* estimation for unsupervised video segmentation. Our approach is based on the intuition that the background region is connected to image boundaries in some way. Therefore we calculate a distance metric for every pixel to the boundary. Compared to the aforementioned techniques, we will show that our method can better deal with complex, non-rigid motion.

We use u to denote the foreground motion saliency of the video. Moreover, u_i and $u_i(p_i)$ denote the foreground saliency for frame i and for pixel p_i in frame i respectively. To compute the motion saliency estimate, we treat every frame x_i, $i \in \{1, \ldots, F\}$ independently. Given a frame x_i, let $x_i(p_i)$ refer to the intensity values of pixel p_i, and let $f_i(p_i) \in \mathbb{R}^2$ denote the optical flow vector measuring the motion of the object illustrated at pixel p_i between frame i and frame $i + 1$. In addition, let $\mathscr{B}_i$ denote the set of boundary pixels of frame i.

We compute the foreground motion saliency u_i of frame i based on two terms $u_i^{(0)}$ and $u_i^{(1)}$, each of which measures a distance between any pixel p_i of the i-th frame and the boundary $\mathscr{B}_i$. For the first distance $u_i^{(0)}$, we compute the smallest flow direction difference observed between a pixel p_i and common flow directions on the boundary. For the second distance $u_i^{(1)}$, we measure the smallest barrier distance between pixel p_i and boundary pixels. Both of the terms capture the similarity between the motion at pixel p_i and the background motion. Subsequently, we explain both terms in greater detail.

Computing Flow Direction Difference: More formally, to compute $u_i^{(0)}(p_i)$, the flow direction difference between pixel p_i in frame i and common flow directions on the boundary $\mathscr{B}_i$ of frame i, we first cluster the boundary flow directions into a set of K clusters $k \in \{1, \dots, K\}$ using k-means. We subsume the cluster centers in the set

$$\mathscr{K}_i = \left\{ \mu_{i,k} : \mu_{i,k} = \arg\min_{\hat{\mu}_{i,k}} \min_{r \in \{0,1\}^{|\mathscr{B}_i| K}} \frac{1}{2} \sum_{p_i \in \mathscr{B}_{i,k}} r_{p_i,k} \|f_i(p_i) - \hat{\mu}_{i,k}\|_2^2 \right\}. \qquad (1)$$

Hereby, $r_{p_i,k} \in \{0,1\}$ is an indicator variable which assigns pixel p_i to cluster k, and r is the concatenation of all those indicator variables. We update $\mathscr{K}_i$ to only contain centers with more than $1/6$ of the boundary pixels assigned. Given those cluster centers, we then obtain a first distance measure capturing the difference of flow between pixel p_i in frame i and the major flow directions observed at the boundary of frame i via

$$u_i^{(0)}(p_i) = \min_{\mu_{i,k} \in \mathscr{K}_i} \|f_i(p_i) - \mu_{i,k}\|_2^2. \qquad (2)$$

Computing Smallest Barrier Distance: When computing the smallest barrier distance $D_{bd,i}$ between pixel p_i in frame i and boundary pixels, *i.e.*, to obtain

$$u_i^{(1)}(p_i) = \min_{s \in \mathscr{B}_i} D_{bd,i}(p_i, s), \qquad (3)$$

we use the following barrier distance:

$$D_{bd,i}(p_i, s) = \max_{e \in \Pi_{i,p_i,s}} w_i(e) - \min_{e \in \Pi_{i,p_i,s}} w_i(e). \qquad (4)$$

Hereby, $\Pi_{i,p_i,s}$ denotes the path, *i.e.*, a set of edges connecting pixel p_i to boundary pixel $s \in \mathscr{B}_i$, obtained by computing a minimum spanning tree on frame i. The edge weights $w_i(e)$, which are used to compute both the minimum spanning tree as well as the barrier distance given in Eq. (4), are obtained as the maximum flow direction difference between two neighboring pixels, *i.e.*, $w_i(e) = \max\{f_i(p_i) - f_i(q_i)\} \in \mathbb{R}$ where the max is taken across the two components of $f_i(p_i) - f_i(q_i) \in \mathbb{R}^2$. Note that $e = (p_i, q_i)$ refers to an edge connecting the two pixels p_i and q_i. To compute the minimum spanning tree we use the classical 4-connected neighborhood. Intuitively, we compute the barrier distance between 2 points as the difference between the maximum edge weight and minimum edge weight on the path of the minimum spanning tree between the 2 points. We then compute the smallest barrier distance of a point as the minimum of the barrier distances between the point and any point on the boundary.

Computing Foreground Motion Saliency: We obtain the pixelwise foreground motion saliency u_i of frame i when adding the two distance metrics $u_i^{(0)}$ and $u_i^{(1)}$ after having normalized each of them to a range of $[0, 1]$ by subtracting the minimum entry in $u_i^{(\cdot)}$ and dividing by the difference between the maximum and minimum entry. Examples for $u_i^{(0)}$, $u_i^{(1)}$ and the combined motion saliency are visualized in Fig. 2.

We found the proposed changes to result in significant improvements for saliency estimation of video data. We present a careful assessment in Sect. 4.

3.2   Neighborhood Construction

The second important term for diffusion based video segmentation beyond initial estimates is the neighborhood graph G. Classical techniques construct the adjacency matrix using local information, such as connecting a node with its spatial and temporal neighbors, and non-local connections. These methods establish a connection between two nodes as long as their visual appearance is similar.

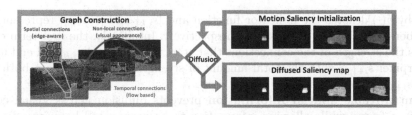

Fig. 3. Graph construnction. In our method, we construct a graph for diffusing the initial motion saliency estimation. Our graph contains (1) edge-aware spatial connections (intra-frame connections), (2) flow-based temporal connections (inter-frame connections and (3) non-local long range connections. We show the initial motion saliency and the diffused saliency map using the constructed graph. We found these three types of connections to help propagate the initial saliency estimation effectively.

In contrast, we compute the neighborhood graph, *i.e.*, the adjacency matrix for graph diffusion, $G = T \times E \times V$ as the product of three components, based on inter-frame information T, intra-frame signals E, and long-range components V, as shown in Fig. 3, and use a variety of cues for robustness. We formally discuss each of the components in the following.

Inter-frame temporal information is extracted from optical flow cues. We connect superpixels between adjacent frames following flow vectors while checking the forward/backward consistency in order to prevent inaccurate flow estimation at motion boundaries.

More formally, to compute the flow adjacency matrix T, consider two successive video frames x_i and x_{i+1} each containing pixel p_i and p_{i+1}, respectively. We compute a forward flow field $f_i(p_i)$ and a backward flow field $b_{i+1}(p_{i+1})$ densely for every pixel p using [21]. Using those flow fields, we define the forward confidence score $c_i^F(p_i)$ at pixel p_i of frame x_i via

$$c_i^F(p_i) = \exp\left(\frac{-\| - f_i(p_i) - b_{i+1}(p_i + f_i(p_i))\|_2^2}{\sigma_2}\right), \tag{5}$$

and the backward confidence score $c_i^B(p_i)$ at pixel p_i of frame x_i via

$$c_i^B(p_i) = \exp\left(\frac{-\| - b_i(p_i) - f_{i-1}(p_i + b_i(p_i))\|_2^2}{\sigma_2}\right), \tag{6}$$

where σ_2 is a hyper-parameter. Intuitively, this confidence score measures the distance between the pixel p_i and the result obtained after following the flow field into frame x_{i+1} via $p_i + f_i(p_i)$ and back into frame x_i via $p_i + f_i(p_i) + b_{i+1}(p_i + f_i(p_i))$. Taking the difference between pixel p_i and the obtained reprojection results in the term given in Eqs. (5) and (6). We use the confidence scores to compute the connection strength between two superpixels $s_{i,k}$ and $s_{i+1,m}$ in frame i and $i+1$ via

$$T(s_{i,k}, s_{i+1,m}) = \sum_{p \in s_{i,k}} \frac{\delta(p + f_i(p) \in s_{i+1,m}) c_i^F(p)}{|s_{i,k}| + |s_{i+1,m}|} + \sum_{p' \in s_{i+1,m}} \frac{\delta(p' + b_{i+1}(p') \in s_{i,k}) c_{i+1}^B(p')}{|s_{i,k}| + |s_{i+1,m}|}. \tag{7}$$

Hereby $\delta(\cdot)$ denotes the indicator function and $|s_{i,k}|$ and $|s_{i+1,m}|$ represent the number of pixels in $s_{i,k}$ and $s_{i+1,m}$, respectively. Intuitively, the first term compares the strength of the connections that start in superpixel $s_{i,k}$ and end up in superpixel $s_{i+1,m}$ with the total amount of strength originating from both $s_{i,k}$ and $s_{i+1,m}$. Similarly for the second term.

Intra-frame spatial information prevents diffusion across visual edges within a frame, while allowing information to be propagated between adjacent superpixels in the same frame if they aren't separated by a strong edge.

More formally, to find the edge aware spatial connections E, we first detect the edge responses frame-by-frame using the training based method discussed in [10]. Given edge responses, we calculate the confidence scores $A(s)$ for all superpixel s by summing over the decay function, i.e.,

$$A(s) = \frac{1}{|s|} \sum_{p \in s} \frac{1}{1 + exp(\sigma_w \cdot (G(p) - \epsilon))}. \tag{8}$$

Hereby, $G(p) \in [0, 1]$ is the edge response at pixel p. σ_w and ϵ are hyperparameters, which we fix at $\sigma_w = 50$ and $\epsilon = 0.05$ for all our experiments.

We calculate the edge-aware adjacency matrix E by exploiting the above edge information. Specifically,

$$E(s_{i,k}, s_{i,m}) = \frac{1}{2}(A(s_{i,k}) + A(s_{i,m})), \tag{9}$$

if $s_{i,k}$ is spatially close to $s_{i,m}$, *i.e.*, if the distance between the centers of the two superpixels is less than 1.5 times the square root of the size of the superpixel.

Long range connections based on visual similarity allow propagating information between superpixels that are far away either temporally or spatially as long as the two are visually similar. These long-range connections enable the information to propagate more efficiently through the neighborhood graph.

More formally, to compute the visual similarity matrix V, we find those superpixels that are most closely related to a superpixel $s_{i,m}$. To this end, we first perform a k nearest neighbor search. More specifically, for each superpixel $s_{i,m}$ we find its k nearest neighbors that are within a range of r frames temporally. To compute the distance between two superpixels we use the Euclidean distance in the feature space.

We compute features $f(s)$ of a superpixel s by concatenating the LAB and RGB histograms computed over the pixels within a superpixel. We also include the HOG feature, and the x and y coordinate of the center of the superpixel.

Let the k nearest neighbors of the superpixel $s_{i,m}$ be referred to via $N(s_{i,m})$. The visual similarity matrix is then defined via

$$V(s_{i,m}, s) = \exp\left(\frac{-\|f(s_{i,m}) - f(s)\|_2^2}{\sigma}\right) \quad \forall s \in N(s_{i,m}), \tag{10}$$

where σ is a hyper-parameter and $f(s)$ denotes the feature representation of the superpixel s. Note that we use the same features to find k nearest neighbors and to compute the visual similarity matrix V. In this work, we refrain from using deep net based information even though we could easily augment our technique with more features.

To address the computational complexity, we use an approximate k nearest neighbor search. Specifically, we use the fast implementation of ANN search utilizing the randomized k-d forest provided in [37].

4   Experiments

In the following, we present the implementation details, describe the datasets and metrics used for evaluation, followed by ablation study highlighting the influences of the proposed design choices and comparisons with the state-of-the-art.

4.1   Implementation Details

For the proposed saliency estimation algorithm, we set the number of clusters $K = 3$ for modeling the background. For neighborhood graph construction described in Sect. 3.2, we found $k = 40, r = 15, \sigma = 0.1, \sigma_2 = 2^{-6}, \sigma_w = 50$ to work well across datasets. The number of diffusion iterations is set to 25. In the supplementary material, we show that the performance of our method is reasonably robust to parameter choices.

The average running time of our approach on the DAVIS dataset, including the graph construction and diffusion is about 8.5 s per frame when using a single PC with Intel i7-4770 CPU and 32 GB memory. Extracting superpixels and feature descriptors takes about 1.5 and 0.8 s per frame, respectively. We use the implementation by [21,47] for computing optical flow, which takes about 10.7 s per frame, including both forward flow and backward flow.

4.2 Datasets

We extensively compare our proposed technique to a series of baselines using the DAVIS dataset [42] (50 video sequences), the SegTrack v2 dataset [33] (14 video sequences), and the FBMS-59 dataset [39] (22 video sequences in the test set). These datasets are challenging as they contain nonrigid deformation, drastic illumination changes, cluttered background, rapid object motion, and occlusion. All three datasets provide pixel-level ground-truth annotations for each frame.

4.3 Evaluation Metrics

Intersection Over Union ($\mathcal{J}$): The intersection over union (IoU) metric, also called the Jaccard index, computes the average over the dataset. The IoU metric has been widely used for evaluating the quality of the segmentation.

Contour Accuracy ($\mathcal{F}$) [42]: To assess the segmentation quality, we compute the contour accuracy as $\mathcal{F} = \frac{2PR}{P+R}$, where P and R are the matching precision and recall of the two sets of points on the contours of the ground truth segment and the output segment, calculated via a bipartite graph matching.

Table 1. Contribution of different components of our algorithm evaluated on the DAVIS dataset. Our algorithm with inter-frame, intra-frame connections, long range connections, and focused diffusion (denoted as FDiff) enabled performs best and achieves an IoU of **77.56%**.

Connections			FDiff	IoU (%)
Inter-frame	Intra-frame	Long range		
-	-	-	-	57.52
✓	-	-	-	62.75
-	✓	-	-	62.13
-	-	✓	-	72.38
✓	✓	-	-	65.01
✓	-	✓	-	72.70
-	✓	✓	-	74.13
✓	✓	✓	-	74.34
✓	✓	✓	✓	**77.56**

Temporal Stability ($\mathscr{T}$) [42]: The temporal stability is measured by computing the distance between the shape context descriptors [3] describing the shape of the boundary of the segmentations between two successive frames. Intuitively, the metric indicates the degree of deformation required to transform the segmentation mask from one frame to its adjacent frames.

Subsequently we first present an ablation study where we assess the contributions of our technique. Afterwards we perform a quantitative evaluation where we compare the accuracy of our approach to baseline video segmentation approaches. Finally we present qualitative results to illustrate the success and failure cases of our method.

4.4 Ablation Study

We assess the resulting performance of the individual components of our adjacency defined neighborhood in Table 1. The performance in IoU of the motion saliency estimation in our approach (with all the connections disabled) is 57.52%. We analyze the effect of the three main components in the adjacency graph: (1) inter-frame flow based temporal connections T, (2) intra-frame edge based spatial connections E and (3) long range connections V.

The improvements reported for saliency estimation and neighborhood construction motivate their use for unsupervised video segmentation. Besides, we apply a second round of 'focused diffusion,' restricted to the region which focuses primarily on the foreground object, to improve the results. The effects of the focused diffusion (denoted 'FDiff') can be found in Table 1 as well, showing significant improvements.

In Table 1, the checkmark '✓' indicates the *enabled* components. We observe consistent improvements when including additional components, which improve the robustness of the proposed method.

4.5 Quantitative Evaluation

Evaluation on the DAVIS dataset: We compare the performance of our approach to several baselines using the DAVIS dataset. The results are summarized

Table 2. The quantitative evaluation on the DAVIS dataset [42]. Evaluation metrics are the IoU measurement $\mathscr{J}$, boundary precision $\mathscr{F}$, and time stability $\mathscr{T}$. Following [42], we also report the recall and the decay of performance over time for $\mathscr{J}$ and $\mathscr{F}$ measurements.

	Semi-supervised										Unsupervised							
	SEA	HVS	JMP	FCP	BVS	OFL	CTN	VPN	MSK	**OURS-S**	NLC	MSG	KEY	FST	FSG	LMP	ARP	**OURS-U**
Deep features	-	-	-	-	-	✓	✓	✓	✓	-	-	-	-	-	✓	✓	-	-
$\mathscr{J}$ Mean $\mathcal{M}$ ↑	0.556	0.596	0.607	0.631	0.665	0.711	0.755	0.750	<u>0.803</u>	**0.810**	0.641	0.543	0.569	0.575	0.716	0.697	<u>0.763</u>	**0.776**
$\mathscr{J}$ Recall $\mathcal{O}$ ↑	0.606	0.698	0.693	0.778	0.764	0.800	0.890	0.901	<u>0.935</u>	**0.946**	0.731	0.636	0.671	0.652	0.877	0.829	**0.892**	0.886
$\mathscr{J}$ Decay $\mathcal{D}$ ↓	0.355	0.197	0.372	**0.031**	0.260	0.227	0.144	<u>0.093</u>	0.089	0.102	0.086	<u>0.028</u>	0.075	0.044	**0.017**	0.056	0.036	0.044
$\mathscr{F}$ Mean $\mathcal{M}$ ↑	0.533	0.576	0.586	0.546	0.656	0.679	0.714	0.724	<u>0.758</u>	**0.783**	0.593	0.525	0.503	0.536	0.658	0.663	<u>0.711</u>	**0.750**
$\mathscr{F}$ Recall $\mathcal{O}$ ↑	0.559	0.712	0.656	0.604	0.774	0.780	0.848	0.842	<u>0.882</u>	**0.928**	0.658	0.613	0.534	0.579	0.790	0.783	<u>0.828</u>	**0.869**
$\mathscr{F}$ Decay $\mathcal{D}$ ↓	0.339	0.202	0.373	**0.039**	0.236	0.240	0.140	0.136	<u>0.095</u>	0.115	0.086	0.057	0.079	0.065	<u>0.043</u>	0.067	0.073	**0.042**
$\mathscr{T}$ Mean $\mathcal{M}$ ↓	<u>0.137</u>	0.296	**0.131**	0.285	0.316	0.239	0.198	0.300	0.189	0.212	0.356	0.250	**0.190**	0.276	0.286	0.689	0.352	<u>0.243</u>

Table 3. The attribute-based aggregate performance comparing unsupervised methods on the DAVIS dataset [42]. We calculate the average IoU of all sequences with the specific attribute: appearance change (AC), dynamic background (DB), fast motion (FM), motion blur (MB), and occlusion (OCC). The right column with small font indicates the performance change for the method on the remaining sequences if the sequences possessing the corresponding attribute are not taken into account.

Attribute	NLC [13]	MSG [5]	KEY [31]	FST [40]	FSG [25]	LMP [49]	ARP [30]	OURS-U
AC	0.54 +0.13	0.48 +0.08	0.42 +0.19	0.55 +0.04	**0.73** -0.02	0.67 +0.03	<u>0.73</u>+0.04	0.72 +0.07
DB	0.53 +0.15	0.43 +0.15	0.52 +0.07	0.53 +0.06	<u>0.67</u>+0.05	0.57 +0.16	**0.70** +0.08	0.66 +0.15
FM	0.64 +0.00	0.46 +0.14	0.50 +0.12	0.50 +0.12	0.69 +0.04	0.67 +0.05	<u>0.73</u>+0.05	**0.75** +0.04
MB	0.61 +0.04	0.35 +0.29	0.51 +0.08	0.48 +0.14	0.65 +0.10	0.64 +0.08	<u>0.69</u>+0.11	**0.74** +0.06
OCC	0.70 -0.09	0.48 +0.10	0.52 +0.08	0.53 +0.07	0.65 +0.10	0.70 -0.01	<u>0.71</u>+0.08	**0.81** -0.05

in Table 2, where we report the IoU, the contour accuracy, and the time stability metrics. The best method is emphasized in bold font and the second best is underlined. We observe our approach to be quite competitive, outperforming a wide variety of existing unsupervised video segmentation techniques, e.g., NLC [13], MSG [5], KEY [31], FST [40], FSG [25], LMP [49], ARP [30]. We also evaluate our method in the semi-supervised setting by simply replacing the saliency initialization of the first frame with the ground truth. Note that it is common to refer to usage of the first frame as 'semi-supervised.' Our unsupervised version is denoted as **OURS-U** and the semi-supervised version is referred to via **OURS-S** in Table 2. Semi-supervised baselines are SEA [1], HVS [17], JMP [14], FCP [43], BVS [36], OFL [52], CTN [27], VPN [26], and MSK [41]. Note that OFL uses deep features, and CTN, VPN, MSK, FSG, and LMP are deep learning based approaches. We observe our method to improve the state-of-the-art performance in IoU metric by 1.3% in the unsupervised setting and by 0.7% in the semi-supervised case. Note that beyond training of edge detectors, no learning is performed in our approach.

In Table 3, we compare the average IoU of all DAVIS sequences, clustered by attributes, e.g., appearance change, dynamic blur, fast motion, motion blur, and occlusion. Our method is more robust and outperforms the baselines for fast motion, motion blur and occlusion. In particular, our method performs well for objects with occlusion, outperforming other methods by 10% for this attribute.

Evaluation on the SegTrack v2 Dataset: We assess our approach on the SegTrack v2 dataset using identical choice of parameters. We show the results in Table 4. We observe our method to be competitive on SegTrack v2. Note that the reported performance of NLC differs from [13] as in the evaluation in [13] only a subset of the 12 video sequences were used. We ran the code released by [13] and report the results on the full SegTrack v2 dataset with 14 video sequences. The results we report here are similar to the ones reported in [48].

Table 4. Performance in IoU on SegTrack v2 dataset [33].

Sequence	KEY [31]	FST [40]	NLC [13]	FSG [25]	Ours
BIRDFALL	0.490	0.014	0.565	0.380	**0.649**
BIRD OF PARADISE	0.922	0.837	0.814	0.699	**0.937**
BMX	0.630	0.621	0.754	0.591	**0.847**
CHEETAH	0.281	0.396	0.518	**0.596**	0.518
DRIFT	0.469	0.811	0.741	**0.876**	0.829
FROG	0.000	0.629	0.713	0.570	**0.832**
GIRL	**0.877**	0.441	0.860	0.667	0.846
HUMMINGBIRD	0.602	0.335	0.624	**0.652**	0.464
MONKEY	0.790	0.699	**0.823**	0.805	0.739
MONKEYDOG	0.396	0.523	**0.525**	0.328	0.381
PARACHUTE	**0.963**	0.839	0.859	0.516	0.937
PENGUIN	0.093	0.074	0.139	**0.713**	0.240
SOLDIER	0.666	0.453	0.692	0.698	**0.800**
WORM	**0.844**	0.705	0.782	0.506	0.800
Average IoU	0.573	0.527	0.672	0.614	**0.701**

Table 5. Performance in IoU on FBMS-59 test set [39].

	NLC [13]	POR [59]	POS [28]	FST [40]	ARP [30]	**OURS**
Average IoU	0.445	0.473	0.542	0.555	0.598	**0.608**

Table 6. Performance comparisons in IoU on the initialization on the DAVIS and SegTrack v2 datasets.

Training?	DAVIS					Segtrack v2			
	NLC	FST	FSG	LMP	**Ours**	NLC	FST	FSG	**Ours**
	-	-	✓	✓	-	-	-	✓	-
Initial saliency	0.402	0.456	**0.602**	0.569	0.575	0.419	0.389	**0.530**	0.424

Evaluation on the FBMS Dataset: We evaluate our method on the FBMS [39] test set which consists of 22 video sequences. The results are presented in Table 5. We observe our approach to outperform the baselines.

Comparisons of the Saliency Estimation: To illustrate the benefits of the proposed motion saliency estimation, we compare the performance of the proposed initialization with other approaches in Table 6 and observe that the proposed saliency estimation performs very well. Note that the saliency estimation in our approach is unsupervised as opposed to FSG and LMP which are trained on more than 10,000 images and 2,250 videos, respectively.

4.6   Qualitative Evaluation

Side-by-Side Comparison: Next we present qualitative results comparing our algorithm to competing methods on challenging parts of the DAVIS dataset. In Fig. 4 we provide side-by-side comparisons to existing methods, *i.e.*, APR [30], LMP [49], FSG [25], and NLC [13]. We observe our approach to yield encouraging results even in challenging situations such as frames in BMX-TREES (Fig. 4, first row), where the foreground object is very small and occluded, and the back-

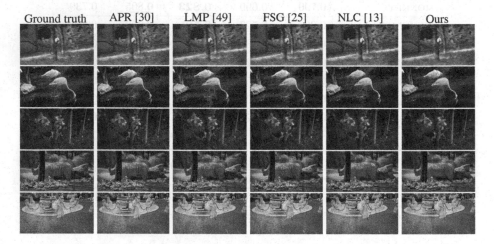

Fig. 4. Comparison of our algorithm and other unsupervised methods on sequence BMX-TREES (1st row), FLAMINGO (2nd row), LIBBY (3rd row), RHINO (4th row), and DANCE-JUMP (5th row) of the DAVIS dataset.

Fig. 5. Visual results of our approach on the sequences SWING (1st row), SOAPBOX (2nd row), DRIFT-STRAIGHT (3rd row), and DANCE-TWIRL (4th row) of the DAVIS dataset.

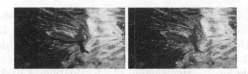

Fig. 6. Failure case. Groundtruth vs. our result.

ground is very colorful, and in FLAMINGO (Fig. 4, second row), where there is non-rigid deformation, and the background object is similar to the foreground object. We refer the interested reader to the supplementary material for additional results and videos.

Success Cases: In Fig. 5, we provide success cases of our algorithm, *i.e.*, frames where our designed technique delineates the foreground object accurately. We want to highlight that our approach is more robust to challenges such as occlusions, motion blur and fast moving objects as the attribute-based aggregate performance in Table 3 suggests.

Failure Modes: In Fig. 6, we also present failure modes of our approach. We observe our technique to be challenged by complex motion. Since our method mainly relies on motion and appearance, water is classified as foreground due to its complex motion (MALLARD-WATER).

5   Conclusion

We proposed a saliency estimation and a graph neighborhood for effective unsupervised foreground-background video segmentation. Our key novelty is a motion saliency estimation and an informative neighborhood structure. Our unsupervised method demonstrates how to effectively exploit the structure of video data, *i.e.*, taking advantage of flow and edges, and achieves state-of-the-art performance in the unsupervised setting.

Acknowledgments. This material is based upon work supported in part by the National Science Foundation under Grant No. 1718221, 1755785, Samsung, and 3M. We thank NVIDIA for providing the GPUs used for this research.

References

1. Avinash Ramakanth, S., Venkatesh Babu, R.: SeamSeg: video object segmentation using patch seams. In: Proceedings of the CVPR (2014)
2. Badrinarayanan, V., Galasso, F., Cipolla, R.: Label propagation in video sequences. In: Proceedings of the CVPR (2010)
3. Belongie, S., Malik, J., Puzicha, J.: Shape matching and object recognition using shape contexts. PAMI (2002)
4. Brendel, W., Todorovic, S.: Video object segmentation by tracking regions. In: Proceedings of the ICCV (2009)

5. Brox, T., Malik, J.: Object segmentation by long term analysis of point trajectories. In: Daniilidis, K., Maragos, P., Paragios, N. (eds.) ECCV 2010. LNCS, vol. 6315, pp. 282–295. Springer, Heidelberg (2010). https://doi.org/10.1007/978-3-642-15555-0_21

6. Brutzer, S., Hoeferlin, B., Heidemann, G.: Evaluation of background subtraction techniques for video surveillance. In: Proceedings of the CVPR (2011)

7. Cheng, H.T., Ahuja, N.: Exploiting nonlocal spatiotemporal structure for video segmentation. In: Proceedings of the CVPR (2012)

8. Costeira, J., Kanande, T.: A multi-body factorization method for motion analysis. In: Proceedings of the ICCV (1995)

9. Criminisi, A., Cross, G., Blake, A., Kolmogorov, V.: Bilayer segmentation of live video. In: Proceedings of the CVPR (2006)

10. Dollár, P., Zitnick, C.L.: Structured forests for fast edge detection. In: ICCV (2013)

11. Elgammal, A., Duraiswami, R., Harwood, D., Davis, L.: Background and foreground modeling using nonparametric kernel density estimation for visual surveillance. In: Proceedings of the IEEE (2002)

12. Elhamifar, E., Vidal, R.: Sparse subspace clustering. In: Proceedings of the CVPR (2009)

13. Faktor, A., Irani, M.: Video segmentation by non-local consensus voting. In: BMVC (2014)

14. Fan, Q., Zhong, F., Lischinski, D., Cohen-Or, D., Chen, B.: JumpCut: non-successive mask transfer and interpolation for video cutout. In: SIGGRAPH (2015)

15. Fragkiadaki, K., Zhang, G., Shi, J.: Video segmentation by tracing discontinuities in a trajectory embedding. In: Proceedings of the CVPR (2012)

16. Galasso, F., Nagaraja, N., Cardenas, T., Brox, T., Schiele, B.: A unified video segmentation benchmark: Annotation, metrics and analysis. In: Proceedings of the ICCV (2013)

17. Grundmann, M., Kwatra, V., Han, M., Essa, I.: Efficient hierarchical graph-based video segmentation. In: Proceedings of the CVPR (2010)

18. Haymanand, E., Eklundh, J.O.: Statistical background subtraction for a mobile observer. In: Proceedings of the ICCV (2003)

19. Hu, Y.T., Huang, J.B., Schwing, A.G.: MaskRNN: instance level video object segmentation. In: Proceedings of the NIPS (2017)

20. Hu, Y.T., Huang, J.B., Schwing, A.G.: VideoMatch: Matching based Video Object Segmentation. In: Proc. ECCV (2018)

21. Hu, Y., Song, R., Li, Y.: Efficient coarse-to-fine patchmatch for large displacement optical flow. In: Proceedings of the IEEE Conference on Computer Vision and Pattern Recognition (2016)

22. Irani, M., Anandan, P.: A unified approach to moving object detection in 2d and 3d scenes. PAMI (1998)

23. Irani, M., Rousso, B., Peleg, S.: Computing occluding and transparent motions. IJCV (1994)

24. Jain, S.D., Grauman, K.: Supervoxel-consistent foreground propagation in video. In: Fleet, D., Pajdla, T., Schiele, B., Tuytelaars, T. (eds.) ECCV 2014. LNCS, vol. 8692, pp. 656–671. Springer, Cham (2014). https://doi.org/10.1007/978-3-319-10593-2_43

25. Jain, S.D., Xiong, B., Grauman, K.: FusionSeg: learning to combine motion and appearance for fully automatic segmention of generic objects in videos. In: Proceedings of the CVPR (2017)

26. Jampani, V., Gadde, R., Gehler, P.V.: Video propagation networks. In: Proceedings of the CVPR (2017)

27. Jang, W.D., Kim, C.S.: Online video object segmentation via convolutional trident network. In: Proceedings of the CVPR (2017)
28. Jang, W.D., Lee, C., Kim, C.S.: Primary object segmentation in videos via alternate convex optimization of foreground and background distributions. In: Proceedings of the CVPR (2016)
29. Keuper, M., Andres, B., Brox, T.: Motion trajectory segmentation via minimum cost multicuts. In: Proceedings of the ICCV (2015)
30. Koh, Y.J., Kim, C.S.: Primary object segmentation in videos based on region augmentation and reduction. In: Proceedings of the CVPR (2017)
31. Lee, Y.J., Kim, J., Grauman, K.: Key-segments for video object segmentation. In: Proceedings of the ICCV (2011)
32. Lezama, J., Alahari, K., Sivic, J., Laptev, I.: Track to the future: Spatio-temporal video segmentation with long-range motion cues. In: Proceedings of the CVPR (2011)
33. Li, F., Kim, T., Humayun, A., Tsai, D., Rehg, J.M.: Video segmentation by tracking many figure-ground segments. In: Proceedings of the ICCV (2013)
34. Li, W., Viola, F., Starck, J., Brostow, G.J., Campbell, N.D.: Roto++: accelerating professional rotoscoping using shape manifolds. In: SIGGRAPH (2016)
35. Lovász, L.: Random walks on graphs: a survey (1993)
36. Maerki, N., Perazzi, F., Wang, O., Sorkine-Hornung, A.: Bilateral space video segmentation. In: Proceedings of the CVPR (2016)
37. Muja, M., Lowe, D.G.: Fast approximate nearest neighbors with automatic algorithm configuration. In: International Conference on Computer Vision Theory and Application (2009)
38. Nagaraja, N., Schmidt, F., Brox, T.: Video segmentation with just a few strokes. In: Proceedings of the ICCV (2015)
39. Ochs, P., Malik, J., Brox, T.: Segmentation of moving objects by long term video analysis. PAMI (2014)
40. Papazoglou, A., Ferrari, V.: Fast object segmentation in unconstrained video. In: Proceedings of the ICCV (2013)
41. Perazzi, F., Khoreva, A., Benenson, R., Schiele, B., A.Sorkine-Hornung: Learning video object segmentation from static images. In: Proceedings of the CVPR (2017)
42. Perazzi, F., Pont-Tuset, J., McWilliams, B., Gool, L.V., Gross, M., Sorkine-Hornung, A.: A benchmark dataset and evaluation methodology for video object segmentation. In: Proceedings of the CVPR (2016)
43. Perazzi, F., Wang, O., Gross, M., Sorkine-Hornung, A.: Fully connected object proposals for video segmentation. In: Proceedings of the ICCV (2015)
44. Price, B.L., Morse, B.S., Cohen, S.: LIVEcut: learning-based interactive video segmentation by evaluation of multiple propagated cues. In: Proceedings of the ICCV (2009)
45. Rao, S.R., Tron, R., Vidal, R., Ma, Y.: Motion segmentation via robust subspace separation in the presence of outlying, incomplete, or corrupted trajectories. In: Proceedings of the CVPR (2008)
46. Ren, Y., Chua, C.S., Ho, Y.K.: Statistical background modeling for non-stationary camera. PRL (2003)
47. Revaud, J., Weinzaepfel, P., Harchaoui, Z., Schmid, C.: EpicFlow: edge-preserving interpolation of correspondences for optical flow. In: Computer Vision and Pattern Recognition (2015)
48. Tokmakov, P., Alahari, K., Schmid, C.: Learning video object segmentation with visual memory. In: Proceedings of the ICCV (2017)

49. Tokmakov, P., Alahari, K., Schmid, C.: Learning motion patterns in videos. In: Proceedings of the CVPR (2017)

50. Torr, P.H.S., Zisserman, A.: Concerning Bayesian motion segmentation, model averaging, matching and the trifocal tensor. In: Burkhardt, H., Neumann, B. (eds.) ECCV 1998. LNCS, vol. 1406, pp. 511–527. Springer, Heidelberg (1998). https://doi.org/10.1007/BFb0055687

51. Tsai, D., Flagg, M., Rehg, J.: Motion coherent tracking with multi-label MRF optimization. In: Proceedings of the BMVC (2010)

52. Tsai, Y.H., Yang, M.H., Black, M.J.: Video segmentation via object flow. In: Proceedings of the CVPR (2016)

53. Tu, W.C., He, S., Yang, Q., Chien, S.Y.: Real-time salient object detection with a minimum spanning tree. In: Proceedings of the CVPR (2016)

54. Vijayanarasimhan, S., Grauman, K.: Active frame selection for label propagation in videos. In: Fitzgibbon, A., Lazebnik, S., Perona, P., Sato, Y., Schmid, C. (eds.) ECCV 2012. LNCS, vol. 7576, pp. 496–509. Springer, Heidelberg (2012). https://doi.org/10.1007/978-3-642-33715-4_36

55. Wang, T., Collomosse, J.: Probabilistic motion diffusion of labeling priors for coherent video segmentation. IEEE Trans. Multimed. (2012)

56. Wei, Y., Wen, F., Zhu, W., Sun, J.: Geodesic saliency using background priors. In: Fitzgibbon, A., Lazebnik, S., Perona, P., Sato, Y., Schmid, C. (eds.) ECCV 2012. LNCS, vol. 7574, pp. 29–42. Springer, Heidelberg (2012). https://doi.org/10.1007/978-3-642-33712-3_3

57. Xiao, F., Lee, Y.J.: Track and segment: an iterative unsupervised approach for video object proposals. In: Proceedings of the CVPR (2016)

58. Yuan, C., Medioni, G., Kang, J., Cohen, I.: Detecting motion regions in the presence of a strong parallax from a moving camera by multiview geometric constraints. PAMI (2007)

59. Zhang, D., Javed, O., Shah, M.: Video object segmentation through spatially accurate and temporally dense extraction of primary object regions. In: Proceedings of the CVPR (2013)

Temporal Relational Reasoning in Videos

Bolei Zhou$^{(\boxtimes)}$, Alex Andonian, Aude Oliva, and Antonio Torralba

MIT CSAIL, Cambridge, USA
{bzhou,aandonia,oliva,torralba}@csail.mit.edu

Abstract. Temporal relational reasoning, the ability to link meaningful transformations of objects or entities over time, is a fundamental property of intelligent species. In this paper, we introduce an effective and interpretable network module, the Temporal Relation Network (TRN), designed to learn and reason about temporal dependencies between video frames at multiple time scales. We evaluate TRN-equipped networks on activity recognition tasks using three recent video datasets - Something-Something, Jester, and Charades - which fundamentally depend on temporal relational reasoning. Our results demonstrate that the proposed TRN gives convolutional neural networks a remarkable capacity to discover temporal relations in videos. Through only sparsely sampled video frames, TRN-equipped networks can accurately predict human-object interactions in the Something-Something dataset and identify various human gestures on the Jester dataset with very competitive performance. TRN-equipped networks also outperform two-stream networks and 3D convolution networks in recognizing daily activities in the Charades dataset. Further analyses show that the models learn intuitive and interpretable visual common sense knowledge in videos (Code and models are available at http://relation.csail.mit.edu/.).

1 Introduction

The ability to reason about the relations between entities over time is crucial for intelligent decision-making. Temporal relational reasoning allows intelligent species to analyze the current situation relative to the past and formulate hypotheses on what may happen next. For example (Fig. 1), given two observations of an event, people can easily recognize the temporal relation between two states of the visual world and deduce what has happened given only two video frames[1].

Temporal relational reasoning is critical for activity recognition, forming the building blocks for describing the steps of an event. A single activity can consist of several temporal relations at both short-term and long-term timescales. For example, the activity of *sprinting* contains the long-term relations of crouching at the starting blocks, running on track, and finishing at end line, while it also includes the short-term relations of periodic hands and feet movement.

---

[1] Answer: (a) Poking a stack of cans so it collapses; (b) Stack something; (c) Tidying up a closet; (d) Thumb up.

© Springer Nature Switzerland AG 2018
V. Ferrari et al. (Eds.): ECCV 2018, LNCS 11205, pp. 831–846, 2018.
https://doi.org/10.1007/978-3-030-01246-5_49

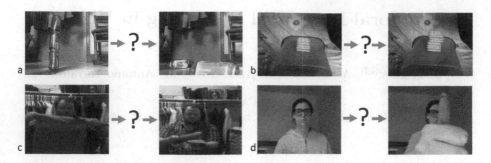

Fig. 1. What takes place between two observations? (see answer below the first page). Humans can easily infer the temporal relations and transformations between these observations, but this task remains difficult for neural networks.

Activity recognition has been one of the core topics in computer vision. However, it remains difficult due to the ambiguity of describing activities at appropriate timescales [1]. Many video datasets, such as UCF101 [2], Sport1M [3], and THUMOS [4], include many activities that can be recognized without reasoning about the long-term temporal relations: still frames and optical flow are sufficient to identify many of the labeled activities. Indeed, the classical two-stream Convolutional Neural Network [5] and the recent I3D Network [6], both based on frames and optical flow, perform activity recognition very well on these datasets.

However, convolutional neural networks still struggle in situations where data and observations are limited, or where the underlying structure is characterized by transformations and temporal relations, rather than the appearance of certain entities [7,8]. It remains remarkably challenging for convolutional neural networks to reason about temporal relations and to anticipate what transformations are happening to the observations.

In this work, we propose a simple and interpretable network module called Temporal Relation Network (TRN) that enables temporal relational reasoning in neural networks. This module is inspired by the relational network proposed in [7], but instead of modeling the spatial relations, TRN aims to describe the temporal relations between observations in videos. Thus, TRN can learn and discover possible temporal relations at multiple time scales. TRN is a general and extensible module that can be used in a plug-and-play fashion with any existing CNN architecture. We apply TRN-equipped networks on three recent video datasets (Something-Something [9], Jester [10], and Charades [11]), which are constructed for recognizing different types of activities such as human-object interactions and hand gestures, but all depend on temporal relational reasoning. The TRN-equipped networks achieve very competitive results even given only discrete RGB frames, bringing significant improvements over baselines.

1.1   Related Work

Convolutional Neural Networks for Activity Recognition. Activity recognition in videos is a core problem in computer vision. With the rise of deep convolutional neural networks (CNNs) which achieve state-of-the-art performance on image recognition tasks [12,13], many works have looked into designing effective deep convolutional neural networks for activity recognition [3,5,6,14–16]. For instance, various approaches of fusing RGB frames over the temporal dimension are explored on the Sport1M dataset [3]. Two stream CNNs with one stream of static images and the other stream of optical flows are proposed to fuse the information of object appearance and short-term motions [5]. 3D convolutional networks [15] use 3D convolution kernels to extract features from a sequence of dense RGB frames. Temporal Segment Networks sample frames and optical flow on different time segments to extract information for activity recognition [16]. A CNN+LSTM model, which uses a CNN to extract frame features and an LSTM to integrate features over time, is also used to recognize activities in videos [14]. Recently, I3D networks [6] use two stream CNNs with inflated 3D convolutions on both dense RGB and optical flow sequences to achieve state of the art performance on the Kinetics dataset [17]. There are several important issues with existing CNNs for action recognition: (1) The dependency on beforehand extraction of optical flow lowers the efficiency of the recognition system; (2) The 3D convolutions on sequences of dense frames are computationally expensive, given the redundancy in consecutive frames; (3) Since sequences of frames fed into the network are usually limited to 20 to 30 frames, it is difficult for the networks to learn long-term temporal relations among frames. To address these issues, the proposed Temporal Relation Network sparsely samples individual frames and then learns their causal relations, which is much more efficient than sampling dense frames and convolving them. We show that TRN-equipped networks can efficiently capture temporal relations at multiple time scales and outperform dense frame-based networks using only sparsely sampled video frames.

Temporal Information in Activity Recognition. For activity recognition on many existing video datasets such as UCF101 [2], Sport1M [3], THUMOS [4], and Kinetics [17], the appearance of still frames and short-term motion such as optical flow are the most important information to identify the activities. Thus, activity recognition networks such as Two Stream network [5] and the I3D network [6] are tailored to capture these short-term dynamics of dense frames. Therefore, existing networks don't need to build temporal relational reasoning abilities. On the other hand, recently there have been various video datasets collected via crowd-sourcing, which focus on sequential activity recognition: Something-Something dataset [9] is collected for generic human-object interaction. It has video classes such as 'Dropping something into something' and 'Pushing something with something'. Jester dataset [10] is another recent video dataset for gesture recognition. Videos are recorded by crowd-source workers performing 27 kinds of gestures such as 'Thumbing up' and 'Swiping Left'. Charades dataset is also a high-level human activity dataset that collects videos by asking crowd workers to perform a series of home activities and then record themselves [11]. For recognizing the complex activities in these three datasets, it is crucial to integrate temporal relational reasoning into the networks. Besides, many previous works model the temporal structures of videos for action recognition and detection using bag of words, motion atoms, or action grammar [18–22]. Instead of designing temporal structures manually, we use a more generic structure to learn the temporal relations in end-to-end training.

Relational Reasoning and Intuitive Physics. Recently, relational reasoning module has been proposed for visual question answering with super-human performance [7]. We focus on modeling the multi-scale temporal relations in videos. In the domain of robot self-supervised learning, many models have been proposed to learn the intuitive physics among frames. Given an initial state and a goal state, the inverse dynamics model with reinforcement learning is used to infer the transformation between the object states [23]. Physical interaction and observations are also used to train deep neural networks [24]. Time contrast networks are used for self-supervised imitation learning of object manipulation from third-person video observation [25]. Our work aims to learn various temporal relations in videos in a supervised learning setting. The proposed TRN can be extended to self-supervised learning for robot object manipulation.

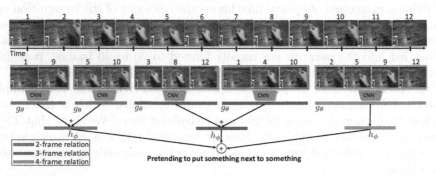

Fig. 2. The illustration of Temporal Relation Networks. Representative frames of a video (shown above) are sampled and fed into different frame relation modules. Only a subset of the 2-frame, 3-frame, and 4-frame relations are shown.

2   Temporal Relation Networks

In this section, we introduce the framework of Temporal Relation Networks. It is simple and can be easily plugged into any existing convolutional neural network architecture to enable temporal relational reasoning. In later experiments, we show that TRN-equipped networks discover interpretable visual common sense knowledge to recognize activities in videos.

2.1   Defining Temporal Relations

Inspired by the relational reasoning module for visual question answering [7], we define the pairwise temporal relation as a composite function below:

$$T_2(V) = h_\phi\Big(\sum_{i<j} g_\theta(f_i, f_j)\Big) \tag{1}$$

where the input is the video V with n selected ordered frames as $V = \{f_1, f_2, ..., f_n\}$, where f_i is a representation of the ith frame of the video, e.g., the output activation from some standard CNN. The functions h_ϕ and g_θ fuse features of different ordered frames. Here we simply use multilayer perceptrons (MLP) with parameters ϕ and θ respectively. For efficient computation, rather than adding all the combination pairs, we uniformly sample frames i and j and sort each pair.

We further extend the composite function of the 2-frame temporal relations to higher frame relations such as the 3-frame relation function below:

$$T_3(V) = h'_\phi\Big(\sum_{i<j<k} g'_\theta(f_i, f_j, f_k)\Big) \tag{2}$$

where the sum is again over sets of frames i, j, k that have been uniformly sampled and sorted.

2.2   Multi-Scale Temporal Relations

To capture temporal relations at multiple time scales, we use the following composite function to accumulate frame relations at different scales:

$$MT_N(V) = T_2(V) + T_3(V)... + T_N(V) \tag{3}$$

Each relation term T_d captures temporal relationships between d ordered frames. Each T_d has its own separate $h_\phi^{(d)}$ and $g_\theta^{(d)}$. Notice that for any given sample of d frames for each T_d, all the temporal relation functions are end-to-end differentiable, so they can all be trained together with the base CNN used to extract features for each video frame. The overall framework is illustrated in Fig. 2.

2.3   Efficient Training and Testing

When training a multi-scale temporal network, we could sample the sums by selecting different sets of d frames for each T_d term for a video. However, we use a sampling scheme that reduces computation significantly. First, we uniformly sample a set of N frames from the N segments of the video, $V_N^* \subset V$, and we use V_N^* to calculate $T_N(V)$. Then, for each $d < N$, we choose k random subsamples of d frames $V_{kd}^* \subset V_N^*$. These are used to compute the d-frame relations for each $T_d(V)$. This allows kN temporal relations to be sampled while run the base CNN on only N frames, while all the parts are end-to-end trained together.

At testing time, we can combine the TRN-equipped network with a queue to process streaming video very efficiently. A queue is used to cache the extracted CNN features of the equidistant frames sampled from the video, then those features are further combined into different relation tuples which are further summed up to predict the activity. The CNN feature is extracted from incoming key frame only once then enqueued, thus TRN-equipped networks is able to run in real-time on a desktop to processing streaming video from a webcam.

3 Experiments

We evaluate the TRN-equipped networks on a variety of activity recognition tasks. For recognizing activities that depend on temporal relational reasoning, TRN-equipped networks outperform a baseline network without a TRN by a large margin. We achieve highly competitive results on the Something-Something dataset for human-interaction recognition [9] and on the Jester dataset for hand gesture recognition [10]. The TRN-equipped networks also obtain competitive results on activity classification in the Charades dataset [11], outperforming the Flow+RGB ensemble models [11,26] using only sparsely sampled RGB frames.

The statistics of the three datasets Something-Something dataset (Something-V1 [9] and Something-V2 [27] where the Something-V2 is the 2nd release of the dataset in early July 2018) [9,27], Jester dataset [10], and Charades dataset [11] are listed in Table 1. All three datasets are crowd-sourced, in which the videos are collected by asking the crowd-source workers to record themselves performing instructed activities. Unlike the Youtube-type videos in UCF101 and Kinetics, there is usually a clear start and end of each activity in the crowd-sourced video, emphasizing the importance of temporal relational reasoning.

Table 1. Statistics of the datasets used in evaluating the TRNs.

Dataset	Classes	Videos	Type
Something-V1	174	108,499	Human-object interaction
Something-V2	174	220,847	Human-object interaction
Jester	27	148,092	Human hand gesture
Charades	157	9,848	Daily indoor activity

3.1 Network Architectures and Training

The networks used for extracting image features play an important factor in visual recognition tasks [28]. Features from deeper networks such as ResNet [29] usually perform better. Our goal here is to evaluate the effectiveness of the TRN module for temporal relational reasoning in videos. Thus, we fix the base network architecture to be the same throughout all the experiments and compare the performance of the CNN model with and without the proposed TRN modules.

We adopt Inception with Batch Normalization (BN-Inception) pretrained on ImageNet used in [30] because of its balance between accuracy and efficiency. We follow the training strategies of partial BN (freezing all the batch normalization layers except the first one) and dropout after global pooling as used in [16]. We keep the network architecture of the MultiScale TRN module and the training hyper-parameters the same for training models on all the three datasets. We set $k = 3$ in the experiments as the number of accumulated relation triples in each relation module. g_ϕ is simply a two-layer MLP with 256 units per layer, while h_ϕ is a one-layer MLP with the unit number matching the class number. The CNN features for a given frame is the activation from the BN-Inception's global average pooling layer (before the final classification layer). Given the BN-Inception as the base CNN, the training can be finished in less than 24 h for 100 training epochs on a single Nvidia Titan Xp GPU. In the Multi-Scale TRN, we include all the TRN modules from 2-frame TRN up to 8-frame TRN (thus $N = 8$ in Eq. 3), as including higher frame TRNs brings marginal improvement and lowers the efficiency.

3.2   Results on Something-Something Dataset

Something-Something is a recent video dataset for human-object interaction recognition. There are 174 classes, some of the ambiguous activity categories are challenging, such as 'Tearing Something into two pieces' versus 'Tearing Something just a little bit', 'Turn something upside down' versus 'Pretending to turn something upside down'. We can see that the temporal relations and transformations of objects rather than the appearance of the objects characterize the activities in the dataset.

The results on the validation set and test set of Something-V1 and Something-V2 datasets are listed in Table 2a. The baseline is the base network trained on single frames randomly selected from each video. Networks with TRNs outperform the single frame baseline by a large margin. We construct the 2-stream TRN by simply averaging the predicted probabilities from the two streams for any given video). The 2-stream TRN further improves the accuracy on the validation set of Something-v1 and Something-v2 to **42.01%** and **55.52%** respectively. Note that we found that the optical stream with average pooling of frames used in TSN [16] achieves better score than the one with the proposed temporal relational pooling so we use 8-frame TSN on optical flow stream, which gets 31.63% and 46.41% on the validation set of Something-V1 and Something-V2 respectively. We further submit MultiScale TRN and 2-stream TRN predictions on the test set, the results are shown in Table 2a.

We compare the TRN with TSN [16], to verify the importance of temporal orders. Instead of concatenating the features of temporal frames, TSN simply averages the deep features so that the model only captures the co-occurrence rather than the temporal ordering of patterns in the features. We keep all the training conditions the same, and vary the number of frames used by two models. As shown in Table 2b, our models outperform TSNs by a large margin. This

Table 2. (a) Results on the validation set and test set of the Something-V1 Dataset (Top1 Accuracy) and Something-V2 Dataset (Both Top1 and Top5 accuracy are reported). (b) Comparison of TRN and TSN as the number of frames (fr.) varies on the validation set of the Something-V1. TRN outperforms TSN in a large margin as the number of frames increases, showing the importance of temporal order.

	Something-V1		Something-V2	
	Val	Test	Val	Test
Baseline	11.41	-	-	-
MultiScale TRN	34.44	33.60	48.80/77.64	50.85/79.33
2-Stream TRN	42.01	40.71	55.52/83.06	56.24/83.15

	TRN	TSN
2-fr.	22.23	16.72
3-fr.	26.22	17.30
5-fr.	30.39	18.11
7-fr.	31.01	18.48

(a)　　　　　　　　　　　　　　　　　　(b)

result shows the importance of frame order for temporal relation reasoning. We also see that additional frames included in the relation bring further significant improvements to TRN.

3.3   Results on Jester and Charades

We further evaluate the TRN-equipped networks on the Jester dataset, which is a video dataset for hand gesture recognition with 27 classes. The results on the validation set of the Jester dataset are listed in Table 3a. The result on the test set and comparison with the top methods are listed in Table 3b. MultiScale TRN again achieves competitive performance as close to 95% Top1 accuracy.

Table 3. Jester dataset results on (a) the validation set and (b) the test set.

	Val
Baseline	63.60
2-frame TRN	75.65
3-frame TRN	81.45
4-frame TRN	89.38
5-frame TRN	91.40
MultiScale TRN	**95.31**

	Test
20BN Jester System	82.34
VideoLSTM	85.86
Guillaume Berger	93.87
Ford's Gesture System	94.11
Besnet	94.23
MultiScale TRN	**94.78**

(a)　　　　　　　　　　　　　　　　　　(b)

We evaluate the MultiScale TRN on the recent Charades dataset for daily activity recognition. The results are listed in Table 4. Our method outperforms various methods such as 2-stream networks and C3D [11], and the recent Asynchronous Temporal Field (TempField) method [26].

The qualitative prediction results of the Multi-Scale TRN on the three datasets are shown in Fig. 3. The examples in Fig. 3 demonstrate that the TRN model is capable of correctly identifying actions for which the overall temporal ordering of frames is essential for a successful prediction. For example, the turning hand counterclockwise category would assume a different class label when shown in reverse. Moreover, the successful prediction of categories in which an individual *pretends* to carry out an action (e.g. 'pretending to put something into something' as shown in the second row) suggests that the network can capture temporal relations at multiple scales, where the ordering of several lower-level actions contained in short segments conveys crucial semantic information about the overall activity class.

This outstanding performance shows the effectiveness of the TRN for temporal relational reasoning and its strong generalization ability across different datasets.

Table 4. Results on charades activity classification.

Approach	Random	C3D	AlexNet	IDT	2-Stream	TempField	Ours
mAP	5.9	10.9	11.3	17.2	14.3	22.4	**25.2**

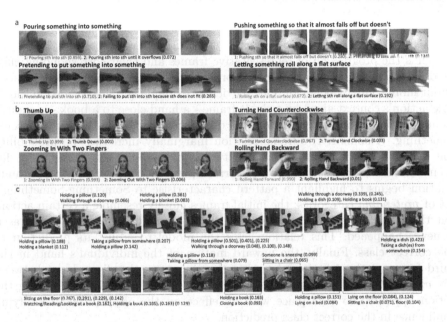

Fig. 3. Prediction examples on (a) Something-Something, (b) Jester, and (c) Charades. For each example drawn from Something-Something and Jester, the top two predictions with green text indicating a correct prediction and red indicating an incorrect one. Top 2 predictions are shown above Charades frames.

3.4   Interpreting Visual Common Sense Knowledge Inside the TRN

One of the distinct properties of the proposed TRNs compared to previous video classification networks such as C3D [15] and I3D [6] is that TRN has more interpretable structure. In this section, we have a more in-depth analysis to interpret the visual common sense knowledge learned by the TRNs through solving these temporal reasoning tasks. We explore the following four parts:

Representative Frames of a Video Voted by the TRN to Recognize an Activity. Intuitively, a human observer can capture the essence of an action by selecting a small collection of representative frames. Does the same hold true for models trained to recognize the activity? To obtain a sequence of representative frames for each TRN, we first compute the features of the equidistant frames from a video, then randomly combine them to generate different frame relation tuples and pass them into the TRNs. Finally we rank the relation tuples using the responses of different TRNs. Figure 4 shows the top representative frames voted by different TRNs to recognize an activity in the same video. We can see that the TRNs learn the temporal relations that characterize an activity. For comparatively simple actions, a single frame is sufficient to establish some degree of confidence in the correct action, but is vulnerable to mistakes when a transformation is present. 2-frame TRN picks up the two frames that best describe the transformation. Meanwhile, for more difficult activity categories such as 'Pretending to poke something', two frames are not sufficient information for even a human observer to differentiate. Similarly, the network needs additional frames in the TRNs to correctly recognize the behavior.

Thus the progression of representative frames and their corresponding class predictions inform us about how temporal relations may help the model reason about more complex behavior. One particular example is the last video in Fig. 4: The action's context given by a single frame - a hand close to a book - is enough to narrow down the top prediction to a qualitatively plausible action, unfolding something. A similar, two-frame relation marginally increases the probability the initial prediction, although these two frames would not be sufficient for even human observers to make the correct prediction. Now, the three frame-relation begins to highlight a pattern characteristic to Something-Something's set of *pretending* categories: the initial frames closely resemble a certain action, but the later frames are inconsistent with the completion of that action as if it never happened. This relation helps the model to adjust its prediction to the correct class. Finally, the upward motion of the individual's hand in the third frame of the 4-frame relation further increases the discordance between the *anticipated* and *observed* final state of the scene; a motion resembling the action appeared to take place with no effect on the object, thus, solidifying confidence in the correct class prediction.

Temporal Alignment of Videos. The observation that the representative frames identified by the TRN are consistent across instances of an action category suggests that the TRN is well suited for the task of temporally aligning videos with one another. Here, we wish to synchronize actions across multiple videos by establishing a correspondence between their frame sequences. Given several video instances of the same action, we first select the most representative frames for each video and use their frame indices as "landmark", temporal anchor points. Then, we alter the frame rate of video segments between two consecutive anchor points such that all of the individual videos arrive at the anchor points at the same time. Figure 5 shows the samples from the aligned videos. We can see different stages of an action are captured by the temporal relation. The temporal

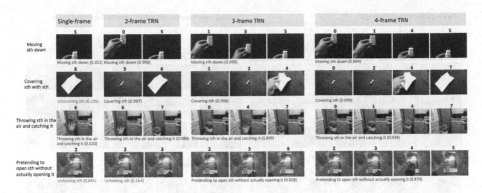

Fig. 4. The top representative frames determined by single frame baseline network, the 2-frame TRN, 3-frame TRN, and 4-frame TRN. TRNs learn to capture the essence of an activity only given a limited number of frames. Videos are from the validation set of the Something-Something dataset

alignment is also an exclusive application of our TRN model, which cannot be done by previous video networks 3D convNet or two-stream networks.

Importance of Temporal Order for Activity Recognition. To verify the importance of the temporal order of frames for activity recognition, we conduct an experiment to compare the scenario with input frames in temporal order and in shuffled order when training the TRNs, as shown in Fig. 6a. For training the shuffled TRNs, we randomly shuffle the frames in the relation modules. The significant difference on the Something-Something dataset shows the importance of the temporal order in the activity recognition. More interestingly, we repeat the same experiment on the UCF101 dataset [2] and observe no difference between the ordered frames and shuffled frames. That shows activity recognition for the Youtube-type videos in UCF101 doesn't necessarily require the temporal reasoning ability since there are not so many casual relations associated with an already on-going activity.

To further investigate how temporal ordering influences activity recognition in TRN, we examine and plot the categories that show the largest differences in the class accuracy between ordered and shuffled inputs drawn from the Something-Something dataset, in Fig. 6b. In general, actions with strong 'directionality' and large, one-way movements, such as 'Moving something down', appear to benefit the most from preserving the correct temporal ordering. This observation aligns with the idea that the disruption of continuous motion and a potential consequence of shuffling video frames, would likely confuse a human observer, as it would go against our intuitive notions of physics.

Interestingly, the penalty for shuffling frames of relatively static actions is less severe if penalizing at all in some cases, with several categories marginally benefiting from shuffled inputs, as observed with the category 'putting something that can't roll onto a slanted surface so it stays where it is'. Here, simply learning the coincidence of frames rather than temporal transformations may be sufficient

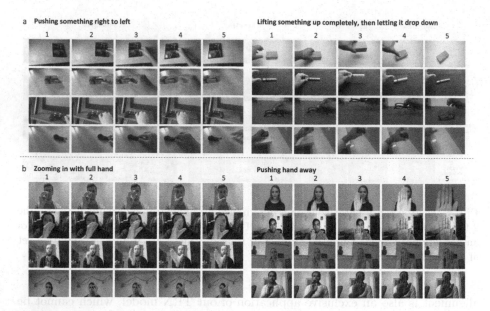

Fig. 5. Temporal alignment of videos from the (a) Something-Something and (b) Jester datasets using the most representative frames as temporal anchor points. For each action, 4 different videos are aligned using 5 temporal anchor points.

for the model to differentiate between similar activities and make the correct prediction. Particularly in challenging ambiguous cases, for example 'Pretending to throw something' where the release point is partially or completely obscured from view, disrupting a strong 'sense of motion' may bias model predictions away from the likely alternative, 'throwing something', frequently but incorrectly selected by the ordered model, thus giving rise to a curious difference in accuracy for that action.

The difference between TSN and TRN is at using different frame feature pooling strategies, where TRN using Temporal Relation(TR) pool emphasizes on capturing the temporal dependency of frames while TSN simply uses average pool to ignore the temporal order. We evaluate the two pool strategies in detail as shown in Table 5. The difference in the performance using average pool and TR pool actually reflects the importance of temporal orders in a video dataset. The tested datasets are categorized by the video source, where the first three are Youtube videos, the other three are videos crowdsourced from AMT. The base CNN is BNInception. Both of the models use 8 frames. Interestingly, the models with average pool and TR pool achieve similar accuracy on Youtube videos, thus recognizing Youtube videos doesn't require much temporal order reasoning, which might be due to that activity in the randomly trimmed Youtube videos doesn't usually have a clear action start or end. On the other hand, the crowdsourced video has just one activity with clearly start and end, thus temporal relation pool brings significant improvement.

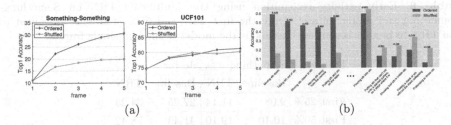

(a)   (b)

Fig. 6. (a) Accuracy obtained using ordered frames and shuffled frames, on Something-Something and UCF101 dataset respectively. On Something-Something, the temporal order is critical for recognizing the activity. But recognizing activities in UCF101 does not necessarily require temporal relational reasoning. (b) The top 5 action categories that exhibited the largest gain and the least gain (negative) respectively between ordered and shuffled frames as inputs. Actions with directional motion appear to suffer most from shuffled inputs.

Table 5. Accuracy on six video datasets for models with two pool strategies.

Dataset	Youtube videos			Crowdsourced videos		
	UCF	Kinetics	Moments	Something	Jester	Charades
Num. Classes	101	200	339	174	27	157
Average Pool	82.69	**63.34**	24.11	19.53	85.41	11.32
TR Pool	**83.83**	63.18	**25.94**	**34.44**	**95.31**	**25.20**

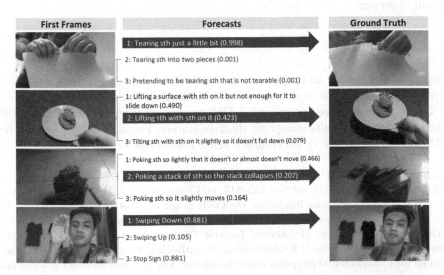

Fig. 7. Early recognition of activity when only given the first 25% frames. The first 25% of each video, represented by the first frame shown in the left column, is used to generate the top 3 anticipated forecasts and corresponding probabilities listed in the middle column. The ground truth label is highlighted by a blue arrow which points to the last frame of the video on the right.

Table 6. Early activity recognition using the MultiScale TRN on Something-Something and Jester dataset. Only the first 25% and 50% of frames are given to the TRN to predict activities. Baseline is the model trained on single frames.

Frames	Something		Jester	
	Baseline	TRN	Baseline	TRN
First 25%	9.08	11.14	27.25	34.23
First 50%	10.10	19.10	41.43	78.42
Full	11.41	33.01	63.60	93.70

Early Activity Recognition. Recognizing activities early or even anticipating and forecasting activities before they happen or fully happen is a challenging yet less explored problem in activity recognition. Here we evaluate our TRN model on early recognition of activity when given only the first 25% and 50% of the frames in each validation video. Results are shown in Table 6. For comparison, we also include the single frame baseline, which is trained on randomly sampled individual frames from a video. We see that TRN can use the learned temporal relations to anticipate activity. The performance increases as more ordered frames are received. Figure 7 shows some examples of anticipating activities using only first 25% and 50% frames of a video. A qualitative review of these examples reveals that model predictions on only initial frames do serve as very reasonable forecasts despite being given task with a high degree of uncertainty even for human observers.

4 Conclusion

We proposed a simple and interpretable network module called Temporal Relation Network (TRN) to enable temporal relational reasoning in neural networks for videos. We evaluated the proposed TRN on several recent datasets and established competitive results using only discrete frames. Finally, we have shown that TRN modules discover visual common sense knowledge in videos.

Acknowledgement. This work was partially funded by DARPA XAI program No. FA8750-18-C-0004, NSF Grant No. 1524817, and Samsung to A.T.; the Vannevar Bush Faculty Fellowship program funded by the ONR grant No. N00014-16-1-3116 to A.O.. It is also supported in part by the Intelligence Advanced Research Projects Activity (IARPA) via Department of Interior/ Interior Business Center (DOI/IBC) contract number D17PC00341. The U.S. Government is authorized to reproduce and distribute reprints for Governmental purposes notwithstanding any copyright annotation thereon. Disclaimer: The views and conclusions contained herein are those of the authors and should not be interpreted as necessarily representing the official policies or endorsements, either expressed or implied, of IARPA, DOI/IBC, or the U.S. Government.

References

1. Sigurdsson, G.A., Russakovsky, O., Gupta, A.: What actions are needed for understanding human actions in videos? arXiv preprint arXiv:1708.02696 (2017)
2. Soomro, K., Zamir, A.R., Shah, M.: UCF101: a dataset of 101 human actions classes from videos in the wild. In: Proceedings of CVPR (2012)
3. Karpathy, A., Toderici, G., Shetty, S., Leung, T., Sukthankar, R., Fei-Fei, L.: Large-scale video classification with convolutional neural networks. In: Proceedings of CVPR (2014)
4. Gorban, A., et al.: THUMOS challenge: action recognition with a large number of classes. In: CVPR Workshop (2015)
5. Simonyan, K., Zisserman, A.: Two-stream convolutional networks for action recognition in videos. In: Advances in Neural Information Processing Systems, pp. 568–576 (2014)
6. Carreira, J., Zisserman, A.: Quo vadis, action recognition? A new model and the kinetics dataset. arXiv preprint arXiv:1705.07750 (2017)
7. Santoro, A., et al.: A simple neural network module for relational reasoning. arXiv preprint arXiv:1706.01427 (2017)
8. Lake, B.M., Ullman, T.D., Tenenbaum, J.B., Gershman, S.J.: Building machines that learn and think like people. Behav. Brain Sci. **40**, 1–101 (2016)
9. Goyal, R., et al.: The "something something" video database for learning and evaluating visual common sense. In: Proceedings of ICCV (2017)
10. Twentybn jester dataset: a hand gesture dataset (2017). https://www.twentybn.com/datasets/jester
11. Sigurdsson, G.A., Varol, G., Wang, X., Farhadi, A., Laptev, I., Gupta, A.: Hollywood in homes: crowdsourcing data collection for activity understanding. In: Leibe, B., Matas, J., Sebe, N., Welling, M. (eds.) ECCV 2016. LNCS, vol. 9905, pp. 510–526. Springer, Cham (2016). https://doi.org/10.1007/978-3-319-46448-0_31
12. Krizhevsky, A., Sutskever, I., Hinton, G.E.: Imagenet classification with deep convolutional neural networks. In: Advances in Neural Information Processing Systems, pp. 1097–1105 (2012)
13. Zhou, B., Lapedriza, A., Xiao, J., Torralba, A., Oliva, A.: Learning deep features for scene recognition using places database. In: Advances in Neural Information Processing Systems, pp. 487–495 (2014)
14. Donahue, J., et al.: Long-term recurrent convolutional networks for visual recognition and description. In: Proceedings of the IEEE Conference on Computer Vision and Pattern Recognition, pp. 2625–2634 (2015)
15. Tran, D., Bourdev, L., Fergus, R., Torresani, L., Paluri, M.: Learning spatiotemporal features with 3D convolutional networks. In: Proceedings of CVPR (2015)
16. Wang, L., et al.: Temporal segment networks: towards good practices for deep action recognition. In: Leibe, B., Matas, J., Sebe, N., Welling, M. (eds.) ECCV 2016. LNCS, vol. 9912, pp. 20–36. Springer, Cham (2016). https://doi.org/10.1007/978-3-319-46484-8_2
17. Kay, W., et al.: The kinetics human action video dataset. arXiv preprint arXiv:1705.06950 (2017)
18. Gaidon, A., Harchaoui, Z., Schmid, C.: Temporal localization of actions with actoms. IEEE Trans. Pattern Anal. Mach. Intell. **35**(11), 2782–2795 (2013)
19. Pirsiavash, H., Ramanan, D.: Parsing videos of actions with segmental grammars. In: Proceedings of the IEEE Conference on Computer Vision and Pattern Recognition, pp. 612–619 (2014)

20. Wang, H., Schmid, C.: Action recognition with improved trajectories. In: Proceedings of ICCV, pp. 3551–3558 (2013)
21. Gaidon, A., Harchaoui, Z., Schmid, C.: Activity representation with motion hierarchies. Int. J. Comput. Vis. **107**(3), 219–238 (2014)
22. Wang, L., Qiao, Y., Tang, X.: MoFAP: a multi-level representation for action recognition. Int. J. Comput. Vis. **119**(3), 254–271 (2016)
23. Agrawal, P., Nair, A.V., Abbeel, P., Malik, J., Levine, S.: Learning to poke by poking: experiential learning of intuitive physics. In: Advances in Neural Information Processing Systems, pp. 5074–5082 (2016)
24. Pinto, L., Gandhi, D., Han, Y., Park, Y.-L., Gupta, A.: The curious robot: learning visual representations via physical interactions. In: Leibe, B., Matas, J., Sebe, N., Welling, M. (eds.) ECCV 2016. LNCS, vol. 9906, pp. 3–18. Springer, Cham (2016). https://doi.org/10.1007/978-3-319-46475-6_1
25. Sermanet, P., Lynch, C., Hsu, J., Levine, S.: Time-contrastive networks: self-supervised learning from multi-view observation. arXiv preprint arXiv:1704.06888 (2017)
26. Sigurdsson, G.A., Divvala, S., Farhadi, A., Gupta, A.: Asynchronous temporal fields for action recognition (2017)
27. Mahdisoltani, F., Berger, G., Gharbieh, W., Fleet, D., Memisevic, R.: Fine-grained video classification and captioning. arXiv preprint arXiv:1804.09235 (2018)
28. Sharif Razavian, A., Azizpour, H., Sullivan, J., Carlsson, S.: CNN features off-the-shelf: an astounding baseline for recognition. In: Proceedings of the IEEE Conference on Computer Vision and Pattern Recognition Workshops (2014)
29. He, K., Zhang, X., Ren, S., Sun, J.: Deep residual learning for image recognition. In: Proceedings of the IEEE Conference on Computer Vision and Pattern Recognition, pp. 770–778 (2016)
30. Ioffe, S., Szegedy, C.: Batch normalization: Accelerating deep network training by reducing internal covariate shift. In: International Conference on Machine Learning, pp. 448–456 (2015)

Author Index

Printed in the United States
By Bookmasters

Printed in the United States
By Bookmasters